Dictionary
of American
Religious
Biography

DICTIONARY
OF AMERICAN
RELIGIOUS
BIOGRAPHY_____

SECOND EDITION,
Revised and Enlarged

Henry Warner Bowden

GREENWOOD PRESS _____
Westport, Connecticut • London

Library of Congress Cataloging-in-Publication Data

Bowden, Henry Warner.
Dictionary of American religious biography / Henry Warner Bowden.
—2nd ed., rev. and enl.
p.   cm.
Includes bibliographical references.
ISBN 0–313–27825–3 (alk. paper)
1. Religous biography—United States—Dictionaries.   2. United
States—Biography—Dictionaries.   I.   Title.
BL72.B68   1993
209'.2'2—dc20   92–35524
[B]

British Library Cataloguing in Publication Data is available.

Copyright © 1993 by Henry Warner Bowden

Library of Congress Catalog Card Number: 92–35524
ISBN: 0–313–27825–3

First published in 1993

Greenwood Press, 88 Post Road West, Westport, CT 06881
An imprint of Greenwood Publishing Group, Inc.

Printed in the United States of America

The paper used in this book complies with the
Permanent Paper Standard issued by the National
Information Standards Organization (Z39.48–1984).

10 9 8 7 6 5 4 3 2 1

CONTENTS

PREFACE

The purpose behind issuing a revised, enlarged edition of this dictionary is to enhance its value and usefulness for both scholars and general readers alike. Such a hope is based on tangible proof that for more than fifteen years readers of different ages and backgrounds have found its content helpful in their own inquiries. Additional materials, together with thorough updating of original entries, will make the work even more valuable as a guide to learning.

This volume is still the only single reference work that correlates information on American religious figures from all chronological periods and most denominational or theological affiliations. Its content has been expanded more than twenty percent: With the addition of 125 new biographies, this volume now contains a total of 550 people who figured importantly in American religions. Previous typographical errors in text, bibliography, and cited dates have been corrected, so the present volume is now even more accurate and reliable than the high standards achieved at its first printing. Over 350 of the original entries have been revised, either in terms of their content or in citing new publications in the bibliographies following each entry. These emendations plus an end-of-volume general bibliography covering major themes provide the latest scholarship regarding critical interpretations and recent biographical studies. The end result affords trustworthy data on individuals who stem from all geographical sections of our country, follow varying vocations, and acknowledge many different ethnic identities.

Brevity may be the soul of wit, but it is the bane of biography. Space limitations have curtailed the length of each sketch in order to include more entries. In each one of them the author has pursued three aims: (1) to summarize basic information on every individual as accurately as possible, (2) to incorporate vital statistics within sound interpretive judgments, and (3) to present all data in a manner that stimulates further inquiry. By doing this, it is hoped that advanced scholars as well as beginning students might use the volume profitably. It gives reliable information as a handy refresher for those already familiar with persons discussed in the entries. At the same time, its format is plain enough to help those approaching the material for the first time.

Details descriptive of each person's vital statistics and career precede the narrative discussion. All dates have been revised to fit the New Style (Gregorian) calendar currently in use. Bibliographical citations follow each narrative sketch, with Part A comprising works by the individual under consideration and Part B listing references about that person. Part A lists a maximum of six book-length publications. Many authors wrote a great deal more, but six representative works will lead students to a more comprehensive search of their own. In Part B the secondary materials have similar limitations. Standard reference works are listed in abbreviated form; an explanatory key to the symbols is provided at the end of this preface. All pertinent references within this list of standard works have been printed. No more than five published biographies, usually the latest and the most accurate, have been included as additional aids to continuing study. In this revised edition many earlier listings in Part B have been deleted in order to include more recent works appearing in the past decade. Thus each entry gives a compact summary of available material, both by and about every historical figure.

It is always a challenge to choose entries for a dictionary such as this. Who was significant or unique enough to include, who too commonplace to omit? One criterion was to discuss only those who were deceased before 1 July 1992. This facilitated overviews of entire careers in each case, but it also proved frustrating because a solid dozen of worthwhile entries were held in abeyance just because of actuarial circumstances. Still, difficult choices had to be made about myriads of historical figures, and the final tally reflects the author's own judgments regarding each individual's impact on contemporaries and long-range effectiveness.

Another guideline used throughout the project was the conviction that religion studies in this country have too long been dominated by a consensus viewpoint. This collection of entries has been put together on the assumption that religious expressions through five hundred years of American experience have been rich, both in complexity and diversity, from the beginning. No religious leaders have been excluded because they did not fit a preconceived standard of orthodox belief or acceptable behavior. The only thesis undergirding this work is that pluralism has been an element of religious experience on this continent from earliest times to the present.

At the end of the twentieth century we are now realizing that Protestant Christianity, controlled by ordained white males, never enjoyed exclusive rights over American citizens with religious interests. Still, the majority of entries in this dictionary reflect that image simply because of the numeric imbalance. But simple recognition of the evidence calls for more discussion of women, Native

Americans, Blacks, Asians, laypeople in many walks of life, and voices of several minority gospels. This revisionist historical perspective tries to present the full panoply of diverse strains found in what Philip Schaff called the ''motley sampler'' of competing religions in this country. And in going beyond Christian denominations, one must admit theists, freethinkers, transcendentalists, and many cultists as qualified representatives of religion in our collective past. Whether they are considered orthodox or heretical, participants in mainstream culture or misfits, they contributed expressions of astonishingly creative diversity in American religion, and all of them merit inclusion here.

So what follows is a wide sampling of religious activities, voices, and deeds exemplified in the dynamic context of individual lives. The dictionary does not contain all the people worthy of mention—no single volume ever will—but those it does consider were vital and energetic, people with a purposeful intensity that led to effective action. For some, this zeal found expression in founding new religious groupings; for others it strove to perpetuate established traditions and to manage familiar institutions successfully. Many were reformers, visionaries, thinkers, and doers. Others were charlatans and con artists who endangered both themselves and the welfare of their followers. Figures in each generation have served dutifully in traditional patterns, while others have followed new visions, constructed new bodies of thought, called for justice, and bled for freedom; and some, alas, have bilked the gullible. But the good and the bad, the ponderous and the mystical, the steady and the flashy are all representative figures in the kaleidoscope of components that make up religion in this country, past and present. The list of participants ranges from leathery circuit riders to pallid philosophers, from sectaries and dreamers to social activists and cosmic-minded citizens of the world. All changed life around them to an appreciable degree, and each of them teaches us something about ourselves.

Henry Warner Bowden
Rutgers University

ABBREVIATIONS FOR STANDARD REFERENCE SOURCES

AAP *Annals of the American Pulpit*, ed. William B. Sprague, 9 vols. (New York, 1857–69; 1969).

DAB *Dictionary of American Biography*, ed. Allen Johnson and Dumas Malone, 20 vol. (New York, 1928–37; Four Supplements, 1944–74).

EJ *Encyclopedia Judaica*, 16 vols. (Jerusalem, 1971).

NAW *Notable American Women, 1607–1950: A Biographical Dictionary*, ed. Edward T. James *et al.*, 3 vols. (Cambridge, MA, 1971).

NCAB *National Cyclopedia of American Biography*. 55 vols. (New York, 1892–1974; Current Series, volumes A-L, 1930–72).

NCE *New Catholic Encyclopedia*. 15 vols. (New York, 1967).

NYT *New York Times*, 1851 to present.

SH *New Schaff-Herzog Encyclopedia of Religious Knowledge*, ed. Samuel M. Jackson *et al.*, 12 vols. (New York, 1908–12; Grand Rapids, MI, 1949–50).

UJE *The Universal Jewish Encyclopedia*, ed. Isaac Landman, 10 vols. (New York, 1939–43).

Dictionary
of American
Religious
Biography

Biographies

A

ABBOT, Francis Ellingwood (6 November 1836, Boston, MA—23 October 1903, Beverly, MA). *Education:* B.A., Harvard Coll., 1859; studied at Harvard Div. Sch., 1859–60; graduated from Meadville Sem., 1863; Ph.D., Harvard Univ., 1881. *Career:* headmaster, girls' school, Meadville, PA, 1860–63; minister, Dover, NH, 1864–69; minister, First Independent Society, Toledo, OH, 1869–73; editor, *The Index*, 1870–80; headmaster, boys' school, New York, 1880–81; headmaster, boys' school, Cambridge, MA, 1881–92; active retirement, 1892–1903.

The national Unitarian Conference formulated a statement of beliefs in 1865, but Abbot, as a young minister of that denomination, argued for less restrictive terminology. The "Lordship of Jesus" was too confining a principle for his antiauthoritarian tastes, so he led the liberal faction in an attempt to express their religious impulse along freer lines. In 1867 he helped create the Free Religious Association as a focal point for those who thought even Unitarian orthodoxy to be unhealthily restrictive. Within a year he became involved in court action to retain his New Hampshire pastorate; though a majority of the congregation supported his radical ideas, conservatives won the case and forced Abbot's resignation. Thereafter he was an avowed nonsectarian. Religious truth for him implied the necessary rejection of all dogmatic authority, any reliance on revelation whether in scripture or creed. His libertarian viewpoint, on which he was doggedly insistent throughout life, held that truth was open to every individual. The free inquiry of science provided a broad avenue for each person to learn about God on a sound, rational basis. In so arguing, he contributed to the ferment of religious ideas in late nineteenth-century American thought and represented one of the earliest attempts to create an empirical theology that used Darwinian naturalism as its point of departure.

Through pages of *The Index*, semiofficial weekly of the Free Religious Association, and then in full volumes on scientific theism, Abbot elaborated his ideas. He viewed the universe as thoroughly intelligible—an intelligent organism in which every component, including man, experienced a gradual process of self-realization. This world and truth from God about it (not intuition or subjective idealism) constituted the real basis for moral improvement. As human reason apprehended God by a purely rational analysis of nature, God was seen to be an absolute, objectively real personality. Moreover the same order of personality existed in humanity, connected to God by a concentric hierarchy of varying existences in an integrated chain of being. Human consciousness thus coincided, to a small degree, with the divine. Beginning with finite divinity, man as a progressive being could hope for eventual perfection. This "free religion" looked to the infinite humanity of God as the noblest form of theism, while it substantiated that conception in the eternal absolutes of Nature. Such ideas were unacceptable to Transcendentalists and idealists alike, rebuttal appearing in the latter instance as a strong critique from *Josiah Royce. But Abbot defended his empirical epistemology as well as the religion of humanity against every dissent. Then, unexpectedly, he committed suicide by taking poison at his wife's gravesite, an act singularly out of keeping with the philosophical system he had constructed over a number of decades.

Bibliography:

A.   *Scientific Theism* (Boston, 1885, 1888); *The Way Out of Agnosticism, or The Philosophy of Free Religion* (Boston, 1890); *The Syllogistic Philosophy, or Prolegomena to Science*, 2 vols. (Boston, 1906).
B.   NCAB 24, 113–14; DAB 1, 11–12; NYT 25 Oct 1903, 11; Sydney E. Ahlstrom, *The Scientific Theist: A Life of Francis Ellingwood Abbot* (Macon, GA, 1987).

ABBOTT, Lyman (18 December 1835, Roxbury, MA—22 October 1922, New York, NY). *Education*: B.A., New York Univ., 1853; read law and passed N.Y. bar exam, 1856; read theology and ordained as Congregationalist minister, Farmington, ME, 1860. *Career*: practiced law, 1853–59; minister at Terre Haute, IN, 1860–65; secretary of American Freedmen's Union Commission, 1865–69; minister at New York, NY, 1865–69; contributor to *Harper's Magazine* and *Independent*, 1869–71; editor, *Illustrated Christian Weekly*, 1871–76; editor, *Christian Union*, 1876–93; minister at Plymouth Church, Brooklyn, NY, 1888–99; editor, *Outlook*, 1893–1922.

As lecturer, author, preacher, and newspaper editor, Abbott succeeded in spreading his ideas as widely as any religious spokesman of his time. He was always interested in the major goals of social reform, human liberty, temperance, and morality in national life, even when these commitments found expression in partisan programs. He came to support the Northern cause in a divided state during the Civil War and afterwards worked to rehabilitate the South, especially in the areas of education and non-sectarian moral training for those recently emancipated. Abbott's ideas about Christian duty in society were forcibly stated in his many writings and editorial responsibilities. His wide, informal reading in religious topics allowed him to move beyond many commonly held beliefs of the day, but his social views tended to remain closer to midstream acceptability. He was a strong backer of Theodore Roosevelt and championed that politician's socio-economic programs for almost two decades, eventually to the detriment of his own influence and popularity. During World War I, he helped shape the bellicosity of public opinion by urging a Christian rationale for preparedness, mobilization, the Espionage and Sedition Acts, even advocating war crimes trials in opposition to Woodrow Wilson's more lenient policies. For forty-six years, his editorials in the *Christian Union* and then the *Outlook* (the name was changed in 1881 when *Henry Ward Beecher ceased affiliation with it) reached over 100,000 subscribers and affected their ideas on moral issues in public questions.

Abbott never tried to maintain any system of thought as part of an unchanging religious heritage, and his effectiveness in popularizing liberal theology was as important as editorializing on social issues. His response to skepticism and declining faith due to modern sciences was an attempt to develop the spiritual life through free theological inquiry, wherever that pursuit led. As a result of that positive approach, Abbott was able to incorporate many aspects of Darwinian thought and Biblical criticism into a reformulation of Christian affirmations. His new views did not depend on biblical literalism, miracles, or natural evidence to vindicate religious faith. They tended, rather, to an evolutionary understanding of inspiration, salvation, individual spiritual development, churches, and Christian society. His acceptance of the main features of naturalistic science and history made Abbott essentially an apologist for necessary adaptations, not a radical thinker. In contrast to more conservative theology, however, he found it neither necessary nor tenable to emphasize the divinity of Jesus, vicarious atonement, or a strict separation of natural and supernatural forces. By a constant outpouring of writing and speaking on these matters, Lyman Abbott helped great numbers of people to an acceptance of new views about religion within an evolutionary framework, without the complete destruction of their faith.

Bibliography:

A. *The Evolution of Christianity* (Boston, 1892); *Christianity and Social Problems* (Boston, 1896); *The Theology of an Evolutionist* (Boston, 1897); *The Great Companion* (New York, 1904); *Reminiscences* (Boston, 1915; 1923); *What Christianity Means to Me: A Spiritual Autobiography* (New York, 1921).

B. SH 1, 7; NCAB 1, 473; DAB 1, 24–25; NYT 23 Oct 1922, 1; William W. Sweet, *Makers of Christianity: From John Cotton to Lyman Abbott* (New York, 1937); Ira V. Brown, *Lyman Abbott: Christian Evolutionist* (Cambridge, MA, 1953; Westport, CT, 1970).

ABDU'L-BAHA (23 May 1844, Teheran, Iran—28 November 1921, Haifa, Israel).

In nineteenth-century Iran, a visionary of the Shi'ite sect of Islam announced that he was al-Bab ("The Gateway"), a divine messenger who would inaugurate Allah's peaceable kingdom among men. Later he declared that the Koranic laws of prophet Mohammed were superseded by his own, which comprised a new faith known as Baha'ism. After the Bab was executed, an exiled disciple entitled Baha'-U'llah claimed to be the one whose advent al-Bab had proclaimed. Prison and governmental interference did not prevent his writing *Kitab-i Aqdas*, the fundamental scripture of Baha'is. His eldest son, Abbas Effendi, became the greatest apostle of Baha'ism. Through his lecturing and writing the religion reached its most definitive expression, while his missionary zeal established centers for its doctrine on three continents. With the title of Abdu'l-Baha ("Servant of God") he was able to overcome internal opposition and gain recognition as the authoritative interpreter of his father's teachings. For a long time the Baha'i faith was embroiled in Turkish politics, but beginning in 1909 it was allowed to stand solely on its merits as a religious philosophy. Missionaries had preceded Abdu'l-Baha to the western world; in 1911–12 he visited congregations himself to cultivate the faith already planted. Beginning at London and then Paris, he spread wisdom in lectures spoken in Persian, translated into languages appropriate for the audience. From April to December of 1912, he toured North America. In churches and synagogues as well as rented halls, he addressed followers in New York and Boston through Chicago to San Francisco and Los Angeles. By this means he consolidated individuals into a community that has grown in every subsequent decade.

The teachings of Baha'ism seek a rational harmony for mankind and the religions supported by segments of the human family. God has revealed himself through various manifestations including Moses, Jesus, Mohammed, and Baha'-U'llah. These figures serve as mirrors of God; they reflect supplementary images of a single source. In addition to espousing this syncretistic theology, Baha'is advocate world peace, universal education, social equality, and the eradication of all prejudices. They see the earth as one homeland where there should be equality for all persons, male and female. They seek disinterested cooperation, mutual aid, and protection for all. Within a half century of Abdu'l-Baha's visit, American followers have built an imposing temple at their headquarters in Wilmette, Illinois, in addition to establishing over 500 local assemblies throughout the country.

Bibliography:

    A.   *Paris Talks* (London, 1912); *The Promulgation of Universal Peace*, 2 vols. (Chicago, 1922–25); *The Memorials of the Faithful* (Haifa, 1924); *Selected Writings of Abdu'l-Baha*, translated by Shoghi Effendi (Wilmette, IL, 1942).
    B.   M. H. Phelps, *Life and Teachings of Abbas Effendi* (New York, 1903); Isabel F.

Chamberlain, *Abdul Baha on Divine Philosophy* (Boston, 1918); H. M. Balyuzi, *Abdu'l-Baha: The Centre of the Covenant of Baha' u'llah* (London, 1971).

ADAMS, Hannah (2 October 1755, Medfield, MA—15 December 1831, Brookline, MA). *Career*: author, historian, scholar of religion, 1784–1831.

A distant cousin to the presidential branch of the family, Adams found that she inherited her father's frail health as well as his retentive intellect and love of books. She attended school only sporadically, but she supplemented her own voracious reading with tutorials in Latin, Greek, and philosophy from ministerial students who boarded at her home. By the 1780s she became intrigued by a British publication that surveyed world religions, and she determined to produce her own. The earliest title of her attempt to portray each religion without bias announced her work as "an alphabetical compendium of the various sects which have appeared in the world from the beginning of Christianity to the present day." Another revealed it as "a dictionary of all religions and religious denominations: Jewish, Heathen, Mohameton, and Christian, both ancient and modern." This activity made Adams one of the first women in America to choose writing as a profession. And her wide reading wedded to scrupulous accuracy also made her a pioneer and foundress of the history of religions as a scholarly discipline in this country. In truth, she was more a compiler than analyst, but her careful work nurtured later efforts to view all religions from a single perspective.

Health and finances were always problematic, but Adams persisted in her researches to such an extent that by 1805 her eyesight was severely damaged. At that time she also became involved in a controversy with *Jedidiah Morse concerning copyright or "rivalry" between competing publications. The details regarding two histories of New England are obscure, but discussion soon moved beyond such small confines. Most Boston intellectuals were inclined toward the liberal side in questions regarding Unitarian tendencies in the established Congregational church of Massachusetts. They championed Adams' side of the question because they admired her independent, questioning spirit. They were also indisposed to support Morse because he was a staunch defender of Calvinist thought and conservative church policies. As bitter charges increased with every exchange, the woman author retired from public debate, but she continued to publish books on Christianity and biblical studies which sustained her eminence as an intellect whose zeal for truth refused to be governed by the social constraints of her day.

Bibliography:

A.   *A View of Religions* (Boston, 1784 and many subsequent editions); *A Summary of the History of New England from the First Settlement at Plymouth to the Acceptance of the Federal Constitution* (Dedham, MA, 1799); *The Truth and Excellence of the Christian Religion* (Boston, 1804); *The History of the Jews from the Destruction of Jerusalem to the Nineteenth Century*, 2 vols. (Boston, 1812); *Letters on the Gospels*

(Cambridge, MA, 1824); *A Memoir of Miss Hannah Adams, Written by Herself* (Boston, 1832).

B. NCAB 5, 459–60; DAB 1, 60–61; NAW 1, 9–11.

ADDAMS, Jane (6 September 1860, Cedarville, IL—21 May 1935, Chicago, IL). *Education*: graduated from Rockford Coll., 1881; studied at Woman's Medical Coll. of PA, 1881–82. *Career*: director, Hull House, 1889–1935.

Looking back on years of social work, Addams surmised that she first became concerned about the urban poor in 1883 during a convalescent tour of European cities. Returning there in 1887, with *Ellen Gates Starr as a traveling companion, she determined by 1889 to do something about the social problems resulting from industrialization. Later the same year she rented a decaying mansion in Chicago's 19th Ward and started meeting immediate needs in the community. Addams was motivated by humanitarian benevolence and genuine love of people, but more importantly she was a pioneer in using corrective action to replace simple charity. Her work probed for a new social ethic which transcended the old code of individualistic morality. Over the years she attracted talented assistants and coordinated a great number of activities including a day nursery, a gymnasium, clubs for boys and girls, a dispensary, cooking and sewing classes, a cooperative boardinghouse, and outlets for both music and drama. Thousands of people, most of them immigrants took advantage of this program that offered no religious instruction but sought to affirm the sanctity of each person's ideas and abilities.

The injustice of tenements and sweatshops, the cruelty of poverty and prejudice, made Addams a crusader for changing the causes of such conditions. She championed the labor movement and urged legislation for industrial safety. She advocated child labor laws and used her influence to help create in Illinois the first state court for juveniles in 1899. Some wealthy patrons withdrew their support because of her outspoken pro-union position, and others were dismayed at her thoroughgoing pacifism. In 1915 Addams was the chief instigator of the Women's Peace Party, and four years later she became chair of the Women's International League for Peace and Freedom. Her transparent good will eventually won over most critics, and in her last decades recognition of her contributions spread widely. As co-recipient she became in 1931 the first American woman to receive the Nobel Peace Prize. In her varied attempts to achieve racial equality, social justice, and peace she always sought to reconstruct social relationships by drawing on the potential good in human hearts.

Bibliography:

A. *Democracy and Social Ethics* (New York, 1902); *Newer Ideals of Peace* (Chautauqua, NY, 1907); *The Spirit of Youth and the City Streets* (New York, 1909); *The Long Road of Woman's Memory* (New York, 1916); *The Excellent Becomes the Permanent* (New York, 1932); *Forty Years at Hull House* (New York, 1935).

B. DAB 21, 10–13; NAW 1, 16–22; NYT 22 May 1935, 1; James Weber Linn, *Jane Addams* (New York, 1935).

ADLER, Cyrus (13 September 1863, Van Buren, AR—7 April 1940, Phila-
delphia, PA). *Education:* B.A., Univ. of Pennsylvania, 1883; Ph.D., Johns
Hopkins Univ., 1887. *Career:* member, Department of Semitics, Johns Hopkins
Univ., 1887–93; librarian, Smithsonian Institution, 1892–1905; assistant sec-
retary, Smithsonian, 1905–08; president, Dropsie Coll., 1908–40; president,
Jewish Theological Sem., 1924–40.

Many of the institutions founded in this country to preserve the life and learning
of traditional Judaism were successful because of Adler's unstinting support.
Perhaps his most effective trait was an ability to organize structures necessary
to accomplish tasks and then to lead men of differing temperaments in common
pursuit of those goals. Boards, committees, and commissions too numerous to
mention are a gauge of his dedication to augment the religious heritage that he
absorbed in his uncle's Philadelphia home. He helped in forming the Jewish
Publication Society of America (1888), serving on its executive committee and
editorial board. Between 1892 and 1917, he served as the architect and coordinator of a group of experts, which produced a new authoritative translation of
the Hebrew Bible. Through skilled diplomacy, sincerity, and even temper he
secured the cooperation of Reform (*Kaufmann Kohler) and Conservative (*Solomon Schechter) scholars alike. Adler was the main force behind founding the
American Jewish Historical Society in 1892, and beginning in 1910 he edited
the *Jewish Quarterly Review* for thirty years. Though not a rabbi, he served as
vice-president of the United Synagogue of America after its inception in 1913
and worked through many channels to promote its objectives. Those included
loyalty to the Torah and its historical exposition, continued observance of Sabbath
and dietary laws, maintaining the traditional character of synagogue worship
with Hebrew as the language of prayer, and preserving awareness of Israel's
past and hopes for its eventual restoration.

Through personal religious commitment and acquired training, Adler was
continually involved in furthering the cause of biblical scholarship. He built the
program of Dropsie College into one that excelled in the study of Hebrew and
cognate fields. But the school that best afforded him status as a leader in traditional ways was the Jewish Theological Seminary in New York. Adler helped
persuade his friend, Solomon Schechter, to come from England and serve as the
reorganized seminary's president in 1902. He worked closely with that Conservative leader, and as a Trustee raised funds to create one of the most comprehensive libraries in the world. He became acting president after Schechter's death
in 1915 and by 1924 was recognized in name for long having been in fact a
guiding force in the institution. Adler was also involved in projects to secure
aid for Jews in central and eastern Europe. His main concern was their welfare
and security, not Zionism or any particular nationalist position. A member of
the American Jewish Committee, Adler did not agree with the policies of *Stephen S. Wise and the American Jewish Congress. His last years offered satisfaction at seeing so many Conservative endeavors flourish in his native land,

yet there was growing apprehension and a sense of being less than effective in problems regarding European Jewry.

Bibliography:

A. *Lectures, Selected Papers, Addresses*, ed. Edward D. Coleman and Joseph Leider (Philadelphia, 1933); *I Have Considered the Days* (Philadelphia, 1941).

B. SH 1, 44, NCAB 41, 16–17; DAB 22, 5–7; UJE 1, 488–89; EJ 2, 272–74; NYT 8 Apr 1940, 1; Abraham A. Neuman, *Cyrus Adler: A Biographical Sketch* (New York, 1942.)

ADLER, Felix (13 August 1851, Alzey, Germany—24 April 1933, New York, NY). *Education*: B.A., Columbia Coll., 1870; Ph.D., Heidelberg, 1873. *Career*: rabbi, Temple Emanuel, New York, 1873–74; professor of Hebrew and Oriental Literature, Cornell Univ., 1874–76; minister, Ethical Culture Society, New York, 1876–1908; professor of Political and Social Ethics, Columbia Univ., 1902–33.

Trained to succeed his father as rabbi of a Reform temple, Adler quickly outdistanced his constituents and subsequently abandoned the restraints of clerical identification to follow an independent course. He thought that sectarian ideologies impeded religious progress, and he adopted a careful neutrality regarding confessional differences, pragmatically convinced that beliefs were secondary to action. Adler preferred the broader stream of spiritual evolution, which he discerned leading to universal ethical idealism, rejecting ideas of a personal God, and concentrating on the moral good within human nature. He drew inspiration from ancient Hebrew prophets who had criticized human failings with such moral fervor. Added to that was Jesus' conception of inner purity. These supplemental emphases on human potential were strands that the ethical philosopher combined and then superseded by pointing to a compendium of idealized ethical reality. Through all his writings and programs, Adler maintained an intense moral conviction that this metaphysical reality was ultimate and more genuine than the natural world or its lower forms of organized religious practice. He spent the greater part of his life persuading others that they should try to mold their family, vocation, and social surroundings in conformity to the ethical and spiritual nature of this exalted paradigm.

In 1876, Adler formed the Ethical Culture Society, a model organization that embodied his ideas about religious endeavor and facilitated their implementation in educational and philanthropic work. Its objective was to welcome the unchurched from all backgrounds and provide means for moral activity that would at once serve and reform society. Among its early practical concerns were child welfare, medical care for the poor, visiting nurses, and reform in labor relations, slums, and city politics. Adler was a pioneer in progressive methods of modern education, instituting free kindergartens and vocational training schools, which were widely copied. His institute for child study was one of the first such associations in the country. His books and many articles in the *International Journal of Ethics* (1890) helped spread the basic thrust of ethical culture. During the 1880s, similar societies were established in major American cities (Philadelphia, Chicago, St. Louis) and abroad, attesting to the general acceptance of this liberalized perspective. Filling roles as spokesman and agent, Adler's life exhibited an understanding of religion as social utility led by the high ideals men could attain by searching for the right.

Bibliography:

A.   *Creed and Deed: A Series of Discourses* (New York, 1877, 1972); *The Moral Instruction of Children* (New York, 1892); *Life and Destiny* (New York, 1903); *The Religion of Duty* (New York, 1905); *An Ethical Philosophy of Life* (New York, 1918); *The Reconstruction of the Spiritual Ideal* (New York, 1924).
B.   SH 1, 44; NCAB 23, 98; DAB 21, 13–14; UJE 1, 91–92; EJ 2, 276; NYT 26 Apr 1933, 15; Robert S. Guttchen, *Felix Adler* (Boston, 1974); Benny Kraut, *From Reform Judaism to Ethical Culture: The Religious Evolution of Felix Adler* (Cincinnati, 1979); Horace L. Friess, *Felix Adler and Ethical Culture: Memories and Studies* (New York, 1981).

AINSLIE, Peter (3 June 1867, Dunnsville, VA—23 February 1934, Baltimore, MD). *Education*: studied at Transylvania Coll., 1886–89. *Career*: minister, Calhoun Street Christian Church (later, Fulton Street Christian Temple), Baltimore, MD, 1891–1934; editor, *Christian Union Quarterly*, 1911–34.

Son and grandson to preachers with whom he shared the same name, Ainslie decided on a ministerial career while still a youth. Ill health caused him to foreshorten his studies, but this did not prevent his ordination in the Disciples of Christ. In his early professional years he strove to expand activities in his denomination. During his decades of work in Baltimore he erected a new church building at a new site and established eight branches or missionary stations in the metropolitan area. Disciples ideology has always been concerned about ecumenical outreach, and though he continued to acknowledge his denominational affiliation, Ainslie moved increasingly within this perspective to a more inclusive viewpoint. As early as 1910 he startled some conference members when he called for a world fellowship of all Christians. The following year he established the *Christian Union Quarterly*, which he edited until his death as a means of furthering ecumenical concerns. By 1924 he persuaded congregants to adopt a policy of open membership in his local church, a tangible affirmation of the equality of all Christians before God.

Local changes had their place, but Ainslie knew that more comprehensive measures were needed to achieve a lasting reunion among churches. As early as 1910 he inaugurated a fifteen-year presidency of the Council on Christian Union of the Disciples of Christ, a group which in 1916 became the Association for the Promotion of Christian Unity. As faithful delegate to conferences that eventually resulted in the World Council of Churches, he attended ecumenical discussions at Constance (1914), The Hague (1919), Geneva (1920), Copenhagen (1922), Stockholm (1925), and Lausanne (1927). During World War I he served on Andrew Carnegie's Church Peace Union and thereafter became an administrator of the World Alliance for Promoting International Friendship Through the Churches. An opponent of war, Ainslie also called for conciliation between Christians and Jews in this country plus better relations between black and white segments of the population. Such ideas warranted his election in 1927 as president of the Christian Unity League for Equality and Brotherhood. Throughout this full and active life he also managed to lecture widely and write a dozen books while fulfilling pastoral responsibilities for more than four decades.

Bibliography:

A.   *Plain Talks to Young Men on Vital Issues* (St. Louis, 1897); *Studies in the Old Testament* (St. Louis, 1907); *The Message of the Disciples for the Union of the Church, including their Origin and History* (New York, 1913); *Working with God; or, The Story of a Twenty-five Year Pastorate in Baltimore* (St. Louis, 1917); *The Scandal of Christianity* (New York, 1929); *Some Experiments in Living* (New York, 1933).

B.   DAB supp. 1, 15–16; Finis S. Idleman, *Peter Ainslie: Ambassador of Good Will* (Chicago, 1941).

ALBRIGHT, Jacob (1 May 1759, Montgomery County, PA—18 May 1808. Lebanon County, PA). *Career*: farmer and tile maker, 1785–96; itinerant Methodist exhorter in PA, MD and VA, 1796–1803; itinerant minister in PA. 1803–08; bishop, Evangelical Association, 1807–08.

Having no formal education, Albright (originally Albrecht) learned his father's craft of making bricks and supported himself for life with that trade. He had been baptized in the Lutheran church but showed no serious concern regarding spiritual matters until the deaths of several children around 1780. Thus softened by grief, he became aware of his own sinfulness, a condition that in turn effected a change of heart. On realizing how forgiveness was his through faith, he claimed in later sermons that all former anguish receded as peace flooded into his newborn soul. Experience of this sort convinced Albright there was something lacking in the customary practices of Lutheranism, and he began attending Methodist classes at a neighbor's home. Slowly he adopted Methodist doctrine as his own, receiving a license by 1796 to spread that emphasis among German-speaking villages down the Shenandoah valley. He delivered his simple message wherever opportunity allowed, urging listeners in school-houses, mills, general stores, and private houses to accept the salvation that yielded a Christian witness of virtual perfection. Repentance, voluntary conversion, and the duty of following a sanctified life—this was the gospel he preached to share with others the blessing made so forcible in his own experience.

Pointing out individual sin was one thing, but criticizing the lethargy or permissive moral standards of local churches was quite another. Albright viewed his early preaching as supplementary to that of ordained ministers; in time he found it both natural and necessary to form independent units for the mutual edification of his scattered followers. This caused clergymen from Reformation traditions to denounce him as a false prophet, a charge occasionally touching off mob violence. But by 1803, several evangelical gatherings grew strong enough to comprise an assembly of German Methodists. In that year Albright was declared their ordained pastor with appointive power over preaching circuits. Apparently such action did not strain relations with leaders of the larger Methodist church because the German minister never withdrew from the parent body, nor was his license revoked by it. Still, language was an obstacle to full cooperation. *Francis Asbury was opposed to the use of German because he thought it would soon die out; Albright knew it to be the only means of reaching most inhabitants in his region. So without any thought of starting a new denomination, the first annual conference of what came to be known as the Evangelical Church was held in 1807—Wesleyan in doctrine and polity, German in language and culture. Albright, the chief figure behind its formation, was elected first bishop. Though death occurred shortly thereafter, survivors following his example soon placed incipient sectarians on a solid denominational footing.

Bibliography:

B.   SH 1, 111; NCAB 11, 114; DAB 1, 136–37; NCE 1, 266; Reuben Yeakel, *Albright and his Co-Laborers* (Harrisburg, PA, 1877); Robert S. Wilson, *Jacob Albright: The Evangelical Pioneer* (Myerstown, PA, 1940).

ALBRIGHT, William Foxwell (24 May 1891, Coquimbo, Chile—19 September 1971, Baltimore, MD). *Education*: B.A., Upper Iowa Univ., 1912; Ph.D., Johns Hopkins Univ., 1916. *Career*: acting and then formal director, American Schools of Oriental Research, Jerusalem, 1920–29 and 1933–36; professor of Semitic Languages, Johns Hopkins Univ., 1929–58; professor emeritus, 1958–71.

Born to Methodist missionary parents, Albright matured in austere physical surroundings after the family returned to this country. Hardships could not deter his will to learn, however, and by dint of talent, discipline, and stubborn effort he became proficient in ancient languages and history. In the year he earned his academic degree he was also drafted and sent to Palestine to perform ''limited service'' in the U.S. Army. He remained there after the armistice, studying on a fellowship in 1919, and his career began to take an entirely new direction. Instead of concentrating on Hebrew and Arabic, he slowly moved into the field of archaeology and directed excavation projects with systematic procedures rarely used before his time. Albright placed archaeological study of the Holy Land on a new footing, causing observers to respect it as a seriously empirical science. In addition to supervising expeditions during the 1920s, he was a member of the University of California's exploration of Sinai (1947–48) and chief archaeologist on the South Arabian Expedition (1950–51).

At Johns Hopkins University Albright created the dominant school of Old Testament scholarship in America, an eminence maintained for decades. More

than simply reporting the results of excavations, he revolutionized the understanding of biblical writings by synthesizing textual references to reliably dated
artifacts. His work helped place biblical literature in cultural settings that lent
deeper significance to ideas thus placed in context. Always interested in how
additional discoveries could enrich knowledge of religious texts, he was one of
the first scholars to write extensively on the Dead Sea Scrolls in 1947. Over the
course of his life he produced more than eight hundred books and articles on
the ways archaeological data corrected and confirmed ideas about the Bible.
Among membership in dozens of learned societies, Albright held high office in
the American Oriental Society, the International Congress of Orientalists, the
Archeological Institute of America, the International Organization of Old Testament Scholars, and the Society of Biblical Literature. Degrees conferred by a
score of universities and fellowships in European institutes further substantiate
the importance of this individual who was pivotal in making biblical archaeology
a systematic discipline.

Bibliography:

A.   *Excavations and Results at Tell el-Ful* (New Haven, 1924); *The Archaeology of
Palestine and the Bible* (New York, 1932); *From the Stone Age to Christianity: Mon-
otheism and the Historical Process* (Baltimore, 1940); *Archaeology and the Religion of
Israel* (Baltimore, 1942); *The Bible after Twenty Years of Archeology, 1932–1952* (Pitts-
burgh, 1954); *History, Archeology and Christian Humanism* (New York, 1964).
B.   NCAB 56, 221–23; NYT 20 Sep 1971, 28.

ALEXANDER, Archibald (17 April 1772, Rockbridge County, VA—22 October 1851, Princeton, NJ). *Education*: studied theology with William Graham,
Lexington, VA, 1789–91. *Career*: itinerant missionary for the Synod of VA,
1792–94; minister, Briery, VA, 1794–98; president, Hampden-Sydney Coll.,
1796–1806; minister, Third Presbyterian Church, Philadelphia, 1806–12; professor of Didactic and Polemic Theology, Princeton Sem., 1812–51.

Not openly irreligious nor preternaturally pious, Alexander grew up in the
austere habits of frontier life with the slight formal education it afforded. At the
age of seventeen he experienced conversion true to revivalistic form, an indication
that Awakening sympathies did not cease to exist in western Virginia after mid-
century. He pursued studies with his mentor at Liberty Hall Academy (now
Washington and Lee University), preparing with the means available for a ministry that covered almost sixty years. The great talent he brought to the task was
not scholarship, however, but evangelical zeal couched in a direct, effective
preaching style. Even after he was called from early pastorates to a college
presidency, preaching continued to receive most of his attention. By 1806, he
accepted the invitation to head one of the four Presbyterian churches in Philadelphia, ministering to Scotch-Irish parishioners employed mostly in the city's
shipyards. Alexander became a pioneer in using laymen for city missions. By
1808, he formed an Evangelical Society, which directed efforts to spend Sunday

evenings in classes and prayer groups among the poor. Those activities and extemporaneous speaking of extraordinary power quickly made him a valuable fixture in the metropolis, permanent seat of his denomination's General Assembly.

Theological education traditionally consisted of private tutelage under an ordained minister for a time sufficient to pass examination for licensing. During an extended tour (1801) of New England, Alexander noticed how such an uncoordinated training system had produced theological diversity to the point of confusion, not to mention serious error. The question of improving educational methods had been debated by Presbyterians in their national meetings since 1805, when Congregationalists established the first distinct seminary in this country. All agreed that reading with individual pastors was an inadequate preparation for future ministers, but few suggested a definite remedy. In 1808, Alexander called for several schools to provide men adequately trained for their tasks as leaders in church and society. Others, including *Samuel Miller, echoed his plea, and Princeton Theological Seminary emerged slowly (1812) after years of committee work. Alexander was elected its first professor, teaching the entire course of study until Miller joined him as colleague in December of 1813. For over three decades, Alexander made Princeton the source of Presbyterian orthodoxy. His work together with that of student *Charles Hodge and their two sons perpetuated the view of sound, rationally defended Christian beliefs for generations. Theological conservatism earmarked part of his impact on the nineteenth century, but more personal gifts of spiritual counseling, eloquent preaching and pastoral wisdom survived in numbers of young men whose lives he shaped.

Bibliography:

A.   *A Brief Outline of the Evidences of the Christian Religion* (Princeton, 1825); *The Canon of the Old and New Testaments Ascertained* (Princeton, 1826); *Evidences of the Authenticity, Inspiration and Canonical Authority of the Holy Scriptures* (Philadelphia, 1836; New York, 1972); *Biographical Sketches of the Founder and Principal Alumni of the Log College* (Princeton, 1845); *A History of the Israelitish Nation* (Philadelphia, 1852); *Outlines of Moral Science* (New York, 1852).

B.   AAP 3, 612–26; SH 1, 121–22; NCAB 2, 22; DAB 1, 162–63; NCE 1, 299; James W. Alexander, *The Life of Archibald Alexander* (New York, 1854).

ALLEN, Ethan (21 January 1738, Litchfield, CT—12 February 1789, Burlington, VT).

Economic circumstances deprived Allen of formal schooling, but he maintained a lively interest in philosophical questions and published toward the end of his life a controversial treatise on religion. His fame rests largely on military accomplishment, primarily the capture of Fort Ticonderoga for the Continental Army in 1775. Revolutionary politics led directly to radical religious views in Allen's case, he exemplified the dissatisfaction many citizens felt regarding authoritarian structures. Beginning as an Arminian opponent of Calvinism, he gradually developed a militant anti-Christian position that criticized established beliefs in uncompromising language. He wanted to shatter the smug platitudes of Congregationalism, deflating both the superstitious message and personal arrogance found among clerics in his region. In the name of reason, he gibed at the idea of biblical inspiration; miracles, revelation, or atonement were foreign to cycles of nature as he discerned them. His book on reason and faith, a compilation of manuscripts written over decades, denounced reliance on the Bible, orthodox churches, and the influence ministers had customarily exerted in American society.

Affirmations of intellectual liberty and rational inquiry predominated on the positive side of Allen's views. He thought that aspects of God were disclosed to men as they correctly interpreted the natural order. Harmony in nature evidenced a regulating agent who provided beneficial environments for all creatures. Knowledge of that intricate universe and man's moral freedom in it led Allen to endorse a vaguely described universalism as the general character of his reasonable religion. But he was more rebel than builder. He could detect weaknesses in current beliefs more easily than clarify an alternative position. The categories of God's perfections and human immortality constantly intrigued him, but "Christian" was a name he avoided, while "deist" left him unsure as well. His work (most of it accidently destroyed in a printer's shop fire) was disavowed by many deists who wished to retain biblical elements in their systems. Of course for those relying fully on revelation, he became a target for all they considered heretical and profane. While his struggle for rational ideals did not materially affect the thought or behavior of most Americans, it symbolized a growing edge of free thought that resisted the political and intellectual control wielded by Christian churches in New England.

Bibliography:

A. *Reason the Only Oracle of Man; Or, A Compenduous System of Natural Religion* (Bennington, VT, 1785).

B. NCAB 1, 45–47; DAB 1, 188–89; Hugh Moore, *Memoir of Col. Ethan Allen* (New York, 1892); John Pell, *Ethan Allen* (Boston, 1929); Stewart H. Holbrook, *Ethan Allen* (New York, 1940); Charles A. Jellison, *Ethan Allen: Frontier Rebel* (Syracuse, NY, 1969).

ALLEN, Richard (14 February 1760, Philadelphia, PA—26 March 1831, Philadelphia, PA). *Career*: various jobs and itinerant preaching in DE, MD, PA and NJ, 1781–86; businessman and lay preacher, Philadelphia, 1786–99; deacon, Bethel Church, Philadelphia, 1799–1816; Bishop, African Methodist Episcopal Church, 1816–31.

As one born into slavery and released (probably 1781) to purchase his freedom, Allen knew from first-hand experience the difficulties facing Negroes who tried to become effective participants in American society. He very early associated freedom with the evangelical message of Methodism and stressed religion as the basic impetus for his many contributions to the welfare of black parishioners and community affairs. He worked at various occupations to support a large family, but that did not distract him from the main task of preaching, using St. George's Church in Philadelphia as headquarters for his itinerancy. In 1787, Allen and other black members left that church because of discrimination at the hands of white coreligionists who did not accept them as equals. For several years, he conducted services wherever he could, often under the auspices of the Free African Society. That organization had too many Quaker tendencies for Allen, however, and despite much opposition he was the primary agent in founding Bethel Church, dedicated by *Francis Asbury in 1794, chartered two years later and receiving final legal recognition in 1816. In the latter year, Bethel hosted the first General Conference of sixteen black congregations, which consecrated Allen as the first bishop of the first racially distinct denomination in this country—the African Methodist Episcopal (AME) Church.

Education, economy, and union were the keys to success in any long-range efforts among blacks for self-determination. Allen knew this and concentrated his efforts in areas that could foster moral discipline and cohesion among his people. Some observers assumed that he was more interested in consolidating his own power than in uniting black Methodism, though this was not always the case. The bishop's aggressive dedication to a vision often made it difficult to work with him, and *James Varick for one found it necessary to set up Methodist Zion churches as alternative structures. But Allen learned from mistakes and mellowed. A strong vanguard of ministers emerged from small, lower income constituencies, and the AME organization expanded its base as a stable denomination. It served as the fundamental agency utilized by Blacks for economic cooperation and social welfare, ranging from the charitable distribution of food and clothing to hiding runaway slaves. Allen was primarily concerned with the spiritual development of those under his care, but he did not divorce such priorities from the totality of black needs, as witness his vigorous opposition to the American Colonization Society. By 1830, the AME Church had missions in Canada, Haiti, and West Africa; but it exerted a much greater impact at home on the growing community of freedmen in northern states. The bishop's labors as preacher, disciplinarian, and mediator built it into a striking example of theological and institutional coherence under exclusively black leadership.

Bibliography:

A. *The Life, Experience and Gospel Labors of the Rt. Rev. Richard Allen, Written by Himself* (Philadelphia, 1793 and many subsequent editions to 1960).

B. NCAB 13, 200–01; DAB 1, 204–05; Charles H. Wesley, *Richard Allen: Apostle of Freedom* (Washington, 1935); Marcia M. Mathews, *Richard Allen* (Baltimore, 1963); Carol V. R. George, *Segregated Sabbaths: Richard Allen and the Emergence of Independent Black Churches* (New York, 1973); E. Curtis Alexander, *Richard Allen: The First Exemplar of African American Education* (New York, 1985).

ALTHAM, John (1589, Warwickshire?, England—5 November 1640, St. Mary's City, MD).

There is little exact information about Altham's early life, even regarding his surname, as references often called him Gravener. He is thought to have entered the Society of Jesus in 1623 and after education on the Continent returned to England as a secret missionary in Devon. Part of the earliest contingent of Maryland settlers, he was appointed to that field by Jesuit superiors who responded to an appeal from the territory's proprietor, *Cecilius Calvert. Altham, along with *Andrew White and one lay brother, accompanied the first two shiploads of colonists, which reached the New World in 1634. He helped explore the Chesapeake Bay and Potomac estuary, ministering to varied needs as plantations slowly developed in tidewater sections of the colony. Parochial responsibilities to Catholic residents in the fort known as St. Mary's City occupied part of his time, but additional interests included the conversion of Protestants and evangelical work among native Indians. Missionary journeys to neighboring tribes combined with constant witness amid the English-speaking population to produce a life of both physical hardship and spiritual rewards. He was particularly successful in establishing Catholicism on Kent Island, an area of strategic location claimed by authorities in Virginia as well as Maryland. His years of sacrifice had just begun to yield converts in encouraging numbers when he died of yellow fever.

Bibliography:

B.   DAB 1, 231–32.

AMES, Edward Scribner (21 April 1870, Eau Claire, WI—29 June 1958, Chicago, IL), *Education:* B.A., M.A., Drake Univ., 1889, 1891; B.D., Yale Div. Sch., 1892; postgraduate study, Yale Univ., 1892–94; Ph.D., Univ. of Chicago, 1895. *Career:* professor of Philosophy and Education, Butler Coll., 1897–1900; at various ranks, professor of Philosophy, Univ. of Chicago, 1900–35; minister, Hyde Park (later University) Church of the Disciples, Chicago, 1900–40; editor, *The Scroll,* 1925–51; dean, Disciples Divinity House, 1927–45; active retirement, 1945–58.

Though his intellectual pilgrimage occasioned many ideological changes, Ames always held that his psychology of religion corresponded to basic attitudes in the denomination he served, the Disciples of Christ. His attempts to provide an interpretation of religious values congruent with modern currents of scientific thinking still protested against dogmatic scholasticism and sectarian divisions. In traditional Disciple style, he sought to unite believers by discarding creeds, encouraging individual liberty, and emphasizing religious experience as necessary for practical ethical living. As minister for four decades, college professor, and widely read philosopher, Ames also contributed in no small measure to the spread of modernistic theology in the first third of the twentieth century. He was influenced by reading *William James, developing his approach on the shared conviction that psychology was the conditioning science by which all branches of theology had to be amended. Beginning with that concentration on an empirical understanding of religious faith, Ames went on to apply it in concrete situations. Within a context of demonstrably beneficient values, meaning could then be given to old doctrinal labels. He found salvation to be ethical, a life process that signifies realization of the soul's natural powers. Heaven was participation in this divine realization here and now; hell was simple failure, suffering degrees of ignorance and perverted desires. Christians could manifest faith by recognizing the ideal human achievement in Christ, adjusting subsequent efforts through repentance in approximating that ideal. Such practical considerations of personal religious affirmation left little room for thoughts about trinity, virgin birth, miracles, substitutionary atonement, or an afterlife.

Psychology gave Ames the means of avoiding doctrinal mazes, emphasizing instead those sources that gave men strength and guidance for worthwhile living. An appreciation of such values and a willingness to work for them were sufficient tokens of the religious life. Ames' empirical, pragmatic approach was grounded on the view that the only reality men ever know is that which comes through the experience of living. In his version of idealistic humanism, doctrinal categories were understood in terms of their function in the experience of human life. The soul was the qualitative character of one's personality. God was not an objective entity in space-time, but rather something known through discerning the values of life implemented in the social process. Common elements of human decency such as health, security, friendship, knowledge, justice, beauty, and the promise of a better society for future generations were derived from the never-ending search for real and enduring values. His focus on religion as human striving—a present, active, and indeed divine objective—yielded the conclusion that enough good remained in it to make it the pursuit worth human affirmation.

Bibliography:

A. *The Psychology of Religious Experience* (Boston, 1910); *The Divinity of Christ* (Chicago, 1911); *The Higher Individualism* (New York, 1915); *The New Orthodoxy* (Chicago, 1918); *Religion* (New York, 1929); *Letters to God and the Devil* (New York, 1933).

B. Van M. Ames (ed.), *Beyond Theology: The Autobiography of Edward Scribner Ames* (Chicago, 1959).

ANDREW, James Osgood (3 May 1794, Wilkes County, GA—2 March 1871, Mobile, AL). *Career*: itinerant Methodist minister in GA and SC, 1813–16; minister at Wilmington, NC, 1817–20, Augusta, GA, 1820–21, Savannah, GA, 1822–23, Charleston, SC, 1824–28, and Greensborough-Athens, GA, 1829–32; bishop of the Methodist Episcopal Church, 1832–46; bishop of the Methodist Episcopal Church, South, 1846–66; retirement, 1866–71.

A raw backwoods boy with meager educational attainments, Andrew exhibited leadership qualities at an early age. He was licensed to preach at eighteen and within ten years became Presiding Elder in one of the largest districts of southern Methodism. Neither his preaching nor writing was particularly outstanding; the work of pastoral care and sound advice to other ministers were areas where he made the greatest contributions. As bishop he was constantly on the move, presiding at quarterly meetings and nurturing the steady maturation of pastors who in turn applied greater wisdom to their congregations. For years he conducted visitations over half the country, from Baltimore to Martha's Chapel in east Texas. He had little use for agitators, northern or southern, in religion or politics. His primary concern was the salvation of souls and providing adequate ministerial care for Christian living in the framework of Methodist discipline. Participation in the board of trustees for Emory College (opened 1839) was another indication of those evangelical objectives. Ecclesiastical strife was painful to him and, though he was later charged with dividing the church, Andrew sacrificed himself for decades in service to a denomination which was the fastest growing in the nation.

The obstacle to national service was slavery; try as he might, Andrew could not avoid it. When his first wife died (1842), two servants became his property, but he took steps to resettle or free them in another state. Two years later the problem reappeared because his second wife owned a number of slaves, which also belonged to the bishop by right of common property. Northern Methodists marshaled enough anti-slavery sentiment at the General Conference in 1844 to force the issue. They passed a resolution (110 to 68) demanding that Andrew stop exercising episcopal functions until his connection with slavery ended. Southern delegates refused to let their section of the church be controlled by outside spokesmen. They admitted slavery was a moral evil but claimed that an abolitionist stance would ruin their influence with slaveholders and waste whatever good they had begun with the slave population. So that sectional bloc met in 1845, with Andrew as one of the two bishops presiding, to approve a Plan of Separation designating conferences in slave states an independent body. Episcopal work in the new denomination continued much the same as in the old. A moderate in all things, Andrew would not defend slavery or espouse abolition, and he watched helplessly as fire-eating politicians inched the nation closer to war. When the South was invaded, he encouraged (but not heartily) the Confederacy to defend itself in a just cause. His main task during wartime was to remind ministers that salvation and the care of parishioners still had top priority. Hampered by partial paralysis after 1863, he received superannuated status three years later, saddened toward the end by knowledge that he could not respond to duty as he had for so long.

Bibliography:

A. *Family Government: A Treatise on Conjugal, Parental, Filial and Other Duties,* (Charleston, SC, 1847 and many subsequent editions); *Miscellanies* (Louisville, KY, 1854).

B. SH 1, 172; NCAB 1, 521; DAB 1, 277–79; NYT 5 Mar 1871, 5; George G. Smith, *The Life and Letters of James Osgood Andrew* (Nashville, 1882).

ARMSTRONG, Samuel Chapman (30 January 1839, Hawaiian Islands—11 May 1893, Hampton, VA). *Education*: B.A., Williams Coll., 1862. *Career*: officer, Union Army, 1862–65; agent, Freedmen's Bureau, 1866–72; instructor, Hampton Institute, 1868–93.

A son of missionary parents, born on the Island of Maui, Armstrong was subject to continuing influences of Christian nurture. After attending Oahu College for two years he finished his education in New England where *Mark Hopkins inspired him with high ideals. The Civil War was raging when he graduated, and even though he was not an American citizen, Armstrong enlisted with most of his classmates in the northern army. Leadership qualities were quickly noticed as the young officer moved from captain to colonel, experiencing a time of capture and parole in the process. Black soldiers were being organized into separate units by 1863, and Armstrong was given the unpopular assignment of commanding one of them. As colonel of the Ninth Colored Regiment he soon came to admire the capacity of such men. They in turn respected his discipline which gave them self-respect and courage enough to face stiff combat around Petersburg, Virginia. When the war ended, Armstrong received brevet rank as brigadier general; his Negro troops then saw action along the Mexican border, but he was not interested in warfare that lacked a clear humanitarian purpose.

In Armstrong's view, the war had been fought to free human beings from slavery; all his later work centered on efforts to improve the quality of life for black men and women so recently made American citizens. He worked for the Freedmen's Bureau which tried to supply rudiments of needed food, jobs, medicine, and education for thousands of ex-slaves set adrift in the South. Though he was not overly admiring of frequent church attendance or the frills of worship services, he made a lasting contribution by bringing religious principles to bear on the lives of those in his charge. "The General," as others called him, was very much interested in developing energetic Christian character in young black Americans who could then lead their own people to embody moral virtues in private and public life. In 1867, he approached the American Missionary Association for aid, which allowed the Hampton Normal and Industrial Institute for Negroes to begin classes a year later. Mental and manual training was combined to help students see the value of honest labor while giving them profitable skills for later employment. Armstrong spent two-thirds of his time away from the school in search of funds, but as a teacher he continually emphasized the complementary virtues of industry and learning. His efforts on their behalf allowed many black Americans the opportunity to acquire confidence in themselves while they formed habits in keeping with Protestant expectations of moral development. After 1891, the General was incapacitated by strokes, but he worked as much as possible for a people whose future seemed full of promise.

Bibliography:

B.   NCAB 38, 427–28; DAB 1, 359–60; NYT 12 May 1893, 6; Edith A. Talbot, *Samuel Chapman Armstrong* (New York, 1904).

ASBURY, Francis (20 August 1745, near Hamstead Bridge, England—31 March 1816, Spotsylvania, VA). *Career*: lay preacher and blacksmith, 1763–66; itinerant minister in England, 1766–71; itinerant minister (general assistant after 1772), American colonies, 1771–84; superintendent (bishop after 1787), American Methodist Church, 1784–1816.

Apprentice blacksmiths rarely become bishops, but it was not without reason that Asbury rose to virtually apostolic stature as leader of America's first independent church. His indefatigable ministry extended over forty-five years and stamped Methodism with evangelical characteristics discernible more than a century later. As armed conflict loomed in the Revolutionary period, Methodists were generally suspect because of their founder's political sympathies. Despite that, Asbury was the only one of Wesley's appointees who remained in the country, albeit sometimes in hiding. Travel was restricted, but as a non-combatant he continued to preach among local meetings in Delaware and Maryland. By the time political separation was recognized, Asbury had consolidated his leadership of most Methodists, even on the point that Anglican priests or those similarly ordained could rightly administer the sacraments. In 1784 *Thomas Coke arrived from England with powers to provide such ordination. Asbury insisted that lay preachers meet the same year to discuss future plans, and the Christmas Conference at Baltimore was largely the result of his efforts. Sixty men convened and adopted an episcopal polity with elders and deacons, the discipline, liturgy and hymns of English Methodism, and, for doctrine, Wesley's twenty-four articles of religion. They also decided unanimously to elect Asbury and Coke as superintendents, a title that Asbury soon changed to bishop. Even though Wesley deplored the name, Asbury used the office to exercise benevolent despotism in building American Methodism into the most efficient religious organization on the continent. As the Episcopal church declined, the Methodist bishop's forces exerted themselves and inaugurated a season of extraordinary growth.

Bad food, worse roads, no comforts of home, exposure to dangers of health and physical safety—in enduring all these, Asbury demanded no more sacrifices of his clergymen than he did of himself. A bishop on horseback, he exemplified the itinerant ministry, which he saw as crucial in reaching scattered pioneers in addition to those in more densely populated areas. Circuit-riding was as much the key to Methodist success as their gospel of free grace. Asbury traveled incessantly to preach that gospel, covering an estimated 300,000 miles and delivering approximately 16,500 sermons. He was not known for stirring eloquence, but the compelling zeal with which he spoke had its effect. Resourceful in debate and inured to harsh conditions, he blanketed the seaboard, visiting preachers and laymen witnessing in taverns, jails, or homes as chance offered. An early advocate of camp meetings, he eagerly supported revivals as a means of evangelical outreach. More than 4,000 preachers received ordination from his hands, and he presided over 224 separate annual conferences. His health was always precarious, and waning strength forced him to accept an associate bishop.

In 1808 *William McKendree became what Asbury always called his assistant. Still he followed a daily regimen that would have consumed a lesser man, and death came while fulfilling missionary labors as duty defined them.

Bibliography:

A.   *The Doctrines and Discipline of the Methodist Episcopal Church in America With Explanatory Notes by Thomas Coke and Francis Asbury* (Philadelphia, 1789); *The Journal and Letters of Francis Asbury*, 3 vols. (New York, 1852); ed. Elmer T. Clark, J. Manning Potts, and Jacob S. Payton (Nashville, 1958).

B.   AAP 7, 13–28; SH 1, 308–09; NCAB 6, 293–95; DAB 1, 379–83; NCE 1, 929; George G. Smith, *Life and Labors of Francis Asbury* (Nashville, 1898); Ezra S. Tipple, *Francis Asbury: The Prophet of the Long Road* (New York, 1916); Herbert Asbury, *A Methodist Saint: The Life of Bishop Asbury* (New York, 1927); William L. Duren, *Francis Asbury: Founder of American Methodism* (New York, 1928); L. C. Rudolph, *Francis Asbury* (Nashville, 1966).

B

BABCOCK, Rufus (18 September 1798, Colebrook, CT—4 May 1875, Salem, MA). *Education*: B.A., Brown Univ., 1821; studied theology with William Staughton, Washington D.C., 1821–23. *Career*: tutor, Columbian Coll., 1821–23; minister, Poughkeepsie, NY, 1823–26; associate minister, First Baptist Church, Salem, MA, 1826–33; president, Waterville Coll., 1833–36; minister, Spruce Street Baptist Church, Philadelphia, 1836–40; minister, Poughkeepsie, NY, New Bedford, MA, and Paterson, NJ, 1840–75.

After growing up as the son of a Baptist minister and attending that denomination's largest school, Babcock, not unnaturally, entered clerical service in the same ecclesiastical tradition. Through the years he preached at several important churches and became second president of what is now known as Colby College, pursuing teaching responsibilities with great energy until poor health forced him to resign. Thereafter he proved a valued leader in denominational affairs, providing guidance as increased membership made Baptists a body whose proportions and significance were nationally recognized. By 1841, he founded (and edited until 1845) the *Baptist Memorial*, a monthly periodical that fostered a sense of denominational heritage by means of historical sketches as well as current religious news. He was also president for many years of the Baptist Publication Society and served as district secretary for that agency in Philadelphia. In larger contexts, he bridged the gap between strictly sectarian concerns and interdenominational cooperation in areas of common interest. By personal example and frequent exhortation, he insisted that churches of his persuasion shared basic goals with other denominations. Babcock served three terms as corresponding secretary of the American and Foreign Bible Society, an office that involved extensive traveling to solicit popular support. For some time, he held a similar position in the American Sunday School Union, stressing again common objectives to be secured through voluntary cooperation of local churches. Thus he signified increased acculturation among Baptists, and a gradual development of attitudes away from sectarian independence toward greater participation in mainstream evangelical Protestantism.

Bibliography:

A. *Tales of Truth for the Young* (Philadelphia, 1837, 1846); *The Emigrant's Mother* (New York, 1859); he edited but was virtual author of *Forty Years of Pioneer Life: Memoir of John Mason Peck* (Philadelphia, 1864; Carbondale, IL, 1965).
   B.   NCAB 8, 405.

BACKUS, Isaac (9 January 1724, Norwich, CT—20 November 1806, Middleborough, MA). *Career*: Congregationalist minister, Middleborough, MA 1748–56; Baptist minister, Middleborough, MA, 1756–1806.

As a Connecticut farmboy with no formal schooling, Backus did not question the Standing Order, which supported only Congregational churches through taxation. He had been baptized as an infant into one such church, but by 1741 a dramatic conversion experience caused him to change his views along both theological and ecclesiastical lines. "New Light" filled his soul, and the importance of that personal event was so central to identity as a Christian that he agreed with others who restricted church membership to participants in similar conversions. For the better part of eighty years, it had been the practice of New England churches to baptize the children of parents who were not themselves full communicants. In the flush of enthusiasm about personal religious experience during the First Great Awakening, many began to reject the old half-way covenant and insist on a single standard for membership. The end result of this new reformation was schism, and by 1745 the latter-day puritans emerged as "Separates," claiming to be not a new sect but a pure form of the established church. Lawful associations of churches thought such precipitate action dangerous to the Standing Order and sought to repress sectarianism for the good of society. Backus was among those subject to fines or imprisonment for daring to challenge orthodox practices. Thus he learned an early lesson about the pressure an ecclesiastical body could apply through civil magistrates to enforce its own view of proper ecclesiology.

Political power could not dissipate the energy of separatist Congregationalism, and Backus spent years laboring for its growth. The whole question of "believer's baptism" troubled him, however, and by 1751 he came slowly to the conclusion that infant baptism had no scriptural warrant and that immersion was the proper mode for consenting adults. After much parish dissension and sharp controversy, he openly adopted Baptist principles, leading a remnant of his congregation to form another unit in that denomination. Baptists had no legal place in the New England scheme of things. For the next half century, Backus worked to rectify that situation, eventually winning recognition as one of the chief protagonists of religious liberty in colonial America. He objected to tax-supported churches and chafed under the system of certification whereby Baptists could have their ministerial rates remitted. Distinguishing between freedom and mere toleration, he argued in pamphlets, reports, and petitions that the purity of religion must be safeguarded by separating churches entirely from state control. As spokesman for Massachusetts Baptists, he presented a memorial in 1774 to the First Continental Congress, asking for a declaration of full religious liberty. He also served as a delegate in 1780 to draft a state constitution, defending as vigorously as ever the independence of local churches on grounds of theological rectitude, not efficient civil government. Backus ended his days as an elder statesman who protested against civil control of religion until the end, just a few decades before the dream became a statutory reality at long last in Massachusetts.

Bibliography:

A.   *The Bond-woman and the Free* (Boston, 1756); *A Seasonable Plea for Liberty of Conscience* (Boston, 1770); *An Appeal to the Public for Religious Liberty Against the Oppression of the Present Day* (Boston, 1773); *A History of New England, with Particular Reference to . . . Baptists*, 3 vols. (Boston and Providence, 1777–96; rev. ed. Newton MA, 1871; New York, 1969); *Government and Liberty Described and Ecclesiastical Tyranny Exposed* (Boston, 1778); *Truth is Great and Will Prevail* (Boston, 1781).

B.   AAP 6, 54–58; NCAB 7, 223; DAB 1, 468–72; Alvah Hovey, *Memoir of the Life and Times of the Rev. Isaac Backus* (Boston, 1859); Thomas B. Maston, *Isaac Backus: Pioneer of Religious Liberty* (Rochester NY, 1962); William G. McLoughlin, *Isaac Backus and the American Pietistic Tradition* (Boston, 1967); Stanley Grenz, *Isaac Backus: Puritan and Baptist* (Macon, GA, 1983).

BACON, Leonard (19 February 1802, Detroit, MI—24 December 1881, New Haven, CT). *Education*: B.A., Yale Coll., 1820; B.D., Andover Sem., 1823; postgraduate study, Andover, 1823–24. *Career*: minister, First Congregational Church, New Haven, CT, 1824–81; editor, *Independent*, 1848–61; acting professor of Theology and Church History, Yale Div. Sch., 1866–81.

Though Bacon was born the son of a missionary in Old Northwest Territory, his heritage and lifelong concern was New England Congregationalism. As minister of Center Church in New Haven (emeritus after 1866), he exerted great influence on issues in his own denomination and contributed significantly to questions of social reform in the culture at large. He conceived of service in broader social avenues to be an extension of his ministry, working for decades as journalist and public speaker to exert a moral force on the body politic. Of all the issues addressed, none was more important than slavery. Bacon was adamantly opposed to the institution, though he supported neither abolition as a strategy nor its tactics of abuse. He sympathized more with the Colonization Society as a means of ending slavery to the mutual benefit of white and black citizens. Gradual emancipation and transportation of freedmen to Liberia were causes for which he wrote pamphlets, raised funds, and defended in debate. Still, as he sought to avoid recriminations through irenic discussion, he wrote extensively to arouse public opinion from its apathy on the most urgent moral topic of his day. After the Civil War, Bacon lent the weight of his authority to anti-liquor forces in controversies over temperance, but that focus did not achieve the prominence of earlier disputes regarding basic human freedom.

Within church circles Bacon was known as a reconciler and a diplomatic statesman who sought ecclesiastical strength through greater historical self-consciousness. Early in life he had been a partisan of New School theology, but as years passed he belittled the differences between schools of thought. He emphasized the great and acknowledged verities of Christianity rather than disputable formulations; grace, more important than a church or creed, served as mediator through which salvation was made possible. Much of Bacon's diplomatic skill can be understood as a consequence of this tolerant, inclusive view of theologies' witnessing to the same Saviour. But while confessional preferences could be minimized, he did not anticipate the demise of historic denominations. Nonsectarian cooperation should not result in the absorption of any traditional group. In 1801, Presbyterians and Congregationalists had formed a Plan of Union to facilitate their efforts in evangelizing the West. Subsequent events favored a one-sided Presbyterian growth, and many besides Bacon called for a return to more exclusively denominational activities. As chief spokesman for Connecticut churches and senior editor of the new paper championing Congregational independence, the New Haven pastor was long a galvanic presence in denominational affairs. He urged cooperative programs of evangelical reform in American society, but only for those based on autonomous local churches that controlled their own doctrine and chose their arena of moral action.

Bibliography:

A. *A Plea for Africa* (New Haven, 1825); *Thirteen Historical Discourses* (New Haven, 1839); *Slavery Discussed in Occasional Essays* (New York, 1846); *The Genesis of the New England Churches* (New York, 1874; 1972).

B. SH 1, 416; NCAB 1, 176; DAB 1, 479–81; NYT 25 Dec 1881, 9; Theodore D. Bacon, *Leonard Bacon: A Statesman in the Church* (New Haven, 1931).

BAINTON, Roland Herbert (30 March 1894, Ikeston, England—13 February 1984, New Haven, CT). *Education*: B.A., Whitman Coll., 1914; B.D., Yale Div. Sch., 1917; Ph.D., Yale Univ., 1921. *Career*: instructor (1920–23), assistant professor (1923–32), associate professor (1932–36) of Church History, and Titus Street Professor of Ecclesiastical History (1936–62), Yale Univ.; professor emeritus, 1962–84.

As a young immigrant, first to Vancouver and then to the state of Washington, Bainton was greatly affected by the pacifist views of his father, a Congregationalist minister. As a lifelong conscientious objector he served in the Quaker unit of the American Red Cross during World War I, and though he became a Congregationalist clergyman in 1927, he was also an affiliated member of the Society of Friends, his wife's denomination. He served on the American Friends Service Committee during later wars and was a member of the Fellowship of

Reconciliation. In addition to these activities, teaching and writing were the most efficient means by which Bainton made an impact on life around him. He lectured for more than forty years at Yale and spoke to captivated audiences around the world. He published more than thirty books, nineteen of them after retirement, several of which were translated into a dozen languages. Most of his studies centered on the sixteenth and seventeenth centuries, but his topics actually ranged from early Christianity to contemporary times. In all those works he tried to bring the past alive through factual reporting and a sprightly, readable style. Most important he labored to glean fundamental principles from earlier experience in order to enrich modern life with lessons drawn from previous example.

Three basic themes permeate all of Bainton's reflections on what Christianity has to offer modern civilization. The first was peace, seeking freedom from the violence and cruelty of war. He erroneously but emphatically declared that early churches were uniformly pacifist, and therefore the only Christian position regarding modern warfare and nuclear weapons was absolute pacifism. Secondly he championed freedom of thought and speech, lauding the process of open discussion and critical search for truth. Bainton held that all attempts to clarify ideas were signs of a healthy society where diversified debate was preferable to stultifying uniformity. Finally he argued that true Christianity nurtured religious toleration, the freedom to associate with others of like conscience. Oppression in the name of some orthodoxy always proved to be harmful to victims, their persecutors, and the culture which all of them shared. His many appeals for peace and greater understanding for others were motivated by a conviction that the cross and the stake were incompatible, that coercion could never foster genuine spiritual affirmation.

Bibliography:

A.   *Here I Stand: A Life of Martin Luther* (Nashville, 1950); *The Travail of Religious Liberty: Nine Biographical Studies* (Philadelphia, 1951); *The Reformation of the Sixteenth Century* (Boston, 1952); *Christian Attitudes Toward War and Peace: A Historical Survey and Critical Re-evaluation* (New York, 1960); *Erasmus of Christendom* (New York, 1969); *Roly: Chronicle of a Stubborn Non-Conformist*, ed. Ruth C.L. Gritch (New Haven, 1988).

B.   NYT 14 Feb.1984, D26.

BAIRD, Robert (6 October 1798, near Pittsburgh, PA—15 March 1863, Yonkers, NY). *Education:* studied at Washington Coll., 1816–17; B.A., Jefferson Coll., 1818; graduated from Princeton Sem., 1822. *Career:* taught at Princeton Academy, 1822–28; agent of NJ Missionary Society, 1828–29; agent of American Sunday School Union, 1829–34; agent of American and Foreign Christian Union and related organizations, 1834–55, 1861–63.

The combined themes of evangelical missionary work and social service through public information help unify many of the activities that Baird pursued. He founded and was principal of a grammar school for five years after finishing seminary training. As agent for the New Jersey Missionary Society, he cooperated with a program to supply every family in the state with a Bible, and he did much through published suggestions to lay the foundations for a state-supported system of common schools. From 1829 to 1834 he served the American Sunday School Union by traveling through most of the settled areas of the nation, establishing schools and reporting on the religious conditions in each section. Having been ordained a Presbyterian minister in 1828, Baird's activities as spokesman and agent indicate his commitment to religious values that were based on knowledge, training, and well-informed principles.

In 1834 Baird accepted a position from an association that sought to advance the Protestant cause in France. For the next twenty-nine years he toured, wrote, and lectured on behalf of toleration for Protestants, especially in southern European countries. His other major interest was a transatlantic version of the American Temperance Society. He made repeated journeys, including ones to such capitals as Rome, Moscow, and Stockholm, and distributed hundreds of thousands of books in the interests of prohibition. His original agency, the French Association, developed into the Foreign Evangelical Society and then became the American and Foreign Christian Union; Baird was its agent through all those changes, which marked a general drift toward ecumenical cooperation among evangelical denominations. He identified himself as an early advocate of the Evangelical Alliance, frequently attending and addressing those sessions as did *Philip Schaff, another international ecumenist. Altogether he crossed the Atlantic eighteen times and traveled over three hundred thousand miles to further the interests of religious freedom, sobriety, and Protestant evangelicalism.

While Baird promoted various causes like the Sunday School, temperance unions, and Bible distribution in Europe, he was often called upon to answer questions about his native land. By 1840, he began to put such information into book form, and it became one of the most important nineteenth century discussions of religious conditions in the New World. His essentially accurate and comprehensive interpretation of Protestant dominance in American life before the Civil War captured its elemental qualities. The voluntary principle (church support after separation of church and state), evangelical revivalism, social relevance through reform agencies, and sound theological foundations were seen both as positive achievements and the basis for more successes in the future. Baird also reflected largely negative ideas about immigration, slavery and racial tensions, minority groups, and dissent. In these areas too, he drew from a common store of American religious notions, and his articulation of them helped clarify and perpetuate those mental habits far beyond the circumstances that originally formed them.

Bibliography:

A. *A View of the Mississippi Valley* (Philadelphia, 1832); *Histoire des Sociétés de Tempérance des Etats-Unis d'Amérique* (Paris, 1836); *Religion in America* (Edinburgh, 1843; New York, 1844; rev. ed. 1856; New York, 1969; crit. abr. 1970); *Sketches of Protestantism in Italy* (Boston, 1845; 1847); *The Progress and Prospects of Christianity in the United States* (London, 1851).

B.   NCAB 8, 171; DAB 1, 511–12; NYT 17 Mar 1863, 8; Henry M. Baird, *The Life of the Rev. Robert Baird, D.D.* (New York, 1866).

BALLARD, Edna Wheeler (1886, Burlington, IA—10 February 1971, Chicago, IL).

Before the "I Am" movement was inaugurated in the early 1930s, Edna Ballard had already indicated sustained interest in theosophical ideas. Together with her husband *Guy, for whom she left the concert stage in 1916, she explored doctrines of swamis, Rosicrucians, Christian Science, and other sources of the occult. Belief in her husband's spiritual visions came easily; when multitudes of people also showed positive response, she coordinated operations into a well-regulated organization. She and Guy, together with their son Donald, traveled across the country as "accredited messengers" of the Ascended Masters, filling the largest auditoriums of major cities as they lectured on revelations from the transcendental realm. Within the movement she was known as "Lotus," a name derived from one of her previous existences. She was undoubtedly the dominant figure in planning and controlling mass meetings which publicized the new-yet-ancient religion. Small ten-day classes for concentrated study were begun (1934) in larger cities and met with astonishing success. In less than a year, one such gathering at Los Angeles attracted 6,000 students. Between 1935 and 1938, her managerial ability pushed both classes and mass rallies to their apex. Despite mounting criticism from a hostile press, she conducted colorful, elaborately staged sessions which drew capacity crowds and persuaded many that a new age of truth had dawned.

Difficulties in the "I Am" movement rose to crisis proportions in 1939 when Guy Ballard, the original spokesman, died. Most believers had thought that accredited messengers would not die but rather ascend to the level of bliss where Saint Germain, Jesus, and other masters resided without physical disabilities. The movement never recovered from Guy's death, in spite of Edna's reassurances that he had indeed ascended to the plane of incorporeal, luminous consciousness. But virtually insuperable difficulties emerged in 1940 when she and several others were indicted for fraudulent solicitation of funds. After two trials in as many years, she was found guilty on seven counts and forbidden the use of mail service in connection with "I Am" activities; these findings were reversed on final appeal to the Supreme Court in 1946. But court proceedings caused an enormous decline of support among once numerous followers. She continued to head up the organization as before, supervising all the radio programs, bookshops, and study centers through which doctrine was methodically disseminated. As a medium through whom Saint Germain spoke, she transmitted messages in the monthly *Voice of the I Am*. She also helped establish facilities for annual ceremonies at Mount Shasta, site of the movement's earliest revelations. Though badly discredited by lawsuits and attendant publicity, she remained leader of the group and helped keep it alive to the present day.

Bibliography:

A.   Listed as co-author with Guy Ballard: *The Book of David, or "I Am" in the Bible* (Los Angeles, 1937); *Ascended Master Light* (Chicago, 1938); *The "I Am" Discourses* (Chicago, 1949).

BALLARD, Guy Warren (28 July 1878, near Newton, KS—31 December 1939, Los Angeles, CA).

Little is known about Ballard's temporal life except for general knowledge that he traveled the American West in pursuit of various gold mine and oil well schemes. But adherents of his teachings were not interested in his personal background because they considered him a transmitter of ancient truths unaffected by individual circumstances. In 1930 he claimed to have experienced a vision near Mount Shasta in northern California; the aftermath of that event produced a remarkably popular religious phenomenon that flourished for over a decade and survives today with membership of more modest proportions. The content of his initial revelation came from Saint Germain, an eighteenth-century historical figure commonly referred to in theosophical groups; on the transcendental level, he was the spiritual master who gave Ballard insight into primeval wisdom. Ballard in turn unveiled those mysteries by publishing highly readable volumes on the subject and thus launched the "I Am" movement. In a gnostic perspective, he taught that true faith calls believers away from the chains of the physical world. The "I Am Presence" resides above all lesser existence. Beneath that level of pure Being and yet beyond mere human life is a realm of "Ascended Masters" who had been human at one time but transcended such limitations by purifying their lives. By means of special revelations from Saint Germain and Jesus, he sought to help others understand what vast resources of cosmic power were available for their use in realizing the divine spark within them.

The goal of life, as Ballard communicated what he learned from Ascended Masters, was to break the bonds of human entanglement and reach the higher plane of unconditioned joy. Borrowing terminology from classical Hinduism, he maintained that "I Am," like Brahman, poured light and intelligence into human hearts. If persons resisted those spiritual impulses to act in worldly ways, light was withdrawn and "death" occurred as a result. But each person was born anew to try again in never ceasing attempts to purify daily thoughts and action. The law of karma, inviolable in meting out consequences of good or bad action, could be utilized to escape from carnal fetters. Ballard insisted that individuals could rise above the cosmic wheel of existence with its cycle of rebirths because the "Mighty I Am Presence" as well as the Ascended Masters offered help in the process. The supreme source of all life was grounded in each person, and on grasping that fact through correct diet, morality, and proper concentration, one's causal body became luminous, ascending to join those who had already risen above temporality. There was great ambiguity (and no little anxiety) on the question of whether one realized this state after "death" or whether decay of the body was a sign of shortcoming. Late in the year 1939,

Ballard's own death caused many to reject his doctrine, and the movement began to disintegrate from that point on.

Bibliography:

A. *Unveiled Mysteries* (Chicago, 1934); *The Magic Presence* (Chicago, 1935); *"I Am" Adoration and Affirmations* (Chicago, 1935); *"I Am" Decrees* (Los Angeles, 1937); *Ascended Masters Discourses* (Chicago, 1937).

BALLOU, Adin Augustus (23 April 1803, Cumberland, RI—5 August 1890, Milford, MA). *Career:* minister, Universalist church, Milford, MA, 1824–27 and 1828–31; minister, Universalist church, New York City, 1827–28; editor, *Independent Messenger*, 1831–39; president, Hopedale Community, 1841–52; minister, Hopedale Unitarian Parish, 1841–80.

At the age of twelve Ballou joined a conventionally orthodox church and within six years performed acceptably as a preacher. He studied the ideas of Universalism in order to attack it more effectively, but, instead of determining which weaknesses to assail, he became its advocate. A voracious reader and persuasive speaker, he had considerable influence on Universalist and Unitarian thought as these liberal denominations began to emerge in the early national period. Most notably Ballou clashed with his kinsman, *Hosea Ballou, on the question of future punishment. Both parsons agreed that all souls would eventually be reconciled with a God who would not inflict eternal punishment on them. But whereas Hosea argued that there would be no punishment for anyone beyond this life, Adin held that a limited amount of future punishment had to apply or else no one would respect God's moral law. The prospect of retribution (but not damnation) would reinforce moral standards and induce people to accord them greater respect. Together with six others he founded in 1831 the Massachusetts Association of Universalist Restorationists and edited its magazine to further its views. It never grew much and was disbanded ten years later.

In addition to doctrine Ballou was interested in putting religion into practice, especially in areas where it could combat cultural evils such as intemperance, slavery, and war. By 1841 he succeeded in creating a joint-stock company to manage Hopedale Community, the first of many utopian experiments in nineteenth century America. He was convinced that human social arrangements could flourish if based on Christian principles. Holiness and happiness could be attained, and this was best pursued through farming. Additional helps were light industries and prohibition of alcohol, together with no participation in any civil affairs at all, especially military ones. The experimental community grew for almost three decades, adding acreage and participants even after its first president retired from office. In 1856, however, two major stockholders redefined the enterprise along blatantly capitalistic lines, and the utopian dream faded. The moral core of the old altruistic venture slowly merged with the local Unitarian church which Ballou served as minister until the last decade of his serious, energetic life.

Bibliography:

A.   *Christian Non-Resistance, in All Its Important Bearings, Illustrated and Defended* (Philadelphia, 1846); *An Exposition of Views Respecting the Principal Facts, Causes, and Peculiarities Involved in Spiritual Manifestations, Together with Interesting Phenomenal Statements and Communications* (Boston, 1852); *Practical Christian Socialism* (Hopedale, MA, 1854); *Primitive Christianity and Its Corruptions*, 3 vols. (Boston, 1870–1900); *Autobiography of Adin Ballou*, completed and edited by William S. Heywood (Lowell, MA, 1896); *History of the Hopedale Community, from Its Inception to Its Virtual Submergence in the Hopedale Parish*, edited by William S. Heywood (Lowell, MA, 1897).

B.   NCAB 7, 558–59; DAB 1, 556–57.

BALLOU, Hosea (30 April 1771, Richmond, NH—7 June 1852, Boston, MA). *Education*: private study at home; studied at Quaker academies in Richmond and Chesterfield, NH, 1790–91. *Career*: minister, Dana, MA, 1794–1803; minister, Barnard, VT, 1803–09; minister, Portsmouth, NH, 1809–15; minister, Salem, MA, 1815–17; minister, Second Universalist Society, Boston, 1817–52; editor, *The Universalist Magazine*, 1819–21; co-editor, *The Universalist Expositor*, 1830–32.

Few preachers relished controversy more than Ballou, and in defending his ideas about salvation he became the chief formulator of tenets known as American Universalism. Developing his ideas out of a Calvinist Baptist background, the young itinerant minister was influenced by the writings of *Ethan Allen, which challenged orthodoxy with reason, and those of *Charles Chauncy, which stressed God's benevolence and Christ's role as mediator. By 1805, Ballou had formed his theology around a conception of atonement in radical contrast with theories of salvation for an elect few. Through treatises, pamphlet debates, and public discourses, he aided the process of humanizing thoughts of God and mitigating the harsh features of theology in New England. He wanted to rescue Christianity from the odium that distorted doctrines and unreasonable interpretations of the Bible had brought upon it. By restoring the central emphases of religion's true import, Ballou thought he could both silence critics and bolster the faith. One example was the trinitarian definition of God—unreasonable in itself and not founded solidly enough on the Scriptures to satisfy skeptical minds—so Ballou argued that it was better to leave past mistakes and view God as unitary and Christ as his divine agent. His apologetics written for the common man showed that Universalism had a theological affinity with Unitarianism, but in fact the two groups remained socially and institutionally apart for many years.

Also unscriptural and unbelievable were doctrines that sin and punishment are infinite or that God himself might die to satisfy an eternal principle of justice. Ballou held that sin is misery, a serious burden that prevented the happiness of moral agents until God in his power overcame it. He considered such a view of sin and its consequences sufficient answer to those who charged universalist faith with libertarian tendencies. But at the same time, sin's great weight was lifted by the limitless and unchanging love of God. He did not punish an innocent victim in Christ but rather sent him to acquire sinfulness through incarnation. God disciplined Christ with death and indicated in that act the way by which all humanity benefited from his providence. Christ suffered with men, not instead of them, and all approached the future state with hope of eventual reconciliation. Ballou taught that salvation is possible for all because God uses every event to bring about good. Christ was an unmistakable sign that the spirit of reconciliation was abroad, bringing about a renewal of love that overcame sin. Fifty years of preaching this gospel of love were effective in spreading wider circles of change in religious thought and affiliation. At the time of Ballou's death, the small denomination had acquired a newspaper, educational institutions, and an assembly of 500 ministers.

Bibliography:

A. *Notes on the Parables of the New Testament* (Randolph, VT, 1804; enl. ed., 1812); *A Treatise on Atonement* (Randolph, VT, 1805); *A Series of Lecture Sermons* (Boston, 1819); *Select Sermons* (Boston, 1832); *An Examination of the Doctrine of Future Retribution* (Boston, 1834); *A Voice to Universalists* (Boston, 1849).

B.   SH 1, 429; NCAB 5, 487–88; DAB 1, 557–59; Maturin M. Ballou, *Biography of Rev. Hosea Ballou* (Boston, 1852); Thomas Whittemore, *Life of Rev. Hosea Ballou* (4 vols. Boston, 1854–55); Oscar F. Safford, *Hosea Ballou* (Boston, 1889); John C. Adams, *Hosea Ballou and the Gospel Renaissance of the Nineteenth Century* (Boston, 1903); Ernest Cassara, *Hosea Ballou: The Challenge to Orthodoxy* (Boston, 1961).

BANGS, Nathan (2 May 1778, Stratford, CT—3 May 1862, New York, NY). *Career*: itinerant minister, Upper Canada, 1801–04; itinerant minister, Province of Quebec, 1804–12; minister and presiding elder in NY, 1812–20; agent, Methodist Book Concern, 1820–36; secretary, Methodist Missionary Society, 1836–41; president, Wesleyan Univ., 1841–42; minister, several churches in NY, 1842–52; active retirement, 1852–62.

Frontier conditions afforded few educational opportunities, but Bangs acquired enough learning to become thoroughly perplexed by rival arguments about free will; Methodist itinerants led him from this state of anxiety after lengthy discussions. Once that crisis was passed, he volunteered to help others who might be enmeshed in similar struggles over salvation and moral resolve. For more than a decade, he rode circuits from Niagara to Quebec, spreading the gospel of free grace so effectively that many considered him the founder of Methodism in the lower St. Lawrence valley. Though largely self-taught, he was a diligent student who became an able polemicist for his denomination's doctrinal emphasis. His sermons and books were widely noted for their power, if not their polish, especially when concentrating on what he called the pernicious influence of Calvinism. Doctrines of predestination or individual election were, he held, contrary to every human experience ranging from the biblical record to natural reason. More importantly, they thwarted evangelical preaching at every turn—

partially awakened minds temporized while waiting for the "effectual call" they had been taught to expect; those feeling a call acknowledged no responsibility for moral conduct; backslidden converts were overly confident of ultimate safety and failed to repent. Bangs hoped to end such thinking by thorough exposition of their faults. As an advocate of freedom in institutional forms as well as personal agency, he also worked for years to abolish (1818) church tax laws in Connecticut, which had supported a Calvinistic establishment for far too long.

It is fitting that Bangs is regarded as father of the Methodist Missionary Society because his whole life was spent in expanding facilities for evangelistic outreach. He chaired meetings that formed the Society, served as first presiding officer, and drafted its constitution. From its inception in 1819, he helped stabilize programs providing basic financial support for ministers who could not collect the allowance conferences allotted them. In this manner the Society made it possible for preachers to continue work among Indians, Blacks, and the poor without constant worries about how to provide for their own families. This bureau, more than any other, helped preserve the denomination's contact with common people, keeping the gospel alive where it was needed instead of just where congregations could afford to pay for it. Then too, Bangs was instrumental in raising standards of ministerial education far above that of the common man. By 1844, he succeeded in having theological training requirements written into the Book of Discipline. As chief agent of the Book Concern, he renovated its entire system of printing and distribution. He also served as editor of major journals (among them *Methodist Magazine*, 1820–28; *Christian Advocate and Journal*, 1828–32), increasing an appetite for literary accomplishment in his church. Of course he never ceased his steady regimen of preaching while pursuing these additional activities. Though officially superannuated at the age of seventy-five, he continued his ministerial labors until almost the very end.

Bibliography:

A. *The Errors of Hopkinsianism Detected and Refuted* (New York, 1815); *The Reformer Reformed* (New York, 1816); *Letters to Young Ministers* (New York, 1826); *An Authentic History of . . . Missions* (New York, 1832); *A History of the Methodist Episcopal Church*, 4 vols. (New York, 1838–40).

B. NCAB 9, 429–30; DAB 1, 574–75; Abel Stevens, *Life and Times of Nathan Bangs* (New York, 1863); Alexander H. Tuttle, *Nathan Bangs* (New York, 1909).

BARNES, Albert (1 December 1789, Rome, NY—24 December 1870, Philadelphia, PA). *Education*: B.A., Hamilton Coll., 1820; graduated from Princeton Sem., 1824. *Career*: minister, Morristown, NJ, 1825–30; minister, First Presbyterian Church, Philadelphia, PA, 1830–67; retirement, 1867–70.

During early years of building a reputation as revivalist and social reformer, Barnes deliberately molded a theology which he thought compatible with Scripture, common sense, and the progressive development of modern times. In 1829, he preached a famous sermon contradicting several points which conservative Calvinists had championed in the face of increasing evangelicalism. His explicit doctrines fanned the flames of a long smoldering theological controversy, and for decades he served as one of the most notable spokesmen on the New School side of that debate. In denying that men were guilty of Adam's original sin, he held that persons were sinful through exercising their own will, not by imputation. To rectify sin, he spoke of unlimited atonement, full and free, to those who would embrace the general promise of salvation. In keeping with basic emphases in the Second Great Awakening, he urged sinners of their own volition to repent and accept the grace available to all. If anyone perished due to hardness of heart, he warned that it was because they, not God, determined the outcome. In 1830, Philadelphia conservatives charged him with doctrinal error in his rejecting original sin, denying substitutionary atonement for the elect only, and implying unregenerate persons had some ability to cooperate in their own salvation. In the 1831 General Assembly, party warfare broke out over Barnes' liberal preachments, resulting in his acquittal. Defeat roused the Old School to greater efforts in combating unsound doctrine and lax discipline. A second phase of the same battle (1835–36) reached much the same conclusion, which hardened into a denominational split by 1837. Theological considerations seem to have predominated in this first of many institutional divisions based on social as well as intellectual factors in antebellum America.

The same humanistic doctrines of liberty informing Barnes' theology also motivated his efforts toward social reform. As a temperance advocate in his first pastorate, he virtually put the local liquor industry out of business. Sunday closing laws received his perennial support as did opposition to theaters and ballroom dancing. He was actively interested in Christian education, backing everything from better Sunday Schools to the new Union Theological Seminary (1836), which was established by liberals as an academy independent of all official church control. He also wrote a series of immensely popular commentaries on the New Testament, Psalms, and Isaiah, spreading New School ideas further as those volumes sold over a million copies. Another area where Barnes performed outstanding service was in the antislavery campaign. Basic Christian truths regarding the nature and destiny of man plus natural human rights achieved under republican government had made, he argued, slavery of human beings a manifest moral absurdity. But despite such exhortation from their leaders, New School Presbyterians took few practical steps to end slavery. After that issue was resolved by civil war, Barnes worked to heal the old wounds of institutional separation. When the reconciled factions met in common session again in 1870, they convened in the Philadelphia church led by one who had done much to push earlier tensions to the breaking point.

Bibliography:

A. *Notes Explanatory and Practical on the Scriptures*, 11 vols. (Philadelphia, 1832–53); *Sermons on Revivals* (Philadelphia, 1841); *An Inquiry into the Scriptural Views of Slavery* (Philadelphia, 1846); *The Way of Salvation* (Philadelphia, 1855); *The Atonement* (Philadelphia, 1859); *Lectures on the Evidences of Christianity in the Nineteenth Century* (New York, 1868).

B. SH 1, 488; NCAB 7, 360; DAB 1, 627–29; NYT 27 Dec 1870, 5.

BARTON, Clara (25 December 1821, Oxford, MA—12 April 1912, Glen Echo, MD). *Education*: studied at home and public schools before 1836; studied at Liberal Institute, Clinton, NY, 1852. *Career:* taught schools around North Oxford, MA, 1836–52; taught schools, Hightstown and Bordentown, NJ, 1853–55; clerk, U.S. Patent Office, 1855–57, 1860–61; director, volunteer relief agency, 1861–65; superintendent, Missing Persons Bureau, 1865–69; associated with International Red Cross, 1869–72; convalescence in England and Dansville, NY (after 1876), 1872–81; president, American National Red Cross, 1881–1904; retirement, 1904–12.

Clarissa Harlowe Barton, or ''Clara'' as she preferred to be called, emerged from humble origins in rural New England to achieve recognition as one of the nation's greatest humanitarians. From the age of fifteen, when she began teaching in local schools, to that of eighty-three, when she resigned from the largest national philanthropic society, most of her life was spent in service to others. Circumstances, not anticipation, seem to have led Barton to the work long associated with her name. In the first months of the Civil War, she found it impossible to ignore the suffering of casualties and the poor conditions in military hospitals. Her most effective contribution was that of securing supplies and improving logistics to get help where it was needed. Her most important motivation was a deep sense of compassion for human misery and a sense of obligation to do something about it. Through wars and other catastrophies, she always considered it her humanitarian charge not to desert the needy but to stay and suffer with them. She forgot her own infirmities in efforts to comfort others, as demonstrated by her work during the Franco-Prussian War when doctors had prescribed a long period of rest for her in Switzerland. Reared in Universalist surroundings, Barton was not affiliated with any religious institution, nor did she rationalize her activities with a creed. But her life of dedicated service embodied the principles of mercy and charity; which many held basic to practical religious witness.

There were many like Barton who gave of themselves in times of crisis, but she had the foresight and determination to organize such efforts on a continuing basis. By 1881, she succeeded in persuading governmental officials to align this country with the Swiss-based Red Cross, an international relief institution begun in 1863. She was named the first president of the American branch of the Red Cross and directed its operations in alleviating the hardships of victims of hurricanes, yellow fever, forest fires, railway accidents, famine, and wars, providing the essentials for survival and the necessities for rebuilding. As the voluntary organization grew and met each challenge, Barton's stature as a moral figure was increasingly recognized. She was a living example of sacrifice and helped create a national awareness of the need for relief institutions of comprehensive proportions. Often headstrong and self-reliant, she was not one to accept criticism easily. Her last controversial years as president ended in acrimonious debate over authority and appropriation of funds, but in the final analysis everyone acknowledged her unselfish, pioneering efforts to meet fundamental human needs.

Bibliography:

A. *The Red Cross: A History* (Washington, DC, 1898; subsequent editions entitled *The Red Cross in Peace and War*, 1899 and 1912); *A Story of the Red Cross* (New York, 1904); *Story of My Childhood* (New York, 1907).

B. NCAB 15, 314; DAB 2, 18–21; NAW 1, 103–08; NYT 13 Apr 1912, 13; Percy H. Epler, *The Life of Clara Barton* (New York, 1915); Mabel T. Boardman, *Under the Red Cross Flag* (Philadelphia, 1915); William E. Barton, *The Life of Clara Barton*, 2 vols. (Boston, 1922); Ishbel Ross, *Angel of the Battlefield* (New York, 1956).

BAYLEY, James Roosevelt (23 August 1814, Rye, NY—3 October 1877, Newark, NJ). *Education*: studied at Amherst Coll., 1831–33; B.A., Trinity Coll. (CT), 1835; studied at Sem. of St. Sulpice, 1842–43. *Career*: rector, St. Andrew's Episcopal Church, New York, 1840–41; vice-president, St. John's Coll. (NY), 1844–48; secretary to the bishop of New York, 1848–53; bishop of Newark, 1853–72; archibishop of Baltimore, 1872–77.

After serving for a year as an Episcopal priest at a church in Harlem, Bayley withdrew for further study. He had become perplexed over various conceptions of the church found among larger circles of the Anglican community, especially those fostered by Oxford divines who initiated the Tractarian controversy. While in Europe he became convinced that Roman Catholicism embodied the proper view of church life and was received into its communion in 1842. Within two years, he was again ordained to the priesthood, this time in a church that eventually appointed him as primate in the oldest, most prestigious American see. But the bulk of his important contributions was made before that time in the diocese of Newark, which then comprised the whole state of New Jersey. As first bishop in the newly created diocese, Bayley organized an administrative structure providing strong, efficient guidance for those under his care. He worked energetically to build churches and parochial schools, recruit priests, secure funds from missionary societies, and prepare young men for the ministry. To that end he also established Seton Hall (1856) and a nascent seminary, Immaculate Conception. He counseled his people by means of frank pastoral letters and continued such direction with frequent visitations. Wise statesmanship combined with decisive action helped lay the foundations of orderly church government in a geographical area where membership grew faster than personnel could keep pace with it.

Several younger churchmen who later made their mark in American Catholic history obtained firsthand experience under Bayley's leadership. The bishop made *Bernard J. McQuaid rector of his cathedral and then president of Seton Hall. He also financed advanced theological study for *Michael A. Corrigan because he recognized potential there. Bayley was interested in religious affairs beyond his own diocese, which had grown to impressive proportions. For decades he solicited funds as a staunch supporter of the American College in Rome. When the Second Plenary Council met in 1866, he participated in its attempts to safeguard doctrine and promote uniform discipline for all parts of the nation. He attended the General Council of the Vatican (1869–70) where he did what he could as part of the anti-infallibilist party. A conservative believer himself, he did not argue that papal infallibility distorted the deposit of faith; in his view it was simply inopportune to declare such a tenet. At the end, though, he acquiesced and voted for the proclamation. By the time he became the eighth archbishop of Baltimore, Bayley had passed the peak of his accomplishments. He set to work with a will, but poor health intervened in all those later efforts. Still he met responsibilities moderately well and secured (1876) the aid of *James Gibbons as coadjutor. Though his strength lay primarily in coordinating the affairs of complex organizations, he found time amid demanding duties to visit the sick, administer sacraments, and share with others the common gift of faith.

Bibliography:

A. *Sketch of the History of the Catholic Church on the Island of New York* (New York, 1853); *Memoirs of Simon Gabriel Bruté* (New York, 1860).

B. SH 2, 17; NCAB 1, 487–88; DAB 2, 73–74; NCE 2, 183; M. Hildegarde Yeager, *The Life of James Roosevelt Bayley* (Washington, DC, 1947).

BEECHER, Edward (27 August 1803, East Hampton, NY—28 July 1895, Brooklyn, NY). *Education*: B.A., Yale Coll., 1822; studied at Andover Sem., 1824–25. *Career*: headmaster, Hartford Academy, 1822–24; tutor, Yale Coll., 1825–26; minister, Boston, 1826–30; president, Illinois Coll., Jacksonville, IL, 1830–44; minister, Boston, 1844–55; editor, *Congregationalist*, 1849–53; minister, Galesburg, IL, 1855–71; assistant editor, *Christian Union*, 1871–73; retirement, occasional preaching and writing, 1871–95.

The Beecher family lived close to basic issues in the development of American culture for two generations, and their responses often spoke the mind of Protestants who wished to build the Republic into a Christian civilization. Edward absorbed many ideas regarding the dangers of Unitarianism and Catholicism from his father, *Lyman, but his reaction was more positive. He saw truth in classic affirmations of human sinfulness and divine sovereignty, yet he also agreed that principles of honor required God to act according to man's standards of justice and fair play. Beecher sought to adjust orthodox Calvinistic tenets to contemporary intellectual and social realities and work thereby towards a new theological synthesis. Publications on sin and atonement sustained over a period of fifty years contributed to that end. He came to see human life as an extension of a preceding existence where men had sinned and made themselves susceptible to eternal punishment. At the same time he believed reconciliation to be within reach and emphasized human regeneration in cooperation with a benevolent God who limited himself and suffered on man's behalf. As circumstances dictated, Beecher became involved with extending this abstract principle of justice, originally applied to individuals, until it covered the question of social justice as well.

The worst of social abuses was slavery, and by the 1830s many clergymen were beginning to reject colonization and gradual emancipation in favor of abolition as the means of dealing with the evil. In November of 1837, Beecher's ministerial friend and newspaper editor, *Elijah P. Lovejoy, was murdered in Alton, Illinois, while defending himself against a mob intent on destroying his printing press. Lovejoy was the protagonist in the event, but Beecher was its chief interpreter, and his theological analysis galvanized more clergy into action for the cause of social justice. Through his narrative of the tragedy and in subsequent reflections, Beecher formed a conception of "organic sin," which defined the reason and object of further reform efforts. It was possible in his view to denounce institutionalized immorality while not condemning individuals who, through moral ignorance, had acquiesced in a reprehensible system. He argued that God's law was the fundamental law of the universe and, when human constitutions contravened that standard of justice, nations were bound to repeal compromises with evil practice and disengage from corporate sin. Evangelical abolition thus found a major spokesman who could articulate a rationale broad enough to include supporters otherwise divided. Beecher could never forget Alton, and all his later activities were undergirded by the conviction that persons who experienced the holiness of God were compelled to assault the corruption they saw about them in society.

Bibliography:

A. *Narrative of Riots at Alton* (Alton, IL, 1838; New York, 1965); *Baptism, with Reference to Its Impact and Modes* (New York, 1849); *The Conflict of Ages* (Boston, 1853, and many subsequent editions); *The Papal Conspiracy Exposed* (Boston, 1855); *The Concord of Ages* (New York, 1860); *History of Opinions on the Scriptural Doctrine of Retribution* (New York, 1878).

B. SH 2, 24; NCAB 3, 128; DAB 2, 128; NYT 29 July 1895, 1; Robert Merideth, *The Politics of the Universe: Edward Beecher, Abolition, and Orthodoxy* (Nashville, 1963).

BEECHER, Henry Ward (24 June 1813, Litchfield, CT—8 March 1887, Brooklyn, NY). *Education*: B.A., Amherst Coll., 1834; B.D., Lane Sem., 1837. *Career*: minister of Presbyterian churches in Lawrenceburg, IN, 1837–39; Indianapolis, IN, 1839–47; minister, Plymouth Congregational Church, Brooklyn, NY, 1847–87; editor, *Independent*, 1861–63; *Christian Union*, 1870–81.

Some popular preachers are notable for their dramatic oratory or appealing message, others for personal traits that achieve rapport with audiences; Beecher had all these qualities. After a decade in the Midwest, where he mastered elocution, metropolitan centers vied for his services. He chose Brooklyn, "city of churches," and rapidly became one of the most conspicuous clergymen in national life. He did not pay much attention to conventionalities in the pulpit or out of it, and crowds flocked to hear him. His picturesque, witty sermons (published weekly after 1859) were undergirded by sincere moral earnestness, not uncommon in a Beecher. He was never really interested in theology and thought a sermon effective only if it created an emotional atmosphere that touched the vital experiences of those who heard it. With that goal in mind, he employed great expository facility and a fertile imagination to convey simple truths to many followers. Beecher minimized theological differences in religion and sought freedom of expression outside denominational confines. In 1882, his church withdrew from Congregational association because he wished no institutional questions raised about his views on christology, miracles, future punishment, and evolution. Contagious high spirits, a genial disposition, and lack of ostentatious piety made his embodiment of middle class values all the more palatable.

While the content of sermons had a religious lesson, more often than not Beecher organized them around topics of current social interest. He was an advocate of mild reforms but tended to avoid controversial measures, usually joining causes after they had become popular. Often governed by expediency more than sacrificial dedication, he broached no new ideas and initiated no correctional movements. Yet an ability to reflect majority sentiment linked his name with every major issue from antislavery to industrial reform. Most of his socio-political opinions were based on a peculiarly American confidence in freedom, progress, and the possibilities that human nature could attain in a free society. For that reason Beecher supported reform in principle but remained moderately conservative in practice. His callous attitudes about poverty and labor disputes are particularly indicative of a tendency to lag behind the times. Liberal statements and cautious action made Beecher an appealing figure despite careless habits with clothes, money, and friends. Between 1872 and 1876, he was implicated in a complex scandal with Mrs. Josephine Tilton, one of his parishioners. Court action ended in a hung jury; church members backed him to the end. With a reputation somewhat tarnished, he nevertheless enjoyed a popularity and influence not often equalled by an American clergyman.

Bibliography:

A. *Seven Lectures to Young Men* (Indianapolis, 1844); *Star Papers*, 2 vols. (New York, 1855–58); *Eyes and Ears* (Boston, 1863); *Freedom and War* (Boston, 1863); *Yale Lectures on Preaching*, 3 vols. (New York, 1872–74); *Evolution and Religion* (New York, 1885).

B. SH 2, 24–25; NCAB 3, 129–30; DAB 2, 129–35; NCE 2, 220–21; NYT 9 Mar 1887, 1; Lyman Abbott, *Henry Ward Beecher* (Hartford, 1887); Joseph Howard, *Life of Henry Ward Beecher* (Philadelphia, 1887); Paxton Hibben, *Henry Ward Beecher: An American Portrait* (New York, 1927, 1942); William G. McLoughlin, *The Meaning of Henry Ward Beecher* (New York, 1970); Clifford E. Clark, Jr., *Henry Ward Beecher: Spokesman for a Middle-Class America* (Urbana, IL, 1978).

BEECHER, Lyman (12 October 1775, New Haven, CT—10 January 1863, Brooklyn, NY). *Education*: B.A., Yale Coll., 1797; read theology under *Timothy Dwight, 1797–98. *Career*: minister, Presbyterian church of East Hampton, Long Island, 1799–1810; minister, Congregational church, Litchfield, CT, 1810–26; minister, Hanover Street Congregational church, Boston, MA, 1826–32; minister, Second Presbyterian Church, Cincinnati, OH, 1833–43; president, Lane

Sem., Cincinnati, OH, 1832–50; semi-retirement, lecturing, and writing, 1851–63.

Beecher had the distinction of confronting several major issues in the early national period with a conservative point of view, yet he was realistic enough to accept the general drift of events and adapt to changed circumstances as a means of continuing spiritual leadership. For example, he struggled to maintain the Standing Order in Connecticut; but after church and state were officially separated there in 1818, he became reconciled to voluntaryism and found it to be the best thing that ever happened to churches. He tried to eradicate social abuses like dueling and intemperance, but his chief reason for being identified as a conservative was a militant defense of Trinitarian theology in the face of burgeoning Unitarianism in New England. Called to Boston to pursue that battle, Beecher found himself embroiled in another controversy, which demonstrated his flexible common sense. Powerful revivals were attracting attention in the "burned over district" of New York, particularly those being conducted by *Charles G. Finney. In 1827, Beecher opposed Finney's "new measures," but within a few years he admitted the worth of the evangelist's campaigns and invited him to hold services in Boston.

While ministering to the specific needs of parishioners and preaching for genuine revivals within the churches, Beecher retained a Puritan's concern for the larger questions of religion in society. One area that increasingly vexed him was that of immigration and the alarming growth of Roman Catholicism in a land where Protestants had long enjoyed an unchallenged position of cultural influence. Beecher was disturbed for the nation's welfare, in both coastal cities and in the new West, as the country struggled to absorb foreigners of alien faith with no training in democratic procedures. His fiery sermons on the subject, several being delivered while visiting Boston in 1834, apparently helped incite mob action and the burning of an Ursuline convent and school in August of that year. Catholicism continued to grow, as did Unitarianism. Beecher was never reconciled to what he considered threats to evangelical Protestantism, nor was he particularly successful in counteracting non-evangelicals' increased numbers and social eminence. Another problem in which he was less than effective had to do with slavery and the mounting enthusiasm for abolition. Beecher was president of Lane Theological Seminary when a vocal minority under the leadership of *Theodore D. Weld denounced the temporizing of its faculty in 1834 and moved to Oberlin College. The president was not directly at fault, but the incident did not enhance his reputation as one who led the way in reforming social evils with religious benevolence.

The irony of Beecher's conservative reaction to many religious issues is that he was thought too liberal in theology and in 1835 had to weather a trial for heresy. He was not one to cleave strictly to any denominational definition of orthodoxy because it was more important in his view to apply the essentials of evangelical Christianity as different occasions demanded. Theology was not his main concern, and Beecher usually preferred a pragmatic application of the spirit over the letter of various formulations. Yet his long association with *Nathaniel W. Taylor and their common view of man's ability to repent in response to God's grace brought strong criticism from rigid Calvinists. His many activities as pastor, revivalist, educator, and social reformer filled a complex ministry. The key to all his dynamism was a strong conviction that Christian values stemming from the experience of redemption could and should be applied to the morals and social dealings of men.

Bibliography:

A. *A Plea for the West* (Cincinnati, 1832); *Views in Theology* (Cincinnati, 1836); *Works*, 3 vols. (Boston, 1852–53); Charles Beecher (ed.), *Autobiography, Correspondence, Etc., of Lyman Beecher, D.D.*, 2 vols. (New York, 1864–65; new ed., Barbara Cross, Cambridge, MA, 1961).

B. SH 2, 25; NCAB 3, 126–28; DAB 2, 135–36; NYT 12 Jan 1863, 5; Lyman B. Stowe, *Saints, Sinners, and Beechers* (New York, 1934); George M. Marsden, *The Evangelical Mind and the New School Presbyterian Experience* (New Haven, 1970); Stuart C. Henry, *Unvanquished Puritan: A Portrait of Lyman Beecher* (Grand Rapids, MI, 1973); James W. Fraser, *Pedagogue for God's Kingdom: Lyman Beecher and the Second Great Awakening* (Lanham, MD, 1985); Vincent Harding, *A Certain Magnificence: Lyman Beecher and the Transformation of American Protestantism, 1775–1863* (Brooklyn, NY, 1991).

BEISSEL, Johann Conrad (April 1690, Eberbach, Germany—6 July 1768, Ephrata, PA). *Career:* recluse and leader of the Seventh Day Dunkers, Ephrata, PA, 1732–68.

Orphaned at an early age and apprenticed to a baker, Beissel espoused pietistic habits to which he was already naturally inclined. He associated with a number of inspirationist sects in Germany but kept his own counsel as to particular rigors in holy living. By 1720, he emigrated from the Palatinate to Pennsylvania where he assisted Peter Becker, a weaver and Baptist minister at Germantown. The young man had always tended towards an independent spiritual life, aided by isolation, continence, and poverty. Though he joined through baptism with Becker's group from 1722 to 1728, his preference for solitude and independent vigils did not make him a cooperative follower. He was an ascetic at heart, setting an example for a number of like-minded individuals who changed his anchoritic existence (beginning in 1721) into a monastic community. As early as 1727, Beissel had caused no little disturbance by stating the conviction that Saturday was the proper day for worship. As a result his followers were known as Seventh Day Dunkers; celibate orders within the sect comprised Solitary Brethren and Spiritual Virgins. No later than 1732, the loosely organized party settled at Ephrata where Beissel, now with the name of Friedsam Gottrecht, divided his time between contemplation and recruitment. Administration of those resident lagged. By mid-century, though, several hundred members made the name of Ephrata one of considerable interest to German settlers throughout the region.

Celibacy remained a uniform practice among those who sought perfection under Beissel's leadership. There was some sharing of property, the semblance of a rule (weekly confessions), and fluctuating emphases on poverty; but physical continence was stressed constantly. Self-denial was requisite for service to God. Even conjugal relations were thought to be sinful and thus an abomination in God's sight. Beissel taught that anyone with serious interests in religion must conquer the flesh and move to spiritual ecstasies instead. His mind was fixed on heaven, which his melodious hymns described in veiled, esoteric language. But he was negligent about daily necessities for communal existence, and the order was torn by a series of inner struggles. Beissel preferred composing hymns or treatises on human depravity while the community, dependent on him to a fault, suffered from lack of coordination. Schism frequently occurred (one notable example, Israel Eckerle), but the founder held the majority together through his lifetime. Decline set in after his death. By 1814, only four adherents continued their old regimen, unable to find new disciples in a land where action was almost universally deemed more beneficial than contemplation. Still for a time the community and its fascinating leader presented the anomaly of monasticism on the Protestant frontier.

Bibliography:

A. *Die Ehe das Zuchthaus fleischlicher Menschen* (German edition, Philadelphia, 1730; English edition, Ephrata, 1785); *Mystische Und sehr geheyme Sprueche* (Philadelphia, 1730); *Das Gesäng Der einsamen und verlassenen Turtel-Taube* (English edition, Lancaster, PA, 1903).

B. NCAB 7, 497; DAB 2, 142–43; Joseph M. Hark (transl.), *Chronicon Ephratense* (Lancaster, PA, 1889); Walter C. Klein, *Johann Conrad Beissel: Mystic and Martinet* (Philadelphia, 1942).

BELL, Bernard Iddings (13 October 1886, Dayton, OH—5 September 1958, Chicago, IL). *Education*: B.A., Univ. of Chicago, 1907; S.T.B., Western Sem., 1912. *Career*: vicar, St. Christopher's Episcopal Church, Oak Park, IL, 1910–13; dean, St. Paul's Cathedral, Fond du Lac, WI, 1913–18; chaplain, U.S. Navy, 1917–19; president, St. Stephen's Coll., 1919–33; professor of Religion, Columbia Univ., 1930–33; preaching canon, St. John's Cathedral, Providence, RI, 1933–46; canon, Cathedral of Saints Peter and Paul, Chicago, IL, 1946–54; active retirement, 1954–58.

After enduring a long siege of religious skepticism through his early student years, Bell drew on those experiences to become an influential commentator on spiritual problems in modern culture. His position at several Midwestern churches provided avenues for fruitful service, but education proved to be the field which attracted most attention. Beginning in 1919, he presided over St. Stephen's College, a small denominational school on the Hudson River badly in need of funds. During his tenure as "warden" there, he helped raise over one million dollars and, more importantly, renovated basic curricular programs. Resisting tendencies to make students accept mediocrity or conform to anonymous crowd pressure, he stressed individualism and independent thought. Indeed, as a critic of contemporary civilization, he charged that schools failed generally to give students an understanding of priorities or to help them think about values on their own. Churches shared the blame for this widespread state of illiteracy, and Bell repeatedly issued trenchant analyses of poor ecclesiastical leadership. The root of the problem, he maintained, lay in overemphasized materialistic goals, which cheapened human standards and fashioned educational methods to achieve only secular success. In sermons, lectures, articles, and twenty books he called for better education, reinvigorated by churchmen who thought the gospel still played a part in shaping current social values. With these convictions he served as a consultant to the Episcopal bishop of Chicago and represented his diocese on the University of Chicago campus as well as other institutions in the area. Failing eyesight forced him to resign in 1954, but he continued until the end to advocate serious reappraisals of intellectual priorities.

Bibliography:

    A.   *Common Sense in Education* (New York, 1928); *Beyond Agnosticism: A Book for Tired Mechanists* (New York, 1929); *Religion for Living: A Book for Postmodernists* (London, 1939); *The Altar and the World* (New York, 1944); *God Is Not Dead* (New York, 1945); *Crisis in Education: A Challenge to American Complacency* (New York, 1949).
    B.   NCAB 43, 202–03; NCE 2, 250; NYT 6 Sep 1958, 17.

BELL, Eudorus N.

For some time before 1908 Bell served as a Baptist minister in Texas; during that year, however, he converted to Pentecostalism and gradually became an important spokesman for particular branches of that movement. He was one of the first to organize local groups, usually indisposed to anything resembling denominational structure, into a larger association for purposes of coordinating missionary activity. In 1909 he led the ''Apostolic Faith Movement'' and in 1911 merged his following with the Church of God in Christ under bishop *Charles H. Mason. Two years later, these white pentecostals from Texas to Alabama withdrew from Mason's church, using temporarily the same name yet issuing separate ministerial credentials. Finally in April of 1914, they held a nation-wide convention at Hot Springs, Arkansas. At this meeting, three-hundred delegates formed themselves into a harmonious body confessing standard pentecostal doctrines such as baptism by the Holy Ghost and speaking in tongues. But their view of holiness or sanctification was deliberately outside the Wesleyan tradition. Declaring sanctification to be a progressive rather than an instantaneous experience, they embodied a theological distinctiveness which has continued to the present time. This convention also constructed an executive committee, with Bell as president instead of bishop, to administer what amounted to a new American denomination: a General Council of the Assemblies of God. Its emergence marked the end of interracial experimentation among pentecostals, and its strength precluded doctrinal unity or hope for eventual reunion of various holiness sects.

A more serious ideological controversy erupted just as the newly formed Assemblies of God began to consolidate institutional foundations. Bell's part in subsequent discussions was less than consistent, but in the last analysis he provided the leadership that kept most churches within traditional conceptions of theological orthodoxy. Some preachers held that trinitarian definitions of God were wrong; titles of Father, Son, and Holy Ghost were simply names applicable to the single person of Christ. Rejecting baptism performed under tripartite formulas, they called for new sacraments with a "Jesus only" orientation. In 1915, Bell called a conference to combat this unitarian heresy. He also published several articles against such beliefs in *Word and Witness*, the official Assembly periodical which he edited. But shortly thereafter he shocked his co-religionists by espousing the new theory and submitting to rebaptism. By 1916, he reversed his opinion and once again accepted a trinitarian description of the Godhead. Since he was still the most powerful individual among church leaders, the General Council of 1916 adopted a "statement of fundamental truths," which precluded any unitarian faction of "Jesus only" adherents. As a result of this declaration, more than one hundred congregations, including 156 out of 585 clergymen, separated from the trinitarian Assembly. Despite such losses, the denomination maintained its stability and quickly became one of the largest pentecostal-holiness groups in the nation.

Bibliography:

B.   Vinson Synan, *The Holiness-Pentecostal Movement in the United States* (Grand Rapids, MI, 1971).

BELLAMY, Joseph (20 February 1719, Cheshire, CT—6 March 1790, Bethlehem, CT). *Education*: B.A., Yale Coll., 1735; studied theology with *Jonathan Edwards, Northampton, MA, 1735–37. *Career*: minister, Bethlehem, CT, 1738–90.

The longest, most resilient theological tradition in American religious history has been Calvinism, and after his mentor Jonathan Edwards, Bellamy was the ablest spokesman who perpetuated that system into yet another generation. During the early years of the First Great Awakening, he established himself as a powerful itinerating evangelist in colonies surrounding Connecticut, but he soon settled into a single pastorate that remained his for over half a century. There he preached, taught, and published materials which developed New Divinity concepts to full maturity. While justly considered one of Edwards' earliest and most influential disciples, Bellamy revised several categories as he sought to explain the ways of God to men. Audiences of his time were thought to possess more enlightened consciences; consequently, he softened the harsher aspects of election and divine sovereignty to make them congruent with prevailing notions of reasonable justice. God was defined as a moral governor, one who permitted but did not actively cause sin to exist in His creation. Such a theodicy showed creatures their need for God while correspondingly it enhanced the capacity of divine mercy. The controversial theologian went on to argue that sin and redemption thus glorified God more than any bleak condition of uniform sinlessness ever could.

God conceived as ethical, universal lawgiver made it possible for Bellamy to introduce a new understanding of the atonement. Borrowing from the Dutch thinker, Hugo Grotius, he held that punishment of sin resulted not from God's wrath as an offended sovereign, but from more humane consequences of His enforcing the moral dictates of universal law. Sin caused death because it was a moral outrage; Christ's atoning sacrifice did not satisfy an angry deity but rather expressed God's love in effecting reconciliation for the well-being of the entire universe. In this perspective Bellamy did not stress unity between Adam and subsequent individuals, nor did he dwell on an organic imputation of sin. Daily failures were enough to convince men of the need for grace, and he speculated that atonement might include more human beings than earlier Reform thinkers had surmised. Yet with his expansion of the possibilities for salvation beyond a narrow circle of God's elect, he sternly defended high standards for ecclesiastical membership. Only regenerate persons could belong to the church, and its vital communion services were restricted to visible saints. In so arguing he hoped to avoid the errors of antinomians while defeating Half-Way Covenant compromises at the same time. Such doctrine would, he hoped, sustain the remnant of Israel as it struggled to preserve its heritage against extremes of emotion and rationalism.

Bibliography:

A.   *True Religion Delineated* (Boston, 1750); *Four Sermons* (Boston, 1758); *A Dialogue on the Christian Sacraments* (Boston, 1762); *The Wisdom of God in the Permission of Sin, Vindicated* (Boston, 1769); *A Careful and Strict Examination of the External Covenant* (New Haven, 1770); *Works* 3 vols. (New York, 1811–12).

B.   AAP 1, 404–12; SH 2, 33–34; NCAB 7, 78; DAB 2, 165.

BELLOWS, Henry Whitney (11 June 1814, Boston, MA—30 January 1882, New York, NY). *Education*: B.A., Harvard Coll., 1832; graduated from Harvard Div. Sch., 1837. *Career*: Unitarian minister, Mobile, AL, 1837–39; Unitarian minister, New York, NY, 1838–82; president, United States Sanitary Commission, 1862–78.

With only one year of ministerial experience behind him, Bellows moved to a church in New York City at the rather tender age of twenty-four. But his easy charm and tolerance of differing opinions soon gained him acceptance in many of the religious and social circles there. His church, originally Congregationalist, had by then evolved into a Unitarian Society, later changing its name first to Church of Divine Unity and then to All Soul's Church. In addition to preaching from his own pulpit for forty-four years, Bellows was constantly active in other speaking engagements. He became widely known as an innovative and stimulating thinker who always challenged his audiences with fresh ideas and new causes. Scores of his sermons, addresses, memorials, and discourses were published. In addition, he wrote frequently for the *Christian Inquirer* which he edited for several years after 1847 and for the *Christian Examiner* during a decade of editorship after 1866. He also helped found the National Conference of Unitarian Churches (1865), the Ministers' Institute (1866), and many state and local conferences for clergy in his denomination.

Unitarians have always emphasized the importance of applying religious values to practical situations in everyday life. Bellows exemplified this altruistic civic-mindedness in many ways, but it was nowhere more conspicuous than during the Civil War. When the numbers of sick and wounded mounted to unprecedented heights, Bellows was appalled to learn how inadequate government facilities were for treating patients. Consequently he organized the United States Sanitary Commission and directed its far-flung activities efficiently with great energy. He raised millions of dollars in northern cities, using those funds to purchase and distribute medicines and hygienic items to field hospitals and men in the Union army. Even after the war Bellows contributed to care for veterans and their welfare. This led in turn to championing the cause of civil service reform, and Bellows traveled widely to organize associations dedicated to ending the spoils system in American politics. Through his long career a restless mind sought causes worth supporting, and his zealous activism produced tangible results in many areas where spiritual ideals can do good for humankind.

Bibliography:

A. *Re-Statements of Christian Doctrine in Twenty-Five Sermons* (New York, 1860); *The Old World in Its New Face: Impressions of Europe in 1867–1868*, 2 vols. (New York, 1868–69); *Twenty-Four Sermons Preached in All Souls Church New York*, ed., Russell N. Bellows (New York, 1886).

B. SH 2, 35; NCAB 3, 261; DAB 2, 169; NYT 13 Feb. 1882, 1; Walter Donald Kring, *Henry Whitney Bellows* (Boston, 1979).

BENDER, Harold Stauffer (19 July 1897, Elkhart, IN—21 September 1962, Chicago, IL). *Education*: A.B., Goshen Coll., 1918; B.D., Garrett Sem., 1922; M.A., Princeton Univ. and Th.M., Princeton Sem., 1923; Th.D., Univ. of Heidelberg, 1935. *Career*: at various levels instructor of Bible and Church History, Goshen Coll., 1924–62; editor, *Mennonite Quarterly Review*, 1927–62; member and assistant secretary, Mennonite Central Committee, 1931–62; dean, Goshen Coll., 1933–44; dean, Mennonite Biblical Sem., 1944–62.

The Anabaptist vision of the church emphasizes simple, unassuming charity together with utter nonviolence. Bender spent his many fruitful years helping his fellow Mennonites to understand that vision better and to unite segments of his church in an effective expression of their common beliefs. As part of this program to promote self-understanding, he organized the Mennonite Historical Society the year he returned to his alma mater as instructor. For well over three decades he served on his denomination's board of education, on historical committees, as well as publication agencies that sponsored studies in Anabaptist and Mennonite history. The *Mennonite Quarterly Review*, begun in 1927, also stimulated scholarly inquiry and added substantially to contemporary policy through knowledge of past experiences. The crowning event in ventures of this sort was the *Mennonite Encyclopedia*, which Bender saw through the presses as chief editor. In four volumes published between 1955 and 1959 he coordinated the work of 2,700 different authors on 13,000 articles related to a brand of Christianity too often vilified by more established churches in their three centuries of existence.

Education and historical awareness were important, but Bender ministered to the physical needs of fellow believers too. In 1930, for instance, he interrupted his doctoral studies in Germany to aid Mennonite refugees from Russia, helping to settle them at last in Paraguay. Such relief work went hand in hand with his peace witness. In the decades surrounding World War II he worked vigorously for these causes. His ideas on peace, war, and military service were adopted by his denomination's general conference in 1937. In the aftermath of war he strove in 1948 to re-establish the doctrine and practice of biblical nonresistance. In ''Mennonite Peace Action throughout the World'' he called on groups that had temporarily abandoned their pacifism to return to their historic principle. Bender fostered worldwide cooperation among the many varieties of Anabaptists. He furthered ecumenical understanding through frequent travels and carefully nurtured the idea of world conferences. His labors contributed to a special quickening within his confession and to a greater sense of unity among those who shared it.

Bibliography:

A. *Two Centuries of American Mennonite Literature: A Bibliography of Mennotica Americana, 1727–1923* (Goshen, IN, 1929); *Menno Simon's Life and Writings: A Quadricentennial Tribute, 1536–1936* (Scottdale, PA, 1936); *Conrad Grebel, c. 1498–1526: The Founder of the Swiss Brethren, Sometimes Called Anabaptists* (Goshen, IN, 1950); *These Are My People: The Nature of the Church and Its Discipleship According to the New Testament* (Scottdale, PA, 1962).

BENEZET, Anthony (31 January 1713, St. Quentin, France—3 May 1784, Philadelphia, PA). *Career*: instructor, Germantown Acad., 1739–42; instructor, Friends' English Public Sch., 1742–54; principal and instructor, private female acad., Philadelphia, 1755–66, 1768–84.

After the Edict of Nantes was revoked in 1685, Huguenots found it increasingly difficult to exercise their religious preference in France. The Benezet family left their native Picardy in 1715 for reasons of conscience and eventually spent sixteen years in London where young Anthony became a Quaker. By 1731, he had moved to the New World, engaging in business for a time with his brothers. But teaching, which proved more attractive, led to a series of posts at Friends' schools, culminating with his own attended by daughters of the best families in Philadelphia. In addition to advances in education, including work with deaf-mutes, Benezet made his greatest contribution in the area of humanitarian reform. Largely by means of publishing articles and pamphlets, plus extensive correspondence with influential persons on both sides of the Atlantic, he was able to initiate several philanthropic endeavors. For example, in 1774 he wrote against immoderate use of liquor, starting a chain of events that, through the agency of *Dr. Benjamin Rush, produced some of the earliest temperance activity in this country. Toward the end of his life he began to study the miserable condition of American Indians, calling for amelioration of their plight as he had so often done before in other contexts. His concern to end unjustifiable prejudice and promote human welfare, sustained over five decades, preserved its selfless character throughout that time.

Of all the causes to which Benezet turned his attention, none absorbed him more than the oppression rampant among black slaves. As early as 1750, he was distressed to read of conditions in the West Indies; soon thereafter he met *John Woolman who supplied additional information about practices in southern colonies. Both men were aroused to pity and indignation over what they considered a brutal institution. Benezet was one of the first to broadcast facts regarding slavery, arguing that traffic in human flesh constituted grievous iniquity. Many of his essays were reprinted in England, distributed at various yearly meetings, and sent gratis to members of Parliament. In 1775 he joined others in Philadelphia to form the first American abolitionist society. Arguing that slavery was unlawful, he tried to convince governments, churchmen, and citizens in general to end the enormity. Primarily because of his and Woolman's persuasion, all Pennsylvania Quakers emancipated their slaves in 1774. Within thirteen more years Quakers in every state abandoned the practice. In England his ideas affected national prohibition of trading in slaves, and through his influence on John Wesley's thinking in this regard he indirectly shaped early Methodist attitudes as well. It was disclosed in his will that most of a slender fortune was bequeathed to a school for black children, one where he had taught without salary for years. In this conscientious act, as in so many others, he embodied an undiscriminating desire to improve circumstances for fellow human beings.

Bibliography:

A. *A Caution and Warning . . . on the Calamitous State of the Enslaved Negroes* (Philadelphia, 1766); *An Historical Account of Guinea* (Philadelphia, 1771); *The Mighty Destroyer Displayed* (Trenton, NJ, 1779); *Short Account of the People Called Quakers* (Philadelphia, 1780).

B.   SH 2, 52; NCAB 5, 419; DAB 2, 177–78; Roberts Vaux, *Memoirs of the Life of Anthony Benezet* (Philadelphia, 1817); George S. Brookes, *Friend Anthony Benezet* (Philadelphia, 1937); Wilson Armistead, *Anthony Benezet* (London, 1859; Freeport, NY, 1971).

BERKOWITZ, Henry (18 March 1857, Pittsburgh, PA—7 February 1924, Atlantic City, NJ). *Education*: studied at Cornell Univ., 1872–73; B.A., Univ. of Cincinnati, 1881; graduated from Hebrew Union Coll., 1883. *Career*: rabbi, Sha'are Shomayim Congregation, Mobile, AL, 1883–88; rabbi, B'nai Jehuda Congregation, Kansas City, MO, 1888–92; rabbi, Rodeph Shalom Congregation, Philadelphia, PA, 1892–1921; retirement, 1921–24.

By the time Berkowitz accepted the rabbinate of a large Philadelphia synagogue, his reputation as a follower of *Isaac M. Wise had spread quite far. Graduating in the first Hebrew Union College class, he worked for four decades to foster the growth of Reform Judaism in America. In all his pastoral activities he sought to eliminate outdated forms while retaining a spirit of congregational piety, bringing his followers into the mainstream of liberal thought and practice. By 1897 he had reorganized synagogue school, reduced its number of sessions, made the study of German optional, introduced congregational singing, and established a children's choir. Moreover, he created new pageants for festivals such as Hanukkah and Succoth, adopted the *Union Prayer Book* (parts of which were his own composition) as a standard for corporate worship and opened wider vistas by exchanging pulpits with other rabbis. He was also interested in providing liturgical material in English for domestic services, publishing several popular volumes to serve that purpose. Thoughtful sermons, influential books, and gentle, unobtrusive leadership did much to silence his critics and enhance the vitality of Jewish liberalism in metropolitan centers across the country. He helped establish patterns for steady growth in Reform activity on the concrete level through dynamic pioneering in areas where he thought change strengthened traditional Jewish precepts.

Civic affairs, as well as organized activities outside the local congregation, occupied much of Berkowitz's attention. He often took the lead in promoting humane societies, established united charity fund drives, and served as trustee on dozens of institutional boards concerned with everything from playgrounds to vice control. Public-minded reform efforts also led him to experiment with new types of interfaith cooperation. Within denominational lines, however, his greatest contribution probably was the Jewish Chautauqua Society, dedicated to popularizing the ideal of education among coreligionists. From 1893, the year of its founding, until death he labored as chancellor to formulate annual programs, improve teacher training, and devise syllabi for study groups in Bible reading and other literature. As a leading figure in the Jewish Publication Society, he helped enlarge the sources available for cultural enrichment. He was also a charter member of the Central Conference of American Rabbis, working as its first secretary for several years. Recurring heart attacks forced retirement, but his active mind continued to spread, through articles and books, the ideals of liberal Judaism consonant with a democratic milieu.

Bibliography:

A.   *Bible Ethics* (New York, 1883); *Judaism on the Social Question* (New York, 1888); *The Open Bible*, 2 vols. (Philadelphia, 1890); *Kiddush, or Sabbath Sentiment in the Home* (Philadelphia, 1898); *The New Education in Religion*, 2 vols. (Philadelphia, 1913); *Intimate Glimpses of the Rabbi's Career* (Cincinnati, 1921).
B.   NCAB 22, 55; DAB 2, 219–20; UJE 2, 204–05; EJ 634–35; NYT 8 Feb 1924, 19; Max E. Berkowitz, *The Beloved Rabbi* (New York, 1932).

BESANT, Annie Wood (1 October 1847, London, England—20 September 1933, Adyar, India).

A striking feature of Mrs. Besant's life is the number of faiths through which her spiritual odyssey led. Beginning as the wife of an Anglican vicar, she came in a few years to renounce Christianity altogether, joining a number of socialist societies in an effort to benefit mankind through socio-economic reorganization. By the early 1890s, she embraced theosophical ideas taught by *Helena P. Blavatsky and traveled as missionary of the newly discovered ancient truth to many parts of the world. By 1893 she considered the Theosophical Society at Adyar, India, her home. Authorities in the society held that, through psychic contact with earlier masters (mahatma), they had received letters containing important points of doctrine. Besant supported the claim, and when an American branch of theosophists led by William Q. Judge seceded in 1895, she remained with the larger group and helped develop distinctive emphases in Adyar Theosophy. When the society's president, *Henry S. Olcott, died in 1907, she succeeded him as leader of an international movement. In collaboration with Charles W. Leadbeater she penned speculative treatises, lives of past mahatma, and descriptions of occult initiations. More than thirty books and scores of articles appeared under her name as she tried to extend knowledge of Hindu wisdom and its spiritual message for modern man. To perpetuate her society's views, she helped establish (1912) in southern California a school and community that have influenced the growth of lodges in many other parts of this country. Her dedication to Indian nationalism inspired several leaders such as Mohandas Gandhi, and the Home Rule for India League was another significant expression of her commitment to reformist causes. In addition to institutional effectiveness, Besant's religious values are symbolic of many individuals who both condemned technological materialism and perceived inadequacies in the Judeo-Christian heritage.

Bibliography:

A.   *Annie Besant: An Autobiography* (London, 1893); *Death—and After?* (New York, 1893); *Karma* (London, 1895); *The Ancient Wisdom: An Outline of Theosophical Teachings* (London, 1897); *Initiation: The Perfecting of Man* (London, 1912); *Mysticism* (London, 1914).

B.   SH 2, 72–73; NYT 21 Sep 1933, 19; Geoffrey West, *The Life of Annie Besant* (London, 1929); Theodore Besterman, *Mrs. Annie Besant: A Modern Prophet* (London, 1934); Arthur H. Nethercot, *The First Five Lives of Annie Besant* (Chicago, 1960) and *The Last Four Lives of Annie Besant* (Chicago, 1963).

BETHUNE, Mary McLeod (10 July 1875, Mayesville, SC—18 May 1955, Daytona Beach, FL). *Education*: graduated from Scotia Sem., Concord, NC, 1893; graduated from Mission Training Sch., Moody Bible Institute, 1895. *Career*: president, Bethune-Cookman Coll. (under various names before 1928), 1904–42; president emerita and trustee, 1942–55.

The daughter of former slaves, Bethune learned to value education quite early in life with the aid of a Presbyterian missionary. She went to one of the best institutions available for black women in the region and volunteered for missionary training at Chicago's new Moody Bible Institute. Her plan was to serve in Africa, but the mission board had no place for her. Disappointed in that wish, she determined that Africans in the United States needed Christ and the benefits of learning as much as Negroes in Africa. So she turned to education as a means of religious witness, intellectual development, and social service to her people. After teaching elementary school for a number of years in Georgia and Florida, she began her own modest academy—the Daytona Normal and Industrial School for Girls—in 1904. Meager beginnings were marked by years of struggle. She used crates for desks with charcoal for pencils; a garden supplied lunches sold to construction crews to raise money and buy the vacant lot where a schoolhouse was built. Bethune organized a Sunday School, in addition to day and evening classes, where religious training was blended with basic reading skills. Her vision and iron determination inspired several philanthropists to support her work, which expanded to include a hospital, dormitories, and an increased faculty and student body. The school, which began in her home with five students, merged in 1928 with Cookman Institute to become an outstanding coeducational college for southern black youth. As the institution's president explained in her syndicated newspaper column, "My Day," students entered to learn and departed to serve the needs of society.

Service to fellow black citizens and to wider circles of American society always had priority for president Bethune. She directed relief work for the Red Cross after the hurricane of 1928. Under the Hoover administration, she served on the National Commission for Child Welfare, and under Roosevelt she became a special adviser on minority affairs. As a member of the National Youth Administration (1936–44), she traveled over 40,000 miles through twenty-one states in an average year to supervise programs for black youth. Her influence made grants available for many promising young persons to enter graduate studies. Vice-president of the NAACP and commissioner in the National Urban League, she participated in a host of projects for improvement among her people. In 1935 she founded (president until 1953) the National Council of Negro Women, which coordinated major interests of thousands of black leaders through the depression and war years. In 1952 she realized her original dream of going to Africa (Liberia), not as a missionary but as the nation's envoy, personally chosen by President Truman. Such a designation was appropriate for one who had for the last decade received wide recognition for her many years of distinguished service in fields of human welfare.

Bibliography:

B.   NCAB 49, 118; NYT, 19 May 1955, 29; Catherine O. Peare, *Mary McLeod Bethune* (New York, 1951); Rackham Holt, *Mary McLeod Bethune: A Biography* (New York, 1964).

BINGHAM, Hiram (30 October 1789, Bennington, VT—11 November 1869, New Haven, CT). *Education*: B.A., Middlebury Coll., 1816; B.D., Andover Sem., 1819. *Career*: missionary, Hawaiian Islands, 1819–40; at intervals, minister, New Haven, CT, 1840–63; retirement, 1863–69.

New England Congregationalists first learned about the state of religious affairs in Hawaii from a young native, Obookiah (Opukahaia), who came to America in 1809. Bingham was among those who responded to the missionary impulse engendered by the youth, sailing in 1819 with another ordained minister, two schoolmasters, a physician, a printer, a farmer, and their respective wives. He helped start the earliest mission stations at Honolulu and Lahaina, concentrating initially on royal families to influence the general populace after gaining elitist support. Education proved to be the chief means of introducing Christianity. Bingham reduced local dialects to a twelve-letter alphabet, began compiling a grammar, and taught natives of all ages to read in schoolhouses built for that purpose. He conducted many preaching tours, accompanied by Queen (later regent) Kaahumanu, who urged the new religion on her subjects with great effectiveness. Schools as well as chapels were erected at Hilo and Waimea as the mission program soon touched all the principal islands. Representatives of Yankee morality, the missionaries encountered some resistance in their attempts to burn pre-christian images, prohibit infanticide, and regulate sexual customs. But despite native preferences, they slowly succeeded in establishing behavioral standards more in keeping with the gospel advocated so vigorously. Still, Bingham's most lasting contribution was connected with language. In 1825 he began translating the New Testament; by 1839 he and other colleagues had finished rendering the entire Bible into Hawaiian. With financial aid from the American Tract Society, they printed and distributed 20,000 Bibles plus thousands of testaments and seventy other works—more than 150 million pages in all. Because of his wife's poor health, Bingham obtained a furlough in 1840 and never returned to his evangelical post. At times he was pastor of an African church in New Haven, the city where he spent the bulk of his remaining years. But missionary zeal seems always to have been his main concern, evidenced by the fact that a son, also named Hiram, served with distinction in the Gilbert Islands.

Bibliography:

   A.   *A Residence of Twenty-One Years in the Sandwich Islands* (Hartford, CT, 1847).
   B.   DAB 2, 276.

BIRNEY, James Gillespie (4 February 1792, Danville, KY—25 November 1857, Perth Amboy, NJ). *Education*: B.A., Coll. of New Jersey, 1810; studied law in Philadelphia, PA, 1810–13. *Career*: member, lower house of the Kentucky legislature, 1816–18; representative, first General Assembly of Alabama, 1819; practicing attorney, 1814–45.

Along with inheriting wealth derived from slave labor, Birney also inherited a family repugnance of the system and its abuses. After being admitted to the bar he entered politics at an early age, but opposition to popular national figures such as Andrew Jackson and Henry Clay ended hopes in that direction. Wavering fortunes did not, however, curtail his attitude regarding slavery, and by 1826 he helped pass laws in the state of Alabama against importing new slaves. He also began collecting funds and establishing units of the American Colonization Society, an organization dedicated to restricting slave trade and transporting freedmen back to Africa. Birney traveled in many southern states, lecturing on the merits of emancipation through political action. His ideal at that time was gradual extinction of the system with financial compensation by action of state legislatures. By 1834 he decided that immediate abolition would be less detrimental to both owners and the country, so he joined the American Anti-Slavery Society and served as its executive secretary in 1837.

In the 1830s Birney also freed his own slaves and moved north of the Ohio River. He continued to address large audiences, sometimes braving personal danger from hostile reaction to this, his chosen form of gospel preaching. For a short time he issued the *Philanthropist*, an abolitionist paper whose circulation rose alongside aggressive opposition. As agent of the American Anti-Slavery Society he organized more than six hundred new branches and lobbied in state legislatures to secure emancipation laws. Birney did not go as far as the Garrisonian wing of the abolitionist movement. He changed his expectation of when slavery should end, but he always held to political action as the necessary means for effective action, a course of social change that still preserved the nation's Constitution. In 1840 and 1844 he ran for president as nominee of the Liberty Party, receiving more than seven thousand votes the first time and over sixty-two thousand the second. In 1845 he was crippled after being thrown from a horse, but he wrote much for papers and magazines, these essays often issued later as pamphlets. All these avenues combined to make Birney one of the most conspicuous voices that advocated an end to slavery through political action as well as moral suasion.

Bibliography:

   A.   *The American Churches, the Bulwarks of American Slavery* (London, 1840; New York, 1969); *Letters of James Gillespie Birney, 1831–1857*, 2 vols., ed., Dwight L. Dumond (New York, 1938).
   B.   NCAB 2, 312–13; DAB 2, 291–94; Beriah Green, *Sketches of the Life and Writings*

of James Gillespie Birney (Utica, NY, 1844); William Birney, *James G. Birney and His Times* (New York, 1890).

BLACKBURN, Gideon (27 August 1772, Augusta County, VA—23 August 1838, Carlinville, IL). *Career*: minister, Maryville, TN, 1792–1810; instructor, Indian school, 1804–10; president, Harpeth Acad., Franklin, TN, 1810–23; minister, Louisville, KY, 1823–27; president, Centre Coll., 1827–30; minister, Versailles, KY, 1830–33; supply preacher in IL, 1833–38.

Born on the edge of civilization, west of the Blue Ridge, Blackburn moved with his family in the van of Scotch-Irish migration into eastern Tennessee. There, at fifteen years of age, he joined the Presbyterian church and prepared for the ministry, acquiring an education largely through his own efforts and surpassing that of most pioneers in the region. Farming was his means of livelihood, but he spent as much time as possible preaching to soldiers and settlers. While he located in one place after licensing by the Presbytery, he ranged the countryside, organizing churches or preaching stations within a fifty-mile radius. In many places he spoke with a loaded rifle propped against the pulpit, as ready as the rest of his congregation to meet possible Indian attacks. Blackburn was admired and respected as a courageous Indian fighter in addition to his fervent preaching. But early in the new century, he grew compassionate and sought to convert red men instead of destroying them. Finding little encouragement among local whites, he appealed to the General Assembly in 1803 for funds to begin a school in the Cherokee nation, a people he thought capable of assimilating Christian cultural patterns. Seven years of great sacrifice followed as he solicited money, clothes, and books for about 300 children whom he taught the rudiments of spelling, hygiene, ciphers, and the Shorter Catechism. By 1810, however, his missionary work had drained both health and personal finances to the point of collapse. Nevertheless, it was with great reluctance that he left pastorates and schools in search of better conditions farther west.

While his health mended slowly, Blackburn supervised a private academy. He still placed higher priority on preaching than classroom activities, attested by the establishment of another circuit of rotating Sunday appointments around his new home. Called to large churches in Kentucky, he became even more widely known as an evangelical orator. He appealed directly to the imagination and conscience of his listeners, fitting the mold of revivalistic preaching which emphasized human participation in the drama of salvation. The powerful flow of his descriptive language was so effective, even critics were captivated by his unassuming address, forgetting to notice pronunciation, grammar, the passage of time itself. By 1830 he worked for social reform as well, serving as an agent of the state's temperance society for a time and growing increasingly opposed to slavery. He freed his own slaves save two incorrigibles; those he sold and sent the others to Liberia where life promised more dignity than could be hoped for in white man's America. Blackburn held no stated charge after moving to Illinois, but college trustees employed him to raise funds for their institution. His efforts were not overly successful, though a school bearing his name was established in 1857 on the proceeds. Painfully hampered by cancer of the mouth, he welcomed death as an end to years of pain.

Bibliography:

B.   AAP 4, 43–58; NCAB 13, 543; DAB 2, 314–15.

BLACKWELL, Antoinette Louisa Brown (20 May 1825, Henrietta, NY—5 November 1921, Elizabeth, NJ). *Education*: completed literary course, Oberlin Coll., 1847; completed theological course, Oberlin Coll., 1850. *Career*: lecturer and guest preacher, 1850–53; minister, First Congregational Church, South Butler, NY, 1853–54; social worker, New York City, 1855; wife, mother, author, lecturer, 1856–80; pastor emeritus, All Souls' Unitarian Church, Elizabeth, NJ, 1908–21.

The factor that shaped Brown's education and early career was the simple recognition that she was as bright and capable as any male around her. But the conventions of her time confined women to few occupations. This became graphically clear when the Oberlin faculty refused to grant a preaching license or award her a degree upon completion of theological study because women were expected to remain silent during church services. This stirred her to action rather than acquiescence. For several years she toured "the Yankee belt" from New England to the Midwest, speaking on behalf of temperance, antislavery, and women's rights. In the summer of 1853 she attained considerable notoriety when, as a regularly authorized delegate to the World's Temperance Convention held in New York, she was shouted down for attempting to speak amid a male audience. She also preached as occasions presented themselves, and in 1853 reached a milestone in American religious history. That year she accepted appointment at a small Congregationalist church near her home town and was ordained minister there. Brown thus became the first woman to be ordained in a major Protestant denomination. The question of infant damnation particularly offended her sense of justice and views of a benevolent deity. She embraced increasingly unorthodox views and within a year asked the church to dismiss her from clerical responsibilities. Nevertheless her pioneering effort inspired other women to seek ordination in several denominations. Thereafter she pursued urban social work, wrote for the *Women's Journal*, and served as vice president of the Association for the Advancement of Women. Later generations of feminists honored her efforts and saw symbolic victory in her voting for the first time one year before she died.

In 1856 Brown became Mrs. Samuel C. Blackwell, entering upon a lengthy marriage that enjoyed five surviving children and remarkably supportive attitudes between wife and husband. Alongside domestic duties, Blackwell persisted in studying and writing at least three hours every day. She possessed a creative, inquisitive mind that would not abide theological conventions any more easily than social ones. Early on she rejected ideas of infant damnation and thought of salvation as a cheap rescue from hell. By 1878 she had arrived at ideas of human goodness that progressed through divine benevolence. These convictions accorded best with Unitarianism, and so she embraced that identity as her own. As an early and innovative student of Darwinism, she reconciled her religious beliefs with the findings of that modern science, finding in its evidence, incidentally, that evolution proved a need for further female emancipation. Her devout spirit was always questing beyond timid thoughts and regulations; it exemplified the perennial search for better understanding of the soul and the created order through personal experience and reflection.

Bibliography:

A.   *Woman's Right to Preach the Gospel* (Syracuse, NY, 1853); *Shadows of Our Social System* (New York, 1856); *Studies in General Science* (New York, 1869); *The Sexes Throughout Nature* (New York, 1875); *Philosophy of Individuality; or, The One and the Many* (New York, 1892); *The Making of the Universe: Evolution the Continuous Process which Derives the Finite from the Infinite* (Boston, 1914).

B.   NCAB 29, 129; DAB 2, 319–20; NAW 1, 158–61; NYT 6 Nov 1921, 22; Elizabeth Cazden, *Antoinette Brown Blackwell: A Biography* (Old Westbury, NY, 1983).

BLAIR, James (1655?, Alvah, Scotland—18 May 1743, Williamsburg, VA). *Education*: M.A., Univ. of Edinburgh, 1673; studied theology with William Keith and Laurence Charteris, Edinburgh, 1673–79. *Career*: minister, Cranston, Scotland, 1679–81; clerk, Rolls Office, London, 1682–85; rector, Varina, VA, 1685–94; President, Coll. of William and Mary, 1693–1743; rector, Jamestown, VA, 1694–1710; rector, Bruton Parish Church, Williamsburg, VA, 1710–43.

After two years of rigorous training at Marischal College, an aggressively Calvinistic school in Aberdeen, young Blair proceeded to Edinburgh where, at length, he was ordained a minister in the Church of Scotland. His first pastorate ended abruptly when he refused to sign a test oath acknowledging the English king (James II, a Catholic) to be head of the Scottish church. Three years of secular employment in London allowed him time to meet the city's Anglican bishop, form a lasting friendship, and receive appointment to a rural parish in Henrico County, colony of Virginia. Blair pursued his work there with great diligence, spurred by a zeal amounting to tactlessness as he tried to elevate moral behavior among those whose inclinations were more hedonistic than abstemious. In 1689 he became the first colonial priest to be designated commissary, an office wherein the bishop of London deputized him to supervise general standards for local clergymen; short of power to confirm or ordain, he represented episcopal authority in the New World. As a latitudinarian churchman, the commissary accepted diversity on a variety of theological issues, but he drew the line at tolerating Catholics, Unitarians, and especially Quakers within a proper English domain. Still his experiences were often troubled. He antagonized laymen by requesting more secure financial arrangements for priests. He alienated many clerics by attempting to establish ecclesiastical courts with specific catalogues of offenses and punishments. Across the Atlantic, his only fame was, happily, through volumes of straightforward sermons on moral conduct—popular homilies that remained a standard feature in Anglican libraries for over a century.

In 1690, Commissary Blair summoned the colony's lawful ministers (numbering approximately twenty-four at the time) to consider the low tenor of current religious conditions. One of the lasting results of that meeting was a plan to establish a college that might provide Christian education for local youth and ensure a learned ministry. After spending many tedious months (1691–93) in England, where he gained support from influential friends, Blair finally secured the college's charter and was named its first president. He returned to Virginia and created a classical academy, the initial step toward instruction in philosophy, mathematics, and some of the more practical arts. Despite scant local support, opposition from governmental officials, and one disastrous fire (1705), the president of William and Mary established the strongest tradition of intellectual excellence found in southern colonies before the Revolution. From 1694 onward, Blair was a member of the governor's council, a political arena where his self-interest and ambition for personal gain impeded growth of the established church. He proved a ruthless combatant against all who opposed his will; slowly, mundane battles took precedence over spiritual objectives. Though his motives may not have been mixed as were his actions, this early leader of Virginia's mother church epitomized its struggle between commitment to pastoral service and concern for material advantage.

Bibliography:

A.   *Our Saviour's Divine Sermon on the Mount . . . Explained, and the Practice of it Recommended in Divers Sermons and Discourses*, 5 vols. (London, 1722); 4 vols. (London, 1740).

B.   AAP 5, 7–9; SH 2, 196; NCAB 3, 231–32; DAB 2, 335–37; Parke Rouse Jr., *James Blair of Virginia* (Chapel Hill, NC, 1971).

BLAKE, Eugene Carson (7 November 1906, St. Louis, MO—31 July 1985, Stamford, CT). *Education*: B.A. Princeton U., 1928; studied at New Coll., Edinburgh, Scotland 1929–30; Th.B., Princeton Sem., 1932. *Career*: teacher, Forman Christian Coll., Lahore, India, 1928–29; assistant minister, St. Nicholas Collegiate Church, New York City, 1932–35; minister, First Presbyterian Church, Albany, NY, 1935–40; minister, Pasadena Presbyterian Church, 1940–51; stated clerk of the General Assembly, Presbyterian Church, U.S.A., 1951–58; stated clerk of the General Assembly, United Presbyterian Church in the U.S.A., 1958–66; general secretary, World Council of Churches, 1966–72; president, Bread for the World, 1974–78; active retirement, 1978–85.

A dynamic, vigorous activist in many causes, Blake is probably best remembered for his work in the cause of ecumenism. He first attracted attention as leader of a large Presbyterian congregation in California and a popular voice on regular radio broadcasts which his church sponsored. By mid-century he became the chief executive of his denomination's administrative machinery and guided the organization's affairs for fifteen years. From that position he often engaged in controversial issues, showing that American religious principles should apply effectively to contemporary social issues. Blake used the eminence of his office as spokesman for almost three million Presbyterians to oppose McCarthyism and to speak against the similarly narrow-minded anti-Catholicism of the 1960 presidential election. As president of the National Council of Churches he strove to coordinate the efforts of more than thirty-five million church members in thirty Protestant and Eastern Orthodox denominations along those lines. He figured prominently in civil rights activities throughout the 1960s and criticized American involvement in Vietnam as a wasteful diversion from more pressing matters at home.

In addition to social activism, Blake was a major force for church unity. He was convinced that separate denominations were an offense to divine will as well as a sociological scandal. In a famous sermon delivered in December of 1960 at Grace Cathedral in San Francisco he broached "a proposal toward the reunion of Christ's church" which eventually led to an ongoing Consultation on Church Union, currently involving nine denominations. Blake always maintained that he did not want to replace the tragic division among churches with a single, authoritative organization. But since he opposed ecclesiastical separation and rivalry so vigorously, his critics often pointed out no more than half in jest that this "Presbyterian pope" envisioned the creation of a mammoth "superchurch" to take the place of denominational pluralism. Still, Blake was transfixed by the image of a united Christendom. He was a delegate to the 1948 occasion that formed the World Council of Churches, and after supporting its subsequent activities he became its president eighteen years later. There he welcomed representatives from the third world as churches burgeoned in those new countries. He also facilitated the entry of Russian and other Orthodox churches into the mutually supportive global association. In his many travels and the issues he addressed, he embodied a faith applied directly to the practical needs of his time.

Bibliography:

A. *Christian Faith: Bulwark of Freedom* (Houston, TX, 1956); *He Is Lord of All* (Philadelphia, 1958); *The Church in the Next Decade* (New York, 1966).

B. NCAB I, 142–43; NYT 1 August 1985, A 16; R. Douglas Brackenridge, *Eugene Carson Blake: Prophet with Portfolio* (New York, 1978).

BLAVATSKY, Helena Petrovna (12 August 1831, Ekaterinoslav, Russia—8 May 1891, London, England).

The international wandering and experimental liaisons characterizing successive decades of Madame Blavatsky's search for truth gave an exotic coloration to all her endeavors. While reports of her early life contain many claims difficult to verify, it is certain that her imaginative spirit refused to stay within conventional expectations for marital or religious behavior. She narrowly escaped drowning at sea in 1871 and turned to spiritualism in earnest after that. In 1873 she arrived in New York on a steerage ticket, facing bleak prospects for life on the Lower East Side. Hearing of seances conducted in Vermont, she went there in 1874 and met *Henry S. Olcott, a man who soon became her companion and influential disciple. Their apartments in New York quickly attracted attention as the focal point for mystics and seekers of the occult. In 1875 the Theosophical Society was formed with Olcott as president and Blavatsky modestly in the background as corresponding secretary. But Blavatsky was unmistakably the society's major voice, her publications supplying through the years ideological content for the universal wisdom which it disseminated. By 1878 it was clear the Society was not flourishing; so the madame mystic, now an American citizen, sailed for India to seek alliances with Hindu pundits at first and then major leaders in Buddhism. Her international following proved unruly. Dissension in London and accusations of chicanery in India (both in 1884) caused many to conclude that she was nothing more than a charming, ingenious imposter. Defections were balanced with new converts, and she remained to the end a powerful contributor to theosophy.

It was important to Blavatsky that she distinguish her movement from cheaper attempts of spiritualists to contact psychic phenomena through individual mediums. By contrast she claimed to have received ancient teachings directly from masters (mahatmas) who had developed their spiritual life to an uncommonly high degree. These masters transmitted their thoughts to Blavatsky in the form of letters that inexplicably appeared in her possession. She in turn shared these insights into science and theology with the world. Skeptics charged that much of her writing was plagiarized, but theosophists extolled her ability to summarize their central beliefs. Those beliefs were based on the view that existence stemmed from a single, all-encompassing principle transcending human conception. Individual souls are only aspects of one Oversoul, and they must seek to understand the basic Unknown Root through personal effort during many reincarnations. While she made no extensive claims about her own psychic powers, Blavatsky was convinced there was genuine value in occult mysteries. She also hoped the Society would promote universal human brotherhood, further the comparative study of religions, and investigate the undiscovered powers of nature still faintly understood by men. In the last years she continued to write in London, taking hope that *Annie Besant, a recent convert, would consolidate factions of the wide ranging religious impulse.

Bibliography:

A.   *Isis Unveiled*, 2 vols. (New York, 1877); *The Secret Doctrine*, 3 vols. (London, 1888–97); *Key to Theosophy* (London, 1889); *The Voice of the Silence* (London, 1889); *Theosophical Glossary* (London, 1892); *The Complete Works of H. P. Blavatsky*, ed. A. Trevor Barker, 4 vols. (London, 1933).

B.   SH 2, 199; NCAB 15, 336–37; DAB 2, 361–63; NAW 1, 174–77; NYT 9 May 1891, 1; Arthur Lillie, *Mme. Blavatsky and Her Theosophy* (London, 1895); Carl E. Bechofer-Roberts, *The Mysterious Madame* (New York, 1931); Charles J. Ryan, *H. P.*

Blavatsky and the Theosophical Movement (Point Loma, CA, 1937); Gertrude M. Williams, *Priestess of the Occult* (New York, 1946); John Symonds, *Madame Blavatsky: Medium and Magician* (London, 1959).

BLISS, William Dwight Porter (20 August 1856, Constantinople, Turkey—8 October 1926, New York, NY). *Education:* B.A., Amherst Coll., 1878; B.D., Hartford Sem., 1882. *Career:* minister of Congregational churches in Denver, CO and South Natick, MA, 1882–85; Episcopal rector, Lee, MA, 1885–87; rector, Grace Episcopal Church, Boston, 1887–90; rector, Church of the Carpenter, Boston, MA, 1890–94; traveling lecturer, Christian Socialist Union, 1894–98; rector, Church of Our Saviour, San Gabriel, CA, 1898–1902; rector, Amityville, NJ, 1902–06; special investigator, U.S. Bureau of Labor, 1907–09; rector, West Orange, NJ, 1910–14; student, pastor and YMCA worker in Switzerland, 1914–21; rector, St. Martha's Episcopal Church, New York, 1921–25.

Born to missionary parents who spent fifty years among Armenians in the Ottoman Empire, Bliss returned to this country for education and subsequent pastoral service. After a brief term as Congregationalist minister he joined the Episcopal church, inaugurating forty years of innovative work in that denomination's efforts to advance social reforms. His first rectorship at Lee, Massachusetts, was in a factory town which forced him to consider the relation between churches and workers alienated from religion. Influenced by the ideas of Charles Kingsley, Frederick D. Maurice, and other Anglican socialists, he advocated mild programs of Christian socialism at a time when American clergymen seemed universally opposed to such activities. He joined the Knights of Labor and in 1887 ran for lieutenant-governor on the Labor Party ticket. In 1890 he broke fresh ground by founding a new kind of church community; Boston's Christian Socialist Church of the Carpenter became an inner city experimental center where he tried to apply New Testament teachings as he understood their relation to social problems. Embodying a persistent moral energy, he lectured widely in the U.S., Canada, and England in an effort to convince church leaders of their social responsibility. His publicity campaigns in ecclesiastical circles served to heighten awareness of conditions endemic to industrial society, while his practical work on local levels generated specific welfare programs congruent with a liturgical perspective.

In addition to taking the initiative in local programs and speaking tours, Bliss also founded a number of larger groups that furthered the cause of social reform. In 1889 he helped organize the first Christian Socialist Society and served as its secretary. Ten years later he became president of the National Social Reform League. During this era he also cooperated with *William R. Huntington in organizing the Church Association for the Advancement of the Interests of Labor. By 1909 he had formed a long, fruitful relationship with *Josiah Strong and his American Institute of Social Service. He also collaborated with Strong to produce an important Social Gospel publication, *Studies in the Gospel of the Kingdom*. Another significant contribution on the informational side was his compilation of an *Encyclopedia of Social Reform* (1898), which ran to many editions. Other duties included editorship of *The Dawn* (1889–96), monthly organ of the Christian Socialist Society, and *The American Fabian* (1895–96). Not known for his scholarship but as a tireless propagandist, Bliss continued to champion Christian ideology as a basis for concrete amelioration of social distress. His writings together with sermons and a wide range of churchly activities stressed the importance of the working poor as a special focus for modern gospel witness.

Bibliography:

A.   *A Handbook of Socialism* (New York, 1895).
B.   SH 2, 204; NCAB 20, 91–92; DAB 2, 377–78; NYT 9 Oct 1926, 17.

BOEHM, John Philip (November, 1683, Hochstadt, Germany—29 April 1749, Hellertown, PA). *Career*: schoolmaster for the Reformed congregation at Worms (1708–15) and Lambsheim (1715–20), Germany; itinerant Reformed minister (after 1725) and farmer, Whitpain, PA, 1720–49.

Reformed churches among German colonists in Pennsylvania were not formed as a result of missionaries sent from the fatherland. A dozen of the earliest ones were founded by a former schoolteacher turned farmer who could not refuse the entreaties of his neighbors. Shortly after emigrating (1720), Boehm began conducting worship services at his home; he finally yielded (1725) to the repeated urging of friends and openly declared himself a minister. Regular worship according to Reformed standards developed quickly thereafter, and Boehm was a faithful pastor to many of those congregations. He preached and administered sacraments principally at Falkner Swamp, Skippack, and Whitemarsh, but his itinerary extended over 100 miles, a circuit he traveled every month for twenty years. In 1727 George M. Weiss, a university-educated and regularly ordained minister, upon coming to America challenged Boehm's qualifications for pastoral office. Boehm was stung by such criticism because it contained an element of truth. He appealed his case to the Dutch Reformed Classis of Amsterdam, which ruled in his favor, recommending ordination to avoid future charges on that score. Accordingly in 1729 he was ordained in New York at the hands of Dutch clergymen and inaugurated a period of close cooperation with their church lasting until 1792. Weiss professed reconciliation but slighted the earlier preacher's work and prevented any material help from Holland for almost two decades.

Founding churches and ministering to their needs was sufficient to preserve Boehm's name in the annals of Reformed history, but another significant contribution lay in preserving their loyalty to traditional standards of the faith. The most serious threat to this loyalty was posed by *Nicholas L. Zinzendorf, who toured eastern Pennsylvania in 1741–42 with hopes of uniting all German evangelicals into a single church. He proposed a Union Synod that would combine all sects into a true apostolic body, patterned after the Moravians whom he represented. The new synod also began appointing clergymen and issued a new catechism. Boehm denounced not only the arbitrary manner in which Zinzendorf presumed to break with traditional authorities but also the meager content of his experimental ecumenism. Far from wishing to dissolve ties with the Classis of Amsterdam, Boehm argued that his churches' existence depended on continued relations with that body and on the Heidelberg Catechism as a guideline for their common belief. Tested church procedures were always high among his priorities, and his able defense of them preserved historical continuity in a setting where innovation appealed to many other groups. In 1747 he was instrumental in forming, with the help of *Michael Schlatter sent by Dutch authorities the year before, the Coetus of Pennsylvania. Through that governing body and his continued preaching, he laid the basis for strong Reformed witness in the middle colonies.

Bibliography:

A. *Getreuer Warnungsbrief an die Hochteutsche Evangelische Reformirte Gemeinde und all deren Glieder in Pennsylvanien* (Philadelphia, 1742).

B. DAB 2, 404–05; NCE 2, 630; Henry S. Dotterer, *John Philip Boehm* (Philadelphia, 1890); William J. Hinke (ed.), *Life and Letters of the Rev. John Philip Boehm* (Philadelphia, 1916; New York, 1972).

BOEHM, Martin (30 November 1724, Lancaster County, PA—23 March 1812, Lancaster County, PA). *Career*: minister, Mennonite Society, Pequea, PA, 1756–77; bishop, 1759–77; independent itinerant preacher, 1777–1800; bishop, Church of the United Brethren in Christ, 1800–12.

There was little consideration of vocational aptitude when Boehm was first designated as minister of his local Mennonite society. A farmer like most of his neighbors, he was chosen instead by lot. This casual beginning left him doubtful about his pastoral qualifications, but a conversion experience in 1758 enabled him to preach thereafter with great power and authority. In 1761 Boehm traveled extensively among German-speaking churches in Pennsylvania, Maryland, and Virginia. In the Shenandoah Valley he encountered *George Whitefield and witnessed Great Awakening enthusiasms that accorded closely with his personal convictions. By the mid–1770s criticism began to mount regarding his vigorous revival preaching and his association with people in other denominations. Admonitions to conform had no effect, and in 1777 Mennonite clergy excommunicated Boehm for what they perceived to be unorthodox doctrine and liberal attitudes. This action further strengthened his views, and he preached more actively as an independent evangelist who drew large crowds of German-speaking Americans in the central colonies.

One of the many people who heard Boehm preach was *Philip W. Otterbein, a Dutch Reformed minister, and the pair immediately formed a lasting collaborative friendship. After years of small, preliminary associations, the two pastors formed in 1800 the Church of the United Brethren in Christ. At that time each of the co-founders also became bishops of the United Brethren. In a parallel set of events, a Methodist class had been meeting in Boehm's home since 1775.

Other members of his family belonged to that religious group, and in 1802 the aging bishop and preacher added his name to the rolls as well. While he did not leave the United Brethren, he was at the same time a powerful force in spreading Methodism throughout central Pennsylvania. After fifty-five years of evangelical activities his life finally came to an end. Bishop *Francis Asbury delivered a memorial sermon on his behalf, commemorating a life whose single-minded energies had greatly affected three separate denominations.

Bibliography:

B.   NCAB 21, 137–38; DAB 2, 405–06; Henry Boehm, *Reminiscences, Historical and Biographical, of Sixty-four Years in the Ministry* edited by Joseph B. Wakeley (New York, 1865).

BOOTH, Evangeline Cory (25 December 1865, London, England—17 July 1950, Hartsdale, NY). *Career*: principal of Training College, Clapton, and commander of field operations in London, 1888–95; field commissioner in Canada, 1896–1904; field commissioner in the U.S., 1904–34; general of the International Salvation Army, 1934–39; active retirement, 1939–50.

The year in which "little Eva" Booth was born marked the time when her father left Methodism to found a separate movement known as the Salvation Army. She grew up within that organization, absorbing her family's emphasis on personal religious commitment, strict moral principles, and compassion for social outcasts. By the age of fifteen she was on the streets selling *War Cry*, the Army newspaper, and two years later she was in charge of her own preaching station. Never doctrinaire in her feminist convictions, she quietly followed the example of her mother and proved that women could be as successful as men in winning souls. She also gained no small reputation as a troubleshooter, arguing her cause before mobs and magistrates who opposed the work of salvation. After additional years of service in England, Booth was transferred to Canada in 1896 to supervise operations there. Under her able leadership, the Army's fundamentally spiritual ministry remained in contact with those on a social level that others seemed unable or unwilling to reach. In rough conditions from Toronto to the Klondike, she helped spread a gospel message through agencies which brought relief to the poor and needy. Extensive efforts in providing rescue homes, food depots, temporary residence facilities, and rehabilitation centers were the practical means used to give reformed lives moral purpose again.

Unlike several of her brothers and sisters, Evangeline Booth obeyed orders from headquarters without serious opposition. In 1904 she was moved to the United States and began a period of service eventually spanning thirty years. The Army's normal habits were easily adapted to the American custom of voluntary support, and the new commander quickly secured broad financial backing for her many programs. Expanded social service was probably the most noticeable aspect of diversified work which the Army pursued. Hospitals, industrial homes, unemployment bureaus, bread lines, prison work, emergency disaster relief, and old age homes indicated some of the organization's concerns. During World War I, the tremendous scope of activities was enlarged even further to include care for American soldiers in France. During the 1920s, Booth reluctantly participated in reforms within the Army that caused some personal strain but proved beneficial to the entire movement. In 1929 she voted to depose her brother (second general, appointed by his father) and helped set the rule that new generals be elected rather than chosen by their predecessor. In 1934 she was chosen by such an election to become the fourth general, and only woman, to head up the international agency. She was also the last of the Booths to lead the Army and the last commander in this country to symbolize personally an institution that continues to serve the downtrodden.

Bibliography:

A. *Love Is All* (New York, 1908); *The War Romance of the Salvation Army*, with Grace L. Hill (Philadelphia, 1919); *Toward a Better World* (Garden City, NY, 1928).

B. NCAB B, 127–29; NAW 1, 204–7; NYT 18 Jul 1950, 29; Philip W. Wilson, *General Evangeline Booth of the Salvation Army* (New York, 1948); Herbert A. Wisbey, Jr., *Soldiers Without Swords: A History of the Salvation Army in the United States* (New York, 1955).

BOUDINOT, Elias (1802?, near Rome, GA—22 June 1839, Park Hill, Indian Territory, now OK). *Education*: studied at mission school, Cornwall, CT, 1818–22; studied at Andover Sem., 1822–23. *Career*: spokesman for the Cherokee Nation, 1823–35; editor, *Cherokee Phoenix*, 1828–35.

Tribal lands in the southern Appalachians had been home for Iroquoian-speaking Cherokees long before white settlers entered those mountains. In the early 1800s, a young native named Galagina began to emerge as a leader who could combine red and white cultures for the benefit of his people. Galagina, or Buck Watie as he was sometimes called after his father, was sent by missionaries to schools in New England. There he adopted the name of Elias Boudinot, a school patron, and absorbed ideas that might improve life among Cherokees on his return. Further training at Andover gave him the intellectual tools necessary for converting other members of his nation and guiding their selective borrowing of white cultural patterns. One of his more lasting contributions centered on a translation, begun in 1823, of the New Testament into Cherokee. A few years earlier another tribesman, Sequoyah, had created an alphabet for their language, and Boudinot used that in collaboration with Samuel A. Worcester to render the gospels into native speech. The project continued for many years, extending beyond Boudinot's untimely death. His easy transference from one culture to the other was indicated in 1824 when he proposed marriage to Harriet Gold, a white girl living near the old missionary school in Connecticut. This occasioned, not for the first time, a furor of race prejudice. The controversy over miscegenation did not end when the couple was united in 1826 and anticipated years of service in Georgia.

Working for the general uplift of his people, Boudinot counseled, wrote, and raised funds on their behalf. He edited the *Cherokee Phoenix*, the first newspaper ever printed for any American Indian tribe. Its contents (written mostly in English with perhaps 25% in Cherokee) advanced public education, increased the influence of Christian moral standards, and gave considerable impetus to national solidarity. Boudinot had begun life as a worshiper of aboriginal religious figures, but on his return from New England he was a vital force in spreading Christian principles as an alternative. He also wrote the first novel in the Cherokee tongue, depicting the virtues of such acculturating changes. His influence was great among kinsmen until 1835, when he signed the Treaty of New Echota, a document that sold tribal lands and agreed to national removal beyond the Mississippi River. Though he did not understand the intentions behind that fraudulent transaction, Boudinot with his friendly attitudes regarding whites was blamed for the disastrous result. After three years' resistance, Cherokees were forced at the point of bayonets to evacuate their homeland and follow (1838) a "trail of tears" to the West. Vengeful warriors responded by assassinating the red man who had so confidently urged the adoption of white values.

Bibliography:

A. *An Address to the Whites* (Philadelphia, 1826); *Poor Sarah, or The Indian Woman* (New Echota, GA, 1833); *Letters and Other Papers Relating to Cherokee Affairs* (Athens, GA, 1837).

B. NCAB 19, 224–25; DAB 2, 478–79; Ralph H. Gabriel, *Elias Boudinot, Cherokee and his America* (Norman, OK, 1941).

BOWNE, Borden Parker (14 January 1847, Leonardville, NJ—1 April 1910, Brookline, MA). *Education*: B.A., Univ. of the City of New York, 1871; studied at Paris, Halle, and Göttingen, 1873–75; M.A., Univ. of the City of New York, 1876. *Career*: minister at Whitestone, NY, 1872–73; asst. professor of Modern Languages at Univ. of the City of New York and religious editor of *The Independent*, 1875–76; professor of Philosophy, Boston Univ., 1876–1910; dean of Graduate School, Boston Univ., 1888–1910.

During the last half of the nineteenth century many Christian assumptions about the natural world and human life were being challenged by the implications of modern science. Bowne's central activity in that context was to place ideas drawn from faith on a steady yet flexible philosophical foundation. He attempted to synthesize, not resist, the facts and methods of science, molding them into a unified, idealistic basis in philosophy. His thought had a liberalizing influence primarily among fellow Methodists, and aspects of it were developed by two theological students, *Edgar S. Brightman and *Albert C. Knudson. But his many years of university teaching and an impressive publication record spread his ideas beyond denominational lines, laying the philosophical groundwork for much of Liberal theology in America. The fact that he was tried and acquitted on doctrinal matters in 1904 is incidental to his career and bears mentioning only because it was the last significant investigation by Methodists into the alleged heresy of one of its ministers.

As a philosopher Bowne was concerned with refuting materialistic and naturalistic views of the world, in a manner similar to Rudolph H. Lotze, under whom he studied in Germany. In place of those mechanistic conceptions of reality, he posited the existence of a single, ideal ground of being which allowed for constant laws in natural events but did not lead to determinism. He could not accept any view that the world was a meaningless compound of atoms and a blind interaction of their forces. On the contrary, he insisted that objects of the material order were expressions of ideas and those ideas the product of one infinite, omnipresent energy which continually supports objective reality. Such a view provided intelligibility to the natural order, rescuing it from a mechanistic interpretation of endless changes and making it quite compatible with modern physics.

Just as naturalistic systems were inadequate to account for categories such as knowledge, substance, or causality, Bowne was convinced that impersonalistic systems of thought could not provide the unitary agent necessary for intelligent thought and action. His metaphysical orientation, which came to be called "personalism," allowed for thought and thinker on both the theistic and human level. This made objects of the material world intelligible, and it allowed for conceptions of the human self beyond a continuum of mechanistic processes. Bowne's view also provided for individual volition as an element in the complexities of human history. Personalism afforded a perspective that could accept the findings of historical and natural science and still secure faith in God, considering the limited understanding men had gained regarding the ultimate purposes of natural or human events. Bowne's defense of theological idealism renewed the basis for theism and personal ethics that had been impaired by some evolutionists of his day.

Bibliography:

A. *Studies in Theism* (New York, 1879); *Metaphysics: A Study in First Principles* (New York, 1882); *Philosophy of Theism* (New York, 1887); *The Theory of Thought and Knowledge* (New York, 1897); *The Immanence of God* (Boston, 1905); *Personalism* (Boston, 1908).

B. SH 2, 242–43; NCAB 11, 180, DAB 2, 522–23; NYT 3 Apr 1910, II, 11; Charles B. Pyle, *The Philosophy of Borden Parker Bowne* (Columbus, OH, 1910); Francis J. McConnell, *Borden Parker Bowne, His Life and His Philosophy* (New York, 1929).

BOYD, Richard Henry (15 March 1843, Noxubee County, MS—23 August 1922, Nashville, TN). *Education*: studied at Bishop Coll., 1870–72. *Career*: minister, several Baptist churches in TX, 1872–95; corresponding secretary, National Baptist Home Mission Board, 1896–97; corresponding secretary, National Baptist Publishing Board, 1897–1922.

Son to a slave mother and a white planter, this individual grew to manhood being called Dick Gray. Emancipation found him in Texas, and he changed his name to R.H. Boyd while pursuing various jobs with little sense of purpose. But in 1870 he converted to Christianity and determined to enter the Baptist ministry. He had learned the rudiments of spelling and reading largely on his own, and this allowed him to profit from concentrated training at a school founded and operated by the Home Missionary Society of New York. Thereafter he organized many Baptist churches, appealing particularly to former slaves, and forming them into the first association of Negro Baptists in the state. By the mid–1870s Boyd was elected superintendent of Baptist missions for the black population in Texas, and he quickly became the general convention's most conspicuous black leader. White Baptists in Texas, as in other southern states, were quite content to let black Baptists establish separate denominational structures. By the 1890s Boyd capitalized on this independence by starting a new publishing operation for black Baptist Sunday Schools. This use of published material soon led to more ambitious designs and influential activities.

In 1896 Boyd was elected secretary of the home mission board which was responsible for missions to black citizens throughout the country. He did not remain at that post for long, but his enlarged vision and his move from the confines of one state to a prominent position in a denomination of national proportions remained part of his subsequent career. That career centered on the publication board of the National Baptist Convention, a printing venture that he nursed through early economic difficulties and built into a powerful source of Negro Baptist literature. It issued the first such literature ever published, providing among other things lessons for religious education, guidebooks for pastors, and hymnals. Some denominational leaders clashed with Boyd over administering the agency. By 1915 a lawsuit vindicated Boyd, and he kept the efficient organization under his forceful control. But vindication brought no reconciliation with denominational authorities, and he withdrew from the national convention. This departure constituted the nucleus of the American National Baptist Convention, Incorporated. Over time this group has become the second largest black Baptist denomination in the country.

Bibliography:

A.   *The National Baptist Hymnal: Arranged for Use in Churches, Sunday Schools and Young People's Societies*, edited by R.H. Boyd (Nashville, 1903); *Ancient and Modern Sunday-school Methods: Their Origin, Organization, Government, Officers and Literature* (Nashville, 1909); *National Baptist Pastor's Guide* (Nashville, 1915); *A Story of the National Baptist Publishing Board* (Nashville, 1915).

B.   DAB 2, 528.

BRADFORD, William (March, 1590, Austerfield, England—9 May 1657, Plymouth, MA). *Career*: governor, Plymouth Colony, 1621–33; 1635; 1637, 1639–43, 1645–57.

Descended from yeoman stock in Yorkshire, young Bradford disappointed his guardians by exercising independent judgment in regard to religious matters. By the age of sixteen he had become a Separatist, joining the small Puritan band which met at *William Brewster's house in Scrooby. His serious mien and private study of Scripture led to responsible posts in the congregation, but he remained through life a layman. He weathered the unsettled period of 1607–09, accompanying other dissenters from England to the Dutch city of Leyden in search of religious freedom. While he supported himself there by working in textiles, Bradford read extensively in theological literature and became trusted as a pious mainstay of the church. By 1619 he agreed with those who determined to secure more favorable circumstances for Puritans in the New World, sailing with the first contingent one year later on the *Mayflower*. Landfall in Massachusetts was not expected, nor was the severe winter and lack of provisions which their foundered ship, *Speedwell*, would have supplied. But despite these hardships and personal loss (wife drowned, 1620), he survived along with half the original colonists. John Carver, the first governor, died in early spring, and Bradford was chosen to succeed him. Except for a few years of rotation, he served in that office for the rest of his life, usually without salary and often to the benefit of fellow immigrants. He never held spiritual office, but his practical reliability and wise leadership made him the leading Pilgrim founder of Plymouth.

Religious tolerance and relations with neighboring powers were problems Bradford eventually had to face, but the immediate one was famine. Though foodstuffs were scarce through 1622, the Pilgrims survived hard times, acknowledging providential protection in a situation where similar ventures had ended in ruin. At the same time Bradford was shrewd enough to recognize a more local agent of deliverance and carefully nurtured friendly alliances with Massasoit, sachem of the Wampanoag nation on his borders. That relationship was an essential element in the colony's early defense and growth. The governor's Indian policy, at once generous and firm, laid the basis for decades of relatively peaceful red-white interchange. His attitude about religious differences was equally benign. Not committed in principle to indifferent toleration, he nevertheless thought it arrogance for any man or church to claim it had sounded the full depths of God's word. Thus Catholic visitors (1650) were received with courtesy, and the vote was not restricted to church members in this first New England plantation. Plymouth developed slowly, overshadowed by the larger domain of Massachusetts Bay. Bradford represented his people in common enterprises for protection and trade, and he often defended their rights for separate autonomy modeled after congregational polity. In addition to active participation in daily affairs, his journals, poems, and copybooks have preserved the tenor of life in a group forced by external pressures to a new beginning.

Bibliography:

A. *History of Plymouth Plantation*, ed. William T. Davis (New York, 1908); ed. Worthington C. Ford (Boston, 1912); ed. Samuel E. Morison (New York, 1952).

B. NCAB 7, 368–69; DAB 2, 559–63; NCE 2, 743–44; James Shepard, *Governor*

William Bradford (New Britain, CT, 1900); Albert H. Plumb, *William Bradford of Plymouth* (Boston, 1920); Bradford Smith, *Bradford of Plymouth* (Philadelphia, 1951).

BRAINERD, David (20 April 1718, Haddam, CT—9 October 1747, Northampton, MA). *Education*: studied at Yale Coll., 1739–42; studied theology with Jedediah Mills, Ripton, CT, 1742. *Career*: Society in Scotland for the Propagation of Christian Knowledge (SSPCK) missionary to Indians in NY, PA and NJ, 1742–47.

By his own account Brainerd was of a somber and melancholy disposition, suffering before the age of eight terrible fears of death. With his father dying in that year and his being completely orphaned by 1732, the young man turned ever inward to the consolations of religion. But the rigorous doctrine of salvation through election afforded cold comfort to one who was almost pathologically obsessed with matters of the soul. His inner tumult did not subside until 1739. Once he admitted that all expiatory works of merit were unavailing in face of a sovereign God, then solace broke through and transformed his life into one of witness with only occasional lapses into despair. That same year Brainerd entered Yale, a preparatory step for the ministry that he espoused despite shy, retiring manners. He approved of the Awakening sermons advanced by such preachers as *Jonathan Edwards and *George Whitefield, making unadvisedly harsh comparisons between their work and clergymen at Yale. One such remark came to the attention of president Thomas Clap, who demanded an apology; Brainerd refused and was expelled. Still his missionary zeal to spread the gospel was unaffected. A way opened in 1742 for him to pursue the goal of self-immolation while preaching Christ crucified as man's only comfort. The Society in Scotland for the Propagation of Christian Knowledge (SSPCK) commissioned him to work among Algonkian Indians at Kaunaumeek in the province of New York.

Brainerd's missionary activities were not a marked success. He did not stay in one place long enough to learn a native language, become familiar with aboriginal customs, or gain acceptance from those he sought to convert. In 1744, after being ordained by the Presbytery of New York, he was transferred to a site on the Delaware River. The following year saw him in central New Jersey, first at Crossweeksung (Crosswicks) and then Cranberry (Cranbury). These latter villages were scenes of relative encouragement to the evangelist. For once his gloomy journal referred to ready listeners and scores of Indians who requested further instruction—a genuine revival of unexpected proportions and duration. But Brainerd was dogged by poor health, a tubercular condition which caused him to leave the mission in his brother's care. He revisited Northampton and spent a few waning months nursed by his fiancee, Jerusha, one of Jonathan Edwards' daughters. Edwards was so impressed with the dying missionary's diary that he published it as an example of selfless Puritan virtue. It quickly became a minor classic, serving both as a devotional handbook for introspective mystics and a stimulus to further missionary work. His posthumous influence was probably greater in a number of fields than his practical achievements had been in life.

Bibliography:

B. AAP 3, 113–17; SH 2, 251; NCAB 2, 253; DAB 2, 591–92; *An Account of the Life of the Late Reverend Mr. David Brainerd*, ed. Jonathan Edwards (Boston, 1749); many subsequent editions under varying titles, the latest, ed. Philip E. Howard (Chicago, 1949); Richard E. Day, *Flagellant on Horseback* (Philadelphia, 1950); David Wynbeek, *David Brainerd: Beloved Yankee* (Grand Rapids, MI, 1961).

BRANHAM, William Marrion (6 April 1909, near Burkesville, KY—24 December 1965, Amarillo, TX). *Career*: independent Baptist evangelist, 1933–65.

Born and raised in grinding poverty, Branham worked at several odd jobs before returning to set up a new Baptist church in his home town of Jeffersonville Indiana. Friends contributed a tent for meetings, and the preacher whose career was launched in that obscure manner eventually became the most famous and popular of all pentecostal-charismatic leaders in the twentieth century. But times were difficult at first, with meager finances and sparse audiences. Things began to change in May of 1946, however, when Branham claimed to have been visited by an angel who gave him the divine gift of healing. This capacity seemed vindicated almost immediately at revival meetings in St. Louis, Missouri. Word of miraculous cures spread rapidly, and attendance at Branham's services mushroomed as he moved to increasing triumphs in Arkansas, Louisiana, Texas, Arizona, and California. Though the preacher remained an ordained Baptist all his life, most of his support came from Assemblies of God and Pentecostal churches. People affiliated with those denominations hungered for demonstrations of God's miraculous powers, and Branham seemed to meet those needs. In 1950 a famous photograph was released, showing a halo over the revivalist's head. Skeptics dismissed the aberration, but followers saw in it confirmation of their leader's special status. Hundreds of thousands attended meetings held by this modest, poorly educated man who filled the largest halls and stadiums in the country.

Many younger evangelists tried to legitimize their bids for fame by claiming Branham as their model. Few matched his personal humility, though, and none of them labored as hard through hours of prayer for the sick as did he. Followers thrilled at every story of new healings, angelic visions, psychiatric as well as physical diagnoses, and mystical sayings. Rumors persisted that even the dead had been raised in special circumstances. Such popularity began to falter in the late 1950s. Branham was himself meek and unpretentious, but his campaign managers were less scrupulous and used revival funds for their own gain. In 1956 the federal government launched investigations into campaign funding, and this created bad publicity for the revivals. Attendance also waned because Branham preached controversial doctrine with increasingly authoritarian emphasis. His "Jesus only" formulations of oneness in the godhead alienated the more orthodox minded. When he died as a result of an automobile accident, perhaps the best nonjudgmental observation made was that, compared to the glib business techniques of promotional evangelism, his honest, naive simplicity had merely become outdated.

Bibliography:

B. Gordon Lindsay in collaboration with William Branham, *William Branham: A Man Sent from God* (Jeffersonville, IN, 1950); C. Douglas Weaver, *The Healer-Prophet, William Branham: A Study of the Prophetic in American Pentecostalism* (Macon, GA, 1987).

BRAY, Thomas (1656, Marton, England—17 February 1730, London, England). *Education*: B.A., All Souls Coll., Oxford Univ., 1678; M.A., Hart Hall, Oxford Univ., 1693. *Career*: curate and family chaplain, Shropshire and Warwickshire, 1678–90; rector, Sheldon, England, 1690–96; American commissary for the bishop of London, 1696–1706; rector, St. Botolph Without, London, 1706–30.

William of Orange and Mary Stuart became in 1689 the first British monarchs whose coronation featured an oath to maintain Protestantism as established by law in their realm. In the American colony of Maryland, that turn of events encouraged Anglicans to press the Bishop of London for closer supervision of religion in their midst. As a result Bray was appointed commissary, an office in which he served for a decade to augment and perpetuate English missionary efforts in the New World. While recruiting personnel for colonial parishes, he soon learned that only the poorer clergy could be persuaded to leave their native land. They were unable to buy books, but without competent libraries they could not be useful to the design of their mission. Bray decided to provide those libraries, affording the basis for educated leadership in succeeding generations. By 1699 his efforts resulted in the formation of the Society for Promoting Christian Knowledge (SPCK), a group which contributed thousands of volumes to parochial collections. The SPCK began approximately fifty libraries in colonial plantations from New York to the Carolinas and Bermuda, with predominant concentration in Maryland. As commissary, Bray visited Maryland in 1700 at his own expense for a brief, intensive period of work. He circulated supervisory letters, conducted a tour of inspection, disciplined clergymen and laid plans for missionary expansion. His overriding concern was to have Anglican worship established by royal authority as the colony's one religious standard. He was more instrumental than any other individual in securing that objective in 1702.

On his return from inspecting colonial churches, Bray found that missionary work had expanded to the point of requiring a separate institution to support it. In 1701 he obtained a charter for the Society for the Propagation of the Gospel (SPG) in Foreign Parts. Throughout the eighteenth century, the SPG was the life blood of the Church of England on American shores. That mechanism of Bray's engineering supplied funds and manpower to sustain the comforts of religion that geography and sectarianism threatened to destroy. After resigning his post as episcopal assistant, Bray kept working for the cause of missionary outreach. He continued to emphasize the importance of libraries at home and abroad. Toward the end of his life he formed a third corporation notable for its effects in the New World. "Dr. Bray's Associates," as it was called, made significant advances in instructing Negro children, converting the local Indian population, and supporting the establishment of Georgia colony. Clearly the Anglican commissary's organizational activities influenced American religion long after he set them in motion.

Bibliography:

A. *Catechetical Lectures* (Oxford, 1696); *Bibliotheca Parochialis* (London, 1697); *A General View of the English Colonies in America with Respect to Religion* (London, 1698); *A Memorial Representing the Present State of Religion on the Continent of North America* (London, 1700).

B. DAB 2, 610–11; Bernard C. Steiner (ed.), *Rev. Thomas Bray: His Life and Selected Works* (Baltimore, 1901; New York, 1972); Henry P. Thompson, *Thomas Bray* (London, 1954).

BRECK, James Lloyd (27 June 1818, Philadelphia County, PA—30 March 1876, Benicia, CA). *Education*: B.A., Univ. of Pennsylvania, 1838; B.D., General Sem. (NY), 1841. *Career*: Episcopal missionary priest in WI, 1841–50, in MN, 1850–67, and in CA, 1867–76.

By the age of sixteen, Breck had dedicated himself to missions, a calling he pursued effectively for thirty-five years. While studying in a Long Island preparatory school run by *William A. Muhlenberg, he was influenced by new emphases on liturgical renewal, a sacramental resurgence also receiving attention in seminary. Those directives combined in the young student to produce a return to rigorous discipline in both personal and ecclesiastical life. In 1841 he responded to a call from bishop Jackson Kemper, volunteering for mission work on the sparsely settled prairies of Wisconsin. That setting gave him the opportunity to build on tendencies absorbed from the Oxford Movement and institute a celibate brotherhood for Episcopalians, ideals dormant in that denomination since the sixteenth century. He considered asceticism to be fundamental in a return to apostolic tasks; by 1842 Nashotah House provided the focus for regular recitation of canonical hours, manual labor, and extensive missionary work among pioneering families in the region. Self-denial was the cornerstone of monasticism, and Breck continued to follow the stern discipline even when his original companions abandoned it for a secular ministry. He traveled widely, hundreds of miles on foot and thousands on horseback, to develop schools or administer sacraments. Postulants for orders were attracted in increasing numbers to the establishment. Breck reluctantly assumed the presidency of all Nashotah enterprises, where life at the altar was deemed more important than evangelical preaching.

New mission fields beckoned, however, and Breck would not stay in an administrative position that lacked the challenge of new beginnings. In 1850 he moved farther northwest, attempting to found another monastic society. But the ascetic ideal itself had begun to pall; within five years the doughty missionary took a wife even as he persisted in ministerial labors. He concentrated on work among Indians of the Ojibway nation, building stations at Gull Lake (St. Columba) and at Leech Lake. Since he had long determined to endure harsh conditions as a soldier of Christ, his fortitude won admiration from native peoples. One of his converts, Enmegahbowh, became the first Ojibway ordained (1859) into Episcopal orders, in which office he served his people for six decades. Breck built another system of boarding schools and a theological seminary (Seabury) in the area between St. Paul and Faribault. Then for a third time he traveled to new mission territory, this time by ship to San Francisco. There he cooperated with the resident bishop in plans for extending the witness of their communion along three thousand miles of coastline. And, since the education of youth was always a pressing need together with that of supplying trained clergymen, his major contribution lay once again in founding more schools. California filled Breck with a great sense of urgency because it was not a wilderness and already so populous. Its many opportunities for ecclesiastical growth gave him room enough for continued sacrifice, which inspired others to follow a similar course.

Bibliography:

B.   DAB 3, 3–4; Charles Breck (ed.), *The Life of the Reverend James Lloyd Breck, Chiefly from Letters Written by Himself* (New York, 1883); Theodore I. Holcombe, *An Apostle of the Wilderness* (New York, 1903).

BRENGLE, Samuel Logan (1 June 1860, Fredericksburg, IN—20 May 1936, Scarsdale, NY). *Education*: A.B., Indiana Asbury (later DePauw) Univ., 1883; studied at Boston Univ., 1885. *Career*: itinerant Methodist minister in IN, 1884; independent evangelist, 1886; cadet and then officer in the Salvation Army, 1897–1931.

After founders of a movement succeed in getting initial momentum under way, the continuing success of either ideas or institutions depends on successors devoted to the cause. Brengle was one of those latter stalwarts, and his dedicated service of more than three decades to the Salvation Army helped keep its original zeal alive. He spent a few rather vaguely focused years in Methodist evangelism, but in 1885 he came to a sharp and vivid understanding of personal holiness. Shortly thereafter he felt a strong call to volunteer for William Booth's hardy band of witnesses who preached private salvation and served the urban downtrodden with equal energy. Brengle was one of the few ordained clergy to serve in the Army, and yet his vigorous exhortations epitomized the movement's early emphases well into the twentieth century. He urged staff members to strive after Wesleyan holiness, though he never endorsed speaking in tongues. As he rose in the ranks, he served mostly in New England states, working eventually in Chicago and San Francisco as well, plus ten foreign countries. Always noted for sermons with fire and bite, this sprightly and irrepressible evangelist helped keep Salvation Army work true to its early witness. Such work, he said, brought him joy, peace, and a world of fun.

Bibliography:

A. *Helps to Holiness* (London, 1896); *Heart-Talks on Holiness* (London, 1897); *The Way of Holiness* (New York, 1902); *The Soul-Winner's Secret* (New York, 1904); *When the Holy Ghost Came* (London, 1909); *Resurrection Life and Power* (London, 1925).

B. NYT 21 May 1936, 23; Clarence W. Hall, *Samuel Logan Brengle: Portrait of a Prophet* (New York, 1933).

BREWSTER, William (1560, Nottinghamshire, England—10 April 1644, Plymouth, MA). *Career*: retainer to William Davison, ambassador to Holland, 1583–89; bailiff and postmaster, Scrooby, England, 1590–1608; printer, Leyden, Holland, 1609–19; colonist and church elder, Plymouth, New England, 1620–44.

After an undetermined period of study at Peterhouse, Brewster entered the service of a gentleman active in foreign affairs for the Crown. He worked successfully in diplomatic circles for several years, but those activities ended when his patron incurred the queen's displeasure. By 1590 Brewster was comfortably settled at Scrooby, apparently inheriting both the social position and job occupied earlier by his father. He supported the Church of England, as might be expected of one holding a government position, but at the same time he sympathized with those who called for further reform. When James I became king and religious toleration was restricted, Brewster gravitated more toward Puritan convictions. He saw ministers suspended and silenced, preachers to whom he had listened with great spiritual profit. Convinced by 1606 that those persecuted leaders were more faithful to gospel purity than the courts and canons forcing them into conformity, he left the national church and cast his lot with separatists. His house became the meeting place for the small band of nonconformists, but as dangers mounted he fled with the rest to Amsterdam and then to Leyden. In Holland the congregation drew up a covenant of seven articles, constituting themselves a church faithful to sound doctrine and independent disciplinary authority. John Robinson was named its pastor while Brewster was appointed ruling elder, a position which he filled dutifully for the rest of his life.

By 1619 it was clear to Elder Brewster and others that the English flock must find a haven other than the Low Countries. After protracted negotiation, in 1620 a grant of land near the Hudson River was allowed them by the Virginia Company, and plans were quickly made for emigration to the New World. The *Mayflower* brought the Pilgrim colonists to Cape Cod Bay instead of to their designated tract, but they decided to settle there and prepare for winter already hard upon them. Brewster's elemental usefulness emerged during that first season when scurvy and starvation reduced the group by half. He spared no pains to help the needy, nursing the sick and standing watch through all hardships. As the only church officer present, he conducted worship services as well, expounding Scripture and conducting prayer services with the faithful. Brewster was not ordained and thus did not baptize or celebrate communion, but for nine years he was the only ecclesiastical authority in his colony to furnish spiritual nourishment for the gathered saints. His presence was steady and substantial, like a wheel horse that carried the weight of practical affairs during troubled times. Though technically not a minister, he nurtured the congregation and guided its daily conduct for over two decades of its American existence.

Bibliography:

B.   SH 2, 264; NCAB 7, 30–31; DAB 3, 29–30; Ashbel Steele, *Chief of the Pilgrims: The Life and Time of William Brewster* (Philadelphia, 1857); Dorothy Brewster, *William Brewster of the Mayflower: Portrait of a Pilgrim* (New York, 1971).

BRIGGS, Charles Augustus (15 January 1841, New York, NY—8 June 1913, New York, NY). *Education*: studied at the Univ. of Virginia, 1857–60; studied at Union Sem., NY, 1861–63; studied at Berlin, 1866–69. *Career*: minister, Roselle, NJ, 1870–74; professor of Hebrew and Cognate Languages, Union Sem., NY, 1874–91; professor of Biblical Theology, Union Sem., 1891–1904; professor of Theological Encyclopedia and Symbolics, Union Sem., 1904–13.

In the last decades of the nineteenth century, Briggs was the leading Old Testament scholar among Presbyterians and probably among all the country's Christians interested in Bible study. His work in Berlin under Isaac A. Dorner, founded on the conviction that historical critical methodology could provide a comprehensive biblical theology, opened up new vistas for him. After a short pastorate, he assumed the duties of provisional professor at New York's Union Seminary and enhanced the reputation of that institution for the next thirty-nine years. From the beginning he held the view that using reasonable scientific methods in biblical study, on questions about authorship for example, would not endanger the supernatural character of revelation. But there was within Presbyterianism at that time a widespread opposition to that liberal approach, strong enough to control the General Assembly and reject those of special competence, like Briggs, as detrimental to sound beliefs. He was also connected with those favoring a revision of the Westminster Confession, another position that led conservatives to view him with misgiving.

In 1891 Briggs was transferred to a newly established chair of biblical theology and precipitated an important controversy with his inaugural address. He noted that many feared historical criticism because it seemed to produce nothing but agnosticism, but he countered such trepidations with assurances that God had revealed Himself continually to men by means of three fountains of divine authority: the Bible, the Church, and human Reason. In the same address, Briggs discussed his conception of redemption, insisting that it was a process of sanctification which extended beyond death to ultimate perfection. He also emphasized a similar process of progressive moral development in Israel's history, from Noah and Abraham to Jesus of Nazareth. Bitter reaction erupted immediately. Charges of heresy were raised, and an intricate process of inquiry, trial, and appeals devolved over the general issues of: (1) equating Bible, church, and reason as coordinate sources of divine revelation, (2) preaching progressive sanctification, and (3) rejecting verbal inspiration and the textual inerrancy of original (autograph) biblical documents. The last charge stemmed from Brigg's scornful rejection of a definition of inspiration and Scriptural authority formulated by professors at Princeton Seminary, including *Benjamin B. Warfield.

The case went through many phases until 1893 when the General Assembly found Briggs guilty and suspended him from the ministry. Another brief was prepared regarding his friend and defendant, *Henry P. Smith of Lane Seminary, which resulted in victory for the prosecution. Union Seminary was also censured for continuing on its faculty someone with such dangerous inclinations, a declaration which highlighted that institution's commitment to academic freedom and modern research methods. Briggs labored for another two decades in that congenial atmosphere, producing many lasting works on higher criticism. He wrote commentaries and exegesis, translated documents of the early church, and served as co-editor of two scholarly landmarks, the *International Theological Library* and the *International Critical Commentary*. In 1899 he became a priest in the Episcopal denomination and served in that capacity as well as being an effective educator to another generation of theological students.

Bibliography:

A. *The Authority of Holy Scripture: An Inaugural Address* (New York, 1891); *Bible Church and Reason* (New York, 1892); *The Messiah of the Gospels* (New York, 1894); *The Messiah of the Apostles* (New York, 1895); *General Introduction to the Study of Holy Scripture* (New York, 1899); *History of the Study of Theology*, 2 vols. (New York, 1916).

B. SH 2, 270–71; NCAB 7, 318–19; DAB 3, 40–41; NCE 2, 802; NYT 9 Jun 1913, 1; George L. Prentiss, *The Union Theological Seminary: Its Design and Another Decade of its History* (Asbury Park, NJ, 1899); George H. Shriver (ed.) *American Religious Heretics* (Nashville, 1966); Mark S. Massa, *Charles Augustus Briggs and the Crisis of Historical Criticism* (Minneapolis, 1990).

BRIGHTMAN, Edgar Sheffield (20 September 1884, Holbrook, MA—25 February 1953, Newton Center, MA). *Education*: B.A. and M.A., Brown Univ. 1906, 1908; S.T.B. and Ph.D., Boston Univ., 1910, 1912; studied at Berlin, 1910–11, and Marburg, 1911–12. *Career*: professor of Philosophy, Nebraska Wesleyan Univ., 1912–15; professor of Ethics and Religion, Wesleyan Univ. (CT), 1915–19; professor of Philosophy, Boston Univ. 1919–53.

Theistic philosophy has had its defenders among twentieth century thinkers, but none based theism more solidly on a personalistic footing than Brightman. Led in that direction by *Josiah Royce, he also drew heavily on *Borden P. Bowne, a philosopher whose name adorned Brightman's professorship after 1924. Through four decades of teaching, fourteen books, and over 200 articles, he became the leading American exponent of personalist idealism. Brightman viewed reality as a world of persons; their experiences provided the only reliable information for understanding other aspects of the cosmos. While critics thought its epistemology was too subjective, this system held that all metaphysical hypotheses were extrapolations of data received through personal experience. Each person was a self-conscious unity of complex activities, capable of moral purpose and religious sensitivity. Brightman also held that God and human personalities were distinct entities, each with their own capabilities and spheres of action. In that manner he avoided having individuals lose their distinctiveness by absorption into a single Absolute. At the same time he provided a groundwork for making rational conclusions about the attributes and power of God.

The experiences that Brightman found pertinent to theology yielded a conception of God as an ultimate, processive Creator. Eternal and self-sufficient, God was not tied to the biological world as humans are, but still there were limits that prevented Him from existing simply as an unbounded entity of amorphous proportions. In that special sense God was finite, governed by limitations similar to those of His creatures. Human experience pointed to a God not of completed goodness or perfection but to one of inexhaustive creative processes, changing constantly to achieve His purposes. As the human learning experience continued to unfold for Brightman, he discerned further attributes emerging in God's personality. His will was unfailingly good, but the natural world stood as another limitation of His capacities. Waste and pain, for example, are circumstances God would not have created voluntarily. Their existence shows that God is struggling under conditions not of His choosing but which He will eventually overcome. Human sin is another factor that limits God and challenges His persistent salutary designs. In Brightman's view, the personalities of God and man are strong but tragic; they suffer but persevere. In the last analysis Brightman was not dismayed by the limits of unachieved purposes or evil conditions. Rather he was encouraged by the tenacity of divine will and the resourceful energy of a living God.

Bibliography:

A. *Immortality in Post-Kantian Idealism* (Cambridge, MA, 1925); *The Problem of God* (New York, 1930); *Moral Laws* (New York, 1933); *Personality and Religion* (New York, 1934); *The Future of Christianity* (New York, 1937); *Persons and Values* (Boston, 1952).

B. NCAB 41, 38–39; NCE 2, 802–03; NYT 27 Feb 1953, 21; James J. McLarney, *The Theism of Edgar Sheffield Brightman* (Washington, DC, 1936).

BROADUS, John Albert (24 January 1827, Culpeper County, VA—16 March 1895, Louisville, KY). *Education*: graduated from Univ. of Virginia, 1850. *Career*: private tutor, Fluvanna County, VA, 1850–51; minister, Charlottesville, VA, 1851–59; instructor in Greek and Latin, 1851–53, and chaplain, 1855–57, Univ. of Virginia; professor of New Testament Interpretation and Homiletics, Southern Baptist Sem., 1859–62, 1865–95; preacher in local churches, Greenville, SC, 1862–65; president, Southern Baptist Sem., 1889–95.

After joining three other professors to form the first faculty of Southern Baptist Seminary established at Greenville, South Carolina, Broadus was dismayed to see the Civil War threaten its extinction. Classes were suspended during the conflict, but with great determination faculty members began to rebuild their institution as soon as possible. Broadus emerged as the most effective instrument in that attempt, serving as agent to rally support for the school and embodying its ideal of high intellectual standards for the general elevation of Baptist scholarship. Physical deprivation was a constant concern for decades; professors could rarely expect full salary, and students often wondered if classes would convene the following term. But perhaps a more serious obstacle to seminary growth was widespread opposition to ministerial education. Broadus helped create a more receptive attitude regarding educated clergymen as a professional class, while at the same time he itinerated from Texas to Maine in search of funds for such theological training. In 1877 the seminary was moved to Louisville, Kentucky, a more centrally located city which drew students in such numbers that future stability was assured. In sermons, lectures, and scholarly publications, the seminary's professor of Bible became foremost among those who grappled with New Testament criticism in his denomination. He blended mastery of ancient languages with a reverent approach to holy writ, producing commentaries and classroom instruction calculated to preserve pious habits backed by vast stores of erudition. Many other institutions of higher learning tried to secure the luster of his name as their president, but he was tenaciously loyal to the one place where he could instill future Baptist leaders with both evangelical zeal and a love of learning.

Bibliography:

A. *A Treatise on the Preparation and Delivery of Sermons* (Philadelphia, 1870, and many subsequent editions); *Lectures on the History of Preaching* (New York, 1876); *Sermons and Addresses* (Baltimore, 1886); *Commentary on Matthew* (Philadelphia, 1887); *Jesus of Nazareth* (New York, 1890).

B. SH 2, 272; NCAB 18, 430; DAB 3, 59; Archibald T. Robertson, *Life and Letters of John Albert Broadus* (Philadelphia, 1901).

BROOKS, Phillips (13 December 1835, Boston, MA—23 January 1893, Boston, MA). *Education*: B.A., Harvard Coll., 1855; B.D., Protestant Episcopal Sem. (VA), 1859. *Career*: rector, Philadelphia, 1859–69; rector, Trinity Episcopal Church, Boston, 1869–91; bishop of Massachusetts, 1891–93.

In most instances preaching does not receive much notice among denominations where liturgy provides more tangible riches, but Brooks packed Episcopal churches and made them ring with pulpit oratory. Known for style and felicity of expression even in his school days, he became one of the most eloquent and highly esteemed clergymen of his time. He declined an offer to serve as head of the new Episcopal Theological School (1866) and similarly rejected a professorship with chaplaincy at Harvard (1881) because he preferred to stay with his church and nourish its growing congregation. After being destroyed in the great Boston fire of 1872, Trinity Church was relocated and designed along striking architectural lines. It was completed in 1877 and provided physical surroundings as notable as the meetings housed within it. Brooks was not an innovative thinker, and he did not adopt new modes of public address. His gift was rather an ability to reduce important issues to simple terms and then convey them to others through an infectious personal affirmation of their truth. He did not wish to attain a rational faith, reconcile science and religion, or combat materialistic philosophy with arguments. Stressing the aesthetic and emotional elements more than intellectualism, Brooks preached as he understood the Christian life, communicating something of the liberty and abundance men could find in its spiritual power. Through imagination, subtle humor, and compelling expositions, he spoke of Christianity not as a system of doctrine but as a force capable of transforming individual lives.

Three sermons every Sunday were common for the popular orator who set new standards of ministerial eloquence. Through wide reading, especially in Samuel T. Coleridge, Frederick D. Maurice, and *Horace Bushnell, Brooks came to a conception of faith in God that transcended the limits of creedal statements and sought expression in everyday living. He made Bible passages come alive and helped audiences gain a fresh understanding of the present reality of gospel truths. Many listeners attested to his ability to restate standard beliefs and rescue them from doubts, conflicting claims, or liberalized descriptions which depleted their mystery. Brooks was not just an effective speaker. He had experienced the faith he preached and stood before congregations as an embodiment of what he wished to share. On numerous occasions his unifying theme was to remind listeners of the undiscovered potential in human nature and of the nearness of God in each individual. Through most of his life Brooks was tolerant rather than appreciative of bishops and ecclesiastical administration, but at length he came to view the office as a means of further service and accepted episcopal appointment, working effectively during the brief time remaining.

Bibliography:

A. *Lectures on Preaching* (New York, 1877); *The Influence of Jesus* (New York, 1879); *Sermons Preached in English Churches* (New York, 1883); *Twenty Sermons* (New York, 1886); *The Light of the World* (New York, 1890); *The Law of Growth* (New York, 1902).

B. SH 2, 274; NCAB 2, 304; DAB 3, 83–88; NYT 24 Jan 1893, 1; Alexander V. G. Allen, *Life and Letters of Phillips Brooks*, 2 vols. (New York, 1900); William Lawrence, *The Life of Phillips Brooks* (New York, 1930); Raymond W. Albright, *Focus on Infinity* (New York, 1961).

BROWN, William Adams (29 December 1865, New York, NY—15 December 1943, New York, NY). *Education*: B.A. and M.A., Yale Univ., 1886 and 1888; B.D., Union Sem. (NY), 1890; studied in Berlin, 1890–92; Ph.D., Yale Univ., 1901. *Career*: instructor and professor of Systematic Theology, 1892–1930, and Professor of Applied Christianity, 1930–36, at Union Sem.; active retirement, 1936–43.

Graduate study in Germany under Adolf Harnack was the culmination of Brown's theological training, a long process that prepared him for four decades of teaching at Union Seminary. He became one more voice among twentieth century christocentric liberals who struggled to formulate religious principles compatible with both denominational traditions (Presbyterian in his case) and secular standards of a scientific age. Following Harnack's lead in this task, he sought to discern and teach the essence of Christianity. He did not linger over questions of God's existence because belief was thought to be primarily a matter of inner certitude, rising from experience not arguments. The more important focus was Christ who revealed the moral attributes of God as Father. Transcendental elements in theology were overshadowed by the more concrete emphasis on God as an ever-present spirit who guided all that happened to a wise and holy end. Brown's conception of the moral qualities in God's nature was grounded in a utilitarian framework. In his view the legitimacy of belief rested on the practical consequences of ethical living. Men's lives were transformed; hope was possible in the face of despair; good could emerge from faulty conditions. These observations made for a theology that was consistent with historical Christian symbols and still free to affect contemporary social problems.

The systematic articulation of liberal ideas in theology was a major achievement through the years, but Brown also sought practical outlets for his convictions about the ethical focus of a living faith. His activities regarding urban problems contributed more than teaching to his reputation as a leading churchman. Tenement slums (Union Settlement, 1895); reform in city government (1904), labor unions, and free speech; higher education; and public service—all these were areas which spawned commissions and agencies engaging his energies for a lifetime. After 1920 he tried to continue wartime patterns of interchurch cooperation and work for gains in the wider sphere of world ecumenism. Through the years, as theologian and social activist, Brown became the dean of American ecumenical leaders. In 1925 he led his countrymen at the Universal Christian Council for Life and Work; two years later he served on the executive committee of the World Conference on Faith and Order. Ideological conviction and pragmatic necessity caused him to work indefatigably for greater unity among churches of varying confessional, national, and ethnic backgrounds. In 1937 he again represented American ecumenists at Oxford and worked through the next year to secure acceptance of the provisional constitution for the World Council of Churches. His thought and activities for over half a century were consistent in pursuing cooperative efforts in the name of principles which all Christian groups could endorse.

Bibliography:

A.   *Christian Theology in Outline* (New York, 1906); *Modern Theology and the Preaching of the Gospel* (New York, 1914); *Beliefs That Matter* (New York, 1928); *The Church: Catholic and Protestant* (New York, 1935); *A Teacher and His Times* (New York, 1940); *Toward a United Church: Three Decades of Ecumenical Christianity* (New York, 1946).

B.   DAB 23, 110–11; NCE 2, 825; NYT 16 Dec 1943, 27; Samuel McC. Cavert and Henry P. Van Dusen (eds.) *The Church Through Half a Century: Essays in Honor of William Adams Brown* (New York, 1936).

BROWNSON, Orestes Augustus (16 September 1803, Stockbridge, VT—17 April 1876, Detroit, MI). *Career*: Universalist minister, Litchfield, Ithaca, Geneva, and Auburn, NY, 1826–29; political activity, Workingmen's Party, 1828–31; independent minister, Ithaca, NY, 1831–32; Unitarian minister, Walpole, NH and Canton, MA, 1832–36; minister, Society for Christian Union and Progress, 1836–43; editor, *Boston Quarterly Review*, 1838–42; editor, *Brownson's Quarterly Review*, 1844–65, 1873–75.

Religious history abounds with stories of adult conversions, but few individuals acted so decisively or as often as did Brownson. From Presbyterianism at nineteen years of age to Roman Catholicism at forty-one, he sought the best foundations for developing human nature and organizing society to secure happiness for mankind. In a life seldom free from inner turbulence, Brownson symbolized the intellectual mobility and spiritual questing characteristic of many in the early national period. At times under the influence of *William E. Channing and then *Ralph W. Emerson he became influential as a Unitarian and then Transcendentalist reformer. He wrote with great zeal and no small ability in advocacy of his successive viewpoints, all of which consistently stressed the relationship between religion and social betterment. Brownson was long a champion of the industrial proletariat, seeking their good through activities as diverse as philosophical discussions and Jacksonian politics. Gradually he came to view human progress as a joint product of God and man in nature. This realignment led him to a new appreciation of Christ as mediator of the communion sought after;

finally, the corporate church, in this case the Roman institution, emerged as his concept of the most tangible promise of divine communion and ultimate meaning. Always one to act on the strength of his convictions, he entered the Roman Catholic church in October of 1844 and did not change his affiliation thereafter.

For a brief time after this last conversion Brownson accepted the standard doctrinal and ecclesiastical tenets of his new spiritual home. He soon returned to intellectual independence and published opinions which alienated many in the church and the country in general, lessening his impact on current thought. Still convinced that religion and politics were inseparable, he boldly stated that Catholicism was the best fulfillment of American ideals. But these ideals were defined conservatively, Brownson not declaring for the Union or antislavery until 1860. He later adopted more liberal views of democracy, especially strict separation of church and state, that aroused much hierarchical opposition. Attacks leveled against parochial schools, Irish immigrants, Jesuits, and political despotism in the papal states did not endear him to coreligionists; defenses of papal authority in doctrinal matters ruined his standing among the Protestant majority. Through an enormous literary production, Brownson left the record of a vigorous mind that grappled openly with important questions; but the mercurial quality of his thought eventually diminished the prestige one might expect as his due.

Bibliography:

A. *New Views of Christianity, Society and the Church* (Boston, 1836); *Essays and Reviews* (New York, 1852); *Spiritualist Rapper: An Autobiography* (Boston, 1854); *The Convert, or Leaves from My Experience* (New York, 1857, 1877); *The American Republic: Its Constitution, Tendencies and Destiny* (New York, 1865); Henry F. Brownson (ed.), *Works*, 20 vols. (Detroit, 1882–87).

B.   SH 2, 281; NCAB 7, 197; DAB 3, 178–79; NCE 2, 827–29; NYT 18 Apr 1876 7; Henry F. Brownson, *Life of Orestes Brownson*, 3 vols. (Detroit, 1898–1900); Arthur M. Schlesinger, Jr., *Orestes A. Brownson: A Pilgrim's Progress* (Boston, 1939, 1966); Theodore Maynard, *Orestes Brownson: Yankee, Radical Catholic* (New York, 1943); Hugh Marshall, *Orestes Brownson and the American Republic* (Washington, DC, 1972); Thomas R. Ryan, *Orestes A. Brownson: A Definitive Biography* (Huntington IN, 1976).

BRUTÉ DE RÉMUR, Simon William Gabriel (20 March 1799, Rennes, France—26 June 1839, Vincennes, IN). *Education*: graduated from Coll. of Medicine, Paris, 1803; graduated from Sem. of St. Sulpice, Paris, 1808. *Career*: professor of Theology, Rennes, 1808–10; professor of Philosophy, St. Mary's Sem. (MD), 1810–12; professor, Mount St. Mary's Coll. (MD), 1812–15; president, St. Mary's Coll. (MD), 1815–18; professor, Mount St. Mary's Coll., 1818–34; bishop of Vincennes, 1834–39.

Raised in an affluent bourgeois family, Bruté anticipated receiving royal patronage until the French Revolution changed his family's fortunes. But as an outstanding medical student, he still seemed destined for a lucrative practice among those of high social position. Dreams of missionary sacrifice intervened, however, and the young doctor from Brittany entered the Sulpician seminary to prepare for service in China or India. After ordination he was assigned instead to teaching in his home district, though only briefly because he soon volunteered for the American field in response to *Benedict J. Flaget who had come to France seeking men of his caliber. On reaching the New World, Bruté found no post in the wilderness; someone with his training was needed more urgently by the large Catholic population around Baltimore. As pastor and teacher he worked for almost a quarter-century in Maryland, residing mostly at Emmitsburg where small institutions prepared the way for solid Catholic advance in the early national period. There he also met *Elizabeth B. Seton, founder of the Sisters of Charity, with whom he immediately struck a bond of mutual respect and friendship. He served unofficially as spiritual director of the order as long as he remained at "the Mountain." Often restless and moody to the point of being considered eccentric, he nevertheless inspired students with a zeal for prayer and study. He also influenced Catholic action in larger areas through correspondence with more public figures such as *John England of Charleston and *John Hughes of Philadelphia. His information regarding points of canon law or theology lay behind many of their efforts to defend the church in open debate.

Even though Bruté had the reputation of being a free spirit with no capacity for managing practical affairs, he was made first bishop of Vincennes, a frontier district comprising eastern Illinois and all of Indiana. Once responsibility was forced on him, he proved a highly successful organizer among the 25,000 nominal Catholics scattered along the Wabash. The last five years of his life were ones of unrelieved hardship, but in that time he raised the number of priests from two to twenty-five, established twenty-seven churches, and inaugurated a seminary, college, and girls' academy. Travel was physically painful for him, but he visited every part of the diocese, preaching in halting English never sufficiently mastered. He recruited priests from France, including German-speaking ones from Alsace, and while in Vienna interested the Leopoldinen-Stiftung in his mission. One of his main concerns lay in catechizing the young; through such instruction he often won parents back to the church while ensuring faithful adherence by the next generation as well. He also ministered to Christian Indians, notably the Potawatomi nation, until their forcible removal in 1837. By the time of his death, his pioneering efforts had helped plant Catholicism more securely as a respected minority group in midwestern states.

Bibliography:

B.   NCAB 12, 413–14; DAB 3, 188–89; NCE 2, 842; James R. Bayley, *Memoirs of the Rt. Rev. Simon Wm. Gabriel Bruté* (New York, 1861); Mary S. Godecker, *Simon Bruté de Rémur* (St. Meinrad, IN, 1931); Theodore Maynard, *The Reed and the Rock: Portrait of Simon Bruté* (New York, 1942).

BRYAN, William Jennings (19 March 1860, Salem, IL—26 July 1925, Dayton, TN). *Education*: B.A., Illinois Coll., 1881; graduated from Union Law Coll., Chicago, 1883.

The Progressive Era witnessed the rise of many notable figures dedicated to social reform; of these none commanded more popular attention than Bryan whose spellbinding oratory helped define public issues for over two decades. His deep humanitarianism and sense of justice were fashioned by a fundamental identity with the underdog, sustained throughout by a Protestant moralism which made righteousness and justice coterminous. As the "great commoner," Bryan spoke for farmers and laborers, leading crusades on their behalf and articulating the sentiments of thousands who lacked words to express themselves. His speeches, often lay sermons couched in evocative rhetoric, repeatedly moved audiences to adopt causes he advocated. His plea that corporate wealth should not be allowed to crucify labor on "a cross of gold" launched a political career of national proportions. He ran unsuccessfully for president (1896, 1900, 1904) on the Democratic ticket and served (1913–15) under Woodrow Wilson as Secretary of State in efforts to implement his views of peace, sound economics, and fair business practices. His activities in political office were geared to the conviction that Christian morality could be enhanced through legislation. Society could be remade along more equitable lines if basic tenets of biblical ethics informed the guidelines of social improvement. This religious ideal underlay all the Nebraska lawyer's many labors to influence the course of human good.

After 1915 Bryan had passed the zenith of his powers, but a narrowed constituency still followed his leadership in a final struggle to protect American society from corruption. Persuaded that theological liberalism threatened to destroy the fundamental verities of Christian belief, he often entered the lists to defend truth against special interests. His own religious principles corresponded fairly well to those doctrines associated after 1910 with the name "Fundamentalism." Convinced that Darwinism was a menace to home, church, and school, he helped draft (1923) a bill for the Florida legislature that prohibited teaching evolution in public schools and offered his services as prosecuting attorney in any case where such a law was challenged. In 1925 the state of Tennessee (one of five with the law) charged John T. Scopes with violating its anti-evolutionary statute. Clarence Darrow tried to defend Scopes by arguing the validity of natural science as worthwhile knowledge. Bryan won the battle but lost the war because he showed fundamentalism to be essentially reactionary. He died shortly after the trial, but his brand of conservatism remained a strident voice to be reckoned with. In the last analysis, his ideals had become increasingly embattled due to an inability to adjust to new social forces that were shaping an America alien to his experience and expectations.

Bibliography:

A.   *The Prince of Peace* (Chicago, 1909); *The Bible and Its Enemies* (Chicago, 1921); *In His Image* (New York, 1922); *Orthodox Christianity versus Modernism* (New York, 1923); *Christ and His Companions* (New York, 1925); *The Memoirs of William Jennings Bryan* (Philadelphia, 1925).

B.   NCAB 19, 453–55; DAB 3, 191–97; NYT 27 Jul 1925, 1; John C. Long, *Bryan: The Great Commoner* (New York, 1928); Paxton Hibben, *The Peerless Leader* (New York, 1929); Paul W. Glad, *The Trumpet Soundeth: William Jennings Bryan and his*

Democracy, 1896–1912 (Lincoln, NE, 1960); Paolo E. Coletta, *William Jennings Bryan: Political Evangelist, 1860–1908* (Lincoln, NE, 1964); Lawrence W. Levine, *Defender of the Faith* (New York, 1965).

BUCHMAN, Frank Nathan Daniel (4 June 1878, Pennsburg, PA—7 August 1961, Freudenstadt, Germany). *Education*: B.A., Muhlenberg Coll., 1899; studied at Mt. Airy Sem., 1899–1902. *Career*: minister, Overbrook, PA, 1902–05; director, Luther Hospice, Philadelphia, 1905–09; secretary for YMCA at Pennsylvania State Coll., 1909–15; lecturer, Hartford Sem., 1916–21; agent for Moral Re-Armament, 1921–61.

After years of service as pastor and founder of the first Lutheran settlement house in Philadelphia, Buchman left for a European tour following arguments with his managerial advisers. During that trip abroad (1908) he underwent something approaching conversion to a new purpose; it became clear that spiritual experiences could actually change people, and he felt called to spread such influences to as many human lives as possible. Representing no new sect and preaching no new gospel, he began a broadly defined evangelical campaign on college campuses, wartime prison camps, and countries of the Far East. Buchman's message was one of Christian renaissance based on idealistic objectives of absolute love, honesty, purity, and unselfishness. He stressed the need for surrender of human wills to the will of God. Continuous contact with the Divine through prayer, Bible reading, and listening to the Holy Spirit would disclose that will, allowing every follower to witness for Christ as he worked to bring others within God's influence. The well-traveled evangelist was convinced that vital, dedicated lives could be the foundation of a new social order under the dictatorship of God. He found that large meetings were less congenial than intimate gatherings, or "house parties," where he converted many influential persons to his point of view. In such informal settings he laid the basis for a new religious movement which attracted considerable attention between the two great wars of this century.

In 1921 Buchman arrived at Oxford University with nothing more than a letter of introduction and a quasi-messianic sense of destiny. His success with students during that year launched the First Century Christian Fellowship, or the "Oxford Group Movement," changed in 1938 to Moral Re-Armament. Still utilizing techniques of private conversation, group confessions, and silent meditation, he persuaded increasing numbers of individuals to amend their lives. But as time passed, Buchman gravitated toward aristocratic patrons, finding more satisfactions in influencing highly placed politicians than in ministering to the masses. Missionary work has rarely been conducted in more luxurious surroundings as he sought out prestigious followers accustomed to money and power, with better results in Britain than the United States. He urged a God-guided crusade to prevent war by means of a moral awakening, running a race with time to remake nations before it was too late. In 1938–39 those ideas had some effect in formulating appeasement policies related to Axis powers. They also became associated with profascist sympathies in opposition to what was viewed as godless communism. By 1950 the movement's slogans and its chief proponent had outlived their time of widespread public interest.

Bibliography:

A.   *Remaking the World* (New York, 1949).

B.   NCAB B, 405–06; NCE 2, 845–46; NYT 9 Aug 1961, 1; Peter Howard, *The World Rebuilt: The True Story of Frank Buchman* (New York, 1951) and *Frank Buchman's Secret* (Garden City, NY, 1961); Garth Lean, *Frank Buchman: A Life* (London, 1985).

BURKE, John Joseph (6 June 1875, New York, NY—30 October 1936, Washington, DC). *Education*: B.A., St. Francis Xavier Coll., 1896; S.T.B. and S.T.L., Catholic Univ., 1899 and 1901. *Career*: member, Congregation of St. Paul the Apostle, 1896–1936; editor, *The Catholic World*, 1904–22; general secretary, National Catholic Welfare Conference ("Council" until 1923), 1919–36.

In keeping with the ideals of Paulist Fathers, the monastic community to which he belonged for forty years, Burke tried in various capacities to serve religion and country. Convinced that publishing was an efficient means of Christian witness in modern times, he pioneered in founding the Paulist Press and presided (as co-founder) over the Catholic Press Association. For years his chief goal was to provide outlets for capable, intelligent expressions of faith, hoping thereby to deepen piety among the faithful as well as influence the whole of American culture. Literary pursuits proved to be a rewarding task, but the coming of World War I brought new challenges and work in larger fields. Early in the war, Burke established the Chaplain's Aid Society to supply priests who visited the troops; by 1917 he conceived of a larger organization to be responsible for protecting and furthering all Catholic interests. The National Catholic War Council (NCWC) thus emerged from his initiative, and he served as executive officer to coordinate the church's resources in support of the war effort. In addition to his Council work, which made him one of the best known churchmen in the country, he also directed the "Committee of Six." This group, comprising one Catholic, one Jew, and four Protestants, advised the Secretary of War on programs related to religious matters in the armed forces. It was largely because of activities in this latter office that Burke was awarded the Distinguished Service Medal in 1919. He accepted it for action congruent with his universal faith grounded at the same time in principles of American democratic life.

After the war Burke found himself at the head of an organization able to mobilize Catholic resources, but with no program for peacetime activities. At his suggestion the old NCWC was continued, settling on the name National Catholic Welfare Conference (NCWC) serving as a clearing house for voluntary work between dioceses. More than that, he made the complex of offices an innovative source of Catholic action applied to pressing contemporary issues. As general secretary he functioned under a board of four bishops and correlated the separate programs of departments, which focused on social action, immigrants, lay organizations, and legal advice. Quite often he represented Catholic opinion in the nation's capital as lawmakers consulted him on church teaching related to social problems. He proved a staunch defender of *John A. Ryan's platform, issued (1919) by NCWC as the "Bishops' Program of Social Reconstruction." For more than two decades he defended the ideals of minimum wage, public housing, collective bargaining, and fair tax laws. Social justice found in him a skillful advocate—one who was led by spiritual ideals and could implement practical plans with telling effect. He thought of Catholic action in society as both a religious and civic accomplishment, one that strengthened personal virtue, family life, and republican citizenship. Among those who publicly acknowledged his distinguished contributions was Pius XI, who in 1936 made him a domestic prelate, an honor never before given to a member of a religious community in this country.

Bibliography:

    A.   *Christ in Us: Meditations* (Philadelphia, 1934); *Pray for Us: A Collection of Prayers for Various Occasions* (New York, 1936); *Lent and the Mass* (New York, 1936).
    B.   DAB 22, 72–74; NYT 31 Oct 1936, 19. John Sheerin, *Never Look Back: The Career and Concerns of John J. Burke* (New York, 1975).

BURROUGHS, Nannie Helen (2 May 1878?, Orange, VA—20 May 1961, Washington, DC). *Career*: editor, *The Christian Banner*, 1896–97; janitor, Washington, DC, 1897–99; bookkeeper, Washington, DC, 1899–1900; secretary, Foreign Mission Board, National Baptist Convention, 1900–09; secretary (1900–47) and president (1948–61), National Baptist Woman's Convention.

Hard times instilled a work ethic in Burroughs that characterized all her activities as educator, civil rights advocate, and religious leader. Poverty was one thing, but racial prejudice compounded her difficulties. Despite graduating with honors from the District of Columbia school system and achieving an excellent rating on civil service exams, she was told that there were no vocational opportunities for black women other than menial jobs. In 1900 she electrified the largest national convention of black Baptists with a speech, "Hindered from Helping," that pointed out the waste of unused talent among women. Shortly thereafter, in time spared from her work at the convention's headquarters in Louisville, Kentucky, she organized the Woman's Industrial Club. There she sponsored classes in practical skills such as shorthand, typing, and bookkeeping, in sewing, cooking, and millinery. Such exemplary work led to Burroughs' election as corresponding secretary of the National Baptist Woman's Convention, an auxiliary agency formed to nurture missionary activity through training and fund raising. This became one of the most important focal points of her life, and as she traveled thousands of miles to accomplish its work she became the agency's guiding spirit and leading influence.

In 1906 Burroughs succeeded in furthering the other major interest in her life:

a school dedicated to educating young black women. That year she persuaded the Woman's Convention to pledge support for such a school, and in 1909 what is presently called the National Training School for Women and Girls opened in Washington, D.C., with Burroughs as president. From modest beginnings the institution grew rapidly, shaping in its first fifty years thousands of young women from every state in the nation and from South Africa and the Caribbean as well. There Burroughs taught her charges that self-help can combat segregation and discrimination. She strongly emphasized the connection between education and the development of spiritual qualities. Religious character could knit women in Christian sisterhood, and outstanding performance could overcome stereotypes related to gender and ethnic identity. In larger outlets she contributed significantly to the National Association of Colored Women. But mostly in the supplementary fields of missionary support and pioneering education, she enhanced the work of the largest black Baptist denomination in this country and augmented the heritage of black contributions to American culture.

Bibliography:

B. NAW 4, 125–27; NYT 22 May 1961, 31; William Pickens, *Nannie Burroughs and the School of the Three B's* (New York, 1921); Earl L. Harrison, *The Dream and the Dreamer* (Washington, DC, 1956).

BUSHNELL, Horace (14 April 1802, Bantam, CT—17 February 1876, Hartford, CT). *Education*: B.A., Yale Coll., 1827; studied at Yale Law Sch., 1829–31; B.D., Yale Sem., 1833. *Career*: school teacher and journalist, CT and NY, 1827–29; tutor, Yale Coll., 1829–31; minister, North Congregational Church, Hartford, CT, 1833–59; travel, convalescence and continued writing, 1859–76.

On the verge of entering private legal practice, Bushnell underwent a conversion experience which led him to accept preaching as a better calling. His ministry covered twenty-six years in a single church (with some time spent in travel for health reasons), though his theologizing continued after retirement and the influence of his monumental writings spread far beyond Hartford. He was unimpressed with the attempts of many colleagues who strove to maintain traditional patterns of thought in a new intellectual climate. The striking innovations of Bushnell's ideas aroused a great deal of factional criticism during his own time, but he was later recognized as the father of American religious liberalism. Prompted by Coleridge and German idealists, he began with a conception of language that changed accepted views of creeds and Scripture in addition to theological discourse. To him all words were metaphors, evocative of meaning but not exact in content or communicative ability. Language bore historically conditioned connotations, and doctrinal statements as well as everyday speech had to be understood within that context of inexactitude. Attempts to describe religious experiences could never fully succeed because all words, indeed thoughts themselves, were social phenomena more than timeless truths. Consequently, Bushnell tried to avoid religious controversy, preferring the role of conciliator and apologist instead of strident reformer.

Another area where he saw indistinct boundaries rather than sharp dichotomies was the religious life itself. Christian nurture was all-important in his view of family, church, and nation. Refusing to condone the mechanisms of revivalistic philosophy, he held that a properly nurtured person need not distinguish between being saved and unsaved nor ever remember a time of being outside the organic structure of Christian society. Bushnell extended his contextual view of social patterns to a similar relationship between natural and supernatural realms. Nature was a created world where phenomena interacted on the basis of constant laws. The supernatural was not part of that chain of cause and effect, but neither did it act on nature from outside. The supernatural was consubstantial with, yet distinguishable from, the natural sphere. There was a constant action and reaction between the two; taken together they constituted the one true system of God's providence. Such a perspective allowed Bushnell freedom to reach new conclusions regarding human nature and its eventual redemption.

Of all the theological categories with which Bushnell struggled to reach fresh insight, none was more important to him than the atonement. Reconciliation, which was crucial for understanding central doctrines of the church, played a significant part in his interpretation of the Union's ultimate purpose during the Civil War. That signal promise of redemption was made possible by Christ's vicarious sacrifice, an objective action complementing the more important subjective work of re-engaging the world's love and reuniting it to Eternal Life. Bushnell explicitly rejected the traditional idea that crucifixion had an effect on God's attitude, causing Him to be more merciful toward sinners. The process began and took effect outside such mechanistic conceptions of material causality. Christ's ritual offering produced a change in human beings, not in the mind of God. As supernatural forces acted in and through the natural sphere, so man was regenerated by the atoming work of Christ in a manner similar to the promptings of other creative human impulses. Such ideas opened the way for many other thinkers to emphasize morality and social progress instead of penal theories in depicting salvation. Bushnell's complex thought inaugurated a new era. Measured in terms of both intrinsic merit and subsequent impact, he ranks with *Jonathan Edwards and *Reinhold Niebuhr as one of the three foremost Protestant theologians in American history.

Bibliography:

A.   A Discourse on Christian Nurture (Boston, 1847); God in Christ (Hartford, 1849); Christ in Theology (Hartford, 1851); Nature and the Supernatural (New York, 1858); Sermons for the New Life (New York, 1858); The Vicarious Sacrifice (New York, 1866).

B.   SH 2, 318–19; NCAB 8, 303; DAB 3, 350–54; NCE 2, 910; NYT 18 Feb 1876, 4; Mary B. Cheyney, Life and Letters of Horace Bushnell (New York, 1880, 1969); Theodore T. Munger, Horace Bushnell: Preacher and Theologian (Boston, 1899); Warren S. Archibald, Horace Bushnell (Hartford, 1930); Barbara M. Cross, Horace Bushnell: Minister to a Changing America (Chicago, 1958); William A. Johnson, Nature and the Supernatural in the Theology of Horace Bushnell (Lund, Sweden, 1963).

C

CABRINI, Frances Xavier (1 July 1850, Sant' Angelo Lodigiano, Italy—22 December 1918, Chicago, IL). *Education*: studied under Daughters of the Sacred Heart, Arluno, 1863–68. *Career*: teacher in public schools, Vidardo, 1872–74; teaching and supervising an orphanage, Codogno, 1874–80; prioress and mother-general (permanent after 1910), Missionary Sisters of the Sacred Heart, 1880–1917.

Maria Francesca Cabrini dreamed of giving her life to missionary activity and adopted the name of Frances Xavier in anticipation of that apostolate. She was refused entry into one order for health reasons. After several years of difficulties in a faltering convent, she inherited its nucleus and was made superior of a new missionary order which expanded rapidly. Though she wished to be sent to China, work among Italian immigrants in the New World was considered a more pressing need. In 1889 Mother Cabrini and a small group of sisters were welcomed to New York by *Michael A. Corrigan, who aided their work in the "Little Italy" section of that city. By establishing a school and orphanage and by daily contact with people in tenements and alleyways, they helped immigrants retain something of their Catholic heritage. Much of their considerable effect on the unchurched cannot be measured, but it was not ineffective in rescuing abandoned children and in easing the despair of newcomers who sought adjustment to conditions of ghetto life. Hospitals, convents, schools, and always more orphanages are the means of gauging the missionary zeal of these sisters and their leader. They are also an indication of Mother Cabrini's vision, faith, and determination to care for those whom she accepted as divinely appointed charges.

Good intentions succeed only when one has the means to act upon them, and the mother-general possessed diplomatic skill, financial resourcefulness, and managerial acumen to a remarkable degree. She was able to move her base of operations to West Park, New York, in 1890 and thereafter extend her ministry among those who worked in the mines, docks and mills of major American cities. Undeterred by physical hardships or worries about an uncertain future, she eventually spread her work in Nicaragua, Chile, and Argentina, counting at her death an estimated 4,000 daughters in sixty-seven religious houses. Mother Cabrini was constantly alert to chances for accomplishing additional charitable work. She crossed oceans thirty times, repeatedly traversed her new home (naturalized citizenship, 1909) by rail, and crossed the Andes on muleback to secure missionary objectives. Though poor health slowed her itinerary in later years, there was no abatement of purpose. When death claimed the diminutive leader, her teaching and charitable institutions continued without serious decline because of the long-term plans she had wisely provided. In an unusually short time Mother Cabrini was nominated, beatified (1938), and canonized (1946) as a saint, the first citizen of the United States to be so designated. Feast day, 22 December.

Bibliography:

B.   NCAB 27, 476–77; DAB 21, 146–48; NCE 2, 1039; NAW 1, 274–76; Theodore Maynard, *Too Small a World: The Life of Francesca Cabrini* (Milwaukee, 1945); Pietro Di Donato, *Immigrant Saint: The Life of Mother Cabrini* (New York, 1960); Achille Mascheroni, *Madre Cabrini: La Sante che Scopri gli Italiani in America* (Rome, 1983).

CADBURY, Henry Joel (1 December 1883, Philadelphia, PA—7 October 1974, Bryn Mawr, PA). *Education*: B.A., Haverford Coll., 1903; M.A., Ph.D., Harvard Univ., 1904, 1914. *Career*: professor, at various ranks, of Biblical Literature, Haverford Coll., 1910–19; professor, at various ranks, of Biblical Literature, Andover Sem., 1919–26; professor of Biblical Literature, Bryn Mawr Coll., 1926–34; professor of Divinity, Harvard Div. Sch., 1934–54; lecturer at Quaker School of Graduate Study, Wallingford, PA, 1954–72.

The outer calm of an academic life centered on Biblical and historical studies did not disclose Cadbury's commitment to public service. Larger questions of peace and human welfare occasioned by two European wars provided a setting in which he contributed distinctive, religious leadership for over six decades. As a student of Quaker history, he catalogued a great number of unpublished manuscripts by *George Fox and wrote essays signed "Now and Then" for denominational journals. He was also director of the Andover-Harvard Library (1938–54), which developed under his care into one of the finest collections of religious literature in the country. Many of his publications on biblical themes were considered valuable advances at the time of their appearance. He worked with eight other scholars to produce the Revised Standard Version of the New Testament, appearing in 1946, and a new translation of the Apocrypha, 1957. But while placing a priority on scholarly accomplishment throughout his many years as a teacher, Cadbury was more interested in translating gospel tenets into living principles. He was a distinguished academician who went beyond intellectual concerns to practical efforts on behalf of causes in which he believed deeply.

As early as 1912 Cadbury began attending the Winona Lake Peace Conferences, an agency focusing on one of his dominant interests. This led to a National Peace Committee in 1915 and, when the United States entered World War I two years later, to the establishment of an emergency organization for Quaker humanitarian aid. Cadbury was one of the primary agents behind the American Friends Service Committee (AFSC) from its inception. His brother-in-law, *Rufus M. Jones, was its first chairman, but he was closely associated with its work at all times. During the first thirty years of its activities, Cadbury's spiritual guidance played a strong role as the AFSC spent over sixty million dollars to relieve suffering and privation in needy countries. As one who envisioned peace through world brotherhood, he often criticized anti-German hysteria during wartime. He claimed that overt hatred made America incapable and unworthy of achieving durable peace; it would only lay the basis for future wars. As a result of stating such ideas in 1918, he was dismissed from his post at Haverford, but as chairman of the AFSC (1928–34 and 1944–60) he accepted the Nobel Peace Prize, awarded in 1947 jointly to British and American Friends. This committee was only one of many to which he brought a capacity to evoke consensus on spiritual objectives, all these in keeping with his dedication to scholarship, service, and fellowship.

Bibliography:

A. *National Ideals in the Old Testament* (New York, 1920); *The Making of Luke-Acts* (New York, 1927); *The Peril of Modernizing Jesus* (New York, 1937); *The Book of Acts in History* (London, 1955); *John Woolman in England* (London, 1971); *Friendly Heritage* (Norwalk, CT, 1972).

B. NYT 9 Oct 1974, 46; Margaret Hope Bacon, *Let This Life Speak: The Legacy of Henry Joel Cadbury* (Philadelphia, 1987).

CAIN, Richard Harvey (12 April 1825, Greenbrier County, VA (now WV)— 18 January 1887, Washington, DC). *Education*: studied at Wilberforce Univ., 1860. *Career*: elder and presiding elder, various African Methodist Episcopal conferences, 1862–80; state and national congressman in SC, 1868–70, 1873–75, and 1877–79; bishop, AME Church, 1880–87.

Born to free Negro parents who soon moved the family to Ohio where Cain first worked aboard steamboats, he was converted in 1841 and three years later received a Methodist license to preach. Dissatisfaction with conditions in that denomination led shortly to a new affiliation: the African Methodist Episcopal Church. Ordination as deacon came in 1859, and after a short period of study elevation to elder came in 1862 at the hands of bishop *Daniel A. Payne. Cain served conferences in Iowa, Missouri, and New York, but in 1865 he was assigned a southern post in order to nurture churches among recently emancipated slaves. In South Carolina this clergyman sought to improve the social and political status of black people in addition to elevating their spiritual condition. Asked to represent them in larger society, he was a member of the 1868 South Carolina constitutional convention and served in the state Senate for two subsequent years. He also twice represented the state in the U.S. House of Representatives. Throughout such activities he maintained a reputation for honesty and an emphasis on high moral standards in public service.

A national reputation stemming from political life, enhanced by vigorous literary efforts in various periodicals, inevitably brought Cain to the attention of his denomination's top leaders. In 1880 he was elected a bishop and assigned to the ninth episcopal district, comprising the conferences of Louisiana, Texas, and West Texas. There he continued his demonstrated interests in religious growth, adding two new annual conferences, and in education as well, serving for a time as president of Paul Quinn College in Waco. In 1884 he was transferred to the first episcopal district which contained the conferences of Philadelphia, New Jersey, New York, and New England. There he continued to supervise affairs with probity and diplomatic finesse. His consolidating abilities helped the AME church to maintain its lead as one of the largest and most influential black denominations in American religious history.

Bibliography:

    B.   DAB 3, 403–04.

CALLAHAN, Patrick Henry (15 October 1865, Cleveland, OH—4 February 1940, Louisville, KY). *Career*: salesman, Glidden Varnish Co., 1888–92; sales manager and president (after 1910), Louisville Varnish Co., 1892–1940.

After study at the Spencerian Business School in Cleveland, Callahan made rapid progress in commercial affairs. As a Catholic layman interested in the religious aspects of social reform he became one of the leading proponents of industrial partnership and welfare capitalism. In 1915 he worked with *John A. Ryan to construct a profit-sharing plan for his employees. After implementation, he lectured extensively to promote this plan, which divided surplus revenue between stockholders and workers. In addition to wide travel he wrote articles for popular journals, explaining the innovative concept that workers have substantial property rights in manufacturing corporations sustained by their labor. In subsequent decades he continued activities in this area by serving on the National Child Labor Commission and the Catholic Conference on Industrial Problems. During World War I he was chairman of the Knights of Columbus Committee on War Activities, coordinating that group's ministrations to servicemen with such effectiveness, Pius XI designated him (1922) the first American honored as a Knight of the Order of St. Gregory the Great. But tangible progress in social issues gave him more satisfaction than honorific titles. For many years he served on committees dedicated to racial harmony, attempting to end prejudice in ecclesiastical administration and local politics. Another sphere where he made important advances was that of inter-faith conciliation, and in that capacity he helped organize the National Conference of Christians and Jews. Other causes of his were less popular with rank and file Catholic laymen. He was, for example, a staunch advocate of prohibition and, besides supporting the Eighteenth Amendment, represented the United States at the Geneva Conference on Alcoholism. He also backed *William J. Bryan in many of his ideas regarding fundamentalist beliefs, particularly during the 1925 Scopes trial. But in most cases he was a leader of liberal causes, drawing his motivation from Catholic tradition and applying it with creative energy in the American context.

Bibliography:

B.   DAB 22, 86–88; NCE 2, 1077; NYT 5 Feb 1940, 17; William E. Ellis, *Patrick Henry Callahan (1866–1940): Progressive Catholic Layman in the American South* (Lewiston, NY, 1989).

CALVERT, Cecilius (1606, London, England—30 November 1675, London, England).

After graduating from Oxford in 1621 young Calvert disported himself as a gentleman adventurer, though his family's conversion to Catholicism ended opportunities for high office in England. He became second Baron of Baltimore in 1632 and continued attempts initiated by his father to found a haven for religious refugees in the New World. Two years later the *Ark* and the *Dove* sailed for territory north of Virginia. Under Calvert's instructions the colony of Maryland pursued from the very beginning a careful policy of religious toleration for all inhabitants. With a blend of expediency and personal conviction, the lord proprietor urged colonists to accept confessional diversity as a practical necessity, cooperating with neighbors regardless of their beliefs. He also invited Jesuits to build self-supporting missions in the colony, a move which brought *Andrew White and *John Altham for pioneering work among Indians, slaves, and immigrants alike. On the death of his brother, he appointed a Protestant governor, William Stone, who continued Calvert's benevolent attitude regarding freedom of belief. In 1649 an assembly of Protestants and Catholics passed an "Act Concerning Religion," drafted by the proprietor with the intent of perpetuating open tolerance through statutory enactment. Such freedom did not extend to blasphemers or those denying the divinity of Christ, but in the main it was an unprecedented declaration of magisterial forebearance. Unfortunately for the Catholic minority, Virginia Puritans under William Claiborne wrested control of affairs from Calvert's lieutenants and reversed conditions by 1654. In that year the assembly was forced to disfranchise Catholics, thus ending two decades of experimentation in tolerance by Calvert whose ideals ran ahead of common expectations in his day.

Bibliography:

B.   NCAB 7, 331–32; NCE 2, 1086; William H. Browne, *George Calvert and Cecilius Calvert: Barons of Baltimore* (New York, 1890).

CAMPANIUS, Johan (15 August 1601, Stockholm, Sweden—17 September 1683, Frösthult, Sweden). *Education*: studied theology at Univ. of Upsala, ?– 1633. *Career*: chaplain, Swedish legation to Russia, 1634; schoolmaster, Norrt-älje, Sweden, 1635–?; chaplain and preceptor, Stockholm Orphans' Home, ?– 1642; minister to Swedish settlers in DE, 1642–48; minister, Frösthult and Hernevi, Sweden, 1649–83.

A few Swedish Lutheran ministers had preceded Campanius to work among colonists of the lower Delaware valley, but he was deservedly the best known of those who nurtured the gospel there. Arriving at Fort Christina (now Wilmington) early in 1643, he provided both word and sacrament to scattered settlers who were slowly making headway in the territory of New Sweden. For several years there was no central place for corporate worship; so he visited all cabins ranging as far upriver as Fort New Gothenburg. One of the few tangible reminders of those travels is a gilded silver chalice, brought from the old country at his own expense, with which he celebrated the eucharist for isolated communicants. Missionary activity among local Indians of the Delaware nation was another field of ministerial endeavor where Campanius made notable beginnings. He gained a fairly accurate knowledge of their language and preached with some effect. More importantly he transliterated their vocabulary, numerals, and common phrases for later missionaries. Experience in such materials enabled him to translate the Lutheran Catechism into the Algonkian dialect spoken by Delawares. The manuscript, though not printed until 1696, represents one of the earliest attempts by a European to reduce an American tongue to writing. He also observed native folkways and recorded them in his journal, preserving some anthropological data while perpetuating the widespread misconception that Indians had descended from ancient Hebrew tribes. By 1647 he confessed to the archbishop of Stockholm that he was weary of his New World charge. Conscious of his responsibilities as the sole resident priest, he also petitioned the consistory to designate ministerial replacements. Three others were sent to continue services until the Swedish tract was comandeered by Dutch forces in 1655.

Bibliography:

B.   DAB 3, 445.

CAMPBELL, Alexander (12 September 1788, Ballymena, Ireland—4 March 1866, Bethany, WV). *Education*: study at home and in his father's school; studied at Univ. of Glasgow, 1808–09. *Career*: minister, Brush Run, PA, 1812–40; editor, *The Christian Baptist*, 1823–30; editor, *The Millennial Harbinger*, 1830–66; president, Bethany Coll., 1840–66.

The movement to restore apostolic simplicity to American religious practice originated with *Thomas Campbell, while his son Alexander consolidated that impetus with lasting ideological and institutional structures. The younger Campbell followed his father to this country, joining the free Association of Christians as minister of the Brush Run church in 1812. His convictions about immersion as the proper mode of baptism led the group to join the Redstone Baptist Association, but in 1826 theological tension ended that arrangement. By 1827 Campbell emerged as leading spokesman for the Disciples of Christ, a vigorous new denomination despite its intention of overcoming denominational pluralism. The Disciples thought of themselves not as another sect but as a gathering of believers content with the single name, Christian. The early years of Campbell's ministry were marked by a contentious zeal to argue points of doctrine with all comers. After his first public debate in 1820, he warmed to the task, and disputations became a major outlet for spreading his views on baptism, early creeds, the relative merits of Catholicism, and evidences of Christian belief. He traveled through midwestern and southern states, winning converts primarily from Baptist churches but capitalizing wherever revivalistic emphases stressed conversion experience and simple biblicism. His journals brought additional attention to his ideas and helped make the "Campbellites" one of the fastest growing religious organizations of the early national period.

As Campbell's preaching brought more and more followers, his early censoriousness gave way to a more statesmanlike concern for ecclesiastical harmony and growth. In 1832 his group united with the Christian Connection, led prominently by *Barton W. Stone. Though their internal organization was not complete until 1849, the Disciples of Christ can be said to have assumed denominational status by the earlier date. Campbell continued to lecture, edit, travel, and write on a host of subjects; to those tasks he added that of building a college to supply more learned ministers for new churches. The new churches were his predominant concern, though by his own definition they embodied no innovations or distinctive tenets. They existed to restore the pure religion of apostolic times. Generations of church history had encrusted the plain gospel of primitive Christianity with elaborate creeds, theological speculation, and unscriptural practices. Campbell sought an end to those aberrations and called for a return to original, undistorted piety. Particular manifestations of that untrammeled religion included a rudimentary liturgy, weekly communion, and local autonomy of each church led by elders and deacons. Underneath all those specifics lay a reliance on biblical authority for all activities, proscribed or advocated. The central objective of the Disciples of Christ as well as their chief methods for accomplishing them have remained virtually constant for over a century. The influence of this early leader can still be traced in current activities.

Bibliography:

A. *Psalms, Hymns and Spiritual Songs* (Bethany, VA, 1834); *The Christian System in Reference to the Union of Christians and the Restoration of Primitive Christianity* (Cincinnati, 1835; New York, 1969); *A Debate . . . on Christian Baptism* (Lexington, KY, 1844); *Christian Baptism* (Bethany, VA, 1851); *Popular Lectures and Addresses* (Philadelphia, 1863); *Familiar Lectures on the Pentateuch* (Cincinnati, 1867).

B. SH 2, 370–72; NCAB 4, 161; DAB 3, 446–48; NCE 2, 1111–12; NYT 11 Mar 1866, 5; Robert Richardson, *Memoirs of Alexander Campbell*, 2 vols. (Philadelphia,

1868–70); Jesse R. Kellems, *Alexander Campbell and the Disciples* (New York, 1930); Robert F. West, *Alexander Campbell and Natural Religion* (New Haven, 1948); Harold L. Lunger, *The Political Ethics of Alexander Campbell* (St. Louis, 1954); Granville Walker, *Preaching in the Thought of Alexander Campbell* (St. Louis, 1954).

CAMPBELL, Thomas (1 February 1763, County Down, Ireland—4 January 1854, Bethany, WV). *Education*: B.A., Univ. of Glasgow, 1786; graduated from theological school, Whitburn, Scotland, 1791. *Career*: a succession of ministerial and teaching posts in Ireland, PA, OH, VT and WV, 1786–1852.

There have been many Christian churchmen to propose various solutions regarding sectarian diversity, but few went as far as Campbell in acting on their principles. In 1807 he came to this country for combined reasons of poor health and low political fortune. Settling in western Pennsylvania, he continued his identification as Presbyterian minister, though the relationship proved to be a short-lived one. Campbell was perturbed by the evil of Christian division, the party spirit it engendered as well as the dearth of liberty, charity, and fellowship found between opposing factions. He was committed to the ideal of brotherhood rather than denominational loyalty and exhibited an indifference to ecclesiastical rules, causing some Presbyterians to challenge his place among them. By 1809 he was censured for being too open with communion practices; as a result he withdrew from Presbyterian affiliation and continued to plead for interchurch union on a large scale. His vision went beyond the confusion of contemporary groupings with their conflicting shibboleths and well-intended creeds. He sought to unite believers by destroying all manufactured systems of human opinion and restoring the peaceful simplicity of primitive Christianity. Reunion would come, in his view, through the elementary process of returning to the univocal source of faith.

By September, 1809, a small group of followers joined with Campbell to form the Christian Association of Washington, using the name of their township as a sole distinguishing feature. In later decades this organization became another unit in the lengthening list of denominations in America, but at its inception there was no intention to form a new church or compete as an optional ecclesiastical form. Instead, the group merely issued a "declaration and address" to advertise itself as a local congregation of believers who were faithful to uncorrupted gospel standards. Within two years the first church in this Association, formed at Brush Run in Pennsylvania's Washington County, expressed the wish that other like-minded associations would emerge in voluntary response to the example of primitive Christian witness. For Campbell, the Bible was sufficient basis for restoring pure Christianity because it revealed God's will and served as an adequate rule of faith. Members of the reconstituted apostolic church declared that where the Scriptures spoke, they spoke, and silence was the only response to questions where no scriptural warrant provided an answer. In that manner all could come firmly to the original ground of religious truth and take up things just as the apostles left them. As the movement, which sought a new reformation, gained wider support, the elder minister shifted burdens of leadership to his son, *Alexander. The young clergyman contributed materially to the gradual development of the Disciples of Christ, but Thomas Campbell stands as its originator and early inspiration.

Bibliography:

B.   DAB 3, 463; Alexander Campbell, *Memoirs of Elder Thomas Campbell*, 2 vols. (Cincinnati, 1861); Lester G. McAllister, *Thomas Campbell: Man of the Book* (St. Louis, 1954).

CANNON, James, Jr. (13 November 1864, Salisbury, MD—6 September 1944, Chicago, IL). *Education*: B.A., Randolph-Macon Coll., 1884; B.D., Princeton Sem., 1888; M.A., Coll. of New Jersey, 1890. *Career*: minister, ME Church, South, Charlotte circuit, VA, 1888–89; Newport News, VA, 1889–91; Farmville, VA, 1891–94; principal of Blackstone Female Institute, 1894–1911, 1914–18; superintendent of Southern Assembly at Lake Junaluska, NC, 1911–14; bishop, Methodist Episcopal (ME) Church, South, 1918–38; retirement, 1938–44.

The bulk of Cannon's ecclesiastical activities took place in public arenas rather than ones normally applying to churches. He was a minister in the Southern Methodist Church and served as one of its bishops for two decades, but most of his work did not directly affect the growth of that denomination. His most important goals throughout life were broad issues of social reform, particularly the temperance movement, and he concentrated an amazing amount of energy on efforts to win success in that crusade. Recognized early for his strong will and combative temperament, Cannon advanced his ideas and his own importance as editor of the *Methodist Recorder* (1894–1903), editor and owner of the *Baltimore and Richmond Christian Advocate* (begun 1904) and as founder of the *Richmond Virginian* (begun 1910). Through these pages he was able to wage battles against liquor interests, help achieve temperance legislation in the state, and at the same time consolidate his position as the leading Methodist in Virginia.

As bishop, Cannon's chief responsibility was the supervision of missionary work in Mexico, Cuba, Brazil, and the Congo. He often traveled to those sites as well as to European cities in the name of the World League against Alcoholism, Near East Relief, the World Missionary Conference, the World Conference on Faith and Order, and the Universal Christian Conference on Life and Work. He was named to the executive committee of the Anti-Saloon League in 1902 and became actively involved with the Federal Council of Churches from its inception in 1908. Cannon succeeded in winning an overwhelming victory for his primary interest in 1914 when his native state adopted prohibition, and he then became the most effective lobbyist in Washington for the cause that was embodied in the Eighteenth Amendment. His political influence reached its peak when he campaigned against Alfred E. Smith, Democratic presidential candidate in 1928. Because Smith was Catholic and ''wet'' due to alliance with liquor interests,

Cannon helped swing Virginia and four other southern states to the Republican side for the first time since the Reconstruction Era.

In 1929 Cannon's prestige began to wane due to scandal and public charges of moral dereliction. These included misusing campaign funds, hoarding flour during World War I, stock market speculation, and adultery for two years with Helen McCallum before she became his second wife. In the course of five publicity-filled years of Senate investigations, inquiries by a Methodist trial board and retaliatory libel suits, Cannon was eventually declared not guilty of wrongdoing. In the eyes of many, however, he was not exonerated, and his once powerful influence in church and national life came to an end. The bishop proved himself to be tough-minded and calm under pressure, whether advocate or defendant, and he usually commanded respect while unable to elicit friendship. He remained dedicated to the larger ideals that informed his life and died, fittingly, while attending meetings of the Anti-Saloon League.

Bibliography:

A.   Richard L. Watson, Jr. (ed.), *Bishop Cannon's Own Story* (Durham, 1955).

B.   NCAB 35 129–30; DAB 23, 131–33; NYT 7 Sep 1944, 23; Virginius Dabney, *Dry Messiah: The Life of Bishop Cannon* (New York, 1949; Westport CT, 1970).

CARROLL, John (8 January 1735, Upper Marlboro, MD—3 December 1815, Baltimore, MD). *Education*: graduated from St. Omer Coll., Flanders, 1753; completed training in the Society of Jesus at Watten, Liege, and Bruges, 1753–71. *Career*: private ministerial practice in MD and VA, 1774–84; Vicar Apostolic for the U.S., 1784–89; bishop of Baltimore, 1789–1808; archbishop of Baltimore, 1808–15.

Events beyond the control of American Catholics, including papal suppression of Jesuits in 1773 and colonial rebellion against British authority in 1776, threatened to stunt the early progress of Catholicism in the English colonies. Carroll returned home in 1774 after long residence in Europe to cope with the unsettled circumstances, proving himself eventually to be the chief architect of Catholic growth in the new republic. One achievement in those early years was success in protecting Jesuit holdings and preserving the Society's distinctiveness as a "select body of clergy" until restoration in 1814. When he became the first native son appointed as superior of missions, his powers were hardly greater than those enjoyed while living on family estates and pursuing an itinerant ministry. He tried with mixed results to discipline unruly parishes that conducted affairs autonomously and laid the basis for conflicts over trusteeism in the nineteenth century. Churches with local preferences exercised control over priests of varied foreign origins, creating potential schisms from Boston to Georgia. For all his problems with congregational democracy, Carroll was attached to the principles of religious liberty and proclaimed toleration as the situation best suited to ecclesiastical growth in the new nation. His strong commitment to separation of church and state set a precedent followed by many successors in seeking cordial relations with the federal government.

After consecration as the first resident American bishop, Carroll began the solid administrative work that facilitated expansion on adequate foundations. He faced problems of an immense territorial jurisdiction, an uncertain number of nominal Catholics, and much confusion over lines of episcopal authority. Despite these unpromising portents, his leadership brought renewal to church life in several tangible areas. He was a great patron of schools, religious and secular, providing admirably for the future by securing the aid of Sulpician fathers who founded St. Mary's Seminary in 1791. Since religious orders were also his concern, the bishop encouraged many to locate where need called for their services. Work with the new order founded by his spiritual charge, *Elizabeth B. Seton, was particularly satisfying. Probably the most far reaching institutional action took place in calling the first national synod. In 1791 Carroll met with twenty priests of seven nationalities to build a canonical structure that regulated discipline, liturgy, and procedures for choosing future prelates. When division of his diocese created four new sees in 1808, the archbishop continued supporting orthodox doctrine and efficient practices which caused American Catholicism to be counted a proper provincial representative of the universal faith.

Bibliography:

A. *An Address to the Roman Catholics of the United States of America* (Annapolis, MD, 1784); *The John Carroll Papers*, 3 vols., edited by John O. Hanley (Notre Dame, IN, 1976).

B. SH 2, 426; NCAB 1, 480–82; DAB 3, 526–28; NCE 3, 151–54; John G. Shea, *The Life and Times of the Most Rev. John Carroll* (New York, 1888); Peter Guilday, *The Life and Times of John Carroll*, 2 vols. (New York, 1922; Westminster, MD, 1954); Annabelle M. Melville, *John Carroll of Baltimore: Founder of the American Catholic Hierarchy* (New York, 1955).

CARTWRIGHT, Peter (1 September 1785, Amherst County, VA—25 September 1872, Pleasant Plains, IL). *Career*: itinerant Methodist minister in KY, TN, OH and IN, 1803–24; itinerant minister and farmer in IL, 1824–72; member, state legislature, 1824–40.

Society was open and moral standards were low in southern Kentucky when the Cartwright family moved there in 1793. As a young man Peter reveled in the widespread horse races and gambling until he was converted (1801) in a revival. He quickly dedicated himself to Methodist preaching with the zeal formerly spent in pursuit of pleasure. For almost seventy years after that, he embodied the attitudes and methods representative of backwoods preachers as they spread evangelical Christianity through midwestern pioneer society. He scorned formal theological training as a requirement for the ministry, claiming that Methodists could set things on fire while other clergymen were still collecting their degrees and negotiating salaries. Cartwright read the Bible diligently, prayed regularly, and spoke as his ardent nature led him; that was training enough to conquer sin. Licensed as an exhorter before his seventeenth birthday, the "Kentucky boy" rode circuit in that and surrounding states as he received ordination as deacon (1806) and elder (1808). His simple message of free salvation and rigorous ethical conduct was delivered in sermons of great emotional power. Preaching Methodism was a joyous task of using rugged speech to save souls from evil and other sects. Cartwright's wit, homespun homilies, and plain manners contributed significantly to camp meetings and local revivals. But common sense did not let him condone those excesses which occasionally broke out at times of high spiritual excitement.

Building the church, not spiritual ecstasy, was the itinerant's major objective. As early as 1812 Cartwright was named presiding elder in his local conference, and he worked dutifully for institutional growth during the next five decades. Except for rare occasions of ill health, he presided over annual ministerial sessions, encouraging colleagues to persevere in their common missionary enterprise. Beginning in 1816 he was appointed delegate to the General Conference, a quadrennial affair of national scope in which he participated until 1864. Cartwright was a mobile, self-reliant westerner in religion and social views. He became an inflexible opponent of slavery, transferring to Illinois primarily to get away from that pernicious system. Elected (1824) by Sangamon district residents to represent them in state politics, he was reelected over *Abraham Lincoln in 1832 but then defeated (1846) by Lincoln in a race for U.S. Congress. The General Conference of 1844 revolved around slavery, and despite heated arguments Cartwright labored to hold Methodist factions together. In the end he was unable to do so, siding with the antislavery party rather than sacrifice freedom to unity. As an aging itinerant, he chafed at younger ministers who did not stress evangelical preaching but preferred moderate spiritual nurture in settled locations. Yet his outdated methods continued without appreciable decline long after frontier conditions had given way to new cultural patterns.

Bibliography:

A. *Autobiography of Peter Cartwright*, ed. W. P. Strickland (Cincinnati, 1856); ed. Charles L. Wallis (Nashville, 1956); *Fifty Years as a Presiding Elder*, ed. W.S. Hooper (Cincinnati, 1871).

B.   SH 2, 430; NCAB 6, 61–62; DAB 3, 546–48; NCE 3, 172; NYT 27 Sep 1872, 5; Helen Hardie Grant, *Peter Cartwright, Pioneer* (New York, 1931); Sydney Greenbie and Marjorie B. Greenbie, *Hoof Beats to Heaven*, (Penobscot, ME, 1955).

CARUS, Paul (18 July 1852, Ilsenburg, Germany—11 February 1919, La Salle, IL). *Education*: studied at Greifswald and Strassburg; Ph.D., Tübingen, 1876. *Career*: editor, *Open Court*, 1887–1919; editor *Monist*, 1890–1919.

Though he was the son of a prominent theologian and superintendent of the Prussian state church, Carus represented liberal philosophers of his day who tried to make natural science the touchstone of their intellectual system. He lived for a while in England (1881–84), after resigning a teaching post in Dresden because of conflicts over his religious views, and then sought greater freedom of action in America. Shortly after arriving, he proved himself a capable editor for *Open Court*, a new and ambitious journal which encouraged fresh ideas in religion, science, and related fields. The significance of Carus' prodigal genius is that virtually every aspect of knowledge was relevant to his comprehensive perspective. The magazine, changed soon into a weekly, became a forum for discussing ideas about God and the soul, life and death, the origin of man, and the nature of morality. Its self-consciously advertised central purpose was a thoroughgoing reformation of religion under the influence of science. Carus enlivened the publication by also including articles on travel, Asian literature, Greek drama, and German philosophy. His own writing listed more than fifty books, with translations of Chinese religious and ethical treatises in addition to original compositions. He was instrumental in reprinting inexpensive editions of philosophical classics and in issuing new works on the growing edge of scientific discovery. By these means he gained wide popular influence in developing more rational attitudes about religion in twentieth-century America.

In his own symbiotic collection of ideas, Carus maintained allegiance to a resilient monism. He found a basic identity between laws of nature and of the mind. Material and intellectual sciences presented objective truths which could be systematized into a harmonious viewpoint leading to more effective action. All forms of thought were eternal types, and the entire system of formal thoughts constituted what he referred to as divinity. Borrowing an ancient title, Carus said that God was more properly the Logos, that sum of forms that conditions the cosmic order and governs the universe. Under such a divinity, philosophy could embrace all natural functions, and religion gave man sentiments to affirm the rational process. Instead of providing a category for intangible, spiritual experiences, Carus rejected the transcendent. The soul was a mode of intellectual perception, and immortality was the survival of one's worldly influence. In the last analysis his comprehensive system had no lasting impact on major religious institutions nor on philosophy within academic circles. He slighted epistemological difficulties and sought to include too many incompatible tendencies, but his mental ventures were symbolic of a growing religious diversity in modern times.

Bibliography:

A. *Fundamental Problems* (Chicago, 1889); *The Gospel of Buddha* (Chicago, 1894); *Buddhism and its Christian Critics* (Chicago, 1897); *The Soul of Man* (Chicago, 1900); *God: An Enquiry and a Solution* (Chicago, 1908); *Philosophy as a Science* (Chicago, 1909).

B. NCAB 14, 476; DAB 3, 548–49; NYT 15 Feb 1919, 11.

CARY, Lott (1780?, Charles City County, VA—10 November 1828, Monrovia, Liberia). *Career*: employee, Shockoe Tobacco Warehouse, Richmond, VA, 1804–20; Baptist minister, Sierra Leone and Liberia, 1821–28.

The only child of a slave couple, Cary was nurtured in a home of strong Baptist piety which his father embodied. By 1804, however, he moved to Richmond and, as he described it, led a prodigal life of profanity and intoxication. This dissolution ended in 1807 when he experienced Christian conversion and joined the predominantly black First Baptist Church in town. Equally important, he taught himself to read and write, acquiring capacities that earned him greater responsibilities and higher wages at work. By 1813 he had earned enough to purchase his freedom together with that of his two children, his wife being deceased. That same year Cary was licensed to preach, and he held many effective worship services among Negroes in districts around Richmond. Influenced by the sermons of *Luther Rice, he became interested in missionary outreach and the possibility of building Baptist churches in other countries. To this end he helped organize the Richmond African Missionary Society, serving for five years as its secretary. The funds it collected from poor blacks in central Virginia went to the evangelical programs of the Baptist General Convention.

After months of serious deliberation in 1819 Cary volunteered for work in Africa, and the Baptist Board of Foreign Missions accepted him in May of the same year. After a year of intensive study he was ordained and with other colonists formed the nucleus of what would become the first Baptist church in West Africa. The party traveled under the auspices of the American Colonization Society and arrived in Sierra Leone before mid-1821. Colonists faced many difficulties over the years, particularly over land ownership and disease, hostile neighbors without, and bickering leaders within. Cary provided much stability through trying times, serving multiple needs in the roles of educator, pastor, and medical adviser. The congregation slowly grew as the faith flourished among colonists and natives alike. After several early clashes with colonial officials, he was by 1826 named as a trusted governmental agent and dedicated himself to defense of the area. While packing cartridges for one such defense, he was fatally injured by an accidental explosion and died two days later.

Bibliography:

    B.   AAP 6, 578–87; DAB 3, 555.

CASE, Shirley Jackson (28 September 1872, Hatfield Point, Canada—5 December 1947, Lakeland, FL). *Education*: B.A., Acadia Univ., 1893; M.A., Acadia Univ., 1896; B.D., Yale Div. Sch., 1904; Ph.D., Yale Univ., 1906. *Career*: instructor in Greek, New Hampton Literary Institute, 1897–1901; instructor in New Testament Greek, Yale Div. Sch., 1905–06; professor of History and Philosophy of Religion, Bates Coll., 1906–08; at various ranks professor of New Testament Interpretation, Univ. of Chicago, 1908–17; professor of Early Church History and New Testament Interpretation, Univ. of Chicago, 1917–25;

professor of the History of Early Christianity, 1925–38; professor of Religion, Florida Southern Coll., and dean of the Florida Sch. of Religion, 1940–47.

Having been raised in the Free Baptist tradition may be a reason why Case developed liberal attitudes about religion and epitomized open-minded inquiry throughout a lifetime of scholarship. He put early training in mathematics to work by teaching at two academies in his native New Brunswick province. In 1897 he moved to New Hampshire, teaching Greek and serving as pastor of the local community church. While studying biblical languages at Yale he also served as minister in neighboring Congregational churches. But historical interests gradually won out over textual ones, and Case soon gained enough notice to be invited to the University of Chicago. As he progressed through the ranks there his many important publications took effect in intellectual circles, and his eminence contributed to making Chicago one of the premier centers of learning in this country. His work embodied a particular socio-historical method of analysis which some called the "Chicago School" approach to materials in history, theology, and New Testament studies. This viewpoint, to which Case adhered but did not create single-handedly, stressed rigorous attention to evidence and sensitivity to the environment surrounding events—the full social, economic, political, philosophical, and psychological context—as they unfolded.

Historical knowledge did more than provide an accurate understanding of why religious developments occurred the way they had; it freed contemporaries from worry about confining themselves within previously set standards. Case perceived Christian events of any period as the record of people working out their own understanding of God, human nature, sin, salvation, ethics, and destiny. All varieties of faith were answers to spiritual needs shaped by specific times and cultures. Answers thus environmentally conditioned were not absolutes to be copied. They were only examples of prior faith, and Case encouraged people to transcend such static devices and to live on the edge of continuing quest and change. History taught the limits of earlier religious formulations and released people from conformity to any derivative, external authority. Case urged Christians in his day to search for their own spiritual affirmations in light of contemporary experience, and in articulating this liberal attitude he represented one of the most influential Protestant viewpoints extant in the first quarter of this century.

Bibliography:

A. *The Evolution of Early Christianity: A Genetic Study of First-Century Christianity in Relation to Its Religious Environment* (Chicago, 1914); *The Social Origins of Christianity* (Chicago, 1923); *Jesus through the Centuries* (Chicago, 1932); *The Social Triumph of the Ancient Church* (New York, 1933); *The Christian Philosophy of History* (Chicago, 1943); *The Origins of Christian Supernaturalism* (Chicago, 1946).

B. NCAB 36, 152; DAB supp. 4, 151–53; NYT 7 Dec 1947, 76: Louis B. Jennings, *The Bibliography and Biography of Shirley Jackson Case* (Chicago, 1949); William J. Hynes, *Shirley Jackson Case and the Chicago School: The Socio-Historical Method* (Chico, CA, 1981).

CAYCE, Edgar (18 March 1877, near Hopkinsville, KY—3 January 1945, Virginia Beach, VA). *Career*: psychic diagnostician, 1901–45.

There are some indications that Cayce wanted to be a minister but as a sixth-grade dropout in rural Kentucky, he had neither the finances nor aptitude for training in such a career. Instead, in his early years he worked on farms, as a shoe salesman, insurance agent, bookstore clerk, and photographer. By 1900, though, acquaintances began to take him seriously as a visionary and healer. His reputation spread, and he spent almost a half century using his powers to help needy persons who consulted him. Cayce responded to direct questions passed on to him by his wife or trusted friends while he was asleep. At appointed times, normally twice a day, he would sleep or lie in a trance. Then he would deliver "readings," not new revelations but what he considered messages from Universal Consciousness whose thought streamed through him as a medium. This subconscious clairvoyance, or the Information, was often a surprise to the waking Cayce, and he readily admitted that he was perplexed at this God-given power which overcame his own fallibility.

As a humble individual full of self-doubts, Cayce never profited from his mystic gift. He read the Bible every day, taught Sunday School, and helped others only when asked. Many did ask, and over the years he produced readings that diagnosed health problems, prescribed dietary regimens, dealt with psychic disorders, and predicted future events such as wars, earthquakes, and changes in governments. He spoke, moreover, of reincarnations, the early history of Israel, and the lost civilization of Atlantis. Enough of his diagnoses and predictions proved true to silence many skeptics and to develop a wide following. Over fifteen thousand of his readings have been collected in the Association for Research and Enlightenment. All of them show his deep concern to keep physical conditions in close touch with spiritual awareness and this spirituality close to faith in God who worked out His will and purpose through the natural universe. Definitely not the head of a personality cult, Cayce urged everyone to remain, like himself, cooperative with the Divine Mind that communicated through subconscious experience.

Bibliography:

B.   NYT 4 Jan 1945, 19; Jess Stearn, *Edgar Cayce: The Sleeping Prophet* (Garden City, NY, 1967); Harmon H. Bro, *Dreams in the Life of Prayer: The Approach of Edgar Cayce* (New York, 1970); Edgar E. and Hugh L. Cayce, *The Outer Limits of Edgar Cayce's Power* (New York, 1971); Mark A. Thurston, *Experiments in a Search for God: The Edgar Cayce Path of Application* (Virginia Beach, VA, 1976); W. H. Church, *Many Happy Returns: The Lives of Edgar Cayce* (San Francisco, 1984).

CHANDLER, Thomas Bradbury (26 April 1726, Woodstock, CT—17 June 1790, Elizabethtown (now Elizabeth) NJ). *Education*: B.A., Yale Coll., 1745; studied theology with *Samuel Johnson, 1745–47. *Career*: schoolteacher, Woodstock, CT, 1745–47; lay reader and catechist, St. John's Church, Elizabethtown, NJ, 1747–51; rector, St. John's 1751–90.

While a student at Yale, Chandler came under the strong Episcopalian influences begun there by *Timothy Cutler. Before he completed theological preparation or reached the canonical age of ordination, he started serving at the church with which he was associated for an eventual total of forty-three years. After receiving orders in England, he returned to that Anglican parish and worked at several adjoining missionary stations as well. He was content with established ways in the Church of England. In 1763 when *George Whitefield appeared in town, Chandler refused to let the evangelist preach in his church. Revivals would, he feared, interrupt the tranquility of parish life, and though many agreed with his priorities, the decision caused some resentment in his flock. Chandler was a leading advocate of establishing Anglican bishops in the American colonies. His publication to that effect in 1767 provoked widespread controversy in both religious and political circles. One spirited reply came from the pen of *Charles Chauncy who presented a long list of objections to resident bishops. Prolonged exchanges continued to keep the priest's name in public view.

In addition to being an ardent churchman Chandler was also a staunch Loyalist. He warned against republican thought as disloyal to legitimate government, and he denounced revolutionary sentiment as nothing less than lawlessness. In 1774 he wrote "The American Querist," a pamphlet protesting rebellious acts in the colonies. The following year he published an even more forceful defense of the status quo in a piece called "What Think Ye of Congress Now?" This attack on actions taken by the Continental Congress made Chandler notorious as a voice for conservatism in church and government. It also made him unwelcome in areas where republican convictions predominated. Consequently he took temporary leave of his church and lived as an exile in England from 1775 to 1785. During that time he studied, wrote, and enjoyed the company of many highly placed friends. His health declined seriously, however, and though he returned to his old parish, he rarely officiated there any longer. In 1786 he was offered the bishopric of Nova Scotia, but poor health forced him to decline the honor. By the time of his death he had helped instill in the American Episcopal church that element of traditionalism which had characterized most of its adherents in colonial times.

Bibliography:

A. *An Appeal to the Public in Behalf of the Church of England in America* (New York, 1767); *The Appeal Defended; or, the Proposed American Episcopate Vindicated* (New York, 1769); *The Appeal Further Defended: In Answer to the Farther Misrepresentation of Dr. Chauncy* (New York, 1771); *The Life of Samuel Johnson* (New York, 1805).

B. AAP 5, 137–42; DAB 3, 616.

CHANNING, William Ellery (7 April 1780, Newport, RI—2 October 1842, Bennington, VT). *Education*: graduated from Harvard Coll., 1789; private theological studies, Cambridge, MA, 1801–02. *Career*: tutor, private family in Richmond, VA, 1798–1800; minister, Federal Street Congregational Church, Boston, 1803–42.

Men with retiring dispositions are hardly ever recognized as leaders of controversial movements, but Channing is an exception to the rule. His sermons and writings were widely influential in defining basic emphases in the liberal theology of his day. Much of that new outlook had to do with optimistic expectations regarding human nature and a rejection of Calvinistic strictures on human ability. His sermons were mixed, however, with high Arian statements about Jesus' divinity, and some chose to attack the liberals on trinitarian rather than anthropological grounds. Channing sought tolerance for a spectrum of opinions, but by 1815 he was drawn into the debate and came to be regarded as the most prominent spokesman for American Unitarianism. He put forth no new doctrines but was able to synthesize the varied preferences of many and give coherence to the first generation of an emerging denomination. Beginning with the word of God, found in Scripture and interpreted within limits of reasonableness, he was careful to stress the supernatural element in Christianity. The gentle preacher was just as emphatic in declaring that he could find no scriptural basis for doctrines of a jealous God, human depravity, the vicarious sacrifice of an innocent Jesus, or election by grace. Consequently his gospel included ideas of God whose goodness was paramount and of humanity which could act responsibly, free to develop its essential goodness toward ultimate perfection. By 1819 these tenets became the manifesto of New England Congregationalists who were largely misunderstood and maligned as Unitarians.

The central point of Channing's theology was human dignity, and his primary concern about religious activity was in attaining a moral excellence which affected the collective life and temper of men. Man's nature was basically the same as God's, according to this perspective, and the moral grandeur of Jesus indicated how men might follow ethical ideals to perfect themselves while aiding the general progress of society. As a preacher Channing tried to guide others by pointing out their moral obligations to each other and to the community at large. This capacity led him to speak against slavery and other social abuses, but such condemnations were not his forte. He wished to reform the inner man by moderate appeals to the divine promptings in everyday experience, thinking that external changes would follow naturally. As a historical figure, Channing was a significant connecting link between some of the rationalistic principles of the Enlightenment and the warmer religious impulses of Romanticism. He reflected many of the attitudes about man and the natural world that found expression in America as Transcendentalism. At another point of transition, he was both an independent liberal who kept his own counsel and one who revered the central principles of biblical Christianity common to Protestantism. But he was most effective for personal qualities, and those about him were inspired by his optimistic faith and modest persuasiveness.

Bibliography:

A.   *Discourses, Reviews and Miscellanies* (Boston, 1830); *Discourses* (Boston, 1832); *The Works of William E. Channing, D.D.*, 8th ed., complete, 6 vols. (Boston, 1848, and many subsequent editions).

B.   AAP 8, 360–84; SH 3, 3–4; NCAB 5, 458–59; DAB 4, 4–7; William H. Channing,

Memoir of William Ellery Channing, with Extracts from his Correspondence and Manuscripts, 3 vols. (Boston, 1848); John W. Chadwick, *William Ellery Channing* (Boston, 1903); Robert L. Patterson, *The Philosophy of William Ellery Channing* (New York, 1952); David P. Edgell, *William Ellery Channing* (Boston, 1955); Jack Mendelsohn, *Channing the Reluctant Radical* (Boston, 1971).

CHAPMAN, John Wilbur (17 June 1859, Richmond, IN—25 December 1918, New York, NY). *Education*: studied at Oberlin Coll., 1876–77; B.A., Lake Forest Coll., 1879; B.D., Lane Sem., 1882. *Career*: minister, Liberty, IN, 1882–83; minister, Schuylerville, NY, 1883–85; minister, First Reformed Church, Albany, NY, 1885–90; minister, Bethany Presbyterian Church, Philadelphia, 1890–92 and 1895–99; urban evangelist, 1892–95; minister, Fourth Presbyterian Church, New York, 1899–1902; secretary, Presbyterian Committee on Evangelism, 1902–18.

Early pastorates in two denominations gave Chapman opportunities for displaying considerable energy and organizing skill. He was drawn into city revivals by his classmate and longtime friend, *Benjamin F. Mills, but the major impetus in that direction came from *Dwight L. Moody. The aging evangelist made Chapman his protege because, of all those pursuing the course of mass conversions, apparently he thought the hope of American revivalism was wrapped up in the young minister from Philadelphia. For three decades beginning in 1890 his message was consistent, offering a broad appeal for individuals from various persuasions to respond in Christian affirmation. Since he was no stickler for creeds or denominational boundaries, Chapman never tried to persuade persons to join a Presbyterian church during his city-wide meetings. But he thought it was important for everyone to be thoroughly informed about and loyal to some church or other. In the main, though, he preached a simple gospel which held forth the essentials of salvation for all who would accept it. He preached Christ's atoning death as sufficient for redemption, repentance toward God, and a life of practical Christian conduct, allowing free preference for denominations within that framework. The central objective was salvation of souls, and all his scriptural exposition of christocentric theology stressed that point. Additional emphasis on prayer and personal dedication of co-workers brought divine power to evangelical sessions often thought to be manifest in numbers of new converts.

The message which Chapman delivered with no little success on three continents offered no doctrinal innovations. His primary significance lay in contributions helping to standardize the sophisticated techniques of urban evangelism. Among these procedures perhaps none was more important than the "simultaneous campaign" in which the visiting evangelistic team was aided by twenty to forty of a city's resident clergymen. Interdenominational support was supplemented with a saturation program of publicity, newspaper coverage, weeks of meetings, prayer services, songfests, special consultations, quiet hours, noonday prayers for businessmen, and preaching almost daily. Such methods usually brought gratifying results, even when they could not match the truly spectacular successes of Boston (1909) and Chicago (1910). Once the complicated problems of logistics were worked out, the city-wide crusades produced great numbers of new church members in every English-speaking country around the world. Chapman and a corps of local ministers counted the program a triumph if crowds signed decision cards or came forward to dedicate their lives to higher principles and more wholesome conduct. The traveling evangelist continued to work in this fashion as a specialist for his own denomination in the larger setting of missions to urban population. He died after emergency surgery, two years after physicians had warned him to slow the pace of almost ceaseless activity.

Bibliography:

A. *The Power of a Surrendered Life* (New York, 1897); *The Secret of a Happy Day* (Boston, 1899); *Revivals and Missions* (New York, 1900); *Present Day Evangelism* (New York, 1903); *The Problem of the Work* (New York, 1911); *When Home Is Heaven* (New York, 1917).

B.   SH 3, 7; DAB 4, 19; NYT 26 Dec 1918, 11; Ford C. Ottman, *J. Wilbur Chapman* (Garden City, NY, 1920); John C. Ramsay, *John Wilbur Chapman: The Man, His Methods and His Message* (Boston, 1962).

CHASE, Philander (14 December 1775, Cornish, NH—20 September 1852, Jubilee, IL). *Education:* B.A., Dartmouth Coll., 1795. *Career:* schoolteacher and Episcopal missionary in NY, 1795–99; rector, Poughkeepsie and Fishkill, NY, 1799–1805; rector, New Orleans, LA, 1805–11; rector, Hartford, CT, 1811–17; bishop of Ohio, 1818–31; president, Kenyon Coll., 1824–31; semi-retirement in Gilead, MI, 1831–35; bishop of Illinois, 1835–52.

Descended from two generations of Congregationalist deacons, Chase became an Episcopalian while at college. He served for over five decades as evangelist for the orderly worship and apostolic order which he found so convincing in the Book of Common Prayer. Missionary pioneering was a fundamental motivation in all his affairs, drawing him from comfortable city parishes to the challenge of dioceses in midwestern states. Chase became the first bishop of Ohio, and he provided aggressive leadership for work there as population grew faster than ministers could cope with it. He was convinced that westerners must supply their own priests conformable to the low church, evangelical practices held in deliberate opposition to romanizing tendencies found in some eastern sectors. In 1824 he traveled to England in search of funds for a college, which was strongly opposed by fellow bishop, *John H. Hobart, who doubted the wisdom of both the enterprise and its leader. Chase remained undaunted in the face of odds which he overcame with charm and patience, together with the aid of several aristocratic patrons. Kenyon College bore the name of its chief benefactor; the town of Gambier designated another. But the missionary bishop proved to be a better founder than manager. His early habits of single-handed responsibility made it difficult to delegate authority to others, and many resented his domineering control over every detail. His paternalistic manner seemed imperious to a growing body of clergymen who asked for new diocesan rules that would mitigate episcopal absolutism. Always sensitive to criticism, he resigned rather than submit to cooperation with others in ruling a growing diocese.

For almost five years Chase returned to farming the land, a vocation loved since boyhood, but the old missionary impulse could not be stilled. In 1835 three ministers with thirty-nine communicants in Illinois called him to be their first bishop, and once again he accepted the task of transforming meager beginnings into an opportunity for church development. Another tour of England produced enough money to raise a second college, named Jubilee this time (founded 1839, chartered 1847). As stern as ever, the pioneering bishop worked indefatigably to organize churches on the prairie, carrying the gospel to frontier hamlets and making the evangelical side of his denomination effective through education. He was justly proud of the fact that Kenyon and Jubilee were the only schools in the whole Mississippi valley where Episcopal priests could be trained. It was also gratifying to see that, within a decade of his coming, twenty-five priests shepherded 500 communicants, a membership figure which doubled again by 1848. But his crusty authoritarianism was still a source of tension; Chase could build better than he could govern. The seniority system made him presiding bishop at General Conventions from 1844 to 1850, but by then feeble health began to take its toll. Still he officiated at ceremonies until almost the end, preaching from a chair in service of a church he did much to extend.

Bibliography:

A.   *Reminiscences: An Autobiography*, 2 vols. (Peoria, IL, 1841–44; Boston, 1848).
B.   AAP 5, 453–62; NCAB 7, 1–2; DAB 4, 26–27; Laura C. Smith, *The Life of Philander Chase* (New York, 1903).

CHAUNCY, Charles (1 January 1705, Boston, MA—10 February 1787, Boston, MA). *Education:* B.A., Harvard Coll., 1721. *Career:* minister, First Congregational Church, Boston, 1727–87.

The content of eighteenth century liberal theology developed along lines best understood by contrasting it with alternative viewpoints. Chauncy was an acknowledged leader in this intellectual movement, which revised traditional religion to make it congruent with new optimism about human ability. For sixty years in Boston's prestigious First Church, he shaped a theology from Puritan and Enlightenment elements, setting precedents for further growth in the next generation of New England ministers. While not a one-sided rationalist, Chauncy gave reason highest place in religious life because it could integrate all experiences into an orderly whole conducive to godliness. During the First Great Awakening he became an implacable critic of such preachers as *George Whitefield on the ground that he aroused emotions instead of reaching the minds of his hearers. He did not grasp *Jonathan Edwards' important distinction between emotion and religious affections but insisted that everything in the irrational category was subordinate to reasonable faith. Revivalistic enthusiasm was also repugnant because it stressed spiritual assurance as opposed to the means of grace provided by church ordinances; it contrasted faith and works as if they were opposites. Chauncy vigorously defended his view of good works and orderly progress toward a more perfect understanding of scriptural truths as preferable to the vagaries of revival hysteria. In both a theological and an institutional sense he represented conceptions of covenantal duty at variance with the New Divinity men who followed Edwards. Reason and order were more important to him than the unsettling results of a disproportionate stress on faith.

As early as 1762 Chauncy had begun to think that salvation would be granted to all men. Unlike his more outspoken friend, *Jonathan Mayhew, he quietly explored doctrines of election for two more decades before rejecting the view of eternal damnation as too extreme. He believed in an essentially benevolent deity who communicated happiness to the whole created order. With such a profound faith in the goodness of God, he could not conclude that man was made to suffer indefinitely or that divine power was insufficient to rectify human sin. The wicked would be punished after death, he said, for a time proportionate to their moral depravity. From one perspective, suffering was punishment for evil, but it was also a process of regeneration, delivering the soul from misery acquired through sinful behavior. Such a view stood in marked contrast to Old Calvinists, but Chauncy found it easier to reconcile with the essential goodness of God, justice for creatures under providential care, and Christ's passion as a means to secure it. After careful searching of the Bible, whose literal authority he never questioned, he was happy to revise a doctrine which traditionally consigned so great a number of the human race to eternal misery. Though admitting men would inevitably sin, he labored unstintingly to persuade them that orderly Christian habits would ultimately fit them for happy immortality.

Bibliography:

A. *Enthusiasm Described and Caution'd Against* (Boston, 1742); *Seasonable Thoughts on the State of Religion in New-England* (Boston, 1743); *Twelve Sermons* (Boston, 1765); *The Benevolence of the Deity, Fairly and Impartially Considered* (Boston, 1784); *The Mystery hid from Ages and Generations, made Manifest by the Gospel-Revelation* (London, 1784; New York, 1969); *Five Dissertations on the Scripture Account of the Fall* (London, 1785).

B. AAP 8, 8–13; SH 3, 22–23; NCAB 5, 168; DAB 4, 42–43; Edward M. Griffin, *Old Brick: Charles Chauncy of Boston; 1705–1787* (Minneapolis, 1980); Charles H. Lippy, *Seasonable Revolutionary: The Mind of Charles Chauncy* (Chicago, 1981).

CHEVERUS, Jean Louis Lefebre de (28 January 1768, Mayenne, France—19 July 1836, Bordeaux, France). *Education*: studied at Coll. of Louis-le-Grande and Sem. of St. Magloire, Paris, 1781–90. *Career*: assistant priest, Notre Dame de Mayenne, France, 1791–92; tutor in French and Mathematics, Wallingford, England, 1792–94; priest, Tottenham Chapel, London, 1794–96; priest and missionary in MA, 1796–1810; bishop of Boston, 1810–23; archbishop of Bordeaux, 1826–36; cardinal, 1836.

As with many victims of anticlerical outbursts in the French Revolution, de Cheverus fled first to England and then to the United States. He arrived in Boston and, though he volunteered for missions in the interior wherever else bishop *John Carroll chose to place him, he remained in the northeast, associated with a congregation begun in 1784 by French and Irish Catholics. He made his way on pastoral rounds with becoming modesty, walking long distances whenever possible and avoiding ostentation at all times. He strove to make his ministry self-sustaining, whether as missionary to native American tribes such as the Passamaquoddy or Penobscots in Maine or to scattered families of the faithful in the Boston area. De Cheverus sought to make himself useful in his host community, and his mild manners often won friendly responses from the Protestant majority. His selflessness also impressed local citizens, especially during the yellow fever epidemic of 1798. He had to endure some anti-Catholic prejudice, however. In 1800, for example, he faced both civil and criminal charges for having performed a marriage ceremony. Residual bigotry notwithstanding, he was quickly exonerated.

In 1808 when Carroll's huge jurisdiction was divided, de Cheverus was named the first bishop of Boston, receiving actual consecration two years later. His diocese included all of New England, and yet he eschewed the pomp that some thought accrued to his new status and responsibility. He continued to dress modestly and walked whenever he could on missionary tours and visits. In addition to serving his needs as a dwelling, his small house doubled as a seminary and a hospital. De Cheverus helped Catholics increase in piety and numbers, but his greatest contribution lay in fostering friendly relations between his flock and the Protestants who dominated cultural affairs. He also made warm friends with other clergy, particularly *William E. Channing who corresponded with the cardinal archbishop for the rest of his life. When he was summoned back to France, it seemed the whole city lamented his departure, paying him rich tribute in farewell ceremonies. He proved to be equally effective as pastor and diocesan administrator in his native land, earning again the people's affection. An indication of the esteem in which he was held can be found in the claim that all of France mourned at his death.

Bibliography:

    B.   NCAB 6, 331–32; DAB 4, 61–62; NCE 3, 555–56; Andre J. M. Hamon, *Life of the Cardinal de Cheverus, Archbishop of Bordeaux and formerly Bishop of Boston, in Massachusetts*, translated from the French by Robert M. Walsh (Philadelphia, 1839); Anabelle M. Melville, *Jean Lefebre de Cheverus, 1768–1836* (Milwaukee, 1958).

CLARK, Francis Edward (12 September 1851, Aylmer, Canada—26 May 1927, Newton, MA). *Education*: B.A., Dartmouth Coll., 1873; B.D., Andover Sem., 1876. *Career*: minister, Williston Congregational Church, Portland, ME, 1876–83; minister, Phillips Congregational Church, Boston, 1883–87; president, United Society of Christian Endeavor, 1887–1925; editor *Christian Endeavor*

World (*Golden Rule* before 1897), 1886–1919; president, World's Christian Endeavor Union, 1895–1925.

An orphan at seven years of age, the boy whom friends called Frank was raised by an uncle, establishing a relationship later formalized by a legal change of surnames from Symmes to Clark. He also chose the vocation of his adoptive parent and spent early pastoral years in common chores that ranged from composing sermons to financing new buildings for a rapidly expanding congregation. The young clergyman had a knack for reaching young people; he soon made a noticeable impact on the adolescent population with down-to-earth lectures on topics such as the gambling den, trash in print, king alcohol, plus other threats to Christian character. In 1881 he went one step further and organized the youth of his church into a formal body self-consciously dedicated to strengthening practical religious action. The movement soon to be known around the world as Christian Endeavor was based primarily on its founder's strong convictions regarding the importance of converting children at an early age and training their habits through involvement in church affairs. While remaining nondenominational, it emphasized close cooperation with churches in support of all moral or philanthropic reforms, Christian missions, and programs encouraging good citizenship. Clark decided that his efforts to work up this form of Christian nurture accomplished more good than other ministerial contributions, so he gave it full concentration after 1887. Under his promotional guidance, the movement grew to proportions of astounding size and geographical distribution.

Local Christian Endeavor societies were accepted in most Protestant denominations because they helped revitalize their Sunday Schools and provide a format where young people could achieve needed recognition. By 1921 over 80,000 of these unions had been formed, comprising millions of members in forty countries. Annual conventions (biennial after 1901) were held to further general ideals of Christian witness; probably the largest was convened in 1895 when 56,000 delegates registered in huge tents on Boston Common. Clark attended these meetings as well as countless sessions on regional levels, speaking and advising on ways to develop moral fiber in the next generation. He also edited the movement's paper, which reached a circulation of 100,000. Extensive travels took him to every continent as he circled the globe three times and preached in almost every state of the American Union. His tours of major cities, including those in Canada and Europe, amounted to evangelical campaigns in which he promoted the cause of youthful participation in church extension. He was constantly in demand and met obligations as long as good health endured. But the rigors of constant travel began to tell by 1925, forcing him to relinquish control of future activities into the hands of associates.

Bibliography:

A. *Looking Out on Life* (Boston, 1892); *A New Way Around an Old World* (New York, 1901); *Training the Church of the Future* (New York, 1902); *The Christian Endeavor Manual* (Boston, 1903); *Christian Endeavor in All Lands* (Philadelphia, 1906); *Memories of Many Men in Many Lands* (Boston, 1922).

B.   SH 3, 125; NCAB 13, 51–52; DAB 4, 126–27; NYT 27 May 1927, 23; Eugene F. Clark, *A Son's Portrait of Dr. Francis E. Clark* (Boston, 1930).

CLARKE, James Freeman (4 April 1810, Hanover, NH—8 June 1888, Boston, MA). *Education*: B.A., Harvard Coll., 1829; B.D., Harvard Div. Sch., 1833. *Career*: minister, Louisville, KY, 1833–40; editor, *Western Messenger*, 1836–39; minister, Church of the Disciples, Boston, 1841–50; convalescence and travel, 1850–54; minister, Church of the Disciples, Boston, 1854–88.

As a young Unitarian minister who sought to spread the transcendental ideals of his persuasion farther west, Clarke accepted the invitation of a small congregation in Kentucky. Only after arriving there did he begin to count slavery among the wrongs to be righted in a general program of social and moral progress. He slowly formed antislavery convictions and, while editor of a monthly, the *Western Messenger*, spread his ideas through the region. He did not promote any specific means of dealing with the problem, but from the beginning there was a strong emphasis on human bondage as an evil system that somehow had to be eradicated. Slavery was monstrous because it inevitably produced cruelty for servants and demoralization for their owners. After returning to Boston, Clarke expanded his thoughts into calm, deliberate addresses, speaking of slavery as a national sin. He urged that working for its termination was the moral obligation of all citizens, despite apparent indications to the contrary like the Fugitive Slave Law and the Dred Scott decision. In his view, religion was dedicated to freeing all the oppressed, and he persevered in the cause even when some charged that his advocacy would eventually destroy the Union. The question of human liberty was more compelling to him than political compromise. Through sermons, public resolutions, articles in the *Christian Examiner*, and other civic acts Clarke worked for decades to arouse antislavery feeling in New England.

Abolition was only one of the areas in which Clarke pursued his conception of the ministry, endeavoring to permeate the larger circles of society with religious influence. Boston's Church of the Disciples, organized to allow freedom of belief for all members, served as a center for such activities. Its Wednesday evening meetings allowed free discussion on issues of interest, providing a forum for topics that ranged from prison reform to botany, from predestination to supplying rifles for Kansas freesoilers. Not always in the best of health, Clarke spent many months at his wife's parental home in Meadville, Pennsylvania, preaching there occasionally and furthering work in the Unitarian seminary. In 1865 he was a central figure in forming the National Conference of Unitarian Churches and, as a moderate trusted by both sides, was chosen the first speaker to address that organization. After 1867 he was an adjunct professor at Harvard Divinity School and gave weekly lectures on doctrine and world religions that contributed to the growing interest in historical scholarship. His influence is best seen in a variety of activities intent upon applying religious ideals to improvement in law, literature, science, and society.

Bibliography:

A. *Orthodoxy: Its Truths and Errors* (Boston, 1866); *Steps of Belief* (Boston, 1870); *Ten Great Religions*, 2 vols. (Boston, 1871–83); *Anti-Slavery Days* (New York, 1884); *Manual of Unitarian Belief* (Boston, 1884); *Every-Day Religion* (Boston, 1886).

B. SH 3, 126–27; NCAB 2, 186; DAB 4, 153–54; NYT 9 June 1888, 4; Edward E. Hale (ed.), *James Freeman Clarke: Autobiography, Diary and Correspondence* (Boston, 1891; New York, 1968); John W. Thomas, *James Freeman Clarke: Apostle of German Culture in America* (Boston, 1949); Arthur S. Bolster, Jr., *James Freeman Clarke* (Boston, 1954).

CLARKE, John (8 October 1609, Westhorpe, England—28 April 1676, Newport, RI). *Career*: minister and physician, Newport, RI, 1639–52; diplomatic agent for RI in England, 1652–64; minister and physician, Newport, RI, 1664–76.

There is no clear evidence that Clarke received a formal education, but his mastery of languages, medicine, and theology indicate an admirable preparation for the contingencies of colonial life. Having already formed Separatist convictions in England, he emigrated to Massachusetts Bay at a time (1637) when Puritan leaders had begun restricting the limits of religious diversity. He immediately sided with *Anne Hutchinson and other supporters of a covenant of grace, all of whom the Massachusetts authorities condemned as antinomian. Within months he began searching for a place where dissenters might retire, first in New Hampshire then near the colony of *Roger Williams who welcomed them enthusiastically. By 1638 Clarke together with several other settlers bought the island of Aquidneck from neighboring Indians and established the town of Portsmouth; a year later he helped found Newport on the southern tip of their purchase, renamed Rhode Island, a location which he considered home for the rest of his life. The local church designated him their minister or "teaching elder," a capacity wherein he served faithfully through the course of almost forty years. Sometime between 1641 and 1648, the congregation declared acceptance of Baptist principles. The minister was known for strong Calvinistic inclinations, and at his urging Newport parishioners endorsed the limited atonement doctrine of Particular Baptists. His activity as spiritual leader and political benefactor helped further the cause of tolerance for heterodox religious patterns in townships surrounding Narragansett Bay.

Respect for the rights of individual conscience in religious matters was an ideal Clarke supported as thoroughly as did his fellow colonist, Roger Williams. In 1651 he was arrested and fined £ 20 for conducting an unauthorized worship service in Lynn, Massachusetts. In response to such persecution he wrote a short treatise, enlarging it to book length the next year in order to portray the suffering incurred while defending issues of private judgment. This book did much to win British sympathy for the cause of toleration in Rhode Island. At that time, Clarke was in London with Williams for the purpose of obtaining a new charter for their colony—one which would not only confirm the land grant but assure religious liberty as well. Williams returned to the New World in 1654, but Clarke remained to treat with both Commonwealth and Stuart administrations until a new charter was acquired in 1663. His patient diplomacy, no less than his skill at drafting constitutional clauses, resulted in lawful protection of religious freedom. As long as citizens did not disturb civil peace or use their liberty to licentiousness, they would not be molested for differences of opinion on doctrinal questions. Upon returning to Newport, Clarke resumed his ministerial labors, serving too as member of the General Assembly (1664–69) and three terms as deputy governor (1669–72). After that, he withdrew from the political arena in which he had long embodied the idea that civil states were best maintained when they provided full liberty in matters concerning religion.

Bibliography:

A. *Ill Newes from New England, or A Narrative of New England's Persecutions* (London, 1652).

B. AAP 6, 21–26; SH 3, 127; NCAB 7, 346–47; DAB 4, 154–56; Thomas W. Bicknell, *Story of Dr. John Clarke* (Providence, RI, 1915).

CLARKE, William Newton (2 December 1841, Cazenovia, NY—14 January 1912, Deland, FL). *Education*: B.A., Madison Coll. (now Colgate Univ.), 1861; graduated from Hamilton Sem., 1863. *Career*: minister, Keene, NH, 1863–69; minister, Newton Center, MA, 1869–80; minister, Montreal, Canada, 1880–83; professor of New Testament Interpretation, Toronto Baptist Coll., 1883–87; minister, Hamilton, NY, 1887–90; professor of Christian Theology, Colgate Sem., 1890–1908; lecturer in Ethics, Colgate Sem., 1908–12.

It is important to notice that Clarke began systematizing his theological views after having served in a number of Baptist pastorates for almost three decades. Practical experience lay behind his ideas, which had a formative influence on major facets of Protestant liberalism, including its methodological dictum that theology is an expression of the human spirit. Following careful revision of lecture notes, he issued in 1898 an outline of Christian thought, the first systematic American treatise based on an acceptance of biblical criticism, historical change, and scientific knowledge of the natural world. The large volume proved an immediate success, running to twenty editions, in less than that number of years. It was widely acclaimed by those who had broken with outmoded doctrinal statements and yet adhered to values they wanted explained in contemporary idioms. Clarke's work filled a need by providing continuity with earlier confessional patterns without sacrificing rational integrity under current circumstances. He began with the evidence of human experience because man as the bearer of God's image disclosed all the divine attributes worth knowing in modern life. In discussing God's nature, he emphasized those qualities which Jesus as representative man had stressed in his own ministry. With a fairly low Christology, he held that Jesus was the man through whom God's spirit found such complete expression; His self-consciousness continued to be normative for understanding the content of revelation.

All the qualities of divine-human encounter that Clarke emphasized in his theology were grounded in what he saw as Jesus' religious experience, a universal pattern for others to follow. From that perspective he viewed God as a loving father, anticipating the needs of His children and always ready to welcome repentant prodigals. His holiness was conceived in terms of moral excellence with love as its greatest expression; there was no distinct end set apart for divine righteousness, dualistically separate from God's mercy and graciousness. Both aspects of His ethical personality helped conform the child to the father. Whether God punished or forgave, all action was consistent within the supreme purpose of redemption, a long-range plan for which divine wisdom and power augured success in spite of every obstacle. Indeed, Clarke brimmed with optimism regarding human improvement, holding that man, though persistently self-willed, was still developing as chief product of the evolutionary process. Even the presence of evil in private or social experience was part of God's beneficial purposes, nourishing good tendencies in people as they progressed to greater realization of their potential. These general tenets placed little priority on sacraments, corporate worship in a gathered church, or ethical imperatives; but they embodied the ideals of many who used cultural mores as a component in forming religious ideas.

Bibliography:

    A.   *Commentary on the Gospel of Mark* (Philadelphia, 1881); *An Outline of Christian Theology* (New York, 1898); *What Shall We Think of Christianity?* (New York, 1899); *The Use of the Scriptures in Theology* (New York, 1905); *The Christian Doctrine of God* (New York, 1909); *Sixty Years with the Bible* (New York, 1912).

    B.   SH 3, 128; NCAB 22, 264–65; DAB 4, 164; NCE 3, 918; NYT 16 Jan 1912, 13; Emily S. Clarke, *William Newton Clarke* (New York, 1916); Claude L. Howe, *The Theology of William Newton Clarke* (New York, 1980).

CODY, John Patrick (24 December 1907, St. Louis, MO—25 April 1982, Chicago, IL). *Education*: graduated from St. Louis Preparatory Sem., 1926; Ph.D., S.T.D., and D.C.L., North American Coll., Rome, Italy, 1928, 1932, and 1936. *Career*: Assistant director, North American Coll., and staff member, Vatican Secretariat of State, 1933–38; secretary and chancellor to archbishop of St. Louis, 1938–50, auxiliary bishop of St. Louis, 1947–54; bishop coadjutor of St. Joseph, MO, 1954–56; coadjutor and then full bishop of Kansas City–St. Joseph, 1956–61; coadjutor and then full archbishop of New Orleans, 1961–65; archbishop of Chicago, 1965–82; cardinal, 1967–82.

While still a young priest on the staff of the Roman Curia, Cody learned much about the uses of ecclesiastical power. Those experiences helped his rise to prominence among American prelates, high placement that brought both fame as champion of a liberal cause and notoriety as a conservative autocrat. In his early years as diocesan administrator (dates and titles being imprecise because of differences between titular and actual responsibility) he also gained a reputation for hard work, skill at fund raising, and zeal to nurture church growth. In 1961 Cody was transferred to the See of New Orleans as assistant to the archbishop, receiving appointment as Apostolic Administrator the following year. In fact he exercised all archipiscopal authority from his arrival until he succeeded to the office in 1964. As such he attracted national attention by his unequivocal advocacy of racial integration and for his swift implementation of that view in the parochial school system. His firm stand and bold policy served notice that temporizing, half-way measures were no longer good enough. He refused to yield to racist opponents, going so far as to excommunicate several core agitators. His uncompromising methods quickly aligned a Deep South diocese with the liberal cause supported in his church and country.

Success in that controversy, and undoubtedly with help from old friends in Rome, soon led to appointment as sixth archbishop of Chicago, the nation's largest Catholic diocese. It became increasingly clear that Cody was a traditional hierarch whose regal and arbitrary manner fit poorly with post–Vatican II policies. The Association of Chicago Priests had been organized as an advisory group, hoping to democratize administrative procedures, but Cody's resistance to shared governance turned the body into an adversary instead. In 1971 the priests voted by a narrow margin to censure their superior for not adequately reporting their views and for ignoring their concerns about reform. It was Cody's sad fate to witness a decline in church attendance, the departure of one-third of his priests from their vocation, and a widespread decrease of respect for episcopal authority. In 1981 it was also alleged that he misappropriated diocesan funds, perhaps up to one million dollars, to aid a lifelong friend and distant relative. Such charges probably hastened his death and ended his personal demonstration of confusing power as a means of accomplishing good with power as an end in itself.

Bibliography:

B.   NCE 18, 101; NYT 26 Apr 1982, B 15; Charles W. Dahm, *Power and Authority in the Catholic Church: Cardinal Cody in Chicago* (Notre Dame, IN, 1981).

COFFIN, Henry Sloane (5 January 1877, New York, NY—25 November 1954, Lakeville, CT). *Education*: B.A., Yale Coll., 1897; studied at Edinburgh, 1897–99, and Marburg, 1899; B.D., Union Sem. (NY), 1900. *Career*: minister, Bedford Park Church, New York, 1900–05; associate professor of Practical Theology, Union Sem., 1904–26; minister, Madison Avenue Presbyterian Church, New York, 1905–26; president, Union Sem., 1926–45; active retirement, 1945–54.

After studying at some of the best schools on two continents, Coffin began preaching in a rented hall over a butcher shop. Because of the transparent reality of his own spiritual life and the honesty with which he approached intellectual problems in religion, he rapidly made a name for himself as a gifted liberal thinker. Sharing many of the attitudes current at the turn of the century, he called for a restatement of Christian doctrines in the light of modern scientific discoveries. He accepted the results of biblical scholarship and asked others to search for truth with an open mind, following such ideas wherever they might lead. While still aware of human sin and not overly optimistic about eradicating it, he nevertheless urged Christians collectively to remake society. Faith in God's forgiveness made him distinctly evangelical in emphasis. Yet he avoided shallow liberalism, which reduced Jesus to a human example and the Bible to one among many guidebooks, replacing sacrificial atonement with human effort. He remained loyal to what he saw as essentials of Christian belief, expounding them in books of sermons which affected many thoughtful persons who might otherwise have felt out of place in contemporary churches.

As an exponent of liberal Christianity, Coffin's activities often found a more institutional form of expression. After 1910 he became a leader among those who resisted fundamentalist attempts to confine Presbyterianism within rigid confessional definitions. He was an outspoken protagonist for theological diversity, defending *Harry E. Fosdick not only on principle but because he agreed with him and then later *Reinhold Niebuhr when they did not agree on much of anything. In 1924 he was one of the primary agents behind the "Auburn Affirmation," which declared loyalty to the Presbyterian confession of faith but claimed a right to interpret it along with the Scriptures as individuals saw fit. Further, he and three hundred other ministers rejected biblical inerrancy while they denied that the General Assembly had constitutional grounds to control his belief in central facts such as biblical inspiration, incarnation, atonement, resurrection, and the continuing life of Christ, but he resisted dictation of any theory as to how those facts must be interpreted. He labored throughout life for mutual toleration and an inclusive church. His election as moderator of the General Assembly in 1943 signaled an agreeable end to controversy over those principles. After succeeding *Arthur C. McGiffert as president of Union Seminary, he worked there to provide a continuing atmosphere of open inquiry into various ways gospel insights could be applied to current social and intellectual questions. He also labored for decades to aid the nascent ecumenical movement, foreseeing a time when denominations would be less important than the single God they served and the common goals they pursued.

Bibliography:

A.   *The Creed of Jesus* (New York, 1907); *Some Christian Convictions: A Practical Restatement in Terms of Present-Day Thinking* (New Haven, 1915); *A More Christian Industrial Order* (New York, 1920); *The Meaning of the Cross* (New York, 1931); *Religion Yesterday and Today* (Nashville, 1940); *God Confronts Man in History* (New York, 1947).

B.   NCAB E, 134–35; NYT 26 Nov 1954, 29; Morgan P. Noyes, *Henry Sloane Coffin: The Man and His Ministry* (New York, 1964).

COFFIN, Levi (28 October 1789, near New Garden, NC—16 September 1877, Avondale, OH). *Career*: merchant, Newport (now Fountain City), IN, 1826–47; merchant, Cincinnati, OH, 1847–62; independent agent for freedmen, 1862–67; retirement, 1867–77.

By accounts in his own reminiscences, Coffin became aware of slavery and its cruelties when only seven years old. His Quaker parents and grandparents refused on principle to sanction the practice, but in young Levi that conviction rose to the more forthright expression of abolitionism. Persuaded that slavery was the most important moral issue of his day, he argued against quietistic religion which concentrated exclusively on inner feelings. In a modest but inflexible way, he criticized any faith that ignored tasks in the real world as Pharisaic and not worth preserving. His residence in Indiana soon provided the opportunity for putting such an activistic orientation into practice because it lay in the path of the "underground railroad." Slaves escaping from southern regions traveled by night in desperate attempts to reach Canada or other territory beyond the reach of slavehunters. There routes converged on Coffin's home in Newport, and the conscience-bound Quaker fearlessly aided refugees there for more than twenty-five years. Hardly a week went by without his helping runaways traveling singly or by the wagonload by giving them shelter, clothing, and the means for further progress—all this at private expense. His practical ministry benefited an estimated 3,500 persons and won him unofficial recognition as "president" of the underground railroad.

Not all Quakers in the state approved of helping runaway slaves, but Coffin refused to compromise and made the town of Newport a hotbed of abolitionism. The Indiana Yearly Meeting of Friends repeatedly censured his activity, and in 1842 it separated the local congregation from larger affiliation. These pronouncements created tension, protests, and appeals over an extended period of time, but Coffin remained a steadfast friend to the oppressed. In Cincinnati he met *Harriet B. Stowe and gave her many specifics for her classic tale of runaways, *Uncle Tom's Cabin*, finding later that he had been incorporated into the story himself. When the Civil War altered conditions for black Americans, he organized (1863) the Western Freedmen's Aid Commission. Thousands of former slaves were suddenly thrown on their own resources by the liberating northern armies. Coffin made several visits in war zones down the Mississippi to distribute supplies and money among the pitiable dependent freedmen. He also toured northern cities, arousing sympathy and generous support for the latest phase of Negro humanitarianism. In 1864 he helped organize a freedmen's aid society in England that contributed over one hundred thousand dollars within a single year. Though he retired shortly after attending the 1867 International Anti-Slavery Convention in Paris, his lifework demonstrated one way in which inner light could find expression in practical action.

Bibliography:
A. *Reminiscences of Levi Coffin* (Cincinnati, 1876; New York, 1968).
B. NCAB 12, 124; DAB 4, 268–69; NYT 17 Sep 1877, 4.

COKE, Thomas (9 October 1747, Brecon, Wales—3 May 1814 on shipboard bound for Ceylon). *Education*: B.A., M.A., D.C.L., Jesus Coll., Oxford Univ., 1768, 1770, 1775. *Career*: burgess and bailiff, Brecon, 1769–71; Anglican curate, South Petherton, 1771–77; Methodist minister, London, 1778–83; superintendent (bishop after 1787), American Methodist Church, 1784–1814.

The Methodist connection received an unusual candidate for its ministry in 1777—Coke brought with him a doctorate in civil law and seven years' experience as ordained priest in the Church of England. The young clergyman had been dismissed from his living for too much enthusiasm in sermons and headstrong parish administration, but his sound faith combined with zeal for good works made a favorable impression on John Wesley, guiding light of evangelical Methodists. Coke soon became Wesley's trusted confidant, accepting in 1784 the responsibility to superintend church work in the newly independent United States. After much deliberation he accepted ordination, not out of a sense of canonical propriety, but on the practical ground that designation as the founder's representative was necessary to make his mission successful. Soon after arriving in America he met *Francis Asbury, and together they convened the "Christmas Conference" of Methodist ministers at Baltimore in December of 1784. Coke carried credentials to ordain Asbury as joint superintendent of the American mission without wider consultation. He did not appreciate the democratic preferences of his New World brethren, nor could he see any significance in demands that the conference elect him and Asbury to office. Nevertheless he acquiesced in such procedures, established cordial relations with his more popular counterpart and tried to remain on good terms with leaders on both sides of the Atlantic.

Extending missions was Coke's primary objective, and he expended great efforts during nine tours of America to foster the growth of Methodism from Nova Scotia to Antigua. He sustained the rigors of prolonged itinerancy, left off wearing a clerical gown, held meetings at the unaccustomed time of midday, and in numerous other ways adapted to new circumstances in order to spread the gospel. In one area he did not compromise, however, for slavery was something he continually opposed. As early as 1784 he persuaded the conference to threaten slaveholders with excommunication if they persisted in their ways. Compromises occurred among Methodists later, but Coke remained an irritating witness to human liberty in this regard. There were continuous disputes with Asbury over other policies in this country's first independent church, with Asbury usually prevailing. Coke's conception of the office of bishop permitted an exercise of power which the American church would not accept. By 1808 the struggles between conference and bishop had reached a stalemate, and while Coke remained nominally an American bishop, he relinquished virtually all New World activities. But all the while he kept the respect of most American churchmen through tireless labors for their common cause. He was burdened with affairs in England, increasingly so after Wesley's death in 1791, and devoted the major portion of his time to overseas missions. Death came while he sought wider opportunities in that field.

Bibliography:

A.   *The Life of the Rev. John Wesley* (London, 1792); *Four Discourses on the Duties of the Gospel Ministry* (Philadelphia, 1798); *A Commentary on the Holy Bible*, 6 vols. (London, 1801–07); *An Account of the Rise, Progress, and Present State of the Methodist Missions* (London, 1804); *Extracts of the Journals of the Late Rev. Thomas Coke* (Dublin, 1816).

B.   AAP 7, 130–42; SH 3, 153; NCAB 10, 89; DAB 4, 279–80; Joseph Sutcliffe, *Memoirs of the Late Rev. Thomas Coke* (Dublin, 1816); Samuel Drew, *Life of the Rev. Thomas Coke* (London, 1817); Warren A. Candler, *The Life of Thomas Coke* (Nashville, 1923); John A. Vickers, *Thomas Coke: Apostle of Methodism* (London, 1969).

CONNOR, Walter Thomas (19 January 1877, Center [now Rowell], AR—26 May 1952, Fort Worth, TX). *Education*: B.A., Baylor Univ., 1906; Th.B., Southwestern Baptist Sem., 1908; studied at Rochester Sem., 1908–10; studied at Univ. of Chicago, 1910; studied at Southern Baptist Sem., 1914. *Career*: schoolteacher and minister, Jones County, TX, 1899–1901; minister, Eagle Lake, TX, 1903–04; professor of Theology, Southwestern Baptist Sem., 1910–49; retirement, 1949–52.

After turning from early plans to be a foreign missionary, Connor dedicated himself to teaching in an institution built on ground just two generations removed from wilderness. He also found himself servicing a denomination still largely unaccustomed, if not decidedly hostile, to an educated ministry. But in the rapidly growing Southwest region, he articulated major theological emphases which characterized almost all evangelical groups in addition to most Texas Baptists. His experiences at the seminary during its struggle with poor financial support paralleled ecclesiastical development in the area, covering a span of four decades which saw the amalgamation of voluntary associations into closely knit, aggressive denominations, eager to perpetuate their religious views. Connor became known as a "people's theologian" because his simple writing style communicated descriptive definitions of Christian realities to the average person. Though he occupied a position somewhere right of center, he always employed conservative categories with enough devotional spirit to avoid the legalistic dogmatism or hidebound literalism so prevalent among Fundamentalists. In an atmosphere noted for its anti-intellectualism, he defended full investigation of theological matters and did much to embody the search for academic excellence at a school where religious fervor often predominated over scholarship.

Over the years Connor's religious thought matured in a search to provide adequate rationale for theological affirmations. He began by attempting to state biblical truths with logical precision and finality; he ended by concluding that truth is a functional guide which lends perspective during one's continual spiritual growth. As he sought to understand the meaning of biblical language, it became apparent the Bible was not a rigid oracular source of timeless propositions. Scripture was rather the creative source of Christianity that had to be understood through human reason and personal religious experience, with dynamic vehicles of knowledge more promising than the sterile process of deduction. This emphasis on a flexible, empirical structure for traditional beliefs made Connor's theology instrumental in rescuing local religious debates from the extreme positions of both radical liberals and conservatives. He discussed Christology before conceptions of revelation or the attributes of God because the historical personality of Christ gave focus to every important category. For example he retained predestinarian belief in God's choosing whom He would save, but he stressed a primacy of love over holiness. The Trinity was more an analogy than essential to divine character; the church was secondary to individual grace, not dispenser of it. Finally in an area where eschatology loomed large in evangelical thought, he modestly affirmed a postmillennial view but declared all such notions inconsequential for effective daily living. He pursued light to see how to walk, not a finished philosophy of the universe.

Bibliography:

A.   *A System of Christian Doctrine* (Nashville, 1924); *Revelation and God* (Nashville, 1936); *Personal Christianity* (Grand Rapids, MI, 1937); *The Faith of the New Testament* (Nashville, 1940); *The Gospel of Redemption* (Nashville, 1945); *The Work of the Holy Spirit* (Nashville, 1949).

B.   Stewart A. Newman, *W.T. Connor: Theologian of the Southwest* (Nashville, 1964).

CONWELL, Russell Herman (15 February 1843, South Worthington, MA— 6 December 1925, Philadelphia, PA). *Education*: studied at Yale Coll., 1860– 62; studied law privately and at School of Law, Albany Univ. (NY), 1865. *Career*: officer, Union Army, 1862–65; practiced law, Minneapolis, MN, 1865– 68; semi-retirement and convalescence, 1868–70; reporter and editor, *Boston Traveller*, businessman, practiced law, Boston, 1870–80; minister, Lexington, MA, 1880–82; minister, Grace Baptist Church, Philadelphia, 1882–1925; president, Temple Univ. 1888–1925.

The entrepreneurial character of Conwell's life was evident long before he decided to assume the vocation of minister. Certain crises in his life—severe wounds in the Civil War and the death of his first wife—turned his thoughts to religious matters; but up to 1879 he was just another successful businessman who taught Bible classes in local churches and worked with the YMCA. Then a more clerical course was set, and in the early 1880s he came to a struggling church in Philadelphia that soon became one of the city's largest Protestant congregations, popularly known as the Baptist Temple. Conwell's ministry was not known for evangelistic fervor but for its promotion of educational and social concerns as well as preaching and individual counseling. It was popular and successful to have church life as the locus for suppers and choir concerts, committee work and prayer meetings, fairs, and study classes. Conwell began providing free night school classes in the church basement with volunteer teachers. By 1888 this enterprise developed into Temple University, a source of higher education for indigent students and industrious working men and women who wished to better themselves. It later added schools of law, dentistry, and medicine (founding or greatly aiding three hospitals) to benefit the larger community even further. Conwell's energetic leadership in all these programs was guided by a pastoral conception of service to others in as many areas as practicable.

In circles beyond local attention, Conwell was famous as an orator. He spoke extemporaneously and gave little thought to preparing remarks for an occasion, but his speeches were widely appreciated for their vivid descriptions of people and places and for their emphasis on moral uplift. He filled his delivery with anecdotes and simple stories, but included a full measure of practical advice. He sought to instruct and inspire audiences by means of this aspect of his ministry. Conwell hoped to increase the welfare of his listeners by urging them to develop capacities within themselves, to stay active, branch out, and try to succeed despite seeming obstacles. The best known of all his addresses was "Acres of Diamonds," delivered over 6,000 times during a span of forty years, the proceeds of which went to educational support for deserving students. Conwell's message of self-help, industry, and success struck a responsive chord in the minds of thousands of people inhabiting industrial America. His ideas both reflected and helped articulate this country's emphasis on religious activism and its close association with cultural values.

Bibliography:

A. *Woman and the Law* (Philadelphia, 1876); *Acres of Diamonds: How Men and Women May Become Rich* (Philadelphia, 1890, and many subsequent editions); *Observation* (New York, 1917); *What You Can Do With Your Will Power* (New York, 1917); *Effective Prayer* (New York, 1921); *Unused Powers* (New York, 1922).

B. SH 3, 263; NCAB 3, 29; DAB 4, 367–68; NYT 7 Dec 1925, 21; Albert H. Smith, *The Life of Russell H. Conwell* (Boston, 1899); Agnes R. Burr, *Russell H. Conwell and His Work* (Philadelphia, 1917; rev. ed. 1926).

COOK, Joseph (26 January 1838, Ticonderoga, NY—25 June 1901, Ticonderoga, NY). *Education*: studied at Yale Coll., 1858–61; B.A., Harvard Coll., 1865; B.D., Andover Sem., 1868; post-graduate theological study, Andover Sem., 1868–69; travel and study in Europe, 1871–73. *Career*: acting minister, First Congregational Church, Lynn, MA, 1869–71; lecturer and author, Boston, MA, 1874–95; retirement, 1895–1901.

Originally named Flavius Josephus but shortening it to Joseph for convenience, Cook pursued theological studies at some of the best schools on two continents. He never received ordination, however, and chose to spread his ideas by freelance lecturing instead, a medium in which he eventually won international repute. By 1875 his speaking at a traditional Monday prayer meeting in Boston had attracted such large audiences, the capacious Tremont Temple was used to seat them. Crowds came to hear him discourse on general themes such as biology, heredity, marriage, labor, socialism, and a host of current events. He purported to command the latest scholarship in religion and science; newspaper coverage made him a nationally known figure who spoke with reassuring self-confidence if not scientific accuracy. He was also interested in the social implications of Christianity and did much to publicize that reformist impulse in the last quarter of the nineteenth century. While discussing modern developments in science, Cook was staunchly, vehemently orthodox. He lashed out against those who tried to dilute traditional theology by using evolutionary theories or biblical criticism. But at the same time he was no obscurantist and often helped audiences understand that science or modern philosophies were not enemies to religious truth. Lecture invitations came from every major city in the English-speaking world. He conducted a highly successful global tour in 1880–83 and planned another in 1895. But while in Australia a debilitating stroke caused him to end the campaign prematurely and return home to forced retirement. Four years later he improved enough to resume part of his activities, continuing for a brief time longer that eloquence which had inspired many to think seriously about their faith and modern intellectual trends.

Bibliography

A.   *Boston Monday Lectures*, 11 vols. (Boston, 1877–88).
B.   SH 3, 265; NCAB 2, 260–61; DAB 4, 371–72; NYT 26 Jun 1901, 7; Steven R. Pointer, *Joseph Cook: Boston Lecturer and Evangelical Apologist* (Lewiston, NY, 1991).

CORRIGAN, Michael Augustine (13 August 1839, Newark, NJ—5 May 1902, New York, NY). *Education*: studied at St. Mary's Coll. (DE), 1853–55; B.A., Mount St. Mary's Coll. (MD), 1859; D.D., North American Coll., Rome, 1864. *Career*: professor of Dogmatic Theology and Sacred Scripture, Seton Hall Sem., 1864–68; president, Seton Hall Coll., 1868–76; bishop of Newark, 1873–80; bishop coadjutor of New York, 1880–85; archibishop of New York, 1885–1902.

A succession of administrative posts gave increasing opportunity for Corrigan to display his genius for getting things done. As a member of the first graduating class at the American College in Rome, he was qualified for priestly service, but he returned home to face larger managerial tasks. His abilities in this area were recognized by *James R. Bayley, who appointed him vicar-general in 1870 to supervise affairs in the statewide diocese. Three years later Corrigan followed Bayley as diocesan ordinary. While at Newark and later in New York, he was remarkably energetic in developing all facets of Catholic life. He stressed methodical organization, frequent visitations, financial solvency, and a missionary outreach to the immigrant population. Under his guidance more churches were built; parochial schools, hospitals, orphanages, industrial homes, and a host of other charitable institutions were erected. Discipline and efficiency characterized the growth of Catholicism under vigilant administrative care. As one faithful to the statutes of his church's plenary councils, he fostered development through strict conformity to forms of ecclesiastical regulation. In his view, healthy religious institutions had a bright future as long as their doctrines and customs were based on sound hierarchical principles of legal sanction.

As a legist, Corrigan emphasized the place of lawful authority in institutional development; on a personal level he was convinced that obedience produced qualities of high moral value. He also stressed the importance of humility, fostering it in himself and expecting to find it in those under his jurisdiction. One priest who failed sufficiently to embody such virtues was *Edward McGlynn, a pastor whose support of public schools and social experimentation raised Corrigan's opposition. In 1887 the archbishop admonished, then suspended the outspoken priest. By charging him with deviance from established attitudes regarding education and socialism, Corrigan acquired the reputation of staunch conservative, one who would not tolerate irregularities where canon law applied. After much negotiation McGlynn was reinstated in 1895, but the archbishop continued to represent the conservative wing of American Catholicism in his day. Together with his old friend and fellow prelate, *Bernard J. McQuaid, he stood against parishioners' belonging to secret societies, whether these were labor unions or harmless fraternal orders. He severely criticized school plans which failed to build a strong parochial system without relying on public funds. The dangers of compromising with secular culture were also visible to him, and he repeatedly warned against attitudes resembling "Americanism" as it was being called in Europe. Because of these controversies, the more reactionary side of Corrigan's activities has eclipsed his successful administration of a large archdiocese. In addition to remembering his severe insistence on lawful development, one should bear in mind his devotion to daily office, steady habits, and scholarly refinement.

Bibliography:

B.   SH 3, 275; NCAB 1, 196; DAB 4, 450–52; NCE 4, 352–54; NYT 6 May 1902, 1; John M. Farley (comp.), *Memorial of the Most Reverend Michael Augustine Corrigan* (New York, 1902); Frederick J. Zwierlein (ed.), *Letters of Archibishop Corrigan to Bishop McQuaid* (Rochester, NY, 1946); Robert Emmett Curran, *Michael Augustine Corrigan and the Shaping of Conservative Catholicism in America, 1878–1902* (New York, 1978).

COTTON, John (4 December 1584, Derby, England—23 December 1652, Boston, MA). *Education*: B.A., M.A., Trinity Coll., Cambridge Univ., 1603, 1606; B.D., Emmanuel Coll., Cambridge Univ., 1613. *Career*: Fellow and sometime dean, Emmanuel Coll., 1607–12; rector, St. Botolph's Anglican Church, Boston, England, 1612–33; minister, Congregational Church, Boston, MA, 1633–52.

With a brilliant intellectual record behind him at Cambridge and a comfortable pastorate in Lincolnshire, Cotton could have anticipated preferment as a distinguished clergyman in the Church of England. By 1615, however, his Puritan convictions began to appear in sermons and in modifications of liturgical practice.

He was treated leniently by his bishop for twenty years, but the accession of William Laud to Canterbury in 1633 produced strictures in ecclesiastical policy that made it difficult for dissenters to retain their appointments. Instead of compromising his theology, Cotton accepted the hard road of exile. Upon arriving in the newly-planted Massachusetts Bay colony he was immediately asked to accept the ministerial office of teacher in the church there. He labored in that post for the rest of his life and acquired high standing among the first generation of colonial leaders. Cotton was an able writer who did much to defend the doctrinal foundations of Congregational polity through logic, history, and biblical exposition. He figured in almost all the major decisions affecting the religious standards of New Englanders. One signal contribution was to serve on a tripartite committee which deliberated over models of church government. Though his suggestions were not followed by the Synod as much as those of Richard Mather, he helped substantially to draft the Cambridge Platform of 1648, a document serving as the basis of congregational organization in Massachusetts until the nineteenth century.

Two controversies reveal Cotton's position on crucial matters of Calvinist theology and civil law. *Roger Williams had been arguing for years that magistrates could not legitimately be used to enforce conformity in matters of religious scruple. Cotton was instrumental in effecting Williams' banishment (1635) and thereafter conducted a lengthy *guerre de plume* with him over questions of conscience and coercion. He articulated very well the dominant view that secular power ought to ensure obedience to true doctrines and practices, even to the point of executing incorrigible dissenters. Another episode centered on the essential question of salvation. Cotton had long stressed the unconditional nature of election, and his emphasis on personal experience of regenerating grace helped make confession of such an event requisite for membership in New England churches. But some of his disciples such as *Anne Hutchinson went to extremes and excluded outer sanctity in favor of inner feelings. Cotton finally came to see that such religious enthusiasts threatened to dissolve the linked covenants of grace and works. Whatever his ideas before 1637, he sided with majority opinion at Hutchinson's trial and publicly denounced her prideful errors. With his reputation somewhat diminished, he continued to work to the end of his days in fostering a holy commonwealth amid wilderness surroundings.

Bibliography:

A.   *The Way of Life* (London, 1641); *The Pouring Out of the Seven Vialls* (London, 1642); *The Bloudy Tenent, Washed and Made White in the Bloud of the Lambe* (London, 1647); *The Way of Congregational Churches Cleared* (London, 1648); *Of the Holinesse of Church-members* (London, 1650); *A Treatise of the Covenant of Grace* (London, 1659).

B.   AAP 1, 25–30; SH 3, 278; NCAB 7, 27–28; DAB 4, 460–62; NCE 4, 368; Williston Walker, *Ten New England Leaders* (New York, 1901); Larzer Ziff, *The Career of John Cotton: Puritanism and the American Experience* (Princeton, 1962); Everett H. Emerson, *John Cotton* (New York, 1965).

COUGHLIN, Charles Edward (25 October 1891, Hamilton, Ontario, Canada— 27 October 1979, Bloomfield Hills, MI). *Education*: B.A., St. Michael's Coll., Univ. of Toronto, 1911; studied for the priesthood, St. Basil's Sem., Toronto, 1911–16. *Career*: instructor, Assumption Coll., Sandwich, Ontario, 1916–23; assistant pastor, St. Leo's Church, Detroit, 1923–24; pastor, North Branch, MI, 1924–26; pastor, Shrine of the Little Flower Church, Royal Oak, MI, 1926–66; enforced retirement, 1966–79.

After a youthful stint as a member of the Congregation of Priests of St. Basil, Coughlin left the order and transferred to Detroit as a secular priest in 1923. There he quickly made a name for himself as a compelling preacher and effective promoter, fame enough to be chosen pastor of a new church in Royal Oak dedicated to recently canonized St. Therese, the "Little Flower of Jesus." There Coughlin built a parish from the ground up, using a flair for publicity and a new communications medium: radio. Beginning with a local station in 1926 and confining himself strictly to religious topics, Coughlin developed widespread positive response. He soon added new outlets for Sunday broadcasts, and as the Great Depression deepened, he became known as "the radio priest" who addressed between ten to forty million people per week. Greatly troubled by the poverty and despair he saw around him, Coughlin began addressing social problems, denouncing bolshevism and socialism as enemies of real justice and prosperity. By 1935 he had become a national figure, and it was necessary to employ one hundred clerks to answer his mail and tabulate contributions from Protestants and Jews as well as Catholics. He championed the downtrodden and criticized the exploiters; he offered simple explanations and hope to the frustrated and fearful; most of all he had charisma that led people to believe in him.

A career that began with compassion for the plight of the unemployed ended with increasingly controversial attacks against Wall Street, international bankers, Jews, Communists, and the New Deal. Coughlin held millions enthralled by his magnetic voice and Irish brogue, but he confused the roles of priest, and demagogue to the point where one could not be distinguished from the other. In his magazine, *Social Justice* (1936–42) and his organization, National Union for Social Justice (1934–36) which tried to influence national politics, Coughlin inveighed against F. D. Roosevelt and International bankers as the roots of contemporary unrest. By the late 1930s he supported a Christian Front movement which openly baited Jews and blamed them for all of society's woes. This pro-Nazi brand of Christianity became embarrassing to Roman Catholic officials, but Coughlin continued to align his volatile messages more closely to propaganda fabricated in Germany. Actually, Catholic opinion was split, with some archbishops and laity supporting his controversial attitudes and others denouncing it. But governmental pressure finally induced key members of the church hierarchy to cooperate in silencing the fiery popular spokesman. As a dutiful son of Roman polity, Coughlin submitted to discipline and subsided into virtual anonymity for the last decades of his life.

Bibliography:

B.   NCE 18, 108–09; NYT 28 Oct. 1979, 44; Charles J. Tull, *Father Coughlin and the New Deal* (Syracuse, 1965); Sheldon Marcus, *Father Coughlin: The Tumultuous Life of the Priest of the Little Flower* (Boston, 1973); Alan Brinkley, *Voices of Protest: Huey Long, Father Coughlin and the Great Depression* (New York, 1983).

CRAPSEY, Algernon Sidney (28 June 1847, Fairmount, OH—31 December 1927, Rochester, NY). *Education*: studied at St. Stephen's Coll., 1867–69; B.D., General Sem., 1872. *Career*: assistant minister, St. Paul's Chapel, New York, NY, 1872–79; minister, St. Andrew's Church, Rochester, NY, 1879–1906; travel, occasional lecturing and writing, state parole officer (after 1914), 1906–27.

Ordained as an Episcopal priest in 1873, Crapsey was appointed to the staff of New York's Trinity Church for seven years, a large urban parish where he had served as deacon the year before. He accepted the invitation of a small, struggling church in Rochester and labored there for twenty-eight years, until 1906 when he was forced to resign his ministry. In the interim, however, he made impressive strides in increasing his number of communicants, fostered a parochial school, and contributed to social service by various "institutional church" methods. One of Crapsey's fundamental concerns was the application of moral influences upon civic affairs. Many of the statements used against him within a theological frame of reference were actually made in the context of lecturing on social and economic reforms. He was well liked in Rochester for his interests in church unity and moral reform, often sharing tasks in the city with *Walter Rauschenbusch, another clergyman of similar views. But prominence and popularity were not enough to obviate charges of heresy and subsequent dismissal from an influential pulpit.

Discussion of Crapsey's views became widespread after publication of thirteen Sunday evening lectures, issued under the title *Religion and Politics*. He was not greatly interested in doctrine and referred only indirectly to the creedal aspects of early Christianity. His personal attitude was that the spiritual impetus of creeds were more important than their historical factuality. Crapsey placed primary emphasis on social reform, urging that churches become more scientific, democratic, and socialistic in pursuit of that moral commitment. With such a modernist viewpoint, the humanity of Jesus could be used as a powerful example of moral action, and outdated disputes over his virgin birth or divine nature need not detain those wishing to act on Christian principles. Nevertheless, others in the diocese of Western New York brought him to trial for casting doubt upon beliefs that Jesus was divine, that he was conceived by the Holy Ghost, was born of a virgin, was raised from the dead, or was part of the Trinity. The main question in this case was one of creedal traditionalism, not biblical literalism which provoked many similar trials in that era. Crapsey was convicted and lost appeals because he did hold such views, maintaining what he called a "spiritual" allegiance to creeds he thought vulnerable to historical criticism. He refused to recant, was deposed, and ceased to have much direct influence on American Christianity except through visiting lectureships and publishing. There were no heresy trials for others in the Episcopal ministry of similar persuasion; none resigned in sympathy with his position; there were no repercussions in the denomination's seminaries. The episode was significant because it raised the questions of personal freedom to interpret traditional tenets of the faith and of ecclesiastical authority to preserve that faith by repression. Crapsey's conviction did not retard the growth of modernist attitudes, nor did it revise his church's generally tolerant policy on doctrinal matters. His example was one that pointed up the difficulties involved in absorbing scientific standards and historical criticism within an ancient structure of ideas.

Bibliography:

A.   *A Voice in the Wilderness* (New York, 1897); *The Greater Love* (New York, 1902); *Religion and Politics* (New York, 1905); *The Re-Birth of Religion* (New York, 1907); *The Last of the Heretics* (New York, 1924).

B.   NCAB 14, 174–75; DAB 4, 513–14; NYT 1 Jan 1928, 19; George H. Shriver (ed.), *American Religious Heretics* (Nashville, 1966).

CROSBY, Frances Jane (24 March 1820, Southeast, NY—12 February 1915, Bridgeport, CT). *Education*: studied at the New York Institution for the Blind, 1835–43. *Career*: taught at NYIB, 1843–58; hymn writer and lecturer, 1864–1915.

Despite the fact that she was blind from earliest childhood, or perhaps because of it, Fanny Crosby became a well-known poetess and one of the most beloved hymn writers in America. While a student and then instructor at a special school for the blind she gained notice for a retentive memory and facility for composing verse. In 1850 Crosby experienced a religious awakening during revival meetings held in New York City. Many of her poems reflected the sort of piety which she shared with others of that day. In 1858 she married Alexander Van Alstyne, resigned her teaching position, and moved to Maspeth on Long Island. But after the death of their child a year later, the couple moved back to Manhattan and slowly drifted apart. Beginning new work with W.B. Bradbury in 1864, then with Biglow and Main after 1868, she collaborated with publishers of Sunday School hymnbooks. At times she provided words to melodies given her, but most often she wrote poems which others set to music. Many such songs became popular in the next decade, and when evangelist *Dwight L. Moody and his song leader *Ira D. Sankey used them in 1876, her hymns began to influence huge American audiences.

In the last decades of the nineteenth century Crosby was known as the queen of hymn writers. By modern standards her work might be considered mawkish or too sentimental. But their simple, homey appeal struck a responsive chord in Victorian culture. Their informal ballad style broke away from the staid, formal approach of earlier periods, touching deep emotions in singers and listeners alike. Instead of dismissing her words as maudlin or saccharin, audiences thrilled to them as the essence of genuine, heartfelt Christianity. Crosby composed thousands of such poems in her career that spanned many decades. Some of the favorites are: "Safe in the Arms of Jesus," "Pass Me Not, O Gentle Savior," and "Blessed Assurance, Jesus is Mine." These and hundreds more gave her great renown during her lifetime, and they are still sung all over the world.

Bibliography:

A.   *The Blind Girl and Other Poems* (New York, 1844); *Monterey and Other Poems* (New York, 1851); *Bells at Evening and Other Verses* (New York, 1897); *Fanny Crosby's Life-Story, By Herself* (New York, 1903); *Memories of Eighty Years* (Boston, 1906).

B.   NCAB 7, 65–66; DAB 4, 567; NAW, 1, 411–12; NYT 13 Feb 1915, 9; Samuel Trevena Jackson, *Fanny Crosby's Story of Ninety-Four Years* (New York, 1915); Bernard Ruffin, *Fanny Crosby* (New York, 1976).

CRUMMELL, Alexander (1819, New York, NY—12 September 1898, Point Pleasant, NJ). *Education*: B.A., Queen's Coll., Oxford Univ., 1853. *Career*: missionary in West Africa, professor of Intellectual and Moral Science, Coll. of Liberia, 1853?–1873?; rector, St. Luke's Church, Washington, DC, 1873?– 1893?

During most of his lifetime, Crummell endured the trials of being a Black in white man's America, but he did so with knowledge that his father had been an African prince. His schooling was avant garde for the time, including an inter-racial experiment at Canaan, New Hampshire, until townspeople destroyed it; he then studied at the innovative Oneida Institute. Though he was refused entry into General Theological Seminary because he was a Negro, Crummell became an Episcopal priest in 1842 and served intermittently among his own people in New York and Providence, Rhode Island. He sought wider fields of service in England and, after patrons sponsored his studies at Oxford, was encouraged to foster religious developments in the colony of Liberia. He labored there for approximately two decades before returning to this hemisphere. Based at St. Luke's parish in the nation's capital, he supported many efforts around the country to raise the general cultural standards of his race. He was convinced that education afforded the surest means of elevating Blacks to full participation in American life, and he constantly urged young people to seek scholarly ex-cellence. A lasting monument to this dedication is the American Negro Academy, an exclusive group limited to forty members that he founded in 1897. Since that time the Academy has included outstanding spokesmen of the Negro intelli-gentsia, and their learned papers on religion, educational philosophy, economics, and political affairs have opened new vistas in those fields. Father Crummell's pioneering work did not create an educated gentry as he hoped, but it provided a format where spiritual influence could join profitably with impulses to achieve elemental social improvement.

Bibliography:

A.   *The Future of Africa* (New York, 1862); *The Greatness of Christ and Other Sermons* (New York, 1882); *Africa and America* (Springfield, MA, 1891; New York, 1969).

B.   NCAB 5, 553; Gregory U. Rigsby, *Alexander Crummell: Pioneer in Nineteenth-century Pan-African Thought* (New York, 1987); John R. Oldfield, *Alexander Crummell (1819–1898) and the Creation of an African-American Church in Liberia* (Lewiston, NY, 1990).

CULLIS, Charles (7 March 1838, Boston, MA—18 June 1892, Boston, MA). *Career*: homeopathic physician and minister, 1865–92.

It is perhaps pertinent to his career that Cullis experienced delicate health as a child and hovered near invalid status through most of his life. After clerking briefly in a Boston mercantile establishment, he studied medicine privately and began a practice that concentrated on the poor and on incurables. He heard stories about faith cures from Germany, Switzerland, and England and soon came to believe that such miracles were possible in Boston too. In 1865 he founded a home for consumptives, the first of six erected in his hometown area. Cullis was a sincere believer in curing through faith, and the popular response to his activities made him a leader in nineteenth century enthusiasm for this approach to illness. New England was not the only location of his philanthropic efforts. He also founded curing homes in Boynton, Virginia, Oxford, North Carolina, and Alameda, California, plus two in India. He helped train others to administer faith cures and built orphanages as well as housing for nursing deaconesses.

Grove Hall near Boston was probably the best known place where Cullis welcomed patients. He also began a ministry at Beacon Hill Church, then went on to attract large audiences at the Lewis Mission and the Cottage Street Church. In 1873 he established Faith Training College to consolidate practical instruction, incorporating medical science to its fullest extent and using practical procedures as much as possible. And throughout each summer he conducted revival services at vacation spots in New Hampshire and Maine. Opponents in more conventional pulpits attacked him, as did several skeptical physicians, but Cullis kept his dignity and made no reply to either theological or scientific criticism. Great numbers of the general population found enough worth in his activities to sustain him for decades. He said he never solicited donations, but sufficient voluntary gifts were always forthcoming to support his many charitable projects. He made honest use of the money, too, and died a poor man because he refused to withhold part of the funds for himself. Many of the institutions failed upon his death because no provision had been made for support other than occasional contributions. While there was no strong connection between Cullis and the emergence of Christian Science, similar emphases at the same period undoubtedly helped favorable public opinion as *Mary B. Eddy publicized her teachings.

Bibliography:

A.   *Faith Cures*; *or, Answers to Prayer in the Healing of the Sick* (Boston, 1879); *More Faith Cures* (Boston, 1881); *Other Faith Cures* (Boston, 1885); *Tuesday Afternoon Talks* (Boston, 1892).

B.   DAB 4, 587–88; William H. Daniels (ed.), *Dr. Cullis and His Work* (Boston, 1885).

CUMMINS, George David (11 December 1822, near Smyrna, DE—26 June 1876, Lutherville, MD). *Education*: B.A., Dickinson Coll., 1841. *Career*: Methodist circuit rider, 1842–45; assistant rector, Christ Episcopal Church, Baltimore, MD, 1845–47; rector, Christ Church, Norfolk, VA, 1847–53; St. James's Church, Richmond, VA, 1853–54; Trinity Church, Washington, DC, 1855–58; St. Peter's Church, Baltimore, MD, 1858–63; Trinity Church, Chicago, IL, 1863–66; assistant bishop of Kentucky, 1866–73; bishop of the Reformed Episcopal Church, 1873–76.

Since his widowed mother was Methodist, Cummins grew up largely under that denomination's influence. He joined the church himself while at college and preached for a few years thereafter under the supervision of the Baltimore Conference. But a growing preference for ordered worship led him in 1845 to become an Episcopalian, his father's preference. Ordained deacon that same year and priest in 1847, Cummins quickly gained fame as a noted speaker. Many of his sermons were printed, and prestigious churches sought to make him an ornament in their pulpits. By mid-century he grew increasingly disturbed by conservative developments within his communion, attitudes stemming ultimately from the Oxford Movement in England. He agreed with other Evangelicals or Low Church advocates such as *Charles P. McIlvaine who opposed emphases put forth by Ritualists or the High Church party. An issue of minor irritance was the Ritualists refusal to change any wording in the Book of Common Prayer or to allow alternate phrasing. Cummins favored revision and was willing to cooperate with all denominations in sharing a common faith in a universal Christ. His openness to other forms of Christianity contrasted sharply with the competitiveness and exclusivism harbored by many church authorities in his day.

Conservative churchmen used theology to restrict access to salvation. They argued that the true church existed only within episcopalian polity, that ministers were priests, set apart from mere laypersons by their sacerdotal office, that the communion table was an altar upon which the body and blood of Christ is repeatedly sacrificed, and that Christ is physically present in the element's of the Lord's Supper. Cummins disagreed with all of these ideas. He tried to use his authority as assistant bishop to counteract what he saw as dangerous errors. But High Church sacramentalism and the spirit of denomination superiority were more than he could deal with effectively. In 1873 he participated in a joint communion service with ministers of several other churches. This brought sharp criticism from within his own denomination, and so he reluctantly concluded that he could no longer exert any good influence there. In December of that same year he and some other disaffected liberals formed the Reformed Episcopal Church. Cummins served as first bishop of this new church which spread to Canada and England during the unexpectedly short remainder of his life.

Bibliography:

A. *A Sketch of the Life of the Rev. William M. Jackson* (Washington, DC, 1855); *Life of Mrs. Virginia Hale Hoffman, late of the Protestant Episcopal Mission to Western Africa* (Philadelphia, 1859); *Mission Service Book: Recommended for Use in the Reformed Episcopal Church* (Philadelphia, 1874).

B. SH 3, 321; NCAB 7, 57–58; DAB 4, 599–600; NYT 29 Jun 1876, 10; A.M. Cummins, *Memoir of George David Cummins, D.D. First Bishop of the Reformed Episcopal Church* (Philadelphia, 1878).

CUSHING, Richard James (24 August 1895, Boston, MA—2 November 1970, Boston, MA). *Education*: studied at Boston Coll., 1913–15; graduated from St. John's Sem. (MA), 1921. *Career*: curate, Roxbury and Somerville, MA, 1921–22; assistant and director, Society for the Propagation of the Faith, Boston, 1922–39; auxiliary bishop of Boston, 1939–44; archbishop of Boston, 1944–70; cardinal of Boston, 1958–70.

Leadership in New England's oldest, best established archdiocese required spiritual resources and native talent. Cushing added hard work and iron determination to these qualities and became one of the nation's most prominent ecclesiastical figures during the middle third of the twentieth century. The public knew him primarily as a fund raiser, constantly seeking more resources for the institutions and programs that supported Catholic life in the Boston area. Expenditures in a normal year averaged between eight and eleven million dollars, and Cushing worked steadily without fanfare or vacation in order to meet financial obligations. Another image by which all people recognized the archbishop was his accessibility. Open and unpretentious, he made himself available as a priest and made others feel at ease with his informality. His speeches were often earthy and unsophisticated, narrowing the distance between hierarchy and laymen and lowering psychological restraints to allow fuller cooperation. Cushing was a man of the people, and his self-deprecating accomplishments on their behalf augmented work that had been placed on a solid footing before his appointment.

Priorities and goals of the private Cushing were not as easily noticed, but they lend greater understanding to the whole man. Throughout his life he maintained an intense commitment to the cause of missions, particularly those in Latin America. Much of Cushing's fund raising was for world missions, and he supplied money for buildings together with a "lend lease" program of volunteer priests for understaffed territories. Though denied the privilege, he asked to be relieved of office and allowed to work in mission stations himself. Another major concern was poverty. Cushing remembered his own youth and acted as father to the poor in slums from South Boston to Chile. As Vatican II inaugurated changes in the church, he accepted many reforms as long overdue. He gave strong support to conducting the liturgy in English, argued for declarations of wider religious toleration, and welcomed more lay participation in ecclesiastical affairs. The cardinal disliked many worn out mannerisms that were tied to the old authoritarian days and urged renewal with a spirit of ecumenism that bolstered the inner strength of Catholicism. While moving with the times, he nonetheless opposed trends that encouraged dissent with the pope, lay election of bishops, birth control, or street demonstrations to secure civil rights. He never ceased denouncing communism and even saw its influence in the Supreme Court ban on reading the Bible in schools. All in all, his pronouncements on public issues were unpredictable, but their internal consistency was grounded in a concern for the poor, the unchurched, and those of every denomination responsive to religious impulses.

Bibliography:

A.   *Call Me John: A Life of Pope John XXIII* (Boston, 1963).

B.   NYT 3 Nov 1970, 1; John H. Fenton, *Salt of the Earth: An Informal Portrait of Richard Cardinal Cushing* (New York, 1951); Joseph Dever, *Cushing of Boston: A Candid Portrait* (Boston, 1965); John H. Cutler, *Cardinal Cushing of Boston* (New York, 1970).

CUTLER, Timothy (31 May 1684, Charlestown, MA—17 August 1765, Boston, MA). *Education*: B.A., Harvard Coll., 1701. *Career*: Congregational minister, Stratford, CT, 1710–19; rector, Yale Coll., 1719–22; rector, Christ Episcopal Church, Boston, MA, 1723–65.

After almost a decade of participation in Connecticut church affairs, Cutler was made presiding officer of the colony's highest academy, recently settled at New Haven. But there, in the institution dedicated to perpetuating orthodox standards, he dismayed ministerial colleagues by challenging the fundamental tenets on which American Puritanism had been established. The principal vehicle used in reaching such startling apostasy was a library, seven hundred volumes lately added to the college including works by Locke, Newton, and liberal Anglican divines. Cutler delved deeply into these treasures and formed a discussion group comprising several clergymen favorably impressed with the new learning. By 1722 the rector of Yale, its only tutor and a former tutor, *Samuel Johnson who was minister in a nearby town, had concluded that their ordination was invalid. Convinced that proper ecclesiastical authority resided in bishops rather than independent assemblies of dissenting ministers, they resigned their offices and sailed for Britain to receive holy orders from appropriate hands. Cutler became a symbol in Anglican circles for an anticipated wave of new conversions to the Church of England. As such he was given honorary degrees and returned to his native land a missionary of the Society for the Propagation of the Gospel (SPG). For his erstwhile Congregationalist friends, he epitomized defection to all they hoped to forestall by establishing the New England Way. Preventive measures were taken by requiring that future teachers at Yale subscribe to the Saybrook Platform, a confessional antidote to Arminian and prelatical corruptions.

During forty years as priest of newly erected Christ Church in Boston, Cutler functioned as one of the most vigorous spokesmen for Episcopal prerogatives. His conversion to Anglicanism did not include an attitude of tolerant comprehensiveness often found in that denomination. He did not, for example, favor the itinerant ministry of *George Whitefield, Anglican like himself but one given to Calvinistic emphases and an enthusiastic preaching style. His adherence to episcopal polity was unbending, and he authored repeated pleas that a bishop be placed in the colonies for purposes of co-ordinating their efforts. He also harbored high Tory inclinations in politics, arguing for a strong combination of royalist and episcopal authority as the power structure best suited to conditions of his day. As far as positive theological development was concerned, he allowed for some cautious enlargement of man's rational and moral abilities. Fresh conceptions in the Age of Reason combined in him to indicate modest progress toward Christian rationalism. Lockean epistemology and Newtonian cosmology gave new dimensions to his sermons, only four of which ever appeared in print. After 1756 his ministry was greatly hampered by palsy, but he remained to the end a staunch embodiment of British authoritarianism.

Bibliography:

B.   AAP 5, 50–52; NCAB 1, 165; DAB 5, 14–15.

D

DABNEY, Robert Lewis (5 March 1820, Louisa County, VA—3 January 1898, Victoria, TX). *Education*: studied at Hampden-Sidney Coll., 1836–37; M.A., Univ. of Virginia, 1842; graduated from Union Sem. (VA), 1846. *Career*: missionary minister, Louisa County, VA, 1846–47; minister, Tinkling Spring, VA, 1847–53; professor of various subjects in history, polity, and theology, Union Sem. (VA), 1853–83; chaplain and officer, Confederate Army, 1861–62; professor of Philosophy, Univ. of Texas, 1883–94; retirement, 1894–98.

The conservative pattern of Dabney's Old School Presbyterian views was already established before war and its aftermath made them rigid. He maintained unbending loyalty to a social and creedal past, and from his influential position as theologian in the Southern Presbyterian Church's major seminary, Dabney was the most important factor in shaping the character of that denomination for decades. He was devoted to ante-bellum southern life, claiming that its activities and modes of thought had been refined to a cultural pinnacle. Reconstruction policies led him to embittered resistance against change. He lamented the loss of former grandeur and loathed alien rule with its universal suffrage and other attempts to secure civil rights for freedmen. For years he seriously considered emigration, supporting various plans for removal to Brazil or Australia in an attempt to save the true, spiritual South. Such projects were eventually abandoned, and Dabney remained to influence southern Protestants through teaching and writing, exercising leadership in a church whose social prominence was greater than its numerical strength. In this connection he was also a forceful opponent of any proposed reunion with the northern branches of Presbyterianism.

The area where Dabney had perhaps the greatest effect as conservative spokesman was in theology. He agreed in virtually every aspect with the Calvinistic system propounded by *Charles Hodge of Princeton, adding that strict adherence to creed and discipline were virtues in themselves. On a philosophical level Dabney's major work took place in the areas of epistemology and world view. Beginning with Darwinian controversies, he broadened the debate to cover all positivistic and materialistic rubrics in natural science. There was nothing in his analysis of scientific hypotheses that could disprove faith assumptions about final causes, but he still considered them inimical to religion. Evolutionary speculations were just pretexts for the materialism and sensuality that natural man harbored as a result of original sin. Dabney worked to bolster doctrinal and biblical orthodoxy in the face of attempts to raise new questions, some of these being broached by former friend, *James Woodrow of Columbia Seminary. At Union Seminary the influence of Dabney's strong arguments remained long after his tenure there, and when he moved to Texas for reasons of health, he was largely responsible for building similar convictions into the Austin School of Theology. By 1890 the old veteran was infirm and blind, but that did not prevent continued lectures that showed how much he was still at war with most developments of his age.

Bibliography:

A. *Life and Campaigns of Lieutenant-General Thomas J. Jackson* (New York, 1866); *Defense of Virginia and the South* (New York, 1867); *Treatise on Sacred Rhetoric* (Richmond, 1870); *Syllabus and Notes of the Course of Systematic and Polemic Theology* (Richmond, 1871); *Sensualistic Philosophy of the Nineteenth Century Examined* (New York, 1875); *Practical Philosophy* (Kansas City, MO, 1897).

B. SH 3, 340; NCAB 2, 26; DAB 5, 20–21; Thomas C. Johnson, *The Life and Letters of Robert Lewis Dabney* (Richmond, 1903).

DAVENPORT, James (1716, Stamford, CT—10 November 1757, near Pennington, NJ). *Education*: B.A., Yale Coll., 1732; studied theology in New Haven, CT, 1732–35. *Career*: minister, Southold, NY, 1738–44; minister of several churches in NJ, 1744–57.

As the First Great Awakening gathered momentum, some preachers were led by its enthusiasm to advocate radical positions regarding spiritual experience and the personal holiness stemming from it. None of these was more notable than Davenport, whose whirlwind revivals left divided churches wherever he happened to preach. After two obscure years on Long Island, he emerged in 1740 as a prophet who claimed to embody special divine gifts. Itinerating from Philadelphia to Boston, he received endorsements from many eminent clergymen, such as *Gilbert Tennent and *George Whitefield, but his extravagant language and excessive emotionalism soon made them wonder if such work really came from God. Davenport had no doubts whatsoever, pressing a stark insistence on conversion experience as proof of salvation. When local clergy demurred, he denounced them as unregenerate, increasingly so until he told audiences he would rather see them drink poison than have them listen to a blind, unconverted minister. Further, he claimed that God gave him the unique power to discern whether persons were truly saved or not, regardless of their protestations. Such charismatic zeal caused many to suspect he was mentally deranged, but his unrelenting emphasis on spiritual impulses strengthened the growth of Strict Congregationalists, sectarians who placed intuition over intellectual content and common order in religion.

By 1741 Davenport began urging congregations to separate from ministers who opposed his conception of divine imperatives. Confusion, division, and ill-will followed in his train as he rebuffed delegations of fellow Presbyterians who asked him to follow a more moderate course. Within a year Connecticut passed a law suppressing itinerancy, and when Davenport violated its strictures, he was arrested and tried in Hartford. After listening to hours of his ranting about private revelation, the General Assembly found him *non compos mentis* and ordered deportation. One month later he appeared in Boston where even pro-revival preachers were apprehensive about the havoc he had created. A similar trial ensued, which Davenport welcomed because of the martyrdom it conferred, and once again a grand jury declared him insane. His own church placed him on probation late in 1742, but in a few months he caused another sensation in New London, Connecticut, by burning books and other luxuries that hindered spiritual perfection. Then with an eccentric despondency some take as evidence of neurosis, he repented of his riotous ways. Publishing an open confession and retractation in 1744 he repudiated his former arrogance; many individuals who had responded to his sectarian holiness tendencies remained in that pattern of religiosity after he moved to New Jersey. But even there his way was not smooth. The congregation at what was then called Hopewell petitioned for his dismissal shortly before he died.

Bibliography:

B.   AAP 3, 80–92; DAB 5, 84–85.

DAVENPORT, John (April 1597, Coventry, England—15 March 1670, Boston, MA). *Education*: studied at Merton Coll., Oxford Univ., 1613–15; B.D., Magdalen Coll., Oxford Univ., 1625. *Career*: private chaplain near Durham, England, 1615–16; curate, Church of St. Lawrence Jewry, London, 1619–24; vicar, St. Stephen's Church, London, 1624–33; independent minister, Amsterdam and Rotterdam, Netherlands, 1633–37; minister, New Haven colony, 1639–68; minister, First Congregational Church, Boston, 1668–70.

As an Anglican divine in London, young Davenport was known more for his heroism during the plague of 1625 than for Puritan sympathies. But gradually through conversations with friends such as *John Cotton and *Thomas Hooker he adopted theological views at variance with the national church. So like many others, he fled to Holland in 1633 when William Laud's archepiscopacy promised relentless enforcement of conformity. Preaching to refugee congregations across the Channel was a trying experience too, full of personal conflicts with resident ministers, notably John Paget, who jealously guarded their positions. In 1637 he sailed for America aboard the *Hector*, arriving in Massachusetts with a colonizing party that contained many of his London parishioners. Less than a year later, they chose land first occupied during the Pequot War. The independent colony was originally named Quinnipiac but became New Haven after 1640 and followed the rule of Puritan commonwealths established elsewhere in the New World. As first pastor of the settlement, Davenport held fast to the vision of churches reserved exclusively for the elect; these individuals in turn controlled civil matters to insure the proper place of religious influence in daily life. In keeping with his view of righteous government, church membership was requisite for voting or holding office in New Haven territory.

Changes slowly modified the ideal church-state relationship in New England colonies, occurring earlier in nearby townships and eventually in New Haven as well. Davenport resisted each development in a series of frustrating skirmishes. The chief difficulty, as he and other patriarchal statesmen saw it, was a general wish to relax qualifications for church membership. Children of visible saints were baptized as a matter of course, but when they failed to achieve full membership by professing a mature faith later on, this left the status of their children very much in doubt. The New Haven minister was strenuously opposed to "Half-Way Covenant" suggestions that the third generation receive baptism without their parents' progressing to full membership first. Disputes about high standards of religious affiliation naturally involved struggles over widening the base of enfranchised citizenry. Here again Davenport argued against compromising the Puritan regulations already in force. In practical terms he fought incorporation into the larger, more permissive colony of Connecticut; but in 1662 New Haven lost the battle. Thus embattled by change, he eagerly accepted a call to Boston where orthodoxy might still be defended in its finest stronghold. His New Haven church twice refused to release him, but this fact was concealed from the Boston congregation. When finally disclosed, it split the church and darkened an aging minister's last days with charges of deception. Perhaps anxiety over a fading ideal led him to connive at questionable tactics, hoping to perpetuate by any means a system he believed divinely ordained.

Bibliography:

A.   *A Catechism Containing the Chief Heads of Christian Religion* (London, 1659); *The Saint's Anchor-hold in All Storms and Tempests* (London, 1661); *Another Essay for Investigation of the Truth in Answer to Two Questions, Concerning 1. The Subject of Baptism 2. The Consocation of Churches* (Boston, 1662).

B.   AAP 1, 93–98; SH 3, 360–61; NCAB 1, 161–62; DAB 5, 85–87.

DAVIES, Samuel (3 November 1723, near Summit Ridge, DE—4 February 1761, Princeton, NJ). *Education*: graduated from Samuel Blair's private academy, Fagg's Manor, PA, 1746. *Career*: Presbyterian minister, Hanover County, VA, 1748–59; president, Coll. of New Jersey, 1759–61.

Settlers in the Virginia piedmont had different social and religious tastes from those who lived on plantations in the tidewater region. Anglicanism was officially the colony's only sanctioned religion, but it did not satisfy the multiple human demands placed on it from all sides. As an alternative to church attendance, pious laymen began meeting in homes to read devotional works. Presbyterians responded to reports of such readinghouses by sending Davies, a young ordinand who became the foremost organizer of dissenting churches and chief advocate of religious freedom. Civil authorities were indisposed to grant licenses to nonconformist churches. Fighting a long, hard legal battle to obtain licenses for seven churches of his own denomination, Davies created the opening wedge for complete toleration which came later in the century. He argued on practical grounds that religious needs were not being sufficiently met by the monopolizing Church of England. Another line of reasoning was that the royal Toleration Act (1689) permitted freedom of worship in British colonies as well as in the homeland. Investigations, lawsuits, and petitions continued along those lines until 1753 to 1755 when Davies and *Gilbert Tennent were sent to England to raise funds for the struggling College of New Jersey. While in London the young Virginia minister presented his case and won a favorable ruling. Thereafter a degree of toleration was granted to colonial dissenters, enough to encourage proselytizing and the permanent organization of evangelical churches.

Hanover County was the primary focus of Davies' preaching activities, though he traveled throughout the colony to build up a strong Presbyterian membership. In 1775 he was instrumental in establishing the Hanover Presbytery, his denomination's first association of continuing effectiveness in the South. Recognized quite early as a preacher of stirring power, his evangelical fervor helped perpetuate the emphases of the First Great Awakening. Davies was unquestionably New Side in his sympathy for revivals and personal experience as the core of Christian affirmation. His sermons contributed to that cause, winning him no small reputation as an orator of substantial accomplishment on both sides of the Atlantic. Fame as an evangelist led to an offer of the college presidency at Princeton. At first Davies declined but accepted one year later. His removal to New Jersey left no educated Presbyterian minister in Virginia, and many of those originally awakened by his efforts found their way into local Baptist churches. His brief tenure at the small New Side college was distinguished for success in raising standards for entrance and graduation. Precarious health had been a personal burden for decades; during one of those bouts death ended a short life dedicated to church service and the expansion of Christian influence in American culture.

Bibliography:

A. *The State of Religion among the Protestant Dissenters in Virginia* (Boston, 1751); *Virginia's Danger and Remedy* (Glasgow, 1756); *The Good Soldier* (London, 1756); *The Duty of Christians to Propagate their Religion among the Heathens* (London, 1758); *Sermons on Important Subjects*, ed. Albert Barnes, 3 vols. (New York, 1841, and many subsequent editions).

B.   AAP 3, 140–46; SH 3, 366; NCAB 5, 465; DAB 5, 102–03; George W. Pilcher (ed.), *The Reverend Samuel Davies Abroad* (Urbana, IL, 1967); George W. Pilcher, *Samuel Davies: Apostle of Dissent in Colonial Virginia* (Knoxville, TN, 1971).

DAVIS, Andrew Jackson (11 August 1826, Blooming Grove, NY—13 January 1910, Watertown, MA).

By his own admission Davis received only haphazard training in church and schoolhouse, with no regular attendance at either institution. At the age of seventeen, however, he began to exhibit clairvoyant powers which attracted wide attention. Under the influence of hypnotism (mesmerism or animal magnetism), the young man convinced many that he could read newspapers blindfolded, diagnose ailments, and converse with the spiritual world. On one occasion in 1844 he experienced what he called a "flight through space" wherein he became aware of an eternal communion between human life and natural forces, all harmonized under God's providential plan. He also felt himself influenced by departed persons such as Emmanuel Swedenborg who aided his understanding of indwelling essences and vital elements of harmonious life. By means of such visions Davis became known as the "Poughkeepsie Seer" and over the next fifty years helped formulate some of the basic principles of modern spiritualism. His first book was published from lectures delivered while in a hypnotic trance; the twenty-six subsequent volumes were written outside that medium because Davis found he could enter higher psychic states at will. In addition to writings, which contributed much of the spiritualist terminology still used today, he practiced as a physician of both mind and body in Boston until 1909. His emphasis on personal regeneration and social reconstruction made him one of the most widely read exponents of spiritualist philosophy in the nineteenth century.

The Harmonial Philosophy, as Davis envisioned it, was based on a belief that the productive power of all existence is enthroned in a central sphere, the circumference of which is the boundless universe. This power is what all mankind calls Deity, recognizing its primary attributes as love and wisdom. Before man can know himself or be happy, he must realize that all manifest substances are emanations from this Great Celestial Center. Plants and minerals, planets and stars are representatives of the spiritual universe, everlasting forms of the order and wisdom found in the Divine Mind. In such a system Davis preached that personal errors and social mistakes could be rectified if individuals would cultivate their true relation with Nature, the next level of general existence emanating from divine power. He foresaw an ultimate reformation in society because of this new spirit, one through which the world could be renovated and all beings in their hierarchical order could stand in harmony with others. All beings with their distinctive natures could cooperate as organs in a single body, giving reciprocal assistance in order to promote the mutual good. In these and a plethora of other ideas the "Poughkeepsie Seer" encouraged readers to seek the good in themselves that corresponded to the beneficial essence of all things.

Bibliography:

A. *Principles of Nature* (New York, 1847); *The Great Harmonia*, 5 vols. (Boston, 1852–66); *The Pentralia* (Boston, 1856); *The Magic Staff* (Boston, 1857); *A Stellar Key to the Summer Land* (Boston, 1867); *Views of our Heavenly Home* (Boston, 1878).

B. NCAB 8, 442; DAB 5, 105; NYT 14 Jan 1910, 9.

DAY, Dorothy (8 November 1897, Brooklyn, NY—29 November 1980, New York, NY). *Education*: studied at Univ. of Illinois, 1914–16. *Career*: social activist and journalist, 1933–80.

From her early years onward, Day showed a strong love of letters, both in voracious reading and in writing her thoughts. This alone did not lead her to adopt a bohemian lifestyle, but while in college the exciting ideas of socialist and anarchist writers opened vistas which she explored with some abandon. After many travels, journalistic assignments, and demonstrations for socialist causes, Day entered the Roman Catholic church in late 1927. When she met *Peter Maurin six years later, her life received not new meaning or orientation, but new focus. With this Catholic visionary she pursued old ideals of social and economic justice, now joined to specific ways of expressing them in a distinctive style of living.

Earlier experience in writing for communist and socialist tabloids gave Day a solid background for establishing *The Catholic Worker* in 1933. She wrote a column in this penny monthly for fifty years. There she championed the poor, the homeless, and the jobless, supporting at the same time such causes as unilateral disarmament, racial justice, trade unions, and cooperative farms. Day responded to bread lines and picket lines by urging works of mercy, a combination of faith and social action made tangible in urban "houses of hospitality" and rural communes. For her this kind of voluntaristic communalism nurtured Christian love and made it real to the down-and-out who needed it most. Within a decade there were forty houses of hospitality and six communal farms. As an alternative to the modern welfare state this unstructured version of charity and agrarianism was a minor element in Catholic social reform thought. But Day remained steadfast in her vision. In her simple piety and voluntary poverty she practiced what she preached. True to her chosen apostolate until the end, she died at Maryhouse, a haven for homeless women which she maintained on the Lower East Side of Manhattan.

Bibliography:

A. *From Union Square to Rome* (Silver Spring, MD, 1938); *House of Hospitality* (New York, 1939); *The Long Loneliness: An Autobiography* (New York, 1952; rev. ed., 1982); *Loaves and Fishes* (New York, 1963); *On Pilgrimage: The Sixties* (New York, 1973).

B. NCE 18, 113–14; NYT 1 Dec. 80, D 12; William D. Miller, *A Harsh and Dreadful Love: Dorothy Day and the Catholic Worker Movement* (New York, 1973); Nancy L. Roberts, *Dorothy Day and the Catholic Worker* (Albany, NY, 1984); Jim Forest, *Love*

Is the Measure: A Biography of Dorothy Day (New York, 1986); Robert Coles, *Dorothy Day: A Radical Devotion* (Reading, MA, 1987).

DE SMET, Pierre Jean (30 January 1801, Termonde, Belgium—23 May 1873, St. Louis, MO). *Career*: novice, Society of Jesus, Whitemarsh, MD, 1821–23 and Florissant, MO, 1823–27; treasurer, St. Louis Coll. (MO), 1827–33; travel and recuperation, Belgium, 1833–37; superior of western missions, 1838–46; procurator and secretary to father provincial, St. Louis, 1846–73.

For over two centuries Jesuits were the most effective missionaries among American Indians, and De Smet promoted that cause more than any other single individual. After lengthy preparation in the order's spiritual discipline (and a short time of indecision because of health problems), he began work with cultural units relatively unchanged by contact with whites. In 1838 the Potawatomi nation around Council Bluffs, Iowa, was his first charge, but soon more distant tribes made themselves known. Envoys of the Flathead group in Oregon came to ask that a "blackrobe" be sent to baptize and instruct their people. De Smet led exploration parties through the northwest mountains in 1840 and 1841 to find advantageous sites for permanent mission settlements. He was largely responsible for establishing St. Mary's mission in the Bitterroot valley among the Flatheads. After making peace with their traditional enemies, the Blackfoot nation, he founded (1844) missions in the Columbia and Willamette valleys as well. These activities gave De Smet the reputation of missionary to native Americans, but he was actually more effective in publicizing and raising funds for those who stayed with the work as a full-time vocation. He traveled over 180,000 miles in efforts to collect men and material for New World missions, crossing the Atlantic nineteen times in search of aid. His reportorial travelogues stimulated interest in evangelical outreach while providing some of the most accurate information about indigenous customs in their natural settings.

Superiors in the Jesuit order were not favorably impressed with De Smet's adventures in the wild. He was reduced to the daily routine of a clerk and confined to local affairs around St. Louis. But his good relations with Indians of the Great Plains made him a natural choice for negotiating peace treaties. Father De Smet had always been able to endure physical hardships cheerfully, a quality admired by red men. He also treated their customs and values with genuine respect, tolerating instead of destroying lifestyles he hoped to reform. For those reasons he was accepted as friend by many nations, trusted more than any other white man. He often served as peacemaker, mediator, and counselor to agents of the federal government. In 1851, 1858–59, and 1868 he helped secure temporary agreements between the Osage, the Sioux, and the encroaching white population. Warriors who vowed to kill the first white to enter their village welcomed the esteemed "blackrobe" into camp. In 1870 De Smet established a mission among the Sioux, though he did not live to see it flourish. He was valued by whites who often sought his advice but seldom followed it; he was trusted by red men who saw in him virtues few others embodied. His dedication to missions is still in evidence from the Pacific to the Dakotas.

Bibliography:

A. *Letters and Sketches* (Philadelphia, 1843); *Oregon Missions* (New York, 1847); *Voyage au Grand Desert en 1851* (Brussels, 1853); *Cinquante Nouvelles Lettres* (Paris, 1858); *Western Missions and Missionaries* (New York, 1863; Shannon, Ireland, 1972); *New Indian Sketches* (New York, 1865).

B. NCAB 11, 453–54; DAB 5, 255–56; NCE 4, 804; Hiram M. Chittenden and Alfred T. Richardson, *Life, Letters and Travels of Father Pierre-Jean De Smet*, 4 vols. (New York, 1905, 1969); E. Laveille, *Life of Father De Smet*, trans. Marian Lindsay (New York, 1915); H. Margaret, *Father De Smet: Pioneer Priest of the Rockies* (Milwaukee, 1940).

DICKINSON, Jonathan (22 April 1688, Hatfield, CT—7 October 1747, Elizabeth, NJ). *Education*: B.A., Yale Coll., 1706; independent theological study, 1706–08. *Career*: minister, Elizabeth, NJ, 1709–47; president, Coll. of New Jersey, 1746–47.

When young Dickinson was called to minister in a church at Elizabethtown, as it was then known, he added strength to the English Puritan wing of Presbyterianism which sought greater effectiveness in the middle colonies. Placed alongside that minority in the denomination were Scotch-Irish clergymen who wished to erect more vital religious standards by means of rigorous discipline in both doctrine and ecclesiastical structure. Dickinson dealt with those tensions with such patience and moderation that he emerged as the most respected denominational spokesman of his generation. As early as 1722 he upheld the view that genuine church renewal could come only from spiritual rebirth, not legal requirements. Still there were those who tried to make all Presbyterian ministers subscribe to the Westminster symbols, confession, and both catechisms, as a way of ending corruption. The Elizabethtown pastor argued instead that the Bible rendered other rules unnecessary. If extra-biblical formulations such as creeds or directories were raised to the level of law, then it implied Scripture was insufficient for Christian faith. If human statements superceded the Bible and were made binding, there would be nothing left by which to test orthodoxy. Indeed, he warned, creeds might cease being guides for faith and become ends in themselves, leading churchmen to use coercive power to achieve conformity of belief. By such arguments he persuaded enough colleagues to compromise on the subscription issue. In 1729 the Adopting Act emphasized creedal uniformity, but its distinction between essential and nonessential articles together with allowance for mental reservations made it a victory for anti-subscriptionists.

A similar situation in which Dickinson showed himself to be a champion of freedom for dissenters was related to Anglicanism. Missionaries for the Society for the Propagation of the Gospel (SPG) such as *Samuel Johnson defended the priority of episcopacy as both theologically proper and constitutionally best suited to orderly church life; but Dickinson proved a competent opponent in that arena. His detached, rational analysis of episcopal claims covered a wide range of material including biblical exegesis, church history, and theological presuppositions. In a pamphlet war of long duration, he attacked the foundations of episcopacy and did much to crystalize libertarian sympathies in the American colonies. He was also one of the most prominent Calvinist theologians of his time, achieving an international reputation second only to *Jonathan Edwards. Agreeing with New Side proponents who insisted that "assurance" was possible regarding spiritual experience, he defended at the same time more traditional conceptions of salvation as a lengthy process. Like Edwards he distinguished between a state of true grace and mere enthusiasm, holding that the fruits of conversion should demonstrate a person's regeneration. When his diplomatic efforts to prevent schism among Presbyterians failed in 1741, he sided with the pro-revivalists and served as moderator of the Synod of New York formed in 1745. An advocate of learning for ministers who would support revivals, he helped obtain (1746) a college charter. Classes were held in his home until death claimed this first president of the school subsequently moved to Princeton.

Bibliography:

A.   *The Reasonableness of Christianity* (Boston, 1732); *The True Scripture-Doctrine Concerning Some Important Points of Christian Faith* (Boston, 1741); *A Display of God's Special Grace* (Boston, 1742); *Familiar Letters . . . upon . . . Subjects in Religion* (Boston, 1745, and many subsequent editions); *A Second Vindication of God's Sovereign Free Grace* (Boston, 1748); *Sermons and Tracts* (Edinburgh, 1793).

B.   AAP 3, 14–18; SH 3, 419–20; NCAB 5, 463; DAB 5, 301–02.

DIVINE, Father (1877?, Hutchinson Island, GA—10 September 1965, Woodmont, PA).

Obscure historical data prevent an accurate description of Father Divine, but that concerns only outsiders; time means nothing within the cult, and adherents are not inclined to scrutinize the temporal career of one they believe to be God himself. Apparently his original name was George Baker, while another used in the early days was Major J. Devine. Appellations aside, after a brief mission episode in Baltimore and a brush with the law in Georgia, by 1919 Father Divine had established himself in Sayville, Long Island, thus beginning a ministry whose emphases remained fairly constant during the next forty-five years. It has always been a mystery how he was able to provide food, lodging, and other practical aids for his followers, but he did it lavishly, and such a feature is one key to the group's appeal. In 1933 the Father Divine Peace Mission Movement was transferred to Harlem, and then in 1942 a large estate outside Philadelphia became the center for branches established in most northern cities. The man behind it all was reverenced as God incarnate by the faithful (whose numbers are difficult to estimate) and though he did not proclaim the status as part of his message, he accepted popular adulation without demur. A weekly paper, *New Day*, recorded every word and deed for those closely aligned with the deified personage. His taste for $500 silk suits, extensive real estate holdings, and an interracial marriage did not lessen the intense devotion of his followers, nor could death alter their serene conviction that he is God. He is still considered spiritually present in the movement, directing every detail as before.

The Peace Mission was founded by a black man with some charismatic presence, but its success was due more to ethical teachings and communal spirit. By 1936 a platform with fourteen planks had been formed to deal with economic and social activities. Base passions such as prejudice, lust, and selfishness were proscribed in addition to a list including cosmetics, movies, and tobacco. But the most significant tenets emphasized racial equality, as Father Divine's religion abolished color barriers among believers. Even words like "white" or "Negro" were forbidden, and followers lived together in harmony under a leader who refused to acknowledge distinctions of race. The collective held no formal worship services nor did it have any clergy, creed, scripture, or membership rules. Meetings were the occasion for songs, impromptu sermons, and banquets as a form of communion. While enjoining celibacy and fraternity, the religion functioned as a protective environment which satisfied the socio-economic needs of many trapped in urban despair.

Bibliography:

B.   NYT 11 Sep 1965, 1; Robert A. Parker, *The Incredible Messiah: The Deification of Father Divine* (Boston, 1937); Arthur H. Fauset, *Black Gods of the Metropolis* (Philadelphia, 1944, 1971); Sara Harris and Harriet Crittenden, *Father Divine: Holy Husband* (Garden City, 1953); Kenneth E. Burnham, *God Comes to America: Father Divine and the Peace Mission Movement* (Boston, 1979); Robert Weisbrot, *Father Divine and the Struggle for Racial Equality* (Urbana, IL, 1983).

DIXON, Amzi Clarence (6 July 1854, Shelby, NC—14 June 1925, Baltimore, MD). *Education*: B.A., Wake Forest Coll., 1874; studied at Baptist Sem., Greenville, SC, 1875–76. *Career*: Baptist minister, Mount Olive, NC, (1874–75), Chapel Hill, NC (1876–79), Ashville, NC (1879–82), Baltimore, MD (1882–90), Brooklyn, NY (1890–1901), Boston, MA (1901–06), Chicago, IL (1906–11), London, England (1911–19), and Baltimore, MD (1921–25).

Literature was scarce in the post-Civil War South, but Dixon devoured all he could find, especially the Bible and sermons by Spurgeon, because he too planned to be a Baptist preacher. His zeal for conversions was apparent from the first, and he viewed the mounting number of successful pastorates as increased means to achieve the same end: make each church a soul-saving center. In 1885 he heard *Dwight L. Moody for the first time; after that he became a strong auxiliary in urban revival efforts, preaching at Moody's request in Chicago (World's Fair, 1893), Tampa (embarkation depot, American troops, 1898), and serving as minister of his nondenominational church for five years. He also met *Adoniram J. Gordon whose premillennial ideas influenced his thinking during the 1890s.

But his primary concern throughout life was in reaching the unconverted masses of mankind with a simple message of Christian salvation available for those who would accept it. At times he thought of church life as a springboard to work in the surrounding community, as in temperance endeavors which he vigorously pursued for a number of decades. In the main, however, he was not interested in social reform itself because only the gospel could meet the deepest aspects of human problems. It was easier to reach the body, he argued, by curing the soul rather than vice versa, and to reform a person's character was far more important an objective than effecting some change in the environment.

With top priority given to personal conversions, Dixon engaged in few doctrinal debates or controversies related to larger cultural issues. But several major developments did attract his attention because they threatened the central orientation of preaching and the simplistic faith it sought to nourish. Darwinism together with biblical criticism drew his ire; "evolution" became symbolic of a state of mind which popularized the modernist's empty gospel and turned colleges into hotbeds of infidelity or refrigerators of indifference. Dixon's rather anti-intellectual response to new thought patterns consisted of stressing personal religious experience, daily prayer, and devotional use of Scripture as the best protection against modern liberalism. Beginning in 1909 he was asked by a California businessman to help compile and edit a series of books setting forth the basic principles of sound Christian belief. Within a year the first one appeared, inaugurating a twelve volume series entitled *The Fundamentals: A Testimony*. They were sent free of charge to some 200,000 ministers, missionaries, YMCA secretaries, and Sunday School superintendents around the world. Dixon resigned on leaving for England, but the final volume came out in 1915, renewing the faith of many whose association with the series gave rise to the name, "fundamentalist." Looking back on this effort to stem the tide of destructive skepticism, the famous preacher considered it one of the most satisfactory accomplishments of his ministry.

Bibliography:

A. *Heaven on Earth* (Chicago, 1897); *Light and Shadows of American Life* (New York, 1898); *Evangelism Old and New* (New York, 1905); *Present Day Life and Religion* (Cleveland, OH, 1905); *The Young Convert's Problems and Their Solution* (Boston 1906); *Back to the Bible* (London, 1912).

B. SH 3, 459; NCAB 39, 194; Helen C. A. Dixon, *A. C. Dixon: A Romance of Preaching* (New York, 1931).

DRAPER, John William (5 May 1811, St. Helens, England—4 January 1882, Hastingson-Hudson, NY). *Education*: studied at University Coll., London, 1829–32; M.D., Univ. of Pennsylvania, 1836. *Career*: professor of Chemistry and Natural Philosophy, Hampden-Sidney Coll., 1836–39; professor of Chemistry, New York Univ., 1839–81; professor of Chemistry (and Physiology after 1850), NYU Medical Sch., 1841–81.

Nurtured in a Wesleyan manse and encouraged by his clergyman father to dabble in chemistry and astronomy, Draper embraced modern scientific procedures as a way of life. He pursued medical studies for a while, but his father's death caused the family to emigrate to America. Eventually he graduated with a medical degree and soon joined the scientific faculty at New York University. Draper experimented with radiant energy, making several advances in the study of heat and light as well as in photography. His interest in physics supplemented his work in the fields of physiology and general medical practice. From this eminence he did much to popularize science among people of the Victorian era, extolling the spirit of free inquiry and the tangible results derived from it. In an intellectual history of western civilization he made much of the advance of human knowledge and repeatedly criticized all attempts to stifle the temperament of open investigation. He saw entrenched authority as the obstacle to intellectual progress, and conversely a willingness to explore new vistas as the key to human progress.

In his most famous book Draper chronicled this antagonism as basically a conflict between religion and science. Through the centuries institutionalized religion, especially the Roman Catholic church, had attempted to hold back scientific advances. Bold thinkers like Copernicus, Kepler, Bruno, and Galileo had been martyrs for science, victims of papal tyranny over human minds. In his own day Draper noted similar clashes between fundamentalists, who defended faith in supernatural causes, and liberals, who inclined toward rationalist categories and naturalistic explanations. He was particularly emphatic in defending evolutionary hypotheses and biblical criticism against those who interpreted the Bible literally. Darwinism and higher criticism were in his view simply the latest examples of the liberating quest for greater understanding in western culture. Seeking divinity in the general order of the universe, Draper was immensely successful in voicing the spirit of modern rational progress. He attacked standard religious formulations not out of malice but because he gave priority to intellectual freedom and the practical humanitarian results that such liberty could achieve.

Bibliography:

A. *Human Physiology, Statistical and Dynamical* (New York, 1856); *A History of the Intellectual Development of Europe* (New York, 1862); *Thoughts on the Future Civil Policy of America* (New York, 1865); *History of the American Civil War*, 3 vols. (New York, 1867, 1868, 1870); *History of the Conflict between Religion and Science* (New York, 1874).

B. NCAB 3, 406–07; DAB 5, 438–41; NYT 11 Jan 1882, 8; Donald Fleming, *John William Draper and the Religion of Science* (Philadelphia, 1950).

DREXEL, Katharine (27 November 1858, Philadelphia, PA—3 March 1955, Cornwells Heights, PA). *Career*: foundress and mother superior, Sisters of the Blessed Sacrament for Indians and Colored People, 1891–1937; retirement, 1937–55.

The millionaire banker's home in which young Katharine grew up was marked as much by Catholic piety as by luxury. While she was educated with the customary private tutors, conducted through grand tours of Europe, and brought out at a debutante's ball, her spiritual life developed inclinations contrasting with secular enjoyment. Thus it is not surprising to find that she turned from inherited wealth to a life of poverty and service. After an audience with Leo XIII in 1887, at which time he suggested that she enter missionary work, Drexel suffered great inner turmoil regarding a vocation. Two years later she became a postulant in the novitiate of the Sisters of Mercy. In 1891 she was allowed to establish a new order dedicated to service among black and red Americans who did not receive the usual benefits of modern society. Mother Mary Katharine slowly began collecting a congregation which served primarily as teachers in Indian schools from the Dakotas to Arizona. Work among Pueblos and Navajos was strengthened in places where Franciscans had begun missions two centuries earlier. In addition to making large donations to the Bureau of Catholic Indian Missions, the mother superior built convents and staffed schools in the Southwest to extend Catholicism while aiding cultural development. Spurning a life of ease in preference for one of self-effacing labor, she touched literally hundreds of thousands of under-privileged children.

While Sisters of the Blessed Sacrament pursued apostolic activity in southwestern states, their foundress was also concerned to inaugurate work in the South. She had already donated funds to *John LaFarge's Catholic Interracial Group in New York, but the plight of black children in Tennessee and Louisiana needed more immediate aid. Beginning in Nashville and New Orleans she established a number of schools which over the years imparted faith, learning skills, and culture to their young charges. In the latter city she founded (1915) Xavier University, the first and only Catholic university designated for Negro students. For years her duties consisted of visitations throughout the order's far-flung field of operations. But in 1935 a heart attack forced her to curtail her strenuous life, even to step down as superior two years later. After that she entered two decades of eucharistic contemplation to replace the constant travel of former times. As an invalid in the Motherhouse she pursued a daily round of prayer, mysteries of the rosary, and stations of the cross. Aided by such an example, her sisters continued the educational work. By the time Mother Katharine died, fifty-one convents flourished in twenty-one states where nuns conducted forty-nine elementary schools and twelve high schools. Over twelve million dollars had been poured out by the banker's daughter who sought to accomplish some good while resources and time gave her opportunity. Pronounced venerable, 26 January 1987.

Bibliography:

B.   NCE 4, 1059–60; NYT 4 Mar 1955, 23; Katherine Burton, *The Golden Door: The Life of Katharine Drexel* (New York, 1957); Consuela M. Duffy, *Katharine Drexel* (Philadelphia, 1966).

DU BOSE, William Porcher (11 April 1836, near Winnsboro, SC—18 August 1918, Sewanee, TN). *Education*: graduated from Military Coll. of South Carolina, 1855; M.A., Univ. of Virginia, 1859; studied at Episcopal Sem., Camden, SC, 1859–61. *Career*: officer and chaplain, Confederate Army, 1861–65; rector, St. John's Church, Winnsboro, SC, 1865–67; rector, Trinity Church, Abbeville, SC, 1868–71; chaplain and professor of Moral Science (1871–94), professor of New Testament Language and Interpretation (1894–1908), professor emeritus (1908–18), Univ. of the South, 1871–1918.

Converted while attending a military academy known as "The Citadel," Du Bose persisted for a lifetime in attempts to understand and then teach such Christian doctrine as could be assimilated to contemporary thought. His priestly endeavors were also constant through half a century, but it was his intellectual creativeness that made him one of the most notable Episcopal spokesmen of modern times. While much of his work went unnoticed beyond a circle of devoted students at Sewanee, his emphasis on change within traditional categories placed him in the forefront of those seeking to revitalize orthodoxy. He found it natural to conceive of life as process, historical development, and personal transformation following evolutionary lines of progress. But with that perspective Du Bose still thought there was unitive truth in Scripture and a singleness of mind in the one Church which God appointed as His witness on earth. Just as he was confident that God's creativity was not obscured in the process of evolution, so His redemptive power was not impaired by the fact that it was visible only through humanity, an imperfect reflection of divine purpose. As theologian he sought to proclaim the biblical conception of salvation with guidelines set by the ecumenical faith of apostolic churches. The technical aspects of theological disputes did not interest him; he saw life as more important than doctrine, content more vital than verbal formulation. Largely through study of St. Paul, he came to stress the universal, humanistic qualities of Christianity rather than the rigid formalism so often found in churches reliant on creeds.

The incarnation was central to all categories of Du Bose's thought, giving coherence to his emphasis on the church and relevance to his stress on evangelical faith. Particular incarnation occurred when God was embodied in the man Jesus Christ, a divine fact antecedent to every believer's sensible experience of it. But far from being exhausted in that individual person, incarnation was generically present in humanity. God's action in visible reality was part of the cosmic process, which incorporated Christian events into a single scheme where natural, rational, and divine truth formed an organic whole. Du Bose could find no break between supernatural and natural orders; Christ was not merely a celestial being but rather the same as Adam, just as earth and heaven constituted one arena of life. His appreciation of New Testament authority and the catholic witness of one ecumenical Church came from recognizing that truth is a corporate possession. Knowledge of God's message is a never-ending process in which no person comprehends the entire truth nor understands perfectly that portion within his grasp. As teacher and author he urged others to determine their private faiths within the larger context of divine economy deposited in churches. True to his own admonitions, he continually pursued greater affirmation of God's revelation, observing that Truth is not personal truth when it ceases to be plastic, and ageless faith is vital faith only in the making.

Bibliography:

A. *The Soteriology of the New Testament* (New York, 1892); *The Ecumenical Councils* (New York, 1897); *The Gospel in the Gospels* (New York, 1906); *The Gospel According to St. Paul* (New York, 1907); *The Reason of Life* (New York, 1911); *Turning Points in My Life* (New York, 1912).

B.   SH 4, 16; NCAB 18, 43; DAB 5, 472–73; NYT 22 Aug 1918, 11; Theodore D. Bratton, *The Life and Thought of the Reverend William Porcher DuBose* (New York, 1936); John O. F. Murray, *DuBose as a Prophet of Unity* (London, 1942).

DUBOURG, Louis Guillaume Valentin (14 February 1766, Cap François, Santo Domingo—12 December 1833, Besançon, France). *Education*: studied at Coll. of Guyenne, ?–1784; studied at Sem. of St. Sulpice, Paris, 1786–88?. *Career*: Sulpician instructor, Issy, France, 1788–92; president, Georgetown Coll. (MD), 1796–98; missionary and educator, Havana, Cuba, and Baltimore, MD, 1798–1803; superior, St. Mary's Coll. (MD), 1803–12; administrator apostolic, Diocese of Louisiana, 1812–15; bishop of Louisiana, 1815–26; bishop of Montauban, France, 1826–33; archibishop of Besançon, France, 1833.

Birth in the West Indies to aristocratic parents provided for refined upbringing and educational advantages in France, opportunities on which Dubourg capitalized to prepare well for clerical service. Records of his studies at St. Sulpice were destroyed in the Revolution, but we know that he was ordained around 1788, taught for a time at a Sulpician training center near Paris, fled to Bordeaux and then Spain because of anti-ecclesiastical revolutionary sentiment, finally sailing to Baltimore in 1794. His major interest throughout various circumstances lay in education, the instructional aspect of religion that began with early influences among the church's youth and broadened to include moral as well as doctrinal guidance for adults. In each of his many North American locations he established schools to facilitate this high priority missionary objective; present universities in Baltimore, St. Louis, and New Orleans trace their origins to his initial efforts. He was also personally instrumental in encouraging *Elizabeth B. Seton to organize a new monastic community near his college in Maryland. Over the years, Dubourg imported several orders of religious to staff his educational enterprises. Lazarist fathers, Ursuline sisters, and notably *Philippine Duchesne, with her Order of the Sacred Heart, came at his urging to strengthen the place of religious work along a St. Louis-Flourissant continuum in Missouri. Such work laid the basis for slow expansion of Catholicism in the huge diocese considered the Southwest of its day. By 1826 its bishop had established forty new parishes, built two cathedrals, and founded numerous academies as evidence of modest but steady growth in trans-Mississippi territories.

When Dubourg was named by *John Carroll to administer Catholic affairs in Louisiana, the diocese had been without a bishop for a decade. French priests there would not submit to an American hierarchy and forced the new bishop to reside in St. Louis rather than New Orleans as principal locus for his see. By 1820, however, he was able to win enough support from down-river clergy to inaugurate a more peaceable era. Those early years unwittingly afforded the chance to visit all parts of the far-flung diocese, and Dubourg met every challenge with hardy, enterprising zeal. Recognizing the need for more adequate missions to Indians along the Missouri River, he persuaded a group of Belgian Jesuits to accept this task. One of those who responded was *Pierre-Jean de Smet, pioneering missionary and friend to nations ranging from the Dakota to the Flathead. He also labored without ceasing among the white population, struggling to counteract ignorance about the true faith not unmixed with prejudice against the Roman embodiment of it. Small gains were made as sacraments became more available and as education dispelled indifference. But supervisory rivalries broke out again in 1824 when he made Joseph Rosati bishop coadjutor. Dissension eroded confidence in his ability to control subordinates, and he was allowed to resign. Appointment to large jurisdictions in France gave some consolation, while it removed him from demands for vigorous leadership needed in less settled conditions of the western world.

Bibliography:

    B.   NCAB 4, 435–36; DAB 5, 473–75; NCE 4, 1081; Annabelle M. Melville, *Louis William DuBourg: Bishop of Louisiana and the Floridas*, 2 vols. (Chicago, 1986).

DUCHESNE, Rose Philippine (29 August 1769, Grenoble, France—18 November 1852, St. Charles, MO). *Career*: entered Order of the Visitation of St. Mary, Grenoble, 1788–92; private charitable work, 1792–1804; member, Society of the Sacred Heart, 1804–52; secretary general of the Order, Paris, 1815–18; missionary in the United States, 1818–52.

As one who thought often of a religious vocation, especially the apostolate of foreign missions, Sister Duchesne readily assimilated herself to the common life and discipline of Visitandine tradition. Anti-ecclesiastical outbursts during the French Revolution obliged her to resume the appearance of secular pursuits, but she was faithful to the order's rule and tried to revive its institutions after the Terror had passed. Failing this, she joined the Society of the Sacred Heart, becoming through the years one of its chief architects in Paris and in the New World. She possessed great strength and patience under trial and failure. Her stamina and determination were a source of encouragement to other sisters as they made a newly created order one of the foremost teaching orders in America's heartland. Arriving at St. Louis, Missouri, in August of 1818, Mother Duchesne and her small following expected to establish schools for Indian girls. The mercurial bishop, *Guillaume V. Dubourg, sent them instead to the rude town of St. Charles where they lived in a log house and conducted school for the village children, in 1819 they were moved to Florissant and put to work in more schools, also founding there the first novitiate for training American religious in the Society. Other schools were established in Louisiana (1821–25) together with an orphanage, academy, and parish school in St. Louis (1827). All of the projects were dependent upon Mother Duchesne and the aid of her practical friend, the new bishop, Joseph Rosati.

Always inclined to penances and mortification, Mother Duchesne was hard in judging herself. She considered much of her activity to be a failure because it did not reach the Indians for whom she had originally planned missionary work. Still the order slowly enlarged its solid foundations. Her rigorous discipline and inability to speak English did not help the schools grow very quickly, and she often said that prayer was the most effective contribution she could make to the growth of the church. When she was finally allowed to work among Indians, that life of prayer had a significant impact on those she wished to influence. In 1841, at the age of seventy-two, she lived for a short while among the Potawatomis at Sugar Creek, Kansas. Their admiration for her severe offices is seen in the fact that their name for her was "Woman-Who-Prays-Always." After one year, she was recalled to the St. Charles convent and passed the last decade of her life with acts of exemplary humility in the place where the American mission had begun. Mother Duchesne was beatified in 1940, and canonized, 3 July 1988.

Bibliography:

    B.   DAB 5, 477–78; NCE 4, 1088–89; NAW 1, 524–26; Marjory Erskine, *Mother Philippine Duchesne* (New York, 1926); Louise Callan, *Philippine Duchesne: Frontier Missionary of the Sacred Heart* (Westminster, MD, 1957); Catherine M. Mooney, *Philippine Duchesne: A Woman with the Poor* (New York, 1990).

DUNSTER, Henry (1609, Bury, England—27 February 1659, Scituate, MA). *Education*: B.A., M.A., Magdalene Coll., Cambridge Univ., 1631, 1634. *Career*: schoolmaster and curate, Bury, England, 1634–40; president, Harvard Coll., 1640–54; minister, Scituate, MA, 1655–59.

The earliest record of Dunster's existence is a baptismal notice dated November, 1609, in a Lancashire village church. After acquitting himself well at university, he returned to minister among those townspeople but emigrated in 1640, apparently because of nonconformist principles. Within three weeks of arriving in the Bay Colony, he was appointed the first president of Harvard, a college created four years earlier. The institution had been proposed by founding fathers who wished to advance learning; further, they dreaded leaving an illiterate ministry to serve churches after their generation, and it was Dunster's major achievement that the stated objectives were realized. He immediately collected scattered students and set them to work. Administrative statutes and degree requirements copied from medieval patterns at Cambridge were enacted as he fashioned the struggling school into a genuine college. In 1642 the first commencement was held, and by 1650 the resourceful president was able to secure a charter for his promising academy. But with foundations laid for future growth, change occurred from an unanticipated theological development. In 1653 Dunster refused to have his new son baptized because he had concluded such practice was not authorized by scripture. He argued, on positive ground, that only penitent believers should receive the ordinance. A public outcry arose because most clergymen feared, on negative ground, that he might embody the subversive tendencies of Anabaptists. Such circumstances forced his resignation and removal to a pastorate in Plymouth County where he soon died without bitterness or compromise.

Bibliography:

B.   AAP 1, 125–26; SH 4, 31; NCAB 6, 409–10; DAB 5, 524; Jeremiah Chaplin, *The Life of Henry Dunster* (Boston, 1872); Samuel Dunster, *Henry Dunster and His Descendants* (Central Falls, RI, 1876).

DWIGHT, Timothy (14 May 1752, Northampton, MA—11 January 1817, New Haven, CT). *Education*: graduated from Yale Coll., 1769; further resident study, Yale Coll., 1769–71. *Career*: tutor, Yale Coll., 1771–77; chaplain, American Revolutionary Army, 1777–78; farmer, teacher, state legislator 1781–83; supply preacher, Northampton, MA, 1778–83; minister and schoolmaster, Greenfield Hill, CT, 1783–95; president, Yale Coll., 1795–1817.

With the advantages of family connection, inherited property, and precocious intellectual capacity, Dwight quickly became a respected figure in public affairs. Though years of hard study painfully affected his eyesight, his teaching ability was renowned long before he succeeded *Ezra Stiles as president of Yale. Accomplishments as a preacher, hymn writer, and poet gave further promise that central objectives which he set for the small college would be secured. With a clear vision of what Yale should become, Dwight used flexible methods together with energetic leadership and more discipline than the school had seen for a decade to achieve those ultimate purposes. Under his administration attempts were finally successful in establishing professional schools for studying medicine and theology, while additional faculty expanded the curriculum in many undergraduate areas. As president he lectured to the senior class and preached to all students twice on Sundays, discharging those spiritual duties with pastoral assiduity. He met youthful irreligion by encouraging open debate on the subject; in 1802 his discourses produced a campus revival, convincing many to adopt orthodox beliefs and join the ranks of learned Calvinistic divines. Federalist politics was also valued as a defense against social decay, and students did not escape without an introduction to strong opinions about the excesses of Jeffersonian democracy.

Young men were only a fraction of the audience Dwight reached through writing and speaking to defend the cause of orthodox Christianity. He was convinced that proofs refuting fashionable notions spread by deists could demonstrate the genuineness and authenticity of Scripture. Attacking the nature of infidel philosophy, he waged a bold campaign against *Thomas Paine and other rationalist authors because they represented to him nothing less than atheism. Confronting their blasphemous insinuations with a battery of rebuttals, he proved himself to be a firm defender of traditional patterns, whether theological or social. But Dwight did not conform strictly to the ideas of *Jonathan Edwards, his grandfather; rather he occupied a mediating position between Old Calvinism and New Divinity. He influenced *Nathaniel W. Taylor, who liberalized theology much more explicitly, but it is impossible to place him in a single theological camp. Inclined toward Scottish epistemology and a positive appreciation of man's moral ability, Dwight helped define religion as a system of duties in which persons participated responsibly. Still, the moral implications of religion were a consequence of its grounding in revelation, and the president's major impact on his generation resulted from an articulate battle against skepticism in favor of a sound body of Calvinist doctrine.

Bibliography:

    A.   *The Conquest of Canaan: A Poem in Eleven Books* (Hartford, 1785); *Theology Explained and Defended*, 5 vols. (Middletown, CT, 1818); *Travels in New England and New York*, 4 vols. (New Haven, 1822); *Sermons*, 2 vols. (New Haven, 1828).
    B.   AAP 2, 152–65; SH 4, 41; NCAB 1, 168; DAB 5, 573–77; NCE 4, 1129; Charles E. Cunningham, *Timothy Dwight, 1752–1817: A Biography* (New York, 1942); Kenneth Silverman, *Timothy Dwight* (New York, 1969); Stephen E. Berks, *Calvinism versus Democracy: Timothy Dwight and the Origins of American Evangelical Orthodoxy* (Hamden, CT, 1974).

DYER, Mary (?–1 June 1660, Boston, MA).

The earliest document mentioning the name of Mary Barrett records her marriage to William Dyer at London in October, 1633. Two years later, the couple had settled in Massachusetts Bay Colony, finding general acceptance by citizens together with membership in the Puritan church established there. Soon after that time, however, difficulties began to emerge which eventually led to impassioned religious debate and severe action. Divergence of opinion came to the surface when *Anne Hutchinson argued with increasing emphasis that salvation through grace could be separated from salvation through works. Mary Dyer was similarly persuaded that the Holy Spirit dwelled in regenerated saints, making a covenant of grace the only essential concern for God's elect. The colony's church leaders tried to reason with, silence by edict, and finally banish Hutchinson for spreading such dangerous ideas. In 1637 William Dyer was disenfranchised for associating with those harboring views inclining toward heresy. But Mary remained true to her friend; when Anne was expelled from church in 1638, she was the only person to accompany her out of a group eager to forestall antinomianism. The Dyers were themselves excommunicated and banished in turn. They moved to Rhode Island where greater tolerance provided an atmosphere of relative tranquility. By 1652 they traveled again to England, where Mary was attracted to the teachings of *George Fox. Since the doctrine of Inner Light dwelling in individual believers was not dissimilar to ideas she already held, conversion to Quakerism seemed as valid as it was natural.

In 1657 Mary Dyer returned to the New World, convinced more than ever that she must testify effectively for her new faith. After arrival in Boston, she was imprisoned for violating a law passed the year before against professing Quaker beliefs. Her husband secured her release, but he was unable to confine her preaching. In 1658 she was expelled from New Haven, and during the summer of 1659 Boston authorities jailed her again for visiting Friends already incarcerated there. All of them were expelled with the warning that return was punishable by death. They returned in September, 1659, as one said, to look the bloody law in the face; consequently all were condemned to die. Within a month William Robinson and Marmaduke Stephenson were hanged while Mary Dyer was given a last minute reprieve. Not impressed with leniency, she reluctantly spent the winter preaching on Long Island. She felt a divine impulse behind her mission and longed to offer up her life as a martyr. Entering Boston for a fourth time in defiance of the law, she was again sentenced to death at the end of May, 1660, with execution carried out the following day. The orthodox community thought of her as an obstinate heretic whose death would hopefully deter future aberrations. Dissenters held rather that her resolute action was the right thing to do because it stemmed from deep inner certitude. Whether motivated by obedience to divine will or a wish to achieve statutory freedom of conscience, her sacrifice was indicative of first generation Quaker witness to truth as they saw it.

Bibliography:

B.   NCAB 11, 438; DAB 5, 584; NAW 1, 536; Horatio Rogers, *Mary Dyer . . . the Quaker Martyr* (Providence, RI, 1896).

E

EDDY, Mary Baker (16 July 1821, Bow, NH—3 December 1910, Brookline, MA). *Education*: private tutoring, 1830–34; studied at Sanbornton Academy (NH), 1842; studied with Phineas P. Quimby, Portland, ME, 1862, 1864. *Career*: itinerant teaching in MA, 1866–75; minister, Christian Science Association, Lynn, MA, 1876–81; minister, Church of Christ (Scientist), Boston, 1881–1910.

Mary Morse Baker experienced lifelong health problems which gave her ideas a focus that eventuated in a major American religious phenomenon. Nervous illness and depressions of uncertain diagnosis were her lot through four decades until she met Phineas P. Quimby, a healer who gave relief and a hint of new directions to follow. After Quimby's death in 1866, she emerged as a teacher and healer, building on his thoughts and shaping the tenets of health through Christian Science. After several years of wandering, estrangement, and some good fortune she settled at Lynn, Massachusetts, and began successful classes. Three marriages, two ended by deaths, were incidental to the work that began to take shape in 1875 when public services were first held and the earliest edition of her authoritative textbook appeared.

Like many before her, Mrs. Eddy thought she held the key to understanding Scripture in its proper sense. The resulting doctrine was not in her view a product of human speculation but rather the fullness of God's self-disclosure. Basic to her convictions was the affirmation that God is All, the only Being, and that the Eternal Mind is the source of all genuine existence. Human life is a corollary of this truth if it is perceived spiritually as a divine reflection of God. Those not evaluating existence in spiritual terms were making a serious mistake because, Mrs. Eddy taught, the so-called world of the senses is unreal. Conceptions such as matter, sin, pain, disease, and death are illusions of the mortal mind. Reliance on the senses produced an erroneous dualism of spirit and matter, leading to experiences of disease and pain caused by the mind alone. Salvation as interpreted by Christian Science comes by the Eternal Mind, making it possible to overcome illusions of sin and sickness and to banish their outward appearance. In keeping with this general perspective, Mrs. Eddy addressed those who thought they were suffering from afflictions, urging them to abandon pharmaceutics and take up ontology.

The institutional framework which Mrs. Eddy consolidated through the years was effective in perpetuating ideas initiated by her writings and remarkable teaching ability. The first Christian Science Association was formed in 1876; by 1886 so many new churches existed that a national association was needed to coordinate them. In 1892 this framework was reorganized, with all powers over doctrine and property concentrated in a small directorate. This board of directors passed on all applications for membership to the Mother Church, and it supervised the activities of branch societies, their practitioners, and expositions authorized for teaching purposes. Practitioners were trained under auspices of the Massachusetts Metaphysical College from 1881 to 1899 and after that by means considered appropriate to the directorate. Printed matter issued by the *Christian Science Journal* (monthly, 1883), the *Sentinel* (weekly, 1898) and the *Monitor* (daily, 1908) aided in disseminating the new denomination's ideas. By 1889 Mrs. Eddy secluded herself from day to day involvement with church matters, but she did not cease attempts to provide her following with stable institutional forms, structures which are further evidence of her lasting work.

Bibliography:

A. *Science and Health, with Key to the Scriptures* (Boston, 1875, and many subsequent revised editions); *Retrospection and Introspection* (Boston, 1891); *Manual of the Mother Church* (Boston, 1895); *Miscellaneous Writings* (Boston, 1896); *Christian Healing and the People's Idea of God* (Boston, 1909).

B. SH 4, 73; NCAB 3, 80–81; DAB 6, 7–15; NAW 1, 551–61; NYT 5 Dec 1910, 1; Georgine Milmine, *The Life of Mary Baker Eddy and the History of Christian Science* (New York, 1909); Edwin F. Dakin, *Mrs. Eddy: The Biography of a Virginal Mind* (New York, 1929); Ernest S. Bates and John V. Dittemore, *Mary Baker Eddy: The Truth and the Tradition* (New York, 1932); Hugh A. S. Kennedy, *Mrs. Eddy: Her Life, Her Work, and Her Place in History* (San Francisco, 1947); Robert Peel, *Mary Baker Eddy: The Years of Discovery; . . . Trial; . . . Authority,* 3 vols. (New York, 1966; 1971; 1977).

EDWARDS, Jonathan (5 October 1703, East Windsor, CT—22 March 1758, Princeton, NJ). *Education*: B.A., Yale Coll., 1720; postgraduate study of theology, Yale Coll., 1721–22. *Career*: minister, Presbyterian church, New York, 1722–23; tutor, Yale Coll., 1724–26; minister, Congregational church, Northampton, MA, 1726–50; minister, Stockbridge, MA, 1751–58; president, Coll. of New Jersey, 1758.

Of all religious thinkers in the American experience, none is more prominent than Edwards, who combined practical insight, imagination, and intellectual discipline to an outstanding degree. After a brief pastorate in New York, he returned to Yale, which had been without sufficient direction since 1722. He labored there with credit to both himself and the institution, but readily accepted an invitation to become junior colleague of his grandfather, the venerable *Solomon Stoddard. Rounds of ministerial duties occupied him for almost a quarter-century; in the aftermath of revivals at Northampton, however, Edwards began changes in church practice which eventually produced his expulsion. For twenty years he had accepted his grandfather's habit of serving communion to those not yet proclaiming firsthand conversion experience as well as to those who did. His heightened appreciation of ecclesiastical offices for the regenerate caused him to "fence the Lord's table" more exclusively, disconcerting many in the parish accustomed to laxer standards. After much wrangling over breach of contract, the church voted (200 to 23) to dismiss their pastor. He moved to a nearby village, where his charge included speaking through an interpreter to Housatonic Indians. At this time he also completed four of his greatest theological treatises. Upon the death of his son-in-law, he was elected president of the college at Princeton, indicating hopes that he would perpetuate revivalist impulses in succeeding generations of Calvinist preachers. He died from the effects of smallpox vaccination only months after his arrival.

Two intellectual currents blended in Edwards to produce a notable synthesis of eighteenth century thought. He wrote primarily as one defending classic Reformed doctrines of the Puritan tradition, but he was far ahead of contemporaries in employing new perspectives from the Age of Reason. After reading John Locke and Isaac Newton at an early age, he used their modern categories to re-emphasize man's dependence on God—a position endemic to a Calvinistic theory of salvation. He stressed the arbitrary and absolute character of divine election together with the immediacy of God's operations in the human soul. With relentless logic he argued for the innate corruption of mankind, taking proofs from Scripture and his own observations. Throughout these apologetic tracts, he set forth the complete right of God to deal with creatures as He saw fit, to exercise absolute sovereignty regarding a selective salvation of undeserving sinners. Yet with these theological strictures, Edwards admitted that God had effected surprising conversions in Massachusetts churches. He defended strong religious emotions associated with the First Great Awakening, affording some of the most balanced considerations of that exciting period and the new energies it built upon.

More important than the philosophic rigor of his doctrinal works, Edwards articulated a mystic appreciation of God's metaphysical nature to round off his comprehensive theological system. A sense of the glory of the divine Being dominated his thought much more than occasional references to sinners in the hands of an angry God. Edwards was enthralled with the sense of God's majestic presence, not with man's submission to infinite authority. Love of God was assent to being, in general, and true virtue consisted in love of all beings proportionate to their rank on the scale of existence. Love of archangels was properly more than that of earthworms, and love of God stemmed from recognizing His ultimate place as the ground of all being. Love for being less wide than this, springing from narrower motives, could not be true benevolence. Above all his other intellectual gifts, Edwards had, and could communicate to others, a vision of the glory of God that transfigured human life. That vision pointed to a beauty of spirit in the Puritan clergyman more remarkable than all the doctrinal achievements noted by later students.

Bibliography:

A. *A Faithful Narrative of the Surprising Work of God* (London, 1737; New Haven, 1972); *A Treatise Concerning Religious Affections* (Boston, 1746; New Haven, 1959); *A Careful and Strict Inquiry into the Modern Prevailing Notions of the Freedom of the Will* (Boston, 1754; New Haven, 1957); *The Great Christian Doctrine of Original Sin Defended* (Boston, 1758; New Haven, 1970); *Two Dissertations* (Boston, 1765); *The Works of President Edwards*, ed. Sereno E. Dwight, 10 vols. (New York, 1829–30).

B. AAP 1, 329–35; SH 4, 80–81; NCAB 5, 464–65; DAB 6, 30–37; NCE 5, 183–84; Alexander V. G. Allen, *Jonathan Edwards* (Boston, 1889); Ola E. Winslow, *Jonathan Edwards* (New York, 1940); Perry Miller, *Jonathan Edwards* (New York, 1949); Conrad Cherry, *The Theology of Jonathan Edwards: A Reappraisal* (New York, 1966); Harry S. Stout, *Jonathan Edwards and the American Experience* (New York, 1988).

EDWARDS, Jonathan, Jr. (26 May 1745, Northampton, MA—1 August 1801, Schenectady, NY). *Education*: B.A., Coll. of New Jersey, 1765; studied theology with *Joseph Bellamy, Bethlehem, CT, 1765–66. *Career:* tutor, Coll. of New Jersey, 1767–69; minister, New Haven, CT, 1769–95; minister, Colebrook, CT, 1796–99; president, Union Coll., 1799–1801.

As a boy, the younger Edwards grew up in western Massachusetts, learning to speak Mohegan better than English while his famous father was afforded enough time to write theological treatises. Though both parents died when the youth was only thirteen, friends enabled him to finish his education preparatory to service as a Congregationalist minister. The Connecticut church that called him was a divided and contentious one; his coming only served to create new problems where the old ones were bad enough. Many in that congregation wanted their new pastor to baptize children of members who scarcely participated in formal worship, but he strongly opposed anything resembling the half-way covenant. Qualifications for membership were the same, he insisted, as those for full communion. As a result of that adamant policy, church attendance began to dwindle. Another reason for declining numbers lay in the dry, abstruse sermons that Edwards dispensed on controverted points of Christian belief. Questions raised by deistic critics occupied much of his attention, and he informed audiences of proper rebuttals in an exhibition of truth destitute of verbal adornment. His reasoning was always closely confined to the topic, following rigid demonstrations that resembled pure mathematics, a subject which fascinated him avocationally throughout life. In time the church became so small, it was forced to dismiss him for lack of funds.

Diligent adherence to doctrinal consistency was more a measure of success for Edwards than currying the favor of a popular following. Though not as effective as *Samuel Hopkins or *Joseph Bellamy, he still must be counted among those who contributed materially to the spread of systematic Edwardsean theology. Among his notable emphases was a governmental theory of atonement, contrasted with the satisfaction hypothesis that made God seem too ruthless in punishing sinners. Instead of holding that Christ's death was suffering in payment of a debt which God exacted for sin, Edwards viewed the work of Christ to be a demonstration of how the natural world was regulated by moral government. Atonement for sin was enacted in conformity to moral law, which was the divine creation of a benevolent governor, not an arbitrary sovereign power. Of course this was not new doctrine, but it gained wider acceptance through his advocacy. As early as 1791, he created no little stir by inveighing against the slave trade, becoming one of the first New England divines to do so. He also argued tenaciously in defense of eternal punishment and won recognition as a scholar suited to assume the presidency of a college. In addition to his own publications, he edited several of his father's manuscripts, which appeared in four printed volumes. After brief tenure as a teacher, he unexpectedly fell victim to an attack of fever which deprived him of speech, of reason at intervals, and finally of life.

Bibliography:

A. *The Salvation of All Men Strictly Examined* (New Haven, CT, 1790); *The Works of Jonathan Edwards . . . Late President of Union College*, ed. Tryon Edwards, 2 vols. (Andover, MA, 1842).

B. AAP 1, 653–60; SH 4, 82–83; NCAB 7, 169–70; DAB 6, 37–38; Robert L. Ferm, *Jonathan Edwards the Younger: A Colonial Pastor* (Grand Rapids, MI, 1976).

EELLS, Cushing (16 February 1810, Blandford, MA—17 February 1893, Tacoma, WA). *Education:* B.A., Williams Coll., 1834; B.D., East Windsor (CT) Theol. Inst., 1837. *Career:* agent for the American Board of Foreign Missions in Oregon Territory, 1838–48; school-teacher and Congregationalist minister, OR and WA, 1848–93.

While still a divinity student in what later became Hartford Seminary, Eells volunteered for missionary service among the Zulu tribes of southeastern Africa. Warfare in that region prevented his departure, so he accepted the invitation of pioneers in Oregon to join their evangelical work. By the summer of 1838, he arrived with a few other missionaries at the station founded by *Marcus and *Narcissa Whitman. For a decade, the Eells family settled with Spokan Indians at a place called Tshimakain. These Interior Salish natives, a distant branch of Algonkian linguistic stock, were a docile people who proved to be tractable but slow learners. Despite language difficulties, the missionary held frequent worship services, reading Scripture and explaining it as far as possible through an interpreter, singing, and praying to provide object lessons for his audience. Eells was realistic about not expecting rapid progress; he knew that his simple instruction on a child's level would not quickly develop into the virtues of mature

Christianity. Still he persevered, trying at the same time to be an example of industry in hopes of civilizing and elevating those around him. Work among the Spokan was not an outstanding success, but it did not result in disaster. When the Whitmans were massacred in 1847, the Spokan mission remained peaceful. Yet neighboring Cayuse were so hostile, the station was abandoned one year later, to the apparent disappointment of resident Indians. Later trips allowed for some renewed religious activity, but it did not continue on a permanent basis again.

For several years Eells drifted from one post to another, farming and teaching in various academies to support himself until the Mission Board sent new directives. By 1855 he dropped formal connection with the parent organization because it suggested that he move to Hawaii. He decided to stay in the Northwest and help the white population instead of entering a new field with all the language problems that entailed. Two schools in which Eells labored became institutions of higher learning; Tualitin Academy grew into Pacific University, and the resuscitated Whitman mission built a college in 1860. He often traveled to preach in small gatherings where the opportunity offered, almost always without pay. In later years he was minister to some congregations at Colfax, Medical Lake, Sprague, Half Moon, and Cheyney, some of the first Congregationalist churches north of the Snake River. He also contributed a large portion of his slender income to build churches and hire others to staff them. In his view, schools and churches were congruent institutions that strove for the same cultural objectives. Educational as well as ecclesiastical beginnings through his agency had been placed on solid ground by the time Washington became a state in 1889. In his waning years "Father Eells" wintered mostly on the Skokomish reservation near Puget Sound, spending summer seasons east of the Cascades as a self-supporting home missionary without commission. Some persons he met in such travels had not heard a Protestant sermon in two decades, and knowledge of that circumstance drove him for the entire fifty-five year period of his life's work.

Bibliography:

B.   Myron Eells, *Father Eells* (Boston, 1894).

EINHORN, David (10 November 1809, Dispeck, Germany—2 November 1879, New York, NY). *Education*: rabbinical diploma, Yeshiva at Fürth, Germany, 1826; studied at Erlangen, Würzburg, and Munich. *Career*: rabbi, Birkenfeld, Germany, 1842–47; rabbi, Mecklenburg-Schwerin, Germany, 1847–51; rabbi, Har Sinai Congregation, Baltimore, MD, 1855–61; rabbi, Keneseth Israel Congregation, Philadelphia, PA, 1861–66; rabbi, Adath Jeshurun Congregation, New York, NY (Temple Beth-El after merger in 1874), 1866–79; retirement, 1879.

Reform Judaism had its beginnings in Germany, and rabbis like Einhorn brought it to American shores providing a vigorous leadership that made it the dominant form of Jewish practice for half a century. After having received traditional Talmudic training, he began to espouse liberal views and attended several secular universities. This was viewed as defection by Orthodox leaders, and they succeeded in blocking his appointment to a synagogue for over a decade. Later in Hungary, pressure was exerted to close his temple. But Einhorn grew increasingly articulate in defense of the new interpretations of Judaism and participated in important conferences of the Reform Verein at Brunswick, Frankfurt, and Breslau in the 1840s. During the next decade, he worked out a theological basis for all his suggestions about adjusting Jewish life to modern conditions.

In 1855 Dr. Einhorn came to America where he continued the work as scholar and theologian that had already won him recognition as a prominent spokesman for Reform. In his first year at Baltimore he criticized *Isaac M. Wise for his views on the Talmud and quickly attracted attention as leader of the radical wing in this country. He began issuing *Sinai* (1856–62), a German monthly in which he published his most important sermons and topical views. Another significant contribution of the period was a prayer book which shortened and modified traditional services, omitted references to sacrifices, translated all the Hebrew into German, and added many original German prayers. His liturgical arrangements were largely incorporated into the compromise *Union Prayer Book* (1892 and 1895), which superseded it. Interestingly, while abandoning Hebrew, he insisted that Reform ideas depended on preservation of the German language, even through the succeeding generation. Einhorn was an outspoken abolitionist and had to flee Baltimore in 1861 to escape a pro-slavery mob. Subsequent to that he served as rabbi to large congregations in Philadelphia and New York, not retiring from an active ministry until shortly before his death.

Einhorn's ideas about Reform Judaism tried to avoid the shallow arrogance of rationalists and the hollow ceremonialism of the Orthodox, insisting rather that the essence of Mosaic patterns lay in a living, growing faith. He perceived a continuous development within the life of a chosen people that could progress beyond old forms and still lead men to greater moral perfection because it was founded on the spirit, not the letter, of divine revelation. He sought not a reformed cultus, but a reformed Jewish heart, a reinvigorated belief in God, and a restitution of the Sabbath as Israel's tower of strength. In 1869 he was instrumental in defining the main outlines of the American Reform impetus at a conference in Philadelphia. That meeting declared the Messianic hope to be universalistic, not nationalistic, and Israel's dispersion to be a fulfillment of its mission. It eschewed attitudes reverential to the sacrificial cult and the Aaronic priesthood, urged further acceptance of vernacular prayers, sought to elevate the status of women, and denounced requiring circumcision for identification as a Jew. The meeting's pronouncements impressed the Jewish world on both sides of the Atlantic and laid the basis for an even more emphatic manifesto that stemmed from the Rabbinical Conference at Pittsburgh in 1885.

Bibliography:

    A. *Princip des Mosaismus und dessen Verhältnis zum Heidenthum and Rabbinischen Judenthum* (Leipzig, 1854); *Olath Tamid* (Baltimore, 1856; enl. ed., 1858); *Ner Tamid* (Philadelphia, 1866); *David Einhorns Ausgewählte Predigten und Reden*, ed. Kaufmann Kohler (New York, 1880); *David Einhorn Memorial Volume: Selected Sermons and Addresses*, ed. Kaufmann Kohler (New York, 1911).
    B.   NCAB 12, 380; DAB 6, 65; UJE 4, 27–28; EJ 6, 531; NYT 4 Nov 1879, 5.

ELIOT, John (August 1604, Widford, England—21 May 1690, Roxbury, MA). *Education*: B.A., Jesus Coll., Cambridge Univ., 1622. *Career*: supply minister, Boston, MA, 1631–32; minister, Roxbury, MA, 1632–90.

By 1630 it was clear to many English Nonconformists that difficult years lay ahead of them because of Archbishop Laud's policy of attrition directed against puritans of every stripe. Eliot prudently emigrated to the New World and settled into a parish where the pure gospel could be followed without episcopal interference. In addition to ministerial duties among his countrymen, he turned his attention to Algonkian-speaking native Americans, becoming in time one of the few Christian missionaries to merit the title "apostle to the Indians." From the start communication was difficult; Algonkian tribes such as the Massachuset and Wampanoag had no written language, no dictionary, no grammar for an outsider to study. After years of labor with native tutors, Eliot succeeded in creating all of these. He manifested the distinctive Puritan emphasis on correct doctrine and supplied the means of training Indian converts in good knowledge of scripture, that indispensable source of Protestant religious nurture. Through the decades he translated psalms, catechisms, and books on godly living into the local tongue. Finally in 1663 his greatest literary achievement appeared: the entire Bible was printed in Algonkian for what he envisioned as successive generations of believers led by their own learned ministry. Thus the basis was laid for a sustained effort to preach and reform, educate and civilize Indians into the way of life defined by European standards of righteousness.

While continuing his parish responsibilities in Roxbury, Eliot began missionary tours among the Massachuset nation, preaching his first sermon in their language in 1646. Conversions came slowly and for a variety of reasons, but the number of baptized followers gradually mounted. These Praying Indians, as they were called, accepted much more than a system of religious propositions. They conformed to English modes of dress and personal hygiene; men learned to till the soil while women turned to spinning as models of frugal industry; their family life, economics, and recreation adapted to Old World expectations as the process of acculturation developed under Eliot's guidance. All these changes occurred in a setting that contrasted sharply with indigenous habits, namely in permanent villages whose streets and houses were patterned after English designs. The first town for Praying Indians was Natick (begun 1651) and at the height of missionary influence, fourteen sanctuaries for native Christians were built. The unremitting zeal of Eliot and funds from abroad authorized by an act of Parliament in 1649 helped the enterprise flourish. Much of this work was destroyed in 1675 when warfare with the Wampanoag chieftain, King Philip, caused white colonists to suspect peaceful catechists of collusion. Hundreds died in concentration camps, their towns were burned, and evangelical work was virtually obliterated by bellicose hysteria. Despite these impediments, some converts remained faithful, and Eliot continued to minister among their scattered, broken bands.

Bibliography:

A. *A Late and Further Manifestation of the Progress of the Gospel amongst the Indians in New-England* (London, 1655); *A Further Account of the Progresse of the Gospel* (London, 1660); *Mamusee Wunneetapanatamwe Up-Biblum God*, or *The Indian Bible* (Cambridge, MA, 1663).

B. AAP 1, 18–23; SH 4, 108–09; NCAB 2, 419–23; DAB 6, 79–80; Nehemiah Adams, *The Life of John Eliot* (Boston, 1847); Convers Francis, *Life of John Eliot: The Apostle to the Indians* (Boston, 1896); David Chamberlain, *Eliot of Massachusetts* (London, 1928); Ola E. Winslow, *John Eliot: Apostle to the Indians* (Boston, 1968).

ELY, Richard Theodore (13 April 1854, Ripley, NY—4 October 1943, Old Lyme, CT). *Education*: studied at Dartmouth Coll., 1872–73; B.A., Columbia Univ., 1876; Ph.D., Heidelberg Univ., 1879. *Career*: lecturer and associate professor of Political Economy, Johns Hopkins Univ., 1881–92; director, School of Economy, Political Science, and History, Univ. of Wisconsin, 1892–1925; director, Institute for Research in Land Economy and Public Utilities, Northwestern Univ., 1925–32; president, Institute for Economic Research and School of Land Economy, Columbia Univ., 1937–43.

The son of devout Presbyterians, both of whom maintained a strong concern for social reforms, Ely continued that heritage with professional sophistication. After some graduate study at Halle, the prize-winning student came into his own by discovering economics as a field of specialization, acquiring increased expertise at Heidelberg and then Berlin. He quickly adopted the historical perspective on economic matters, viewing them as changing and relative to local conditions as opposed to fixed absolutes that applied mechanically to all situations. This dynamic view allowed Ely to support liberal reforms of his day against the laissez-faire doctrine of vested interests. Economic principles were not governed by natural law, he argued, and policies regarding property and wages had to be integrated into specific societies where state control directed the organic evolution of all citizens into a cooperative commonwealth. Such perspectives made him a champion of organized labor in this country. He held that economic science, not theology, demonstrated the need for higher wages, shorter working hours, slum clearance, and child education instead of child labor.

Behind his intellectually based advocacy of social improvements, Ely was also motivated by religious and ethical impulses. This made him an outstanding lay supporter of the Social Gospel in his day. He was recognized as the dean of American economists and blended this prestige with humanitarian concerns in 1885 as one of the principal founders of the American Economics Association. After joining the Episcopal church he cooperated with *William D. P. Bliss in 1891 to found the Episcopal Social Union, a group which sought fruitful ways of accomplishing things ''for the good of man and the glory of God.'' It was the earthly mission of Christianity to redeem social relations and to awaken the conscience of churches as a means of producing communal harmony in keeping with Christian principles. As years went by, Ely moved from concerns about labor strife to questions of land use and corporate responsibility for natural resources. In all his activity from the Progressive era to that of the New Deal, from the Knights of Labor to questions of national forests and mineral reserves, he remained faithful to ideas of stewardship, a custodial obligation for both the earth and the welfare of its inhabitants.

Bibliography:

A.   *The Past and Present of Political Economy* (Baltimore, 1884); *The Labor Movement in America* (New York, 1886); *The Social Aspects of Christianity, and other Essays* (New York, 1889); *Outlines of Economics* (New York, 1893 and many subsequent editions); *The Social Law of Service* (New York, 1896); *Ground Under Our Feet: An Auto-biography* (New York, 1938).

B.   NCAB B, 204–05; DAB supp 3, 248–51; NYT 5 Oct 1943, 25; Benjamin G. Radar, *The Academic Mind and Reform: The Influences of Richard T. Ely in American Life* (Lexington, KY, 1966).

EMBURY, Philip (September 1728, Ballingrane, Ireland—August 1773?, Washington County, NY).

A second generation refugee from the Rhineland Palatinate, Embury was raised a Lutheran in Ireland but espoused Wesleyan convictions in 1752. He soon became an active class leader in County Limerick, learning carpentry as a trade and preaching as local opportunity allowed. Proposed as an itinerant in 1758, he was placed on the reserve list probably because of his plans to marry. Two years later he and a small band of Palatines sailed aboard the packet *Perry* for New York. Embury may have attempted some preaching, but there is no evidence of continued effort; indeed, several of his children were baptized in the Lutheran church during this interim. But by 1766 his cousin, *Barbara Heck, was so exasperated at the low spiritual condition of her fellow immigrants that she persuaded the reluctant carpenter to resume preaching. Classes were held in his home, then in a rented room, finally in a narrow loft designed for rigging sails. Though Embury was not an official minister, he stands as the first Wesley-trained exhorter to organize a church in the American colonies. The loft on William Street grew crowded, thanks to the aid of ''Captain'' Thomas Webb, who also preached there. By 1768 a separate building was erected on John Street, with Embury delivering the chapel's dedicatory sermon in October of that year. Official missionaries soon began to arrive from Britain, honorably releasing the original minister, who was still a layman, from such responsibilities. By 1770 he rejoined his countrymen on a farm up the Hudson valley, still preaching among them each Sabbath and organizing Wesleyan societies around Camden, Salem, and Ashgrove. Death occurred before he could consolidate much of this missionary activity, but he held a place of considerable significance in the first crucial years of Methodist beginnings in the New World.

Bibliography:

B.   AAP 7, 1–3; SH 4, 119; NCAB 3, 523; DAB 6, 125–26; NCE 5, 301.

EMERSON, Ralph Waldo (25 May 1803, Boston, MA—27 April 1882, Concord, MA). *Education*: B.A., Harvard Coll., 1821; studied at Harvard Div. Sch., 1825–26. *Career*: instructor in private school, Boston, 1821–25; minister, Second Congregational Church, Boston, 1829–32; travel and study in Europe, 1832–33; private life with travel for lectures, Concord, 1833–82.

As son of an eminent Boston cleric, Emerson fulfilled expectations by attending Harvard and preparing for the Unitarian ministry. That comprised the extent of his orthodoxy, however, because he emerged after resigning a pastorate in 1832 as one of the chief critics of his denomination as well as the larger assumptions of American Protestantism. Emerson's facility for poetic expression was vehicle to his moral imagination and distinctive views of the natural world, qualities which made him an outstanding spokesman for the Transcendentalist movement in this country. He was not self-consciously the leader of a school of thought, but over decades of formulation he became sage, seer, and articulate embodiment of new religious conceptions, which greatly affected liberal theology for the rest of the century. His essentially monistic perspective held that all things proceed from the same creative spirit; nature is the product of one mind and will whose activity is discernible everywhere. Awareness of this supreme law evoked in man a religious sentiment constituting his highest happiness. Instead of allowing separations between man and God, he argued that it was better to see the universe as an ever new creation where men lived by moral principles known through intuition. Miracle was not interruption in such a world, but at one with the blowing clover and falling rain. The shining laws of virtue were so ordered that the world mirrored the soul. His holistic vision comprehended both laws of gravity and purity of heart, rounding all into a coherent system of duty, science, beauty, and joy.

While controversy was not the context in which Emerson chose to express himself, much of his reforming message was framed in a way that made it inevitable. In 1838 he urged prospective ministers at Harvard to cast behind them all restraints of conformity in order to acquaint men at first hand with Deity. He called for no new cultus nor a softening of doctrines because such weak measures were still tied to authoritarian patterns. His indictment of orthodoxy stemmed not so much from its being in error as from its stultifying effect on individual communion with the Over Soul. Emerson called for nothing less than a fundamental change of heart, a consent to Being that cannot be taught through history or heritage. His humanitarian affirmation of Jesus stressed the early example of vibrant moral truth, a capacity open for all to appropriate. But Jesus was not a final authority any more than scriptures, churches, or creeds. At bottom, nothing was sacred but the integrity of divine reason immanent in every person. He urged freedom in both religion and society to permit individual realization of whatever potentialities lay within human souls. Prevailing authorities were naturally shocked by Emerson's challenge, but his emphasis on religious affections struck a responsive note in many who were alienated by spiritual restrictions of their day. There is more than a grain of truth in the observation that he is the only citizen of the New World worthy of having his name ranked with Plato.

Bibliography:

A.   *The Complete Works of Ralph Waldo Emerson*, ed. Edward W. Emerson, 12 vols. (Boston, 1903–04); *Journals of . . . Emerson*, ed. Edward W. Emerson and Waldo E. Forbes, 10 vols. (Boston, 1909–14); *The Letters of . . . Emerson*, ed. Ralph L. Rusk, 6 vols. (New York, 1939).

B.   NCAB 3, 416–18; DAB 6, 132–41; NCE 5, 302–03; NYT 28 Apr 1882, 1; James E. Cabot, *Memoir of Ralph Waldo Emerson*, 2 vols. (Boston, 1887); George E. Woodberry, *Ralph Waldo Emerson* (New York, 1907); Ralph L. Rusk, *The Life of Ralph Waldo Emerson* (New York, 1949); Sherman Paul, *Emerson's Angle of Vision* (Cambridge, MA, 1952); Stephen E. Whicher, *Freedom and Fate* (Philadelphia, 1953).

EMMONS, Nathaniel (1 May 1745, East Haddam, CT—23 September 1840, Franklin, MA). *Education*: B.A., Yale Coll., 1767; studied theology with Nathan Strong, Coventry, CT, and John Smalley, Berlin, CT, 1767–69. *Career*: unattached supply preacher, 1769–73; minister, Franklin, MA, 1773–1827; retirement, 1827–40.

Of all those perpetuating Edwardsean emphases in theology, Emmons was regarded by many to be the boldest thinker among them. That reputation probably accrued more because of his fearless expression than of his creative formulation of opinions. But his influential preaching helped shape the Hopkinsian version of New England theology. In addition to producing volumes of systematically arranged, didactic sermons, he trained upwards of one hundred men for the Congregationalist ministry, educating more students than any other individual of his generation. Emmons' preaching stressed standard doctrines, including the sole causality of God. Good or bad human conduct was, he held, a series of exercises of which God was the immediate agent. He also believed that God had put an inclination toward evil in Adam's heart, an area affecting volition not the rational faculties. For that reason sin lay in the sinning, consisting of exercises freely willed on man's part while in keeping with the providential guidance of things. He gave less weight than his intellectual predecessors to depraved nature or inherited dispositions, but liberals such as *Timothy Dwight thought he made God unfairly responsible for sin. Emmons adjusted Calvinism to nineteeth century idioms somewhat, but his ideas retained a basically conservative cast while making room for evangelical concentration on redemptive experience.

Questions of ecclesiastical policy formed another realm where Emmons made a lasting impact. In 1803 it was proposed that Massachusetts Congregational churches form a state association similar to the pattern which had long existed in Connecticut. Emmons spoke out strongly against such a measure, insisting that the full power of church government remain in the hands of local membership where it had traditionally resided. He epitomized the democratic quality of Congregationalism in arguing that no higher judicatory should be allowed to override the decisions made by a duly recognized, autonomous body. In a telescopic prediction notable for hyperbole if not historical accuracy, he warned that association led to consociation, then successively to Presbyterianism, Episcopalianism, and Roman Catholicism. The 1803 proposal was defeated, simultaneously preserving separatism and preventing national cooperation in the denomination. A strong missionary program for western territories also suffered as a result. Within the state, however, Emmons was an active supporter of home missions and edited for a time the *Massachusetts Missionary Magazine*. He retired from active preaching when old age began to tell on him, but he continued to express himself on current topics with a vigor characteristic of all his declamations.

Bibliography:

A.   *The Works of Nathaniel Emmons*, ed. Jacob Ide, 6 vols. (Boston, 1842–45).

B.   AAP 1, 693–706; SH 4, 121; NCAB 5, 141; DAB 6, 150–51; NCE 5, 308; Edwards A. Park, *Memoir of Nathaniel Emmons* (Boston, 1861).

ENGLAND, John (23 September 1786, Cork, Ireland—11 April 1842, Charleston, SC). *Education*: studied law, 1800–02; studied for the priesthood at Coll. of Carlow, Ireland, 1802–08. *Career*: cathedral lecturer, chaplain to convent, reformatory, and prison, inspector of schools, Cork, Ireland, 1808–12; rector, Bandon, Ireland, 1817–20; bishop of Charleston, SC, 1820–42.

As a young Irish priest, England became embroiled in resisting a plan by which the British government could control nominations to episcopal sees. Fame as a successful agitator won him transferal to an isolated pastorate in a Protestant village, and his elevation to bishop was popularly understood as a move by aristocratic prelates to rid themselves of an irreconcilable democrat. Reaching this country in 1820 he found that his diocese, comprising both the Carolinas and Georgia, contained no more than 5,000 scattered Catholics, five missionary priests, and a few nondescript buildings. He began immediately to rectify matters for his followers, providing instruction with a new missal and catechism, affording greater encouragement through constant visitations. When nativist attacks on his church caused some to worry about the place of Catholicism in American life, England was quick to answer. In 1822 he founded the *United States Catholic Miscellany*, the first Catholic newspaper in America, and wrote or edited most of its material for two decades. The bishop was a prolific, provocative journalist whose pen was never idle in refuting calumnies against his coreligionists. The paper made him a national figure. Negro slavery was another matter, however, and though he may have found the system personally repugnant, England did not advocate democracy to the point of supporting abolition. He argued that his church sought to protect the rights of bondmen while it sanctioned their lowly status, noting ironically that most of them fared better than Irish peasants. Still he tried to improve their condition with a free school (1835), but slaveowners soon put an end to that libertarian venture.

The growth of Catholic institutions was high among the bishop's priorities and he worked indefatigably to develop native-born clergy for an American branch of the universal church. In 1825 he established a seminary, organized a diocesan community of religious in 1829, and later (1833) imported Ursuline nuns to supplement educational and charitable programs. As one favorable to democracy, he had no difficulty in working with both clerical and lay delegates to construct a diocesan constitution. The "trusteemania" wracking churches in Richmond, Philadelphia, and New York did not reach such proportions in Charleston; nor did England find it disagreeable to cooperate with trustees for the sake of internal harmony. But for all this, he was considered radical by much of the hierarchy, particularly by archbishop *Ambrose Maréchal to whom England probably represented revolutionary tendencies already experienced in his Gallic homeland. England in turn thought the French ecclesiastics were an obstacle to Catholic advance in this country, and he urged appointment of more Irish clergy to posts of leadership. He persisted in asking that provincial councils be called to formulate broad policy guidelines. Four such meetings were convened in his lifetime. During the last years he grew pessimistic over slight Catholic growth despite large numbers of new citizens and left a legacy of great determination to see that the immigrant kept the faith.

Bibliography:

A.   *The Works of the Right Reverend John England*, ed. Ignatius A. Reynolds, 5 vols. (Baltimore, 1849); ed. Sebastian G. Messmer, 7 vols. (Milwaukee, 1908).

B.   NCAB 5, 28–29; DAB 6, 161–63; NCE 5, 352–53; Peter Guilday, *The Life and Times of John England, 1786–1842: First Bishop of Charleston*, 2 vols. (New York, 1927, 1969); Joseph L. O'Brien, *John England, Bishop of Charleston: The Apostle to Democracy* (New York, 1934); Dorothy F. Grant, *John England; American Christopher* (Milwaukee, 1949); Patrick Carey, *An Immigrant Bishop: John England's Adaptation of Irish Catholicism to American Republicanism* (Yonkers, NY, 1982).

EVANS, Warren Felt (23 December 1817, Rockingham, VT—4 September 1889, Salisbury, MA). *Education*: studied at Middlebury Coll., 1837–38; studied at Dartmouth Coll., 1838–40. *Career*: Methodist minister in NH and MA, 1844–64; practitioner and teacher of mental curing, Boston and Salisbury, MA, 1867–89.

After serving in a number of small Methodist churches for two decades, Evans was slowly drawn to conceptions of Christian truth that existing denominations refused to take seriously. After 1863 when a nervous disorder was cured by Phineas P. Quimby, he became a proponent of the view that healthy bodies are effected by purified souls. He associated briefly with a Swedenborgian church (1864–69) and thereafter searched independently for a metaphysical structure to support his central convictions. Evans was the first American mental healer to publish his ideas; those literary efforts, comprising unique formulations plus acquaintance with a wide range of philosophical, religious, and scientific authors, had a formative influence on later developments in New Thought. His understanding of the intimate connection between physical health and spiritual well-being was based on the correspondence of natural and spiritual worlds. Material entities have counterparts in the ideal world that correspond to the essence of reality. In fact, God is the only Reality or Central Life from whom all things emanate and to whom they return. Evans discerned this Pure Infinitude manifested in the Christ principle, in man's rational soul, and in all nature. After developing this monistic ontological conception, he concluded that the visible universe is an imaginary scene, something with apparent existence but having reality only in the mind. Such ideas unlocked the deeper mysteries of Christianity and disclosed how one could rise above materialism to return to the intuition of pure thought.

The historical Jesus did not exhaust the Evans' perspective, because all men are included in the being of Divine Man. Jesus was the greatest exemplar of realizing that one is part of a larger whole, and he still mediates as individuals progress toward perfection of religious truth. Evans grounded his philosophy in both modern idealism and ancient precedents when he declared that thought alone is actually existent. The body is, at length, unreal, an illusory prison of the soul that confines man's true nature within artificial material limits. As a practitioner of mental cure, Evans held disease to be not so much physical derangement as a manifestation of abnormal mental states. All disease corresponded to mistaken ideas; it vanished when false notions were replaced by true ones. Anyone suffering acute pain or distress had to realize that the deepest reality of illness is mental, not physical. The aim, then, of what he called "phrenopathic practice" was to help people reject bondage to their senses by recognizing their true nature. That was the first step on the pathway to health and spiritual awareness. Through a series of practical methods, not miracles, Evans attempted to help persons live in accord with natural laws and enhance their spiritual being. His writings are an important link between transcendentalists of an earlier day and "Christian Science," a term he employed fifteen years before it came into vogue with the teachings of *Mary B. Eddy.

Bibliography:

A.   *The Mental-Cure* (Boston, 1869); *Mental Medicine* (Boston, 1872); *Soul and Body* (Boston, 1876); *The Divine Law of Cure* (Boston, 1876); *The Primitive Mind Cure* (Boston, 1885); *Esoteric Christianity and Mental Therapeutics* (Boston, 1886).
B.   NCAB 22, 429–30; DAB 6, 213–14.

EWING, Finis (10 June 1773, Bedford County, VA—4 July 1841, Lexington, MO). *Career*: farmer, Logan County, KY, 1794–1800; licensed preacher and revivalist, 1800–10; part-time minister, Lebanon, KY, 1812–20; minister, New Lebanon, MO, 1820–36; minister, Lexington, KY, 1836–41.

Growing up on the Tennessee frontier without much formal education, Ewing married the daughter of a Revolutionary War hero and settled down as a prosperous farmer in Kentucky by 1794. The couple joined a Presbyterian church in nearby Russelville, though the decision reflected more social conformity than religious conviction. But *James McGready was minister there, and when the great period of revivals began to break out in 1800, Ewing experienced a vivid conversion under his pastor's preaching. That same year he volunteered to exhort, counsel, and speak wherever allowed in order to increase the spiritual quickenings that soon rose to gratifying numbers. Ordained by the Cumberland presbytery in 1803 he proved to be an indefatigable worker for revivals. He spoke with tangible power at hundreds of camp meetings and in more settled congregations. Some Presbyterians opposed the revivals, however, and criticized the creation of ministers such as Ewing who had no academic training. The main problem, though, was that many pro-revival preachers had reservations about the doctrine of predestination as stated in the Westminster Confession, customary theological standard for Presbyterians. Since revivalists were more inclined to emphasize free will and human initiative in the reception of grace, conservatives in the Synod of Kentucky tried to silence them by dissolving the Cumberland presbytery in 1806.

Enthusiasm for continuing what they viewed as God's work led Ewing and others to persevere in evangelical efforts. By 1810 they revived the Cumberland presbytery as an independent body; further success in conversions and recruitment led in 1813 to the Synod of Cumberland and in the following year to a full-fledged Cumberland Presbyterian Church. Ewing was recognized as one of the founders of this new denomination, along with Samuel King and Samuel McAdow, and he became its most influential early leader. He presided over church meetings and fostered all of its expanding concerns. He championed its theological position against Calvinists and Arminians alike and was the principal author of the *Circular Letter* that explained Cumberland doctrine as a revision of the Westminster Confession. By 1820 he followed migrating Kentuckians into Missouri where he continued to labor unceasingly in organizing more churches. Religious work was more a vocation than a profession for Ewing. Finances from his farm allowed him time for preaching, and after 1836 placement as Register of a Land Office in Missouri did the same. By the time of his death several generations acknowledged "Father Ewing" as the central figure in their denomination's origins and an essential contributor to its rapid success.

Bibliography:

A.   *A Series of Lectures on the Most Important Subjects in Divinity* (Fayetteville, TN, 1827; several rev. and enl. eds., Nashville, TN, 1870).

B.   SH 4, 235; NCAB 11, 423; DAB 6, 233–34; F.R. Crossitt, *The Life and Times of Rev. Finis Ewing* (Louisville, KY, 1853).

F

FAHS, Sophia Blanche Lyon (2 August 1876, Hangchow, China—17 April 1978, Hamilton, OH). *Education*: B.A. Wooster Coll., 1897; studied at Univ. of Chicago, 1901–02; M.A. Columbia Univ., 1904; B.D. Union Sem. (NY), 1926. *Career*: high school teacher, Wooster, OH, 1897–99; traveling secretary, Student Volunteer Movement, 1899–1901; lecturer in Religious Education, Union Sem. (NY), 1927–44; editor (1937–54) and consultant (1954–64), New Beacon Series in Religious Education, 1937–64; active retirement, 1964–78.

Born to missionary parents in China but reared principally in Ohio, Sophia Lyon developed strong views about personal religious effectiveness long before she married similar-minded Charles H. Fahs in 1902. As a mother of four and greatly interested in religious education, she became increasingly dissatisfied with instructional methods currently employed by most churches. After much reading, independent thinking and attempts to answer her own children's questions, she concluded that fresh approaches were needed to develop honest, emotionally healthy religion among the young. Testing her new methods at Teachers College Sunday School, the Union School of Religion and finally Riverside Church, all in New York, Mrs. Fahs pioneered in improving religious education by taking seriously the psychology of child development. Beginning with Bible stories and real life dramas, she avoided abstract ideas in preference for specific details which conveyed vivid, accurate information. She sought to relate curriculum to the child's own growing experience, one which helped each one mature at their own pace by assimilating larger circles of relationships with others. Adjusting her lessons to the life situations of various students, she deliberately tried to counteract the prevailing attitude: "Except ye become as grownups, ye cannot enter the kingdom of God." In 1927 she became one of the first women ever appointed to the faculty of Union Theological Seminary. Another mark of her eminence is that a remarkably popular series of juvenile books (*Martin and Judy*) were used by many Protestant denominations and several liberal Jewish schools as well.

Innovative techniques in religious instruction led Fahs by the early 1930s to revise her ideas about the content of such education. She found that many contemporary problems were not dealt with in the Bible, and consequently additional sources were necessary as basic texts. The Bible was not really a children's book; attempts to convey truth without mystification called for reducing the importance of Scripture if not abandoning it altogether. After years of practical experience she concluded that religious education for the science-oriented child of modern times was best pursued by emphasizing an open, growing spiritual awareness. Proper learning could not take place if faith was considered a static body of knowledge, already completed before young people appropriated it. Furthermore, she thought Christianity to be only one of many expressions of the truth. Students should not be limited arbitrarily to a single heritage in their independent search for meaning and individual fulfillment. By 1937 this perspective led her to join the American Unitarian Association (merged with Universalists, 1961), but even there some critics charged that she evacuated all positive content from confessional contexts. Nevertheless she persisted in writing, experimenting and conducting teachers' workshops to encourage a complex number of approaches toward sound pedagogical accomplishment. Her efforts spanning more than six decades were a significant factor in defining modern educational needs from the child's point of view.

Bibliography:

A.   *Red, Yellow and Black* (New York, 1918); *Beginnings of Earth and Sky* (Boston, 1937); *Jesus: The Carpenter's Son* (Boston, 1945); *Today's Children and Yesterday's Heritage* (Boston, 1952); *The Old Story of Salvation* (Boston, 1955); *Worshipping Together with Questioning Minds* (Boston, 1965).

B.   NYT 19 Apr 1978, II, 10.

FEEHAN, Patrick Augustine (29 August 1829, Killenaule, Ireland—12 July 1902, Chicago, IL). *Education*: studied at Castle Knock Coll., 1845–47; graduated from Maynooth Coll., 1852. *Career*: instructor, Carondelet Sem., 1852–53; assistant pastor, St. John's Church, St. Louis, MO, 1853–54; president, Carondelet Sem., 1854–58; pastor, St. Michael's Church, St. Louis, MO, 1858–59; pastor, Church of the Immaculate Conception, St. Louis, MO, 1859–64; bishop of Nashville, 1865–80; archibishop of Chicago, 1880–1902.

The five year seminary course at Ireland's famed College of Maynooth prepared Feehan well for the trials of parish life. But more important than scholarly ability, he added a sense of self-sacrifice and devotion to duty that made his ministry particularly effective among those he touched. As pastor in St. Louis, he became widely known for charitable activity among the sick and poor, helping all those needful in either mind or body. During the Civil War he administered sacraments to soldiers brought north from the battlefields. He comforted the dying and converted many through simple acts of kindness. By war's end he was chosen to restore order in the chaotic diocese of Nashville, devastated by war and demoralized by military occupation. There were only three secular priests in Tennessee when he arrived; together they began the slow task of rebuilding churches, recruiting more clergy, and planning for future growth. The new bishop greatly aided Sisters of Mercy in their educational establishments. He labored hard to extend the whole range of religious institutions, which both served church members and won new followers in the process. Perhaps no example of his leadership can equal that exhibited during the yellow fever and cholera epidemics at Memphis (1873, 1878). In those trying times his personnel gained unprecedented, lasting respect for Catholicism because of their work to alleviate the suffering of others.

As first archbishop of Chicago, Feehan brought much needed administrative stability to that rapidly expanding jurisdiction. During his twenty-two years there, the Catholic population increased fourfold (to 800,000), and under his farsighted planning the institutions kept pace with population. With sound financial backing, he inaugurated a vast building program; hospitals, orphanages, and homes for the aged met some of the need. But education was the archbishop's chief concern, one given added force by deliberations in the Third Plenary Council of 1884. He was firmly opposed to state-controlled schools or any other form of education which neglected moral and religious training for the child. Parochial schools mushroomed at his instigation, growing from 88 to 166 and containing almost 63,000 students by the end of his tenure. Chicago had become a polyglot metropolis; Feehan hoped slowly to blend Italian, Polish, German, and Czechoslovakian immigrants into a homogenous citizenry, but he did not rashly order them to abandon nationalistic customs at once. Under the rule of one church he permitted the continuance of various languages in local congregations. In this instance, as in many others, his mild administrative technique was conservative, tempered with personal humility and contagious good will. A friend to laymen as well as clerical subordinates, he finished out his days trying to advance the interests of the church in dutiful service to God and neighbor.

Bibliography:

    B. NCAB 9, 80–81; DAB 6, 311–12; NCE 5, 875–76; NYT 13 Jul 1902, 13; Cornelius J. Kirkfleet, *The Life of Patrick Augustine Feehan* (Chicago, 1922).

FILLMORE, Charles Sherlock (22 August 1854, near St. Cloud, MN—5 July 1948, Lee's Summit, MO). *Career*: director, Unity School of Christianity, 1889–1933; editor, *Unity (Modern Thought* and other titles before 1895), 1889–1933.

Life was not too successful for Fillmore in jobs such as office clerk, teamster or in the boom and bust extremes of real estate. After the health of his wife, *Myrtle, began to improve in 1886, he made a serious study of the metaphysical wisdom which she insisted was at the root of her recovery. Through a long process of doubt and testing, conviction slowly came. At the same time he saw a practical demonstration of spiritual truth when his rheumatic leg, crippled since a boyhood accident and worn in a brace, began to heal. By 1889 he and his wife had determined their real vocation: sharing with others the peace of mind, inner harmony, and mental health they had experienced. Most of Charles' ideas were compatible with traditional Christian tenets, though an admixture of theosophy, mind-cure, and reincarnation gave larger scope to his thinking. His voluminous writing in magazines, tracts, and a dozen books spread a gospel of human perfectibility patterned after Christ's example. He emphasized the potential for good, or "spiritual ethers," latent in humanity. If one's life were unified with the Christ mind in prayer, then energies could be released to produce health and prosperity in abundance. He offered himself as evidence; by affirming unity with the infinite energy of the one true God, he perpetually retained youthful vigor. Going beyond his wife's view of death, he taught a doctrine of immortality for those who obeyed the laws of right thinking and right living. Death could be conquered in the present incarnation, after which the spiritually adept would join the Mind behind all minds.

Individuals who sought fulfillment similar to the Fillmores contacted them for help. That help was freely given, especially in prayer and counsel on practical difficulties. The Unity School of Christianity was founded in 1889 (incorporated, 1903, as a nonprofit organization) to facilitate this aid. Charles' ideas were not at all esoteric; in fact the many enterprises connected with his name developed primarily as ways to make the School's teachings more readily available. He insisted that Unity operations constituted a school, not another sectarian church, whose teachings simply added extra dimensions to more familiar religious tenets. Within a few decades, however, hundreds of local Unity Centers functioned as churches, holding regular services in major cities. With headquarters in Kansas City, Missouri, teachers were trained to serve these units as ministers. Financial support came through unsolicited contributions, and mounting income warranted larger buildings, an immense publishing empire, and a large agricultural tract with cheap homes for those agreeing with Unity ideals. Millions of correspondents contacted officials over the years. Literature and prayers at set times of the day were a source of comfort to casual acquaintances as well as devoted followers. By 1933 Mr. Fillmore began turning over direction of the School's many affairs to his two surviving sons. He retired from what had amounted to a pulpit (held since 1893), remarried, and conducted speaking tours from Illinois to southern California. Until the end his keen faith in metaphysical healing remained a vital force in the movement, which continues to flourish.

Bibliography:

    A. *Christian Healing* (Kansas City, MO, 1909). *Talks of Truth* (Kansas City, MO, 1926); *The Twelve Powers of Man* (Kansas City, MO, 1930); *Jesus Christ Heals* (Kansas City, MO, 1939); *Atom-Smashing Power of the Mind* (Kansas City, MO, 1949); *The Revealing Word* (Kansas City, MO, 1959).

B.   NCAB B, 58–59; DAB 24, 270–72; Hugh D'Andrade, *Charles Fillmore: Herald of the New Age* (New York, 1974).

FILLMORE, Myrtle Page (6 August 1845, Pagetown, OH—6 October 1931, Lee's Summit, MO). *Education*: studied at Oberlin Coll., 1868–69. *Career*: schoolteacher, Clinton, OH, 1869–75, and Denison, TX, 1875–78; co-editor, *Unity (Modern Thought* and other titles before 1895), 1892–1923; editor, *Wee Wisdom*, 1893–1923.

Experience in the life of this individual (née Mary Caroline Page) were catalytic in founding the Unity School of Christianity. She had been troubled for years by tuberculosis until 1886 when lectures by a disciple of *Emma C. Hopkins marked the turning point of her life. It suddenly became clear that since she was a child of God, sickness was not part of her inheritance. She perceived her health steadily improving as a result of that striking insight; after complete recovery she devoted herself to helping others see the "beautiful law" of spiritual healing. Through her suffering she reached the conclusion that God was a supreme power who could, by means of fixed laws, overcome all disabilities, material and spiritual. Her conviction was an inspiration to others, and she served as an avenue of harmonious strength for everyone contacting her over the years. Mrs. Fillmore embodied proof that concepts usually categorized under the rubric of New Thought could produce wondrous effects in human lives. Her message was disseminated largely through the mails, in articles written for the Unity School's publications and in private correspondence. She answered thousands of letters from persons who sought advice or spiritual consolation. All her many writings contained a special blend of ideals, which made her thought distinctive and gratifying to a large, popular following.

The heart of Mrs. Fillmore's ministry lay in prayer. Together with her husband, *Charles, she was in every sense the co-founder and mutual guide of Unity School operations, but practical efforts through prayer for those asking it remained her forte. By 1891 the Society of Silent Unity gave form to what she called a sanctuary of continuous prayer in which all could participate. In this simple, hopeful faith she accepted the material world as real but stressed the power of prayerful thought to overcome its problems. Mental healing and prosperity would, she hoped, help build a new humanity strengthened in knowledge of divine laws as expressed in right thinking and right living. Another aspect of her beliefs rested on reincarnation. She thought of death as simply laying aside the physical body for a time, a temporary break in the conscious connection with material existence. It did not imply an end of spiritual existence or exclusion from further corporeal life. Rebirth occurred when the divine urge prompted one to build another physical temple for more earthly experiences. This faith was sustained by practical results in her own life, and she labored selflessly to share the benefits with others. Correspondents through the Midwest and Pacific coast were governed by her counsel while the institution based on family leadership continues to the present.

Bibliography:

A. *Myrtle Fillmore's Healing Letters* (Kansas City, MO, 1936).
B. NAW 1, 617–19.

FINLEY, James Bradley (1 July 1781, NC—6 September 1856, Cincinnati OH). *Career*: itinerant Methodist minister in OH, 1809–56.

The son of a Presbyterian minister itinerating in southern colonies, Finley was born at a place in North Carolina lost to historical record. The family soon moved west, trying locations in Kentucky and then Ohio, where young Finley came to love the wild freedoms of frontier life. If we can rely on his reminiscences, he grew up rugged and resourceful, a crack shot and ready to brawl at the drop of a hat. But his pioneering was not completely undisciplined; he received a thorough drilling in Latin and Greek at his father's classical academy, thus acquiring an education better than most frontiersmen whose company he chose. He also learned enough about practicing medicine to be known as a doctor, but his delight was hunting in the vast Ohio woodlands. In 1801 he attended a revival at Cane Ridge, Kentucky, and fell under conviction of sin. For the next seven years he felt called to preach but hesitated to accept such a serious vocation. After alternating periods of depression and abandon, unable to resist any longer, he finally joined the Methodist church in 1808 and began his first appointment on the Scioto circuit one year later. Since he was already hardened to backwoods conditions, the ordeals encountered as a traveling preacher posed no new hazard. Finley ministered faithfully for decades, wearing his wolfskin hat and leather hunting shirt to preach in cabins, barns, or courthouses. Like hundreds of others he prayed and exhorted wherever possible to apply the benefits of his office.

Following the Methodist custom of tending a different circuit almost every year, Finley served his denomination's churches in Ohio during a ministry spanning fifty years. He honored the wishes of bishop *William McKendree by consolidating mission work among the Wyandot Indians. These peoples were remnants of the Huron nation which fled south after defeat in 1649 by the Iroquois. Finley had favored Indian customs as a boy and found it easy to assimilate himself to them again as a missionary. From 1820 to 1827 one of his main responsibilities was to teach them essentials of the white man's moral and social patterns. Other duties over the years included posts as district superintendent, chaplain at the state penitentiary, and representative to General Conferences. Finley was elected eight times to attend those conventions where he debated issues of national importance. One such issue was slavery, a topic on which he held strong convictions. He was polite in address but inflexible in purpose, insisting that Methodists could not sanction human bondage. It was his resolution which passed the Conference of 1844 and required *James O. Andrew to suspend episcopal functions until his slaves were freed. Of course he did not intend to produce a sectional split within the church, but that price was worth paying to avoid compromising on the slavery question. Finley continued all his pastoral duties, preaching by the end of his life to vastly increased congregations in cities where only villages once had stood.

Bibliography:

A. *History of the Wyandott Mission* (Cincinnati, 1840); *Memorials of Prison Life* (Cincinnati, 1850); *Autobiography of Rev. James B. Finley* (Cincinnati, 1853); *Sketches of Western Methodism* (New York, 1854, 1969); *Life Among the Indians* (Cincinnati, 1857).

B. AAP 7, 531–33; NCAB 12, 557; DAB 6, 389–90.

FINNEY, Charles Grandison (29 August 1792, Warren, CT—16 August 1875, Oberlin, OH). *Career*: schoolteacher, Henderson, NY, 1808–12; schoolteacher in NJ, 1814–16; studied and practiced law, Adams, NY, 1818–21; revivalist principally in NY, 1821–32; minister, Second Free Presbyterian Church, New York, 1832–36; minister, Broadway Tabernacle, New York, 1836–37; professor of Theology, Oberlin Coll., 1835–75; minister, First Congregational Church, Oberlin, OH, 1835–72; president, Oberlin Coll., 1851–66.

At the age of twenty-nine, Finney abandoned a promising law practice after receiving what he called a retainer from Jesus Christ to plead His cause. In so doing he inaugurated a new era in American revivalism. Largely self-taught in previous studies, he brought the same independence of mind to theological education where he worked out his own views through private study of Scripture. He was ordained a Presbyterian in 1824 but never ascribed to Calvinistic tenets as perceived through any recognizable interpretation. Beginning as an evangelist in small towns and gaining fame and notoriety enough to draw invitations from larger cities, he preached a gospel emphasizing every individual's ability to repent. Finney provided a rationale more clearly than anyone else in his generation to end predestinarian thinking among revivalists of the early national period. It was as easy to choose right, he held, as it was to continue in the wrong. Christ's death removed the burden of sin, but there was no passive regeneration. His own conversion experience confirmed the idea that all men could repent by deliberate choice and be saved immediately; damnation was reserved for those who willfully rejected God's benevolent amnesty. Finney also set new standards for pulpit oratory. His logical arguments, expressive language, and urgent appeals for decisions persuaded thousands to respond with unexpected fervor. His exclusive concentration on salvation gave new form to the revival sermon too, eliminating everything that distracted listeners from the central objective of personal acceptance of Christ as Saviour.

Orthodoxy was what Finney considered acceptable to reason and experience; on that pragmatic ground he developed techniques for promoting conversions which have survived in professional evangelism to this day. Some of his "new measures" produced a sensation, causing liberals such as *Lyman Beecher initially to disclaim association with rude western customs. Allowing women to pray in public or making direct appeals to persons in the audience affronted the good taste of many. The use of protracted meetings and the anxious bench seemed to others theologically unsound, but Finney defended all those procedures because they helped force individuals to make a definite faith commitment without delay. He also adopted much of the perfectionism inherent in Second Great Awakening enthusiasm, maintaining that sin and holiness cannot exist in the same person. It was possible to reach such a peak of Christian experience that one could overcome moral weakness and live, in effect, without serious failings. Finney concentrated on reforming individuals rather than society and treated complex issues such as slavery with a pietistic optimism relevant to millennial conceptions instead of practical circumstances. His insistence that churches keep themselves at a revival pitch yielded an institutionalized outlet for pietistic fervor. An emphasis on practical results eclipsed theological subtleties but provided an effective method of renewal and church growth. The pragmatic test of new conversions became a major aspect of Protestant vitality, remaining a factor long after the passing of the acknowledged dean of modern evangelism.

Bibliography:

A. *Lectures on Revivals of Religion* (New York, 1835); *Sermons on Various Subjects* (New York, 1835); *Sermons on Important Subjects* (New York, 1836); *Lectures on Systematic Theology*, 2 vols. (New York, 1846–47; London, 1851); *Memoirs* (New York, 1876); *Lectures to Professing Christians* (Oberlin, OH, 1880).

B. SH 4, 316–17; NCAB 2, 462–64; DAB 6, 394–96; NCE 5, 928; NYT 17 Aug 1875, 4; George F. Wright, *Charles Grandison Finney* (Boston, 1891); Frank G. Beardsley, *A Mighty Winner of Souls* (New York, 1937); William G. McLoughlin, *Modern Revivalism* (New York, 1959); Nancy Hardesty, *Your Daughters Shall Prophesy: Revivalism and Feminism in the Age of Finney* (Brooklyn, NY, 1991).

FISK, Wilbur (31 August 1792, Brattleboro, VT—22 February 1839, Middletown, CT). *Education*: studied at Univ. of Vermont, 1812–13; B.A., Brown Univ., 1815; studied law, Lyndon, VT, 1815–16. *Career*: private tutor near Baltimore, MD, 1816–17; itinerant Methodist minister in VT and MA, 1818–25; principal, Wesleyan Acad., 1826–30; president, Wesleyan Univ., 1830–39.

Before 1800 Methodist preachers had a general reputation for meager intellectual training, compensating in zeal for what they lacked in education. But Fisk was college bred and gave a tone of greater sophistication to his denomination's activities in New England. Poor health constantly hampered his work; pulmonary hemorrhaging brought him close to death many times. Despite such trials, he preached on circuit in addition to serving as presiding elder (1823–25) in eastern Vermont. The General Conference elected him bishop in 1828, but health was one reason he gave for declining. The other reason was a desire to pursue educational objectives already in progress at the Wilbraham, Massachusetts, academy where he taught. Education for prospective ministers and for well informed lay leadership was Fisk's primary vocational interest. As the first president of Wesleyan University, he advanced the cause of learning among his charges while at the same time retaining a pastoral solicitude for their piety and morals. He opposed creating seminaries for ministerial education, saying that theological training occurred through practical experience instead of concentrated courses. Still, his advocacy of study helped create educational societies in many local conferences.

Lectures, fund-raising tours, and preaching constituted the element in which Fisk felt at home. He was also drawn into several debates but proved a reluctant participant. Some of his printed sermons caused mild theological disputes with Calvinists and Universalists. In 1835 he spoke out against the methods of abolitionists; while not approving of slavery, his social conservatism was taken by many to imply proslavery sentiments. This fact made him acceptable to both northern and southern constituencies of the church, and it led to another election as bishop in 1836. Again he declined because of health. On the more positive side, he was long a promoter of temperance, battling liquor interests at every turn. He also supported missionary efforts to spread Methodist witness abroad, especially to deported freedmen in Liberia, Mohawks in Canada, and Flatheads in Oregon. Always frail, he gained a short lease on life in 1835 with a convalescent tour of Europe. He learned a great deal from major universities there about ways to improve conditions at Wesleyan; yet death came before there was enough time to realize his pioneering efforts in liberal education.

Bibliography:

A. *Calvinistic Controversy* (New York, 1835); *Travels on the Continent of Europe* (New York, 1838).

B. AAP 7, 576–87; SH 4, 320; NCAB 3, 177; DAB 6, 415–16; Joseph Holdich, *The Life of Wilbur Fisk* (New York, 1842); George Prentice, *Wilbur Fisk* (Boston, 1890).

FLAGET, Benedict Joseph (7 November 1763, Contournat, France—11 February 1850, Louisville, KY). *Education*: studied at Clermont (university) 1779–81, (seminary) 1781–83; studied at Issy, 1783–86. *Career*: taught theology at Nantes and Angers, 1786–89; missionary priest, Vincennes, Northwest Territory, 1792–95; teacher and administrator, Georgetown Coll., 1795–98; private tutor, Havana, Cuba, 1798–1801; teacher at St. Mary's Coll., Baltimore, 1801–08; bishop of Bardstown (Louisville after 1841), KY, 1808–50.

Among its unexpected consequences, the French Revolution produced a number of émigré clergy who sought safety and new opportunities in mission fields of the Americas. One such priest, a Sulpician professor of dogmatic theology, reached Baltimore in 1791 and soon found himself in a rude outpost of the universal church. But even there, Flaget labored much to build up numbers of the faithful. At his first Christmas in Vincennes, he was able to persuade only twelve out of 700 nominal Catholics to receive communion. Working through children and then their parents, he slowly won many back to more frequent pious observance. Flaget moved to a succession of teaching posts but discovered to his dismay in 1808 that he had been appointed the first bishop in Kentucky.

With great reluctance he finally accepted jurisdiction over an immense territory that eventually yielded eleven new dioceses during his lifetime. He spent the greater portion of his early episcopacy on horseback, traveling hundreds of miles per month to visit the sick, hear confessions, and administer the sacraments. The frontier, comprising eight future states, held scattered Catholics whom Flaget served with unflagging endurance, giving instruction, discipline, and consolation where needed. He took his own advice to seek rest in heaven, not before, and spent all his energy (except for an extended European tour, 1835–39) to consolidate the western plantings of Catholicity.

As bishop, Flaget supervised the growth of small churches and log chapels, established educational institutions including colleges and a seminary (St. Thomas), and furthered work among Indians and non-Catholics. He encouraged the building of convents, schools, orphanages, and infirmaries with sisterhoods to staff them and lay societies to supply their needs. In 1819 he dedicated at Bardstown the first cathedral west of the Alleghenies and in 1849 laid the cornerstone of a more imposing one at Louisville. He was proud of the fact that one could witness, amid the austere conditions of frontier life, an exact recapitulation of Roman liturgy accompanied by solemn Gregorian chants. At the age of forty-one, Flaget had applied for entry into a Trappist monastery; forty-four years later, he made it possible for Trappists to locate a permanent residence in his diocese at Gethsemani. The fatigue of constant travel, exposure to disease (cholera, 1833), and the cares of office did not quickly wear down this strong missionary. His years of practical activity laid the foundations for Catholic growth and stability at a time that witnessed far greater expansion of Protestant denominations in the same region.

Bibliography:

B.   NCAB 6, 333–34; DAB 6, 445–47; NCE 5, 956–57; Abbe Desgeorge, *Monseigneur Flaget, Eveque de Bardstown et Louisville: Sa Vie, son Esprit et ses Vertus* (Paris, 1851); Martin J. Spalding, *Life, Times and Character of the Right Reverend Benedict Joseph Flaget* (Louisville, 1852; New York, 1969).

FOSDICK, Harry Emerson (24 May 1878, Buffalo, NY—5 October 1969, Bronxville, NY). *Education*: B.A., Colgate Univ., 1900; studied at Colgate Sem., 1900–01; B.D., Union Sem. (NY), 1904; M.A., Columbia Univ., 1908. *Career*: minister, First Baptist Church, Montclair, NJ, 1904–15; part-time instructor, Union Sem., 1908–15; professor of Practical Theology, Union Sem., 1915–34; associate minister, First Presbyterian Church, New York, 1919–25; minister, Park Avenue Baptist Church (Riverside Church after 1931), 1926–46; active retirement, 1946–69.

During the 1920s, conflicts between theological liberals and fundamentalists moved from narrow academic circles to wider arenas of public awareness. This was perhaps best indicated by reactions to Fosdick's sermons, the most effective expression of moderate Protestant liberalism for over two decades. As a ministerial student Fosdick had been greatly influenced by *William N. Clarke and the writings of *Walter Rauschenbusch. Following their lead, he stressed themes such as the indwelling presence of God in man and the world. These provided a basis for social action in addition to beliefs in Christ's divinity, human immortality, and a generally optimistic view of cultural progress. He was one of the first preachers to recognize the possibilities of radio, and after 1922 increased his audience by broadcasting Sunday worship services. His wide dissemination of liberal ideas made him a major figure in relating selected Christian teachings to scientific standards of the twentieth century. Though ordained a Baptist, Fosdick was invited to serve as guest preacher in a large Presbyterian church. His sermon "Shall the Fundamentalists Win?" (1922) served notice that fundamentalist rigidities in biblical interpretation and doctrinal platform could not flourish without rebuttal. For a time he became the storm center of theological dispute. Opposition led by *William J. Bryan clamored to have him removed from office, and a total of twelve overtures were made to the Presbyterian General Assembly for that purpose. In 1923 he offered to resign, but the church refused to let him go. Two years later he did resign instead of submitting himself to ecclesiastical authority or a specific creedal formula.

The events which seemed a victory for sectarian orthodoxy actually allowed Fosdick to move into his most influential period as a Protestant spokesman. The church he served moved to the Morningside Heights section of New York and assumed a deliberate interdenominational, interracial, international stance. Fosdick's insistence that no creedal requirements or modes of baptism should bar membership made him an ecumenical pioneer on the practical level. Riverside Church became a place of religious instruction and social service, an imposing edifice distinctive for its ideology as well as its architecture. Fosdick directed a great number of different programs in a community church where confessional differences did not hinder common worship or social action in the nation's largest city. Most of his ideas remained the same, though economic depression and wars made him less optimistic about social redemption. But he changed radically on the war question. In 1917 he supported entry into the European theater, repented during the subsequent decade, and proved an outspoken pacifist thereafter. In retirement he kept a busy schedule of speaking and writing. For an additional twenty years he looked expectantly to future events rather than dwell upon the memory of past eminence.

Bibliography:

A.   The Meaning of Prayer (New York, 1915, and many subsequent editions); Christianity and Progress (New York, 1922); The Modern Use of the Bible (New York, 1924); The Secret of Victorious Living (New York, 1934); On Being a Real Person (London, 1943); The Living of these Days: An Autobiography (New York, 1956).

B.   NCAB E, 266–67; NYT 6 Oct 1969, 1; Robert M. Miller, Harry Emerson Fosdick: Preacher, Pastor, Prophet (New York: 1985).

FOX, Emmet (30 July 1886, Ireland—13 August 1951, Paris, France). *Career*: lecturer, International New Thought Alliance, Great Britain, 1928–31; minister, Church of the Healing Christ, New York, 1931–51.

After studying for several years at Stamford Hill Jesuit College near London, Fox became a successful electrical engineer largely through his own efforts. But all his spare time was given over to reading New Thought materials, a realm of spiritual exploration which he found more compatible with personal experience than the Catholicism of his parental home. He attended metaphysical lectures as early as 1914 but matured slowly in developing concepts; by 1928 he began speaking under New Thought auspices and within three years became pastor in New York of the largest congregation of that persuasion in the world. Using facilities such as the Astor Hotel, Hippodrome, and finally Carnegie Hall, Fox spoke to capacity crowds about the basic principles of hope and truth as he envisioned them. The most important spiritual law from which everything else derived meaning was a conception of God as the infinite and undefinable Creator of all things. Referred to alternately as Mind (in metaphysics) or Cause (in natural science), this source of all existence could be known through prayer and communication with Its various attributes: life, truth, intelligence, soul, spirit, principle, and ultimately love. The enigmatic preacher assured packed audiences including pilgrims from all over the United States that man's progress is measured by assimilation to this law of perfect harmony. God is the Law of Being; man's understanding of and obedience to that basic principle was the key to harmonizing body, soul, and mind.

It seems on the surface of things that human nature comprised four elements—physical, emotional, intellectual, and spiritual—but Fox insisted there was an essential unity within them. As individuals progress in spiritual knowledge, the first three categories are merged into the final one, the eternal self, and they discover their oneness with Divine Being. Indeed, the true purpose of life is for men to become aware of themselves as focal points of God's self-expression, bringing His ideas into concrete manifestation. Each person under Fox's influence was urged to achieve full realization of one's soul as an individualization of God, to sense the peace and harmony that comes through unity with every other living creature. Physical healing was an aspect of Divine Science that the pastor did not neglect, but it was always considered an external sign of more important spiritual growth. Fox conducted weekly healing services while he led followers to the higher objective of experiencing the glory of God in themselves, building the "house magnifical" of spiritual consciousness. Through private prayer or silent meditation similar to Quaker meetings he sought to help persons discover God's presence in their everyday affairs, at their point of greatest need. Instead of miracles or instantaneous wealth, he offered them strength based on faith, a format primarily for living *right* now and living right *now*. References to life after death were kept to a minimum though he personally looked forward to reincarnations as an eternal aspect of God the True Being.

Bibliography:

    A. *The Sermon on the Mount* (New York, 1934); *Power through Constructive Think-ing* (New York, 1940); *Sparks of Truth* (New York, 1941); *Make Your Life Worth While* (New York, 1946); *Alter Your Life* (New York, 1950); *Stake Your Claim* (New York, 1952).
    B. NYT 18 Aug 1951, 11; Harry Gaze, *Emmet Fox: The Man and His Work* (New York, 1952).

FOX, George (July 1624, Drayton, England—January 1691, London, England). *Career*: itinerant Quaker preacher and author, 1648–91.

The modest beginnings of a weaver's son gave little indication that Fox's preaching would add another sect to the puritanical wing of reform-minded English churches. Apprenticed as shepherd and shoemaker, he had the time to think seriously about religious questions which he was inclined to consider from early childhood. By 1643 brooding over such matters led to periods of depression followed by redoubled efforts to find spiritual consolation. After three more years with no solace in searching Scripture and varied evangelical opinions, Fox con-cluded that the stamp of God's spirit could be effectively known only by inward acquaintance. He perceived that every man received by nature a measure of inner light which, if followed, would lead to the Light of Life itself. Because of that spiritual principle, he rejected the doctrine of human depravity, proclaim-ing instead the equality of men before God. Since direct access to the throne of grace was possible, he refused to be confined to biblical revelation or outward ceremonies of the faith such as creeds, sacraments, national churches, or a hireling ministry. The revolutionary freedom of Divine Light had social impli-cations as well; the promptings of religious experience led him to defy such customs as taking an oath, observing formal modes of speech, removing his hat when expected (e.g., in court), or supporting war efforts. Those responding to the new spiritualist message were known as Children of Light, or Friends of Truth, shortened to Friends, nicknamed Quakers.

The powerful appeal of inner certitude drew to Quaker meetings a variety of seekers and visionaries who worshiped God with little verbal or physical restraint. Outsiders regarded them as fanatics gone mad, but reviling and persecution only heightened their zeal to follow the truth of Divine Light wherever it led. It was Fox's second major contribution to regulate the mystics whom he had attracted. His discipline of silence at worship services had a sobering influence, while the interlocking system of meetings he devised produced a stronger sense of corporate responsibility. Cohesion and stability on the institutional level was apparent at the first Yearly Meeting in 1669, though there was still room enough for private affirmations of unspecified content. Despite long periods of imprisonment, Fox persisted as preacher, organizer, and pamphleteer to spread his gospel of un-mediated religious experience. In 1672 to 1673 one of his missionary journeys brought him to the Western Hemisphere where hardy witnesses had already settled in several colonies. A thin scattering of Quaker meetings extended from Portsmouth (later New Hampshire) to Cape Hatteras (later North Carolina), and Fox went about visiting them to consolidate their purpose on American shores. His ministry was generally well received, even theological disputes resulting in greater public knowledge of Quaker ideas. Many new meetings were organized as a result of the founder's efforts, and the faith of New World Friends was strengthened by acquaintance with one who traveled much in Truth's service.

Bibliography:

    A.   *A Journal, or Historical Account of the Life . . . of . . . George Fox* (London, 1694), ed. Norman Penney (Cambridge, 1911), ed. John L. Nickalls (Cambridge, 1952); *The Works of George Fox*, 8 vols. (Philadelphia, 1831).
    B.   SH 4, 348–49; NCAB 7, 10; NCE 5, 1047–48; Thomas Hodgkin, *George Fox* (Boston, 1896); Rufus M. Jones, *George Fox: Seeker and Friend* (London, 1930); Alfred N. Brayshaw, *The Personality of George Fox* (London, 1933); Vernon Noble, *The Man in Leather Breeches: The Life and Times of George Fox* (New York, 1953); Douglas Gwyn, *Apocalypse of the Word: The Life and Message of George Fox* (Richmond, IN, 1986).

FRELINGHUYSEN, Theodorus Jacobus (November 1692, Hagen, Germany—?1748). *Career*: minister Embden, Holland, 1717–18; subrector, Latin Acad., Enkhuizen, Holland, 1718–19; minister to Dutch Reformed churches in the Raritan Valley, NJ, 1720–?48.

As the son of a Reformed pastor and himself a ministerial candidate, Frelinghuysen added Dutch to his Westphalian German apparently to profit from Calvinist orthodoxy as expounded by theologians in Holland. After two brief pastorates in the Low Countries, he sailed for America to serve Dutch congregations for almost thirty years in the area surrounding New Brunswick, New Jersey. Domine Frelinghuysen brought with him a strong determination to build up the piety and morals of his new parishioners while mitigating the formalism too commonly found in Reformed churches. He was loyal to the Heidelberg Catechism but also employed methods and evangelistic zeal that attracted attention soon after disembarking. Primary emphasis lay on conversion with attendant conviction of sin, genuine repentance, and reliance in faith on the Holy Spirit for regeneration. Beyond that he stressed an upright moral life sustained by private devotions. The minister's concern for the inner spirituality of church discipline was so great, he laid down strict requirements for admission to communion. By demanding evidence of conversion he hoped to make persons more aware of church life as the seat of piety, informed beliefs and acceptable manners. Some resented his arbitrary handling of disciplinary questions, but he encouraged lay participation enough to foster growth in each of his eight missions.

Within his own denomination Frelinghuysen was considered more eccentric than saintly. Laymen embittered by his excommunication appealed to conservatives in New York for vindication. Those ministers, Henry Boel for example, feared the excesses of religious emotionalism and took issue with many of the young Domine's unauthorized practices. Controversy flashed between factions in the church for a decade after 1723 until peace, not accord, was sorted out by compromise. In the larger circles of American life, Frelinghuysen stands as one of the inaugurating agents of the First Great Awakening. Though his travels were circumscribed, his attitude regarding the importance of tangible religious experience corresponded to that of more famous revival preachers. His influence did not spread as far as that of fellow New Brunswick minister, *Gilbert Tennent, but his evangelical activities (especially 1739–40) helped stimulate later developments in the middle colonies. He also trained several young men for clerical service and caused no small perturbation by ordaining them without permission, seeking thereby greater local autonomy for Dutch churches on American soil. For ten years he supported plans to organize a Coetus under the jurisdiction of the Classis of Amsterdam to supervise affairs in the New World. It was created in 1747, but he did not live to see it improve the quality of Reformed churches. Unaccountably, knowledge about the date of his death and gravesite is lacking.

Bibliography:

A.   *Sermons*, trans. William Demarest (New York, 1850).

B.   AAP 9, 8–15; NCAB 12, 329; DAB 7, 17–18; NCE 6, 143; Peter H. B. Frelinghuysen, *Theodorus Jacobus Frelinghuysen* (Princeton, 1938); James Tanis, *Dutch Calvinistic Pietism in the Middle Colonies: A Study in the Life and Theology of Theodorus Jacobus Frelinghuysen* (The Hague, 1968).

FRIEDLAENDER, Israel (8 September 1876, Kovel, Poland—5 July 1920, Kamenets Podolskiy, Ukranien S.S.R.). *Education*: studied at the Hildesheimer Rabbinical Sem. and Univ. of Berlin, 1895–1900; Ph.D., Univ. of Strassburg, 1901. *Career*: privatdozent for Semitic Languages, Univ. of Strassburg, 1902–04; Sabato Morais Professor of Biblical Literature and Exegesis, Jewish Sem., 1904–20.

Born in the Russian sector of Poland, raised in Warsaw, educated in Berlin, and employed predominantly in New York, Friedlaender seemed to epitomize the adage that the star of empire makes its way ever westward. By 1900 he had discarded plans for a rabbinical career and concentrated instead on Semitic languages. He was particularly interested in Judeo-Arabic literature and culture, more breadly in historical relations between Judaism and Islam. He wrote many valuable essays on historical and linguistic topics, especially on the lifework and influence of Maimonides in such prestigious journals as the *Jewish Quarterly Review* and *Journal of the American Oriental Society*. While based in New York City, Friedlaender also taught at Dropsie College in Philadelphia and lectured on history at Hebrew Teacher's Institute. As a member of the United Synagogue of America and chair of the Bureau of Jewish Education, he implemented strong convictions about the importance of education in giving Jewish youth an identity and in securing their loyalty to the faith. He was passionately devoted to the survival of Jews and Judaism, seeing ultimate triumph as an organic union of education in the best of surviving traditions, continuing religious practice, and nationalism.

Interest in the last category made Friedlaender an untiring worker for the Zionist cause. Greatly influenced by Ahad Ha-Am, he thought of Palestine as a land of promise for all people: for Jews and everyone else who looked for human progress through a higher, better social order. His brand of Zionism envisioned a thriving Jewish community in the old homeland, not necessarily a politically independent state. Judaism was centered on religion as a way of life, and, while placing Jerusalem at the heart of Jewish culture, he saw nothing wrong with widespread settlement, favoring "Palestine plus the Diaspora." Such ideas moved Friedlaender to seek reconciliation between the Federation of American Zionists and the American Jewish Committee, opposing groups on whose executive boards he served with equal sincerity. Shortly after World War I ended, he went personally to supervise distribution of funds to Jewish war sufferers in Europe. Attempting to alleviate the misery stemming from disease, starvation, and programs, he and fellow worker, rabbi Bernard Cantor, were murdered by Bolshevik guerrillas. A phrase he once wrote about someone else also applied to him: the important turns of history are not made by philosophers but by martyrs.

Bibliography:

A. *The Heterodoxies of the Shiites in the Presentation of Ibn Hazm* (New Haven, 1909); *The Political Ideal of the Prophets* (Baltimore, 1910); *Jewish-Arabic Studies* (Philadelphia, 1912); *Die Chadhirlegende und der Alexanderroman: Eine sagengeschichte und literatur-historische Untersuchung* (Leipsig, 1913); *Jews of Russia and Poland: A Bird's Eye View of Their History and Culture* (New York, 1915); *Past and Present: A Collection of Jewish Essays* (Cincinnati, 1919).

B.   DAB 7, 32–33; EJ 7, 179.

FROTHINGHAM, Octavius Brooks (28 November 1822, Boston, MA—27 November 1895, Boston, MA). *Education*: B.A., Harvard Coll., 1843; graduated from Harvard Div. Sch., 1846. *Career*: minister, North Church, Salem, MA, 1847–55; minister, Unitarian Society, Jersey City, NJ, 1855–59; minister, Third Unitarian Society (after 1875 the Independent Liberal Church), New York 1859–79; independent writer, 1879–95.

As the son of a Unitarian minister, Frothingham was acquainted since childhood with the more conservative aspects of his religious tradition. But a preference for open inquiry into spiritual matters eventually made him leader of the radical wing of late nineteenth century Unitarianism. Frothingham first drew attention to himself in 1854 by criticizing northern compliance with the Fugitive Slave Law. In a sermon entitled, "The New Commandment" he rebuked complacency regarding the capture and return of runaway slaves. Notoriety in reformist politics led to pastorates in New Jersey and New York where he also became known as one of the most outstanding intellectual preachers of his day. For Frothingham churches were places of worship, of course, but more importantly they were arenas for mental challenge and encounters with faiths of all kinds. He said his task was to sift out the divine wisdom to be found in every viewpoint. He used the term "radical faith" to show that he sought truth, not dogma. In an inclusive theism based on transcendentalist philosophy he resisted distinctions drawn between God and humanity, the infinite and the finite, the natural and the supernatural. The only real gulf lay between human and animal elements in each person, and his goal was to elicit the good in people for the benefit of themselves and others.

Detractors of this rather vague and superficial optimism thought Frothingham was edging toward heresy. In an attempt to provide guidelines for standard beliefs and to set limits for subsequent speculation, ministers such as *Henry W. Bellows organized a National Conference of Unitarian clergy. Frothingham was highly suspicious of any centralization of power and an imposition of creedal restrictions. Accordingly, he helped organize the Free Religious Association in 1867 and served as its first president until 1878. Opposed to dogmatism and external control, this loose collection of free churches announced that its objectives were to promote the interests of pure religion, to encourage the scientific study of theology, and to increase fellowship in the spirit among those who wished it. Frothingham also expressed these ideals in his writing. He edited *The Index* from 1870 to 1880, after which time the paper became the official organ of the FRA. He wrote for several other journals as well, commenting on religious, political, and literary subjects. Of lasting importance are his publications of biographies and an early history of his denomination, tracing developments from its origin to the period of his own controversial involvement.

Bibliography:

A. *Story of the Patriarchs* (Boston, 1864); *The Religion of Humanity* (New York, 1873); *Life of Theodore Parker* (New York, 1874); *The Cradle of Christ: A Study of Primitive Christianity* (New York, 1877); *Recollections and Impressions, 1822–1891* (New York, 1891).

B. SH 4, 402; NCAB 2, 423; DAB 7, 44; J. Wade Caruthers, *Octavius Brooks Frothingham: Gentle Radical* (University, AL, 1977).

FULLER, Charles Edward (25 April 1887, Los Angeles, CA—19 March 1968, Pasadena, CA). *Education*: B.S., Pomona Coll., 1910; graduated from Bible Institute of Los Angeles, 1923. *Career*: manager, Southern California Citrus Packing Association, 1912–18; minister, Calvary Church, Placentia, CA, 1926–32; executive director, Gospel Broadcasting Association, 1933–68; president, Fuller Evangelistic Foundation, 1943–68; president, board of trustees, Fuller Sem., 1947–68.

With a college degree in chemistry, Fuller worked for a year in gold mining operations near Sacramento. He returned to southern California and helped his father invest in orange groves, moving to supervisory positions with large citrus firms when his own ventures failed. In 1917 he experienced a deeply felt conversion to Christianity and began studying the Bible on his own. Others met with him in regular sessions at his home in Placentia, and this formed the core of Calvary Church, an interdenominational, evangelical congregation which he founded and served as pastor. Before the church was formed, however, Fuller attended the Bible Institute of Los Angeles (BIOLA), where he was greatly influenced by the conservative theology of *Reuben A. Torrey. He was ordained into the Baptist ministry in 1925, but one year prior to that he began the type of activity that would make him familiar to millions of people. In 1924 he made his first radio broadcast, speaking twice a week under BIOLA auspices. By 1927 he was convinced that radio ministry was his lifework and thus dedicated himself to evangelical outreach through this modern medium.

At first Fuller's independent radio broadcasts derived from church services in Placentia, where a few stations carried both morning and evening sessions on Sundays and Thursday meetings as well. Within four years the setting moved to Long Beach Auditorium, attracting more stations to beam out ''The Pilgrim Hour'' on Sunday mornings and a gospel hour in the evening. By 1935 services from this arena seating four thousand participants had become ''The Old Fashioned Revival Hour'' and achieved a national hookup two years later. By the early 1940s Fuller's program of hymns, letters of testimony, and folksy sermons reached an estimated twenty million people a week through a thousand stations on the Mutual Network. When Mutual refused in 1944 to broadcast any religious program after noon, the Old Fashioned Revival Hour was so popular, independent stations picked it up, and in 1949 the American Broadcasting Company gave it further stability, sending its message around the world. Fuller was a mild fundamentalist and literalist in his approach to questions about theological matters and biblical interpretation. At the height of his popularity he founded a seminary to shape later generations of evangelists who would defend and perpetuate views such as his.

Bibliography:

B.   NYT 21 Mar 1968, 47; Wilbur M. Smith, *A Voice for God: The Life of Charles E. Fuller, Originator of the Old Fashioned Revival Hour* (Boston, 1949).

FULLER, Richard (22 April 1804, Beaufort, SC—20 October 1876, Baltimore, MD). *Education*: graduated from Harvard Coll., 1824. *Career*: practiced law in SC, 1825–31; minister, Baptist church of Beaufort, SC, 1832–47; minister, Seventh Baptist Church, Baltimore, MD, 1847–71; minister Eutaw Place Baptist Church, Baltimore, 1871–76.

Raised in a wealthy family that was nominally Baptist, Fuller entered college with an eye toward legal practice. He proved to be a good student, but after two years poor health, which some feared as tuberculosis, caused him to leave school. His excellent performance, though truncated, nevertheless warranted granting him a diploma when his class graduated. After a few years as an attorney Fuller reconfirmed membership in the Baptist church in 1831 and shortly afterward began preaching. He possessed an eloquence that soon gained him national attention. While ministering to a hometown congregation he also attracted notice through printed media. In 1839 he published some articles in the Charleston *Courier* in favor of prohibiting alcoholic beverages. Incidental statements in these essays aroused Catholic bishop *John England, and the two engaged in a protracted exchange about Baptists and Catholics, freedom and constraint. Similarly in 1844 Fuller supplied the *Christian Reflector* of Philadelphia with arguments justifying slavery by appeal to scripture. These efforts were answered by fellow Baptist *Francis Wayland, with the full debate issued the following year as a book.

The slavery issue proved tragic for Baptists, and Fuller was present at the triennial convention that witnessed permanent separation over regional priorities. He moved to Baltimore where he could minister to people of both Northern and Southern sympathies. There he tried to reconcile factions and alleviate distress caused during the Civil War and Reconstruction period. His mediating work was helpful, but Fuller inclined more south than north. In 1859 and 1861 he served as president of the Southern Baptist Convention, preaching its very first annual sermon in 1846. After the war he urged the convention to support seminary training for ministers, especially in the area of biblical studies. In 1872 he also urged greater attention to home missionary work, including outreach to the black population whom Baptists seemed to have abandoned after Appomattox. His efforts to meet such ideals were minimally successful; his conciliatory diplomacy was even less so. Good will on his part and on that of a few others could not knit Baptists back together again, and reunion has still not occurred another century later.

Bibliography:

A. *Letters Concerning the Roman Chancery* (Baltimore, 1840); *Domestic Slavery Considered as a Scriptural Institution* (New York, 1845); *Baptism and the Terms of Communion: An Argument* (Baltimore, 1850); *Sermons* (New York, 1860); *Sermons by Richard Fuller, Preached during his Ministry with the Seventh and Eutaw Place Baptist Churches, Baltimore, 1847–76*, 3 vols. (Philadelphia, 1877).

B. SH 4, 409; NCAB 23, 291–92; DAB 7, 62–63; James H. Cuthbert, *Life of Richard Fuller* (New York, 1879).

FULLER, Sarah Margaret (23 May 1810, Cambridgeport, MA—19 July 1850, shipwreck off Fire Island, NY). *Career*: teacher, Temple School, Boston, MA, 1836–37; teacher, Greene Street School, Providence, RI, 1837–39; teacher, private classes, Boston, 1839–41; joint editor, *Dial*, 1840–42; literary critic, *New York Tribune*, 1844–46; foreign correspondent, 1846–50.

With Puritan ancestors and a strong preference for intellectual pursuits, Fuller embodied the best qualities of the Unitarian, Transcendentalist movement as it developed in her day. Her facility with languages, witty conversation, and earnest search for high ideals soon made her a fixture in Boston society. In the 1820s she formed lasting friendships with such luminaries as *Frederic Henry Hedge, *James Freeman Clarke, and Bronson Alcott. After teaching classical and modern languages in several academies, she launched her own school for a while, gaining considerable attention for her "conversations" or socratic exchanges which she used to clarify ideas and values. In this work she did much to advance the cause of higher education for women and their more general claim for equal rights as citizens. By 1840 Fuller worked with *Ralph Waldo Emerson and *George Ripley to publish *Dial*, a quarterly journal intended to further awareness of Transcendentalism. She was a major contributor to the periodical's pages, and her many writings helped crystallize the content and objectives of the philosophical-religious point of view.

In all her musings Fuller sought a more profound understanding of the forces that comprised the universe around her. She wanted a wider and richer appreciation of the "divine spirit of creation" that activated all things. A life of philosophic purpose called out for higher sentiments, and the most important object in life was continuous growth. Free creativity and practical action were guidelines which led to greater spiritual truth and personal improvement. In 1846 an opportunity arose for her to make a long-desired tour of Europe. While in Italy she became embroiled in the Roman Revolution (1847–1849) and enamored of a well-born but poor Italian revolutionary, Giovanni Angelo, Marchese d'Ossoli. As supporters of Mazzini, the couple organized republican forces, administered hospitals, and endured the deprivations of wartime alongside other idealists. Around mid–1849 the couple announced their marriage, at which time Fuller, with a son who was at least a year old, began using the title, Marquesa. As the revolution collapsed due to French intervention, Fuller wrote a history of the debacle. The family traveled to America in 1850 in hopes of finding a publisher, but the ship foundered and sank within sight of land. The body of neither parent was discovered.

Bibliography:

A. *Woman in the Nineteenth Century* (Boston, 1844); *Papers on Literature and Art* (New York, 1846); *At Home and Abroad*, edited by A. B. Fuller (Boston, 1856); *Life Without and Life Within*, edited by A. B. Fuller (Boston, 1859); *The Writings of Margaret Fuller*, selected and edited by Mason Wade (New York, 1941); *The Letters of Margaret Fuller*, edited by Robert N. Hudspeth, 5 vols. (Ithaca, NY, 1983–88).

B. NCAB 3, 28–29; DAB 7, 63–66; NAW 1, 678–82; Mason Wade, *Margaret Fuller: Whetstone of Genius* (New York, 1940); Madeline B. Stern, *The Life of Margaret Fuller* (New York, 1942; rev. ed., Westport, CT, 1991); Joseph Jay Deiss, *The Roman Years of Margaret Fuller* (New York, 1969); Margaret Vanderhaar Allen, *The Achievement of Margaret Fuller* (University Park, PA, 1979); David Watson, *Margaret Fuller: An American Romantic* (New York, 1988).

FURMAN, Richard (9 October 1755, Esopus, NY—25 August 1825, High Hill, SC). *Career*: minister, Charleston, SC, 1787–1825.

Raised in a family which moved South soon after his birth, young Furman was a precocious student who learned much at home without the benefit of formal instruction. He also dedicated himself to the Baptist ministry quite early, and before his nineteenth birthday crowds gathered to hear the ''boy preacher'' deliver gospel messages. During the Revolutionary War, he supported colonial independence with such eloquence that British authorities put a price on his head. But he avoided Cornwallis' troops and conducted missionary work in relative safety along the North Carolina-Virginia piedmont. On returning to his adopted state, he became an outstanding spokesman in denominational affairs throughout the region. As early as 1785 he initiated procedures for organizing the Charleston Baptist Association; five years later he represented a more general constituency at the South Carolina Constitutional Convention where he helped secure religious freedom for all churches. Through the years he developed widespread influence among coreligionists by virtue of magnetic personal qualities. When Baptists formed a Triennial Convention (1814) to support the missionary efforts of *Adoniram Judson and *Luther Rice, Furman was chosen president, a unanimous decision repeated in 1817. He strongly advocated the use of centralized authority in both government and ecclesiastical structures, but such a Federalist orientation did not long survive him in politics or denominational patterns. In the field of education, however, he made a more lasting contribution. For several decades he urged churchmen to recognize the need and to provide means for adequate training of the next generation's clergy. He also superintended work to collect funds for that purpose while convincing Georgia and Carolina Baptists to pool their interests in building a single educational facility. Fifteen months after he died, an academy and theological school was established, soon to bear the name of one who had substantially aided its foundation.

Bibliography:

B.   AAP 6, 161–65; NCAB 12, 292; DAB 7, 76–77; James A. Rogers, *Richard Furman: Life and Legacy* (Macon, GA, 1985).

G

GANNETT, Ezra Stiles (4 May 1801, Cambridge, MA—26 August 1871, near Boston, MA). *Education*: B.A., Harvard Coll. graduated from Harvard Div. Sch., 1823. *Career*: assistant and then minister, Federal Street Unitarian Church, Boston, MA, 1824–42 and 1842–69; secretary, American Unitarian Association, 1825–31; president, A.U.A., 1847–51.

After distinguishing himself at college and seminary, Gannett was called shortly after ordination to assist *William E. Channing at one of the most eminent churches in Boston. He excelled in pastoral duties, but his contributions in larger issues were even better known. In 1825 he played a significant role in organizing the American Unitarian Association, the institutional focal point for liberals in New England Congregationalism. Serving as its first secretary and later as president, Gannett provided steady administrative leadership as Unitarianism emerged fully and explicitly as a separate denomination in this country. Despite the fact that in 1840 a paralytic stroke crippled his right leg, he continued meeting the demands of a full, rigorous schedule. He was instrumental in founding the Benevolent Fraternity of Churches, an organization that supported ministry among the urban poor. Again serving as secretary and president (1857–62) he helped guide this agency which became Boston's principal Unitarian missionary society. His conspicuous leadership qualities were further displayed in printed media where he helped edit the *Scriptural Interpreter* (1831–35), the *Monthly Miscellany of Religion and Letters* (1839–43), and most importantly the *Christian Examiner* (1844–49).

In addition to executive talent Gannett was also known for his eloquence, a gifted extemporaneous speaker whose sermons and discourses were savored when either heard or reproduced in newspapers or pamphlets. As an advocate of moderate theological views, what he called "old-fashioned Unitarianism," he opposed Transcendentalists like *Theodore Parker in the denomination. Instead of relying on intuition and novelty in religious thought as they did, Gannett preferred scriptural precedent for ideas and emphasized an unchanging gospel centered on Christ's miraculous influence on human conduct. He epitomized solid endorsement of beliefs in the fatherhood of God and human brotherhood achieved through faith in Christ as a moral exemplar. To these he added profound commitment to the reality of spiritual values and the possibilities of improving human lives through individual effort. These principles warrant considering him a bellwether on antebellum moralism in the northern United States of his day. Always committed to the causes of peace, education, temperance, and personal righteousness, he died in a train accident while on his way to fulfill yet another preaching engagement.

Bibliography:

B.   NCAB 10, 149–50; DAB 7, 122–23; NYT 28 Aug 1871, 4; William Channing Gannett, *Ezra Stiles Gannett, Unitarian Minister in Boston, 1824–1871* (Boston, 1875).

GARNET, Henry Highland (23 December 1815, New Market, MD—12 February 1882, Monrovia, Liberia). *Education*: studied at Noyes Aca., 1834–35; studied at Oneida Institute, 1836–40. *Career*: minister, Liberty Street Presbyterian Church, Troy, NY, 1843–48; missionary for the United Presbyterian Church of Scotland in Jamaica, 1853–56; minister, Shiloh Presbyterian Church, New York, 1856–64; minister, 15th Street Presbyterian Church, Washington, DC, 1864–66; consul-general, Liberia, 1881–82.

Starting life as a slave and subsequently experiencing many forms of racist abuse made Garnet a fierce abolitionist and advocate of human rights. He escaped to freedom with his family at the age of nine and sought to improve himself through education. By 1834 he and *Alexander Crummell became the first black pupils admitted to an experimental school in New Hampshire, but protesting whites destroyed the academy less than a year later. After finishing studies in upstate New York, Garnet was ordained a Presbyterian clergyman and served a number of important ministerial posts. His real fame, though, lay in reform activities for a number of causes on the national and international level. These included social justice, world peace, women's rights, and temperance. But such objectives were eclipsed by his real passion: freedom, dignity, and equality for Negroes wherever they lived.

As early as 1843 Garnet attracted attention for his radical and militant ideas about ending slavery. That year he addressed the National Convention of Free People of Color, held in Buffalo, New York. There he stated forthrightly that slavery had to be resisted by force and ended at once rather than terminating it gradually through moral suasion. His ''call to rebellion'' against oppression did not shrink from armed uprisings and slaves' executing their masters, if necessary. Conservatives at the convention did not support such extreme sentiments, but Garnet earned a reputation for fiery oratory and forceful measures. He often lectured for the American Anti-Slavery Society. He also served as president of the African Civilization Society and was chaplain to three colored regiments during the Civil War. In 1865 he was the first black minister invited to preach a sermon in the House of Representatives. In that address he advocated morality, industry, and thrift as the means of Negro self-help and political strength. His disappointment with Reconstruction compromises led him to support colonization efforts in the back-to-Africa movement. Diplomatic appointment to Liberia promised to further that goal, but he died before putting those lifelong dreams into practical action.

Bibliography:

   A.   *The Past and Present Condition and the Destiny of the Colored Race* (Troy, NY, 1848); *A Memorial Discourse* (Philadelphia, 1865).
   B.   NCAB 2, 414; DAB 7, 154–55; NYT 11 Mar 1882, 5; James M. Smith, *Sketch of the Life and Labors of Rev. Henry Highland Garnet* (Washington, DC, 1865); Earl Ofari, *"Let Your Motto Be Resistance": The Life and Thought of Henry Highland Garnet* (Boston, 1972).

GARRETTSON, Freeborn (15 August 1752, Harford County, MD—26 September 1827, New York, NY). *Career*: itinerant Methodist minister, 1775–1827.

In retrospect, Garrettson said that his childhood was carnal and pleasure loving, filled with pursuits irrelevant to his eternal welfare. He was not licentious by any standard, but from a post-conversion viewpoint the preacher decried a misspent youth. In his early twenties the young man heard *Francis Asbury and other Methodist itinerants, deciding under their influence to associate with that wing of the Anglican establishment. By 1775 a concern for the salvation of others manifested itself, and Garrettson began an evangelical ministry which lasted more than fifty years. At the same time he freed slaves inherited on the family estate, but did so on impulse without any serious convictions about the matter. In subsequent years he developed an aggressively negative policy regarding the institution of slavery, proposing legislation for gradual emancipation and favoring repatriation as the ultimate solution for both races. But preaching the riches of free redemption was his major interest, not social reform. He traveled extensively to deliver the living word in major circuits and raised new churches where he could.

Antislavery principles made Garrettson unpopular in many southern quarters, but his pacifism during the Revolution created even more of a stir. He refused to bear arms, an act of conscience always disconcerting in wartime, and his nominal connection with the Church of England raised the question of Tory sympathies. He also declined to swear allegiance to new state governments (Virginia, 1777). During the next several years his circuit-riding did not abate, but he was often threatened by prison and incidents of mob violence. Shortly before the Christmas Conference of 1784, he was the courier who sped like an arrow to outlying districts, summoning Methodists to their first declaration of independent status. After two years' missionary work in Nova Scotia, he returned to the American heartland, serving for decades as presiding elder and preacher at large. The Conference inexplicably refused to make him superintendent; nevertheless, his administrative contributions to the early church were substantial. He married into a wealthy family and settled (1800) at Rhinebeck on the Hudson River. His home became a haven for traveling preachers as well as a base for increased evangelism in northern territory. Spiritual and ecclesiastical activities diffused Garrettson's influence over a number of states, but his most important achievement was unquestionably the extension of Methodism in New York.

Bibliography:

A.   *The Experience and Travels of Mr. Freeborn Garrettson* (Philadelphia, 1791); *A Dialogue Between Do-Justice and Professing-Christian* (Wilmington, DE, 1820).

B.   AAP 7, 54–63; NCAB 10, 480–81; DAB 7, 166–67; Nathan Bangs, *The Life of the Rev. Freeborn Garrettson* (New York, 1830).

GARRISON, James Harvey (2 February 1842, near Ozark, MO—14 January 1931, Los Angeles, CA). *Education*: B.A., Abingdon Coll., 1868. *Career*: infantryman, then officer, Union Army, 1861–65; associate minister, Macomb, IL, 1868–72; editor, *The Christian-Evangelist* (under various titles before 1882), 1869–1912; editor emeritus, 1912–31.

While in college, Garrison sought membership as a Disciple of Christ because he thought Christian unity was the greatest ideal he could work for in the world. He figured prominently in church affairs during the next sixty years and exerted a moderating influence in controversies that marked the most turbulent period of his denomination's history. As editor of a journal known variously as *The Gospel Echo* or *The Christian*, he built it from a monthly to a weekly paper and by 1874 had based it at St. Louis, the geographical center of Disciple activity. By 1884 circulation figures reached 25,000 and remained there as the *Christian-Evangelist* surpassed the *Christian Standard* (by 1907) as the denomination's most representative periodical. It is difficult to enumerate concrete results stemming from Garrison's efforts to defend moderation in important questions. But for a half century his contributions to debates provided specific content in issues of formative significance among Disciples who grappled with modernity. For example, he refused to censure independent thought in biblical scholarship, adopting neither indiscriminate hostility nor wholesale acceptance of its conclusions. He continued to espouse many conservative tenets, such as inerrancy and the virgin birth, but declined making them tests of orthodox orientation. Indeed he was so favorable to open inquiry into Scripture, he engaged *Herbert L. Willett (in 1899) to write articles that might bridge the gap between higher criticism and uninitiated laymen. Instead of resisting all scientific advance, it was more important to avoid intellectual isolationism which was draining the church of vitality and relevance.

The problem of isolationism emerged even more clearly in questions related to unity among Christians, the overriding ideal of Garrison's entire editorial ministry. He was opposed to infant baptism and accepted immersion as the pattern demanded by New Testament precedent. But since he thought God was the ultimate judge of persons, he would not say all those unimmersed would be damned or all those duly baptized, saved. He remained an outspoken opponent of "open membership" but would not categorically denounce churches which accepted converts if they had been baptized by some method other than immersion. Unfortunately he alienated conservatives and liberals alike by insisting that unity was more important than particular modes of ritual. The primary goal was, in his mind, to restore the spirit of harmony found in the undivided church of apostolic times. Abandoning rigid legalism, he argued that Disciples should not make their exclusivism a stumbling block to ecumenical witness. Garrison was unable to prevent isolationists from splitting into digressive factions (1906, 1926), but he was largely responsible for denominational cooperation with larger groups, especially the Federal Council of Churches in 1908. In retirement he continued to write his popular editorials, entitled "The Easy Chair," in response to widespread acceptance of his ideas as weighty opinion in church circles.

Bibliography:

A. *Alone with God* (St. Louis, 1891); *Half-Hour Studies at the Cross* (St. Louis, 1895); *Helps to Faith: A Contribution to Theological Reconstruction* (St. Louis, 1903); *The Holy Spirit* (St. Louis, 1905); *The Story of a Century* (St. Louis, 1909); *Memories and Experiences* (St. Louis, 1926).
B.   NCAB 18, 276; William E. Tucker, *J. H. Garrison and Disciples of Christ* (St. Louis, 1964).

GARVEY, Marcus Mosiah (17 August 1887, St. Anne's Bay, Jamaica—10 June 1940, London, England).

Within the space of a decade Garvey created the first mass movement among American Negroes to arouse pride in black identity and demands for social justice. After experiencing job discrimination by whites in the Caribbean and London (1912–14), he returned to Jamaica and organized the Universal Negro Improvement Association (UNIA). In 1916 he came to the U.S. alone and unknown; three years later his followers numbered more than a million. With messianic zeal to uplift Blacks everywhere, Garvey utilized a flambouyant personality and gifted oratory to stir the loyalty of black urban masses. His impressive ceremonies, business ventures and broad philosophical vision nourished group-consciousness with phenomenal, though short-lived, success. He was convinced that Blacks could never count on equal treatment from whites. Consequently his many activities, including the weekly *Negro World* (1918–33), steamships on the Black Star Line (1919–22), and international conventions of the UNIA, were coordinated aspects of a single goal: black liberation. The motto of "One God! One Aim! One Destiny!" made him one of this country's early advocates of black nationalism. He urged repatriation to Africa for the redemption of his ancestral home. While his ideas did not echo the old colonization societies, they fostered a dream of pan-African solidarity strong enough to compel justice for Blacks in every nation. On the strength of such goals he built the largest and most powerful all-black organization known in the world at that time.

The religious groundwork beneath Garvey's comprehensive social program was psychologically important as a factor in its success. He urged Blacks to worship God conceived in a racial likeness to themselves. Too long they had thought of Christianity in terms of the hypocritical system represented in white churches, sanctioned by a white god and motivated by white values. In an attempt to end the theological dominance of European symbols, Garvey conceived of a Negro deity whose image was dramatized in the physical beauty and characteristics of free black men. In 1921 the African Orthodox Church was established with former UNIA chaplain George A. McGuire (an Episcopal priest) receiving appointment as bishop. During the next few years *The Negro Churchman* fleshed out ideas for a genuine black church whose art featured a black madonna and child, black angels, and saints. The attitude of one believer, that no white man would die on a cross for Blacks, indicates why the church looked to a Negro Christ who saved members from a white devil. The response to Garvey's call for an all-black religion was largely negative, whether from clergymen, the press, or black intelligentsia. Yet his use of black religious images had great pragmatic value in stimulating racial confidence. The advances begun under his leadership created a frame of mind on which the Black Muslims later capitalized. Garvey was indicted for mail fraud (1922), imprisoned (1925), and deported (1927). He did not realize many specific goals, but his vision remained a source of inspiration to black nationalists who still revere his name.

Bibliography:

A. *Philosophy and Opinions of Marcus Garvey*, ed. Amy Jacques-Garvey, 2 vols. (New York, 1923–26, 1969); *The Tragedy of White Injustice*, ed. Amy Jacques-Garvey (New York, 1927).

B. NYT 12 June 1940, 4; Edmund D. Cronon, *Black Moses: The Story of Marcus Garvey and the Universal Negro Improvement Association* (Madison, WI, 1955); Amy Jacques-Garvey, *Marcus Garvey* (Kingston, Jamaica, 1963); Adolph Edwards, *Marcus Garvey, 1887–1940* (London, 1967); Elton C. Fax, *Garvey: The Story of a Pioneer Black Nationalist* (New York, 1972); Edmund D. Cronon (ed.), *Marcus Garvey* (Englewood Cliffs, NJ, 1973); Randall K. Burkett, *Garveyism as a Religious Movement: The Institutionalization of a Black Civil Religion* (Metuchen, NJ, 1978).

GIBBONS, James (23 July 1834, Baltimore, MD—24 March 1921, Baltimore, MD). *Education*: graduated from St. Charles Coll. (MD), 1857; graduated from St. Mary's Sem. (MD), 1861. *Career*: curate, mission pastor, and volunteer chaplain in Baltimore area, 1861–65; secretary to *Martin J. Spalding, Baltimore, 1865–68; vicar apostolic of NC, 1868–72; bishop of Richmond, VA, 1872–77; archibishop of Baltimore, 1877–1921; cardinal, 1886–1921.

The last decades of the nineteenth century were particularly crucial ones for the growth of American Catholicism, and the church was fortunate indeed to have a man of Gibbons' stature as ordinary in its premier see. His guidance through myriad problems of internal stability and sensitive issues related to broader cultural questions helped place the church on a sound footing as it received the status of full independence in 1908. The capacity for effective Catholic action in a modern setting was due in no small measure to his tactful leadership. Thoughtful and sympathetic to the good points in all sides of disputes, the second American cardinal won the admiration of almost all the nation's hierarchy. His judgment was often sought on theological and public questions where he displayed wisdom, virtue, and executive ability, showing at times that he could even accept defeat gracefully. His analysis of Catholicism in American culture was astute. As a priest he ministered constantly to aspects of people's lives that were basic to faith and morality. Moving with the same pastoral concern to a wider range of activities, he spoke with some alarm about divorce, declining Sabbath observance, increasing materialism, public corruption, problems of the poor, political fraud, and inadequate educational programs. Through writing, addresses, and episcopal functions connected with the eminence of his office, Gibbons' contributions to his church and country had no parallel.

A partial list of general topics indicates the complexity of affairs with which Gibbons had to deal: labor organizations, secret societies, charges of trusteeism and investigatory visits by apostolic delegations, school controversies (where he defended *John Ireland), care for soldiers during wartime, and comfort for the bereaved at home. The cardinal was consultant and adviser to presidents. He maintained a voluminous correspondence, much of it international, dealing with the manifold problems facing the church in differing contexts. In most of these labors he was sustained by the good will of other ecclesiastical notables, gathered by him in one place at the Third Plenary Council (1884) and contacted at their local jurisdictions through frequent exchange of ideas. One exception to this rule was New York archbishop, *Michael A. Corrigan, whose inclinations were usually more conservative and whose diocese posed something of a rival power base.

One of Gibbons' most important contributions had to do with unity. As immigrant groups came to the New World, they wished to perpetuate familiar customs acquired in previous surroundings. This natural tendency led to theological and nationalistic conflicts among English-speaking Catholics dominated by the Irish and growing numbers of German, Polish, and Italian portions of the faithful. The continued use of German language was singularly vexing. Gibbons deplored dissension that weakened the church's cohesion, and he met divisiveness by refusing to make distinctions in governmental procedures or to grant special privileges to any national segment. The incipient denominationalism contained in "Cahenslyism" (named after Peter P. Cahensly, general secretary of the St. Raphael's Society to aid German Catholicism) found a determined foe in the cardinal of Baltimore. Another legacy was Gibbons' work over thirty-five years to sustain the Catholic University of America, serving as chancellor after 1885 to raise funds, recruit an outstanding faculty, and encourage religious houses to associate with the institution. As a patriot and firm believer in democratic principles he spoke positively about dual allegiance to American life and Catholic faith, finding that it led to involvement in the "Americanism" imbroglio. A close identification between church and country was reprehensible to Roman officials, but criticism in this confusing realm did not detract from the substantial dedication Gibbons continued to manifest as servant and guide.

Bibliography:

A.   *The Faith of Our Fathers* (Baltimore, 1876); *Our Christian Heritage* (Baltimore, 1889); *The Ambassador of Christ* (Baltimore, 1896); *Collections and Recollections in the Life and Times of Cardinal Gibbons*, ed. John Reily, 10 vols. (Martinburg, WV, 1890–1904); *Discourses and Sermons* (Baltimore, 1908); *A Retrospect of Fifty Years* (Baltimore, 1916; New York, 1972).

B.   SH 4, 484; NCAB 29, 77–79; DAB 7, 238–42; NCE 6, 466–68; NYT 25 Mar 1921, 1; Allen S. Will, *The Life of Cardinal Gibbons*, 2 vols. (New York, 1922); John T. Ellis, *The Life of James Cardinal Gibbons: Archbishop of Baltimore, 1834–1921*, 2 vols. (Milwaukee, 1952); Arline B. Tehan, *Prince of Democracy: James Cardinal Gibbons* (Garden City, NY, 1962).

GINZBERG, Louis (28 November 1873, Kovno, Lithuania—11 November 1953, New York, NY). *Education*: studied at the Univ. of Berlin; Ph.D., Univ. of Heidelberg, 1898. *Career*: editor, *Jewish Encyclopedia*, 1900–03; professor of Talmud and Rabbinics, Jewish Sem., 1902–53.

Descended from generations of distinguished rabbis, especially on his mother's side, Ginzberg received solid rabbinic training in Lithuanian yeshivot. After secular education in German universities he came to America in 1899, answering an invitation from Hebrew Union College. That invitation was subsequently cancelled, and in a short time he found placement at Jewish Theological Seminary whose more conservative perspective coincided happily with that of the young Talmudic scholar. Through the years he demonstrated vast erudition regarding the contents of both Babylonian and Jerusalem talmudim. Much of his learning was literally encyclopedic, and he contributed more than 400 articles to the *Jewish Encyclopedia*. In 1919 Ginzberg helped found the American Academy for Jewish Research and served as its president from 1929 to 1941. The scope of his interests was great, including the origins of halakah (law) and haggadah (tradition) as well as the literature of geonic times, dating approximately 500–1050. In both his voluminous writings and in instructing generations of future rabbis he stressed that true understanding of religious life was possible only when the mind's knowledge blended with sympathies that came from the heart.

Also blending yeshiva studies with historical, critical analysis, Ginzberg was one of the first scholars to apply methods of literary criticism to rabbinic literature. His introduction and commentary on edited manuscripts provided comprehensive explorations of historical questions. He traced the development of halakah plus rabbinic theology and the emergence of specific rituals through Jewish history.

He correlated knowledge from rabbinical texts with external books, Hellenistic literature, early Christian writings, various translations and exegesis, and the Kabbalah. He also mastered similar knowledge of the evolution of haggadah, synthesizing information from Talmud, Midrash, and extra-rabbinic sources. Through these researches he uncovered many lost Jewish legends, publishing several volumes on maxims and parables in addition to the lives of heroes, prophets, and the fathers of Israel. It was said in tribute to his eminence that, if error due to lack of study was a sin, then the ever-studious Ginzberg was a saint.

Bibliography:

A.   *Die Haggada bei den Kirchenvätern und in der apokryphischen Litterature* (Berlin, 1900); *The Legends of the Jews* 7 vols., translated by Henrietta Szold (Philadelphia, 1909–38); *Geonica* 2 vols. (New York, 1909); *Students, Scholars, and Saints* (Philadelphia, 1928); *Geonic and Early Karaitic Halakah* (New York, 1929).

B.   EJ 7, 584–85; UJE 4, 613–14; NYT 12 Nov 1953, 31; Eli Ginzberg, *Keeper of the Law: Louis Ginzberg* (Philadelphia, 1966).

GLADDEN, Solomon Washington (11 February 1836, Pottsgrove, PA—2 July 1918, Columbus, OH). *Education*: B.A., Williams Coll., 1859. *Career*: minister, Brooklyn, NY, 1860–61; minister, Morrisania, NY, 1861–66; minister, North Adams, MA, 1866–71; editorial staff, *Independent*, 1871–75; minister, Springfield, MA, 1875–82; minister, First Congregational Church, Columbus, OH, 1882–1914; semi-retirement, 1914–18.

No Protestant minister better epitomized theological change and emerging social conscience than Washington Gladden, whose career spanned six decades and two wars—one fought to preserve the Union and the other, democracy. He was never inclined to accept the fixed categories of Calvinism and gradually moved away from them. The writings of *Horace Bushnell aided in this process, and Gladden became close friends with the theologian who formed many of the seminal ideas later applied to social contexts. Through his various practical duties as pastor, Gladden also embodied in a positive way many liberal attitudes about biblical criticism and a lack of regard for orthodox definitions. He was a topical, not a systematic, thinker who tried to deal with problems as he met them, using Christian principles insofar as they helped alleviate the situation. The pragmatic approach was more characteristic of his style than theoretical considerations, and humanitarian impulses won out over a scholarly treatment of issues. His willingness to experiment was a significant ingredient in Gladden's success as a popular spokesman whose duty led into controversial areas. By linking theological liberalism with a strong interest in social concerns, he remained near the center of Social Gospel ideology and deserves the reputation as one of the movement's main instigators.

Gladden was fond of saying that his pragmatic social theology had been hammered out on the anvil of daily use. He saw that urban growth and industrial reorganization caused new problems for which there were no standard answers, these on a magnitude that could not allow Christian ethics to remain inside the realm of private practice. Through more than thirty-eight books, 114 articles, and countless speeches, he narrowed his criticism of American culture to specific issues related to labor-management relations, taxation, political corruption, racial bigotry, and religious sectarianism. He did not advocate any single formula for improvement but usually won the respect of all disputants in attempts to work out solutions from within a framework of Christian principles. He was an early leader in urging interdenominational cooperation on a pragmatic basis, and because of moral convictions too, in order to accomplish the larger tasks of social reform. That moderate, ecumenical spirit won him the enmity of those unwilling to admit Negroes, Catholics, and Jews to a legitimate place in national life. Gladden's lasting influence was that of supplying a sustained interpretation of the nature and direction of social change, together with a response based on his understanding of the churches' message of hope in that context. As one whose moral conscience could not avoid confronting the social injustices of modern society, his activities were a major factor in creating a level of religious awareness in community affairs not attained before.

Bibliography:

A.   *Applied Christianity: Moral Aspects of Social Questions* (New York, 1886); *Social Salvation* (New York, 1902); *Christianity and Socialism* (New York, 1905); *The Christian Pastor and the Working Church* (New York, 1907); *The Church and Modern Life* (New York, 1908); *Recollections* (Boston, 1909); *Present Day Theology* (Columbus, OH, 1913).

B.   SH 4, 492–93; NCAB 10, 256; DAB 7, 325–27; NYT 3 Jul 1918, 13; Jacob H. Dorn, *Washington Gladden: Prophet of the Social Gospel* (Columbus, OH, 1966); Richard D. Knudten, *The Systematic Thought of Washington Gladden* (New York, 1968).

GOLDSTEIN, David (27 July 1870, London, England—30 June 1958, Boston, MA). *Career*: director, Catholic Truth Guild, 1906–35; director, Catholic Campaigners for Christ, 1935–58.

Raised by Dutch-Jewish parents who came to America within a year of his birth, Goldstein received his education at synagogues, public academies, and at the Hebrew Free School of New York City. At a very early age he also followed his father into the cigar making trade and remained a lifelong member of the Cigar Makers' International Union. Members of that profession were at the forefront of labor union activities in this country, and this may explain why the young craftsman joined the Socialist Labor Party when he moved to Boston in 1888. In addition to his own work he lectured extensively for eight years, extolling the virtues of social and economic justice which his party advocated. During that time he ran unsuccessfully for mayor of Boston, the first to do so on the Socialist Labor ticket. At that time he also met Mrs. Martha Moore Avery whose interest in social problems drew them together. Her influence on Goldstein was considerable and manifested itself in different ways through the rest of his life. Not least of these facets was his resignation from the Socialist party in 1903 and his writing two subsequent books denouncing that orientation.

The second and more striking instance of Mrs. Avery's influence occurred in 1905 when Goldstein was baptized into the Roman Catholic faith at Boston's Immaculate Conception Church. The following year he inaugurated his own brand of evangelical outreach. The organization's name changed, but its approach continued the same for more than fifty years. Instead of following the usual procedures of large audiences, choral music, fervid preaching, and emphasis on conversion statistics, Goldstein developed a modest but effective person-to-person approach. He remained a layman and trained hundreds of others to reach people directly through personal contact and quiet conversation—not the standard manner of urban evangelism in the twentieth century. In this context he spent twenty-five years lecturing across the country in support of his evangelical methods. He also served as a determined apologist, defending his church against attack. Between 1945 and 1958 he supplied a column to the *Boston Pilot*, the diocesan newspaper. Among other acknowledgements of his contributions to the church, in 1955 Pope Pius XII made him a Knight of St. Gregory.

Bibliography:

A. *Socialism: The Nation of Fatherless Children* (Boston, 1903); *Bolshevism: Its Cure* (Boston, 1919); *Campaigning for Christ* (Boston, 1924); *Campaigners for Christ Handbook* (Boston, 1924); *Autobiography of a Campaigner for Christ* (Boston, 1936); *Letters Hebrew-Catholic to Mr. Isaacs* (St. Paul, MN, 1943).

B. NCE 6, 601–02; NYT 1 Jul 1958, 31.

GOOD, James Isaac (31 December 1850, York, PA—22 January 1924, Philadelphia, PA). *Education*: B.A., Lafayette Coll., 1872; B.D., Union Sem. (NY), 1875. *Career*: minister, German Reformed churches in York, PA (1875–77), Philadelphia, PA (1877–90), and Reading, PA (1890–1905); professor of religion, Ursinus Coll., 1890–1924; professor of theology, Central Theol. Sem., 1907–24.

While in his third pastorate Good began teaching, thus inaugurating the second and ultimately more significant part of his career. In 1893 he became dean of a theological school that had evolved from a college department, and five years later he moved his divinity students to a campus in downtown Philadelphia. By 1907 several elements merged to form Central Theological Seminary, located in Dayton, OH, and Good taught church history and liturgics there every fall semester. Each spring he lectured to undergraduates at Ursinus, and since he never married, such periodic shifts of residence were rather easily accomplished. During twenty-five summer vacations Good became a seasoned traveler in Europe, tracing the roots of Calvinism among the Germans, Dutch, and Swiss. In the course of those travels he made extensive notes that served a foundations for large publications on the origin and history of Reformed ecclesiastical traditions. He also made arrangements for documents and archival deposits to be copied and transported to libraries in the United States, thus to a considerable degree enhancing German Reformed historical scholarship in this country.

Good served on many of the larger managerial structures in his denomination, including the presidency of the General Synod from 1911 to 1914. Interested to some extent in ecumenical activities, he participated in the Reformed Alliance and the World Alliance of Reformed and Presbyterian Churches. In almost every facet of theology, Good was a thoroughgoing and undaunted conservative. He was content with the commonplace understanding of scripture, creeds, and historical experience which most people in his denomination held. He had no use for what he called the wild speculations of biblical criticism. In his view critical analysis was a threat to adequate faith and successful ministry. Liberalism tore the Bible apart and eroded the sure foundations on which Reformed theology rested. Good denounced references to evolution and to any other developmental process that attempted to explain the past. He also rejected the notion that Christianity needed to deal with social problems as part of its witness. He viewed innovations as signs of deteriorating faith, and his response was to confront those threats with an uncompromising reliance on beliefs formulated hundreds of years prior to his own age.

Bibliography:

A. *The Origins of the Reformed Church in Germany* (Reading, PA, 1887); *History of the Reformed Church in Germany, 1620–1890* (Reading, PA, 1894); *History of the Reformed Church in the United States, 1725–1792* (Reading, PA, 1899); *Famous Women of the Reformed Church* (Philadelphia, 1901); *Famous Missionaries of the Reformed Church* (Baltimore, 1903); *History of the Reformed Church in the U. S., in the Nineteenth Century* (New York, 1911).

B. NCAB 5, 360; DAB 7, 375–76; NYT 23 Jan 1924, 17; Carl H. Gramm, *The Life and Labors of the Reverend Prof. James I. Good, D.D., LL.D., 1850–1924* (Webster Groves, MO 1944).

GOODSPEED, Edgar Johnson (23 October 1871, Quincy, IL—13 January 1962, Los Angeles, CA). *Education*: B. A., Denison Univ., 1890; studied at Yale Univ., 1890–91; B.D. and Ph.D., Univ. of Chicago, 1897 and 1898. *Career*: schoolteacher, Morgan Park Academy and South Side Academy, Chicago, IL, 1891–92 and 1894–98; at various ranks, professor of Bible and Patristic Greek, Univ. of Chicago, 1902–37; professor emeritus, 1937–62.

Some individuals are fortunate enough never to deviate from activities chosen early in life, and in Goodspeed's case he continued to enjoy an initial love of classical languages, specializing in New Testament Greek later on. This facility, together with enlightened encouragement from the University of Chicago, made him one of the outstanding American biblical scholars in the twentieth century. For two years after earning his last degree he continued to study pre-Christian and early Christian texts at the universities of Oxford and Berlin. He advanced in mastery of Hellenic and Semitic literature even further while establishing personal friendships with prominent authorities in the field. Goodspeed became particularly fascinated with the task of deciphering the texts of Greek papyri and acquired invaluable knowledge of them at museums in Berlin, Cairo, Dresden, and the Hague. His philological research deepened, and his nurturing influence in this country helped spread more thoroughgoing knowledge of the original gospel languages and their cultural settings. Over his career he published more than fifty books, together with almost two hundred articles on facets of paleology and biblical literature.

On the academic side Goodspeed enhanced decades of scholarly inquiry into manuscripts and ancient texts. In 1923 he issued one of the first translations of the New Testament into contemporary English. His knowledge of the latest texts together with their historical provenance plus his passion for precise meaning and willingness to accept American idiomatic speech made this translation a bestseller. Its trustworthy scholarship, put forth in simple and straightforward English appealed to both critical and casual readers. Between 1930 and 1946 Goodspeed served as one of nine committee members who revised the American Standard Version of the Bible, producing the Revised Standard Version that eventually appeared in 1952. He also published other important contributions such as a harmony of the synoptic gospels, a gorgeous rendition of Codex 2400 of the Greek New Testament, and several important studies of apocryphal literature. Good health prolonged his years long after retirement, and he remained active with his pen in both popular writings and scrutinies of the most esoteric focus.

Bibliography:

A.   *The New Testament: An American Translation* (Chicago, 1923); *Things Seen and Heard* (Chicago, 1925); *The Meaning of Ephesians* (Chicago, 1933); *The Story of the Bible* (Chicago, 1936); *How to Read the Bible* (Philadelphia, 1946); *Matthew: Apostle and Evangelist* (Philadelphia, 1959).

B.   NCAB 52, 481–82; NCE 6, 629–30; NYT 14 Jan 1962, 84; James Harrell Cobb and Louis B. Jennings, *A Biography and Bibliography of Edgar Johnson Goodspeed* (Chicago, 1948); James I. Cook, *Edgar Johnson Goodspeed: Articulate Scholar* (Chico, CA, 1981).

GORDON, Adoniram Judson (19 April 1836, New Hampton, NH—2 February 1895, Boston, MA). *Education*: B.A., Brown Coll., 1860; B.D., Newton Sem., 1863. *Career*: minister, Jamaica Plain, MA, 1863–69; minister, Clarendon Street Baptist Church, Boston, 1869–95.

When Gordon became the pastor of a large urban Baptist church, he confronted the familiar circumstances of an affluent congregation whose religious interests were only partially stimulated. The young preacher soon reinvigorated public worship with lively sermons and with audience participation in singing, prayers, and responsive readings. He also fostered periodic revivals, his church becoming the center of evangelical influence that sometimes extended as far as the central Atlantic states. Around Boston, Gordon supported many philanthropic causes like settlement houses, prohibition, women's rights, protection for immigrants (Chinese in this case), and the defense of public schools against parochial competition. His activities as a minister in the town made him worthy of note.

But concern for the underprivileged at home did not compare with his desire to aid foreign missions. Gordon served on the executive committee of the American Baptist Missionary Board from 1871 to 1894 (chairman after 1888) and became particularly interested in China and the Congo. He had long been associated with *Dwight L. Moody because of joint revival endeavors. After attending Moody's summer conferences at Northfield, Gordon became a perennial fixture there and figured in the beginnings of the Student Volunteer Movement in 1886. Shortly after that, in 1889, he established his own vehicle for training men and women in practical missionary techniques, the Boston Missionary Training-School, a small but dedicated seminary which later bore his name.

Gordon's sense of urgency about missionary field work was enhanced by his premillennial beliefs. Along with many other Protestant evangelicals of his day, he expected the second coming of Christ at any moment, and that was a powerful motive for spreading the gospel while there was still time. Gordon was convinced that current historical events were portents of the end foretold in biblical prophecy. He interpreted Scripture literally and had no sympathy with optimistic views of human improvement or social progress. As one whose prominence in the millenarian movement went beyond denominational lines, he attended many Niagara Bible conferences and the American Bible and Prophetic Conferences during the last two decades of his life. His monthly journal, *Watchword*, founded in 1878, became one of the unofficial organs to disseminate millennialist expectations. Belief in Christ's imminent return and anticipations of a consummating spiritual fellowship in the one true Church gave both fervor and continuity to his varied ministry.

Bibliography:

A. *In Christ, or The Believer's Union with His Lord* (Boston, 1872); *Grace and Glory* (Boston, 1881); *The Twofold Life* (Boston, 1883); *Ecce Venit* (New York, 1889); *Ministry of the Spirit* (Philadelphia, 1894); *Yet Speaking* (New York, 1897).

B. SH 5, 24; NCAB 11, 263; Ernest B. Gordon, *Adoniram Judson Gordon: A Biography* (New York, 1896).

GORDON, George Angier (2 January 1853, Oyne, Scotland—25 October 1929, Brookline, MA). *Education*: B.D., Bangor Sem., 1877; B.A., Harvard Coll., 1881. *Career*: minister, Second Congregational Church, Greenwich, CT, 1881–84; minister, Old South Congregational Church, Boston, 1884–1929.

An eighteen-year-old immigrant newly arrived from Aberdeenshire, Gordon sought to preserve religious ties by associating with a Presbyterian church. He soon became acquainted with its minister, Luther H. Angier, who recognized in the boy potential for a life of clerical service. With pastor Angier's encouragement and financial aid, Gordon achieved high academic distinction first at seminary, then college. He adopted Angier as his middle name in gratitude for years of support. Though he came from a Calvinist theological heritage, he became an outspoken liberal, and some members of Old South Church in Boston wondered whether they had chosen a new minister wisely. He did not scruple to criticize traditional ideas when they were found to be out of keeping with current trends. The doctrine of arbitrary election, for example, was unacceptable. Instead of limited atonement he insisted that the gospel was available to everyone, at least until man in his free moral agency chose to accept it or not. He argued for the dignity and worth of human life instead of universal depravity, and the Fall was insufficient in his view to account for moral disorder. Over the years, though, Gordon proved to be a solid spiritual guide, a forthright defender of orthodoxy as it could be expressed in idioms of modern learning. His sermons emphasized standard liberal themes such as the fatherly attributes of God, individual responsibility in religious affirmations, and the genuine possibility of ethical progress. They spread ideas with increasing effectiveness in a congregation which grew over the decades.

Of all Gordon's pronouncements in modern religious thought, none was more striking than his Christology. He appreciated contemporary tendencies to stress the kinship between God and man, offering a view of eternal humanity in God and aspects of infinite significance in human existence. But he insisted that there was a fundamental distinction between those two orders of life that man's presumption tended to obscure. Jesus was a historic figure, the perfection of humanity, whose work showed by example the union which others might hope to experience. But behind the historical character, Gordon asserted, stood the eternal, pre-existent Son of God. Following a favorite theologian, Origen of Alexandria, he described God as an ineffable society within Himself where trinitarian and incarnational ideas still retained powerful relevance. Christ was uniquely divine, the indispensable medium for man's salvation, and lesser christological definitions robbed Christianity of its central focus. As a christocentric liberal, Gordon did not emphasize Jesus' sacrificial death as much as his moral example, but his resonant apology for divinity warned against further drift into humanism. Most of his preaching and writing on such themes continued until 1927 when semi-retirement gradually ended a long teaching ministry.

Bibliography:

    A. *The Christ of To-Day* (Boston, 1895); *Immortality and the New Theodicy* (Boston, 1897); *The New Epoch for Faith* (Boston, 1901); *Ultimate Conceptions of Faith* (Boston, 1903); *Through Man to God* (Boston, 1906); *My Education and Religion: An Autobiography* (Boston, 1925).
    B. SH 5, 24; NCAB 22, 307–08; DAB 7, 419–21; NYT 26 Oct 1929, 17.

GRACE, Charles Emmanuel (25 January 1881, Brava, Cape Verde Islands—12 January 1960, Los Angeles, CA). *Career*: bishop, United House of Prayer for All People, 1926–60.

After assuming a name indicative of his function more than his origins, "Daddy Grace" rose to prominence as charismatic leader of a radical pentecostal-holiness sect. Descended apparently from Portuguese and African ancestry, he did not admit to being a Negro; the greater portion of his followers nevertheless came from black ghettos in economically depressed urban areas. By 1926 he organized his first house of prayer in Charlotte, North Carolina, working up the seaboard to Newark, New Jersey, where he found another broad base of support. As bishop of the church he did not claim divine status, as did his cultic rival *Father Divine, but an emphasis on personal mediation was so strong, God was virtually forgotten. In fact, with double meaning to his words, he asserted that if one sinned against God, Grace could save the individual; but if one sinned against Grace, not even God's power could help. He preached that Grace was the only provision for salvation because all must receive Grace through faith. It was wrong, he argued, to worship God in heaven while ignoring Grace on earth. To clarify priorities, he assured audiences that Grace had given God a vacation and would take care of all difficulties which appeared in human experience before God's return. But sharp distinctions between the two were ultimately misleading because wherever Grace was visibly present on earth, God was invisibly there as well, rewarding the faithful in myriad tangible ways.

Adherents to the Grace cult received benefits in many concrete forms, the most important of which was probably healing. There were also ecstatic worship services with Bible reading, exhortations, brass bands, and frenzied dancing; sometimes the leader himself would appear at these meetings, and followers would shower him with dollar bills or rose petals. Additional helps for patrons took the form of church cafeterias and retirement homes, but personal testimonies always emphasized healing as the main reason for converting. Grace apparently cured hundreds of persons who attested to his remarkable ability. Even his *Grace Magazine* supposedly had curative powers; selling for ten cents and applied directly to the body, it was held to be a remedy for everything from chest colds to tuberculosis. Then too he sold a wide range of commodities such as toothpaste, soap, and cold cream—nostrums containing the hint of medicinal value in addition to their normal properties. Frequent donations of worldly goods were encouraged to continue Grace's church activities plus his flamboyant life style, in which followers participated vicariously. Annuities and gifts mounted to impressive proportions. Some have estimated membership figures as high as three million people spread through sixty cities with national headquarters in Washington, D.C. That total is probably too large, but the movement is substantial and has retained its vitality despite the death of its founder and struggles for power among his successors.

Bibliography:

B. NYT 13 Jan 1960, 47.

GRANT, Frederick Clifton (2 February 1891, Beloit, WI—11 July 1974, Gwynedd, PA). *Education*: studied at Lawrence Coll., 1907–09; studied at Nashotah House, 1909–11; B.D., General Sem., 1913; S.T.M. and Th.D., Western Sem., 1916 and 1922. *Career*: curate, St. Luke's Episcopal Church, Evanston, IL, 1917–20; rector, Trinity Church, Chicago, IL, 1921–24; editor, *Anglican Theological Review*, 1924–55; dean, Bexley Hall Div. Sch., 1924–26; librarian and professor of Systematic Theology, Berkeley Div. Sch., 1926–27; president, Western (Seabury-Western after 1933) Sem., 1927–38; professor of Biblical Theology, Union Sem. (NY), 1938–59; active retirement, 1959–74.

Modern developments in the specialized study of ancient scriptures found in Grant an independent thinker who furthered both the cause of scholarship and its application to contemporary religious practice. After early years of institutional administration, wherein he showed flashes of real talent, an offer from Union Seminary in New York made it possible to resume the research and teaching he loved best. Through that medium he imparted an infectious joy for study, embodying a positive and intellectual tradition which permeated the rigors of theological training with a rich, firm faith. As a distinguished New Testament scholar, he covered many fields with unusual thoroughness. Early interest in the life of Jesus led him to significant work in synoptic gospel studies; then he pursued questions related to the Jewish background of Christian origins, including both rabbinical and intertestamental writings; finally he conducted inquiries into the larger context of Hellenistic-Roman religions and their impact on emergent Christianity. In an effort to furnish the English-speaking world with the latest German scholarship, he translated important works by Rudolf Bultmann (1934), Johannes Weiss (1937), and Martin Dibelius (1939). He also served for years on the committee which produced (1946) the Revised Standard Version of the New Testament. An active churchman dedicated to his denomination as well as the universal community, he sought to relate biblical theology to people's everyday needs. In keeping with these goals he served as one of the four Anglican observers at the Second Vatican Council. For almost a half century he helped advance textual criticism together with the more personal qualities of religious life as illumined by such biblical study.

Bibliography:

A.   *New Horizons of the Christian Faith* (Milwaukee, 1928); *The Gospel of the Kingdom* (New York, 1940); *An Introduction to New Testament Thought* (New York, 1950); *The Gospels: Their Origin and Their Growth* (New York, 1957); *Ancient Judaism and the New Testament* (New York, 1959); *Rome and Reunion* (New York, 1965).

B.   NYT 13 July 1974, 26.

GRATZ, Rebecca (4 March 1781, Philadelphia, PA—27 August 1869, Philadelphia, PA). *Career*: secretary, Philadelphia Orphan Asylum, 1819–59; president, Hebrew Sunday School Society, 1838–64.

Born into a well-to-do merchant family Gratz showed early interest in local philanthropic endeavors. By the age of twenty she helped organize the Female

Association for the Relief of Women and Children in Reduced Circumstances and served for a time as secretary of that charitable organization. In 1815 she helped establish the Philadelphia Orphan Asylum, over whose affairs she presided with gentility and wisdom for forty years. Another institution to which she contributed was the Female Hebrew Benevolent Society, perhaps the central facilitating agency for her ideas about social welfare and certainly the main outlet for such work by women of her station. In 1850 Gratz wrote a letter to the *Occident*, a monthly magazine published in Philadelphia. Signing herself "a daughter of Israel," she advocated erecting an institutional system to care for those threatened with disintegrating family life. Largely through her efforts, the Jewish Foster Home and Orphan Asylum was begun in 1855 to meet that need. This and several other forms of social work allowed her to make positive contributions as American culture developed in the early national period.

Religious education for Jewish children was another interest that Gratz pursued over her long philanthropic career. As early as 1818 she conducted school for a small number of children in her own home. That venture was short-lived, but she gave the cause high priority in later years. Finally in 1838 she established the Hebrew Sunday School Society, the first of its kind in America and prototype for all others well into the twentieth century. With funds from the Female Hebrew Benevolent Society and staffing from Mikveh Israel, her family's synagogue begun by *Gershom M. Seixas, boys and girls from all parts of the Philadelphia Jewish community were welcome free of charge. Evidence of her dedication to such work is the fact that Gratz served as the Society's president until she was 83 years old. She never married but raised the nine children of her deceased sister. It has long been believed that she was the pattern for Sir Walter Scott's heroine of the same name in his novel, *Ivanhoe*. There is only meager and tenuous support for the claim, however, and she is better remembered not for her admitted physical beauty but for her more amply manifest spiritual qualities and broadly applied humanitarian zeal.

Bibliography:

B.   NCAB 10, 130; DAB 7, 505–06; NAW 2, 75–76; David Philipson (ed.), *Letters of Rebecca Gratz* (Philadelphia, 1929); Rollin G. Osterweis, *Rebecca Gratz: A Study in Charm* (New York, 1935).

GRAVES, James Robinson (10 April 1820, Chester, VT—26 June 1893, Memphis, TN). *Career*: schoolteacher, Kingsville, OH, 1840–42; schoolteacher, Jessamine County, KY, 1842–43; Baptist preacher in OH, 1843–45; editor, *The Tennessee Baptist*, 1846–89; retirement, 1889–93.

Early years on an unproductive Vermont farm did not allow Graves more than rudimentary schooling, but he compensated for that deficiency through intense private study. In 1842 he became a Baptist preacher and pastored churches at undetermined intervals for most of his life; his chief vocation, though, was journalism. He used the press to encourage sound doctrinal opinion, defending truth as he saw it and denouncing opponents with the single-minded truculence of a zealot. Beginning in 1848 he began publicizing ideas loyal to a rigid, exclusive conception of Baptist ecclesiology. Though he did not originate such thoughts or even coin the phrase, "old landmarks," Graves was the dominant figure in the Landmark movement which precipitated controversy in Southern Baptist circles for over half a century. In 1851 he convened at Cotton Grove, Tennessee, the mass meeting whose resolutions declared the manifesto of Landmarkism. By 1859 his paper had become the largest Baptist weekly in the world, sending some 13,000 subscribers a constant barrage of trenchantly polemical writing. After the Civil War, he developed a more conciliatory manner but did not soften in ideology. He moved the paper from Nashville to Memphis and from that base toured southern states as a platform speaker of considerable persuasiveness. His fame continued even after 1889, when a stroke confined him to a wheelchair. At that time he relinquished all interest in the paper, though it kept his name on the masthead until he died.

Doctrines and historical claims in Landmarkism sought to defend what were regarded as distinctive principles of Baptist existence. Graves articulated those ideas with a force that shaped attitudinal characteristics of local congregations, perpetuating them in some areas to the present time. Basic to their perspective was the belief that Baptist churches were a genuine apostolic institution; since the time of Christ, faithful followers had constituted the true church in unbroken succession by means of adult baptism and congregational polity. The valid work of God found visible expression in voluntary associations, having no temporal head such as bishops or assemblies, preserving without coercion the original doctrines and ordinances of primitive usage. A single deviation from this list of features, for example by Methodists or Campbellites whom Graves vehemently criticized, was enough to invalidate a church's presumed acceptability. Consequently, the negative side of Landmarkism gave it more prominence than positive assumptions. Baptists of this persuasion refused to recognize other "religious societies" as true churches because either their baptism, leadership, or organizational structure was wrong. They refused to exchange pulpits, permit fellowship with other professing Christians, or even admit that any institutional framework other than their own could benefit humanity in its quest for salvation. While such views did not extend to all Southern Baptists, they greatly stimulated denominational self-consciousness well into the twentieth century.

Bibliography:

A.   *The Great Iron Wheel: or, Republicanism Backwards, and Christianity Reversed* (Nashville, TN, 1855); *The Bible Doctrine of the Middle Life* (Memphis, TN, 1873); *Old Landmarkism: What Is It?* (Memphis, TN, 1880); *Inter-Communion of Churches Unscriptural, Deleterious, and Productive of Evil Only* (Memphis, TN, 1881); *The Work of Christ in the Covenant of Redemption: Developed in Seven Dispensations* (Memphis, TN, 1883).

B.   DAB 7, 507–08.

GRAY, James Martin (1851, New York, NY—21 September 1935, Chicago, IL). *Career*: rector, First Reformed Episcopal Church, Boston, 1879–94; independent evangelist, 1894–1904; professor of English Bible, Moody Bible Inst., 1904–35; dean and president (after 1908), Moody Bible Inst., 1904–34; editor, *Moody Bible Institute Monthly*, 1907–35.

The early background of Gray's life is unaccountably obscure, but his earliest known institutional affiliation discloses an evangelical religious orientation. As Episcopal minister of a low church reformist congregation, he stressed biblical preaching over ritualism and soon won the friendship of leading revivalists in Boston such as *Adoniram J. Gordon. Through Gordon he met *Dwight L. Moody who repeatedly engaged him as instructor at the Bible Institute in Chicago and at summer conferences held for students in Northfield, Massachusetts. Gray's emphasis on city revivalism together with careful Bible study ultimately led to a permanent relationship with the growing midwestern school. He originally expected to spend four months of every year in Chicago, with the remaining eight months left for preaching and extension work. But no other deans could be found to complement such an arrangement; so he found himself associated with the school as solitary administrator on a twelve month basis. As it turned out he supplied the longest, most stable leadership for the Institute since its founding and in the course of thirty years placed it on solid administrative foundations. For decades he served as supply preacher at the Moody Memorial Church in Chicago, helping to perpetuate in yet another way the fervent evangelical witness of urban revivalism.

In addition to influencing generations of students in the classroom, Gray's literary efforts contributed much to the development of a fundamentalist consensus in the early years of this century. His lectures on historic evidences of Christianity were used as a textbook in Bible institutes other than his own. He had an ability to answer destructive critics in simple terms laymen could understand, and in several widely distributed pamphlets denounced the follies of evolution, ecumenical movements, and eucharistic conferences. In one notable exchange he printed deliberate rebuttals to *Harry E. Fosdick, defending traditional doctrines regarding the virgin birth, plenary inspiration of the original Scriptures, substitutionary atonement, and a premillennial interpretation of Christ's second coming. But Scripture was his primary concern as teacher and expository evangelist. He thought there was a self-witness inherent in revelation that withstood all the doubting raised by textual critics. Instead of treating Scripture as a human document, he recommended that the faithful begin reading at Genesis and follow the Holy Spirit as it progressively unveiled the timeless meaning of God's Word. Continuous, prayerful reading strengthened his conviction as to the integrity and plenary inspiration of the whole Bible; it enlarged his vision about the divine plan of dispensational truth, and most of his instructional work exhibited such views to others. For that reason he was invited to contribute articles to *The Fundamentals* as a modern spokesman who would not yield the tenet of biblical inerrancy.

Bibliography:

A. *Synthetic Bible Studies* (Cleveland, OH, 1900); *Primers of the Faith* (New York, 1906); *Great Epochs of Sacred History* (New York, 1910); *Christian Workers' Commentary on the Old and New Testaments* (New York, 1915); *Prophecy and the Lord's Return* (New York, 1917); *Steps on the Ladder of Faith* (New York, 1930).
  B.   William M. Runyan, *Dr. Gray at Moody Bible Institute* (New York, 1935).

GREELEY, Dana McLean (5 July 1908, Lexington, MA—13 June 1986, Concord, MA). *Education*: B.S., Harvard Coll., 1931; S.T.B., Harvard Div. Sch., 1933. *Career*: Unitarian minister, Lincoln, MA (1932–34), Concord, NH (1934–35), and Boston, MA (1935–58); secretary, American Unitarian Association, 1945–53; president, A.U.A., 1958–61; president, Unitarian-Universalist Association, 1961–69; Unitarian minister, Concord, MA, 1970–86.

In 1961 the American Unitarian Association merged with the Universalist Church of America, and Greeley was named the first president of this new denomination. This culmination ended a lengthy process of discussions and studies begun with an accord known as the Free Church Fellowship in 1934, just two years after Greeley was ordained as a Unitarian minister. The two churches increasingly realized their common tradition of religious freedom and local autonomy as they issued a joint hymnal in 1937, formed a Council of Liberal Churches in 1953, and appointed in 1955 a commission to study consolidation seriously. Plebiscites in 1959–60 approved the plan. Choosing Greeley to head the new union proved to be a wise decision because he excelled in diplomacy and equitable judgment. When he became president of the American Unitarians in 1958, it had been the first contested election in the church's 133 year history, but he succeeded in holding religious factions together. There were serious differences between those who wanted explicit references to the Jewish-Christian tradition and others who encouraged free thought and wished to unite liberals of all persuasions. Greeley took the middle ground and hoped that his church, while not severing its ties with Protestant Christianity, could still serve as a bridge between Christian and non-Christian worlds.

In addition to activities that nourished ecclesiastical growth, much of Greeley's efforts were directed to problems in contemporary culture. He was convinced that a vital faith manifested itself best by relating dynamically to the major social concerns of the day. As a consequence of this practical religious motivation he became a leading voice in this century's civil rights movement. He served on the Unitarian Service Committee and on several urban leagues, as trustee for several colleges, orphanages, and old age homes, as member of the Massachusetts Council of Churches, and as participant on many projects concerning community welfare or service. Greeley was a fervent seeker after peace as well as freedom. He helped found and co-chair the World Conference on Religion and Peace in addition to serving on the administrative board of the Inter-Religious Peace Commission. His many contributions in this area acquired more tangible form when a foundation for peace and justice was organized and named in his honor, just two months before his death.

Bibliography:

A.   *Toward Larger Living: Sermons on Personal Religion* (Boston, 1944); *A Message to Atheists* (Boston, 1948); *25 Beacon Street and Other Recollections* (Boston, 1971); *Know the Concordians* (Concord, MA, 1975).
    B.   NYT 14 June 1986, 32.

GRIMKÉ, Angelina Emily (20 February 1805, Charleston, SC—26 October 1879, Hyde Park, MA).

Firsthand experience with slavery brought Angelina Grimké slowly to the iron conclusion that it was wrong. As her sister *Sarah had done earlier, she left the Episcopal church in 1826 and, after a year's sojourn among Presbyterians, became a Quaker as the only honest option left. She was reluctant to leave South Carolina, but by 1829 Philadelphia was her home, and she began attending antislavery meetings soon thereafter. By 1835 both sisters were fully committed to abolition, with the more eloquent Angelina being the first to accept invitations to address women regarding the issue. She also wrote an appeal for southern women to speak out against a criminal system which contravened both divine justice and the Declaration of Independence. The erstwhile aristocrat gained a reputation for earnest, forceful speeches presented with a magnetic style that captivated audiences. Her knowledge and moral suasion were so great that she was invited to address mixed audiences, becoming one of the first American women to do so. In 1838 she accomplished a similar first by addressing the Massachusetts legislature and presenting it with an antislavery petition signed by 20,000 women. But so intense was the opposition to her speaking in public, it became necessary to defend women's rights as well as the abolitionist cause. Both sisters found that working for the liberation of slaves became ineluctably linked with exertions to secure their own freedom.

The gifted speaker who attracted wide notice for moral convictions about race relations discovered that she was also involved in the question of women's rights. Thus she became one of the first Americans to present a reasoned case for the legal and social emancipation of women. With great dignity and compelling logic she argued that women were moral, intelligent, and responsible human beings who needed a voice in forming the laws by which they were governed. Though her primary concern was over slavery, for a short while she formed part of the original generation of feminist leaders. In 1838, to the dismay of many who thought it would curtail her reformist work, she married *Theodore D. Weld, another famous antislavery spokesman. After 1840 she was often ill; the combined distractions of convalescence, domestic life, and Weld's own health problems after 1844 did bring about a semi-retirement from public life. Through the 1850s and 1860s Angelina found some satisfaction in teaching, translating, and writing for newspapers. But the time of her greatest impact on national life was during the 1830s when she remarked to her sister that abolitionist women were turning the world upside down.

Bibliography:

A. *Appeal to the Christian Women of the South* (New York, 1836); *Letters to Catherine E. Beecher* (Boston, 1838); *Letters of Theodore Dwight Weld, Angelina Grimké Weld and Sarah Grimké, 1822–1844*, ed. Gilbert H. Barnes and Dwight W. Dumond, 2 vols. (New York, 1934).

B. NCAB 2, 325; DAB 7, 234–35; NAW 2, 97–99; Theodore D. Weld, *In Memory: Angelina Grimké Weld* (Boston, 1880); Catherine H. Birney, *The Grimké Sisters: Sarah and Angelina Grimké* (Boston, 1885); Gerda Lerner, *The Grimké Sisters from South Carolina* (Boston, 1967); Katharine D. Lumpkin, *The Emancipation of Angelina Grimké* (Chapel Hill, 1974).

GRIMKÉ, Francis James (4 November 1850, near Charleston, SC—11 October 1937, Washington, DC). *Education*: B.A., Lincoln Univ., 1870; studied law at Lincoln Univ. (1870–71 and 1872–73) and at Howard Univ. (1874–75); B.D., Princeton Sem., 1878. *Career*: graduate instructor and financial agent, Lincoln Univ., 1871–72; minister, Fifteenth Street Presbyterian Church, Washington, DC, 1878–85 and 1889–1928; minister, Laura Street Church, Jacksonville, FL, 1885–89.

As the second son of Nancy Weston, a mulatto slave, and Henry Grimké, brother to *Angelina and *Sarah Grimké, the young man grappled early with the uncertainties of illegitimacy and servant status. His half-brother sold him to a Confederate officer during the Civil War, but after manumission at the end of the conflict benefactors sent him and his brothers to a liberal school in Pennsylvania. There Grimké excelled and thus came to the attention of his aunts who publicly acknowledged their relation to him and subsidized his education. For a time he studied law like his elder brother, Archibald, but in time he chose to enter the Presbyterian ministry instead. After customary seminary training he was ordained in 1878 and settled into a pastorate that lasted for half a century, except for a four-year interlude occasioned by health problems. The church in rapidly urbanizing Washington attracted the elite of Negro society, and Grimké soon became an outstanding leader among his people, notable for both a powerful intellect and eloquent sermons.

Late nineteenth century America exhibited an ugly intransigence against blacks, and Grimké spoke out boldly against every form of racist prejudice. Lynchings, disfranchisement, and Jim Crow legislation made emancipation seem a mockery, but the Presbyterian pastor rallied other Afro-American clergy in the capital city to fight those abuses. Grimké advocated character formation and moral integrity as the basis on which American Negroes could achieve equality with whites. Through hard work, industrial education, and respect for authority black citizens could insist upon parity among others because they deserved it. The Christian ministry could function in this struggle as the conscience of society as well as the fundamental source of moral instruction. As the years went by, Grimké became less interested in accommodation and more of a gadfly, impatient at slow progress and insistent about more tangible changes. His prophetic ardor did not diminish with the years. His cogent reminders that all believers should be equal in the church continued through his lifetime and after it to trouble temporizers in his denomination and in society at large.

Bibliography:

A. *The Works of Francis James Grimké*, ed., Carter G. Woodson, 4 vols. (Washington, DC, 1942).

GRIMKÉ, Sarah Moore (26 November 1792, Charleston, SC—23 December 1873, Hyde Park, MA).

Social reformers of high moral principle are not often willing to sacrifice wealth and high status. But Sarah Grimké was exceptional in refusing to accept the privileges of an aristocratic heritage because they were based on slave labor. She was also alienated by social patterns which placed her in subordinate rank, allowing enough education for polite society but forbidding other topics like Latin, philosophy, and law, which were reserved for men. Her deep revulsion at injustices suffered by slaves led to some attempts at relieving their condition, but family pressure frustrated those mild versions of reform. In 1819 Sarah became acquainted with Quakers while accompanying her father in Pennsylvania and New Jersey. She read the works of *John Woolman several times and found that he expressed her own convictions about the cruelty of human bondage. By 1821 she left plantation life altogether, moved to Philadelphia, and two years later braved ostracism by joining the Society of Friends. Led by the example of *Lucretia Mott, she tried for a short time to become a Quaker minister, but personal timidity and a halting speaking style created generally unfavorable receptions at local meetings. With antislavery crusading still the leading passion in her life, her sympathy for the cause continued to grow despite the fact that most Philadelphia Quakers were reluctant to endorse reform. By 1836 she refused further association with them because of what she considered unconscionable temporizing with the evil.

Though she was not as bold or fluent as her younger sister, *Angelina, Sarah moved to New York and cast her lot with the abolitionists. She wrote a stirring appeal to southern clergymen, urging them to take the initiative in opposing slavery. Another of her publications rebutted the argument that slavery in biblical times justified its continuance. An indifferent response to such ideas convinced her that she must begin public lectures for the antislavery cause, even though it was not customary for women to conduct themselves in that manner. For nine months in 1838, Sarah and her sister toured New England on behalf of abolition, arousing at the same time considerable excitement over the side issue of whether women had the right to say anything about public issues. For a brief time she stood in the front lines of both the antislavery struggle and the controversy over women's rights in American society. By 1840 she no longer occupied a central place in those related fields, preferring to live quietly with her sister and brother-in-law. Teaching school became a second vocation during the 1850s and 1860s, as the family home moved to various towns in New Jersey and Massachusetts. Causes which she originally championed had taken different directions by the time of her death, but none could forget that Sarah Grimké was among the first female antislavery agents.

Bibliography:

A. *An Epistle to the Clergy of the Southern States* (New York, 1836); *Letters on the Equality of the Sexes and the Condition of Woman* (Boston, 1838).

B. See listings under Grimké, Angelina Emily.

GRISWOLD, Alexander Viets (22 April 1766, Simsbury, CT—15 February 1843, Boston, MA). *Career*: rector, Plymouth, Harwinton, and Northfield, CT, 1795–1804; rector, St. Michael's church, Bristol, RI, 1804–30; rector, St. Peter's church, Salem, MA, 1830–35; Episcopal bishop, Eastern Diocese, 1811–43.

Young Griswold had hoped to attend Yale college, but reprisals against his family during the Revolution made it impossible to pay for formal schooling. He married early and became a farmer, reading in his spare time on a wide variety of subjects. By 1794 friends persuaded him to prepare for orders, and he was ordained an Episcopal priest less than two years later. Work in early parishes was supplemented by farm labor in summer and schoolteaching in winter. He performed such tasks dutifully for years, viewing the office as an obligation rather than one where ministering to others was a joyful vocation. As something of a formalist, he manifested little piety and mentioned the prayer book more than the Bible in homilies. His preaching usually illustrated moral precepts, instead of spiritual truths, that might serve as the fountainhead of living godliness. But consecration as bishop at the age of forty-six produced an inner crisis. Serious thoughts about the duties of a Christian minister struck home for the first time, and after that Griswold was a changed man. He became decidedly evangelical in his preaching; those under his jurisdiction were urged to stress personal experience in religious devotions; a general awakening occurred in his diocese, marking an increase in piety among the growing numbers of church members. As a leading exponent of low-church, evangelical attitudes, he emphasized gospel preaching with slightly more priority than sacraments or creedalism.

When Griswold became bishop of the "Eastern District," a diocese comprising all of New England except Connecticut, he faced a vast territory which held only twenty-four parishes. It was largely due to his durable energy and executive ability that the number of Episcopal churches grew to one hundred by 1840. He issued many pastoral letters wherein the missionary duty of every church was a dominant theme. Societies for developing Sunday Schools and greater dissemination of religious literature were encouraged. He cooperated with interdenominational societies to increase Bible distribution. In 1820 he was the principal agent behind founding at general convention the Domestic and Foreign Missionary Society. Griswold labored tirelessly for his widespread diocese, making frequent visitations at great physical sacrifice to himself. He was usually self-effacing but stood firm in exercising canonical authority when occasion demanded. Still, Episcopal communions expanded under his care mostly because of the tact and moderation with which he guided their endeavors. After 1835 he also served as presiding bishop. No successor was appointed when the venerated ordinary died because he had performed his tasks so well. By that time the extension of churches was so great, five dioceses were created where only one had stood before.

Bibliography:

A.   *Convention Addresses* (Middlebury, VT, 1827); *Discourses on the Most Important Doctrines and Duties of the Christian Religion* (Philadelphia, 1830); *The Reformation: A Brief Exposition of Some of the Errors and Corruptions of the Church of Rome* (Boston, 1843); *Remarks on Social Prayer-Meetings* (Boston, 1858).

B.   AAP 5, 415–25; NCAB 4, 78–79; DAB 8, 7–8; John S. Stone, *Memoir of the Life of the Rt. Rev. Alexander Viets Griswold* (Philadelphia, 1844).

H

HAAS, Francis Joseph (18 March 1899, Racine, WI—29 August 1953, Grand Rapids, MI). *Education*: studied at St. Francis Sem. (WI), 1904–13; studied at Johns Hopkins Univ., 1920–21; Ph.D., Catholic Univ., 1922. *Career*: curate, Holy Rosary parish, Milwaukee, WI, 1913–15; professor of English, St. Francis Sem., 1915–19; professor of Sociology and dean of college departments at Marquette Univ., 1922–31; editor, *Salesianum*, 1922–31; president, National Catholic Sch. of Social Service, 1931–35; rector, St. Francis Sem., 1935–37; dean, Sch. of Social Science, Catholic Univ., 1937–43; bishop, Diocese of Grand Rapids, MI, 1943–53.

Practical action in the area of labor-management relations was a form of religious witness which Haas developed to a remarkably effective degree. Wide experience and clear statement of spiritual motivations made him one of the American priests most closely identified with twentieth-century Catholic thought on social justice. In that context, he often argued that American citizens had a right to industrial peace, full production of goods, and security of livelihood. He wrote many pamphlets on the question of equitable labor practices, many of them published by the Paulist Press under auspices of the Social Action Department of the National Catholic Welfare Conference. Those publications maintained that economic slavery was the chief modern obstacle to persons' enjoying their God-given destiny of freedom. To remedy this, he envisioned cooperative production systems in which personal initiative and private enterprise would not be abolished but rather harnessed as means of promoting the common good. While head of the National Catholic School of Social Services, established by fellow social activist *John J. Burke, he sought to instill in participants the ideal of genuine harmony in socio-economic terms. This goal took concrete form in his mind, including fair distribution of goods and balance between price and income, together with recurrent collective bargaining as a safeguard for corporate interests and personal liberty.

As a labor relations expert, Haas repeatedly proved himself to be a master of conciliation. Early in his arbitration activity, he successfully ajudicated disputes of truckers and newspaper workers in Wisconsin. He was also a long-time advocate of national policies regarding old age pensions and social security benefits. He belonged to literally dozens of associations which sought progress in causes ranging from international peace to racial harmony as facets of one central objective: social justice. During the Great Depression he performed yeoman's service on a continental scale. In 1933 he became a member of the Labor Advisory Board, which functioned under the National Recovery Act. Moving to the U.S. Department of Labor in 1935 as a special strike mediator, he is said to have successfully settled over 1,500 disputes in that capacity. Such work demonstrated, he said, the triumph of democracy. In 1943 he combined membership on countless other boards with becoming chairman of the embattled Committee on Fair Employment Practices. He immediately began utilizing that office to end racial discrimination in trades unions and industries, but elevation to a bishopric terminated the work before it accomplished much. For the last decade of his life, he administered diocesan affairs with the same energy and fairness that had characterized his activities in larger circles of national life.

Bibliography:

A. *Shop Collective Bargaining: A Study of Wage Determination* (Washington, DC, 1922); *Man and Society: An Introduction to Sociology* (New York, 1930).

B. NCAB D, 34; NCE 6, 875; NYT 30 Aug 1953, 88; Thomas E. Blantz, *A Priest in Public Service: Francis J. Haas and the New Deal* (Notre Dame, IN, 1982).

HAMMOND, Lily Hardy (24 September 1859, Newark, NJ—24 January 1925, New York, NY).

After culminating her private education with study at Brooklyn's Packer Institute, Lily Hardy married a minister and returned to the South, her ancestral home. For decades she was a leading proponent of more effective social service programs among Southern Methodists. Working particularly through the Women's Missionary Council of that denomination she tried to show in practical ways how saving souls also implied the task of changing physical conditions. Mrs. Hammond spoke of local problems as part of the moral dilemma germane to all modern societies. She spoke with great sensitivity regarding issues of race prejudice found in southern states, but these immediate difficulties were interpreted in a larger context of universal human values. The order of the day, she said at a time when few dared raise their voice, was to face social problems soberly and solve them in the light of principles found in religious faith. With that moral impulse, she confronted most of the tough issues in post-Reconstruction times: Jim Crow discrimination, mob violence, labor peonage, and poverty. Calling for wider horizons, she asked whites to lay aside, not their wish for racial separation, but their prejudice. In that spirit she singled out better housing and education as keys to Negro improvement. Personal hygiene, vocational training, and moral leadership could help give black Americans the backbone every race needs to acquire self-respect. Moreover she called on southern women as a whole to mold strong families out of which an improved society would emerge. Mothers were the most important influence on succeeding generations because through example and instruction they provided the ideals needed for human reform. Every race has potential for greater development, she urged, and Christian mothers held the promise of such progress. Her liberal attitude on racial harmony did not extend to equality; race consciousness was inevitable, and separate-but-equal facilities for Blacks seemed an acceptable relationship. But in the early decades of this century, even modest suggestions for reform were ahead of common notions, and they helped move public opinion toward a higher standard of social justice.

Bibliography:

A. *The Master-Word: A Story of the South Today* (New York, 1905); *In Black and White: An Interpretation of Southern Life* (New York, 1914, 1972); *In the Garden of Delight* (New York, 1916); *In the Vanguard of a Race* (New York, 1922, 1972); *Missionary Heroes* (Nashville, 1925).
B. NYT 25 Jan 1925, II, 7.

HANDSOME LAKE (1735, village of Gano'wages on the Genesee River, NY—10 August 1815, Onondaga Reservation, NY).

The Seneca nation was the westernmost of five original "longhouses" that comprised the Iroquois League. Their power centered in New York state and extended as far as the upper Ohio valley and Canada, where they came into contact with Jesuit missionary *Isaac Jogues in 1642. The Iroquois were caught between the larger struggles of France and England, however, and gradually suffered attrition. By the time Handsome Lake was born, or Ganio'dai'io as he was called in Iroquoian, the era of Seneca dominance and prosperity was coming to an end. By 1787 the warrior tradition had been disrupted, hunting territories were opened to white settlement, their far-flung political league was reduced to impotence, and religious customs were slowly abandoned as inapplicable or no longer relevant. The end result of such a trend seemed to be the dissolution of a once cohesive way of life through the slow decay of disillusioned individuals.

Handsome Lake embodied along with many others the despair and rootlessness occasioned by the decline of his nation's culture. For a time he turned to whiskey and other aimless pursuits to assuage the loss of identity, but his most important response eventually provided his people with the moral fiber necessary for cohesion and survival. In 1799 he began experiencing a series of visions or revelations from four beings who told of the Creator's will. These revelations formed the basis of a new religious awareness, Gai'wiio' or "Longhouse Religion," which Handsome Lake preached for the last sixteen years of his life. It consisted of moral and social reforms that preserved Iroquoian culture, forming Indian life around an Indian religion. The new code afforded a framework for revitalized native values in the face of alien hostilities.

There were four main tenets at the base of the new message, four acts which angered the Creator and threatened to alienate Him altogether. These actions denounced by Handsome Lake were: (1) evil to oneself, particularly the use of alcohol, (2) witchcraft and (3) poison that spread malicious destruction to others, and (4) herbs that produced abortions and sterility. Generalizing on these tenets, the Seneca prophet urged his people to stop wasting their own lives in corruption, to cease working for ill effects among their tribesmen, and to accept the responsibility for building a new generation by means of marital fidelity and a strong home life. In the face of defeat, frustration, and poverty, a new gospel of self-respect arose to reject despair and affirm many of the values that had originally made the Iroquois great. It slowly won followers among the Six Nations as a revitalizing force, and by 1861 the Gai'wiio' religion was the only form in which some old traditions survived into modern times.

Bibliography:

B.   Arthur C. Parker, *The Code of Handsome Lake, the Seneca Prophet* (Albany, 1913); Anthony F. C. Wallace, *The Death and Rebirth of the Seneca* (New York, 1969).

HARKNESS, Georgia Elma (21 April 1891, Harkness, NY—21 August 1974, Claremont, CA). *Education*: B.A., Cornell Univ., 1912; Ph.D., Boston Univ., 1923. *Career*: high school teacher, Schuylerville, NY, 1912–14, and Scotia, NY, 1914–18; professor of Religious Education, Elmira Coll. for Women, 1923–37; professor of History and Literature, Mt. Holyoke Coll., 1937–39; professor of Applied Theology, Garrett Sem., 1939–50; professor of Applied Theology, Pacific Sch. of Religion, 1950–61; active retirement, 1961–74.

It was unusual for a woman in the early decades of this century to pursue theological studies, but Harkness pioneered in the field with unobtrusive ability and sustained competence. Her publications mounted to a total of thirty-six volumes, in which she exhibited a gift for combining sound scholarship with concern for basic human needs in religion. She did not write for professional colleagues but sought rather to make difficult doctrines plain enough for the average person to understand. In a manner not at all simplistic, she conveyed an evangelical approach to theological questions as an aid for laymen to improve their potential witness. She understood the modern world but reaffirmed tenets of a trinitarian faith in the face of atomic bombs, politics of fear, personality crises, and a decaying sense of community. Though she was the first woman named to a theological professorship, she kept the practical interests of nonspecialists in mind as she developed thoughts with appreciable practicability. Many of her devotional works dealt with the inner spiritual life where she offered guides for private prayer as well as meditations on the Bible, apostolic history, and doctrine centering on the Holy Spirit. Books of poems and prayers of her own composition complemented a strong emphasis on God as revealed through Christ (primarily), the natural world, and human experience.

Private devotions served to strengthen Harkness' loyalty to the institutional aspects of religious practice. She devoted years of service to the Methodist church, in which she was reared, and was fittingly recognized (1947) as one of the ten most influential living Methodists. As early as 1926 she had been designated a local elder, but that did not mean full ordination. While not a militant feminist, she persistently advocated equal clerical status for qualified women in the church. Ironically enough, when this became possible after 1956, she declined it. She had been one of the leading agents in counteracting male domination in religious institutions but refused to break her association with the laity by joining the ministerial ranks. This did not hamper her work in larger organizations. She participated six times as delegate to the General Conference of the United Methodist Church. Beginning in 1937 (Oxford) and then in 1952 (Lund), she brought creative insights to bear on ecumenical conferences regarding Life and Work. As delegate to the World Council of Churches (Amsterdam, 1948; Evanston, 1954) she was instrumental in drafting statements on social and economic issues. Of all the public questions in which she had a hand, probably none attracted more attention than her stand in 1950 protesting the use of atomic weapons, whether in retaliation or for strategic purposes. In sermons, books or the classroom, on Methodist boards or ecumenical commissions, Harkness contributed much to religious thought and practice during her lifetime.

Bibliography:

A. *Dark Night of the Soul* (New York, 1945); *Understanding the Christian Faith* (New York, 1947); *Christian Ethics* (New York, 1957); *Beliefs That Count* (New York, 1961); *Grace Abounding* (Nashville, 1969); *Women in Church and Society* (Nashville, 1971).

B. NYT 22 August 1974, 36.

HARPER, Frances Ellen Watkins (24 September 1825, Baltimore, MD—22 February 1911, Philadelphia, PA).

Frances Watkins was born to free Negro parents, but their deaths caused her to be raised by an uncle in whose school she developed both literary ability and a passion for cultural progress through education. As early as 1845, some of her writing was published—poems of modish sentimental tone and earnest content which eventually made her the most popular black poet since Phillis Wheatley. After several years of teaching near Columbus, Ohio (1850–52), and Little York, Pennsylvania (1852–54), she became deeply involved in the antislavery movement. Her facility with words made her an eloquent spokeswoman who stirred hundreds of audiences with moral fervor and forceful oratory. Employed initially by Maine antislavery societies, she toured that state denouncing the Fugitive Slave Law as an abomination which all men should defy. For another five years (1856–60), she lectured in states from New York to Ohio on the abolition platform. Her home in Philadelphia became an important station in the underground railroad; fugitives always found in her a sympathetic friend who encouraged their efforts with words and all forms of material aid. Her sacrifice of money, time, talent, and energy was natural as well as unassuming because she thought it an elemental act for the cause of freedom. Antislavery was an impulse common to all persons of decency, and she insisted that her part in it was not a duty but a right.

In 1860 Miss Watkins married Fenton Harper and settled on a farm in central Ohio, to the regret of abolitionists who considered her removal a great loss to the cause. But her husband died in 1864, and Mrs. Harper began lecturing again, this time impressing postwar listeners with the opportunities presented them by emancipation. She made extended tours of southern states, speaking to Negro and mixed audiences on the importance of education as a means of cultural improvement. Like an itinerant evangelist, she embodied the new gospel of education, castigating ignorance as an evil and upholding instruction as a divinely appointed remedy. She felt particularly attracted to freedwomen in the South who sorely needed the rudiments of homemaking skills together with a simple command of reading and writing. This moral sense of doing things to improve her race led Mrs. Harper into many fields. Though denominationally associated with Unitarians, she helped organize Sunday Schools for all children and participated actively in programs of the African Methodist Episcopal (AME) Church. Later in life her general concern for moral uplift focused on the Women's Christian Temperance Union. She gave able direction to temperance work among black Americans for almost a decade and then went on to head up other national associations with educational goals. She also participated in the movement for woman's suffrage, but her lasting contribution lay in efforts for ethnic improvement through various avenues of learning.

Bibliography:

A. *Poems on Miscellaneous Subjects* (Boston, 1854); *Moses: A Story of the Nile* (Philadelphia, 1869); *Poems* (Philadelphia, 1871); *Sketches of Southern Life* (Philadelphia, 1872); *Iola Leroy, or Shadows Uplifted* (Philadelphia, 1892).
B. NAW 2, 137–39.

HARPER, William Rainey (24 July 1856, New Concord, OH—10 January 1906, Chicago, IL). *Education*: B.A., Muskingum Coll., 1870; Ph.D., Yale Univ., 1875. *Career*: principal, Macon Masonic Coll., 1875–76; tutor and principal of preparatory school, Denison Univ., 1876–79; instructor in Hebrew, Baptist Union Sem., 1879–86; professor of Semitic Languages, Yale Univ., 1886–91; head of Semitic Department and president, Univ. of Chicago, 1891–1906.

From his earliest years Harper exhibited a precocious ability to master languages. He was particularly fascinated with Hebrew, and two years after graduating from college at the age of fourteen he held classes there in that subject.

Private study together with formal training at Yale provided familiarity with Greek, Latin, Sanskrit, and German in addition to a half dozen cognate Semitic tongues. During his early years as a teacher in boys' schools Harper slowly reached an important religious decision. His family was affiliated with United Presbyterians, but in 1876 he became a Baptist. He had a tremendous capacity for hard work, and his enthusiasm for study was contagious. Those qualities would have led to imminence of some sort in any event, but his identity with Baptists also helped shape his career in Chicago. While teaching at a denominational seminary there, Harper broached the idea of conducting a summer school. That proved so successful, he developed correspondence courses and textbooks for those who could not travel. He launched two journals: *Hebrew Student* (later named *Biblical World*) and *Hebraica* (later named *American Journal of Semitic Languages and Literature*). He was also associated with educational work at Chautauqua summer gatherings, showing that a different focus for labor was vacation enough for him.

By 1890 it was evident that John D. Rockefeller was going to endow a great university and that he wanted fellow-Baptist Harper to be its first president. Harper accepted on condition that the new institution begin as a full-fledged university, not just a well-equipped college that might someday grow into one. He displayed a talent for organization, administration, and fund raising. But much more important, Harper instilled the University of Chicago with a spirit of open inquiry and academic freedom. He had little interest in theological controversies and wanted the Divinity School at his university to ease tensions among denominational conservatives by exemplifying an honest search for truth. He built an institution that showed students how to think, not what to believe. That university remains important today because it still honors Harper's conviction that neither individual, state, nor church has the right to interfere with the search for truth.

Bibliography:

A.   *Introductory Hebrew Method and Manual* (Chicago, 1885); *The Priestly Element in the Old Testament: An Aid to Historical Study* (Chicago, 1902); *Religion and the Higher Life* (Chicago, 1904); *A Critical and Exegetical Commentary on Amos and Hosea* (New York, 1905); *The Trend in Higher Education* (Chicago, 1905).

B.   SH 5, 158–59; NCAB 11, 65–67; DAB 8, 287–92; NYT 11 Jan 1906, 9; Thomas Wakefield Goodspeed, *William Rainey Harper: First President of the University of Chicago* (Chicago, 1928); James P. Wind, *The Bible and the University: The Messianic Vision of William Rainey Harper* (Atlanta, GA, 1987).

HAVEN, Gilbert (19 September 1821, Malden, MA—3 January 1880, Malden, MA). *Education*: B.A., Wesleyan Univ., 1846. *Career*: schoolteacher, Amenia, NY, 1846–51; minister in Northampton, Wilbraham, Westfield, Roxbury, and Cambridge, MA, 1851–61; chaplain, Union Army, 1861; minister, Boston, 1863–67; editor, *Zion's Herald*, 1867–72; bishop of the Methodist Episcopal Church, 1872–80.

In 1850, one year before Haven was licensed to preach, a fugitive slave law was passed by Congress to ease sectional tensions. That compromise legislation transformed the young idealist into a staunch abolitionist who went on to become one of the most outspoken exponents of racial equality in his generation. As a clergyman who had not abandoned the old New England view of national covenant with God, he also embodied a millennial hope of inaugurating the final era of human brotherhood. From that perspective he preached salvation from all sin—personal, social, and national. He appealed to a higher law opposing popular sovereignty, claiming that divine will was greater than political authority, urging national repentance and reaffirmation of undiscriminating liberty for all men. But on the tangible level, Haven called for more than acceptance of a principle; he wanted absolute social equality even to the point of racial amalgamation. Many considered him radical to the point of madness on this score, but he thought it the only logical conclusion of full emancipation. In all his activities, as minister, military chaplain, editor, and bishop, he vigorously pursued this end. In pursuit of benefits for freedmen, he was one of the first to discern that racism no less than slavery had to be overcome. Through the last two decades of his life he battled against color caste, a massive prejudice in white America that eventually thwarted much of his effort for further reform.

When slavery ended, it became clear to Haven that racism was a more pervasive, insidious enemy of new social ordering. As episcopal representative of northern Methodism, he was based at Atlanta and toured southern conferences in a postwar crusade against caste in the churches. His uncompromising opposition to segregation did not endear him to many in the South, but he criticized laws which excluded Blacks from politics, established racially separate schools, or prevented intermarriage. He often proved an embarrassment to northern colleagues in such agitation, but that did not prevent his support of full and open fraternization between races in everything ranging from worship to eating facilities. Haven wished to help freedmen find sound economic bases to accompany their political fights, though he made no lasting contribution toward achieving that goal. He solicited funds and recruited northern teachers for a while, but his efforts consisted largely of exhortation rather than practical programs. After contracting malaria on a visit to Liberia (1876), he was forced to adopt an attenuated schedule of duties. While he still wrote often about equal rights, it was his bitter fate to witness the end of Reconstruction policies, the establishment of white supremacy in virtually every aspect of American culture, and the imposition of color barriers even in his own church.

Bibliography:

A.   *The Pilgrim's Wallet* (Boston, 1866); *National Sermons* (Boston, 1869; New York, 1969); *Father Taylor, the Sailor Preacher* (New York, 1871).

B.   SH 5, 172; NCAB 13, 261–62; DAB 8, 407–08; NYT 5 Jan 1880, 1; William H. Daniels (ed.), *Memorials of Gilbert Haven* (Boston, 1880); George Prentice, *The Life of Gilbert Haven* (New York, 1883); William Gravely, *Gilbert Haven: Methodist Abolitionist* (Nashville, 1973).

HAYGOOD, Atticus Greene (19 November 1839, Watkinsville, GA—19 January 1896, Oxford, GA). *Education*: B.A., Emory Coll., 1859. *Career*: minister of the Methodist Episcopal Church, South, at several churches in GA, 1859–70; chaplain, Confederate Army, 1861; secretary, Southern Methodist Sunday Schools, 1870–75; president, Emory Coll., 1875–84; editor, *Wesleyan Christian Advocate*, 1878–82; agent, John F. Slater Fund, 1884–91; bishop of the Southern Methodist Church, 1890–93; retirement, 1893–96.

Reared in a pious, well-to-do Methodist home, Haygood decided for the ministry early enough to obtain a provisional license before graduating from college. He supported the Confederacy in pulpits and briefly as military chaplain, but patriotism motivated him more than any particular ideas about slavery. Through the war years he was a pastor and presiding elder, doing what he could to continue the routine of church life under straitened conditions. As director of Sunday School programs for Southern Methodists, he sought to improve the content of lesson materials by means of new books and a teacher's magazine. Pursuing the goal of education, he accepted the presidency of his alma mater and worked mightily to overcome its financial disabilities. Haygood succeeded in enlarging Emory's endowment, raised new buildings, and doubled the student body. One of his lasting contributions was to instill in young southerners the determination to acquire collegiate training. In addition to preparing men for secular leadership he inspired many to volunteer for missionary stations in China where his sister was already serving with distinction. He also influenced religious thought locally through the major Methodist weekly paper. His editorial task led him to consider events of the late Reconstruction era, and his response had far-reaching effects.

The free, black American was a person in whom Haygood found much to admire. By 1881 he concluded that slavery had been a crime the South was well rid of. He argued that Negroes had the right to live where they chose, to own land, and to receive equal treatment alongside whites under common law. While he asked whites to recognize the justice of black liberation, he urged Blacks to improve themselves through industry, education, and religious integrity. Such ideas about brotherhood were well in advance of their time, and they provoked a storm of criticism from unreconstructed southerners. Yet they impressed many as a voice of the new South that could secure justice and well-being for all its citizens. In 1882 Haygood was elected bishop but declined (the first in his church ever to do so) because he was afraid some thirty ministerial students would falter if he left Emory. Eventually he did move from the college to direct work for a Negro educational fund, advocating a host of projects intended to teach and elevate those whom he called brothers in black. Again in 1890 he was offered a bishopric which he accepted. For three years he resided in Los Angeles and directed efforts to build Methodist churches throughout the Pacific Conference.

His attitude regarding northern churches was friendly, but until poor health forced him to retire, he labored for the cause of Southern Methodism which he loved so well.

Bibliography:

   A.   *Our Brother in Black: His Freedom and His Future* (Nashville, 1881); *Sermons and Addresses,* (Nashville, 1883); *Pleas for Progress* (Nashville, 1889); *The Man of Galilee* (Cincinnati, 1889).
   B.   NCAB 1, 520; DAB 8, 452–53; NYT 20 Jan 1896, 5; Elam F. Dempsey, *Atticus Green Haygood* (Nashville, 1940); Harold W. Mann, *Atticus Greene Haygood: Methodist Bishop, Editor and Educator* (Athens, GA, 1965).

HEALY, James Augustine (6 April 1830, near Macon, GA—5 August 1900, Portland ME). *Education*: graduated from Coll. of the Holy Cross, 1849; studied at Sulpician Sem., Montreal, Canada, 1849–51; graduated from Sulpician Sem., Paris, France, 1854. *Career*: Priest, Diocese of Boston, 1854–75; bishop of Portland, ME, 1875–1900.

Raised initially on a plantation in Jones County, Georgia, Healy was one of several children born to an Irish immigrant father and a mulatto slave mother. State law made such a union technically illegal, but both parents regarded the marriage as genuine and honored it until they died two decades later. Schooling began at Quaker academies in New York and New Jersey, but when Healy decided on the priesthood, he entered Catholic institutions. By the time he graduated from Holy Cross, he was first in his class. Then he acquired seminary training in French-speaking Canada for two years and took minor orders there, studying for three more years on the continent and receiving ordination at the cathedral of Notre Dame de Paris in 1854. Called to Boston, he served in many capacities, including staff membership at Angel Guardian House, assistant pastor at St. John's Church, and the diocese's first chancellor. Besides those duties he was also the bishop's secretary (1854–57), rector of the cathedral (1857–66), and pastor of St. James Church (1866–75) where he built a new edifice.

While in Boston Healy was also actively involved in social welfare work. He played a decisive role in the Home for Destitute Catholic Children, St. Anne's Foundling Home, and the House of the Good Shepherd. His interest in civic affairs also found outlet in work with the Catholic Laymen's Union. In addition to such activities he was known as a redoubtable pulpit orator. Excellence in all these fields led to favorable notice within the hierarchy, and in 1875 Healy was chosen the next bishop of Portland, a diocese encompassing all of Maine and New Hampshire. In light of his family background, many wondered if someone with "indelicate blood" would be welcomed in Portland. After a few early difficulties the new bishop proved to be a model prelate well loved by his people. He added 60 new churches and 68 mission stations, doubling the number of priests too, as Canadian immigrants swelled the Catholic population. Healy also contributed to canon law in the American church at the Baltimore Council of

1884. The following year he supervised division of his responsibilities along state lines, keeping his old see and erecting a new one in Manchester, New Hampshire. In broader areas he served as consultant regarding neighboring Native Americans, the Abenaki tribe, for the Interior Department's Bureau of Indian Affairs. For a quarter of a century he demonstrated how people of all ethnic backgrounds could eventually reach the highest posts in American Catholicism.

Bibliography:

B.   NCAB 10, 242; NCE 6, 964; Albert S. Foley, *Bishop Healy: Beloved Outcaste* (New York, 1954).

HECK, Barbara Ruckle (1734, Ballingrane, Ireland—17 August 1804, near Prescott, Canada). *Career*: American Methodist lay supporter, 1760–74.

Born into a family of German refugees from the Palatinate, young Ruckle was strongly influenced by Wesleyan preaching and piety, as were many in the local countryside. She joined a Wesleyan society at the age of eighteen and married Paul Heck some few years later. In 1760 the couple moved to New York. For a time her fervor and that of her co-religionists seemed to wane; whatever quiet worship was observed at home, there was no open evangelism. Things changed in 1766, however, when Heck visited friends and saw a card game in progress. She rebuked the frivolous gamesters, burned the cards, and immediately beseeched her cousin, *Philip Embury, to resume preaching. Her exhortations led to organization of the first Methodist society in town and is generally accepted as the beginnings of that denomination in this country. The following year she helped acquire a rigging loft for public services, and in 1768 her efforts facilitated erection of Wesley Chapel, the first American church building raised for that faith. It became the center of early Methodism and served as headquarters for *Joseph Pilmore when he arrived a year later as an officially authorized missionary.

Shortly after Pilmore's arrival Heck and her family moved north to the Lake Champlain area. There too she was instrumental in organizing the first Methodist society in the region. But Heck's loyalist sympathies shortened their stay, and by 1774 they moved to Sorel, Canada, near Montreal. A subsequent move to Ontario placed them in Augusta township where they organized yet another pioneering Methodist society and settled for good in a home that became a haven for itinerant preachers. Heck was typical of many sturdy, often anonymous, women who spread Methodism in its early years. She held no official position, but she was zealous for the spiritual welfare of her family and neighbors. Before ministers arrived to sanction evangelical activities, her beneficial presence had already prepared the way. She touched hearts by words and personal example, accomplishing spiritual victories before formal institutions came along to sustain them. For this she has been widely recognized as the "Mother of Methodism in America."

Bibliography:

B.   NCAB 13, 115–16; DAB 8, 493; NAW 2, 174–75; William H. Withrow, *Barbara Heck: A Tale of Early Methodism* (Cincinnati, 1895).

HECKER, Isaac Thomas (18 December 1819, New York, NY—22 December 1888, New York, NY). *Education*: private study while holding various jobs, particularly in family bakery, 1830–44; novitiate in Redemptorist order, Belgium, 1845–46; further training in Holland, 1846–48, and England, 1848–49. *Career*: Redemptorist missionary in America, 1851–57; superior, Congregation of Missionary Priests of Saint Paul the Apostle, 1858–88.

Spiritual wanderers often move from one affiliation to another without ever finding a true sense of fulfillment. This was not the case with Hecker, who remained after conversion a loyal son of the Catholic church and founded its most distinctively American religious order. Forced to leave school at an early age and work in his brothers' bakery, he showed an intellectual curiosity about fundamental issues in politics, philosophy, and theology. Baptized a Lutheran and associated for a time with Methodism, in 1841 his life took a different turn when he met *Orestes Brownson, another seeker whose religious odyssey resembled his own in many ways. On Brownson's advice, Hecker spent six months at Brook Farm in 1843, searching for enlightenment and spiritual solace but finding little. He sojourned briefly at Bronson Alcott's Fruitlands and also with the Henry D. Thoreau family. In all, though, he was repelled by the lonely individualism characteristic of Transcendentalist thinkers. In 1844 he became a Catholic and a year later was admitted to the Redemptorist order, adding the name of Thomas at that time. After training and ordination in Europe, Father Hecker served for six years as a missionary priest among German immigrants in New York. At the urging of several colleagues, he traveled to Rome in 1857 to request the creation of an English-speaking branch of Redemptorists for the purpose of converting non-Catholic countrymen. Since he had come without permission, there was some danger of being expelled from the order, but after several anxious months Pius IX released him and his friends (all converts) from former vows and suggested that they form a new missionary order.

The new monastics, popularly known as Paulist Fathers, adopted a rule in 1858, designated Hecker their superior and in the same year persuaded archbishop *John J. Hughes to sanction their activities. A primary objective was the conversion of Protestants, a goal patterned after their collective experience and a desire to share with others the haven they had reached. Quite early, Hecker recognized the value of disseminating apologetic literature. In 1865 he began the *Catholic World*, a monthly which he edited the rest of his life. The next year he organized the Catholic Publication Society (later the Paulist Press) to facilitate distributing tracts on a national scale. In 1870 he began the *Young Catholic* for juveniles and was well on the way to realizing plans for a Catholic daily newspaper when failing health curtailed his activities. After 1871 he was an invalid, yet he remained the soul of missionary endeavor and continued writing to accomplish the order's main purpose. His work presented Catholicism as the answer to man's religious quandry. He conceived of the church as essentially democratic and portrayed it as a guarantor of republican ideals. In this regard Hecker stood within a tradition of American Catholic thought, which tried to convince men that the Roman church was not the enemy of liberty. His ideas were subsequently misrepresented in the European debate over "Americanism," but that should not detract from one who tried to present his church's teachings in a manner understandable to the modern world.

Bibliography:

A.   *Questions of the Soul* (New York, 1855); *Aspirations of Nature* (New York, 1857); *The Church and the Age* (New York, 1887).

B.   SH 5, 196; NCAB 9, 166–67; DAB 8, 495; NCE 6, 982–83; Walter Elliott, *The Life of Father Hecker* (New York, 1891, 1972); Charles Maignen, *Études sur l'Américanisme; Le Père Hecker, Est-il un Saint?* (Paris, 1898); Henry D. Sedgwick, *Father Hecker* (Boston, 1900); Joseph McSorley, *Father Hecker and his Friends* (St. Louis, 1952); Vincent F. Holden, *The Yankee Paul: Isaac Thomas Hecker* (Milwaukee, 1958).

HEDGE, Frederic Henry (12 December 1805, Cambridge, MA—21 August 1890, Cambridge, MA). *Education*: B.A., Harvard Coll., 1825; B.D., Harvard Div. Sch., 1829. *Career*: minister, West Cambridge, MA, 1829–35; minister, Bangor, ME, 1835–50; minister, Providence, RI, 1850–56; minister, First Unitarian Church, Brookline, MA, 1857–72; editor, *Christian Examiner*, 1857–61; professor of Ecclesiastical History, Harvard Div. Sch., 1857–76; professor of German Literature, Harvard Coll., 1872–84; retirement, 1884–90.

The Transcendentalist wing of American Unitarianism found in Hedge a seminal thinker who helped articulate many fundamental assumptions of the movement. As time passed, it became clear that he was also a moderate who tried to anchor his denomination within explicitly Christian conceptions. A major perspective which he shared with other transcendentalists was the view of reality admitting no sharp dualities. There was one world of nature and spirit wherein the single, all-present power of God worked as equally in the sod as in the souls of men. Divine will was revealed in laws of gravitation as well as in those of moral obligation. Hedge also thought human nature contained an uncorrupted faculty through which divine grace could operate as an immanent force, cultivating man's spirit by natural processes. All things proceeded by stages of growth, whether in physical or moral development, and regeneration was accomplished by educating the latent good in individuals until it gained ascendency. Progress came by harmonizing the forces of the soul, during which process the preacher used Christ's example to illumine moral counsels potentially within everyone. There was also a social corollary to this developmental definition of salvation. Every personal effort made some contribution to the groundwork of society, and cooperation was possible at all levels of interdependence. Social improvement through reason and a sense of reciprocity was unquestionably within human capabilities, approaching a true commonwealth of interests.

Similar ideas led many Unitarians to radical departures, confessionally and institutionally, in their denomination, but Hedge remained a self-styled "enlightened conservative." He believed that mankind was bound in a natural, involuntary process of continuous perfection. True reformers, then, were those who accepted this divine ordering of things and cooperated with it instead of creating new orders from human invention. He refused to be aligned exclusively with any particular clique in the church, insisting that instantaneous reform could not be achieved through agitation. Hedge represented transcendentalism in a dialectical sense. He distinguished between the discursive activities of science and the intuitive ground of religious conviction, claiming both were necessary for bringing man's whole powers to fruition. Since he thought the nucleus of truth emerged after juxtaposing contrary elements of opposing viewpoints, he presented all sides of a question in hopes of at last mirroring the truth for his hearers. This blend of rationality and intuition made the pastor-turned-professor a distinguished churchman. He embodied for many a perspective which kept intellectuals from conformity to outmoded orthodoxies, while at the same time it prevented rejecting corporate religion altogether.

Bibliography:

A. *Reason in Religion* (Boston, 1865); *The Primeval World of Hebrew Tradition* (Boston, 1870); *Ways of the Spirit and Other Essays* (Boston, 1877); *Atheism in Philosophy* (Boston, 1884); *Martin Luther and Other Essays* (Boston, 1888).

B. SH 5, 196–97; NCAB 8, 271–72; DAB 8, 498–99; NYT 23 Aug 1890, 4; Orie W. Long, *Frederic Henry Hedge: A Cosmopolitan Scholar* (Portland, ME, 1940); Ronald V. Wells, *Three Christian Transcendentalists* (New York, 1943, 1972); George H. Williams, *Rethinking the Unitarian Fellowship with Protestantism: An Examination of the Thought of Frederic Henry Hedge* (Boston, 1949).

HENDERSON, Charles Richmond (17 December 1848, Covington, IN—29 March 1915, Charleston, SC). *Education*: B.A., Univ. of Chicago, 1870, B.D., Baptist Union Sem., 1873; Ph.D., Univ. of Leipzig, 1901. *Career*: minister, First Baptist Church, Terre Haute, IN, 1873–82; minister, Woodward Avenue Baptist Church, Detroit, MI, 1882–92; university chaplain and at various ranks professor of Sociology, Univ. of Chicago, 1892–1915.

While still a student at the original University of Chicago, Henderson ministered to a small church near the stockyards. There at first hand he learned about the harsh economic and social realities that confronted the poor. During his pastoral service in two churches, a decade each, he retained an abiding interest in social problems and in the various attempts to meet human needs through charitable institutions. Evidence of this perennial concern are his presiding over the 26th National Conference of Charities in 1898–99 and the United Charities of Chicago in 1913. Henderson readily understood that charity alone was not enough. Alleviating immediate needs could reduce suffering, but it was more important to change the fundamental conditions that produced those needs in the first place. On his return to the University of Chicago, newly resuscitated by *William R. Harper, he became a pioneer in social studies which attempted basic reforms in community conditions. In sixteen books and over one hundred articles he combined academic materials with practical suggestions for improving social conditions. His work blended religious concern for human welfare with scientific information to attempt progressive realization of a Social Gospel.

There are at least four distinct categories among Henderson's widespread interests. Most broadly he was concerned about labor disputes, and he often tried to arbitrate strikes and settle disagreements between management and workers. He was an early investigator of conditions in the workplace and pioneered studies of occupational diseases, employee insurance, and industrial legislation. Neglected children were a third lifetime concern of his, and he served on administrative boards of several orphanages. Lastly, he was probably most notable as an authority on penology. Henderson made extensive studies of penal institutions and reformatories in order to improve their management and their ultimate objective. His presidency of the National Prison Association (1901–02), representing the United States at the International Prison Commission (1909), and presiding over the International Prison Congress (1910) attest to his eminence in the field. More contributions were expected from this spiritually motivated social reformer, but he died unexpectedly while on a vacation intended to restore health shattered by overwork.

Bibliography:

A.   *The Development of Doctrine in the Epistles* (Philadelphia, 1890); *An Introduction to the Study of the Dependent, Defective, and Delinquent Classes* (Boston, 1893); *Social Elements, Institutions, Characters, Progress* (New York, 1898); *Practical Sociology in the Service of Social Ethics* (Chicago, 1902); *Social Duties from the Christian Point of View: A Textbook for the Study of Social Problems* (Chicago, 1909); *The Cause and Cure of Crime* (Chicago, 1914).

B.   NCAB 11, 75; DAB 8, 524–25; NYT 30 Mar 1915, 11.

HENKEL, Paul (15 December 1754, Rowan County, NC—27 November 1825, New Market, VA). *Career*: itinerant evangelist in VA, NC, TN, KY, OH and IN, 1783–1823.

While growing up among fellow German-Americans in what later became West Virginia, Henkel acquired better than average acquaintance with orthodox Lutheran writings. He was a cooper by trade and supported a large family by that means throughout his lifetime, but conducting religious services always claimed higher priority. Prayer meetings or Bible classes in neighboring homes offered many opportunities for him to focus on spiritual values; by 1781 he preached his first sermon, in German then in English, and resolved on a pattern of missionary endeavor spanning forty years. The Ministerium of Pennsylvania (which licensed him 1783, ordained 1792) provided some financial aid, but most of his evangelical travels were made at his own expense. An indefatigable traveler, he preached, baptized, and formed congregations in a wide arc of frontier territory. Another significant aspect of his work was that of organizing clergymen to administer proper ecclesiastical ordinances. In 1803 he helped found the North Carolina Synod, a structure providing regular discipline and mutual support but more importantly a body able to withstand the extreme emotionalism of current revivals. Returning to Virginia by 1806, he began distributing books produced by his son's printshop—the first and, for many years, the only Lutheran publishing house in the nation. The Joint Synod of Ohio (1818) and the Synod of Tennessee (1820) were two more direct results of Henkel's energetic itinerancy. They also embodied his strong personal antipathy to liberal ideas put forward by *Samuel S. Schmucker and his General Synod. Schmucker hoped to achieve a union of all evangelical churches, but Henkel resisted cooperation because he wished to avoid the theological compromise implied by such an alliance. His strict adherence to doctrinal symbols, such as the Augsburg Confession, helped lay institutional foundations for a strong confessional movement which later flourished in many branches of American Lutheranism. A paralytic stroke slowed activities after 1823, but, within limitations, he continued to preach and write until six weeks before his death.

Bibliography:

A.   *Eine kurze Betrachtung der Heil. Taufe und Abendmahl* (Neumarket, VA, 1809); *Das Neu Eingerichtete Gesang-Buch* (Neumarket, VA, 1810); *The Christian Catechism* (New Market, VA, 1811).

B.   AAP 9, 92–95; DAB 8, 538–39.

HERRON, George Davis (21 January 1862, Montezuma, IN—9 October 1925, Munich, Germany). *Career*: minister, Lake City, MN, 1883–92; minister, Burlington, IA, 1892–93; professor of Applied Christianity, Iowa Coll., 1893–99; political and literary activity, U.S. and Europe, 1900–25.

Early pastorates in Congregational churches provided Herron with the medium through which he first began calling for social reform. Having no college or seminary training, he filled the deficiency with a strong conviction that he was somehow personally chosen to help regenerate the social order. His public criticism of economic oppression led to a teaching post (Grinnell College after 1909) where he analyzed relations between Christian ethics and social conditions. For a time he attracted national attention by concentrating on genuine abuses, but his unbridled criticism of implicated persons alienated a great many followers. Herron's messianism often made him feel he was above human conventions. The rectitude of his purpose made it unnecessary to observe common expectations in marriage and capitalism, two coercive institutions he hoped to renovate by personal antagonism. Public outcry against his religio-economic heresy, not to mention domestic irregularity, led him to resign his professorship. In 1901 his wife sued for divorce on uncontested grounds of desertion, and he married Carrie Rand, daughter of his chief financial supporter. For a combination of reasons, he was then deposed from the Congregational ministry. From that time onward he considered his home to be an estate at Fiesole in the Italian countryside where the scope of his agitation for social change increased rather than diminished.

By the turn of the century Herron had joined the Socialist Party with a view to developing Christian Socialism as a plank in its platform. For almost two decades he exercised wide influence among international theorists who sought to translate gospel teachings into practical terms for the benefit of humanity. His motivations remained fundamentally religious to the end, even though he abandoned any self-conscious use of Christian terminology by 1910. He lectured often and campaigned for Eugene V. Debs' presidential candidacy, but his doctrinaire attitude made it difficult to cooperate with organized movements in either religion or politics. The compromises necessary for group action were repugnant to him, and so his major contribution lay in literary efforts. Books and articles flowed from his pen, covering all ethical considerations involved in political issues. He grew increasingly one-sided, however, and broke with Socialists because they would not condemn Germany in World War I. Altering his original pacifism, he became a staunch friend of the Allies, using his European connections to facilitate British and Italian diplomacy. He helped persuade the German government to capitulate in 1918 largely on the strength of hopes for a League of Nations. While the Treaty of Versailles was a severe disappointment, he nevertheless urged its ratification as the best one could hope for. Intense work during those war years broke his health; neither his idealism nor physical condition ever completely recovered.

Bibliography:

A. *The Larger Christ* (New York, 1891); *The Christian State* (Boston, 1895); *Between Caesar and Jesus* (New York, 1899); *The Day of Judgment* (Chicago, 1904); *The Menace of Peace* (London, 1917); *Germanism and the American Crusade* (New York, 1918).

B. NCAB 9, 277; DAB 8, 594–95; NYT 11 Oct 1925, II, 5.

HESCHEL, Abraham Joshua (1907, Warsaw, Poland—23 December 1972, New York, NY). *Education*: Ph.D., Univ. of Berlin, 1933. *Career*: professor of Jewish Philosophy and Rabbinics, Hebrew Union Coll., 1940–45; professor of Jewish Ethics and Mysticism, Jewish Sem. of America, New York, 1945–72.

The son and grandson of Hasidic rabbis, descended from Talmudic scholars going back to the sixteenth century, Heschel seemed destined by birth for a lifework in religious thought. After classical rabbinic training blended with a secular degree, he taught at Jewish institutes of higher learning in Berlin, Frankfurt, and Warsaw, being expelled from Germany in 1938 and fleeing Poland two months before the Nazi invasion. In 1940 he began lecturing in American Reform circles, but five years later he found a more congenial atmosphere at the seminary for Conservative Judaism in New York. By 1951 his writings began to attract wide attention because they spoke to the general condition of modern humanity. He thought that much of the doubt and rootlessness characterizing contemporary man was due to a denial of transcendence. This estrangement from religion resulted not from intellectual perplexity but from man's failure to experience that dimension of reality where divine-human encounters took place. In response to such conditions, Heschel forged a philosophy preserving the substance of Jewish tradition while articulating it in contemporary idioms including process metaphysics and existentialist ontology. He hoped thus to provide conceptual tools for grasping divine reality while at the same time evoking an appreciation of the holy dimension in daily life. Talmudic views of Torah and revelation yielded for him an authentic theology, the basis for applying traditional sources of religious vitality to questions modern man must face. Linking ancient heritage with new problems, he established continuity between the prophets, Maimonides, Hasidic piety, and the 1967 Six Day War.

Life is not meaningful unless it serves an end beyond itself; Heschel repeatedly emphasized that point in an attempt to revivify a basic theme in biblical thought. In all his writings, scholarly and devotional, he alluded to the living God of the Bible who is neither philosophical abstraction nor psychological projection but a reality with intense concern for His creatures. With this fundamental tenet, he went on to describe the full dimensions of being human, a condition acknowledging both the fragility and the nobility of life. The ability to rise to life's holy dimension was, he maintained, the root of human freedom. More particularly, a capacity to transcend egocentric interests in loving response to divine guidance was the essence of Jewish observance; failures and successes in this regard constituted the drama of Jewish history. Late in his life Heschel began discussing these insights in relation to concrete problems such as prayer, symbolism, youth, aging, racial justice, civil rights, interfaith dialogue, and the State of Israel. In the creative tension between law and spontaneity—*halacha* and *haggada*—he taught men how to accept true human existence, holding a vision of meaning defined by a reality beyond the power of human contrivance.

Bibliography:

A. *Man Is Not Alone: A Philosophy of Religion* (New York, 1951); *Man's Quest for God* (New York, 1954); *God in Search of Man: A Philosophy of Judaism* (New York, 1955); *The Prophets (New York, 1962); The Insecurity of Freedom* (New York, 1965); *Israel: An Echo of Eternity* (New York, 1969).

B. UJE 5, 344; EJ 8, 425–27; NYT 24 Dec 1972, 40; Fritz A. Rothschild (ed.),

Between God and Man: An Interpretation of Judaism, from the Writings of Abraham J. Heschel (New York, 1959); Franklin Sherman, *The Promise of Heschel* (Philadelphia, 1970).

HEWIT, Augustine Francis (27 November 1820, Fairfield, CT—3 July 1897, New York, NY). *Education*: B.A., Amherst Coll., 1839; studied at the Theological Institute of Connecticut, 1840–42; studied theology with Patrick N. Lynch, 1846–47. *Career*: deacon, Episcopal church, 1843–46; Roman Catholic priest and vice principal, Charleston Collegiate Institute, 1847–48; member, Congregation of the Most Holy Redeemer, 1849–58; member, Missionary Society of St. Paul the Apostle, 1858–97; superior general, 1889–97; editor, *Catholic World*, 1866–74.

Christened Nathaniel Augustus, the son of a Congregationalist minister, Hewit was licensed in 1842 to preach but left the denomination within a year. After studying theology with an Episcopal rector he was ordained deacon in that church and served for three years. Greatly influenced by the Oxford movement, he was persuaded by John Henry Newman that true apostolic succession resided only in the Catholic church. So in 1846 Hewit joined that denomination, receiving his first communion on Easter Sunday, and after adopting a new name prepared for ordination into the priesthood the following year. After a brief stint in southern states he joined the Redemptorists in Baltimore, taking his vows in 1850 and pursuing missionary efforts for eight years. While a Redemptorist Hewit met *Isaac Hecker and several other Protestant converts to Catholicism. In 1858 these monks were allowed to form a new order dedicated to spreading their faith among the non-Catholic population. As the Paulists grew during the second half of the nineteenth century Hewit was second only to Hecker as the order's most influential member. He wrote the first constitutions of the new society and trained its candidates. For years he taught theology and philosophy at the Paulist seminary in New York City.

Whenever Hecker was absent because of poor health, Hewit served as superior of the group. It was a natural step, then, for him to become the second superior general after Hecker's death in 1888. In that capacity he pledged Paulist support for the Catholic University of America, a new educational venture begun in the District of Columbia. He established a Paulist house of studies on the campus, making it the first religious order affiliated with the university. This later became St. Paul's College and was an additional adornment to St. Thomas Aquinas College, another project sponsored by Paulists. Hewit extended operations to the west coast, erecting in 1894 a missionary house in San Francisco. In 1896 he founded the Catholic Missionary Union to facilitate outreach to Protestants, and in 1891 he laid the foundations of what eventually became the Paulist Press. Hewit was a prolific writer, and for several decades he found outlet for his talent as staff member of *Catholic World*. In most of his books he had a genuinely pastoral concern to explain Catholicism to his countrymen. Through those efforts he embodied the early ideals of his order and became one of the foremost Catholic apologists of his era.

Bibliography:

A.   *Problems of the Age, with Studies in St. Augustine on Kindred Topics* (New York, 1868); *Memoir of the Life of the Rev. Francis A. Baker, Priest of the Congregation of St. Paul* (New York, 1868); *Light in Darkness: A Treatise on the Obscure Night of the Soul* (New York, 1871); *The King's Highway: or, The Catholic Church the Way of Salvation, as Revealed in the Holy Scriptures* (New York, 1874); *Lectures on the Catholic Doctrine of the Church in Holy Scripture, and the Tradition of the First Four Centuries* (Washington, DC, 1890); *The Teaching of St. John the Apostle to the Churches of Asia and the World* (New York, 1895).

B.   NCAB 11, 358, DAB 8, 604; NCE 6, 1092–93; Joseph P. Flynn, *The Early Years of Augustine F. Hewit, C.S.P.* (Washington, DC, 1945).

HICKS, Elias (19 March 1748, Hempstead, NY—27 February 1830, Jericho, NY). *Career*: farmer and carpenter, Jericho, NY, 1771–1830; recorded minister, Society of Friends, 1778–1830.

Born to the modest customs of a Quaker farming community on Long Island, Hicks easily absorbed its quiet piety and embodied those characteristics through fifty years of active ministry. After undergoing a religious crisis in 1774, he reached a deeper sense of reconciliation with God and dedicated himself to whatever use the Spirit might have for him. He began preaching and serving on committees, working at every level of Quaker life from Preparative to Yearly Meetings. In the course of itinerant visits to conduct worship and provide counsel for local societies, Hicks traveled over forty thousand miles, reaching groups as far away as Virginia, Indiana, and Canada. He was a soul-stirring orator who impressed many with his message of salvation as the birth, life, and government of Christ in the soul. It was possible to perform significant service in quietist meetings too, but Hicks was most influential as a powerful speaker who spread the doctrine of God's self-revelation in human experience. While stressing inward communion, he also emphasized the plain virtues of industry, temperance and peace in attempts to speak to the condition of his listeners. His willingness to let God lead individuals to right conduct, together with his acceptance of human reason as a means of discerning truth, made Hicks' doctrine attractive to many followers. More than one generation of Friends acknowledged his leadership in questions of personal ethics and liturgical procedure.

The state of society in post-revolutionary America made for a great deal of political and intellectual uncertainty. Most Quakers responded by insisting on greater regulation of beliefs and conduct through the use of Scripture and application of church discipline. Hicks also wished to combat worldliness and spiritual lethargy, but he did so by holding more tenaciously to the Inner Light and its sure promptings. If all good things rose from within oneself, he was convinced that external standards like the Bible and orthodox theology would prove to be unnecessary obstacles to the essence of Quaker vitality. The evangelicals thought Hicks' spiritual individualism was too loose and rejected it as insufficient for meeting contemporary problems. There was some disagreement over specific issues, but the two parties were basically at odds over the proper means of achieving religious insight and perpetuating a body of common truths. By 1827 those irreconcilable differences produced a separation into Orthodox and Hicksite branches of the Society that has lasted to the present. While not solely to blame for creating the controversy, Hicks was accurately understood as the dominant spokesman for that branch which sought to protect itself from the world by withdrawing from it.

Bibliography:

A. *Observations on the Slavery of the Africans and Their Descendants* (New York, 1811); *A Series of Extemporaneous Discourses* (Philadelphia, 1825); *Journal of the Life and Religious Labours of Elias Hicks, written by himself* (New York, 1832, 1969).

B. SH 5, 274; NCAB 11, 464; DAB 9, 6–7; NCE 6, 1096; Henry W. Wilbur, *The Life and Labors of Elias Hicks* (Philadelphia, 1910); Rufus M. Jones, *The Later Periods of Quakerism*, 2 vols. (London, 1921; Westport, CT, 1970); Bliss Forbush, *Elias Hicks: Quaker Liberal* (New York, 1956); Robert W. Doherty, *The Hicksite Separation* (New Brunswick, NJ, 1967); H. Larry Ingle, *Quakers in Conflict: The Hicksite Reformation* (Knoxville, 1986).

HIGGINSON, Francis (1586, Claybrooke, England—6 August 1630, Salem, MA). *Education*: B.A. and M.A., St. John's Coll., Cambridge Univ., 1610 and 1613. *Career*: curate, Claybrooke, 1615–17; lecturer, St. Nicholas, 1617–27; minister, Salem, MA, 1629–30.

The early years of Higginson's Anglican ministry show no apparent inclination towards Puritan reform. By 1627, however, he was deprived of clerical office because of an acquired sympathy with nonconformist principles. The local bishop allowed him to continue minimal duties in his native Leicestershire, but Archbishop Laud insisted that his license be withdrawn. Hearing that proceedings had begun against him in a court of high commission, he volunteered for service in New England. In 1629 he was appointed by governors of the Massachusetts Bay Colony as minister for one of their settlements. He sailed in the *Talbot*, reaching Naumkeag (later Salem) in the summer of that same year. Higginson was chosen to serve as teacher of the Salem church in conjunction with Samuel Skelton, who was appointed pastor. Since their clerical status was somewhat in doubt, a covenant was drawn up by the local congregation to sustain the validity of their ministerial functions. Emphases in their polity and confession of faith were decidedly Puritan but not Separatist. Higginson claimed that he never intended to leave the Church of God in England, only the corruptions found in it. Nonseparating congregationalism found early establishment in his brief ministry, which death terminated within a year. His beginnings set precedent for the great migration of churchly minded Puritans soon to follow his example.

Bibliography:

A. *New-Englands Plantation. Or, A Short and True Description of the Commodities and Discommodities of that Countrey* (London, 1630; Salem MA, 1908).

B. AAP 1, 6–10; NCAB 1, 380; DAB 9, 11–12; Thomas W. Higginson, *Life of Francis Higginson* (New York, 1891).

HITCHCOCK, Edward (24 May 1793, Deerfield, MA—27 February 1864, Amherst, MA). *Education*: studied at Yale Div. Sch., 1820. *Career*: principal, Deerfield Acad., 1816–19; minister, Conway, MA, 1821–25; professor of Chemistry and Natural History, Amherst Coll., 1825–45; president, Amherst Coll., 1845–54; professor of Natural Theology and Geology, Amherst Coll., 1854–64.

Since family resources could not afford the cost of formal education, Hitchcock hired out as a farm laborer to pay for college. In the meantime he developed a fondness for natural history and mathematics, which taught him the value of exact, disciplined thinking. Overzealous pursuit of such studies ruined his school plans, however, producing a state of chronically poor health and weak eyesight. Loosely associated with the local Unitarian church since childhood, he chose more trinitarian views after mature reflection and entered the Congregationalist ministry in a nearby town. But five years later the church dismissed him at his own request because ill health intervened again. Though he expected to live only a brief time longer, he accepted a science professorship at Amherst, a post which he filled with distinction for almost four decades. As a scientist Hitchcock contributed to many ventures beyond the campus. He initiated a geological survey of Massachusetts and produced the first relevant data (1830–33, 1837–41) for that pioneering effort. In 1840 he led the way for establishing the American Association for the Advancement of Science. Many papers on quartz conglomerates, river terraces, and fossil footprints brought additional notice as a naturalist of no slight accomplishment. He accepted the presidency of Amherst more out of a sense of duty than willingness, but sacrifice for that institution relieved its financial embarrassment while adding buildings and increasing its academic reputation.

As professor and president, Hitchcock exhibited a paternalistic concern for the religious welfare of his students. In his lectures he took pains to show that knowledge of the natural world could lead to a strengthened faith, not an eroded skepticism too often found among scientists. His main purpose was to illustrate by scientific facts the principles of natural theology. Though never robust in health, he was a prolific writer, producing more than twenty-four volumes based on the premise that natural and revealed religion afforded mutual confirmation. Whether conducting Thursday afternoon Bible class or tracing the evidence of glacier movement, he used all data to proclaim the handiwork of a providential designer. For Hitchcock there was no conflict between geological findings and scriptural accounts of creation; science was useful in disclosing moral as well as natural laws that operated in the universe. For generations of students and countless readers of his books he detailed ways in which geology gave proof of divine benevolence in a fallen world preserved through miraculous interventions. He stood at the threshold of a new intellectual era, one wherein scientific research did not easily conform to traditional notions of natural theology. But while he did not influence the content of later debates, his belief in compatibility between secular and religious knowledge has continued in chastened form to present times.

Bibliography:

A. *Elementary Geology* (New York, 1841, and many subsequent editions); *Religious Lectures on Peculiar Phenomena* (Amherst, MA, 1850); *The Power of Christian Benevolence* (Philadelphia, 1851); *The Religion of Geology and its Connected Sciences* (Glasgow, 1851; Boston, 1852); *Religious Truth Illustrated from Science* (Boston, 1857); *Reminiscences of Amherst College* (Northampton, MA, 1863).

B. NCAB 5, 308–09; DAB 9, 70–71; NYT 6 Mar 1864, 5.

HOBART, John Henry (14 September 1775, Philadelphia, PA—12 September 1830, Auburn, NY). *Education*: studied at the Coll. of Philadelphia, 1788–91; B.A., Coll. of New Jersey, 1793; studied theology with *William White, Philadelphia, 1796–98. *Career*: curate, Oxford and Perkiomen, PA, 1798–99; curate, New Brunswick, NJ, 1799–1800; curate, Hempstead, NY, 1800–01; assistant minister, Trinity Church, New York, 1801–11; assistant bishop of New York, 1811–16; bishop of New York, 1816–30; professor of Pastoral Theology and Pulpit Eloquence, General Sem. (NY), 1821–30.

Aggressive leadership for high church Episcopalians was supplied by Hobart, whose early consecration evidenced the trust many placed in his abilities. He began exercising virtually complete episcopal authority in 1811 because of the diocesan bishop's poor health. Within his 46,000 square mile jurisdiction (including New Jersey until 1815), he was the most significant agent in rebuilding a denomination which had suffered particularly heavy losses during revolutionary conflict. Hobart was a forcible preacher who stirred flagging missionary interest in church extension. He traveled thousands of miles on visitations by stage, canal boat, and horseback, ministering to the needs of Oneida Indians as well as to white settlers who rapidly populated the state. While not a vindictive man, he was overly sensitive to criticism and intolerant enough of opposition that his manner often bordered on the autocratic. On the positive side, such energy produced results of far reaching consequence in church development. For example he was instrumental in founding a theological society (1806) which produced the first general seminary for adequate ministerial training. He established a Bible and Common Prayer Book Society (1809) which still distributes religious literature today. In 1810 he began a tract society; in 1817 a Protestant Episcopal Press came into being, and he began the first diocesan newspaper that same year, *The Churchman's Journal*. By these means, together with persuasive oratory and the stated duties of his office, the bishop worked to augment a sense of dedication among those with whom he came in contact.

Institutional efficiency and a passion for souls were external marks of Hobart's conviction that his church embodied the best of evangelical truth and apostolic order. He was ecumenically minded enough to cooperate with other religious groups, but he thought any unified principles, feelings, or language uttered with one voice to praise God would be those already current among churchmen of his persuasion. The true church was in his conception a divine institution, adhering at all essential points to the faith, ministry, and worship which distinguished the community in apostolic times. The three orders of bishop, priest, and deacon received their authority from Christ through the apostles and their successors in unbroken descent from the New Testament period. Doctrines and observances, sacraments and canon law, all these came to Hobart in uninterrupted historical succession, and he was determined to maintain their integrity for human good as they were originally intended. While thus undeniably a high churchman, he believed that the efficacy of faith and order rested on Reformation principles of justification as a free gift of grace. He held that liturgical elements only symbolically represented flesh and blood, claiming further that the word, "sacrifice" was foreign to early worship. So in his own way he tried to blend formalism with some evangelical aspects of American Protestantism. He died while on visitation, spreading that version of piety incorporated within tangible forms of expression.

Bibliography:

A. *A Companion for the Altar* (New York, 1804); *An Apology for Apostolic Order and Its Advocates* (New York, 1807); *The Nature of the Ministry* (New York, 1815); *The Churchman* (New York, 1819); *Sermons on the Principal Events and Truths of Redemption,* 2 vols. (New York, 1824); *The Correspondence of John Henry Hobart,* ed. Arthur Lowndes, 6 vols. (New York, 1911–12).

B. AAP 5, 440–53; SH 5, 302; NCAB 1, 514–15; DAB 9, 93–94; NCE 7, 42; John F. Schroeder, *Memorial of Bishop Hobart* (New York, 1831); John McVickar, *The Early Life and Professional Years of Bishop Hobart* (Oxford, 1838); John N. Norton, *Life of the Rt. Rev. John Henry Hobart* (New York, 1857).

HODGE, Charles (28 December 1797, Philadelphia, PA—19 June 1878, Princeton, NJ). *Education*: B.A., Coll. of New Jersey, 1815; graduated from Princeton Sem., 1819; studied Hebrew with Joseph Banks, Philadelphia, 1819–20; studied at Paris, Halle, and Berlin, 1826–28. *Career*: instructor and professor of Oriental and Biblical Literature, 1820–40, and professor of Exegetical and Didactic Theology, 1840–78, at Princeton Sem.; editor, *Biblical Repertory*, 1825–71.

During the nineteenth century, Calvinistic theology increasingly lost adherents either because persons in new social and intellectual conditions found it unacceptable or their attempts to preserve it through modification redefined it beyond recognition. This was not the case at Princeton Seminary where Hodge epitomized the unwavering fidelity to confessionalism long associated with that institution. Patterning himself after mentor and ideal, *Archibald Alexander, he waged theological warfare for over fifty years in defense of Reformed dogmatics. Hodge considered theologizing to be a simple process of inductive reasoning (after the manner of Scottish common sense realism) on facts contained in Scripture, the source of verbally inspired, infallible religious truth. Beyond that, he was content to elaborate and defend most of the standard categories formulated in the Westminster Confession. He was convinced that its magisterial affirmations were superior to proposed alterations prompted by trends in biblical criticism, revivalistic enthusiasm, or evolutionary philosophy. It was a matter of pride and mark of loyalty to claim that a new idea never originated in the seminary while his influence reigned there. And that influence went far beyond the 3,000 students who were personally affected through the years; readers on both sides of the Atlantic appreciated the erudition of his books as well as the commanding position of his journal (a quarterly of unstable title but mostly *Biblical Repertory* and *Princeton Review*). Reviews, essays, classroom exercises, and sermons—all these were vehicles by which Hodge exerted a powerful conservative force in American Protestantism.

All of Hodge's activities were guided by the ideal of constancy to established patterns, whether contemplating new doctrine or a new tailor. He adhered to accepted standards of excellence and resisted any change as a departure from them. As an Old School Presbyterian, he fought proposals to modify his church's organizational structure or to cooperate with other denominations on common boards of home missions. After Presbyterians split in 1837, he remained with the conservative wing and welcomed its gravitation toward Princeton, while New School thinkers looked to Union Seminary (NY) for leadership. Biblical inerrancy and rigid confessionalism were so important that he opposed, unsuccessfully, the move to reunite (1869) both Schools in the northern states. For decades Hodge was a conservative presence in Presbyterianism to be reckoned with. He affected matters pertaining to polity, doctrinal standards, exegesis, theological training, and social effectiveness. While not the founder of a specific school of thought, he embodied a change-resistant suspicion of innovation that prized accepted traditions and concentrated on extending them through massive learning. One measure of his lasting influence is that such a spirit of conservatism remained within the seminary long after his passing.

Bibliography:

A. *A Commentary on the Epistle to the Romans* (Philadelphia, 1836); *The Constitutional History of the Presbyterian Church in the United States*, 2 vols. (Philadelphia, 1839–40); *The Way of Life* (Philadelphia, 1841); *Systematic Theology*, 3 vols. (New York, 1871–72); *What Is Darwinism?* (New York, 1874).

B. SH 5, 305–06; NCAB 10, 245; DAB 9, 98–99; NCE 7, 44; Alexander A. Hodge, *The Life of Charles Hodge* (New York, 1880, 1969).

HODUR, Francis (2 April 1866, Zarkack, Poland—16 February 1953, Scranton, PA). *Education*: studied at Univ. of Jagielon; graduated from St. Ann's Collect, Univ. of Crakow. *Career*: priest, Catholic churches in Scranton and Nanticoke, PA, 1893–97; independent Polish Catholic priest, Scranton, PA, 1897–1904; bishop, independent synod, 1904–07; bishop, Polish National Catholic Church, 1907–53.

One year after reaching this country in 1892, Hodur was ordained a priest and began ministering to congregations of Polish-speaking immigrants like himself. Just as many national groups had done before them, the Polish churches sought to control their own affairs through local boards of trustees. For most foreign-born laymen the issue centered on ethnic independence from a predominately Irish and German hierarchy. For American Catholics in general, particularistic tendencies among the Poles violated canons laid down by the councils of Baltimore and threatened to shatter the ideal of one faith for all peoples. In 1897 the Sacred Heart parish in Scranton was obliged to transfer its deed to the diocesan property office. But unlike similar controversies, this did not end the affair. Hodur led his group in building a new church, St. Stanislaus, which the bishop refused to bless because it was unauthorized. While appeals went to Rome for final arbitration in the struggle, Polish communicants continued to support the separatist organization rather than regularly appointed places of worship. Finally Hodur was excommunicated for following such an obstinate course of minority group autonomy, but the groundwork had been laid for permanent schism in American Catholicism. By 1904 enough disaffected Polish groups had followed suit to form a synod and elect Hodur their bishop. Within the next three years a structure of even larger scope was formed to consolidate both ethnic self-sufficiency and continuity with traditional doctrine.

Troubles of a similar nature had emerged in Chicago around 1895. Anton Koslowski led a schismatic group of Polish Catholics in forming their own institutions; when Koslowski died in 1907, Hodur provided the guidance necessary to unite both structures and establish the Polish National Catholic Church. He was consecrated bishop of that body the same year. The Polish Church is distinguished from the Roman one primarily by its use of Polish in the liturgy together with lay control of property and clerical appointments. There are also differences regarding sacraments, feast days, and creedal orientations. As patriarch of the new church Hodur was responsible for superintending the seminary (Savonarola, established 1904) and presiding over synodical meetings. Additional duties included that of producing all church publications and consecrating other bishops (9 during his lifetime) to supervise four territorial jurisdictions. He also founded the Polish National Union (a fraternal and insurance society), as well as a home for the aged. For the last eight years of his life he suffered total blindness, but that did not prevent his preaching every Sunday until one week before his death. By 1950 his ecclesiastical unit claimed more than 250,000 members in 165 parishes in this country and Canada, with mission stations in Poland itself.

Bibliography:

B.   DAB supp. 5, 304–06; NYT 17 Feb 1953, 34.

HOGAN, William (1788, Ireland—3 January 1848, Nashua, NH). *Career*: priest in Limerick, Ireland, 1814?–1819; priest in New York, 1819–20; priest in Philadelphia, 1820–23; lecturer, author, and lawyer, NC, GA, MA and NH, 1824–48.

Little is known of Hogan's early years, except that he was dismissed from seminary on disciplinary grounds and yet received ordination in the diocese where his uncle served as vicar general. On coming to this country, he worked for a time in churches along the Hudson but moved, without permission of his bishop, to Philadelphia in 1820. There he formed a strong alliance with lay trustees of St. Mary's Cathedral and became their leader in the best known struggle between laymen and episcopal authority in American Catholic history. Later that same year he attacked Henry Conwell, new bishop and himself recently arrived in the city, for attempting to exercise any power over local church committees. Hogan resorted to underhanded tricks (forgery) and open defiance in his fight to establish democratic government in Catholic circles. Despite warnings and finally excommunication in 1821, he advocated an "American Catholic Church" which allowed congregations to select their own pastors without episcopal supervision. In 1822 the Pennsylvania Supreme Court decided against the trustees' claim that each congregation was an autonomous body, but Hogan persisted in his independent course at St. Mary's for another year. He left the church in 1823 (resigned, 1824) and began lecturing on Catholic abuse of power to Protestant gatherings. Twice married in subsequent years, he also practiced law, edited a Boston newspaper, served as consul to Cuba, and printed a number of scurrilous anti-Catholic pamphlets. Trusteeism, or "Hoganism" as many called it, did not collapse with the abdication of its volatile spokesman. Philadelphia trustees continued to choose their own priests until 1831 when *Francis P. Kenrick as coadjutor effectively quelled trustee republicanism. But manifestations of local autonomy were widespread until mid-century when state laws allowed bishops to hold ecclesiastical property in their name and thus preserve hierarchical control over priests and lay communicants alike.

Bibliography:

A.   *Popery . . . Auricular Confession and Popish Nunneries* (Hartford, CT, 1856).
B.   NCE 7, 47; Francis E. Tourscher, *The Hogan Schism* (Philadelphia, 1930).

HOLMES, Ernest Shurtleff (21 January 1887, Lincoln, ME—7 April 1960, Los Angeles, CA). *Career*: lecturer, Metaphysical Institute of CA, 1917–25; dean, Institute of Religious Science and Philosophy, 1927–60.

Though straitened family circumstances precluded a formal education, Holmes read widely in the realm of New Thought and eventually became one of the movement's most popular spokesmen. After several years on the lecture circuit with his brother Fenwicke, he was persuaded to settle in southern California and organize audiences along more permanent institutional lines. By 1927 he was head of a group which offered systematic instruction in his distinctive intellectual synthesis, one that also spelled out practical methods for implementing such ideas on a functional level. At the same time he launched a monthly magazine, *Science of Mind*, soon the best known of all New Thought periodicals, which made the term "mental science" familiar to millions of readers in this country and abroad. After 1932 he guided the Church of Religious Science, a body claiming 100,000 members in approximately seventy congregations scattered over the country. Within this setting Holmes sought to promote consciousness of Mind, Unseen Power, or Essential Cause because it was the Uncreated Source binding all life together. Once persons established a dynamic relationship with this Divine Being, they would be able to experience beneficial results. The subconscious human mind could align itself with Universal Mind and thereby unlock reliable, lawlike powers of the natural order. Creative energy was thus released; the greater one's understanding of this truth, the more power available to achieve desired ends such as health, happiness, and enjoyment of the good life. Holmes relied a great deal on Bible reading in his study courses, and he urged explicitly Christian moral behavior. But he also held that his message lay at the heart of every major religion, regardless of confessional differences. Always flexible in his attempt to increase knowledge of transcendental verities, he did not insist on his own ideas as a standard for others. Nevertheless he proved to be a persuasive teacher who developed a following of considerable size and impressive longevity.

Bibliography:

A.   *Science of Mind* (New York, 1926; rev. ed., 1938, and many subsequent editions); *The Bible in the Light of Religious Science* (New York, 1929); *Pray and Prosper* (Los Angeles, 1944); *Words That Heal Today* (New York, 1949); *You Will Live Forever* (New York, 1960).

B.   NYT 9 Apr 1960, 23.

HOLMES, John Haynes (29 November 1879, Philadelphia, PA—3 April 1964, New York, NY). *Education*: B.A., Harvard Coll., 1902; S.T.B. Harvard Div. Sch., 1904. *Career*: Unitarian minister, Third Religious Society, Dorchester, MA, 1904–07; Unitarian minister (associate until 1912), Church of the Messiah, New York, 1907–21; independent minister, Community Church, New York, 1921–49; retirement, 1949–64.

With a lineage counting three generations of leadership in Unitarian circles, Holmes' choice of the ministry seemed as natural as it was full of promise. He tried to make religion effective in human lives, and came to the conclusion over several years that it must constitute a practical social program instead of a system of theology. In his opinion, churches had become ineffectual and out of touch with the real problems of modern man, offering empty phrases in place of concrete suggestions for public welfare. Holmes' religious motivation consisted basically in a theistic humanism where appropriate goals for churches corresponded to secular organizations seeking human improvement. In such a perspective, church and society were aspects of a single fabric; by 1921 the logic of that position led to an abandonment of distinctive religious identity altogether. Holmes remained minister of the same congregation for forty-two years, but after 1921, as Community Church, it had no Christian implications in its covenant. The unity of all men was emphasized, as Jews, Chinese, Catholics, Indians, and Protestants were welcomed under common worship of a universal father. The minister of that uniquely comprehensive church became an outstanding proponent of social reform in scores of unpopular causes. As vice-president of the NAACP after 1909 he fought for racial justice; for years (1929–38) he worked with other civic leaders to combat Tammany Hall and its corrupt political machine in New York; with a rapid, powerful speaking style, he inveighed against abuses ranging from industrial capitalism to intemperance, advocating radical innovations in socialistic cooperation. He may have been overly optimistic about trends in modern society, but there was no mistaking his belief that obstacles could be surmounted by reason and moral suasion.

Of all the social questions on which Holmes expressed notable opinions, perhaps none was more outstanding than pacifism. After 1914 he preached against the growing spirit of militarism in this country, warning that civil liberties would suffer from war hysteria. He denounced military conscription and made his church a counseling center for conscientious objectors. He was one of the main figures who formed the American Civil Liberties Union to prevent further erosion of personal freedom in wartime conditions. Many denounced him as a traitor for saying Germans were still included in the family of God's children. But these animosities notwithstanding, he continued to speak out bravely against prejudice, nationalism, and war. He often joined forces with rabbi *Stephen S. Wise to promote reform or common humanitarian interests. By 1929 he became a strong supporter of cultural Zionism because peaceful, bi-national settlement in Palestine seemed the most workable solution for world Jewry. As years went by, he was increasingly hampered by Parkinson's disease but was able to write for some time after retirement. He never lost his sunny expectations for human betterment, even though to his chagrin many in a later generation had begun to espouse a theology called neo-orthodoxy.

Bibliography:

    A.   *The Revolutionary Function of the Modern Church* (New York, 1912); *Is Death the End?* (New York, 1915); *Is Violence the Way out of our Industrial Disputes?* (New York, 1920); *Palestine Today and Tomorrow* (New York, 1929); *The Sensible Man's View of Religion* (New York, 1933); *Rethinking Religion* (New York, 1938).
    B.   NCAB 15, 273–74; NYT 4 Apr 1964, 1; Carl H. Voss, *Rabbi and Minister* (Cleveland, OH, 1964).

HOOKER, Thomas (7 July 1586, Marfield, England—7 July 1647, Hartford, CT). *Education*: B.A., M.A., Emmanuel Coll., Cambridge Univ., 1608, 1611. *Career*: fellow and catechist, Emmanuel Coll., 1611–18; rector, Esher, 1620–26; lecturer, Church of St. Mary, Chelmsford, 1626–30; emigré minister, Holland, 1630–32; minister Newtown (now Cambridge), MA, 1633–36; minister Hartford, CT, 1636–47.

A reputation for evangelical sermons in Surrey and Essex made Hooker suspect in the eyes of Anglican authorities. Rather than appear before a court of inquiry to answer questions about Puritan sympathies, he fled to Holland, settling as minister in Delft. But he saw no bright prospect in the Low Countries; so when members of his old congregation of Chelmsford extended an invitation, he agreed to join them as pastor in the New World. Arriving in Boston with *John Cotton on the *Griffin* in 1633, Hooker was reunited with his parishioners. He brought luster to the region as one of the best preachers in New England. His powerful expositions of gospel tenets laid bare the anatomy of spiritual experience for all to understand. His pithy phrases externalized the subjective mood of Puritan piety and taught with great psychological insight the ways of daily righteousness. In addition to being a physician of the soul, Hooker's leadership qualities also made him a prime figure in establishing a new colony. Desires for land, wider franchise, more regulation of civil magistrates, and fewer restrictions on church membership caused a small exodus to central Connecticut in 1636. As one of the founders of Hartford, Hooker helped draft (1639) its Fundamental Orders, a covenant grounding both ecclesiastical and secular government in popular consent. He argued that authority came from the people who elected officials and set limits on their power. To this extent the colony's first minister can be said to have planted seeds of democracy which grew to more vigorous expressions in a later era.

With only slight modifications regarding popular liberty, Hooker's ideas about establishing a holy commonwealth were essentially the same as those regnant in Massachusetts. Activity throughout his American ministry exemplified the New England Way, and some of his publications served as official defenses of New World Congregationalism. While still a pastor at Newtown he was chosen by Bay Colony authorities to argue (1635) against *Roger Williams, whose ideas about religious freedom were considered subversive to social cohesion. He also sat (1637) as co-moderator during the trial of *Anne Hutchinson, another libertarian who threatened to rend the socio-religious fabric which he valued. Probably one of the best indications of Hooker's status as patriarch among original colonists is the fact that he presided at Cambridge when efforts were made to provide a single standard for orthodox churches. Congregationalists on both sides of the Atlantic found it necessary to distinguish their ecclesiology from left-wing Separatists who abandoned religious uniformity and from right-wing Presbyterians who made uniformity a weapon against local autonomy. For two years Hooker was active in synodal deliberations toward that important end. Delegates to the meeting dispersed to avoid a virulent epidemic in 1647; as one of its victims, the minister from Hartford did not see the culmination of his work, collected with that of other statesmen, in the Cambridge Platform of 1648.

Bibliography:

A.   *The Soules Preparation for Christ* (London, 1632); *The Soules Humiliation* (London, 1637); *Four Godly and Learned Treatises* (London, 1638); *A Survey of the Summe of Church Discipline* (London, 1648); *The Saints Dignitie and Dutie* (London, 1651); *The Application of Redemption*, 2 vols. (London, 1656–57).

B.   AAP 1, 30–37; SH 5, 361; NCAB 6, 279–80; DAB 9, 199–200; NCE 7, 132; George L. Walker, *Thomas Hooker: Preacher, Founder, Democrat* (New York, 1891); Frank Shuffleton, *Thomas Hooker, 1586–1647* (Princeton, 1977).

HOPKINS, Emma Curtis (2 September 1853, Killingly, CT—25 April 1925, New York, NY).

Few records give information about the early life of Emma Curtis, but we know that she studied at Woodstock Academy in Connecticut, taught there for a while, and in 1874 entered upon a brief, unrewarding marriage. By 1883 she had moved to Boston and enrolled in the Christian Science course of *Mary B. Eddy. Made a practitioner three months later, Mrs. Hopkins became a trusted lieutenant in the Boston church and served as editor (1884–85) of the *Christian Science Journal*. Within another year, however, relations deteriorated between the two religious thinkers; Mrs. Hopkins consulted sources other than Mrs. Eddy's writings, and her independent quest for spiritual truth created an impossible situation. In 1886 she moved to Chicago where she established the Christian Science Theological Seminary (1887), a separate institution for promulgating teachings similar to those of her mentor. As president of the seminary and principal writer for the magazine, *Christian Metaphysician* (1887–97), she developed a wide following among persons interested in mind cure or the realization of God in all living things. Mrs. Eddy repudiated her erstwhile pupil for being an upstart, denouncing her incorrect teachings and unprincipled claims as well as immature or misleading demonstrations. But Mrs. Hopkins' supporters acclaimed her as the most effective teacher they ever heard. In many instances, it was asserted, invalids attended her class to emerge completely well at the end. She dwelt so continuously in matters of the spirit, they held that her mere presence could heal or fill listeners with the reviving energy of new life.

A subtle blend of charismatic personality and cogent metaphysics made Mrs. Hopkins one of the most compelling spiritualist teachers of her day. Her published works together with classes at the seminary created a sphere of influence which eventually spread from Boston to San Francisco. While her thought was not determinative in the systems of other spiritualists, she influenced at least fourteen such leaders and stands at the headwaters of New Thought in modern America. Revered as the "teachers' teacher," her efforts had considerable impact on men and women who founded their own separate metaphysical groups. Probably the most notable among those she influenced were *Charles and *Myrtle Fillmore, founders of the Unity School of Christianity, Mrs. Fillmore was healed by a student of Mrs. Hopkins, and the two Missourians made frequent trips to Chicago for study with their acknowledged master of ancient wisdom. Mrs. Hopkins imparted to them, as to all her students, an eclectic view of biblical teachings, mysticism, and the sayings of philosophers from many traditions. Her emphasis on the mystical element helped establish that perspective as a major aspect in variations collectively called New Thought. Her concentration on metaphysical interpretations of Christian Scripture tended to place subsequent groups on a firmer biblical basis than those preceding her work. Toward the end of her life she retired from public lectures, but private lessons in New York kept alive the influence which motivated others to search for God inside themselves.

Bibliography:

A. *High Mysticism*, 12 vols. (Philadelphia, 1920–22); 13 vols. (Cornwall Bridge, CT, 1928–35).
B. NAW 2, 219–20.

HOPKINS, Mark (4 February 1802, Stockbridge, MA—17 June 1887, Williamstown, MA). *Education*: B.A., Williams Coll., 1824; studied medicine at Berkshire Medical Inst., 1829. *Career*: tutor, Williams Coll., 1826–28; professor of Moral Philosophy and Rhetoric, Williams Coll., 1830–36; president, Williams Coll., 1836–72; professor of Intellectual and Moral Philosophy, Williams Coll., 1872–87.

After exploring the possibilities of law or medicine as a useful profession, Hopkins entered his real element by returning to Williams as its professor of philosophy. His decision indicated not only a preference for small town virtues over the materialistic pursuits of city life; it also represented an emphasis on spiritual values in liberal education, which he helped popularize for almost six decades. He shaped the minds and hearts of thousands of young men for whom modern society was made less bewildering in transition from inherited patterns. Hopkins endured as a teacher of solid convictions in which there were no unanswered questions and no unfulfilled visions, only duty to sound doctrine and high purpose. The environment fostered at Williams under his presidency stressed piety as much as learning and moral truth even more than scientific advance. Souls were as important as minds, and Hopkins based much of his policy on the conviction that lasting human interests could be promoted only by firm grounding in religion. Not an adventurous or speculative thinker, he prolonged the influence of familiar ideas by giving them the vigor of fresh endorsement. He was also guardian of tested virtues, an instructor of the Westminster Catechism who found salvation compatible with material prosperity. While optimistic about progress in all the manifold appliances of civilization, he tempered enthusiasm with knowledge that human sinfulness had a long, tenacious history. New England traditions spoke through him as he lectured against spiritual pitfalls such as skepticism, naturalism (Darwin), Transcendentalism, and Romanism in addition to the moral danger of alcohol and vice. After resigning the college's highest office to younger leaders, he embodied till death the ideal that education should mold men of good character rather than concentrate exclusively on intellectual accomplishment.

Bibliography:

A. *Lectures on the Evidences of Christianity* (Boston, 1846); *Lectures on Moral Sciences* (Boston, 1862); *The Law of Love and Love as Law* (New York, 1869); *An Outline Study of Man* (New York, 1873); *Strength and Beauty* (New York, 1874); *The Scriptural Idea of Man* (New York, 1883).

B. SH 5, 363; NCAB 6, 237–38; DAB 9, 215–17; NYT 18 June 1887, 1; Franklin Carter, *Mark Hopkins* (Boston, 1892); John H. Denison, *Mark Hopkins: A Biography* (New York, 1935); Frederick Rudolph, *Mark Hopkins and the Log* (New Haven, 1956).

HOPKINS, Samuel (17 September 1721, Waterbury, CT—20 December 1803, Newport, RI). *Education*: B.A., Yale Coll., 1741; studied theology with *Jonathan Edwards, Northampton, MA, 1741–42. *Career*: minister, Housatonic (now Great Barrington), MA, 1743–69; minister, First Congregational Church, Newport, RI, 1770–1803.

As was the custom for ministerial students in those days, Hopkins read theology in the home of an established pastor after graduating from Yale. Later, during his first pastorate, he had the opportunity to converse at great length (1751–58) with Jonathan Edwards, that early host who was forced from Northampton to modest tasks at nearby Stockbridge. A lasting friendship resulted, and the young disciple became principal systematizer of his mentor's capacious theological genius. Hopkins was a man of sedentary habits, an indefatigable student who inherited Edwards' library and brought comprehensive reasoning powers to doctrines comprising the New Divinity. Never known for success as a preacher, his writing defended "Consistent Calvinism" with such trenchant insight that in many quarters it was known equally well under the name of "Hopkinsianism." By and large it contained the main features of Edwards' Calvinism, emphasizing the sovereignty of God who does all things for his own glory and for the general good of creation. A governmental theory of atonement, love as the epitome of human virtue, and sin as the occasion of God's displaying mercy were ancillary categories in this scheme of doctrine. It presented a formidable body of ideas to critics and supporters alike.

Important modifications made Hopkins' work more than a simple collation of tenets formulated by an earlier thinker. Like Edwards he said that man should learn to find his place in God's world, living for the good of the whole. But he did not include the concept of God as Being, and he sharpened the general view of disinterested benevolence to a stern maxim: one should be willing to be damned if it counted for the greater glory of God. Hopkins also stressed actual sinning more than the state of original sin, defining human failure as grounded essentially in selfishness. The process of salvation began with regeneration, an imperceptible action of the Holy Spirit that inclined certain persons toward greater knowledge of God. Then one could participate actively with a regenerate human will in conversion, a deliberate turning from sin to embrace virtue and truths of the Gospel. In this manner Hopkins unwittingly gave more freedom to human volition. He made Calvinism an instrument of defense against Arminian critics while the metaphysical heart of positive adoration faded into the background. Yet the concepts of disinterested benevolence and personal reform had strong implications for practical action. Evangelical revivals drew strength from his theology by applying the system to human ability to change through conversion. Social reforms also benefited, and Hopkins led the way standing as one of the first Congregationalists to denounce slavery, this done amid shipping magnates who flourished by such trade. Judging from its consistency and long-range effect, his work extended an influence far beyond the limited confines of a single New England congregation.

Bibliography:

A. *Sin... an Advantage to the Universe* (Boston, 1759); *The True State and Character of the Unregenerate* (New Haven, 1769); *An Inquiry into the Nature of True Holiness* (Newport, 1773); *A Dialogue Concerning the Slavery of the Africans* (Norwich, CT, 1776); *A Treatise on the Millennium* (Boston, 1793; New York, 1972); *System of Doctrines Contained in Divine Revelation, Explained and Defended,* 2 vols. (Boston, 1793).

B. AAP 1, 428–35; SH 5, 363–64; NCAB 7, 154–55; DAB 9, 217–18; Stephen West, *Sketches of the Life of the Late Samuel Hopkins* (Hartford, 1805); John Ferguson, *Memoir of the Life and Character of Rev. Samuel Hopkins* (Boston, 1831); Edwards A. Park, *Memoir of the Life and Character of Samuel Hopkins* (Boston, 1854).

HOSIER, Harry (1750?, near Fayetteville, NC—May 1806, Philadelphia, PA). *Career*: Methodist exhorter, 1780–1805.

Not much is known about Hosier's origins because in those days few people noted the birth of just another slave. It seems that by the age of thirty he lived near Baltimore and had either been given his freedom or had bought it. As a convert to Methodism he soon met *Francis Asbury, possibly as early as 1773 but definitely by 1780. By that latter year "Black Harry" was rapidly gaining a reputation for powerful and effective preaching. He never learned to read or write, but his retentive memory and remarkable eloquence moved audiences as no other speaker could. Hosier traveled often with Asbury and did much to recruit the black population, freedmen as well as slaves, into the fledgling Methodist church. Moreover, he proved to be as effective with white listeners as with blacks. His dramatic exhortations on sinfulness and redemption through faith affected persons of all stations in life and helped make Methodism one of the most integrated denominations at that time. Some individuals attended his meetings out of curiosity, but in the end they agreed with even well-educated ministers who called Hosier one of the best preachers in the world and certainly the greatest natural orator in America.

When Methodists officially declared themselves to be a separate denomination in 1784, Hosier was present at the momentous Christmas Conference. Thereafter he traveled with and preached alongside several pioneer Methodists from the Carolinas to New England. Though small and slightly built, he always had a tremendous impact on audiences in every region because of his unusual skill and oratorical gifts. There is some credibility to the claim that Hosier was the first African-American to be licensed as a Methodist preacher in this country. But that claim to seniority aside, there is no proof at all of his ordination, and Hosier was never officially recognized as a member of the clergy. Perhaps because of this subordinate status he suffered periods of depression late in life. In the end, though, he conquered excessive drinking and recovered a faith that met death with confidence. Unlike his colleague *Richard Allen who organized the African Methodist Episcopal Church, Hosier remained with the original group all his life and gave invaluable service in its outreach to all kinds of people.

Bibliography:

B.   Warren Thomas Smith, *Harry Hosier: Circuit Rider* (Nashville, 1981).

HUBBARD, Lafayette Ronald (13 March 1911, Tilden, NE—24 January 1986, Creston, CA). *Education*: studied at George Washington Univ., 1930–32. *Career*: head, Church of Scientology, 1954–86.

It is wise to keep in mind that most reports about L. Ron Hubbard contain unsubstantiated claims. Basic matters like public events can be verified; skepticism is the best policy regarding statements issuing from the private sector alone. After several years of writing science fiction and adventure stories for pulp magazines, Hubbard published in 1950 a lengthy work on mental health which became a bestseller. In that year he also created the Hubbard Dianetic Research Foundation, and after several tries at organizing a religion he established in 1954 the Church of Scientology of California. Other churches or therapeutic centers appeared in major American cities and spread to Europe and most English-speaking countries, their success largely due to Hubbard's enthusiasm, organizational ability, and salesmanship. Standard religious services have little place in these churches, but members accept a highly structured system of beliefs that avoid mysticism and concentrate on a type of science which promises reliable, predictable results. Scientology presents the classic characteristics of a cult: offering salvation through secret knowledge and dominated by a single leader who claims monopoly over such information.

Scientology teaches that humans are "thetans," immortal life forces who have inhabited many bodies over vast stretches of time. During previous lives thetans have experienced painful events, or "engrams," which are stored in their subconscious. The purpose of dianetic therapy is to help persons raise engrams to the level of conscious awareness and thus reduce the ill effects they have been causing amid present circumstances. A trained "auditor" uses a device called an "E-meter" to treat applicants who wish to rid themselves of debilitating engrams. Novices, or "preclears," pay substantial fees to the church centers for treatment in hopes of becoming "clear." In 1963 the Federal Food and Drug Administration challenged these quasi-medical claims. Psychotherapists opposed such ideology too, and in 1984 the Internal Revenue Service revoked the Church's tax-exempt status. Law suits in many countries, together with denunciations from many disaffected former members caused the fortunes of Scientology to fluctuate dramatically. Such adverse publicity led Hubbard to announce his resignation as head of the Church in 1966, but he remained in charge of its many lucrative activities until death. Today's adherents claim that the organization has as many as six million followers worldwide; skeptics grant less than a third of that number.

Bibliography:

A. *Dianetics: The Modern Science of Mental Health* (New York, 1950, many reprints); *Science of Survival: Simplified, Faster Dianetic Techniques* (Wichita, KS, 1951, many reprints); *Dianetics: The Evolution of a Science* (London, 1966, many reprints); *Introduction to Scientology Ethics* (East Grinstead, England, 1968, many reprints); *Dianetics Today* (Los Angeles, 1975, many reprints); *What Is Scientology* (Los Angeles, 1978, many reprints).
B. George Malko, *Scientology: The Now Religion* (New York, 1970); Russell Miller, *Bare-Faced Messiah: The True Story of L. Ron Hubbard* (New York, 1987); Bent Corydon and L. Ron Hubbard, Jr., *L. Ron Hubbard: Messiah or Madman?* (Secaucus, NY, 1987).

HUGHES, John Joseph (24 June 1797, Annaloghan, Ireland—3 January 1864, New York, NY). *Education*: studied at Mount St. Mary's Coll. and Sem., 1819–26. *Career*: rector, St. Joseph's Church, 1827–32, and St. John's Church, Philadelphia, 1832–38; bishop coadjutor, Diocese of New York, 1838–42; bishop of New York, 1842–50; archbishop of New York, 1850–64.

Many young men emigrated to the New World because of economic or social pressures, but Hughes left Ireland to fulfill his intention of becoming a priest. Tenacious in pursuit of that vocation, he succeeded in being appointed to a parish just when the trusteeism controversy was reaching its apex. Questions of whether laymen or bishops selected personnel, administered discipline, and determined ecclesiastical policy were strong ones in many dioceses. Hughes was emphatic that the priesthood was a divine office to be controlled by church authorities, not a human occupation regulated by democratic legislation. Experiences accumulating from a curacy to those as the first archbishop of New York convinced him in principle that churches should be guided by a spiritual hierarchy. Through adroit practical maneuvers and appeals for popular support he was able to rescue Catholic administration from the more divisive aspects of democracy. A bold and skillful leader, he helped reduce trustee power around Philadelphia. In his own diocese, he crushed it by modifying state property laws, setting a pattern for resolving conflicts nationwide. Yet he insisted that his faith was compatible with the republican nation and often rose to defend Catholicism against nativist calumny. He relished debate for good causes, refusing to suffer in silence when his countrymen or church was under attack. One public debate (1832–35) with John Breckinridge, a Presbyterian minister, made Hughes a national figure. He founded a newspaper (*Catholic Herald*, 1833) and a tract society which served to counterbalance nativism while they gave immigrants increased self-respect.

Controversial speeches on issues of public importance made Hughes the most prominent voice among American Catholics for three decades. During the 1840s his activity related to public education raised questions which have remained part of our cultural history ever since. The immediate struggle began over equitable distribution of funds for local schools, but it stemmed from basic views regarding the nature and goals of education. He argued that public schools were dominated by Protestant bias, forcing on Catholic children distorted interpretations of their heritage and depriving them of sound religious guidance as a foundation for other training. In the swirl of politics and religious antagonism, Hughes tried to overcome prejudice as well as alleviate the financial burden of poor Catholic families. The end result was disappointing to all concerned; public schools were more thoroughly secularized while Hughes moved reluctantly to a full-fledged parochial school program. As archbishop he often traveled abroad, soliciting funds and recruiting clergy for his large jurisdiction. He imported many religious societies to promote work in education and in a number of charities. Tremendous institutional growth was evidence of his managerial abilities, including a business acumen which overcame heavy debts in the diocese. Still his public image was the main feature of leadership among Irish Americans. One of his last appearances among them was to appeal for calm in the draft riot of July, 1863, thus serving, while close to death, in ways to help both church and country.

Bibliography:

A. *Controversy between Rev. Messers. Hughes and Breckinridge on the Subject, "Is the Protestant Religion the Religion of Christ?"* (Philadelphia, 1833); *The Complete Works of the Most Rev. John Hughes*, ed. Lawrence Kehoe, 2 vols. (New York, 1865).

B. SH 5, 388; NCAB 1, 193–95; DAB 9, 352–55; NCE 7, 196–98; John R. G. Hassard, *Life of the Most Reverend John Hughes: First Archbishop of New York* (New York, 1866, 1969); Henry A. Brann, *Most Reverend John Hughes* (New York, 1892).

HUNTINGTON, Frederic Dan (28 May 1819, Hadley, MA—11 July 1904, Hadley, MA). *Education*: B.A., Amherst Coll., 1839; graduated from Harvard Div. Sch., 1842. *Career*: minister, South Congregational Society, Boston, 1842–55; editor, *Monthly Religious Magazine*, 1845–59; chaplain and professor of Christian Morals, Harvard Coll., 1855–60; rector, Immanuel Episcopal Church, Boston, 1861–69; bishop of Central New York, 1869–1904.

From the time when his parents were denied communion because of their Unitarian beliefs, Huntington sought to avoid the bitterness often caused by ecclesiastical bigotry. In his sixty-two ministerial years, first in association with the Unitarian denomination and then as an Episcopal priest, he tried to win others to the larger Christian perspective that improved their personal lives and benefited society without reference to parties or factionalism. His early decades were spent among liberal Congregationalists around Boston, where Huntington gained influence as preacher, journalist, and teacher. But through the 1850s he became distressed over transcendental emphases which he thought detrimental to the whole foundation of the denomination's theology. There were too many opportunities for private discernment of truth to suit him and not enough reliance on revelations already recorded in Scripture. When the debate shifted away from interpretations of holy writ altogether to new sources of religious inspiration, Huntington was hardly able to support his Unitarian colleagues any longer. He slowly moved away from those who recognized no binding authority or even guidelines in historical beliefs, ordinances, and institutions. By 1859 he was led to affirm the divinity and redemptive function of Christ, a correspondingly trinitarian definition of the godhead, and a divinely authorized polity based on apostolic succession. While the Episcopal church did not embody those principles without retaining some faults, Huntington's removal to that body was more congruent with his matured theology, and it gave new scope for his catholic zeal.

As rector of a new parish in Boston, Huntington became notable for missionary activity, for efforts to spread beliefs he found convincing, and for attempts to meet basic needs of those around him. During the rest of his life, he sought to make churches helpful to all people, the downtrodden as well as the affluent. When he was made bishop and moved to Syracuse, New York, he continued welfare and mission work, having as a special pastoral care the Onondaga tribe of Iroquois who still resided in the state. His unpretentious manner put people at ease, and his efforts to build new churches bore fruit in many small towns as well as cities. From his early stress on the dignity of man, to a continued emphasis on ethics as part of salvation achieved through action in the present life, Huntington was always interested in the social aspects of religion. He did pioneering work in applying Christian principles to labor-management relations, politics, and business, and urged fellow clergy to do the same. As industry and urban population grew, Huntington was already concentrating on practical matters enough to supply some of the early ideas which culminated in the Social Gospel.

Bibliography:

A. *Sermons for the People* (Boston, 1856); *Divine Aspects of Human Society* (Boston, 1858; New York, 1891); *Christ and the World* (New York, 1874); *The Fitness of Christianity to Men* (New York, 1878); *Christ in the Christian Year and in the Life of Man*, 2 vols. (New York, 1878–81).

B. SH 5, 412; NCAB 3, 363; DAB 9, 413–14; NYT 12 Jul 1904, 1; Arria S. Huntington, *Memoir and Letters of Frederic Dan Huntington* (Boston, 1906); George C. Richmond, *Frederic Dan Huntington* (Rochester, NY, 1908).

HUNTINGTON, William Reed (20 September 1838, Lowell, MA—26 July 1909, Nahant, MA). *Education*: B.A., Harvard Coll., 1859; studied theology with *Frederic D. Huntington, Boston, MA, 1859–62. *Career:* instructor in Chemistry, Harvard Coll., 1859–60; curate, Emmanuel Church, Boston, 1861–62; rector, All Saints' Church, Worcester, MA, 1862–83; rector, Grace Episcopal Church, New York, 1883–1909.

As a local church figure, Huntington spent over four decades in the routine of pastoral care and administration, providing leadership in the broad church tradition of evangelical sermons plus sacraments without undue reliance on ritual. Beyond his own parishes, he augmented Episcopal work in city missions and general community welfare. Beginning in 1871 he came to be an acknowledged floor leader in the House of Deputies at triennial General Conventions, taking active part in temperance resolutions and attempts (successful in 1889) to revive the order of deaconess. But within denominational lines his most significant contribution lay in revising the 1789 Book of Common Prayer (BCP). In 1877 he worked on a committee which dealt with isolated problems of liturgical usage. Three years later he spearheaded a drive to end piecemeal alterations and deal with them in a comprehensive, coherent fashion. As coordinating secretary of three subcommittees he worked unremittingly to enhance not doctrinal change but enrichment in forms of worship. Always something of a poet, he had a fine instinct for liturgical expression, which appeared in judicious refinement of old prayers as well as several entirely new collects. The work was accepted in 1883, reviewed after 1886, and finally ratified in 1892, a monument to his patient, persuasive skill. It is indicative of his long-range influence that Edward L. Parsons, later bishop and main force behind the 1928 revised BCP, first acquired liturgical interests as his curate in New York.

As early as 1865, in a sermon on ''American Catholicity,'' Huntington exhibited strong concern for church union. His 1870 book on the subject became a classic ecumenical document which set forth a structural basis for ending the scandal of divided Christendom. The church was, he argued, a tangible representative of the kingdom of God, but Roman Catholics overemphasized it while Puritan critics failed to appreciate the central place of church life; rationalists and modernists distorted its meaning beyond recognition. In suggesting a platform, or ''quadrilateral,'' of essentials on which churches could agree, Huntington gave an outline for most ecumenical discussion to the present time. Within dimensions of a simple creed, varied worship, and generous polity he advocated: (1) Holy Scripture as the rule and ultimate standard of faith, (2) Apostles' and Nicene creeds as sufficient statement of that faith, (3) two sacraments, baptism and the supper, instituted by Christ, and (4) episcopacy as the keystone or focal point of governmental unity. In 1886 these articles were adopted by the General Convention as constituting the best single hope for union of churches in America. Three years later the Lambeth Conference sanctioned them as expressive of worldwide Anglican policy. Many denominations responded favorably to overtures for union based on the quadrilateral, but negotiations foundered on arguments over the episcopacy. Pioneering efforts of such ecumenical thinkers as Huntington have borne greater fruit in twentieth century developments, when the validity of ministerial offices could be separated from their present form or historic origins.

Bibliography:

A. *The Church Idea: An Essay Toward Unity* (New York, 1870, and many subsequent editions); *Conditional Immortality* (New York, 1878); *The Causes of the Soul* (New York, 1891); *A National Church* (New York, 1898); *Four Key Words of Religion* (New York, 1899); *A Good Shepherd* (New York, 1906).

B. SH 5, 412–13; NCAB 38, 131–32; DAB 9, 420–21; NYT 27 July 1909, 7; John W. Suter, *Life and Letters of William Reed Huntington: A Champion of Unity* (New York, 1925).

HUTCHINSON, Anne Marbury (1591, Alford, England—?August 1643, New Netherland Colony).

The Massachusetts colony to which Hutchinson emigrated in 1634 was troubled over royal attempts to control the enterprise and internal resistance of Puritan plans for building a holy commonwealth. Still the lady, wife of a prosperous merchant, made herself useful in Boston society with open friendliness and compassionate acts as a visiting nurse. Before leaving England, she had already formed definite ideas on central theological points, including the relative merits of grace and works in salvation. She had been influenced in such doctrines by *John Cotton, a Lincolnshire minister whose Puritan convictions led him to sail for the New World in 1633. Cotton tried to modify an emphasis on sanctified living as evidence of inward grace; while still enjoining moral effort, he stressed intuitional awareness of election as more important. Hutchinson shared this viewpoint but developed it far beyond Cotton's intent and produced a crisis in the New England conception of institutionalized righteousness. She inferred that the gift of God's grace implied an actual indwelling of the Holy Ghost, providing sanctification already and rendering the secondary externals of conventional morality minimally applicable. Through private conversations and then well-attended meetings in her home she argued against a covenant of works. Salvation was assured to those who experienced mystical union with God. In light of that certainty, evidence of sanctification was superfluous. By 1636 her sharp distinction between covenants of grace and works found parallel alignment in political factions, weakening theology and society by admitting no compromise.

Those accustomed to regulating human life in secular as well as religious matters considered Hutchinson's one-sided visions dangerously akin to Antinomianism. They charged that her attitude produced subjectivism in religion while it yielded social anarchy. Fears of that sort led to a series of inquiries and finally a trial where she was accused of traducing ministers in following their vocational duties. At General Court she parried every legal thrust with wit and vivacious competence, very nearly clearing herself entirely. But toward the end of the session, she made the astonishing announcement that God had privately revealed He would destroy her persecutors. Association with lawless sedition was bad enough, but extra-biblical revelation was even worse, particularly when it promised destruction of the entire Puritan state. Officials immediately pronounced sentence of banishment, to be carried out the following spring. During the winter of 1637–38 Hutchinson spread ideas which increasingly alarmed local clergymen; even John Cotton tried to dissuade his erstwhile disciple from error. But by March, the Boston church, a majority of whom had once been her friends, formally excommunicated her for heresy. The Hutchinson family moved to Rhode Island and flourished there until 1642. Anne then settled in the Dutch colony along Long Island Sound where Indians killed her and all but one small daughter. While she was not a champion of religious liberty, she did embody the ideal of placing individual conscience above the restraints of authoritarian social structures.

Bibliography:

B.   NCAB 9, 148–49; DAB 9, 436–37; NAW 2, 245–47; Winnifred K. Rugg, *Unafraid: A Life of Anne Hutchinson* (Boston, 1930); Helen Augur, *An American Jezebel* (New York, 1930); Edith Curtis, *Anne Hutchinson* (Cambridge, 1930); Reginald P. Bolton, *A Woman Misunderstood* (New York, 1931); Emery J. Battis, *Saints and Sectaries* (Chapel Hill, NC, 1962); Selma R. Williams, *Divine Rebel: The Life of Anne Marbury Hutchinson* (New York, 1981).

I

INGERSOLL, Robert Green (11 August 1833, Dresden, NY—21 July 1899, Dobbs Ferry, NY). *Career*: practiced law, Shawneetown, IL (1854–57), Peoria, IL (1857–61 and 1863–79), Washington, DC (1879–85), and New York (1885–97); officer, the Union Army, 1861–63; lecturer on religious topics, 1856–99.

Birth in a Congregationalist manse and stern rearing by a widower father did not endear Ingersoll to the theory or practice of Christianity. Early experiences of hellfire preaching produced in him a deeply etched horror of ideas such as damnation and the supernatural basis on which they were defended. Reading in search of more adequate values, he finally concluded that unless ideals were grounded on reason, observation, and experience, they were empty claims, detrimental to human progress. Speculation about the origin of the universe, existence of God, truth of the Bible, divinity of Christ, or immortality of the soul never produced sure knowledge. Ingersoll spent almost four decades of his life touring the country, spreading such ideas and welcoming the title of religious agnostic. His witty, daring eloquence drew large audiences. For a time it seemed that a lucrative law practice and his oratory would lead to success in politics, but the reputation of antagonist to established religion ended those ambitions. His popular lectures struck out against the mental tyranny engendered by religious spokesmen, denouncing as well the ignorance and fear that resulted from their influence. Suffering in the name of some hypothetical future existence was unacceptable to this free-thinking iconoclast. He attracted national attention by exposing some of the limitations in Christian belief. Discussions on gods, ghosts, "some mistakes of Moses," heresies, myth and miracles, biblical inerrancy, and "the creed of science" set his listeners to thinking, some to reject him outright, others to broaden their theological horizons.

While most people remembered Ingersoll for destructive attacks on superstition and dogma, these stemmed from positive motives. He wished to free men from the wasteful oppression of belief in order to promote more rational pursuit of happiness in this world. His activities took the form of a crusade, spreading the gospel of humanism in which man was seen as a power and end in himself. As an evangelist of rational thought, Ingersoll hoped to shed light in dark places, destroying falsehood to make room for individual liberty. He was convinced that science was potentially the instrument of making a heaven in this life. Liberated persons could be their own redeemers, building a society where jus .ice might be achieved and individual tranquility become a concrete realization. Most American citizens were disturbed by his facile criticisms of their confessional sentiments; in the last analysis his platform performances served as symbolic protests rather than strong impulses for new humanitarian commitments. But his vision of a democratic world where liberty and science could create the good society remains a compelling ideal in the history of religious thought.

Bibliography:

A.   *The Works of Robert Ingersoll*, ed. Clinton P. Farrell, 12 vols. (New York, 1900); *The Letters of Robert G. Ingersoll*, ed. Eva I. Wakefield (New York, 1951).

B.   NCAB 9, 255–56; DAB 9, 469–70; NYT 22 Jul 1899, 3; Cameron Rogers, *Colonel Bob Ingersoll* (Garden City, NY, 1927); C. H. Cramer, *Royal Bob* (Indianapolis, 1952); Joseph Lewis, *Ingersoll the Magnificent* (New York, 1957); Orvin Larson, *American Infidel: Robert G. Ingersoll* (New York, 1962); David D. Anderson, *Robert Ingersoll* (New York, 1972).

IRELAND, John (11 September 1838, Burnchurch, Ireland—25 September 1918, St. Paul, MN). *Education*: graduated in classics from college at Meximieux, France, 1857; graduated from seminary at Montbel, France, 1861. *Career*: chaplain, Union Army, 1861–62; curate, cathedral at St. Paul, MN, 1861–67; rector, cathedral at St. Paul, 1867–75; bishop (coadjutor, 1875–84), diocese of St. Paul, 1875–88; archbishop of St. Paul, 1888–1918.

Vigorous, frank, and outspoken, St. Paul's first archbishop was an outstanding controversialist for the ideals which he thought his church and country embodied for the betterment of mankind. As an ecclesiastical administrator, Ireland was dutiful in building facilities necessary for religious care in his diocese, but his activities in larger issues drew most attention to his name. He was an early and lasting advocate of progressive reform in urban affairs. The issues of temperance and its related concern for family stability, race relations and the genuine need for desegregation programs, labor-management arbitration, and the continuing problem of just wages for workers—all these were questions in which Ireland was a bold and energetic champion for constructive change that benefited the common man. Aside from disputes that involved doctrinal considerations, the bulk of the archbishop's work applied in areas where religious concerns bore upon the cultural welfare of all members of society.

Education was a field to which Ireland devoted much of his time, speaking for the liberal Catholic side in ensuing debates. In an 1891 address which explained his opposition to exclusively secular education, he announced support for compulsory state schools but added that religious instruction was also a basic ingredient in training children. Some of his remarks caused bitter reaction among those who wished to maintain control over all subjects in parochial schools, a group led by Jesuits and New York archbishop, *Michael A. Corrigan. Ireland was willing to cooperate with the state in joint educational projects, approving a plan in two towns within his diocese, Faribault and Stillwater. During the year 1891–92, parochial buildings were rented and state funds were used for teaching secular subjects; after school hours, religious personnel used the same setting for worship and religious instruction. Charges were made that such a plan threatened to supplant the Catholic school system, and Ireland was forced to defend his liberality in the press, eventually going to Rome for discussions with authorities there. His loyalty to Catholic education and his flexibility in new circumstances were vindicated, but the plan fell through and stands now as just one episode in a continuing dilemma.

As early as the Third Plenary Council of 1884, Ireland was known for eloquent declarations that the principles of his church were harmonious with those of the republic. He urged that American Catholics could be loyal to the hierarchy and still adopt more democratic, individualistic patterns of action to meet social needs. In 1891 he wrote an introduction to a biography of *Isaac T. Hecker, in which he praised such virtues in the man whom he saw as typical of the modern priest, capable of solving contemporary problems. American Catholics, sensitive to the charge of foreignism, acclaimed his stand; French Catholics and some Americans, embroiled in different issues, seized upon it as a threat to traditional channels of clerical eminence. "Americanism" became the symbol for a complex and emotional debate on both sides of the Atlantic. Conservatives saw Ireland as the potential head of a schismatic church, democratic in structure and reductionist in theology. He and his faithful friend, *James Gibbons, defended themselves as best they could against overblown claims, but in 1899 the pope acted to settle the matter. *Testem Benevolentiae* condemned any departure from the deposit of faith or moral teachings and anything that sought to minimize or reinterpret doctrines in order to accommodate to new conditions and win converts. Ireland responded immediately that he too repudiated such errors and that the "American heresy" was not held by any serious Catholic in his country. This disavowal notwithstanding, the bewildering set of events was seen as a victory for conservative forces; and perhaps because of his place in the controversy, Ireland was never elevated to the cardinalate.

Bibliography:

A. *L'Eglise et le Siècle* (Paris, 1894); *The Church and Modern Society: Lectures and Addresses* (Chicago, 1896).

B. NCAB 9, 226; DAB 9, 494–97; NCE 7, 610–13; NYT 26 Sep 1918, 13; Cuthbert Soukus, *The Public Speaking of Archbishop John Ireland* (St. Cloud, MN, 1948); Edwin

V. O'Hara and Richard Purcell, *Archbishop Ireland: Two Appreciations* (St. Paul, MN, 1949); James H. Moynihan, *The Life of Archbishop John Ireland* (New York, 1953); Marvin R. Oconnell, *John Ireland and the American Catholic Church* (St. Paul, MN, 1988).

IVES, Levi Silliman (16 September 1797, Meridan, CT—13 October 1867, Manhattanville, NY). *Education*: studied at Hamilton Coll., 1816; studied theology with *John H. Hobart, New York, 1819–22. *Career*: missionary curate and rector, Batavia, NY, Philadelphia and Lancaster, PA, 1823–27; assistant rector of Christ Church and rector of St. Luke's Church, New York, 1827–31; bishop of North Carolina, 1831–52; agent for Catholic charities, New York, 1854–67.

Reared in a Presbyterian family, Ives entered college with plans to serve as a minister of that denomination. But illness forced him to return home where he gradually developed views found articulated to his satisfaction in the Episcopal communion. After almost two decades of priestly endeavor under the guidance of his mentor and father-in-law, *John H. Hobart, he was named second bishop of North Carolina. There he worked with great energy, conducting visitations, building schools, recruiting a small number of dedicated clergymen, and establishing missions which extended into Tennessee as part of his jurisdiction until that state became a separate diocese in 1834. The new bishop continued his church's work with plantation slaves; while compliant with their subordinate status, he nevertheless encouraged owners to provide for the means of salvation among black workers, organizing them into separate rather than integrated congregations. In 1845 a farm and training school was established at Valle Crucis to prepare candidates for holy orders. At that mountain mission he founded the Brotherhood of the Holy Cross, a semimonastic order based on a regimen of devotional practices rarely associated with Protestant religious principles. Further, the brotherhood embodied many of Ives' high church predilections which favored auricular confession, veneration of saints, and belief in transubstantiation. In 1848 opposition to such innovations had become so widespread that the brotherhood was dissolved, and it was necessary for the bishop to provide his diocesan convention with written assurance of his orthodoxy.

That did not, however, mark the end of debates over acceptable doctrine nor of Ives' personal odyssey in spiritual orientation. At some time in the ensuing four years he concluded that the Episcopal church was not a branch of the primitive, truly catholic Body of Christ where sacraments were still valid. But he pursued a vacillating course, protesting loyalty to a denomination while holding private views at variance with it. After obtaining a leave of absence, the troubled bishop embarked for Europe and within three months was received into the Roman Catholic church on 25 December 1852. Ives was the only American Episcopalian in high office who converted to Catholicism. The decision was welcomed by many in his former church as an end to equivocation; it was noticed with equal favor by Roman officials as an indication of ecclesiastical probity. Concerning the legalities involved, he resigned by letter to his diocese but was formally deposed by the Episcopal House of Bishops for not acting in conformity to canon law. As a Catholic layman he taught rhetoric at Fordham (college and seminary) and worked for several charitable agencies such as the New York Catholic Protectory, which he founded in 1863. The last fifteen years of his life were not outstanding in public accomplishments, but they were sustained by a conviction of having at last resolved inner conflicts regarding the true faith.

Bibliography:

A. *The Apostles' Doctrine and Fellowship* (New York, 1844); *The Obedience of Faith* (New York, 1849); *Trials of a Mind in its Progress to Catholicism* (New York, 1854).

B. SH 6, 71; NCAB 5, 409; DAB 9, 521–22; NCE 7, 776–77; NYT 14 Oct 1867, 5; John O'Grady, *Levi Silliman Ives* (New York, 1933).

J

JACKSON, Sheldon (18 May 1834, Minaville, NY—2 May 1909, Asheville, NC). *Education*: B.A., Union Coll., (NY), 1855; B.D., Princeton Sem., 1858. *Career*: Presbyterian missionary, Indian Territory, 1858–59; minister, La Crescent, MN (1858–64) and Rochester, MN (1864–69) while missionary in WI and MN, 1859–69; superintendent for Presbyterian Board of Home Missions (PBHM) in MT, WY, UT, CO, NM and AZ, 1869–82; editor, *Rocky Mountain Presbyterian*, 1872–82; business manager for PBHM in NY, 1882–84; superintendent for PBHM in AK, 1884–1909; editor, *North Star*, 1887–97.

An emphasis on missionary activity was so strong in Jackson's early training, he hardly considered any vocation other than field work for the Presbyterian church. His first assignment at a school for Choctaw Indians in Spencer, Oklahoma, was challenging enough, but attacks of malaria made it necessary to seek another location. During the next decade he served at two churches in Minnesota, which provided a base for constant itineration over a tract covering 13,000 square miles. Jackson was indefatigable in labors to develop and extend churches on the growing edge of frontier settlement. He recruited ministers, solicited aid for his "raven fund," and distributed money and boxes of clothing to support ministerial efforts in the American heartland. As superintendent of missions in a region amounting to half of the nation's territory, he helped organize seven presbyteries and three synods after having founded most of the churches comprising them. Aggressive work in mining towns or among Pima Indians did not receive high priority from most Presbyterians, but Jackson had the ability to arouse great interest in the cause of such missions. Neither risk nor meager funds could deter his tireless energy in starting new ventures, and his missionary canvassing left permanent establishments from the Mexican border to the Arctic circle. His pioneering editorial work on the magazine which became the *Pres-*

byterian Home Missionary (after 1882) also served to focus attention on the needs of struggling churches west of the Missouri.

As early as 1877 Jackson visited Alaska to see about starting missions there. In the decades following official appointment, he helped supervise development of cultural as well as religious facilities from Sitka to Point Barrow. One of his many capacities was governmental superintendent of public schools (after 1885), and he traveled widely to begin elementary instruction for children of all races. Tribes of the Tlingit nation, whaling stations, logging towns, Eskimo villages— he considered all these part of his missionary responsibility. In a sparsely settled land, all Christian efforts were bound by common ties; he was friend to Moravian and Catholic missionaries in addition to all Protestant groups which had representatives in the wilderness. Schools and churches were primary implements of Jackson's evangelical concern, but in 1891 he initiated another practical contribution for native Alaskan welfare. In that year he began importing herds of reindeer from Siberia to feed the Eskimo population. It also proved to be the most effective means of achieving the old missionary objective of encouraging aboriginal hunters to adopt the more settled life of herdsmen. Jackson made thousands of speeches, prepared twenty annual reports on education, and traveled almost a million miles to advance the cause of Christian civilization in Alaska. He delivered his last address on the subject just a few days before undergoing surgery from which he never recovered.

Bibliography:

A.   *Alaska and Missions on the North Pacific Coast* (New York, 1880).

B.   SH 6, 73; NCAB 9, 251–52; DAB 9, 555–56; Robert L. Stewart, *Sheldon Jackson* (New York, 1908); J. Arthur Lazell, *Alaskan Apostle: The Life Story of Sheldon Jackson* (New York, 1960).

JAMES, William (11 January 1842, New York, NY—26 August 1910, Chocorua, NH). *Education*: studied at Lawrence Scientific Sch., Harvard Coll., 1861–63; M.D., Harvard Med. Sch., 1869. *Career*: professor at various ranks of Physiology, Philosophy, and Psychology, Harvard Univ., 1872–1907.

American religious liberalism received one of its greatest articulations by an individual not connected with preaching or theologizing. James developed his ideas through a long, varied educational process of scientific pursuits which culminated in philosophical reflections on God and the religious aspect of life. The personal and practical accent in his writing represented a broad contemporary tendency shared by many thinkers; his lucid exposition made him the spokesman for an untold number of others. It was natural for James to reconcile subjective feelings with scientific method because he valued basic principles of psychology more than the discovery of new facts. As he became more absorbed in deeper problems of morals and metaphysics, strong empirical elements remained operative. This is best seen in his insistence that personal religious experience is the proper point of departure for any discussion of spiritual affirmations. The variety of religious experiences made for a multiplicity of beliefs. These were dictated by practical preferences stemming from various feelings and resolves in human nature. Since the moral will was essentially partisan, James argued for a pluralism in belief linked with a thoroughgoing voluntaristic individualism. The motives and reasons for every choice could be justified in rational scientific discourse. Underlying all these tenets was the fundamental conviction that, in questions of uncertain resolution, there was more likelihood of getting at the truth by believing than by doubting.

The individual's right freely to believe as he chose did not define truth, and James made one of his most important contributions by addressing that problem. He held that truth is an attribute of ideas, not of reality. Truth pertains to ideas as they fulfill the purpose for which they were invoked. So one tests the meaning of a concept by examining the consequences it has for experience and conduct instead of speculating about absolutes. James had slowly formulated this eminently practical approach to cognition over a period of thirty years, but late in his intellectual development he coined its lasting title: pragmatism. Meaning and utility are inextricably joined, validated by experience and justified through effective action. Many popularizers vulgarized James' epistemology by saying any belief that worked was true, or all religions were equal because they were utilitarian for adherents. James never reached those conclusions himself, but he did have a relativistic view of the world that emphasized plasticity and adaptation in human knowledge. Change, freedom, and no absolute standards for meaning characterized his thought. Those qualities made him a powerful influence on the empirical, experiential idealism as expressed by liberal activists of the twentieth century.

Bibliography:

A. *Principles of Psychology*, 2 vols. (New York, 1890); *The Will to Believe* (New York, 1897); *The Varieties of Religious Experience: A Study in Human Nature* (New York, 1902); *Pragmatism: A New Name for Some Old Ways of Thinking* (New York, 1907); *The Meaning of Truth* (New York, 1909); *A Pluralistic Universe* (New York, 1909).

B. SH 6, 94; NCAB 18, 31–34; DAB 9, 590–600; NCE 7, 815–16; NYT 27 Aug 1910, 7; Emile Boutroux, *William James* (London, 1912); Julius S. Bixler, *Religion in the Philosophy of William James* (Boston, 1926); Ralph B. Perry, *The Thought and Character of William James*, 2 vols. (Boston, 1935; abr. ed. New York, 1954); Max C. Otto, *William James* (Madison, WI, 1942); Bernard P. Brennan, *The Ethics of William James* (New York, 1961).

JARRATT, Devereux (17 January 1733, New Kent County, VA—29 January 1801, Dinwiddie County, VA). *Career*: rector, Bath Parish, Dinwiddie County, VA, 1763–1801.

As was the case with many young men who delighted more in gamecocks and racehorses than morning prayers, Jarratt grew up in Anglican Virginia with little thought to religion. But an awakened sensitivity to that sphere, together with reading and the advice of concerned friends, eventually led him to a vital faith. Though most of his spiritual consultants were Presbyterians, Jarratt decided that the Church of England offered a wider field of opportunity for his services. Consequently he sailed for London in 1762 for ordination and returned within a year to minister in one parish for the better part of four decades. That local parish was not the only center of activity; he itinerated through dozens of counties in Virginia and North Carolina, traveling as much as 600 miles per trip in addition to his regular duties. He was often shocked to hear fellow clergy ridicule or burlesque the most sacred doctrines of Christendom. By contrast he sought to counteract spiritual decay with evangelical preaching, spreading the message of repentance and rebirth in two colonies. It was an uphill battle, but Jarratt braved the hostile reaction of other Anglican priests and condemned their worldliness. Between 1764 and 1772, his emphasis on vital religious experience caused widespread awakenings of pietistic fervor. He in turn was denounced as a visionary and dissenter, but he remained in the established church, virtually a solitary figure who kept the revivalistic spirit alive.

Exhorters of the Wesleyan connection were making headway in Virginia by 1773, and Jarratt readily blended his efforts with theirs. He became a close friend of *Francis Asbury and cooperated closely with the Methodist itinerants sent into his district. Since he perceived they did not threaten to leave the established church, he welcomed their work as a means of quickening the religious life in Anglican circles. Jarratt prized vital faith as the nucleus of Christian living, but he also had a strong sense of the nurturing influence which church life, its sacraments, and pastoral care, provided for new believers. While Methodist preachers received his continual support, he urged converts to align themselves with the duly constituted ecclesiastical structure as well. In 1784, when Methodists became a separate religious organization, Jarratt was less cordial regarding them. He had been isolated by unsympathetic Anglicans and now felt betrayed by Methodists who chose independence at the expense of loyalty to tradition. Nevertheless, as deism, wartime conditions, and sectarianism mitigated his effectiveness, he continued the pietistic witness so long associated with his name.

Bibliography:

    A.   *Sermons on Various and Important Subjects*, 3 vols. (Philadelphia, 1793–94), *Thoughts on Some Important Subjects in Divinity* (Baltimore, 1806); *The Life of the Reverend Devereux Jarratt, . . . Written by Himself* (Baltimore, 1806; New York, 1969).
    B.   AAP 5, 214–22; NCAB 10, 118; DAB 9, 616–17.

JEFFERSON, Thomas (13 April 1743, Goochland (now Albemarle) County, VA—4 July 1826, Albemarle County, VA).

Of all those who shaped national policies regarding the relation between religion and government perhaps none was more influential than Jefferson. He did so from a perspective which conceived of religion primarily as moral action. Wary of metaphysical ideologies, he was particularly opposed to Calvinism because its demoralizing dogmas rendered men powerless to affect their own conduct. God had formed men as moral agents, he contended, in order to promote the happiness of those with whom they were placed in society. Goodness consisted in treating others with honesty, benevolence, and respect for individual rights, especially freedom of conscience. Jefferson was convinced that the most sublime code of ethics produced with these ends in view had been that of Jesus of Nazareth. He considered himself a real Christian because he ardently admired that prophet's central principles. Christianity was not a deposit of otherworldly knowledge; it afforded, rather, a useful method of propagating tenets ultimately deriving their validity from nature. In keeping with his deist understanding of history, he held that the pure lessons of Christian morality had been overladen with superstitions in subsequent centuries. But he was certain the words of Jesus could be distinguished from later accretions as easily as diamonds descried in a dunghill. Misunderstandings and ambiguities ("amphibologisms" he called them) could be stripped away until the common truths of social benevolence were clear for all to follow. The basically intelligible nature of God, man's communal existence, and the highest moral teachings happily converged to yield this result.

In religious questions having consequences outside the realm of social utility, Jefferson allowed for diversity because he was indifferent to what he termed "opinion." If persons believed in one god or twenty, their views had no effect on the body politic, and all could exist in innocuous variegation. Religion on this level, he argued, is a matter which lies solely between men and their deity; they are accountable to no public authority for particularities in faith or worship. Similarly, the legislative powers of government apply to actions only, not opinions, and therefore have no right to intrude upon religious institutions. Magistrates should be interdicted from prescribing any exercise or from assuming any authority pertaining to religious discipline. Thus separation of church and state would make for true freedom of religion, not just toleration of sectarians at the sufferance of orthodoxy. As early as 1779, Jefferson drafted an Act for Establishing Religious Freedom for consideration by the Virginia Assembly. With the aid of fellow statesman, James Madison, this bill finally passed in 1786, placing all churches in the state on an equal basis. Such ideas also played a part in giving form to the first constitutional amendment, becoming a national statute in 1791. Jeffersonian principles were unmistakably the guidelines that prevented the federal government from making any law respecting an establishment of religion or prohibiting the free exercise thereof.

Bibliography:

A. *The Writings of Thomas Jefferson*, ed. Andrew A. Lipscomb, 20 vols. (Washington, DC, 1903); *The Works of Thomas Jefferson*, ed. Paul L. Ford, 12 vols. (New York, 1904–05); *The Papers of Thomas Jefferson*, ed. Julian P. Boyd, 19 vols. (Princeton, NJ, 1950–).

B.   NCAB 3, 1–5; DAB 10, 17–35; Gilbert Chinard, *Thomas Jefferson* (Boston, 1929); Karl Lehmann, *Thomas Jefferson: American Humanist* (New York, 1947); Henry W. Foote, *The Religion of Thomas Jefferson* (Boston, 1947, 1960); Robert M. Healey, *Jefferson on Religion in Public Education* (New Haven, 1962); Dumas Malone, *Jefferson and His Time*, 5 vols. (Boston, 1948–74).

JOGUES, Isaac (10 January 1607, Orléans, France—18 October 1646, Mohawk Territory, now Auriesville, NY). *Education*: studied as novice in the Society of Jesus at Rouen, 1624–26, La Flèche, 1626–29, and Paris, 1633–36. *Career*: instructor in grammar at Rouen, 1629–33; missionary among Huron and Iroquois, 1636–46.

As a Jesuit novice, Jogues hoped for missionary assignment to either Constantinople or Ethiopia, but contact with priests returning from New France directed his attention to the New World. Six weeks after reaching Quebec in 1636, he was transported to lands inhabited by the Iroquoian-speaking Wyandot nation, called Huron by the French. For five years he lived there, serving in mission stations which held some promise of making a significant impact on surrounding native patterns. Explorations in 1641 took him as far west as Sault Ste. Marie where he introduced gospel preaching in new outposts. During the next year, however, his life was radically changed by the Mohawks, one of the five nations constituting the Iroquois League. Jogues was captured together with René Goupil, a *donné* or lay assistant, and both were taken by long marches back to Iroquois territory (now central New York). Starvation, the gantlet, ingenious torture, and execution at sunrise was the usual fate of prisoners. This case appeared to be no exception. Goupil quickly succumbed, but the priest was allowed to live, existing as a servant who worked with mutilated hands under the constant possibility of death. Despite these hardships, he persisted in religious devotions and succeeded in baptizing over sixty children at the enemy camp. In 1643 *Johannes Megapolensis and other Dutch officials at Fort Orange (Albany) effected his escape. By Christmas he was safe in France, celebrating mass after the pope made special allowance for his inadequate but exemplary physical condition.

By early 1644 Jogues had returned to Canada, drawn by a vision of sacrifice and martyrdom common to missionaries. Ondessonk (''Bird of Prey''), as he was named in Iroquoian, threw himself into pastoral labors to edify both Indian converts and his Jesuit colleagues. He also served as ambassador for the French government during the short season of 1645 to secure peace with Mohawk representatives. After the treaty was signed, he received permission to enter Iroquois territory as the first missionary to reside there. Factions of Mohawk warriors did not honor the peace agreement; as soon as Jogues and another assistant entered their region, they subjected them to punishments more cruel than before. The former servant announced his intention to live as a simple minister, but several clans were not mollified by such modesty. His captors could not distinguish between evangelical motivations and the fact that he embodied an alien culture which threatened their own. They thought his pyx contained demonic powers, and they charged him with witchcraft that brought disease to native peoples. He was taken to Ossernenon where a small band of zealots killed him before tribal elders could decide his fate. News of his martyrdom prompted fellow Jesuits to similar acts of sacrifice, and it advanced the cause of missions in France as well. Father Jogues was beatified in 1925, canonized in 1930.

Bibliography:

B.   DAB 10, 74–75; Felix Martin, *The Life of Father Isaac Jogues* (New York, 1885); Francis Talbot, *Saint among Savages* (New York, 1935); Glenn D. Kittler, *Saint in the Wilderness* (Garden City, NY, 1964).

JOHNSON, Samuel (14 October 1696, Guilford, CT—6 January 1772, Stratford, CT). *Education*: graduated from Yale Coll., 1714. *Career*: school-teacher, Guilford, CT, 1714–16; tutor, Yale Coll., 1716–19; Congregational minister, West Haven, CT, 1720–22; Anglican rector, Stratford, CT, 1723–54, 1764–72; president, King's Coll., New York, 1754–63.

During college years and his early experience as minister in Connecticut's Standing Order, Johnson had little reason to question accepted ideas regarding ecclesiastical authority or theology. But his avid reading habits kept him abreast of fresh intellectual currents from Europe; the adjustments he made through a lifetime of learning became a leading example of colonial society growing more complex in its behavior and motivations. Johnson chose a pastorate near New Haven where Yale had recently deposited its library. Together with *Timothy Cutler, rector of Yale, he became acquainted with a great spectrum of church history and modern theology that raised questions about the exclusive validity of Congregational teachings. By 1722 both of them, along with Yale's only tutor converted to Anglicanism, journeyed to England for ordination and returned as missionaries of the Society for the Propagation of the Gospel (SPG). Johnson dedicated (1724) the first church for Episcopal worship in his home colony, encountering no small opposition there as that communion's only representative. Popular reception of his attitudes was not enhanced by the fact that he grew increasingly distrustful of democracy, whether applied to secular or sacred matters. He was a vigorous advocate of establishing bishops in the colonies, arguing that they would foster sound doctrine and canonical discipline. As independence loomed ever closer, he disclosed Tory sympathies by saying bishops could also maintain political subordination to the Crown.

New philosophical and theological emphases were other elements of enlightenment which Johnson helped introduce in the colonies. Not an original thinker, he nevertheless responded to the more cosmopolitan views of British rationalists. He adopted an aggressively Arminian position regarding human ability. His anti-Calvinist controversy with *Jonathan Dickinson, Presbyterian minister of Elizabethtown, New Jersey, did much to advertise new sciences compared to old traditions. In fact all his writings in ethics or theology were informed by revelation but based on the primary foundations of reason and nature. He was also an early exponent of idealistic philosophy, disseminating ideas of friend George Berkeley in several treatises. By 1749 those publications won him an offer to become president of the University of Pennsylvania, but Johnson declined. Still, he could not long avoid eminence in the educational field, accepting the presidency of King's College (later Columbia) for nine years. He made some lasting curricular reforms and used the college as another means of recommending the benefits of natural religion under Episcopal auspices. But the new institution did not flourish under its first administration, suffering from few students, slender means, and frequent disruption due to smallpox in the area. Finally the philosopher-educator retired as priest once again in his former parish, to spend the remaining years in reading and reflection which had been his favorite occupations through life.

Bibliography:

A. *Elementa Philosophica* (Philadelphia, 1752); *Samuel Johnson: His Career and Writings*, ed. Herbert and Carol Schneider, 4 vols. (New York, 1929).

B. AAP 5, 52–61; SH 6, 221; NCAB 6, 341; DAB 10, 118–19; Thomas B. Chandler, *The Life of Samuel Johnson* (New York, 1805); Eben E. Beardsley, *Life and Correspondence of Samuel Johnson* (Hartford, 1873); Joseph J. Ellis, *The New England Mind in Transition: Samuel Johnson of Connecticut, 1696–1772* (New Haven, 1973).

JONES, Charles Colcock (20 December, Liberty County, GA—16 March 1863, Pleasant Grove, GA). *Education*: studied at Andover Sem., 1827–29; B.D., Princeton Sem., 1830. *Career*: minister, First Presbyterian Church, Savannah, GA, 1831–32; home missionary, Liberty County, GA, 1832–36 and 1839–47; professor of Ecclesiastical History and Church Polity, Columbia Theol. Sem., 1837–38 and 1848–50; corresponding secretary, Presbyterian Board of Domestic Missions, 1850–53; stated supply, Pleasant Grove, GA, 1853–63.

There is some irony in the fact that Jones was born at his father's plantation called "Liberty Hall" because as an adult he owned well over one hundred slaves. Yet as a rich planter he also perceived moral dilemmas in the slave system and strove to solve them. He was the epitome of the conscience-stricken slaveholder who sought ways to improve conditions among Blacks, eventually to pave the way for their manumission. His Presbyterian training convinced him that religious instruction and spiritual nurture lay at the heart of all such endeavors. So, when poor health forced a resignation from the pulpit in 1832, he organized the Association for the Religious Instruction of the Negro in order to further these missionary ends. He solicited funds from sympathetic whites and enlisted the cooperation of black religious leaders, building a rather effective network of evangelical activity with their aid. He wrote catechisms to guide teaching activities, and he publicized the work as an inducement for others to found similar institutions. In 1850 his advocacy of Negro evangelism reached national proportions, and he acquired the sobriquet of "Apostle to the Blacks."

It may be true that Jones helped awaken citizens to the religious plight of the Negro, but there were flaws and limitations to his perspective. He saw the abuses of slavery, but he still defended the institution and wanted only to alleviate malpractice in the system. He was respected as a pioneer in a sensitive moral area, but he insisted that cultural advancement depended on, and could only be derived from, improvements in spiritual welfare. Within that framework Jones assumed that the status of blacks could rise only to the degree that they became more like their white masters. This self-serving brand of religious outreach failed to transform slaves into independent, self-disciplined individuals or copies of the "civilized" society which oppressed them. Jones' association of religious instruction may have been the consuming work of his life, but the program compromised with slavery and never met its ultimate goals or lived up to its youthful ideals.

Bibliography:

A. *A Catechism for Colored Persons* (Charleston, SC, 1834 with revised editions after 1837 entitled *Catechism of Scripture Doctrine and Practice: For Families and Sabbath Schools, designed also for the Oral Instruction of Colored Persons); The Religious Instruction of the Negroes in the United States* (Savannah, GA, 1842); *Suggestions on the Religious Instruction of the Negroes in the Southern States* (Philadelphia, 1847); *The History of the Church of God during the Period of Revelation* (New York, 1867).

B. Robert Manson Myers (ed.), *The Children of Pride: A True Story of Georgia and the Civil War* (New Haven, 1972).

JONES, James Warren (13 May 1931, Crete, IN—18 November 1978, Jonestown, Guyana). *Education*: studied at Indiana Univ., 1949–52. *Career*: minister, Peoples Temple Christian Church, Indianapolis, IN, 1956–65; Ukiah, CA, 1965–77; Jonestown, Guyana, 1977–78.

Developing a flair for both preaching and humanitarian zeal as a teenager, Jim Jones began pastoral work in a Methodist church as early as 1952. He was always something of an outsider but used this marginal status to recruit a following drawn from the fringes of society. By 1956 his people evolved into an independent church, emphasizing charismatic prophecies, pentecostal speaking in tongues, and healing miracles. In 1960 the Disciples of Christ accepted this group into its denomination. Jones made humanitarian ideals the central focus of all his religious emphases, though he continued to use healing and tongues to placate segments of his constituency. Most people were drawn by his sympathy for the poor and disadvantaged, the victims of racism and social inequality. To combat these ills he advocated an integrated church family, meals for the aged and jobless, interracial adoptions, and greater recognition of human rights. As his movement drew more followers he developed cooperative routines that blended church members into a divinely inspired socialist commune. Many devoted years of labor, their life savings, children, and themselves to this closed community. The strongest attraction was shared love of a common cause and a mutual appreciation of each other.

In California Jones spread his influence from the "nuclear free" zone at Ukiah to urban areas such as Los Angeles and San Francisco. He controlled these satellite churches with increasingly obvious signs of a disturbed personality.

Before long his message made little use of the Bible and proclaimed instead that the God within everyone was especially present in Jones himself, a living prophet and healer. His benevolence had an underside of cruelty and manipulation; his compassion hid cunning and his genius, madness. He escalated demands on followers, cajoling and threatening them to tighten control over their lives. He isolated them from the outside world and through bonding rituals together with reportedly cruel discipline made them totally dependent on him as their cultic leader. Finally, seeking to avoid American social ills and produce a socialistic Eden in a new land, the majority of Peoples Temple moved to South America. After threats of defection from some members of the commune, the paranoid Jones induced the church to commit mass suicide. The faithful obediently drank a grape flavored drink laced with potassium cyanide, and a total of 913 bodies were found. Jones died from a gunshot wound in his left temple.

Bibliography:

B.   Stephen C. Rose, *Jesus and Jim Jones* (New York, 1979); Shiva Naipaul, *Black and White* (London, 1980); James Reston, Jr., *Our Father Who Art in Hell* (New York, 1981); Ethan Feinsod, *Awake in a Nightmare, Jonestown: The Only Eyewitness Account* (New York, 1981): Tim Reiterman with John Jacobs, *Raven: The Untold Story of the Rev. Jim Jones and His People* (New York, 1982).

JONES, Jenkin Lloyd (14 November 1843, Llandyssil, Wales—12 September 1918, Chicago, IL). *Education*: graduated from Meadville Sem., 1870. *Career*: minister, Unitarian church, Winnetka, IL, 1870–71; minister, All Souls Church, Janesville, WI, 1871–80; secretary, Western Unitarian Conference, 1875–84; secretary, Western Unitarian Sunday School Society, 1874–80; editor, *Unity*, 1878–1918; minister, All Souls Church, Chicago, IL, 1882–1905; director, Abraham Lincoln Center, 1905–18.

While still an infant Jones emigrated with his family from native Cardiganshire to rural Wisconsin. He served for three years in the Union artillery during the Civil War and struggled thereafter to acquire a theological education in Pennsylvania. Graduating and receiving ordination in 1870 he returned to the Midwest for a vigorous career of religious leadership and social reform. Within two years he began writing liberal Sunday School lessons and continued to do so for a decade. In 1875 he became a functionary of the Western Unitarian Conference and used that office until 1884 to guide the modernist elements of his denomination. This group became known as "Unity men" because of the weekly newspaper which Jones co-founded in 1878 and edited for the rest of his life. The Western Conference insisted on taking independent steps regarding a number of issues, a policy which led to frequent clashes with the American Unitarian Association and its administrators in Boston. This liberal wing of the denomination conducted energetic missionary enterprises in the heartland between the mountains from Ohio to Colorado. In 1882 Jones reorganized an old church in Chicago into All Souls Church, and then in 1905 caused it to declare a nonsectarian position in favor of pursuing a settlement-house program for urban welfare.

The basis on which Jones sought to improve human life moved increasingly from references to God and Christ to those of an evolving human spirituality and pure thought. He wanted little to do with creeds, hoping rather to inspire people with ethical appeals and a catholic spirit that embraced the good in all humankind. Motivations of this nature led him to play a central role from 1892 to 1893 in the World's Parliament of Religions. That convocation of religious leaders from around the globe, held in conjunction with the Columbian Exposition at Chicago, stressed the noble and beneficial elements which could be found in a universalistic outlook. Jones sought to further such a perspective as general secretary of the Congress of Religion between 1894 and 1905. He was also a staunch pacifist and was on the board of directors of the Church Peace Union. He consistently opposed America's entry into World War I, and his persistence in *Unity* editorials caused the Postmaster General to suspend the paper in 1918, just before the dynamic and controversial activist finally rested from his many efforts.

Bibliography:

A.   *Religions of the World*, 7 vols. (Chicago, 1893); *Word of the Spirit to the Nation, Church, City, Home and Individual* (Chicago, 1894); *Jess: Bits of Wayside Gospel* (New York, 1899); *A Search for an Infidel: Bits of Wayside Gospel* (New York, 1901); *Nuggets from a Welsh Mine* (Chicago, 1902); *Love for the Battle-torn Peoples: Sermon-Studies* (Chicago, 1916).
   B.   SH 6 225; NCAB 14, 161–62; DAB 10, 179–81; NYT 13 Sep 1918, 11.

JONES, Robert Reynolds Davis (30 October 1883, Skipperville, AL—16 January 1968, Greenville, SC). *Education*: studied at Southern (later Birmingham Southern) Univ., 1901–04. *Career*: revivalist, 1895–1968; president, Bob Jones Coll. (later Univ.), 1926–64.

Energy, zeal, and a way with words gained Jones local fame as a "boy preacher" before he was in his teens. He conducted his first revival at the age of twelve and quickly attracted invitations to conduct similar services in larger towns. The Methodist church granted him a license to preach when he was fifteen, but Bob Jones was always too independent to accept that denomination's discipline or educational requirements. People came to hear him because his message was commonplace and his style, captivating. An artist with words, he held audiences spellbound while he hammered away at sin both real and imagined. Jones drew increasingly larger crowds as he matured. He began to travel widely and was called "the *Billy Sunday of the South." In addition to delivering typical sermons on sin and salvation, he also warned listeners about such debilitating vices as liquor, gambling, and Roman Catholicism. He spoke not from careful training or calm reflection but rather from strong convictions. Those fundamental opinions carried many with him, putting converts in churches, closing saloons, and leading thousands simply to "live the right way."

The type of evangelical fervor Jones embodied expressed itself as often by what it opposed as by what it advocated. Sensing that moral values were eroding as American culture became more secularized, Jones fought to preserve the values he had absorbed as a boy. He regarded Protestant liberalism as an abomination, perhaps not as corrupt as Catholicism, but still dangerous because it departed from the fundamental truths of biblical literalism. In an effort to protect young people from such deviations and train them properly, he founded Bob Jones College at St. Andrews, Florida, in 1926. Financial problems forced a move to Cleveland, Tennessee, in 1933; then with elevation to university status in 1947 the enterprise moved to Greenville, South Carolina. Like its founder, the school stood without apology for conservative religion and old-time morality. It was also one of the most intransigent institutions of higher education to resist racial integration. Its regimented student life bore the stamp of its founder, giving off constant reminders that compromise with liberal thought, the ecumenical movement, or churches unlike themselves were a sellout to Satan. Instead of teaching humility or love for one's enemies, this brand of Christianity teaches aggressive attitudes of suspicion and censoriousness.

Bibliography:

A. *Bob Jones' Sermons* (Montgomery, AL, 1911); *Comments on Here and Hereafter* (New York, 1942); *Things I Have Learned: Chapel Talks by Bob Jones, Sr.* (New York, 1944); *Bob Jones' Revival Sermons* (Wheaton, IL, 1948).

B. DAB supp. 8, 303–05; NYT 17 Jan 1968, 47; Melton Wright, *Fortress of Faith: The Story of Bob Jones University* (Grand Rapids, MI, 1960); R. K. Johnson, *Builder of Bridges: The Biography of Dr. Bob Jones, Sr.* (Murfreesboro, TN, 1969).

JONES, Rufus Matthew (25 January 1863, South China, ME—16 June 1948, Haverford, PA). *Education*: B.A., Haverford Coll., 1885; studied at Heidelberg, 1887; at Univ. of Pennsylvania, 1893–95; at Harvard Univ., 1900–01; at Oxford, 1908. *Career*: teacher, Providence, RI, 1887–89; principal, Oak Grove Sem., Vassalboro, ME, 1889–93; professor of Philosophy at various ranks, Haverford Coll., 1893–1934; professor emeritus, 1934–48; editor, *The American Friend*, 1894–1912; recorded minister, Society of Friends, 1890–1948.

A single vocation among those of teacher, editor, historian, Quaker minister, or coordinator of humanitarian relief work would usually demand all of an individual's resources; Jones filled the dimensions of those roles with outstanding results in each area. While in college he read the works of *Ralph W. Emerson which led him to reaffirm the basic religious tendencies of his early training. Years of study brought knowledge about mysticism which, added to his own personal experiences, gave Jones a deep certainty of the reality of God's love and the possibility of man's response to it. Much of his enormous literary output was spent in interpreting the inner life so essential to Quaker vitality, relating that in turn to other mystical movements found in Christian history. Philosophical and psychological discussions of those spiritual experiences allowed for wider understanding of the general phenomena, enlightening some and encouraging others to wait for the Spirit in a similar manner. Through years of teaching, Jones helped many discover richer meaning in life by finding God revealed in the finite. He embodied a serene optimism that stemmed from what he called a mutual and reciprocal correspondence of human and divine spirits. His personality evinced, as a consequence, the fundamental conviction that such inner communion provided the means of meeting contemporary needs in religious and social contexts.

One of those contexts had to do with reform in the Society of Friends because Jones thought the fourteen yearly meetings too decentralized to recognize common ties. In an attempt to reconcile evangelical and liberal factions, he drafted a Uniform Discipline and a unifying statement of beliefs, both of which began to be generally accepted by 1900. He viewed his church as a movement, not an institution bound to earlier formulas, eager to try new approaches and widen the area of light among mankind. An expression of that attitude which affected millions of people around the world was the American Friends Service Committee (AFSC), in large measure a product of Jones' vision. As chairman of the AFSC (1917–28, 1935–44) he guided efforts to feed children from Belgium to Russia and to alleviate human suffering wherever possible. Jones poured his thought and energy into this channel as a service of love in wartime, in retrospect judging it the most important thing he did. When the Committee received a Nobel Prize in 1947, it was in no small degree a tribute to the modest Friend who tried to manifest inner faith in practical ways.

Bibliography:

A.   *Social Law in the Spiritual World* (Philadelphia, 1904); *Studies in Mystical Religion* (London, 1909); *The Later Periods of Quakerism* (London, 1921; Westport, CT, 1970); *The Trail of Life in the Middle Years* (New York, 1924); *Pathways to the Reality of God* (New York, 1931); *The Testimony of the Soul* (New York, 1936).

B.   SH 6, 225–26; NCAB 38, 301–02; NCE 7, 1097–98; NYT 17 Jun 1948, 25; David Hinshaw, *Rufus Jones: Master Quaker* (New York, 1951); Elizabeth G. Vining, *Friend of Life: The Biography of Rufus M. Jones* (Philadelphia, 1958).

JONES, Samuel Porter (16 October 1847, Chambers County, AL—15 October 1906, near Perry, AR). *Career*: lawyer in GA, 1868–72; Methodist minister in GA, 1872–80; agent, North Georgia Conference Orphan's Home, 1880–92; urban evangelist, 1892–1906.

By the time Jones was twenty-five, he had ruined his law practice with an addiction to alcohol, finding no better work than stoking furnaces for twelve hours a day. But in 1872 he stopped drinking to honor his father's dying request, professed Christianity one week later, and began preaching on a Methodist circuit in northern Georgia later that same year. He soon became known as a speaker of uncommon ability; by 1885 his practical, incisive preaching carried him beyond the confines of a denominational pastorate to wider opportunities found in urban evangelism. *Thomas D. Talmage invited him to conduct a revival in Brooklyn, and from there he went on to every major city, North and South, drawing capacity crowds to hear sermons of startling uniqueness. Jones deliberately used blunt, homely language in his addresses to broach matters on a level common men could understand. Some complained that his use of slang in the pulpit was irreverent, his anecdotes coarse; but with wit and invective, he held audiences spellbound. Plain speech and unvarnished aphorisms proved so effective, Jones became one of the best known religious figures of his day, earning notice as ''the Moody of the South.'' His message combined popular entertainment with civic reform. As modern Christians faced the uncertainties of urban growth, he presented the right and wrong on every issue, demanding that the religious element of each city form itself into an army of righteousness to resist the advances of sin. Conversion for him was essentially reform in moral conduct, deeds rather than beliefs, confessions, or an experience of grace. In that light he became famous as a vigorous advocate of prohibition, denouncing saloons with all the fire of a reformed drunkard. Other personal vices such as profanity, gambling, and Sabbath breaking also came under blistering attack. Until the end of his life he sought to convince others that resolve to lead a better life was adequate proof of conversion. He died on a train which carried him home from such a revival campaign in Oklahoma City.

Bibliography:

    A. *Sermons*, 2 vols. (Chicago, 1886); *Quit Your Meanness* (Cincinnati, 1886); *Sam Jones' Sermons*, 2 vols. (Chicago, 1896); *Popular Lectures* (New York, 1909); *Lightning Flashes and Thunderbolts* (Louisville, 1912); *Revival Sermons* (New York, 1912).
    B. SH 6, 226; NCAB 13, 438; DAB 10, 199; NYT 16 Oct 1906, 9; Laura M. Jones, *The Life and Sayings of Sam P. Jones* (Atlanta, 1906); Walt Holcomb, *Sam Jones* (Nashville, 1947).

JUDSON, Adoniram (9 August 1788, Malden, MA—12 April 1850, on shipboard bound for the U.S.). *Education*: B.A., Brown Univ., 1807; B.D., Andover Sem., 1810. *Career*: missionary to Burma, 1811–50.

New England was the cradle of American foreign missions, and though Congregationalists were the first denomination to send envoys to the Far East, one of their original number made all his notable achievements as a Baptist. In 1810 Judson was among the first volunteers for missionary work. After accepting a commission to preach Congregationalist Christianity in Burma, he and his wife studied the standard practice of baptizing infants, the better to defend it amid English Baptist colleagues in the field. But the end result was that both of them rejected sprinkling infants in preference for immersion after individuals beyond the age of discretion requested it. By 1812 Judson had himself been immersed. After notifying home authorities of his new views, most friendships and all funds were withdrawn, but the Baptist Triennial Convention soon (1814) responded by supporting his Burmese mission. Work to establish Christian teaching in the new land faced imposing obstacles, not the least of which were governmental opposition and popular indifference. Hostilities between Burma and England (1824–25) were disastrous to the effort, causing him to be imprisoned along with most other foreigners in execrable physical conditions for seventeen months.

Still he persevered, moved the mission to Maulmein in 1827, and founded a center for evangelical activities which long survived him.

Conversions were few and slow in coming. Judson's lasting accomplishments were more literary and symbolic than statistical. Others reported that the Burmese would sit unaffected and go away unimpressed with what they heard, but Judson continued to master their language. He began writing pamphlets which contained essential gospel truths, distributing them gratis to anyone who would accept them. After many years of labor he published a full translation of the Bible in 1834 and further utilized his knack for languages by issuing a complete Burmese-English dictionary in 1849. The personal toll for such work was heavy. Health was always a problem, with fever, blinding headaches, and family deaths causing him to suffer periods of morbid self-denial and deep melancholy. But his impact on the American religious consciousness was tremendous. After thirty-three years in Asia, Judson returned for a brief stay in his native land, finding that he was a legendary figure to most Protestants. Thousands had read his reports, regularly printed in religious journals. His missionary addresses from Boston to Philadelphia stirred renewed dedication to the evangelical enterprise among northern Baptists. As he returned to spend the last years in what by then had become his home, it was apparent that he had begun an endeavor whose future and stability was something larger than his own doing. Recurring illness demanded another voyage to America, but he died shortly after embarking.

Bibliography:

B.   AAP 6, 607–20; SH 6, 257–58; NCAB 3, 92–93; DAB 10, 234–35; NCE 8, 46; Francis Wayland, *A Memoir of the Life and Labors of the Rev. Adoniram Judson*, 2 vols. (Boston, 1853); Edward Judson, *The Life of Adoniram Judson* (New York, 1883); Stacy R. Warburton, *Eastward! The Story of Adoniram Judson* (New York, 1937); Courtney Anderson, *To the Golden Shore: The Life of Adoniram Judson* (Boston, 1956); Joan J. Brumberg, *Mission for Life . . .* (New York, 1980).

K

KALLEN, Horace Meyer (11 August 1882, Berenstadt, Germany—16 February 1974, Palm Beach, FL). *Education*: B.A., Harvard Coll., 1903; Ph.D., Harvard Univ., 1908. *Career*: lecturer in English, Princeton Univ., 1903–05; lecturer in Philosophy, Harvard Univ., 1908–11; instructor in Logic, Clark Coll., 1910; instructor in Philosophy and Psychology, Univ. of Wisconsin, 1911–18; professor, New School for Social Research, 1919–52; research professor of Social Philosophy, New School for Social Research, 1952–69; active retirement, 1969–74.

The philosophical views which Kallen championed were far removed from his background as a rabbi's son whose boyhood dream was to be a novelist. But he was greatly influenced by *William James and others at Harvard who posed the intriguing task of relating inherited religious traditions to modern science. The end result of that intellectual venture comprised a body of ideas on man, nature, and society distinctive for its emphasis on individual freedom. In a radically empirical approach, Kallen accepted the undiscriminated immediacy of all experiences, giving precedence to no interpretive pattern which dogmatists might claim as normative. He viewed the universe with no passion for unity, admitting there was a variety of systems but no single integrative factor. On the practical level he urged that every person must choose or invent a system with which to survive in a world where chance and individuality constituted basic reality. Group life was also part of such a concatenated pluralism; cultural units existed as parts of a federated union of peoples. Kallen held that his attitude toward life was compatible with the insights of science and naturalistic humanism, values which he personally espoused. As men tried to realize their potential in a world shared with other natural creatures, it was possible to believe in life despite death, in goodness despite evil, and to work at bringing about improvement through vigilant effort. He thought science and democracy had a power approaching holiness because they best approximated the goals of human betterment.

The basic premises of Kallen's philosophy were applied to concrete problems such as civil liberty and minority rights, the search for peace amid war and economic depression, the role of education in a democracy, and the utility of aesthetics in western civilization. In all these situations he gave a rationale for cultural pluralism which orchestrated the differences of groups as each pursued its objectives while living in a common environment. He was one of the founders of the New School for Social Research where studies of cultural pluralism received much attention. His theories were particularly useful for the Jewish community as it struggled to preserve distinctive usages in the American melting pot. Kallen himself was more naturalistic than traditional in his outlook, but he worked for decades in service of such Hebraic organizations as the American Jewish Congress. He was a constant advocate of Jewish settlement in Palestine where the heritage of a cohesive cultural unit could develop free from persecution. On a much larger scale he served on scores of committees to further progress in international relations, labor unions, city planning, higher education, science, and culture. He influenced a large number of students through teaching and reached wider audiences with manifold publications. All his activities centered on positive values for free peoples in an open, tolerant society.

Bibliography:

A. *Culture and Democracy in the United States* (New York, 1924, 1970); *Why Religion?* (New York, 1927); *Judaism at Bay: Essays toward the Adjustment of Judaism to Modernity* (New York, 1932, 1972); *Individualism: An American Way of Life* (New York, 1933); *Art and Freedom*, 2 vols. (New York, 1942); *The Education of Free Men* (New York, 1949).

B. UJE 6, 298; EJ 10, 712–13; NYT 17 Feb 1974, 66; Sidney Hook and Milton R. Konvitz (eds.) *Freedom and Experience* (Ithaca, NY, 1947); Sidney Ratner (ed.) *Vision and Action* (New Brunswick, NJ, 1953).

KAPLAN, Mordecai Menahem (11 July 1881, Swenziany, Lithuania—8 November 1983, New York, NY). *Education*: B.A., City Coll. of New York, 1900; M.A., Columbia Univ., 1902; rabbinate, Jewish Sem., New York, 1902. *Career*: rabbi, Congregation Kehilath Jeshurun, 1903–09; principal, Teachers Institute of the Jewish Sem., New York, 1909–31; dean, Teachers Institute, 1931–46; professor, Rabbinical Sch. of the Jewish Sem., New York, 1910–63; active retirement, 1963–83.

Though stemming from an Orthodox Jewish family, Kaplan pursued a secular education alongside theological studies. He absorbed the pragmatic philosophy and sociological emphases that developed early in this century, and these helped shape his distinctive ideas on Judaism in contemporary times. Amid the challenges that caused many immigrants to abandon their religion, Kaplan tried to redefine Judaism in realistic ways that made renewal possible. He viewed Judaism primarily as a civilization, a group consciousness that was the source of values, especially religious ones. Such ideas made it difficult for him to serve an Orthodox congregation, and so in 1916 he helped organize the Jewish Center in New York City. Six years later he established a more congenial Society for the Advancement of Judaism, a congregation and community center that encouraged participation in Jewish life as the way to make beliefs vital in modern society. Kaplan's ideas about the mutual interdependence of religious values and cultural nexus were well known by 1935 when he institutionalized his program in the Jewish Reconstructionist Foundation, issuing that same year a biweekly periodical featuring Reconstructionism in its title too.

This school of thought tried to reinvigorate all types of Judaism by emphasizing pragmatic adaptation to new circumstances. Reconstructionism viewed Orthodox Judaism as doomed because it treated tradition as infallible. It disapproved of Reform Judaism as well because it made too radical a break with the past, rejecting still useful rituals and opposing Zionist nationalism. In efforts to show others how traditions could be reworked for modern needs Kaplan helped produce a *New Haggadah for the Passover Seder* in 1941 and a *Sabbath Prayer Book* in 1945. In those aids to worship and in countless other writings he defined Jews not as a chosen people but as a group whose salvation lay in their ethical ideals. He taught that God was not a supernatural force but the cultural seed of spiritual growth; scriptures were not divinely inspired but evidence of the Jewish quest for meaning, value, and purpose. By 1945 the Union of Orthodox Rabbis had become so alarmed at the liberties Kaplan took with cherished ideas, it officially condemned his activities and placed him under ban. But still this vigorous thinker sought unity in Jewish action, not divisiveness; by the same token he was not deterred by criticism or opposition. He resisted the thought of founding a separate denomination, but in 1954 he helped establish the Federation of Reconstructionist Congregations, an agency that listed over fifty associated groups by the time of his death. In 1968 the nascent denomination opened the Reconstructionist Rabbinical College in Philadelphia, another step in solidifying this version of Judaism as a distinctive option in pluralistic America.

Bibliography:

A. *Judaism as a Civilization* (New York, 1934); *The Meaning of God in Modern Jewish Religion* (New York, 1936); *The Future of the American Jew* (New York, 1949); *Judaism Without Supernaturalism* (New York, 1958); *The Greater Judaism in the Making* (New York, 1960); *The Purpose and Meaning of Jewish Existence* (Philadelphia, 1964).

B. UJE 6, 311; EJ 10, 752–53; Ira Eisenstein and Eugene Kohn (eds.), *Mordecai M. Kaplan: An Evaluation* (New York, 1952); Richard Libowitz, *Mordecai Kaplan and the Development of Reconstructionism* (New York, 1984); Emanuel S. Goldsmith and Mel Scult (eds.), *Dynamic Judaism: The Essential Writings of Mordecai M. Kaplan* (New York, 1985).

KEANE, John Joseph (12 September 1839, Ballyshannon, Ireland—22 June 1918, Dubuque, IA). *Education*: graduated from St. Charles' Coll. (MD), 1862; graduated from St. Mary's Sem. (MD), 1866. *Career*: curate, St. Patrick's Church, Washington, DC, 1866–78; bishop of Richmond, VA, 1878–88; rector, Catholic Univ. of America, 1887–96; consultant (titular archbishop), Congregation of the Propaganda, Rome, 1897–99; archbishop of Dubuque, IA, 1900–11; retirement, 1911–18.

With outstanding oratorical skills and a zealous concern for the welfare of parishioners, Keane's rise to ecclesiastical prominence seemed as natural as it was rapid. Rarely did an assistant pastor move directly into a bishopric, but as he succeeded *James Gibbons at Richmond, his assiduous work with Catholic programs there confirmed the promise many prelates saw in him. In addition to supporting the usual charities and diocesan societies, he increased the church's contact with less familiar areas ranging from greater evangelism among Negroes to better public relations with Protestants. After the Third Plenary Council he was appointed to a committee responsible for establishing a national university for the denomination. Thus from its planning stage, Keane was identified with Catholic University as promoter, fund raiser, and original rector. In 1886 he accompanied *John Ireland to Rome, forming lifelong bonds of friendship with him in the process, and secured papal approval of the proposed institution. As its chief administrator he gained wide recognition for the new school, which in turn drew much of its élan from his vigorous leadership. While in that position he exerted, together with Gibbons and Ireland, considerable episcopal influence on questions regarding the place of Catholicism in American life.

Liberalism in American Catholic circles took many forms during the 1880s and 1890s, but, whatever the issue, Keane usually advocated accommodation to cultural change. He supported Ireland's experimental cooperation with public schools, so much so that their names were used interchangeably by conservatives who denounced their dangerous proclivities. Along with Gibbons, he helped defend the Knights of Labor because the union's work to improve conditions among poor workingmen was respectable and just. He opposed Cahenslyism (enclaves in German or other ethnic groups) as potentially schismatic, urging instead the gradual Americanization of all immigrants into cultural homogeneity. Such attitudes drew unrelenting fire from those who feared liberal tactics would compromise the very birthright of Catholic fidelity. Keane was most vulnerable of the triad of liberals, so conservative pressure focused more on the university rector than on archbishop or cardinal. As a result, curial authorities removed him from office in 1896, compensating with a sinecure in Rome that amounted to exile. In less than three years he was allowed to return to this country on a begging tour for Catholic University. Shortly thereafter he was given another diocese for whose development he worked as long as strength allowed. By 1909, however, debilitating health problems set in, and he soon found it necessary to resign. Though he lingered on for several years, he did not regain that vigor manifest at a time when he gave ''Americanism'' part of its distinctive content.

Bibliography:

B.   SH 6, 303–04; NCAB 6, 285; DAB 10, 267–68; NCE 8, 139–40; NYT 23 June 1919, 18; Patrick H. Ahern, *The Life of John J. Keane: Educator and Archbishop, 1839–1918* (Milwaukee, 1955).

KEITH, George (1638?, Peterhead, Scotland—27 March 1716, Edburton, England). *Education*: M.A., Marischall Coll., Aberdeen Univ., 1685. *Career*: minister, Society of Friends, 1664–95; headmaster, Quaker school, Philadelphia, 1689–92; independent minister, London, 1695–1700; Society for the Propagation of the Gospel (SPG) missionary in the American colonies, 1702–04; Anglican rector, Edburton, 1706–16.

Early converts to Quakerism brought a variety of strengths with them, but few proved as able in defense of the new sect as former Presbyterian Keith. His zeal soon made him a close associate of *George Fox and *William Penn with whom he toured continental Europe on a missionary journey in 1677. By 1685 frequent imprisonment caused him to sail for America where he continued his versatile service to those sharing commonly intuited truths. But Keith emphasized the need for objective content in Quaker thought and constantly sought ways to establish its orthodoxy by formulating theological standards. He did not hesitate to use Scripture and the historical Jesus as tangible guidelines for articulating the substance of faith. With a naturally contentious manner, he minced no words in saying that the doctrine of inner light could never provide the full range of ideas needed for organizational stability. When preachers in the Philadelphia Yearly Meeting resisted both the manner and matter of his arguments, he attacked them publicly. Ambition also played a part in Keith's attempt to speak for all Quakers, but instead of succeeding Fox he threatened the small community with factionalism. By 1692 a schismatic group known as "Christian Quakers" or "Keithites" charged their parent church with lax discipline and doctrinal heresy. Responding to such open rebellion, the majority of Quakers disowned the separatist, who promptly appealed to London for vindication.

After years of bitter struggle, English Quakers finally (1695) repudiated Keith for personal acts of mischievous separatism. He in turn quit them, renting a hall in London where he preached, baptized, administered communion, and launched a vigorous pamphlet war against his erstwhile friends. Anglicanism became increasingly attractive as an alternative to the lack of structure in private Christianity. Consequently in 1702, Keith's spiritual pilgrimage culminated with ordination in the Church of England, but his role as religious controversialist did not end. He returned to the colonies as agent for the SPG, conducting with *John Talbot the first of many Anglican missionary tours. He traveled from Maine to North Carolina, contending with Quakers all the way and winning many to his point of view. The Episcopal church benefited greatly from his labors, especially in the middle colonies, though Friends did their best to protect themselves from charges of formless dogma. The old Keithites slowly dispersed; some rejoined the Quakers while the rest opted for either Anglican or Baptist congregations.

Keith ended his days in tranquility, content with a comprehensive belief system which he had sought for years.

Bibliography:

A. *Immediate Revelation not Ceased* (Amsterdam, 1668); *The Universal Free Grace of the Gospell Asserted* (Amsterdam, 1671); *Quakerism no Popery* (Aberdeen, 1675); *The Deism of William Penn and his Brethren . . . Exposed* (London, 1699); *The Standard of the Quakers Examined* (London, 1702); *A Journal of Travels from New Hampshire to Caratuck* (London, 1706).

B. AAP 5, 25–30; SH 6, 307; DAB 10, 289–90; Ethlyn W. Kirby, *George Keith* (New York, 1942).

KENRICK, Francis Patrick (3 December 1796, Dublin, Ireland—8 July 1863, Baltimore, MD). *Education*: studied at the Coll. of Propaganda, Rome, Italy, 1814–21. *Career*: professor of Theology, St. Thomas Sem., Bardstown, KY, 1821–30; bishop coadjutor of Philadelphia, 1830–42; bishop of Philadelphia, 1842–51; archbishop of Baltimore, 1851–63.

After brilliant success in studies at Rome, Kenrick was ordained in 1821 and volunteered for work in the American midwest. Under the leadership of bishop *Benedict J. Flaget he lectured on theology and church history in the seminary at Bardstown and taught Greek in the nearby college as well. In 1829 he attended the first Catholic provincial council in Baltimore, where he served as secretary, and heard the assembled prelates discuss the problems of trusteeism. As part of the solution, delegates persuaded Rome to appoint Kenrick as auxiliary to Henry Conwell, the aging and embattled bishop of Philadelphia. So in 1830 Kenrick was consecrated titular bishop of Arath and traveled to Philadelphia, determined to confront the Catholic laity who wanted to control his church as well as Protestant detractors who wanted to destroy it. In the first case he defeated unruly laypersons by placing one church, St. Mary's, under interdict until its trustees admitted the bishop alone had authority to assign pastors to parishes. In 1832 he had a diocesan synod pass laws to prevent recurring difficulties, including one that placed all property and donations in the name of the bishop.

Parochial education received Kenrick's strong support, and he helped build Villanova and St. Joseph's colleges plus St. Charles Borromeo seminary. He also criticized reading from a Protestant Bible in public schools, and this precipitated another outbreak of nativist hostility. In 1844 anti-Catholic mobs burned St. Michael's and St. Augustine's churches, but the moderate bishop prevented his flocks from retaliating. This restraint caused some parishioners to murmur, but such firm patience attracted many converts to the faith and ultimately contributed to improved relations between denominations. In 1851 Kenrich became the sixth archbishop of this country's oldest see. The following year he was named apostolic delegate and presided over the American church's first plenary council. In 1858 he introduced the forty hours devotion to enrich liturgical practices. A man of many scholarly interests, he translated both Old and New

Testaments into English and was known as the leading moral theologian of his day. Supporting causes like temperance and poor relief, he succeeded in being a bishop to everyone, showing in his ministry that Catholicity could serve native and immigrant alike in a comprehensive embrace of ethnic and cultural groups.

Bibliography:

A.   *The Primacy of the Apostolic See, and the Authority of the General Councils, Vindicated* (Philadelphia, 1838); *Theologia Dogmaticae* 4 vols. (Philadelphia, 1839–40); *The Catholic Doctrine on Justification, Explained and Vindicated* (Philadelphia, 1841); *Theologia Moralis* 3 vols. (Philadelphia, 1841–43); *A Treatise on Baptism* (Philadelphia, 1843); *A Vindication of the Catholic Church* (Baltimore, 1855).

B.   SH 6, 319; NCAB 1, 485–86; DAB 10, 339–40; NCE 8, 155–56; Hugh J. Nolan, *The Most Reverend Francis Patrick Kenrick, Third Bishop of Philadelphia, 1830–51* (Washington, DC, 1948).

KIMBALL, Spencer Wooley (28 March 1895, Salt Lake City, UT—5 November 1985, Salt Lake City, UT). *Education*: studied at Gila Junior Coll., 1910–14; Brigham Young Univ., 1914; Univ. of Arizona, 1917. *Career*: stake clerk and counselor to the president of St. Joseph Stake, 1918–38; president, Mt. Graham Stake, 1938–43; member, Council of the Twelve Apostles, 1943–73; president, Church of Jesus Christ of Latter-day Saints, 1973–85.

In his early years Kimball conducted himself as a solid, reliable citizen of southern Arizona. He worked as a teller in banks (1918–27), manager of an insurance and realty company (1927–43), secretary of an irrigation company (1935–43), and part owner of a broadcasting company (1935–85). Additionally he served on city councils, advised retirement boards, and encouraged youth organizations. But his consuming passion was Mormon missions. Early in life he sacrificed formal schooling for work in the East Missouri Conference. By the 1950s he was traveling extensively to enhance missionary outreach in Latin America, Europe, and particularly in this country among native Americans. His evangelical zeal was contagious, and membership rolls soon rose to over four million, including people of all races and colors. Missions were the key to Kimball's church becoming a truly worldwide religion, and the missionary-minded apostle chafed at anything that hindered such vindicating growth.

For the first century of the church's existence authorities had refused to include men of African descent in the priesthood. Kimball was concerned quite early about this discriminatory practice. When he became the twelfth president of the church in 1973, the logic of his lifelong evangelism bore significant fruit in both idea and concerted action. After much prayer and deliberate consultation with Council members Kimball issued a revelation in June of 1978 that opened the Mormon priesthood to Mormon believers. This repeal of a harmful exclusionary practice relieved many church members who empathized with the civil rights movement of the 1960s and who were embarrassed by anachronisms in their faith. Abandoning the practice of denial was even more welcome to black men who wished to advance in their chosen ecclesiastical context. Mormon leadership has made great strides since then in integrating such willing personnel and in using black talent in important posts. Kimball's enlightened compassion and inclusive vision contributed greatly to expanding the positive concept of Christian universalism.

Bibliography:

A.   *The Miracle of Forgiveness* (Salt Lake City, 1969); *Faith Precedes the Miracle* (Salt Lake City, 1972); *Proclaiming the Gospel: Spencer W. Kimball Speaks on Missionary Work*, edited and arranged by Yoshihiko Kikuchi (Salt Lake City, 1988).

B.   NYT 7 Nov 1985, D7; Edward L. Kimball and Andrew E. Kimball, Jr., *Spencer W. Kimball: Twelfth President of the Church of Jesus Christ of Latter-day Saints* (Salt Lake City, 1977).

KING, Martin Luther, Jr. (15 January 1929, Atlanta, GA—4 April 1968, Memphis, TN). *Education*: B.A., Morehouse Coll., 1948; B.D., Crozer Sem., 1951; Ph.D., Boston Univ., 1955. *Career*: minister, Montgomery, AL, 1954–59; associate minister, Ebenezer Baptist Church, Atlanta, GA, 1959–68; president, Southern Christian Leadership Conference, 1957–68.

One hundred years after slavery was abolished in this country black Americans were still treated as second-class citizens, especially in the South. One of their number, a Baptist minister with extraordinary rhetorical ability, captured the national imagination for a decade as he spoke authoritatively about the relation of Christian conscience to civil rights. While a graduate student King had been greatly impressed with the writings of *Walter Rauschenbusch and *Reinhold Niebuhr. The former encouraged him to think that social evil could actually be eliminated; the latter helped expose false optimism in the early Social Gospel and gave a certain political realism in assessing social conditions or power structures. King also drew lessons from Mohandas Gandhi, profiting from the Indian reformer's experience with nonviolent tactics which could implement his own liberal Protestant theology. With the early cooperation of the Fellowship of Reconciliation, King blended theoretical assumptions that nonviolence was morally superior with concrete demonstrations that it worked. Passive resistance to social oppression was not just a viable technique, he came to see, but rather the most productive means of achieving social improvement. Perhaps King's most significant contribution went beyond eschewing violence. It lay in his ability to lead masses who raged at injustice into peaceful protests instead of destructive outbursts. He persuaded thousands that racism and hatred could be overcome with the power of love, the oppressor worn down through a capacity to suffer.

Suffering indignities in order to redeem oppressors had a noble ring to it, but King's larger success came in organizing the black community into a force strong enough to compel change. Beginning with the bus boycott (1955–56) in Montgomery, Alabama, he found himself thrust into leadership roles. His eloquent mixture of moral exhortation and solemn resolve led many to work for improved voter registration, for equal opportunity in hiring practices, and for more open housing. King was not the only spokesman in such crusades, but he became the symbol of peaceful demonstrations which began to show results in schools, ballot boxes, and lunch counters. The high point of public effectiveness probably occurred at a Washington, D.C. rally in the summer of 1963. Years of racial segregation, economic exploitation, and political domination lay behind his words as they momentarily transported 250,000 people with a dream of justice and freedom for all. Yet as the years wore on, younger leaders began questioning whether it was better to receive violence than to inflict it. King's moral suasion was not able to provide all movements for black fulfillment with an overarching set of goals or methods. As he continued to work on behalf of the poor in major cities, North and South, an assassin's bullet ended a declining career. But popular emotion released by the murder expanded the significance of his activities to martyr proportions, creating a legendary aura which moves beyond mere biography.

Bibliography:

A. *Stride Toward Freedom: The Montgomery Story* (New York, 1958); *Strength to Love* (New York, 1963); *Why We Can't Wait* (New York, 1964); *Where Do We Go from Here: Chaos or Community?* (New York, 1967); *Trumpet of Conscience* (New York, 1968); *The Measure of a Man* (Philadelphia, 1968).

B. NYT 5 Apr 1968, 1; Lerone Bennett, Jr., *What Manner of Man* (Chicago, 1964); Lionel Lokos, *House Divided* (New Rochelle, NY, 1968); William R. Miller, *Martin Luther King, Jr.: His Life, Martyrdom, and Meaning for the World* (New York, 1968); Coretta S. King, *My Life with Martin Luther King, Jr.* (New York, 1969); David L. Lewis, *King: A Critical Biography* (New York, 1970).

KING, Thomas Starr (17 December 1824, New York, NY—4 March 1864, San Francisco, CA). *Career*: minister, Universalist church, Charlestown, MA, 1846–48; minister, Hollis Street Unitarian Church, Boston, MA, 1848–60; minister Unitarian church, San Francisco, CA, 1860–64.

The early death of his father, a Universalist minister, seriously curtailed King's educational plans. Largely self-taught and working at odd jobs, he nevertheless succeeded in intellectual pursuits and by 1842 was principal of a grammar school in Medford, Massachusetts. By 1846 he was ordained as a Universalist minister and accepted a call to his father's church in Charlestown. In the following year he also developed a penchant for lecturing in the lyceum circuit on a wide variety of topics. Lecturing and pastoral activity complemented each other in his public life, and it would be difficult to say which was more important to him or influential in larger social settings during the next two decades. His religious views were flexible enough, and indeed convictions between the two groups were compatible enough, that he had no difficulty moving from a Universalist to a struggling

Unitarian church in 1848. His energy and versatile rhetorical techniques soon made that Boston congregation a ringing success. His immense popularity on the speaker's platform made him a welcome lecturer from Bangor, Maine, to St. Louis and Chicago in the Midwest. Such travels convinced him that moving even farther west was his destiny.

In 1860 King accepted an invitation to lead Unitarian efforts in California, and in doing so he became the chief missionary of his denomination to the Pacific coast. There he again won fame as a lecturer in addition to a clergyman. Since his church emphasized applying religious principles in secular contexts, it seemed natural for him to blend gospel insights with such topics as "Goethe," "Socrates," and "The Lost Arts." King was a key figure in establishing Unitarianism in California, but his contribution in another sphere was equally significant. As civil war loomed on the horizon in 1861, he canvassed the new state to keep its citizens loyal to the federal government. His powerful speeches, such as "Washington and the Union," did much to persuade residents to support the northern side in the conflict. Then, as a member of the U.S. Sanitary Commission, he helped collect material for the physical and spiritual welfare of soldiers in the field. As a pioneer for both church and country he was memorialized later when the Starr King School for Religious Leadership, a Bay area Unitarian seminary, was erected in 1904.

Bibliography:

A. *The White Hills: Their Legends, Landscape, and Poetry* (Boston, 1959); *Patriotism and Other Papers*, edited by Richard Frothingham (Boston, 1864); *Christianity and Humanity*, edited by Edwin P. Whipple (Boston, 1877).

B. NCAB 4, 472; DAB 10, 403–05; NYT 5 Mar 1864, 3; Charles W. Wendte, *Thomas Starr King: Patriot and Preacher* (Boston, 1921); Richard Frothingham, *A Tribute to Thomas Starr King* (Boston, 1921); Arnold Compton, *Apostle of Liberty: Starr King in California* (Boston, 1950).

KINO, Eusebio Francisco (1 August 1645, Segno, Italy—15 March 1711, Magdalena, Mexico, later AZ). Entered novitiate of Jesuit order, 1665; studied at Freiburg, Ingolstadt and München, 1665–70; instructor in grammar, Innsbruck, 1670–73; studied theology at Ingolstadt, 1673–77; assigned to missions in New Spain, 1678; arrived in Mexico, 1681; missionary and cartographer, Atondo expedition, Lower CA, 1683–85; missionary in Pimeria Alta, 1687–1711.

There is irony in Kino's title as "Apostle of Sonora and Arizona" because he had trained for years to prepare himself as a missionary to China. When he was allowed to join a group assembling in Cadiz in 1678 to be sent to America and Asia, it was necessary for the men themselves to sort out their destinations. By the simple but disappointing process of drawing lots, Kino was designated for Mexico, not the Far East. Shortly after arriving there, he was attached as head of the Jesuit mission within a larger expedition to Lower California. He succeeded in the intial stages of missionary work among the relatively primitive native peoples. He also explored the territory extensively, sending many maps, letters, and reports to Mexico City and Europe. Drought caused the end of the missionary and colonizing enterprise in 1685.

After a brief interlude, Kino entered upon further evangelical work that was to mark his career with lasting fame: he became chief missionary to the Pima Indians in northern Mexico. Beginning with headquarters at Mission Dolores in 1687, he labored for almost a quarter century to establish and cultivate missions in the San Miguel, Magdalena, Altar, Sonoita, Santa Cruz, and San Pedro river valleys. He baptized an estimated 4,500 Pimas during that time and contributed to the pacification as well as the spiritual needs of several generations. Father Kino traveled as far as the Gila and Colorado Rivers on the north and made important contributions to cartography and further exploration. Instead of returning to Lower California, he sent cattle and other supplies in support of missions when they were renewed there. His maps and calculations helped prove that California was not an island, and he planned to open a road around the head of the Gulf; this dream was realized later by *Junípero Serra. Kino introduced stock raising to the economy of the region and pioneered in planting wheat and other European foodstuffs. His efforts among native Americans brought them important material aspects of European culture and at the same time acquainted Indians with the more universal teachings of Christianity.

Bibliography:

A. *Kino's Historical Memoir of Pimeria Alta*, trans. and ed. Herbert E. Bolton (Berkeley, 1919, 1948); *Kino Writes to . . . the Duchess of Aveiro*, ed. Ernest J. Burrus (St. Louis, 1965).

B. DAB 10, 419–20; NCE 8, 201–02; Rufus K. Wyllys, *Pioneer Padre: The Life and Times of Eusebio Francisco Kino* (Dallas, 1935); Herbert E. Bolton, *Rim of Christendom: A Biography of Eusebio Francisco Kino, Pacific Coast Pioneer* (New York, 1936); Charles Polzer, *A Life of Eusebio Francisco Kino: Arizona's First Pioneer and A Guide to His Missions and Monuments* (Tucson, 1968); Ernest J. Burrus, *Kino and Manje: Explorers of Sonora and Arizona* (St. Louis, 1971).

KIRK, Edward Norris (14 August 1802, New York, NY—27 March 1874, Boston, MA). *Education*: B.A., Coll. of New Jersey, 1820; studied law in New York, 1820–22; studied at Princeton Sem., 1822–26. *Career*: agent for the American Board of Commissioners for Foreign Missions, 1826–28; minister, Fourth Presbyterian Church, Albany, NY, 1828–37; travel and preaching in Europe, 1837–39; secretary, Foreign Evangelical Society, 1839–42; minister, Mt. Vernon Congregational Church, Boston, MA, 1842–71.

It was not until Kirk had almost become a lawyer that he converted to Christianity and decided to preach the gospel. An additional year in seminary after graduation helped him make up for what he considered insufficient preparation, but it took years of practice for him to develop as a preacher. Missionary tours from Virginia to Georgia provided the experience in which he mastered homiletic skills to an impressive degree. He was minister of two churches organized especially for him during his lifetime, but the larger sphere of revival activity remained a dominant interest. Kirk was an early advocate of "new measures" in revivalism such as protracted meetings where repetitious services often rescued backsliders or persuaded unrepentant sinners. In keeping with this outlook, he opened his pulpit to *Charles G. Finney when every other church in Albany was closed against him. Through the 1840s and 1850s he conducted evangelical campaigns in major eastern cities, frequently preaching twice a day in churches, colleges, and seminaries. A polished, graceful manner complemented an earnest style of delivery as he repeated simple themes in most sermons. His direct, colloquial language worked effectively with most listeners because it conveyed truths which the speaker so obviously believed himself. In both personal example and content of religious witness, this revivalist added dimensions to characteristic features of the Second Great Awakening.

Revivalism as reform of individual souls often had its counterpart in efforts to improve society on a collective scale. Kirk was no exception to this generalization, as evidenced by his continual support of tract societies, Sunday Schools, and movements to strengthen the quality of public education. On the alcohol question he was particularly active as an early supporter of total abstinence. Not given to halfway measures, his opposition to slavery was another instance of embracing reformist causes when it was unpopular to do so. As early as his Albany days, he spoke against the institution, but by 1854 he came to strong denunciations of all, including clergymen, who condoned slaveholding. He was quite severe toward those who even tacitly helped make slavery a permanent American custom—who allowed some men the freedom to hold others in perpetual servitude. During 1860 he toured his old southern missionary territory in futile hope of winning some to abolitionism. He was wholeheartedly in favor of war, once it became a clear necessity, as a means of preserving the Union and ending slavery. Thinking that northern forces were enforcing divine decrees for national destiny, he cooperated with the U.S. Christian Commission and later the American Missionary Association with their programs to aid freedmen. By the early 1870s, however, he was forced to retire because of throat ailments and gradually failing eyesight, maladies which seriously hampered his closing years.

Bibliography:

A.   *Sermons Delivered in England and America* (New York, 1840); *Lectures on the Parables of Our Saviour* (New York, 1856); *Discourses Doctrinal and Practical* (Boston, 1860); *Lectures on Revivals* (Boston, 1875).

B.   SH 6, 345; NCAB 6, 194; DAB 10, 427–28; NYT 28 Mar 1874, 7; David O. Mears, *Edward Norris Kirk* (Boston, 1877).

KNUDSON, Albert Cornelius (23 January 1873, Grandmeadow, MN—28 August 1953, Cambridge, MA). *Education*: B.A., Univ. of Minnesota, 1893; S.T.B., Boston Univ. 1896; studied at Jena and Berlin, 1897–98; Ph.D., Boston Univ., 1900. *Career*: professor of Church History, Univ. of Denver, 1898–1900; professor of Philosophy and English Bible, Baker Univ., 1900–02; professor of English Bible and Philosophy, Allegheny Coll., 1902–06; professor of Hebrew and Old Testament Exegesis, Boston Univ., 1906–21; professor of Systematic Theology, Boston Univ., 1921–43; active retirement, 1943–53.

A search for vital positive forms of religious faith characterized Knudson's intellectual development even when it meant abandoning specific doctrines learned during boyhood days in a manse. He soon realized how much the world-view underlying traditional beliefs clashed with modern science and remained in a perplexed state of mind until he met his most influential teacher, *Borden P. Bowne. Despairing that epistemology and metaphysics seemed hopelessly polarized, he learned from Bowne how personalistic idealism afforded a view of life more intelligible than materialistic naturalism, common sense realism, or absolute idealism. Knudson became the chief systematizer of personalism, giving polished expression to conceptions which circulated widely in liberal Protestant circles up to World War II. He pursued such an endeavor because it was important to associate theology with theistic philosophy; rational explanations of one's faith were difficult to construct but yielded more respectable results than irrational moralism, pragmatic humanism, or appeals to the authority of miracles and mysticism. Neither supernaturalistic authority nor the moral-emotional nature of man could, he maintained, serve as a substitute for inquiry into the metaphysical foundations of religious belief. Basing all ideas on the experience of one's own selfhood, he built a consistent structure which interpreted God and man in terms of personality.

Reacting to the one-sided intellectualism of earlier theologies, Knudson emphasized the practical basis of theistic belief. Faith in God required voluntary affirmation, and that was as justifiable as believing, for example, that the natural world could be understood. Religion was a fundamental, independent aspect of human experience, autonomously valid and irreducible to other cognitive faculties. In that sphere, men have their only direct acquaintance with the inwardness of their being, a category which illuminates self-consciousness and the unity of personal identity through change. There was no principle of explanation above personality or self for interpreting God and none below it adequate to the task. God as person, not as object known through its physical exterior, could be real to modern man. Knudson also spoke of God as immanent, a causal ground of the universe, but he did not accept *Edgar S. Brightman's theory of divine finitude in that connection. Nevertheless he held that men were free moral beings whose guilt or merit accrued to their own choices. Inherited ideas about original sin, total depravity, and unconditional awareness of God were rejected as philosophical impossibilities, as was the conception that individual souls would eventually be absorbed into the Absolute. Only the pure in heart would see God, and for decades the speculative religious thinker urged morally responsible perseverance toward that end.

Bibliography:

A. *The Religious Teaching of the Old Testament* (New York, 1918); *Present Tendencies in Religious Thought* (New York, 1924); *The Philosophy of Personalism* (New York, 1927); *The Doctrine of God* (New York, 1930); *The Doctrine of Redemption* (New York, 1933); *The Validity of Religious Experience* (New York, 1937).

B. NCE 8, 243–44; NYT 30 Aug 1953, 90.

KOHLER, Kaufmann (10 May 1843, Fürth, Germany—28 January 1926, New York, NY). *Education*: private rabbinical studies, principally in Mainz, Altona, and Frankfurt am Main, 1851–64; studied at gymnasium, Frankfurt, 1862–64; university studies at Munich, 1864–65, and Berlin, 1865–67; Ph.D. Erlangen, 1867. *Career*: rabbi, Beth-El Congregation, Detroit, 1869–71; rabbi, Sinai Congregation, Chicago, 1871–79; rabbi, Temple Beth-El, New York, 1879–1903; president, Hebrew Union Coll., 1903–21; active retirement, New York, 1922–26.

Extensive training in German rabbinical schools and universities helped fashion Kohler into one of the most scholarly proponents of Reform Judaism in America. He acknowledged that Samson R. Hirsch had influenced him greatly, but instead of following his teacher's orthodox reaffirmations he was more attracted by modern science and new methods of historical criticism. His wide-ranging studies, which extended over fifty years, produced major contributions in understanding Judaism from an evolutionary perspective. He always sought to reconcile new knowledge with the old faith, remaining through life a radical critic of forms and a profound believer in essentials. In efforts to harmonize Judaism with modern thought and new social conditions, he saw Reform as a logical outcome of the historical process. Adaptation was not symptomatic of weakness but rather a sign of living faith which constantly tried to be relevant in varying concrete situations. Kohler held that evolution was the master key to what was vital and true in the Jewish spirit. Instead of wooden adherence to ephemeral ceremonies or laws, Judaism was fundamentally the law of truth inscribed on human hearts for all to observe. The rabbi's broad learning and deep conviction combined to proclaim his faith in the One, Holy God who had entrusted to the Jewish people, a priestly nation, the objective of attaining righteousness for all humanity.

As a ministerial candidate fresh from graduate school, young Kohler was considered too liberal by European standards; so he came to this country in 1869 and subsequently filled a number of distinguished posts. He was welcomed by *David Einhorn (became his son-in-law the following year) and entered immediately into the work of buttressing Reform ideals with strong institutional supports. An active participant in the Philadelphia Rabbinical Reform Conference

(1869), he was also a key figure in drafting the Pittsburgh Platform of 1885. His membership in the Central Conference of American Rabbis dates from its inception in 1889, and the stature he maintained in that organization helped determine the course of Reform emphases for decades. Kohler was a writer of prodigious output, publishing in the end more than 2,000 articles and speeches. He collaborated in preparing the *Union Prayer Book* (1892); served (1898–1902) as an associate editor on the committee which printed a new translation of the Hebrew Bible; contributed over three hundred entries while on the board of editors (1901–06) that produced the *Jewish Encyclopedia*. The fact that Kohler succeeded Einhorn as rabbi in New York and then followed *Isaac M. Wise as president of Hebrew Union College gives some indication of his eminence in the Reform movement. His passion for humanitarian Jewish idealism unconfined by nationalistic identifications and his commitment to high educational standards and lasting social justice firmly establish him in the forefront of American religious leaders.

Bibliography:

A. *Backward or Forward* (New York, 1885); *Guide for Instruction in Judaism* (New York, 1899); *Jewish Theology Systematically and Historically Considered* (German edition, Leipzig, 1910; English edition, New York, 1918); *The Origins of the Synagogue and the Church* (New York, 1929); *Studies, Addresses and Personal Papers* (New York, 1931).

B. SH 6, 370; NCAB 13, 396; DAB 10, 487–88; UJE 6, 428–30; EJ 10, 1142–43; NYT 29 Jan 1926, 21.

KRAUTH, Charles Porterfield (17 March 1823, Martinsburg, VA—2 January 1883, Philadelphia, PA). *Education*: graduated from Pennsylvania Coll., 1839; graduated from Gettysburg Sem., 1841. *Career*: minister, Baltimore, MD, Martinsburg, VA, and Winchester, VA, 1841–55; minister, Pittsburgh, 1855–59; minister, Philadelphia, 1859–61; editor, *Lutheran and Missionary*, 1861–67; professor of Systematic Theology, Lutheran Sem., Philadelphia, 1864–83; professor of Philosophy, Univ. of Pennsylvania, 1868–83.

English-speaking Lutherans faced a choice during the middle third of the nineteenth century, and largely because of Krauth's activities most of them remained close to traditional patterns. Modifications in belief and practice were being proposed by pragmatic ecumenists like *Samuel S. Schmucker, but more conservative forces viewed the new ''American Lutheranism'' as too radical a departure from the confessions and constitution of a Reformation church. Krauth became one of the most prominent spokesmen who urged loyalty to central motifs in Lutheran orthodoxy, advocating those ideas through polemical writing and irenic leadership in ecclesiastical affairs. He thought that his denomination contained a theology, polity, and confessionalism binding on its members. The moral obligation to support such foundations could not be ignored, nor could accepted standards be altered by individual opinion or synodal preferences. In the last analysis, he found innovations to be too rationalistic and independent, yielding a new kind of sect with a mutilated confession, a broken historical lineage, and a censorious spirit alien to genuine Lutheranism. Dubious speculations and passing experiments might threaten adherents of a church three centuries old, but Krauth was determined to resist adulteration of received truths. In later decades he defined his ecclesiological position even more strictly, declaring that preaching and communion were open only to members in good standing. A sense of exclusiveness based on loyalty to historical symbols led him to oppose all forms of syncretism and union.

By 1864 it was clear that the General Synod and its lax organization was inadequate to preserve the distinctiveness Krauth and other conservatives wished to maintain. A new seminary was established that same year to produce ministers more conscious of their tradition, and in 1867 the General Council of the Evangelical Lutheran Church was formed to further common purposes. Krauth, youngest professor at the seminary and leading statesman for over a decade, composed the Council's principles on faith and polity. He was also the author of a constitution for congregations which gave them stability in times of change and expansion. Outside the denomination he was known for biblical scholarship and philosophical ability, contributing scores of essays and translations of contemporary German theologians to American intellectual circles. Krauth's teaching and administrative leadership added strength to a movement which perpetuated loyalty to confessional tenets and standards in generations far beyond his own.

Bibliography:

A. *Tholuck's Commentary on the Gospel of John* (translation, Philadelphia, 1859); *The Augsburg Confession* (translation and notes, Philadelphia, 1868); *The Conservative Reformation and its Theology* (Philadelphia, 1871); *Berkeley's Principles of Human Knowledge* (prolegomena and notes, Philadelphia, 1874).

B. SH 6, 381–82; NCAB 1, 349; DAB 10, 502–03; NCE 8, 262; NYT 3 Jan 1883, 5; Adolph Spaeth, *Charles Porterfield Krauth*, 2 vols. (New York, 1898, and Philadelphia, 1909; New York, 1969).

KUHLMAN, Kathryn (9 May 1907, near Concordia, MO—20 February 1976, Tulsa, OK). *Career*: itinerant evangelist with Parrott Tent Revival, 1923–28; independent evangelist, 1928–76.

Descended from generations of Lutherans, Kuhlman as a youth attended both Methodist and Baptist services which her parents preferred. In 1921 at the age of fourteen she joined the Baptists, her father's church, and within two years became part of her brother-in-law's evangelistic troupe. By 1928 she was holding services on her own and shortly thereafter received ministerial credentials from the Evangelical Church Alliance, the only institutional authorization she ever utilized. As the Great Depression deepened, crowds attended her meetings in greater numbers, and in 1934 she settled in Denver, Colorado, and built the Kuhlman Revival Tabernacle. Four years later she courted disaster by marrying a divorced follower, Burroughs A. Waltrip, the scandal splitting her congregation and dogging her subsequent efforts until she left the man in 1946. That same year she established a successful ministry at Gospel Revival Tabernacle in Franklin, Pennsylvania. In 1947 she began making popular half-hour radio broadcasts. These programs usually featured sermons on the beauty of experiencing the Holy Spirit in one's life and then testimonies from people who claimed to have been healed by the Spirit from various ailments. In 1966 Kuhlman moved to Los Angeles and became nationally famous through televised versions of her standard emphases.

The basic ingredient in Kuhlman's message was the Holy Spirit, its significance for internal salvation and external enabling power to serve others. Not to be confused with instantaneous sanctification, her emphasis on biblical gifts of the Spirit focused on the miracles wrought in everyday experience. Over the years this baptism of the Holy Spirit manifested itself at her meetings primarily in healing. Kuhlman always maintained that she never healed anyone; it was only through God's power that people were cured of their diseases. But people claimed that they were cured, despite her refusal to employ such mechanical devices as long lines of supplicants, direct personal prayers, and touching each person to effect a change. This personal integrity set her apart from dozens of health-cure entrepreneurs, and her outreach extended for the first time to many middle-class Protestants and Catholics. Her lasting influence was in democratizing the charismatic movement at mid-century, thus making references to spirit possession more familiar within mainstream American religious circles.

Bibliography:

A.   *I Believe in Miracles* (Englewood Cliffs, NJ, 1962); *God Can Do It Again* (Englewood Cliffs, NJ, 1969); *How Big Is God?* (Minneapolis, 1974); *Nothing Is Impossible with God* (Englewood Cliffs, NJ, 1974); *Never Too Late* (Minneapolis, 1975); *A Glimpse into Glory* (Plainfield, NJ, 1979).

B.   NYT 22 Feb 1976, 48; Helen Kooiman Hosier, *Kathryn Kuhlman: The Life She Led, the Legacy She Left* (Old Tappan, NJ, 1976); Jamie Buckingham, *Daughter of Destiny: Kathryn Kuhlman, Her Story* (Plainfield, NJ, 1976).

L

LA FARGE, John (13 February 1880, Newport, RI—24 November 1963, New York, NY). *Education*: B.A., Harvard Coll., 1901; graduated from Univ. of Innsbruck, 1905; M.A., Woodstock Coll., 1910. *Career*: entered novitiate of Jesuit order, 1905; instructor in languages, Canisius Coll., 1907; instructor in languages Loyola Coll. (MD), 1908; pastor, St. Mary's County, MD, 1911–26; editorial staff, *America*, 1926–63.

After brief service as chaplain in urban hospitals and jails, LaFarge was assigned work in rural Maryland, a district which had been under Jesuit influence since the first white men settled in that territory in 1634. There he served country churches with mixed congregations and followed the standard missionary attempt at providing adequate education among people too poor to pay for it. He also began to realize that black and white communicants needed their religious tradition as a basis for achieving overdue social changes. His new vision of racial cooperation spurred him to a lifelong apostolate in furthering interracial justice, a field which he explored long before it rose to national prominence in the 1950s. As an editor for *America*, a comprehensive weekly review published by the Jesuit order, LaFarge wrote continually on the spiritual and moral aspects of social reconstruction. Synthesizing Catholic doctrine, natural law, and pertinent facts of the American situation, he called for a fundamental renewal of religious life as the key to justice in ecclesiastical as well as secular communities. His point of view received powerful backing in 1931 when Pius XI defined matters essentially the same way in *Quadragesimo Anno*. Slowly he succeeded in spreading the conviction that moral law governed human society, and under such principles the rights of minorities had to be protected. Integral justice and charity was the ideal which he argued would provide full Catholic life for the Negro, one allowing black Americans equal opportunity to fulfill their duty to God and their fellow man.

Under LaFarge's leadership organizations quickly formed to combat segregation in Catholic institutions and to help create saner attitudes regarding minority groups in American culture. By 1934 a small layman's study union grew into the Catholic Interracial Council of New York. Its many efforts to end political and economic discrimination against Negroes made promising gains. With headquarters on Vesey Street it dispensed a monthly *Interracial Review* and encouraged groups in other cities to pursue beneficial change on socio-religious grounds. Forty such organizations combined in 1958 to form the National Catholic Conference for Interracial Justice. For years LaFarge broadcast news of this reform movement through his weekly column, "With Scrip and Staff." He also used those pages, often signed simply as "The Pilgrim," to keep track of other important religious and cultural events pertinent to Catholic enrichment. As early as 1927 he joined the Catholic Association of International Peace and proved a constant supporter of liturgical renewal in the Liturgical Arts Society. All these efforts were sustained by a balance of faith and reason, good will and patience. Until the end he remained optimistic about racial harmony, willing to work constructively for the rule of love, justice, and law.

Bibliography:

A. *The Jesuits in Modern Times* (New York, 1928); *Interracial Justice* (New York, 1937); *The Race Question and the Negro* (New York, 1943; *No Postponement: U.S. Moral Leadership and the Problem of Racial Minorities* (New York, 1950); *The Manner Is Ordinary* (New York, 1954); *The Catholic Viewpoint on Race Relations* (Garden City, NY, 1956).

B. NCAB 49, 155–56; DAB supp 7, 447–48; NCE 8, 314–15; NYT 25 Nov 1963, 19.

LAMY, Jean Baptiste (11 October 1814, Lempdes, France—13 February 1888, Santa Fe, NM). *Education*: studied at Royal College, Petit Seminaire, and Grand Seminaire, Clermont-Montferrand, ?–1838. *Career*: assistant pastor, Chapre, France, 1838–39; missionary priest in OH and KY, 1839–50; vicar apostolic of NM, 1850–53; bishop of Santa Fe, 1853–75; archbishop of Santa Fe, 1875–85; retirement, 1885–88.

After a short stint of parish work in his home diocese of Puy de Dome, Lamy volunteered for the missionary fields of trans-Appalachian America. For eleven years he labored among scattered flocks principally in southern Ohio where his bishop, *John B. Purcell, supervised operations in a vigorous new see. But events in 1848 began to affect his future assignment. In that year Mexico ceded land to the United States, and American bishops petitioned Rome for a transfer of ecclesiastical jurisdiction. With papal approval, Lamy was consecrated (in Cincinnati, 1850) to be apostolic vicar of a territory including New Mexico with large parts of Arizona, Nevada, Utah, and Colorado. Sailing downriver to New

Orleans, he made an extremely hazardous journey (shipwrecked off Galveston) through Texas to his episcopal residence at Santa Fe. Since he arrived before anyone there had heard of the appointment, his credentials were challenged. His reception was less than cordial because he represented the intrusion of Anglo civilization (though he was French) into an area dominated by Hispanic culture for more than two hundred years. Indian and Mexican residents were suspicious of the outsider while many clergy were nothing less than hostile. Lamy met the problem with characteristic resolution: he rode 800 miles south to meet the bishop of Durango and settle the matter of jurisdictions. Successful in establishing good relations with his adjacent diocese, he then set about a slow process of winning the hearts and cooperation of people in that enormous domain.

Consolidating Catholic forces in his neglected area required strenuous activity, constant travel, and unflagging evangelical instruction, all of which Lamy supplied as evidence of a tough, dedicated missionary spirit. Probably the greatest contribution he made was in the fields of education and parish ministry. He made several recruiting expeditions to eastern states and Europe to secure funds or personnel for his territory. By 1852 Sisters of Loretto (Kentucky) laid foundations for Catholic schooling in the Southwest; in 1865 Sisters of Charity built the first hospital and orphanage west of the Pecos. Christian Brothers (1859) and Jesuits (1867) also came at the bishop's invitation to expand the numbers of faithful. Lamy turned most of the administrative work over to his old classmate and vicar general, Joseph P. Machebeuf. He was thus free to increase the clergy fourfold, build 45 new churches, and restore 20 old ones. Held in great esteem by all elements of society, Protestant and Jewish as well as Catholic, he backed every venture for civic or cultural improvement. Contributions from that larger constituency helped build a cathedral in Santa Fe to replace the adobe (1714) church. With the cornerstone laid in 1869, an incomplete structure was dedicated in 1886. By that time the archbishop's pace had begun to lessen enough to warrant retirement near the ecclesiastical center he had done so much to strengthen.

Bibliography:

B.   NCAB 12, 49–50; DAB 10, 566–67; NCE 8, 355–56; Louis H. Warner, *Archbishop Lamy: An Epoch Maker* (Santa Fe, NM, 1936); Paul Horgan, *Lamy of Santa Fe* (New York, 1975).

LANDIS, Benson Young (12 October 1897, Coopersburg, PA—10 November 1966, Scarsdale, NY). *Education*: B.A., Moravian Coll., 1918; M.A. and Ph.D., Columbia Univ., 1923 and 1927. *Career*: instructor, Nazareth Hall Military Academy, 1913–19; associate director of rural surveys, Interchurch World Movement and Institute of Social and Religious Research, 1920–21; managing editor, *Christian Work*, 1921–23; associate secretary, Department of Research and Education, Federal Council of Churches, 1923–46; secretary, FCC Washington

office, 1946–50; editor, *Rural America*, 1923–41; associate director, Department
of Research and Survey, National Council of Churches, 1951–65.

It is indicative of his Moravian heritage that Landis participated so fully in
the ecumenical activities of twentieth century federated churches. Another notable aspect, stemming from a more personal choice, was the importance he
placed on rural life and on church work among agricultural communities. For
twenty years (1929–41) he was executive secretary of the American Country
Life Association. He was also a member of the Rural Sociological Society and
the American Farm Economy Association. As director of an institute on rural
economies he also served as special consultant to the Department of Agriculture
and the National Recovery Administration. Much of his time was spent in trying
to preserve family-size tracts of land against encroachments from huge, industrialized "factory farms." He also furthered the causes of adult education in
rural areas and church programs geared to meeting spiritual and social needs far
away from urban settings. The institutional vehicle for most of his pastoral
impulses was the Federal Council of Churches, whose staff he joined in 1923.
When this cooperative organization became the National Council of Churches
in 1950, Landis continued in place as manager of its department that focused
on town and country church work.

After a period of vigorous advocacy that lasted through the Great Depression,
Landis turned more to providing information that churches needed if they were
to take relevant action. As associate director of the department of research and
survey in the NCC he edited (1953–65) the *Yearbook of American Churches*.
This "bible" of American religious statistics was widely acknowledged to be
the most accurate count of membership in American religious institutions. Other
educational contributions included syndicated columns for Religious News Service, a total of more than eighty journal articles, and at least fifteen books. In
all of these writings Landis returned to themes dear to his heart. There are
recurrent discussions of land management, organized agriculture alongside organized labor, and the needs of rural society in addition to those of the cities.
He also tackled problems like alcohol and crime, consumer protection plans and
questions of wealth in a Christian vocation. Many writings also confirmed his
own denomination's traditional ecumenical emphasis, beginning with interdenominational cooperation, and moving through interfaith discussions in western
countries to better understanding of all religions around the globe.

Bibliography:

A. *Rural Church Life in the Middle West* (New York, 1922); *The Church and Social
Relations* (Boston, 1926); *The Third American Revolution: An Interpretation* (New York,
1933); *A Cooperative Economy* (New York, 1943); *Religion and the Good Society: An
Introduction to Social Teachings of Judaism, Catholicism, and Protestantism* (New York,
1943); *World Religions* (New York, 1957).

B. NYT 11 Nov 1966, 43.

LAS CASAS, Bartolomé de (1474, Seville, Spain—1566, Madrid, Spain). *Career*: priest and social reformer, 1512–66; bishop of Chiapas, Mexico, 1544–66.

As an adventurer bent on acquiring a fortune in the New World, Las Casas was no different from others who forced Indians to work for them by right of conquest. He prospered as a planter on Hispaniola from 1502 to 1506, and even though he took holy orders while studying in Rome between 1506 and 1512, he took part in the conquest of Cuba in 1513. But he soon had a radical change of heart, and in 1514 he shocked his congregation by preaching against mistreatment of the native population. Returning to Spain, he advocated various projects to mitigate the cruelties of *encomienda* labor arrangements and the brutalities of military conquest. Those efforts were generally unsuccessful, and in 1523 a despairing Las Casas entered the Dominican Order. During a decade of seclusion he began writing his famous history and thereby learned that the pen could be his greatest weapon in campaigns to secure justice for native Americans. In the mid 1530s he experimented in Nicaragua and Guatemala with ways of converting natives peacefully to Christianity without the destructive tactics or oppressive presence of Spanish soldiers. Those efforts were unavailing too because most Spaniards felt no compunction at inhumane treatment of Indians.

In 1547 Las Casas was back in Spain, publishing treatises and memorials that denounced the cruelties he witnessed firsthand in the New World. Some of his prose undoubtedly exaggerated the Indians' plight and the conquerors' crimes, but the dogged zeal with which Las Casas pursued his cause began to take effect. His stern indictments had some influence at the Spanish court and were thus a factor in reforms that emerged as the New Laws of 1542. Among other things this legislation created a Council of the Indies, prohibited Indian slavery, forbade creation of new *encomiendas*, and terminated existing ones when their current owners died. Most colonists detested such changes, resisted their implementation, and reviled the crusading friar for causing them problems. When Las Casas spent two years in his diocese in southern Mexico (1545–47), he could not enforce the reforms there. By 1547 he returned to Spain and additional controversies that occupied the rest of his life. In 1550 he debated Juan Gines de Sepúlveda on human rights and conquest as applied to native Americans. More and more propaganda continuously poured from his pen. By the time he died in a Dominican monastery after a half-century of fighting cruelty and injustice, even his detractors acknowledged him as "the apostle of the Indies."

Bibliography:

A.   *The Tears of the Indians*: *Being an Historical and True Account of the Cruel Massacres and Slaughters of Above Twenty Millions of Innocent People, Committed by the Spaniards in the Islands of Hispaniola, Cuba, and Jamaica, etc.* (London, 1656; reprint, Stanford, CA, 1953); *A Relation of the First Voyages and Discoveries Made by the Spaniards in America* (London, 1699); George Sanderlin (ed.), *Bartolomé de Las Casas: A Selection of His Writings* (New York, 1971).

B.   SH 6, 417; NCE 8, 394–95; L.A. Dutte, *The Life of Bartolomé de Las Casas and the First Leaves of American Ecclesiastical History* (St. Louis, MO, 1902); Marcel Brion, *Bartolomé de Las Casas: "Father of the Indians"* (New York, 1929); Lewis Hanke, *Bartolomé de Las Casas: Bookman, Scholar, and Propagandist* (Philadelphia, 1952); Henry R. Wagner and Helen R. Parish, *The Life and Writings of Bartolomé de Las Casas* (Albuquerque, NM, 1967); Pedro Borges, *Quien era Bartolomé de las casas?* (Madrid, 1990).

LATHROP, Rose Hawthorne (20 May 1851, Lenox, MA—9 July 1926, Hawthorne, NY). *Career*: writer and homemaker, 1871–96; volunteer nurse, 1896–1900; Mother Superior, Dominican Congregation of St. Rose of Lima, 1900–26.

The youngest surviving child of well-connected New Englanders, young Hawthorne spent most of her formative years in Europe until she married Londoner, George P. Lathrop, in 1871. The couple lived mostly in New York and Boston for two decades, the husband editing magazines and the wife frequently publishing her own short stories and verse. In 1881 they lost their only child, a five-year-old son, to diphtheria. Both parents had been interested enough in Catholicism to have their son baptized in that faith, and in 1881 they themselves were received into the church. Lathrop left her husband in 1895 because of his difficulties with alcohol (he died three years later), and in the following year she embraced a new vocation that is distinguishable for its compassion and self-effacing service. Inspired by extant nursing institutions and the lives of those who cared for the poor and sick, she determined in 1896 to tend cancer victims and to ease their last days on earth. After training for three months at New York Cancer Hospital, Lathrop established a modest hospice in the slums of the Lower East Side. She survived on contributions from those who learned of her work through publicity which she generated herself by writing articles for newspapers and magazines.

Relief efforts expanded quickly because there were always more patients than volunteer nurses. In 1899 Lathrop became a Dominican tertiary and took the name, Mary Alphonsa. The following year Sister Alphonsa was allowed to place her operation on an ecclesiastically approved basis by founding a religious order and naming it for her favorite saint, St. Rose of Lima. Before 1900 the group had been known by a different name, and most people continued to refer to it as the Servants of Relief for Incurable Cancer. By 1901 the order was able to buy Rosary Hill House in Westchester County and to establish there a mother-house, a novitiate, and cancer ward. Mother Alphonsa concentrated on those who were terminally ill, destitute, and without friends. She received all she could, no matter what race or creed characterized the suffering. Her order was devoted exclusively to nursing and tried to share love and human concern with those who faced dreadful realities. At several clinics her example of practical, selfless piety exhibited a rare religious concern for the whole person, body as well as soul.

Bibliography:

A. *Along the Shore* (Boston, 1888); *A Story of Courage: Annals of the Georgetown Convent of the Visitation of the Blessed Virgin Mary* (Cambridge, MA, 1895); *Memories of Hawthorne* (Boston, 1897).

B. NCAB 9, 194; DAB 1, 227; NCE 8, 411–12; NAW 2, 372–74; James J. Walsh, *Mother Alphonsa: Rose Hawthorne Lathrop* (New York, 1930); Katherine K. Burton, *Sorrow Built a Bridge: A Daughter of Hawthorne* (New York, 1937); Theodore Maynard, *A Fire Was Lighted: The Life of Rose Hawthorne Lathrop* (Milwaukee, 1948).

LATOURETTE, Kenneth Scott (9 August 1884, Oregon City, OR—26 December 1968, Oregon City, OR). *Education*: B.S., Linfield Coll., 1904; B.A., M.A., Ph.D., Yale Univ., 1906, 1907, 1909. *Career*: traveling secretary, Student Volunteer Movement for Foreign Missions, 1909–10; instructor, Yale in China, Chang-sha mission, 1910–12; instructor, Reed Coll., 1914–16; instructor, Denison Univ., 1916–21; professor of Missions and Oriental History, Yale Div. Sch., 1921–53; active retirement, 1953–68.

Interest in the YMCA caused Latourette to abandon plans for a law degree and prepare instead for the mission field. After several years' academic preparation, he served briefly in China, but poor health forced a return to this country in 1912. It did not end his concern for the worldwide enterprise of Christian missions, however, and over the next five decades he fashioned historical studies around that central theme. His expertise in Oriental history quickly earned the respect of secular scholars. High standards of accuracy were a basic feature which he used to bolster his ideas about the religious significance of historical trends. Latourette is renowned as one who compiled a wealth of church historical materials, particularly regarding the modern age; he shall also be recognized as a chief twentieth-century apologist for a Christian interpretation of history. More than eighty books expounded facets of his thinking in this general area. The ideal of pure scientific objectivity was not, he discovered, ultimately attainable, and so he utilized a complex mixture of ideas to produce what he considered satisfactory historical narratives. Three elements comprised his studies: carefully verified facts, rational interpretations of the evidence, and insights provided by personal faith. Latourette thought that such studies could remain useful on the level of general information while at the same time speak to larger questions of Christian hope and a providential future.

The optimistic interpretation which Latourette brought to historical records was temporally and geographically comprehensive. He insisted that the impact of Christianity should be viewed from a worldwide perspective, not just from its effect on western Europe during recent times. As its religious influence spread through the world in a series of advances and recessions, the historian concluded that it had been truly a vital, beneficial force among men. The emergence of new movements from within indicated vitality; reform in standards of human decency pointed to its cultural value. Even though some critics thought modern forces had curtailed the influence of Christian witness, Latourette did not counsel despair. His conclusion of faith, supported by fact and interpreted by reason, was that Christianity had never been more significant to more persons than during the last 150 years. Missions at home and abroad continued to expand the operations of what he saw as a young, vigorous religion. Latourette furthered the cause of missions as writer, teacher, and administrator at Yale. Other forms of service included many trusteeships and guest lectures as well as contributions to missionary organizations and projects within his Baptist denomination. Retirement did not slow his activities, and he was full of prospects for the future when an unknown motorist accidentally struck him down.

Bibliography:

A. *A History of the Expansion of Christianity*, 7 vols. (New York, 1937–45); *Anno Domini: Jesus, History and God* (New York, 1940); *A History of Christianity* (New York, 1953); *Christianity in a Revolutionary Age*, 5 vols. (New York, 1958–62).

B. NYT 1 Jan 1969, 21.

LEE, Ann (29 February 1736, Manchester, England—8 September 1784, Watervliet, NY).

All forms of human depravity including war, disease, poverty, and oppression are the result of concupiscence. This was the distinctive doctrine preached by Ann Lee (changed from Lees) who did not doubt that evil was rooted in sexual cohabitation. As early as 1758 she had become mildly attracted to a group of former Quakers who emphasized Christ's imminent return. Their ecstatic utterance and eccentric worship, which had already earned them the name "Shakers," provided her with a vehicle for subsequent developments. After marriage in 1762 she bore four children, all of them dying in infancy. By 1772 her bravery under persecution and direct religious visions led to recognition as leader of the small sect. While in prison she claimed to have received a divine commission to complete Christ's earthly work, preaching a gospel of freedom from bondage to the flesh. Mother Ann declared that one could be released from carnal lust by means of confession and celibacy. Salvation consisted of spiritual rebirth and rigorously abstinent habits, products of an internal resurrection which was the true meaning of millennial expectations. The Second Coming was embodied in her for all to see and available also for individual appropriation at will. Once one had risen from the "Adamic plane" of existence to the more exalted level of life, all the faithful were to enjoy equal status. No profane measurement of money, race, or sex could apply within pure communities where persons shared tasks and goods in common. These teachings were delivered on the assumption that Christ spoke directly through "Ann the Word." Eventually the group made little distinction between their leader's role as prophetess and that of female messiah.

By 1774 the United Society of Believers in Christ's Second Coming, consisting of nine members, reached the New World. Two years later they acquired a tract of land at Niskeyuna (later Watervliet), New York, and settled into a life of communitarian celibacy. Circumstances forced their pooling of resources and strict obedience to regulated life, patterns later canonized into principles which made the Shakers one of the most outstanding socialist experiments of the nineteenth century. During the last four years of her life, Mother Ann initiated public campaigns to expand her following in New York and New England. Shaker leaders were able to attract many converts from Baptist groups where revivals had stirred an interest in millennialism and perfectionism. By the time of her death or passing to a higher state, eleven colonies had been established. A total of eighteen were founded before the Civil War, each sharing a rule and liturgy centered on her revelations and the belief that Christ's Second Coming was a present reality among the faithful. The Mother of New Creation was thought to be continually among them as they sustained for generations a religious association bound together by communal principles.

Bibliography:

B.   SH 6, 438; NCAB 5, 132–33; DAB 11, 95–96; NAW 2, 385–87; Rufus Bishop, *Testimonies of the Life, Character, Revelations and Doctrines of Our Blessed Mother Ann Lee* (Hancock, MA, 1816): Frederick W. Evans, *Ann Lee* (Mt. Lebanon, NY, 1858); Edward D. Andrews, *The People Called Shakers* (New York, 1953); Nardi R. Campion, *Ann the Word: The Life of Mother Ann Lee, Founder of the Shakers* (Boston, 1976).

LEE, Jesse (12 March 1758, Prince George County, VA—12 September 1816, Hillsborough, MD). *Career*: farmer and local preacher in NC, 1777–80; itinerant minister in NC and VA, 1780–83; formally appointed minister on circuits in VA, MD, NJ, NY and CT, 1784–89; itinerant minister and presiding elder in New England, 1790–97; assistant to *Francis Asbury, 1797–1800; presiding elder, VA and MD districts, 1801–16; chaplain, U.S. House of Representatives, 1809–13, and U.S. Senate 1814–15.

Methodism originated with British missionaries, but the crucial manpower came from leaders such as Lee who extended the new church into every state of the republic. He is representative of those early itinerants whose plain manners and lack of formal education gave them more rapport with common folk than foreign appointees ever achieved. Like many others, his family followed a common pattern of nominal association with Anglicanism until a search for vital religious experiences led them to join the Methodist connection. At the age of seventeen Lee began a ministry covering more than four decades, laboring with blunt and dogged persistence for the salvation of those around him. His independent character and dedication to moral standards was evident from the first. In 1780 the North Carolina militia drafted his services, but he refused to bear arms on grounds of conscience. He drove supply wagons as alternative duty and improved the time by preaching with great effect. After the war he rode circuit in several states. In 1784 *Francis Asbury gave official sanction to clerical habits already well formed, at length presiding over his ordination as deacon (privately) and elder (publicly) in 1790. By that time, Lee had begun pioneering work in

New England where his denomination received little encouragement from local Congregationalists. Years of toil and hardship saw the establishment of six circuits and brought him recognition as one of the foremost Methodist apostles in that region. In 1797 he became Asbury's assistant, visited churches, attended conferences, and for three years performed all the functions of bishop except that of ordaining. He narrowly missed being named bishop in 1800, losing a runoff election to *Richard Whatcoat.

Independent attitudes regarding ecclesiastical authority may have cost Lee a bishopric. While his spirit may have reflected popular Methodist attitudes, the outcome of that episcopal contest revealed a clerical preference for order in the church. For quite some time Lee had argued unsuccessfully to reduce the power of bishops. He also tried repeatedly to change parts of the Discipline. Whenever he agreed with the common rule, he enforced it rigorously, but he would not submit nor require adherence by others on those points he found unacceptable. Proud and unbending to the end, Lee remained something distinctively American and yet anomalous in the Methodist code of hierarchical organization. He represented the common man in his simple sermons and unaffected customs. Rude buildings and common dress were always more appropriate to him than opulent churches or canonical gowns. He differed with Asbury on many matters but on balance deserves assessment as his denomination's second most important patriarch. Interested in camp meetings to the very end, he died while attending a revival on Maryland's eastern shore.

Bibliography:

A.   *A Short Account of the Life and Death of the Rev. John Lee* (Baltimore, 1805); *A Short History of the Methodists in the United States of America* (Baltimore, 1810).

B.   AAP 7, 80–87; SH 6, 438; NCAB 13, 187; DAB 11, 112–14; Minton Thrift, *Memoir of the Rev. Jesse Lee: With Extracts from His Journals* (New York, 1823, 1969); Leroy M. Lee, *The Life and Times of the Rev. Jesse Lee* (Louisville, 1848); William H. Meredith, *Jesse Lee: A Methodist Apostle* (New York, 1909).

LEESER, Isaac (12 December 1806, Neuenkirchen, Prussia—1 February 1868, Philadelphia, PA). *Education*: private studies with rabbis at Dulmen and Münster, and in Gymnasium of Münster, before 1824. *Career*: rabbi, Mikveh Israel Congregation, Philadelphia, 1829–50; unaffiliated preaching and literary work, 1850–57; rabbi, Beth-El Emeth Congregation, Philadelphia, 1857–68; president, Maimonides Coll., 1867–68.

At eighteen years of age Leeser moved from Germany to Richmond, Virginia, where he worked in his uncle's store and served as a volunteer teacher in Jewish circles. Four years later he came to public notice by engaging in a literary battle against articles that were defamatory to Judaism. As a result he was invited to serve as rabbi, sometimes the post is designated as hazan, in Philadelphia's oldest Sephardic congregation. Leeser was a traditionalist and did much to stem the tide of Reform, but he was not opposed to change per se. For example, he translated both Sephardic (1837) and Ashkenazic (1848) rituals into English and preached in the vernacular as well, a practice which slowly won gradual acceptance. In 1843 he began editing a monthly, *The Occident and American Jewish Advocate*, a thoroughly conservative magazine that helped stimulate interest in Jewish life and thought throughout the country. Twenty-five volumes of this pioneering journal, which contained much of Leeser's thought, appeared during his lifetime.

Perhaps because he was not trained as a rabbi himself, Leeser made numerous contributions to the foundations of American Jewish education. He wrote and translated many books of instruction for Jewish schools, providing the first Hebrew primer for children in 1838. Toward the end of his life (1867) he was successful in founding Maimonides College, the first school for rabbinical training to appear in America. Perhaps the most significant achievement was his English translation of the Hebrew Bible in 1845, the product of seventeen years' labor. It was widely appreciated for correcting errors of the King James translation and for avoiding christological connotations. That translation was not superceded until 1917. He was also the inspiring force behind many community organizations such as the Jewish Hospital and one of the first Jewish Publication Societies. Not always known for tactful ways, Leeser resigned from Mikveh Israel because of difficulties with his congregation. He nevertheless continued to exert himself in organizing synagogues through the southern and western parts of the country. A new group formed in Philadelphia to rescue him from financial burdens and to provide a center for continuing his work, a ministry dedicated to perpetuating traditional Jewish doctrines and practices.

Bibliography:

A. *Jews and the Mosaic Law* (Philadelphia, 1833); *The Claims of the Jews to an Equality of Rights* (Philadelphia, 1842).

B. NCAB 10, 393–94; UJE 6, 588; DAB 11, 137–38; EJ 10, 1561–62; Henry S. Morais, *Eminent Israelites of the Nineteenth Century* (Philadelphia, 1880).

LELAND, John (14 May 1754, Grafton, MA—14 January 1841, Cheshire, MA). *Career*: itinerant minister, centered in Orange County, VA, 1776–91; itinerant minister, centered in Cheshire, MA, 1792–1841.

Young Leland matured under the advantages of sound elementary schooling and the usual affiliations with Congregationalism, the established church in Massachusetts. By the time he turned eighteen, however, he sought immersion as a Baptist, forsaking worldly pleasures to follow the ministry. Two years later he was licensed to preach and in 1776 moved south with his bride to urge the cause of Baptist principles among Virginians. His largest congregations were located in Mt. Poney, Orange, and Louisa, but he toured the surrounding region extensively in efforts to spread his understanding of gospel grace. These activities were occasionally rewarded by warm, popular responses (especially in 1787), and Leland was regarded as one of the most effective preachers in the state. In addition to evangelism he took a prominent part in debates regarding religious freedom in Virginia. His persuasive powers helped secure passage (1786) of Jefferson's bill disestablishing Anglicanism, and he also supported the federal constitution on assurance that a Bill of Rights would be added to liberty of individual conscience. Leland also worked for freedom in wider circles. He argued that human slavery was wrong because it was inconsistent with the new republican government as well as a violation of fundamental rights of nature. At his instigation, the Baptist General Committee in Richmond adopted (1789) a resolution containing those antislavery ideas.

Politics and theology combined in Leland to produce a strong advocate of freedom in every human sphere. At first a Jeffersonian Republican, then a Jacksonian Democrat, he consistently pursued the same objectives during sixty years of active ministry. In both Connecticut and Massachusetts he struggled to overthrow the Standing Order, serving in the latter state's House of Representatives from 1811 to 1813. Leland did not settle into a single residence after returning north, though Cheshire was most often his home. He criss-crossed New England on lengthy preaching tours, covered much of New York state, and returned several times to Virginia, holding meetings all the way there and back. This itinerant missionizing continued despite the fact that he experienced long bouts of depression. He described it as feeling barren in himself and useless to others, unsure how to address sinners and unable to effect their repentance. But in the face of such misgivings he would always return to his central vocation, finding that conversions followed in due course. He composed hymns, wrote pamphlets and kept evangelical witness alive with many years of faithful proclamation. As a seasoned veteran of the pulpit he was long remembered for labor to promote piety while simultaneously vindicating the civil and religious rights of men.

Bibliography:

A. *The Writings of the Late Elder John Leland*, ed. L. F. Greene (New York, 1845, 1969).

B. AAP 6, 174–86; NCAB 5, 513; DAB 11, 160–61.

LIEBMAN, Joshua Loth (7 April 1907, Hamilton, OH—9 June 1948, Boston, MA). *Education*: B. A., Univ. of Cincinnati, 1926; graduated from Hebrew Union Coll., 1930; studied at Harvard, Columbia, and Hebrew Univs., 1930–31; D.H.L., Hebrew Union Coll., 1939. *Career*: lecturer in Philosophy, Univ. of Cincinnati, 1926–30; instructor in Bible and medieval exegesis, Hebrew Union Coll., 1931–34; rabbi, Temple Israel, Lafayette, IN, 1931–34; rabbi, Kehilath Anshe Maarab Temple, Chicago, IL, 1934–39; rabbi, Temple Israel, Boston, MA, 1939–48.

A brilliant child descended from rabbis on both sides of the family, Liebman studied at college and seminary simultaneously before being ordained in the Reform tradition in 1930. He had a remarkable capacity to speak relevantly to modern anxieties and also to master many of the nuances of medieval Jewish philosophy. In the former vein he was a popular radio preacher on Boston stations and as the voice of "Message of Israel" on NBC and ABC networks between 1939 and 1946. In the latter area he lectured on Jewish literature and culture at a half-dozen universities, even Andover-Newton Theological School where he was the first rabbi to achieve regular faculty status at a Christian seminary. During World War II Liebman served on the National Committee of Education and on the Army and Navy Religious Activities Committee. He also made important and lasting contributions as chair of the Committee for Racial and Religious Understanding organized by the governor of Massachusetts. As a dynamic and forceful speaker he was a popular guest on college campuses. In the few years before his unexpected death he trebled the size of his congregation in Boston. Other activities include support for the Boston Civil Liberties Commission, the United Jewish Appeal and the Jewish Publication Society.

As early as his years in Chicago Liebman felt that his training had not prepared him adequately for helping people face their daily troubles. So he turned increasingly to psychology and in 1946 published a book on his acquired insights. The small volume made him famous almost overnight. In it he maintained that psychiatry and religion are not enemies but rather complementary tools, suitable for creative partnership. Psychiatry can aid spiritual redemption by helping people realize that life is frustrating and inner turmoil, natural. Religion can help people to evaluate their limitations realistically and recover a sense of their own worthiness, to share in each other's frailties and draw on each other's strengths. Liebman's immense best seller helped thousands to gain new insight into personal growth and maturity through a better understanding of their psychic nature. Readers appreciated his work as more human than most books on psychology and more practical than most books on religion. His brand of spiritual counseling helped individuals develop wholesome views about overcoming their guilt as a crucial step in developing affirmative attitudes regarding their personal and social salvation.

Bibliography:

A. *Peace of Mind* (New York, 1946).
B. NCAB 38, 624–25; DAB supp 4, 495–96; NYT 10 Jun 1948, 25.

LINCOLN, Abraham (12 February 1809, near Hodgenville, KY—15 April 1865, Washington, DC).

It is difficult to pinpoint the sources of Lincoln's deep spirituality. During his boyhood the family had associated with various Baptist groups, and in later life he had tangential relationships with Presbyterian and Episcopal bodies. In the main, however, he could not assent without mental reservations to much of what passed for orthodox Christianity. While creeds and arguments over scriptural authority were not to his liking, he still embodied a biblically rooted faith which gradually matured with the pace of his own experiences. By the time he was elected sixteenth president of the United States, he held an abiding conviction that nations and men are instruments through which divine will is accomplished. Lincoln gave people of his day a theological interpretation of the nation's history, one making no self-righteous claims but definitely uniting federal policy with moral purpose. He saw the Civil War as something more than a mundane struggle for political rights; with his prophetic vision it became a test of faith, a judgment on the evil of slavery, and punishment by the Almighty to bring about its removal. Many of the president's public statements lifted northern understanding of the war to a higher level where God's people were seen as chastised for past sins yet made hopeful for mercy that would preserve the covenant once established on these shores. In reminding hearers that divine judgment, though terrible, was altogether true and righteous, he reiterated an ancient belief that men stood before the living God of history who pursued ends of His own choosing.

Both sides, North and South, read the same Bible; both prayed to the same God to invoke His aid against the other. But Lincoln was continually disturbed that some men dared to pray after having derived their wealth from the sweat of other men's brows. The enormity of slavery was so repugnant, he could not remember a time when his opposition to it ever wavered. By 1862 he had transformed a war to preserve the Union into one which sought the nobler objective of freedom for residents in every section. In the Emancipation Proclamation and later speeches, he articulated the American dream of democracy as the last, best hope of earth. Touching on themes unmistakably religious in origin, he lifted northern ideals to the point of declaring that a country which freed the slave would be the providential means of advancing liberty and democracy around the world. At Gettysburg his mention of great battles followed a baptismal pattern wherein he suggested that the nation was dying to past sins in order to rise to a new birth of freedom. Short months before his assassination, he spoke once again of an attitude that fostered sacred motivations within national consciousness. He echoed thousands in swearing a solemn oath registered in heaven to finish the appointed task, to end secession and slavery without malice, to bind up the wounds of wartime with charity toward all involved. A spiritual dedication to national achievements has not been completely lacking in any generation since then.

Bibliography:

A. *The Writings of Abraham Lincoln*, ed. Arthur B. Lapsley, 8 vols. (New York, 1905–06); *The Collected Works of Abraham Lincoln*, ed. Roy P. Basler, 8 vols. (New Brunswick, NJ, 1953).

B. NCAB 2, 65–74; DAB 11, 242–59; NYT 16 Apr 1865, 1; John G. Nicolay and John Hay, *Abraham Lincoln*, 10 vols. (New York, 1890); William E. Barton, *The Soul of Abraham Lincoln* (New York, 1920); Carl Sandburg, *Abraham Lincoln: The Prairie Years, The War Years*, 6 vols. (New York, 1926, 1939); Benjamin P. Thomas, *Abraham Lincoln* (New York, 1952); William J. Wolf, *The Almost Chosen People: A Study of the Religion of Abraham Lincoln* (Garden City, NY, 1959).

LIPSCOMB, David (21 January 1831, Franklin County, TN—11 November 1917, Nashville, TN). *Education*: graduated from Franklin Coll., 1849. *Career*: lay preacher for Disciples of Christ, 1856–1913; editor, *The Christian Advocate*, 1866–1913; instructor, Nashville Bible Sch., 1891–1913; retirement, 1913–17.

Like his father before him, Lipscomb believed from his earliest days that the Bible was an all-sufficient rule for human faith and practice. Scripture embodied God's laws to men who in turn had the opportunity of living in harmony with those laws and their author. As an unostentatious preacher who never considered himself a clergyman in any professional sense of the term, Lipscomb spent almost sixty years advocating a life of absolute trust in Bible teachings. In addition to speaking whenever invited to do so, he wrote constantly on religious topics pertinent to Disciples of Christ followers and exerted a widespread influence, ranging from Kentucky to Texas, and from Georgia to Missouri. Primarily through the printed word, he filled an important place among those who sought to restore New Testament Christianity during the half century following Appomattox. The crowning achievement of his ministry was the school founded in Nashville (now a college bearing his name) where he taught the Bible, free from any theological system. By such means he offered students not empty degrees or other titles but rather the solid foundation on which to build an earnest Christian life. Through annual coverage of both Testaments, he helped pupils discern God's laws and at the same time prevented them from setting up their own judgments as to what constituted right or wrong.

Loyalty to the plain teachings of Scripture also obliged believers to resist departures from that standard, and Lipscomb proved himself to be an adamant foe of foolish notions in modern society. For one thing he was convinced that Christians should take no active part in civil affairs. Firm and unyielding in his stand that true believers should not vote or hold office, he became particularly emphatic during the Civil War that church members should not participate in the fighting. The editor and schoolteacher did not relent on this perennial issue even when fellow Disciple, James A. Garfield, ran for the national presidency in 1880. Another of his targets was instrumental music in churches, a worldly contrivance for which he could find no warrant in primitive customs of worship. Probably the most serious controversy was related to missionary societies or any other association, beyond the local congregation, that sought to spread the gospel. Lipscomb opposed societies because he saw them as a human addition to God's plan of salvation, arguing that they introduced expediency and politics into a sphere where spiritual considerations alone should rule. Many in the denomination interpreted this conservatism as the reaction of a sour obstructionist who insisted on having his own way in church policy. Another view is that he kept alive in the early twentieth century a passion for firsthand religious immediacy despite a gradual drift toward routinizing the sacred in ecclesiastical agencies.

Bibliography:

A. *Queries and Answers*, ed. J. W. Shepherd (Nashville, 1910); *Salvation from Sin* (Nashville, 1913); *Queries and Answers*, ed. M. C. Kurfees (Nashville, 1921).

B. Earl I. West, *The Life and Times of David Lipscomb* (Henderson, TN, 1954); Robert E. Hooper, *Crying in the Wilderness: A Biography of David Lipscomb* (Nashville, 1979).

LIVERMORE, Mary Ashton (19 December 1821, Boston, MA—23 May 1905, Boston, MA). *Career*: language teacher, Charlestown, MA, 1836–38; family tutor, plantation in southern VA, 1839–42; principal, private school in Duxbury, MA, 1842–45; associate editor, *New Covenant*, 1858–69; worker and director, Sanitary Commission, Chicago, 1861–65; editor, *Agitator*, 1869–70; editor, *Woman's Journal*, 1870–72; lecturer on lyceum circuit, 1872–95.

Mary Ashton Rice was born into a Calvinistic Baptist family whose stern moral standards produced within her fears of eternal punishment difficult to assuage. In 1845 she married Daniel P. Livermore, a Universalist minister whose devotion provided a happy home life and whose optimistic theology offered greater hope for salvation. For sixteen years she aided his work in six pastorates and in editing a monthly journal, doing what she could with charitable organizations along the way. In Chicago during the Civil War she applied herself to humanitarian work on a much larger scale and came to national attention as an efficient agent and administrator of Sanitary Commission activities in that region. Together with her friend, Jane C. Hoge, she helped organize over 3,000 local aid societies in northwestern states. With that base, Mary Livermore worked tirelessly to raise funds, surgical supplies, and food supplements for Union Armies. She toured hospitals and troop depots from St. Louis to Vicksburg, providing countless acts of charity for soldiers and issuing intelligent factual reports to government officials who sought to improve conditions in that sector. Like many in her generation, she found that wartime conditions elicited a moral response of heroic proportions which otherwise might not have been achieved.

After the war Mrs. Livermore embraced the cause of woman suffrage with the conviction that politics was the best means of combating social abuses like prostitution, alcoholism, and poverty. Through articles in national magazines, several editorial positions, and lecture tours she worked for twenty-five years to emphasize the role of women in moral reform. She organized the first woman's suffrage convention in Illinois (1868), helped found a stable association in Massachusetts (serving on its executive board and as president, 1893–1903), and was president of the American Woman Suffrage Association, 1875–78. Another of her lasting concerns was temperance. As president of the Massachusetts branch of the WCTU (1875–85) she delivered effective antiliquor sermons in churches and other meetings throughout the state. Her efforts were greatly appreciated by *Frances Willard who acknowledged her as the movement's foremost speaker. In 1895 Mrs. Livermore retired from the lecture circuit but continued to speak occasionally and work with local charity groups. The death of her husband was a great blow to her, and at length she turned to spiritualism, with claimed success, as a means of conversing with him. For many years she suffered from pain in her eyes and welcomed the end that would permit reunion with the man who helped sustain their common moral crusade.

Bibliography:

    A. *What Shall We Do With Our Daughters?* (Boston, 1883); *My Story of the War* (Hartford, 1889); *Story of My Life* (Hartford, 1899).
    B. NCAB 3, 82; DAB 11, 306; NAW 2, 410–13; NYT 24 May 1905, 9.

LIVINGSTON, John Henry (30 May 1746, Poughkeepsie, NY—20 January 1825, New Brunswick, NJ). *Education*: B.A., Yale Coll., 1762; studied law in Poughkeepsie, NY, 1762–64; S.T.D., Univ. of Utrecht, 1770. *Career:* minister, New York, 1770–1810; president and professor of Theology, Queen's Coll., 1810–25.

When Livingston returned to New York after four years' theological study in Holland, he became involved in the question of speaking English in Dutch Reformed churches. Proponents of its use wanted to keep in touch with young people, who were still attached to their ancestral faith but whose first language was now English. Many resisted because for them it symbolized a deterioration of traditional creeds, liturgy, and polity. Livingston was diplomatic enough to remain friendly with both sides, gradually moving policy in the liberal direction. During the next five decades, such conduct was instrumental in placing American Reformed Dutch churches on a stable, independent footing. As early as 1747 a Coetus had been formed in the colonies, still subordinate to the Classis of Amsterdam but too separatist to satisfy conservatives. Those wishing closer links with Europe split from the Coetus in 1764 to form a Conferentie. It was to Livingston's enduring credit that he successfully negotiated a merger of these two factions, reuniting all parties in 1772. The constitution which he drafted was not officially adopted until 1792, but with his careful shepherding, substantial independence and general good will were maintained. He also helped compile doctrinal standards, a hymnbook (1813), and rubrics for common worship in keeping with patterns originally formulated across the Atlantic.

The major portion of Livingston's ministerial labors was expended in New York (except for the Revolutionary period), but he also accepted educational responsibilities which designated New Brunswick, New Jersey, as his final residence. Queen's College, later named Rutgers University, had received a charter from British authorities in 1766; work begun on the academy five years later was interrupted by the war. Finally in 1785 Livingston was made professor of theology, the first office of its kind in this country and one which he occupied along with pastoral chores. After twenty-six years of teaching in the city and on Long Island, he reluctantly agreed to become president of Queen's because it seemed duty demanded it. He viewed his removal to New Brunswick as a species of martyrdom, but at last his professorial activity was grounded in an institutional framework. All the problems of finances, adequate buildings, and sufficient enrollment plagued his administration, and it was difficult to solve them in a satisfactory manner. But with effort and prayer the college grew after modest, sporadic beginnings, becoming strong enough at length to encourage the hope that it would be perpetually useful for the denomination. In his contribution to ministerial education as with other facets of sound ecclesiastical growth, the president achieved almost universal recognition as father of the Dutch Reformed Church in America.

Bibliography:

B. AAP 9, 52–66; SH 7, 2; NCAB 3, 400; DAB 11, 314–15; Alexander Gunn, *Memoirs of the Rev. John H. Livingston* (New York, 1829).

LOVEJOY, Elijah Parish (9 November 1802, Albion, ME—7 November 1837, Alton, IL). *Education*: B.A., Waterville (Now Colby) Coll., 1826; studied at Princeton Sem., 1832–33. *Career*: schoolteacher, China, ME, 1826–27; schoolteacher, St. Louis, MO, 1827–32; editor, *St. Louis Observer*, 1833–36; editor, *Alton Observer*, 1836–37.

With little more than a casual interest in moral values and a willingness to teach school until something better came along, Lovejoy moved west like thousands of other New Englanders to improve his fortune. But like those same compatriots he was susceptible to the spiritual quickenings and appeals for reformist zeal that characterized the Second Great Awakening. Converted in one of those revivals, Lovejoy decided to follow his father into the ministry and after a single year of study was in 1833 licensed to preach by the Philadelphia Presbytery. Returning to Missouri he preached occasionally, but his central duty was supervision of a Presbyterian weekly paper. In its pages he supported most of the causes associated with general benevolence including temperance, distribution of tracts and Bibles, together with other evangelical attempts to improve the moral and educational lives of society. Within a short time, however, Lovejoy became an ardent abolitionist, and his activities regarding the question of slavery brought him increasingly to public attention.

Even though Missouri was a slave state, many of its citizens wished to end the institution through gradual emancipation. Lovejoy had no patience with such delay and half measures. He defied slaveowner and timid reformer alike, antagonizing public sentiment in his paper until 1836 when friends prevailed on him to move to safer environs in Illinois. But even while in transit he attended the Presbyterian General Assembly and denounced equivocating conservatives who would not demand an immediate and universal end to slavery. Settled in Alton, he persuaded *Edward Beecher that abolitionism was the better position, but many others resented his uncompromising position and fiery exhortations. In scarcely more than a year opponents succeeded in destroying three printing presses which Lovejoy used to disseminate antislavery news. He refused to cower before mob action and ordered a fourth press while calling for punishment of his attackers. As the press arrived, friends took up arms to defend it and the paper's editor. Hostile shots were exchanged, and Lovejoy was shot to death in the ensuing fight. His cause did not die with him but rather, as is often the case with martyrs, expanded until it forced the nation to face the question of slavery in an ordeal by fire.

Bibliography:

B. NCAB 2, 328; DAB 11, 434–35; Joseph C. and Owen Lovejoy, *Memoir of the Rev. Elijah P. Lovejoy: Who Was Murdered in Defence of the Liberty of the Press, at Alton, Illinois, Nov. 7, 1837* (New York, 1838); Henry Tanner, *The Martyrdom of Lovejoy: An Account of the Life, Trials, and Perils of Elijah P. Lovejoy* (Chicago, 1881); Merton L. Dillon, *Elijah P. Lovejoy: Abolitionist Editor* (Urbana, IL, 1961); Paul Simon, *Lovejoy: Martyr to Freedom* (St. Louis, MO, 1964).

LYMAN, Mary Redington Ely (24 November 1887, St. Johnsbury, VT—9 January 1975, Claremont, CA). *Education*: B.A., Mt. Holyoke Coll., 1911; B.S., Union Sem. (NY), 1919; studied at Cambridge Univ., 1919–21; Ph.D., Univ. of Chicago, 1924. *Career*: high school teacher, Rockville, CT, 1911–13; general secretary of YWCA, Mt. Holyoke Coll., 1913–16; at various ranks professor of Religion, Vassar Coll., 1920–26; at various ranks professor of Religion, Barnard Coll., 1928–40; dean and professor of Religion, Sweet Briar Coll., 1940–50; dean of women and Morris K. Jesup Professor of English Bible, Union Sem. (NY), 1950–55; active retirement, 1955–75.

As leader of YWCA activities at her alma mater Mary Ely conducted Bible study classes and discovered that she loved it. She soon enrolled at New York's Union Seminary, the only woman in her class, having determined to become a Bible teacher. Though a prize-winning student, she was forced by custom to sit among faculty wives in the balcony and from their view her own graduation ceremony. The prize supported two years of study in England, but prejudice against women scholars was no less abroad. After obtaining a doctorate and teaching for several years at Vassar, she married Eugene W. Lyman in 1926 and enjoyed more than two decades of happy union where family and professional interests blended nicely. The couple moved to Virginia when her husband retired, but Mary Lyman continued to teach and served as dean of Sweet Briar College. Within a year of her husband's death she was in 1949 ordained a Congregationalist minister. And the following year, 1950, she returned to Union Seminary, becoming the first woman to hold a faculty chair in that institution and the first woman to become a full professor at any American theological school.

By the middle of this century an increasing number of women were attending seminaries to prepare for many different kinds of religious vocations. Lyman was both an exemplar for younger women to follow and an advocate of better support for them in schools and parishes. She became particularly well informed on the subject when she served (1948–54) on the Commission on the Life and Work of Women in the Churches, an international committee sponsored by the

World Council of Churches. But her larger interest was to share knowledge and understanding of the Bible, enhanced by critical scholarship, with all Christians. She had a practical concern to nourish people's faith by explaining how the early Christian community had developed and how its records had evolved into the New Testament. Through books, articles, and classes she tried to recapture the world that shaped biblical authors and then to suggest ways in which their thought could be adapted to modern life. After retirement she continued to travel, teach, and serve on many boards and agencies. Finally moving to Pilgrim Place, a community for retired church workers in California, Lyman remained active to the end, participating in speaking engagements, church services, and, as always, Bible study groups.

Bibliography:

A.   *Paul the Conqueror* (New York, 1919); *Knowledge of God in Johannine Thought* (New York, 1925); *The Fourth Gospel and the Life of To-Day* (New York, 1931); *The Christian Epic: A Study of New Testament Literature* (New York, 1936).

B.   NAW 4, 435–37; NYT 11 Jan 1975, 32.

M

McAFEE, Joseph Ernest (4 April 1870, Louisiana, MO—14 March 1947, Princeton, NJ). *Education*: B.A., Park Coll., 1889; studied at Union Sem. (NY), 1889–90; studied at Auburn Sem., 1891–93; B.D., Princeton Sem., 1896. *Career*: at various ranks professor of Greek, Park Coll., 1890–91, 1893–95, and 1896–1900; chaplain and professor of Religion, Park Coll., 1900–06; associate secretary (1906–14) and general secretary (1914–17), Presbyterian Board of Home Missions, 1906–17; secretary, American Missionary Association, 1918–20; community counselor, Univ. of Oklahoma, 1921–23; director of community service, Community Church, New York, 1924–32; active retirement, 1932–47.

After teaching for almost fifteen years at his Presbyterian alma mater, McAfee went on to serve his denomination in the larger field of home missions. In that capacity he discerned an increasing need to define urban evangelical enterprises in ways which took account of social contexts as well as personal needs. In one of his many influential pamphlets issued before World War I, he described an approaching crisis in missionary method. There was too much emphasis, he asserted, on just saving souls and not enough attention paid to organic conceptions of human life within a social fabric. In the first decade of the twentieth century this official spokesman articulated a gradually developing split between conservatives who stressed an individualistic approach to salvation and liberals who maintained that such a scheme was not enough. McAfee called for a broader conception of mission work as social-philanthropic service. He did not agree that a narrowly defined task of saving souls, regardless of their social condition and prospects, was the primary goal of Christian missions. His subsequent activities as counselor in the extension division of a western university and then director of social services in a large New York church attest to the fact that he found gospel witness inextricably related to social work. By the time of the

Great Depression, poor health forced him to retire from active participation in such programs, but for several years thereafter he wrote about missions and the many ramifications of that vocation in modern life.

Bibliography:

A. *Missions Striking Home* (New York, 1908); *World Missions from the Home Base* (New York, 1911); *College Pioneering* (Kansas City, MO, 1938).

B. NYT 15 Mar 1947, 13.

McCABE, Charles Cardwell (11 October 1836, Athens, OH—19 December 1906, New York, NY). *Career*: minister, Putnam, OH, 1860–62; chaplain, Union Army, 1862–64; agent, U.S. Christian Commission, 1864–65; minister, Portsmouth, OH, 1865–68; financial agent, Church Extension Society, 1868–84; corresponding secretary, Missionary Society, 1884–96; bishop of the Methodist Episcopal Church, 1896–1906; chancellor, American Univ. (DC), 1902–06.

An active boy who had farmed and clerked before deciding on the ministry, McCabe was not one for spending much time on study. During his short stay at Ohio Wesleyan he devoted himself to revivals as much as to books and left for his first pastorate without receiving a degree. Shortly thereafter he enlisted as chaplain with the 122nd Regiment of Ohio Volunteers; within a year, events transpired to make him the best-known Methodist preacher of his generation. He was captured (June, 1863) while tending the wounded after brisk action around Winchester. Taken to notorious Libby Prison near Richmond, he continued to preach, sing, and make life tolerable for hundreds of inmates. After being exchanged, he threw himself into the war effort with an inimitable blend of religious fervor and patriotic devotion. His speeches about prison life aided public efforts to ameliorate such conditions. Countless audiences were galvanized by the direct, first-person narratives of one who was always referred to affectionately as Chaplain McCabe. Blessed with a rich baritone singing voice, he helped make ''The Battle Hymn of the Republic'' a rallying cry for those dedicated to the Union. His eloquent speeches evidenced a life of deep feeling and action. They were full of infectious enthusiasm about religion as a vital, joyful experience coupled with civic duty to promote the cause of freedom for all humanity.

After the Civil War, McCabe tried to settle down in a local parish, but larger fields required his forensic talents. Once confiding that he seemed doomed to raise money, he met such mundane responsibilities magnificently. Evangelical zeal matched an indomitable optimism as he campaigned to extend Methodist witness, building churches, retiring mortgages, and floating loans to house new congregations. Always a strong promoter of ecclesiastical growth, he had a ready answer for *Robert G. Ingersoll. When the skeptic charged that Christianity was no longer effective in American life, Chaplain McCabe responded that they were building a new Methodist church every day and planned soon to double the rate.

In the late 1880s he coined the phrase "A Million for Missions," once again firing the public imagination with a purpose for evangelizing the continent and Christianizing the world. He continued the same strenuous pace after being made bishop, a rank which did not impede his forthright approach or unpretentious manner. He drove himself, visiting 100 cities in 27 states in an average year to promote missions in Alaska, China, Mexico, and the Philippines. His eloquent addresses never failed to rouse the faithful to greater efforts while hardened sinners were also added to the ever enlarging fold. The bishop's duties took him to South America (1901, 1902) where he spent himself in characteristic fashion for the growth of Protestantism there. His last years were full of episcopal tasks which he met with unflagging energy until death terminated the work essential for growth in his denomination.

Bibliography:

B.   NCAB 13, 76; DAB 11, 557–58; NYT 20 Dec 1906, 3; Frank M. Briston, *The Life of Chaplain McCabe* (New York, 1908).

McCONNELL, Francis John (18 August 1871, Trinway, OH—18 August 1953, Lucasville, OH). *Education*: B.A., Ohio Wesleyan Univ., 1894; S.T.B. and Ph.D., Boston Univ., 1897, 1899. *Career:* minister West Chelmsford, MA, 1894–97; minister, Newton Upper Falls, MA, 1897–99; minister, Ipswich, MA, 1899–1902; minister, Cambridge, MA, 1902–03; minister Brooklyn, NY, 1903–09; president, DePauw Univ., 1909–12; bishop, Methodist Episcopal Church, 1912–44; active retirement, 1944–53.

Beginning as a student with a strong philosophical turn of mind, McConnell developed ideas into practical courses of action for the church which he represented as pastor and bishop. For a time he was thought of as possible successor to *Borden P. Bowne, his professor in graduate studies, but opportunities in ecclesiastical administration opened the way for wider implementation of their shared religious orientation. In a basically liberal framework, he thought of God as transcendent, self-revealing, and redemptive; but more importantly he asserted through faith that God was immanent in nature and human society. McConnell concentrated on trying to discern and foster divine purposes in concrete events, more so than his mentor Bowne ever did. But he echoed the personalist emphasis by saying that a well thought out system of personal values was necessary for any social program to work. The individual stood at the center of every social system, and McConnell the thinker sought to utilize theistic humanism as a guideline for social action. He fully appreciated God's limitations in the light of human failings, but he still tried to mitigate such evil by aligning practical programs with his conception of divine will. As he gradually came to see the social implications of a personalist orientation, he translated thought into action. In addition, he had the ability to interpret in plain language the relation between religion and social processes. Many audiences in a confused age appreciated his simple, direct attempts to explain the relevance of Christian witness in industrialized America.

Over the course of several decades McConnell acquired national prominence as an outspoken proponent of social reforms. His opinions were not popular with everyone, often conflicting with conservative Methodists or those who thought religion should stay out of secular affairs, but the bishop's activities are examples of practical steps many found useful after Social Gospel enthusiasm had passed its zenith. For instance he spearheaded an interdenominational investigation of the 1919 steel strike at Pittsburgh, helping eventually to secure improvements for workers. As president of the American Association for Social Security, he labored for years to promote the cause of old age pensions and employee disability benefits. Labeled a radical socialist, he doggedly maintained that a Christian social order should provide enough material goods for everyone, sufficient leisure time for personal development, and terminate industrial abuses such as the twelve-hour workday. Amid those practical measures the bishop emphasized democratic processes for dealing with public issues. He was a champion of civil liberties, including free speech and tolerance among all classes, races, nations, and churches. Democracy in social institutions blended with freedom in church life to provide a strong platform for concrete religious influence in public affairs. Through him the corporate body of Christian believers saw ways of applying faith to spheres where personal values led to social service.

Bibliography:

A.   *The Diviner Immanence* (New York, 1906); *Christian Focus* (Cincinnati, 1911); *Living Together: Studies in the Ministry of Reconciliation* (New York, 1923); *The Christlike God* (New York, 1927); *Human Needs and World Christianity* (New York, 1929); *Christian Materialism* (New York, 1936).

B.   NCAB 15, 215; NYT 19 Aug 1953, 29; Harris F. Rall (ed.), *Religion in Public Affairs* (New York, 1937).

McCOSH, James (1 April 1811, Ayrshire, Scotland—16 November 1894, Princeton, NJ). *Education:* studied at Glasgow Univ., 1824–29; M.A., Edinburgh Univ., 1834. *Career:* minister in the Established Church of Scotland, Arbroath, 1834–39, and Brechin, 1839–43; minister in the Free Church of Scotland, Brechin, 1843–52; professor of Logic and Metaphysics, Queen's Coll., Belfast, 1852–68; president, Coll. of New Jersey, 1868–88; president emeritus, 1888–94.

Long periods of training in Scotland's major universities and in the parish ministry gave McCosh ample time to formulate his metaphysical reflections. After 1852 he worked out the basic tenets of an intuitional philosophy which he defended against all systems precluding belief in the supernatural. He maintained that there are certain fundamental principles in the human mind which are sufficient guides to truth, in both cognition and judgment. Such a view was based on, but not derived from, generalizations about individual experience, and it guaranteed the objective authority of the mind's basic structure. Man's essential faculties could not be known directly; it was up to what McCosh called intuition to discern what could not be reduced to lower, materialistic terms. Such an epistemology provided a reliable basis for common truths regarding mind and body, cause and effect, space and time, to name a few. As intuition was confirmed on elementary levels of experience, it allowed the mind to rise with similar assurance to universal, necessary principles regarding the divine origin and government of the world. McCosh thus propounded a view of man and nature in which ideas about transcendent or supernatural categories had the attribute of positive cognition. On that philosophical basis, he could then combat irreligion as inconsistent with both empirical and providential evidence.

Fame as a philosophical defender of revealed religion increased in 1866 when McCosh lectured and preached his way through a tour of this country. Two years later he was invited back to continue his role as educator in a Presbyterian institution by assuming the presidency of Princeton. The college was in critical postwar straits, but through McCosh's administrative ability it soon began steady improvement. In the course of two decades the faculty was doubled and the student body tripled. New buildings were added together with curricular expansion including graduate studies in new schools of art, philosophy, and science. McCosh also contributed significantly to the development of American thought in his positive remarks concerning evolution. As one whose philosophy was confirmed by experience, he always said that the results of scientific investigation were to be welcomed. New ideas emerging from biology were not incompatible with his system nor with biblical faith. In 1870 he stood almost alone in arguing that evolution did not directly or by implication deny the reality of God. He distinguished between main features of the biblical account of creation and its literary form; by so doing he could hold that developmental theories magnified the wonder of God's creation. A beneficent design pervaded the sweeping millennia of evolution, and providence was constantly at work within the process of natural selection. In a time when skepticism or rigid confessionalism was producing bitter intellectual factions, this individual's ideas offered stability and realism as an alternative.

Bibliography:

    A. *The Method of the Divine Government, Physical and Moral* (Edinburgh, 1850); *The Intuitions of the Mind, Inductively Investigated* (London, 1860); *The Supernatural in Relation to the Natural* (Cambridge, 1862); *Christianity and Positivism* (New York, 1871); *Realistic Philosophy*, 2 vols. (New York, 1887); *First and Fundamental Truths* (New York, 1889).

    B. SH 7, 108–109; NCAB 5, 468; DAB 11, 615–17; NYT 17 Nov 1894, 5; William M. Sloane (ed.), *The Life of James McCosh: A Record Chiefly Autobiographical* (New York, 1896); J. David Hoeveler, *James McCosh and the Scottish Intellectual Tradition: From Glasgow to Princeton* (Princeton, 1981).

McGARVEY, John William (1 March 1829, Hopkinsville, KY—6 October 1911, Lexington, KY). *Education*: B.A., Bethany Coll., 1850. *Career*: school-teacher, Fayette, MO, 1850–53; minister, Dover, MO, 1853–62; minister, Main Street Christian Church, Lexington, KY, 1862–67; professor of Sacred History, Coll. of the Bible, 1865–73, 1875–95; editor, *Apostolic Times*, 1869–75; minister, Broadway Christian Church, Lexington, KY, 1871–82; editorial staff, *Christian Standard*, 1893–1911; president, Coll. of the Bible, 1895–1911.

College training did not enable McGarvey to begin preaching immediately after graduation, so he continued to study his Greek New Testament while conducting a boys school. His classroom experience directed by *Alexander Campbell at Bethany had been helpful, but it took several years for him to develop into a speaker of great forensic ability. While in Missouri he divided his time among several churches, considering the ministry to be more evangelical than pastoral. He was energetic in spreading his conception of Christian truth, and his missionary zeal inclined toward theological controversy. McGarvey savored a good stiff debate with a well-informed opponent; one topic of dispute among denominations was the proper mode of baptism, a question for which he thought the only acceptable answer was total immersion. When the Civil War broke out, he criticized secessionists but, more importantly, denounced all Christians who bore arms to end disunion. That unpopular view had little influence on the general populace, other than lowering his reputation, because such opinions were interpreted as either cowardice or treason. McGarvey's judicious transfer to neutralist Kentucky was instrumental in making it the center of Disciples activity in the half century after Campbell's death. He became a leading denominational spokesman there, utilizing pulpit, classroom, and the press. Church work and college life developed under his guidance to embody thoroughly conservative principles. His attitude regarding exclusively Bible-based doctrines and practices served as a strong brake to all modern methods in the brotherhood of Christians.

There were many levels on which McGarvey reacted to modern change. He saw them as cohering within a systematic loyalty to apostolic principles, but in retrospect some issues were more important than others. He was opposed, for example, to instrumental music in churches. No organs, melodeons, or pianos were mentioned in the Bible, and he concluded that their use was therefore prohibited for all time. Through the years there was almost universal acceptance of organs among Disciples, but he refused to compromise, preferring at length (1902) to terminate his eldership rather than withdraw stated convictions. The more basic theme eliciting conservative response had to do with biblical criticism. McGarvey considered it an apologetic duty to discuss the genuineness of New Testament texts, authenticity of authors, or credibility of canonical writings as inspired sources for belief. He welcomed textual analysis but rejected historical criticism because it produced negative, irreligious consequences. Any questioning of the historicity or inerrancy of the Bible was an impeachment on the Christian religion in his eyes. Basing his defense on accepted authorship and literal interpretation, he attacked higher criticism for decades. He contributed widely read essays to the *Christian Standard* in an attempt to reach laymen before specialists could influence them. Too often in those articles he ridiculed personalities as well as the ideas of biblical scholars. Such behavior created enemies and division in his own denomination, but to the end he struggled for his conception of truth rather than popular acceptance of his tactics.

Bibliography:

A.   *A Commentary on the Acts of the Apostles* (Cincinnati, 1863); *Lands of the Bible* (Philadelphia, 1881); *Evidences of Christianity*, 2 vols. (Cincinnati, 1886–91); *Jesus and Jonah* (Cincinnati, 1896); *The Authorship of the Book of Deuteronomy* (Cincinnati, 1902); *Short Essays on Biblical Criticism* (Cincinnati, 1910).

B.   SH 7, 113–14; NCAB 4, 517; DAB 12, 46–47; William C. Morro, *Brother McGarvey* (St. Louis, MO, 1940).

McGIFFERT, Arthur Cushman (4 March 1861, Sauquoit, NY—25 February 1933, Dobbs Ferry, NY). *Education*: B.A., Western Reserve Univ., 1882; B.D., Union Sem. (NY), 1885; studied at Berlin, 1885–86; Ph.D., Marburg, 1888. *Career*: professor at various ranks, Lane Sem., Cincinnati, OH, 1888–93; professor of Church History, Union Sem. (NY), 1893–1927; president, Union Sem., 1917–26; professor emeritus, 1927–33.

The rise of liberal theology in post-Civil War America affected religious thinkers in related disciplines including church history. McGiffert embodied a striking combination of careful scholarship and liberal interpretations in his professional responsibilities, which spanned more than thirty-five years of this period. While studying in Germany he became closely associated with Adolf Harnack who further stimulated interests begun under *Philip Schaff, his seminary professor and academic patron. After some valuable work in translating early church documents, McGiffert published in 1897 a study of apostolic Christianity which caused charges of heresy to be made against him. Some members of the New York Presbytery attempted to show that his volume impugned the authority of Scripture, implied that Christ was mistaken in some of his views, suggested that Christ did not institute the Last Supper, and denied that early Christians held substitutionary theories of the atonement. For his part, McGiffert defended his closely reasoned conclusions as the best ones which evidence could support, but the orthodox branch insisted that history submit to accepted denominational formulations. After prolonged litigation he withdrew from Presbyterianism and became a Congregationalist in 1900. He retained his eminent post at Union, becoming more celebrated and sought after as a result of the whole affair. The liberal direction in which he had been tending was confirmed by these experiences, and he produced eight more books together with forty articles to comprise the most impressive body of modernist religious scholarship in his generation.

While arguing against orthodox-minded contenders, McGiffert maintained that historical investigation should not be subordinated to any set of presuppositions, but his own narratives actually contained a definite theological perspective. One basic hypothesis found in most of his works was that historical change makes religious teachings relative to differing circumstances. Late in life he came to the point of saying there was no continuing essence or variation on common themes in Christian history at all. No creed or doctrinal formulation remains in force very long because changed conditions bring about new questions which men should be free to answer as they are led. He also gave historical backing to the widespread view that religion consists primarily of experiences which deal meaningfully with contemporary problems. Blended with that pragmatic approach to spiritual affirmation were definitions of Jesus as an exemplar of human virtue and thoughts of salvation as a social rather than a personal process. The writing and teaching record compiled by McGiffert before 1916 made his selection as president of Union a popular one. One important action taken in that capacity was to establish closer ties with Columbia University, securing a relationship that provided wider opportunities for succeeding generations of ministerial students. Such efforts in the name of theological education as well as publications acclaimed on two continents sustained McGiffert's reputation as one of the foremost religious luminaries in the first third of this century.

Bibliography:

A. *A History of Christianity in the Apostolic Age* (New York, 1897); *The Problem of Christian Creeds as Affected by Modern Thought* (Buffalo, 1901); *Martin Luther* (New York, 1911); *Protestant Thought before Kant* (London, 1911; New York, 1962); *The Rise of Modern Religious Ideas* (New York, 1915); *A History of Christian Thought*, 2 vols. (New York, 1932).

B. SH 7, 114; NCAB 24, 120; DAB 21, 527–29; NYT 26 Feb 1933, 26.

McGIVNEY, Michael Joseph (12 August 1852, Waterbury, CT—14 August 1890, Thomaston, CT). *Education*: graduated from Niagara Univ., 1873; graduated from St. Mary's Sem., 1876. *Career*: curate, St. Mary's Church, New Haven, CT, 1878–84; pastor, St. Thomas Church, Thomaston, CT, 1884–90.

As the eldest of thirteen children McGivney earned wages for the family in a spoon factory soon after completing public school. He gradually embraced a religious vocation, and his parents were able to eke out payments for a preparatory school (St. Hyacinth) in Canada, college, and theological seminary. Ordination at Baltimore in 1877 came at the hands of its new archbishop, *James Gibbons. Called to assist work in his native state, the energetic new priest threw himself into parish activities. McGivney devoted a great deal of time to sodalities and proved most zealous on the liquor question, organizing a total abstinence society in the church. He was not given to grim sobriety alone, however, and he eagerly promoted fraternal association among church members alongside other interests. This idea grew into plans to bring Catholic laymen together into a mutually supporting society where the benefits of interdependence and common faith would edify all members. So in January of 1882 the young priest and nine parishioners established an association called the Knights of Columbus. Two months later the state of Connecticut recognized the group as a legal corporation and officially sanctioned its charter based on principles of charity, unity, fraternity, and patriotism.

Another aspect of the early Knights, a consequence of McGivney's strong convictions, is that no member could have direct connections with the manufacture or sale of liquor. With the bishop's approval this fraternal organization soon spread throughout the diocese. Extension beyond Connecticut occurred much more slowly, but when the papal delegate approved, growth proceeded rapidly. McGivney remained the inspiring force behind the organization for the rest of his short life. He directed affairs from the crucial positions of corresponding secretary and member of the supreme council. He also served as national chaplain, a post taken by two of his brothers in succession. Currently the Knights of Columbus number approximately two million members. The institution contributes generous sums to charity, hospitals, orphanages, war relief, social welfare, and educational activities. Its myriad projects are a distinctly American expression of Catholic faith in action. Each year its national officers make a pilgrimage to the gravesite of the dynamic curate who gave it impetus more than a century ago.

Bibliography:

B.   DAB 12, 52–53; NCE 9, 18; Maurice F. Egan and John B. Kennedy, *The Knights of Columbus in Peace and War* 2 vols. (New Haven, 1920).

McGLYNN, Edward (27 September 1837, New York, NY—7 January 1900, Newburgh, NY). *Education*: S.T.D., Urban Coll. of the Propaganda, Rome, 1860. *Career*: assistant pastor, St. Joseph's Church, New York, 1860–66; pastor, St. Stephen's Church, New York, 1866–87; president, Anti-Poverty Society, 1887–92; pastor, St. Mary's Church, Newburgh, NY, 1894–1900.

After receiving a doctor's degree at the age of twenty-three, McGlynn devoted himself to an apostolate of parish work instead of teaching. For two decades he served a membership totalling 25,000 persons, more than that comprising some American dioceses at the time. The plight of his poverty-stricken parishioners moved him deeply. Many of his activities consisted simply of attempts to alleviate suffering, so much so that he had little time for developing parochial schools. In 1870 he resisted what he considered educational barriers to absorption of Catholics into mainstream national culture, winning the reputation of ecclesiastical maverick that endured for the rest of his life. Relief through charity for the unemployed seemed a halfway measure to McGlynn, so he began to study economics in hope of finding ways to stanch the flow of continuing poverty. He became convinced that the ideas of Henry George promised a fundamental remedy. The burden of public revenue should be concentrated, he argued, on the communally created value of land. A single tax seemed to promise fair distribution of fiscal responsibility while it lightened the workingman's burden. As early as 1882, officials at Rome ordered the New York priest to end his outspoken support of socialistic theories, but he continued to have regular brushes with authorities on the question. In the main he was prudent enough to obey orders while never acknowledging his archbishop's right to advise him regarding the matter.

In 1886 Henry George ran for mayor of New York. McGlynn planned to campaign for him vigorously, but the new archbishop, *Michael A. Corrigan, forbade him to speak at political rallies. He appeared anyway, and Corrigan suspended him from clerical duties for two weeks. Corrigan would not tolerate even a hint of disobedience, so in January, 1887, he finally removed the priest from his church because of his continued advocacy of single tax schemes. Two days later Rome summoned him to the Vatican, demanding at the same time a full retraction of his views on the land question. A legal adviser responded in defense of the priest's position, but these materials did not reach the pope. Finally a direct order required his presence in Rome within forty days on penalty of excommunication. McGlynn refused to honor the command, pleading reasons of health and protesting innocence. In July, 1887, he was excommunicated. For five years thereafter he served as president of a social reform organization and propounded the single tax doctrine with no decrease of enthusiasm. By 1892 Roman prelates were persuaded that at least this brand of socialism was not contrary to Catholic teaching; as a result, McGlynn was reinstated to the priesthood and allowed to say mass on Christmas Day of that year. In 1893 the restored clergyman had a cordial audience with Leo XIII and remained proud of the fact that he never retracted any views on political economy. During his last years, however, Corrigan placed him in an upstate hamlet to lessen his influence on major events in the metropolitan diocese.

Bibliography:

B.   NCAB 9, 242–44; DAB 7, 53–54; NCE 9, 18–19; NYT 8 Jan 1900, 1; Sylvester L. Malone, *Edward McGlynn* (New York, 1918); Stephen Bell, *Rebel, Priest and Prophet: A Biography of Dr. Edward McGlynn* (New York, 1937).

McGREADY, James (1758?, western PA—February 1817, Henderson, KY). *Education*: studied theology with John McMillan, Canonsburg, PA, 1787–88. *Career*: minister, Orange County, NC, 1790–96; minister, Logan County, KY, 1796–1811; itinerant minister in IN, 1811–17.

As a youth who grew up in North Carolina but returned to his native Pennsylvania for Presbyterian schooling, McGready was one of the first to embody a new spirit of revivalism after the Revolution. He initiated revivals in southern states before crossing the Alleghenies and laid foundations in both areas for the movement known collectively as the Second Great Awakening. His vehement pulpit manner earned him the biblical nickname "Boagernes." Thunderous denunciations of sin either awakened penitence in his listeners, including *Barton

W. Stone who was led thereby to enter the ministry, or they aroused opposition. Reaction to his fierce invective became so strong by 1796, he moved west to "Cumberland country" an area drained by a river of that name in central Kentucky and Tennessee. There he found more indifference to religion than opposition to his style of preaching, and for the next few years he labored hard to spark revivals in his churches. Finally in 1800 a mighty rain of spiritual power began, causing earlier experiences to appear as scattered raindrops before the storm. After a four-day service held at his Red River Church in June of that year, settlers were eager for more exhortation. Within a month, another prolonged session at his Gaspar River Church attracted an audience from one hundred miles around and caused excitement that spread in a manner beyond human contriving. By these circumstances McGready inaugurated the camp meeting, a device born of the need to provide adequate means for ministering to pioneers who traveled great distances to attend open-air services. His innovation established a pattern for thousands of similar meetings which stamped frontier Christianity with distinctive features in the early national period.

Midwestern Presbyterians did not unanimously endorse the new revivals. Some clerics in the Synod of Kentucky charged that McGready and other leaders of Cumberland Presbytery departed from tradition by licensing uneducated preachers. More importantly they charged that revivalists based their message on a modified Calvinism, which contravened the denomination's classical emphasis on human depravity. These criticisms were accurate on both counts, but the pro-revival faction argued such measures were defensible in light of the results they produced. McGready had regularly insisted on a definite experience of rebirth as proof of salvation, and in that context of immediate conversion found no difficulty in calling on sinners to repent while there was still time. By 1805 the Synod suspended a number of ministers who stressed human ability; within a year the outcasts formed a separate Council and, after their appeal to General Assembly was rejected (1809), established the Cumberland Presbyterian Church in 1810. But McGready had no wish for schism. Though inclined to agree with the revivalists, he made his peace with the orthodox party and sought (1809) reinstatement in the Transylvania Presbytery. For almost a decade thereafter he established churches in southern Indiana, fostering the same gospel enthusiasm which characterized his efforts over the previous thirty years.

Bibliography:

A.   *The Posthumous Works of the Reverend and Pious M'Gready*, ed. James Smith, 2 vols. (Louisville, 1831, and Nashville, 1833).

B.   SH 7, 114; DAB 12, 56–57.

McILVAINE, Charles Pettit (18 January 1799, Burlington, NJ—13 March 1873, Florence, Italy). *Education*: graduated from Coll. of New Jersey, 1816; private theological study, 1816–17, 1819–20; studied at Princeton Sem., 1817–19. *Career*: rector, Christ Episcopal Church, Georgetown, DC, 1820–24; chaplain and professor of Ethics, West Point Acad., 1825–27; rector, Brooklyn, NY, 1827–32; bishop of Ohio, 1832–73.

Early in his ministry McIlvaine became known for broad evangelical views which he set forth in stirring sermons. While in Washington and New York he mingled with individuals close to centers of power and grew accustomed to large congregations with the social privileges they afforded. But he sacrificed all that in accepting the invitation to become Ohio's second Episcopal bishop, succeeding *Philander Chase, who resigned after a hot dispute over administrative methods. McIlvaine did not have a robust constitution, and constant travels to scattered parishes in the state taxed his energies severely. Nevertheless he endured hardships of meager resources and primitive conditions to further the church's missionary outreach. Despite possible lessons he might have learned from his predecessor's experience, McIlvaine ruled the diocese with a strong hand. An imperious manner was combined with settled opinions, and his execution of policy seldom faltered. One example of stern administration was a firm refusal to consecrate any church (Columbus, 1846) until its stone altar had been replaced by an honest table with legs. Such actions made the bishop famous as a staunch low churchman who led fights for his faction at every general convention from 1844 to 1871.

In keeping with low church liturgical views, McIlvaine was also a persuasive spokesman for evangelical theology, engaging in a number of controversies which aroused the hostility of some fellow bishops. He harbored special misgivings about the Tractarian movement and in 1840 launched a pamphlet war against theological emphases developed by coreligionists at Oxford. Subjecting their ideas to penetrating analysis, he pronounced emphatically against the direction they indicated. In heavy handed style he condemned them as unscriptural, contrary to Anglican articles of belief, and thoroughly popish in principle. His preference was for the simple message of justification by faith, a stand which viewed any stress on ecclesiology as substituting churches for Christ, priests for the gospel, bondage to superstition for the liberty of an enlightened religion. As a strong advocate of American religious freedom, his greatest fear was not the defection of some to Rome but a penetration of Roman ways into the Protestant Episcopal Church. McIlvaine was able to keep the affection of most of those within his jurisdiction and maintained lasting friendships in England as well as among like-minded clergy whom he met while traveling to restore his health. In those spheres he contributed to debates over religious thought and practice which continued on both sides of the Atlantic through most of the nineteenth century.

Bibliography:

A. *The Evidences of Christianity* (New York, 1832); *Oxford Divinity: Compared with That of the Romish and Anglican Churches* (London, 1841); *Reasons for Refusing to Consecrate a Church Having an Altar Instead of a Communion Table* (Mt. Vernon, OH, 1846); *No Priest, No Sacrifice, No Altar but Christ* (New York, 1850); *Righteousness by Faith* (Philadelphia, 1862).

B. SH 7, 114–15; NCAB 7, 2–3; DAB 12, 64–65; NYT 15 Mar 1873, 7; William

Carus (ed.), *Memorials of the Right Reverend Charles Pettit McIlvaine* (New York, 1882).

McINTYRE, James Francis Aloysius (25 June 1886, New York, NY—16 July 1979, Los Angeles, CA). *Education*: studied at City Coll. of New York and Columbia Univ.; graduated from St. Joseph's Sem., 1921. *Career*: employee, H. L. Horton and Co., 1902–15; assistant priest, St. Gabriel's Church, New York, 1921–23; assistant chancellor and then chancellor, archdiocese of New York, 1923–34 and 1934–41; auxiliary bishop of New York, 1941–45; archbishop coadjutor of New York, 1946–48; archbishop of Los Angeles, 1948–70; cardinal, 1953–70; priest, St. Basil's Church, Los Angeles, 1970–79.

Because his mother died early McIntyre was raised by a cousin and began work at the age of thirteen to care for his invalid father. By early in this century he assumed posts of increasing responsibility in a Wall Street investment firm. His prospects for becoming a partner were good, but in 1915 his father died, and this allowed him to revive thoughts of entering the Catholic priesthood, a vocation he had considered while still an altar boy. Ordained in 1921 McIntyre was soon asked to work at the chancery office because of his financial expertise. His administrative efficiency contributed to a rapid rise in authority, the pope as well as newly arrived archbishop *Francis J. Spellman recognizing his sterling managerial qualities. By 1940 he was named titular bishop of Cyrene and auxially to Spellman. Five years later he became Vicar General of the diocese and assumed additional powers together with fresh responsibilities for the see's finances, its parochial schools, expanding parishes, and charitable institutions.

In 1948 McIntyre was for the first time assigned somewhere other than his beloved New York. In moving to the west coast he inherited a diocese comprising more than 9,000 square miles and over 600,000 parishioners cared for by less than 700 priests. Within a few years he achieved an impressive array of developmental changes. He doubled the number of parishes and tripled the schools, succeeding meanwhile in having state taxes on religious institutions repealed. His vigorous secretariats and commissions revamped educational, charitable, and welfare activities while augmenting the attention paid to the growing number of Spanish-speaking inhabitants of southern California. In 1953 McIntyre became the fourth cardinal in American history and the first prelate from western states to be so elevated. In the 1960s he attended all sessions of the Second Vatican Council, arguing strongly for continued use of Latin in worship and against any changes in the Mass. He opposed moreover any further democratization of episcopal conferences. Despite such conservative views, his jurisdiction implemented mandated changes earlier than did many other dioceses in the country. After taking the unusual step of retiring from the cardinalate, he spent his last few years performing simple priestly duties at an inner-city church in the heart of his former archdiocese.

Bibliography:

    B.   NCE 18, 286–87; NYT 17 Jul 1979, D 15.

McKAY, David Oman (8 September 1873, Huntsville, UT—18 January 1970, Salt Lake City, UT). *Education*: B.A., Univ. of Utah, 1897. *Career*: member, Council of the Twelve Apostles of the Church of Jesus Christ of Latter-day Saints, 1906–70; president, 1951–70.

For two years after graduating from college McKay served as a missionary of the Mormon church in the British Isles. Evangelical work was a normal expectation among males of that institution, but in this case it disclosed a feature that would characterize priorities and labors over another seventy years. Education was an additional interest, and McKay contributed effectively to an array of Sunday School boards and churchwide educational activities between 1906 and 1934. Also in 1906 he was elected an apostle, ascending to the highest level of Mormon leadership and, at the age of thirty-three, becoming the youngest individual to do so. In 1934 he began to serve as second counselor to the president of the church, renewing that function again in 1945 when another president assumed office. Part of his responsibilities included management of the church's commercial properties, large holdings that involved railroads, newspapers, hotels, banks, insurance companies, and real estate. These assets also facilitated his civic activities that touched on the Red Cross, colleges, hospitals, and welfare programs that especially benefited children.

In 1950 McKay was made senior apostle, and the following year the annual conference sustained him as the church's ninth president. He became known as the "missionary president" because of his great influence in guiding Mormonism into successful global outreach. As early as 1920 he toured mission stations around the world, traveling over 62,000 miles in thirteen months. Shortly thereafter (1922–24) he was president of all European missions. Expanding missionary efforts was one of his top priorities, and in the years of his presidency the number of missionaries increased from 2000 to 12,000. Fruits of such efforts soon demanded new buildings and support facilities, and McKay became the most traveled of presidents as he visited new communities and dedicated chapels, tabernacles, and temples. Another measure of his importance is that enrollment in churches around the world grew under his leadership to almost three million members. He was a popular president who led by example, emphasizing the importance of personal witness over doctrinal niceties. Looking back on many decades of faithful service, he said he thought his greatest achievement was in making the church a truly worldwide organization.

Bibliography:

A. *Ancient Apostles, Written for the Deseret Sunday School Union* (Salt Lake City, 1918); *Gospel Ideals: Selections from the Discourses of David O. McKay* (Salt Lake City, 1953); *Cherished Experiences: From the Writings of David O. McKay* (Salt Lake City, 1955); *Treasures of Life* (Salt Lake City, 1962); *True to the Faith: From the Sermons of David O. McKay* (Salt Lake City, 1966); *Man May Know for Himself: Teachings of President David O. McKay* (Salt Lake City, 1967).

B. NCAB 56, 479–81; DAB supp. 8, 408–09; NYT 19 Jan 1970, 1; Llewelyn R.

McKay, *Home Memories of President David O. McKay* (Salt Lake City, 1956); Jeanette McKay Morrell, *Highlights in the Life of President David O. McKay* (Salt Lake City, 1966); Francis M. Gibbons, *David O. McKay: Apostle to the World, Prophet of God* (Salt Lake City, 1986).

McKENDREE, William (6 July 1757, King William County, VA—5 March 1835, near Gallatin, TN). *Career*: itinerant minister in VA, 1788–96; presiding elder, VA and MD, 1796–99; presiding elder, Western Conference, 1800–08; bishop, American Methodist Church, 1808–35.

Little is known of McKendree's early years because he was reluctant to speak about them, even the fact that he served as adjutant in the Continental Army. Converted at the age of thirty, he began to preach shortly thereafter, educating himself on horseback through hours of prayer and Bible reading. His first presiding elder was *James O'Kelly, who won him temporarily to the view that bishop *Francis Asbury's ambition would ruin the church. McKendree supported O'Kelly in his attempts to reform episcopal government until 1792, but in that year he became reconciled to Asbury and cooperated with the Methodist patriarch on friendly terms until his death, in 1816. After that early interlude, he became a staunch defender of episcopal authority, regarding it to be the backbone of an efficient itinerancy system. As a circuit rider he was never idle or silent in proclaiming the riches of redemption as he experienced them. He won respect in communities where he preached, while fellow clergymen grew confident in his abilities as they saw them displayed. In 1800 he began to supervise missionary activities in the huge Western Conference which covered Kentucky and Tennessee together with all settlements west of the Ohio and along the Natchez Trace. As pioneers moved into these valley basins, he and a handful of preachers kept pace with population growth, loyal to Wesley's doctrine and discipline as the best means of coping with unprecedented opportunity for evangelical awakening.

In less than eight years McKendree was elected bishop at the General Conference held in Baltimore, becoming the first native American to receive that office. His field of labor spread from Maine to Missouri, and he traveled constantly to preside over conferences which coordinated church extension on a national scale. Content to endure hardship, he proved indefatigable during years that marked tremendous growth for Methodists. To enhance good will among the clergy he began consulting with local presiding elders before assigning preachers to their annual posts. This "cabinet" procedure remained long in force and helped lessen jealousy over the bishops' arbitrary powers. At the General Conference of 1812 he delivered the first episcopal address which evaluated his work and general church conditions, instituting by that action another device for mutual accountability in managerial relations. Always dedicated to evangelical outreach, he helped organize the Missionary Society in 1819; the following year he began recruiting agents for Indian missions, particularly among the Five Civilized Nations in southern states and the Wyandots in Ohio. After 1820 his health began to decline, but he continued to function as senior bishop for another decade. In his simple, forceful way he encouraged multitudes to perpetuate the old methods which were rapidly transforming Methodists into the largest American denomination.

Bibliography:

B.   AAP 7, 160–72; NCAB 10, 224; DAB 12, 85–86; Robert Paine, *Life and Times of William McKendree*, 2 vols. (Nashville, 1869, 1880); Elijah E. Hoss, *William McKendree: A Biographical Study* (Nashville, 1914).

McPHERSON, Aimee Semple (19 October 1890, near Ingersoll, Canada—27 September 1944, Oakland, CA). *Career:* co-worker in revivals, 1908–10; missionary to China, 1910–11; itinerant revivalist, 1916–23; minister, Angelus Temple, Los Angeles, 1923–44.

Aimee Elizabeth Kennedy exchanged her childhood Salvation Army orientation for Pentecostal emphases at a revival led by Robert J. Semple whom she married within a year (1908). Mrs. Semple was accepted as a regular preacher of the Full Gospel Assembly in 1909, and the couple soon left for missionary service in China. Mr. Semple died within months of their arrival; the wife and new mother returned to this country with determination to continue evangelical work. Two unhappy marriages followed (Harold S. McPherson, 1912–21, and David L. Hutton, 1931–35), but they did not prevent her from conducting tent revivals in Canada, up and down the eastern seaboard, and across the nation. By 1923 Mrs. McPherson had made nine transcontinental tours, preaching a gospel of pietism and faith healing in major cities. Also by that year the central edifice of the International Church of the Foursquare Gospel (incorporated 1927) was completed, and "Sister Aimee" began attracting a following which eventuated into a new denomination. She was the most widely known woman evangelist of her day, with speaking tours, sermons published in *Bridal Call*, and early use of radio contributing to that effect. But she also possessed genuine managerial ability, founding a Bible College (Lighthouse, 1926), welfare agencies, and a chain of 400 churches in her lifetime. Between 1926 and 1936 the evangelist was involved in scandal and law suits over control of the church, but those incidents did not alienate the millions who heard and the thousands who subscribed to her message.

Some of Mrs. McPherson's success was probably due to her flair for the dramatic which led to flamboyant dress and theatrical worship services. But a more important factor was her preaching that stressed love and forgiveness in Christ together with a strong anticipation of speedy return. Negative doctrines of sin and punishment were submerged in preference for simple, cheerful assurances that personal salvation was possible to those who wished it so. Her gospel of love and individualistic fulfillment was called "Foursquare" because it was based on a typology of four roles in Jesus' ministry: (1) Saviour of the world, (2) Baptizer of the Holy Spirit, (3) Healer of human infirmities, and (4) the returning King of kings. Emphasis on personal salvation, joined with conservative views on theological and social innovations, appealed to many, and the varied programs of Angelus Temple flourished despite controversial headlines. Sister Aimee's sincere efforts to meet her people's needs were inspirational to them, and she continued after a nervous breakdown in 1930 to strengthen churches in the corporation through periodic visitations. She died on such a journey from an overdose of barbiturates that was ruled to be accidental, leaving administration of the organization to her son.

Bibliography:

A. *This is That: Personal Experiences, Sermons and Writings* (Los Angeles, 1919; rev. ed. 1923); *Divine Healing Sermons* (Los Angeles, 1921); *In Service of the King: The Story of My Life* (New York, 1927); *The Holy Spirit* (Los Angeles, 1931); *Give Me My Own God* (Los Angeles, 1936).

B. NCAB 35, 229; DAB 23, 497–99; NCE 9, 43–44; NAW 2, 477–80; NYT 28 Sep 1944, 19; Nancy B. Mavity, *Sister Aimee* (Garden City, 1931); Lately Thomas, *Storming Heaven* (New York, 1970); Robert Bahr, *Least of All the Saints: The Story of Aimee Semple McPherson* (Englewood Cliffs, NJ, 1979).

McQUAID, Bernard John (15 December 1823, New York, NY—18 January 1909, Rochester, NY). *Education*: studied at Chambly Coll., Montreal, Canada, 1839–43; studied at St. Joseph's Sem., Fordham, NY, 1843–48. *Career*: rector, St. Vincent's Church, Madison, NJ, 1848–53; rector, St. Patrick's Cathedral, Newark, NJ, 1853–68; president, Seton Hall Coll., 1857 and 1859–68; bishop of Rochester, NY, 1868–1909.

After losing both parents by the age of ten, McQuaid was led by Sisters of Charity in their orphanage to train for the priesthood. He went on to become a model of efficient ecclesiastical administration at a time when native-born clergymen began to outweigh imported talent in American Catholicism. From his early days as missionary, preacher to urban congregations, and college president, he gave all his energy to promote the religious welfare of his people. Probably no other area indicates this zeal for proper spiritual development among parishioners more than work in educational institutions. In New Jersey he was instrumental in establishing (1859) a mother house for the Sisters of Charity, enabling them to teach in the diocese. Leaving his post at Seton Hall to serve as first bishop of Rochester, he organized the Sisters of St. Joseph there for educational purposes. Parochial schools were, to him, the foundation of adequate training in religious principles, so much so that McQuaid often refused absolution to parents who insisted on sending their children to public schools. He also established sixty-nine parishes within his jurisdiction, in addition to founding orphanages, teacher training programs, and a Young Men's Catholic Institute. By 1893 St. Bernard's Seminary crowned all his efforts to build a self-sufficient complex of mutually supporting institutions for clergy and laymen alike. Diocesan projects flourished because their ordinary fostered them with a selfless devotion matched only by his strong determination to succeed once objectives were clearly defined.

As vicar-general (1866–68) for ailing bishop *James R. Bayley, McQuaid quickly made a name for himself as a strict disciplinarian. He was a terror to delinquent priests who threatened disruption of normal parish life through bad personal example or administrative ineptitude. Controversies in the newly formed see at Rochester confirmed him in authoritarian habits, and he sided often with *Michael A. Corrigan against liberal forces he considered ruinous to sound Catholic development. He opposed, for instance, the creation of Catholic University because he feared it would encourage unduly liberal tendencies. Like many other American prelates, he spoke against proclaiming the dogma of papal infallibility in 1870 but accepted the decree after promulgation. As a conservative adhering closely to the letter of canon law, he was strongly opposed to secret societies at a time when many other bishops adopted more lenient policies. All his suspicion and hostility against liberals such as *John Ireland came boiling to the surface in 1894; during a close election for a place on the New York Board of Regents (which he lost) he bitterly denounced Ireland in outbursts that caused Rome to admonish him for displaying such intemperate judgment in public. McQuaid reached a semblance of peace with Ireland in 1905, but neither resistance nor pleas for moderation could lessen his rigid control over matters he thought central to conservative progress in his church.

Bibliography:

B. NCAB 12, 141–42; DAB 12, 163–64; NCE 9, 44–45; NYT 19 Jan 1909, 9; Frederick J. Zwierlein, *The Life and Letters of Bishop McQuaid*, 3 vols. (Rome and Louvain, 1925–27) and *Letters of Archbishop Corrigan to Bishop McQuaid and Allied Documents* (Rochester, NY, 1946); Norlene M. Kunkel, *Bishop Bernard J. McQuaid and Catholic Education* (New York, 1988).

MACHEN, John Gresham (28 July 1881, Baltimore, MD—1 January 1937, Bismarck, ND). *Education*: B.A., Johns Hopkins Univ., 1901; graduate study, Johns Hopkins Univ., 1901–02; B.D., Princeton Sem., 1905; studied at Marburg and Göttingen, 1905–06. *Career*: professor, at various ranks, of New Testament, Princeton Sem., 1906–29; secretary, YMCA in France, 1918–19; professor of New Testament, Westminster Sem., 1929–37.

Spokesmen for conservative Christian views abounded at the turn of the twentieth century, but none surpassed Machen for clarity of expression or tenacity of purpose. By 1920 he had become disturbed over indications that the Presbyterian church was drifting away from its gospel moorings, denying or avoiding truths it had held for so many years. In an atmosphere where he perceived indifference to historic creeds, Machen contributed polemical books and articles in an effort to buttress the faith as he knew it. He was particularly reluctant to abandon fundamental affirmations like the virgin birth, the verbal inspiration of scriptural authors which made the Bible free from error, the vicarious atonement of Christ, and the physical resurrection of the body. These doctrines were facts in his view, not theories to be evaluated or held with mental reservations. He considered such liberal permissiveness on the nature of belief to constitute a new religion altogether, distinct from the foundations and content of Christianity. Anyone who subscribed to beliefs differing from his description of orthodoxy should not be allowed to remain members of churches that were loyal to their heritage.

By 1924 Machen was convinced that Presbyterianism was drifting farther away from the true faith, and he found less determination in the General Assembly to prevent it. Still he did not stop expressing his version of acceptable theology, nor did he cease to represent a minority group whose prospects for affecting policy in the denomination were dim. When Princeton Seminary reorganized its authority structure in 1929, indicating a theological preference as well, he resigned his post and provided part of the scholarly core for Westminster Theological Seminary that was subsequently built in Philadelphia. He became concerned over doctrinal laxity among the church's foreign missionaries, criticizing *Robert E. Speer for allowing unsound ministers to go forth with an imperfect gospel message. As a result of that controversy he set up the Independent Board for Foreign Missions. The General Assembly proscribed that action in 1934; when Machen continued to support it, he was judged guilty a year later of violating ordination vows, and his standing in the denomination was revoked. After that break he acted as a primary agent in founding the Presbyterian Church of America in 1936. This group itself suffered from schism over millennial beliefs, and the majority group was renamed the Orthodox Presbyterian Church in 1939. Machen remained true to his convictions until the end, writing for the new church's organ, *The Presbyterian Guardian* (begun 1935), and accepting invitations at whatever personal hardship to explain his church's doctrinal stand.

Bibliography:

A. *The Origin of Paul's Religion* (New York, 1921); *Christianity and Liberalism* (New York, 1923); *What is Faith?* (New York, 1925); *The Virgin Birth of Christ* (New York, 1930); *The Christian Faith in the Modern World* (New York, 1936); *The Christian View of Man* (New York, 1937).

B. NYT 2 Jan 1937, 11; Ned B. Stonehouse, *J. Gresham Machen: A Biographical Memoir* (Grand Rapids, MI, 1954); Henry W. Coray, *J. Gresham Machen: A Silhouette* (Grand Rapids, MI, 1981).

MACINTOSH, Douglas Clyde (18 February 1877, Breadalbane, Canada— 6 July 1948, Hamden, CT). *Education*: B.A., McMaster Univ., 1903; Ph.D., Univ. of Chicago, 1909. *Career*: instructor in philosophy, McMaster Univ., 1903–04; professor of Biblical and Systematic Theology, Brandon Coll. (Manitoba), 1907–09; professor, at various ranks, of Theology and

Philosophy of Religion, Yale Div. Sch., 1909–42; active retirement, 1942–48.

After two years as a Baptist minister in his native province of Ontario, Macintosh discovered while at college that philosophical inquiry was more to his liking. But he never lost interest in the apologetic aspects of Christian faith as he became one of the most important modernist theologians in twentieth-century American Protestantism. His intellectual pilgrimage ranged from traditionalism through empiricism to what he eventually called critical monism, a metaphysical system which preserved the essence of inherited beliefs made harmonious with modern scientific knowledge. Through almost four decades of teaching and in a dozen books, Macintosh tried to restate the Christian message in terms amenable to his own age, systematizing an ''untraditional orthodoxy'' to confirm its fundamental reasonableness. He began with religious experience as the epistemological basis for constructing an empirical theology. By this means he hoped to support belief while counteracting doubts endemic to philosophical skepticism and historical uncertainty. He tried to show how it was possible to derive reliable theories about God from religious experience in the same way other sciences developed hypotheses from sensory data. In addition to teaching, he served in Europe as chaplain in the Canadian Army (7 months, 1916) and as a YMCA worker with American forces (1918). As a result he became an outspoken pacifist, expressing views which caused the U.S. Supreme Court to deny (1931) him citizenship in a celebrated legal dispute. These activities indicate some of the practical side of one known primarily for speculative thought.

An adequate theology must, according to Macintosh, be established on empirically verified knowledge; unless ideas are grounded in rational, observable evidence, they will not be taken seriously in the modern scientific world. But there is also a pragmatic element in religious thought where men postulate the reality of God, freedom, and immortality. These presuppositions, practical necessities which justify moral intuitions of the self, are not derived from, but must be consistent with, scientific data. On a third level Macintosh appealed to historical evidence about the life and work of Jesus for further knowledge of divine revelation. Finally, on the highest and most comprehensive level, he tried to synthesize all empirical sciences including theology into one metaphysical system. Beliefs at this point were not as demonstrable as those based directly on observed reality or functional experience, but they were nonetheless congruent parts of a reasonable faith. Macintosh was content to call such tenets permissible surmises, rational probabilities which rounded out the body of ideas based on sound epistemological foundations. The result of applying this religious point of view to life was moral optimism. It held that human efforts stemming from good will could help change the world. This representational system of observations and postulates filled the mind with ideas while it also encouraged action to improve conditions among men. Such a combination of thought and deed was useful to many who sought to put the old faith in new terms.

Bibliography:

A.   *Theology as an Empirical Science* (New York, 1919); *The Reasonableness of Christianity* (New York, 1925); *The Pilgrimage of Faith in the World of Modern Thought* (Calcutta, 1931); *Social Religion* (New York, 1939); *The Problem of Religious Knowledge* (New York, 1940); *Personal Religion* (New York, 1942).

B.   DAB 24, 524–26; NCE 9, 35; NYT 7 July 1948, 46; Preston Warren, *Out of the Wilderness: Douglas Clyde Macintosh's Journeys through the Grounds and Claims of Modern Thought* (New York, 1989).

MACKAY, John Alexander (17 May 1889, Inverness, Scotland—9 June 1983, Hightstown, NJ). *Education*: M.A., Univ. of Aberdeen, 1912; B.D., Princeton Sem., 1915; studied at Univ. of Madrid, 1915–16; studied at Univ. of Bonn, 1930. *Career*: founder and principal, Anglo-Peruvian Coll., Lima, Peru, 1916–25; administrator, South American Federation of YMCAs, 1926–32; secretary, Board of Foreign Missions, Presbyterian Church in the U.S.A., 1932–36; president and professor of Ecumenics, Princeton Sem., 1936–59; adjunct professor of Hispanic Thought, American Univ., 1961–64; active retirement, 1964–83.

After ordination into the Presbyterian ministry at his native Inverness in 1916, Mackay left wartorn Europe to serve in South America as an educational missionary for the Free Church of Scotland. He devoted two decades to work there: first in establishing a secondary school in Peru, then in YMCA work in Uruguay and Mexico, and finally holding special responsibility for Presbyterian missions in Latin America. Those experiences stood him in good stead when in 1936 he took on the more explicitly educational task of directing one of America's most important theological seminaries. From that position he succeeded in smoothing over tensions on campus as well as in the denomination as a whole resulting from squabbles over fundamentalism in the 1920s. Mackay was determined to restore theology and philosophy to their rightful place at the center of ministerial training. His efforts in this area slowly improved the scholarly reputation of the faculty and made the seminary's program more academically sound. In 1940 he introduced a doctoral program, and in 1944 founded *Theology Today*, a journal that quickly became a leading forum of contemporary religious thought. His greatest contribution was perhaps in making it possible for the seminary to grow beyond parochial identity and become an interdenominational center of learning for students from many countries.

Ecumenical vision is what sustained Mackay through the years of his presidency. He served on the provisional committee of the World Council of Churches from 1946 to 1948 and sat on the central steering committee for six years after its official organization in Amsterdam. Also in 1948 he began an eleven-year term as chair of the International Missionary Council. Like many of his colleagues in the first half of the twentieth century, Mackay was motivated by ideals of interchurch harmony and cooperation in both education and evangelism. He traveled extensively in Latin America and Southeast Asia for these causes and did much to recommend their widespread adoption.

Bibliography:

A. *The Other Spanish Christ: A Study in the Spiritual History of Spain and South America* (London, 1932); *A Preface to Christian Theology* (New York, 1941); *Christianity on the Frontier* (London, 1950); *Ecumenics: The Science of the Church Universal* (Englewood Cliffs, NJ, 1964); *His Life and Our Life* (Philadelphia, 1964); *Christian Reality and Appearance* (Richmond, VA, 1969).

B.   NYT 10 Jun 1983, D 19.

MAHAN, Asa (9 November 1799, Vernon, NY—4 April 1889, Eastbourne, England). *Education*: graduated from Hamilton Coll., 1824; graduated from Andover Sem., 1827. *Career*: minister, Pittsford, NY (1829–31), Cincinnati, OH (1831–35), Jackson, MI (1855–57), and Adrian, MI (1857–60); president, Oberlin Coll., 1835–50; professor and then president, Adrian Coll., 1860–71; editor, *The Divine Life*, 1871–89.

While still quite young Mahan delighted in religious discussions and matters related to salvation. He readily accepted orthodox Calvinism whose soteriology denied human will any effective role, but a spiritual crisis at the age of seventeen reversed his convictions. Thereafter he advocated a free-will doctrine where individuals ultimately determined their own destiny. He taught school during winter months and participated quite actively in Second Great Awakening revivals from 1824 to 1832. In 1829 he was ordained in the Congregational church and ministered to three churches of that denomination, the fourth pastorate in Cincinnati being Presbyterian. While in that city he also served as a trustee of Lane Seminary and criticized the institution when it forbade students to discuss the question of slavery. In 1835 he became the first president of Oberlin College, founded two years previously. His reputation regarding slavery was instrumental, alongside the influence of *Theodore D. Weld, in the transfer of many Lane students to Oberlin and the establishment of a School of Theology at the fledgling academy.

As the years passed Mahan threw himself into college work and helped give the school some of the distinctive characteristics for which it became justly famous. Emphasizing both free will and the possibilities of human perfection, he made Oberlin a major source of nineteenth century revival preachers and social reformers. He also established a policy from the beginning not to discriminate against prospective students because of their color or ethnic identity. He was also quite proud of the fact that his school was the first in the country to award degrees to women under the same conditions as applied to men. In 1850 he resigned from Oberlin in order to head a group that planned to erect a new university in Cleveland, Ohio. Those plans proved abortive, and so in 1855

Mahan returned to church work. Teaching philosophy and another college presidency followed in Michigan. In 1871 he retired to England in order to complete several writing projects. There he continued to preach to large audiences, and he also edited a monthly magazine in addition to publishing several volumes on philosophical and religious topics.

Bibliography:

A.   *Scripture Doctrine of Christian Perfection* (Boston, 1839); *Doctrine of the Will* (Oberlin, OH, 1845); *Science of Moral Philosophy* (Oberlin, OH, 1848); *The Science of Natural Theology* (Boston, 1867); *Out of Darkness into Light* (Boston, 1876); *Autobiography: Intellectual, Moral, and Spiritual* (London, 1882).

B.   SH 7, 130; NCAB 2, 461–62; DAB 12, 208–09; Edward H. Madden and James E. Hamilton, *Freedom and Grace: The Life of Asa Mahan* (Metuchen, NY, 1982).

MAKEMIE, Francis (1658, near Ramelton, Ireland—1708, Accomac, VA). *Education*: studied at Univ. of Glasgow, 1676–80. *Career*: Presbyterian missionary in middle colonies, principally MD and VA, 1683–1708.

Records of Makemie's early activities, his study and ministerial candidacy, are sketchy because the 1680s were times when Charles II made it dangerous to be a Presbyterian. But we know that he received ordination in 1682 and sailed for the New World within a year to answer a call for missionary work on the eastern shore of Chesapeake Bay. He supported himself with mercantile enterprises while giving the larger portion of his time to evangelical travels. Scattered sources indicate that he concentrated on North Carolina in 1683 to 1684, Virginia in 1684 to 1685, and the island of Barbados in 1696 to 1698. The remaining time was spent south of Delaware where Makemie established some of the earliest Presbyterian churches in the country. By 1698 his itinerancy ended when marriage brought an estate of considerable property, but comfortable surroundings did not distract him from regular duties in a church at Rehoboth, Maryland, which he served for the rest of his life. While in Britain (1704–05) he recruited other clergymen to help staff the growing number of preaching stations. In 1706 he took the lead in organizing these ministers (seven in all) into the Presbytery of Philadelphia, the first such official body on this side of the Atlantic. The fact that he was chosen to preside as the assembly's first moderator gives additional weight to his unchallenged place as chief among the founders of American Presbyterianism.

Beginning in 1690 various representatives of the Anglican persuasion seemed less willing to tolerate nonconformists in outlying colonies than they were required by law to do at home. Makemie twice confronted that widespread prejudice and helped set precedents which matured into full religious liberty about a century later. As a vigorous exponent of doctrines found in the Westminster Confession, he published a catechism to disseminate Calvinistic principles wherever interested parties could be found. Unfortunately no copy of the catechism has survived, but in 1682 *George Keith, onetime Quaker touring southern provinces as an

Anglican missionary, chanced upon it only to discover what he considered grave errors. Makemie was challenged to a public debate on the merits of their respective creeds, but the Presbyterian leader declined. Nevertheless he issued a printed defense of his position, an early example of freedom to dissent which received favorable support from *Increase Mather because of its reverent and judicious opinions. Freedom to preach nonconformist convictions was threatened in another way when Lord Cornbury, governor of New York, imprisoned him for six weeks in 1707 on a charge of speaking without a license. In fact Makemie had been licensed in 1699, and he won a notable courtroom victory by demonstrating his compliance with England's Toleration Act. His arguments for religious diversity embarrassed Cornbury, contributed to his recall, and helped create wider latitude for dissenting churches in several colonies during the early eighteenth century.

Bibliography:

A.   *An Answer to George Keith's Libel* (Boston, 1694); *A Narrative of a New and Unusual American Imprisonment of Two Presbyterian Ministers* (Boston, 1707).
B.   AAP 3, 1–4; SH 7, 135–36; NCAB 11, 384; DAB 12, 215–16; NCE 9, 92; Littleton P. Bowen, *The Days of Makemie* (Philadelphia, 1885); Isaac M. Page, *The Life Story of Rev. Francis Makemie* (Grand Rapids, MI, 1938); John Montieth Barkley, *Francis Makemie of Ramelton: Father of American Presbyterianism* (Belfast, 1981).

MALCOLM X (19 May 1925, Omaha, NE—21 February 1965, New York, NY).

Malcolm Little learned very early that the white man's world was a hostile one. His earliest memory was of his house being burned by racists (1929), and suspicion always lingered that his father was murdered (1931) because he supported the back-to-Africa doctrines of *Marcus Garvey. Even his genealogy was violated by the fact that his grandmother had been raped by a white man. Malcolm was a gifted student in high school, but despite excellent grades he was advised to learn carpentry rather than think of college. He dropped out of school and drifted into crime, becoming at times pimp, addict, pusher, and small time burglar. In 1946 he was sentenced to a ten-year term for robbery and soon encountered ideas which turned his life around completely. While in prison he began reading material preached by the Black Muslims, or more properly the Nation of Islam. He corresponded with the group's leader, *Elijah Muhammad, and was converted to the new faith. In 1953 when probationed, he was fond of saying that Christianity had put him in jail but Islam had led him out a reformed man.

Christianity was a white man's device to enslave the Blacks, and all surnames were evidence of that fact. As a result of such thinking, he declared his new name to be Malcolm X and adopted the Muslim puritanical code of ethics. These two elements, black pride and functional group ethics, were key elements of Muslim preaching which Malcolm X articulated with remarkable persuasiveness.

After a short apprenticeship he was made minister of Mosque No. 7 in Harlem, gaining there a reputation for intense, stern denunciations of white injustice. Whether on street corners or in college debates, he spoke wittily and at times with cold fury in delivering his judgment. Black men were the first on earth, he held, superior to others; yet, they allowed themselves to be subjugated by a devilish race of whites. Liberal institutions in America were bankrupt, and integration was a fraud. Separatism and self-help through Allah's will were the only answers. Black suffering would end only when political power and economic improvement gave men enough leverage to force social change. This was the root of Malcolm X's doctrine and the basis of his appeal to persons tired of abuse, eager for new hope.

Malcolm X was one of the most cogent thinkers among black militants, but there was a larger aspect to his religious vision. He was also known as El-Hajj Malik El-Shabazz, one interested in the universal brotherhood of Islam instead of the black racist orientation of Black Muslims. During 1963 to 1964 his suspension from mosque functions only crystalized a break long in the making. Thereafter he began to internationalize his struggle for the black man's human rights. He became less doctrinaire and softened the uncompromising rhetoric which frightened so many black bourgeois leaders. While formulating a wider appeal for the Organization of Afro-American Unity in the name of world brotherhood, he was murdered for reasons still undetermined. Many were quick to see a correspondence between his explosive speech and violent end, but the quality of his leadership came increasingly to be recognized. He was a rare breed of man whose presence was irreplaceable and whose mature religious heritage was tragically aborted.

Bibliography:

A.   *The Autobiography of Malcolm X*, assisted by Alex Hadley (New York, 1965); *Malcolm X Speaks: Selected Speeches and Statements*, ed. George Breitman (New York, 1966).

B.   NYT 22 Feb 1965, 1; Louis E. Lomax, *To Kill a Black Man* (Los Angeles, 1968); George Breitman, *The Last Year of Malcolm X: The Evolution of a Revolutionary* (New York, 1968); John H. Clarke (ed.), *Malcolm X: The Man and His Times* (New York, 1969); Peter Goldman, *The Life and Death of Malcolm X* (New York, 1973).

MANN, Horace (4 May 1796, Franklin, MA—2 August 1859, Yellow Springs, OH). *Education*: B.A., Brown Univ., 1819; studied law, Litchfield, CT, 1821–23. *Career*: practiced law, Dedham, MA, 1823–33, and Boston, 1833–37; member, Massachusetts state legislature (House, 1827–33; Senate, 1833–37), 1827–37; secretary, state board of education, 1837–48; editor, *Common School Journal*, 1838–48; member, U.S. House of Representatives, 1848–53; president, Antioch Coll., 1853–59.

After Mann became successful in law and politics, he was given the opportunity of serving his native state in the field of education. His primary reason for accepting was a desire to benefit society; another was because it allowed him the chance to combat deficiencies under which he had been reared. Public schools had fallen into serious disrepair by 1837, and it was largely due to Mann's fervent reforming zeal that they improved over the next decade. In practical terms he established a minimum school year, doubled appropriations for buildings and equipment, increased the salary and professional training of teachers, and made free secondary education a tangible reality in the state. On the theoretical side he issued annual treatises to the legislature on the purpose and value of education. Copies of those reports influenced school planning in a great number of states. In addition to that major category, Mann was an early supporter of state hospitals and mental health care; he actively combated slavery, liquor, tobacco, lotteries, profanity, and dancing. There was little formal connection between such crusades and his religious upbringing, but to the end he remained a puritan without a theology, dedicated to improving human conditions. He believed that men could better themselves through education, achieving higher levels of social harmony with enlightened leadership.

Nondenominational religious motivations undergirded much of what Mann sought to accomplish in society. All his childhood reminiscences indicate deep emotional turmoil resulting from the Calvinistic preaching of local minister *Nathaniel Emmons. Repelled by those torments promised for anyone dying unconverted, he came to regard Christianity as an ethical system rather than a message of salvation. Eventually he espoused deistic views associated with natural theology and joined the Unitarian church. But it was not so much the nature of religion as its role in society that marked him as an influential figure in an increasingly secularized environment. Mann argued that sound morality, civic mindedness, and personal character befitting republican citizenship did not rest on sectarian foundations. He wanted to rescue education from theological conflicts, but clerical opponents charged him with instituting godless schools where discipline and dogma failed to receive proper attention. Mann countered by admitting that Bible readings without comment, together with common-denominator humanistic principles, were still a valuable factor in normal schools. But he refused to specify any denominational form of moral code and thus sparked bitter debates over the place of religion in public life. Mann's experience served as the prototype for similar controversies in almost every other state. His pioneering thought made significant strides in an issue which has not yet been resolved.

Bibliography:

A. *Lectures on Education* (Boston, 1850); *Life and Works of Horace Mann*, ed. Mary T. P. Mann, 3 vols. (Boston, 1865–68), ed. George C. Mann, 5 vols. (Boston, 1891).

B. NCAB 3, 78–79; DAB 12, 240–43; NCE 9, 163–64; Albert E. Winship, *Horace Mann the Educator* (Boston, 1896); Burke A. Hinsdale, *Horace Mann and the Common School Revival in the United States* (New York, 1898); George A. Hubbell, *Horace Mann*

(Philadelphia, 1910); Raymond B. Culver, *Horace Mann and Religion in the Massachusetts Public Schools* (New Haven, 1929); Louise H. Tharp, *Until Victory: Horace Mann and Mary Peabody* (Boston, 1953).

MANNING, James (22 October 1738, Piscataway, NJ—29 July 1791, Providence, RI). *Education*: B.A., Coll. of New Jersey, 1762. *Career*: minister, Morristown, NJ, 1763; minister, Warren, RI, 1764–70; president and professor of Languages, Rhode Island Coll., 1765–91; minister, First Baptist Church, Providence, RI, 1770–91.

In the aftermath of First Great Awakening revivalism, Baptist leaders of the Philadelphia Association began in 1762 to think of a college that would train ministers for their expanding denomination. Within a year they chose Manning to supervise those educational efforts to be based in Rhode Island, because its permissive attitude toward religions offered more opportunity for growth than that found in any other colony. By 1764 the college (Brown University after 1804) received a charter and two years later set up operations in the president's manse at Warren; in 1770 it moved to more amenable surroundings at Providence. From the first it pursued liberal policies regarding admission and governance, though majority control rested in Baptist hands. Manning's sacrifices on behalf of this fledgling institution caused virtually everyone to call him founder of the first Baptist school built to elevate intellectual character among clergymen of that persuasion. He solicited funds pursuant to erecting buildings, presided over daily problems with considerable administrative skill, and planned for long-range developments which comprehended education in terms far beyond the limits of theology. During the Revolution, classes were suspended (1776–83), but after the war he reconverted barracks and hospital into recitation rooms again. His long term of office guided the school through its formative stage, providing a trained ministry for local churches as well as cultural enrichment for the new nation.

Though he always gave priority to duties as pastor and preacher, responsibilities to which he was faithful during all the years of higher office, Manning greatly influenced the larger circles of public affairs. In theological questions he embodied a staunch Calvinism and helped foster growth of that orientation among New England Baptists; by the time of his death Calvinists constituted an overwhelming majority in the denomination. In 1767 the Warren Association emerged at his instigation, comprising a means of promoting both harmony within denominational lines and mutual aid to combat oppression resulting from legal strictures in adjacent colonies. Following arguments originally outlined by *Isaac Backus, he often spoke against the "Standing Order" in Massachusetts and Connecticut. In 1774 he presented a memorial to the Continental Congress, pleading for greater religious toleration in New England. While such attempts to enlarge civil and religious liberties were not immediately successful, they added weight to a movement that eventually triumphed in 1833. Manning also served a term (1786) in the U.S. Congress, returning home to advocate acceptance of the federal constitution with its amendments declaring religious freedom as a national standard. In political, cultural, and philanthropic endeavors he proved a constant source of leadership, attentive to each capacity as relevant to a full gospel ministry.

Bibliography:

B.   AAP 6, 89–97; SH 7, 163; NCAB 8, 20–21; DAB 12, 249–51; Reuben A. Guild, *Early History of Brown University Including the Life, Times and Correspondence of President Manning* (Providence, RI, 1897).

MARÉCHAL, Ambrose (28 August 1764, Ingres, France—29 January 1828, Baltimore, MD). *Education:* studied classics and law, Univ. of Orléans, 178?–87; studied at Sulpician Sem., Orléans, 1787–89; studied at Sulpician Sem., Bordeaux, 1789–92. *Career:* missionary priest in MD, 1792–99; professor of Theology, St. Mary's Sem. (MD), 1799–1801; professor of Philosophy, Georgetown Coll., 1801–02; professor at various diocesan seminaries in France, 1803–11; professor of Theology, St. Mary's Sem. (MD), 1812–17; archibishop of Baltimore, 1817–28.

Though he studied law for a time to please his parents, Maréchal could not long resist more urgent inclinations to enter the priesthood. As a Sulpician he helped develop Catholic education in this country, receiving commendation from bishop *John Carroll before superiors recalled him to France. There he labored for almost a decade until Napoleon expelled Sulpicians from all French seminaries. He transferred once again to America and became one of the most prominent émigré clergymen of his era. Though he apparently shunned high office, refusing episcopal nomination in New York and Philadelphia, by 1817 it was impossible to avoid being named coadjutor in Baltimore. But the bills concerning such appointment did not arrive before the death of Leonard Neale, Carroll's successor in 1815. Consequently Maréchal was elevated directly to the office of archbishop, inaugurating, as third metropolitan, a ten-year period of vigorous management and stormy debate within his farflung diocese. He quarrelled bitterly with resurgent Jesuits (reinstated, 1814) over ownership of property, such as venerable Whitemarsh Manor. Trusteeism was another issue plaguing a number of local churches; the Gallic archbishop moved wherever possible to squelch what he regarded as rampant democracy, an impulse fatal to both discipline among priests and sacramental virtue among the laity. His strong action in that context aroused no little resentment. Irish and German parishioners feared domination by a ''foreign'' hierarchy, and they often suspected Maréchal's administrative decisions as attempts to perpetuate French control. One critic, *John England, bishop of Charleston, repeatedly asked for a provincial council to deal with common problems and establish equitable procedures. But the archibishop refused, apparently thinking it better to keep his prelates in isolation than to allow them participation in conciliar decisions. Such cooperation was desperately needed, however, and within a year of his death the first council met to determine uniform ground rules for a church rapidly becoming the nation's largest denomination.

Bibliography:

B.   NCAB 1, 482–83; DAB 12, 279–80; NCE 9, 197–98.

MARQUETTE, Jacques (1 June 1637, Laon, France—18 May 1675, near Ludington, MI). *Education:* entered novitiate in Jesuit order, Nancy, 1654; studied philosophy at Pont-à-Mousson, 1657–59; studied Algonkian at Trois Rivières, Canada, 1666–68. *Career:* taught in Jesuit schools at Auxerre, 1656–57, Reims, 1659–61, Charleville, 1661–63, Langres, 1663–64, and Pont-à-Mousson, 1664–65; missionary to various Indian tribes in Canada, 1669–75.

Judging from reminiscences about his childhood, Marquette seems always to have intended becoming a missionary. The Society of Jesus was long a formative influence to that end too, beginning with his residence as a boarding school student at nine years of age. The usual educational process which he followed as a novice was interrupted in 1665 because mission fields had opened once again in New France. Instead of completing studies in theology, the prematurely ordained priest labored to master Algonkian, a linguistic stock basic to the majority of American aborigines. What is more, he learned to respect Indian patterns of culture. Patience and understanding had been salient characteristics of every Jesuit mission enterprise, and his mentor Gabriel Druillettes instilled the same ideals in this new volunteer before he pushed farther west. By 1668 he was judged ready to assume responsibilities at Sainte Marie du Sault, the crossroads between Lake Superior and Lake Huron frequented by a score of nations but dominated by the Ojibway. Marquette moved in the next year to Chequamegon Bay at the western end of Lake Superior, continuing a mission named La Pointe du Saint Esprit. There he ministered to several tribes, especially the Kiskakon branch of the Ottawa nation and a scattered remnant of Huron. He did what he could to inculcate Christian morality among them, teaching modesty, devotion, and attention to daily offices. But after two years he admitted that his charges had improved little for all his effort.

The main reason for abandoning Saint Esprit in 1671 was not discouragement or isolation; it was apprehension that hostile Sioux would destroy the settlement at any moment. Marquette led his group back to the confluence of lakes, choosing an island (Mackinac) between Lake Michigan and Lake Huron where he built the mission of Saint Ignace. He continued working with the Ottawa there for two years, but his thoughts turned increasingly to the Illinois, a nation southwest of his station with whom he had some earlier contact. In 1673 he received permission to accompany Louis Jolliet in exploration of that unknown territory. Together with five other Frenchmen they traced the Mississippi River as far south as the mouth of the Arkansas. From their calculations it was possible to determine that the huge watershed drained into the Gulf of Mexico instead of the Gulf of California as some cartographers had thought. On the return voyage Marquette re-established contact with the friendly Illinois and promised to begin a mission as soon as possible. Though his health began to fail, he traveled south from Green Bay in the winter of 1674–75 and reached the Kaskaskia village in early spring. He had hardly begun the Immaculate Conception mission there by celebrating Easter mass when another serious illness made it necessary to leave for Saint Ignace. Death occurred before that destination was reached.

Bibliography:

B.   SH 7, 191–92; NCAB 12, 220–21; DAB 12, 294–95; NCE 9, 254; Reuben G. Thwaites, *Father Marquette* (New York, 1902); Agnes Repplier, *Père Marquette* (Garden City, NY, 1929); Joseph P. Donnelly, *Jacques Marquette* (Chicago, 1968); Raphael N. Hamilton, *Father Marquette* (Grand Rapids, MI, 1970).

MARSH, James (19 July 1794, Hartford, VT—3 July 1842, Colchester, VT). *Education*: B.A., Dartmouth Coll., 1817; B.D., Andover Sem., 1822. *Career*: tutor, Dartmouth Coll., 1818–20; professor of Oriental Languages, Hampden-Sydney Coll., 1823–26; president, Univ. of Vermont, 1826–33; professor of Moral and Intellectual Philosophy, Univ. of Vermont, 1833–42.

For the first eighteen years of his life Marsh did not expect or wish to follow any vocation other than farming. Circumstances changed abruptly in his family, however, and he found himself in college where studies began to quicken unexpected interests. A conversion experience in 1815 gave additional purpose to his extensive reading program, producing by 1824 a ministerial candidate of thorough philosophical preparation. He taught for a time in Virginia, hoping that plans for a seminary would come to fruition, but when the University of Vermont asked him to become its fifth president, he considered it his duty to accept. Marsh was not an outstanding speaker who could further the interests of his institution by improving its public image. But in his unpretentious way he elevated the quality of instruction through personal example, introducing, as well, important reform measures for both curricular content and student discipline. Another area in which he wielded appreciable influence had to do with revival techniques. Since he shunned extravagant displays of emotion by nature and habit, his sense of propriety found ''new measures'' in the church shockingly out of place. As an outspoken opponent of strenuous emotionalism, he greatly affected public opinion in his region. This and other instances show how he was able to guide a populace already inclined to emphasize the more deliberative aspects of religious discourse.

From his college days Marsh had been impressed with new philosophical tendencies which he thought would bolster traditional Congregationalist beliefs. Yet for all his interest in perpetuating orthodoxy, he did not find the familiar Scottish realism a satisfactory perspective for understanding it. An early fascination with the Cambridge Platonists led to admiration for emphases usually categorized as Romanticism, and it was in this area that he advanced the ferment of religious thought in ante-bellum New England. To supply a more adequate foundation for inherited beliefs, he introduced many strains of thought from Europe to his American contemporaries. In 1829 he brought out an edition of Coleridge's *Aids to Reflection* with his own introductory essay, a thoughtful piece which stimulated several budding intellectuals including *Ralph W. Emerson. He also translated (1833) Herder's *Spirit of Hebrew Poetry* and other selections of value to the Transcendentalist movement. This was an unanticipated result, but Marsh stood as an important transitional figure who represented a form of religious modernism at home in established churches. The ideas and scholarship he encouraged continued long after his preliminary work to affect variegated emphases on metaphysics, social reform, and personal salvation.

Bibliography:

    B.   AAP 2, 692–704; NCAB 2, 40; DAB 12, 299–300; Joseph Torrey, *The Remains of the Rev. James Marsh . . . with a Memoir of his Life* (Burlington, VT, 1843).

MARSHALL, Daniel (1706, Windsor, CT—2 November 1784, Columbia County, GA). *Career*: farmer and Congregationalist deacon in CT, 1726–47; missionary to Mohawks in PA and NY, 1747–48; lay exhorter near Winchester, VA, 1748–54; itinerant Baptist minister, VA and NC, 1754–58; minister Abbott's Creek Baptist Church, NC, 1758–62; minister, Horse Creek Baptist Church, SC, 1763–71; minister, Kiokee Creek Baptist Church, GA, 1772–84.

For over twenty years Marshall occupied positions of respect and trust in local Connecticut circles. Then, in 1745, the preaching of *George Whitefield transformed his life. Once touched by direct spiritual experience, he became an outspoken advocate of the new awakening blended with additional ingredients of strong millennial expectation. He sold all his property and left comfortable surroundings for missionary work among the Indians. With wife and children he lived beside longhouses of the Mohawk nation in upper reaches of the Susquehanna valley. After eighteen months there were encouraging signs of success, but native warfare caused his mission to deteriorate beyond repair. Admitting failure, he turned southward and joined his brother-in-law, *Shubal Stearns, who persuaded him to accept immersion as the proper mode of Christian baptism. By 1754 Marshall had begun to preach the doctrines championed by Baptist churches; when his family, together with Stearns and others, moved to central North Carolina, he continued to spread the gospel as he now understood it. His missionary spirit never flagged. Having only a rudimentary education, he made up for poor training with zeal and tremendous drive. The rapid spread of Baptist churches in territory from Virginia to Georgia was greatly aided by his efforts.

The churches organized by Marshall and fellow backwoods exhorters were denominated Separate Baptist. Others in contrast to them were called Regular Baptist, associating themselves with Philadelphia as a base of operations and adhering to rigidly Calvinist theology, orderly preaching plus dignified worship.

These less zealous Baptists did not welcome the noisy, emotional Separates. The latter group carried a reputation for illiteracy and bizarre pulpit mannerisms; they gave more place to human initiative and, not least among their characteristics, allowed women a prominent place in religious activities. Marshall's second wife, Martha Stearns, was a singularly gifted woman who embodied the best qualities of piety and elocution which vindicated her role in church services. Her work gave able support to Separate Baptist evangelism, adding strength to her husband's widespread success. As early as 1758 Marshall set his course for Georgia. In spite of difficulties with civil authorities there, he returned again and again as a dissenting preacher. After a nine-year ministry in South Carolina he settled in Georgia and organized (1772) the first Baptist church in the colony. Wartime conditions were adverse to evangelical activity, but he endured the Revolution with staunch republican loyalty. One of his last acts as patriarch of gospel ideals was to organize the Georgia Association, originally composed of six Baptist churches which served as the nucleus for vital expansion in future years.

Bibliography:

B.   AAP 6, 59–61; DAB 12, 308.

MASON, Charles Harrison (8 September 1866, Bartlett, TN—17 November 1961, Memphis, TN). *Education*: studied at Arkansas Baptist Coll., 1893–94. *Career*: minister, Lexington, MS, 1897–1907; senior bishop, Church of God in Christ, 1907–61.

Active originally in Baptist churches, Mason began emphasizing holiness doctrine shortly after three months of college experience convinced him that salvation was not to be found in schooling. By 1897 his evangelical work centered in Mississippi where he founded the first "Church of God in Christ" in an abandoned cotton gin. Drawing on proof-texts from both Testaments and standard holiness ideas about the body as a temple of the Holy Spirit, he stoutly urged that men should conduct themselves in perfect righteousness all their days. Membership increased under the influence of this forceful black exhorter, but within a decade another potent factor affected numerical growth. In 1907 Mason traveled to Los Angeles because stories about *William J. Seymour's remarkable revivals made him seek a new blessing in the spirit. Shortly thereafter he experienced a pentecostal baptism of the Holy Ghost, manifested in the usual signs of speaking in tongues and healing the sick. In that same year he organized the first general assembly of similarly minded black preachers, using the name of his church as symbol for all, with general headquarters at Memphis, Tennessee. Elected bishop and given plenipotentiary power, Mason supervised the movement with a wisdom that enhanced development of a significant ethnic-religious force. He gathered about him numbers of clergymen able to strengthen their churches by converting, sanctifying and healing through the power of faith. The denomination paper, *Whole Truth*, instructed its readers in traditional pentecostal holiness doctrines. By 1933 churches had been established among the black population in every state of the Union largely by means of bishop Mason's adroit leadership. Further institutional growth crowned the founder's last years; after his death a lenghty (1964–68) dispute over authority resulted in a more democratic form of government. Authority regarding doctrine and discipline now resides in the General Assembly with an executive board attending to daily administrative affairs.

Bibliography:

B. German R. Ross (ed.), *History and Formative Years of the Church of God in Christ* (Memphis, TN, 1969).

MATHER, Cotton (12 February 1663, Boston, MA—13 February 1728, Boston, MA). *Education*: B.A., Harvard, Coll., 1678. *Career*: minister, Second Congregational Church, Boston, MA, 1685–1728.

Standing in line of succession from two eminent New England divines, *John Cotton and *Increase Mather, young Mather was not indifferent to the responsibility such an inheritance placed on him. It could be said that anxiety over being faithful to his spiritual patrimony is the key to understanding his complex and apparently contradictory personality. He was quick to learn the pious habits that were part of Puritan education but also quick to prompt others to emulation; he was often regarded by peers as an overbearing prig. After graduating from Harvard he assisted his father's ministry, joining him officially some years later and making most of his contributions during the elder Mather's lifetime. He shared Increase's convictions on most issues and acted largely as a younger participant in second generation leadership. The dominant aspect of Mather's many activities was a pastoral concern to edify those who followed him. Throughout an intensely energetic lifetime he preached, wrote, fasted, and exhorted to continue the New England Way as a model of godliness. He was often unlovable but constantly industrious, authoring the staggering total of some 450 books on a host of subjects. All forms of learning and ministerial care were geared to maintaining the level of excellence already achieved by American Puritanism. Thus humility was mixed with pride, a recognition of continuing sin with the self-righteousness of having conquered it. But in attempts to apply established doctrine and procedures to changing conditions, he also served as a transitional figure who anticipated many eighteenth century religious emphases.

The place of religion in cultural affairs was an area to which Mather gave high priority. He won popular support in opposing Edmund Andros as royal governor, but his status declined in subsequent quarrels with the Phips administration. His conservative efforts in that sphere seem to indicate a desire that orthodoxy maintain its accustomed dominance in politics, not a personal wish to acquire power for its own sake. The witchcraft controversy at Salem Village (1692) was one in which he had only tangential influence, yet his defense of court verdicts rebounded later to his discredit. He was acutely sensitive to a decline of religion among the younger generation; rigid admonitions against laxity was however the main response. When he was not chosen president of Harvard (1701), he devoted himself to a number of alternative societies, including the Yale corporation, in hopes they might better continue proper Christian teaching. His plans for church cooperation declined as new procedures were adopted, notably at Charlestown and Brattle Street Church. Yet he never dismissed a vision of church unity, defining it more along lines of pietistic rather than juridical consensus in later years. His respect for new learning was genuine; as one of the first colonial members of the Royal Society of London he made a bold defense of inoculation against smallpox in 1721. To the end he embodied most traditional attitudes, but ministerial promptings led him to interpret moral principles in ways conducive to the new century's growing spirit of individualism.

Bibliography:

A. *The Wonderful Works of God Commemorated* (Boston, 1690); *A Midnight Cry* (Boston, 1692); *Christianus Per Ignem* (Boston, 1702); *Magnalia Christi Americana: The Ecclesiastical History of New England from its First Planting* (London, 1702; Hartford, 1852; New York, 1967); *Bonifacius: An Essay Upon the Good* (Boston, 1710); *Winter Piety* (Boston, 1712).

B. AAP 1, 189–95; SH 7, 248; NCAB 4, 232–33; DAB 12, 386–89; NCE 9, 460–61; Samuel Mather, *The Life of the Very Reverend and Learned Cotton Mather* (Boston, 1729); William B. O. Peabody, *Life of Cotton Mather* (Boston, 1836); Barrett Wendell, *Cotton Mather* (New York, 1891); Robert Middlekauff, *The Mathers: Three Generations of Puritan Intellectuals, 1596–1728* (New York, 1971); David Levin, *Cotton Mather: The Young Life of the Lord's Remembrancer, 1663–1703* (Cambridge, MA, 1978).

MATHER, Increase (21 June 1639, Dorchester, MA—23 August 1723, Boston, MA). *Education*: B.A., Harvard Coll., 1656; M.A., Trinity Coll., Dublin, 1658. *Career*: chaplain, English garrison on Guernsey, 1659–61; supply preaching in MA, 1661–64; minister, Second Congregational Church, Boston, 1664–1723; president, Harvard Coll., 1685–1701.

It is indicative of the American Puritan mind that Mather considered England his chief frame of reference until a Stuart was restored to the throne. After it became clear that he would have to accept Anglicanism in order to gain influential office, Massachusetts appeared more attractive as the remaining haven of Congregational control. After returning to what was now viewed as home, he exercised a ministry of sixty years which sought primarily to maintain traditional standards as taught by the founding fathers. His many publications (130 books and pamphlets) and skillful preaching brought recognition as one of the foremost divines of his generation. But contributions to issues beyond the parish made his work distinguished for its diplomacy and realism. In 1662 most New England ministers favored a relaxation of rules for church membership, arguing the acceptability of baptizing infants if only one of their grandparents had been a full communicant. Mather opposed the Half-Way Covenant as a compromising double standard which condoned the non-communicant status of parents. But within a few years he was convinced that churches could not prosper unless requirements were lowered enough to increase membership. By 1675 he wrote two volumes defending the practice. In 1688 he went to London and spent three years negotiating for a new colonial charter. His persuasive, adroit sessions with two kings produced a settlement which retained much of the local representative assembly's power, even while it accepted a franchise based on qualifications other than church membership.

As colonial society diversified, Mather lamented the decline of religious zeal in the commonwealth. Efforts in synod and pulpit served to remind citizens of their sins, proclaim fast days, and suggest remedies which looked more to the past than to the future. Despite jeremiads about apostasy, such Mather-led activity did little to affect prevailing trends. One episode in which Mather was more effective had to do with the witchcraft frenzy at Salem Village in 1692. He did not question the reality of witches but cautioned against undue stress on them. More importantly he argued forcefully against emphasizing spectral evidence as a means of identifying guilty persons. His personal influence with Governor Phips and his convincing discourses were instrumental in ending the executions before they got completely out of hand. Nevertheless his prestige began to decline. He was associated with the unpopular new charter, an appointed governor, and old guard maneuvers to preserve a bygone theocracy. His renown as theologian and statesman was diminished, but to the end he was a noted leader in the councils of a waning clerical party that struggled to preserve its view of national righteousness.

Bibliography:

A.   *The Life and Death of . . . Mr. Richard Mather* (Cambridge, MA, 1670); *A Discourse concerning Baptism* (Cambridge, MA, 1675); *A Brief History of the War with the Indians* (Boston, 1676); *The Call from Heaven* (Boston, 1679); *New England Vindicated* (London, 1688); *Cases of Conscience concerning Evil Spirits* (Boston, 1693).

B.   AAP 1, 151–59; SH 7, 248; NCAB 6, 412–13; DAB 12, 390–94; NCE 9, 460–61; Cotton Mather, *Parentator: Memoirs of . . . Increase Mather* (Boston, 1724); Samuel Mather, *Memoirs of the Life of . . . Increase Mather* (London, 1725); Kenneth B. Murdock, *Increase Mather: The Foremost American Puritan* (Cambridge, MA, 1925); Robert Middlekauf, *The Mathers: Three Generations of Puritan Intellectuals, 1596–1728* (New York, 1971); Mason I. Lowance, Jr., *Increase Mather* (New York, 1974).

MATHEWS, Shailer (26 May 1863, Portland, ME—23 October 1941, Chicago, IL). *Education*: B.A., Colby Coll., 1884; B.D., Newton Theol. Inst. 1887; studied at Berlin, 1890–91. *Career*: professor at various ranks of Rhetoric, History, and Political Economy, Colby Coll., 1887–90, 1891–94; professor of New Testament, 1894–1906, professor of Historical and Comparative Theology, 1906–33, and dean, 1908–33, Chicago Div. Sch.; editor, *The World Today*, 1903–11; editor, *Biblical World*, 1913–20; active retirement, 1933–41.

The faith of a modernist sometimes emerges slowly; in Mathews' case it developed through a process of socio-historical studies covering a span of over twelve years. As professor and dean at Chicago he helped shape the course of liberal religious thought in its relation to contemporary intellectual standards, particularly modern science. He stressed a historical approach to Christian doctrines, viewing them not as timeless truths but rather as reflections of cultural patterns which gave them initial expression. Inherited ideas received fresh meanings as they were assimilated to new needs. Different circumstances gave birth to new insights, and those were expressed in various idioms found in changing intellectual frameworks. Mathews argued, as did many liberals, that individual experience and the developmental process were more important than appeals to a metaphysical system or revelation as authoritative standards. He moved beyond mediating liberalism, however, by adopting inductive scientific methods as the only means of identifying legitimate values in traditional orthodoxy for his own day. Theology for him did not involve loyalty to earlier formulations because each was relative to its cultural setting. For modern man he was convinced that its function was to articulate Christian hopes, using Jesus as symbolic of all religious altrium, and to provide guidance for men in their cosmic environment. Belief in God was defensible when it aided human conceptions of the vital, personality-evolving elements of that environment to which man was organically related.

Despite his radical theological conclusions, which abandoned much of traditional Christianity, Mathews remained a staunch supporter of churches. He thought of them not as guarantors of confessional certainty but as the only groups able to effect a readjustment of values in industrial society. The writings of *Washington Gladden and *Josiah Strong furthered his appreciation of the churches' responsibility to apply Christian teachings to social problems. His interest in the function of religion in this area led to an early statement of the biblical basis for Social Gospel activity. He remained a devoted Baptist all his life and was instrumental in organizing the Northern Baptist Convention, serving as president in 1915. His irenic modernism provided, he hoped, a vantage point for understanding the appeal of living Christian witness, regardless of special creeds or polities. Evidence of his larger view is seen in the fact that he served as president of the Federal Council of Churches from 1912 to 1916. Interdenominational missions in Chicago's inner city, boards for improved race relations, summer work with the Chautauqua Institution—all these received long and sustained attention. His ecumenical vision extended abroad, too, where he attended conferences at Stockholm (Life and Work, 1925) and Lausanne (Faith and Order, 1927). Though modernism began to fade during his retirement years, it did not mitigate his basic perspective on the historical development of religious ideas.

Bibliography:

A. *The Gospel and the Modern Man* (New York, 1910); *The Faith of Modernism* (New York, 1924); *The Atonement and the Social Process* (New York, 1930); *The Growth of the Idea of God* (New York, 1931); *Immortality and the Cosmic Process* (Cambridge, MA, 1933); *New Faith for Old: An Autobiography* (New York, 1936).

B.   SH 7, 250; NCAB 11, 74–75; DAB 23, 514–16; NCE 9, 461; NYT 24 Oct 1941, 23; Miles H. Krumbine (ed.), *The Process of Religion* (New York, 1933; Freeport, NY, 1972); Joseph H. Jackson, *Many But One* (New York, 1964); Charles H. Arnold, *Near the Edge of the Battle* (Chicago, 1966).

MAURIN, Aristide Peter (9 May 1877, Oultet, France—15 May 1949, Newburgh, NY). *Career*: novice in the Christian Brothers, Paris, France, 1893–1903; promoter of Sillonist social reform in France, 1903–09; homesteader and unskilled laborer in Canada and the United States, 1909–33; writer and lecturer for *The Catholic Worker*, 1933–49.

Peasant origins in the Languedoc region of southern France gave Maurin a capacity for viewing life's problems in elemental terms. His apostolate in the Christian Brothers was defined in terms of modest accomplishments in primary school education. As he became more interested in socio-economic questions, he gained release from the monastic order and joined the reformist organization led by Marc Sangnier. By 1909 he shipped for the New World, unsure about school and political agitation, but still seeking cogent answers to human difficulties. The middle period of Maurin's life was characterized by rootlessness, wandering from Alberta to Pennsylvania, working at a dozen knockabout jobs in wheatfields, coke ovens, and ferryboats. By 1925 he found himself in New York, making ends meet by tutoring French lessons and pursuing what amounted to a lay apostolate of poverty. Late in 1932 he met *Dorothy Day, a Catholic convert and trained journalist, whom he persuaded to start a newspaper to provide religious perspective on social conditions for the man in the street. *The Catholic Worker* first appeared the following May with 2,500 copies; in three months it grew to ten times that number, and within a year mounted to 110,000. Maurin wrote for the paper every month in his succinct, memorable style, contributing to the burgeoning movement for Catholic welfare which it symbolized. He also made frequent lecture tours, urging a special blend of spiritual humanitarianism and Christian self-help in a time of social depression.

Basic themes in Maurin's thought stemmed from his agrarian roots and peaceful traditions of Catholic charity. In deliberate contrast to the Red Revolution of Marxism with its class-consciousness and inherent strife, he suggested a Green Revolution. It began with study clubs to clarify thinking on social questions including unemployment and its remedy. While ideas were being discussed, he urged that charitable works for the needy be practiced daily. Most important among them were houses of hospitality for the hungry and farming communes where jobless persons could find new beginnings. Maurin drew on the riches of Catholic tradition to propose steps whereby he could be his brother's keeper. He would not accede to a philosophy of bigness, labor unions, and state regulation, preferring rather one of small crafts, decentralization, and Christian communism. With the catch phrase "cult, culture, cultivation," he pursued the familiar theological objectives of good for the soul, mind, and body. Liturgical renewal developed alongside soup kitchens within this grassroots collection of laymen as

Catholic social reform sought to meet human needs in all phases of life. As one of the movement's central figures, Maurin inspired others with his simple views, emphasizing the land, brotherhood, and the church. It was fitting that this selfless individual was buried in a castoff suit and consigned to a donated grave.

Bibliography:

A. *Easy Essays* (New York, 1936, and many subsequent editions); *Catholic Radicalism: Phrased Essays for the Green Revolution* (New York, 1949).

B. NCE 9, 507–08; DAB 24, 561–63; NYT 17 May 1949, 25; Arthur Sheehan, *Peter Maurin: Gay Believer* (Garden City, NY, 1959); Marc H. Ellis, *Peter Maurin: Prophet in the Twentieth Century* (New York, 1981).

MAYHEW, Jonathan (8 October 1720, Martha's Vineyard, MA—9 July 1766, Boston, MA). *Education*: B.A., Harvard Coll., 1744; postgraduate study at Harvard Coll., 1744–47. *Career*: minister, West Congregational Church, Boston, 1747–66.

Advocates of reasonable religion found an outspoken champion in Mayhew whose rather brief ministry at Boston complemented the work of fellow liberal, *Charles Chauncy. He was ostracized by the orthodox clergy in town but persisted for almost two decades to follow theological paths largely in advance of his time. Traditional Calvinism was often his target, with preachers of the First Great Awakening serving as catalysts who moved him to outline an alternative pattern of thought and action. Revivalists denounced attempts to make belief rational while Mayhew sought rather to eliminate all mystery from religion, especially conundrums which defied human reason. He acknowledged that the Bible was infallible but insisted, following John Locke, that man's rational experience must validate revelation. In such a context he declared belief in a single Godhead and refused to meddle further with the deity's interior nature. By 1775 he had rejected trinitarian teachings which deified Jesus because they eclipsed the supreme glory of God the Father. At the same time, in true Arian fashion, he refused to reduce Jesus to mere human status. His sermons were widely read on both sides of the Atlantic as he extolled a pre-existent Mediator whose sacrificial death aided man's salvation by reminding him of the dignity inherent in God's laws.

Salvation according to Calvinists was a matter of unconditional election for sinners who were destitute of personal goodness. Mayhew on the other hand blasted doctrines such as reprobation as unscriptural and a horrible blasphemy against God who was truly a benevolent diety. With unrestrained vigor he struck at the root of evangelical New Divinity by rejecting notions that all-powerful grace saved just a few helpless, depraved beings. He never tired of defending free will and human effort in each person's search for salvation that was available to everyone, holding that saving grace pertained in a way congruent with good works. His advocacy of human striving prompted a debate with *Samuel Hopkins, but both were American Whigs and stood in firm agreement on political questions. Mayhew became involved with the Society for the Propagation of the Gospel (SPG), criticizing it for sending missionaries to parts of New England already settled with Congregationalist churches. He also sparked a heated controversy in 1763 when he charged that plans to establish Anglican bishops in the New World would restrict colonial freedoms. Theological and political liberty were closely aligned in this liberal spokesman. As early as 1750 he laid some of the theoretical groundwork which supported the movement for independence. Men were duty bound, in his view, to obey a king who ruled justly. But if royal authority proved tyrannical, then citizens had the right to resist such arbitrary oppression in the name of civil liberty. Mayhew's governmental theories, as well as his religious affirmations, were compatible with rational inquiry embodied in principles of the Enlightenment. He furthered such tendencies in sermons and the printed word, but death came before his ideals reached their height of popularity.

Bibliography:

A.   *Seven Sermons* (Boston, 1749; New York, 1969); *Sermons* (Boston, 1755); *Christian Sobriety* (Boston, 1763).

B.   AAP 8, 22–29; SH 7, 264; NCAB 7, 71; DAB 12, 454–55; Alden Bradford, *Memoir of the Life and Writings of Rev. Jonathan Mayhew* (Boston, 1838); Charles W. Akers, *Called Unto Liberty: A Life of Jonathan Mayhew* (Cambridge, MA, 1964); John Corrigan, *The Hidden Balance: Religion and the Social Theories of Charles Chauncy and Jonathan Mayhew* (New York, 1987).

MAYS, Benjamin Elijah (1 August 1895, Epworth, SC—28 March 1984, Atlanta, GA). *Education*: B.A., Bates Coll., 1920; M.A. and Ph.D., Univ. of Chicago, 1925 and 1935. *Career*: Mathematics instructor, Morehouse Coll., 1921–24; minister, Shiloh Baptist Church, Atlanta, GA, 1921–24; English instructor, State Coll. of SC, 1925–26; executive secretary, Urban League, Tampa, FL, 1926–28; national student secretary, YMCA, 1928–30; director of research, Institute of Social and Religious Research, NY, 1930–32; dean, Sch. of Religion, Howard Univ., 1934–40; president, Morehouse Coll., 1940–67; member, Board of Education, Atlanta, GA, 1967–81.

By his own account, Mays' earliest childhood memory was that of a white mob looking for a Negro to lynch. That psychological scar, reinforced by incidents of physical discrimination later on, caused this educational and spiritual leader to combat racism all his life. He responded to racial discrimination with emotional fire; he proposed solutions drawn from religious vision; but the chief means utilized between these two poles was the human intellect trained to utilize persuasion. Mays possessed such intellectual talents, evidenced by his rise from rural poverty to success at northern schools. His posts in the Urban League and YMCA set the tone for all subsequent opposition to racist issues. He shunned extremists of all sorts and chose to work within existing social patterns, arguing that American freedoms were real for black as well as white citizens. All that was needed was to realize the full potential of what was already there. Universal suffrage was essential, and calm reason could see that all peoples deserved fair and equal opportunity for jobs, education, and health services. He sought these goals, not just for desegregation, but to better integrate people of all races through mutual love and respect. This religious quality in his passion for civil rights led *Martin Luther King, Jr., to call Mays his spiritual mentor.

Morehouse College remains the center of all circles of Mays' influence. In later years of his presidency and thereafter, he served on national boards (Ford Foundation), international committees (YMCA, World Council of Churches, Baptist World Alliance), and was consultant at the White House (J. F. Kennedy, L. B. Johnson). But Morehouse was the place where he shaped the minds and character of black youths who perpetuated his ideals and expanded them. There for almost three decades he urged the importance of moral integrity and responsible social leadership alongside the highest intellectual standards. He had no patience with complacency or mediocrity because he saw these as leading to moral corruption and social hypocrisy. He embodied high principles himself and taught through example as much as through public utterance. Early on, in 1944, he was elected the first black vice-president of the Federal Council of Churches of Christ in America. Toward the end, in 1970, he became the first black president of the Atlanta Board of Education. Through all these affairs he strove to achieve greater social harmony through Christian principles.

Bibliography:

A.   *The Negro's Church* (written with Joseph W. Nicholson, New York, 1933; 1969); *The Negro's God as Reflected in His Literature* (Boston, 1938); *Seeking to be Christian in Race Relations* (New York, 1957); *Disturbed about Man* (Richmond, VA, 1969); *Born to Rebel: An Autobiography* (New York, 1971).

B.   NYT 29 Mar 1984, D23.

MEGAPOLENSIS, Johannes (1603, Keodyck, Holland—14 January 1670, New York, NY). *Career*: minister of parishes including Schorel, Holland, 1634–42; minister, Rensselaerswyck (now Albany), NY, 1642–49; minister New Amsterdam (now New York), 1649–70.

Jan van Mekelenburg was born to Catholic parents in northern Holland but converted to the Reformed faith when approximately twenty-three years old. The Latinized version of his name appears first as a parish minister and then as one bound to patroon Kiliaen van Rensselaer for clerical duties at his upriver estate on the Hudson. There Dominie Megapolensis labored in rude surroundings for six years, having some effect on the rough manners of local inhabitants through exemplary piety and earnest preaching. After his term of service expired, he planned to return to Europe, but the congregation at New Amsterdam prevailed on him to remain, and he assumed a pastorate that lasted the rest of his life. As part of a general program for doctrinal instruction, he drew up an abbreviated catechism; in 1656 the Classis of Amsterdam commended his diligence but declined to print his manuscript because it did not correspond to the uniform symbols which that ruling body wished to apply within its world-wide jurisdiction. Through the years Megapolensis proved not only a wise shepherd in spiritual matters but a steady counselor on affairs of state as well. In 1664 he was one of those who persuaded governor Peter Stuyvesant that military resistance to English forces would be futile, and he helped negotiate terms of surrender. Soon thereafter he swore allegiance to the British Crown and continued his church work which flourished under a generous protectorate accorded no other communion under the new regime.

Service to the Dutch population was only one aspect of Megapolensis' larger Christian witness in the New World. Soon after arriving at Rensselaerswyck, he established friendly relations with Mohawk Indians, one of the five Iroquois-speaking nations who came annually to trade at Fort Orange. He learned the rudiments of their language and became one of the earliest missionaries to visit palisaded towns in the interior, hoping to spread the gospel there. In 1642 his influence with Mohawk chieftains proved beneficial to *Isaac Jogues, a Jesuit who had been captured earlier in the year. Megapolensis helped barter for the priest's release and secured his safe return to France. Another instance of humane concern for the plight of others occurred in 1654 when a band of Jewish refugees came into port from Brazil. The Dutch pastor helped see to their protection and welfare, even as he advised that no other coreligionists be allowed to enter the colony. He also opposed letting Lutherans conduct public worship in New Amsterdam, protesting by letter in 1654 and resisting three years later the man sent to build a church in his province. Though his ministry was occasionally softened by kind deeds for men of other faiths, the Dominie championed conformity to Reformed standards, and the bulk of his activity evinced loyalty to that orientation.

Bibliography:

A. *A Short Account of the Mohawk Indians* (Alkmaar, 1644; Amsterdam, 1651; English translations: Philadelphia, 1792; New York, 1857).

B. AAP 9, 1–3; SH 7, 276; NCAB 12, 420–21; DAB 12, 499–500.

MENCKEN, Henry Louis (12 September 1880, Baltimore, MD—29 January 1956, Baltimore, MD). *Career:* newspaperman, *Baltimore Morning Herald*, 1899–1906; newspaperman, Baltimore *Sunpapers*, 1906–48; writer and editor, *The Smart Set*, 1908–23; writer and editor, *The American Mercury*, 1924–33.

As a newspaper reporter and editor, Mencken developed a capacity for expressing opinions on everything from philology to prohibition. Between 1911 and 1915 he wrote a column known as ''The Free Lance'' and acquired the reputation of a scathing, exuberant critic of all he thought wrong with the contemporary scene. His aim was to combat, chiefly through ridicule, the established and the accepted. One principal target was religiosity, or tin-pot morality as he called it, because it subsumed much of the sham and cheap conformity that smothered American culture. Mencken's writing was largely misanthropic, not reform-minded, but it had some constructive effect. His alkaline observations provoked angered defense from some, laughter from others, but in the majority of cases readers were led to assess their religious beliefs and attitudes about civic issues. Independent thinking usually decreases the amount of religious posturing in society, and Mencken's blunt efforts to destroy pretense can be seen as a beneficial purgative. As he denounced life, he made others want to live.

In 1925 the trial of John T. Scopes in Dayton, Tennessee, presented to Mencken an epic clash involving principles which he thought worth defending. Personally agnostic about religious beliefs, he moved from the question of evolution to underlying issues of tolerance and freedom of thought. Mencken discerned in the person of *William J. Bryan an epitome of the fatuous American boob, and he pilloried the counsel for the prosecution with concentrated fury. Bryan and the fundamentalists embodied what Mencken despised most. He depicted them as mean, holding that a minority had no rights, obscurantists, clinging to old-time religion as superior to the intellect, and parochial, preferring local roots to city life. His mocking coverage of the trial contributed to the decline of Fundamentalism as a respected viewpoint in the 1920s. With the depression and New Deal, events began to move at an accelerated pace, which Mencken found difficult to monitor. His complaints about hundreds of details took on a note of querulousness, providing more bombast than bite. Late in 1948 he suffered a paralyzing stroke that prevented him from reading or writing effectively thereafter. But until the end he was still able to cast a sardonic eye at efforts falling short of his standards, including, no doubt, a biographical sketch like this.

Bibliography:

A. *Prejudices* (*First* through *Sixth Series*; New York, 1919–27); *Treatise on the Gods* (New York, 1930); *Treatise on Right and Wrong* (New York, 1934); *Happy Days* (New York, 1940); *Newspaper Days* (New York, 1941); *Heathen Days* (New York, 1943).

B. NCAB A, 388–89; NYT 30 Jan 1956, 1; Isaac Goldberg, *The Man Mencken* (New York, 1925); Edgar Kemler, *The Irreverent Mr. Mencken* (Boston, 1950); William Manchester, *Disturber of the Peace* (New York, 1950); Charles Angoff, *H. L. Mencken: A Portrait from Memory* (New York, 1956); Carl Bode, *Mencken* (Carbondale, IL, 1969).

MENDES, Henry Pereira (13 April 1852, Birmingham, England—20 October 1937, Mt. Vernon, NY). *Education:* private Hebraic studies; studied at University Coll., London, 1870–72; M.D., New York Univ., 1884. *Career:* rabbi, Manchester, England, 1875–77; rabbi, Shearith Israel Congregation, New York, 1877–1920; retirement, 1920–37.

Descended from long lines of rabbis in the Sephardic tradition of enlightened orthodoxy, Chaim Mendes continued that emphasis as hazan and teacher in New York for over four decades. Throughout his life he was concerned about the more inclusive aspects of Jewish life and contributed to projects which met both sectarian and social needs. He was active in attempts to safeguard Jewish interests in legislation regarding schools, immigration, and Sunday business. At his instigation the Montefiore Hospital was begun, and other facilities were established to care for crippled children, deaf-mutes, and the blind. All of these tangibles were elements of Mendes' conviction that Israel comprised a living totality, not just a creed alongside others. In keeping with this idea he was an early advocate of Zionism, cooperating with the Federation of American Zionists and traveling to several European congresses. But Mendes was basically committed to "cultural" or "spiritual" Zionism, a wide range of opinions which stressed revitalization of the inner resources of Judaism. He did not side with any of the competing arguments about establishing a Jewish state and thus remained outside the major debates of his day. The quality of life in communities, wherever they were located, was more important to him than the various diplomatic maneuvers most Zionists thought necessary.

Contributions to cultural enrichment often took the form of writing, and Mendes was prolific in this genre. He was a founder of the *American Hebrew* and published many articles, poems, and translations in its early pages. Pamphlets, plays, books for children also appeared together with many hymns and music, both supplied by the author. He also worked as a consulting editor for the *Jewish Encyclopedia* and cooperated with the Jewish Publication Society in its preparation of a modern translation of the Bible. As conservative forces sought stronger institutions, Mendes worked closely with *Sabato Morais to establish the Jewish Theological Seminary of America (1887). He served on its board of advisors, lectured for a time on Jewish history and was interim president from 1897 to 1902. The New York Board of Jewish Ministers (1882) and the more widespread Union of Orthodox Jewish Congregations (1898) were established under his guidance. He served as secretary of the former group for more than twenty years, as president of the latter from 1898 to 1913. These and many other activities were the daily round of a generous and energetic individual who bolstered loyalty to orthodox standards until poor health forced him into retirement and long periods of convalescence.

Bibliography:

A.   *Jewish History Ethically Presented* (New York, 1898); *Looking Ahead: Twentieth Century Happenings* (London, 1899); *Jewish Religion Ethically Presented* (New York, 1905); *Derech Hayim: The Way of Life* (New York, 1934).

B.   NCAB 39, 621–22; DAB 22, 452–53; UJE 7, 479–80; EJ 11, 1343–44; NYT 21 Oct 1937, 23; David deS. Pool, *H. Pereira Mendes: A Biography* (New York, 1938).

MERTON, Thomas (31 January 1915, Prades, France—10 December 1968, Bangkok, Thailand). *Education*: studied at Cambridge Univ., 1933–34; B.A., M.A., Columbia Univ., 1938, 1939. *Career*: instructor in English, St. Bonaventure's Coll., 1940–41; member, Reformed Cistercians of the Strict Observance, or Trappists (Master of Students, 1951–55, Master of Novices, 1955–65), 1941–68.

Merton's life was one of constant search for union with God, a twentieth-century version of Augustinian restlessness that did not end with his entering a Catholic religious order. Nominally an Anglican in his youth, he sought meaning and a sense of vocation during his years as student, college teacher, and settlement house worker in Harlem. Shortly after conversion in 1938, he decided that there was a deeper involvement with reality in monastic contemplation than in frequent attendance at mass or in worldly distractions. He chose an order known for its solitude and rules of silence, entering Our Lady of Gethsemani Abbey near Bardstown, Kentucky, to seek deeper communion with God in the company of like-minded men. But the definite commitment of a Trappist was not enough to satisfy Brother Louis, as he was called within the order. He continued to climb along the seven-storied purgatory of human experiences in search of the perfect vision that has led mystics in every age. Merton's autobiography (best-seller in 1949) and journals provide an unusually lucid portrait of one soul's pilgrimage through darkness toward the light.

There was little intent at the beginning to influence individuals considering a religious vocation, acquire a prominent place in American letters, or become a respected critic of social conditions, but Merton accomplished all these things from within his monastic setting. He originally entered to save his soul and become a saint. His superiors assigned him to tasks in teaching, research, and translation. Instead of finding obscurity Merton found that he wrote more than ever before, and during those twenty-seven years almost fifty books together with three hundred articles appeared over his name. Without his wishing it Merton was established as a major commentator on religion and society. From sophisticated agnostic to monk, he moved full circle to see that by leaving the world he was more genuinely associated with it in a contributive way than before.

The restless energy of Merton's mind led him to write on many topics, and in his dialogue with a wide reading public on issues in the secular sphere none were more important to him than social justice and pacifism. His searching comments on the Black Americans' struggle for recognition of their civil rights and on those seeking peace by nonviolent means are among the best of the 1960s. He also continued to explore different approaches to developing the inner life, becoming a student of oriental monasticism in hopes of supplementing western contemplative traditions. His interest in Zen Buddhism led to a more universal outlook, and in 1968 he received permission to participate in an ecumenical conference in Thailand attended by Buddhist monks as well as Asian Cistercians. He wrote of new insights acquired there and new friendships made. But all the questing was stopped short, when he accidentally touched a fan with faulty wiring in his room and was electrocuted.

Bibliography:

A. *The Seven Storey Mountain* (New York, 1948); *The Sign of Jonas* (New York, 1953); *No Man Is an Island* (New York, 1955); *New Seeds of Contemplation* (New York, 1961); *Seeds of Destruction* (New York, 1964); *Zen and the Birds of Appetite* (New York, 1968).

B. NYT 11 Dec 1968, 1; James T. Baker, *Thomas Merton: Social Critic* (Lexington, KY, 1971); John J. Higgins, *Merton's Theology of Prayer* (Spencer, MA, 1971); Dennis Q. McInerny, *Thomas Merton: The Man and His Work* (Washington, DC, 1974); Peter Kauntz, *Thomas Merton as Writer and Monk: A Cultural Study, 1915–1951* (Brooklyn, NY, 1990).

MICHEL, Virgil George (26 June 1890, St. Paul, MN—26 November 1938, Collegeville, MN). *Education*: B.A., Ph.B., M.A., St. John's Univ. (MN), 1909, 1912, 1913; S.T.B., Ph.D., Catholic Univ. of America, 1917, 1918; studied at International Benedictine Coll. of St. Anselm (Rome), 1924; studied at Louvain, 1924–25. *Career:* entered novitiate, Order of St. Benedict, 1909; teacher and administrator, St. John's Univ., 1918–24; editor, *Orate Fratres*, 1926–30, 1936–38; missionary work among Ojibway Indians, northern MN, 1930–33; teacher and administrator, St. John's Univ., 1933–38.

Originally named George Francis, and taking that of Virgil upon entering the Benedictine order in 1909, Michel was the outstanding spokesman for liturgical renewal among American Catholics during his brief lifetime. His abbot provided some understanding of trends relatively unknown in the English-speaking world, but it was after returning from Louvain that Michel became chief intellectual leader of efforts to make the liturgy a vital component in contemporary church life. At his urging, St. John's Abbey took up the work that made it the center of such spiritual and cultural endeavor in America. In 1926 the Liturgical Press and a bi-monthly, *Orate Fratres* (changed to *Worship* in 1952) were founded to spread ideas about the movement which slowly awakened interest in restoring a usable, living pattern of worship. Michel was a prolific writer with many books, articles (over 700), editorials, and pamphlets issued under his name to publicize a reassessment of the sacraments. Extensive correspondence marked another facet of tireless attempts to promote genuine revival in worship, not spiritually irrelevant changes in ceremony. At the core of renewal was his belief that Christ continued his redemptive life through the Catholic liturgy and, because of it, through the persons whom it incorporated into the mystical body of a sacrificed saviour. This reaffirmation of life's spiritual center in liturgical experience led naturally and forcefully to a meaningful apostolate in the larger circles of human society.

Participation in the active life of Christ and his church was the beginning point for Michel to integrate phases of social thought and action. He repeatedly argued that liturgy was not just for the religious and the diocesan clergy but for laity as well who shared in the priesthood of Christ. Priest led others to an active, intelligent contact with Christ in the liturgy; they in turn worked as part of the church to extend the kingdom of God, redeeming atomized and secularized conditions around them. By these motivations Michel helped stimulate others to creative activity in social programs during the 1930s. After Pius XI issued *Quadragesimo Anno* in 1931, Dom Virgil spoke often about restructuring society on an adequate philosophical basis that preserved spiritual values and humanized economic practices. He called for a return to Thomistic categories as a sound basis for adequate treatment of social problems, contributing somewhat to a scholastic renaissance in the middle decades of this century. Philosophy would clarify the ends to pursue, and social science would suggest means, while liturgical riches provided life to the whole. Michel devoted what time and talents he had in service of these principles.

Bibliography:

A. *Philosophy of Human Conduct* (Minneapolis, 1936); *Christian Social Reconstruction* (Milwaukee, 1937); *The Liturgy of the Church* (New York, 1937); *Our Life in Christ* and a second volume *The Christian in the World* in collaboration with the monks of St. John's Abbey, (Collegeville, MN, 1939).

B. DAB 22, 454–56; NCE 9, 800–01; NYT 27 Nov 1938, 48; Paul B. Marx, *Virgil Michel and the Liturgical Movement* (Collegeville, MN, 1957); R.W. Franklin, *Virgil Michel: An American Catholic* (Collegeville, MN, 1988).

MILLER, Perry Gilbert Eddy (25 February 1905, Chicago, IL—9 December, Cambridge, MA). *Education*: Ph.B. and Ph.D, Univ. of Chicago, 1928 and 1931. *Career*: at various ranks, professor of English and American Literature, Harvard Univ., 1931–63; officer, U.S. Army, 1942–45.

After attending college for a time in 1922, Miller left to experience life in a variety of pursuits that included acting and the merchant marine. While in what was then the Belgian Congo he developed a desire to understand what lay at the core of America's productive greatness. This led him back to studies and to Puritanism as the fundamental root of this country's beginnings. Ironically, several professors advised him to choose other topics because the field of Puritan studies had been so thoroughly covered, there was nothing of significance left to do. During the next three decades Miller rejuvenated the study of Puritanism, opened its content more thoroughly than anyone before him, and set new standards of scholarship for succeeding generations to emulate. Some of the new topics he uncovered included the logical architectonic of Peter Ramus and the centrality of covenant, or federal, theology in the Puritan system. He also discussed more familiar categories such as regeneration and sanctification from new angles of vision. Beyond that he provided fresh, provocative biographical studies of crucial figures like *Jonathan Edwards and *Roger Williams.

The basic interest that Miller had regarding Puritans lay in their ideas. As people of this persuasion came to America in order to complete the Reformation and, as a city set on a hill, provide Europe with a model, their ideas were central in determining their behavior. So Miller concentrated on what Puritans perceived to be the nature of reality and the limits of human capacity, what they thought about grace and salvation, and how they contemplated the true church and its place in a holy commonwealth. His wider studies took him to analysis of ideas among the Transcendentalists, in literary figures such as Poe and Melville, and basic conceptions abroad in nine-teenth century American culture. But it is in Puritan studies that he concen-trated most, issued the greatest number of publications, and earned a lasting reputation. Some observers found it odd that, as a self-proclaimed atheist, he chose such an intensely religious group of people as his subject matter. That did not detract from his fascination with their vigorous minds or their integrated systems of thought. And it did not prevent him from stimulating further Puritan studies for the rest of modern times.

Bibliography:

A.   *Orthodoxy in Massachusetts*, 1630–1650 (Cambridge, MA, 1933); *The New England Mind: The Seventeenth Century* (New York, 1939); *Jonathan Edwards* (New York, 1949); *The New England Mind: From Colony to Province* (Cambridge, MA, 1953); *Roger Williams: His Contribution to the American Tradition* (Indianapolis, 1953); *Errand into the Wilderness* (Cambridge, MA, 1956).

B.   DAB supp 7, 537–38; NYT 10 Dec 1963, 43.

MILLER, Samuel (31 October 1769, near Dover, DE—7 January 1850, Princeton, NJ). *Education*: B.A., Univ. of Pennsylvania, 1789; studied the-ology with John Miller, Dover, DE, 1789–91 and with Charles Nisbet, Car-lisle, PA, 1791–92. *Career*: supply preacher, Dover and Duck Creek, DE, 1792–93; associate minister, First Presbyterian Church, New York, 1793–1813; professor of Ecclesiastical History and Church Government, Princeton Sem., 1813–50.

When Miller was called as Presbyterian minister in New York, he served in a collegial relationship with two (later three) congregations. His first years were taken up with preparing sermons and following a round of pastoral concerns, but as years went on he developed an enviable literary reputation. Many of his discourses were issued in pamphlet form, covering a variety of topics such as slavery, temperance, Masonry, the French Revolution, and suicide. Another subject was prompted by vigorous claims put forth by high church Episcopalians of the city, particularly *John H. Hobart. In response to assertions that episcopal churches made all other dissenters or schismatics, Miller politely yet firmly (and repeatedly) defended the idea that presbyters stemmed from authorization equally ancient and valid. Another of his writings grew from his practice of reviewing annual events in a new year's sermon. His first lengthy study consisted of an ambitious review of the eighteenth century, including its ethics, politics, the-ology, natural science, and mechanical arts in addition to advances in scholarship, fine arts, and human rights. The reputation gained through this undertaking made him a likely committee member when Presbyterians began investigating the question of founding a theological seminary. After years of urging, such an institution was begun in 1812 at Princeton, New Jersey. *Archibald Alexander became at once its first professor, but in the following year the New York minister who had written so much to advocate its establishment was appointed Alexander's solitary colleague.

Throughout his many years as professor of church history (and often homiletics), Miller tried self-consciously to shift from sermons to careful lectures. He was convinced that a study of history gave evidence of the reality of vital religion while it proved that Protestant doctrines of grace had been legitimately derived from the Word of God. A scholarly understanding of the past also provided examples for both warning and pious emulation, teaching through all ages that one should not despair over the fate of true believers. In all pedagogical exercises, Miller was dutiful in preserving adherence to orthodox views and strict Presbyterian regulations. He had no sympathy with Hopkinsianism or other New England errors and resisted association with them in various interdenominational missionary societies. Miller was not without ecumenical spirit, but he usually expressed it within the boundaries of his own church, and only a select portion of that. While not opposed to revivals, he stood against ''new measures'' and the Pelagian tendencies of New School theology. For a time he tried to conciliate *Albert Barnes and other liberals, but by 1835 their persistent radicalism caused him to admit firmer measures were necessary. After 1837 he was a staunch Old School Presbyterian who labored faithfully to strengthen religious propriety as he saw it. He worked until the end for greater integrity in church offices as well as excellence of personal performance in them.

Bibliography:

A.   *A Brief Retrospect of the Eighteenth Century*, 2 vols. (New York, 1803); *Letters on Clerical Manners and Habits* (New York, 1827); *Life of Jonathan Edwards* (Boston, 1837); *The Primitive and Apostolic Order of Christ Vindicated* (Philadelphia, 1840); *Letters from a Father to His Sons in College* (Philadelphia, 1834); *Thoughts on Public Prayer* (Philadelphia, 1843).

B.   AAP 3, 600–12; SH 7, 379; NCAB 7, 152; DAB 12, 636–37; Samuel Miller, *The Life of Samuel Miller*, 2 vols. (Philadelphia, 1869).

MILLER, William (15 February 1782, Pittsfield, MA—20 December 1849, Low Hampton, NY). *Career:* farmer, Poultney, VT, 1803–13; officer, VT militia, 1810–13 and U.S. Army, 1813–15; farmer, Low Hampton, NY, 1815–49; lay Adventist preacher, 1831–47.

The ferment of millennial expectations was quite strong during Second Great Awakening excitement, and no preacher gave it more intensity than Miller. His background as a poorly educated army officer and pronounced deist made this seem unlikely. But with a conversion experience in 1816, he began studying the King James version of Scripture in order to settle lingering doubts about contradictory evidence for religious faith. As he progressed, it became increasingly clear to him that the Bible taught a physical return of Christ to earth. Using Archbishop Ussher's chronology of the creation (4004 B.C.) and the heuristic device of reading ''days'' as calendar years, he concluded that the Second

Coming would occur sometime around 1843. Fearing error, Miller was hesitant about voicing his opinion and continued to search biblical passages for another fifteen years. But at length (1831) he felt compelled to preach on the matter. The Baptist church he attended soon gave him a license (1833), and his pulpit mastery together with elaborate charts began drawing large crowds. The stirring message of God's coming wrath quickened many revivals. After 1839 Miller's ideas were publicized by Joshua V. Himes who used newspapers such as *The Midnight Cry* and *Signs of the Times* to disseminate adventist views even farther. Comets and meteor showers in 1843 were seen by many as portents of the end. Thousands flocked to hear the simple traveling preacher who spoke with calm authority about the Day of the Lord. A small minority whipped themselves into a frenzy of extraordinary behavior; most waited in quiet anticipation, certain of their fate on Judgment Day.

The time of predicted cleansing passed without incident. Miller, confessing that this calculations of prophetic periods had been faulty, responded by naming a corrected estimation of Christ's arrival. The day named was 22 October 1844, and anticipation rose higher than ever before. Unfounded rumors spread that adventists indulged in immoral practices and gathered on hilltops in white robes to await the end. It is true that some defied convention by speaking in tongues or liquidating their worldly goods, but most "Millerites" did not indulge in such activity. On 23 October reaction set in after the "Great Disappointment"; the majority of followers returned to former pursuits, their ardor for the millennium substantially cooled. Miller and hard core believers continued to expect Christ's return in the immediate future, though they no longer mentioned a specific time. In April, 1845, they met in Albany, New York, to perpetuate an Adventist collectivity. Miller was considered titular head of the movement, but his importance was figurative rather than tangible. He felt uncomfortable as a sectarian leader preferring to see persons with adventist convictions in other denominations rather than Adventism as a separate church. Perhaps that is why he did not try to hold followers together as disputes over theological emphasis or interpretation produced one splinter group after another. Still he attended annual conferences and preached occasionally until he lost his eyesight shortly before the end.

Bibliography:

A. *Evidence from Scripture and History of the Second Coming of Christ* (Troy, NY, 1836; many subsequent editions); *Dissertation on the True Inheritance of the Saints* (Boston, 1842); *Remarks on Revelation* (Boston, 1844); *Apology and Defense* (Boston, 1845).

B. SH 7, 379; NCAB 6, 542–43; DAB 12, 641–43; NCE 9, 855; Sylvester Bliss, *Memoirs of William Miller* (Boston, 1853; New York, 1971); Francis D. Nichols, *The Midnight Cry* (Washington, DC, 1944); Robert Gale, *The Urgent Voice: The Story of William Miller* (Washington, DC, 1975).

MILLS, Benjamin Fay (4 June 1857, Rahway, NJ—1 May 1916, Grand Rapids, MI). *Education*: B.A., Lake Forest Univ., 1879. *Career*: Congregational minister, Cannon Falls, MN and Greenwich, NY, 1878–84; Congregational minister, Rutland, VT, 1884–86; Congregational evangelist, 1886–97; independent minister, Boston, MA, 1897–99; minister, First Unitarian Church, Oakland, CA, 1899–1903; minister, Los Angeles Fellowship, 1904–11; minister, Chicago Fellowship, 1911–16.

Raised the son of an Old School Presbyterian minister and a mother who had seen missionary service in India, Mills' choice of a clerical vocation seemed as natural as it was promising. By 1886 he devoted himself to full time evangelism, gradually emerging as one of the most prominent urban revivalists in that era. His artlessly simple sermons, without eloquence or overwrought passion, won an estimated 500,000 converts during a decade of successful preaching. Another important factor in his campaigns was their technical efficiency; leaving nothing to chance, he carefully engineered the advance preparation, choirs, committees of volunteer workers, and necessary financing. His "district combination plan" constituted a new phenomenon in modern revivals, but in 1893 Mills began to change the content of his message. Influenced by the social reform ideas of *George D. Herron, he enlarged his perspective to include a more universal interpretation of the gospel. Whereas individual repentance and private morals had comprised his earlier goals, by 1897 he began to advocate concepts such as the brotherhood of all men, organic salvation of society, and righteousness defined as civic cooperation. In that same year he formally disavowed orthodox Christianity because it seemed his expectation of genuine awakening would never occur in standard denominational settings. Further, he felt drawn to a more social vision of redemption and in these universalized religious views he no longer considered the Bible to be the exclusive source of divine revelation. First in Boston and then on the west coast, he launched several associations to sustain his new program of Christian socialism.

A gospel of hope permeated Mills' new plans for regenerating the social order. He believed that the new perspective made possible not only a reorientation of individual lives but a restructuring of the environment as well. Mild premillennial convictions substantiated his belief that the world was improving, that God's kingdom would soon be established through human agency. In keeping with those expectations he became a strong critic of capitalism, exploitation of workers, and the conservative Christianity which abetted these customary social practices. It was more important, he argued, to support municipal ownership of utilities than to insist on enforcing outdated codes of blue laws. Social gospel advocates such as *Washington Gladden endorsed Mills in his new preaching, but few tangible results came from his efforts. After founding two independent religious societies, he concluded that the universal principles of religion fell short of a genuinely redemptive gospel. So in 1915 he sought admission to the Presbytery of Chicago and returned to more orthodox formulations of human salvation. His pilgrimage through various attitudes regarding individual and social reform point to the dilemma of Protestantism, with its tensions or limitations, as it confronted evil in the guise of twentieth century civilization.

Bibliography:

A. *Victory Through Surrender* (Chicago, 1892); *God's World and Other Sermons* (New York, 1894); *Twentieth Century Religion* (Cambridge, MA, 1898); *The Divine Adventure* (Los Angeles, 1905).
B.   SH 7, 379; NCAB 14, 178; DAB 13, 2–3; NYT 2 May 1916, 13.

MILLS, Samuel John (21 April 1783, Torringford, CT—16 June 1818, on shipboard bound for the U.S.). *Education*: B.A., Williams Coll., 1809; B.D., Andover Sem., 1812. *Career*: agent for the CT and MA Home Missionary Societies, 1812–13, 1814–15; agent for the American Colonization Society, 1817–18.

Though his religious nurture in a Congregationalist manse was strong and supportive, Mills originally planned to be a farmer. But he underwent a conversion experience common to many in evangelical Protestantism and became one of the first in his generation to express interest in missions beyond the United States. He sparked a religious revival after entering Williams College in 1806 and helped focus attention on the cause of missions throughout his stay there. In that same year he and several companions constituted the nucleus of a missionary vanguard, formed at a modest prayer meeting hastily convened under a haystack during a thunderstorm. While in seminary, Mills talked incessantly about foreign missions. In 1810 he joined with *Adoniram Judson and two others to petition the Massachusetts General Conference of established ministers for aid in pursuing their objectives. The consequence of that student-initiated movement was the formation of the American Board of Commissioners for Foreign Missions, an evangelical body still active. Poor health prevented his being sent with the first contingent in 1812, so Mills turned to the home front instead. In two separate excursions, he traveled in a large triangle from New York to Louisiana, Georgia, and back to New England. While preaching and distributing Bibles (including French Testaments in New Orleans), he collected information regarding western territories, which he viewed as greatly in need of religious influence. The general situation prompted him to promote the cause of domestic benevolent societies as much as he once had done in creating support for foreign missions.

Greater distribution of religious literature was an important means by which Mills sought to pursue his ministerial calling. He seems to have been an unimpressive speaker, but his energetic determination and organizing ability made some headway in inaugurating cooperative efforts. For example he was instrumental in persuading several denominational groups to merge in 1816, forming the American Bible Society. Dutch Reformed and Presbyterian churches pooled their resources under his guidance to establish the United Foreign Missionary Society. For a time he also turned his attention to the urban poor, whom he described as living in sottish ignorance and deep impiety. Once again the chief method of working among them was tract circulation. In 1817 Mills found another practical outlet, this time for Negro freedmen through the agency of the American Colonization Society. He agreed that independent status for Africans, Christianized under American slavery and transported back to their homeland, would serve a double purpose: evangelism and social tranquility for all concerned. With that in mind he visited western Africa to purchase land for the colonizing venture, territory which eventually became Liberia. Taken suddenly ill with fever, he died on the return voyage and was buried at sea.

Bibliography:

B.   AAP 2, 566–72; SH 7, 380; NCAB 13, 187; DAB 13, 15–16; NCE 9, 856; Gardiner Spring, *Memoirs of the Rev. Samuel J. Mills* (New York, 1820); Thomas C. Richards, *Samuel J. Mills* (Boston, 1906).

MOODY, Dwight Lyman (5 February 1837, Northfield, MA—22 December 1899, Northfield, MA). *Career*: shoe clerk, Boston, 1854–56; shoe salesman, Chicago, 1856–61; agent, Christian Commission, 1861–65; officer, Chicago Sunday School Union and YMCA, 1865–71; itinerant evangelist, 1871–99.

No one was more instrumental in developing enthusiasm for urban revivalism than this dynamic preacher, a poorly educated businessman who turned evangelist and labored with his song leader, *Ira D. Sankey, for over a quarter-century. Moody early made a name for himself in Chicago as a dedicated layman interested in organizing Sunday schools, one of which formed the nucleus of his base of operations, the Illinois Street Independent Church. He was also long associated with the practical and spiritual ministry of the YMCA. During the Civil War he served in a similar capacity. By 1870 he was noted as an able executive, successful fund-raiser, and tireless worker for the religious welfare of those in his vicinity.

But gradually he moved from institutional service to a pulpit career. Moody often traveled for the joint purpose of preaching and securing contributions for the YMCA, but in Great Britain his sermons began to register astounding effects. He conducted an extended campaign there in 1873–75 (others in 1881 and 1891–92) which attracted a large and responsive following. Though he was never ordained in any denomination, Moody, as a simple preacher, returned to this country a famous evangelist and launched a long series of revival campaigns. Huge crowds filled the largest auditoriums or specially constructed facilities in every major northern and midwestern city. Counting the millions who attended and thousands who professed conversion to Christianity, the Moody team restored the place of revivals in American religion and enhanced it beyond standards set earlier in the century. In an effort to nurture the lives of converts and prepare others for the cause of evangelical witnessing, Moody founded secondary schools for young women (1879) and men (1881) in his home town. In Chicago he began the more advanced Bible Institute for Home and Foreign Missions (1889), a thriving seminary which was later named after him. Two young men influenced by Moody and his institutions' ecumenical missionary thrust were *Reuben A. Torrey and *John R. Mott.

Much of the key to Moody's success lay in his optimistic message of salvation and the direct, earnest style in which he delivered it. He always stressed the willingness of God to save every individual who would decide freely to accept the gift of grace. His emphasis was usually confined to the rescue of souls, not doctrinal rigidities, the relevance of religion to social questions, or the welfare of specific denominations. Always direct and vivid in his speech, Moody never let his audiences become overwrought with emotion. Compared to some revivalists of the day, his sermons were lively but not extravagant. They contained the simple, heartfelt message of spiritual redemption offered for all, a theme that has come to characterize modern revivalism.

Bibliography:

A.   *How to Study the Bible*, (New York, 1875); *Selected Sermons* (Chicago, 1881); *The Way to God* (Chicago, 1884); *Prevailing Prayer* (New York, 1885); *Bible Characters* (Chicago, 1888); *The Great Redemption* (Chicago, 1889).

B.   SH 7, 491–92; NCAB 7, 244; DAB 13, 103–06; NCE 9, 1102–03; NYT 23 Dec 1899, 4; William R. Moody, *The Life of Dwight L. Moody* (New York, 1900); Arthur P. Fitt, *Moody Still Lives* (New York, 1936); Emma M. Powell, *Heavenly Destiny* (Chicago, 1943); Richard K. Curtis, *They Called Him Mister Moody* (Garden City, NY, 1962); James F. Findlay, *Dwight L. Moody: American Evangelist, 1837–1899* (Chicago, 1969).

MOON, Charlotte Digges (12 December 1840, near Scottsville, VA—24 December 1912, Kobe, Japan). *Education*: B.A., Valley Union Sem. (now Hollins Coll.), 1857; M.A., Albemarle Female Institute, 1861. *Career*: schoolteacher, Danville, KY (1869–70) and Cartersville, GA (1870–73); Southern Baptist missionary in China, 1873–1912.

Raised on a plantation in Albemarle County by a Presbyterian father and a Baptist mother, Moon proved to be as precocious and as accomplished as her siblings. She was skeptical about religion in early years, but in 1859 she was converted at a revival held by *John A. Broadus and made Baptist piety the center of life thereafter. After the death of her father she helped manage the farm and for several years taught in schools for girls. But she yearned for an outlet of greater service and felt thwarted by the policy of the Southern Baptist Foreign Mission Board which refused to commission unmarried women. In 1872 this policy was reversed, however, and Edmonia, one of Moon's sisters, became the first appointee under the new rule. The following year she too received an appointment and joined her sister in China. Except for occasional furloughs she spent the remaining forty years of her life in Shandong (formerly Shantung) province, at the major city of Penglai (formerly Tengchow or P'englai) or the inland village of Pingdu (formerly P'int-tu). Her educational and evangelical activities were continuously helpful to both native hosts and other American female missionaries whom she trained in her home.

As an ardent advocate of missionary activities in foreign countries Moon remained an important figure in her native land. She wrote a steady stream of letters and articles publicizing the cause and asking for help. In 1888 in a letter to Baptist women of the South she suggested a special Christmas offering for the sake of missions. The idea caught on, and enough funds were raised in that initial effort to send three additional missionaries to China. Moon also urged more organized control over missionary activities, and at her urging the Women's Missionary Union was formed as an auxiliary to the convention's mission board. Since then the W.M.U. has provided massive financial aid for evangelical endeavors overseas. Revolution and famine in 1911 brought severe hardships in China. Faithful to the end, the aging missionary shared her meager substance with local citizens, actually starving alongside them and dying from complications caused by malnutrition. In 1918 her denomination officially proclaimed the Lottie Moon Christmas Offering for Foreign Missions, thereby recognizing her as the "patron saint" of such sacrificial activities and acknowledging her contribution in that field.

Bibliography:

B. NAW 2, 570–71; Una Roberts Lawrence, *Lottie Moon* (Nashville, 1927); Catherine B. Allen, *The New Lottie Moon Story* (Nashville, 1980).

MORAIS, Sabato (13 April 1823, Leghorn, Italy—11 November 1897, Philadelphia, PA). *Career*: teacher for Bevis Marks Congregation, London, 1846–51; rabbi, Mickveh Israel Congregation, Philadelphia, 1851–97; professor of Biblical Literature, Maimonides Coll., 1867–73; president and professor of Bible, Jewish Theological Sem., 1887–97.

After pursuing private Talmudic studies with several Italian rabbis, Morais taught Hebrew for five years at a Jewish orphans' school in London before entering his American rabbinate. He placed great emphasis on education through many channels, helping to revive Hebrew letters in this country and turning his own home into an academy where many influential leaders of the next generation were trained. When his teaching at Maimonides College terminated with the institution in 1873, he had hopes of cooperating with *Isaac M. Wise and Hebrew Union College to aid Jewish higher learning. But the Pittsburgh Platform (1885) was too radical a departure from tradition for him, and he became increasingly troubled over the destructive tendencies of Reform. Morais was gentle and not inclined to dispute philosophical points, but he was adamant in considering the Torah inviolate because of its divine origin. He was not an original thinker but a man of deep moral sincerity whose broad vision led other conservatives to acknowledge his leadership in defending traditional ways. By 1887 this more orthodox-minded group succeeded in establishing Jewish Theological Seminary as an institution for training rabbis along conservative lines. Morais was chosen its first president, a fitting post for one who exerted himself during a span of fifty years to maintain familiar patterns in Judaism.

There were few lines of demarcation between Orthodox and Conservative Jews in Morais' time, and he did not follow any specific guidelines in dealing with current issues. Soon after arriving in America, he became a bold exponent of antislavery views and denounced the evil in polished Sephardic cadence. A half dozen Jewish periodicals, including the *American Hebrew* and *Occident*, received his articles on this and many other topics. Every charitable enterprise in Philadelphia felt the strength of his support, and in the 1880s when Russian refugees began arriving, he was particularly energetic in seeing to their adjustment and relocation. Morais built up through the years no small capacity in biblical exegesis. In addition to professorial duties and efforts at composing Hebrew verse, he translated the book of Jeremiah for the new Bible sponsored by the Jewish Publication Society. By combining scholarship, dignified leadership on moral issues, and selfless efforts to meet practical needs of humanity, Morais won the respect of his coreligionists and that of other citizens as well.

Bibliography:

    A. *Italian Hebrew Literature*, ed. Julius H. Greenstone (New York, 1926).

    B. NCAB 10, 170; DAB 13, 149–50; UJE 7, 638–40; EJ 12, 294–95; NYT 13 Nov 1897, 7; Henry S. Morais, *Sabato Morais: A Memoir* (Philadelphia, 1898).

MORRISON, Charles Clayton (4 December 1874, Harrison, OH—2 March 1966, Chicago, IL). *Education*: B.A., Drake Univ., 1898. *Career*: minister, Clarinda and Perry, IA, Chicago and Springfield, IL, 1892–1908; editor, *The Christian Century*, 1908–47; editor, *Pulpit* 1929–56; editor, *Christendom*, 1935–41; retirement, 1956–66.

In 1909 Morrison bought a small, insolvent religious newspaper named *The Christian Century* at a sheriff's sale. Over the course of four decades he transformed it from an organ servicing his denomination, the Disciples of Christ, into the leading nondenominational journal of Protestant opinion in this country. From his editorial offices in Chicago he became known around the world as a leading Christian journalist who pursued his vocation to the higher level of general public interests. He had no patience with secondary issues or poor writing. As editor he demanded that correspondents write with authority on major questions, championing causes and emphasizing the central place of religion in culture. He repeatedly indicated in specific contexts how churches and their ministerial leadership should become more involved in current issues, not withdrawing from relevant questions but rather locating places where a forthright stand could be taken to advance the effectiveness of religion in human lives. Morrison was a crusader, willing to polarize opinion because he believed gospel truths applied to the full range of society and its problems. His shrewd sense of choosing timely topics, his knack for encouraging writers of innovative zeal, his precisely worded articles on movements of international significance—all these characteristics stemmed from the view that Protestantism had a fundamental place in human culture and that nothing lay outside a perspective informed by Protestant insight.

Over the years Morrison emerged as a vigorous thinker regarding the nature of the church and its mission in the world. Never one to avoid declaring his position on contemporary issues, he criticized mass revival campaigns led by *William A. "Billy" Sunday because of their ephemeral effect on individual piety. He also spoke out frequently against a preoccupation with social reforms because it lacked solid theological content. On a more positive note, he was a perennial advocate of outlawing war. This question of Christian pacifism was so essential to his outlook, he urged adherence to the Kellogg Briand Pact (1928) long after it ceased to be viable, much to the dismay of *Reinhold Niebuhr and others who published *Christianity and Crisis* as an alternative to Morrison's isolationist viewpoint. But ecumenism was the area where his thought had lasting impact. Convinced that ultracongregationalist sentiments were inadequate, unreflective of the past, and incapable of meeting the future, he pressed relentlessly to heal the brokenness of the church. His ecumenical vision began with the 1910 World Missionary Conference and developed appreciably through the 1948 formation of a World Council of Churches. Throughout the intervening years, he helped spread theological and ecclesiastical understanding considered necessary for union of separate bodies. Long after he relinquished control of his paper, it continued to emphasize a central concern for informing readers how to embody the mission and unity of one church in a world of divided loyalties.

Bibliography:

A.   *The Meaning of Baptism* (Chicago, 1914); *The Outlawry of War: A Constructive Policy for World Peace* (Chicago, 1927); *The Social Gospel and the Christian Cultus* (New York, 1933); *What is Christianity?* (New York, 1940); *The Unfinished Reformation* (New York, 1953).

B.   NCAB 52, 276; NYT 4 March 1966, 33.

MORSE, Jedidiah (23 August 1761, Woodstock, CT—9 June 1826, New Haven, CT). *Education*: graduated from Yale Coll., 1783; studied theology under *Jonathan Edwards Jr. and Samuel Wales, New Haven, 1783–85. *Career*: teaching and preaching in CT, GA, and NJ, 1785–89; minister, First Congregational Church, Charlestown, MA, 1789–1819; editor, *Panoplist*, 1805–10; semiretirement, New Haven, CT, 1819–26.

For thirty years, liberal ministers in the Boston area had to contend with a vigorous defender of Calvinist orthodoxy who remained lodged in their vicinity like a thorn in the flesh. Morse did more perhaps than any other individual to initiate the doctrinal dispute which forced Unitarians into open disagreement with traditional Congregational beliefs. He was much occupied with upholding an orthodox body of New England theology and Federalist politics as its counterpart, opposing any compromise which allowed churches to drift toward heresy or republicanism. In 1803 he urged that Harvard appoint as divinity professor someone of sound theological convictions; when a liberal acceded to the chair two years later, he brought the covert struggle into the open by printing a severe criticism of the proceedings. The battle at Harvard was lost, but Morse was a formidable antagonist who continued the war, consolidating Hopkinsians and Old Calvinists into a coalition to resist further Unitarian advances. As publisher of the *Panoplist*, he relentlessly attacked the views of many who wished to avoid controversy. He also worked closely with *Leonard Woods in the monumental task of founding Andover Seminary (1808), the first institution of its kind in this country and a lasting testimony to their party's conservative zeal. The result of these polemic efforts was that by 1815 each theological camp had become so rigid, hopes for a unified Congregationalist platform were no longer feasible.

There were other activities besides doctrinal wrangling in which Morse laid claim to fame. For many years an amateur collector of geographical data, he published a series of books, maps, and gazetteers that gained him early recognition as the father of American geography. He was convinced of the benefits of disseminating religious literature and helped found the New England Tract Society (1814) as well as the larger American Bible Society (1816). Missionary fervor lay behind much of his work, whether of positive or negative connotation, and he served for nine years on the American Board of Commissioners for Foreign Missions. After troubles in his own parish led to his resignation in 1819, he did not remain idle. At the request of the federal government he investigated conditions among Indian nations along U.S. borders with a view toward improving their religion and culture. His report was understandably full of white bias but aroused in its readers a deep interest in sharing the blessings of civilization and Christianity with heathen tribes to the west. To the end of his days, Morse represented an embattled orthodoxy, opposed to departures which increasingly came to characterize the post-revolutionary era.

Bibliography:

A.   *The American Universal Geography*, 2 vols. (Boston, 1793); *The American Gazeteer* (Boston, 1797); *Review of American Unitarianism* (Boston, 1815); *An Inquiry into the Right to Change the Ecclesiastical Constitution of the Congregational Churches of Massachusetts* (Boston, 1816); *Report to the Secretary of War . . . on Indian Affairs* (New Haven, 1822).

B.   AAP 2, 247–56; NCAB 13, 353; DAB 13, 245–47; William B. Sprague, *Life of Jedidiah Morse* (New York, 1874); James K. Morse, *Jedidiah Morse: A Champion of New England Orthodoxy* (New York, 1939).

MOTT, John Raleigh (25 May 1865, Livingston Manor, NY—31 January 1955, Orlando, FL). *Education*: studied at Upper Iowa Univ., 1881–85; Ph.B., Cornell Univ., 1888. *Career*: student secretary (1888–1915) and general secretary (1915–31), International Committee of the Student Volunteer Movement, 1888–1920; general secretary (1895–1920) and chairman (1920–28), World's Student Christian Federation; chairman, International Missionary Council, 1928–46; active retirement, 1946–55.

As a Methodist layman who decided he could do more good working with college students than in a pastorate, Mott grew along with the magnitude of his task to reach worldwide stature. When he was hardly more than a student himself he began touring the country as secretary of the YMCA intercollegiate movement. Over the next few years he expanded operations on groundwork laid by *Luther D. Wishard, his friend and mentor. At the same time he was deeply involved with student volunteers for foreign missions, a group which met at summer conferences in *Dwight L. Moody's Northfield, Massachusetts home. Mott brought his administrative efficiency to bear on that movement as well, and over succeeding decades he furthered interdenominational missionary efforts with zeal matched by confidence of ultimate success. In 1895 one of his greatest achievements came to fruition in the World's Student Christian Federation. The international organization hoped to unite student Christian movements throughout the world by exchanging information, deepening spiritual life and extending the kingdom of Christ through the witness of young people. Though he was continually plagued with seasickness, Mott traveled extensively (1.7 million miles) on behalf of the federation. His repeated world tours for missions and YMCA work made his name synonymous with an evangelism determined to overcome geographical, linguistic, and cultural barriers.

Mission work on an international scale led Mott to see the value of cooperation between different churches. The practical task of meeting evangelical needs made him one of the strongest American proponents of ecumenism in the twentieth century. He helped prepare for the World Missionary Conference which met at Edinburgh in 1910; during the ensuing decade he served as chairman of its continuing committee. In 1937 he presided at Oxford over the first Faith and Order Conference as it formulated guidelines for later ecumenical agreements. After 1938 he served as vice-chairman of the provisional committee which pursued its efforts for churchly cooperation despite the disruptions of global warfare. In 1948 their work was crowned by the formation in Amsterdam of the World Council of Churches. Mott was appointed one of its first presidents, a title later made honorary and given him for life. His single-minded devotion to world missions and ecumenical activity to accomplish the goal made him a fitting recipient of the Nobel Peace Prize in 1946. He remained active until almost the end, spurred by the vision of converting all nations within the space of his own generation.

Bibliography:

A. *The Evangelization of the World in This Generation* (New York, 1900, 1972); *The Students of North America United* (New York, 1903); *The Future Leadership of the Church* (New York, 1909); *The World's Student Christian Federation: Origin, Achievements, Forecast* (New York, 1920); *The Present-Day Summons to the World Mission of*

Christianity (Nashville, 1931); *Addresses and Papers of John R. Mott*, 6 vols. (New York, 1946–47).

B.   SH 8, 30; NCAB 44, 346–47; NCE 10, 43; NYT 1 Feb 1955, 29; Basil J. Mathews, *John R. Mott: World Citizen* (New York, 1934); Galen M. Fisher, *John R. Mott: Architect of Co-operation and Unity* (New York, 1952); C. Howard Hopkins, *John R. Mott, 1865– 1955: A Biography* (Grand Rapids, MI, 1979).

MOTT, Lucretia Coffin (3 January 1793, Nantucket, MA—11 November 1880, Roadside, PA). *Career:* Quaker minister, 1821–80; president, American Equal Rights Association, 1866–69.

The importance of Lucretia Mott's life cannot be measured by institutional offices but by the causes which she supported in various ways, her consistency sustained over half a century and the depth of moral purpose which led to such action. As a Quaker preacher who agreed with *Elias Hicks in 1827 that religious thought should be free from any version of orthodoxy, Mott devoted her life to theological and social forms of emancipation. Though she developed views of God and man that resembled Unitarianism, doctrines were not stressed as much as the practical application of Jesus' teachings. She believed in human goodness and worked to realize that potential in the public as well as private sphere. In 1825 she became concerned about slavery and by 1831 had adopted the Garrisonian position that immediate emancipation was the only practical solution. Strengthened by her husband's support, Mott urged freedom for black Americans when it was unpopular for anyone, let alone a woman, to do so. She was an auxiliary force to abolitionist societies, serving on their executive committees after women were allowed to participate. She helped organize the Anti-Slavery Convention of American Women and stood bravely when a mob burned its meeting hall in 1838, conducting herself equally well in a similar incident two years later. Runaway slaves could always rely on finding practical aid at her home. After emancipation, she continued to work on their behalf, pressing for Negro suffrage and providing necessities, such as school supplies for freedmen in the South.

Freeing Blacks from human bondage was the paramount issue to Mrs. Mott for decades, but it could not be separated from the more universal oppression of women. Because of her Quaker background where women were allowed a voice in religious affairs, she refused to bow to the widespread prejudice that public activities were disallowed. Together with *Elizabeth C. Stanton she helped organize the first women's rights convention at Seneca Falls, New York, in 1848, and continued thereafter to expose the injustices under which her sex suffered in educational, economic, and political matters. Unlike many of her sister activists, she did not consider the right to vote as the essential point of their general struggle for equality. Annual conventions on women's rights could always count on Mott's active support through stirring speeches and practical advice. She did not take sides in 1869 when leading feminists split into factions, preferring to work for the larger ideals which all of them followed. Continuing for the last twelve years without her husband, she was active in reform projects large and small, providing the next generation with an example of commitment and tenacity that was not lost on it.

Bibliography:

A. *A Sermon to the Medical Students* (Philadelphia, 1849); *Discourse on Woman* (Philadelphia, 1850).

B. NCAB 2, 310–11; DAB 13, 288–90; NAW 2, 592–95; NYT 12 Nov 1880, 5; Anna D. Hallowell (ed.), *James and Lucretia Mott: Life and Letters* (Boston, 1884); Lloyd C. M. Hare, *The Greatest American Woman: Lucretia Mott* (New York, 1937); Otelia Cromwell, *Lucretia Mott* (Cambridge, MA, 1958); Dorothy Sterling, *Lucretia Mott: Gentle Warrior* (Garden City, NY, 1964); Margaret Hope Bacon, *Valiant Friend: The Life of Lucretia Mott* (New York, 1980).

MUHAMMAD, Elijah (7 October 1897, Sandersville, GA—25 February 1975, Chicago, IL). *Career*: itinerant laborer, 1913–23; factory worker, Detroit, MI, 1923–29; assistant minister, Temple of Islam, Detroit, 1930–34; itinerant missionary, Nation of Islam, 1934–42; imprisonment, 1942–46; chief minister, Nation of Islam, Chicago, IL, 1946–75.

Elijah (or Robert, according to some sources) Poole was one of thirteen children born to a poverty-stricken ex-slave who supplemented farming with preaching in local Baptist churches. He left home at the age of sixteen and worked at odd jobs or on railroad gangs until moving to the automotive assembly plants of postwar Detroit. There he met and quickly became a disciple of Wallace D. Fard, a black man like himself who taught that Islam was the true faith of so-called Negroes, a potentially great nation scattered and oppressed in white man's America. After adopting the surname Muhammad in place of his "slave name," he rose to eminence in nearby Temple No. 1 as the people known as Black Muslims began to gather strength. Fard disappeared without a trace in 1934; Muhammad proclaimed himself divinely appointed "Messenger of Allah," an office making him both custodian of revelation and head of all the faithful in America. Schism resulted from struggles for power in the movement, and "Prophet" Muhammad was forced to move to Chicago, then to the east coast where he spent seven years defending himself against rival factions as well as building up loyal followers in major cities. He was jailed from 1942 to 1946, charged with violating the Selective Service Act, but prison gave him martyr status. On returning to Chicago, he emerged as undisputed leader of the Nation of Islam, a racially separate religious body now grown to significant proportions. His Mosque No. 2 became the spiritual center of a national membership ranging between an estimated 50,000 to a quarter million persons.

Black Muslims based their corporate identity on the exclusive truth of Islam, the vital quality of self-knowledge and the essential factor of self-sufficiency. Such maxims caught the imagination of young Blacks, usually uneducated and stemming from economically desperate social strata, who found new meaning for their lives amid conditions shaped by white domination with its Christian rationalizations. They were able to believe that the original human race had been black; whites appeared as mutations, an intellectually inferior and morally depraved collection of devils compared to dark-skinned peoples. Muhammad insisted that his religion did not preach race hatred but simply spoke the truth as borne out by historical experience. In the last years of his life he began to moderate the anti-white tone of Muslim ideology, but it functioned for three early decades as a rallying point for black pride. More importantly, its puritanical moralism, strict authoritarianism, and program of economic self-improvement gave adherents a dignified cohesiveness rarely achieved under Christian auspices. At Muhammad's urging, strong moral codes were enforced. Alcohol, tobacco, and narcotics are forbidden; adultery, juvenile delinquency, and other crime is virtually non-existent. Lives radically changed under these sanctions have silenced many critics who doubted the spiritual basis of this reform movement. The impulse for religio-cultural independence also expresses itself in supplying material goods for the faithful. Farmland, transport systems, banks, schools, restaurants, stores, publishing companies—all attest to the fact that Black Muslims are determined to maintain a separate way of life, one structured by their honored prophet whose religious vision had no place for cultural servitude.

Bibliography:
    A. *The Supreme Wisdom*, 2 vols. (Chicago, n.d.); *Message to the Blackman in America* (Chicago, 1965); *How to Eat to Live* (Chicago, 1967).
    B. NYT 26 Feb 1975, 1.

MUHLENBERG, Henry Melchior (6 September 1711, Einbeck, Germany— 7 October 1787, Trappe, PA). *Education*: graduated from Univ. of Göttingen, 1738; studied theology under Gotthilf Francke while a teacher at Waisenhaus, Halle, 1738–39. *Career*: assistant minister and inspector of orphanage, Grosshennersdorf, Germany, 1739–41; minister, united Lutheran congregations, Philadelphia, New Hanover, and New Providence (Trappe), PA, 1742–79.

The first German Lutheran congregation was organized in America around 1703 in the vicinity of Philadelphia. Thirty years later additional immigrants had created a number of scattered churches which petitioned the fatherland for trained ministers to provide discipline and sacraments under acceptable standards. After many delays Muhlenberg was sent in 1742 by pietist leaders at Halle, largely because *Nikolaus L. Zinzendorf was making inroads among Lutherans for the Moravian cause. Arriving in the New World unheralded, Muhlenberg soon gained control over pastors of dubious character and began the endless task of planting churches among dispersed settlers. He looked beyond his three local congregations because of a determination to work for the larger cause of American Lutheranism, pursuant to which he traveled from New York to Georgia during forty-five years of dedicated labor. While he preached mostly to Germans who lived between the Hudson and Potomac rivers, he soon began ministering to

Dutch and English colonists as well, each in their own language. Frequent travel to administer sacraments and to preach the gospel as rooted in the unaltered confessional symbols of Augsburg was the mainstay of Muhlenberg's effort to foster an independent, self-sustaining church system. His itinerant visits which carefully tended to religion's external scaffolding and its spiritual edifice contributed to a steady growth of faithful communicants. Muhlenberg may have seemed only a missionary pastor in the eyes of his superiors at Halle, but enterprise, talent, and boundless energy made his work equal to that of a bishop.

Probably Muhlenberg's greatest single achievement along institutional lines came in 1748 with the organization of Lutheran clergymen into the Pennsylvania Ministerium, the first permanent synod in this country. In that same year he helped prepare a uniform liturgy. He also compiled basic tenets for an ecclesiastical constitution which most churches adopted in 1761. Much of the work on a hymnal (published by the Ministerium in 1786) came from his pen. He traveled wherever needed to baptize and exhort, organizing new congregations while strengthening existing ones. Often his judicious presence was used to arbitrate disputes among coreligionists or between them and other confessions. He labored to recruit ministers from Europe and more importantly to develop the calling among local personnel. His pastoral zeal slowly made itself an important molding force within the culture of German settlers. Because of loyalty to the house of Hanover he tried to remain neutral during the Revolution. But one of his sons served as a general in the Continental Army, and another became a distinguished congressman. Their sympathies reflected majority opinion more than did the old preacher's. Poor health forced him into retirement but did not entirely end those labors which made Muhlenberg the patriarch of Lutheran churches in America.

Bibliography:

A. *The Journals of Henry Melchior Muhlenberg*, trans. and ed. Theodore G. Tappert and John W. Doberstein, 3 vols. (Philadelphia, 1942–58); *Heinrich Melchior Mühlenberg: Selbstbiographie, 1711–43*, ed. William Germann (Allentown, PA, 1881).

B. AAP 9, 4–13; SH 8, 36–38; NCAB 5, 499; DAB 13, 310–11; NCE 10, 64–65; Martin L. Stoever, *Memoir of the Life and Times of Henry Melchior Muhlenberg* (Philadelphia, 1856); William J. Mann, *Life and Times of Henry Melchior Mühlenberg* (Philadelphia, 1887); Paul A. W. Wallace, *The Muhlenbergs of Pennsylvania* (Philadelphia, 1950); Leonard R. Riforgiato, *Missionary of Moderation: Henry Melchior Muhlenberg and the Lutheran Church in English America* (Lewisburg, PA, 1980).

MUHLENBERG, William Augustus (16 September 1796, Philadelphia, PA— 8 April 1877, New York, NY). *Education*: B.A., Univ. of Pennsylvania, 1815; studied theology under *William White in Philadelphia, 1815–18. *Career*: curate, Christ Church, Philadelphia, 1817–20; rector, Lancaster, PA, 1820–26; supply rector, Flushing, NY, 1826–28; principal, Flushing Institute, 1828–46; professor, St. Paul's Coll., 1837–46; rector, Church of the Holy Communion, New York, 1846–58; pastor-superintendent, St. Luke's Hospital, New York, 1857–77.

Although a German Lutheran heritage stemmed from his great-grandfather, *Henry M. Muhlenberg, the younger Muhlenberg began attending Episcopal services at the age of nine and grew up comfortably within that communion. His education in cosmopolitan Philadelphia brought contact with varying churches from Quaker to Catholic, helping to confirm in him an ecumenical mindedness which undergirded some of his most notable activities. He was an accomplished musician and poet who furthered aesthetic reforms in liturgical practice by adding hymns and prayers from many Christian traditions to standard denominational fare. From his hints for catholic union in 1835 to a paper read before the Evangelical Alliance in 1873, Muhlenberg urged the confederation of major Protestant groups in America. His memorial at an Episcopal General Convention in 1853 was probably the most important single factor in stimulating debate over ecumenical goals. He suggested that bishops streamline their administrative procedures and initiate liturgical and canonical changes in order to work with clergy of all denominations in representing the gospel among men from all strata of society. The ecclesiastical bases for such cooperation already existed, and the memorialist advocated them for common action. He was confident that the Apostles' Creed could serve as a unifying theological base; shared Bible lessons and hymns could permit similar worship; a council on joint affairs could manage related activities; and finally, though he was less sanguine about it, a common pattern of ordination might be achieved to facilitate interchurch exchanges of service. The Muhlenberg memorial did not gain significant backing when first offered, but it stimulated thought in that direction and anticipated later developments.

While at the height of his influence in New York, Muhlenberg published a weekly, *The Evangelical Catholic* (1851–53), which avoided party strife and emphasized matters of practical Christian action among the poor. In designing his parish along institutional church lines, he provided a model for many others in urban areas. In 1845 (formal constitution, 1853) he organized the Sisterhood of the Holy Communion and thereby furthered his great interest in religious education. By 1858 the order's work in a dispensary had expanded to become St. Luke's Hospital, an institution which gave assistance to all who needed it. Another venture was St. Johnland, a large community on Long Island where Muhlenberg experimented with forms of Christian socialism, accepting participants with a nonsectarian policy. By the end of his life he had spent all his inherited wealth on projects of serious, practical religious witness, dying in poverty at St. Luke's.

Bibliography:

A.   *Christian Education* (Flushing, NY, 1840); *An Account of St. Johnland* (New York, 1870); *Evangelical Catholic Papers*, comp. Anne Ayres, 2 vols. (New York, 1875–77).

B.   SH 8, 51; NCAB 9, 199; DAB 13, 313–14; NYT 9 Apr 1877, 5; Anne Ayres, *Life and Work of William Augustus Muhlenberg* (New York, 1880; rev. ed. 1884); William W. Newton, *Dr. Muhlenberg* (New York, 1890); Alvin W. Skardon, *Church Leader in the Cities: William Augustus Muhlenberg* (Philadelphia, 1971).

MULLINS, Edgar Young (5 January 1860, Franklin County, MS—23 November 1928, Louisville, KY). *Education*: graduated from Texas A&M Coll., 1879; B.D., Southern Baptist Sem., 1885; studied at Johns Hopkins Univ., 1891–92. *Career*: minister, Harrodsburg, KY, 1885–88; minister, Baltimore, MD, 1888–95; associate secretary, Southern Baptist Foreign Mission Board, 1895–96; minister, Newton Center, MA, 1896–99; president, Southern Baptist Sem., 1899–1928.

Though his father and grandfather had been Baptist preachers, young Mullins graduated from college with plans for the legal profession rather than preaching. But a conversion experience led to seminary training, then a series of pastorates in which he became known for vigorous, lucid sermons. At the height of his intellectual powers, he was asked to accept the presidency of Southern Baptist Theological Seminary, an institution recently torn by denominational controversy. With great patience and no little diplomacy he slowly built the seminary's following into unified support. Under his leadership, steps were taken to establish three new professorships, inaugurate a theological quarterly (the *Review and Expositor*), and increase endowment substantially. He executed all presidential duties with considerable administrative skill, but probably his greatest contribution lay in teaching theology. For years he had been forced to simplify his thoughts for general audiences; in the classroom it was possible to investigate systematically every aspect of religious topics among students with a similar taste for thoroughness. Mullins helped raise the theological level of ministerial students in his denomination by means of such lectures in addition to several books which defended conservative theology in an irenic spirit. His moderate views had a widespread impact on the thought of Southern Baptists, particularly in the area of preserving evangelical faith, despite problems raised by modern science. In affairs extending beyond the seminary, which moved outside downtown Louisville at his direction, he presided over the Southern Baptist Convention from 1921 to 1924. In 1923 he was also made president of the Baptist World Alliance and in that capacity labored for the rest of his life to promote harmony among worldwide constituents in the name of cooperative progress amid modern challenges.

Bibliography:

A.   *Why is Christianity True?* (Chicago, 1905); *Baptist Beliefs* (Louisville, 1912); *Freedom and Authority in Religion* (Philadelphia, 1913); *The Life in Christ* (New York, 1917); *The Christian Religion in its Doctrinal Expression* (Philadelphia, 1917); *Christianity at the Cross Roads* (Nashville, 1924).

B.   SH 8, 52–53; NCAB 21, 115; DAB 13, 322–23; NYT 24 Nov. 1928, 17; Isla M. Mullins, *Edgar Young Mullins: An Intimate Biography* (Nashville, 1929); William E. Ellis, ''*A Man of Books and a Man of the People*''*: E.Y. Mullins and the Crisis of Moderate Southern Baptist Leadership* (Macon, GA, 1985).

MUNDELEIN, George William (2 July 1872, New York, NY—2 October 1939, Mundelein, IL). *Education*: B.A., Manhattan Coll., 1889; graduated from St. Vincent's Sem., 1892; D.D., Urban Coll. of Propaganda, Rome, 1895. *Career*: associate secretary to the bishop of Brooklyn, 1895–97; chancellor, diocese of Brooklyn, 1897–1909; auxiliary bishop of Brooklyn (titular bishop of Loryma), 1909–15; archbishop of Chicago, 1915–39; cardinal, 1924–39.

After gaining a reputation for administering successful building programs in his home diocese, Mundelein was named the third archbishop of Chicago, a midwestern metropolis that afforded many opportunities for thinking and acting big. There he became a noted fund-raiser and careful planner as Catholicism spread through the suburbs. Under his supervision hundreds of new churches were built, together with schools for secondary education, hospitals, orphanages, convents, and rectories. Another indication of his corporation management skill was the Associated Catholic Charities, founded in 1917 to coordinate all the different welfare and support programs that distributed aid to the needy. At that time Mundelein also established a preparatory seminary, named for his predecessor James E. Quigley, which by 1925 had become the largest in the country. His most ambitious project was to create a major seminary to train priest for the growing archdiocese and neighboring areas. In 1920 he founded Saint Mary of the Lake Seminary forty-five miles northwest of Chicago, and over the next fourteen years he erected fourteen buildings at a cost of ten million dollars. In 1924 both the locale and the seminary changed their names to Mundelein as a tribute to their patron who had just been named cardinal.

Descended from immigrants himself, Mundelein was typically enthusiastic about the process of Americanization. He discouraged continuing ethnic identity among parishioners and urged all Catholics to designate themselves only through their religion and their American citizenship. This emphasis on assimilation caused particularly bitter reactions from Polish Catholics in the archdiocese. As counterbalance the prelate hosted the 28th International Eucharistic Congress in 1926, and it was a spectacular success, marred though it was by a torrential downpour. More than a million of the faithful, including 12 cardinals, 64 archbishops, and 8,000 priests, attended this, one of the largest religious assemblies in history. Mundelein often spoke on behalf of the poor and championed the cause of labor. Both his deep patriotism and liberal economic views made him a strong supporter of President Franklin D. Roosevelt and New Deal measures. He criticized *Charles E. Coughlin and took pains to say that isolationism and anti-Semitism were not genuine Catholic doctrine or sentiment. He was also a sharp critic of Fascism, coining the phase that Hitler was an "Austrian paperhanger." This dynamic, direct leader was devoted to his church, country, and people. He died seven months after attending the enclave that made Pius XII pope.

Bibliography:

A.   Two Crowded Years (Chicago, 1918); Letters of a Bishop to His Flock (New York, 1927).

B.   NCAB 15, 36; DAB supp. 2, 477–79; NCE 10, 70–71; NYT 3 Oct. 1939, 1; Paul R. Martin, The First Cardinal of the West (Chicago, 1934); Edward R. Kantowica,

Corporation Sole: Cardinal Mundelein and Chicago Catholicism (Notre Dame, IN, 1983).

MUNGER, Theodore Thornton (5 March 1830, Bainbridge, NY—11 January 1910, New Haven, CT). *Education*: B.A., Yale Coll., 1851; B.D., Yale Div. Sch., 1855; studied at Andover Sem., 1855. *Career*: minister, Dorchester, MA, 1856–60; minister, Haverhill, MA, 1864–69; interim minister, Providence, RI, 1869–71; minister, Lawrence, MA, 1871–75; minister, San Jose, CA, 1875–77; minister, North Adams, MA, 1877–85; minister, United Congregational Church, New Haven, CT, 1885–1900; retirement, 1900–10.

During the years of his first pastorate, Munger entered a period of theological unrest which led him to resign for purposes of further study and a possible change of denomination. For some time he was attracted to the continuity, catholicity, and broad church fellowship found among Episcopalians, but he decided eventually that theological certainty was not within the purview of any institutional structure. He remained a Congregationalist, serving a number of churches and defending the cause of honest search in religious thought for himself and many others. His liberal ideas were greatly influenced by *Horace Bushnell, a personal friend whom Munger revered and whose theology he did much to publicize. Their thoughts coincided at so many points, it is difficult to distinguish between the two. After Bushnell's death in 1876, Munger tried self-consciously to continue his basic attitudes regarding the message of Christian nurture in the daily experiences of human life. He kept alive for another generation the ideal of tolerance in men's common search for religious truth, not in systems of divinity but through all categories of modern thought.

One example of Munger's concern for intellectual freedom can be seen in his reaction to the Burial Hill Declaration of 1865. Representatives of Congregational churches had met in that year at Plymouth, Massachusetts, to define their denomination's inclusive affirmations. Munger spoke for a minority which perceived the effort as just another attempt to prevent change by imposing the authority of a rigid creed on speculative minds. He rejected creedal qualifications for church membership and argued that theology was too easily used as a test, preventing cooperation among fellow Christians in their larger task of witnessing to the gospel. The self-centered spirit of denominational distinctiveness was foreign to his conception of the ministry, and Munger labored to counteract all such exclusionist tendencies. His sermons and writings were marked by an ecumenically minded wish to avoid party factions and concentrate on the major issues shared by Christians of every creed. The irenic, open-ended approach of this individual was sustained by the sympathies essential to late nineteenth century Protestant Liberalism, and he embodied that outlook for over fifty years of public life.

Bibliography:

A. *The Freedom of Faith* (Boston, 1883); *The Appeal to Life* (Boston, 1887); *Character through Inspiration* (Boston, 1897); *Horace Bushnell: Preacher and Theologian* (Boston, 1899); *Essays for the Day* (Boston, 1904).

B. SH 8, 53; NCAB 31, 339–40; DAB 13, 327–28; NYT 12 Jan 1910, 9; Benjamin W. Bacon, *Theodore Thornton Munger: New England Minister* (New Haven, 1913).

MURRAY, John Courtney (12 September 1904, New York, NY—16 August 1967, New York, NY). *Education*: B.A. and M.A., Boston Coll., 1926 and 1927; S.T.L., Woodstock Sem. (MD), 1934; S.T.D., Gregorian Univ., Rome, 1937. *Career*: instructor, Ateneo De Manila, Philippines, 1927–30; professor of Theology, Woodstock Sem., 1937–67; editor, *Theological Studies*, 1941–67; associate editor, *America*, 1945–46.

For centuries the Roman Catholic position on church-state relations was accepted by its theologians without substantial modification. But in 1942 a young American Jesuit began questioning the place of his church in democratic society, producing in time (1948–54) some of that denomination's most constructive ideas on the role of religion in modern culture. The standard conception against which he worked assumed that the purpose of states is to promote the general welfare of citizens, including cultural and moral dimensions of life. As man's highest socio-political organization, the state is obligated to see that men worship God according to correct procedures, grant no rights to erroneous religion, and regulate itself according to divine guidance. The ideal of a Catholic state, where church teachings molded both religious and civic action, was a widely accepted theory. It found varying application in countries from Spain to the United States, but it remained an ideal for universal emulation. Murray slowly dissociated himself from that mentality, which he called too defensive and incapable of charitable cooperation with non-Catholics in the political sphere. He did not agree that spiritual ends beyond the natural order were the single basis for cooperative action in society. Human reason could achieve partial solutions for a state's citizens without compromising the Catholic faith held by some of the population. The common ground of rational purposes afforded charitable tolerance, especially in a country where irreducible religious heterogeneity was a concrete and perpetual reality. While disappointing in an ultimate sense, pluralistic circumstances did not make coexistence altogether useless.

The central focus of Murray's thought was on formulating principles of ecclesiastical political theology, valid enough to cover all contingencies and dependent on none of them. He sought to defend the unchanging spiritual authority of the church while indicating how it could adapt to divergent temporal orders. In doing so he stressed the indirect power of religion in, not over, civic affairs. Within the spiritual realm, church authority was direct and exclusive; in the workaday world it had an indirect effect by virtue of influencing the conduct of believers. Murray valued this kind of incidental power because of its limitation: there could not be a state church or a religious government under such a scheme.

This view coincided with his general observation that no ideal realizations were possible on the changing political level. Since there were no lasting mundane standards, the church could remain apart from governmental alliances, applying religious teachings to human life as one political reality succeeded another. Murray's theology was a marked departure from traditional European patterns, and while not supported unanimously by American Catholics, it presented itself as a self-conscious, contemporary alternative. The high point of his influence came in 1965 when the Second Vatican Council adopted a decree on religious freedom. He was the chief architect of that document, which opened avenues for mutual tolerance and common effort among men of good conscience.

Bibliography:

A.   *We Hold These Truths: Catholic Reflections on the American Proposition* (New York, 1960); *The Problem of God: Yesterday and Today* (New Haven, 1964); *The Problem of Religious Freedom* (Westminster, MD, 1965).

B.   NYT 17 Aug 1967, 37; Thomas T. Love, *John Courtney Murray: Contemporary Church-State Theory* (Garden City, NY, 1965); Donald E. Pelotte, *John Courtney Murray: Theologian in Conflict* (New York, 1976); Lawrence Brandt, *John Courtney Murray and Religious Liberty* (Rome, 1983); Robert W. McElroy, *The Search for an American Public Theology: The Contribution of John Courtney Murray* (New York, 1989).

N

NETTLETON, Asahel (21 April 1783, Killingworth CT—16 May 1844, East Windsor, CT). *Education*: B.A., Yale Coll., 1809; studied theology with Bezaleel Pinneo, Milford, CT, 1809–11. *Career*: evangelist for Western Association of New Haven, 1811–17; evangelist for Consociation of Litchfield County, 1817–22; convalescence and occasional preaching, 1822–34; part-time lecturer and evangelist, 1834–44.

After several years as a farmer, Nettleton was converted in 1801 and decided to leave the land for volunteer service as a foreign missionary. But local opportunities in evangelistic work opened for him, and he responded to them instead, concentrating his efforts mostly in Connecticut without ever settling into a pastorate. Welcomed by many Congregational clergy of the state, he embodied a form of revivalism that followed eighteenth-century Edwardsean patterns more than those prevalent in the Second Great Awakening. He was careful to avoid highly emotional topics; nevertheless converts multiplied as he poured out awful doctrines of total depravity, personal election, and the sovereignty of divine grace. Such preaching, which did not paralyze but rather promoted favorable response, appeared all the more remarkable because he was not exceptionally gifted as speaker or thinker. His deliberately unsensational methods influenced thousands of persons to join churches while they fostered greater cooperation among those who already belonged. The evangelist's direct approach included house-to-house visits and private conversations with townspeople on religious matters. Inquiry meetings and catechetical instruction for converts added to his effective manner of confronting individuals with God's truth. In 1822 he contracted typhus and never fully recovered. But as far as strength permitted, he continued to encourage steady, godly habits which in his view derived from properly conducted revivals.

By the time Nettleton had reached a measure of success through preaching traditional Calvinistic doctrines, new ideas and techniques associated with evangelist *Charles G. Finney came into vogue. The New England revivalist was perturbed by Finney's modern contrivances, declaring them to be false in theory, contrary to fact, and dangerous in consequences. High-pressure sermons did nothing more than stimulate the feelings of ignorant persons; he thought such practices were fit only for Methodists or Ranters because they excited temporary passions and fostered spiritual pride. This opened the door to extravagances which departed from Scripture, allowed for censorious self-confidence, and ignored the salutary checks of a humble conscience. Siding with *Bennet Tyler, he also opposed intellectual revisions known generally as "New Haven Theology." Consequently Nettleton helped form the Connecticut Pastoral Union in 1833 and backed its theological institute (later Hartford Seminary), which emerged a year later. Poor health caused him to decline a professorship there, but he lectured occasionally and preached in neighboring churches. Ironically his attempts to diminish self-righteousness through the doctrine of election often produced the opposite result. Despite his preaching the supreme excellency of divine attributes, public sentiment increasingly supported the idea that man participated in salvation as well as God. Moralism and self-interest were prevalent characteristics of his age; the inability to affect them is a mark of how far Puritan piety had declined by that time.

Bibliography:

B.   AAP 2, 542–54; SH 8, 127; DAB 13, 432–33; Bennet Tyler, *Memoir of the Life and Character of Rev. Asahel Nettleton* (Hartford, CT, 1844).

NEUMANN, John Nepomucene (28 March 1811, Prachatitz, Bohemia [now Czechoslovakia]—5 January 1860, Philadelphia, PA). *Education*: studied at diocesan sem., Budweis, Bohemia, 1831–33; studied at archiepiscopal sem., University of Prague, 1833–35. *Career*: missionary priest, Williamsville, NY, 1836–40; member, Congregation of the Most Holy Redeemer: novice, 1840, full vows, 1842; missionary priest in MD, PA, VA, OH, 1840–44; rector, St. Philomena's Church, Pittsburgh, 1844–47; vice regent and superior, C. SS. R., 1847–49; rector, St. Alphonsus Church, Baltimore, 1849–52; bishop of Philadelphia, 1852–60.

In retrospect, the fact that Neumann was born on Good Friday and named for his country's patron saint may be taken as a portent of his own saintliness. After completing theological studies he was thwarted in becoming a priest because there were already too many of them in his home region. Consequently he accepted aid from the Leopoldinen-Stiftung, a missionary society based in Vienna, and traveled to America, reaching New York in 1836 and receiving ordination shortly thereafter. For four years he worked among German-speaking immigrants in upstate New York, especially around Buffalo. There he impressed everyone with traits of both humility and dogged determination. Accepting the privations of a sparsely settled area, he established churches and schools as means of retaining the Catholic faith in American society. In 1840 Neumann joined the Redemptorist Fathers, the first person to be professed in this country. After more missionary work in several states he also rose to prominence in Redemptorist administrative affairs. This ability, together with considerable pulpit eloquence, led to his being selected as fourth bishop of Philadelphia.

German-Americans felt they were not adequately represented in the hierarchy, and so Neumann's placement in what was then the largest diocese in the nation was particularly welcome. His short tenure was full of accomplishments in new construction and efficient organization. As an energetic supervisor he visited every church and mission station once a year. He helped organize parochial education into an orderly and comprehensive system, building more than a hundred schools toward that end. At Glen Riddle he established a preparatory seminary and significantly improved standards at St. Charles Borromeo, the most advanced institution in the diocese. In addition to organizing eighty new parishes, he began construction of an imposing cathedral, Saints Peter and Paul. Noted for his pastoral letters and personal devotional practices, he nurtured Catholic life in general by writing two catechisms that were endorsed by American bishops at their First Plenary Council in 1852. Nominated for the process of canonization a few decades after his death, Neumann was named blessed in 1963 and pronounced a saint in 1977. He became the first American male and the first American bishop to be so honored. His feast day is 19 June.

Bibliography:

B.   NCAB 5, 232; DAB 13, 435–36; NCE 10, 364–65; Michael J. Curley, *Venerable John Nuemann, C. SS. R., Fourth Bishop of Philadelphia* (Washington, DC, 1952); James J. Galvin, *Blessed John Neumann, Bishop of Philadelphia*, (Baltimore, 1964); Tom Langan, *Harvester of Souls: John Neumann* (Huntington, IN, 1976); Robert H. Wilson, *St. John Neumann, 1811–1860: Fourth Bishop of Philadelphia* (Philadelphia, 1977).

NEVIN, John Williamson (20 February 1803, near Shippensburg, PA—6 June 1886, Lancaster, PA). *Education*: B.A., Union Coll., 1821; graduated from Princeton Sem., 1826. *Career*: instructor at Princeton Sem., 1826–28; convalescence, 1828–30; professor of Biblical Literature at Western Sem., Allegheny, PA, 1830–40; professor of Theology at Mercersburg Sem., Mercersburg, PA, 1840–53; president of Marshall Coll., located in the same town, 1841–53; retirement for reasons of health, 1853–61; lecturer and then president (1866) of Franklin and Marshall Coll., Lancaster, PA, 1861–76; retirement, 1876–86.

Born and educated within Presbyterianism, Nevin transferred his creedal affirmation to another branch of Reformed theology when he moved to Mercersburg in 1840. His preaching and educational activities were effective inside denominational lines, but they were not as outstanding as his contributions to general theological development in the Reformed tradition and in larger circles of American religious thought. He worked to restore an understanding of the church, its sacraments, and the catholic historical heritage that had been abandoned by an overemphasis in this country on revivalistic emotionalism. In 1849 he became the first editor, and until 1853 the chief contributor, to the *Mercersburg Review*, a quarterly journal which served as an important vehicle for what came to be known as "Mercersburg theology."

As early as 1843 Nevin launched a vigorous attack on the "new measures" of *Charles G. Finney and the superficialities which he thought revivalists were encouraging. By contrast, he stressed the intelligent piety embodied in theological structures like the Heidelberg Catechism as well as more genuine attitudes of corporate worship found in liturgies of Reformation churches. Stimulated by the likeminded *Philip Schaff, Nevin also wrote books on such topics as the mystical presence and Calvin's doctrine of the Eucharist, ecclesiology, historical creeds, and the importance of continuity in church forms, both confessional and liturgical. He stood as a strong example of reasoned and emphatic rebuttal to the revivalism and experimental innovations that characterized much of American religious practice. The accumulated weight of all his writings stressed the importance of traditional church life as a guide and stimulus for individual spiritual development. His preference for the catholic and churchly traditions since the sixteenth century provided minority opposition to pragmatic innovations and helped stabilize theological adaptation to new circumstances in American life.

Bibliography:

A.   *The Anxious Bench* (Chambersburg, 1843; rev. and enl. 2nd ed., 1844); *The Mystical Presence: A Vindication of the Reformed or Calvinistic Doctrine of the Holy Eucharist* (Philadelphia, 1846, 1867); *The History and Genius of the Heidelberg Catechism* (Chambersburg, PA, 1847); *The Church* . . . (Chambersburg, PA, 1847); *The Apostles' Creed: Its Origin, Constitution and Plan* (Mercersburg, PA, 1849); *The Doctrine of the Reformed Church on the Lord's Supper* (Mercersburg, PA, 1850).

B.   NCAB 5, 256; SH 8, 130; DAB 13, 442–43; Theodore Appel, *The Life and Work of John Williamson Nevin* (Philadelphia, 1889; New York, 1969); James H. Nichols, *Romanticism in American Theology: Nevin and Schaff at Mercersburg* (Chicago, 1961).

NEWTON, Joseph Fort (21 July 1876, Decatur, TX—24 January 1950, Philadelphia, PA). *Education*: studied at Southern Baptist Sem., 1895–97. *Career*: minister, First Baptist Church, Paris, TX, 1897–98; assoc. minister, Nonsectarian Church, St. Louis, MO, 1900–03; minister, People's Church, Dixon, IL, 1903–08; minister, Liberal Christian Church, Cedar Rapids, IA, 1908–16; minister, City Temple, London, England, 1916–19; minister, Church of the Divine Paternity, New York, 1919–25; Episcopal layreader, deacon, and priest, Memorial Church of St. Paul, Overbrook, PA, 1925–30; co-rector, St. James's Church, Philadelphia, 1930–35; special Preacher to the Associated Churches of Philadelphia, 1935–38; rector, Church of St. Luke and the Epiphany, Philadelphia, 1938–50.

Texas Baptists are noted for conservative ways and unimaginative thinking, but Newton moved in the opposite direction. He was largely self-taught, and widespread reading led him quite early to question a religion based on threats and thunderings about human depravity. This liberal attitude led him on a spiritual pilgrimage that sought a faith able to satisfy the mind and sanctify the heart. Newton wanted to emphasize the positives in religious thought, nurturing the good in perspective and in human fellowship. He was indifferent to theological points that separated churches, finding sectarianism absurd, and he was quite willing to let sleeping dogmas lie. In his opinion, most doctrinal disputes were as dull as ditch water, and he said the poets taught more about religion than did theologians. Throughout his ministry in three separate denominations he stressed one central theme: the love of God is the origin and end of human life. It fills human experience with tenderness, tenacity, and final triumph. As lecturer, writer, and preacher this ecumenical churchman emphasized the good in human nature in simple, lucid English. He developed ever wider circles of popular support by decrying creedal requirements and holding up instead the vital experiences of life and faith that touch everyone.

This buoyant, somewhat mystical, and always romantic optimism stayed with Newton as he moved from Baptist churches to Universalist ones and finally to the Episcopalian communion. In 1925 he decided that Episcopalianism was the best possible compromise between arid liberals and acrid conservatives, a church that provided common ground on which all could worship together. It provided a genial home for his wider activities too. These included frequent writings as associate editor for *The Christian Century* and "Everyday Living," a column for a syndicated newspaper chain. In 1939 a poll that queried twenty-five thousand clergy declared Newton to be one of the five most prominent ministers in the country. Congruent with his positive outlook on human abilities he was a 33rd degree Mason, served as chaplain, helped establish the National Masonic Research Society, and edited *The Master Mason*. In all these efforts he tried to celebrate the worth of life, to find meaning and purpose in all human experience, and to find in religion that which sustained people through their suffering and bore them victory.

Bibliography:

A. *What Have the Saints to Teach Us?* (New York, 1914); *The Sword of the Spirit: Britain and America in the Great War* (New York, 1918); *The New Preaching: A Little Book about a Great Art* (Nashville, 1930); *His Cross and Ours* (New York, 1941); *River of Years: An Autobiography* (Philadelphia, 1946); *The One Great Church: Adventures of Faith* (New York, 1948).

B. NCAB 38, 70; DAB supp 4, 627–29; NYT 26 Jan 1950, 27.

NIEBUHR, Helmut Richard (3 September 1894, Wright City, MO—5 July 1962, Greenfield, MA). *Education*: studied at Elmhurst Coll., 1912; graduated from Eden Sem., 1915; M.A., Washington Univ. (MO), 1918; B.D., Yale Div. Sch., 1923; Ph.D., Yale Univ., 1924; studied at Berlin and Marburg, 1930. *Career*: newspaper reporter, Lincoln, IL, 1915–16; minister, St. Louis, MO,

1916–18; instructor in Theology and Ethics, Eden Sem., 1919–22, 1927–31; president, Elmhurst Coll., 1924–27; professor, at various ranks, of Theology and Ethics at Yale Div. Sch., 1931–62.

In attempting to characterize the profound impact Niebuhr made on a wide range of religious thought, perhaps the best description is that he approached theology from the standpoint of ethical and historical reflection. In doing so he was influenced by the writings of Ernst Troelsch who had grappled with the problems of historicism and helped him appreciate the contextual nature of religious affirmations. As one who was also largely sympathetic to neo-orthodox theology, Niebuhr moved beyond a trenchantly Barthian position to retain elements of liberal thought as well. He embodied a commitment to the continuing relevance of creeds and biblical symbols, but at the same time he represented freedom from orthodox traditions by protesting against isolation of churches and by insisting on historical criticism of customary beliefs. As a Christian ethicist who understood better than most the historically conditioned relativity of knowledge, he urged that the meaning of church teachings could be rediscovered in contexts which made them relevant to contemporary culture. His critical orthodoxy was a form of confessionalism, but it avoided both self-defensive apologetics and any conflation of expression with content. Confessional forms of religious thought were points of view, not absolutes, and they did not attribute ultimacy to symbols themselves instead of to the God who is viewed in faith. From this perspective it made sense to discuss the historical dynamics of belief acquired through evolutionary, revolutionary processes, more so than to contemplate doctrines expressed as conceptual packages outside an encounter with real events.

While Niebuhr did not build a system of religious thought, he developed a distinctive perspective applicable to many themes. He thought that the radically monotheistic nature of God made it possible to accept the relational situation of revelation and values. Since faith knew of an absolute standpoint, the believers' context and knowledge were necessarily partial; each person could hold the truth, but none could contend dogmatically that his version was whole. Such theological existentialism allowed for continuing reformation, a dialogue of mutual correction where new ideas were permitted to reinterpret, not replace, classic statements. From that perspective he published some of the most creative sociohistorical analyses of the Christian past, clarifying typological patterns in their limited contexts. For his own day, Niebuhr called for a resymbolization of the message of life and faith in One God. In so doing he was confident that a rejuvenated Christian monotheism would dethrone loyalty to pretentious absolutes short of the Principle of Being itself. Yet it would affirm the relative worth of categories in full panoply of creation. From this viewpoint Niebuhr tried to deal positively with ecclesiastical confessions in a world of historical flux. He held that churches must consider their inner meaning in connection with actual experience in varying social contexts. Similarly, he spoke of the relativism confronting individuals who lived by faith. Existential personalism was a basic motif in his ethics as well as an emphasis on moral action as response to culturally conditioned demands. Many expected him to pull together ideas fashioned over forty years' teaching, but he died a year before retirement with the magnum opus still unfinished.

Bibliography:

A. *The Social Sources of Denominationalism* (New York, 1929); *The Kingdom of God in America* (New York, 1937); *The Meaning of Revelation* (New York, 1941); *Christ and Culture* (New York, 1951); *Radical Monotheism and Western Culture* (New York, 1960); *The Responsible Self* (New York, 1963).

B. NCAB 47, 64–65; NCE 10, 462; NYT 6 Jul 1962, 25; Paul Ramsey (ed.) *Faith and Ethics: The Theology of H. Richard Niebuhr* (New York, 1957); John D. Godsey, *The Promise of H. Richard Niebuhr* (Philadelphia, 1970); James W. Fowler, *To See the Kingdom: The Theological Vision of H. Richard Niebuhr* (Nashville, 1974); Lonnie D. Kliever, *H. Richard Niebuhr* (Waco, TX, 1977).

NIEBUHR, Karl Paul Reinhold (21 June 1892, Wright City, MO—1 June 1971, Stockbridge, MA). *Education*: graduated from Elmhurst Coll., 1910; graduated from Eden Sem. (MO), 1913; B.D., Yale Div. Sch., 1914; M.A., Yale Univ., 1915. *Career*: minister, Detroit, MI, 1915–28; associate professor of Philosophy of Religion, Union Sem. (NY), 1928–30; professor of Applied Christianity, Union Sem., 1930–60; editor, *Christianity and Crisis*, 1941–66; active retirement, 1960–71.

Thirteen years as Evangelical and Reformed minister in Detroit developed a social conscience in Niebuhr which blended a realistic assessment of concrete situations with liberal expectations for improving them. He was strongly influenced by social gospel heritage as well as empirical, pragmatic strains in American religious thought, but he wrestled with them from the standpoint of Lutheran piety, emphasizing themes of human sin and justification. These elements plus firsthand experience with labor strikes, race riots, and global warfare combined in him to produce the most fertile theological mind of the twentieth century. His critical appropriation of Protestantism was not primarily exegetical but rather a mixture of biblical insights and penetrating analysis of present circumstances. From such a perspective he unfolded the relevance of theological affirmations to daily living. In discerning the signs of the times, he grew with them, moving generally to the left politically while remaining on the theological right. A Socialist Party candidate for congressional office in 1930, he changed to a moderate supporter of New Deal policies by 1940. A pacifist in 1919, he became by 1939 one of the first to call for resistance to Fascism. In these and countless other activities he embodied an attempt to reform present social abuses on the basis of wide-ranging philosophical reflection.

In all his relating of theology to social sciences, Niebuhr emphasized the incompleteness of modern man and his confused social arrangements. He did this because he saw sin as a basic, though not necessary, fact of life. The ambiguities and idolatries which pervaded human experience grew out of men's attempts to transmute their partial selves into an infinite good. Niebuhr dropped some of his biblical imagery in later writings, but he continued to point out man's egotism and pride as permanent features of existence. On the individual level, man had the ability to transcend selfish inclinations, finding an adequate life in love of God and service to others. On the corporate level, men could not sublimate their collective egotism to the point of working for altruistic goals at their own expense. A review of human history bore out the observation that the pervasiveness of sin made social perfection impossible. Standing on that ground, Niebuhr criticized overconfidence in progress assuming man's goodness as well as reform ideologies, such as Marxism, which denigrated the individual to historical forces. His brand of Christian realism was neither utopian nor doctrinaire, but it always anticipated demonic possibilities in every new form of humanistic endeavor.

Pessimism was not, however, the end result of Niebuhr's stern reminder that sin permeated the contingencies of nature. Through the complex experience of grace, man could learn to sacrifice himself for others. God in Christ, over man and in him, provided resources which man did not have himself, enabling him to become what he truly ought to be. Yet this grace was seen to be more available than operative in the realist's evaluation of ethical activity. In the social sphere, justice rather than love was the goal to seek, and Niebuhr insisted that awareness of sin made political action necessary. Far from concluding in despair or quietism, he argued that politics is the element wherein social moralists should strive to attain justice. It could never be fully achieved, but justice approximated a state of harmony among groups in which freedom and equality were realized as far as possible. Power was necessary to enforce such compromises, and proximate answers to insoluble problems were the only options available. Inevitable conflicts, and difficult choices between lesser evils characterized situations depending on the capacity of groups to agree on arbitrated settlements. Justice was more procedural than substantive for Niebuhr, but he urged that man must continually reach for fuller expressions of it, even while admitting that his major hope lay beyond history altogether.

Bibliography:

A.   *Leaves from the Notebook of a Tamed Cynic* (New York, 1929); *Moral Man and Immoral Society* (New York, 1932); *An Interpretation of Christian Ethics* (New York, 1935); *The Nature and Destiny of Man*, 2 vols. (New York, 1941–43); *The Children of Light and the Children of Darkness* (New York, 1944); *The Structure of Nations and Empires* (New York, 1959).

B.   NCAB G, 468–69; NYT 2 Jun 1971, 1; Charles W. Kegley and Robert W. Bretall (eds.), *Reinhold Niebuhr: His Religious, Social and Political Thought* (New York, 1956); Gordon Harland, *The Thought of Reinhold Niebuhr* (New York, 1960); June Bingham, *Courage to Change* (New York, 1961); Gabriel Fackre, *The Promise of Reinhold Niebuhr* (Philadelphia, 1970); Ronald H. Stone, *Reinhold Niebuhr: Prophet to Politicians* (Nashville, 1972); Richard Fox, *Reinhold Niebuhr: A Biography* (New York, 1985).

NORRIS, John Franklyn (18 September 1877, Dadeville, AL—20 August 1952, Keystone Heights, FL). *Education*: B.A., Baylor Univ., 1903; Th.M., Southern Baptist Sem., 1905. *Career*: minister, McKinney Avenue Baptist Church, Dallas, TX, 1905–08; minister, First Baptist Church, Fort Worth, TX, 1909–52; minister Temple Baptist Church, Detroit, MI, 1935–51; editor, *The Baptist Standard*, 1906–09; editor, *The Fundamentalist* (earlier known as *The Fence-Rail* and *The Searchlight*), 1909–52.

Hard times in childhood, including poverty and an abusive father, made J. Frank Norris a driven man. His ambition to be successful made it possible to finish academic training in record time and to build struggling churches into powerful congregations. But part of him also led to expressing a variety of strong opinions and dealing harshly with anyone who stood in his way. The two sides of his personality annealed, manifesting an utter confidence that his views were absolute truth and that their defense was a righteous crusade. This combativeness accompanied a genuine evangelical concern, and his melodramatic sermons always ended with an altar call for uncommitted souls to embrace the faith. At bottom, though, the churches Norris led were preaching centers based on his flamboyant personality. And he flourished on the notoriety that controversy brought him. In 1914 a local pastor's conference expelled him because he constantly criticized other ministers. By 1922 a county association of Baptists excluded him as a threat to peace and unity. In 1924 the Baptist General Convention of Texas ousted him and his church for noncooperative actions. And yet the following year Norris claimed that his congregation was the largest Baptist church in the world.

All the contention mentioned thus far hinged on Norris's belief in the autonomy of local churches and his opposition to denominational machinery. He also embodied an unwavering commitment to biblical literalism, the central importance of personal redemption, and the premillennial return of Christ. These concerns led him in 1935 to organize a church for transplanted southerners in Detroit, Michigan. Thereafter he traveled thousands of miles each week, speaking at Fort Worth and Detroit on alternate Sundays. During his turbulent career Norris was charged with arson and perjury (1912) and murder (1926) but was acquitted both times. He became stridently anti-communist in the 1930s and an equally forceful advocate of Zionism in the 1940s because it fit his premillennial expectations. But striking at wrongs was always easier than nurturing the good. He saw nothing but religious error, moral decay, and political ruin in the New Deal, the Federal Council of Churches, and the Baptist World Alliance. This contentious, domineering individual battled for what he saw as the truth, but he left a record of acrimony, strife, and division. His bitterness and sensationalism made him one of the most controversial figures in American religious history.

Bibliography:

A. *The Gospel of Dynamite: Messages that Resulted in over 700 Conversions* (Ft. Worth, n.d.); *Infidelity Among Southern Baptists Endorsed by Highest Officials* (Ft. Worth, n.d.); *The Federal Council of Churches Unmasked* (Ft. Worth, n.d.).

B. DAB supp. 5, 516–17; NYT 21 August 1952, 19; Louis Entzminger, *The J. Frank*

Norris I Have Known for Thirty-four Years (Ft. Worth, 1946); E. Ray Tatum, *Conquest or Failure? Biography of J. Frank Norris* (Ft. Worth, 1966).

NORTON, Andrews (31 December 1786, Hingham, MA—18 September 1853, Newport, RI). *Education*: B.A., M.A., Harvard Coll., 1804, 1809. *Career*: tutor, Bowdoin Coll., 1809–10; tutor, Harvard Coll., 1811–12; editor, *The General Repository and Review*, 1812–13; lecturer and librarian, Harvard Coll., 1813–19; professor of Sacred Literature, Harvard Coll., 1819–30; active retirement, 1830–53.

The liberal position of one generation often becomes, by standing still, the conservative force reacting to change in the next. Norton was a good example of the fate meted to consistency, emerging as a brash young liberal in 1812 but acquiring the reputation as "pope of Unitarianism" within three decades. In the earlier years he was outspoken in criticizing trinitarian orthodoxy and inaugurated a new era of controversy with the lead article of his short-lived journal. He was more willing than moderates such as *William E. Channing to declare his liberalism outside the mainstream of New England theology. In keeping with that forthright stance, Norton played a leading role in organizing the American Unitarian Association in 1825. While a professor at Harvard he began some of the earliest work on biblical criticism in this country. His conception of the task was limited to hermeneutics, one which avoided the harder questions being asked in Europe regarding historicity and authorship. The essential task for him was to demonstrate that the gospel records presented an authentic account of Jesus Christ who, as God's messenger, had established the bases of true religion. All his scholarship was founded on Lockean principles which accepted biblical teachings as timeless, rational truths to be understood by means of careful study. Since marriage had brought enough wealth to make early retirement possible, the professor left teaching in order to devote himself full time to such study.

Many charged that Unitarianism was only a halfway house to infidelity, but Norton was determined to arrest the development of critical opinion while it still retained the elements of basic Christianity. He did not doubt that everything essential to true religion could be found in the gospels, nor did he lack confidence in his ability to discern it. Change began to occur, however, when younger liberals appealed to scriptures less and less in substantiating their theological orientation. He took strong exception to those who theorized that it was unnecessary to rely on miracles as proof of biblical authority. Younger thinkers drew their ideas from a transcendentalist conception of man and the world, but Norton considered such idealist epistemology, stemming from either Germany or England, to be inimical to sound belief. Indeed he flatly charged anti-Lockean innovators with deliberate infidelity. His speech in 1839 against new forms of thought was commonly interpreted as a rejoinder to *Ralph W. Emerson's Divinity School address of the previous year. Placing an ultimacy on conceptual (not verbal) revelation, he defended the finality of Christianity as opposed to relativism. He rejected attempts to bridge the sharp distinction between nature and the supernatural because it implied pantheism. But those tendencies paled in comparison to the transcendentalists' worst mistake: claiming intuitive perception of Christian truth. Norton denounced Emerson, *Theodore Parker, and others because their subjectivism led to unacceptable conclusions. He represented the old guard in scolding both perspective and content in what constituted a major debate within the young denomination.

Bibliography:

A. *Statement of Reasons for Not Believing the Doctrines of Trinitarians* (Boston, 1833); *The Evidences of the Genuineness of the Gospels*, 3 vols. (Boston and Cambridge MA, 1837–44); *Tracts Concerning Christianity* (Cambridge, MA, 1852); *Internal Evidences of the Genuineness of the Gospels* (Boston, 1855).

B. AAP 8, 430–35; SH 8, 194; NCAB 7, 63–64; DAB 13, 568–69.

NOYES, John Humphrey (3 September 1811, Brattleboro, VT—13 April 1886, Niagara Falls, Canada). *Education*: B.A., Dartmouth Coll., 1830; studied law, Chesterfield, NH, 1830–31; studied at Andover Sem., 1831–32; studied theology at Yale Coll., 1832–34. *Career*: communitarian religious leader, Putney, VT, 1836–48 and Oneida, NY, 1848–80; active retirement, 1880–86.

Emotions released in revival services of the 1830s sometimes led to extremes in both ideas and action. Noyes was a product of those fervid times, embodying some of the most radical doctrines of his day. While still a theological student (1833), he was licensed to preach in one of New Haven's free churches, a congregation which preferred more uninhibited worship than traditional patterns would allow. That license was revoked and he was dismissed from Yale within a year because he claimed personally to have reached a level of absolute sinlessness. But such conventional impediments could not restrain his dedication to perfectionism; it remained the basic principle which guided his activities for over half a century. After several fruitless attempts to interest other evangelists in his doctrine, he returned to Vermont and established a small following known as Bible Communists. Noyes' ideas hinged on the conviction that the Second Coming of Christ had already occurred in 70 A.D. That spiritual return had abolished the old law of sin, inaugurating an era when perfection was possible for all who would accept the new life of divine inspiration. The Kingdom of God reigned within, and neither Mosaic nor civil codes were binding on those led by their perfect understanding of God's will. The chief means of disseminating such doctrines was through publishing. Journals and public correspondence spread this particular brand of perfectionism through the "Yankee Belt" where revival enthusiasm was at a peak. Members were added to the community, but its symbolic significance was always more important than its size.

The Bible Communists, who placed all their goods in common, flourished as a model social experiment. But their notoriety came from practicing complex marriage within the family of believers. As early as 1837 Noyes declared that monogamy, with its exclusivism, quarreling, and jealousy, was incompatible with perfectionism. Free love or multiple associations among true believers was a manifestation of their superiority to customs of the old dispensation. By 1846 the surrounding communities became so scandalized at Noyes' antinomianism that they filed charges of adultery. He fled to central New York, and the sect moved shortly thereafter. Life in the Oneida colony was regulated according to communitarian principles. It was widely publicized as a financial success and a showplace for Noyes' opinions regarding selective breeding among his followers. By 1877 the aging leader stepped down in favor of a ruling committee; three years later a decision was reached to change the entire group into a joint-stock company. Members returned to monogamous marriage at that time and adopted more capitalistic habits in several small industries. Noyes avoided pending legal action by emigrating to Canada. Today only the name Oneida survives as a reminder of the impact religious enthusiasm can have on forms of social organization.

Bibliography:

A.   *The Berean: A Manual for the Help of Those who Seek the Faith of the Primitive Church* (Putney, VT, 1847; NY, 1969); *Bible Communism* (Oneida, NY, 1848); *Confessions of John H. Noyes* (Oneida, NY, 1849); *Salvation from Sin the End of Christian Faith* (Wallingford, CT, 1869); *History of American Socialisms* (Philadelphia, 1870); *Male Continence* (Oneida, NY, 1872; New York, 1969).

B.   NCAB 11, 238–39; DAB 13, 589–90; NYT 14 Apr 1886, 2; George W. Noyes (ed.), *Religious Experience of John Humphrey Noyes* (New York, 1923) and *John Humphrey Noyes: The Putney Community* (Oneida, NY, 1931); Robert A. Parker, *Yankee Saint: John Humphrey Noyes and the Oneida Community* (New York, 1935); Constance N. Robertson (ed.), *Oneida Community*, 2 vols. (Syracuse, 1970–72); Robert D. Thomas, *The Man Who Would Be Perfect: John Humphrey Noyes and the Utopian Impulse* (Philadelphia, 1977).

O

OCCOM, Samson (1723, Mohegan, CT—14 July 1792, New Stockbridge, NY). *Education*: studied at private school of *Eleazar Wheelock, Lebanon, CT, 1743–47. *Career*: schoolmaster and minister to Montauck Indians, Long Island, 1749–64; fund raising tour to England, 1766–68; itinerant minister to Indian tribes in New England, 1768–84; minister to Mohegans, Brothertown Tract, NY, 1784–92.

By his own account Occom was reared in heathenish ways, perhaps no more so than other unchurched youth of the time, but as an Indian he was self-conscious about it. Born into the Mohegan tribe of the once-great Pequot nation, he found it possible to assimilate the white man's ways to a remarkable extent. Converted around 1740, he began to study the intricacies of English, Latin, and Hebrew immediately thereafter. His potential for the ministry came to the attention of *Eleazar Wheelock who invited him to study at his school in the township of Lebanon. Poor health and eyestrain made it impossible for Occom to attend college, but licensed as a Presbyterian preacher he began instructional work among Indians on Long Island. He had a natural affinity with native groups and preached to them in their own languages with considerable results. In 1759 he received full ordination, a status he maintained proudly for the rest of his life. At the suggestion of *George Whitefield he traveled to England with another companion to raise funds for more extensive Indian missions. His sermons attracted great crowds, including many who came out of curiosity but stayed to donate freely because of the preacher's words. In the end he collected more than £12,000 and returned home anticipating a new era in mission work among fellow tribesmen.

Touring England was the turning point in Occom's life because it gave him a greater sense of independence. Perhaps the adulation of British audiences puffed up an ego which had long resented condescension from white ministers; for whatever reason though, his later life was marked by conflicts with former friends. Wheelock urged him to live among Indians in primitive settings, the better to secure native converts while they were undisturbed in their own cultures. Occom resisted that suggestion and chafed at his patron's interference. When Wheelock moved his charity school north to found Dartmouth College in New Hampshire, opening it to whites instead of Indians, Occom's bitterness became implacable. He claimed that the money obtained for Indian missions was being used for purposes which belied its origin. Instead of an alma mater for native students he saw the new college as nothing better than another alba mater. After 1771 strained relations between the two clergymen led to permanent separation. Occom remained in New England, preaching when he could to tribal groups but living in poverty, indulging in occasional self-pity and excessive drinking. He tried to defend his people's lands from white encroachment, but by 1773 it was clear that removal was necessary to save what was left of native life from complete destruction. After the Revolution, he was instrumental in transferring remnants of former nations to central New York. After much labor on their part he spent a final decade among them, respected by the local Presbytery and admired by neighbors as one who kept his dignity while living in two cultures.

Bibliography:

A. *A Choice Collection of Hymns and Spiritual Songs* (New London, CT, 1774).

B. AAP 3, 192–95; DAB 13, 614–15; William D. Love, *Sampson Occom and the Christian Indians of New England* (Boston, 1899); Leon B. Richardson, *An Indian Preacher in England* (Hanover, NH, 1933); Harold W. Blodgett, *Samson Occom* (Hanover, NH, 1935).

O'CONNELL, Denis Joseph (28 January 1849, Donoughmore, Ireland—1 January 1927, Richmond, VA). *Education*: studied at St. Charles Coll. (MD), 1868–71; D.D., Urban Coll. of the Propagation of the Faith, 1877. *Career*: assistant pastor, St. Peter's Cathedral, Richmond, VA, 1877–83; rector, North American Coll., Rome, 1885–95; rector, Church of Santa Maria Rome, 1895–1903; rector Catholic Univ. of America, 1903–09; auxiliary bishop of San Francisco, 1909–12; bishop of Richmond, 1912–26.

As an immigrant in South Carolina with two uncles serving as examples O'Connell showed early signs of a priestly vocation. The vicar apostolic of that region, *James Gibbons, recognized quality in the young man and encouraged his progress through a ministry of great significance to American Catholicism. After acquitting himself well in theological studies at Rome, he served for a while in parish duties. But superiors thought O'Connell was more valuable near the centers of power, and by 1883 he began serving in various capacities as Gibbons' trusted agent. Two years later he returned to Rome as rector of the college which had been his home for half a decade. Education was part of his responsibility, but more importantly he served as a discreet intermediary who furthered American interests at the papal court. His diplomatic presence was influential in representing new world views on such issues as the Knights of Labor, Cahenslyism, Henry George, parochial schools, apostolic delegates, and the "Americanist" controversy. He was more supportive of liberal policies identified with Gibbons and *John Ireland than those of conservative bishops. As a result, conservatives grew suspicious of his maneuverings and criticized his handling of the college. Their lack of confidence caused him to step down, remaining a beleaguered symbol of liberalism in virtual oblivion.

Appointment as third rector of the Catholic University of America brought O'Connell back into the mainstream of religious developments on this side of the Atlantic. His administration provided much needed academic, monetary, and organizational stability to the deteriorating institution. It was on the verge of complete collapse (especially after financial disaster in 1904), but Monsignor O'Connell effected a slow revival of its energies and promise. He increased student enrollment by adding undergraduate instruction to the university's program; constitutional difficulties were ironed out to rectify internal deficiencies in organization; and the quality of faculty personnel was markedly improved. Academic procedures were regularized on a creditable basis while ways were actively pursued to achieve a united front in American Catholic educational systems. Perhaps the rector's most important contribution was the establishment of an annual diocesan collection whereby all Catholics could support their university through regular giving. Many considered O'Connell top candidate to succeed Gibbons in Baltimore, but the years passed him by. He served for a time on the west coast and then returned to Richmond, diocese of his first pastoral labors. By 1921 old age made a cardinalate unlikely; so he continued to fill his round of duties until failing health caused him to resign shortly before the end.

Bibliography:

B.   NCAB 15, 65; NCE 10, 635–36; NYT 2 Jan 1927, II, 9; Colman J. Barry, *The Catholic University of America, 1903–1909: The Rectorship of Denis J. O'Connell* (Washington, DC, 1950); Gerald P. Fogarty, *The Vatican and the Americanist Crisis: Denis J. O'Connell, American Agent in Rome, 1885–1903* (Rome, 1974).

O'HARA, Edwin Vincent (6 September 1881, near Lanesboro, MN—11 September 1956, Milan, Italy). *Education*: studied at St. Thomas Coll. (MN), 1898–1900; studied at St. Paul Sem. (MN), 1900–05; studied at Catholic Univ., 1910; studied at Catholic Inst., Paris, France, 1918. *Career*: pastor, St. Mary's Cathedral (assistant until 1911), Portland, OR, 1905–20; pastor, St. Mary's Church, Eugene, OR, 1920–28; instructor in Sociology, Catholic Univ., 1929–30; bishop, Great Falls, MT, 1930–39; bishop, Kansas City, MO, 1939–56.

As a priest facing industrial problems in his west coast parish, O'Hara quickly adapted to the needs he saw around him. Humanitarian concerns were a natural extension of pastoral activities, and he became deeply involved in debates regarding Catholic teachings on the rights of labor. By 1913 a committee which he chaired issued its report, leading the way for Oregon to enact some of the earliest legislation establishing minimum wages for women and minors. Washington and California passed bills the same year using verbatim terminology. These bills led to court tests which O'Hara as chairman of the Oregon Industrial Welfare Commission, helped steer to final confirmation by the Supreme Court. Moving smoothly from urban to rural problems, the young pastor achieved even greater prominence in his concern for Catholicism in country districts. For a decade after 1920, he directed the Rural Life Bureau of the National Catholic Welfare Conference, stressing the need for adequate religious education in farming communities. In 1921 he issued a tabloid, *St. Isidore's Plow (Catholic Rural Life* after 1924), to pool the efforts of Catholic ruralists and to propagandize the movement. By 1923 he placed their work on a permanent basis through the National Catholic Rural Life Conference. Connected with these general activities for proper education was his successful campaign in Oregon against compulsory attendance in public institutions. Parochial schools soon began to flourish after the law was declared unconstitutional in 1925.

Educational aspects of Catholic witness had highest priority in O'Hara's ministry, and his elevation to bishop opened new avenues for work along those lines. He immediately inaugurated a Confraternity of Christian Doctrine by which church teachings and moral values were expounded on a regular basis in his diocese. By 1933 he helped establish a national Confraternity headquarters at Catholic University, seeing further that the first national congress was held two years later. He then initiated two seminal projects related to the church's conception of religious truth based on tradition and revelation. Beginning in 1935 he supervised a committee charged with revising the Baltimore Catechism, a document which had remained substantially unchanged since 1855. Under his direction, 150 bishops and theologians collaborated with educational experts to produce a catechism of sound orthodoxy that would also present instructional material meaningfully to young minds. Through his initiative, the document appeared with general approbation in 1941. Also in 1935 O'Hara instigated a committee to revise the outdated Douai-Rheims version of the English Bible. Though he took no part in the actual revision, he shepherded an unwieldy group of scholars and secured the necessary patronage from American prelates. In addition he played a central role in preparing (1947–54) an approved version of sacramental rites in English, a third essential for Catholic education and one designed to encourage more lay participation in the liturgy. His death occurred en route to an international liturgical congress where he hoped to learn more about extending the faith by modern use of ancient rubrics.

Bibliography:

A.   *Catholic Pioneer History of Oregon* (Portland, OR, 1911); *The Church and the Country Community* (New York, 1927).

B.   NCAB 43, 26; NCE 10, 660–61; NYT 12 Sep 1956, 37; James G. Shaw, *Edwin Vincent O'Hara: American Prelate* (New York, 1957).

O'KELLY, James (1735?, Ireland?—16 October 1826, southern VA). *Career:* farmer, 1759–78; itinerant minister, Methodist connection, 1778–84; presiding elder, Methodist church, 1785–92; itinerant minister, The Christian Church, 1793–1826.

Nothing is known for certain about the birth or formative years of O'Kelly's life. The earliest existing record lists him as a Methodist preacher in 1778, after he had apparently farmed with considerable success, fought on the patriot side during the Revolution, and converted to Christianity under Wesleyan exhortation. After 1784 he rose to great prominence in southern Virginia, influencing other ministers with his deep piety and forcible leadership qualities. But as Methodism gradually formed efficient institutional patterns, O'Kelly became restive. He was opposed to anything which restricted local ministers and viewed the introduction of bishops in his church as a despotic maneuver bordering on popery. He became increasingly alarmed at the actions of *Francis Asbury, claiming that his dictatorial conduct was a violation of the office delegated him. There had been earlier tension over questions of administering the sacraments and slaveholding in the churches, but the chief issue was whether bishops were to be tolerated in republican America. In 1792 O'Kelly presented a resolution to modify Asbury's power of appointment; the measure was soundly defeated, and so its author withdrew from Methodist affiliation. By 1794 his minority following constituted themselves as "The Christian Church," acknowledging no head but Christ, no creed or discipline save the Bible, no slavery among its constituents. For the rest of his life this undaunted denominational leader preached under new auspices the same gospel he had always advocated. By 1809 some 20,000 adherents could be counted, and they recognized congregations in New England based on similar restorationist principles. The Christian Church lasted until 1931 when it merged with Congregationalists, following that group and others into larger merger as the United Church of Christ in 1957.

Bibliography:

A. *Essay on Negro-Slavery* (Philadelphia, 1784, 1789); *The Author's Apology for Protesting Against the Methodist Episcopal Government* (Richmond, VA, 1798); *A Vindication of the Author's Apology with Reflection on the Reply* (Raleigh, NC, 1801); *The Divine Oracles Consulted* (reprint: Hillsboro, NC, 1820); *Letters from Heaven Consulted* (reprint: Hillsboro, NC, 1822); *The Prospect Before Us* (reprint: Hillsboro, NC, 1824).

B. SH 8, 230; NCAB 13, 282–83; DAB 14, 7–8; Wilbur E. MacClenny, *The Life of Rev. James O'Kelly* (Raleigh, NC, 1910; Indianapolis, IN, 1950).

OLCOTT, Henry Steel (2 August 1832, Orange, NJ—17 February 1907, Adyar, India). *Education:* studied at the Univ. of the City of New York, 1847; studied law, New York, 1865–68. *Career:* experimental farming in OH, NJ, and NY, 1849–59; associate agricultural editor, *New York Tribune*, 1859–61; officer, Union Army, 1861–65; practiced law, New York, 1868–78; president, The Theosophical Society, 1875–1907; editor, *The Theosophist*, 1879–1907.

A man of variegated pursuits, Olcott worked in a number of fields before he became founder and president of The Theosophical Society. His parents had raised him a Presbyterian, but maternal uncles opened up the world of spiritualism which he found infinitely more fascinating. His interest in esoteric wisdom continued on a rather amateur level until 1874, when he met *Helena P. Blavatsky and turned into a serious disciple of religious mysteries. The following year he and H.P.B., as she preferred to be called, were primary agents in founding a society for the study of ancient wisdom. Olcott said the purpose of theosophy was to recover the laws of nature known to the Chaldeans and Egyptians. The group comprised a fraternity of persons concerned with collecting and diffusing such knowledge, furthering the goal of brotherhood for all humanity. Through knowledge of spiritual teachings, astral light from the ancients, he hoped also to free the public mind from theological superstition and its subservience to material science. He thought of Society members as simple investigators, of earnest purpose and unbiased mind, who sought truth wherever perceived. In his eclectic approach nothing had final authority, neither Vedas, Bible, nor Darwin; everything was open for consideration by one's personal judgment and inner vision.

Practical contributions to stability in the theosophical movement were Olcott's greatest achievements. He traveled extensively in the United States (especially 1901), Europe, and Asia to extend branches from headquarters in India. At the time of his death, 600 existed in forty-two countries. After dispelling early suspicions that his motives concealed another colonialist trick, he helped revive popular interest in Hindu philosophy together with Sanskrit literature. In Ceylon he embraced Buddhism, declaring that he considered it identical with Aryan wisdom in the Upanishads and at one with all ancient faiths. "The White Buddhist," as he was known in that island kingdom, struggled for years to gain more religious freedom for his coreligionists in the face of British reluctance to grant it. Education in traditional teachings was seriously lacking; so he composed a catechism which reached millions through publications in over twenty languages. He also provided a compromise platform for establishing more cordial relations between Mahayana forms of Buddhism (especially in Japan) and Theravada schools (Burma and Ceylon). His administrative skill within Theosophy was patient and firm, smoothing petty jealousies while maintaining the larger goal of enlightenment by individualistic quest. By means of clairaudient messages, the president gave his society a constancy permitting adherents in both hemispheres to seek guidance from sources thought to be essentially one.

Bibliography:

A. *People from the Other World* (Hartford, CT, 1875); *A Buddhist Catechism* (Colombo, Ceylon, 1881; many subsequent editions); *Theosophy, Religion and Occult Science* (London, 1885); *Old Diary Leaves*, 6 vols. (New York, 1895–1935).

B. NCAB 8, 464–65; DAB 14, 10–11; NYT 18 Feb 1907, 9; Howard Murphet, *Hammer on the Mountain* (Wheaton, IL, 1972).

OLIN, Stephen (2 March 1797, Leicester, VT—16 August 1851, Middlebury, CT). *Education*: graduated from Middlebury Coll., 1820. *Career*: professor of Ethics and Belles Lettres, Franklin Coll. (later Univ. of Georgia), 1827–33; president, Randolph-Macon Coll., 1834–37; president, Wesleyan Univ., 1842–51.

After pushing his delicate health beyond the breaking point in college, Olin moved to a warmer climate in hopes of regaining his strength. For a time he taught at Tabernacle Academy near Abbeville, South Carolina, and there with the gentle encouragement of neighbors he converted to Methodism. In 1824 he was admitted on trial as a preacher, but the rigors of itinerancy were more than his poor physical condition could endure, and he was forced to conduct a settled ministry. College teaching proved to be a more amenable vocation, and in 1828 Olin was elevated to the office of elder, receiving ordination at the hands of bishop *William McKendree. Shortly thereafter he became the president of a pioneering Methodist College in Virginia. For more than two decades he did much to strengthen his denomination's interest in education, particularly in theological training. Several of his influential articles in the *Christian Advocate and Journal* argued persuasively for better intellectual standards among clergy and laity alike. Between 1837 and 1841 he traveled in Europe and the Near East for health reasons, but after assuming the presidency of Wesleyan University he made that institution the strongest center for higher learning in the Methodist church.

By the early 1840s controversies over slavery had produced crises in several major American denominations. In 1844 Olin attended the Methodist General Conference where his church separated on this tragic question along regional lines. Since he had lived for so many years in the South, he was asked to serve on the committee charged with finding a basis of agreement between pro-slavery and anti-slavery factions. The obstacles to reconciliation were insurmountable, however, and no matter how much he hoped to prevent rupture, he finally voted on the anti-slavery side and watched the church slip apart. Immediately afterwards Olin strove to reunite the separated branches, activity that was not successful until almost a century later. He also pursued wider ecumenical ventures in 1846, helping to establish the Evangelical Alliance in the United States and serving as a delegate to the world congress in London. Through these means he helped Methodism to emerge from its revivalist origins to expand into a full range of mature institutions.

Bibliography:

A.   *Travels in Egypt, Arabia Petraea, and the Holy Land*, 2 vols. (New York, 1843); *The Works of Stephen Olin*, 2 vols. (New York, 1852); *The Life and Letters of Stephen Olin*, 2 vols. (New York, 1853); *Greece and the Golden Horn* (New York, 1854).

B.   AAP 7, 685–99; SH 8, 236; NCAB 9, 429; DAB 14, 13–14.

O'REILLY, John Boyle (28 June 1844, near Drogheda, Ireland—10 August 1890, Hull, MA). *Career*: editor, *Pilot*, Boston, MA, 1870–90.

Like many young Irish patriots, O'Reilly joined (1863) the Fenian revolutionary movement to free his homeland from British rule. He was arrested for treason in 1866 and after two years at hard labor was sentenced to twenty more in an Australian penal colony. Escaping from that institution took a bit of doing, but after many adventures the dauntless political refugee finally reached America late in 1869. Within a few months he was at work again in journalism through which he became a dominant influence in Irish Catholicism on this continent. O'Reilly had suffered enough under intolerance to detest it in any of its many guises. He made his newspaper a voice for mutual respect among religious faiths and ethnic enclaves found in modern cities. Irish Americans were particularly encouraged to preserve their traditional heritage while actively pursuing assimilation in the larger patterns of New World culture. Education, Irish colonization, and the Catholic Union of Boston found in him a staunch supporter. He also defended oppressed minorities such as Jews, Indians, and Negroes. In the latter case he was accused of inciting them to open violence, but he urged Blacks to defend themselves against Jim Crow laws and lynch mobs. He lost few opportunities to remind the public that no race ever won fair play from Anglo-Saxons without fighting for it. Whether in editorials or poems for which he was widely famous, the Catholic layman brought piety and a sense of common decency to bear in fighting against prejudice wherever it was encountered.

Bibliography:

A. *Songs, Legends and Ballads* (Boston, 1878); *Statues in the Block* (Boston, 1881); *In Bohemia* (Boston, 1886).

B. NCAB 1, 428–29; DAB 14, 53–54; NCE 10, 741; NYT 11 Aug 1890, 1; James J. Roche, *Life of John Boyle O'Reilly* (New York, 1891); William G. Schofield, *Seek for a Hero* (New York, 1956); Francis G. McManamin, *The American Years of John Boyle O'Reilly* (Washington, DC, 1959).

OTTERBEIN, Philip Wilhelm (3 June 1726, Dillenburg, Germany—17 November 1813, Baltimore, MD). *Career*: preceptor, Herborn, 1748–52; vicar, Ockersdorf, 1749–52; minister in PA: Lancaster, 1752–58, Tulpehocken, 1758–60, Frederick, 1760–65, and York, 1765–74; minister, Baltimore, 1774–1813.

After studying for an undetermined length of time at the seminary in Herborn, Otterbein returned there to offer pietistic training for other young ministers. In his first church he aroused a degree of opposition because of unaccustomed zeal in disciplining parishioners and in attempts to organize Bible classes for laymen. So when *Michael Schlatter toured the Palatinate in 1752, recruiting volunteers for the colonies, Otterbein decided to try his vigorous conception of Christianity in the New World. For the next sixty-one years he stood as a leading example of pietist influences grounded in pastoral work. In his first American pastorate, he recognized even more clearly that vital religion consisted in neither the private revelations of sectarian mysticism nor the comfortable morality of workaday society. He stressed, rather, genuine change of heart, a religion of grace mediated through God's word found in Scripture and the Heidelberg Catechism. Further spiritual nourishment for his flock came by means of private prayer meetings, regular fasting, strict attendance at Sunday worship, and confessional interviews before holy communion. In that manner, pastor Otterbein sought to intensify the personal faith of those under his public care. And with those guidelines he also helped define an alternative to both the subjectivism found nearby at Ephrata and the empty formalism found too often in churches of the fatherland.

Throughout his American ministry, Otterbein was a member of the German Reformed Coetus of Pennsylvania. He was regarded as a "fit person" for the Coetus and always thought of himself in that connection. But at the same time he participated in a nonsectarian religious movement which grew into independent denominational status after his death. By 1767 he met Mennonite preacher *Martin Boehm and admitted that their common emphasis on evangelical doctrine sought identical objectives. Seven years later he became a close friend of Methodist itinerant *Francis Asbury—close enough to participate in his consecration as superintendent in 1784. Both of these acquaintances show that Otterbein valued the brotherhood of evangelical preachers more than strict observance of denominational loyalty. He promoted the growth of nonsectarian fellowship among ministers because it fostered a wider network of preaching in the middle seaboard frontier. In 1789 an informal group was formed to encourage such purposes; eleven years later Otterbein and Boehm accepted positions of superintendent in what they called the Vereinigte Bruderschaft zu Christo. Just seven weeks before he died the German Reformed pastor ordained Christian Newcomer, a young preacher who developed the Church of the United Brethren in Christ into a separate institution. Thus a simple society formed originally to invigorate established churches grew unintentionally into an organization which added to the competing bodies characteristic of American religious pluralism.

Bibliography:

B. SH 8, 287; NCAB 10, 504; DAB 14, 107–08; NCE 10, 814; Augustus W. Drury, *The Life of Rev. Philip William Otterbein* (Dayton, OH, 1884); Arthur C. Core and Ehrhart Lang, *Philip William Otterbein: Pastor, Ecumenist* (Dayton, OH, 1968); John S. O'Malley, *Pilgrimage of Faith: The Legacy of the Otterbeins* (Metuchen, NJ, 1973).

OUTLER, Albert Cook (17 November 1908, Thomasville, GA—1 September 1989, Bradenton, FL). *Education*: B.A., Wofford Coll., 1928; B.D., Emory Univ., 1933; Ph.D., Yale Univ., 1938. *Career*: minister, Baxley, GA, 1928–30; minister, Pineview, GA, 1930–32; minister, Gordon, GA, 1932–34; minister, Macon, GA, 1934–35; instructor to associate professor of Theology, Duke Univ., 1938–45; associate and full professor of Theology, Yale Univ., 1945–51; professor of Theology, Southern Methodist Univ., 1951–79.

Growing up in a Methodist parsonage led Outler to a lifelong interest in the practical good of local ministry and the healing work of pastoral counseling. With the aid of academic training he added interest in intellectual history: doctrinal development in the early Christian period and more specifically the distinctive formulations of his own Wesleyan tradition. From those perspectives Outler grew into an effective voice and vital figure in the modern ecumenical movement. After professorial stints at Duke and Yale, he returned to the South and helped establish the Perkins School of Theology as a strong institution of higher learning. He attended Methodist quadrennial conferences for decades and served on numerous task forces. His denominational leadership was particularly effective as chair of the Commission on Doctrine and Doctrinal Standards which helped clarify the church's position on historical and pastoral theology. Results of this momentous undertaking were adopted in 1972. As a member of the educational board of the Wesley Works Project, Outler contributed a biography of John Wesley, supervised the work of collaborating scholars, and edited nine volumes of Wesley's own *Works*.

Religious learning was a necessary ingredient and an adequate means to ecclesiastical reform. Outler added to that cerebral preparation a generous heart and boundless enthusiasm for ecumenical good will. In 1952 he attended the third meeting of the Faith and Order conference at Lund, Sweden. In 1963 he served as vice-chair of the fourth conference at Montreal, Canada. That duty coincided with one of the most important of Outler's duties: a Protestant observer at the Second Vatican Council. He was also Methodist delegate to the third assembly of the World Council of Churches in New Delhi, India, vice-president of the Commission on Ecumenical Affairs, and in 1964 chair of the Ecumenical Study and Liaison Committee. In all these areas, this kind and gentle figure tried to nurture mutual understanding among different Christians and to aid appreciation of various traditions through discovery of commonly held emphases and objectives. He urged wider latitudes in interpreting scripture and broader acceptance of different traditions that stemmed from a central historical core. He enriched the study of patristics, clarified the Wesleyan tradition, and enhanced ecumenical cooperation by embodying the highest ideals found in all three areas.

Bibliography:

A. *Psychology and the Christian Message* (New York, 1954); *The Christian Tradition and the Unity We Seek* (New York, 1957); *John Wesley* (New York, 1964); *Methodist Observer at Vatican II* (Westminster, MD, 1967); *Evangelism in the Wesleyan Spirit* (Nashville, 1971); *Theology in the Wesleyan Spirit* (Nashville, 1975).

OXNAM, Garfield Bromley (14 August 1891, Sonora, CA—12 March 1963, White Plains, NY). *Education*: B.A., Univ. of Southern California, 1913; S.T.B., Div. Sch. of Boston Univ., 1915. *Career*: Methodist minister, Poplar, CA, 1916; minister, Church of All Nations, Los Angeles, CA, 1917–27; professor, Div. Sch. of Boston Univ., 1927; president, DePauw Univ., 1928–35; bishop, Methodist Church, 1936–60.

As a defender of labor interests while in college and his early pastorates, Oxnam perpetuated ideals of the Social Gospel after it ceased to exist as an identifiable movement. He sympathized with most liberal causes and urged them through sermons, writings, and a forceful personality. In 1926 he visited the Soviet Union and admired attempts to achieve social and economic parity there. He also served as secretary of the World Peace Commission and for more than a decade was a member of the Methodist Federation for Social Service. These activities led some as early as 1934 to charge him with being part of a "red" network in this country. Church leaders were apparently not intimidated, though, showing their appreciation of Oxnam's abilities by electing him bishop slightly more than a year later. In addition to meeting local responsibilities in successive bishoprics based in Omaha (1936–39), Boston (1939–44), New York (1944–52), and Washington, DC (1952–60), he chaired his denomination's General Boards of Education (1939–44) and Missions (1944–52). Ecumenical interests were always part of his ministry too, including service as president of the Federal Council of Churches of Christ in America (1944–46) and the National Council of Churches (1950). He was also one of the six founding presidents of the World Council of Churches, holding that office from 1948 to 1954.

A vigorous and dynamic personality, Oxnam was not one to shrink from controversy. He disturbed many American Catholics by criticizing the Franco regime in Spain and by pointing out the lack of religious freedom in South American countries. Furthermore he opposed federal aid to parochial schools, and he attacked the idea of sending an American emissary to the Vatican. To those ends in 1948 he helped found Protestants and Other Americans United for Separation of Church and State. Still, his liberalism attracted more attention than these conservative escapades. During the McCarthy era Oxnam's concern for peace, international harmony, and workers' rights led to charges of his being a Communist sympathizer. He was named in investigating committees and denounced in Congress as one who "served God on Sunday and the Communist front for the balance of the week." In July of 1953 he appeared before the House Un-American Activities Committee, challenging the constitutionality of its methods which smeared individuals without solid evidence. An able church administrator before that episode, he became known thereafter as a defender of American civil rights and a champion of decency and fair play in all spheres of life.

Bibliography:

A. *The Ethical Ideals of Jesus in a Changing World* (New York, 1941); *Preaching in a Revolutionary Age* (New York, 1944); *Labor and Tomorrow's World* (New York, 1945); *The Church and Contemporary Change* (New York, 1950); *I Protest* (New York, 1954); *A Testament of Faith* (Boston, 1958).

B. NCAB, G234; DAB supp. 7, 596–98; NCE 10, 847; NYT, 14 Mar 1963, 16; Robert Moats Miller, *Bishop G. Bromley Oxnam: Paladin of Liberal Protestantism* (Nashville, 1990).

P

PAGE, Kirby (7 August 1890, Fred, TX—16 December 1957, La Habra, CA). *Education*: B.S., Drake Univ., 1915; studied at Univ. of Chicago, 1915–16; studied at Columbia Univ. and Union Sem. (NY), 1918–20. *Career*: assistant secretary YMCA, Houston, TX, 1907–11; student minister, Church of Christ, Montieth, IA, 1912–15; minister, Morgan Park Church of Christ, Chicago, IL, 1915; secretary, YMCA in England and France, 1916–17; minister Ridgewood Heights Church of Christ, Brooklyn, NY, 1918–21; independent speaker and writer, 1921–57; editor, *The World Tomorrow*, 1926–34.

Though ordained in 1915 as a Disciples of Christ minister, Page filled the roles of lecturer and author more than that of local pastor. After early work with the YMCA he served for a time as private secretary to *John R. Mott from whom he undoubtedly developed a more global perspective. He also accompanied Sherwood Eddy on evangelical campaigns in China, Korea, and Japan. In 1921, with enabling financial support from Eddy, he inaugurated a career as observer of international affairs, world markets, and the relevance of Christian witness in those secular arenas. During the next three decades Page made over twenty fact-finding trips to Russia, the Near East, northern Africa, India, China, Japan, and the Philippines. His views on socio-economic problems appeared in a great many publications: more than 40 books, another 8 either edited or co-authored, plus 5 volumes of collected pamphlets and essays. He wrote for *The World Tomorrow* and after 1935 was a contributing editor for *The Christian Century*. Those avenues provided opportunities for the social prophet and evangelist to display his other qualities as theologian and activist.

The most noticeable and durable of Page's many interests was his advocacy of pacifism. From 1916 onward he was associated with the Fellowship of Reconciliation, serving for a time as its vice chair and cooperating as well with the

American Friends Service Committee. In the years following World War I he scolded the community of nations for their belligerent follies and moral anarchy, warning that such myopic selfishness would only lead to further fighting. As early as 1922 he was instrumental in persuading the Federal Council of Churches to issue a statement regarding the pacifist responsibility of churches. That same coordinating agency distributed 53,000 copies of his 1923 book on the causes and consequences of war to clergy throughout the country. In 1937 he helped organize the Emergency Peace Campaign through which he promoted his lifetime ideal: peace despite the growing Nazi menace. Page envisioned a new economic order where considerations of human welfare superseded those of private wealth. He warned against aggression of all kinds and sought to nurture a more harmonious world. His vigorous efforts in that direction earned for him recognition as an itinerant social evangelist for peace.

Bibliography:

A.   *War: Its Causes, Consequences and Cure* (New York, 1923); *Dollars and World Peace* (New York, 1927); *Living Creatively* (New York, 1932); *The Personality of Jesus, Then and Now* (La Habra, CA, 1950); *Kirby Page, Social Evangelist: The Autobiography of a 20th Century Prophet for Peace*, edited by Harold E. Fey (Nyack, NY, 1975).

B.   NCAB 47, 607–08; NYT 18 Dec 1957, 35.

PAINE, Thomas (29 January 1737, Thetford, England—8 June 1809, New York, NY).

Perhaps it was a Quaker upbringing that gave Paine deep respect for private convictions, but his acquired knowledge of contemporary philosophy also made liberty paramount in the age of enlightenment. Since he was afforded only the rudiments of formal education, a fact his detractors were quick to point out, he maintained an obscure existence in England as minor official and tradesman from 1757 to 1774. Then he tried his fortune in the New World where writing reformist tracts became his acknowledged metier. Two pamphlets of 1776 in support of the Revolution, *Common Sense* and *Crisis*, won Paine the reputation of advocate for democratic government. His widely circulated treatises affected thousands of American colonists whom he urged to change human destiny by their example. After various practical services during the war, he tried farming for a time but returned to Europe by 1787. In Paris after 1789, he wrote as a popularizer of world revolution, primarily with *Rights of Man* in 1791 and 1792, until he was imprisoned (1793–94) when Girondist allies fell from power. Then he formed a small Theophilanthropist society, a forerunner of many such humanistic organizations for ethical advance which sought to replace Christianity with reasonable religion. Returning to America in 1802, Paine continued his interests in religious reform, much to the dismay of erstwhile companions and of course all orthodox believers. He associated with *Elihu Palmer because their ideologies coincided, but in the main his declining years were heavy with poverty, poor health, and social ostracism. That allowed a degree of satisfaction because it left him free to hold ideals with the uncompromising zeal of a visionary.

As far as religious thought is concerned, Paine's lucid essays contained a standard deistic credo mixed with fiery indictments of historical institutions. In the *Age of Reason* (two parts, 1794 and 1796), he reiterated beliefs in one God and no more, human happiness beyond this life, equality among men, and religious duties consisting of attempts to establish justice, mercy, and the well-being of fellow creatures. The existence of God was based, in good enlightenment fashion, on arguments from design and causation in the cosmos. Christian ideas as well as others masked in revelation were, in his opinion, decidedly inferior to those derived from the complex order governing an immense creation. Paine also went into lengthy analysis of Scripture to prove with a host of objections that both testaments were untrustworthy. In characteristic overstatement, he railed against "priestcraft," charging that all churches were human inventions to enslave credulous minds and wield unnatural power. Christian apologists responded to such propaganda with the misplaced accusation of atheism. But in fact this egalitarian agitator represented a rational deism and workable moral system which declined slowly under the onslaught of evangelical revivals and Federalist politics.

Bibliography:

A. *Life and Writings of Thomas Paine*, ed. Daniel E. Wheeler, 10 vols. (New York, 1908); *The Life and Works of Thomas Paine*, ed. William M. Van der Weyde, 10 vols. (New Rochelle, NY, 1925).

B. SH 8, 299–300; NCAB 5, 412–13; DAB 14, 159–66; NCE 10, 866–67; James Cheetham, *The Life of Thomas Paine* (New York, 1809); Moncure D. Conway, *The Life of Thomas Paine*, 2 vols. (New York, 1892); Mary A. Best, *Thomas Paine* (New York, 1927); Joseph Lewis, *Thomas Paine* (New York, 1947); Audrey Williamson, *Thomas Paine: His Life, Work and Times* (London, 1973).

PALMER, Benjamin Morgan (25 January 1818, Charleston, SC—28 May 1902, New Orleans, LA). *Education*: studied at Amherst Coll., 1832–34; B.A., Univ. of Georgia, 1838; B.D., Columbia Sem. (SC), 1841. *Career*: schoolteacher, McPhersonville and Mt. Pleasant, SC, 1834–36; minister, Savannah, GA, 1841–43; minister, Columbia, SC, 1843–53; minister, First Presbyterian Church, New Orleans, LA, 1856–1902.

Pulpit oratory has long been an effective means of shaping public opinion in the South, and in his generation, Palmer was an acknowledged master of that medium. His ministry in three major cities together with frequent contributions to the *Southern Presbyterian Review*, which he helped establish in 1847, expressed attitudes widespread among average citizens. On racial questions, particularly, he both influenced and reflected the popular mind. He argued that it was the providential trust of southern people to conserve and perpetuate the institution of slavery. After condemning abolitionists as undeniably atheistic, he rebuked all legislative attempts to settle disputes in an area which could be determined only by divine intervention. He also advocated secession to resist what he saw as an attack on constitutional freedom in states, churches, and family life. Self-preservation and concern for protecting the slaves themselves required southerners to unite in opposing foreign intervention. During the war, Palmer worked hard to bolster morale among soldiers as well as those on the home front. After one speaking tour in the summer of 1863 an officer remarked that he was more valuable to the southern cause than a brigade of infantry. His ideas regarding race relations, formulated before conflict but hardened in wartime, bespoke a prevailing sectional attitude which lasted for another hundred years.

Forty-seven presbyteries convened at Augusta, Georgia, late in 1861 to form a separate ecclesiastical unit. Palmer, chosen first moderator of the southern Presbyterian church, labored for the rest of his life to preserve its distinctive existence. Voicing ideas of his friend and mentor, *James H. Thornwell, he spoke often about the spiritual nature of the church. Doctrines and practices must be based exclusively on scripture, not on cultural preferences or governmental pressure. Southern Presbyterians could retain their pure vision only through isolation; reunion with northern churches would bring compromise and certain ruin in its train. During the 1880s Palmer opposed attempts to establish cordial relations between the two general assemblies. Doctrinal differences played a part, but the major stumbling block was race again. Some northern presbyteries consisted of black churches while many others had mixed congregations; contact with such practices was unthinkable for persons with Palmer's convictions. He thought it essential that races live in separate groups, each with their own churches, schools, and leadership. Any prolonged or extensive contact between them spelled disaster for both. So racial fears combined with theology to form ecclesiastical policy, one pervasive enough to sustain denominational separation well into the twentieth century.

Bibliography:

A. *The Life and Letters of James Henley Thornwell* (Richmond, VA, 1875; New York, 1969); *Sermons*, 2 vols. (New Orleans, 1875–76); *The Family in Its Civil and Churchly Aspects* (Richmond, VA, 1876); *The Threefold Fellowship and the Threefold Assurance* (Richmond, VA, 1902).

B. AAP 4, 341–48; SH 8, 324; NCAB 11, 481; DAB 14, 175–76; Thomas C. Johnson, *The Life and Letters of Benjamin Morgan Palmer* (Richmond, VA, 1906).

PALMER, Elihu (7 August 1764, Canterbury, CT—7 April 1806, Philadelphia, PA). *Education*: B.A., Dartmouth Coll., 1787; studied theology with John Foster, Pittsfield, MA, 1787. *Career*: Presbyterian minister, Newtown, NY, 1788–89; Baptist minister, Philadelphia, 1790–91; Universalist minister, Philadelphia, 1791; practiced law in Philadelphia, 1793; independent deist preacher, 1793–1806.

The normal expectation for Palmer's ministry as a promising college graduate was abruptly altered when his liberal opinions came to light. His denial of original sin and the divinity of Jesus resulted in ejection from one pulpit after another until he emerged as a fully militant, anti-Christian radical. For a time he studied law in western Pennsylvania, but shortly after being admitted to the bar, a yellow fever epidemic took his eyesight. So he returned to his original vocation and preached at a number of religious societies embracing what he called reasonable beliefs. Palmer became one of the most conspicuous antagonists to what deists considered the degrading superstitions of traditional Christianity. He argued that the Bible offered no internal evidence that proved its divine authority; to accept it as the word of God was the highest pitch of extravagance. Doctrines claiming miraculous origin strained credulity while they insulted native intelligence with their content. Commonly accepted ideas about God made him a vengeful tyrant who delighted in punishing innocent creatures. The prevalent view of mankind as inherently wicked and deserving of endless punishment contravened the self-respect for which Nature had designed men. Palmer asserted further that Moses, Mohammed, and Jesus were all imposters, two of them murderers in fact and the other one in principle. These three and their unnatural religious systems had cost the world more human blood than all other fanatics combined. The corrupt tenets of revealed religion had disgraced the character of men and robbed them of happiness, taking advantage of ignorance to dominate minds instead of encouraging free use of reason.

The twin curses of superstition and despotism could be met effectively, according to Palmer's optimistic way of thinking, by the sane application of reason and republicanism. As the American Revolution had created political emancipation, so education and reason could bring about freedom from religious tyranny. Pursuant to this end he founded a deistic society (known under a succession of names) in New York where he spoke on Sunday evenings; branches in Philadelphia and Baltimore also provided settings for his advocacy of religion on the basis of reason alone. As editor of two short-lived weeklies, *Temple of Reason* (1801–03) and *Prospect: View of the Moral World* (1803–05), Palmer struggled to place deism on a sound institutional footing. He was an indefatigable campaigner for religion seen from a natural perspective. He welcomed the friendship of *Thomas Paine whose similar attitudes complemented his own. Honest and outspoken to the point of tactlessness, Palmer was unrelenting in efforts to place republican religion on a foundation beyond the reach of human corruption. But his gospel of liberty and reason was viewed by most church leaders with alarm. Within his own lifetime, reliance on reasonable religion was outdistanced by evangelical versions of traditional Christianity, an emphasis which accelerated in subsequent generations.

Bibliography:

A. *Principles of Nature; or, A Development of the Moral Causes of Happiness and Misery among the Human Species* (New York, 1802); *Posthumous Pieces* (London, 1826).

B. DAB 14, 177–79; Kerry S. Walters, *Elihu Palmer's Principles of Nature: Text and Commentary* (Wolfeboro, NH, 1990).

PALMER, Phoebe Worrall (18 December 1807, New York, NY—2 November 1874, New York, NY). *Career*: lay Methodist evangelist, 1837–74; editor, *Guide to Holiness*, 1862–74.

At the age of nineteen Phoebe Worrall married Walter C. Palmer, a New York physician, and built their home life around simple Methodist piety with which both were already familiar. By 1835 she began participating in meetings held in her sister's home on Tuesdays, small gatherings where she soon directed services of Scripture reading, prayer, and personal testimony. On the strength of Wesley's example coupled with her own experience she quietly spread the perfectionist doctrine of "entire sanctification." All spiritual attainments described in the Bible were within reach of truly dedicated persons, the spring of every motive could be pure, and one could be certain that consecration of self would be wholly accepted by God. In Mrs. Palmer's view this holiness was immediately available through faith in Christ. Conversion brought the first blessing of grace, while complete consecration to Christ as God's altar brought the second blessing of immediate sanctification to those serving as divine vessels. Some demurred by saying belief alone was not enough; others such as *Nathan Bangs criticized her "altar phraseology." But few Methodists, including many bishops and presiding elders whom she impressed, denied the doctrine of sanctification. With their cooperation and her personal witness hopes for immediate sanctification by faith spread to all areas touched by the Second Great Awakening. As a female evangelist in Tuesday Meetings or in camp revivals, she embodied a romantic optimism in keeping with scriptural formulas. Her ideas did not verge on intuitive experience or mystical revelation but rather stressed a rational confidence that God would honor promises made in His written Word.

Convictions about her own spiritual state led Mrs. Palmer to expressions of that consummate love in service to humanity. Rather than withdrawing to private ecstasy, she became one of the most vigorous pioneers in social reform activity, distributing tracts in the early 1840s, contributing materially to poor relief in prisons and orphanages. By far her most important effort was a mission built in New York's Five Points district. There she established (1850) a model Protestant welfare institution, maintaining a chapel, schoolrooms, baths, and rent-free apartments for local families. She was also instrumental in organizing the Ladies Christian Association (later Union) which conducted prayer meetings, Bible classes, and boarding houses in urban slums in addition to providing rescue homes for delinquents and asylums for the deaf. Mrs. Palmer remained neutral on one great issue of her day, slavery. The otherworldly aspects of her consecration permitted compassion for the poor but not overt agitation for social change, as exemplified in the antislavery impulse. She also avoided association with the emergent feminist movement yet defended by cogent arguments the right of women to participate fully in church work. Her influence on Methodists—clergy as well as laymen—was both profound and lasting. Her popular writings had an even greater impact on a generation seeking the elusive goal of human perfection through spiritual experience.

Bibliography:

A. *The Way of Holiness* (New York, 1845); *Present to My Christian Friend: Entire Devotion to God* (New York, 1845); *Faith and its Effects* (New York, 1846); *Incidental Illustrations of the Economy of Salvation: Its Doctrines and Duties* (New York, 1855); *Promise of the Father* (Boston, 1859); *Pioneer Experiences: The Gift of Power Received by Faith* (New York, 1867).

B. NAW 3, 12–14; Richard Wheatley, *The Life and Letters of Mrs. Phoebe Palmer* (New York, 1876); Thomas C. Oden (ed.), *Phoebe Palmer: Selected Writings* (New York, 1988).

PARHAM, Charles Fox (4 June 1873, near Muscatine, IA—29 January 1929, Baxter Springs, KS). *Education*: studied at Southwest Kansas Coll., 1890–93. *Career*: Methodist supply preacher, Eudora, KS, 1893–95; independent evangelist, 1895–1929; editor, *Apostolic Faith*, issued sporadically between 1899–1929.

As a teenager Parham said that he felt called to be a preacher even before he had a conversion experience. At college he deviated from the ministry to medicine, and his childhood rheumatic fever returned. Once he vowed again to preach in 1891, he claimed to be "instantly healed," and that confirmed his vocation. He sought truth largely through his own study of Scripture and developed a modest following by combatting both sin and sickness. Parham never claimed to be a healer; those who came to him could be healed through faith in God's power to accomplish miracles. By the turn of this century he had established a Bible college in Topeka, Kansas, together with myriad projects associated with a settlement house. In 1901 revivals at Topeka led him to formulate ideas that came to be recognized as the foundation of the modern Pentecostal movement. He also published the first periodical for adherents and organized the first interstate camp meetings and conferences. His recurrent themes emphasized the importance of a definite conversion, sanctification or holiness in everyday living, and divine healing from all sickness. Parham moved beyond those points to link speaking in tongues with a second baptism by the Holy Spirit and finally with identity as part of the "Bride of Christ," a select body of believers who would meet God in rapture as the millennium began.

In his own view, Parham thought speaking in tongues was an inspired ability to speak a recognizable language as a means of conducting missions. This view, known as xenoglossa, was rejected by most Pentecostals after 1910 because people under divine influence usually spoke no known tongue. They manifested glossolalia instead, using speech understood by no one except those whom God allowed to interpret it. In 1905 Parham taught Bible classes in Houston, Texas, where he influenced *William J. Seymour, a black preacher who made glossolalia famous a year later in Los Angeles at the Azusa Street Mission. But Parham was recognized as the movement's early founder, and his first book in 1902 expounded the group's theological structure. A scandal in 1907 involving charges of homosexuality led to relative obscurity during the last two decades of his life.

But while other dynamic leaders took the movement in several different directions, many competing institutions today still rely on Parham's ideas as their basic intellectual heritage.

Bibliography:

   A.   *Kol Kare Bomidbar: A Voice Crying in the Wilderness* (Kansas City, MO, 1902; Joplin, MO, 1944); *The Everlasting Gospel* (n.p., 1919–20); Robert L. Parham (ed.), *Selected Sermons of the Late Charles F. Parham and Sarah E. Parham* (Baxter Springs, KS, 1941).
   B.   Sarah E. Parham, *The Life of Charles F. Parham* (Joplin, MO, 1930; Birmingham, AL, 1977); James R. Goff, Jr., *Fields White Unto Harvest: Charles F. Parham and the Missionary Origins of Pentecostalism* (Fayetteville, AR, 1988).

PARKER, Daniel (1781, VA—1844, IL).

Few specifics about Parker survive, but it is known that he was born in Virginia and became an active Baptist preacher along the Tennessee-Kentucky line in the early 1800s. By 1817 he moved to southern Illinois where he spent his remaining years as a stern, conservative spokesman in the denomination. For more than two decades he was the storm center of a controversy over Christian missions that wracked almost every Baptist association west of the Alleghenies. In an effort to spread gospel witness both to Americans on the frontier and to persons in foreign lands, many voluntary societies had been formed to sustain such activity. But Parker stood for thousands who opposed missions in either field. For one thing, he argued in an 1820 pamphlet, mission societies were man-made organizations contrary to scriptural directives. These interchurch boards also posed a threat to the democratic government considered basic to local Baptist autonomy. Moreover, societies insisted on advanced education for their missionaries; Parker rejoined that God alone prepared the preacher, and it was blasphemy to seek further improvement through education. A final flaw in mission programs was their need for money, an imposition which antimissionists viewed as a tax on western churches to support misbegotten schemes of ecclesiastical power. All these sentiments lay behind those who resisted organized evangelism. Mission work, said the Illinois preacher, rebelled against the king of Zion, violated the government of gospel churches, and thus forfeited any right to develop concerted action in the sphere of religion.

An additional factor undergirded Parker's attack on missionary endeavor. He adhered to hyper-Calvinistic views including a predestinarian fatalism which rendered evangelical efforts useless. The non-elect could never receive salvation, he said, and no amount of preaching would affect their status. In 1826 he expounded these ideas in a doctrine known as "Two-Seeds-in-the-Spirit," providing innovative terminology but thoughts common to rigid Calvinism. God had created Adam and Eve with good seed emanating from divine origins. After man's fall from grace, however, "seeds of the serpent" were also planted in Eve. Subsequent generations of mankind stem from one of these two sources, good and evil or elect and non-elect, deriving their nature from one of these progenitors. Parker could then argue that it was folly to waste missionary effort on the wicked because they were constitutionally unable to experience redemption. In a like manner, he held God would save good persons at times and in ways of His own choosing. It was presumptuous to usurp God's place by attempting to save those who are inevitably evil. The "Two Seeds" theory did not gain widespread acceptance among midwestern Baptists, but it helped butress antimission convictions which arose for a host of reasons. Parkerism, a salient focus of such attitudes, proved to be a cause of much dissension during the early national period.

Bibliography:

    B.   Benajah H. Carroll, *The Genius of American Anti-Missionism* (Louisville, KY, 1902).

PARKER, Quanah (1845?, Cedar Lake, TX—23 February 1911, Cache, OK).

Indians of the American plains counted no man fully mature until he had distinguished himself in battle by either killing or counting coup on the enemy. Quanah ("Fragrant") grew up in the Quohada tribe of the Comanche nation, a portion which maintained those traditional values after most others had submitted to white dominance. Though he was only half Indian biologically speaking (his mother, Cynthia Ann Parker, a captive for eleven years), he fully embodied Comanche cultural patterns, and in 1867 rose by prowess to become one of their most influential chieftains. He refused to accept the Medicine Lodge Treaty (1867) which pacified most of the southern plains tribes. During the ensuing decade he rallied warriors of his own nation together with many Cheyenne and Kiowa to terrorize white settlers. Traditional affirmations defined by violence were combined with a sense of desperation, producing a fighting force intent on preserving native ways of life. Most of the skirmishing ended by mid-1875, though some stragglers held out through the next winter in base camps on the Llano Estacado. Quanah could see that open resistance spelled eventual disaster for the red man; so the Shoshonean-speaking leader turned to other means of protecting his people's culture.

After surrendering at Fort Sill in 1875, Quanah adopted his mother's surname and settled down to assimilate manners of the hated white man. He adopted domestic habits of agriculture, lived in an impressive house, and developed the reputation of a shrewd businessman. He persuaded his tribe to lease grasslands to neighboring stock breeders, adding a large source of additional income for Comanche welfare. Through all his conforming to white cultural expectations, he still held to native customs such as plural wives and aboriginal religious ideology. One of the most important mechanisms for this accommodation process was peyote religion. The peyote button (peyotl or mescal) of a certain cactus found in the Rio Grande valley had long been used as a stimulant and for its healing properties. Toward the end of the nineteenth century a religion emerged among defeated Indian groups, organized around its use. Quanah Parker was a prominent figure in his nation who influenced the spread of this religion through the Oklahoma reservations. Worshippers usually gathered at night to pray, eat peyote buttons, sing, and meditate. Their ethics, called "following the Peyote Road," corresponded to white patterns of frugality, industry, and temperance. Native symbols of the Great Spirit, Thunderbird, and Peyote Woman fit easily with Christian symbols. Visions induced by peyote gave tangible support to traditional religious ceremonialism, while their private, peaceful character allowed for greater accommodation in white society. By the time Parker died, peyoteism had become institutionalized as the Native American Church, a syncretistic movement of tremendous importance for the perpetuation of fundamental Indian religion and cultural identity.

Bibliography:

B.   DAB 15, 294; Zoe A. Tilghman, *Quanah: The Eagle of the Comanches* (Oklahoma City, 1938); Clyde L. and Grace Jackson, *Quanah Parker: Last Chief of the Comanches* (New York, 1963).

PARKER, Theodore (24 August 1810, Lexington, MA—10 May 1860, Florence, Italy). *Education*: private study, passed all examinations at Harvard Coll. as nonresident, 1830–31; graduated from Harvard Div. Sch., 1836. *Career*: teacher in private school, Watertown, MA, 1831–33; minister West Roxbury, MA, 1837–46; minister, Twenty-Eighth Congregational Society, Boston, 1846–59.

New England contained many agents of theological ferment in the 1830s and 40s, but none was more outstanding than Parker who dismayed even fellow Unitarians with his bold pronouncements. Influenced by the friendship and counsel of *William E. Channing and through omnivorous reading in twenty languages, he set a standard of intellectual rigor which placed him on the growing edge of liberal affirmations. By 1841 he declared it possible to distinguish between transient and permanent aspects of Christianity, and in defining them won the ostracism of most coreligionists. Parker reasoned that all cultures and human opinions had added their weight to God's fundamental work, obscuring it in the process. Two accretions which he was particularly anxious to dispose of had to do with christological definitions and the authority of Scripture. It was no longer necessary, he argued, to accept man's ideas as the doctrine of God; liberals were everywhere free to seek truth from any source that afforded it and to respect Jesus for his teachings, not his nature. Parker refused to accept the Bible, with all the uncertainties about its origins, as the sole channel of revelation just as he declined to verify the authenticity of Jesus' message by means of creedal formulae. Forms and doctrines would always fluctuate, but the truth of God's word in individuals' hearts sanctioned genuine religion. He preached the love of man and God, to be lived on the single unassailable conviction that God does exist. Doing the best thing from high motives, finding cause for action in the voice of God who spoke through the experience of all pious men—this was the core and validation of simple, unmediated Christianity. Such was his startling perspective which led through a variety of debates and reform projects, even to the point of breaking the law.

Believing that ministers should speak on everything of national or cultural concern, Parker became highly visible as a champion of reformist causes. He organized societies, served on committees, lectured, wrote, and preached on a wide range of topics involving problems and persons of every station. Often intemperate in speech and manner, no issue excited him more than slavery, and for fifteen years this was the core of a militant Christian philanthropy. The Boston minister was implacable in opposition to the peculiar institution. He urged resistance to laws which supported it and was indicted for civil disobedience. He protected fugitive slaves in his home and served as a secret backer of John Brown, approving of his plans for insurrection. Whatever the particular need, Parker threw himself into the swirl of things to be done and gave unselfishly in hope of achieving a higher good. Education, economics, politics, and morality filled his concern because he saw them as activities where men could apply the principles of good that were harbored within them. Ill health caused him to seek recovery in travel, but he did not live to see slavery ended in a manner congruent with its violent past.

Bibliography:

A.   *A Discourse of Matters Pertaining to Religion* (Boston, 1842); *Sermons of Theism, Atheism and the Popular Theology* (Boston, 1853); *Collected Works*, Centenary Edition, 15 vols. (Boston, 1907–13).

B.   SH 8, 359–61; NCAB 2, 377–78; DAB 14, 238–41; John Weiss, *The Life and Correspondence of Theodore Parker*, 2 vols. (New York, 1864, 1969); Octavius B. Frothingham, *Theodore Parker* (Boston, 1874); John W. Chadwick, *Theodore Parker: Preacher and Reformer* (Boston, 1900); Henry S. Commager, *Theodore Parker: Yankee Crusader* (Boston, 1936); John E. Dirks, *The Critical Theology of Theodore Parker* (New York, 1948).

PARKHURST, Charles Henry (17 April 1842, Framingham, MA—8 September 1933, Ventnor, NJ). *Education*: B.A., Amherst Coll., 1866; studied at Halle, 1869–70, and Leipzig, 1872–73. *Career*: high school principal, Amherst, MA, 1867–69; instructor, Williston Sem. (MA), 1870–71; minister, Congregational church, Lenox, MA, 1874–80; minister Madison Square Presbyterian Church, New York, 1880–1918; retirement, 1918–33.

When Parkhurst accepted a pastorate in New York, he brought the studious habits of one who preached from written manuscripts and cared for little else than the spiritual needs of those in his congregation. But in 1891 he was made president of the Society for Prevention of Crime, an office which briefly thrust him to public influence as a social reformer. Early the next year he caused a sensation by charging that there was an alliance between politicians, policemen, and criminals operating in the city. Denouncing them as "a lying, rum-soaked, libidinous lot," he called for serious investigation of crime at its roots rather than superficial prosecution of minor figures. Parkhurst was then embarrassed to admit that his accusations had been based on rumor. In the ensuing months he frequented saloons, brothels, and gambling dens to collect facts personally. Armed with a sheaf of affidavits, he mounted the pulpit once again to prove his case; this time public opinion rose to new heights and caused official inquiries into charges of corruption. By 1894 many politicos had been discredited, Tammany Hall outvoted, and reformed government reinstated, albeit for a short while. For two decades thereafter Parkhurst was considered one of the city's most effective clergymen, though he never took the lead in civic affairs again. In 1918 his resignation was occasioned by a merger of his church with two other downtown congregations, and he entered a period of secluded inactivity.

Bibliography:

    A.   *Our Fight with Tammany* (New York, 1895); *The Sunny Side of Christianity* (New York, 1901); *A Little Lower than the Angels* (New York, 1908); *The Pulpit and the Pew* (New Haven, 1913); *My Forty Years in New York* (New York, 1923).
    B.   SH 8, 361; NCAB 4, 402–03; DAB 14, 244–46; NYT 9 Sep 1933, 13.

PASSAVANT, William Alfred (9 October 1821, Zelienople, PA—3 June 1894, Pittsburgh, PA). *Education*: graduated from Jefferson Coll., 1840; graduated from Gettysburg Sem., 1842. *Career*: minister of Lutheran churches, Baltimore, MD (1842–43) and Pittsburgh, PA (1844–55); staff member, *Lutheran Observer*, 1842–48; editor, *The Missionary*, 1848–61.

In his early years Passavant was strongly influenced by his seminary professor, *Samuel S. Schmucker, and thus he naturally supported liberal attitudes in American Lutheranism. Missionary outreach was one of his consuming interests, and he worked in that capacity while still a student at Gettysburg. Licensed by the Maryland Synod in 1842, he was ordained the following year and moved shortly thereafter to Pittsburgh where he remained active for the next half century. He helped organize the Pittsburgh Synod in 1845 and exercised a dominant influence on its procedures for decades. But due to a long friendship with *Charles P. Krauth he slowly withdrew his sympathy for liberal ideas and adopted a conservative position known in his day as "Old Lutheranism." In 1848 he established a monthly magazine to promote the cause of home missions, and over the years this journal provided an outlet for Krauth's theological emphases as well. In 1856 *The Missionary* became a weekly, and in 1861 it merged with *The Lutheran*, published in Philadelphia. Writing and editing were one of Passavant's persistent activities, and in 1881 he established another publication, *The Workman*, supervising its production for the rest of his life. Through such efforts he became the most widely known Lutheran cleric in the midwestern region. And as such he gave considerable prestige to conservatives when in 1867 they organized a General Council of the Evangelical Lutheran Church in North America.

As minister of the first English-speaking Lutheran church in Pittsburgh, Passavant nurtured denominational growth among Americanized segments of the population. But he also gave substantial aid to German and Scandinavian missionaries who ministered to immigrants who had only recently arrived. Another of his interests lay in the area of philanthropy, and he worked prodigiously for a number of causes. In 1849 he was instrumental in bringing deaconesses from Kaiserswerth, Germany, to serve as nurses. He founded a hospital in Pittsburgh for their work and established other hospitals in Milwaukee, Chicago, and Jacksonville, Illinois. He founded orphanages in Zelienople and Germantown, Pennsylvania, in Rochester and Mt. Vernon, New York, and in Boston, Massachusetts. Further, he was instrumental in founding Thiel College (1870) in Greenville, Pennsylvania, and Chicago Lutheran Theological Seminary (1891) in Illinois. Labors in support of all these institutions kept the clergyman busy through long years of service, and these in turn helped consolidate Lutheranism as a stable and effective American denomination.

Bibliography:

B.   SH 8, 368; DAB 14, 289–90; George H. Gerberding, *Life and Letters of W. A. Passavant, D.D.* (Greenville, PA, 1906).

PASTORIUS, Francis Daniel (26 September 1651, Sommerhausen, Germany—?1720, Germantown, PA). *Education*: studied at Altdorf, 1668–70, Strassburg, 1670–72, and Jena, 1673–74; J.D., Altdorf, 1676. *Career*: practiced law, Windsheim, 1676–79; private tutor, 1680–82; agent for the Frankfurt Land Company, 1683–1700; mayor and clerk, Germantown, 1683–1707; schoolmaster, Germantown, 1702–19.

Born in a well-to-do Lutheran family and educated in the best German universities of his day, Pastorius was equipped for social leadership. His training in jurisprudence provided experienced guidance for settlement in the New World while other attainments enhanced the survival of Teutonic culture for generations to come. Success in business held little attraction for him; when he met Philipp J. Spener, it became clear that their common quest for spiritual regeneration offered rewards worth whatever sacrifices it might demand. After accompanying (1680–82) a young nobleman on his Wanderjahre through much of western Europe, Pastorius decided that traditional customs excluded genuine toleration of religious dissenters. Accordingly he put his legal talents to work for sectarian emigrants gathered at Frankfurt and Krefeld. In 1683 he sailed for *William Penn's proprietary estate, acting for assorted Mennonites, Pietists, and Quakers who sought a haven there. While he cannot be considered the sole instigator of such colonization, he was definitely a central figure in establishing Germantown, the first permanent German settlement and gateway for subsequent population from the fatherland. As one of the town's chief citizens, he was frequently elected mayor or clerk where his scholarly training was put to good use and his sense of duty served the community well.

As one of the leading intellectuals among first generation immigrants, Pastorius helped broaden their cultural horizons. A pietistic Lutheran who increasingly frequented Quaker worship services, he also contributed to religious developments in the area. In 1688 he joined three neighbors in sending their Monthly Meeting a written protest against slaveholding, the first to appear in American history. Pastorius was a prolific writer who produced early transatlantic documents on law, medicine, science, theology, agriculture, and history. He accumulated an immense store of manuscript materials which retain something of the variety of colonial life. His encyclopedic commonplace book, called fittingly the "Beehive," furnishes an insight into both the author and his fascination with New World phenomena. In addition to writing what was probably the original schoolbook in Pennsylvania, an elementary primer, he composed reams of verse in Latin, German, and English. Practical achievements guided by sound judgment, this was the daily service of one who shaped policy for school, church, and civil government.

Bibliography:

A. *Four Boasting Disputers of This World Briefly Rebuked* (New York, 1697); *Umstandige Geographische Beschreibung Der zu Allerletzt erfundenen Provintz Pensylvaniae* (Frankfurt, 1700).

B. NCAB 11, 352; DAB 14, 290–91; Marion D. Learned, *The Life of Francis Daniel Pastorius* (Philadelphia, 1908).

PATTON, Francis Landey (22 January 1843, Warwick, Bermuda—25 November 1932, Warwick, Bermuda). *Education*: studied at Knox Coll. and Univ. of Toronto, 1858?–62; graduated from Princeton Sem., 1865. *Career*: minister, New York, NY, 1865–67; minister, Nyack, NY, 1867–70; minister, Brooklyn, NY, 1871; professor of Didactic and Polemic Theology, Sem. of the Northwest (now McCormick Sem.), 1872–81; editor, *The Interior*, 1873–76; minister, Chicago, IL, 1874–81; professor of the Relations of Philosophy and Science to the Christian Religion, Princeton Sem., 1881–88; president, Princeton Univ., 1888–1902; president and professor of Religion, Princeton Sem., 1902–13; retirement, 1913–32.

For a period of almost fifty years Patton sought to improve the general quality of religion by concentrating primarily on its instructional aspects. His various roles as clergyman, author, and educator joined to promote Christianity within traditional channels maintained by the Presbyterian church. Though his conservatism derived from positive motivations, at times it made him appear narrow and reactionary. In 1874 he brought charges of heresy against *David Swing, a fellow minister in Chicago who resigned from the denomination when Patton insisted on continuing litigation. Again in 1891 he was vocal in opposing the views of *Charles A. Briggs whose work in biblical criticism at New York's

Union Seminary created a stir in varied intellectual circles. But despite these conspicuous struggles in the name of rigid orthodoxy, Patton's more basic goal was to establish defensible grounds for thoughtful belief amid contemporary circumstances. As professor and president of first the university then the seminary at Princeton, he steadily pursued that goal. His lectures on ethics to senior classes (1886–1913), discourses at Sunday chapel on the philosophy of religion, together with irenically worded publications helped build a reputation wherein he was known as "the grand old man of Presbyterianism." Under his administration, the two schools succeeded in expanding their conceptions of educational responsibility. He greatly improved professorships, library space, laboratory equipment and diversified curriculum at the university which formally adopted that institutional title in 1896. At the seminary he continued the tradition of conservative adherence to historical formularies, a part of that academy's perspective since its founding. Deteriorating health caused him to retire from public life, but even though near-blindness made traveling difficult, he often returned to Princeton for annual lectures.

Bibliography:

A. *The Inspiration of the Scriptures* (Philadelphia, 1869); *A Summary of Christian Doctrine* (Philadelphia, 1898); *Fundamental Christianity* (New York, 1926).
B. SH 8, 393; NCAB 5, 468–69; DAB 14, 315–16; NYT 27 Nov 1932, 34.

PAYNE, Daniel Alexander (24 February 1811, Charleston, SC—29 November 1893, Wilberforce, OH). *Education*: studied at Gettysburg Sem., 1835–37. *Career*: schoolteacher, Charleston, SC, 1829–35; minister of Presbyterian church, East Troy, NY, 1837–38; schoolteacher, Philadelphia, 1840–42; minister, Israel Church, Washington, DC, 1843–45; minister, Bethel Church, Baltimore, 1845–50; travel as historiographer for the African Methodist Episcopal (AME) Church, 1850–52; bishop, AME Church, 1852–93; president, Wilberforce Univ., 1863–76.

The son of a free black father and Catawba Indian mother, Payne was orphaned early in life. He struggled hard to educate himself, and by 1829 succeeded in opening a school for black children in his native city. A state law prohibiting the education of Negroes closed his flourishing academy six years later; after that he traveled north and accepted a scholarship offered by Lutheran students who sought to expand their church's mission program. Payne did not graduate from Gettysburg Seminary because poor eyesight curtailed his studies, but the training received there had far reaching effects on his later work. After a few desultory years of preaching and teaching he decided to join the African Methodist Episcopal (AME) Church, despite its reputation for opposition to educated ministers. Almost immediately he opened a campaign against illiteracy among fellow clergymen. Though many were hostile to the idea, he emphasized education as a means of improving not only clerical leadership but the general quality of Christian life for all church members. By 1844 he persuaded the General Conference to adopt a course of study for all ministers. Later efforts produced a Book Concern, Sunday Schools, and a Missionary Department for fostering educational projects in the denomination. In 1862, all his concern for adequate training was focused at Wilberforce University, an institution just acquired by the AME Church and the first college to thrive under black leadership. As president, Payne was the first Negro in America to hold such an office. He guided it through a decade of financial insecurity, built its curriculum, and opened the way for coeducational, nonsectarian instruction as a basis for forming Christian character.

After attending the General Conference of 1844, which some consider the turning point of AME fortunes, Payne quickly made himself a dominant figure in determining church policy. Many urged him to accept nomination as bishop, an office for which he thought himself unfit but finally accepted out of a sense of duty. For forty-one years thereafter he tried to maintain the church's government, discipline, and doctrine as he originally found it. He presided over a period of tremendous expansion, not unmarred however by jurisdictional squabbles, racial tensions, and controversies related to social justice. In decades following the Civil War he helped consolidate gains caused by greater concern for freedmen. Upon election as bishop, there were about 2,000 ministers for 50,000 communicants; at his death, there were over 4,000 clergy for approximately 500,000 members. Payne functioned as elder statesman during this time of growth, and much of its stability was due to his resourceful administration. By 1876, though, he reluctantly yielded some control to younger men. They ignored his cautious advice against proliferating small colleges and sending missionaries with inadequate supplies. Still, when he attended the first Methodist ecumenical conference at London in 1881, every branch of the church paid tribute to his many years of distinguished service.

Bibliography:

A.   *A Treatise on Domestic Education* (Cincinnati, 1885); *Sermons* (Nashville, 1888; New York, 1972); *Recollections of Seventy Years* (Nashville, 1888; New York, 1968); *History of the African Methodist Episcopal Church* (Nashville, 1891).

B.   SH 8, 423; NCAB 4, 188; DAB 14, 324–25; Charles S. Smith, *The Life of Daniel Alexander Payne* (Nashville, 1894); Josephus R. Coan, *Daniel Alexander Payne: Christian Educator* (Philadelphia, 1935).

PEABODY, Francis Greenwood (4 December 1847, Boston, MA—28 December 1936, Cambridge, MA). *Education*: B.A., Harvard Coll., 1869; S.T.B. Harvard Div. Sch., 1872; studied at Halle, 1872–73. *Career*: minister, First Parish Unitarian Church, Cambridge, MA, 1874–79; lecturer in Ethics and Homiletics (1880–81), professor of Theology (1881–86) and professor of Christian Morals (1886–1913), Harvard Div. Sch., 1880–1913; active retirement, 1913–36.

Utilizing a well-developed theological sensitivity, Peabody became one of the first American clergymen to recognize that moral issues arising from social problems were a central factor in modern life. Consequently in his capacity as educator he introduced the earliest systematic treatment of Christian social ethics into a seminary curriculum. For over forty years he remained a pioneering thinker in this new field, defending the priority of biblical guidelines as ones within which viable solutions could be fashioned. By 1906 his advocacy of sociological studies had expanded courses to a full program of graduate and undergraduate instruction. The Bible had a central place in his response to current problems because he was convinced that Jesus' teachings held the key to worldly progress. As God transformed the inner vision of human beings, they in turn were motivated as agents to establish the Kingdom of God amid present circumstances. Peabody recommended several reform measures based on this mild, optimistic strain of Christian humanitarianism. Like many before him he urged that everyone participating in capitalistic enterprises be morally concerned about the stewardship of wealth. Further, he justified organized labor, supported efficient welfare programs, low rent housing for the poor, and vocational training such as *Samuel C. Armstrong's experimental academy, Hampton Institute. In all these meliorative reforms Peabody attacked the preoccupation with materialism or commercialism by comparing those values with spiritual priorities maintained in the Christian tradition. The institutional church played a minor role in his thought because arguments over creed, polity, and discipline too often diverted humanitarian impulses. Instead of tying religion to rigid forms, he held it rather to be an ideal freely appropriated by all who wished to build a better world. Long after retirement, the former seminary professor continued to spread these ideas through eloquent sermons and popular volumes on social ethics.

Bibliography:

A. *Jesus Christ and the Social Question* (New York, 1900); *Jesus Christ and the Christian Character* (New York, 1905); *The Approach to the Social Question* (New York, 1909); *The Christian Life in the Modern World* (New York, 1914); *The Apostle Paul and the Modern World* (New York, 1923); *The Church of the Spirit* (New York, 1925).

B. SH 8, 425; DAB 22, 518–19; NYT 30 Dec 1936, 22.

PECK, John Mason (31 October 1789, Litchfield, CT—14 March 1858, Rock Spring, IL). *Career*: Baptist missionary in MO, IL and IN, 1817–58.

Doubts about infant baptism caused Peck to leave Congregationalism for affiliation with Baptists in 1811, shortly after the birth of his first child. He soon obtained a license to preach and, after studying theology for a year in Philadelphia, moved to St. Louis (1817) where he established a mission. The enterprise foundered, but in 1822 he became an agent of the Massachusetts Baptist Missionary Society which supported him with the princely sum of five dollars a week, if he could collect it from local patrons. Giving equal time to territories on both sides of the Mississippi, he labored vigorously to foster the institutional frame work necessary for continuing evangelistic efforts. Peck was more interested in the organizational aspects of the ministry than in revival preaching; under his industrious leadership, Baptists learned the value of organizing denominational activities along rational lines. He shared the basic conviction that visible conversion experience initiated Christian living, but for him it was just as important to channel religious witness by means of churches, schools, newspapers, national regulatory agencies, and sound financial planning. As early as 1819 he helped establish a seminary (Shurtleff College after 1835) which was the first institution of higher learning in Illinois. In addition to itinerating thousands of miles per year, he wrote countless sermons, edited two denominational papers (1829–39, 1849) and worked to build the facilities that buttressed civilization in the new West.

Social change of an unprecedented nature was occurring in the early national period as east coast emigrants mingled with settlers coming directly from Europe. Peck was eager to supply appropriate means of instilling middle-class morality in that burgeoning context, alert to both dangers and opportunities present in frontier life. Within his own denomination such action was resisted by an antimission faction which stressed local autonomy to the point of making associational responsibility impossible. He struggled for a lifetime against those elements preferring minimal organization with undefined channels of authority. Indeed a main feature of Peck's ministry was the way in which he grappled with two antagonistic tendencies: genuine belief that free consent of individuals was the only proper basis for government, civil or ecclesiastical, and practical knowledge that men were free only when they consented to the discipline afforded by authoritative structure. He was also taken with a vision that the American West was God's new Zion, constituting a prairie republic where democracy nurtured by Christian institutions would spread to the ultimate benefit of all humanity. These deep convictions sustained him as he tried to show that men living in community can achieve cooperative objectives when they follow creative ideals that transcend parochial interests.

Bibliography:

A. *Gazetteer of Illinois* (Jacksonville, IL, 1834); *A New Guide for Emigrants to the West* (Boston, 1836); *Life of Daniel Boone* (Boston, 1847); *"Father Clark," or the Pioneer's Preacher* (New York, 1855); *Forty Years of Pioneer Life: Memoir of John Mason Peck*, ed. Rufus Babcock (Philadelphia, 1864; Carbondale, IL, 1965).

B. DAB 14, 381–82; Matthew Lawrence, *John Mason Peck: The Missionary Pioneer* (New York, 1940).

PENN, William (14 October 1644, London, England—30 July 1718, Ruscombe, England). *Education*: studied at Christ Coll., Oxford Univ., 1660–62; studied at Saumur, France, 1663–64; studied law at Lincoln's Inn, 1665. *Career*: proprietary governor of PA, 1682–92, 1694–1718.

It was natural to see the son of an English naval hero enter Oxford; it was less common to find him suspended for having developed puritanical, nonconformist sympathies. Penn was directed to study at a Huguenot college on the Loire, to make the grand tour, and finally to perform military service; but all were futile attempts to distract him from serious concern for spiritual rectitude. By 1667 his puritanism developed through doubt and crisis to a Quaker confrontation with the Christ within. After that time much of his activity centered on using tongue and pen to spread Quaker doctrines. On missionary trips to Holland and Germany (1670, 1677, 1685) and in pamphlets eventually numbering over 150, he denounced worldly pursuits as fatal amusements. He urged listeners to avoid the fruits and fashions of the world because they were bound for fiery retribution. But while many Friends withdrew from the world altogether, Penn determined to struggle for a more liberal government in England. He was neither quietistic nor apocalpytic in social outlook. Still as a restorationist visionary he definitely sought for procedures that would transform present conditions. His preaching added to the public witness of Quaker emphases, but favorable connections with the Stuart monarchy opened a way for more practical efforts on their behalf in the New World.

In 1681 Penn accepted a grant of American land in lieu of specie payment from Charles II for debts owed his family. The chief motivation for undertaking the colonization of Pennsylvania was religious—hoping to build an ideal Christian society as an example to other nations. Since forces of the old order had proved intractable in England, he turned to new territory where a consensual model of the heavenly kingdom might be established. This holy experiment found tangible expression in the 1682 Frame of Government. The constitution was not radically egalitarian, but it did provide for personal liberties under the leadership of a responsible elite. More importantly, it assured that all believers in God would not be molested on matters of faith nor would they be compelled to frequent any particular church. With no militia, oaths in court, or any place for atheists among its citizens, Pennsylvania appeared to be a haven for persecuted idealists seeking to embody a social utopia. By the late 1680s its proprietor came to admit that even regenerate men needed more coercion than he had thought, but in 1701 another charter reaffirmed most basic freedoms. The colony was also notable in its fair dealings with Indians during the first forty years of contact. Penn himself spent most of his time in England after 1683, harrassed by disputes. He languished for a time in debtor's prison and suffered embarrassment at the conduct of one son. An attack of apoplexy in 1712 left him virtually incapacitated. Yet the memorial of one monthly meeting was not wide of the mark in observing that he could be ranked among the learned and good without straining his character.

Bibliography:

A. *The Collected Works of William Penn*, ed. Joseph Beese, 2 vols. (London, 1726; New York, 1971).

B. SH 8, 449–51; NCAB 2, 274–76; DAB 14, 433–37; NCE 11, 88; William T. Hull, *William Penn* (New York, 1937); Catherine O. Peare, *William Penn* (Philadelphia,

1956); Mary M. Dunn, *William Penn: Politics and Conscience* (Princeton, 1967); Melvin B. Endy, Jr., *William Penn and Early Quakerism* (Princeton, 1973); Hans Fantel, *William Penn: Apostle of Dissent* (New York, 1974).

PENNINGTON, James William Charles (1809, MD—October 1870, Jacksonville, FL). *Career*: schoolteacher, Newtown, NY, and New Haven, CT, 1835–37; minister African Congregational Church, Newtown, NY, 1838–40; minister, African Congregational Church, Hartford CT, 1840–47; minister, First Shiloh Presbyterian Church, New York, NY, 1847–55.

Born a slave on a plantation somewhere on the eastern shore of Maryland, Jim Pembroke escaped in 1830 and fled north to Pennsylvania. There he changed his name, received aid from several Quakers, and began private studies to improve his lot in life. Five years after his escape Pennington acquired enough skills to teach in schools for black children on Long Island and in Connecticut. He studied theology avidly and soon organized a church where his pulpit eloquence attracted immediate attention. The Hartford Central Association of Ministers had no other black members than he, and the fact that they twice chose him as president is an indication of the esteem with which his colleagues held him. As might be expected, Pennington was deeply interested in the slavery question. Some of his printed sermons contain cogent arguments for "The Reasonableness of Abolition" and for the view that "Covenants Involving Moral Wrong Are Not Obligatory Upon Man."

In 1843 Pennington served as a delegate to the World's Anti-Slavery Convention in London. The same year he represented the American Peace Convention at the World's Peace Society, also held in London. There was time moreover for preaching engagements in London, Paris, and Brussels. The Fugitive Slave Law, passed in 1850, caused Pennington to worry that he might be kidnapped and returned to servitude. So he entered negotiations to purchase his freedom and traveled in Europe until 1851 when the financial transaction was satisfactorily completed. But after bright years of social prominence and religious leadership, the final decades of this black clergyman are shadowy and puzzling. After 1855 he is listed on rolls of the Third New York Presbytery as a member without a pastorate. Tentative and inexact references suggest that he resided at times in New York, Connecticut, and Maine, conducting sporadic pastoral activities in those states. His last years seem to have been impaired by excessive drinking. He apparently hoped to organize a black Presbyterian church in Florida, but death overtook him before he succeeded in doing so.

Bibliography:

A.   *Text Book of the Origin and History of the Coloured People* (Hartford, CT, 1841); *The Fugitive Blacksmith; or, Events in the History of James W. C. Pennington* (London, 1844).

B.   NCAB 14, 307; DAB 14, 441–42; Joseph R. Washington, Jr., *The First Fugitive Foreign and Domestic Doctor of Divinity* (Lewiston, NY, 1990).

PERRIN, Norman (29 November 1920, Wellingborough, England—25 November 1976, Chicago, IL). *Education*: B.A., Univ. of Manchester, 1949; B.D. and Th.M., London Univ., 1952, 1956; studied at Kirchliche Hochschule, Berlin, 1956–57; Dr. Theol., Univ. of Göttingen, 1959. *Career*: served in Royal Air Force, 1940–46; minister, Westbourne Park Baptist Church, London, 1949–52; minister, Sketty Baptist Church, Swansea, South Wales, 1952–56; assistant professor of New Testament, Candler Sch. of Theol., Emory Univ., 1959–64; associate and full professor of Bible and Theology, Univ. of Chicago Div. Sch., 1964–76.

After intelligence service during World War II Perrin studied for the ministry and in 1949 received ordination in the Baptist Union of Great Britain and Northern Ireland. Experience in two pastorates confirmed his preference for scholarly research over institutional religion, and after doctoral work in Germany, he emigrated to America where he launched a distinguished academic career. Perrin lived on the cutting edge of New Testament scholarship as it evolved during this century's middle decades. He epitomized the honesty and sincerity of those who strove to understand the meaning of scriptural passages that undergirded most organized forms of Christianity. His general interests included the life of Jesus, the formation of the gospels, and the pre-literary stages of the synoptic gospel tradition. He represented a synthesis of scholarship from Britain (T.W. Manson), Germany (J. Jeremias and R. Bultmann), and the United States (colleagues in many universities, especially his own at Chicago). As time went on he became particularly noted for concern about method. His discriminating use of hermeneutical techniques helped delineate criteria for determining authentic scriptural passages. But he slowly abandoned his early interest in historical authenticity as a basis for faith. Factual matters became less important as the literary symbolism in texts took on a power and meaning of its own.

A desire to learn characterizes any seeker after truth, and a willingness to modify one's views under criticism or convincing argument as a sign of progress. Perrin stood at the forefront of New Testament studies because of these forthright intellectual qualities. The gospel of Mark challenged and fascinated him for years. Through his own publications and his influence on graduate students he created a nascent school of Markan research that continues today. His distinctive interpretations of key scriptural themes have permeated many levels of contemporary ideas about biblical meanings. In Son of Man christology, for instance, he held that such statements were symbolic, not a literal description but a reference to the realities and possibilities of human existence in the world. Another basic theme was the Kingdom of God which he thought could be found wherever God was active in any individual's experience. These key ingredients to Christian discourse in any age were also refreshed by gospel parables. In discussing these Perrin disclosed his own religion as well as his scholarship. The parables of Jesus showed that God is to be experienced directly, shattering the complacency of everyday life. Instead of nourishing traditions with moralizing allegories, the parables defy comfortable habits, disturbing individuals and challenging them to probe for fresh meaning on a personal level.

Bibliography:

A. *The Kingdom of God in the Teaching of Jesus* (London, 1963); *Rediscovery of the Teaching of Jesus* (London, 1967); *The Promise of Bultmann* (Philadelphia, 1969); *A Modern Pilgrimage in New Testament Christology* (Philadelphia, 1974); *The New Testament, An Introduction: Proclamation and Parenesis, Myth and History* (New York, 1974); *Jesus and the Language of the Kingdom: Symbol and Metaphor in New Testament Interpretation* (Philadelphia, 1976).

PHILIPSON, David (9 August 1862, Wabash, IN—29 June 1949, Boston, MA). *Education*: B.A., Univ. of Cincinnati, 1883; graduated from Hebrew Union Coll., 1883; studied at Johns Hopkins Univ., 1884–86. *Career*: rabbi, Har Sinai Congregation, Baltimore, 1884–88; rabbi, Bene Israel Congregation, Cincinnati, 1888–1938; instructor in Semitic languages (1889–91); Homiletics (1891–1905), Reform Judaism (1905–49), Hebrew Union Coll., 1889–1949.

Reform Judaism was brought to the United States by German-speaking rabbis who found religious tolerance amenable to their practices. Second generation leaders came from the ranks of those already settled in this country, and Philipson was one of the most distinguished in that category. On the advice of *Isaac M. Wise he entered Hebrew Union College, graduated among its first class of scholars, and secured a rabbinate while studying Assyriology in Baltimore. By 1885 he proved a contributive spokesman for Reform principles by helping to draft the Pittsburgh Platform, a document which long defined the basic position of liberal synagogues. Returning to the oldest congregation west of the Alleghenies, he served there for fifty years to perpetuate the humanitarian vision of Jewish philanthropy inaugurated by his predecessors. Philipson was a staunch advocate of the compatibility between Reform definitions of religious activity and the main tenets of American citizenship. He denounced all conceptions of Judaism that included a self-conscious separatism, whether this was couched in nationalistic or psychological demands for distinctive existence. Proponents of Zionism were particularly unacceptable to his view of Judaism as a religion congruent with many cultural settings. As events in the twentieth century mounted hardships on European Jews, he admitted that a State of Israel could serve as refuge for displaced persons, but he never saw it as the main center of Hebraic culture.

Practical service in his denomination indicates one of the reasons why Philipson was considered a dean of the American Reform rabbinate. He was chairman of the committee which revised the Union Prayer Book (1913–21) and worked with the board of editors issuing a new translation of the Bible in 1916. Education was an abiding interest, evidenced by the fact that he taught at his alma mater and served continually on its board of governors after 1892. He was president of the Hebrew Sabbath School Union from 1894 to 1903; in the latter year he was instrumental in securing a merger with the American Hebrew Congregations and served as its chairman (elected and honorary) for the rest of his life. He also helped work out plans for the formation of the American Jewish Committee, an all-embracing organization to facilitate educational and philanthropic efforts on a national scale. Hardly an aspect of civic involvement, political reform, charity, or benevolence failed to receive his energetic support. For over half a century he gave practical expression to the liberal tenets constituting his faith in human betterment. An influential member of the Central Conference of American Rabbis (president, 1907–09), he died while attending its annual convocation.

Bibliography:

A. *The Jew in English Fiction* (Cincinnati, 1889); *The Oldest Jewish Congregation in the West* (Cincinnati, 1894); *A Holiday Sheaf* (Cincinnati, 1898); *The Reform Movement in Judaism* (New York, 1907, 1931); *Centenary Papers and Others* (Cincinnati, 1919); *My Life as an American Jew* (Cincinnati, 1941).

B. NCAB B, 302–03; UJE 8, 488–89; NYT 30 Jun 1949, 23.

PIERSON, Arthur Tappan (6 March 1837, New York, NY—3 June 1911, Brooklyn, NY). *Education*: B.A., Hamilton Coll., 1857; B.D., Union Sem. (NY), 1860. *Career*: minister, Binghamton, NY, 1860–63; minister, Waterford, NY, 1863–69; minister, Fort Street Presbyterian Church, Detroit, MI, 1869–82; minister Second Presbyterian Church, Indianapolis, IN, 1882–83; minister, Bethany Tabernacle, Philadelphia, PA, 1883–89; editor, *Missionary Review of the World*, 1888–1911; independent evangelist in England and U.S., 1889–1911.

From his earliest pulpit days Pierson showed a more than common interest in missionary activity. He tried to convince parishioners that preaching had its chief end in the conversion of souls, and churches had their existence in the plain worship of common folk. But successful midwestern pastorates did not satisfy him because they seemed to provide inadequately for spreading the message of salvation. Whereas most wealthy churchgoers wanted artistic sermons in comfortable surroundings, Pierson felt trapped in the indulgent atmosphere of middle class decorum. By 1883 he abandoned such local concerns to concentrate on wider fields, first in a nondenominational Philadelphia tabernacle, then in work for foreign missions as integral components of evangelistic endeavor. Within a few years he became a popular speaker at missionary conferences, especially those held by *Dwight L. Moody at his Massachusetts summer home, Northfield; there his urgent appeals galvanized young listeners and helped launch the Student Volunteer Movement for foreign missions. He also edited a journal for two decades which collated facts and stirred readers with enthusiastic descriptions of missionary advance around the globe. As late as 1910 he crossed the Pacific to stimulate mission activity in the Orient, and though poor health soon forced his return, he continued to write editorials on the subject until two days before he died. As an elder statesman of the world mission cause, he was constantly moved by the thought that countless persons were waiting for salvation and spiritual guidance.

Just as Pierson grew from a small town pastor to an evangelist of unlimited perspective, he also continued throughout life to develop intellectually. In 1878 he was convinced by George Müller, a British minister of recent acquaintance, that premillennialism was taught by Scripture. Thereafter he made the imminent second coming of Christ a central element in his preaching. While offering no specific dates for the advent, he emerged as a leading controversialist in the proposition that Christ would return before inaugurating a thousand-year reign of peace. Millennialism was a key which unlocked mysteries of the Bible; for decades Pierson spoke with great effect on these matters at Niagara Bible Conferences and Bible Institutes across the country. His interest in biblical injunctions led to another ideological change late in life. Through the influence of *Adoniram J. Gordon, his closest friend and fellow missionary advocate, he became convinced that adult baptism was the only practice condoned by Scripture. Consequently in 1896 he was immersed, resigned from the Philadelphia Presbytery, and aroused considerable discussion even among Baptists whose views he adopted. Shortly thereafter he also espoused goals of the "Keswick movement," an English perfectionist group which urged tangible progress in deepening one's spiritual life. These doctrinal changes indicated a vigorous mind at work, trying to enhance the meaning of religion in his personal experience as well as for those to whom he expounded multiple facets of a single gospel.

Bibliography:

    A. *The Crisis of Missions* (London, 1886); *In Christ Jesus, or The Sphere of the Believer's Life* (New York, 1898); *Forward Movements of the Last Half-Century* (New York, 1900); *The Gordian Knot, or The Problem which Baffles Infidelity* (New York, 1902); *God's Living Oracles* (New York, 1904); *The Bible and Spiritual Criticism* (New York, 1905).

    B. SH 9, 53; NCAB 13, 408; DAB 14, 589–90; NYT 4 Jun 1911, 11; J. Kennedy Maclean (ed.), *Dr. Pierson and His Message* (New York, 1911); Delevan L. Pierson, *Arthur T. Pierson* (New York, 1912).

PIKE, James Albert (14 February 1913, Oklahoma City, OK—?3–7 September 1969, Israel). *Education*: studied at Univ. of Santa Clara, 1930–32; B.A., UCLA, 1934; LL.B., UCLA, 1936; J.S.D., Yale Univ., 1938; B.D., Union Sem. (NY), 1951. *Career*: practiced law, Washington, DC, 1938–42; officer, U.S. Navy, 1942–45; rector, Poughkeepsie, NY, 1947–49; chaplain, Columbia Univ., 1949–52; rector, New York, NY, 1952–58; bishop of California, 1958–66; staff member, Center for the Study of Democratic Institutions, Santa Barbara, CA, 1966–69.

For most of his life Pike accepted the theological formulations of the Episcopal church in a conventional manner. Thousands heard him speak as dean of St. John the Divine Cathedral in New York and then as bishop at Grace Cathedral in San Francisco, those audiences finding his ideas on doctrinal issues largely representative of the Episcopal church in this country. But by 1960 Pike began to change, and the rest of his life was symbolic of modern man's search for new religious affirmations. The bishop grew increasingly serious about theology, reflecting at length on its existential function and ontological objective as he sought greater certitude in defining faith. Through this process he became disenchanted with several classical formulations of belief and boldly suggested that they be discarded. He held that God was the only absolute and everything else relative. This being the case, all creeds and ethical codes, all church polities and liturgical forms had to be understood as historically conditioned and only partially true. Proper discrimination would allow for vital faith and still permit the abandonment of outdated ideas as ones to which contemporary man could no longer conscientiously subscribe. Many were distressed to find, however, that among the "excess baggage" Pike wanted to leave behind were the Trinity, virgin birth, and salvation through Christ alone. Reaction to his radical, well-intended suggestions about theological revision came quickly. Specifications for charges of heresy were drawn up, and in 1966 the House of Bishops censured him for irresponsibility in an office of public leadership.

The search for relevance and effectiveness was not confined to theology; at times Pike seemed just as unsettling in his social views. He supported open housing laws, grape pickers' strikes, civil rights marches, ordination of women, and urged more humane treatment for alcoholics and homosexuals. In 1966 one of Pike's sons committed suicide, and his search for meaning took another turn. After resigning as bishop he began experimenting in the realm of psychic phenomena as a means of establishing contact with the dead boy. This added more notoriety to the public image of one driven by inner needs for religious comprehension. While on a study trip in Israel, one more facet of that inner quest which he continually pursued, Pike died in the Judean wilderness after his touring car broke down west of the Dead Sea, too far from help. He achieved no synthesis of new religious ideas, but his search for a faith that withstood modern criticisms was shared by many less willing to admit it in his day.

Bibliography:

A. *Beyond Anxiety* (New York, 1953); *The Church, Politics and Society* (New York, 1955); *Doing the Truth* (Garden City, NY, 1955). *A Time for Christian Candor* (New York, 1964); *What is This Treasure* (New York, 1966); *If this be Heresy* (New York, 1967); *The Other Side: An Account of My Experiences with Psychic Phenomena* (Garden City, NY, 1968).

B. NCAB J, 457–58; NYT 8 Sep 1969, 1; William Stringfellow and Anthony Towne, *The Bishop Pike Affair* (New York, 1967); Hans Holzer, *The Psychic World of Bishop Pike* (New York, 1970); Diane K. Pike, *Search* (Garden City, NY, 1970); William Stringfellow and Anthony Towne, *The Death and Life of Bishop Pike* (New York, 1976).

PILMORE, Joseph (31 October 1739, Tadmouth, England—24 July 1825, Philadelphia, PA). *Career*: lay missionary in Great Britain, 1767–69 and 1776–84; lay missionary in American colonies, 1769–74; rector, United Episcopal Parishes, Philadelphia, PA, 1786–89; assistant rector, St. Paul's Episcopal Church, Philadelphia, 1789–93; rector, St. Paul's Episcopal Church, 1804–25.

When Pilmore was sixteen years old, he was converted at one of John Wesley's preaching services. He took Wesley seriously when he said that such preaching and consequent conversions helped rejuvenate the Church of England. So as he matured Pilmore became one of Wesley's trusted assistants, accompanying him on evangelical tours and preaching himself quite often. In 1769 he volunteered for similar work in America. He and Richard Boardman were the first two authorized Methodist preachers sent to this country. The two men spent most of their time in Philadelphia and New York City, but Pilmore also toured much of the seacoast between Massachusetts and Georgia. Revolutionary sentiments impeded their pastoral efforts, though, because many Anglican ministers, together with lay preachers of Methodist inclination, were staunch Loyalists. As such, they came under increasing criticism and apposition from republican colonists and were forced to leave the scene.

Reaching England in 1774, Pilmore received no assignment for more than a year, but he was soon filling circuits again as a lay preacher. This activity ended abruptly in 1784, however, when John Wesley enacted a Deed of Declaration. This legal document perpetuated "The Conference of the People called Methodists" with arrangements for ordination, discipline, and corporate property. Pilmore felt this act of incipient independence violated earlier pledges to bolster Anglicanism, and so he broke with Wesley over the issue of rival institutions. Shortly thereafter he received ordination as an Episcopal priest at the hands of *Samuel Seabury and devoted the next four decades of his life to the American branch of the Anglican communion. There he held parishes in the urban northeast, serving people with the same genial personal qualities and fervent personal qualities that had characterized his work while identified with the Wesleyan cause. He served on General Convention committees to revise the Book of Common Prayer and to streamline the service of Communion, but his most durable contribution was the warm, heartfelt emotions attached to Christian experience which he nurtured. These elements became lasting characteristics of Episcopal churches in southern and middle Atlantic states.

Bibliography:

A. *Narrative of Labors in South Wales* (Philadelphia, 1825).
B. AAP 5, 266–70; DAB 14, 609–10.

POLK, Leonidas (10 April 1806, Raleigh, NC—14 June 1864, near Marietta, GA). *Education*: studied at Univ. of North Carolina, 1821–23; graduated from U.S. Military Acad., 1827; B.D., Virginia Sem., 1830. *Career*: curate, Richmond, VA, 1830–31; convalescent travel and farming, Europe, NC and TN, 1831–38; Episcopal bishop of the Southwest, 1838–41; bishop of Louisiana, 1841–64; officer, Confederate Army, 1861–64.

Military service seemed a likely prospect for young Polk who gained entry into West Point on the strength of his father's Revolutionary War record. But as a cadet he was greatly influenced by the preaching of chaplain *Charles P. McIlvaine; as a result he resigned his commission after graduation and took steps to become a priest instead of a soldier. After several years of bad health and nonclerical pursuits, his service to American Episcopalianism began in 1838 when he was consecrated by McIlvaine as missionary bishop. His territorial jurisdiction was enormous, comprising five states from Alabama to Texas. At least three visitations were made, each taking six months to cover 5,000 miles. Since there were few clergy in the area, Polk's work was primarily evangelistic, but he also baptized, confirmed, celebrated communion, and organized new congregations whenever opportunities presented themselves. By 1841 he was able to narrow his responsibilities to one state, settling on a sugar plantation where he supervised the labor of four hundred slaves. Churches grew from three to thirty-three under his guidance, but agricultural ventures proved ruinous. In 1853 the bishop turned his plantation over to creditors and pursued his episcopal duties in modest surroundings as rector of Trinity Church at New Orleans. Systematic rounds of pastoral inspection gave substantial impetus to growth as his denomination grew increasingly stronger in southern states.

A concern for educating leaders in those southern states led Polk to campaign for a university—the University of the South—which stands as one of his most lasting achievements. In addition to training young men for the priesthood, he wanted to benefit all levels of society by providing a school for the elite. Sound learning and humane principles would, he hoped, create a genuine aristocracy with qualifications beyond mere wealth. Men trained by such standards would embody a healthful conservatism to counterbalance radical forces which the bishop saw growing to the north. For these and allied reasons Polk's plan (1856) was endorsed by the southern hierarchy. Bishops Stephen Elliott and James H. Otey also played roles in bringing this project to fruition. But their Louisiana colleague was principally responsible for its endowment, constitution and location at Sewanee, Tennessee; the University of the South became a living reality in 1860. In the following year Polk became a corps commander for the Confederacy because he believed that his country, only recently defined by seceding states, was fighting for its sacred freedom. He distinguished himself at the battles of Shiloh, Perryville, Murfreesboro, and Chickamauga. Though he no longer exercised episcopal responsibilities, it was possible to continue reading divine service and at times baptize in the field converts such as John B. Hood and Joseph E. Johnston. A chance cannon shot caused his death while on reconnoiter near Pine Mountain.

Bibliography:

B.   NCAB 11, 341–42; DAB 15, 39–40; William M. Polk, *Leonidas Polk: Bishop and General*, 2 vols. (New York, 1893); Joseph H. Parks, *General Leonidas Polk, C.S.A.: The Fighting Bishop* (Baton Rouge, LA, 1962).

PRATT, Parley Parker (12 April 1807, Burlington, NY—13 May 1857, near Van Buren, AR). *Career*: elder, Church of Latter-Day Saints, 1830–57.

Like many others in the Yankee belt, Pratt moved west with his family to settle new lands in Ohio. He responded favorably to doctrines preached by Reformed Baptist, *Sidney Rigdon, and decided within the year that his real calling was to preach a similar gospel. While on tour through central New York in 1830, he was won over to the Mormon faith because it possessed the revelation, tangible saintliness, and new priesthood for which he had been searching. Pratt's capabilities were quickly recognized by *Joseph Smith as well as other leaders of the growing organization. Ordained an elder in 1830 and made a high priest one year later, he was chosen among the first Quorum of Twelve Apostles in 1835. He accompanied the remnant of Saints from Ohio to Missouri after economic collapse made the move necessary. In Caldwell County west of the Mississippi he helped defend Mormons against ''Gentile'' pillage, only to find himself jailed for his pains. After escaping, he fled with the rest to Illinois. Missionary assignments often took him far afield; he served his church faithfully in those enterprises, preaching, baptizing, and establishing new branches wherever possible. By 1840 Canadian missions led to evangelical work in England where Pratt served for two years as editor of the *Millennial Star*. In addition to publishing their major paper, he helped compile a Mormon hymnbook, including some fifty of his own compositions. As one of the church's luminaries he provided stability after their founder's murder in 1844.

When it became clear that Mormons would have to leave Nauvoo, Illinois, Pratt helped lead the great migration of 1846–47. He headed scouting parties, blazing a trail for *Brigham Young and the larger van's overland trek to the Great Salt Lake. During the first two winters his large family suffered as others did, living mainly on sego lily roots. Once a living was wrested from the difficult land, he served as legislator for the State of Deseret, made a U.S. Territory in 1854. Within the church he opposed Young's move to be made President but eventually submitted rather than cause further schism in the ranks of followers. For a few months during 1851–52 he embarked on an ambitious missionary journey to Chile; language difficulties and local revolution hampered such efforts. The next year he laid one of the cornerstones of the new Temple at Salt Lake City. His preaching and administrative ability were especially fruitful in extending churches throughout California. While in San Francisco he married his twelfth wife, Elenor McLean, a convert whose children had been sent by her irate family back to New Orleans. The next year Pratt allowed Elenor to kidnap her children and meet him on a Cherokee reservation in Arkansas where he was organizing a wagon train for Utah. Hector McLean, Elenor's first husband, accused Pratt of petty larceny, but the Mormon preacher was found innocent. A few miles from town, the vengeful plaintiff murdered Pratt and was not apprehended by sympathetic townspeople. Four months later a large band (121) of pioneers from Arkansas and Missouri were massacred at Mountain Meadows, Utah, an apparent retaliation in which Mormons killed every man, woman, and child over six years of age.

Bibliography:

A. *A Voice of Warning and Instruction to all People* (New York, 1837); *Key to the Science of Theology* (Liverpool, 1855); *Autobiography*, ed. Parley P. Pratt Jr. (New York, 1874); *Writings of Parley Parker Pratt*, ed. Parker P. Robinson (Salt Lake City, 1952).
    B. NCAB 16, 16–17; DAB 15, 175; Reva Stanley, *A Biography of Parley P. Pratt: The Archer of Paradise* (Caldwell, ID, 1937); *The Essential Parley P. Pratt* (Salt Lake City, 1990).

PRIESTLEY, Joseph (13 March 1733, Fieldhead, England—6 February 1804, Northumberland, PA). *Education*: graduated from Daventry Acad., 1755. *Career*: minister, Needham Market, 1755–58; minister and schoolmaster, Nantwich, 1758–61; tutor, Warrington Acad., 1761–67; minister, Leeds, 1767–72; librarian to Lord Shelburne, 1772–80; minister, Birmingham, 1780–91; minister, Hackney, 1791–94; active retirement in America, 1794–1804.

Major British universities did not welcome students from non-Anglican families; so Priestley received his training in the more liberal atmosphere of a dissenting academy. His restless mind pursued knowledge well beyond that introductory phase, however, to reach distinguished accomplishments in religion, politics, and natural science. A speech impediment ruined early efforts to serve as a minister, but teaching school proved more to his liking. He introduced modern history together with scientific topics such as anatomy and botany in secondary education. On the secular side his enduring fame lay in the area of chemical experimentation. He isolated no fewer than nine gases, notably oxygen, and achieved eminence as a Fellow of the Royal Society. Such prestige lent weight to his heterodox religious philosophy. By 1770 he proclaimed forthright Unitarian views and ministered to some of the most liberal congregations in England. After the French Revolution began, he published a defense of republican government which aroused hostility in a public fearful of possible repercussions in British society. In 1791 a mob burned his house and destroyed all personal effects including the library. Three years later he emigrated to America where he was well received by many dignitaries. To his lasting chagrin he was not invited to preach. In 1796 he established a small Unitarian society in Philadelphia, but through the final decade he was primarily occupied with laboratory experiments and writing on a variety of subjects.

The eighteenth century popular mind made little distinction between Unitarianism and atheism, but Priestley never considered himself anything but Christian. He was convinced that what passed for orthodoxy in his day led to either supersition or unbelief. Rational inquiry proved that the apostolic church had been Unitarian, only to be corrupted by an influx of pagan notions. Some of those corruptions were ideas about original sin, predestination, a Trinity, the worship of Christ, and plenary inspiration of scripture. Priestley's religion was thus an attempt to reconstruct beliefs in their original purity, pared of spurious doctrines added through the ages. He believed in God as benevolent creator and governor of the world. The moral teachings of Jesus in addition to his miracles, death, and resurrection were of essential importance to him. He also looked forward to immortality for all men where virtue would be rewarded and vice punished by a righteous providence. In America he presented a marked contrast to such radical deists as *Ethan Allen or *Elihu Palmer. Content to discuss deism in the quiet dignity of gentlemen's homes, he embodied none of the demagoguery bent on spreading new doctrine among the masses. His piety and learning represented a version of enlightened religion able to deflect most of the vituperation which orthodox churches continued to heap on it.

Bibliography:

A.   *An History of the Corruptions of Christianity*, 2 vols. (Birmingham, 1782); *Letters to a Philosophical Unbeliever* (Birmingham, 1787); *Unitarianism Explained and Defended* (Philadelphia, 1796); *The Theological and Miscellaneous Works of Joseph Priestley*, ed. John T. Rutt, 25 vols. (London, 1817–32).

B.   AAP 8, 298–308; SH 9, 254–55; NCAB 6, 148–49; DAB 15, 223–26; NCE 11, 777; Thomas E. Thorpe, *Joseph Priestley* (London, 1906); Anne D. Holt, *A Life of Joseph Priestley* (London, 1931); Frederick W. Gibbs, *Joseph Priestley* (London, 1965); A. Truman Schwartz and John G. McEvoy (eds.), *Motion Towards Perfection: The Achievement of Joseph Priestley* (Boston, 1990).

PRIME, Samuel Irenaeus (4 November 1812, Ballston, NY—18 July 1885, New York, NY). *Education*: B.A., Williams Coll., 1829; studied at Princeton Sem., 1832–33. *Career*: schoolteacher, Cambridge and Sing Sing, NY, 1830–36; schoolteacher, Newburgh, NY, 1836–38; Presbyterian minister, Matteawan, NY, 1838–40; assistant editor, *New York Observer*, 1840–49; secretary, American Bible Society, 1850; editor, *The Presbyterian*, 1851; editor, *New York Observer*, 1851–85.

As the son and great-grandson of Presbyterian ministers, it seemed natural for young Prime to aspire to the clergy. He tried to serve in the traditional manner, especially after licensing in 1833 and ordination two years later, but health problems prevented fulfillment in that capacity. By 1838 the ambitious preacher and pedagogue began to realize that wider horizons beckoned in journalism. Something in his facile pen made it easy to write on a wide range of topics, and most of them quickly appeared in the *New York Observer*, a weekly religious paper with Presbyterian affiliations. Prime soon became a fixture at the journal, often seeing issues through the press single-handedly. He contributed editorials and essays known as the "Irenaeus Letters" issuing opinions in lively prose on a broad scope of current issues. If all his efforts had been reprinted as books, they would have filled an estimated one hundred volumes, but only two, containing choice selections, appeared in 1882 and 1885.

Through the use of both voice and pen Prime became a popular and influential figure in his day. His ministerial consciousness led him to emphasize church affairs, social reforms, and general spiritual needs of society in his paper. Through its pages he touched the thought and sentiment of prominent citizens across the country and helped mold the religious dimensions of popular culture.

His reports on foreign travels drew lessons for improvements at home. His writings on religious and educational endeavors influenced developments in many philanthropic activities that were motivated by Christian benevolence. His counsels on politics and literature strove to uplift social standards by means of more adequate spiritual guidance. Widely read because of these attributes and in great demand as a lecturer, Prime became an arbiter of American taste and a template for national morality during the third quarter of the nineteenth century. His pervasive ethical concern and easygoing manner made such clerical leadership attractive. His popularity points to the success enjoyed by Protestant ministers as dominant cultural voices before industrialization, urbanization, and immigration eroded their status.

Bibliography:

A. *The Old White Meeting House: Reminiscences of a Country Congregation* (New York, 1846); *Thoughts on the Death of Little Children* (New York, 1852); *Travels in Europe and the East* (New York, 1855); *The Power of Prayer* (New York, 1859); *Fifteen Years of Prayer in the Fulton Street Mission* (New York, 1872); *Songs of the Soul: Gathered out of Many Lands and Ages* (New York, 1873).

B. SH 256–57; NCAB 7, 237–38; DAB 15, 228; NYT 19 Jul 1885, 7; Wendell Prime, *Samuel Irenaeus Prime: Autobiography and Memorials* (New York, 1888).

PROVOOST, Samuel (9 March 1742, New York, NY—6 September 1815, New York, NY). *Education*: B.A., King's Coll., 1758; studied at St. Peter's Coll., Cambridge Univ., 1761–66. *Career*: assistant minister, Trinity Church, New York, 1766–71; farmer, East Camp, NY, 1771–84; rector, Trinity Church, New York, 1784–1800; bishop of New York, 1787–1801; retirement, 1801–15.

Baptized in the Dutch Reformed church and descended from several generations in that communion, Provoost's preference for Anglicanism is difficult to uncover. Probably one reason was his frustration at seeing Dutch ministers resist the use of English in worship services, but a more important factor was his experience at college. *Samuel Johnson was president and chief instructor of the new academy; along with other members of the first graduating class, young Provoost was probably influenced by his mentor's emphasis on the fitness of Episcopal doctrine. He prepared for orders in England, received ordination there, and returned to one of the busiest parishes in the New World. But within a few years trouble began to brew for reasons both complex and obscure. The assistant minister's sermons were terse, rational discourses which failed to satisfy those vestrymen who wished to hear preaching of a more evangelical nature. Another factor was related to politics, a sphere determining much of his subsequent activity. Most of the parish was Loyalist in 1770 while Provoost was a zealous patriot. Consequently he dissolved connections with Trinity Church and retired to secular pursuits in Dutchess County. In recognition of his dedication to the American cause he was invited to serve churches in Boston and Charleston, but he declined all opportunities until his old parish welcomed him back in 1784.

An American Episcopal church insistent on securing democratic freedoms seemed to have a strong leader in this republican clergyman.

In 1786 the diocese of New York chose Provoost as its first bishop, a decision reflecting approval of convictions already tested and hopes for future development. But after consecration in England with *William White in 1787, he did not play an important role in forming a strong Episcopal church in this country. Though he was chairman of the committee (4 persons) which drafted a constitution and revised the Book of Common Prayer for American churches, others did most of the work. He objected to overemphasis on episcopal prerogatives, opposing *Samuel Seabury and preventing national union of churches for years because of this issue. The patriot bishop wished less continuity with the complete Anglican tradition and more liberty in American patterns. The General Convention of 1789 was able unanimously to recognize the validity of Seabury's consecration only because Provoost did not attend. Three years later Provoost refused to cooperate with Seabury because he thought too many concessions had been granted the prelatical party. Personal tragedies rather than ecclesiastical controversy soon removed him from active duty. The death of his wife and two sons, one by suicide, caused him to resign all office. The confused House of Bishops protested such unprecedented action even while accepting it by appointing a coadjutor. Provoost appeared in public only once thereafter, agreeing in 1811 to serve as third celebrant at the consecration of *John H. Hobart and *Alexander V. Griswold. The following year he attempted to resume other powers, but the diocese clearly indicated its backing for leaders less inclined to sacrifice diocesan growth to personal considerations.

Bibliography:

B.   AAP 5; 240–45; SH 9, 312; NCAB 1, 513–14; DAB 15, 249–50; John N. Norton, *The Life of Bishop Provoost of New York* (New York, 1859).

PURCELL, John Baptist (26 February 1800, Mallow, Ireland—4 July 1883, Brown County, OH). *Education*: studied at Mount St. Mary's Coll. (MD), 1820–23; studied at Sem. of St. Sulpice, Paris, 1824–27. *Career*: private tutor, Queen Anne's County, MD, 1818–20; professor (president after 1829), Mount St. Mary's Coll., 1827–33; bishop of Cincinnati, 1833–50; archbishop of Cincinnati, 1850–83.

By the time Purcell became second bishop of Cincinnati, population in the old Northwest Territory was increasing at a rate which gave the district happy prospect of more expansion in ensuing decades. He presided over that growth with considerable administrative ability and winning diplomacy, avoiding factionalism between German and Irish ethnic groups as immigration brought additional numbers to their ranks almost daily. For example he sanctioned the establishment of Holy Trinity Church (1834), center of the first German-speaking parish west of the Alleghenies. He also supported a periodical, *Der Wahrheitsfreund* (1837–1907), as a valuable means of spreading Catholic truth among those of the diocese still clinging to old world language and customs. Another important contribution lay in the area of institutional development, especially charitable and educational centers; he imported ten different communities of religious women as well as eight separate monastic orders to help staff those diocesan functions. When Purcell entered Ohio, there were no more than sixteen churches tended by fourteen priests. At the end of his productive tenure there were more than five hundred churches, 480 priests, thirty parochial schools, three colleges and as many seminaries, six hospitals, and almost two dozen orphanages. These tangible expressions of the bishop's pastoral energy indicate how thoroughly he shaped contemporary growth with an eye toward long-range stability.

In addition to providing for the material expansion of Catholicism in midwestern states, Purcell was an outstanding spokesman for his church in issues of wider cultural interest. As a strong temperance advocate, one of his perennial lecture themes was total abstinence from alcohol. In 1836–37 he debated with *Alexander Campbell on popular notions regarding the Roman religion; few converts were made on either side, but the public airing of differences helped somewhat to moderate local nativist hostilities. By 1853 those anti-Catholic prejudices recurred when papal legate, Gaetano Bedini, conducted a tour for purposes of investigating trusteeism. Purcell manifested both physical and moral courage by inviting Bedini to Cincinnati, defending his authority and protecting him from a mob which threatened his life. As a delegate to the First Vatican Council in 1870 he opposed definitions of papal infallibility not only because it seemed inopportune to promulgate such a belief but more than that he objected to clarification of the doctrine itself. He voted against the measure in preliminary ballots and left Rome before its final passage, accepting it only after it occupied the highest theological stage of dogma. The archbishop's last years were clouded by a financial disaster in which four million dollars of private funds were lost through unwise investment procedures. Though the faulty scheme was not his personal responsibility, he accepted the blame and retired to monastic seclusion after 1879. A coadjutor handled diocesan affairs thereafter, but this unfortunate denouement should not be allowed to eclipse all the good accomplished in fifty years of prior service.

Bibliography:

B. SH 9, 364; NCAB 5, 186–88; DAB 15, 266–68; NCE 11, 1029–30; NYT 6 Jul 1883, 1; Mary A. McCann, *Archbishop Purcell and the Archdiocese of Cincinnati* (Washington, DC, 1918).

R

RANSOM, Reverdy Cassius (4 January 1861, Flushing, OH—22 April 1959, Wilberforce, OH). *Education*: studied at Wilberforce Univ., 1881–82; studied at Oberlin Coll., 1882–83; graduated from Wilberforce Univ., 1886. *Career*: minister, Altoona and Hollisdayburg, PA, 1886–88; minister, Allegheny City, PA, 1888–90; minister Springfield, OH, 1890–93; minister, Cleveland, OH, 1893–96; minister, Chicago, IL, 1896–1900; minister, Institutional Church and Social Settlement, Chicago, 1900–04; minister New Bedford, MA, 1904; minister, Boston, MA, 1904–07; minister, New York, NY, 1907–12; editor, *A.M.E. Review*, 1912–24; bishop, African Methodist Episcopal Church, 1924–52.

The culture into which Ransom was born had begun to disavow slavery, but it was far from granting free blacks the same social status as white citizens. As pastor in almost a dozen parishes, many of whose congregations were products of his own organizing zeal, he was an outspoken champion of social and political rights for all Americans. He knew that churches served as a social center in the lives of black people and that religious experience was a strong foundation for developing Afro-American culture. These functions were particularly critical during Ransom's ministry because the black population was leaving rural Southern areas in increasing numbers, moving to northern cities where churches were the only familiar symbols of stability amid bewildering changes. Traditional A.M.E. policies were inadequate to deal with such needs, and Ransom helped modernize the church, causing his denomination to confront problems of social welfare. In speaking out for equal rights and universal franchise during the Jim Crow era, and in calling for better wages, working conditions, housing, and educational opportunities, he served both his faith and all Negro citizens.

Social and political activism were necessary adjuncts to Ransom's image of the church. He believed that Christianity applied to conditions in this world and that the Gospel had to be Social if it was to be truly effective. Such work would help bring about God's plan for a world without racial and social injustice. Such an achievement would benefit all people, but Ransom was especially eager to secure greater elevation and advancement for those of his own race. Widely noted as a gifted orator, he often pointed out that the true test of Christianity and democracy in this country was whether those ideologies treated people of different races equally or not. He was impatient for change and sided with those of the Niagara Movement in opposition to the more accommodating *Booker T. Washington and his Afro-American Council. In 1909 Ransom participated in the organization of the National Association for the advancement of Colored People, and the following year he delivered a keynote address at its formal beginnings. In his later years as bishop, college trustee, speaker, and denominational historiographer he continued to press for reforms and improvements. He lived almost the whole century following emancipation from slavery, and he was vitally involved in struggles to enhance the welfare of both the bodies and souls of his people.

Bibliography:

A.   *School Days at Wilberforce* (Springfield, OH, 1892); *The Spirit of Freedom and Justice: Oration and Speeches* (Nashville, 1926); *The Negro: The Hope or Despair of Christianity* (Boston, 1935); *The Pilgrimage of Harriet Ransom's Son* (Nashville, 1949); *Preface to the History of the A.M.E. Church* (Nashville, 1950).

B.   Calvin S. Morris, *Reverdy Ransom: Black Advocate of the Social Gospel* (New York, 1990).

RAPP, George (1 November 1757, Iptingen, Germany—7 August 1847, Economy, PA).

Johann Georg Rapp had little formal education but was greatly influenced by the writings of such visionaries as Böhme, Spener, and Swedenborg. A linen weaver by trade, he responded more to the spiritual promptings within himself than to formal Lutheran ministrations in the province of Würtemberg. By 1785 Rapp had attracted a following whose resistance to established churches and schools earned them recognition as separatists, with fines, prison, and other restrictions following as a result. Yet the prophet was adamant in preaching his views on spiritual rebirth and rigorously perfectionist ethics. Those who believed as he did formed a small community, purified by God's spirit, waiting eagerly for Christ's return. Rapp thought of his congregation as the bride of Christ, or as the book of Revelation described her, the Sun Woman. Those chosen were to endure special temptation and receive special glory, to have God's name written on each saint and be sealed by angels. ''Father Rapp'' assured his flock that their purity would qualify them as firstfruits in the new Kingdom where they would reign with Christ for a thousand years. He eventually (1807) decided that celibacy was another corollary to millenarian hopes, and he enforced among followers that doctrine which contributed to their ultimate extinction. All those distinctive forms of personal and communal conduct pointed to a basic adventism shared by many religious societies transplanted to the New World.

Radical pietists who hold strong millennial expectations often find communitarian forms of social organization congenial. The celibate, pacifist Rappites who held all goods in common prospered in America despite some internal dissension. Rapp controlled his communistic theocracy with patriarchal solicitude, seconded by his adopted son Frederick Reichert, and received in turn the reverence of most residents. He ruled as duty led him, serving without care for praise or blame, in order to be no idler in God's economy for the righteous. In 1804, Harmony, Pennsylvania, became their home where more than 600 disciples settled to work and await the Second Coming. In 1814 they moved to New Harmony, Indiana, and then in 1825 back to Pennsylvania, residing at last on a remarkably successful tract called Economy. Members of the society were so industrious they grew wealthy, becoming widely known for excellent woolen and distilled products. But Rapp's energetic leadership and moral power were more important factors in the group's continuance. As long as he lived, the religious basis for communitarian harmony kept life in proper perspective. As memories of his ardent chiliasm waned, so did the society's vitality. He preached for the last time on the Sunday before his death and, as an indication of his otherworldly focus, was buried in an unmarked grave.

Bibliography:

A. *Gedanken über die Bestimmung des Menschen* (Harmony, IN, 1824), translated and slightly revised, *Thoughts on the Destiny of Man* (Harmony, IN, 1824).

B. SH 9, 390; NCAB 4, 353; DAB 15, 383–84; NCE 12, 85; John S. Duss, *George Rapp and his Associates* (Indianapolis, 1914); Christiana F. Knoedler, *The Harmony Society* (New York, 1954); William E. Wilson, *The Angel and the Serpent: The Story of New Harmony* (Bloomington, IN, 1964); Karl J. R. Arndt, *George Rapp's Harmony Society, 1785–1847* (Rutherford, NJ, 1965).

RAUCH, Friedrich Augustus (22 July 1806, Kirchbracht, Germany—2 March 1841, Mercersburg, PA). *Education*: studied at Giessen, 1824–26; Ph.D., Marburg, 1827. *Career*: provisional Privatdozent, Giessen, 1828–31; professor of German, Lafayette Coll., 1832; principal of classical school and professor of Biblical Literature, Sem. of the German Reformed Church, York, PA, 1832–35; president and professor, Marshall Coll., 1836–41.

Hegelian philosophical idealism was brought to this country by Professor Rauch who left Germany after difficulties in obtaining a teaching post there. No questions were raised about academic credentials in Pennsylvania synods of the German Reformed church; so he was ordained and quickly established a reputation for classical learning. But contemporary philosophy was the area of greatest impact. His book entitled *Psychology* received more than local attention, evidenced by the fact that it went through five editions within ten years. In that publication he delineated a view of God as Absolute Idea, the basis for comprehending reality in all its manifestations. God as the ultimate identity or synthesis of dialectics was the source of ideas regarding both truth and social justice. The philosophy of Idea led consistently to an understanding of human approximations of truth in formal thought, while it provided an interpretive framework for attempts to embody morality in ethics and aesthetics. Rauch was one of the first exponents of this intellectual perspective in America. In his brief decade of teaching he opened new horizons for students and colleagues alike. When *John W. Nevin joined him at Mercersburg in 1840, he incorporated Rauch's views into what later became a distinctive school of thought. The first president of Marshall College, Rauch was a transitional figure, an early spokesman for German ideological categories which greatly affected the course of religious thought among nineteenth century theologians.

Bibliography:

A. *Psychology, or a View of the Human Soul, including Anthropology* (New York, 1840); *The Inner Life of the Christian* (Philadelphia, 1856).

B. SH 9, 404; NCAB 11, 62–63; DAB 15, 389–90; Howard J. B. Ziegler, *Frederick Augustus Rauch: American Hegelian* (Lancaster, PA, 1953).

RAUSCHENBUSCH, Walter (4 October 1861, Rochester, NY—25 July 1918, Rochester, NY). *Education*: B.A., Univ. of Rochester, 1884; graduated from Rochester Sem., 1886; studied at Berlin, Kiel, and Marburg, 1891–92, 1907–08. *Career*: minister, Second German Baptist Church, New York, 1886–97; professor of New Testament Interpretation, Rochester Sem., 1897–1902; professor of Church History, Rochester Sem., 1902–18.

A pastorate on the edge of slums in New York aroused a passionate social concern in this man who for almost three decades devoted himself to reform. Rauschenbusch had gone to the city with pietistic intentions of saving individual souls, but he confronted harsh conditions of bad housing, unemployment, crime, and disease which caused him to reformulate his ideas in the light of urgent human need. He was further awakened to social crises by secular reformers such as Henry George and advanced theorists in England. The combination of secular and religious views and an ability to analyze concrete situations joined with a broad historical perspective made his insights compelling. Those insights were also produced by a personal synthesis of deep evangelical fervor and commitment to social action. After returning to Rochester, teaching in both German and English divisions of his old seminary, Rauschenbusch was in constant demand as lecturer and writer on topics of current interest. He possessed great rhetorical power, which converted many to the cause and guided their efforts into productive channels. His book of prayers for the working man was an ancillary endeavor that contributed significantly to a new body of devotional literature. Another area of practical achievement was civic reform in his home town where he worked for changes in municipal government and the public school system. After publication of his first book in 1907 he rose quickly to national prominence as a chief spokesman for the Social Gospel movement in America.

While Rauschenbusch drew on sources outside the church to recommend specific reforms, he found a moral impetus within Christianity for urging their implementation. His concern to speak of social ethics in doctrinal terms produced a unique theological position. One aspect was a conception of evil as something tangible to be resisted, not just an inner attitude to be controlled. Abuses could become institutionalized, and Rauschenbusch was perhaps more realistic than many of his generation in recognizing that super-personal forces of evil were a strong adversary to his hopes. But, like most liberals, he remained convinced that sin was a reformable social inheritance. The dominant category of his thought was the Kingdom of God, a concept which invited human participation in redeeming society as the essential tenet of Christian faith. This Kingdom was divine in origin, constituting both a transcendent ideal and an immediate reality. It moved in progressive development toward the unity of mankind organized according to the will of God. By means of that vision Rauschenbusch was able to include churches as aids in the larger movement for social betterment. His ideas, which were representative of progressive sentiments in the early years of this century, won widespread acceptance among those seeking a theology of the Social Gospel. Events toward the end of his life dampened expectations of the coming Kingdom, and, after experiencing great disillusionment during World War I, he died before that conflict inaugurated a new era of social attitudes and religious response.

Bibliography:

A. *Christianity and the Social Crisis* (New York, 1907); *For God and the People: Prayers of the Social Awakening* (Boston, 1910); *Christianizing the Social Order* (New York, 1912); *Dare We Be Christians?* (Boston, 1914); *The Social Principles of Jesus* (New York, 1916); *A Theology for the Social Gospel* (New York, 1917, 1945).

B. SH 9, 405; NCAB 19, 193; DAB 15, 392–93; NCE 12, 94; Dores R. Sharpe, *Walter Rauschenbusch* (New York, 1942); Vernon P. Bodein, *The Social Gospel of Walter Rauschenbusch and its Relation to Religious Education* (New Haven, 1944); Klaus J. Jaehn, *Rauschenbusch: The Formative Years* (Valley Forge, PA, 1976); Paul M. Minus, *Walter Rauschenbusch: American Reformer* (New York, 1988).

RICE, David (29 December 1733, Hanover County, VA—18 June 1816, Green County, KY). *Education*: B.A., Coll. of New Jersey, 1761; studied theology under John Todd, Hanover County, VA, 1761–62. *Career*: minister, Hanover County, VA, 1763–69; minister, Bedford County, VA, 1769–83; minister, Mercer County, KY, 1783–98; minister, Green County, KY, 1798–1816.

Born into a family of simple farmers, nominally Anglican and deliberately non-slaveholding, Rice was shaped by Presbyterian influences during his formative years. The preaching of *Samuel Davies caused him to adopt a ministerial vocation, and shortly after completing theological study coupled with missionary work he settled as pastor of five churches which Davies had previously led. But he seemed driven by a restless, pioneering spirit, moving first to the Virginia mountains and then to open country west of the Alleghenies. No extraordinary emotionalism attended his preaching, but by dint of energetic activity he organized many churches in the new territory. Catechetical instruction and ordinances of regular worship were as important to him as itinerant evangelism. Because of this he attempted to regulate his denomination's participation in camp meeting revivals, preventing scandal, and placing religious vitality on a sound, lasting basis. Honored by many as the founder of Presbyterianism in Kentucky, Rice played a similar role in political advancement. He shared work in the 1792 state constitutional convention and lobbied openly, though futilely, for a clause assuring gradual emancipation of Negro slaves. He was unalterably opposed to slavery, denouncing it as inconsistent with justice and good policy. Whether in sermon or pamphlet form, his cogent arguments against the peculiar institution kept the question alive for decades after the Revolution. He also supported educational excellence, serving as co-founder of Hampden-Sydney College (1775) before he moved west and promoting Transylvania University (1780) for decades as well. Poor health began to slow his activities after the age of sixty-five, but he was still able to tour Kentucky and Ohio (1805–06) for purposes of reporting on general religious conditions to the General Assembly. Suffering from infirmities of age, he preached occasionally as opportunity offered, speaking in public for the last time on his eightieth birthday.

Bibliography:

B. AAP 3, 246–49; DAB 15, 537–38.

RICE, John Holt (28 November 1777, Bedford County, VA—3 September 1831, Hampden-Sydney, VA). *Career*: private tutor in VA and frequently instructor at Hampden-Sydney Coll., 1795–1804; minister, Charlotte County, VA, 1804–12; minister, First Presbyterian Church, Richmond, VA, 1812–23; editor, *Christian Monitor*, 1815–17; editor, *Virginia Evangelical and Literary Magazine*, 1818–28; professor of Theology, Hampden-Sydney Sem. (Union Sem. after 1826), 1823–31.

A young Virginian intent on making something of himself, Rice studied at academies in Lexington and New London as long as his family's slender resources permitted. But he was largely self-taught, following after 1800 a plan of study outlined for him by longtime friend, *Archibald Alexander. After a successful ministry in churches along Cub Creek, where he supplemented income with farming and teaching school, he moved to Richmond and organized the first Presbyterian church in that city. In addition to supplying pastoral care for the small congregation, he turned an energetic hand to Christian endeavors of greater scope. For many years a steady contributor to religious journals in the state, he was finally persuaded to edit the *Evangelical Magazine*. Therein he continued to emphasize standard Calvinism with essays on human depravity, justification by faith and personal holiness as a qualification for happiness. Much the same concern for orthodox doctrine and high morality led Rice to organize the Virginia Bible Society in 1813. Three years later, as a pioneer in such activity, he was invited to assist in founding the national society for distributing Scripture to needy persons. Religious literature and fervent preaching would, he hoped, produce revivals where greater numbers of individuals accepted the gospel as guide to private virtue. By stressing the personal quality of church action he helped create an attitude regarding "the spirituality of the church" that prevented southern Presbyterians from grappling with social issues for much of the nineteenth century.

Revivals proved to be the leading edge of church expansion, and, recognizing this, Rice became a leading promoter of mission activities throughout his native state. In 1819 he organized the Young Men's Missionary Society which aided Presbyterian evangelists until 1864 when the work was absorbed into larger institutional machinery. In 1831 he drafted an important overture to the General Assembly, arguing that the entire church was a missionary society; all members were thus responsible for converting others around the world. Six years after his death the Presbyterian Board of Foreign Missions was created on the basis of such thinking. Still, missionaries needed training, and Rice's most notable achievement lay in the field of theological education. As early as 1792 the Hanover Presbytery had resolved to put aside funds for ministerial preparation. Finally a separate school for theology was established in 1823 with Rice as its first professor. He diligently met the tasks of raising funds, erecting buildings and increasing the number of students. By 1826 the General Assembly placed its supportive control over the southern seminary which received considerable approbation of its teaching perspective. The Bible was used as central text, with all supplementary instruction drawn from the Westminster Confession. Learned piety was encouraged while unprofitable speculation had no place in exegesis or sacred rhetoric. In this manner the earliest professor hoped to establish a nucleus around which a great seminary could grow to benefit the South and enlarge the borders of Christendom.

Bibliography:

B.   AAP 4, 325–41; NCAB 2, 27; DAB 15, 541–42; William Maxwell, *A Memoir of the Rev. John H. Rice* (Philadelphia, 1835).

RICE, Luther (25 March 1783, Northborough, MA—25 September 1836, Edgefield County, SC). *Education*: B.A., Williams Coll., 1810; studied at Andover Sem., 1810–12. *Career*: Congregationalist missionary agent in India, 1812–13; Baptist missionary agent in America, 1813–36.

Even during college days Rice felt a need to preach abroad, an evangelistic calling strong enough to make him one of the original group sent to India in 1812 by the newly created American Board of Commissioners for Foreign Missions. On shipboard, however, he met often with co-worker, *Adoniram Judson, to study the question of baptism, its proper mode, and applicability to infants. Soon after arrival in India, he followed Judson in being rebaptized because both had become convinced that immersion of mature believers was closest to scriptural teaching. Returning to America the next year, he severed relations with the Congregationalist board and turned to Baptists for support, confronting them with the fact that missionaries of their persuasion were already in the field. Rice generated widespread interest in missionary endeavors, meeting enthusiastic response as he traveled up and down the east coast from Boston to Savannah. By 1814 his efforts found expression in a General Convention, founded to meet triennially and coordinate Baptist activities insofar as local agencies contributed to them. As agent of the Convention he itinerated constantly, soliciting funds, organizing support, and reporting on the work as it progressed. He also helped recruit men of ability, notably *John M. Peck, who were willing to sacrifice for expansion of their denomination's evangelical activities. Probably no other figure of the time approached his dedication for active missions which simultaneously created greater awareness of that work among churchmen at home.

In the course of a few years Rice persuaded executives of the Triennial Convention to expand their horizons to include work among Indians, Negroes, and white settlers on the American frontier. He was also determined to provide more learned clergymen for Baptist churches. For that reason he played a major role in the establishment of a denominational publishing house, two journals, and a tract society. More importantly he was a leading figure behind Columbian College (1821) which many hoped would become a national center for theological training as well as for other professions. Rice spent half his time collecting money for the college, the other half promoting missions. With imprudent zeal he allowed plans to outdistance resources, and the school ran heavily into debt. Critics began to say he spread himself too thinly, as indeed had the entire program of the Triennial Convention. By 1826 reaction set in; foreign missionary concern was reinstated as the single reason for Baptist cooperation, while home missions and education were left to regional or state initiative. After that, Rice devoted himself exclusively to the college, still traveling thousands of miles each year without official status, in response to a missionary calling which had always been his chief motivation.

Bibliography:

    B.   AAP 6, 602–07; SH 10, 25; NCAB 3, 75; DAB 15, 542–43; NCE 12, 474; James B. Taylor (ed.), *Memoir of the Reverend Luther Rice* (Baltimore, 1841; Nashville, 1937); Evelyn W. Thompson, *Luther Rice: Believer in Tomorrow* (Nashville, 1967).

RIGDON, Sidney (19 February 1793, Piny Fork, PA—14 July 1876, Friendship, NY). *Career*: Baptist minister, Warren, OH, 1819–20; Baptist minister, Pittsburgh, PA, 1820–24; tanner in OH, 1824–26; unattached minister in OH, 1826–28; Campbellite minister, Mentor, OH, 1828–30; elder, Church of Latter Day Saints, 1830–44; president, Church of Christ, 1845–76.

Evangelistic fervor in the early national period caused many to expect a reestablishment of conditions prevailing in the apostolic church. Rigdon was one such restorationist who transferred his allegiance from Baptist churches to those led by *Alexander Campbell because they corresponded more closely to his expectations. Preaching reformation, restoration, and the coming millennium, he gathered a small following about him. In 1830, however, he and most of his colony were converted from Disciples of Christ to Mormons, baptized as Latter Day Saints since their doctrine best captured eschatological tendencies. Rigdon quickly became an influential counselor in the church's inner circle, spokesman for the prophet *Joseph Smith and organizer of the ruling structure which gave more regularity to institutional development. Acknowledged as a Mormon seer, he preached extensively to win converts; he helped build the first temple in Kirtland, Ohio, and then fled with the rest to Missouri (1838) when economic collapse made it impossible to stay east of the Mississippi. As one of Smith's trusted lieutenants, he contributed to the body of Mormon theology, especially through "Lectures on Faith" incorporated into the official *Doctrines and Covenants*. Some claimed that he helped fabricate the *Book of Mormon*, but Rigdon denied to the end of his life any connection with authorship of the church's basic text. In Nauvoo, Illinois, he continued to serve the faithful, more as postmaster than prophet after 1840, but still in positions of trust and responsibility.

As years went by, differences between Rigdon and Smith came into sharper focus. Rigdon was at times a brilliant speaker but not a good administrator; his behavior was often eccentric, and many elders feared he would bring the church to ruin. By 1842 Smith became convinced he was aiding the Saints' enemies. The fact that he strongly opposed the new practice of plural marriage was additional proof of his drift toward apostasy. Nevertheless he expected to be made guardian of the church after Smith was murdered in 1844. When he was outmaneuvered by *Brigham Young and the council of Twelve, his sulking criticism of ecclesiastical policies led to excommunication. Convinced that the council was misleading true believers, Rigdon persuaded a few of them to follow him instead. In 1845 at Pittsburgh they constituted themselves the "Church of Christ," disowning western Mormons and claiming legitimate descent from prophet Smith whom they continued to revere. The schismatic group never flourished despite its president's attempts through prophecy and ritual to give it vitality. Most dissident Mormons gravitated toward the "Reorganized Church of Latter Day Saints," while Rigdon, unable to tolerate subservient status in any large institution, found his constituency melting away beneath him. In 1863 he refused a proffered reconciliation with Brigham Young and the Utah Mormons, living his later years in bitter poverty and obscurity.

Bibliography:

B.   NCAB 16, 15; DAB 15, 600–01; NYT 24 Jul 1876, 2; F. Mark McKiernan, *Voice of One Crying in the Wilderness: Sidney Rigdon, Religious Reformer* (Lawrence, KS, 1971).

RIGGS, Stephen Return (23 March 1812, Steubenville, OH—24 August 1883, Beloit, WI). *Education*: B.A., Jefferson Coll., 1834; studied at Western Sem., 1834–35. *Career*: minister, Hawley, MA, 1836–37; missionary agent, Lac qui Parle (1837–43, 1846–54), Travers des Sioux (1843–46), and Hazlewood (1854–62), MN, 1837–62; missionary superintendent, Beloit, WI, 1862–83.

A facility with languages brought Riggs to the attention of commissioners for the American Board of Foreign Missions. Translations were needed to extend gospel efforts among the Dakota nation, sometimes called Sioux by outsiders, and he dedicated forty-five years to that mission work. Living first with the Wahpeton band in prairie settlements 200 miles from Fort Snelling, he gradually spread the ideal of elementary education through the Yankton and Teton tribes as well. Riggs embodied the common Christian conviction that religion and civilization might advance simultaneously to ameliorate conditions of Indian life. He sought to end native ways which in his view amounted to barbarism. Clearly savage ignorance had to be corrected, and he set about the task with amiable efficiency. Of primary interest were schools for the children where they learned to recognize their own language in print. Expanding beyond that, he tried to introduce agricultural methods and white living standards as avenues to higher levels of Christian civilization. An adage indicative of his mission's objective was that the gospel of soap formed a necessary adjunct to the gospel of salvation. During this first twenty-five years in southern Minnesota there was a modicum of positive response, but in 1862 events threatened to end the mission altogether.

As early as 1857 serious difficulties had arisen between Dakota tribesmen and U.S. commissioners, inept government officials whom Riggs blamed for letting the trouble get out of hand. Annuities failed to arrive; faced with starvation the Indians raided supply depots, bringing reprisals in turn. Finally in August of 1862 a general uprising broke out with Little Crow at its head. While destruction spread between Spirit Lake and Yellow Medicine Agency, Riggs' flock was attending worship services in a church forty miles away. Most Christian Indians refused to fight, notably Paul Mazakootemane an elder at Hazlewood who helped whites escape the area. But peaceful red men were herded together with the rest after white armies defeated the hostile forces; they faced prison and removal because of guilt by association. Ironically these circumstances proved to be the setting for rapid evangelical advance among the warriors. Many reasoned that their native power or ''Wakan'' had been broken by white intervention, and they turned to the newcomer's religion as a superior force. Riggs welcomed this revival at Mankato prison, encouraging conversions and education among adults over the next three years. After his charges were relocated along the Missouri River, he visited them every summer. During winter months he translated essential educational tools including primers, grammars, dictionaries, and a geography text. He also rendered Scripture into the vernacular, beginning with selections in 1842, the New Testament in 1865, and the entire Bible (*Dakota Wowapi Wakan*) in 1880. Such material could have provided the basis for a native American church, but they appeared too late to serve that purpose. The cohesion and integrity of native culture had passed before great numbers of people could form distinctive Christian expressions in their own manner.

Bibliography:

A.   *The Dakota First Reading Book* (Cincinnati, 1839); *Grammar and Dictionary of the Dakota Language* (New York, 1852; Washington, DC, 1890); *Dakota Odowan: Hymns in the Dakota Language* (New York, 1853); *Tah-koo Wah-kan, or The Gospel among the Dakotas* (Boston, 1869; New York, 1972); *Mary and I: Forty Years with the Sioux* (Chicago, 1880).

B.   SH 10, 37, NCAB 3, 119; DAB 15, 605–06.

RILEY, William Bell (22 March 1861, Greene County, IN—5 December 1947, Golden Valley, MN). *Education*: B.A. and M.A., Hanover Coll., 1885 and 1888; graduated from Southern Baptist Sem., 1888. *Career*: minister, Calvary Baptist Church, Chicago, 1893–97; minister, First Baptist Church, Minneapolis, 1897–1942; president, Northwestern Schools, 1902–47.

After serving a number of small pastorates in Kentucky, Indiana, and Illinois, Riley moved to Chicago, and it was there that he became aware of how serious the liberal-conservative controversy had become in his denomination. He consistently sided with the conservatives and used his considerable preaching abilities to uphold the basic tenets of fundamentalist theology. He proved to be an effective evangelist, conducting revivals across the country and speaking at Bible conferences. He also published over sixty books and countless articles to articulate his rather inflexible body of ideas. All other affirmations rested on the verbal inerrancy of Scripture. Since the Bible could be taken literally, Riley also championed doctrines of the Trinity and the deity of Jesus. This divinity was necessary because humanity was hopelessly lost in sinfulness and could be saved only by the substitutionary, atoning death of a Savior. This made individual redemption possible, and additional belief in bodily resurrection gave converts hope for the physical return of Christ which would usher in the millennium. Liberals sought to modify or redefine these conceptions, and Riley soon became a dominant voice among those who resisted the threats of modernism.

Orthodoxy unsupported by vigorous action produced an anemic religious condition, in Riley's view, and he fostered several practical programs to prove his point. In 1902 he began the first in a series of educational institutions that trained people in conservative Protestantism. The Northwestern Bible and Missionary School provided pastors for small churches in Minnesota and surrounding states. In 1938 Riley added the Northwestern Evangelical Seminary to meet the need for orthodox leadership in urban congregations. A college emerged in 1944 to offer study of the liberal arts under proper evangelical auspices. More important, however, Riley led the way in founding the World's Christian Fundamentals Association in 1919 and serving as its president for the next decade. In this capacity he showed himself to be an ecclesiastical politician who put Fundamentalism on an organized basis. Beyond that he lobbied for anti-evolution laws in several states, and in 1925 it was Riley who secured *William J. Bryan as counsel for the prosecution in the famous Scopes trial. Over much of his lifetime this gifted but censorious leader contributed to religious polarization in American culture.

Bibliography:

A.   *The Perennial Revival: A Plea for Evangelism* (Chicago, 1903; rev. ed., 1933); *The Menace of Modernism* (New York, 1917); *Christ the Incomparable* (New York, 1924); *Inspiration or Evolution* (Cleveland, OH, 1926); *My Bible: An Apologetic* (Grand Rapids, MI, 1937); *The Conflict of Christianity with Its Counterfeits* (Minneapolis, 1940).
B.   DAB supp. 4, 691–92; Marie A. Riley, *The Dynamic of a Dream: The Life Story of Dr. William B. Riley* (Grand Rapids, MI, 1938); William Vance Trollinger, Jr., *God's Empire: William Bell Riley and Midwestern Fundamentalism* (Madison, WI, 1990).

RIPLEY, George (3 October 1802, Greenfield, MA—4 July 1880, New York, NY). *Education*: B.A., Harvard Coll., 1823; B.D., Harvard Div. Sch., 1826. *Career*: tutor, Harvard Coll., 1823–24; minister, Purchase Street Unitarian Church, Boston, 1826–41; director, Brook Farm, 1841–47; editor, *The Harbinger*, 1845–49; literary editor, *New York Tribune*, 1849–80.

Unitarian liberalism found a mild supporter in Ripley who participated in many of the activities marking the rise of Transcendentalism. He was a member of the Transcendental Club, organized at his home in 1836, and he helped edit the *Dial* during its first year, 1840–41. Friend to *Ralph W. Emerson and *Orestes A. Brownson, he too believed in an order of truths transcending the sphere of external senses. Through preaching and journalism he helped direct attention to a higher sphere where the soul could appropriate truth by intuitive perception, where nature and grace were cooperating elements in the process of gradual human improvement. He finally resigned his ministry to pursue more directly the goals of social and intellectual reform. In 1841 Ripley established a farming cooperative in West Roxbury, nine miles from Boston. Brook Farm was modeled after the New Testament social order, hopeful of striking a balance between manual labor and intellectual refinement, plain living and high thinking. Despite expectations that it would inspire others to follow a pattern of common property and mutual toleration, the institution declined into heavy debt. Ripley moved on to a distinguished career in journalism in which he shaped public opinion about new authors ranging from Hawthorne to Darwin. He also did most of the work on the *New American Cyclopedia* (16 vols., 1858–63). All his efforts—essayist, social experimenter, critic, encyclopedist—fit a single theme of trying to enlighten and improve the condition of mankind.

Bibliography:

A.   *Discourses on the Philosophy of Religion* (Boston, 1836); *Letters . . . on the Latest Form of Infidelity* (Boston, 1840).
B.   NCAB 3, 453–54; DAB 15, 623–25; NYT 5 Jul 1880, 5; Octavius B. Frothingham, *George Ripley* (Boston, 1882); Lindsay Swift, *Brook Farm: Its Members, Scholars and Visitors* (New York, 1900); Henry L. Golemba, *George Ripley* (Boston, 1977).

ROBERTS, Benjamin Titus (25 July 1823, Gowanda, NY—27 February 1893, Cattaraugus, NY). *Education*: B.A., Wesleyan Univ., 1848. *Career*: minister to several Methodist churches in western New York state, 1850–58; general superintendent, Free Methodist Church, 1860–93.

After several years of studying law Roberts underwent a deeply moving conversion experience in 1844 and devoted himself to the Methodist ministry. In 1848 he was admitted on probation to the Genesee Conference, and his preaching was acceptable enough to warrant ordination as deacon in 1850 and advancement to the office of elder two years later. As with many adult converts he was particularly fervent in urging holiness of both heart and life on his listeners, embracing Wesley's doctrine of Christian sanctification as his own. By contrast, he criticized those around him for departing from early Methodist virtues. Laymen and ministers alike were disturbed when Roberts denounced ostentatious churches, gaudy clothing, membership in secret societies, and worst of all: compromise on the question of slavery. He wrote a stinging newspaper article called "New School Methodism" and in 1857, his clerical colleagues responded by charging him with "insubordination and contumacy" at their annual conference. During the following year the article was reprinted and widely circulated; so in 1858 the conference of ministers expelled their fellow preacher for manifesting excessive reformist zeal.

Official disapproval did not cause Roberts to curtail his activities or to modify his ideals. By 1860 he organized the Free Methodist Church with its first congregation based in Pekin, New York. For more than three decades he served as the new denomination's bishop, providing vigorous leadership as a pioneering church builder. During those same years (1860–93) he published and edited a paper, *The Earnest Christian*, editing another named *The Free Methodist* for a time (1886–90) too. In addition to much travel, preaching, and administration of conferences, he presided over missionary boards and influenced his followers to allow for ordination of women as full-fledged ministers. In 1866 he was instrumental in providing both women and men with training for denominational service by establishing a seminary at North Chili, New York. Through the years his combination of sincere piety and stable administration consolidated Free Methodists as an effective component in the ever-increasing number of American religious institutions.

Bibliography:

A. *Fishers of Men; or, Practical Hints to Those Who Would Win Souls* (Rochester, NY, 1878); *Why Another Sect: Containing a Review of Articles by Bishop Simpson and Others on the Free Methodist Church* (Rochester, NY, 1879); *Ordaining Women* (Rochester, NY, 1891); *Holiness Teachings, Compiled from the Editorial Writings of the Late Rev. Benjamin T. Roberts*, by Benson Howard Roberts (North Chili, NY, 1893); *Pungent Truths: Being Extracts from the Writings of the Rev. Benjamin Titus Roberts*, compiled and edited by William B. Rose (Chicago, 1912).

B.   DAB 16, 2–3; Benson Howard Roberts, *Benjamin Titus Roberts: Late General Superintendent of the Free Methodist Church* (North Chili, NY, 1900).

RODEHEAVER, Homer Alvan (4 October 1880, Union Furnace, OH—18 December 1955, Winona Lake, IN). *Career*: music director, William E. Biederwolf evangelical campaigns, 1905–10; music director, William A. Sunday evangelical campaigns, 1910–31; president, Rodeheaver, Hall-Mack Publishing Co., 1911–55.

Music, in the forms of both group singing and solos, has become an integral part of urban evangelism in this century, and Rodeheaver was a crucial figure in this development. He emerged from small-town and modest-income origins, studying occasionally at Ohio Wesleyan University but never taking a degree. By 1905 his mellow baritone voice and expertise with the trombone secured professional appointment as song leader with a well-known revivalist. Rodeheaver quickly showed himself to have stage presence, a quality that made him platform manager of all proceedings before massed audiences. He soon transferred to *Billy Sunday's revival team and became internationally famous for his activities in that capacity. Using the more modern gospel songs which he preferred, he led some of the largest singing groups ever assembled in this country, many numbering over one and two hundred thousand. National radio networks such as NBC and CBS also broadcast his popular community song programs.

Modern American evangelists have often blended doing good with doing well, and Rodeheaver was no exception to this general tendency. As a means of helping other song leaders while also supporting himself financially, he founded a printing company which eventually became the world's largest publisher of gospel music. He helped shape generations in popular religious culture by deciding which hymns and choruses to include in the songbooks. He also issued recordings of gospel songs as well as special piano arrangements of sheet music. By the 1950s his company sold more than a million books per year. This entrepreneurial success allowed Rodeheaver to expand even further. He established a summer school and conference on sacred music that was held each August at Winona Lake, Indiana, a favorite gathering place for evangelists. He also converted some of his holdings in Florida into a boys ranch, thus providing a haven for underprivileged youths. These and many other enterprises indicate how altruism and business success were twin phenomena in this century's most eminent evangelicals.

Bibliography:

A.   *Great Revival Hymns* (Chicago, 1911); *Song Stories of the Sawdust Trail* (New York, 1917); *Awakening Songs: For the Church, Sunday School, and Evangelistic Services* (Chicago, 1917); *Twenty Years with Billy Sunday* (Nashville, 1936); *Southland Spirituals* (Chicago, 1936); *New Awakening Songs: A New Song Book for Use in all Departments of Church Work* (Chicago, 1936).

ROGERS, Mary Joseph (27 October 1882, Roxbury, MA—9 October 1955, New York, NY). *Education*: B.A., Smith Coll., 1905; teacher's diploma, Boston Normal Sch., 1909. *Career*: teaching assistant, Smith Coll., 1906–08; school-teacher, Boston, MA, 1909–12; voluntary secretary, Catholic Foreign Mission Society of America, 1912–25; mother general, Foreign Mission Sisters of St. Dominic (after 1954, Maryknoll sisters of St. Dominic), 1925–47; retirement, 1947–55.

Originally named Mary Josephine, the same as her mother, Rogers grew up expecting to teach biology in secondary schools. At college she noticed that Protestant students knew more about their churches' missionary activities than she or others did about Catholic work. So, with the help of James A. Walsh she formed a study club and was gradually drawn to missions during the following years. In 1911 Walsh was authorized to establish the Catholic Foreign Mission Society of America, better known as Maryknoll Missionaries, deriving that name from its location near Ossining, New York. The following year Rogers volunteered to work as secretary for the new organization and to continue editing its magazine, *Field Afar*. Within a short time she was acknowledged leader among the women volunteers, and in 1914 the group received recognition from the Holy See as a special society. In 1920 it attained canonical status as a diocesan religious community of the Third Order of St. Dominic. In 1925, during the first regular chapter of this group destined to become the largest congregation of American Catholic women devoted to missions, Rogers was elected mother general. She continued to be re-elected annually until she finally declined reappointment in 1947.

It was one of Rogers' basic convictions that worship of God is best expressed through service to human beings. The Maryknoll Sisters began acting on that principle as early as 1920 when they opened an orphanage and school for Japanese-Americans in Los Angeles. The following year six sisters embarked for work in China. In 1932 the mother general established a college (now named for her) to train missionaries in various ways of being useful while still respecting the cultural standards of host populations. The following year she also built a cloistered house for those who wished to support Maryknoll efforts through prayer and the contemplative life. By mid-century there were well over a thousand missionary sisters placed in more than eighty missions in almost twenty countries in Asia, Africa, Latin America, and the United States. This program resulted from the broad vision and strong faith of a leader who remained a vital, constructive personal influence long after relinquishing office. Such efforts culminated in 1954 when the order was given its present name and awarded the status of Pontifical Institute.

Bibliography:

    B.   DAB supp 5, 581–82; NAW 4, 590–91; NCE 12, 556–57; NYT 10 Oct 1955, 27; Jeanne M. Lyons, *Maryknoll's First Lady* (New York, 1964); Camilla Kennedy, *To the Uttermost Parts of the Earth: The Spirit and Charisma of Mary Josephine Rogers* (Maryknoll, NY, 1987).

ROYCE, Josiah (10 November 1855, Grass Valley, CA—14 September 1916, Cambridge, MA). *Education*: B.A., Univ. of California, Berkeley, 1875; studied at Leipzig and Göttingen, 1875–76; Ph.D., Johns Hopkins Univ., 1878. *Career*: instructor of Literature and Composition, Univ. of California, Berkeley, 1878–82; member at various ranks of the Philosophy Department, Harvard Univ., 1882–1916.

As a philosopher always interested in religious questions, Royce placed ideas about God, the natural world, and human action within an idealistic metaphysics. His influence as teacher and author was given impetus by a combination of impressively rigorous thought and intense religious devotion. Against naturalistic and mechanistic views of the material world, which could not retain any viable theistic concepts, Royce posited the necessity of an Absolute or Perfect Mind. Such an entity provided in his view the only lasting basis for ideas like knowledge, reality, and meaning to rely upon. His fundamental beginning point, like that of most idealists, was that things are known with assurance only through the mind. Even the scientific experiences of empirical investigation are ultimately mental, and to avoid categorizing such knowledge as mere conjecture, Royce held that one must conclude the mind is essential for certitude. He argued further that reality lies beyond individual minds and thus implies the mental inclusiveness of an Absolute, deeper than any single experience of it. Along similar lines, he reasoned that the plurality of forces in nature implied a unifying power to give them meaning; error or partial truth demonstrated the need for universal, perfect truth; evil or gradations of goodness led to an ultimate goodness. All these epistemological considerations were for him valid indications that belief in God was defensible in the kind of world described by modern physics.

On the more practical level of moral philosophy, Royce addressed himself to a number of important issues such as value, freedom, and obligation, but none was more central than that of the self and its relation to community. He thought that self-realization could not be attained independently of the social context of which individuals were always a part. It was not possible to formulate a complete set of principles to enable the moral agent to act unerringly in every concrete situation, but Royce especially emphasized the concept of loyalty as a guide for correct action. He maintained that individuals thought and acted in more enriching and fulfilling ways in community endeavors than in isolated actions taken by themselves. Loyalty and cooperation with the common interests of human groups, particularly Christian churches, were interpreted as positive values toward self-realization; isolated individualism was seen as disruptive selfishness. The conception of community and human nature contained in this position had a degree of usefulness for Liberal theology in its day and survived to provide some of the groundwork for neo-orthodox thought as well.

Bibliography:

A. *The Religious Aspect of Philosophy* (Boston, 1885); *The Spirit of Modern Philosophy* (Boston, 1892); *The Conception of God* (New York, 1895); *Studies of Good and Evil* (New York, 1898); *The World and the Individual*, 2 vols. (New York, 1900–01); *The Problem of Christianity*, 2 vols. (New York, 1913).

B. SH 10, 106; NCAB 25, 356–57; DAB 16, 205–11; NYT 15 Sep 1916, 11; John E. Smith, *Royce's Social Infinite* (New York, 1950); Vincent Buranelli, *Josiah Royce* (New York, 1964); Bruce Kuklick, *Josiah Royce: An Intellectual Biography* (Indianapolis, 1972); John Clandenning, *The Life and Thought of Josiah Royce* (Madison, WI, 1985); Frank M. Oppenheim, *Royce's Mature Philosophy of Religion* (Notre Dame, IN, 1987).

RUSH, Benjamin (4 January 1746, Byberry, PA—19 April 1813, Philadelphia, PA). *Education*: B.A., Coll. of New Jersey, 1760; M.D., Univ. of Edinburgh, 1768. *Career*: professor of Chemistry, Coll. of Philadelphia, 1769–91; professor of the Institutes of Medicine and Clinical Practice (1792–96) and professor of Theory and Practice (1796–1813), Univ. of Pennsylvania; staff member, Pennsylvania Hospital, 1783–1813.

Using revised dates for the current Gregorian calendar, Rush's proper birthday is listed above. But those looking for color in biography may note that the old style places his birth on Christmas Eve, 1745. His career was varied and distinguished, including the practice of medicine from 1769 onwards, interest in politics which led to his signing the Declaration of Independence, and instructional posts at institutions that evolved into the University of Pennsylvania. Through all of these avenues Rush pursued the cause of social reform, and his general humanitarian interest in public affairs undergirded his many benevolent activities. He had no strong denominational preference, thinking that it was more important to advance the general objects of Christianity in society at large. Doctrine separated people into competitive sects; he wanted the best religious impulses to unite in the struggle to make America virtuous. Some of his earliest appeals to social morality took the form of essays published in Philadelphia magazines. These often survived for decades in the form of tracts that supported reform movements grown to huge proportions in the next century.

Several of the causes which Rush espoused touched the consciences of Quakers, Unitarians, and later more populous groups such as the Methodists. In 1773 he wrote against slavekeeping and helped the next year to organize a society for promoting its abolition. Interestingly, he himself owned a slave until 1797. In the 1780s he became a noted advocate of prison reform, condemning capital punishment and recommending "penitentiaries" where prisoners could repent of their misdeeds. Far more important, though, was his work regarding temperance in alcohol consumption. As early as 1772 he wrote essays on "the pernicious effects of ardent spirits," appealing to human reason and pointing out the problems that such drink caused in the mind and body. He finally concluded that people taken with drink could not be reached through rational argument, and so he transferred the cause to religious organizations in hopes they could reform individuals through spiritual and emotional appeals. Viewed from either perspective, Rush is justly recognized as the "instaurator" of the American temperance movement, a reform element that struggled for more than a century to restrict alcohol and thus improve public morality in this country.

Bibliography:

A.   *Sermons to Gentlemen upon Temperance and Exercise* (Philadelphia, 1772); *Essays, Literary, Moral, and Philosophical* (Philadelphia, 1798); *Medical Inquiries and Observations*, 4 vols. (Philadelphia, 1809); *A Memorial Containing Travels through Life or Sundry Incidents in the Life of Dr. Benjamin Rush . . . Written by Himself* (Philadelphia, 1905).

B.   NCAB 3, 333; DAB 16, 227–31; Harry G. Good, *Benjamin Rush and His Services to American Education* (Berne, IN, 1918); Nathan G. Goodman, *Benjamin Rush, Physician and Citizen, 1746–1813* (Philadelphia, 1934); David Freeman Hawke, *Benjamin Rush: Revolutionary Gadfly* (Indianapolis, 1971); John M. Kloos, Jr., *A Sense of Deity: The Republican Spirituality of Dr. Benjamin Rush* (New York, 1990).

RUSSELL, Charles Taze (16 February 1852, Allegheny, PA—31 October 1916, near Pampa, TX). *Career*: independent minister, Pittsburgh, PA, 1872–1909; editor, *The Watch Tower and Herald of Christ's Presence* (intermittently *Zion's Watch Tower*), 1878–1916; president, Watch Tower Bible and Tract Society, 1884–1916; independent minister, Brooklyn, NY, 1909–16.

Born in what is now a suburb of Pittsburgh, young Russell interrupted his modest schooling to help run the family dry goods business. He had been reared under Calvinistic tutelage but soon rebelled against most traditional ideas, especially the doctrine of eternal punishment. After years of independent Bible study, he began promulgating his own interpretation of Scripture and formed the nucleus of what grew to be a worldwide religious phenomenon. Literature quickly became the chief means of disseminating his doctrine; one early book alone sold over five million copies while the aggregate of his writing exceeded fifteen million copies in thirty languages. In addition to this most important activity of publishing biblical exposition, "Pastor Russell," as adherents called him, traveled incessantly, averaging 30,000 miles annually to build up congregations across this country, Canada, and Europe. As he spread his biblical description of millennial dawn, or the divine plan of the ages, followers hailed him as the seventh and last messenger of God's dispensations for heaven and earth. Names for his 1,200 churches varied in confusing abundance, but Russellites, Millennial Dawnists, or International Bible Students have now been generally termed Jehovah's Witnesses. Their founder did not spare himself in efforts to publicize saving truth among as many as would receive it. His death came unexpectedly while pursuing another transcontinental evangelical campaign.

Central to all of Russell's ideas about God, salvation, and the future was the fundamental tenet that Christ had already returned to earth in 1874. This was not a physical occurrence but rather a spiritual manifestation inaugurating a new age in which God's kingdom would be established. In addition to vindicating the name of Jehovah-God and redeeming obedient believers, Christ as filial prophet of the solitary Almighty was sent to build a Theocracy in the world. This invisible reign began in 1914, and faithful followers were sent forth to preach judgment on all nations. The supreme element of Jehovah's Witness millennial expectation is that a final battle will soon be fought to confirm the rightful rule of divine power. God, Christ, and all the holy angels will wage war against the forces of unrighteousness under Satan in the battle of Armageddon. Evil will be destroyed while humans witness, but do not participate in, the struggle. After goodness triumphs, God's faithful remnant will prosper for a thousand years, after which time Satan will again be loosed to test human loyalty. Those who succumb to temptation will not be tormented; instead they along with their leader will experience a merciful (and literal) liquidation. The righteous will live forever on a renovated earthly paradise where there is no sickness, poverty, pain, or injustice. By means of finely meshed quotations from Scripture, Russell spurred his following with hopes for this imminent day of retribution. When he died, leadership of the apocalyptic movement passed to *Joseph F. Rutherford, one who gave it greater institutional stability during times of severe trial.

Bibliography:

A. *Studies of the Scriptures*, 6 vols. (Allegheny, PA, 1886–1904), vol. 7 ed. C.J. Woodworth and G.H. Fisher (Brooklyn, NY, 1917).

B. NCAB 12, 317–18; DAB 16, 240; NCE 12, 730–31; NYT 1 Nov 1919, 11.

RUSSELL, Walter Bowman (19 May 1871, Boston, MA—19 May 1963, Waynesboro, VA).

There were many vocations at which Russell excelled before he developed a mystic turn of mind. Author of a series of children's books, self-taught organist and composer, illustrator then art editor for fashion magazines, real estate speculator, and sports enthusiast—all these successes were secondary to his fame as an artist. He was in popular demand to paint portraits and after turning to sculpture in the 1920s received commissions to execute busts of many important public figures. But at this same time Russell had also begun to experience inner illumination, a new religious perception of things which he described in print and eventually institutionalized in a foundation that survives to the present time. He claimed to have received innersensory enlightenment from God, a higher cosmic consciousness allowing him to teach others the true nature of reality. From that perspective he assured readers he could penetrate the secrets of the atom as well as comprehend all the nebulae of space. Vital knowledge regarding ways in which the invisible universe controls visible life was his; consequently his teachings stressed the important process of space becoming matter and then moving by myriad channels into space again. In 1949, the year of marriage to his second wife and religious co-worker Lao Stebbing, he established the Walter Russell

Foundation, changed in 1957 to the University of Science and Philosophy. Based at their estate, "Swannanoa," in the Blue Ridge Mountains, the couple developed a correspondence course on the wisdom derived from Cosmic Consciousness. A large number of publications, including periodic charts of the physical elements undergirding a distinctive cosmological perspective, were offered to participating students. There was no emphasis on organized groups, but correspondents from around the world remained in touch with the Virginia headquarters of this movement.

Bibliography:

A. *The Universal One* (New York, 1926); *The Russell Genero-Radiative Concept* (New York, 1930); *The Secret of Light* (New York, 1947); *The Message of the Divine Illiad*, 2 vols. (New York, 1948–49); *The Russell Cosmogony: A New Concept of Light, Matter and Energy* (Waynesboro, VA, 1953); *The One-World Purpose* (Waynesboro, VA, 1960).

B. NYT 20 May 1963, 31.

RUTHERFORD, Joseph Franklin (8 November 1869, Booneville, MO—8 January 1942, San Diego, CA). *Career*: president, Watch Tower Bible and Tract Society, Brooklyn, NY, 1917–42.

After brief service on a Missouri circuit court, "Judge" Rutherford settled down to practice law in the midwest. Some time before 1909 he was converted to the teachings of *Charles T. Russell and became legal adviser to the group known as Jehovah's Witnesses. As second president he continued the practice of spreading doctrine through the printed word. In time his voluminous publications superceded those of Russell and set forth a large body of thought outlining orthodoxy for the movement built around his famous slogan, "millions now living will never die." His thought was determinative for a quarter-century; but more importantly his personal leadership in institutional crises gave tangible cohesion to a loosely organized doctrinal affiliation. Jehovah's Witnesses (official title, 1931) tried to withdraw from political and social superstructures in order to preserve their Christian purity. During wartime this neutral (not pacifist) attitude angered the general citizenry and helps explain why Witnesses have been one of the most persecuted American religious groups in the twentieth century. In 1917 Rutherford was indicted for obstructing the war effort, by counseling young men to refuse the draft and not salute the flag. A nine months' prison term only enhanced his position as denominational spokesman. His unwavering loyalty to religious principle also made a significant contribution to civil rights in this country. Another issue which both antagonized outsiders and consolidated those within the group was inter-church relations. Protestant and Catholic groups were not, in his view, truly Christian. They were pious frauds teaching partial truths that did more harm to genuine biblical witness than frank hostility. The Judge repeatedly attacked other denominations, challenged them to public debate and warned followers against collaborating with the ungodly.

Usually reserved and aloof, in old age he grew as uncommunicative with colleagues as he had urged them to be with other groups. Still, his tenacious leadership had been effective during formative years when it was most needed.

Bibliography:

A. *The Harp of God* (Brooklyn, 1921); *Deliverance* (Brooklyn, 1926); *Government* (Brooklyn, 1928); *Prophecy* (Brooklyn, 1929); *Salvation* (Brooklyn, 1939); *Children* (Brooklyn, 1941).

B. DAB 23, 678–79; NYT 11 Jan 1942, 46.

RYAN, John Augustine (25 May 1869, Vermillion, MN—16 September 1945, St. Paul, MN). *Education*: graduate in classical curriculum, St. Thomas Sem. (MN), 1892; graduate in clerical curriculum, St. Paul Sem. (MN), 1898; S.T.D., Catholic Univ. of America, 1906. *Career*: professor of Moral Theology, St. Paul Sem., 1902–15; professor, at various ranks, of Political Science and Moral Theology, Catholic Univ. of America, 1915–39; director, Department of Social Action, National Catholic Welfare Conference, 1919–45.

As a farm boy on Minnesota's prairies Ryan, christened Michael John, was early associated with Populism and politics. He became aware of the plight of labor after reading *Rerum Novarum* in 1894 and for the next fifty years was a major force behind Catholic action in American social reform. A theologian and economic analyst, teacher and lobbyist, Ryan published sixteen books, dozens of pamphlets, and hundreds of articles to educate citizens of all religious persuasions about the need for correcting basic injustices which too long had oppressed the common man. His doctoral dissertation and first book established him as a primary figure in the ethical and economic aspects of minimum wage legislation, a fundamental concern for just compensation which stood at the core of all his related activities. Ryan argued that a just wage was the worker's right, derived from his personal dignity and essential needs. Such a right to exchange labor for enough wages to meet personal want and support a family in frugal comfort carried the moral sanction of commutative justice, not fluctuating estimates of labor's merit or vague concepts of negotiable equity. The rights of labor and capital to achieve a cooperative and mutually beneficial arrangement were to be protected and sustained under governmental auspices, the state being viewed as an instrument for the good of all instead of a privileged few.

Stubborn, abrupt, and yet persuasive in his manner, at length Ryan succeeded in winning sympathetic listeners in a setting traditionally conservative and reluctant to act in these matters. Beginning in 1917, he edited for some time and wrote constantly in the monthly *Catholic Charities Review* and for *Catholic Action*, both vehicles for his own ideas and the National Conference of Catholic Charities. But the National Catholic Welfare Conference (renamed 1923) was his most effective locus for disseminating information and urging further action. Ryan's Department of Social Action in this postwar replacement of an ad hoc council provided a permanent bureau to coordinate social services, stimulate legislative reforms, facilitate study of current problems and recruit young men and women for service. Within that framework he was the main author in 1919 of a document usually called the "Bishop's Program of Social Reconstruction," one of the first statements with American Catholic episcopal backing that called for definite action to ensure more social justice in this country. Again through him in 1935 the NCWC issued a plea for a new economic order with fuller organization of labor and more consumer cooperatives to replace the haphazard conditions and sufferings witnessed through the depression. Ryan (monsignor after 1933) continued to work at countless tasks, many of them allied with recovery aspects of the New Deal and programs of a president who counted him as a friend and whom he was to survive by only five months.

Bibliography:

A. *A Living Wage: Its Ethical and Economic Aspects* (New York, 1906, and many subsequent editions); *Distributive Justice: The Right and Wrong of Our Present Distribution of Wealth* (New York, 1916, and many subsequent editions); *Social Reconstruction* (New York, 1920); *Declining Liberty and Other Papers* (New York, 1927); *Seven Troubled Years* (Ann Arbor, MI, 1937); *Social Doctrine in Action* (New York, 1941).

B. NCAB C, 190; DAB 23, 679–82; NCE 12, 767; NYT 17 Sep 1945, 19; Patrick W. Gearty, *The Economic Thought of Monsignor John A. Ryan* (Washington, DC, 1953); Francis L. Broderick, *The Right Reverend New Dealer: John A. Ryan* (New York, 1963).

S

SANFORD, Elias Benjamin (6 June 1843, Westbrook, CT—3 July 1932, Middlefield, CT). *Education*: B.A., Wesleyan Univ. 1865. *Career*: Methodist minister, Thomaston, CT, 1865–67; minister, First Congregational Church, Cornwall, CT, 1868–72; newspaper work and supply preacher, Northfield and Thomaston, CT, 1872–82; minister, Congregational church, Westbrook, CT, 1882–94; secretary, Open and Institutional Church League, 1895–1900; general secretary, National Federation of Churches and Christian Workers, 1900–08; corresponding secretary, Federal Council of Churches (FCC), 1908–13; honorary secretary, FCC, 1913–32.

Though raised and educated in Methodist surroundings, Sanford did not embody the attitude of sectarian exclusiveness which characterized many denominational spokesmen in his formative years. His first church opened its doors to Congregationalist townspeople who had no minister at the time, and subsequent affiliation with that polity involved, he found, no change in theology or basic creedal affirmations. Thus his earliest pastoral experiences confirmed an ideological orientation which stressed cooperation among Christian groups in pursuit of common religious objectives. While poor health caused him to withdraw at times from clerical responsibility, he became a steady contributor to interdenominational journals. As an advocate of Christian unity, his primary goal was to change prevailing attitudes regarding sectarian competition. American churches in his view were passing from a period of theological polemic to one where they might serve one God through united effort. Sanford did not envision institutional change as much as an emerging unity of spirit. Instead of creating a pattern to enforce conformity of belief, government, or worship, he wished only to enhance ways in which churches could give practical expression to their oneness in Christ. Under the aura of acknowledging one Shepherd who cared for one flock, there could still be diversity of forms. But at the same time he repeatedly urged that such diversity should be maintained within unity of Protestant action.

In concrete terms Sanford sought more than just a sentimental expression of good will across denominational lines. The problems confronting churches in modern America, especially social issues brought on by industry and urbanization, were too big for separate groups to solve. So he called for federated action—unselfish cooperation in shared programs wherein unified effort could secure common goals better than separate groups could pursue them—this latter pattern often with duplicate, wasted motion. Sanford was more than fifty years old before he began putting his persuasive arguments into a practical plan of action. But in 1895 he put his diplomatic organizing genius to work and provided leadership which eventually culminated in founding the Federal Council of Churches (FCC). In 1905 he helped formulate the constitution for such a voluntary federation, sanctioned by representatives of twenty-nine denominations at an interchurch meeting in New York. Three years later, thirty-three denominations voted the FCC into formal existence at Philadelphia. As one who had worked for interdenominational comity for thirty prior years, he labored in this highest ecumenical structure to make cooperation a tangible reality. Until poor health once again forced resignation he sought both to clarify the churches' conception of a single mission and to lead the way in actually federating their efforts along lines of common endeavor.

Bibliography:

A. *A History of Connecticut* (Hartford, CT, 1887, 1922); *Origin and History of the Federal Council of the Churches of Christ in America* (Hartford, CT, 1916); *A History of the Reformation* (Hartford, CT, 1917).

B. SH 10, 203; NCAB 24, 256–57; DAB 16, 347–48; NYT 4 Jul 1932, 11.

SANKEY, Ira David (28 August 1840, Edinburgh, PA—14 August 1908, Brooklyn, NY).

Joining the local Methodist church when he was fifteen, Sankey quickly rose to prominence as choir leader, Sunday School superintendent and director of the YMCA. He served for a time (1861–63) in the Union Army, returning home to work for the next seven years either as tax collector or assistant in his father's bank. Church music was always his primary interest, however, and he remained active in that sphere. After meeting *Dwight L. Moody in 1870, he was so impressed with the evangelist's program that he moved to Chicago to become his full-time music director. They became an inseparable team, augmenting the scope of urban revivals to tremendous proportions through their cooperative efforts. Between 1873 and 1875 they made a grand tour of England where they acquired an international reputation for successful evangelical techniques. Sankey was a valuable asset in those revival meetings. While his voice was not exceptional, he had an ability to impress audiences with singing marked by clarity, resonance, and moving sincerity. Accompanying himself on the organ, he delivered renditions of favorite hymns with strong dramatic force. His gospel singing was one of the main features which heightened the impact of Moody's revival campaigns.

In addition to making substantial contributions toward personal conversions to Christianity, Sankey helped influence American hymnody in subsequent generations. Along with several other authors (notably Philip P. Bliss), he published a series of *Gospel Hymns*, immensely popular song books which broke circulation records in their genre. In these hymnals, Sankey compiled 704 texts with over seven hundred choral settings. His work best embodies the content and emphases of the late-nineteenth-century gospel hymn movement. He included some examples from each era of Protestant singing but drew heavily on earlier revival songs, keeping their patterns of simple verse and rousing refrains. All of them were arranged along infectious melodic contours of smooth harmony and mild chromaticism. While he composed few lyrics, the music of many favorite songs came from his pen. He shaped a popular religious art form adopted by the majority of white, middle-class churches in northern cities. As that emphasis was slowly outgrown in metropolitan areas during the twentieth century, it held its own in rural churches, predominantly in the South. Sankey's activities were brought to a close by blindness in 1903, but his influence continued long after that.

Bibliography:

    A.   *Sacred Songs and Solos* (London, 1873, and many subsequent editions); *Gospel Hymns Nos. 1 to 6 Complete* (Chicago, 1895); *My Life and the Story of the Gospel Hymns* (Philadelphia, 1906).
    B.   SH 10, 204–05; NCAB 7, 244–45; DAB 16, 352–53; NYT 15 Aug 1908, 7; Edgar J. Goodspeed, *Moody and Sankey in Great Britain and America* (New York, 1876); Elias Nason, *The American Evangelists, Dwight L. Moody and Ira D. Sankey* (Boston, 1877).

SATOLLI, Francesco (21 July 1839, Marsciano, Italy—8 January 1910, Rome, Italy). *Education*: studied at Sem. of Perugia, 1853–62. *Career*: professor of Philosophy, Sem. of Perugia, 1862–70; instructor, Abbey of Monte Cassino, 1870–75; rector, Marsciano, 1875–80; professor of Theology, Coll. of the Propaganda, Rome, 1880–92; papal ablegate in the U.S., 1892–93; apostolic delegate in the U.S., 1893–96; archpriest, Lateran Basilica, Rome, 1896; prefect, Congregation of Studies, Rome, 1897–1910.

As a personal favorite of Pope Leo XIII, Satolli received several preferential appointments to implement policies formulated by the Holy See. On three occasions he served as papal representative in the United States, and the second of those visitations (1892–96) coincided with a time of momentous transition in American Catholic history. For decades he had been known as a leading exponent of neo-scholasticism, stressing the importance of Thomas Aquinas in modern thought and publishing a five-volume compendium to elaborate that doctrinal system. But it was primarily his function as the pope's deputy that made western prelates notice the titular archbishop of Lepanto. Indicating a determination to exercise independent leadership, he resolved the *Edward McGlynn case shortly after arriving in 1892. Within the year he absolved the excommunicated priest and reinstated him in his former archdiocese, securing cooperation if not approbation from *Michael A. Corrigan, metropolitan of that jurisdiction. He also gave limited sanction to *John Ireland's experiments in Minnesota that bypassed the necessity for parochial schools. As long as Catholic children attending public schools also received religious instruction by supplementary means, he conveyed papal approval to such plans. While he still encouraged building more parochial schools, he permitted flexible arrangements between bishops and local school boards. By 1893 the issue was more symbolic than practical, but the envoy's attitude helped establish a significant option in the ongoing debate on this topic.

When the office of Apostolic Delegate became a permanent fixture in 1893, Satolli was named its first occupant. During early years in that position he seems to have favored the programs of liberal officials such as *James Gibbons who maintained cordial relations with the Italian archbishop (cardinal, 1895) throughout his term of office. American Catholic leaders held strong differences over the relation of their church to a bewildering variety of freedoms possible under republican government. They argued over "Americanization," or the compatibility of Catholicism with pluralistic voluntaryism, as heatedly as they contested the school issue. Initially, Satolli backed the liberal wing, affirming that the church would thrive under democratic principles. But by 1895 he inexplicably gravitated to the conservative bloc of American bishops. Without destroying a spirit of cooperation with Gibbons, he increasingly voiced opinions long defended by Corrigan. In the final analysis he emerged as a potent factor in perpetuating the view that Catholics should hold to their European traditions, resist assimilation into Protestant-republican culture, and preserve loyalty to Rome as a badge of religious distinction. After returning to Italy he helped draft *Testem Benevolentiae* (1899), which condemned extreme republicanism in ecclesiastical practices. His presence in the New World was of short duration, but the decidedly conservative tenor of his actions set guidelines for American Catholicism that lasted well into the twentieth century.

Bibliography:

A. *Loyalty to Church and State* (Baltimore, 1895; New York, 1972).
B. NCE 12, 1098.

SAVAGE, Minot Judson (10 June 1841, Norridgewock, ME—22 May 1918, Boston, MA). *Education*: graduated from Bangor Sem., 1864. *Career*: missionary in CA, 1864–67; Congregational minister, Framingham, MA, 1867–69; minister First Congregational Church, Hannibal, MO, 1869–73; minister, Third Unitarian Church, Chicago, IL, 1873–74; minister Church of the Unity, Boston,

MA, 1874–96; minister, Church of the Messiah, New York, NY, 1896–1906; retirement, 1906–18.

It was not until after several years into his ministry that Savage began to have serious doubts about received doctrine in his denomination. He proved to be a dynamic leader, making his flock the largest Congregational church in Missouri, but he increasingly questioned the static notions in orthodox thought. After a long process during which he read seriously in church history, biblical criticism, and evolutionary science, he converted to Unitarianism in 1872. Moving to Boston, he hit his stride as one of the greatest preachers of the era and attracted huge audiences. Savage spoke without notes or text, delivering lucid addresses in a dignified manner that seemed to penetrate each listener directly. His sermons were circulated in series known as the "Unity Pulpit" and then the "Messiah Pulpit" collections. They also provided the basis of many of his books which often went through several printings. He edited a *Unitarian Catechism* and with a collaborator put together a set of *Sacred Songs for Public Worship* for denominational use. These activities made the great pulpit orator one of the most popular and influential Unitarian figures of the late nineteenth century.

Several themes recur in Savage's sermons and books. The one with which he struggled most was the modern evolutionary hypothesis, and his successful resolution of that problem served as a guideline to many others who were similarly troubled. Accepting evolution in physical science meant, he argued, accepting it in theology and social philosophy too. This did not destroy true Christian values, however; it only forced people to distinguish between the passing and the permanent in matters of faith and morals. Change was inevitable, and Savage reminded listeners that they could remain optimistic about goodness in life because they could turn from non-essential matters to those of permanent worth. Human beings were the culminating point of cosmic evolution, and belief in a transcendent, eternal power gave life meaning and purpose. Theism was sound, based on both abstract reason and direct experience. Trust in Providence led to love of humanity, and such an ideal led in turn to faith in immortality. Savage was forced by poor health to retire in 1906, but he spent another decade publishing his uplifting views of reassurance about current affairs and of invitation to improve them through further humanitarian reform.

Bibliography

A.   *Christianity, the Science of Manhood* (Boston, 1873); *Belief in God: An Examination of Some Fundamental Theistic Problems* (Boston, 1881); *Beliefs about the Bible* (Boston, 1883); *The Evolution of Christianity* (Boston, 1892); *Jesus and Modern Life* (Boston, 1893); *Life Beyond Death* (New York, 1899).

B.   SH 10, 213–14; NCAB 1, 35; DAB 16, 389–90.

SCHAFF, Philip (1 January 1819, Chur, Switzerland—20 October 1893, New York, NY). *Education*: studied at Tübingen, 1837–39, and Halle, 1839–40; obtained the lic. theol., Berlin, 1840–41. *Career*: Privatdozent, Berlin, 1842–44; professor of Church History and Biblical Literature, Mercersburg Sem., Mercersburg, PA, 1844–63; secretary to the NY Sabbath Committee, 1864–69;

visiting lecturer in church history and biblical languages at Andover, Drew, Union, and especially Hartford Sems., 1868–71; professor of various subjects in theology, scripture, and history at Union Sem. (NY), 1870–93; retirement, 1893.

Schaff's most important contribution lay in teaching and writing historical studies of Christianity that ranged from biblical times to his own age. His work was informed by a conception of developmental change that drew strength from events in the past and yet stressed the possibility of future improvement. While studying at Tübingen he was influenced along these lines by Ferdinand C. Baur's general perspective on historical development, more than he was ever willing to admit. As a student and a young instructor at the University of Berlin, he was befriended by Johann A. W. Neander, a warmly pious man who also had a significant effect on Schaff's character and intellectual maturation. When he assumed duties at the German Reformed seminary in Mercersburg, Pennsylvania, he became associated with *John W. Nevin, a vigorous theologian who combined with Schaff to give ''Mercersburg theology'' a distinctive emphasis on historical traditions that occasioned strong responses, both positive and negative.

As early as 1844 he began articulating ideas about the dialectical process of advancement in history and the many opportunities this held for beneficial change in religion. Some American ministers in the Reformed tradition held a much more static interpretation of church history; they also resented Schaff's friendly attitude toward Roman Catholicism as part of a single Christian heritage. Nativistic and ideological antipathies combined in this faction to attempt a suppression of the young German professor's continental ideas. In 1845 charges of heresy were made, along with cries of ''popery,'' but Schaff was completely exonerated, both in his broad ecclesiastical outlook and in his dynamic view of historical change. These views remained essentially the same through his long career. Over eighty publications bear his name, and these monumental labors as well as his ideas helped create an appreciation for critical scholarship in this country. One of the best consequences of that stimulus was the American Church History Series (1893–97) a thirteen-volume shelf of denominational histories, which he initiated and guided through the early stages.

Throughout his studies, travels, and variegated activities, Schaff was profoundly motivated by an ecumenical vision. He was convinced that Protestantism and Catholicism would eventually progress to a higher form, an ''evangelical catholicism'' that abandoned the vices and capitalized on the virtues of each persuasion. To further that end, he lectured, wrote, and organized to promote understanding among the various branches of Christianity. He participated in the endeavors of the Evangelical Alliance and worked from 1866 to 1873 to organize its American chapter and to convene an international conference in New York. The idea behind all his activities on committees for creedal revision and modern biblical translations was that mutual understanding provided common ground for tolerance and cooperation. Most of Schaff's historical research and his instrumental founding of the American Society of Church History in 1888 were based on this irenic ecumenical perspective. As if to illustrate the priority of ecumenism, he attended the World's Parliament of Religions in Chicago, against medical advice, and spoke one last time about the reunion of Christendom which had shaped so many of his pursuits.

Bibliography:

A.   *The Principle of Protestantism, As Related to the Present State of the Church* (Chambersburg, 1845; Philadelphia, 1964); *What is Church History? A Vindication of the Idea of Historical Development* (Philadelphia, 1846); *Bibliotheca Symbolica Ecclesiae Universalis: The Creeds of Christendom* (New York, 1877); *Christ and Christianity* (New York, 1885); *History of the Christian Church*, 6 vols. (New York, 1882–92); *Theological Propaedeutic: A General Introduction to the Study of Theology* (New York, 1892).

B.   SH 10, 223–25; NCAB 3, 76–77; DAB 16, 417–18; NYT 21 Oct 1893, 2; David Schaff, *The Life of Philip Schaff, In Part Autobiographical* (New York, 1897); George H. Shriver, *Philip Schaff: Christian Scholar and Ecumenical Prophet* (Macon, GA, 1987); Klaus Penzel, ed., *Philip Schaff, Historian and Ambassador of the Universal Church: Selected Writings* (Macon, GA, 1991).

SCHECHTER, Solomon (7 December 1847, Focsani, Rumania—19 November 1915, New York, NY). *Education*: rabbinic and secular studies, Vienna, 1875–79; talmudic and secular studies Berlin, 1879–82. *Career*: private tutor, London, 1882–90; lecturer in Talmudics, Cambridge Univ., 1890–92; reader in Rabbinics, Cambridge Univ., 1892–1902; professor of Hebrew, University Coll., London, 1899–1902; president, Jewish Theol. Sem., New York, 1902–15.

Schneur Zalman, the son of a Hasidic ritual slaughterer, received careful rabbinic training from an early age. Because of great intellectual promise, he moved rapidly from the ghetto of a backward, anti-Semitic country to advanced schools of Germanic historical scholarship. He advocated the critical, scientific study of Jewish traditions, the Wissenschaft des Judentums as it was called in his Berlin Hochschule, but added a piety discernible in all his writings. At the request of Claude G. Montefiore in 1882, he moved to England where he began publishing essays on the rich heritage revealed in Jewish documents already on British soil. More lasting fame was achieved, however, when he discovered a tremendous cache of manuscripts and fragments (100,000) stored in the Genizah synagogue at Cairo, Egypt. The entire collection, deposited at Cambridge University, became the source of new studies ranging from forgotten sects to missing literary classics. On the basis of these materials, Schechter furthered the scholarly understanding of Judaism as seen by its own adherents. His explication of various topics included Hebrew attitudes regarding the Torah, the Kingdom of God, Israel as a chosen nation, and reverence for tradition. Published works in Hebrew, German, and English strengthened the quiet determination of many leaders to preserve the best of Judaism while not opting for either Orthodox or Reform branches of the faith.

By 1902 Schechter acceded to persistent requests that he become president of Jewish Theological Seminary in New York. Under his guidance the reorganized institution attracted a young, vigorous faculty and grew into one of the most important centers of Jewish learning in modern times. Through graduates of the seminary, as well as in his books, Schechter was able to spread basic ideas about Conservative Judaism, a combination of devotion to tradition and flexible attitudes about innovation as circumstances might demand. His conception of "Catholic Israel" was grounded in the view that authority resided in a living body, not in books of Law or Scripture. The community of Israel had an inner unity, a general consensus affirmed by loyal Jews, which sustained collective consciousness. That consensus made for genuine cohesiveness and provided the basis for creative change in ritual or observances while it preserved continuity with ancient beliefs. Such a conception lay behind Schechter's efforts to found Agudath Jeshurun, a union for promoting traditional Judaism in this country which in 1913 emerged as the United Synagogue of America. He also had a positive appreciation for the spiritual, cultural aspects of Zionism, finding it the best impediment to complete assimilation in WASP social patterns. His major work concentrated on building Conservative Jewish thought and practice on the American continent, objectives which the seminary has continued through successive generations.

Bibliography:

A. *Aboth of Rabbi Nathan* (London, 1887); *Studies in Judaism*, 3 vols. (Philadelphia, 1896–1924); *The Wisdom of Ben Sira* (Cambridge, 1899); *Some Aspects of Rabbinic Theology* (New York, 1909); *Documents of Jewish Sectaries*, 2 vols. (Cambridge, 1910); *Seminary Addresses and Other Papers* (Cincinnati, 1915; New York, 1969).

B. SH 10, 228; NCAB 13, 414; DAB 16, 421–23; UJE 9, 393–94; EJ 14, 948–50; NYT 20 Nov 1915, 13; Norman Bentwich, *Solomon Schechter: A Biography* (Philadelphia, 1938).

SCHLATTER, Michael (14 July 1716, St. Gall, Switzerland—31 October 1790, Chestnut Hill, PA). *Career*: assistant pastor, Wigoldingen, Switzerland, 1745; assistant pastor, Lintebühl, Switzerland, 1745–46; minister to Reformed churches, Philadelphia and Germantown, PA, 1746–55; superintendent, English charity schools, 1755–57; chaplain, British Army, 1757–59; semi-retirement, Chestnut Hill, PA, 1759–90.

Evidence regarding Schlatter's ministerial studies is obscure, suggesting that he acquired university training in Leyden and Helmstedt but received greater theological knowledge through private tutorials in his home parish. By 1746 he volunteered for missionary activities in the New World. For a decade he was the most important factor in developing German Reformed churches into viable denominational status. After that time he lapsed into a partially active status in which he did not utilize his many gifts, but the latter period should not be allowed to obscure initial achievements essential for church growth. Cooperating with earlier ministers such as *John P. Boehm, he labored tirelessly amid congregations harboring Protestant principles brought from the fatherland. Within a year of his arrival, Schlatter was instrumental in organizing the first Coetus of Reformed churches in Pennsylvania. The synod consisted of four clerics and twenty-seven elders, supervised by the Reformed Church of Holland. Ministering to widely scattered churches appealed to this restless missionary. He averaged 2,000 miles a year in travels from the Hudson River to the Shenandoah Valley, preaching at least three sermons a week. In 1751 he made successful appeals in Europe for more aid to American missions. Dutch sources granted annual stipends for five years, while he personally recruited six German pastors to foster Reformed tenets among the faithful.

Education was another of Schlatter's perennial concerns. In 1753 he again traveled to Europe in search of aid for Pennsylvania schools. Two years later, however, he ended formal association with the Coetus in order to supervise schools financed by a British evangelistic society. That decision terminated his influence among German Americans. Advocates of Teutonic culture resisted English schools because they suspected ulterior motives. They wanted neither Anglican religious instruction nor Tory political loyalties in their schools, and Schlatter was blamed for complicity in those imagined objectives. Such criticism, added to jealousy of his eminence as pioneer minister, was fanned to heated controversy by local newspapers. Schlatter quit in disgust and found a measure of solitude by serving as chaplain with British forces during the French and Indian War. After action in Nova Scotia, he returned to farming and preaching near Philadelphia. He never mended relations with the Coetus but continued ministering as he pleased for several decades, viewing at a distance the ecclesiastical development he had done much to initiate.

Bibliography:

B.   SH 10, 239–40; DAB 16, 435–36; NCE 12, 1134; Henry Harbaugh, *The Life of Rev. Michael Schlatter* (Philadelphia, 1857).

SCHMIDT, Nathaniel (22 May 1862, Hudiksvall, Sweden—29 June 1939, Ithaca, NY). *Education*: studied at Stockholm Univ., 1882–84; M.A., Madison (now Colgate) Univ., 1887; studied at Univ. of Berlin, 1890. *Career*: minister, Swedish Baptist Church, New York, NY, 1887–88; associate professor of Semitic Languages and Hellenistic Greek, then professor of Semitic Languages and Literature, Colgate Univ., 1888–90, then 1890–96; professor of Semitic Languages and Oriental History, Cornell Univ., 1896–1932; professor emeritus, 1932–39.

Indicating the religious liberalism that influenced his future, Schmidt's unorthodox father defied the law requiring Lutheran baptism for his son. Despite the fact that he served briefly in a Baptist church, he was much more at home in speculative and reformist circles usually associated with the Ethical Culture Society. Such attitudes blended easily with historical and literary critical analysis which Schmidt applied to biblical materials. He emerged at the turn of this century as a man of prodigious learning as well as one with a bold, innovative turn of mind. He contributed some 1,500 articles for the second edition of the

New International Encyclopedia. In 1904 he directed the American School of Archeology in Jerusalem, and the following year he led an exploration of the Negev and the Kadesh Barnea region. When archeological procedures matured and several institutions merged to form the American School of Oriental Research, he sat on its board of trustees. In 1914 he was president of the Society of Biblical Literature and Exegesis, and in 1931 he filled the same office for the American Oriental Society. As a writer, teacher, and popular public speaker he demonstrated how solid scholarship could undergird a broad humanistic approach to the intellectual and ethical aspects of religion.

Most of Schmidt's work concentrated on biblical topics. He was at the forefront of those in the generation who applied the principles and methods of historical and literary criticism to the Bible. In addition to that central focus he provided a Syllabus of oriental History, consisting of several volumes on the history of Syria, pre-Islamic Arabia, Egypt, Ethiopia, and India. One of his more controversial works was a study of the life and teachings of Jesus of Nazareth. Typical of his liberal perspective, and of his thoroughgoing attention to the sources, he held that Jesus was a religious genius but altogether a human being who never claimed the title of Messiah for himself. His study encouraged many contemporaries to suggest further modifications in commonly accepted christological definitions. Schmidt longed for improvements in current religious organizations, and he envisioned an ideal religion in future times. At that point there would be no dogmas or creeds. In a world union of voluntary participants the emphases would be on ethical principles backed by scientific knowledge. This ideal fired the imagination of the scholar as he ranged from archeology to esthetics, from manuscripts to moral fellowship.

Bibliography:

A. *The Prophet of Nazareth* (New York, 1905); *The Messages of the Poets: The Books of Job and Canticles and Some Minor Poems in the Old Testament* (New York, 1911); *Ibn Khaldun: Historian, Sociologist, Philosopher* (New York, 1930); *The Coming Religion* (New York, 1930).

B. SH 10, 252; DAB supp 2, 596–97; UJE 9, 411; NYT 1 Jul 1939, 1.

SCHMUCKER, Samuel Simon (28 February 1799, Hagerstown, MD—26 July 1873, Gettysburg, PA). *Education*: graduated from Univ. of Pennsylvania, 1819; graduated from Princeton Sem., 1820. *Career*: minister, environs of New Market, VA, 1820–26; professor, Gettysburg Sem., 1826–64; president, Pennsylvania (now Gettysburg) Coll., 1832–34; retirement, 1864–73.

Raised in a Lutheran parsonage, Schmucker added theological scholarship to basic pietistic attitudes and emerged as one of the most competent ecclesiastical statesmen of his time. As early as 1820 he helped establish the General Synod, a pioneering organization among American Lutherans, and he remained through life in the forefront of its attempts to renew Christian witness by means of greater denominational vitality. He took a leading part in founding the church's seminary and classical school (raised to college level in 1832); as professor in the former institution he shaped ideas within the Synod for decades. In addition to writing the earliest English volume on Lutheran systematic theology, he compiled hymnbooks and catechisms, drafted constitutions, and suggested liturgical guidelines in service of denominational traditions which he genuinely admired. Deeply loyal to his Reformation heritage he sought to strengthen Lutheranism in this country through increased unity. As congregations were organized in the process of westward emigration, he tried to secure their association with the General Synod. At the same time he fostered, with visits and frequent correspondence, a stronger sense of fraternity between Evangelical communions on both sides of the Atlantic. As professor, author, and activist, none was more influential than he in encouraging fraternal cooperation during the early national period.

If different portions of the Lutheran church could work together, Schmucker reasoned that all Protestant denominations might approach a more general consensus regarding their common mission. In 1838 he penned a landmark appeal to American churches, calling for greater federation of programs and setting the ideological tone for organizational developments which came to fruition in the twentieth century. The limits of his plan were clear. Wary of centralized control, he proposed only an advisory council which would embody a visible expression of shared principles while symbolizing an end to narrow party spirit. He did not look for an amalgamation of various traditions nor even interference in the judicial sovereignty of historic entities. His plan of union envisioned something more than an association of like-minded individuals (such as the Evangelical Alliance of 1846, which he attended) and something less than a merger of separate church bodies. He sought voluntary cooperation within American Protestantism, an ecumenical witness manifest on local levels by sacramental and ministerial interchange. But as Lutherans from the Old World arrived in ever increasing numbers, Schmucker found himself among an unpopular minority. His party of "American Lutherans" defended broad affiliation, while the more conservative "Old Lutherans" insisted on staunch confessionalism grounded in the 1580 Book of Concord. In 1864 he resigned from the seminary which had itself grown unresponsive to his direction. Thereafter he maintained contact with other ecumenical spokesmen but was virtually repudiated in his own confessional circle.

Bibliography:

A.   *Elements of Popular Theology* (Andover, MA, 1834); *Fraternal Appeal to the American Churches* (New York, 1838; Philadelphia, 1965); *Psychology: Elements of a New System of Mental Philosophy* (New York, 1842); *The American Lutheran Church, Historically, Doctrinally and Practically Delineated* (Springfield, OH, 1851; New York, 1969). *The Lutheran Manual of Scriptural Principles* (Philadelphia, 1855); *The True Unity of Christ's Church* (New York, 1870).

B.   SH 10, 254; NCAB 5, 100–01; DAB 16, 443–44; NCE 12, 1139–40; Peter Anstadt, *Life and Times of Rev. S. S. Schmucker* (York, PA, 1896); Abdel R. Wentz, *Pioneer in Christian Unity* (Philadelphia, 1967).

SCOFIELD, Cyrus Ingerson (19 August 1843, Lenawee County, MI—24 July 1921, Douglaston, NY). *Career*: private, Confederate Army, 1861–65; clerk, land claims office, St. Louis, MO, 1866–68; lawyer, KS (1869–75), and MO (1875–82); minister, First Congregational Church, Dallas, TX, 1882–95 and 1902–07; minister, East Northfield, MA, 1895–1902; active retirement, 1907–21.

Reared by Episcopalian parents who migrated from southern Michigan to central Tennessee, Scofield showed little interest in religion during the first half of his life. After distinguished service as a Confederate orderly, he moved west to study law, eventually practicing successfully enough to secure election for the Kansas state legislature (1870) and receive appointment as U.S. Attorney for the district (1873). But in 1879 he was converted to Christianity through the friendly assistance of a fellow lawyer; that decision turned him in new directions which in time made a deep impression on conservative Protestants in many American denominations. Almost immediately he volunteered for YMCA work in St. Louis while he began studying the Bible with James H. Brookes, a well known minister of the city. As pastor in Dallas, under auspices of the Congregational Home Mission Board, then as lecturer at Niagara Bible Conferences, Scofield quickly became a popular interpreter of biblical texts. While minister of *Dwight L. Moody's church in Massachusetts, he was also president of the Northfield Bible Training School where he influenced great numbers of future Bible teachers. By 1895 those educational experiences were objectified in a three-volume correspondence course, one that counted over 10,000 subscribers in the twenty years of his personal management. After 1915 the Moody Bible Institute briefly supervised the course, but in 1929 it formed the central curriculum of Scofield Theological Seminary.

Sermons and lectures constituted only a minor part of Scofield's contribution to conservative appreciation of biblical religion. After decades of intense intellectual effort, conducted without the benefit of ancient languages, he produced *The Scofield Reference Bible* (1909; amplified in 1919, 1966), probably the single most important publication affecting millenarian ideas to the present time. He did not intend to create a commentary but rather through chains of references to let the Bible disclose its truth on various topics. In fact his theological orientation placed distinctive categories and very definite interpretations on a vast network of interlocking scriptural passages. His millenarian, dispensational views gave coherent form to his own system of cross-references and subtly perpetuated that perspective as part of Scripture itself. In all his study of holy writ, Scofield deliberately excluded the entire field of higher criticism because he considered it a tragic devastation of commonly accepted notions about biblical authenticity. He insisted that every word in the English Bible revealed some divine truth, not just data but universal types and symbols fraught with apocalyptic meaning. The meanings he assigned to those references did much to enhance Fundamentalist attitudes regarding scriptural inerrancy; his durable pattern of mutually confirm-

ing verses in both Testaments continues to support premillennial dispensation-
alism in the twentieth century.

Bibliography:

A. *Rightly Dividing the Word of Truth* (New York, 1888, and many subsequent
editions); *No Room in the Inn* (New York, 1913); *The New Life in Christ* (Chicago,
1915); *What Do the Prophets Say?* (Philadelphia, 1918); *Things New and Old* (New
York, 1920); *In Many Pulpits* (New York, 1922).

B. NYT 25 Jul 1921, 13; Charles G. Trumbull, *The Life Story of C. I. Scofield* (New
York, 1920).

SCOTT, Orange (13 February 1800, Brookfield, VT—31 July 1847, Newark,
NJ). *Career*: itinerant Methodist minister in VT, NH, and MA, 1821–30; presiding elder in MA and RI, 1830–35; minister, Lowell, MA, 1836; agent, American Anti-Slavery Society, 1837; minister, Lowell, MA, 1838–40; convalescent
retirement, 1840–41; minister, Lowell, MA, 1841–42; editor and then publishing
agent for *True Wesleyan*, 1843–46.

In the early years of his ministry Scott received attention among New England
Methodists as one who had overcome poor schooling to excel in several pastoral
appointments. But in 1833 he became absorbed in a cause which gave new
directions to life and added the charge of radicalism to his reputation. He was
convinced through reading and attending antislavery lectures that slaveholding
was sinful. Owners usurped the place of God, he argued, by giving themselves
absolute control over other men. Scott quickly developed into an ardent abolitionist led by the vision of immediate emancipation, education for freedmen,
and constitutional provisions to protect their civil rights. For the next fifteen
years he preached repentance from the sin of slaveholding with a fervor stemming
from the same revivalistic sources he used to exhort rejection of other sins on
the road to salvation. He was a strong opponent of colonization schemes, claiming
that they were impractical, unjust, and morally blind to the basic evil of slavery.
In 1835 he contributed several articles to *Zion's Herald* in an effort to win
popular support for immediate abolition. These were the first such arguments
permitted in the paper, but Scott went on to found (1839) the *American Wesleyan
Observer* to make unrestrained pleas for the cause among Methodists. He also
lectured throughout his region and led abolitionist forces at General Conferences
(1836, 1840) in disputes over issues which gradually moved the church toward
sectional division.

Difficulties with more conservative religious leaders were not slow in emerging. Scott denounced those who compromised with slavery in blunt, stinging
terms. Many considered him a reckless incendiary, but he was driven by a need
to make Methodists aware of their complicity in sin. His bishop, Elijah Hedding,
accused him at a district meeting (1838) of endangering church unity by over-
emphasizing the slavery issue; the charges were not sustained. Tension with
hierarchical authority did not subside, however, because Hedding threw legal

obstacles in the way of returning to his church in Lowell, Massachusetts. By 1842 Scott withdrew from Methodist affiliation in a protest combining self-righteousness on the abolition question and opposition to episcopal polity. The next year he presided at a convention in Utica, New York, which formed the Wesleyan Methodist Connection, a group of antislavery churches ranging from Maine to Michigan. He served the secessionist body primarily as agent for its paper, *True Wesleyan*, but his activities for emancipation took a variety of forms. In 1845 he made an extensive tour of western states to spread the abolitionist gospel, and that arduous task sealed his fate. Since he had long suffered from a feeble constitution, it is not overly dramatic to say that he wore himself out, promoting the cause he had espoused so intensely.

Bibliography:

A.   *An Appeal to the Methodist Episcopal Church* (Boston, 1838); *The Methodist E. Church and Slavery* (Boston, 1844); *The Grounds of Secession from the M. E. Church* (New York, 1848, 1971).

B.   AAP 7, 667–71; NCAB 2, 315–16; DAB 16, 497–98; Lucius C. Matlack, *The Life . . . and Memoirs of Rev. Orange Scott* (New York, 1847–48).

SCOTT, Thomas Fielding (12 March 1807, Iredell County, NC—14 July 1867, New York, NY). *Education*: graduated from Franklin Coll. (later Univ. of Georgia), 1829. *Career*: Presbyterian minister, La Grange, GA, Savannah, GA, and Columbia, TN, 1829–42; Episcopal rector, St. James' Church, Marietta, GA, and Trinity Church, Columbus, GA, 1844–54; bishop of Oregon and Washington Territories, 1854–67.

Licensed to preach by Presbyterians while still a college student, Scott pursued missionary work in nearby Hall and Franklin counties while still enrolled in classes. His ministry to Presbyterian churches is not carefully tabulated, but that fourteen-year orientation changed significantly in 1842 when Scott met Episcopal bishops James H. Otey and *Leonidas Polk. Under their personal influence he became intrigued with the questions of legitimate polity and authentic ordination. After months of studying scripture and historical record he concluded that the traditional episcopate was the proper form of church government. This new conviction led him reluctantly to abandon his old denomination and to seek orders in his new one. Ordination as Episcopal deacon in 1843 and as priest the following year inaugurated another decade of pastoral duties, with the years at various places again not recorded with accuracy. Dedication to work in the new ecclesiastical setting brought such attention that he was in 1853 named the first missionary bishop to the territories of Oregon and Washington.

In 1854 Scott was consecrated as the first Episcopal bishop stationed in the far Northwest, and the following year he finally arrived in his vast diocese. For the next thirteen years he expended his life in trying to cope with all the serious handicaps found there. Travel was often quite difficult in the extensive district which sometimes was enlarged to include either California or Idaho upon special jurisdictional requests. Funds were always scarce, and personnel resources were even more a chronic problem. Still, Scott's pioneering endeavors laid the foundations for more noticeable growth later on. The strains of overwork affected his health, and as he traveled to attend a General Convention, he contracted a fever that killed him before he could reach his destination.

Bibliography:

B.   DAB 16, 501–02.

SCOTT, Walter (31 October 1796, Moffat, Scotland—23 April 1861, Mays Lick, KY). *Education*: B.A., Univ. of Edinburgh, 1818. *Career*: schoolteacher (principal after 1820), Pittsburgh, PA, 1819–26; itinerant minister for the Mahoning Baptist Association in OH, 1826–27; minister and editor, principally at Carthage, OH, 1827–44; minister and editor, Pittsburgh, PA, 1844–50; minister, Mays Lick, KY, 1850–52; principal, female academy, Covington, KY, 1852–55; active retirement, 1855–61.

Within a year of arriving on this continent, Scott moved west to grow up with the country. He became associated with a lay minister who taught him to search the Scriptures for literal truth related to church organization and the meaning of baptism. Though he had belonged to the Church of Scotland from infancy, he felt thus converted to Christianity for the first time and was immersed in obedience to biblical instruction. In 1821 he met *Alexander Campbell whose teachings resembled his own maturing theology; he was an independent thinker, but it is fair to say that by 1826 the two men labored for the same evangelical cause. In fact Scott signed some of his early writings "Philip" to signify that he thought of Campbell as the Luther of a new reformation with himself in the role of Melanchthon. Galvanized into action by what he considered new ideas, he made people's ears tingle with sermons proclaiming a gospel recovered from apostolic times. His rich voice, dynamic energy, and compelling language took its toll among listeners. Using every opportunity to preach in churches, wagons, or from courthouse steps, he converted more than 1,000 persons a year for over three decades. The editorial pages of two magazines, *Evangelist* (1832–35, 1838–44) and *Protestant Unionist* (1844–50), gave an additional outlet for disseminating information in the emerging denomination. As Disciples of Christ gradually became a distinct organization, this forceful preacher helped shape its evangelical emphasis which facilitated rapid expansion in succeeding decades.

For Scott a simple, practical plan of salvation disclosed in the New Testament involved three human actions and three divine. Rebelling against his Calvinist heritage, he had no patience with doctrines of human depravity or inability. Having faith was nothing more than believing the evidence presented by Scripture; no election or divine aid was needed for a person to hear, believe, and obey the gospel restored to its original simplicity. As the revivalist and editor explained the salvation theme countless times, reducing and summarizing them in five points, easily tallied on the fingers of one hand. The first was to have faith: believe in the "Golden Oracle" that Jesus is the Christ. Secondly, repent: men are able to turn from their sin if they genuinely acknowledge that Christ is Messiah. The third aspect of human action is baptism: to be immersed is not symbolic of an inner change already accomplished but rather deliberate obedience to a biblical command. Scott held that only after these things are accomplished does God's threefold action come into effect. The fourth step was His immediate remission of sins. Finally a double promise blended gifts of the Holy Spirit on earth with eternal life as the future's glorious prospect. Claiming no creed but plain New Testament truths, Scott and other founders of the Disciples viewed them as the way to salvation and the bond of Christian union. Even in retirement the patriarchal figure preached occasionally, expounding those doctrines which he had persuaded so many to adopt.

Bibliography:

A. *The Gospel Restored* (Cincinnati, 1836); *The Messiahship, or The Great Demonstration* (Cincinnati, 1853).

B. NCAB 2, 342; DAB 16, 502–03; William Baxter, *Life of Elder Walter Scott* (Cincinnati, 1874); Dwight E. Stevenson, *Walter Scott: Voice of the Golden Oracle* (St. Louis, 1946).

SCUDDER, Vida Dutton (15 December 1861, Madura, India—9 October 1954, Wellesley, MA). *Education*: B.A. and M.A., Smith Coll., 1884 and 1889; studied at Oxford Univ., 1884–85. *Career*: at various ranks, professor of English Literature, Wellesley Coll., 1887–1927; active retirement, 1927–54.

When her Congregationalist missionary father drowned less than a year after her birth, the child named Julia Davida returned with her mother to the Dutton homestead in Massachusetts. There she benefited from the advantages of education and culture which gave her long life notable polish and finesse. As a teenager she and her mother joined the Episcopal church, and in 1889 they became part of the Society of Christian Socialists that was sponsored by *William D. P. Bliss. Scudder blended an intelligent analysis of social problems with a private embarrassment over her own privileges. Her many writings about redemption of society and her activities in the Brotherhood of the Carpenter and the Christian Social Union stemmed from both high ideals and a twinge of guilt. These reformist concerns often put her in conflict with administrators of Wellesley College, itself a bastion of status and privilege. The strain that built up in such clashes led to a breakdown in 1901 and a year's travel in Europe for recuperation. Her sympathies for the needy and her enthusiasm for social reform never flagged, however, even in the classroom where she lectured on the foundations of socialist thought in English literature.

By 1911 Scudder became a founding member of the Episcopal Church Socialist League. There she sought to develop a greater sense of social responsibility among the affluent members of her denomination. In rather simple, naive fashion she encouraged the application of Christian principles to industry and the marketplace. By 1919 she had joined the Socialist Party and formed a lasting friend-ship with *Norman M. Thomas. She also organized the Church League for Industrial Democracy, a forum in which liberal churchgoers could discuss various means of achieving social justice. Scudder had supported American participation in World War I, but by 1923 she had a change of heart, joined the Fellowship of Reconciliation, and remained a staunch pacifist thereafter. As professor emer-itus she enjoyed virtually another whole career, becoming an accomplished scholar on early Franciscan history and delivering lectures around the country on the need to deal effectively with social issues. In summers she held courses at Wellesley on Christian Ethics, and at the age of eighty-five she delivered an astute address to the Conference on Christian Social Thinking. Her altruism envisioned social order guided by religious principles, and her practical sense grasped the need for labor unions and political compromises in order to achieve that ideal.

Bibliography:

A.   *The Social Ideals in English Letters* (Boston, 1898; several editions to 1927); *Socialism and Character* (Boston, 1912); *The Church and the Hour: Reflections of a Socialist Churchwoman* (New York, 1917); *The Social Teachings of the Christian Year* (New York, 1921); *On Journey* (New York, 1937); *My Quest for Reality* (Wellesley, MA, 1952).

B.   NCAB 4, 468–69; DAB supp 5, 616–17; NAW 4, 636–38; NYT 11 Oct 1954, 27.

SEABURY, Samuel (30 November 1729, Groton, CT—25 February 1796, New London, CT). *Education*: B.A., Yale Coll., 1748; studied medicine at Edin-burgh, 1752–53. *Career*: missionary for the Society for the Propagation of the Gospel (SPG) in NJ, 1754–57; rector, Jamaica, NY, 1757–66; rector, West-chester, NY, 1766–76; private medical practice and chaplain to British troops, Staten Island and New York, 1776–83; Episcopal bishop of Connecticut, 1784–96.

The aftermath of political revolution in this country raised important questions about churches formerly associated with English rule. Seabury was a prime agent in rescuing Episcopalians from dissolution in those crucial years, but he was not an architect, like *William White, of the balanced polity which most of them eventually adopted. He was rather a vigorous champion of high church principles in liturgy and government, considered by some to be essential for preserving the ancient heritage of orthodox Christianity. His conservative inclinations were known as early as 1774 when he began writing plain, forceful pamphlets in defense of loyalty to the Crown. Because of such Tory views, he was jailed for a time by patriot militia and thereafter sought protection within British lines. Under those circumstances many Episcopalians were not pleased to hear that priests in Connecticut had nominated Seabury in 1783 to be their bishop. He was consecrated in Scotland the following year by three nonjuring bishops, having resorted to them after English prelates questioned their own authority to act. By 1785 the first American bishop was hard at work in his home state, organizing and revitalizing churches in the new diocese. Based at St. James' Church in New London, he inaugurated a missionary program which he pursued with great zeal and administered with virtually unlimited power. He was not popular south of New England, but within his own territory he did much to foster growth.

The first Episcopal general convention was held at Philadelphia in 1785, but Seabury did not attend because he thought too many of its delegates slighted the authority of bishops. Throughout his tenure he stressed the need for a valid episcopacy which retained its traditional prerogatives, free from lay interference. He had little sympathy for modifications of ecclesiastical structure, calling them attempts to make the church episcopalian in orders but presbyterian in government. As an exponent of doctrines developed by nonjuring divines in Scotland and England, he also resisted liturgical changes because they departed from early Christian practice. There were some who wished to omit the Nicene Creed from the book of common prayer and include only an edited version of the Apostles' Creed. Seabury refused to accept such radical suggestions because they would allow Unitarians to claim the church's articles of belief as their own. By 1789 compromises were reached, leaving no more than a vestige of suspicion and recrimination among factions. Seabury acquiesced in lay representation at national conventions and won approval for a separate House of Bishops. He was largely successful in thwarting excisions of the prayer book. Though he may not have approved of all the emphases which later stemmed from his high church convictions, he made it possible for a strong element of Anglo-Catholic piety to flourish during the nineteenth century.

Bibliography:

A. *Discourses on Several Subjects*, 2 vols. (New York, 1793); *An Earnest Persuasive to Frequent Communion* (New Haven, 1789); *Discourses on Several Important Subjects* (New York, 1798); *Letters of a Westchester Farmer*, ed. Clarence H. Vance (White Plains, NY, 1930).

B. AAP 5, 149–54; SH 10, 315–16; NCAB 3, 475; DAB 16, 528–30; NCE 13, 13; Eben E. Beardsley, *Life and Correspondence of the Right Reverend Samuel Seabury* (Boston, 1881); William J. Seabury, *Memoir of Bishop Seabury* (New York, 1908); Herbert Thoms, *Samuel Seabury, Priest and Physician: Bishop of Connecticut* (Hamden, CT, 1962); Bruce E. Steiner, *Samuel Seabury, 1729–1796: A Study in the High Church Tradition* (Columbus, OH, 1971).

SEIXAS, Gershom Mendez (15 January 1746, New York, NY—2 July 1816, New York, NY). *Career*: minister, Congregation Shearith Israel, New York, NY, 1768–76 and 1784–1816; minister, Congregation Mikveh Israel, Philadelphia, 1780–84.

As the first native-born Jewish minister, Seixas performed the services of cantor (hazzan), ritual slaughterer (shohet), and circumciser (mohel) for his congregation. His strictly orthodox religious principles fit well in the old Sephardic synagogue on Mill Street. He was also notable for espousing the patriot cause as events led up to the American Revolution. In 1776, when British forces approached New York, he persuaded the congregation to close its synagogue rather than continue under royalist occupation. Most members fled to Philadelphia, but Seixas took the Torah and other sacred scrolls to Stratford, Connecticut. It is not known how he lived during the next four years. In 1780 he too moved to Philadelphia and helped establish a synagogue there. During its dedication ceremonies the patriot Jewish minister invoked God's blessing on George Washington and the American Congress. There was further evidence of his republican sympathies in 1783 when he protested a recent Pennsylvania religious test act. His criticism of the law said all members of the state assembly had to recognize the divine origin of the New Testament helped modify the statute and thus provided for greater religious freedom.

Returning to New York the following year, Seixas devoted himself to a great number of civic activities in addition to his rabbinical duties. He was famous as the first preacher to deliver English sermons in an American synagogue. In them he supported his country's policies, offered prayers for the state, and lectured Jews on their duties in a democratic regime. In this manner Seixas became widely recognized as the chief spokesman for American Jewry in his day. His presence as one of the few clergy invited to George Washington's inauguration helped enhance that reputation. In 1784 he became one of the incorporators of Columbia College and served as one of its trustees until 1815. He also served for years on the Board of Regents of the state university as well. In 1793 he organized a Hebrew school to serve the larger Jewish community, and there he helped further the next generation's understanding of Hebrew language, literature, and laws. In 1802 he helped establish Hebra Hased Va-Amet, one of the city's first charitable organizations. This one concentrated on relief of the sick and burial of the dead. His own death marked the passing of a public servant who found that adherence to strict religious discipline was compatible with both community and national service too.

Bibliography:

B.   NCAB 4, 531; DAB 16, 564–65; UJE 9, 462–63; EJ 14, 116–17.

SERRA, Junípero (24 November 1713, Petra, Majorca—28 August 1784, near Monterey, CA). *Career*: Entered novitiate in Franciscan order, 1730; lectured in philosophy and then ordained as priest, St. Francis Friary, Palma, Majorca, 1738; received doc. in theol., Lullian Univ., Palma, 1743; professor of Philosophy, Lullian Univ., 1743–49; transferred to Apostolic College of San Fernando in Mex., 1750; missionary in the Sierra Gorda, 1750–58; Apostolic College administrator and missionary, 1758–67; missionary in Lower CA, 1767–69; missionary in Upper CA, 1769–84.

Serra's career was marked by significant activities in teaching, administration, fiery sermons, exploration, and missionary work among various Indian tribes. Baptized Miguel José, he changed his name to Junípero upon entering the Order of Friars Minor. Because of his intellectual accomplishments, he was given the task of philosophical instruction at his seminary before his ordination, and after attaining his doctorate he won great distinction both as professor and as pulpit orator. In 1749 he obtained permission to attach himself to missionary efforts in the New World. He spent nine years among the Pames of the Sierra Gorda region, learned their language and translated the catechism into it. When the Jesuits were removed from their missions because of events in Europe, Serra was appointed in 1767 to superintend Franciscans who continued the work in Lower California begun by *Eusebio F. Kino and others in the Society of Jesus.

The last major event came in 1769, when Serra and other friars joined the Portolá expedition in its efforts to pacify and colonize Upper California. During the course of Serra's presidency nine missions were founded: San Diego (16 July 1769), San Carlos, San Antonio, San Gabriel, San Luis Obispo, San Francisco de Assisi, San Juan Capistrano, Santa Clara, and San Buenaventura. Eventually twenty-one missions were built in California territory to minister to the religious life of Spanish and native peoples alike. Father Serra's records indicate that he baptized more than 6,000 Indians and confirmed more than 5,000. Always a dedicated and energetic supervisor, he made frequent inspections of his missions to counsel and encourage the faithful. On the material side of success, his able management brought prosperity to those surrounding the missions in terms of cattle, grain, and manufactured goods. Using less tangible measures, the missions endured as a monastic example within Mexican culture, a locus of ecclesiastical solace to Spanish Americans, and while the dwindling number of Indians lasted, a source of salvation to them. Serra considered this last group to be his special charge, as his many preaching ventures among Penutian-speaking groups and protests against governmental abuses of their civil rights indicate (e.g., his *Representacion*, 1773). He was convinced that the mission-colony plan of churches, farms, industry, and permanent dwellings was the best means of converting others to Christianity. Father Serra is representative of hundreds of selfless men who devoted their lives to a religious program of salvation, even though such plans produced more benefits for the extension of European culture than the preservation of native ones.

Bibliography:

A. *Writings of Junipero Serra*, ed. Antonine Tibesar (4 vols. Washington, DC, 1955–66).

B. DAB 16, 591–92; NCE 13, 124–25; Omer Englebert, *The Last of the Conquistadors: Junipero Serra, 1713–1784* (New York, 1956); Theodore Maynard, *The Long*

Road of Father Serra (London, 1956); Maynard J. Geiger, *The Life and Times of Fray Junipero Serra, O.F.M., or The Man Who Never Turned Back, 1713–1784* (Washington, D.C., 1959); Winifred E. Wise, *Fray Junipero Serra and the California Conquest* (New York, 1967).

SETON, Elizabeth Ann Bayley (28 August 1774, New York, NY—4 January 1821, Emmitsburg, MD). *Career*: various teaching and boarding house projects in New York and Baltimore, 1804–09; mother superior, Sisters of Charity of St. Joseph, Emmitsburg, MD, 1809–21.

Unforeseen events changed Mrs. Seton's life pattern perhaps more noticeably than in most cases. Happily married and the mother of five children, she was widowed in 1803 while accompanying her husband to Italy on travels intended to restore his health. She was consoled there by Catholic friends whose example awakened an interest in teachings of the Roman church. When she returned to New York in 1804, she was on the threshold of conversion but wavered because her Episcopal rector, *John H. Hobart, strongly opposed such a move. One year later she became a Catholic only to find herself rejected by former friends and faced with the task of eking out an existence under straitened circumstances. In 1808 she moved to Baltimore at the invitation of *Louis G. V. Dubourg and established a school for girls near her Sulpician host's college and seminary. In that city she taught the daughters of leading families, enjoying too the friendship of archbishop *John Carroll who had confirmed her two years earlier. Mrs. Seton had long wished to found a religious community, and the slow process of organization was set in motion under the approving guidance of Carroll. A site for location was finally chosen by 1809, and after vows were made before the archbishop, the small band of American Sisters of Charity moved to their permanent base in the Maryland mountains.

From the first, teaching was foremost in Mother Seton's order. European sisterhoods often stressed work in hospitals or among the poor, but education was the central activity of those in the rude houses at Emmitsburg. A rule for the Sisters of Charity was brought from France, and in 1812 archbishop Carroll affirmed the rubrics, modified to fit American conditions, which are still observed today. Economic hardships and geographic isolation did not intimidate the order's pioneering work in religious education at St. Joseph's Academy. Mother Seton immersed herself in labor for the community and school, supervising the spiritual growth of her teachers as well as their charges. She found peace through industry, preparing textbooks, writing treatises, and translating useful French volumes. Her practical common sense and simple piety shaped the lives of many young women who spread her influence to wider circles. As far as her own spiritual development was concerned, there were several experiences of personal grief and grace which produced palpable results. At length she achieved a level of joyful abandon where she considered herself a simple atom, lost in the immensity of God's plan for his creatures. Such an insight affected all those who knew her. Mother Seton was declared venerable in 1959 and beatified in 1963. She became in 1975 the first native-born American to receive canonization; her feast day is 14 September.

Bibliography:

    B.   NCAB 2, 436; DAB 16, 596–97; NCE 13, 136; NAW 3, 263–65; Charles I. White, *Life of Mrs. Eliza A. Seton* (Baltimore, 1853); Louise Malloy, *The Life Story of Mother Seton* (Baltimore, 1924); Annabelle M. Melville, *Elizabeth Bayley Seton* (New York, 1951); Joseph I. Dirvin, *Mrs. Seton: Foundress of the American Sisters of Charity* (New York, 1962).

SEYMOUR, William J.

Little specific information remains about Seymour's origins except for general knowledge that he was born in Louisiana and moved to Houston, Texas, early in life. There he became a Baptist minister of modest accomplishment until 1905 when he began studying in a pentecostal Bible school led by *Charles F. Parham, recently of Topeka, Kansas. Though Seymour was a Negro, he was allowed to frequent doctrinal classes and absorb standard holiness convictions that full sanctification was a second blessing in God's plan of salvation. But more importantly he also became a strong advocate of Parham's distinctive view that baptism of the Holy Spirit was a third and final experience in divine-human encounters. Glossolalia, or speaking in tongues, was a manifestation of the culminating inner blessing, unmistakable proof that the Holy Ghost resided in those worthy to be chosen its vessel. In 1906 Seymour moved to Los Angeles and soon underwent a personal experience of the third baptism, an event which proved to be the fountainhead of modern American Pentecostalism. For three years his small storefront church on Azusa Street was the focus of an astonishingly powerful spiritual revival. Thousands flocked to interracial gatherings in the mission whose meager surroundings were reminiscent of frontier camp meetings; hundreds of those attending fell under the influence of religious enthusiasm, exhibiting their exaltation in spontaneous personal witness, speaking in tongues, singing and dancing in joyful abandon. Every major form of modern Pentecostalism traces its heritage back to the outpouring of spiritual energies in Elder Seymour's squalid little church. The fact that it occurred without warning in an unpretentious setting seemed to indicate an initiative beyond human control. But the black man who exhorted others to let tongues come forth was acknowledged as the chief inspirational source for subsequent pentecostal activity. Others contributed doctrinal formulations or institutional structures; he served as the catalytic agent and was directly responsible for setting this interracial movement on a path to phenomenal expansion later in the twentieth century.

Bibliography:

    B.   Vinson Synan, *The Holiness-Pentecostal Movement in the United States* (Grand Rapids, MI, 1971).

SHEEN, Fulton John (8 May 1895, El Paso, IL—9 December 1979, New York, NY). *Education*: B.A., St. Viator Coll., 1917; studied for ordination, St. Paul's Sem., 1917–19; S.T.L., J.C.B., Catholic Univ. of America, 1920; Ph.D., Univ. of Louvain, 1923; S.T.D., Collegio Angelico, Rome, 1924. *Career*: priest, St. Patrick's parish, Peoria, IL, 1926; at various ranks professor of Philosophy and Theology, Catholic Univ. of America, 1926–50; national director, Society for the Propagation of the Faith, 1950–66; auxiliary bishop of New York, 1951–66; bishop of Rochester, 1966–69; titular archbishop of Newport, Wales, 1969–79.

Named Peter at his baptism, Sheen took the name of John at confirmation and soon added his mother's family name to complete the way he wished to be addressed. He always wanted to become a Roman Catholic priest and excelled in his studies that prepared him for such a vocation. His main strengths were a flair for public speaking together with a capacity for discussing religious questions in clear, simple terms. As preacher, lecturer, and guest speaker he developed a considerable reputation for eloquence. When Sheen began utilizing mass media as well, his popularity soared to make him one of the most effective evangelists in the history of broadcasting. In 1930 he began regular preaching on "The Catholic Hour," a radio program broadcast nationwide and around the world by short wave. Response to his lucid, uplifting sermons often produced six thousand letters a day. In 1940 Sheen conducted the first religious service on television, and between 1951 and 1957 he lectured weekly with his famous blackboard in the immensely popular "Life Is Worth Living" series. Regular appearance on television facilitated his effectiveness in making converts through expanded missionary efforts, a perennial concern.

Radio and television were not the only means Sheen used in pursuing his mission. He authored nearly seventy volumes on counseling and evangelical themes. He wrote "God Love You," a regular column for the Catholic press, and "Bishop Sheen Writes," a syndicated entry for secular papers. For many years he also edited *Mission*, one of the most widely circulated Catholic magazines. Sheen aroused some early criticism for supporting the royalist cause in the Spanish Civil War and for defending corporal punishment in schools. During his brief stint as bishop of Rochester, many questioned his administrative methods. But he also took early stands against nuclear warfare and the conflict in Vietnam which helped shape public opinion in those directions. He cooperated fully with changes occasioned by the Second Vatican Council, proving himself to be a dutiful son of the church instead of an egotistical publicity hound. Fame did not turn his head, and his favorite task was preaching at Lenten season services at St. Patrick's Cathedral in New York City.

Bibliography:

A. *The Divine Romance* (Washington, DC, 1930); *Old Errors and New Labels* (New York, 1931); *The Cross and the Crisis* (Milwaukee, WI, 1938); *Communism and the Conscience of the West* (Indianapolis, IN, 1948); *Way to Inner Peace* (New York, 1954); *Treasure in Clay: The Autobiography of Fulton J. Sheen* (Garden City, NY, 1980).

B. NCE 18, 474–75; NYT 10 Dec 1979, A1.

SHELDON, Charles Monroe (26 February 1857, Wellsville, NY—24 February 1946, Topeka, KS). *Education*: B.A., Brown Univ., 1883; B.D., Andover Sem., 1886. *Career*: minister, Waterbury, VT, 1886–88; minister, Central Congregational Church (minister-at-large, 1912–15), Topeka, KS, 1889–1919; editor-in-chief, *Christian Herald*, 1920–25; contributing editor, *Christian Herald*, 1925–46.

The son of a peripatetic Congregationalist minister, young Sheldon grew up in a log cabin on the South Dakota prairie where self-reliance and simple moral truths were his daily schooling. As a pastor he later applied those same teachings to new urban conditions, especially in stories written to replace sermons in Sunday evening services. After printing several series in *Advance*, a Chicago-based religious magazine, one narrative attracted phenomenal attention. In it Sheldon discussed modern problems such as slums, labor unrest, political corruption, and social tension related to immigrants or other minority groups. For each situation he urged that people ask themselves, "What would Jesus do?" and then act accordingly. The story appeared in book form as *In His Steps* in 1897 and became a runaway bestseller, second only to the Bible. Because of defective copyright protection, it was pirated by other publishers who pushed sales to at least six million copies in over twenty languages. Sheldon obviously touched a need in popular taste with his writing. He articulated widely held concerns for the moral dilemmas of industrial society, while his uniform, almost superficial, response to every issue challenged individuals to act on a personal basis without waiting for collective programs or institutional change. He wrote more than thirty social gospel novels, but none of them repeated his earlier success. Still he gained no small reputation as an inspirational writer and social commentator from a liberal Protestant viewpoint. In addition to literary pursuits, he lectured on social abuses and their solution based on gospel ethics. For decades an enthusiastic supporter of prohibition, he stumped the country to aid passage of the Eighteenth Amendment. After 1933 he remained active on behalf of pacifism and ecumenism as he advocated simple, New Testament attitudes as palliative to the centrifugal pressures of contemporary existence.

Bibliography:

A.   *The Crucifixion of Philip Strong* (Chicago, 1894); *In His Steps* (Chicago, 1897, and many subsequent editions); *Robert Hardy's Seven Days* (New York, 1899); *Born to Serve* (Chicago, 1900); *Of One Blood* (Boston, 1916); *Charles M. Sheldon: His Life Story* (New York, 1925).

B.   SH 10, 390; NCAB 34, 367–68; DAB 24, 740–42; NYT 25 Feb 1946, 25; Timothy Miller, *Following in His Steps: A Biography of Charles M. Sheldon* (Knoxville, 1987).

SILVER, Abba Hillel (28 January 1893, Sirvintus, Lithuania—28 November 1963, Cleveland, OH). *Education*: graduated from Hebrew Union Coll. and Univ. of Cincinnati, 1915. *Career*: rabbi, Congregation L'Shem Shamayim, Wheeling, WV, 1915–17; rabbi, Temple Tifereth Israel, Cleveland, OH, 1917–63.

After coming to this country in 1902, Silver prepared himself to become the fifth successive generation of his family to enter the rabbinate. He gained a reputation for hard work and devotion to his people, and this won an invitation to serve one of the largest Reform congregations in the United States. While ministering for 46 years in Cleveland, Ohio, he also became known for original thought and graceful expression, raising standards for Jewish pulpit oratory in his own time and thereafter. Silver was active in the Central Conference of American Rabbis and concerned himself with civic affairs as well. He was interested in revising child labor laws and helped pass Ohio's first employment insurance legislation too. He sat on the board of directors of the American Civil Liberties Union. In municipal activities he helped found, served as president, and worked continuously for Cleveland's Jewish Welfare Fund and its Bureau of Jewish Education. Through the war years he also helped direct programs through the United Palestine Appeal and the United Jewish Appeal for Refugees and Overseas Needs.

The passion underlying much of his labor was Silver's commitment to Zionism. Among his many associations in that regard were high office in the Zionist Organization of America, the Zionist Actions Committee, and the American Zionist Emergency Council. He differed with *Stephen S. Wise over whether plans for Jewish statehood should be strident or patient with Allied governments during World War II. This "Silver activists" and "Wise moderates" factionalism almost split American Zionism, but Silver succeeded in retaining much of his original, militant influence. Long known for his brilliant speaking ability, he addressed the United Nations in 1947, urging the Security Council to sanction creation of the state of Israel. The following year his lifelong dream came true, and his stature among Zionists slowly declined after 1948. Over the years he had alienated many with his blunt criticism and impatience, and this loosened his hold on rank and file supporters. New plans for a vigorous Israel also superseded the old combatant, but dwindling influence could not diminish the fact that Silver had played a crucial part in the most formative years of the American Zionist movement.

Bibliography:

A. *Messianic Speculations in Israel from the First through the Seventeenth Centuries* (New York, 1927); *Religion in a Changing World* (New York, 1930); *World Crisis and Jewish Survival* (New York, 1941); *Vision and Victory: A Collection of Addresses, 1942–1948* (New York, 1949); *Where Judaism Differed: An Inquiry into the Distinctiveness of Judaism* (New York, 1956); *Moses and the Original Torah* (New York, 1961).

B. NCAB 50, 614; DAB supp. 7, 688–90; UJE 9, 536–37; EJ 14, 1543–44; NYT 29 Nov 1963, 1; Daniel J. Silver (ed.), *In the Time of Harvest: Essays in Honor of Abba Hillel Silver* (New York, 1963).

SILVER, Eliezer (1882, Abel, Lithuania—February 1968, Cincinnati, OH). *Career*: rabbi, Orthodox congregations, Harrisburg, PA, 1907–25; rabbi, Orthodox congregations, Springfield, MA, 1925–31; rabbi, Orthodox congregations, Cincinnati, OH, 1931–68.

Rabbinical training under the personal supervision of famous teachers in Poland, Lithuania, and Latvia prepared Silver well for his role as prominent leader of Orthodox congregations in the United States. He came to this country in 1907, and for the next eighteen years presided over Chisuk Emuno, Kesher Israel, and Machzike Hadas synagogues in Pennsylvania. While in Massachusetts for a shorter period of time he conducted services at Kodimo, Bney Israel, Beth Israel, and Kesher Israel synagogues. But the one with which he identified for almost four decades was Kneseth Israel in Cincinnati, Ohio. The city had long been the center of Reform Judaism in America, the site of its first college and rabbinical organization. There is some irony, then, in Silver's presence there where he became the leading spokesman for Orthodox Judaism in America. In the 1920s he was elected president of the Union of Orthodox Rabbis in the United States and Canada, and in the 1940s he became a member of the organization's presiding board, serving until death.

From the early days Silver was known for his unusual scholarly abilities. Throughout a long writing career he made many contributions to talmudic and halakhic journals. In 1939 he founded the American branch of Agudath Israel and was elected its first president. That same year he also founded the much more ambitious Vaad Hazzalah and through its offices helped rescue rabbis, scholars, and students from countries occupied by Nazis during World War II. After the war he helped transport Orthodox congregations from behind the Iron Curtain to greater freedom in the West. At that same time he served as an official representative of the U.S. government in Europe and Israel, assisting war refugees and relocating centers of rabbinic learning. After working in international circles, Silver returned home to the congregation so central to his life. There he presided for another two decades and also headed Vaad Hair, the Greater Cincinnati Council of Orthodox leaders, consistently applying dignity, erudition, and zeal to all his duties.

Bibliography:

B.   UJE 9, 537; EJ 14, 1544–45; NYT 9 Feb 1968, 27.

SIMPSON, Matthew (21 June 1811, Cadiz, OH—18 June 1884, Philadelphia, PA). *Career*: Methodist minister in OH and PA, 1834–37; vice-president and science professor, Allegheny Coll., 1837–39; president, Indiana Asbury Univ. (DePauw after 1884), 1839–48; editor, *Western Christian Advocate*, 1848–52; bishop, Methodist Episcopal Church, 1852–84.

Without the aid of formal schooling Simpson acquired a working knowledge of the printing business, law, medicine, and classical languages. By the time he sought admission to the Pittsburgh Conference of Methodist ministers, his practical experience made him useful for service in a variety of fields. He advanced the cause of education for Methodist leaders somewhat, but his main contributions did not lie in scholarship or innovative thought. Public speaking was his element, and he excelled in a form of oratory where persuasion rather than instruction was the primary objective. Simpson had the imagination and verbal capacity to exert an extraordinary power over audiences. His frank, forceful statements could arouse and guide public opinion because he expressed half-articulated ideas nascent in the minds of his listeners. He always identified with the common people, and preaching extemporaneously on great biblical themes never failed to win heartfelt response. During the Civil War he preached patriotism for the Union in a manner which won the respect of President *Abraham Lincoln and many in his cabinet. His popular address, "The Future of Our Country," overwhelmed audiences with its spellbinding oratory and contagious enthusiasm. An evangelist for church and nation, he witnessed in personal testimony for fifty years to further the influence of divine power in human lives.

In addition to eloquence which Simpson used with telling effect for God and country, he employed sound judgment in offices contributing to steady growth in his denomination. As an editor he confronted public issues ranging from the fugitive slave law to temperance resolutions. From the time he was made bishop he supported measures designed to increase lay participation in church governance, an issue successfully completed in 1872. His episcopal duties took him into almost every section of the country, travelling by horse-back and stagecoach when necessary or by railroad and steamboat where industrial advances made it possible. His work with missions in Mexico, Canada, India, and China indicates how American Methodism had become an international church. He also participated in European conferences (1857, 1870, 1875), reaching perhaps the height of representational eminence in 1881, when he delivered the opening sermon at the Methodist Ecumenical Conference in London. More pertinent to tangible results in ecclesiastical statesmanship were efforts to cement relations between northern and southern sections of American Methodism. As early as 1869 Simpson was urged to explore ways of reuniting churches since slavery no longer separated them. His tact and ungainly charm helped produce an agreement in 1876 which moved closer to resolving long-standing problems. As church builder, citizen, and preacher of personal salvation, the bishop spent himself for denominational affairs which he thought comprised excellence in all three fields.

Bibliography:

A. *A Hundred Years of Methodism* (New York, 1876); *Cyclopedia of Methodism* (Philadelphia, 1878); *Lectures on Preaching* (New York, 1879); *Sermons* (New York, 1885).

B. SH 10, 430–31; NCAB 7, 381–82; DAB 17, 181–82; NYT 19 Jun 1884, 4; George R. Crooks, *The Life of Bishop Matthew Simpson* (New York, 1890); Ezra M. Wood, *The Peerless Orator* (Pittsburgh, 1909); Clarence T. Wilson, *Matthew Simpson* (New York, 1929); Robert D. Clark, *The Life of Matthew Simpson* (New York, 1956).

SMITH, Amanda Berry (23 January 1837, Long Green, MD—24 February 1915, Sebring, FL). *Career*: evangelist and missionary, 1870–1912.

There was little in the early stages of Berry's life to indicate that she would become an internationally famous black evangelist. Born in slavery, the oldest girl of thirteen children, with no formal education, and married at the age of seventeen, she had few prospects other than toil and poverty. Since her first husband never returned home after joining the Union Army in 1862, she moved to Philadelphia the following year and married James Smith, a deacon of Old Bethel, the mother church of the African Methodist Episcopal denomination. A move to New York did not bring financial improvement, but there Smith began attending meetings led by *Phoebe W. Palmer. She was deeply impressed with emphases on Christian perfection and the entire sanctification of one's life in this world. In 1868 she experienced spiritual renewal and began to think of speaking about her convictions in public. The following year her husband died (as did the last of five children), thus releasing her for evangelical work in New York and New Jersey. Some A.M.E. ministers resisted allowing a woman to preach, but Smith slowly gained a popular following, especially among white audiences. Between 1870 and 1878 her fervent message won wide respect, and she held large meetings from Maine to Tennessee.

After 1878 Smith spent eleven years abroad. In England (1878–79) she showed particular interest in holiness conferences held at Keswick. In India (1879–81) she spoke effectively to increasingly large audiences. In Africa (1881–90) she labored for both the salvation of souls and the betterment of physical conditions in Liberia. Returning to the United States she continued evangelical campaigns up and down the eastern seaboard. In 1892 she moved to Chicago and, through her friendship with *Frances E. C. Willard, became active in the temperance movement. She also acquired land in the suburb of Harvey where she founded an orphanage. This home for needy young blacks never had adequate funding, but Smith struggled to maintain its operations. In 1912, the year she retired and moved to Florida, the state granted a charter to the Amanda Smith Industrial School for Girls. Modest governmental support kept the institution alive until it was destroyed by fire in 1918, two years after its founder's death.

Bibliography:

A. *An Autobiography: The Story of the Lord's Dealings with Mrs. Amanda Smith, the Colored Evangelist . . .* (Chicago, 1893).

B. NAW 3, 304–05; Marshall W. Taylor, *The Life, Travels, Labors, and Helpers of Mrs. Amanda Smith* (Cincinnati, 1886); M.H. Cadbury, *The Life of Amanda Smith* (Birmingham, England, 1916).

SMITH, Elias (17 June 1769, Lyme, CT—29 June 1846, Boston, MA). *Career*: schoolteacher, Woodstock, VT, 1785–90; itinerant preacher, 1790–98; minister, Baptist church, Woburn, MA, 1798–1801; minister, Christian church, Portsmouth, NH, 1802–08; editor, *Herald of Gospel Liberty*, 1808–18; practitioner of herbal medicine, 1818–46.

Largely self-taught and reared on the New England frontier, Smith exhibited a spirit of stubborn independence and principled tenacity that he acquired as a youth. His parents provided the rudiments of religious training, but in 1785 he underwent a profound religious experience and began to study the Bible and theology intensely. He started preaching to small gatherings in 1790 and two years later was ordained by the New Hampshire Baptist Association. Smith was popular among unsophisticated people in backwoods areas, but the discomforting refinements of urban churches made him increasingly critical of what he considered his denomination's compromises with the world. He condemned Baptists for adopting an unscriptural name, for imposing standards regarding the education and ordination of ministers, and for insisting that members adhere to a uniform body of beliefs. It seemed to him that Baptists had lost their primitive simplicity and replaced their old fervor with a quest for social respectability. By contrast Smith objected to salaried ministers or any professionalism among the clergy. He denounced formal worship services and rejected all associations or organizational structures larger than the local congregation. In 1804 Baptists withdrew fellowship from this firebrand who was broadcasting such disorderly and schismatic principles.

An independent habit of mind led Smith to revise his theology in addition to his ideas about church order. He became convinced that trinitarian doctrine was nothing less than tri-theism and that Calvinistic predestination was too fatalistic. So he attracted a unique following of like-minded adherents, sometimes called ''Smithites,'' but more often ''Christ-ians.'' This movement held no creed but the Bible and rejected all structures and beliefs not found there. Smith was a prolific pamphleteer whose biting criticisms of all churches earned him both notoriety and many enemies. In 1808 he began publishing *The Herald of Gospel Liberty*, the first religious newspaper in the United States. For almost a decade the ''father of religious journalism'' gave vent in this weekly to his own views of Christian simplicity and plausible faith. In 1818 Smith left his own movement and became a Universalist, but after 1830 he effected a partial reconciliation. His lasting significance is symbolic rather than institutional. He spoke for simple piety free from artificial controls, but his opposition to organizational structures prevented any growth or stability among his own body of followers.

Bibliography:

A.   *The Clergyman's Looking Glass* (Boston, 1803); *Three Sermons on Election* (Exeter, NH, 1808); *The History of Anti-Christ* (Portland, ME, 1811); *A New Testament Dictionary* (Philadelphia, 1812); *The Life, Conversion, Preaching, Travels, and Sufferings of Elias Smith, Written by Himself* (Portsmouth, NH, 1816); *The American Physician and Family Assistant* (Boston, 1826).

B.   DAB 17, 258–59.

SMITH, Gerald Lyman Kenneth (27 February 1898, Pardeeville, WI—15 April 1976, Glendale, CA). *Education*: B.A., Valparaiso Univ., 1918. *Career*: minister, various churches in WI and IN, 1917–34; political organizer, 1934–35; traveling speaker, 1936–42; editor, *The Cross and the Flag*, 1942–76; director, Christian Nationalist Crusade, 1947–76.

In 1916 while working his way through college, Smith began preaching at places like Deep River and Gary, Indiana. After graduation his dynamic rhetorical skills took him to larger congregations in Soldiers Grove, Footville, and Beloit, Wisconsin. By the 1920s he served as minister to the Seventh and then the University Place Christian Church in Indianapolis, but in 1929 a change of scene was necessary because his wife contracted tuberculosis. Between 1929 and 1934 he was pastor at the Kings Highway Christian Church in Shreveport, Louisiana, where he developed strong social reform sentiments and met Huey P. Long, then governor of the state. He decided to put his talent for working crowds to political advantage, traveling widely to promote Long's ''Share Our Wealth'' society until his employer was assassinated in 1935. Thereafter Smith spoke wherever invitations led him, delivering a mixture of ideas about religion, nationalism, and social welfare. His message evolved from a campaign against social injustices to a virulent assault on Communists and Jews. Smith was a master of spellbinding oratory, and he used it to glorify the American flag, uphold the Constitution, and defend private property, all in the name of Christianity.

In the heyday of his influence Smith offered easy solutions to those who were oppressed by a faltering economy and threats of war. His speeches and writings stirred passions and aggravated hatreds, though they produced few tangible results. Once friendly with *Charles E. Coughlin because they shared the same prejudices, Smith's magazine, *The Cross and the Flag*, was seen as a successor to Coughlin's *Social Justice*. It was a reactionary hate sheet whose circulation of twenty-five thousand had great impact on the racist ultra-right in promoting a ''White, Christian America.'' First an isolationist, then a star at America First rallies, Smith blended anti-Semitism and anti-Communism in a series of conspiracy theories through the 1960s which he spread through direct mailing campaigns. By 1964 he spent half of each year in semi-retirement in Arkansas, and the following year he commissioned ''Christ of the Ozarks,'' a seven-story cross-like statue of stone and concrete. Four years later he added a passion play to this tourist attraction and subsequently built a religious art gallery and Bible museum. Smith's bigotry and manipulation of popular prejudices was sincere. Far from an aberration, he represents a pervasive tradition in American life that has affected thought and action on this continent since the Puritans hanged witches.

Bibliography:

A. *Is Communism Jewish?* (St. Louis, MO, n.d.); *Too Much and Too Many Roosevelts* (St. Louis, MO, 1953); *Abolish the United Nations: A Handbook for Patriots* (St. Louis, MO, 1953); *The Story of the Statue of the Christ of the Ozarks* (Eureka Springs, AR, 1967); *Besieged Patriot: Autobiographical Episodes Exposing Communism, Traitorism and Zionism from the Life of Gerald L. K. Smith*, edited by Elna M. Smith and Charles F. Robertson (Eureka Springs, AR, 1978).

B. NYT 16 Apr 1976, 30; Leo P. Ribuffo, *The Old Christian Right: The Protestant Far Right from the Great Depression to the Cold War* (Philadelphia, 1983); Glen Jeansonne, *Gerald L. K. Smith: Minister of Hate* (New Haven, 1988).

SMITH, Henry Preserved (23 October 1847, Troy, OH—26 February 1927, Poughkeepsie, NY). *Education*: studied at Marietta Coll., 1864–66; B.A., Amherst Coll., 1869; B.D., Lane Sem., 1872; studied at Berlin, 1872–74, and Leipzig, 1876–77. *Career*: instructor in Church History (1874–75), instructor in Hebrew (1875–76), then professor of Old Testament Exegesis (1877–93), Lane Sem., 1874–93; professor of Biblical Literature and associate pastor, Amherst Coll., 1898–1906; professor of Old Testament Literature and History of Religions, Meadville Sem., 1907–13; librarian and professor of Theology, Union Sem. (NY), 1913–25; retirement, 1925–27.

In his early theological education, including study at two of the best German universities, Smith was not drawn to biblical criticism. During his first years at Lane Seminary he thought it his duty to utilize grammar, lexicon, and concordance for simple expository purposes. Instead of raising troublesome questions it seemed enough to tell students what each biblical author meant in various passages so future ministers could learn what men should believe about God and what duties God required of them. But a sense of professional responsibility made Smith grapple with questions raised by specialists, and in that process he became a liberal despite himself. He faced the facts laid bare by textual and historical research; after that act of intellectual honesty, it was impossible to agree with Presbyterians who adhered to an inerrant canon. Largely because of arguments made by *Benjamin B. Warfield, many affirmed that original autograph manuscripts of the Bible had been without error. But Smith held that the modern exegete was concerned with available texts, not a speculative hypothesis about original sources. In light of current evidence it was clear, for example, that Moses had not authored the entire Pentateuch, Isaiah had not written half of the book ascribed to him, and the historical accounts contained in Kings and Chronicles were irreconcilable. He did not doubt that Scripture still contained the authoritative Word of God and ought to be every Christian's rule of faith and practice, but modern scholarship forced him to admit the book was not without error.

In 1882 Smith published his first statement on modern biblical criticism, a mild defense of Julius Wellhausen's standard work on authorship and dating in Old Testament writings. Some conservatives doubted his orthodoxy, but another decade passed before serious controversy arose. In 1891 *Charles A. Briggs, exponent of biblical criticism at New York's Union Seminary, was charged with heresy; Smith spoke in favor of his fellow student in the 1892 General Assembly and shortly thereafter was presented with similar charges in the Cincinnati Presbytery. His accusers held that he denied the doctrine of verbal inspiration, a view maintaining every statement in Scripture to be literally true. Smith rejoined that such a doctrine was not contained in the Westminster Confession (to which he unfalteringly professed allegiance) nor could it stand the test of known historical facts. By way of rebuttal he charged that his prosecutors had replaced the authority of God with a new rule of Protestant scholasticism, substituting bibliolatry for plenary inspiration. But the vote went against him 31 to 26. Appeal to the 1894 General Assembly was denied, and his principal opponent eventually became president of Lane Seminary. During several years with no official position (1893–98), Smith continued to teach and write important works which helped establish a place for biblical criticism in American academic circles. His trial did much to advertise the issue, but subsequent decades of careful scholarship did more to show how the self-revelation of God was conveyed through the diverse experiences of fallible men.

Bibliography:

A. *Inspiration and Inerrancy* (Cincinnati, 1893); *A Critical and Exegetical Commentary on the Books of Samuel* (New York, 1899); *Old Testament History* (New York, 1903); *The Religion of Israel* (New York, 1914); *Essays in Biblical Interpretation* (Boston, 1921); *The Heretic's Defense* (New York, 1926).

B.   SH 10, 460; NCAB 23, 174–75; DAB 17, 278–79; NYT 27 Feb 1927, 30.

SMITH, Joseph (23 December 1805, near Sharon, VT—27 June 1844, Carthage, IL). *Career*: president, Church of Jesus Christ of Latter-day Saints, 1830–44.

Revivals in the "burned-over district" of upstate New York produced many new forms of religious expression, but none of them became as important in American life as those of Smith, the Mormon prophet. While an impressionable youth, he was confused by the controversies and conflicting claims of rival denominations. No one can determine the extent to which such an environment affected Smith's ideas, but uncertainty arising from the multiplicity of sects led eventually to the conclusion that none of them represented God's will. By the early 1820s his own religious visions gave immediacy and authority to the claim that he was chosen to restore the church of Christ. In one of those visions Smith said the angel Moroni led him to a place where golden plates were buried (Hill Cumorah) and gave him seer stones to make their hieroglyphics intelligible. After three years of translating, he published the *Book of Mormon* in 1830, furnishing those who read it with a history of the true church on American shores after an early migration from Jerusalem. That volume, along with sermons and subsequent revelations, formed the doctrinal basis of a movement which soon began attracting adherents.

Spiritual security among Mormons was derived from access to divine revelation; another factor in the church's growth was its promised economic security. The faithful were organized along communitarian principles which strengthened the group by mutual aid and cooperative regulations. Smith remained the most dynamic presence among growing numbers of followers, but converts like *Sidney Rigdon contributed substantially to the group's intellectual framework and ecclesiastical structure. Viewed from the outside, Mormons were a cooperative society notable primarily for their industry. From within they were a covenantal community, separated from surrounding "Gentiles" by life patterns fashioned according to teachings which the prophet received from on high. Continuing revelation allowed doctrine and organization to evolve over a period of years.

It also made for confusion until the ruling oligarchy (president and quorum of twelve apostles) declared that only presidents could make new ideas binding on the whole church.

Internal stability was achieved slowly, but financial depressions and hostile neighbors forced Smith to move his church several times. At first it seemed that Kirtland, Ohio, would answer their needs. Then the troubled land of northern Missouri became home for many believers. In 1839 a city charter was obtained for Nauvoo, Illinois, and it seemed that the Stake in Zion had found a refuge from persecution. Smith increased his authoritarian claims after 1840, receiving national fame as presidential candidate and general of an independent army. The flow of new teachings continued. By 1843 the practice of plural marriage was disclosed, producing schism within the church and accelerated opposition outside it. While Smith and his brother Hyrum were being held in jail on a minor charge, a mob shot them with the apparent connivance of local authorities. The church's leader became its martyr. Even after death, his genius continued to shape one of the nation's unique religious associations.

Bibliography:

A. *The Book of Mormon* (Palmyra, NY, 1830, and many subsequent editions); *Doctrine and Covenants* (Kirtland, OH, 1835, and many subsequent editions); *The Pearl of Great Price . . . a choice selection from the Revelations and Narrations of Joseph Smith* (Liverpool, 1851); *History of the Church of Jesus Christ of Latter-Day Saints*, 6 vols. (Salt Lake City, 1902–12).

B. SH 8, 9–10; NCAB 16, 1–3; DAB 17, 310–12; NCE 13, 304–05; Lucy M. Smith, *Biographical Sketches of Joseph Smith the Prophet* (Liverpool, 1853; New York, 1969); John H. Evans, *Joseph Smith: An American Prophet* (New York, 1933); Fawn M. Brodie, *No Man Knows My History: The Life of Joseph Smith* (New York, 1945; 1971); Donna Hill, *Joseph Smith: The First Mormon* (New York, 1977); Francis M. Gibbons, *Joseph Smith: Martyr Prophet* (Salt Lake City, 1977).

SMITH, Joseph Fielding (13 November 1838, Far West, MO—19 November 1918, Salt Lake City, UT). *Career*: missionary to Hawaii, 1854–57, 1864–65, 1884–87; missionary, Great Britain and Europe, 1860–63, 1874–75, 1877; member, Council of Twelve Apostles, 1867–1901; president of the Church of Jesus Christ of Latter-day Saints, 1901–18.

Though he was only ten in 1848, four years after his father Hyrum and uncle *Joseph were murdered, young Smith drove an oxcart in the Mormon trek across the plains to Utah. He was nephew to the founder of the new church, but his devotion to the faith and tireless missionary efforts were more important than family connections in his rise to responsible leadership positions. By 1866 he was made an apostle and the following year a member of the Quorum of Twelve. While abroad he presided over many missionary enterprises, including editing the *Millennial Star*. While in Utah he was active in many projects, often associated with the historian's office, and editing *Improvement Era*, the organ for Young Men's Mutual Improvement Associations. In 1880 he was named a counselor to the president of the church, and this appointment was renewed in both 1889 and 1898 when new presidents entered office. Smith was also active in politics, serving many terms on the Salt Lake City council and on separate occasions in both houses of the territorial legislature. He presided over the convention which in 1882 framed a constitution for anticipated statehood and petitioned Congress for admission.

When church president *Wilford Woodruff issued a Manifesto in 1890 suspending the teaching and practice of plural marriage, statehood followed in 1896. Smith himself had six wives and more than forty children, but this change in church policy did not apply retroactively. The issue was still controversial, however, because many Mormons disputed the ruling, and hostile non-Mormons belittled its worth. In 1901 Smith became the sixth president of the church, the first to be born in it and to spend every day of his life under its aegis. He also inherited polygamy as a troublesome issue. In February of 1904 he provided dignified testimony in the U.S. Senate investigation of Reed Smoot, stating that plural marriages were no longer sanctioned by church authorities. Two months later an annual church conference adopted the Worldwide Manifesto which Smith had drafted. This document ended loose observance of polygamy in no uncertain terms, declaring that further such acts were transgressions against the church and subject to discipline from ecclesiastical courts, leading to disfellowship and excommunication. This move laid the matter essentially to rest, and the diplomatic president turned to more pleasant duties. These included strengthening the church's financial and evangelical endeavors, especially in Canada, Europe, and Hawaii. It also involved laying the foundations for better relations with non-Mormon segments of American culture which from then to the present has been more genial to this once-alien faith.

Bibliography:

A. *Gospel Doctrine: Selections from the Sermons and Writings of Joseph F. Smith* (Salt Lake City, 1919).

B. SH 10, 461–62; NCAB 16, 9–10; DAB 17, 313–14; NYT 20 Nov 1918, 15; Francis M. Gibbons, *Joseph F. Smith: Patriarch and Preacher, Prophet of God* (Salt Lake City, 1984).

SMITH, Rodney (31 March 1860, Wanstead, England—4 August 1947, on shipboard bound for the U.S.).

Born into a gypsy family, Smith relied somewhat on the novelty of his origins to attract crowds for revival meetings. He had no formal schooling but learned to preach after 1877 while serving at Salvation Army posts across England. Five years later he was dismissed for an infraction of the rules and, except for four settled years at Hanley (1882–86), turned to general evangelism as a vocation. ''Gipsy Smith'' came to America for the first time in 1889, holding a succession of large revivals in major cities on the east coast. He conducted a number of return engagements mostly in Methodist churches and at their campground in

Ocean City, New Jersey. Encouraged by his friend, *Ira D. Sankey, he sang solos in a pleasing tenor voice to supplement simple sermons which emphasized the place of personal decisions in the process of salvation. While not a sensationalist, Smith conducted himself with an air of romantic originality that attracted curiosity seekers as well as those concerned about the fate of their souls. His persuasive manner on public platforms and in private conversations helped give a characteristic stamp to modern, urban revivalism. Successful evangelizing came to stress almost exclusively the number of new conversions made under the influence of special circumstances and self-conscious oratory.

Bibliography:

A. *Gipsy Smith: His Life and Work, by Himself* (New York, 1902); *As Jesus Passed By* (New York, 1905); *Gipsy Smith's Best Sermons* (New York, 1907); *Bearing and Sharing* (New York, 1913); *Evangelistic Talks* (New York, 1922); *The Beauty of Jesus* (New York, 1932).

B. SH 10, 462; Harold Murray, *Sixty Years an Evangelist* (London, 1937).

SMITH, William (7 September 1727, Aberdeen, Scotland—14 May 1803, Philadelphia, PA). *Education*: M.A., Univ. of Aberdeen, 1747. *Career*: private tutor, Long Island, NY, 1751–53; provost, College and Academy of Philadelphia, 1754–79, 1789–91; rector, Oxford, PA, 1766–77; rector, Chestertown, MD and instructor, Washington Coll. (Kent School before 1782), 1779–89.

After serving for a few years in London as a clerk for the Society for the Propagation of the Gospel (SPG), Smith traveled to the New World in the company of two young gentlemen whom he tutored at their family estate. Trustees of an academy and charitable school in Philadelphia who had read an essay which he composed on education invited him to implement those plans at their small institution. Before accepting, he returned to take Anglican orders in England. He succeeded in raising his school to college level by 1755 and proved to be its most influential architect for two decades. Smith was active in several capacities, exerting vigorous leadership in religion and politics as well as education. He was a strong supporter of British policies versus French interests but alienated many in the Quaker-dominated colonial Assembly in the process. In 1758 his temporary arrest caused students to attend classes in the jailhouse for six months; it also entrenched his loyalty to the Crown. When the Revolution began, Smith was burdened by his loyalist reputation. He temporized by calling for a reconciliation of factions, remaining lukewarm in support of independence and yet sympathetic toward colonial grievances. Despite the fact that one of his sermons, ''The Present State of American Affairs'' (1775), ran to many cheap editions in several languages, he was not regarded as a true patriot. Thus political considerations as well as educational questions were involved in 1779 when the provost's college found its charter revoked.

The collapse of educational and political fortunes in Philadelphia caused Smith to seek an outlet as clergyman in Maryland. He founded another classical school there which also became a college under his leadership. In 1783 he presided over a state convention of Anglican priests, the first group publicly to adopt the new name, "Protestant Episcopal Church." He was prominent in organizing Maryland ecclesiastical affairs and exerted much influence in attempts to weld Episcopal churches into a national union. As an advocate of the more democratic view of episcopacy, he insisted that bishops were no more powerful than other priests except in their capacity to confirm, ordain, and preside at church synods. Despite this conviction, he was able to establish friendly relations with *Samuel Seabury and bring about a modicum of harmony in the 1789 national convention. He worked closely with *William White in revising the Book of Common Prayer, the major portion of which is thought to be his work. As early as 1783, Maryland clergymen named him bishop, a recommendation seconded by the General Convention ten years later, but he was never consecrated. Though he was an able, versatile leader, many opposed him because of an overbearing manner. Charges of public intemperance sealed his fate, but they could not detract from his central place as one of the founders of American episcopacy. In his waning years Smith withdrew from public activities, preaching occasionally and speculating in western land tracts. Control over his college (made the University of Pennsylvania in 1791) and of his church had passed largely from his hands.

Bibliography:

A. *The Works of William Smith*, 2 vol. (Philadelphia, 1803).

B. AAP 5, 158–63; NCAB 1, 340–41; DAB 17, 353–57; Horace W. Smith, *Life and Correspondence of the Rev. William Smith*, 2 vols. (Philadelphia, 1879–80; New York, 1972); Albert Frank Gegenheimer, *William Smith: Educator and Churchman, 1727–1803* (Philadelphia, 1943).

SMYTH, Newman (25 June 1843, Brunswick, ME—6 January 1925, New Haven, CT). *Education*: B.A. and M.A., Bowdoin Coll., 1863 and 1866; graduated from Andover Sem., 1867; studied at Univ. of Berlin and Univ. of Halle, 1869–70. *Career*: minister, Mission Chapel, Providence, RI, 1867–69; minister, First Congregational Church, Bangor, ME, 1870–75; minister, First Presbyterian Church, Quincy, IL, 1876–82; minister, First Congregational Church, New Haven, CT, 1882–1907; pastor emeritus, 1908–25.

After a year of service with the 16th Maine Volunteers near the end of the Civil War, Smyth returned to studies that qualified him for Congregational ordination in 1868. He quickly gained favorable attention for the literary quality of his sermons. Not an impressive orator, what he said had solid content, nevertheless, and his messages delivered with deep personal sincerity drew large audiences for more than four decades. He was also popular because he remained on the cutting edge of theological development at the turn of the century. Through sermons and books he emerged as one of the most constructive theological thinkers of his generation, and as such he helped define the contours of emergent modernism in contemporary American Protestantism. Smyth was also introduced to advances in biblical criticism while he studied in Germany, and he readily embraced its general perspective as well as its specific findings. He also welcomed new discoveries in the physical sciences and amended religious thought by using naturalistic methods as guidelines. In 1881 he was nominated to fill the Abbot Chair of Christian Theology at Andover Seminary, but the Board of Visitors refused to place him on the faculty. Controversy over appointment, and particularly over beliefs about eternal punishment versus future probation, strengthened Smyth's reputation as a theological liberal.

The chief obstacle to more realistic and effective religious thought was what Smyth called "orthodoxism," a stagnation where dogma refused to interact with the world, an ecclesiastical abuse of orthodox ideas. A better approach was to study human nature in its natural, historical, and psychological environments. Identifying realities in the "process of life" defined human needs and failings; this in turn allowed for a truly effective Christian response. Smyth thought that outmoded doctrines, such as Calvin's stipulated innate depravity, were so discredited as to require no refutation. He preferred simply to ignore useless traditions and to consider more constructive issues. His brand of Christian ethics, for example, gave priority to activities generally known as the Social Gospel. The possibilities of ecumenical cooperation also intrigued him, although the 1907 papal encyclicals condemning modernism among Catholics were serious disappointments. Still, he served on various commissions and in 1913 chaired a delegation to England in hopes of reuniting nonconformist churches with Anglicanism. In this country he also sought greater integration between Congregationalists and Episcopalians.

Bibliography:

A.   *Old Faiths in New Light* (New York, 1879); *Personal Creeds; or, How to Form a Working Theory of Life* (New York, 1890); *The Place of Death in Evolution* (London, 1897); *Through Science to Faith* (New York, 1902); *Passing Protestantism and Coming Catholicism* (New York, 1908); *Constructive Natural Theology* (New York, 1913).

B.   NCAB 26, 344–45; DAB 17, 376–77; NYT 7 Jan 1925, 25.

SOCKMAN, Ralph Washington (1 October 1889, Mt. Vernon, OH—29 August 1970, New York, NY). *Education*: B.A., Ohio Wesleyan Univ., 1911; B.D., Union Sem. (NY), 1916; Ph.D., Columbia Univ., 1917. *Career*: secretary, Intercollegiate YMCA, 1911–13; minister, Madison Avenue Methodist Church (Christ Church after 1934), New York, 1917–61; retirement, 1961–70.

An Ohio farmboy educated at a local college, Sockman moved to New York and remained there to become one of the most famous preachers of his generation. Changes introduced early in his single pastorate quickly produced positive results, eventually rescuing a church which had declined in proportion to the fate of its rundown neighborhood. By 1934 the old congregation moved to a new site on Park Avenue where ever-increasing audiences could hear their young minister's popular sermons. There crowds worshiped amid Byzantine elegance in marked contrast to the usual austerity of Methodism, a denominational designation also purposely eliminated upon moving away from the old buildings. In persuading his congregation to open its doors on a non-sectarian basis, Sockman self-consciously followed the example of nearby colleague and fellow liberal, *Harry E. Fosdick. The usual format of his weekly lectures was to comment on current issues, attempting to guide what he called the "moral intelligence" in every individual to sound ethical judgments. The good of each person within the larger goal of beneficial social change were twin concerns of his optimistic, humane moralism. He hoped by thus confronting modern ethical problems to make the urban church intellectually respected, socially responsible, and spiritually re-demptive.

Many noted speakers have gained a national reputation by means of public addresses and literary effort. Sockman became well known through sermons and a large number of books, but the most important key to his popularity was radio. He was one of the first men to use the new device in preaching, and for over thirty-four years his weekly broadcasts were a memorable feature in thousands of American homes. Beginning in 1928 he was the voice of the "National Radio Pulpit," never missing a session as messages were beamed throughout the U.S., Canada, and by short wave to Europe. Such exposure created a nationwide parish, full of listeners who either supplemented their church-going with addi-tional sermons or relied on them as their only source of spiritual meditation. Sockman received an estimated 30,000 letters every year from listeners who sought his advice on scores of moral dilemmas. The dilemma with which he wrestled most often was that of trying to build a better world in an atmosphere of international cooperation. As president of the Church Peace Union (Carnegie Foundation) and the World Peace Commission (Methodist Church) and as a member of the World Council of Church's Central Committee, he worked many years to secure basic objectives for human improvement. Despite open conflicts, cold war, and civil strife in the 1960s, his fundamental hopes for moral progress led him consistently to advocate moral uplift on a nonpartisan basis.

Bibliography:

A. *Suburbs of Christianity* (New York, 1924); *Morals of Tomorrow* (New York, 1931); *The Paradoxes of Jesus* (New York, 1936); *The Highway of God* (New York, 1942); *A Lift for Living* (New York, 1956); *The Meaning of Suffering* (New York, 1961).

B. NCAB G, 197–98; NYT 30 Aug 1970, 65.

SPALDING, John Lancaster (2 June 1840, Lebanon, KY—25 August 1916, Peoria, IL). *Education*: studied at Mount St. Mary's Coll. (MD), 1857–58; B.A., Mount St. Mary's of the West (OH), 1859; S.T.B., American Coll., Louvain, 1862; lic. theol., Louvain, 1864; studied at Rome, 1864–65. *Career*: secretary to the bishop of Louisville, 1865–71; chancellor, Diocese of Louisville, 1871–73; curate, St. Michael's Church, New York, 1873–77; bishop, diocese of Peoria, 1877–1908; retirement, 1908–16.

Ecclesiastical statesman, author, social activist, orator, and innovator—these were only a few of the roles filled by the first bishop of Peoria. Spalding made himself highly visible for over thirty years in a range of tasks that were related to both church and wider interests. His mastery of the spoken and written word spread his views on hundreds of issues over a broad spectrum of public opinion that was not confined to his own denomination. Always concerned to advance the causes of the church to which he was dedicated, the bishop made particularly important contributions in areas concerning education and the place of Catholic citizens in the mainstream of American social development. He had definite opinions as to the role Catholics should play within American pluralism. Mediocrity or opposing views could make him irascible, causing some to be alienated rather than attracted by his manner and program, but the adroitness of his leadership helped bring that vision closer to realization. A paralytic stroke in 1905 effectually ended his long years of service.

Education under proper auspices was the key, in Spalding's consideration, to good conduct and effective action by clergy and laymen alike. He was a strong advocate of parochial school systems, opposing experiments like those of *John Ireland, and labored constantly to improve the general quality of instruction. As early as 1866 he urged the founding of a Catholic university in this country as an alternative to religious training abroad or secular schools at home. His justly famous sermon on the subject at the Third Plenary Council (1884) focused attention on that cause. Spalding joined forces with Ireland, *James Gibbons, and several other notable prelates to help establish the Catholic University of America in 1889.

Spalding, born into a Catholic family with many generations' residence in this country, laid claim to full citizenship without the apologies many church leaders of his day had to make for foreign birth or immigrant parents. His own native heritage was a living refutation to Protestant nativists who claimed his religious tradition could never allow full participation in democratic processes. Spalding proved to be a forceful combatant of the American Protective Association in 1894, defending the identification of Catholic life and complete cooperation with American cultural patterns. His natural acceptance of a brand of Catholicism that could adapt to non-European conditions placed him on the liberal side of the "Americanism" debate. He defended the position that gradual change and innovation were good for the church and its adherents, discoursing on the subject at Rome itself while the controversy raged. Much of Spalding's public life was taken up with various aspects of this general question. His loyalty to church and country embodied by argument and example the New World's pragmatic approach to changing times.

Bibliography:

A. *Essays and Reviews* (New York, 1877); *Religious Mission of the Irish Church and Catholic Colonization* (New York, 1880); *Education and the Higher Life* (Chicago, 1890); *Thoughts and Theories of Life and Education* (Chicago, 1897); *Opportunity, and Other Essays* (Chicago, 1900); *Religion, Agnosticism and Education* (Chicago, 1902).

B. NCAB 10, 44; DAB 17, 422–23; NCE 13, 515–16; NYT 26 Aug 1916, 7; John T. Ellis, *John Lancaster Spalding, First Bishop of Peoria; American Educator* (Milwaukee, 1961); David F. Sweeney, *The Life of John Lancaster Spalding* (New York, 1965); Robert N. Barger, *John Lancaster Spalding: Catholic Educator and Social Emissary* (New York, 1988).

SPALDING, Martin John (23 May 1810, near Lebanon, KY—7 February 1872, Baltimore, MD). *Education*: B.A., St. Mary's Coll. (KY), 1826; B.D., St. Thomas Sem., 1830; S.T.D., Urban Coll. (Rome), 1834. *Career*: rector, Bardstown, KY, 1834–38, 1841–44; president, St. Joseph's Coll., 1838–40; rector, Lexington, KY, 1840–41; vicar-general, diocese of Louisville, 1844–48; bishop (coadjutor, 1848–50), diocese of Louisville, 1848–64; archbishop of Baltimore, 1864–72.

From the days of his youth on a Kentucky farm, Spalding prepared himself for the Catholic priesthood, manifesting an intellectual capacity and spiritual diligence that helped him rise to prominence in the American hierarchy. As a pastor he was always solicitous about the religious needs of his people, and even when administrative duties demanded most of his attention, he did not become aloof but kept a common touch that warmed those about him. Spalding's concern to alleviate human sorrow found outlets in programs too numerous to list, but a constant desire to be of service was one of his chief personal characteristics. He was also a scholar of no little merit, being particularly desirous of recording through books, articles, and speeches a fair interpretation of Catholic history. Even before he succeeded *Benedict J. Flaget at Louisville and then upon becoming Baltimore's seventh archbishop, he was a perpetual advocate of better education as the key to sound growth among the faithful.

Education was only one of the categories about which Spalding took pains, and he proved himself to be a man of practical ability in parochial tasks. The work of recruiting priests, finding sites and work for religious houses, building churches, schools and orphanages, financing charities and dozens of other causes, all these were basic elements of his successful contribution to the progress of the church. He gave strong support to the Catholic Publication Society, established by *Isaac T. Hecker, because it presented a welcome alternative to Protestant book concerns and tract societies as well as providing suitable reading material for the church's growing membership.

The archbishop was also notable as a loyal son of Rome who thought such religious convictions laid the best possible foundation for American citizenship. He defended the Syllabus of Errors in 1864 and was an active participant at the Vatican Council of 1870, approving the declaration of papal infallibility as a principle that strengthened the doctrinal guidance priests could utilize to benefit their flocks. Probably the best example of Spalding's concern to promote development within established channels was the Second Plenary Council of 1866. He laid the groundwork there for a codification of ecclesiastical discipline, canon law, and doctrinal uniformity that could ensure the stability of future growth patterns. The agenda concentrated on internal affairs—the unity, charity, and holy lives of Catholic adherents—indicating the priority of its convenor. He thought that once the base was established for religion and morality, then free civil responsibility naturally followed. Spalding defended loyalty to his church and country under many trying circumstances and, though often hampered by poor health, continued to work for those ideals till the end.

Bibliography:

A. *Sketches of the Early Catholic Missions of Kentucky* (Louisville, 1844; New York, 1972); *Lectures on the General Evidences of Catholicity* (Louisville, 1847); *Life, Times and Character of the Right Reverend Benedict Joseph Flaget* (Louisville, 1852; New York, 1969); *Miscellanea* (Louisville, 1855, and many subsequent editions).

B. SH 11, 33; NCAB 1, 486; DAB 17, 424–26; NCE 13, 517–19; NYT 8 Feb 1872, 5; John L. Spalding, *The Life of the Most Rev. M. J. Spalding, D.D., Archbishop of Baltimore* (New York, 1873); Adam A. Micek, *The Apologetics of Martin John Spalding* (Washington, DC, 1951); Thomas W. Spalding, *Martin John Spalding: American Churchman* (Washington, DC, 1973).

SPANGENBERG, Augustus Gottlieb (15 July 1704, Klettenberg, Germany— 18 September 1792, Berthelsdorf, Germany). *Education*: M.A., Univ. of Jena, 1726. *Career*: assistant in Theology, Univ. of Jena, 1726–32; professor of Religious Education, Univ. of Halle, 1732–33; missionary for Moravian Church, 1733–44; bishop, Moravian Church, 1744–90; retirement, 1790–92.

Born the son of a Lutheran minister, Spangenberg became deeply grounded in the pietistic wing of that confession while at college. But shortly after graduating he showed a preference for simpler, more heartfelt religious impulses not sanctioned within state supported churches. By 1730 he began frequenting Herrnhut, a Moravian settlement protected by *Nikolaus L. Zinzendorf, and finally joined that small group, though it cost him an important professorship at Halle. From 1733 on he served as Zinzendorf's trusted assistant, supervising missionary activities on two continents and following him as bishop of the United Brethren. In the New World he worked for a time in Georgia (1735) but then moved to Pennsylvania (1736–39) where liberal government policies encouraged sectarian immigration. Between 1739 and 1744 he developed a network of missionary stations in Europe. Spangenberg represented a mild, catholic form of Christian witness which emphasized salvations of souls through divine grace. His modest piety did much to overcome reliance on creedal strictures or institutional requirements as the main feature of ecclesiastical alignment. On returning to Bethlehem, Pennsylvania, the northern center of Moravian enterprises, he helped organize semicommunistic settlements which assigned work according to skills and allowed for greater prosperity among the general body of participants. In addition to these "Home" communities, he expanded "Pilgrim" bands to pursue evangelical activities among German neighbors, nearby Indian tribes, and some English audiences as a third mission field.

In 1752 Spangenberg inaugurated further colonizing in southern territories, principally the Wachau (Wachovian) district of North Carolina. He reorganized mission work after 1757 and helped establish usually peaceable relations with Indians on the western fringe of white settlement. Under his guidance the badly managed communitarian economic experiments were gradually abandoned with a minimum of hostile repercussions. More patient than the flamboyant and aggressive Zinzendorf, he proved to be a major stabilizing force in Moravian circles as they were isolated simultaneously by both high and low church orientations. Still, he manifested a willingness to worship with kindred spirits wherever possible; such an attitude brought him recognition from all churches as a dominant figure in American missions. He spent the last three decades of his life in Germany, but residence at Herrnhut did not prevent him from supervising a farflung network of mission endeavor. There he was also consulted as an expert on colonial affairs and wrote several volumes to perpetuate a heritage of inner devotion which he considered central to the Protestant Reformation.

Bibliography:

A. *Leben des Herrn Nichlaus Ludwig Grafen und Herrn Zinzendorf*, 8 vols. (Barby, 1772–75; London, 1838); *Kurzgefasste Historische Nachricht von der Brüderunität* (Frankfort, 1774; London, 1775); *Idea Fidei Fratrum* (Barby, 1779); *Reden an Kinder* (Barby, 1782); *Das Wort von Kreuz* (Barby, 1791); *Vergebung der Sünde* (Barby, 1792).

B. SH 11, 33–34; NCAB 1, 512; DAB 17, 428–29; NCE 13, 519.

SPEER, Robert Elliott (10 September 1867, Huntingdon, PA—23 November 1947, Bryn Mawr, PA). *Education*: B.A., Princeton Univ., 1889; studied at Princeton Sem., 1890–91. *Career*: secretary, Board of Foreign Missions of the Presbyterian Church in the U.S.A., 1891–1937; active retirement, 1937–47.

At the turn of the twentieth century the United States began to assume greater influence in international affairs, and American churches complemented that move with an expansion of missionary activities in foreign countries. Among Presbyterians, Speer embodied that dedication to worldwide evangelization through his writing, recruiting, and administrative leadership of forty-six years, plus ten more after mandatory retirement. He was influenced in this direction by *Dwight L. Moody's Northfield Conferences and by his close friend, *John R. Mott, who also had considerable effect in persuading young people to volunteer for mission service. As secretary of the Presbyterian Board, Speer greatly increased the scale of funding and personnel in his denomination's work. He traveled to Persia, China, Japan, India, through Southeast Asia, and Latin America to gain firsthand knowledge of fieldwork and immediate needs. The interdenominational range of mission work made a strong impression on Speer, and he cooperated with many Christian organizations to support their fundamental unity of purpose and action. His sense of duty to evangelize the world within the span of one generation led to substantial efforts on behalf of practical ecumenism. Churches abroad increased, and churches at home grew closer together under his energetic guidance.

During the 1920s and 1930s, Speer had to face several challenges regarding policy and leadership which reveal some of his basic convictions about missionary work. One had to do with the relation of indigenous churches to American control, particularly the way in which local leadership could survive without continued foreign subsidies and equipment. Speer was emphatic, against the arguments of many, that such groups become self-supporting, self-propagating, and self-governing. He did not want to establish an ecclesiastical colonial system with native groups ever dependent on the resources of outsiders. In another area, critics led by *John G. Machen opposed his right to appoint missionaries whose views were at variance with their fundamentalist conceptions, and Speer was forced to defend himself and those under his supervision. In 1932 a controversy arose over suggestions that the exclusiveness of Christianity be minimized in foreign lands and cooperation with local religions augmented to enhance general moral improvement. Speer responded decisively with a defense of specifically Christian missions for the purpose of establishing churches with confessional distinctiveness. The General Assembly of 1933 voted in overwhelming numbers to endorse both his personal rectitude and the principle of Christian standards as superior to religions in general. After that, Speer continued to function as a powerful spokesman for evangelism that knew no geographical bounds.

Bibliography:

A.   *The Man Christ Jesus* (New York, 1892); *Missionary Principles and Practice* (New York, 1902); *Men Who Were Found Faithful* (New York, 1912); *Rethinking Missions Examined* (New York, 1933); *The Finality of Jesus Christ* (New York, 1933); *Five Minutes a Day* (Philadelphia, 1943).

B.   SH 11, 39; NCAB 36, 267–68; NCE 13, 560; NYT 25 Nov 1947, 29; W. Reginald Wheeler, *A Man Sent from God: A Biography of Robert E. Speer* (New York, 1956).

SPELLMAN, Francis Joseph (4 May 1889, Whitman, MA—2 December 1967, New York, NY). *Education*: B.A., Fordham Univ., 1911; S.T.D., North American Coll., Rome, 1916. *Career*: curate, Roxbury, MA, 1916–18; staff, Cathedral of the Holy Cross, Boston, 1918–22; vice-chancellor, diocese of Boston, 1922–25; attaché, Papal Secretary of State, Rome, 1925–32; auxiliary bishop of Boston, 1932–39; archbishop of New York, 1939–67; military vicar for Army and Navy Forces, 1940–67; cardinal of New York, 1946–67.

The basic pattern of Spellman's life was one of graduated achievement and increased acceptance of responsibility. Even after studying in Rome and filling various posts in the Vatican State Department, he considered Boston his home and looked forward to a life of service in that vicinity. But in 1939 he was named archbishop of New York and assumed supervision of a debt-ridden diocese whose budget and programs exceeded those of most business corporations or an average municipality. The administrative problems of one of the largest and most racially heterogenous districts in the country might have intimidated a man of less stature, but Spellman met every challenge with patience, good will, and genuine ability. One of his main interests was to continue the many Catholic charities begun by his predecessor, and he compiled an impressive record in furthering guidance for the young and relief of suffering for countless others. As an active, energetic prelate he was able to meet the constant demand for funds, raising millions of dollars to renovate old buildings, erect new ones, and still have the means to inaugurate fresh projects in the name of Christian charity. Spellman's whirlwind pace was undergirded by a life of prayer which gave solace and resolve to meet the expectations laid on him. By means of the enterprises begun or expanded under his administration, it can be said that he succeeded in providing for those under his charge.

Activities pursuant to the religious welfare of a metropolitan diocese would be enough to occupy most individuals, but Spellman achieved national fame in larger issues. From the days of his work under Eugenio Pacelli (later Pius XII) in Rome, the American priest developed a close association between freedom and Christian principles with a corresponding repudiation of fascist and communist viewpoints. During World War II, he identified the cause of Allied forces (except Russia) and Christian civilization, rarely deviating from that position for the rest of his life. His supervision of Catholic chaplains in the Army and Navy, a task inherited with the archbishopric, allowed an opportunity for service which endeared him to thousands of G.I.s. He toured the European and Pacific theaters, saying mass and arranging for canteens that ministered to soldiers' spiritual and physical needs. From Anzio to Da Nang the indefatigable cardinal was a favorite of troops in three wars. He admired their bravery and sacrifices, often reminding them of his convictions about the related virtues of American citizenship and Christian witness for which they were fighting. But whether he conferred with presidents and generals or spent quiet hours in a foundling home, the spiritual goals of his many duties were paramount.

Bibliography:

A. *The Road to Victory* (New York, 1942); *Action This Day* (New York, 1943); *No Greater Love: The Story of Our Soldiers* (New York, 1945).

B. NCAB F, 220–21; NYT 3 Dec 1967, 1; Robert I. Gannon, *The Cardinal Spellman Story* (New York, 1962).

SPRING, Gardiner (24 February 1785, Newburyport, MA—18 August 1873, New York, NY). *Education*: B.A., Yale Coll., 1805; studied law in New Haven, CT, 1805; studied at Andover Sem., 1809–10. *Career*: schoolteacher, Bermuda, 1805–07; practiced law, New Haven, CT, 1808–09; minister, Brick Presbyterian Church, New York, 1810–73.

After initial promptings at a Yale revival in 1802, Spring struggled for six years against thoughts of entering the Christian ministry. Finally relenting, he soon became pastor of an urban congregation which retained his services for over six decades. Spring became a fixture in New York affairs, providing weekly sermons of considerable renown, cooperating with a number of civil enterprises, and serving on interdenominational boards which supervised the spread of Bibles (1816), tracts (1825), and home missions (1826). Theologically speaking, he tended to be conservative, but temperamentally he was conciliatory and fair-minded. Metaphysical categories did not interest him very much, and he was only a casual observer of the rise of New Haven theology. He too was unwilling to conclude that God was the author of evil but at the same time did not doubt fallen man's responsibility for a sinful nature as well as for sinful human activity. Sinfulness lay deep in human hearts, a condition symptomatic of thoroughly flawed character instead of mistakes made by the will. Yet for all his Calvinism, Spring acknowledged the silent work of God's grace in revival experiences and even invited *Charles G. Finney to speak at Brick Church in 1827. Ten years later he protested against excluding liberal synods from the Presbyterian General Assembly. When a split occurred, though, he sided with the Old School and remained a member in good standing as long as conservatives existed as a separate group.

Another issue where Spring exerted a moderating influence had to do with slavery. For twenty years after 1839 he opposed the radical tactics of abolitionists, hoping rather to preserve peace and unity with southern leaders. He argued that slavery was recognized by the national constitution; no outside government could impose regulations on states without violating freedoms guaranteed under the federal compact. Spring tried to mitigate bad feelings, in politics and among Presbyterians, but secession forced his hand. Once conflict broke out, he squarely faced the question of rebellion and changed his viewpoint significantly. In May, 1861, he presented resolutions at the Old School General Assembly requiring all presbyteries to declare allegiance to the Union. Many contended through extensive and heated debate that ecclesiastical conduct of religious matters was extraneous to political loyalty. But in the end most delegates voted to uphold the federal government. The "Spring Resolutions" professed unabated loyalty to the United States and all the provisions of its constitution, whereupon representatives of southern presbyteries left silently to form their own denomination that same year. After the war, Spring began to feel the weight of age and increasing blindness from cataracts. But that did not prevent him from making an eloquent plea for reunion of Old and New Schools in 1869, a merger of northern Presbyterians which he lived to see.

Bibliography:

A. *Essays on the Distinguishing Traits of Christian Character* (New York, 1815); *The Attraction of the Cross* (New York, 1846); *The Power of the Pulpit* (New York, 1848); *First Things*, 2 vols. (New York, 1851); *The Glory of Christ*, 2 vols. (New York, 1852; *Personal Reminiscences*, 2 vols. (New York, 1866).

B. SH 11, 57; NCAB 5, 409; DAB 17, 479–80; NYT 20 Aug 1873, 4.

STANTON, Elizabeth Cady (12 November 1815, Johnstown, NY—26 October 1902, New York, NY). *Education*: graduated from Troy Female Sem., 1832. *Career*: co-editor, *Revolution*, 1868–70; president, National Woman Suffrage Association, 1869–90; president, National American Woman Suffrage Association, 1890–92.

Elizabeth Cady had been inclined from childhood to counteract the low status of women, but in the 1840s those random feelings grew into firm resolve. While accompanying her husband, Henry B. Stanton, to antislavery conventions she was dismayed to see that women were not accepted as equals even there. In those circumstances she met *Lucretia Mott who helped free her from the stern Presbyterianism and personal repression to which she had reluctantly conformed. In 1848 she was the main force behind the women's rights convention held at Seneca Falls, New York. Rapidly developing as an effective writer, Mrs. Stanton was instrumental in issuing a declaration of the meeting's sentiments regarding the legal disabilities of women. Of all these, the vote was most important; and Stanton is notable for making the first public demand for woman suffrage in this country. Happily married and the mother of seven, she spent much of her time writing, stumping in political campaigns (especially Kansas in 1867), and speaking on the lyceum circuit (1869–81), crusading for what she considered the inalienable rights of women. For decades after 1851 she collaborated with Susan B. Anthony on feminist projects, among them co-editing the first three volumes of the classic *History of Woman Suffrage* (1881–86). Through politics, journalism and international contacts, Mrs. Stanton helped place the cause of woman's rights before the public in a manner that slowly won adherents to its side.

One aspect of Stanton's ideas set her apart from most women of her day, and it had to do with organized forms of religion. Holding rationalist views of a beneficent God, an orderly universe and individual immortality, she rejected ideas about providential guidance and special revelation. The Bible was a particularly sore point because she thought its injunctions about the submission of women had been misunderstood and used for tyrannical purposes out of all proportion to their context. From her perspective, American churches were nothing less than the bulwark of woman's slavery and the chief obstacle to reform. In addition to private nonconformity, Stanton insisted on raising the issue at women's conventions, introducing resolutions about greater participation in church affairs and usually arousing opposition among suffragists who feared a confusion of objectives. Stanton became a friend of *Robert G. Ingersoll and continued through storms of protest to offer views on religious thought and practice designed to avoid old prejudices with their theological sanctions. Much notoriety came through her outspoken defense of birth control and liberalized divorce laws, but with her religious probing helped women see something of the intellectual freedom available to them. Though contributions in this area were less tangible than her institutional work, Stanton's example helped overcome the psychological conditioning prevalent in her day and displayed some of the opportunities which emancipated minds could seize.

Bibliography:

A. *The Woman's Bible*, 2 vols. (New York, 1895–98); *Eighty Years and More* (New York, 1898).

B. NCAB 3, 84–85; DAB 17, 521–23; NAW 3, 342–47; NYT 27 Oct 1902, 1; Theodore Stanton and Harriot S. Blatch (eds.), *Elizabeth Cady Stanton as Revealed in Her Letters, Diary and Reminiscences*, 2 vols. (New York, 1922); Alma Lutz, *Created Equal: A Biography of Elizabeth Cady Stanton* (New York, 1940); Elisabeth Griffith, *In Her Own Right: The Life of Elizabeth Cady Stanton* (New York, 1984).

STARR, Ellen Gates (19 March 1859, near Laona, IL—10 February 1940, Suffern, NY). *Education*: studied at Rockford Female Sem., 1877–78. *Career*: schoolteacher, Mount Morris, IL, 1878–79; instructor, private girls' school, Chicago, IL, 1879–88; social worker, Chicago, IL, 1889–1929; retirement in convent, Suffern, NY, 1930–40.

After attending a one-room country school and what was later known as Rockford College, Starr supported herself by teaching. In 1888, while touring Europe with *Jane Addams a former classmate, the two young women formed plans for establishing a settlement house to relieve conditions in Chicago's West Side. Addams raised most of the money; Starr made it a joint undertaking by supplying encouragement, direction, and the staying power needed for success. For forty years after 1889, she was associated with Hull House as co-founder and principal coordinator of its cultural activities. With special concern for immigrants arriving in Chicago by ship, she taught them English and the basic principles of democratic citizenship. After reading John Ruskin and Thomas Carlyle, especially their ideas about the place of artistic appreciation in modern industrial societies, she sought to use art as a power to lift human spirits. Literary clubs, art galleries, murals, and folk crafts flourished under her care. She founded in 1894 and became first president of the Chicago Public School Art Society. But in the first decade of this century she concluded that more radical measures were necessary if the artistic quality of life was to survive amid modern commercialism. Consequently she joined the cause of organized labor to eliminate conditions such as slums and sweatshops, low wages and long hours which destroyed man's creative capacity. Experiencing frequent arrests she played a leading role in strikes, especially those of garment workers in 1915–16. Her religious orientation toward such activities had been strong from the beginning, but through the years it took a more definite confessional shape. Nominally Unitarian as a child, she joined the Episcopal church in 1884 and was gradually converted to Roman Catholicism. In 1920 she formally accepted Catholicism at a Louisiana abbey of the Benedictine monastic order. Nine years later she underwent a spinal operation but never fully recovered. Largely confined to her bed, she spent her last years in the Convent of the Holy Child, urging by correspondence those ideas which had motivated so much practical action in four previous decades.

Bibliography:

B.   NAW 3, 351–53; NYT 11 Feb 1940, 49.

STEARNS, Lewis French (10 March 1847, Newburyport, MA—9 February 1892, Bangor, ME). *Education*: B.A., Princeton, Coll., 1867; studied at Columbia Law Sch., 1867–69; studied at Princeton Sem., 1869–70; studied at Berlin and Leipzig, 1870–71; studied at Union Sem. (NY), 1871–72. *Career*: minister, Norwood, NJ, 1873–76; professor of History and Belles Lettres, Albion Coll., 1876–79; professor of Systematic Theology, Bangor Sem., 1880–92.

When Stearns left law school to become a Presbyterian minister like his father, he showed no great interest in revising the traditional ideas constituting theological education. But after a short pastorate and then a professorship in Michigan which he resigned because of eye trouble, theological revision became his chief preoccupation. Following a year's convalescence, he accepted a post at a Congregationalist seminary in Maine and began shaping new emphases in religious thought. The concern for divine sovereignty which Calvinism embodied was not, in his view, the proper center for a theological system. Further its decree of election placed salvation within reach of only part of mankind; he thought the iron ring of its logic was too exclusive, just as its mechanical arguments for theodicy were repellent to modern minds. Stearns held that scholastic Calvinism had overshadowed the scriptural and spiritual aspects of basic Christianity. In 1890 he declined a job at Union Seminary (New York) because it required subscribing to the Westminster Confession, a document which he deemed a millstone around any denomination's neck. Calvinistic ideas and the entire attitude of dogmatism were elements he found out of keeping with vital inquiry into religious truth. He remained at Bangor and broke new ground in the more positive context of adapting beliefs to practical questions related to contemporary life.

Turning from the old supports of miracles and prophecy as evidence of Christian truth, Stearns concentrated on personal experience of redemption. His central doctrine was atonement through Christ, whether in apologetics or systematic exposition, and its christological orientation gave new meaning to doctrines considered from that vantage point. Without compromising belief that Jesus was God in the highest sense, he laid special emphasis on his humanity. The man Jesus was a primary locus for understanding human suffering and for seeing the common ground of universal brotherhood. His life was historical example and present psychological fact to establish the reality of human redemption. God's indwelling presence in the world thus became more important than His transcendence over created spheres. Ethical progress replaced transactions of sin and forgiveness in the field of salvation as all categories were "christologized." Though a liberal, Stearns still thought of himself as orthodox in holding that God controls human destinies enough to shape all ends to His purpose. But he refused to say that differing philosophical opinions should separate brethren or furnish tests of fellowship. Tolerance and innovation were characteristic of his revisionist attitude because every mundane attempt to explain divine-human encounters could not adequately comprehend the divine work of redemptive grace.

Bibliography:

A. *The Evidence of Christian Experience* (New York, 1890); *Present Day Theology* (New York, 1893).
B. SH 11, 72; NYT 10 Feb. 1892, 2.

STEARNS, Shubal (28 January 1706, Boston, MA—20 November 1771, Guilford [now Randolph] County, NC). *Career*: New Light Congregationalist preacher in CT, 1745–51; itinerant Baptist preacher in CT, 1751–54; minister, Sandy Creek Baptist Church, NC, 1755–71.

The influence of quickened religious emphases collectively known as the First Great Awakening led Stearns to accept evangelism as his lifetime vocation. Six years later he became convinced that immersion of adult believers was the only baptismal method sanctioned by the Bible, and so he sought admission as well as ordination under Baptist auspices. After a short period of preaching in New England and northwestern Virginia, he settled with a small band of colonists in central North Carolina. The church formed there in 1755, comprising sixteen members and taking its name from nearby Sandy Creek, was the first Separate Baptist body in the region. As pastor of that congregation for sixteen years, Stearns who proved to have remarkable energy, played a central role in the rapid spread of Baptist principles among backwoods pioneers. In a movement of phenomenal expansion, forty-two new churches and 125 ministers were recruited largely because of his evangelical zeal. He was also principal architect of the Sandy Creek Association (1758), a group not given to centralized ecclesiastical authority but one which did recognize benefits in pooling the resources of particular churches. Stearns was widely known for his animated preaching style, piercing gaze, and contagious emotionalism. Some of his listeners, noting his passionate exuberance together with a musical voice and small physical stature, thought him second only to *George Whitefield as an effective itinerant. Others were startled by his unrestrained gestures and ''holy whine'' or peculiar affectations in the pulpit. But all agreed that he served as a powerful stimulus to revivals along the southern colonial piedmont. Before his coming, denominational activity had been confined within a Calvinistic orientation of modest numerical strength. But his practical example embodied the trend of future development, providing both a theological perspective and an emotional fervency that soon made Baptists the largest religious group in Protestant America.

Bibliography:

B. DAB 17, 548–49.

STEINBERG, Milton (25 November 1903, Rochester, NY—20 March 1950, New York, NY). *Education*: B.A., Coll. of the City of New York, 1924; M.A., Columbia Univ., 1928; graduated from Jewish Theol. Sem., 1928. *Career*: instructor in Classical Languages, Coll. of the City of New York, 1924–25; instructor in Jewish History and Religion, Teachers Institute of the Jewish Theol. Sem., 1926–28; rabbi, Temple Beth El Zedeck, Indianapolis, IN, 1928–33; rabbi, Park Avenue Synagogue, New York, NY, 1933–50.

There were no strong religious traditions affirming Jewishness in Steinberg's immediate family, but the young man grew attached to home observances through his grandparents. In college he developed a love of philosophy, and as he edged toward the idea of becoming a rabbi, he met *Mordecai M. Kaplan. On the whole their interests were compatible, and Steinberg became an early advocate of Reconstruction Judaism. He helped launch *The Reconstructionist* in 1936 and served as an associate editor of the magazine for the rest of his life. He contributed many essays and book reviews to the periodical and wrote several pamphlets for the incipient denomination as well. Jewish cultural organizations also received his attention as he sat on boards of directors or trusteeships. A partial list of his administrative work includes Haddassah, Hillel Foundations, Young Men's Hebrew Associations, the Jewish Welfare Board, the Jewish Publication Society, the Zionist Organization of America, and the Rabbinical Assembly of America.

A heart attack in 1943 forced Steinberg to curtail many of his activities, and he concentrated thereafter primarily on preaching and writing. By that time he had also moved away from Reconstructionism to embrace Conservative Judaism. Reconstructionism had a sound ideology, he said, but it lacked any real appreciation of philosophy. This was the area of Steinberg's genuine interest and of his most profound contributions. He was a deep thinker whose creative mind probed questions such as the nature of God, His relation to history and human experience, the nature of evil, and the relationships between faith and reason. He nurtured a philosophical consideration of Jewish religious traditions, influencing many intellectuals of his day who hovered between assimilation and affirming their Jewishness. Steinberg insisted on the centrality of religion in human life and spoke often of the challenges modern life posed to that orientation. As new ideologies and new forms of anti-Semitism emerged in the twentieth century, he suggested ways of coping with them by invoking the traditional body of doctrine, ethics, and culture called Jewish. Death came at the untimely age of forty-six, but even in a short career he brought high standards of dignity and prestige to the American rabbinate.

Bibliography:

A.   *The Making of the Modern Jew* (Indianapolis, 1934; rev. ed., New York, 1949); *A Partisan Guide to the Jewish Problem* (Indianapolis, 1945); *Basic Judaism* (New York, 1947); *A Believing Jew: The Selected Writings of Milton Steinberg* (New York, 1951); *From the Sermons of Rabbi Milton Steinberg*, edited by Bernard Mandelbaum (New York, 1954); *Anatomy of Faith*, edited by Arthur A. Cohen (New York, 1960).
B.   UJE 10, 44; EJ 15, 364–65; NYT 21 Mar 1950, 29.

STELZLE, Charles (4 June 1869, New York, NY—27 February 1941, New York, NY). *Education*: private theological study, New York, 1890–93; studied at Moody Bible Inst., 1894–95. *Career*: apprentice and journeyman machinist, 1885–93; layworker, Hope Chapel, Minneapolis, MN, 1895–97; layworker, Hope Chapel, New York, 1897–99; minister, St. Louis, MO, 1899–1903; superintendent, Department of Church and Labor, Presbyterian Home Mission Board, 1903–13; columnist, author and public relations agent, New York, 1913–41.

Manual labor was nothing new to Stelzle by the time he entered a machine shop at the age of sixteen. Tenement life on the Lower East Side of New York, with all its human suffering attendant upon poverty, constituted his real education; the compassion he later showed for workingmen and their problems was sustained by a basic identification with his own proletarian origins. After volunteering for the ministry, he learned that applying the gospel to social conditions was an unpopular practice. As long as preachers denounced injustice among the Amalekites, they were considered perfectly orthodox, but as soon as one touched on the same problems among Brooklynites, he was reminded to concentrate on a "simple gospel" less disturbing to modern congregations. Yet Stelzle refused to compromise and became one of the leading spokesmen for church responsibility in urban areas at the turn of this century. No special theories or doctrines lay behind his emphasis. He simply urged that churches had a fundamental obligation to industrial laborers and needed innovative methods to give people an extensive program of practical aid. Much of his activity was spent in mitigating the needless antagonism between social service and evangelism. Full utilization of religious principles required that evangelism be pursued through social channels, touching as many as possible in the lower class population of large cities. In everything from street preaching to arbitrating labor disputes, he taught that Christianity pertained to the environment as well as to the beliefs of those who followed its vital teachings.

Probably the most concrete expression of Stelzle's ministry came in 1903 when the Presbyterian church entrusted him with a special mission to workingmen. For the next decade he worked for the Department of Church and Labor, largely his own creation, in efforts to facilitate cooperation between clergy and the labor force. His office was the first agency with a paid superintendent to conduct an aggressive social gospel campaign. In 1905 he represented his church at meetings of the American Federation of Labor and materially influenced union attitudes regarding local clergymen; four years later he accepted tasks from the Federal Council of Churches in much the same mediating capacity. Another of his lasting contributions was the Labor Temple, a downtown church begun in 1910 to supplement sermons with a variety of forums and self-help classes ranging from medical care to nutrition. He also wrote a syndicated column that ran in hundreds of newspapers. Even conservative estimates show that he spread more religious literature among workingmen than did the total output of sixty tract societies in this country. By 1912, however, budget cuts and theological polarization caused Stelzle to resign his departmental connection. Still, his subsequent work in advertising and public relations continued to stress the practical aspect of Christian witness in a full spectrum of human needs.

Bibliography:

A.   *The Workingman and Social Problems* (New York, 1903); *Messages to the Workingmen* (New York, 1906); *Christianity's Storm Center: A Study of the Modern City* (New York, 1907); *Principles of Successful Church Advertising* (New York, 1908); *The Church and Labor* (New York, 1910); *A Son of the Bowery* (New York, 1926).

B.   SH 11, 76; NCAB C, 160; DAB 23, 733–35; NYT 28 Feb 1941, 19.

STEPHAN, Martin (13 August 1777, Stramberg, Moravia—22 February 1846, Randolph County, IL). *Education*: studied theology at Halle, 1804–06, and Leipzig, 1806–09. *Career*: Lutheran minister, Haber, Bohemia, 1810; minister to Bohemian exiles in Dresden, 1810–37; leader of colonizing party, 1838–39; independent ministry in IL, 1841–46.

Orphaned, and working at the weaver's trade in Breslau, young Stephan met pietists who encouraged him to train for the Lutheran ministry. He had little patience with the full range of topics designated for pastoral education, but he read extensively in theology. By 1810 he became shepherd to a large congregation of Moravian pietists in Saxony, which provided a locus for several religious awakenings. Stephan was highly successful as a preacher; his emphasis on heartfelt emotion together with support for established confessional symbols made his revival movement acceptable to local authorities in both church and state. His strict standards harbored a separatist tendency, however, and a growing contingent attached itself as much to him as to the faith he broadcast. It seems he reluctantly permitted such adulation at first, then expected it as his due. An able organizer, he set up several independent preaching stations, sent out missionaries whom he had trained, and held meetings resembling conventicles which brought him into conflict with the regular clergy of Dresden. In addition to unconventional ecclesiastical behavior, he was also suspected of questionable personal habits. By 1837 these combined factors resulted in his suspension from the ministry. Emigration to America had been a serious consideration among his people for some time. So late in 1838, almost 700 "Stephanites" sailed in five chartered ships to find religious autonomy in the New World.

A conservative minority of the Saxon state church followed Stephan to "new Canaan" in hopes of exercising pure religion there. Many blended a fear of damnation if they stayed behind with expectations of economic improvement if they went. While still on board the *Olbers*, Stephan had himself proclaimed bishop and bursar of the emigration fund as well. Once he became master of both religious and secular affairs for the Gesellschaft, he exercised authority in an increasingly capricious manner. He insisted that immigrants pledge personal subjection to his rule; those who resisted were denounced in emotional tirades so unbridled as to question the bishop's mental stability. Most of the Saxons settled in Perry County, Missouri, but Stephan insisted on a lavish episcopal residence in St. Louis. He invited several women to live with him, indulging private tastes more openly than he had in Germany. Not surprisingly, opposition began to mount. The validity of his office was not questioned, nor was his exercise of civil and religious power. The major sources of opposition came from personal conflicts with other ministers plus several charges of adultery. By the end of May, 1839, Stephan was deposed from office and excommunicated. He was transported across the river to Illinois where he subsisted for only a few years, living in poverty and illness. The once domineering theocrat learned to preach in halting English and served a small church near the village of Red Bud. He tried to resume relations with the colony, but all attempts failed. Within a year after his death, the majority of his erstwhile followers constituted themselves under new leadership as the Missouri Synod Lutheran Church.

Bibliography:

A. *Der Christliche Glaube*, 2 vols. (Dresden, 1825–26).
B. SH 11, 80; Walter O. Forster, *Zion on the Mississippi* (St. Louis, MO, 1953).

STETSON, Augusta Emma (12 October 1842, Waldoboro, ME—12 October 1928, Rochester, NY). *Career*: minister, First Church of Christ, Scientist, New York, 1888–1902; president, New York City Christian Science Institute, 1891–1928.

Marriage and world travel figured in Augusta Simmons' experiences from 1864 to 1884, but those were only prelude to events which made her name noteworthy in American religious history. Early in that latter year she attended a lecture by *Mary B. Eddy who saw in the new convert qualities of leadership potentially beneficial to the growth of Christian Science. After brief tours of successful practice in Maine and Boston, Mrs. Stetson was assigned the task of consolidating missionary efforts in New York. By 1888 the first church was officially incorporated; within two years Mrs. Stetson received formal title as "Reverend" to distinguish her as the most trusted representative among all Mrs. Eddy's students in the area. In 1891 she founded an Institute to spread the faith and train more practitioners. She made her way easily among rich and powerful backers, delighting in opulence as a demonstration of the truth in Christian Science. By 1903 her ministry led to the completion of a massive church edifice, one which overshadowed the Mother Church itself in Boston. Material success combined with personal popularity caused rumors to grow among the envious. Some claimed the New York minister wished to supplant Mrs. Eddy, but she forcibly denied such charges. When the church's oracle demanded (1902) that all ministers (called "Readers") resign after three-year terms, Mrs. Stetson complied. But the directors in Boston were still alarmed at her dominant influence and the threat of schism implied in her wide following.

By 1909 an inquiry was made into Mrs. Stetson's alleged unorthodoxy. It was claimed she taught that sex and procreation were evil, that one's spiritual self could deny physical deeds (i.e., lie under oath), and that she had tried to injure persons by means of malicious animal magnetism. Underlying those charges was a struggle for power which went against her. Later that year both her practitioner's license and church membership were revoked. Despite this she was loyal to Mrs. Eddy, incorporating the foundress' ideas in the doctrines inculcated at the Institute where she continued to teach. After 1910 she did not try to replace Mrs. Eddy but campaigned vigorously to spread her own views. She was disillusioned by litigation in the Mother Church and criticized its spiritual decline in contrast to her own faith. Hundreds of students spread her influence across the country. In the 1920s she began advertising extensively in leading newspapers, magazines (notably the short-lived *American Standard*), and a radio station (WHAP, 1925–28). The content of her public witness was a mixture of Bible readings, sermons, prophecies, American jingoism, anti-Catholic propaganda, and Nordic racial superiority. She remained active until the last months in work which was perpetuated by a dwindling number of coreligionists.

Bibliography:

A. *Poems Written on the Journey from Sense to Soul* (New York, 1901); *Reminiscences, Sermons and Correspondence* (New York, 1913); *Vital Issues in Christian Science* (New York, 1914); *My Spiritual Aeroplane* (New York, 1919); *Sermons . . . and Other Writings on Christian Science* (New York, 1924).

B. NCAB 18, 400–01; DAB 17, 595–96; NAW 3, 364–66; NYT 13 Oct 1928, 15; Altman K. Swihart, *Since Mrs. Eddy* (New York, 1931).

STEVENS, Abel (17 January 1815, Philadelphia, PA—11 September 1897, San Jose, CA). *Career*: Methodist minister, Church Street Church and Bennet Street Church, Boston, 1835–37; minister, Methodist church, Providence, RI, 1838–40; editor, *Zion's Herald*, 1840–52; *National Magazine*, 1852–56; *Christian Advocate and Journal*, 1855–60; Methodist minister, New York City and Mamaroneck, NY, 1861–65; Union Church, Geneva, Switzerland, 1865–88; associate editor, *The Methodist*, 1871–74; retirement, 1888–97.

Burdens of growing up in a large family without a father made it difficult for Stevens to utilize the customary stages of ministerial training. He studied for a time at Wesleyan University, but poor health and lack of funds forced him to withdraw. Still, he gained early notice as a forceful speaker, and at the age of nineteen he served that school as its financial officer. That same year he was admitted on trial by the New England Conference of the Methodist Episcopal Church and soon ministered to two small congregations in Boston. Ordained deacon in 1836 and elder in 1838, Stevens soon proved to be as effective with his pen as he was in the pulpit. This literary ability led to editorships in some of his denomination's most influential and ambitious journals. He became a prolific writer, producing some of the most widely circulated volumes on Methodism in the nineteenth century and contributing to discussions of ecclesiastical policies in pre–Civil War America.

Regulations called for editors to be re-elected by the general conference of ministers, and that situation involved disappointing consequences for Stevens. Though he had long opposed slavery and called himself an abolitionist, he also had tender feelings for slave-owning Methodists in border states. When zealous reformers like *Orange Scott tried to expel all remaining slaveholders from churches affiliated with northern Methodists, Stevens resisted and argued instead for moderation. This mediating stance alienated the radicals, and in 1860 Stevens was not renewed as editor of the important *Christian Advocate and Journal*. He engaged in some journalism thereafter, but his primary activity lay in producing studies of Methodist experience during its first two centuries. Several of his works became classics, especially the seven volumes on the history of his denomination in England and the United States. His extensive research made his books dependable, and his highly readable style made them popular. The last decades of his life, removed from controversy, were more detached and steadily productive than those spent in arguments over the denomination's public image and future direction.

Bibliography:

A.   *Sketches and Incidents, or, A Budget from the Saddle-bags of a Superannuated Itinerant* (New York, 1843); *The History of the Religious Movement of the Eighteenth Century Called Methodism*, 3 vols. (New York, 1858–61); *Life and Times of Nathan Bangs* (New York, 1863); *The History of the Methodist Episcopal Church in the United States*, 4 vols. (New York, 1864–67); *The Women of Methodism* (New York, 1866); *The Centenary of American Methodism: A Sketch of Its History, Theology, Practical System, and Success* (New York, 1866).
B.   SH 11, 88; NCAB 8, 112–13; DAB 17, 604–05.

STILES, Ezra (15 December 1727, North Haven, CT—12 May 1795, New Haven, CT). *Education*: graduated from Yale Coll., 1746; private theological study, New Haven, 1746–49; private study of law, New Haven, 1750–53. *Career*: tutor, Yale Coll., 1749–55; practiced law, 1753–55; minister, Newport RI, 1755–76; minister, Portsmouth, NH, 1777–78; president and professor of Ecclesiastical History, Yale Coll., 1778–95.

Few eighteenth century savants could match the intellectual appetite or accomplishments of Stiles who was justly recognized as the most learned man in New England. At an early age he was fascinated by mathematics, astronomy, and biblical history, developing a taste for scientific inquiry into a host of subjects that ranged from electricity to revelation. His omnivorous, somewhat indiscriminate, curiosity kept him ever alert to new ideas which fostered a tolerance and moderation rare among Congregationalists of his day. As an enlightened liberal he cannot easily be classified among church parties. He sympathized with the declining Old Light Calvinists but did not agree with their attacks on revivals. At the same time he could not condone the hypersensitive New Divinity squabbles over suspected heresies. As his own views progressed from an appreciation of Christianity as a moral system to more evangelical affirmations, Stiles came to adopt a heterodox ecclesiastical position. He stressed saving grace and unmerited salvation but did not presume to distinguish the unregenerate from visible saints. He preached and offered sacraments to all of sober conduct, attempting to include sinners in his church rather than exclude them. With an irenic ecumenism informing his attitudes, he found the coercive orthodoxy of consociations distasteful. As both minister and educator he remained convinced that religious truth would benefit less from uniformity than from a free exchange of doctrinal opinions.

Religious freedom was only one aspect of Stiles' enthusiasm for republican society as it developed in the latter half of his life. He harbored strong patriotic sympathies and supported the Revolution wholeheartedly. Full reliance on popular elections, a wide franchise, separation of church and state, all these were features he thought would make America the envy and model of other nations. Consistent with such principles, he freed his Negro slave (owned, 1756–78) and in 1790 formed a society to promote the liberation of others. Stiles was so thoroughly committed to democratic ideology that he espoused the name of Jacobin after events in France caused many to have second thoughts about the excesses of republicanism. As the seventh president of Yale he contributed significantly to religious training in Connecticut and beyond. Scarce provisions and fluctuating currency during the war years made it difficult to provide steady educational guidance, but by 1784 Stiles had increased enrollment to unprecedented numbers. The activities of study, note taking, lectures, and correspondence never ceased. Even as his body declined with age, his mind continued with undiminished vigor, grasping at the next idea to use in illustration of God's creative bounty.

Bibliography:

A.   *Oratio Funebris* (New London, CT, 1751); *A Discourse on the Christian Union* (Boston, 1761); *The United States Elevated to Glory and Honor* (New Haven, 1783); *A History of Three of the Judges of King Charles I* (Hartford, 1794).

B.   AAP 1, 470–79; SH 11, 97; NCAB 1, 167–68; DAB 18, 18–21; Abiel Holmes, *The Life of Ezra Stiles* (Boston, 1798); Franklin B. Dexter (ed.), *The Literary Diary of Ezra Stiles*, 3 vols. (New York, 1901); Franklin B. Dexter (ed.), *Extracts from the Other Miscellanies of Ezra Stiles* (New Haven, 1916); Isabel M. Calder (ed.), *Letters and Papers of Ezra Stiles* (New Haven, 1933); Edmund S. Morgan, *The Gentle Puritan: A Life of Ezra Stiles, 1776–1795* (New Haven, 1962).

STODDARD, Solomon (27 September 1643, Boston, MA—11 February 1729, Northampton, MA). *Education*: B.A., Harvard Coll., 1662; postgraduate study of theology, Harvard Coll., 1662–65. *Career*: tutor, Harvard Coll., 1666; librarian, Harvard Coll., 1667; chaplain, Barbados, 1667–69; minister, Northampton, MA, 1670–1729.

In the year Stoddard graduated from college, Massachusetts churches reaffirmed a policy of baptizing the children of parents who maintained no stronger link with local saints than their own infant baptism. This "Half Way Covenant" was intended to reaffirm the central place of church membership among God's faithful and thus check the decline of visible piety which many had begun to notice in second generation Puritanism. Taking a cue from the 1662 compromise, young pastor Stoddard slowly began to urge a further relaxation of membership requirements; he finally concluded that open admission to the Lord's Supper was justified as a means of possibly awakening faith in those who participated. Convinced that man was unregenerate, depraved by nature, and saved only through the inscrutable decrees of God, he argued that because of such doctrines it was wrong to insist on proof of conversion as a requisite to communion. Instead of restricting the sacraments to those who could give satisfactory evidence of regeneration, he said persons of every spiritual state (except the openly scandalous) should be allowed to receive the church's ordinances. Assurance of prior conversion should not be required of those participating in the Supper because the solemn ritual itself had a tendency to stir up faith within communicants. Sacraments could be a medium, like public prayer and preaching, through which full realization of divine grace was effected in those whom God chose to save.

Free access to the church's most important communal act was only one of the ways Stoddard sought to recover ecclesiastical vitality. But it was clear that in all his attempts to promote piety, he was not devoted to static forms of worship and found antiquity no authority for continuing outmoded practices. In effect he declared the entire arrangement of Congregational particularism articulated in the Cambridge Platform (1648) to be obsolescent. Calling for flexible innovations to meet new conditions, he hoped that future experience rather than historical precedent would vindicate his decisions. As early as 1679 other Puritan leaders, especially *Increase Mather and his son *Cotton, denounced "Stoddardeanism" as a subversion of proper church order. In an increasingly abusive controversy where personalities often eclipsed substantive issues, they lamented the desecration of orthodox patterns. But despite the pressure of conservative opinion around Boston, Stoddard continued to exert appreciable influence in the Connecticut River valley. In fact many churches of the area followed his example so closely, he was called "pope" in jocular acknowledgment of widespread respect. His ministerial pragmatism stemmed from a general concern to strengthen the faith of his parish by stressing personal religious experience. Pursuing this fundamental emphasis, he witnessed no fewer than five seasons of revival at Northampton. Ironically, his standard of church participation had become so ingrained by 1748 that his grandson *Jonathan Edwards was dismissed as pastor because he tried to raise requirements which the elder minister had done so much to reduce.

Bibliography:

A.   *The Safety of Appearing at the Day of Judgment in the Righteousness of Christ* (Boston, 1687); *The Doctrine of Instituted Churches Explained and Proved from the Word of God* (London, 1700); *The Inexcusableness of Neglecting the Worship of God* (Boston, 1708); *An Appeal to the Learned* (Boston, 1709); *A Guide to Christ* (Boston, 1714); *A Treatise Concerning the Nature of Saving Conversion* (Boston, 1719).

B.   AAP 1, 172–74; SH 11, 100; NCAB 7, 84–85; DAB 18, 59–60; Ralph J. Coffman, *Solomon Stoddard* (Boston, 1978).

STONE, Barton Warren (24 December 1772, near Port Tobacco, MD—9 November 1844, Hannibal, MO). *Education*: graduated from private academy, Guilford, NC, 1793; studied theology under William Hodge, Orange County, NC, 1793–95. *Career*: language instructor, Washington, GA, 1795–96; itinerant preaching, NC, TN, KY, 1796–98; Presbyterian minister, Cane Ridge and Concord, KY, 1798–1803; evangelical work for Christian Church, based in KY, 1804–32; evangelical work for the Disciples of Christ, based in IL, 1832–44.

Converted at the age of nineteen under preachers including *James McGready, Stone decided not to practice law but to enter the ministry instead. With some theological training and many doubts about his fitness for the work, he crossed the Alleghenies under Presbyterian license to conduct worship services. Bourbon County in Kentucky became the center of his operations, and in 1801 the newly ordained minister of Cane Ridge initiated a revival which marked a new era in American religious history. The camp meeting attracted thousands of people, who drew attention by their behavior as well as their numbers. Stone admitted that some practices were eccentric, but on the whole he defended strange manifestations of religious emotion as evidence that God was working among the fallen for spiritual good. By 1803 his Synod began questioning the indecorous excesses which revivals allowed, the low educational standards permitted there, and the Arminian heresy encouraged by open meetings. In that same year, Stone and four others left the Synod, protesting the obvious benefits of revival techniques and championing free salvation over the election doctrine of traditional Calvinism. For a time they constituted the Springfield Presbytery, but in 1804 they decided to abandon denominational labels and take only the name of "Christian" with no creed but the Bible. Stone became the dominant spokesman and steady leader of this new church.

Farming and teaching were extra sources of income, but Stone's real vocation was evangelization. His travels through several states resulted in the steady growth of the Christian Church, or the Stonites as some called them, through individual conversions and sometimes through entire groups' changing their affiliation. The new church which sought to end sectarianism by inclusion was noted for a strictly congregational polity, salvation offered to all who would accept Scriptural warrant for beliefs and adult baptism by immersion. It was no more successful than others in ending the proliferation of differing institutions, but its methods and emphases were suited to the needs of common folk in frontier settings. Stone's influence was extended further through the publication of the *Christian Messenger*, a monthly which he began in 1826 and continued with few interruptions for the rest of his life. Sometime around 1830 he became acquainted with *Alexander Campbell, another ecumenically minded reformer whose ideas coincided with those broadcast by the press and pulpits of the Christian Church. Their common doctrines and practices presented no obstacle to the ideal of church unity; so in 1832 most of the Stonites and Campbellites followed their leaders into merger as the Disciples of Christ. Though he was hampered by paralysis, Stone continued his evangelical activities for another decade and died while on a preaching tour.

Bibliography:

A.   *Atonement: The Substance of Two Letters written to a Friend* (Lexington, KY, 1805); *Addresses to the Christian Churches . . . on several important doctrines of Religion* (Nashville, 1814; rev. ed. Lexington, KY, 1821); *Letters to Dr. James Blythe* (Lexington, KY, 1824); *The Biography of Eld. Barton Warren Stone, written by Himself* (Cincinnati, 1847; New York, 1972).

B.   SH 11, 105; DAB 18, 71–72; Charles C. Ware, *Barton Warren Stone* (St. Louis, 1932); William G. West, *Barton Warren Stone: Early American Advocate of Christian Unity* (Nashville, 1954).

STOWE, Harriet Elizabeth Beecher (14 June 1811, Litchfield, CT—1 July 1896, Hartford, CT).

American citizens became increasingly aware of slavery as a moral issue during the 1850s, with one publication accomplishing that result more dramatically than any other. Its author, daughter of *Lyman Beecher and sister to *Edward and *Henry, was committed to the family tradition of providing ethical guidance whenever possible as a form of public service. Harriet Beecher moved to Cincinnati, Ohio, in 1832 when her father became president of Lane Seminary. Four years later she married Calvin Stowe, a professor at the institution, and lived altogether eighteen years on the border of slaveholding territory. After returning to New England, debates over the Fugitive Slave Law caused her to draw on those earlier experiences and record them in the pages of *Uncle Tom's Cabin*. Mrs. Stowe wrote essentially a parable of life gone awry in the promised land, a romantic reflection on wrongs which God permitted in a universe where good was supposed to triumph. Its enduring features included pathos, exemplary spiritual beauty, one of the first black heroes in American literature, and, underlying everything else, the transforming power of Christian love. The book struck responsive chords within readers who thought of their nation as progressive and yet wrestled with the problem of human suffering sanctioned by law, churches and economic necessity. In the South her name was despised. Many questioned her accuracy or literary ability, but the volume was important as a moral tract which galvanized the consciences of millions who had never before actually felt the abuses of slavery.

Ten thousand copies of her first book were sold in a week. A national sensation overnight, Mrs. Stowe continued for thirty years to write fiction embroidered with themes of faith versus doubt, the struggle of individuals against difficult circumstances, and of Christian duty to amend the world. But subsequent publications never commanded such attention as did her eloquent description of Blacks in their longing for freedom. She was morosely introspective over questions of religion, and her writings provide an insight into the nineteenth century vestiges of Puritan influence. She created a storm of criticism in England by printing allegations that Lord Byron had intimate relations with his sister. Amid charges of scandalmongering she discussed the issue as a matter of public morals, just as she had with slavery, writing her second most disturbing book in an attempt to meet a problem and set it right. The Stowe household was never free from money worries, and as the family mainstay she endured prolonged managerial burdens. Health problems, the deaths of loved ones, and continuing bouts of melancholy added their weight through the years. But the mental faculties which led Mrs. Stowe for a brief while to shape public opinion remained unimpaired until the last decade of her life.

Bibliography:

A.   *Uncle Tom's Cabin, or Life among the Lowly* (Boston, 1852, and many subsequent editions); *Dred, A Tale of the Great Dismal Swamp* (Boston, 1856); *The Minister's Wooing* (New York, 1859); *Oldtown Folks* (Boston, 1869); *Lady Byron Vindicated* (Boston, 1870); *The Writings of Harriet Beecher Stowe*, 16 vols. (Boston, 1896).

B.   NCAB 1, 423–25; DAB 18, 115–20; NAW 3, 393–402; NYT 2 Jul 1896, 3; Charles E. Stowe, *Life of Harriet Beecher Stowe: Compiled from Her Letters and Journals* (Boston, 1890); Forrest Wilson, *Crusader in Crinoline: The Life of Harriet Beecher Stowe* (Philadelphia, 1941); Charles H. Foster, *The Rungless Ladder: Harriet Beecher Stowe and New England Puritanism* (Durham, NC, 1954); Edward Wagenknecht, *Harriet Beecher Stowe: The Known and the Unknown* (New York, 1965).

STRONG, Augustus Hopkins (3 August 1836, Rochester, NY—29 November 1921, Rochester, NY). *Education*: B.A., Yale Coll., 1857; graduated from Rochester Sem., 1859; studied in Berlin, 1859–60. *Career*: minister, First Baptist Church, Haverhill, MA, 1861–65; minister, First Baptist Church, Cleveland, OH, 1865–72; president and professor of Systematic Theology, Rochester Sem., 1872–1912; president emeritus, 1912–21.

Cumulative personal experience together with prayerful study of Scripture gave Strong theological insights which he passed on to students for almost half a century. Struggles against his own sinful nature while in college convinced him that the human heart is essentially cold and lacking in love. But despite such inability he tried without success to work out his own salvation by serving God as he thought everyone should. These attempts led to frustrated recognition that men cannot become Christians any time they wish because all are dependent on God's redemptive grace. He saw Christ's suffering as the single ground of reconciliation with God, and for a long while his preaching stressed the central theme of divine mercy as power sufficient to atone for individual sin. But as he worked to build churches and develop personal virtue, there was no joy in Christian living. He felt spiritually desolate, fighting alone against a world of evil influences until another important truth emerged. Strong had been a minister for years (and not without external signs of success) before he learned about full union between Christ and each believer. The work of Christ for individuals had originally provided solace for eternity, but awareness of Christ in present reality made it possible to serve God with gladness and singleness of heart. The invigorating realization that Christ, united with each person, was the source of endless power acted like a second conversion on the eloquent preacher. He made it the primary focus of his theology.

Shortly before 1870 Strong began expanding his intellectual interests to include science, a field where he dealt creatively with materials that troubled the majority of religious thinkers. This Baptist professor's grappling with Genesis and geology simply broadened his knowledge of the means God used to display His power. It yielded an insight that Christ is not only life for individuals but also the medium through which the world was created and maintained. Then after viewing Christ as deity and creator, Strong developed what he considered a major contribution to theology: Christ organically united with all humanity as its universal saviour. The larger corollary to personal atonement was that all sin from the whole human race was imputed to Christ, the sustainer of life who could not escape its liabilities. Such a doctrine became the core of theology classes at the seminary and sustained decades of interest in foreign missions. Two other principles emerged toward the end of his teaching experience, one pertinent to fundamentalist controversies, the other to the Social Gospel. He concluded that the immanence of Christ made for gradual, inner enlightenment; truth dwells not in outward forms but in inward development of the spirit. And as regeneration of individuals is indispensable in Christianity, it is only the beginning. Christ's spirit also works outwardly to reform all of human society. These doctrines were the result of a vigorous, independent mind which never stopped seeking for truth in divine-human encounters.

Bibliography:

A. *Systematic Theology* (Rochester, NY, 1886; rev. ed., 3 vols., 1907–09); *Philosophy and Religion* (New York, 1888); *Christ in Creation and Ethical Monism* (Philadelphia, 1899); *Miscellanies*, 2 vols. (Philadelphia, 1912); *Popular Lectures on the Books of the New Testament* (Philadelphia, 1914); *A Tour of the Missions: Observations and Conclusions* (Philadelphia, 1918).

B. SH 11, 114; NCAB 12, 514–15; DAB 18, 142–43; NYT 3 Dec 1921, 13; Grant Wacker, *Augustus H. Strong and the Dilemma of Historical Consciousness* (Macon, GA, 1985).

STRONG, Josiah (19 January 1847, Napierville, IL—28 April 1916, New York, NY). *Education*: B.A., Western Reserve Coll., 1869; studied at Lane Sem., 1869–71. *Career*: minister, Cheyenne, WY, 1871–73; instructor and chaplain, Western Reserve Coll., 1873–76; minister, Sandusky, OH, 1876–81; regional secretary, Congregational Home Missionary Society, 1881–84; minister, Cincinnati, OH, 1884–86; secretary, American Evangelical Alliance, 1886–98; president, American Institute (League before 1902) for Social Service, 1898–1916.

After achieving moderate success in several midwestern pastorates, Strong became a national figure in 1885 with the publication of his first book. For the next three decades he spoke and wrote about issues at the core of the Social Gospel movement. His zeal for social reform did much to arouse churches regarding the urban crisis confronting them. His statistical data exhibited dangers ranging from overconcentrated wealth to an alienated working class. Through all his studies of contemporary issues he focused primarily on industrial cities as the locale where problems festered in alarming proportions. His evangelistic motivations concentrated as never before on the urban environment as a matter of ecclesiastical concern. Strong was probably more influential than any other individual of his generation in making churches aware of new conditions and of Christianity's responsibility to alleviate them. He held that the teachings of Jesus had been oriented around an ideal society, "the Kingdom," which had tangible dimensions as a concrete possibility for the present age. Churches existed to extend such a kingdom, generating concern for human welfare and solving civic problems for a higher good. Reformist doctrine in Strong combined with a sense of national destiny based on racism. He thought that God was training Anglo-Saxons for final competition with other races. America in his view was representative of the largest liberty, purest religion, and highest civilization, chosen to benefit less vigorous peoples by imposing its free institutions on them.

Practical action to meet genuine needs raised Strong's version of the Social Gospel above the level of simply publicizing well-turned phrases. He was a pioneer in analyzing social problems and the unprecedented role churches had to play in meeting modern obligations. But more important than foresight, he labored to persuade churches that the magnitude of common dilemmas required unified action. He saw the need for an overarching federation of churches, beyond the jealousies of denominational competition, to facilitate concerted activity. His concrete programs gave appreciable structure to uncoordinated impulses for social service. After 1886 he tried for twelve years to make the Evangelical Alliance into an agency for practical cooperation, but it proved too conservative. In 1898 he organized the League (later, American Institute) for Social Service as a prototype of interdenominational activity. These moves were not comprehensive enough; so he participated wholeheartedly in forming the Federal Council of Churches in 1908. He inaugurated the "Safety First" movement as a method of protecting personal welfare in industry. In this and a number of other definite ways, he broke new ground in America for Christian unity on a practical level.

Bibliography:

A.   *Our Country: Its Possible Future and Its Present Crisis* (New York, 1885; Cambridge, MA, 1963); *The New Era, or The Coming Kingdom* (New York, 1893); *Religious Movements for Social Betterment* (New York, 1900); *The Next Great Awakening* (New York, 1902); *The Challenge of the City* (New York, 1907); *My Religion in Every-Day Life* (New York, 1910).

B.   SH 11, 115; NCAB 9, 416–17; DAB 18, 150–51; NYT 29 Apr 1916, 11.

STUART, George Hay (2 April 1816, County Down, Ireland—11 April 1890, Philadelphia, PA).

Born in a farmhouse twenty miles from Belfast and emigrating to America at the age of fifteen, young Stuart moved directly into business without the advantages of formal education. In a short time he succeeded well enough in banking and dry goods imports to devote most of his time to a multitude of philanthropic endeavors. He helped launch YMCA activities in Philadelphia (1854), and they provided the basis for what he considered in retrospect the most important work of his life. Shortly after the Civil War began, it became apparent that Union soldiers needed more attention than government services could provide. From November, 1861, through December, 1865, Stuart presided over the U.S. Christian Commission, a voluntary body which coordinated a remarkable amount of activity on behalf of those serving in uniform. Under his energetic direction, more than six million dollars were collected and 5,000 volunteers participated without pay in the Commission's programs at camps, hospitals, or battlefields. Reading material was a primary concern: 1.5 million Bibles, 9 million books, and 30 million tracts were distributed in an attempt to keep the gospel alive in wartime. Additional aid to army surgeons and chaplains took many forms. Stuart's executive ability helped solve complex problems while his earnest concern for souls won warm responses wherever he traveled to raise funds or recruit personnel. It was largely due to his efforts that unnumbered conversions occurred in prayer-tents, denominations saw the value of cooperative action on common problems, and laymen were encouraged to demonstrate a Christian witness as they rarely had been before.

Decades of work with the YMCA was only one of many outlets Stuart found to express his deep interest in the practical exercise of religion. He served (1836–61) as superintendent of Sunday Schools at the First Reformed Presbyterian Church in Philadelphia, receiving ordination as ruling elder in that denomination in 1842. As a member of national boards for temperance unions, foreign missions, and Bible distribution, he served with great assiduity. He traveled to Europe ten times for business reasons, improving each occasion by attending sessions of the Evangelical Alliance, Free Church assemblies, and international committees of the YMCA. As early as 1860 he had become friends with *Dwight L. Moody. He helped several times to make arrangements for the evangelist's visits to Philadelphia, and after seeing the immense crowds of 1875 he threw himself increasingly into the cause of urban revivalism. Several times he declined offers to become a Cabinet member in President Grant's administration, but in 1869 he accepted appointment on the Board of Indian Commissioners. As chairman of its purchasing committee, he worked against corruption in supplying reservations and campaigned extensively for fairer treatment of the American red man. Whether his actions were occasioned by emergencies calling for relief or long-standing needs to be met by missionary outreach, his benevolent response did not falter over a half century's duration.

Bibliography:

A. *The Life of George H. Stuart, written by Himself* (Philadelphia, 1890).

B. SH 11, 116; NYT 12 Apr 1890, 2.

STUART, Moses (26 March 1780, Wilton, CT—4 January 1852, Andover, MA). *Education*: B.A., Yale Coll., 1799; studied law in Newtown, CT, 1801–02. *Career*: schoolteacher, North Fairfield, CT, 1799–1800; tutor, Yale Coll., 1802–04; supply preacher, 1804–06; minister, First Congregational Church, New Haven, CT, 1806–10; professor of Sacred Literature, Andover Sem., 1810–48; retirement, 1848–52.

Though he was admitted to the Connecticut bar in 1802, Stuart decided to accept a tutoring position at Yale instead. There he came under the evangelistic influence of president *Timothy Dwight, joined the church within a year and prepared for the ministry with Dwight's supervisory assistance. As spokesman for conservative Calvinistic theology in New Haven, he attracted the notice and friendship of *Jedidiah Morse, to whose militantly orthodox *Panoplist* he contributed several articles. Notoriety in the Boston area led to appointment as professor of Bible at Andover Seminary. It seems that sound creedalism was more a consideration than ability in choosing him, because at this point Stuart knew hardly any Hebrew. Once in the chair, however, he exerted himself mightily to overcome linguistic deficiencies. He compiled a short grammar by 1813 for student use and in 1821 imported a font of special type to print the first Hebrew grammar produced on this side of the Atlantic. German scholarship was another genre recognized as essential for mastery of his field, so without instruction he acquired knowledge of the materials which had revolutionized biblical studies. After years of effort he was acknowledged as America's most distinguished philologist and grammarian. This was accomplishment enough, but on a more comprehensive level he determined to reconcile the new methods of biblical research with traditional theological tenets.

Over the course of almost four decades Stuart lectured to 1,500 ministerial students, seventy of whom became professors or college presidents. All his instructional work was predicated on the conviction that the Bible contained the Word of God in a consistent, unitive fashion. A firm belief in the doctrine of inspiration, plenary but not verbal, preceded and directed all his studies. It was the subject matter found in historical texts which interested him, not variant expressions translated or interpreted through changing idioms. Biblical criticism was a welcome tool because it allowed scholars to discover the original sense of scriptural passages and therefore recover divine truth. Avoiding some of the greatest problems raised by German criticism, he considered it sufficient for proving the inspiration of a document simply to establish its canonical authenticity and the historical genuineness of its author. Exegesis for Stuart on those assumptions rose to the level of attempting to understand the earliest meaning of biblical statements, an exercise which rescued his students from proof-text theologizing. But all his efforts to found an American school of orthodox biblical scholarship met with little success. His conservative friends found pulpit rhetoric to be more effective than classroom exercises in resisting the spread of liberal views. And too, by the time of his death, social issues had eclipsed intellectual categories among many who sought to express vital religion in relevant terms.

Bibliography:

A.   *Letters to the Rev. Wm. E. Channing* (Andover, 1819); *A Hebrew Grammar* (Andover, 1821); *A Commentary on the Epistle to the Hebrews*, 2 vols. (Andover, 1827–28); *Hints on the Interpretation of Prophecy* (Andover, 1842); *A Critical History and Defense of the Old Testament Canon* (Andover, 1845); *A Commentary on the Book of Daniel* (Boston, 1850).

B.   AAP 2, 475–81; SH 11, 116–17; NCAB 6, 244–45; DAB 18, 174–75; John H. Giltner, *Moses Stuart: The Father of Biblical Science in America* (Atlanta, 1988).

SUNDAY, William Ashley (19 November 1862, Ames, IA—6 November 1935, Chicago, IL). *Career*: undertaker's assistant and furniture salesman, 1880–83; professional baseball player, 1883–91; assistant secretary of YMCA, Chicago, 1891–93; assistant revivalist for *J. Wilbur Chapman, 1893–95; independent revivalist, 1896–1935.

"Billy" Sunday was the most flamboyant of urban revivalists during their heyday in the first decades of the twentieth century. While still a ballplayer he grew serious about Christian witnessing and accepted limited teaching responsibilities at Chicago's YMCA. He moved slowly toward evangelistic preaching as a vocation, starting on his own in small Iowa towns and then with his choir leader, Homer A. Rodeheaver, moving on to the tents and tabernacles of larger cities. In 1903 he was ordained as a Presbyterian minister. Sunday had a talent for dramatization, and his magnetic personality which blended sensational speech with theatrical gestures kept audiences spellbound. His salty, idiomatic language made it easy for common folk to empathize with him. An explosive style that could soothe or blister with slang expressions as occasion demanded was the basic ingredient of his wide popular appeal. Decorous critics naturally thought Sunday's antics were too bizarre, but such methods induced thousands to declare themselves converts. The weight of numbers muffled argument about the evangelist's methods or the content of his message.

Beginning with a simple appeal for all to accept the free gift of personal salvation, by 1902 Sunday also turned his attention to the spiritual and cultural fiber of the nation. He denounced a number of evils that blurred the lines of private and public responsibility, but his remedy stirred the passions of a generation with agrarian roots and did not resemble either the Social Gospel or Progressive politics. He remained innocent of theological complexities, offering only moral regeneration as the primary solution to social problems like economic maladjustment, political corruption, urban crime, or social and religious radicals. The liquor interests were a favorite target, and after 1905 his "Booze Sermon" became famous as an appeal to support Prohibition. Sunday also embodied the widespread prejudice about Black Americans, holding them to be spiritual but not social equals. He blamed many problems on immigrant ''Reds'' and wanted to deport all such agitators. These and other convictions were incidental in keeping with those of the Ku Klux Klan, a grassroots movement of nativists whose support he accepted. Making a close identification with Protestant churches and Americanism, he declared that this was not a country for dissenters to live in. The peak years of Sunday's immense drawing power were 1912–17. During wartime his superpatriotic utterances helped fan the flames of that enthusiasm also. He continued thereafter to accept invitations to preach, but failing health and personal sadness in family matters caused a slow decline in labors that extended over forty years.

Bibliography:

A. *Great Love Stories of the Bible* (New York, 1917).
B. NCAB A, 123; DAB 21, 679; NCE 13, 797; NYT 7 Nov 1935, 1; Theodore T. Frankenberg, *The Spectacular Career of Rev. Billy Sunday* (Columbus, OH, 1913); Elijah P. Brown, *The Real Billy Sunday* (New York, 1914); William T. Ellis, *Billy Sunday: The Man and His Message* (Philadelphia, 1914); William G. McLoughlin, *Billy Sunday Was His Real Name* (Chicago, 1955); Lyle W. Dorsett, *Billy Sunday and the Redemption of Urban America* (Grand Rapids, MI, 1991).

SUZUKI, Daisetz Teitaro (18 October 1870, Kanazawa, Japan—12 July 1966, Kamakura, Japan). *Education*: studied at Ishikawa Coll., 1888–89; studied at Imperial Univ., Tokyo, 1891–92. *Career*: schoolteacher, 1889–91; novice in Buddhist monastery, Kamakura, 1892–97; translator for Open Court Press, Chicago, IL, 1897–1909; lecturer in English, Imperial Univ., Tokyo, 1909–14; at various ranks, professor of English, Imperial Univ., Tokyo, 1909–21; professor of English and Buddhist Philosophy, Otani Univ., Kyoto, 1921–40; active retirement, 1940–66.

A gift for languages enabled Suzuki to communicate with individuals in many cultures and religions other than his own. Throughout his long, influential life he combined linguistic facility with spiritual insight to become the foremost interpreter of Zen Buddhism to the western world. As early as 1893 he translated into English a speech which his abbot delivered at the World's Parliament of Religions in Chicago. Four years later he left his novitiate for work in that same city at the firm established by *Paul Carus. For eleven years he helped produce western copies of Pali, Sanskrit, Chinese, and Japanese manuscripts, enriching the quality of scholarship as well as contributing to greater awareness of oriental religious forms. After 1909 he made his home in Japan but pursued a remarkably active round of visiting lectureships; especially during the 1950s he addressed classes at numerous universities in Europe and the United States, receiving unchallenged recognition as chief spokesman for Buddhist principles in the western hemisphere. In a tremendous literary output, he surveyed wide vistas of Mahayana Buddhism in general and from that perspective discussed many facets of Japanese culture. Countless western students have been led to further inquiry in the field of Asian studies because of his stimulating introduction to the life and thought found there. But it was primarily as an interpreter of the enigma called Zen that he served non-Buddhists with unprecedented clarity.

Writing from both intellectual comprehension and personal experience, Suzuki tried to convey the sense of an orientation which lies basically outside the scope of conventional rationality. On one level he made more understandable features of Chinese and Japanese wisdom schools in operation since the sixth century. Their dialogues (mondo) and riddles (koan) had afforded few insights into deeper meanings until Suzuki, as apostle to the west, supplied them. On another level he recommended Zen as a viable option, one in which enlightenment, or satori, provided an orientation for full harmony and the embodiment of truth. He taught followers to avoid the extremes of quietism and aggression in mind and body. After self-assertive efforts were brought to a standstill (through various means according to different schools), Zen practitioners could reach a sense of "passive activity" transcending all opposites and synthesizing them into a higher conception of reality. In this manner persons could find release from sensual or intellectual attachment to earthly things. They could identify with the cosmos and live in harmony with nature instead of withdrawing from it. "The mind that has no abode" is a synonym for satori, and its chief advocate defended such a perspective because it preserved the completeness of each person's spiritual vitality. All his books pointed to something beyond conscious ideas, to a realm where he was convinced Truth existed undefiled and entire.

Bibliography:

A. *Essays in Zen Buddhism*, 3 vols. (London, 1927–34); *The Training of the Zen Buddhist Monk* (Kyoto, Japan, 1934); *Manual of Zen Buddhism* (Kyoto, Japan, 1935); *The Essence of Buddhism* (London, 1947); *Studies in Zen* (London, 1955); *Mysticism: Christian and Buddhist* (New York, 1957).

B. NYT 12 July 1966, 43; A. Irwin Switzer, *D. T. Suzuki: A Biography* (London, 1985).

SWEET, William Warren (15 February 1881, Baldwin, KS—3 January 1959, Dallas, TX). *Education*: B.A., Ohio Wesleyan Univ., 1902; B.D., Drew Sem., 1906; Ph.D., Univ. of Pennsylvania, 1912. *Career*: minister, Willow Grove, PA, 1906–08; minister, Langhorne, PA, 1908–11; instructor, Ohio Wesleyan Univ., 1911–13; professor of History, DePauw Univ., 1913–27; professor of American Christianity, Univ. of Chicago, 1927–46; active retirement, 1946–59.

For more than a generation after 1900 the American frontier was a dominant theme among historical students, and Sweet emphasized its central place in defining characteristics of this country's churches. His writings, which spanned more than thirty years, were sustained by the general conviction that frontier Christianity had winnowed the unsuitable and rewarded the pragmatic. Such adaptability made some denominations (including his own, Methodism) the largest and most influential forces in extending religion throughout the new nation.

By using quantifiable standards in historical interpretation, Sweet reasoned that successful frontier churches were also qualitatively the best, contributing essentials to the current profile of American religious values. He furthered interest in this theme after moving to the University of Chicago, the institution which created the first professorship, concentrating exclusively on American Christianity. Educators before him had begun the process of collecting primary sources, but Sweet excelled in that activity. He made Chicago the largest single repository of frontier records and published (1931–46) large volumes of documents pertinent to the four most active denominations. Lectures at dozens of colleges together with his advising scores of doctoral candidates did much to make the frontier theme a strong influence in his own day. His twenty-seven books have affected countless readers seeking to understand both timeless and locally conditioned elements of their religious heritage.

American Christianity for Sweet had distinctive contours born of its frontier experience. One product of that environment was a concern for social ethics. Morality in the wilderness was loose, and churches were faced with the necessity of upholding standards for new communities. He concluded that the strongest support for social reforms in temperance, abolition, and the Social Gospel came from groups successful in coping with the frontier. Similarly, their circumstances were largely responsible for the modern missionary impulse which found its chief outlet in revivalism. Techniques were developed to reach westering peoples, and consequent preferences for practical, personal elements eclipsed an emphasis on doctrinal, institutional forms. Theology gave way to activism, meeting religious needs for a society in motion. Sweet also thought that religious freedom developed beyond the seaboard; independence in voluntary associations had a corollary in mutual tolerance and ecumenical cooperation, an aspect judged to be America's greatest contribution to religious practice. In the light of subsequent historical investigation, Sweet's reliance on frontier experience was too great. But in his own day he used it as a metaphysical basis to defend moral values which he thought contemporary society threatened to destroy.

Bibliography:

A. *The Story of Religion in America* (New York, 1930, and subsequent editions); *Methodism in American History* (New York, 1933); *Men of Zeal* (New York, 1935); *Makers of Christianity: From John Cotton to Lyman Abbott* (New York, 1937); *The American Churches: An Interpretation* (New York, 1948); *American Culture and Religion: Six Essays* (Dallas, 1951).

B. NYT 5 Jan 1959, 29; James L. Ash, Jr., *Protestantism and the American University: An Intellectual Biography of William Warren Sweet* (Dallas, 1982).

SWING, David (23 August 1830, Cincinnati, OH—3 October 1894, Chicago, IL). *Education*: B.A., Miami Univ. (OH), 1852; studied theology with Nathan L. Rice, Cincinnati, 1852–53. *Career*: instructor in Greek and Latin, Miami Univ., 1853–66; minister, Fourth Presbyterian Church (Westminster until 1869), Chicago, 1866–75; editor, *The Alliance*, 1873–82; editor, *The Weekly Magazine*, 1883–85; minister, Central Church, Chicago, 1875–94.

As classics professor in a small college, Swing performed additional lay ministry by preaching in local churches. The liberal spirit of his sermons attracted wide notice and led to a pastorate in Chicago where he charmed audiences with emphasis on human experience rather than the metaphysical distinctions of formal theology. Possessed of an artistic cast of mind, he delivered addresses which stressed God's goodness and man's possibilities, basing his ideas not on exegesis or exhortation but on an optimistic endorsement of personal liberty. In 1874 *Francis L. Patton, theologian at McCormick Seminary brought formal charges of heresy against the poetic urban preacher. In his search for broader doctrinal ground outside orthodox formulations, Swing had, it was asserted, violated creedal standards set down in the Westminster Confession. His ethical enthusiasm about practical Christian living paid insufficient notice to original sin, the substitutionary theory of atonement, and endless punishment for the damned. The defendant answered each of the charges, though personally indisposed to argue about them, and successfully justified himself in the local Presbytery. After acquittal, it became clear that strict legalists were going to appeal the case; so Swing quietly left the denomination and yielded up his church within a year. Leading citizens of the city rallied around their "professor," a title retained throughout the time he was a fixture in Chicago. Rented theaters and then the Central Music Hall (1880) provided settings where he preached to thousands each Sunday, influencing many others by means of printed sermons in weekly journals. His optimistic liberalism brought invitations to speak in every state including the territory of Alaska. For decades the humanitarian religion he embodied increased the appeal of Protestant moralism. Popular response to it indicated the increasing need for greater adjustment of traditional symbols to contemporary settings.

Bibliography:

A.   *Truths for To-Day*, 2 vols. (Chicago, 1874–76); *Motives of Life* (Chicago, 1879); *Club Essays* (Chicago, 1881); *Old Pictures of Life*, 2 vols. (Chicago, 1894); *Thoughts that will Live*, 2 vols. (Chicago, 1895); *The Message of David Swing to his Generation* (New York, 1913).

B.   SH 11, 190; NCAB 3, 16; DAB 18, 251–52; NYT 4 Oct 1894, 3; Helen S. Starring (ed.), *David Swing: A Memorial Volume* (Chicago, 1894); Joseph F. Newton, *David Swing: Poet-Preacher* (Chicago, 1909).

SZOLD, Henrietta (21 December 1860, Baltimore, MD—13 February 1945, Jerusalem, Palestine). *Career*: teacher in private schools, Baltimore, 1877–92; editor, Jewish Publication Society, 1893–1916; secretary, Federation of American Zionists, 1910–26; president, Hadassah Women's Zionist Organization of America, 1912–26; honorary president, Hadassah, 1926–45.

The eldest child and spiritual heir of a rabbi recently arrived from Hungary, Szold grew up in an environment which cultivated learning in a wide variety of topics. While still in her teens she began writing for Anglo-Jewish newspapers;

her articles on travel, drama, Hebrew literature, and history showed an early interest in preserving the heritage of Judaism. By 1889 such interests took a practical turn, when she helped found an evening school for immigrants pouring into America because of Russian pogroms. From those pupils of all ages she learned about the depths of European anti-Semitism and the hopes some nourished for eventual restoration in a state of Israel. Four years later she joined Hebras Zion, probably the first Zionist society organized on this continent. That same year (1893) she became editor for the Jewish Publication Society through which she issued books to preserve and revitalize Jewish heritage. Toward that same objective she contributed (1901–06) articles for the *Jewish Encyclopedia* and edited (1904–08) the *American Jewish Year Book*. After joining the Federation of American Zionists in 1897 (on executive committee after 1899), she contributed speeches and articles to keep alive the hope of establishing a safe refuge for world Jewry. She served as secretary for the federation after 1910 (gratis until 1916), but then by 1920 gradually began spending more time in Palestine where needs were most pressing.

After a trip to the Near-East in 1909, Szold became more thoroughly involved than ever in supporting humanitarian programs there. In 1912 she founded and was first president of Hadassah, a women's organization of various titles which through the years made tremendous contributions to Jewish welfare. The core of Hadassah activity was medical service; the American Zionist Medical Unit supervised doctors, nurses, dentists, nutritionists, and sanitation experts as they brought a modicum of attention to woefully neglected conditions. Szold was indefatigable in her support of such work, either raising funds or directing operations in the field, and by so doing she made the future of Israel a prime concern for thousands of American Jewish women. After 1927 she was elected to the Palestine Zionist Executive and made responsible for health and educational programs in all settlements. Questions of hygiene, juvenile delinquency, hospitals, and vocational schools were dealt with in her department; tangible aid from the American Hadassah helped achieve her goals in social service projects. Again with Hadassah sponsorship, she directed the Youth Aliyah which rescued some 30,000 young Jews from Germany and Poland between 1933 and 1948. Her realism struck some Zionists as too timid while her stubborn pacifism frustrated more belligerent activists who could not envision a bi-national future for Israel. Still her selfless concern to care for refugees was a basic element in strengthening Jewish cohesiveness in two hemispheres.

Bibliography:

B.   DAB 23, 756–58; UJE 10, 147–48; EJ 15, 665–68; NAW 3, 417–20; NYT 14 Feb 1945, 19; Marvin Lowenthal, *Henrietta Szold: Life and Letters* (New York, 1942); Elma E. Levinger, *Fighting Angel* (New York, 1946); Rose Zeitlin, *Henrietta Szold: Record of a Life* (New York, 1952); Irving Fineman, *Woman of Valor* (New York, 1961).

T

TALBOT, John (1645, Wymondham, England—29 November 1727, Burlington, NJ). *Education*: B.A., Christ's Coll., Cambridge Univ., 1663; Fellow of Peterhouse, 1664–68; M.A., Christ's Coll., Cambridge Univ., 1671. *Career*: rector, Icklingham, Suffolk, 1673–89; rector, Fretherne, Gloucester, 1695–1701; missionary agent for the Society for the Propagation of the Gospel (SPG) in American colonies, 1702–24.

Little is known of Talbot's early life except the bare notations of rectorship in English villages. In 1701 he was chaplain aboard the ship *Centurion* when Quaker-turned-Anglican *George Keith took passage for a missionary tour of the colonies. Talbot was so impressed by opportunities open for him in the New World, he accompanied Keith for two years as one of the earliest agents of the Society for the Propagation of the Gospel (SPG). By 1704 he settled at St. Mary's Church in Burlington, New Jersey, preferring the steady habits of pastor to those of religious controversialist in which Keith excelled. From Burlington he made frequent journeys into Pennsylvania as well as the Jerseys, proving to be an able preacher who helped sustain small groups of Anglican believers almost singlehandedly. An ardent supporter of episcopacy, Talbot worked for twenty years to have a resident bishop appointed on this side of the Atlantic. His high church views (also the suspicion that he sympathized with the deposed house of Stuart) made him unpopular in some quarters, but he persisted in calling for at least a suffragan to direct American missions. During a trip to England (1720–22) he seems to have been consecrated by Nonjuring bishops to the episcopal office, but he never openly exercised such power upon returning. The SPG discharged him for insubordinate conduct, though he protested his innocence and continued priestly functions until he died. On this sketchy evidence it could be said that Talbot was an irregular predecessor of *Samuel Seabury.

Bibliography:

B.   AAP 5, 30–33; NCAB 3, 460; DAB 18, 278–80; Edgar L. Pennington, *Apostle of New Jersey: John Talbot, 1645–1727* (Philadelphia, 1938).

TALMAGE, Thomas DeWitt (7 January 1832, near Bound Brook, NJ—12 April 1902, Washington, DC). *Education*: studied at Univ. of the City of New York, 1850–53; graduated from New Brunswick Sem., (NJ), 1856. *Career*: minister of Dutch Reformed churches in Belleville, NJ, 1856–59, Syracuse, NY, 1859–62, Philadelphia, PA, 1862–69; minister of Presbyterian churches in Brooklyn, NY, 1869–95, Washington, DC, 1895–99; editor, *Frank Leslie's Sunday Magazine*, 1881–89, *Christian Herald*, 1890–1902.

Through a succession of large pastorates, Talmage became one of the most famous public speakers in his generation. Churches prospered under his ministry in the sense that they drew crowds and completed ambitious building programs with income resulting from increased attendance. In Brooklyn, particularly, Talmage was known as a leading clergyman in the city. When his church was destroyed by fire (1872, 1889, and a third time in 1894), immense popular response yielded funds to rebuild the fashionable Tabernacle. By 1891 audiences sometimes exceeded seven thousand, said at the time to be the largest Protestant church in the world. Weekly sermons were widely published in Europe and America for thirty years; at the height of his fame they were carried by a syndicate with outlets in over 3,500 newspapers. He was also ranked among the most successful lecturers of modern times, criss-crossing the nation repeatedly to fill lucrative speaking engagements. Whether he spoke in opera houses, city squares, hotels, or from an open carriage, Talmage drew throngs of people and impressed them with simple messages couched in direct, arresting language. He was fêted in every city, moving easily among the rich and powerful in the upper echelons of society. His magnetic personality had a glamor about it which made contagious an enthusiasm for topics discussed with great artistry.

Both the style and content of Talmage's discourses help account for their positive reception. His delivery was not overly theatrical, but it included enough vivid metaphors and startling gestures to hold listeners spellbound by what was known locally as "Talmagic." As early as 1879 some envious colleagues in the Brooklyn Presbytery accused him of improper preaching methods that threatened to bring religion into contempt. He was narrowly acquitted. From week to week, the principal focus of sermons was not doctrine but a topic of current interest to which he could add an evangelical word. One indication of this approach is that he chose his subject and then found a Bible passage fitting the theme. Talmage had no reluctance to deliver opinions on everything from the Johnstown flood (1888) to electrocution as a means of capital punishment. His ideas usually corresponded to those of a wide cross-section of the populace, another factor enhancing popularity. He had no appreciation of biblical criticism, for example, and spoke the mind of many when he asked why it was necessary to question scriptures which he found perfectly satisfactory. He often brushed aside hard theological issues with a cheerful generality, pleasing to the ear but lessening the doctrinal integrity of Protestantism in industrial America. Still, millions found Talmage attractive, and he pursued an energetic pace without slowing until death came with little warning.

Bibliography:

    A.   *The Abominations of Modern Society* (New York, 1872); *The Marriage Ring: A Series of Discourses* (New York, 1886); *From Manger to Throne: A New Life of Jesus and a History of Palestine* (Philadelphia, 1890); 500 *Selected Sermons*, 20 vols. (New York, 1900); *T. DeWitt Talmage as I Knew Him* (New York, 1912).
    B.   SH 11, 254–55; NCAB 4, 26–27; DAB 18, 287–88; NYT 13 Apr 1902, 7; John Rusk, *The Authentic Life of T. DeWitt Talmage* (Chicago, 1902); Charles F. Adams, *The Life and Sermons of Rev. T. DeWitt Talmage* (Chicago, 1902); Charles E. Banks, *Authorized and Authentic Life and Works of T. DeWitt Talmage* (Chicago, 1902).

TANNER, Benjamin Tucker (25 December 1835, Pittsburgh, PA—15 January 1923, Philadelphia, PA). *Education*: studied at Avery Coll., 1852–57; studied at Western Sem. (PA), 1857–60. *Career*: assistant minister, Presbyterian church, Washington, DC, 1860–61; minister, Alexander mission, Washington, DC, 1862–63; minister, African Methodist Episcopal (AME) Church, Washington, DC, 1863–66; minister, AME Church, Baltimore, MD, 1866–67; principal, AME school, Frederick, MD, 1867–68; editor, *The Christian Recorder*, 1868–84; editor, *AME Church Review*, 1884–88; bishop, AME Church, 1888–1908; retirement, 1908–23.

While Tanner was at college, supporting himself by working part-time as a barber, he converted to Methodism and received a license to preach. After several pastorates, including one short stint among Presbyterians when no other position was available in the Negro community, he began to make a name for himself as a man of letters. His first book on the aim and purpose of African Methodist polity attracted wide notice for its solid scholarship as well as for its literary merit. In the role of editor for two denominational journals, he administered affairs judiciously and built up an appreciable general readership through terse, forceful writing. Recognizing the need for a journal of high intellectual quality, he helped establish the *Church Review*, a quarterly which quickly became one of the leading periodicals in the country. Tanner also participated actively in the structural proceedings of his denomination, serving often as secretary of the General Conference and preaching before annual conferences as opportunity allowed. A strong supporter of the Book Concern, he helped enlarge its scope to supervise all church publications while he was executive officer in 1872. Another mark of the esteem in which fellow clergymen held him is the fact that he represented African Methodist Episcopal (AME) constituents as a fraternal delegate at conferences of the regular Methodist church.

In his first quadrennial assignment as a bishop, Tanner supervised AME activities in Canada, Bermuda, and the West Indies. Later appointments placed him in the northeastern United States where he continued diligent visitations. His exhortations to the faithful stressed loyalty to the church because of beneficial strength derived from it. After reminding black Americans of their slave origins and of the contemporary experience of discrimination, he pointed out that it was only Christian truth which made them truly free. The church was God's instrument to accomplish good, and as members of that church black people had the power to overcome human suffering. In that exalted sense, Bishop Tanner was an advocate of black unit and self-help. He also took the lead in more practical matters related to other churches. In 1901 he attended and presented a paper at the Third Ecumenical Methodist Conference in London. As early as 1892 he had been cooperating with bishop *Henry M. Turner in attempts to unite major black churches. In 1908 he attended the first "Tri-Council of Colored Methodist Bishops," comprising officials from the Colored ME Church, AME Zion, and his own AME organization. In this setting they found it possible to coordinate activities regarding common liturgies, hymnals, and catechisms together with an overall concern for the social condition of black citizens. Tanner was unsuccessful in securing organic union of the three churches, but his work furthered their distinctive status in the religious pluralism of twentieth century America.

Bibliography:

A.   *An Apology for African Methodism* (Baltimore, 1867); *The Negro's Origin, or Is He Cursed of God?* (Philadelphia, 1869); *An Outline of Our History and Government for African Methodist Churchmen* (Philadelphia, 1884); *Theological Lectures* (Nashville, 1894).
B.   SH 11, 272; NCAB 3, 89; DAB 18, 296; NYT 16 Jan 1923, 21.

TAPPAN, Arthur (22 May 1786, Northampton, MA—23 July 1865, New Haven, CT).

Clerking in a hardware and drygoods store at the age of fifteen launched Tappan on a successful mercantile career. After conducting import businesses in Maine and Montreal, he settled in New York (1826) as a wholesale jobber of silk. Wealth accumulated from that enterprise made it possible to exhibit responsible stewardship through a number of benevolent activities. Together with his brother, *Lewis, Tappan was typical of wealthy laymen who used resources to aid philanthropic causes in the early national period. Humanitarian reforms such as those opposing Sabbath violations, liquor, tobacco, and vice found in him a steady supporter. He was also generous with time as well as money in societies sponsoring Sunday schools, home missions, the distribution of Bibles and tracts. Voluntary benevolence became a natural ally of revivalism, and when *Charles G. Finney came to New York, Tappan helped finance his ministry. Construction of the Broadway Tabernacle was also partly the doing of this Presbyterian layman. Since philanthrophy found expression through support for education too, Kenyon College, Auburn Seminary, Andover, and Yale were beneficiaries of his stewardship. He persuaded *Lyman Beecher to become president of Lane Seminary with promises of financial aid, but after 1834 that income was concentrated more heavily at Oberlin College. All these activities were evidence of a concern to use the means at his disposal in support of good morals for personal and public improvement.

Of all the humanitarian causes for which Tappan spent himself, none was more important than antislavery. He expressed mild interest in colonization but by 1833 came to see that it was not sufficient for ending slavery altogether. Within that year he became president of the New York chapter and then the national assembly of abolitionists known as the American Anti-Slavery Society. He urged, in the *Emancipator*, which he helped establish, that the process of emancipation must begin without delay. Though he expected gradual abolition, such ideas were widely viewed as radical and subversive at the time. In 1834 a riotous mob broke up his antislavery convention, going beyond that to ransack both store and home of the presumably fanatical Tappan brothers. Yet they were resolute in the face of gangster tactics and defied threats with an austere moralism blind to danger. By 1840 Arthur proved in another way how vital his role was in the growth of antislavery. He broke with abolitionist William L. Garrison because he thought association with ancillary movements such as women's rights would lessen chances of gaining the primary objective. So he formed the American and Foreign Anti-Slavery Society together with another journal, the *Reporter*, as an agency exclusively for black freedom. Six years later he organized a larger group, the American Missionary Association, to absorb reformist impulses from other societies refusing to take an abolitionist stand. As an executive officer from 1846 until his death, Tappan helped direct the manifold projects of that bureau, seeking practical application of religious precepts for the benefit of society.

Bibliography:

B.   NCAB 2, 320–21; DAB 18, 298–300; Lewis Tappan, *The Life of Arthur Tappan* (New York, 1870); Rebecca J. Winter, *The Night Cometh: Two Wealthy Evangelicals Face the Nation* (South Pasadena, CA, 1977).

TAPPAN, Lewis (23 May 1788, Northampton, MA—21 June 1873, Brooklyn, NY). *Career*: hardware merchant, Boston, 1813–28; silk merchant, New York, 1828–41; commercial-credit rating agent, New York, 1841–49; active retirement, 1849–73.

As early as his Boston days, Tappan busied himself with doing good in local charities while striving to do well in manufacturing and textile speculation. For several years he toyed with Unitarianism but soon reverted to a dynamic Calvinism often seen among middle class reformers of ante bellum America. Joined with his brother *Arthur in business, he also followed his lead in supporting benevolent associations which sought to guide the general advance of civilization through proper religious influences. But mild philanthropy or the distribution of Bibles and tracts did not seem effective enough while one-sixth of the American population was thought to be a marketable commodity. In 1833 both brothers helped establish the first national antislavery society; then in 1840 after a break with William L. Garrison, they began another organization exclusively devoted to Negro emancipation. Arthur usually led the way, but it was Lewis who persevered, serving as treasurer and policy maker of many enterprises. For decades he raised funds, conducted a prodigious correspondence, wrote pamphlets, edited various journals, organized annual conventions, paid bills, and subsidized missionaries. By 1846 he moved to more constructive means of elevating Blacks, founding in that year the American Missionary Association to provide tangible helps for educating freedmen. Serving as a director without salary he worked behind the scenes, attending to all the details that made for efficient, successful operations. In addition to donating much of the monetary assistance out of his own pocket, he sustained a broad vision of social renovation as an extension of religious revival. His efforts were largely confined to prewar years when Christian laymen made heavy contributions to the evangelical war on slavery.

Bibliography:

A.   *The Life of Arthur Tappan* (New York, 1870); *A Side-Light on Anglo-American Relations*, ed. Annie H. Abel and Frank J. Klingberg (Lancaster, PA, 1927).

B.   NCAB 2, 321; DAB 18, 303–04; NYT 23 Jun 1873, 5; Bertram Wyatt-Brown, *Lewis Tappan and the Evangelical War against Slavery* (Cleveland, OH, 1969).

TAYLOR, George Braxton (25 April 1860, Staunton, VA—9 March 1942, Roanoke, VA). *Education*: B.A., Richmond Coll., 1881; B.D., Southern Baptist Theol. Sem. 1886. *Career*: Baptist minister, Fairmont, Mt. Shiloh, and Mt. Plain, VA, 1886–87; Baptist minister, Chapel Hill, NC, 1887–89; associate minister, First Baptist Church, Baltimore, MD, 1889–91; minister, First Baptist Church, Macon, GA, 1891–94; Baptist minister, Liberty and Hebron, VA, 1894–1903; Baptist minister, Enon and Troutville, VA, 1903–40; professor of English Bible, Hollins Coll., 1903–28; chaplain, Hollins Coll., 1903–33; professor emeritus, 1933–42.

Descended from illustrious and dutiful ancestors on both sides of the family, Taylor provides a model example of Baptist minister, educator, and civic-minded patriot. He was ordained in 1886 and served in a great number of churches, most of them in Virginia, adding duties of chaplain and biblical professor toward the end of his career. Taylor was trustee of the University of Richmond and the Southern Baptist Theological Seminary, his old schools, as well as a Baptist orphanage. He moderated the Appomattox Baptist Association and then the Valley Baptist Association. Between 1911 and 1916 he was a member of the Judson Centennial Committee of the Southern Baptist Convention and for years presided over the Virginia Baptist Historical Society. The solemn preservation of historical tradition always interested him, and he labored for a score of committees including that which commemorated the bicentennial of George

Washington's birth. Such a heritage prepared for an anticipated future as well, and in this regard he functioned as delegate to two Baptist World Alliances, in London (1905) and in Berlin (1934).

The ministry of this representative figure spanned more than fifty-five years, but quite early in its course Taylor took a step that eventually became one of his most significant achievements. In 1886 he organized the first Sunbeam Missionary Society, a focal point for children under nine years of age and a means of firing their interest in missions. The young pastor began by sharing his own family's experience in Europe, but the format soon spread quickly to other topics and other churches. It became a source of information about all missionary efforts. By the turn of this century the Women's Missionary Union adopted the Sunbeams and regulated its organization and procedures. Their goal was to create a unit in every church and to set financial goals for contributions to home and foreign missions. As a result schools and churches were built in China and Cuba, the gift of Sunbeams who numbered in their thousands. Taylor supported the growth of his brainchild, writing a column for the *Foreign Mission Journal* with the pen name, ''Cousin George.'' His varied and steady endeavors laid important foundations for education among young people in Baptist churches throughout the South and beyond.

Bibliography:

A. *Virginian Baptist Ministers* 6 vols. (Lynchburg, VA, 1859–1935); *The Life and Letters of Rev. George Boardman Taylor, D.D.* (Lynchburg, VA, 1908); *Southern Baptists in Sunny Italy* (New York, 1929).

B. NCAB A, 312–13; NYT 10 Mar 1942, 19.

TAYLOR, Nathaniel William (23 June 1786, New Milford, CT—10 March 1858, New Haven, CT). *Education*: graduated from Yale Coll., 1807; studied theology under *Timothy Dwight, New Haven, 1808–12. *Career*: minister, First Congregational Church, New Haven, 1812–22; professor of Didactic Theology, Yale Div. Sch., 1822–57.

The Second Great Awakening called for an adjustment of standard Calvinist categories, and none met this need more satisfactorily than Taylor. While still a young man his reputation as an evangelical preacher at Center Church led to an appointment on Yale's new faculty of theology. He labored in that capacity for thirty-five years, affecting the lives of future ministers and missionaries who spread his influence to distant places. Beyond lecturing to students, his articles in the *Quarterly Christian Spectator* were joined with printed sermons to help shape what became known as New Haven Theology. Taylor did not create a new theological framework single-handedly, but he was the most important figure in transition from Edwardsean Calvinism to liberal ideas stemming from revivals. Together with his friend, *Lyman Beecher, he articulated a form of orthodoxy which rationalized the evangelical sympathies many clergymen had already adopted. More conservative spokesmen, such as *Bennet Tyler, thought he conceded too much to Arminianism. But Taylor repeatedly defended the correctness of his views and associated his version of New England theology with broader cultural patterns of nonsectarian revivals, missions, and benevolent reform. Largely due to his efforts, a modified Calvinism was able to keep some distinctive features alive through another half century.

The average citizen in democratic America rebelled against doctrines which precluded free will and responsible moral action. Taylor tried to retain the old context of natural depravity and yet allow for an emphasis on individual decision stressed by revivalistic methods. He believed in both predestination and free agency because the certainty of man's sin carried with it what he called "power to the contrary." God's moral government of the world was the central concept, not divine sovereignty. Taylor argued that freedom of the will was consistent with such a government where man's moral responsibility played a part. Sinners were punished by a just God because they had freely chosen evil; they were not created with a depraved nature preventing any chance of virtue. A nice distinction made it possible to say that man's nature is the occasion of his sinning but does not preclude the opposite result. It is certain that man sins and that he stands in need of salvation. But any number of those actions does not impinge on his essential constitution, which includes practical power to the contrary. Using these dubious qualifications, Taylor rescued the category of God's nature from charges of tyranny and made sin an act of moral failure, one of free human choice gone astray. Revivalists with an Edwardsean heritage benefited from such new thoughts, using them as a certificate of orthodoxy while Arminian measures became their daily practice.

Bibliography:

A. *Essays on the Means of Regeneration* (New Haven, 1829); *Practical Sermons*, ed. Noah Porter (New York, 1858); *Essays . . . upon select Topics in revealed Theology* (New York, 1859); *Lectures on the Moral Government of God*, 2 vols. (New York, 1859).

B. SH 11, 285; NCAB 7, 187; DAB 18, 338–39; NCE 13, 953–54; Sidney E. Mead, *Nathaniel William Taylor, 1786–1858: A Connecticut Liberal* (Chicago, 1942).

TEKAKWITHA, Catherine (1656?, Gandahouhague, Mohawk Territory—17 April 1680, La Prairie de la Madeleine, Canada).

It is a truism in the history of missions that early converts to outside socioreligious patterns tend to have marginal identification with their native culture. In the case of Tekakwitha this was certainly true; her adoption of new ways did not imply a sacrifice of pleasant or meaningful ties with former habits. She was only half Iroquoian, the daughter of a Mohawk warrior and an Algonkian captive, born in a palisaded longhouse of the Turtle clan near present-day Fonda, New York. At the age of four she had been disfigured by smallpox, a disease which impaired her eyesight and left her an orphan. Raised by an uncle, she met Jesuit missionaries as early as 1667; alienation from native preferences grew as she experienced her uncle's bitter opposition to Christianity. Slowly, through secret conversations with Jacques de Lamberville, she determined to espouse the new religion and received baptism on Easter Day, 1676. For months thereafter she endured the contempt and derision of her village for noncomformity to tribal ways, such as refusing to work on Sunday or to marry. In 1677 she was able, through the help of Christian visitors, to escape her past and flee to an Indian mission near the Lachine rapids (Sault St. Louis) in Upper Canada. For the next three years she was allowed full opportunity there to exercise the abstemious virtues to which she had become so passionately attached.

The mission of St. Francis Xavier du Sault, called Caughnawaga by the Indians, became home for Tekakwitha's brief but remarkable life. There on Christmas Day, 1677, she received her first communion. While she contributed her share to the community's economy, the most striking aspect of her witness lay in practicing great personal austerities. She fasted two days a week, performed unrelenting penance and flagellations, keeping until death a private vow of chastity. In 1679 she was allowed to begin a modest convent at the mission patterned after the Hospital Sisters of Ville-Marie in Montreal. Her exemplary habits were an inspiration to Indian neighbors, many of whom revered her as the epitome of a saintly woman. After she died, Jesuits spread stories of her extraordinary life, which served to edify native and French believers alike. Many of the faithful came over the years to pray at her tomb; in time several miraculous cures have been attributed to her intercession. In 1932 nomination for beatification was introduced at Rome for one who did much to embody Catholic piety in colonial New France. Pronounced blessed, 22 June 1980.

Bibliography:

B.   NCE 13, 978–79; NAW 3, 436–37; Ellen Walworth, *The Life and Times of Kateri Tekakwitha* (Buffalo, NY, 1891); Edouard Lecompte, *An Iroquois Virgin: Catherine Tekakwitha* (New York, 1932); Marie C. Buhrle, *Kateri of the Mohawks* (Milwaukee, 1954).

TENNENT, Gilbert (5 February 1703, County Armagh, Ireland—23 July 1764, Philadelphia, PA). *Education*: studied theology with *William Tennent. *Career*: minister, New Castle, DE, 1725–26; minister, New Brunswick, NJ, 1726–43; minister, Second Presbyterian Church, Philadelphia, PA, 1743–64.

After studying medicine for a year, Tennent prepared for the ministry under his father *William, a scholar whose theological ability surpassed all others in the Presbytery of Philadelphia. His first efforts at spreading evangelical awakening had minimal effect, but the friendly encouragement of *Theodorus J. Frelinghuysen, minister of a neighboring Dutch church in New Brunswick, strengthened his resolve. By 1729 revivals began to occur because he increasingly emphasized personal experience of redemption by means of both pastoral counseling and pulpit addresses. For the next decade he formulated a message which comprised most of the basic elements found in Great Awakening preaching. Late in 1740 *George Whitefield asked him to visit New England in hopes that Tennent would continue the revival which the traveling Anglican had started there. Tennent labored for three months in Massachusetts and Connecticut; great crowds and a surprising number of conversions together with considerable tumult followed in the wake of his controversial preaching. He tried to convince listeners they needed regeneration by attacking their false sense of security in formal religion. Those who relied on external supports such as inherited doctrine, routine morality, or catechetical instruction were dangerously complacent in the dead forms of piety. In contrast to presumptuous "carnal security," he called for repentance and humiliation, a new experience of God's power in each human life as it manifested tangible evidence of salvation in renewed virtue. Response to such preaching made his voice second only to Whitefield's as a representative of the new evangelism.

Criticism of spiritual lethargy among laymen was severe enough, but Tennent became more uncompromising when dealing with clergymen. He charged that those who opposed revivals (because they thought spiritual excesses threatened doctrinal stability) did so because they had experienced no inner change themselves. They were no more reliable guides than blind men, shepherds unable to rescue their sheep, unregenerate professionals not worthy of continued allegiance from their churches. Of course such an unreserved indictment stung conservatives into rejoinders of similar quality, and adherents gravitated to either the Old or the New Side in bitter conflict over revivals. By 1741 the New Brunswick Presbytery, composed largely of Log College men who chafed under the authoritarian Philadelphia Synod, declared itself independent of existing superstructures. Four years later Tennent led his faction into forming the Synod of New York, a pro-revival judicature which lasted for thirteen years. During that time revivals became a firmly established phenomenon, and New Side ministers increased three-fold while the Old Side suffered a proportionate decline. In later life, Tennent grew more irenic. Dismayed by the strife he had done so much to engender, he dropped polemics and adopted a more conciliatory approach to denominational brethren. By 1758 the New York and Philadelphia synods were merged, with the chief instigator of their separation serving as moderator. In his few remaining years he worked to foster growth in Presbyterian churches, all of which now explicitly recognized direct, personal experience as requisite to meaningful religion.

Bibliography:

A. *A Solemn Warning to the Secure World* (Boston, 1735); *The Examiner Examined, or Gilbert Tennent Harmonious* (Philadelphia, 1743); *Twenty Three Sermons* (Philadelphia, 1745); *Irenicum Ecclesiasticum, or A Humble Impartial Essay upon the Peace of Jerusalem* (Philadelphia, 1749); *Sermons on Important Subjects* (Philadelphia, 1758).

B. AAP 3, 35–41; SH 11, 299–300; NCAB 8, 73; DAB 18, 366–69; Milton J. Coalter, *Gilbert Tennent, Son of Thunder* (New York, 1986).

TENNENT, William (1673, Ireland?—6 May 1746, Neshaminy, PA). *Education*: graduated from Univ. of Edinburgh, 1693. *Career*: minister, Bedford, NY, 1720–26; minister, Neshaminy, PA, 1727–46.

Though Tennent is traditionally said to have been born in northern Ireland, there is nothing to substantiate that claim. In 1704 he took Anglican orders, apparently to escape severe penalties of a law passed the previous year against Roman Catholics and Presbyterians. But upon emigrating to America in 1718 he renounced both the episcopal polity and Arminian theology which had troubled him so often in the Old World. Presbyterians in Philadelphia immediately accepted him without further ordination requirements, and he proceeded to serve churches of that denomination for almost three full decades. Of a decidedly evangelical frame of mind, his chief significance lies in pro-revival leadership exhibited during those years. He trained three of his sons for the ministry and by 1735 established a small school to expand such tutorial activity. The Philadelphia Synod refused to endorse products of what was derisively called the "Log College," holding that adequate education could be found only in Scotland or New England. Still Tennent's students (21 in all) became a dynamic force in developing special tendencies in American Presbyterianism. His emphasis on education was the impetus behind founding several other institutions of higher learning, notably the College of New Jersey at Princeton (1746). His stress on emotional fervency or the "experimental" element in religion produced clergymen of similar conviction. Led primarily by his son *Gilbert, they formed the bulk of "New Side" Presbyterians in controversies regarding itinerancy, enthusiasm, and ministerial responsibility in the churches. Whether by preaching or teaching, the elder Tennent built foundations for perpetuating an evangelical following in his denomination. No fact attests more clearly to his influence than this: every Presbyterian clergyman prominent in the First Great Awakening, save one, were Log College men.

Bibliography:

B.   AAP 3, 23–27; SH 11, 299; NCAB 5, 469; DAB 18, 369–70; Mary A. Tennent, *Light in Darkness: The Story of William Tennent, Sr. and the Log College* (Greensboro, NC, 1971).

TENSKWATAWA (1768?, Piqua, Mad River area, Shawnee Territory, later OH—November, 1837, Wyandotte County, KS).

Little is known about a young Shawnee named Laulewasika ("Rattle") before the year 1805. Most evidence agrees that he was younger brother to Tecumtha (often misspelled Tecumseh) and led a drunken, dissolute life for decades. But around the age of thirty he announced himself as bearing new revelations from the Master of Life and inaugurated one of the most widespread revivals of native American religion in the nineteenth century. In accordance with shamanistic patterns in his heritage, he claimed to have been taken up into the spirit world and allowed to see the future. His reformist message stemmed from that vision.

Many of its negative aspects embodied attempts to counteract the influence of white culture and prevent further erosion of Indian life. He denounced liquor as the white man's curse, promising that those who continued to drink would be tormented after death in burning pits with mouths afire. He warned Indian women to cease intermarriage; further, every tool and custom of whites from clothes to firearms must be abandoned. On the positive side he called for a return to the pure ethos taught by the Master of Life where all property was held in common and the young worked harmoniously to care for those less fortunate in the nation. If such a reorientation were accomplished, he promised that the red man would regain divine favor and find that happiness their forefathers had known before the white man came.

Great excitement attended the revelations made by the Shawnee prophet who changed his name to Tenskwatawa ("The Open Door"). He urged vigorous crusades against those suspected of practicing witchcraft as well as everyone who collaborated with whites. Representatives from neighboring tribes came to hear his revitalizing doctrines, returning home to spread ideals of aboriginal puritanism throughout the Northwest Territory. Many skeptics remained but they were silenced when he successfully predicted a solar eclipse in June, 1806, and enthusiasm for pan-Indian restorationism spread even more rapidly thereafter. At the peak of his influence, followers could be found among the Seminoles in Florida to the Blackfeet on the plains of Saskatchewan. Tenskwatawa also announced that he had received power to cure diseases, prevent death in battle, restore game animals, and bring the dead to life. These eschatological overtones coincided with the idea of political confederation which his brother had been urging to drive the whites off Indian lands. His religious impulse was an important factor behind native cooperation with the British in the War of 1812 and the Creek War of 1813. But the Prophet's own prestige had been destroyed in 1811 when William H. Harrison burned his town and scattered his forces at the battle of Tippecanoe. He lived for a time as pensioner in Canada, continuing to preach the fading ideal of nationalistic resistance. By 1827 he returned to his people and suffered with them an aftermath of obscurity west of the Mississippi.

Bibliography:

B.   Benjamin Drake, *The Life of Tecumseh and His Brother the Prophet* (Cincinnati, 1841); Edward Eggleston and Lillie E. Seelye, *Tecumseh and the Shawnee Prophet* (New York, 1878); John M. Oskinson, *Tecumseh and His Times* (New York, 1938).

THOMAS, Norman Matoon (20 November 1884, Marion, OH—19 December 1968, Huntington, NY). *Education*: studied at Bucknell Univ., 1901–02; B.A., Princeton Univ., 1905; B.D., Union Sem. (NY), 1911. *Career*: assistant minister and social worker, New York, 1905–11; minister, East Harlem Presbyterian Church and director of "American Parish" interchurch social work, New York, 1911–18; executive secretary, Fellowship of Reconciliation and editor, *The*

World Tomorrow, 1918–22; co-director, League for Industrial Democracy, 1922–37; member of various committees, Socialist party, 1918–55.

Beginning as a progressive Republican, polished enough for upper class status and financially secure through marriage, Thomas slowly developed a compassion for the needs of common men which affected national trends for five decades. His early years as a minister brought him into contact with slum poverty, the inequality and waste of industrial exploitation, and he espoused a humanitarian course of action considered too radical by former friends. He was primarily an evangelist of social reform, pointing out the evils of capitalism, racism, and war, serving as a conscience of the American people while he worked for change and practical implementations of socio-economic justice. Influenced by the writings of *Walter Rauschenbusch and sustained by other Christian socialists like *John H. Holmes, Thomas attracted wide attention by facing problems which most religious organizations were reluctant to notice. Wherever human beings were abused or their rights ignored, he felt morally compelled to join the struggle and do something about it. Christian ethics for Thomas required social change, and he acted whenever possible to raise the sum total of human decency by fostering a society based on cooperation rather than competition. Through the years he did not despair of setbacks or allow easy answers to mellow his critical perspective. Marxist communism was too materialistic and New Deal experimentations were too haphazard to satisfy his ethical convictions. As activist and visionary, he sought changes of a lasting, more profound nature.

After joining the Socialist party in 1918, Thomas quickly made himself known as a vigorous spokesman for reform in a host of causes. He became the party's standard bearer in six presidential elections (1928–48) in addition to running for local office in the state of New York. As his principles gained favor among voters, the two major parties adopted planks from his platform. In this manner Thomas was influential in speeding the passage of fundamental benefits such as health and unemployment insurance, minimum wage laws, old age pensions, and binding arbitration in labor disputes. In addition to writing a large number of books and articles, Thomas edited his own pacifist-socialist magazine, *The World Tomorrow*, and contributed weekly columns to the *New Leader* (1924–35), *Socialist Call* (1935–60), and *New America* (1960–67) in an effort to disseminate reformist ideas. From a textile workers' strike in 1926 to desegregation marches in 1963, he was always on hand to join picket lines. His dramatic arrests in free speech confrontations precipitated changes which are now the legacy of all citizens. He persisted to the end in doing things he thought needed to be done, making choices amid uncertainty, and grounding his action in the belief that a power beyond human measuring moved events towards a goodness dimly understood and imperfectly achieved.

Bibliography:

A. *The Conscientious Objector in America* (New York, 1923; rev. ed., 1927); *As I See It* (New York, 1932); *War: No Glory, No Profit, No Need* (New York, 1935); *A Socialist's Faith* (New York, 1951); *The Prerequisites for Peace* (New York, 1959); *Socialism Re-examined* (New York, 1963).

B.   NCAB C, 259; NYT 20 Dec 1968, 1; Murray B. Seidler, *Norman Thomas: Respectable Rebel* (Syracuse, NY, 1961); Harry Fleischman, *Norman Thomas: A Biography* (New York, 1964; rev. ed., 1969); W. A. Swanberg, *Norman Thomas: The Last Idealist* (New York, 1976).

THOMPSON, Charles Lemuel (18 August 1839, near Cooperstown, PA—14 April, 1924, Atlantic City, NJ). *Education*: B.A., Carroll Coll., 1858; studied at Princeton Sem., 1858–60; B.D., Theological Sem. of the Northwest, 1861. *Career*: minister, Juneau, WI, 1861–62; minister Janesville, WI, 1862–67; minister, Cincinnati, OH, 1867–72; minister, Chicago, IL, 1872–78; minister, Pittsburgh, PA, 1879–82; minister, Kansas City, MO, 1882–88; minister, New York, NY, 1888–98; secretary, Presbyterian Board of Home Missions, 1898–1914; chairman, Home Missions Council of the Protestant Churches, 1908–24.

Reared in the sparsely populated new state of Wisconsin, Thompson learned at an early age to appreciate the efforts of Presbyterian home missionaries. After their example he too prepared for the ministry, first at Princeton where he revered *Charles Hodge and then, following marriage, at a seminary later named McCormick. He struggled through his first pastorates, learning to preach largely by trial and error. He also came to see that the churches' responsibility in a community was larger than to their own membership. Moving from one city to another, he gradually realized that the mission of churches extended beyond theology and internal affairs to embrace larger questions of social significance. Some of his congregations were staid, some full of snap and ginger, but in all of them Thompson felt at home with his broad evangelical doctrine. Though acquainted with conservative Calvinism, he possessed a poetical frame of mind which realized the difficulties in expressing religious truth with linguistic precision. Then too he liked people regardless of their confessional position and deplored the fact that valuable ministers like *David Swing in Chicago or *Charles A. Briggs in New York were charged with heresy. He thought it more important to join forces in evangelistic campaigns than to waste energy fighting over points of ecclesiastical law. With such a liberal outlook he was well suited for mission work on a national scale.

Resigning the pulpit of a fashionable Madison Avenue church, Thompson welcomed the chance to renovate Presbyterian home missions. Conservatives grumbled and funds were meager, but he pressed forward with a vision that all men could be saved by every possible means. He believed the entire country could be converted, made spiritually fit for the great destiny God determined for its future. In the process he sought to abolish all distinction between religious and secular spheres, creating one Christian culture for the benefit of its citizens. He traveled through almost every state, as well as to Puerto Rico and Alaska, to promote such a goal. But he discerned more than geographical expansion in modern missions. New urban conditions called for specialized welfare services if labor, immigrants, and the great unchurched masses were ever to adopt gospel virtues. Thompson was an important influence in highlighting the social aspects of Christian witness in missions which individualistic soul-saving had not an-

ticipated. He also pioneered in urging genuine cooperation between denominational agencies to avoid wasteful competition. As early as 1899 he laid plans
for a national federation of mission work wherein major denominations could
cooperate in specialized programs more effectively. His experimentation helped
prepare the way for a Federal Council of Churches (1908) which stemmed
primarily from missionary impulses. For over sixty years he labored with good
will and optimism to advance a kingdom whose advent he thought virtually at
hand.

Bibliography:

A. *Times of Refreshing: A History of American Revivals* (Chicago, 1877); *Etchings
in Verse* (New York, 1890); *The Presbyterians* (New York, 1903); *The Religious Foundations of America* (New York, 1917); *The Soul of America* (New York, 1919).

B. NCAB 10, 361–62; NYT 15 Apr 1924, 21; Elizabeth O. Thompson (ed.), *Charles
Lemuel Thompson* (New York, 1924).

THORNWELL, James Henley (9 December 1812, Marlborough District, SC—
1 August 1862, Charlotte, NC). *Education*: graduated from South Carolina Coll.,
1831; private study, 1831–32; studied at Harvard Div. Sch., 1834. *Career*:
minister, Lancaster, SC, 1835–38; professor, South Carolina Coll., 1838–40;
minister, Columbia, SC, 1840–41, 1855–61; professor, South Carolina Coll.,
1841–51; president, South Carolina Coll., 1852–55; editor, *Southern Quarterly
Review*, 1855–57; professor of Didactic and Polemic Theology, Presbyterian
Sem., Columbia, SC, 1855–62.

As a defender of Presbyterian standards and a polemical controversialist,
Thornwell was usually identified with conservative views on matters ranging
from creeds to slavery. He attended his first General Assembly in 1837 but,
while approving its resolutions against unorthodox changes, played no conspicuous part in those momentous proceedings. Ten years later he was elected
moderator of the Old School Assembly, an indication of his speedy rise to
ecclesiastical statemanship. In roles as educator, preacher, and man of letters,
Thornwell maintained a strict interpretation of his church's doctrine and principles of government. He disapproved of those who accepted only parts of the
Westminster Confession or who compromised its structures of organization and
discipline. Such subterfuges indicated a decline in doctrinal rectitude, which he
tried to redress by zealous advocacy of orthodox views. Most of his reasoning
followed a pattern which stated general principles and then extrapolated from
them with careful logic, going no farther than precedent allowed. That undeviating method yielded grounds for judging what was permissible thought and
action while exposing unwarranted innovations at the same time. Thornwell's
passion for orthodoxy lay in a sense of duty to truth as defined by the strictest
rules of deduction; all else was susceptible to error.

Probably no southern churchman was more cogent and dignified than Thornwell in defending the institution of slavery. He began by declaring it a political

matter, one which ministers could not categorically enjoin as a duty or condemn as a sin. Beyond that, he sought to refute antislavery arguments. He held that one could denounce only those institutions which the Bible mentioned as intrinsic evils. Since both testaments referred to slavery in order to regulate but not condemn it, abolitionists had no basis for using the Bible as a theoretical support any more than did critics of monarchy, aristocracy, or poverty. General outcries against injustice and oppression were likewise inapplicable because such observations had force only when referring to unlawful domination. Slavery had been sanctioned by Moses and the apostles, according to Thornwell, and it seemed clear that the master-slave relationship was a lawful one in which justice and love could be achieved. He also argued that Africans were providentially placed at a lower level on the chain of being. Their tutelage under white masters in a land secure from pagan influences allowed them the benefits of Christianity and civilization which would help them rise eventually to higher levels of life. For all these reasons, the apologist urged that slavery was not necessarily bad, the South was justified in seceding to protect its social patterns, and southern churches were correct in following suit to serve the new nation.

Bibliography:

A. *The Arguments of Romanists from the Infallibility of the Church and Testimony of the Fathers on Behalf of the Apocrypha, Discussed and Refuted* (New York, 1845); *The Rights and Duties of Masters* (Charleston, SC, 1850); *Our Danger and Our Duty* (Richmond, VA, 1862); *The Collected Writings of James Henley Thornwell*, ed. John B. Adger and John L. Girardeau, 4 vols. (Richmond, VA, 1871–73).

B. SH 11, 433–34; NCAB 11, 33–34; DAB 18, 507–08; Benjamin M. Palmer, *The Life and Letters of James Henley Thornwell* (Richmond, VA, 1875; New York, 1969); James O. Farmer, *The Metaphysical Confederacy: James Henley Thornwell and the Synthesis of Southern Values* (Macon, GA, 1986).

THURMAN, Howard (18 November 1900, Daytona Beach, FL—10 April 1981, San Francisco, CA). *Education*: B.A., Morehouse Coll., 1923; B.D. Colgate-Rochester Div. Sch., 1926. *Career*: Minister, Mt. Zion Baptist Church, Oberlin, OH, 1926–28; professor of Theology, Morehouse Coll., 1928–31; professor of Systematic Theology and dean of the chapel, Howard Univ., 1932–44; minister, Church for the Fellowship of All Peoples, San Francisco, CA, 1944–53; professor of Spiritual Disciplines and Resources, School of Theol., Boston Univ., 1953–65; active retirement, 1965–81.

Raised in the Deep South in a family where one grandmother had been a slave, Thurman experienced the poverty and discrimination so common among Blacks in the early years of this century. But early on he showed promise, attracting favorable notice and incidently pointing to conditions of the time, by becoming the first Negro child in the area to complete an eighth-grade education. From there he went on to Florida Baptist Academy, working as a janitor and at other menial tasks to support his way. At college he expanded his capacities even further and won fame as a skilled debater while participating in most other campus activities too. Thurman was ordained a Baptist minister in 1925, and much of his subsequent career featured preaching and pastoral concerns. In 1935 while making a "Pilgrimage of Friendship" in India he first conceived of an interracial church where genuine religious fellowship could transcend social and economic barriers. That dream came to fruition in 1944 when he founded a church in the Japanese district of San Francisco, a church deliberately and self-consciously open to Africans, Orientals, and Caucasians.

Long noted for his pulpit eloquence, in 1953 Thurman was named by *Life* magazine as one of the twelve greatest preachers of the twentieth century. That same year he accepted a professorship at Boston University, becoming the first full-time black faculty member at that institution. Part of Thurman's religious instruction had an undercurrent of mysticism about it. When his first wife died in 1930, he took a leave of absence from Morehouse and studied with Quaker scholar *Rufus M. Jones at Swarthmore. Many of his articles and books show signs of a deep serenity and devotionalism that was nurtured during those trying times. But there was also a practical aspect to his outlook, a concern to show how Christianity could tackle the problems of modern times and improve things. Thurman urged that religion should be made to work, to grasp high ideals and to take a stand on issues, especially those bearing directly on the poor and disadvantaged. His lectures at scores of universities during retirement years continued to stress the importance of religious action in the vital social sphere. Over the years he thus balanced resources of inner peace with a determination to produce tangible effects in the larger world of cultural affairs.

Bibliography:

A. *Jesus and the Disinherited* (Nashville, 1949); *Deep in the Hunger* (New York, 1951); *Footprints of a Dream: The Story of the Church for the Fellowship of All Peoples* (New York, 1959); *Disciplines of the Spirit* (New York, 1963); *The Luminous Darkness: A Personal Interpretation of the Anatomy of Segregation and the Ground of Hope* (New York, 1965); *With Head and Heart: The Autobiography of Howard Thurman* (New York, 1979).

B. NYT 14 Apr 1981, B 18; Elizabeth Yates, *Howard Thurman: Portrait of a Practical Dreamer* (New York, 1964); Luther E. Smith, Jr., *Howard Thurman: The Mystic as Prophet* (Washington, DC, 1981).

TILLICH, Paul Johannes (20 August 1886, Starzeddel, Germany—22 October 1965, Chicago, IL). *Education*: studied at Berlin (1904), Tübingen (1905), and Halle (1905–07); Ph.D., Breslau, 1911; lic. theol., Halle, 1912. *Career*: chaplain, German Army, 1914–18; privatdozent, Berlin, 1919–24; professor of Theology, Marburg, 1924–25; professor of Theology, Dresden and Leipzig, 1925–29; professor of Philosophy, Frankfurt, 1929–33; professor of Philosophical Theology, Union Sem. (NY), 1933–55; University Professor, Harvard Univ., 1955–62; professor of Theology, Univ. of Chicago, 1962–65.

After having established himself in German universities as a leading theologian, Tillich was fired by the Nazi government and subsequently persuaded by *Reinhold Niebuhr to leave his homeland. Work in America added to his fame as one of the most important sources of theological scholarship in the twentieth century. With a brilliant array of learning and fertile imagination, his writings became a decisive influence in theological development, especially in the area of relating Christian faith to its cultural context. Tillich wanted to correlate kerygma (the unchanging message of faith found in Scripture and tradition) with the contemporary situation and all cultural forms of man's interpretation of himself. The form he found most expressive of modern humanity was existentialist philosophy. Its analysis of man's isolation and despair proved to be a natural ally of those who sought to formulate a response to problems in contemporary human existence. Since religion was the meaning-giving substance of culture, and culture the totality of forms in which the basic concern of religion expressed itself, the theologian was in a good position to correlate human thought into a message compatible with current idioms. But while trying to appreciate the sacramental nurture of Christian grace in culture, he also insisted that no articulation of it could serve as final authority. The search for theological relevance remained constant because conditions changed the way answers made sense.

Within existentialist guidelines, Tillich could see that estrangement, the ambiguity and despair of human existence, was the dominant theme in western culture. He would not fall back on supernaturalism as a response because its dualistic pattern made God an object, an outside power whom men could not know and whose action contravened natural harmony. Agreeing that no breach should be allowed in the natural order, he held that God was the ground or power of all being, "being-itself." Yet God as the ground of all being transcended that which He supported; in a dialectical relationship the eternal was present in the natural, and such an underlying unity was not destroyed even when created beings freely turned away from their ultimate grounding. In the same view man stood as a separate, fallen creature, estranged from essential being in his finitude and despair. This ontological delineation of pure essence and fragmented existence laid the basis for proclaiming a message of hope in present circumstances.

Jesus as the Christ was the key for Tillich in that his example affirmed the possibility of overcoming the anxiety of estrangement. Jesus had fully participated in the tragic element of human existence, but through him God expressed reconciliation, reunion of alienated man with the source of his being. He thus became the New Being in whom Tillich discerned the power of salvation, a power transforming men and making it possible for them to be linked with "being" again. Speaking of incarnation as a relational concept, "eternal God-Manhood," he pointed to the underlying unity of God and mankind (disrupted, but not destroyed, by estrangement) vividly actualized in freedom by Jesus the New Being. As symbol of unity with God, he pointed the way for adequate living. Rather than the misguided self-sufficiency of human autonomy or the finite pretentions of heteronomous institutions, man could properly follow the theonomous ordering of existence with Being itself. In this manner Tillich articulated standard soteriological ideas within an existentialist framework. More than other theologians in his generation, he helped American religious thinkers assimilate the categories of European intellectual processes, moving from confessional isolation to the boundary of secular involvement.

Bibliography:

A. *The Shaking of the Foundations* (New York, 1948); *The Protestant Era* (Chicago, 1948); *Systematic Theology*, 3 vols. (Chicago, 1951–63); *The Courage to Be* (New Haven, 1952); *Dynamics of Faith* (New York, 1957); *On the Boundary* (New York, 1966).

B.   NYT 23 Oct 1965, 1; James L. Adams, *Paul Tillich's Philosophy of Culture, Science, and Religion* (New York, 1965); David H. Kelsey, *The Fabric of Paul Tillich's Theology* (New Haven, 1967); Carl J. Armbruster, *The Vision of Paul Tillich* (New York, 1967); Robert P. Scharlemann, *Reflection and Doubt in the Thought of Paul Tillich* (New Haven, 1969); Leonard F. Wheat, *Paul Tillich's Dialectical Humanism* (Baltimore, 1970); Rollo May, *Paulus: Reminiscences of a Friendship* (New York, 1973).

TITTLE, Ernest Fremont (21 October 1885, Springfield, OH—3 August 1949, Evanston, IL). *Education*: studied at Wittenberg Coll., 1903–04; B.A., Ohio Wesleyan Univ., 1906; B.D., Drew Sem., 1908. *Career*: minister, Christiansburg circuit, OH, 1908–10; minister, Dayton, OH, 1910–13; minister, Delaware, OH, 1913–16; minister, Columbus, OH, 1916–18; minister, First Methodist Church, Evanston, IL, 1918–49.

There have been many preachers notable for eloquence or style, but Tittle achieved prominence because of his concentration on central issues and the evangelical perspective with which he confronted them. As minister of a large suburban congregation, he also served as counselor, pastor, and leader in church conferences; but his lasting fame was grounded on sermons and prayers laboriously prepared for weekly worship services. Tittle did not preach sociology, economic theories, or political reformism; he preached what he understood to be the gospel message of salvation and man's decision in the light of God's will. The pulpit was, in his view, the one place where prophetic utterance survived, and if that office were neglected, Protestantism was virtually impotent. So he spoke as one having vital information about eternal values, and people hungry for religion came to hear. Tittle's sermons were most often God-centered ones that fed personal faith, but they could not avoid application to contemporary issues as well. Themes on grace, redemption, and personal conduct were blended with powerful discourses on war, racial discrimination, and slums. In addition to appearing in books, over 250 sermons were printed in *The First Church Pulpit* and spread the preacher's words outside midwestern centers to make him a national figure.

Tittle was not a crusader looking for causes to promote. He simply could not preach his understanding of the Bible and stand silently by when he thought fellow human beings were being wronged. His greatness lay in the fact that others hearing him could not remain indifferent to the subjects on which he spoke. Another key to prominence was his fearless defense of unpopular convictions, and not insignificantly his church's loyal support despite much adverse publicity. He attacked racism, anti-intellectual fundamentalism, anti-Catholicism, the Ku Klux Klan, and super patriots. He worked for the American Civil Liberties Union (ACLU), the National Association for the Advancement of Colored People (NAACP), and many other humanitarian, ecumenical movements. He supported prohibition but did not place it among the chief virtues; he opposed nativists but did not identify with any political party. In 1928 when all these issues swirled around the presidential campaign, Tittle voted for *Norman Thomas, then and several times thereafter. He received a great deal of abuse for declaring himself a socialist. He supported efforts at relief and recovery during the 1930s, though seldom did he endorse any specific measures or align himself with any European form of socialism. Another cause that won Tittle more disapproval than respect was his firm stand as a pacifist. The madness of war on a global scale led him to resist nationalistic appeals for blind patriotism. The waste of human lives that might have served to benefit society made him an opponent of violence in any form. His thirty-one years of preaching from a single pulpit broadcast his ideas about the gospel and the social implications which he thought it necessarily implied.

Bibliography:

A. *What Must the Church Do to Be Saved?* (New York, 1921); *The Religion of the Spirit* (New York, 1928); *The Foolishness of Preaching* (New York, 1930); *A World that Cannot Be Shaken* (New York, 1933); *A Mighty Fortress* (New York, 1949); *The Gospel According to St. Luke* (New York, 1951).

B. NYT 4 Aug 1949, 23; Robert M. Miller, *How Shall They Hear Without a Preacher? The Life of Ernest Fremont Tittle* (Chapel Hill, 1971).

TOMLINSON, Ambrose Jessup (22 September 1865, near Westfield, IN— 2 October 1943, Cleveland, TN). *Career*: revivalist and minister, Cleveland, TN, 1904–43; general overseer (moderator until 1910), Church of God, 1906– 23; editor, *The Church of God Evangel*, 1910–22; general overseer, (Tomlinson) Church of God, 1923–43; editor, *The White Wing Messenger*, 1923–43.

After four years of missionary preaching in the hills of Tennessee and North Carolina, Tomlinson joined with several others in 1903 to found a Holiness church. He was then ordained and served as moderator of the first general assembly of such ministers held in 1906. Within a year it was decided that their organization should be named the Church of God to indicate its continuity with biblical patterns of faith and worship. Another tenet had to do with healing, based on the belief that God not only forgives sins in the process of rebirth but heals bodies as well. Moderator Tomlinson (lifetime appointment after 1914) preached and prayed for the sick in revival services from Kentucky to Florida.

In 1908 an intense spiritual experience, which he termed baptism by the Holy Ghost, added another element to his message. Reminiscent of the speaking in tongues mentioned in apostolic times, the Church of God came to view the phenomenon as evidence of God's special favor. Of course Tomlinson held that persons could be in a state of grace without ecstatic utterances, but he encouraged listeners to be so attuned to spiritual promptings that demonstrations like Pentecost could be repeated frequently. In advocating the death of man's carnal nature, rebirth in the spirit, and baptism by the Holy Ghost with fire, he taught followers that the power of God did far more than just feed the intellect. For four decades he transmitted this emphasis on direct experience with the Bible alone as a standard for church life and personal conduct.

By 1922 the Church of God counted over 21,000 members in 666 churches with 923 ministers in the organization, but schism threatened from within. A constitution had been adopted the previous year, distributing Tomlinson's considerable power to a larger number of elders and committees. The general overseer considered this introduction of executive officers unacceptable because the Bible was his single rule of polity. No compromise could be reached, so in 1923 Tomlinson gathered up the remnants of a following to continue what he viewed as the true church. Subsequent court action required the two factions to designate respective positions by using "Elders" and "Tomlinson," to qualify their common claim as the legitimate Church of God. For the rest of his life, Tomlinson worked indefatigably to build up his farflung network of holiness congregations. He attended state and district conventions, reorganized a tithing system, recruited for foreign missions, and promoted countless revivals. Intensive effort paid off with appreciable growth in southeastern states, Caribbean Islands, and mission stations dotting the globe. In all his activities from evangelist to editor, he worked to win souls and have them safely housed in the Church where they could be perfected and made ready for the expected coming of the Lord.

Bibliography:
  A.   *The Last Great Conflict* (Cleveland, TN, 1913).
  B.   NYT 3 Oct 1943, 49; Lillie Duggar, *A. J. Tomlinson* (Cleveland, TN, 1964).

TORREY, Reuben Archer (28 January 1856, Hoboken, NJ—26 October 1928, Ashville, NC). *Education*: B.A., Yale Coll., 1875; B.D., Yale Div. Sch., 1878; studied at Leipzig and Erlangen, 1882–83. *Career*: minister, Garretsville, OH, 1878–82; minister, Open Door Congregational Church, Minneapolis, MN, 1883–86; superintendent, Minneapolis City Missionary Society, 1886–89; superintendent, Moody Bible Inst., 1889–1908; independent evangelist, 1908–12; dean, Bible Inst. of Los Angeles, 1912–24; minister, Church of the Open Door, Los Angeles, CA, 1915–24; active retirement, 1924–28.

While still a seminarian, Torrey was inspired by *Dwight L. Moody to think of mass evangelism as his true calling in life. After a few years in local pulpits, he became head of the Chicago Bible Institute (later to receive Moody's name) and minister of the great evangelist's Chicago Avenue Church (1894–1906), both offices substantiating his claim to be direct heir of the Moody revival enterprise. As a preacher of forthright conversion messages together with conventional emphasis on personal morality, he compiled an impressive statistical record. Between 1901 and 1905 he conducted a worldwide campaign, beginning in Australia and culminating in Great Britain. During those years he addressed more than fifteen million people; estimates of conversions range from 30,000 to 100,000, including some 17,000 in London alone when the tour reached its climax in a five-month revival at Royal Albert Hall. Though he did not convey the same personal warmth as Moody did, his emphatic, authoritative sermons had telling effect on large audiences. Some criticized him for too much advance preparation and "commercialized religion," but he continued to draw crowds in major U.S. or Canadian cities until 1911. Even his role as educator was linked to urban evangelism. Most graduates of the two-year training courses at Chicago and Los Angeles were dedicated to mission work among all strata of metropolitan centers.

While his reputation for effective revival preaching grew, Torrey also emerged as a trenchant critic of liberal changes in mainstream Protestant belief. Many of his public lectures showed he was as intent on saving the fundamentals of evangelical faith as on saving souls. His attacks on evolutionary thought and biblical criticism, drawn from his unsettling experience at German universities, were uncompromising enough to link his name with others committed to an aggressively dogmatic conservatism. In keeping with that position he was asked by *Amzi C. Dixon to help compile *The Fundamentals* (1910–15), a twelve-volume set of articles by sixty-four conservative authors. He was also a prominent figure in the Interdenominational Association of Evangelists, a group stridently opposed to science, modernism, and political schemes for progressive social reform. Torrey epitomized the narrow, literalistic perspective which rejected immanentist thinking and social gospel programs because they represented apostasy spreading like a plague through Christendom. He embodied strong premillennial expectations as well and moved with most millenarians into the Fundamentalist camp as debate with liberals became increasingly bitter. His attempt to restate basic truths such as biblical inerrancy, bodily resurrection, Second Advent, and future punishment of the wicked failed to win a wide national following, but his efforts helped provide a framework for conservative affirmations which survive today with unabated vigor.

Bibliography:

A.   *Real Salvation and Whole Hearted Service* (New York, 1905); *How to Succeed in the Christian Life* (New York, 1906); *Difficulties and Alleged Contradictions in the Bible* (New York, 1907); *The Person and Work of the Holy Spirit* (New York, 1910); *The Fundamental Doctrines of the Christian Faith* (New York, 1918); *The God of the Bible* (New York, 1923).

B.   SH 11, 467; NCAB 21, 428; NYT 27 Oct 1928, 19; Robert Harkness, *Reuben*

Archer Torrey: The Man, His Message (Chicago, 1929); Ed Reese, *The Life and Ministry of Reuben Archer Torrey* (East Meadow, NY, 1975).

TOWNSEND, William Cameron (9 July 1896, Downey, CA—23 April 1982, near Waxhaw, NC). *Education*: studied at Occidental Coll., 1914–17. *Career*: missionary in Guatemala, 1917–29; director, Wycliffe Bible Translators Organization, 1935–82.

As a teenager Townsend joined the Presbyterian church, but his lifetime interests and work transcended all denominational limitations. In 1917 while trying to sell Spanish Bibles to native Americans in Guatemala, he noticed that the Indians did not speak Spanish and that nothing was written in Cakchiquel, their local dialect of the Mayan linguistic stock. With no formal training in such a field he labored for twelve years among natives of the western highlands and produced a small grammar as well as a translation of the New Testament. He also encouraged the local people to acquire literacy, as a means to social improvement in addition to personal salvation. Prodigious efforts in this first instance proved to be a model for Townsend's ultimate vision: the Bible made available to every cultural unit around the world, especially those that had been geographically and linguistically isolated for so long. By 1934 he joined with L. L. Letgers to found the Summer Institute of Linguistics, an academic program based in Huntington Beach, California, to train recruits in putting minority languages into written form. The following year missionary linguists formed the Wycliffe Bible Translators Organization, named for the fourteenth century scholar who produced the first English Bible.

The movement begun by Townsend is nonprofit and nonsectarian, comprising today the largest independent Protestant missionary organization in the world. Thousands of its personnel are at work in more than thirty countries, laboring to capture the nuances of 750 languages on paper. They are credited with having done so with at least 150 of them already. A standard task force contains two linguists plus doctors, nurses, and teachers who compile dictionaries and grammars while caring for the local people and teaching them literacy in their native tongue. This process takes an average of fifteen to twenty years to complete, culminating ideally in a literate population with their own Bible. Since much work takes place in remote areas, Townsend established in 1948 the Jungle Aviation and Radio Service (JAARS) to provide logistical support for his teams. He traveled widely, lived among many different peoples, and impressed all of them with his simple goodwill and sincere altruism. The last days of a peripatetic life were spent near JAARS headquarters, the better to nurture the work that still needed doing.

Bibliography:

A.   *Lazaro Cardenas: Mexico Democrat* (Mexico City, 1952); *They Found a Common Language* (New York, 1972); *Remember All the Way* (Huntington Beach, CA, 1975); *A Thousand Trails: The Personal Journal of William Cameron Townsend, 1917–1919* (White Rock, British Columbia, 1984).

B.   NYT 29 Apr 1982, D 23; James and Marti Hefley, *Uncle Cam* (Waco, TX, 1974).

TOY, Crawford Howell (23 March 1836, Norfolk, VA—12 May 1919, Cambridge, MA). *Education*: M.A., Univ. of Virginia, 1856; studied at Southern Baptist Sem., 1859–60; studied at Berlin, 1866–68. *Career*: taught English at Albemarle Female Institute, Charlottesville, VA, 1856–59; professor of Greek, Richmond Coll., 1861; served in Confederate Army as artilleryman, chaplain, and instructor (captured and exchanged after Gettysburg), 1861–65; professor of Greek, Furman Univ., 1868–69; professor of Old Testament, Southern Baptist Sem., 1869–79; literary agent for *The Independent*, 1879–80; professor of Oriental Languages and Biblical Literature, Harvard Univ., 1880–1909; professor emeritus, 1909–19.

If Toy had fulfilled an early ministerial goal, he would have been a missionary to Japan, and this country would have lost a competent linguist, religious scholar, and educator. His omnivorous reading habits led him constantly to new ideas, even while in military prison, and his professorial career was always marked by recognition of his learned accomplishments. Formal study in Germany helped sharpen his intellectual tools and acquaint him with the best in theological scholarship, but it was private investigation in the writings of Darwin, Spencer, and Wellhausen that made Toy's ideas distinctive for his age and cultural setting. As a Baptist in the South, committed to placing beliefs and actions completely on a Scriptural basis, he was eager to interpret that standard correctly. But he was increasingly disturbed about reconciling that position with the findings of modern biblical scholarship, another part of his intellectual maturation which he refused to compromise. By 1875 he had adopted an evolutionary perspective that viewed biblical materials as conveying religious truths in a form proper to their author's times but not confined to a univocal, literal interpretation.

In 1877 the Southern Baptist Seminary moved from Greenville, South Carolina, to Louisville, Kentucky, in an effort to secure greater financial support for theological education. Toy's advanced ideas about interpreting Scriptures did not correspond to those of most Southern Baptists. His conclusions on authorship, dating, and meaning were not beyond those accepted in European circles; for example he suggested that the Servant passages in Isaiah 42 and 53 probably referred to Israel, not to Jesus as Messiah. But such a novelty was enough to upset much of the seminary's constituency. Toy was convinced that his approach helped ease the difficulties his students had with respect to science and the Bible and so continued to teach in that vein despite mounting criticism. Finally, without bitterness he submitted his resignation in 1879, and the Board of Trustees reluctantly accepted it on grounds that the financially insecure institution could not afford to alienate its supporters. That decision set a precedent for confining ministerial training to views held by the majority of Baptists on all questions, usually at the expense of creative theological exploration and intellectual growth.

Toy's activities in the more generous environment of Harvard were the culmination of projects and studies begun long before. He became a voluminous contributor to technical and literary journals, translator, exegete, editor, and cricial commentator. He worked with students in the Divinity School and added new courses in Semitic languages to the undergraduate curriculum. His contacts enlarged, publications mounted, and his influence there as a teacher was widely felt through three decades of energetic application.

Bibliography:

A.   *History of the Religion of Israel* (Boston, 1882); *Quotations in the New Testament* (New York, 1884); *Judaism and Christianity* (Boston, 1890); *A Critical and Exegetical Commentary on Proverbs* (New York, 1899); *Introduction to the History of Religions* (Boston, 1913).

B.   SH 11, 474–75; NCAB 6, 94–95; DAB 18, 621–22; NYT 13 May 1919, 17; George H. Shriver (ed.), *American Religious Heretics* (Nashville, 1966).

TRINE, Ralph Waldo (9 September 1866, Mt. Morris, IL—21 February 1958, Claremont, CA). *Education*: B.A., Knox Coll., 1891; studied at Johns Hopkins Univ., 1891–92.

Shortly before the turn of this century Trine began writing inspirational essays which eventually sold millions of copies. His facile pen spread New Thought doctrines to wider circles of readers, finding eager reception around the world in twenty or more translated editions. The secret of life, he maintained, was that a single principle of Infinite Power lay behind all existence. This self-existent Spirit rules by means of great, immutable laws in the physical universe. Everything from flowers to a thunderstorm manifests the dynamic energy of this one animating source. Building on this comprehensive foundation, he reasoned further that human life was essentially identical with Infinite Power. Once a person realized the vital connection between isolated selves and the True Self, then a flow of divine vitality increased one's quality of life by tremendous proportions. He assured readers that men differed from God only in matters of degree; the moment one fully realized his basic nature, it was possible to improve daily experience just as God improves all creation. With unbounded optimism he promised that the fullness of peace, power, and plenty would flow to those who awakened their interior forces. Accord with fundamental principles of the universe would allow the weak and suffering to become healthy and strong, those in pain to achieve perfect peace, the impotent to exercise power, and the poor to receive plenitude. This message of success-oriented positive thinking ran, he said, like a golden thread through all the world's great religions. Prophets or saviors in each historical tradition embodied the central truth of oneness with Nature. Trine utilized an impressive capacity for poetic expression to keep alive and win new converts for a body of American thought stemming as far back as his namesake, *Ralph W. Emerson.

Bibliography:

A.   *What All the World's A-Seeking, or The Vital Law of True Life, True Greatness, Power and Happiness* (New York, 1896); *In Tune with the Infinite* (New York, 1897, and many subsequent editions); *In the Fire of the Heart* (New York, 1906); *The New Alinement of Life* (London, 1913); *The Higher Powers of Mind and Spirit* (New York, 1917); *My Philosophy and My Religion* (New York, 1921).

B.   NYT 25 Feb 1958, 27.

TRUETT, George Washington (6 May 1867, Clay County, NC—7 July 1944, Dallas, TX). *Education*: B.A., Baylor Univ., 1897. *Career*: high school principal, Hiawassee, GA, 1887–89; financial agent, Baylor Univ., 1890–92; minister, Waco, TX, 1893–97; minister, First Baptist Church, Dallas, TX, 1897–1944.

For years Truett nourished the single ambition of practicing law, but, shortly after moving to Texas with his family, members of a local Baptist church prevailed on him to enter the ministry. Within months his gift for public speaking attracted the attention of officials at Baylor University, the oldest institution of higher education in that state, then under a debt of $92,000. Given the responsibility of raising funds, the young newcomer quickly impressed Texas Baptists with his forceful preaching and contagious determination to save their college. After successful completion of that task he studied at the school while ministering in a nearby church. In 1897 he accepted a call to Dallas and quickly became an influential religious spokesman throughout the Southwest. His preaching was not theatrical, but it rarely failed to stir audiences with its intense, earnest persuasiveness. Truett spoke directly to the hearts of his listeners in simple words that penetrated all who heard him. Often the beauty of gospel themes elevated his sermons to spell-binding eloquence; more often they left the impression of plain truth persons could readily adopt for spiritual profit. In addition to acquiring national recognition as a pulpit orator, Truett contributed to the growth of his denomination and its many programs. In Dallas he solicited vast sums of money for orphanages and old age homes together with a hospital, which formed part of the Baylor Medical Center. After serving the Southern Baptist Convention for three troubled years (1927–30), he was also president of the Baptist World Alliance from 1934 to 1939. In that capacity he toured foreign missions, held regional conferences, and advised ministerial associations, attempting to further the cause of evangelical witness around the globe. In all these larger functions he remained essentially a preacher whose message derived much of its power from his own devotional life.

Bibliography:

A. *We Would See Jesus* (New York, 1915); *A Quest for Souls* (Dallas, TX, 1917); *Follow Thou Me* (New York, 1932).

B. DAB 23, 778–79; NYT 8 July 1944, 11; Powhatan W. James, *George W. Truett: A Biography* (New York, 1939).

TRUTH, Sojourner (1797?, Ulster County, NY—26 November 1883, Battle Creek, MI).

Born a slave sometime in the 1790s, the woman known as "Isabella" passed through the hands of several owners, bore five children, and left her master the year before emancipation became mandatory in New York. By 1829 she moved to Manhattan where association with a religious visionary, Elijah Pierson, soon led to street preaching and work in an asylum for reformed prostitutes. Isabella had infrequently experienced spiritual visions herself, and much of her subsequent activity was based on the conviction that she was following divine commands. In 1833 Pierson's circle of friends, including the ex-slave, invested all their belongings in an experimental commune, an enterprise resulting in Pierson's death and no little scandal two years later. Until 1843, life for Isabella seems to have been relatively tranquil, but once again she began hearing the mystical voice. In response to such prompting she changed her name to Sojourner Truth and began a preaching tour so unorganized it amounted to mendicancy. As she moved through New England on foot, sharing her mystic, benevolent religious sentiments with those who would listen, crowds began to collect around her. Curiosity seekers came for the novelty of seeing a Negro on a public platform; they stayed to learn from the words of an illiterate black woman whose heavy Dutch accent carried home the truths she advocated. With those modest beginnings she soon exerted a widespread influence for major social reforms.

While certainly no friend to the cause of slavery, Sojourner Truth did not begin campaigning for abolition in earnest before 1846. After that she canvassed northern and midwestern states repeatedly, attracting large audiences with her simple, heartfelt speeches, gospel singing, and invincible capacity to refute hecklers. Even threats of mob violence (in Indiana and Kansas) could not intimidate her. After 1851 she also championed women's rights; this crusade did not elicit as strong a personal endorsement as abolition of slavery, but it continually held her interest. In 1865 she worked for the National Freedmen's Relief Association in Virginia, doing what she could to put hospitals, orphanages, and sanitation facilities in order for Blacks unaccustomed to taking care of themselves. She saw the freedmen's need for enough land and employment to escape the serfdom of governmental doles. For years she tried to gather popular support for a Negro state west of the Mississippi, but all overtures to the Grant administration proved fruitless. There was also waning public response to this final project, so she quietly abandoned it in 1875. Her major contribution lay in the prewar years when her colorful personality and personal history confronted people with a plea for basic freedoms which few could treat with indifference.

Bibliography:

B. NAW 3, 479–81; NYT 27 Nov 1883, 2; Olive Gilbert, *Narrative of Sojourner Truth* (Boston, 1850, and many subsequent editions); Arthur H. Fauset, *Sojourner Truth: God's Faithful Pilgrim* (Chapel Hill, NC, 1938; New York, 1971); Hertha E. Pauli, *Her Name was Sojourner Truth* (New York, 1962); Victoria Ortiz, *Sojourner Truth: A Self-Made Woman* (Philadelphia, 1974).

TUCKER, William Jewett (13 July 1839, Griswold, CT—29 September 1926, Hanover, NH). *Education*: B.A., Dartmouth Coll., 1861; B.D., Andover Sem., 1866. *Career*: schoolteacher, Columbus, OH, 1861–63; minister, Manchester, NH, 1867–75; minister, New York, NY, 1875–79; professor of Sacred Rhetoric, Andover Sem., 1880–93; president, Dartmouth Coll., 1893–1909; retirement, 1909–26.

While he was involved in two parish ministries, Tucker only gradually realized that he could help direct the progressive spirit of a new era. First in a Congregational church and then a Presbyterian one, his experiences led him to conclude that education was the sphere most important for offering guidance to modern Christianity. A professorship offered more time to grapple with the new world of thought which posed aggressive intellectual demands on traditional thought and action. Tucker was a staunch advocate of theological advancement, urging that it was every churchman's duty to break up mechanical forms of religious expression to achieve larger truths as affected by modern conditions. He knew that theology should formulate a better understanding of divine workings in the natural world to parallel development from Newtonian to Darwinian conceptions. Historical criticism of early Christian literature disturbed the customary assumptions of some, but he defended it as more consistent with reasonable fact. The extension of religion into new conditions of modern society broke convention in a third area; again he argued that such changes were beneficial because they confronted secular power in the material world with humanizing influences. That brought him full circle to revising creeds with a view to more humanitarian concerns. As associate editor of the *Andover Review*, he worked for years (1884–93) to harmonize inherited scriptural teachings with more rational instincts of faith. A prolonged litigation over the orthodoxy of Tucker and four colleagues did not deter him from attempting new courses of action or of fashioning a progressive orthodoxy to improve the quality of ministerial training.

While at Andover, Tucker helped articulate new social awareness as churches widened their concern to embrace the unemployed as well as the unrepentant. He saw that individualism as a social theory was being overwhelmed by industrialism, producing a collective conception of human life. Instead of charity for the poor and gospel missions for individual salvation, he argued that social justice was needed. Churches should become agents of social service, actively involved in questions of economics, labor, and all the physical needs of life. He introduced new topics into pastoral theology courses to cover such issues as immigration, leisure time, labor unions, capitalism, crime, and disease. He founded one of the first settlement houses in New England; for decades South End House in Boston gave young ministers a taste of practical service while it offered townspeople an example of religious vitality at work in their community. Tucker's program of educational reconstruction continued after he became president of Dartmouth, a college at that time with conservative views and heavily in debt. During his administration he was able to instill new vision, broaden the curriculum, expand facilities, and achieve a virtual great awakening in reforms affecting alumni. In 1907 poor health forced a serious decline in activities, but in retirement his literary efforts yielded several interpretive volumes on his generation which have proved to be some of the more penetrating retrospectives attainable.

Bibliography:

A. *The Making and the Unmaking of the Preacher* (Boston, 1898); *Personal Power* (Boston, 1910); *Public Mindedness* (Concord, MA, 1910); *The Function of the Church in Modern Society* (Boston, 1911); *The New Reservation of Time* (Boston, 1916); *My Generation: An Autobiographical Interpretation* (Boston, 1919).

B. SH 12, 33–34; NCAB 24, 242; DAB 19, 41–42; NYT 30 Sep 1926, 25.

TUCKERMAN, Joseph (18 January 1778, Boston, MA—20 April 1840, Havana, Cuba). *Education*: B.A., Harvard Coll., 1798; studied theology with Thomas Thacher, Dedham, MA, 1798–1801. *Career*: minister, Chelsea, MA, 1801–26; minister-at-large, Boston, 1826–36.

Experiences in a modest pastorate with country surroundings did not lead Tuckerman into championing the cause of social justice. With liberal convictions later categorized as Unitarianism he exerted himself for the poor and sick in his small flock, but there were no deliberate plans to develop a ministry among those neglected in cities. By 1812 he did learn one valuable lesson when he tried to improve the moral condition of seamen. The society for their improvement accomplished little because Tuckerman had no concrete knowledge of the people he wished to serve. He found that tracts and sermons were not enough to protect sailors from a brothel or grog shop. Chronic poor health dogged his efforts, so much so that he resigned the Chelsea congregation because his voice could not bear the strain of preaching twice on Sundays. On moving to Boston he cast around for some way of continuing pastoral activities without pulpit obligations. His old college roommate, *William E. Channing, gave practical direction to such wishes by making him officer in the American Unitarian Association. As salaried missionary for that agency, he became minister-at-large to the unchurched poor in town. This was not the first such work of its kind, but the ailing minister accomplished enough by his labors to be imitated on two continents.

After a short time of trying to do good by visits and conversation, Tuckerman slowly realized that social welfare needed careful planning. He emphasized the social character of Christianity, arguing repeatedly that religion consisted more of action than of contemplation, more of interpersonal responsibility than of a private pact with God. At the same time he was convinced that religious influences were essential to lasting reform; men of good will must seek to improve character while improving physical circumstances. Tuckerman was one of the first welfare theorists who wanted to care for more than needs of the moment, to find reasons behind problems and remedy them by what he called "scientific charity." He probed for the causes of juvenile delinquency, alcoholism, and poverty (a jobless condition with no stigma, unlike pauperism betokening moral laxity). He worked with legislators, city officials, and institutional directors to improve facilities or change methods in dealing with child welfare, jails, insane asylums, and poor relief. In 1834 he produced another innovation by correlating twenty-one forms of charitable work into the Benevolent Societies of Boston.

This was the first American council of social agencies, formed to avoid duplication in services for a city's poor and needy. For a decade, Tuckerman struggled to have affluent citizens recognize their duties to others while he reclaimed the downtrodden to Christian principles. In 1838 he resigned, shattered by disease, exhaustion, and the death of his wife. His own death came while traveling in search of recovery on a voyage to warmer climates.

Bibliography:

A. *Seven Discourses on Miscellaneous Subjects* (Boston, 1813); *Principles and Results of the Ministry-at-Large* (Boston, 1838); *A Memorial of Rev. Joseph Tuckerman* (Worcester, MA, 1888).

B. AAP 8, 345–56; SH 12, 34; NCAB 6, 230–31; DAB 19, 46; Daniel T. McColgan, *Joseph Tuckerman: Pioneer in American Social Work* (Washington, DC, 1940).

TURNER, Henry McNeal (1 February 1834, Newberry Court House, SC— 8 May 1915, Windsor, Canada). *Career*: revivalist for the Methodist Episcopal (ME) Church, South, 1853–57; revivalist for the African Methodist Episcopal (AME) Church, 1858–62; minister, Israel Church, Washington, DC, 1862–63; chaplain, Union Army, 1863–65; presiding elder, AME Church in GA, 1865–67; political activist and minister, Savannah, GA, 1867–76; general manager, AME Book Concern, Baltimore, 1876–80; bishop of the AME Church, 1880–1915.

Born to free parents in the slaveholding South, Turner grew up under conditions of prejudice and ostracism which he fought all his life. He acquired the rudiments of an education after his fifteenth year and worked at menial jobs before obtaining (1853) a license to preach in southern Methodist churches. Even though Turner was a successful revivalist among white and black congregations in several southern states, he transferred (1858) to the African Methodist Church, preferring the added measure of autonomy and self-esteem found there. During the Civil War his ministerial service was expanded by appointment as a military chaplain, the first such office for a black man. He continued in the regular army briefly after the war and worked in the Georgia Freedman's Bureau. But Turner's ambitions for improvement among his people went unfulfilled; so he returned to recruiting members for AME churches which aided both their religious and social betterment. Politics again attracted his attention during the state's reconstruction era, but building churches in Georgia was the forceful preacher's primary objective. Always an energetic and vigorous leader, Turner's sustained activities in ecclesiastical matters won recognition and added authority upon his election to the episcopacy.

By the 1880s it had become clear that legal emancipation did not insure social equality for Blacks in America, and Turner's bitterness was a gauge of his former optimism. Usually gruff and unrefined in the best of circumstances, he often became overpowering in scathing denunciations of a double tragedy: black meekness in the face of white oppression. He boldly advocated a number of educational and missionary projects to enhance self-determination, founding for example the *Southern Christian Recorder* (1889) and the *Voice of Missions* (1892) to publicize and convince his constituents. After civil rights for Blacks were circumscribed by a Supreme Court decision in 1883, he contended that its judges were iniquitous or, if correct, the Constitution was a sham and the nation ungrateful to thousands who died protecting it. As mob violence and lynch law spread through the South, Turner urged church members and Blacks in general to arm for defense. The cyclonic bishop did not abandon Christianity nor its Methodist form of doctrine and discipline, but he did redefine his expectations of American society, eventually deciding that emigration was the only viable solution. The African mission field became an opportunity for simultaneous escape from white dominance and increased cultural development in a free environment. Turner's emigration schemes had few lasting results, but his attacks on social injustice were widely heard. His tenacity in arguing for what he thought to be right maintained a core of awareness in his own church and served to keep the plight of black citizens before a public that was reluctant to provide equality for all its members.

Bibliography:

B.   NCAB 2, 206; DAB 19, 65–66; M. M. Ponton, *Life of Henry M. Turner* (Atlanta, 1917; Westport, CT, 1970); Edwin S. Redkey, *Black Exodus: Black Nationalist and Back-to-Africa Movements, 1890–1910* (New Haven, 1969).

TUTTLE, Daniel Sylvester (26 January 1837, Windham, NY—17 April 1923, St. Louis, MO). *Education*: B.A., Columbia Univ., 1857; B.D., General Sem. (NY), 1862. *Career*: private tutor, 1857–59; curate and rector, Morris, NY, 1862–67; missionary bishop of Montana, 1867–80; bishop of Utah, 1880–86; bishop of Missouri, 1886–1923.

With only five years' experience in a country church, Tuttle was surprised to find himself named missionary bishop before reaching the canonical age of thirty. After satisfying that requirement he set out for his Rocky Mountain jurisdiction which included Idaho and Utah as well as Montana. The mission territory, one of five created by the Episcopal General Convention in 1865, comprised 340,000 square miles and contained not one ordained priest on his arrival. So Tuttle began pioneering work, often preaching in mining towns or stock tenders' stations where a clergyman had never set foot before. Most of his efforts were spent in the region between Salt Lake City and Helena, following an arc that touched Boise. He did not try to convert Indians or Mormons but concentrated on unchurched American citizens who had prior knowledge of Christianity derived from their eastern origins. Many attended his sermons for the novelty of seeing a clerical gown again, but he made some headway against widespread habits of gambling, profanity, and heavy drinking. Still, he baptized more than he buried, and churches slowly developed as a result of the bishop's energetic missionary labor.

After 1869 Tuttle settled with his family in Salt Lake City where he gained respect from Mormon leaders for his general philanthropic endeavors. Schools were the backbone of missionary work, and he was able to organize academies in principal towns where parishes did not as yet exist. Another important institution was St. Mark's Hospital (1872) which ministered to all inhabitants, regardless of confessional distinctions. The well-meaning bishop received cooperation from people in every occupation, finding mutual respect and tolerance almost everywhere because he manifested spiritual concern for each person he met. Strong and durable (though his hearing began to fail), he traveled forty thousand miles by stagecoach in territory that was broken into three bishoprics after he left. He finally acceded to urgent requests from the diocese of Missouri to manage their affairs and brought to St. Louis in 1886 the same broad, evangelical drive which had sustained him in the mountains. After 1903 he also served as presiding bishop, the last to do so by reason of seniority. A new canon was passed in 1919, over his opposition, providing elective procedures for selecting a chief administrator. It was not put into effect, however, until Tuttle's fifty-six years as bishop and two decades as senior official came to an end.

Bibliography:

A. *Reminiscences of a Missionary Bishop* (New York, 1906).
B. SH 12, 44; NCAB 6, 58–59; DAB 19, 75; NYT 18 Apr 1923, 21.

TYLER, Bennet (10 July 1783, Middlebury, CT—14 May 1858, South Windsor, CT). *Education*: B.A., Yale Coll., 1804; studied theology with Asahel Hooker, Goshen, CT, 1805–07. *Career*: schoolteacher, Weston, CT, 1804–05; minister, South Britain, CT, 1808–22; president, Dartmouth Coll., 1822–28; minister, Second Congregational Church, Portland, ME, 1828–34; president and professor of Christian Theology, Theol. Inst. of CT (later Hartford Sem.), 1834–57.

After two decades of service as pastor and educator, Tyler seemed in 1828 ready to enjoy the quiet pleasures of evangelical labor in a large Maine parish. But that year marked a time when antagonistic theological forces were set in motion, precipitating a controversy which at length won him recognition as outstanding spokesman for "Old School" Calvinism. *Nathaniel W. Taylor, professor at a newly organized divinity school in New Haven, initiated the sequence of events by attempting a rational defense of revivals within the Edwardsean tradition. His address "Concio ad Clerum" and subsequent statements made it clear that he thought man's sinfulness was not due to nature, depravity being no essential attribute of the soul. Taylor hoped by such argumentation to show that God does not create in man a sinful nature and then condemn him for actions over which he has no free choice. As early as 1829 Tyler began private correspondence with Taylor regarding the implications of his ideas; eventually the dispute became public, and opinion gravitated to opposite ends of a spectrum. Conservatives in Connecticut thought the humanizing tendencies of "New Haven

Theology'' compromised too much with the philosophical dictates of modern society. In an effort to counterbalance that tendency, forty ministers formed a Pastoral Union in 1833 and resolved to establish a seminary. Eight months later the cornerstone was laid for an institution at East Windsor, providing the means for vigorous Calvinistic instruction in that municipality until operations were transferred to Hartford in 1865.

Though he was known as an ardent conservative and a tenacious opponent in theological debate, Tyler was able to separate personalities from intellectual issues. In all his activity on behalf of orthodox standards made safe against liberal modification, he avoided attacking the authors of ideas he considered erroneous. Because of this diplomatic, high-minded posture, Tyler could highlight serious disagreements in the denomination without creating schism among New England Congregationalists. Speaking for conservatives he made no charges of heresy against the other side; rather he voiced the fear that ideas of New Haven men, if allowed to reach their logical conclusions, would overthrow fundamental principles of traditional Calvinism. Even before *Asahel Nettleton and other Connecticut clergymen persuaded him to leave Maine and join their forces, he had expressed grave doubts about revising established religious thought. Error could creep in unawares, despite the good intentions of revisionists, and once introduced, the bad effects of false ideas were certain to take their toll. Consequently he stood against compromising the old faith, especially its anti-pelagian tenets which gave God absolute sovereignty in salvation and man no free choice in the matter. In so doing he hoped to preserve sound belief based on simple gospel directives. Loyalty to Bible, Calvin, and *Jonathan Edwards was more important to him than attempts at placating contemporary demands for human initiative in social or religious contexts.

Bibliography:

A.   *Letters on the Origin and Progress of the New Haven Theology* (New York, 1837); *A Review of President Day's Treatise on the Will* (Hartford, CT, 1838); *New England Revivals* (Boston, 1846); *Letters to the Rev. Horace Bushnell*, 2 vols. (Hartford, CT, 1847–48); *Lectures on Theology* (Boston, 1859).

B.   SH 12, 46–47; NCAB 9, 87–88; DAB 19, 85–86.

V

VAN DUSEN, Henry Pitney (11 December 1897, Philadelphia, PA—13 February 1975, Belle Meade, NJ). *Education*: B.A., Princeton Univ., 1919; B.D., Union Sem. (NY), 1924; Ph.D., Univ. of Edinburgh, 1932. *Career*: at various ranks, professor of Systematic Theology, Union Sem. (NY), 1926–63; president, Union Sem., 1945–63; active retirement, 1963–75.

There were a great many religious enterprises to which Van Dusen contributed statesmanlike guidance and unflagging energy over the years. Early student work with the YMCA led to concern for the wider field of foreign missions. But service on Presbyterian mission boards was not enough for this individual whose vision extended to churches of every confession. Van Dusen was a leading ecumenist in modern times; his practical ideas became part of the architecture of the World Council of Churches, and he was a central figure at its meetings from 1948 through 1961. Ever since his student days under *William A. Brown he defended liberal theology with a bouyant, unrelenting manner. After becoming president of Union Seminary, he continued to advocate liberal tenets, even when major theological voices favored a variety of positions known collectively as neo-orthodoxy. Under his able direction, the seminary entered a remarkable period of growth. It achieved worldwide significance as an open marketplace for theological values, maintaining a balance between academic rigor and acute awareness of vital ecclesiastical issues. For almost two decades the institution reflected attitudes of its dynamic leader, particularly those which stressed honest questioning and the right of each individual to define truth for himself after careful inquiry.

The forthright, questing spirit which Van Dusen imparted to his students and colleagues during almost fifty years of vigorous witness was also apparent in his manner of dying. He and his wife had long been members of the Euthanasia

Society because they were convinced that individuals had the right to terminate life instead of enduring debilitating old age. Mrs. Van Dusen was severely hampered by arthritis while Mr. Van Dusen had been rendered virtually speechless by a stroke in 1970. Under crippling disabilities they decided not to eke out an existence in a nursing home and so took overdoses of sleeping pills. Their action came after open, candid discussions of suicide, which did not, they firmly held, carry with it any burden of sin. Modern medicine could support life far beyond the point where physical recovery was possible. Acquiescence in helpless old age was not the only response of Christian obedience to such conditions; they believed that a positive decision to terminate life was also suitable, consistent with the promise of resurrection. By so acting, both of them embodied a loyalty to principle, once it had been achieved through careful deliberation. Mrs. Van Dusen died immediately, but the aging churchman lingered for sixteen days until complications ended the sequence originally set in motion by a will not to survive.

Bibliography:

    A. *The Plain Man Seeks for God* (New York, 1933); *God in These Times* (New York, 1935); *World Christianity: Yesterday, Today and Tomorrow* (Nashville, 1947); *Life's Meaning* (New York, 1951); *One Great Ground of Hope* (Philadelphia, 1961); *The Vindication of Liberal Theology* (New York, 1963).
    B. NCAB H, 340; NYT 14 February 1975, 40.

VAN DYKE, Henry (10 November 1852, Germantown, PA—10 April 1933, Princeton, NJ). *Education*: B.A., Princeton Coll., 1873; B.D., Princeton Sem., 1877; studied at Berlin, 1878. *Career*: minister, United Congregational Church, Newport, RI, 1879–82; minister, Brick Presbyterian Church, New York, 1882–1900; professor of English Literature, Princeton Univ., 1900–23; U.S. Minister to Netherlands and Luxembourg, 1913–17; retirement, 1923–33.

Born into the family of a prominent Old School Presbyterian, young van Dyke showed early signs of a more liberal tendency in religious sentiments. Many of his published sermons evinced a simple, personal response to problems of sin and doubt, not concerned with theological exactitude as much as advice for others regarding the benefits of faith. He preferred short creeds combined with long years of service as the way to steer between extremes of modernism and fundamentalism. After 1889 the popular preacher became an outspoken advocate of revising the Westminster Confession. For the next three years he urged the desirability of a shorter, simpler statement of faith which excised some of the more repellant features of Calvinism such as damning unbaptized infants. Van Dyke wanted to stress God's love for the whole world, Christ's atonement for all mankind, the free offer of salvation to every creature. Without mincing words he announced that he did not care if such ideas were not Calvinistic; he knew them to be Christian. He also supported *Charles A. Briggs during that scholar's theological difficulties with the New York Presbytery. In the last analysis he did not persuade many colleagues to his way of thinking, but his defense of free expression within established channels indicates the mediating position he occupied as a pastor interested in a practicable religion.

Two vocations blended in van Dyke's ministry which brought him fame as a literary figure in addition to his role as a liberal Presbyterian clergyman. Through writing he combined the functions of moralist and artist, making it possible to speak to his age far more adequately than preaching would have done. In fiction, poetry, descriptions of faraway lands, and fishing expeditions, his literary productions embodied a distilled version of genteel Protestantism. Many of his works were bestsellers which reflected popular tastes while they helped keep them in force for another generation. With a fluent style not considered ornate or facile in his day, the minister-turned-professor tried to reach the same basic emotions with his stories as he did in addresses delivered from a podium. One central theme recurring in several major writings is the pilgrimage all human souls endure as they move through earthly existence. Van Dyke depicted characters with an artist's appreciation of life so that romance was never distant nor the wonders of nature obscured. He remained a favorite author for many years as he sought to teach spiritual lessons through literature, providing imagination and adventure for those seeking to understand universal truths in a wider perspective.

Bibliography:

A. *The Story of the Other Wise Man* (New York, 1896, and many subsequent editions); *The Gospel for an Age of Doubt* (New York, 1896); *The Blue Flower* (New York, 1902); *The Unknown Quantity* (New York, 1912); *Fighting for Peace* (New York, 1917); *Works*, 17 vols. (New York, 1920–22).

B. SH 12, 139; NCAB 25, 10–11; DAB 19, 186–88; NYT 11 Apr 1933, 19; Tertius van Dyke, *Henry van Dyke* (New York, 1935).

VARICK, James (1750?, near Newburgh, NY—22 July 1827, New York, NY). *Career*: minister (1799–1820), presiding elder (1820–22), and bishop (1822–27), African Methodist Episcopal (AME) Zion Church, 1799–1827.

Little is known about Varick's early life except that his mother was a slave and he became a shoemaker after moving from Orange County to the city of New York. He joined the John Street Methodist Church, founded by *Philip Embury, and attended regular sessions in the gallery set aside for black members. By 1796 the Negro constituency had grown so numerous, they received permission from bishop *Francis Asbury to hold separate meetings when the building was not otherwise in use. This separate society planted the seed of an independent organization; within three years increased numbers led Varick and others to erect another building. "Zion Church" was dedicated in 1800, forming the cornerstone of an ethnically separate ecclesiastical structure whose numbers and geographical expansion make it a significant facet of Methodist history. After some uneasy preliminary years regarding the question of who should conduct services at Zion Church, Varick was ordained by Asbury in 1806, becoming one of the first three black Americans to receive that ministerial status. Growth continued, new churches appeared from Connecticut to Pennsylvania, and relations with the ''Asbury Church'' remained amicable. But fifteen years later it seems that competition with other black leaders, themselves a splinter group from Wesleyan connection, forced the Zion Church to further steps toward institutional autonomy. But these later developments fit smoothly into the original impulse for independence shaped by the Negro shoemaker with a Dutch surname.

By 1820 several churches previously associated with Zion withdrew and joined *Richard Allen who carried the title of bishop from Bethel Church in Philadelphia. In an attempt to maintain current membership alignments, Varick asked Allen to consecrate Zion leaders as bishops for the New York area. Allen refused unless they would submit to his superintendency over a single denominational structure. Rejecting this demand, the New York group called a general conference (1821) and declared their existence as a fully autonomous body, the African Methodist Episcopal (AME) Church (''Zion'' added in 1848 to avoid confusion with Allen's AME organization). Varick became presiding elder and in less than two years was elected bishop. His labors for both church and race, which won public acclaim, continued unabated thereafter. Many of his achievements were related to denominational consolidation, such as his judicious efforts to draft a book of discipline modeled after Methodist doctrine and form of church government. He also helped found schools for black citizens, encouraging in addition many other self-help associations which improved the lot of freedmen and slaves alike. It was a coincidence, but one taken as a tribute to his lifework, that the state of New York abolished slavery two weeks before he died.

Bibliography:

B.   DAB 19, 225–26.

VENIAMINOV, John (26 August 1797, Anga, Russia—31 March 1879, Moscow, Russia). *Education*: graduated from Irkutsk Sem., 1818. *Career*: deacon and Priest, Church of the Annunciation, Irkutsk, Russia, 1817–21: missionary in Alaska, 1823–68; Metropolitan of Moscow, 1868–79.

Since his christening name, Ivan Popov, was the Russian equivalent of ''John Smith,'' this promising seminarian acquired Veniaminov as a distinguishing and honorific appellation. He married a year before finishing theological studies, and this choice confined him to parish work instead of a hierarchical career. In 1824 he and his family arrived on the island of Unalaska, having volunteered for missionary service the year before to continue Russian Orthodox efforts in that far-off edge of the empire. During the next decade he rebuilt the crumbling wooden church, mostly with his own hands, established a school and an orphanage, and expanded Christian service to native Americans and employees of the Russian-American Trading Company. Veniaminov mastered the Fox-Aleut language enough to preach unassisted, created a writing system based on Cyrillic letters, and translated into it catechisms, prayers, and the Gospel of Matthew.

Transferred to Sitka in 1834, he continued to travel throughout his huge domain, often traveling by dog-sled and kayak in order to minister to his charges.

In 1839 Veniaminov traveled to St. Petersburg and Moscow in hopes of improving support for missions in his area. At the time there were only four priests, ruled by the bishop at Irkutsk and sustained physically by secular trade officials. While there he greatly impressed Orthodox administrators with the importance of further missionary activity. He also contributed a great deal of ethnographic information to those who studied native peoples. Early in 1840 he learned that his wife had died several months previously, and so he took monastic vows, adopting the name of Innocent. Since this decision opened new opportunities for authority in the church, Veniaminov was made bishop of Kamchatka, the Kurile and Aleutian Islands that same year. Returning to Sitka in 1841, he added twenty-five new priests to his diocese over the next decade and increased the number of churches and chapels to over sixty. The Aleuts and Tlingits, major native populations in the area, did not increase. The number of converts dwindled from an estimated ten thousand at the high mark to inconsequential numbers as disease and cultural disintegration took their toll.

In 1852 Innocent was made archbishop, and two years later Yakutsk was added to his territory. In 1859 he moved his residence to Amur on the Asian mainland to meet even greater responsibilities. This robust, vigorous, driven man of humble origins was astonished to learn in 1868 of his appointment as successor to the highest office in Russian Orthodoxy. His personal piety, gentle manners, and zeal for missions continued to influence all those within his orbit. Less than a century after his death, the Holy Synod pronounced him a saint, canonizing him on 6 October 1977.

Bibliography:

B.   Paul D. Garrett, *St. Innocent: Apostle to America* (Crestwood, NY, 1979).

VEROT, Jean-Pierre Augustin Marcellin (23 May 1805, Le Puy, France— 10 June 1876, St. Augustine, FL). *Education*: studied at Issy Sem., 1821–28. *Career*: lecturer, Issy Sem., 1828–30; professor of Mathematics and Science, St. Mary's Coll. (MD), 1830–52; pastor, Ellicott's Mills, MD and surrounding chapels, 1852–58; vicar apostolic of FL, 1858–70; bishop of Savannah, GA, 1861–70; bishop of St. Augustine, FL, 1870–76.

Teaching and pastoral work as a Sulpician occupied most of Verot's life, but during one crowded decade he became conspicuous in activities of more widespread importance. After being elevated to episcopal office, he labored to resuscitate Catholicism in Florida, a territory including only one parish besides his own and a string of mission chapels. His identification with people and customs in the South was genuine; no issue discloses this sectional loyalty more than debates over slavery. In 1861 Verot preached a sermon condemning abolitionists as well as the slave trade. He argued that slavery was not evil in itself and could be theologically justified in the abstract. Suggesting a code of duties to protect both slaves and masters, he sustained the property rights of legitimate owners while striving to ameliorate abuses in current practice. The bishop was unmistakably a southern sympathizer who cooperated with the Confederacy as long as it defended what he called principles of justice. But his pastoral concern for all who came within his jurisdiction was manifest when he sent priests to minister among Union prisoners at Andersonville in 1864. Two years later he accepted the end of slavery and inaugurated the strongest missionary program for Negroes in any of the southern states. In establishing integrated worship and special schools for black children, he anticipated the Second Plenary Council's directives on the matter. His progress in ending racial prejudice was slow, but at least he did not avoid the first great social enterprises to attract sustained attention within American Catholicism.

Another issue on which Verot bespoke a minority opinion, this time with a bluntness that won him the epithet *enfant terrible*, had to do with papal infallibility. In 1870 he attended the Vatican Council called by Pius IX and expressed his views with candor enough to provoke strong reactions ranging from derisive laughter to cold anger. At least one-half of the American hierarchy thought it inopportune to proclaim a doctrine regarding papal power, but Verot went beyond that to argue it had no place in apostolic tradition. Infallibility was not long established or persistent in the church's faith; it smacked rather of a temporary whim introduced by ultramontanists. As a bishop in a predominantly Protestant country, he pled for expounding doctrines in softened, moderate tones instead of exaggerating differences by adding to existing dogma. The bishop failed to thwart promulgation of *Pastor Aeternus*, so he along with fifty-four others left Rome before final votes were cast. Once the doctrine was pronounced, however, he was one of the first opponents to accept it and encourage its adoption by believers in his diocese. Through the waning years he continued to foster growth of Catholic institutions, evangelizing and building with a vision more in keeping with the Second Vatican Council than that characterizing the First.

Bibliography:

    B.   NCAB 12, 535; DAB 19, 252–53; NCE 14, 626; Michael V. Gannon, *Rebel Bishop: The Life and Era of Augustin Verot* (Milwaukee, 1964).

VIVEKANANDA (12 January 1863, Calcutta, India—4 July 1902, Belur, India). *Education*: B.A., Univ. of Calcutta, 1881. *Career*: spokesman for Vedantic Hinduism, 1886–97; founder of the Ramakrishna Mission, 1897–1902.

Nerendra Nath Datta, reared in a wealthy family of the kshatriya (military and government) caste, seemed destined by education and cultural expectations to a profession in civil service. But in 1879 he met by chance a mystic priest of Kali who slowly influenced him to seek spiritual insight instead of materialistic success. The young man was an informal disciple of Sri Ramakrishna until 1886, when he formally renounced worldly pursuits to follow vedantic teachings under his master's tutelage. Adopting the name Vivekananda, "he who has the bliss of spiritual discrimination," he quickly excelled as a mendicant monk and student of advaita (non-dualistic) Hinduism. He followed Ramakrishna's example in believing that the time honored ways of religious activity—work, devotion, knowledge, and mysticism—were equally conducive to edification. Similarly he believed that different religious traditions could be synthesized by anyone seriously determined to achieve closer communion with God. In addition to eclecticism, Vivekananda's teachings were based on the conviction that Ramakrishna was a special incarnation for the present age, one who could provide focus for applying religious truths to contemporary human society.

The renaissance of classical Hinduism did not receive much notice in the United States before 1893. In that year Vivekananda attended the Parliament of Religions, held in connection with the Chicago World's Fair, where his dignity and ecumenical spirit made favorable impressions. He proved to be a fitting representative at conferences which emphasized common elements in man's varying religious visions. Expounding Hinduism as the mother of religions, he spoke eloquently not only of Upanishadic wisdom but of broad common ground in the universal human search for spiritual enlightenment. After the Parliament, he founded during the following year a Vedanta Society in New York and from that base lectured in major cities. Appreciative audiences listened to his instructions on vedantic philosophy, devotion, and meditation, all means by which to subordinate sense impulses to spiritual control. Vivekananda built up a loyal following during his American missionary efforts (1893–96, 1899–1900), founding a number of branch societies in metropolitan areas over the continent. On his return to India in 1897, he established the Ramakrishna Mission and was generally acknowledged to be his master's successor in training disciples for future work. The Mission has continued its witness in this country up to the present, giving notice and encouragement that there are many levels on which spiritual questors might find reward.

Bibliography:

A.   *Eight Lectures . . . on Karma Yoga* (New York, 1896); *From Colombo to Almora* (Madras, 1897); *Vedanta Philosophy* (New York, 1899); *My Master* (New York, 1901); *The Complete Works of Swami Vivekananda*, 8 vols. (Calcutta, 1907–51).

B.   SH 12, 219–20; *The Life of Swami Vivekananda: By His Eastern and Western Disciples* (Calcutta, 1912); George M. Williams, *The Quest for Meaning of Swami Vivekananda: A Study of Religious Change* (Chico, CA, 1974).

W

WALKER, Williston (1 July 1860, Portland, ME—9 March 1922, New Haven, CT). *Education*: B.A., Amherst Coll., 1883; B.D., Hartford Sem., 1886; Ph.D., Leipzig, 1888. *Career*: professor of History, Bryn Mawr Coll., 1888–89; professor of Church History, Hartford Sem., 1889–1901; professor of Church History, Yale Univ., 1901–22.

The ideal of studying Christian history according to modern standards of empirical research and rational interpretations found its most eminent American practitioner in Walker. His graduate training in Germany emphasized the exacting methods of primary source work and impressed him with the lasting perspective that political factors usually played the major role in historical causation. By means of publications which appeared over thirty years, Walker served more than any other church historian to have his specialty accepted within secular circles. His methods were the same as other social scientists, and several of the balanced, compact narratives issued from his pen have remained durable classics. He usually avoided controversial interpretations, contenting himself with a spare delineation of events. But one general sympathy welling up in all his studies was a tendency to support freedom instead of repression in religious opinion. A gradual progress toward tolerance appealed to him, and he extolled every step in the direction of democratic humanitarianism which allowed men of all persuasions to follow the dictates of their consciences. Acquaintance with men of similar conviction had an enobling effect on students. Those who left their environs better, freer by their efforts could help present day churchmen to act effectually in meeting demands of their own age.

For all his participation in the quest for historical knowledge as its own reward, Walker was deeply interested in the record of his own denomination. Many of his writings proudly exhibited the rich heritage of Congregationalism even while they disowned large segments of the past which disclosed embarrassing episodes of persecution. Those exceptions notwithstanding, Walker was convinced that the institutional vitality of Congregational churches would keep them in the mainstream of ecclesiastical progress. In 1913 he served on a committee to draft a new constitution for the denomination. He was interested in the cause of Christian unity but urged at the same time that his church remain independent and work to expand its numerical strength for greater effectiveness. Another of his institutional commitments was Yale University, where he participated in restructuring the divinity school and brought sound judgment to bear in administrative posts including dean of the graduate school and provost. He was energetic in support of foreign evangelism too, supervising for a time Yale's Changsha mission in China. All in all, his teaching had a lasting impact on the young men of Yale while his historical volumes furthered an understanding of both the author and his subject matter.

Bibliography:

A. *The Creeds and Platforms of Congregationalism* (New York, 1893; Boston, 1960); *A History of the Congregational Churches in the United States* (New York, 1894); *The Validity of Congregational Ordination* (Hartford, 1898); *Ten New England Leaders* (New York, 1901, 1969); *John Calvin* (New York, 1906); *A History of the Christian Church* (New York, 1918; rev. ed., 1959).
B. SH 12, 257; NCAB 19, 29–30; DAB 19, 366–67.

WALLS, William Jacob (8 May 1885, Chimney Rock, NC—23 April 1975, Yonkers, NY). *Education*: B.A., Livingstone Coll., 1908; B.D., Hood Theol. Sem., 1913; studied at Columbia Univ., 1922; M.A., Univ. of Chicago, 1941. *Career*: Licensed preacher, 1899–1905; minister, African Methodist Episcopal Zion churches, Cleveland, NC (1905–07), Lincolnton, NC (1908–10), Salisbury, NC (1910–13), and Louisville, KY (1913–20); editor, *Star of Zion*, 1920–24; bishop, AME Zion church, 1924–68; senior bishop, 1951–68.

In light of his own difficulties experienced as a licensed preacher (1899), then as ordained deacon (1903) and elder (1905), Walls became a strong advocate of education in his denomination. After such earlier activities he went back to school and earned formal degrees that symbolized his mature attitude regarding intellectual preparation for church work. Vigorous mental training helped contribute to one of his fundamental interests: growth and greater internal strength in the churches under his care. This was also apparent after he was chosen to edit *Star of Zion*, the denomination's weekly newspaper, whose circulation he tripled within four years. As early as 1907 he attended sessions of the World Christian Education and Sunday School Convention, continuing to do so through 1958. When elected bishop Walls nurtured church growth wherever he served, those conferences being scattered throughout the country, concentrated mainly in highly populated urban areas. He served in this manner for forty-four years, being recalled twice by special vote (1960 and 1964) after having passed the statutory age of retirement. When those extra terms ended, he was commissioned as historiographer of the church, and during the last years of his life he produced the most comprehensive and accurate history of the AME Zion church to date.

While primarily concerned about denominational stability Walls was also interested in interdenominational affairs. As early as 1918 he was a fraternal messenger to the general conference of the southern Methodist church, and ten years later he performed a similar role among northern Methodists, both organizations being predominately white. For fifty years after 1921 he represented his church at Ecumenical Methodist Conferences. In 1948 he was a delegate at the organizational meeting of the World Council of Churches, and he continued to perform that function for two decades. In 1950 he led the procession of different church officials as they formally signed the charter of the National Council of Churches in this country. The following year he served as vice president of the World Methodist Conference which encompassed all the different branches of the Wesleyan tradition. After 1956 he was also on the executive committee of the World Methodist Council. In these ways as well as many others Walls successfully combined two important facets of effective church life: inner strength and compassionate outreach.

Bibliography:

A. *J. C. Price: Educator and Race Leader* (Boston, 1943); *The African Methodist Episcopal Zion Church: Reality of the Black Church* (Charlotte, NC, 1974).
B. NYT 24 Apr 1975, 38.

WALTHER, Carl Ferdinand Wilhelm (25 October 1811, Langenchursdorf, Germany—7 May 1887, St. Louis, MO). *Education*: graduated from Univ. of Leipzig, 1833. *Career*: private tutor, Kahla, Germany, 1834–36; minister, Braunsdorf, Germany, 1837–38; minister, Dresden and Johannesberg, MO, 1839–41; minister, Trinity Church, St. Louis, MO, 1841–87; editor, *Der Lutheraner*, 1844–87; professor of Theology, Concordia Sem., 1850–87; editor, *Lehre und Wehre*, 1855–87.

Conflicts with rationalists in his first parish made Walther despondent over the religious state of his native Saxony. Consequently he was ready to emigrate with a large number of pious Lutherans under the leadership of *Martin Stephan, sailing aboard the *Johann Georg* and settling in Perry County, Missouri, by early 1839. After Stephan was expelled that same year for gross misconduct, Walther emerged as leader of the German community. Over the course of four decades he gave Lutheran churches in his area a distinctive theological orientation and polity which continue virtually intact today. Regarding himself as a loyal conservator of Reformation principles, he called for strict adherence to all six of Luther's Confessions. Articles on doctrinal uniformity printed in his bimonthly, *Der Lutheraner*, brought favorable response from like-minded ministers in several areas. By 1847 they met in conservative fellowship to create the "German Evangelical Lutheran Synod of Missouri, Ohio, and Other States," better known by a title adopted one hundred years later: The Lutheran Church—Missouri Synod. Walther served as first president of the institution which deliberately avoided patterns of centralized ecclesiastical machinery known in Germany. It stressed rather a democratic polity that made local congregations autonomous and gave laymen equal voice with their clergy in church affairs. In 1872 his remarkable talent for organization produced an even larger association, the Evangelical Lutheran Synodical Conference, the presidency of which was natural recognition of his eminence as administrative guide.

Immigrants often cling to old beliefs in order to retain a sense of identity amid their new cultural surroundings. Walther may have championed Lutheran confessionalism for that reason, but more importantly he believed the inherited doctrinal system held all essentials for saving faith. The Bible and Luther's confessional guidelines were adequate aids to inner piety as well as sufficient weapons for combatting false religious opinion. Beginning in 1839 a log cabin school was built to foster the growth of traditional doctrine; ten years later it became Concordia Seminary, and Walther instilled a distinctively militant orthodoxy in generations of its ministerial students. In several theological controversies, he applied immense learning coupled with undeviating assurance that his position was the only correct one. His strong, unequivocal views on such matters as the nature of the church, biblical authority, the duty of ministers, and the central role of grace in salvation were widely adopted throughout the Missouri Synod. Indeed, his insistence on loyalty to traditional symbols left a conservative stamp on the denomination which has remained one of its distinguishing characteristics.

Bibliography:

A. *Die Stimme unserer Kirche in der Frage von Kirche und Amt* (St. Louis, 1852); *Die rechte Gestalt einer vom Staate unabhängigen evangelisch-lutherischen Ortsgemeinde* (St. Louis, 1863, 1879); *Die evangelisch-lutherische Kirche die wahre sichtbare Kirche Gottes auf Erden* (St. Louis, 1867, 1891); *Americanisch-lutherische Pastoraltheologie* (St. Louis, 1872); *Lutherische Brosamen* (St. Louis, 1876); *Die rechte Unterscheidung von Gesetz und Evangelium* (St. Louis, 1901).

B. SH 12, 259; NCAB 26, 118–19; DAB 19, 402–03; NCE 14, 793; Diedrich H. Steffens, *Doctor Carl Ferdinand Wilhelm Walther* (Philadelphia, 1917); William G. Polack, *The Story of C. F. W. Walther* (St. Louis, 1935); Lewis W. Spitz, *The Life of Dr. C. F. W. Walther* (St. Louis, 1961).

WARD, Harry Frederick (15 October 1873, Brantford, England—9 December 1966, Palisade, NJ). *Education*: B.A., Northwestern Univ., 1897; M.A., Harvard Univ., 1898. *Career*: minister at various times, Wabash Avenue Methodist Church, 47th Street Methodist Church, and Union Avenue Methodist Church, Chicago, IL, Euclide Avenue Methodist Church, Oak Park, IL, 1899–1912; professor of Social Service, Boston Univ., 1913–18; professor of Christian Ethics, Union Sem. (NY), 1918–41; professor emeritus, 1941–66.

There is some uncertainty as to when Ward was officially ordained a Methodist minister. He was already a lay preacher before immigrating from England in

1891, and he continued that activity while working at odd jobs in Utah and Idaho. Some time between 1899 and 1902 he became a full-fledged clergyman, though, and by the latter date had joined the Rock River Conference in Illinois. During the first decade of this century he served in churches near Chicago's stockyards, and there he learned of the bitter struggles between labor and big business that affected so many people. He sided with the workers and embraced various aspects of socialist thought; this notoriety made him a controversial figure for the next fifty years. Ward's experience and advocacy epitomized the American Social Gospel. He embodied the conviction that the best form of religion was that which motivated believers to unite in social action. In 1907 he was one of the founders of The Methodist Federation for Social Service (now for Social Action). The following year he helped draft The Methodist Social Creed, a document that called for equal rights and complete justice for everyone at all stages of life, one that was later adopted in enlarged form by the Federal Council of Churches.

The economic wrongs that blight human lives were Ward's abiding concern. He used the Jewish-Christian tradition to criticize the sins of acquisitive society and, in the name of the working poor, to demand reforms for their welfare. Beyond that, he also espoused the causes of civil liberties, peace, racial equality, and antifascism. Between 1920 and 1940 he chaired the national board of the American Civil Liberties Union. For a time he also chaired the American League Against War and Fascism (later for Peace and Democracy). Through the Great Depression and past the McCarthy era he issued manifestos and policy statements for the Citizens Committee for Constitutional Liberties. He delivered speeches and circulated petitions for the Religious Freedom Committee. He was a perennial gadfly, filling the unthanked position of social critic and activist for dozens of libertarian causes. He was also looked on as patron saint of the peace movement, and throughout a vigorous retirement he continued to blend faith and citizenship in pursuit of a better life for all of humanity.

Bibliography:

A. *The Social Creed of the Churches* (New York, 1912); *Social Evangelism* (New York, 1915); *The Gospel for a Working World* (New York, 1918); *The New Social Order: Principles and Programs* (New York, 1919); *In Place of Profit: Social Incentives in the Soviet Union* (New York, 1933); *Democracy and Social Change* (New York, 1940).

B. DAB supp. 8, 680–81; NYT 10 Dec 1966, 37.

WARDE, Frances (1810, Abbeyleix, Ireland—17 September 1884, Manchester, NH). *Career*: member, Congregation of Our Lady of Mercy, 1832–84; mother superior, Carlow, Ireland, 1837–43; mother superior, Pittsburgh, PA, 1843–50; mother superior, Providence, RI, 1851–58; mother superior, Manchester, NH, 1858–84.

After spending several years as a Dublin socialite, Warde's true vocation emerged when she met Catherine McAuley, the aunt of a friend. By 1828 the young girl, virtually an orphan, had become McAuley's intimate associate in her charity work with poor children. The settlement house resembled a convent more than a welfare agency from its inception, but it was not recognized as a religious order until 1832. Choosing the name Mary Frances Teresa, Warde became one of its first postulants, and one year later she was the first Sister of Mercy to profess vows before founder McAuley in the first Convent of Mercy at Dublin. During the next half century she helped expand Sisters of Mercy into one of the world's largest congregations of religious women, founding in America more convents and service institutions than any woman in Christian history. By her own daily regimen, she embodied the order's reciprocal goals of contemplation and active service. As spiritual counselor to novices, she proved to be a sound guide within the cloister, while outside it her name became practically synonymous with aid to the poor, sick, and uneducated in every locality. In addition to furnishing an inspiring example of self-sacrifice, her more important contribution lay in a facility for establishing stable institutions that perpetuated religious witness through cumulative activity.

True to the pattern of many early pioneers, Mother Warde laid foundations of new institutions, then moved on to fresh challenges while others remained to augment the scope of apostolic works. She possessed a tender piety which often warmed her colleagues, but she was also a woman of forceful determination to get things done, harboring a singleminded zeal that amounted at times to severity. With great energy and considerable administrative skill she personally established twenty-five convents, a handful of orphanages, and no less than sixty schools on this side of the Atlantic. Many of these in turn served as motherhouses, sending missionaries and teachers to more areas which compounded outlets for service in ever greater proportions. Mother Warde influenced programs in which thousands of Sisters of Mercy spread convents and academies in a network across the entire continent. She accomplished this without regard to hardships, whether they stemmed from meager physical resources or spiritual trials including internal disputes over vocational priorities and anti-Catholic bigotry in American culture. Her favorite work was Christian doctrine classes for adults, and in that medium she was able to count many converts to Catholicism. An apostolate of transparent holiness, expressed in the secular world as charity and teaching, constituted her long years of effort. She persevered in that calling, despite near blindness in old age, until her strength finally gave way.

Bibliography:

B. NCE 14, 810; M. Catherine Garety, *Rev. Mother M. Xavier Warde* (Boston, 1902); Kathleen Healy, *Frances Warde: American Founder of the Sisters of Mercy* (New York, 1973).

WARFIELD, Benjamin Breckinridge (5 November 1851, near Lexington, KY—17 February 1921, Princeton, NJ). *Education*: B.A., Coll. of New Jersey, 1871; B.D. Princeton Sem., 1876; studied at Leipzig, 1876–77. *Career*: assistant minister, First Presbyterian Church, Baltimore, MD, 1877–78; professor of New Testament Exegesis and Literature, Western Sem. (PA), 1878–87; professor of

Didactic and Polemic Theology, Princeton Sem., 1887–1921; editor, *The Presbyterian Review*, 1890–1903.

After graduating from college with high marks in science and mathematics, Warfield announced without prior notice (while traveling in Europe, 1872) that he planned to enter the ministry. He studied at Princeton while *Charles Hodge still reigned over the Old School tradition, and much of his subsequent activity was spent to strengthen conservative resistance to modernist influence in Presbyterian churches. Situated at the storm center of many theological controversies, Warfield covered the whole range of his discipline with widely acknowledged erudition, lending prestige to what has been called a "high Protestant" doctrine of the Bible. For him theology was not based on human reason or implications drawn from personal experience; it stemmed rather from a grammatical-historical exegesis of biblical texts which carried in themselves their own authoritative interpretation. He insisted further that Scripture taught a doctrine of inspiration which made God the author of every physical fact, spiritual injunction, psychological or philosophical principle contained therein. A proved error would destroy such a structure of absolute inerrancy, but Christianity was safe because fundamental errors were impossible to verify. The extreme tenet of his apologetic defense asserted that verbal inspiration had been perfect in the original manuscripts, not present-day copies. In the last analysis, he sought to preserve biblical inerrancy by arguing that the textual discrepancies which critics found were unimportant; the autograph edition had been immaculate, sufficient proof of God's inherent truthfulness.

Over the course of several decades Warfield put his school's defense of biblical literalism in its most explicit and authoritarian form. In addition to shaping more than one generation of Presbyterian leaders in that conservative mold, his ideas dominated the entire General Assembly between 1892 and 1910. During those years the national body officially declared no less than five times that belief in an inerrant original manuscript Bible was essential for membership in the church. There were other aspects of the historic Christian faith which the influential teacher thought still tenable despite modern tendencies to revise them. From Paul and Augustine to Calvin, he discerned a stream of theological development containing the one true hope of the world. Each of these earlier thinkers had emphasized the importance of grace over ecclesiastical forms or routine morality. The finest expression of that evangelical witness was contained in the Westminster Confession, and Warfield battled against every attempt to change its wording. All of his studies, from patristics through the Reformation to modern times, consisted of arguments to show that liberal assumptions departed from sound Christian belief. More than twenty books, pamphlets, articles, and brilliant book reviews kept up a barrage against those who sought to shift priorities within the Calvinistic tradition. Denying the historical maxim that the past is largely irrecoverable, he used history selectively to oppose change, deliberately equating his theology with that of apostolic times.

Bibliography:

A. *An Introduction to the Textual Criticism of the New Testament* (London, 1886); *Counterfeit Miracles* (New York, 1918); *Biblical Doctrines* (New York, 1929); *Christology and Criticism* (New York, 1929); *The Westminster Assembly and its Work* (New York, 1931); *The Inspiration and Authority of the Bible* (Philadelphia, 1948).
B. SH 12, 273; NCAB 20, 59; DAB 19, 453–54; NCE 14, 810–11; NYT 18 Feb 1921, 11.

WASHINGTON, Booker Taliaferro (5 April 1856, Hale's Ford, VA—14 November 1915, Tuskegee, AL). *Education*: B.A., Hampton Inst., 1875; studied at Wayland Sem., Washington, DC, 1878. *Career*: schoolteacher, Malden, WV, 1875–77; instructor Hampton Inst., 1879–81; principal, Tuskegee Inst., 1881–1915.

Born in slavery, the son of a Negro cook and apparently some white man from a neighboring plantation, Washington chose his surname at a later date. He was largely self-taught, acquiring the rudiments of education while working at a salt furnace in West Virginia where his family moved after emancipation. Hampton Institute provided a setting for more formal schooling, and he so impressed *Samuel C. Armstrong, its founder, that he was later invited to be a member of its staff. A real opportunity for independent growth came in 1881, however, when the state of Alabama appropriated slender funding for a Negro normal and industrial school. Named its first principal, Washington over the next three decades was the most important factor in establishing that institution as a place where practical training sustained pride among southern black Americans. Under his supervision one hundred buildings were constructed from bricks made on the premises; two thousand acres of land were acquired; student enrollment grew to 1,500 in almost forty trades and professional programs. He wanted to change patterns of living more than just start another school. The principal insisted on the dignity of common labor and the necessity of personal hygiene, sometimes acting as if the toothbrush were the linchpin of civilization. In larger perspective he wanted to effect a second emancipation, this time from poverty, ignorance, and disease. All his labors sought to convince students that discipline combined with practical skills in agriculture, mechanics, and commerce were the keys to cultural improvement.

By means of work at Tuskegee and speeches to mixed audiences across the country, Washington became recognized as a national spokesman for American Negroes. As early as 1895 he voiced a notable conception of race relations which won wide acceptance in his own day and set a standard for subsequent refinement. He argued that Blacks and whites could remain separate on a social basis while standing together on matters essential to mutual progress. Once the black man had made himself a productive citizen, an educated and landowning worker, then he would be in a strong position to demand political rights to which ability, character, and material possessions entitled him. Washington considered it more important to make people worthy of franchise than to inflame public opinion by agitating for it. Property, skill, and moral integrity led to the ballot; these were objectives as he saw them leading in sequence to eventual equality between the races. Critics charged that such thinking doomed Blacks perpetually to second class status. It accepted social segregation, they argued, and educated Negroes as a pool of skilled laborers to enrich white industrialists. Still, Washington laid the basic principles for black self-help. He identified immediate problems to be solved before larger questions of social status could be realistically assessed. Even the legal action by NAACP leaders built on his foundations more than they broached altogether new issues.

Bibliography:

A.   *The Future of the American Negro* (Boston, 1899); *Up From Slavery* (New York, 1901, and many subsequent editions); *Working with the Hands* (New York; 1904); *The Negro in Business* (Boston, 1907); *The Story of the Negro* (New York, 1909); *My Larger Education* (New York, 1911).

B.   SH 12, 275; NCAB 7, 363–64; DAB 19, 506–08; NYT 15 Nov 1915, 1; Frederick E. Drinker, *Booker T. Washington* (Philadelphia, 1915; New York, 1970); Emmett J. Scott and Lyman B. Stowe, *Booker T. Washington* (New York, 1916); Benjamin F. Riley, *The Life and Times of Booker T. Washington* (New York, 1916); Basil Mathews, *Booker T. Washington* (Cambridge, MA, 1948); Louis R. Harlan, *Booker T. Washington . . . 1856–1901* (New York, 1972).

WATTS, Alan Wilson (6 January 1915, Chislehurst, England—16 November 1973, Mill Valley, CA). *Education*: graduated from King's Coll., Canterbury, 1932; S.T.M., Seabury-Western Theol. Sem., 1948. *Career*: editor, *The Middle Way*, 1934–38; Episcopal chaplain, Northwestern Univ., 1945–50; professor of Comparative Philosophy, American Academy of Asian Studies., Univ. of the Pacific, 1951–57; independent writer and lecturer, 1957–73.

In his pursuit of Eastern wisdom Watts was initially driven by a desire to separate himself from the stifling conventionality of his suburban London upbringing. By 1930 he associated with English Buddhists and flourished in their circle for a decade. Even ordination as an Episcopal priest and a brief stint as campus chaplain did little to deflect him from concentration on the principles of Zen and Taoism. Choosing what he found personally attractive rather than steeping himself in classical traditions, Watts sought to attain harmony and balance in life. He urged that spiritual and physical health could result from a proper alignment of the individual with the forces of nature. Disruptive passions, egocentric preoccupations, and rational thought patterns were obstacles to a serene flow of life based on spontaneity and intuition. Through the years he became increasingly critical of Christianity because of its uncompromisingly exclusivist institutions and creeds. He sought to affirm the world, not deny it, to realize human potential, not dwell on original sin.

There was a core of serious intention within his efforts to enhance greater understanding of Oriental religions, but Watts succumbed to popularizing and became a guru to various forms of counter-culture in the 1950s and 1960s. He basked in the image of pundit to the flower children and adjusted his message to their expectations. By the early 1960s he experimented with drugs in order to expand his consciousness. Admitting in his autobiography that he was an unrepentant sensualist, Watts was an inspiration to those who sought fulfillment in group therapy, chemicals, and sexual promiscuity. Crowds in hundreds of cities flocked to hear his musings. He produced more than twenty-six books to explain and recommend the universal religious principles he found so promising. Many followers used such ideas as rationalizations for rebelling against conformity, and their demands on his time pushed him to exhaustion. Amid an increasingly unhappy domestic life and beset with a chronic alcohol problem, his death from natural causes occurred at the end of yet another lecture tour.

Bibliography:

A. *The Spirit of Zen: A Way of Life, Work and Art in the Far East* (London, 1936); *The Legacy of Asia and Western Man: A Study of the Middle Way* (London, 1937); *The Meaning of Happiness* (New York, 1940); *The Joyous Cosmology: Adventures in the Chemistry of Consciousness* (New York, 1962); *The Two Hands of God* (New York, 1963); *In My Own Way: An Autobiography, 1915–1965* (New York, 1972).

B. NYT 17 Nov 1973, 38; Monica Furlong, *Genuine Fake: A Biography of Alan Watts* (London, 1986).

WAYLAND, Francis (11 March 1796, New York, NY—30 September 1865, Providence, RI). *Education*: B.A., Union Coll. (NY), 1813; studied medicine in Troy, NY, and the city of New York, 1814–16; studied at Andover Sem., 1816–17. *Career*: tutor, Union Coll., 1817–21; minister, First Baptist Church, Boston, 1821–26; professor of Mathematics and Moral Philosophy, Union Coll., 1826–27; president and professor, Brown Univ., 1827–55; minister, First Baptist Church, Providence, 1855–57; active retirement, 1857–65.

Today, Wayland is remembered primarily for reforms in higher education, but during his own time recognition came also from pastoral efforts to set ethical standards in American society. Not often an impressive speaker, especially in the early years, he composed addresses of greatly literary quality which carried moral force in addition to intellectual content. As early as 1823 he attracted wide attention with sermons on topics of current interest such as the propriety of foreign mission work. Offices of minister and college president blended as he lectured to generations of Brown students on the elements of proper conduct. He supported truths of evangelical Christianity by grounding them in a system of natural law and common sense philosophy. With the clarity of a barrister, he expounded moral laws, applying them to both the sphere of individual action and goals of corporate political economy. Wayland articulated the moral substratum of free enterprise capitalism perhaps better than any of his contemporaries. Lectures, Bible classes, and weekly sermons in the campus chapel distinguished his work as an eminent tutor of young men who subsequently influenced American life. For decades his textbooks shaped the attitudes of countless readers in assuming that a certified moral science undergirded individualism, hard work, competition, and self-help as the best forms of social action.

Moral philosophy affected society through human implementation; for that reason Wayland placed great emphasis on spreading sound principles as far as possible among the citizenry. Whether the question was slavery, trades unions, poverty, or fair treatment of American Indians, he perceived all of them as moral issues to be solved with ethical dicta, not through political agitation. In such matters he always sought to reform the human heart and mind instead of forcing conformity by secular legislation. President Wayland worked for civic improvement by serving on committees to supervise hospitals, libraries, and prisons, but his most important activities were connected with Brown. During his administration, he restored student discipline and generally improved educational standards. The system of rote memory drills was replaced with greater reliance on intellectual stimulation, socratic dialogue, and close reasoning. Curriculum was diversified; new buildings were added; the modest institution of Baptist origins grew in numbers and reputation. Wayland brought energy and vision to those innovations which marked his ideas as a significant contribution to collegiate reform. But it was as a teacher that he was most remembered by students for his moral presence and religious instruction.

Bibliography:

A.   *The Elements of Moral Science* (Boston, 1835, and many subsequent editions); *The Elements of Political Economy* (Boston, 1837, and many subsequent editions); *University Sermons* (Boston, 1849); *A Memoir of the Life and Labors of the Rev. Adoniram Judson*, 2 vols. (Boston, 1853); *The Elements of Intellectual Philosophy* (Boston, 1854); *Letters on the Ministry of the Gospel* (New York, 1863).

B.   SH 12, 279–80; NCAB 8, 22–24; DAB 19, 558–60; NYT 2 Oct 1865, 5; Francis Wayland and H. L. Wayland, *A Memoir of the Life and Labors of Francis Wayland*, 2 vols. (New York, 1867, 1972); James O. Murray, *Francis Wayland* (New York, 1891).

WEDEL, Cynthia Clark (26 August 1908, Dearborn, MI—27 August 1986, Alexandria, VA). *Education*: B.A. and M.A., Northwestern Univ., 1929 and 1930; Ph.D., George Washington Univ., 1957. *Career*: director of Christian Education, St. Luke's Episcopal Church, Evanston, IL, 1931–34; field worker and then national director of Episcopal Youth Work, New York, NY, 1934–39; teacher, National Cathedral School for Girls, Washington, DC, 1939–49.

Service in the Episcopal church characterized this laywoman's entire career, professionally at first and then as a volunteer for decades after marriage in 1939. Wedel held quite a large number of posts on executive boards, particularly the Woman's Auxiliary of the Episcopal Church (1946–65) and associate (1965–69) general secretary of the National Council of Churches, she became that organization's first woman president, serving from 1967 to 1972. This belated recognition of the importance of women in churches was also the first contested election. Black delegates nominated Albert B. Cleague, of Detroit, but voting went heavily against him. Wedel was a gifted conciliator, and this capacity together with a doctorate in psychology aided her attempts to coordinate efforts in missionary outreach, ecumenical cooperation, and social action. Her interest in reconciling differences and finding points of common interest between parties was also useful when she served as an official observer at the Second Vatican Council in 1965 and as one of three women consultants at the Lambeth Conference of Anglican Bishops in 1978.

On an international level Wedel participated in meetings of the World Council of Churches from 1954 onward. This service culminated in 1975 when she became one of its presidents, serving until 1983. For many years she also directed the Church Executive Development Board, a training center for ecclesiastical managers. Beyond that she helped direct sensitivity training for people in several professions at the Institute for Applied Behavioral Science. Her approach was not mediatory on all issues, however, and she had strong convictions about abolishing capital punishment, ending the war in Vietnam, recognizing minority rights more adequately, and helping the poor, especially migrant workers and those in the inner cities. Wedel wrote several guides for discussions among church members, with suggestions for further study. Their topics suggest which issues were of continuing interest to her. In these thoughtful pieces she addressed problems of sexual ethics, women's liberation, and more particularly women's ordination. As church executive and as thinker and activist she spoke to the issues current in her time. In them she sought to produce a modicum of beneficial change for progress in the ways churches witnessed to the faith that lived in them.

Bibliography:

B.   NCE 18, 548–49; NYT 28 Aug 1986, B2.

WEIGEL, Gustave (15 January 1906, Buffalo, NY—3 January 1964, New York, NY). *Education*: B.A., Woodstock Coll., 1928; Ph.D., Gregorian Univ., Rome, 1938. *Career*: professor of Dogmatic Theology, Catholic Univ. of Chile, 1937–48; professor of Ecclesiology, Woodstock Coll., 1949–64.

Beginning as a sixteen-year-old novice in the Society of Jesus, young Weigel was schooled in the long, careful training of that order. Following graduate studies, his effectiveness as a teacher (plus dean of the faculty after 1942) in Chile affected a wide range of Catholic action there. When Jesuit officials ordered him to the United States in 1948, he regarded the change as a form of exile. But it allowed him to enter the field of his most striking contribution to American religious history, proceeding tentatively at first and then with contagious enthusiasm for a cause that slowly received greater hierarchical support. Ecumenism among Catholics in the early 1950s was not a point of lively interest. Protestants around the world had been engaged in serious discussions for half a century, but few of Roman affiliation were encouraged by cooperation between those who remained outside the mother church. Weigel became convinced that ecumenism was an integral dimension of his church's earthly mission; he became a prominent figure by means of writing, speaking engagements, and interfaith dialogues as he generated awareness of the potential for church renewal in visible Christian union. Though many developments proceeded to greater fruition after his death, he was in his day part of the vanguard which led American Catholics toward positive views regarding the gradual coalescence of a divided Christendom.

Practical outlets for ecumenical action slowly opened for Weigel as he proved himself one of the first American priests to counteract traditional isolationism. Beginning almost single-handedly, he evinced a new spirit of cooperation at theological workshops, eucharistic conferences and councils on polity. By 1957 he was allowed to attend the Conference on Faith and Order (Oberlin) as an unofficial observer. His own theological orientation was conventionally orthodox, but positive receptivity to developments in Protestant thought opened fresh avenues for religious dialogue. As Catholic authorities warmed to the ecumenical theme, Weigel was appointed (1960) special adviser to Rome's new Secretariat for the Promotion of Christian Unity. This office and other duties at the Second Vatican Council provided an arena for his last, best efforts. He was already acquainted with many representatives of other faiths, and this friendly quality made him natural liaison officer for non-Catholic observers at the Council's sessions. He was invaluable to Protestants and Eastern Orthodox attendants in furnishing translations, interpretation, and personal insights into events as John XXIII urged his bishops to revitalize the church with needed change. Almost daily he added humor and scholarship to press conferences where he described Catholic motivations to Protestants and explained them to Catholics as well. But the strain of so many meetings took its toll, adding weight to medical problems already apparent. It is indicative of his life work that his funeral attracted not only scores of dignitaries but included a mass celebrated by Chilean Jesuits, featuring a hymn by Martin Luther and selections from Russian Orthodox liturgy.

Bibliography:

A. *A Survey of Protestant Theology in Our Times* (Westminster, MD, 1954); *A Catholic Primer on the Ecumenical Movement* (Westminster, MD, 1957); *Faith and Understanding in America* (New York, 1959); *Churches in North America* (Baltimore, 1961); *Catholic Theology in Dialogue* (New York, 1961); *The Modern God: Faith in a Secular Culture* (New York, 1963).

B. NCE 14, 843–44; NYT 4 Jan 1964, 1; Patrick W. Collins, *Gustave Weigel, S.J.: A Pioneer of Reform* (Collegeville, MN, 1992).

WEIGLE, Luther Allan (11 September 1880, Littlestown, PA—2 September 1976, New Haven, CT). *Education*: B.A., Gettysburg Coll., 1900; studied at Lutheran Sem., Gettysburg, 1902–03; Ph.D., Yale Univ., 1905. *Career*: professor of Philosophy (1905–16) and dean (1911–16), Carleton Coll.; Horace Bushnell Professor of Christian Nurture (1916–24), Sterling Professor of Religious Education (1924–49), and dean (1928–49), Yale Div. Sch.; active retirement, 1949–76.

As the son of a Lutheran minister, Weigle conformed to pattern and was ordained in 1903 by the General Synod, the least conservative segment of that multifaceted denomination. He served as minister of a Lutheran church in Bridgeport while pursuing graduate studies at nearby Yale. But when he began teaching in Minnesota in 1905, he attended a Congregationalist church because there were no English-speaking Lutheran churches around. This arrangement continued through life, formalized when he returned to Connecticut by transferring his ministerial standing to the local Congregationalist association. Weigle was profoundly committed to Christian education and to the greater cooperation among believers it could nurture. He prepared a textbook for training Sunday School teachers, issued by the Lutheran Board of Publication, and this led to appointment at Yale where he labored for thirty-four years. In addition to academic contributions there, Weigle worked for Christian unity in wider circles. He was chair of the executive committee of the World's Sunday School Association for thirty years (1928–58) and held a similar position in the American Association of Theological Schools for twenty years (1929–49). For nine years (1941–50) he also chaired the planning committee of the National Council of Churches. Beyond these he was a valuable member of missionary councils, interdenominational agencies, publication societies, and wartime service committees.

Of all these associations, however, Weigle undoubtedly made his greatest contribution through the American Standard Bible Committee. For forty years (1930–70) he chaired this subsection of the International Council of Religious Education that was charged with issuing a modernized edition of the Bible. Weigle agreed that biblical passages needed a fresh translation because modern research, drawing on everything from linguistics to archeology, made it necessary. Another reason was that culture had changed, and original phrases had lost their meaning or used words that no longer retained their earlier content. So Weigle coordinated the efforts of scholars who sought to recapture the meaning behind ancient words and to express that timeless message in contemporary utterance. Forty-four Protestant denominations in America supported this monumental effort. In 1946 the New Testament appeared, and in 1952 the entire Revised Standard Version of the Bible became available. Weigle continued to teach at numerous colleges and seminaries after retiring from Yale, providing further benefits of his rich life for others.

Bibliography:

A. *The Pupil and the Teacher* (Philadelphia, 1911); *The Training of Children in the Christian Family* (Boston, 1922); *American Idealism* (New Haven, 1928); *Jesus and the Education Method* (New York, 1938); *The English New Testament from Tyndale to the Revised Standard Version* (New York, 1949); *The Glory Days: From the Life of Luther Allan Weigle*, compiled by Richard D. Weigle (New York, 1976).

WELD, Theodore Dwight (23 November 1803, Hampton, CT—3 February 1895, Hyde Park, MA). *Education*: studied at Hamilton Coll., 1825; studied at Oneida Inst., 1829–31; studied at Lane Sem., 1832–34. *Career*: traveling evangelist with *Charles G. Finney, 1825–27; evangelist and abolitionist, 1834–40; farmer, Belleville, NJ, 1840–54; schoolteacher, Perth Amboy, NJ, 1854–63; schoolteacher, Lexington, MA, 1864–67; semi-retirement, Hyde Park, MA, 1867–95.

For one who avoided public notice as resolutely as Weld did, his great influence on American antislavery sentiment is matched only by the difficulty in tracing it. Quite early in life he showed a talent for public speaking and, following the example of *Charles G. Finney, devoted that forensic ability to revival campaigns. Before long he was caught in the grip of evangelical logic which progressed through personal perfectionism to social reform along many utopian lines. By 1830 he was accounted the most powerful spokesman for temperance in New York state, and shortly thereafter he began to set the West on fire for the cause of abolition. Faithfully supported by *Lewis Tappan in many ventures, he entered Lane Seminary for more adequate preparation as a minister. In 1832 he was the only student with forthright abolitionist convictions; within two years he converted a majority of the other students and inaugurated welfare programs among the black population of Cincinnati. In defiance of a faculty ultimatum to end such work, fifty-one students left Lane; Weld became an agent for the American Anti-Slavery Society, and most of the other students formed the nucleus of Oberlin College. For two years he toured widely, persuading many to the view that slavery was a moral evil. He avoided large gatherings and manifested no ambition for conspicuous office or lasting reputation. Yet as long as his health was good, he poured himself into antislavery work as no one before him ever had. It is indicative that later antislavery voting patterns largely coincided with areas of his preaching.

By 1836 Weld's voice had become permanently injured, and he shifted from agent to editor of the Anti-Slavery Society. In that capacity he wrote some of the most compelling literature ever produced by abolitionists. His 1839 tract, which indicted the abuses of slavery by drawing on actual accounts in southern newspapers, sold over 100,000 copies in its first year. Always eager to work behind the scenes, he published anonymously, but volumes of his closely reasoned arguments served as leading antislavery material until 1852. In that year *Harriet B. Stowe superseded his influence, admitting all the while that she borrowed both facts and moral indignation from Weld's sources in writing *Uncle Tom's Cabin*. He declined positions on executive committees, but cooperated closely with abolitionist leaders anyway, working to convince others that slavery was a sin in itself and criminality to the Blacks it oppressed. But he had no stomach for politics. As the movement began to split after 1840 over the question of political action, Weld faded into the background. He married another famous advocate of reform, *Angelina Grimké, and settled into more domestic routines. From time to time they participated in various reform schemes—schools, diets, and communitarian projects—but poor health curtailed their activities which had helped launch the most important social reform movement in nineteenth-century America.

Bibliography:

A. *The Bible Against Slavery* (New York, 1837); *The Power of Congress over the District of Columbia* (New York, 1838); *Slavery As It Is* (New York, 1839); *In Memory: Angelina Grimké Weld* (Boston, 1880); *Letters of Theodore Dwight Weld, Angelina Grimké Weld and Sarah Grimké*, ed. Gilbert A. Barnes and Dwight L. Dumond, 2 vols. (New York, 1934).

B.   NCAB 2, 318–19; DAB 19, 625–27; Benjamin P. Thomas, *Theodore Weld: Crusader for Freedom* (New Brunswick, NJ, 1950); Robert H. Abzug, *Passionate Liberator: Theodore Dwight Weld and the Dilemma of Reform* (New York, 1980).

WHATCOAT, Richard (23 February 1736, Quinton, England—5 July 1806, Dover, DE). *Career*: merchant, Wednesbury, England, 1757–69; itinerant Methodist preacher in England, Ireland, and Wales, 1769–84; itinerant Methodist preacher in United States, 1784–1800; bishop, 1800–06.

A product of conventional Anglican probity and observance, Whatcoat did not show much sincere concern for religious matters until 1758 when he began attending Methodist services. After prolonged turmoil regarding death and eternity, he joined John Wesley's movement in 1761 and soon displayed unexpected leadership qualities as class leader, steward, and then exhorter. Success in those capacities led to independent evangelical tours through selected points in the British Isles. He gained a reputation for zealous preaching, gentle personality, and obedience to discipline, all characteristics that epitomized early generations of Methodist preachers. In 1784 Wesley ordained Whatcoat a deacon, then elder the following day. That same year the new minister accompanied Thomas Coke and Thomas Vasey to the United States and helped organize Methodists into an independent church at their Christmas Conference in Baltimore. Since he was one of the few ordained ministers in the new denomination, Whatcoat administered the sacraments to church members in widespread areas up and down the eastern seaboard.

A combination of factors made Whatcoat a valued church leader. His liturgical qualifications suggested appointment as presiding elder over a number of preaching circuits. His patient and tactful demeanor facilitated administration and helped settle disputes with mutual understanding rather than ill feeling. His personal example of kindness and humility inspired many among the clergy and laity alike. For more than fifteen years he organized new Methodist churches from New York to North Carolina. As early as 1786 Wesley suggested his name for bishop, but American churchmen rejected the idea, either for fear of losing *Francis Asbury as bishop or as an expression of their independent frame of mind. He was elected in 1800, though, winning placement as the second bishop of American Methodism over rival *Jesse Lee. He often traveled with Asbury throughout the eastern states and across the Alleghenies as well. Such rigors soon proved too much, and he died while on an episcopal tour, a lasting example of one who wore himself out in pursuit of pastoral duties.

Bibliography:

B.   AAP 7, 92–101; NCAB 13, 180; DAB 20, 36; William Phoebus, *Memoirs of the Rev. Richard Whatcoat* (New York, 1828); Sidney B. Bradley, *The Life of Bishop Richard Whatcoat* (Louisville, 1936).

WHEELER, Wayne Bidwell (10 November 1869, Brookfield, OH—5 September 1927, Battle Creek, MI). *Education*: B.A., Oberlin Coll., 1894; LL.B., Law Sch. of Western Reserve Univ., 1898. *Career*: legal secretary and superintendent, Anti-Saloon League of OH, 1898–1904, 1904–15; general counsel, Anti-Saloon League of America, 1915–27.

In 1893 the first Anti-Saloon League was formed in Oberlin, Ohio, to curtail liquor traffic by urging churches to exert political pressure. Wheeler attended that meeting, still a student at the local college which was then as much a hotbed of temperance reform as it once had been of abolition. After graduation he began working for the League while reading law in Cleveland. The young lawyer soon proved to be a capable political organizer and campaigned for ''dry'' candidates regardless of whatever else they stood for. Wheeler became the driving force behind temperance legislation ranging from local options on the county level to statewide prohibition. As attorney for the League he prosecuted more than 2,000 saloon cases. He successfully defended the constitutionality of such laws against ''wet'' antagonists, some suits reaching even the Supreme Court. His political strategy was fired by unswerving devotion to a single cause. Without allowing energy to diffuse in several directions, he guided temperance activity to increasingly effective results. In 1903 only three states were dry; by 1916 thirty-two states comprising three-fourths of the total population had enacted some restriction on liquor sales. It finally seemed possible that the tough business of political persuasion might bear fruit on a national scale.

''Churches organized against the saloon'' was a slogan with pleasant idealistic overtones, but prohibition also played upon widespread rural suspicion of city life. Wheeler was not above appealing to those deep prejudices nor, after the war began, to nativism if it helped close down German breweries. He lobbied tirelessly for national prohibition and rejoiced to see the Eighteenth Amendment passed in December, 1917. During the next thirteen months he exerted himself further to have states ratify the bill which became law in January, 1919. The ''noble experiment'' had begun, largely due to his efforts. But as temperance armies began to demobilize, Wheeler prepared for the next phase of the crusade. He aided indirectly in passing the Volstead Act, a statute providing for enforcement of the ideal now so popularly acclaimed. For the last eight years of his life the League's chief counsel became virtually indomitable in securing appropriations to enforce total abstinence. He advocated relentless prosecution, severe penalties, and armed intervention by the Army and Navy if necessary. Passionately sincere about the cause which he equated with righteousness, he embodied the sternest aspects of legalistic moralism. He did not live to see the collapse of this last great Protestant effort to shape society in its image, a collapse to which many thought "Wheelerism" contributed rather than prevented.

Bibliography:

A. *The Federal and State Laws Relating to Intoxicating Liquor* (Westerville, OH, 1916).

B. NCAB 20, 13–14; DAB 20, 54–55; NYT 6 Sep 1927, 1; Justin Steuart, *Wayne Wheeler: Dry Boss* (New York, 1928).

WHEELOCK, Eleazar (22 April 1711, Windham, CT—24 April 1779, Hanover, NH). *Education*: graduated from Yale Coll., 1733. *Career*: minister, Second Congregational Church, Lebanon, CT, 1735–70; president, Dartmouth Coll., 1770–79.

Few New England preachers were more enthusiastic than Wheelock in their support of revival efforts later called the First Great Awakening. In addition to parish duties (which some claimed he neglected), he traveled extensively to spread the gospel message and to quicken consciences wherever possible. But his lasting influence stems from educational pioneering instead of evangelism. Wheelock had been preparing boys for college when an event in 1743 opened new vistas for schooling. In that year *Samson Occom, a young scholar from the Mohegan nation, showed by his success that a school for Indians could be an effective means of missionary work among native tribes. Wheelock recruited Indians from his own colony and as far away as New York and New Jersey. At Moor's Charity School (named after benefactor Joshua Moor) he sought to extract children from their cultures, drill them in the rudiments of white industry and religion, and then send them back home as agents of Christian churches to change their original surroundings. Wheelock saw only savagery in native cultures and sought to change them in order to make his redeemer known among the heathen. In that manner, the instructor declared he could turn habitations of cruelty into domestic sanctuaries where the true God could be worshipped. Occom was his star pupil, standing as evidence that the Indian's lot could be improved. No more than sixty youths had attended the school by 1765, with varying results; but whites at home and abroad saw the school's master as a leading missioner among native Americans.

Products of the Indian school failed to meet Wheelock's expectations; some of them died prematurely while others did not pursue the missionary objectives suggested as their role. The venture received a telling blow in 1768 when Sir William Johnson, British representative among the Iroquois, refused to support it any longer. He saw how Wheelock's methods threatened aboriginal life patterns and urged men of the Six Nations to preserve their integrity by resisting religious forms of white imperialism. Wheelock responded by removing his school to the

New Hampshire frontier. In 1769 he obtained a charter for Dartmouth College (named after English patron, the Earl of Dartmouth) and transferred operations north in hopes of satisfying his educational ambitions there. Dartmouth opened its doors to whites as well as natives, much to the dismay of Occom who had raised most of its funds in the name of Indian missions. But Wheelock persisted to run the institution as best he could through hard times and the disruptions occasioned by revolution. The fact that it survived at all is due largely to his dogged will. With no pretensions as a scholar, his good administrative sense brought the school from austere beginnings to a position where it supplied New Light preachers for the northeast frontier.

Bibliography:

    A.   *A Plain and Faithful Narrative . . . of the Indian Charity-School*, 9 vols. (Boston and Hartford, 1763–75).
    B.   AAP 1, 397–403; NCAB 9, 85–86; DAB 20, 58–59; David McClure and Elijah Parish, *Memoirs of the Rev. Eleazar Wheelock* (Newburyport, MA, 1811; New York, 1972); James D. McCallum, *Eleazar Wheelock: Founder of Dartmouth College* (Hanover, NH, 1939).

WHIPPLE, Henry Benjamin (15 February 1822, Adams, NY—16 September 1901, Faribault, MN). *Education*: studied at Oberlin Coll., 1838–39; studied theology with William D. Wilson, Albany, NY, 1847–50. *Career*: merchant, Adams, NY, 1839–49; rector, Zion Episcopal Church, Rome, NY, 1850–57; rector and missionary, St. Augustine, FL, 1853–54; rector, Church of the Holy Communion, Chicago, 1857–59; bishop of Minnesota, 1859–1901.

Delicate health prevented Whipple from attending college for very long, but with his father's help he grew to be both physically and economically stable. Though reared as a Presbyterian he decided to take holy orders in his grandparents' church, receiving ordination as Episcopal deacon in 1849 and as priest the following year. Within a decade his qualities drew the attention of ecclesiastical leaders, and Whipple was named as the first bishop of Minnesota. When he arrived at the diocesan center in Faribault, his youth stood him in good stead as he labored to expand Episcopalian influences in what was still an expanding frontier society. Not an absentee hierarch, Whipple aided church growth by direct visitation and on-the-scene supervision. He made extensive tours, suffering many hardships and often hazardous conditions, to see the people, learn their needs, and determine which next steps to take. Work among white parishioners progressed steadily, but it was contacts with Native Americans that made the bishop internationally famous.

Episcopalian missions to Ojibway Indians already existed before Whipple occupied the new diocese. He strengthened those efforts, especially on the White Earth reservation with the services of trusted Christian leaders such as Good Thunder and Enmegahbowh. In 1860 he also inaugurated evangelical efforts among the eastern Dakotas or Santee Sioux. There he learned first-hand of how the government mismanaged its treaty obligations to Indians. When the resultant "Little Crow's War" broke out in 1862, he sought to protect natives and interceded with Washington authorities on behalf of native prisoners. Thereafter he lobbied for reforms in Indian administration among local agents, legislators, bureaucrats, and successive presidents. Not much advanced beyond other reformers of his day, he advocated allotment of land to individual Indians, adequate schools, and other inducements to assimilating natives into dominantly white social patterns. Whipple gained the nickname, "Straight Tongue," betokening his reputation for opposition to fraud and deceit in any form. His simple, moving eloquence made him popular in Europe as well as this country as he championed the Indians' cause on many speaking tours. Toward the end of a long episcopate, which he began as one of the youngest, he was by seniority the presiding bishop of the American church when he attended the Fourth Lambeth Conference in 1897.

Bibliography:

A. *Five Sermons* (New York, 1890); *Lights and Shadows of a Long Episcopate* (New York, 1899).

B. SH 12, 337; NCAB 4, 58–59; DAB 20, 68–69; NYT 17 Sep 1901, 7: Phillips Endicott Osgood, *Straight Tongue: A History of Henry Benjamin Whipple, First Episcopal Bishop of Minnesota* (Minneapolis, 1958).

WHITAKER, Alexander (1585, Cambridge, England—March 1617, Henrico County, VA). *Education*: B.A. and M.A., Cambridge Univ., 1605 and 1608. *Career*: Anglican minister, colony of VA, 1611–17.

The Puritan credentials of young Whitaker rested not only on his own training at Cambridge but on the fact that his father was Regius Professor of Theology there. After ordination in the Church of England in 1608 he spent several years in parish work in the northern shires. But he was seized by missionary zeal and, foregoing ease and preferment in the old country, volunteered to serve as priest in the new colony of Virginia. He arrived in Jamestown in 1611, disembarking with Sir Thomas Dale, the colony's newly appointed governor. Dale issued stringent new laws regarding discipline and religious observance, and Whitaker's strong Puritanism coincided quite easily with such strictures. The missionary priest established two new parishes, Henricopolis and Bermuda Hundreds, about fifty miles upstream from the mouth of the James River. There he preached twice each Sunday and once on Wednesdays. He provided what spiritual consolation he could to the scattered colonists, efforts which help account for why he is sometimes referred to as "the apostle to Virginia."

Within two years of his arrival Whitaker sent a report entitled "Good News from Virginia" to councilmen on the colony's managing company. In it he commended further settlement, greater attention to religious affairs by sending more Puritan divines and augmented missionary activity among the local native Americans. Work in the last category acquired another title for him: "apostle to the Indians.'' The most famous of such activities took place in 1613 and 1614 when he instructed a young Algonkian maiden in the principles of Christianity. Her name was Matoaka, more widely known as Pocahontas, and Whitaker baptized her prior to her marriage with John Rolfe. Such beginnings with natives and with the increased number of white settlers augured much growth for the Anglican church system planted there. But the missionary priest's tenure was cut unexpectedly short by accidental drowning. Parishes that he organized would have to depend on other volunteers to nurture them into Virginia's mother church.

Bibliography:

B.   NCAB 7, 32; DAB 20, 79–80.

WHITE, Alma Bridwell (16 June 1862, Kinniconick, KY—26 June 1946, Zarephath, NJ). *Education*: studied at Vanceburg Sem. (KY), 1880?; studied at Millersburg Female Coll. (KY), 1881–82. *Career*: schoolteacher in KY and MT, 1880–87; eldress, Methodist Pentecostal Union (Pillar of Fire after 1917), 1901–18; bishop, Pillar of Fire Church, 1918–46.

During her early years Mollie Alma Bridwell sought outlets for religious expression in a number of ways, first as a teacher, then as a lay exhorter and songleader in her husband's Methodist churches. But after experiencing a feeling of entire sanctification or ''second blessing'' in 1893, she was not content to function merely as a subsidiary any longer. She became a preacher in her own right and obeyed what seemed a divine mission to stir up flagging piety in various Colorado churches. Methodist officials criticized her efforts because as a woman she dared to preach and because her brand of religious enthusiasm violated their sense of decorum as a denominational standard. Consequently both man and wife withdrew from Methodist affiliation in 1895 to embark on independent holiness revivals through the mountain states. Jubilant worship and baptism of the Holy Spirit abounded in successive camp meetings for over six years, even as the evangelistic team stressed loyalty to doctrines originating in John Wesley. A few months after followers formed a pentecostal union in 1901, Mrs. White was ordained an officer of considerable influence. The small religious association had no distinctive creedal platform, but its special religious emphasis provided it with grounds for separate existence. By 1917 it was known as the Pillar of Fire Church and named its foundress to be bishop; she became the first woman in such an office in the history of Christendom.

Separate denominations are often identified by a combination of doctrines and practices rather than by a single distinguishing characteristic. Under the forceful guidance of Bishop White, Pillar of Fire adherents accepted the necessity of both conversion and sanctification in Christian living. They looked forward to an imminent Second Coming, practiced faith healing and accepted ordination of ministers from both sexes. Along with a strict Wesleyan belief system they closely regulated personal habits, eschewing tobacco, alcohol, and ostentatious clothing. They also opposed speaking in tongues, regarding most pentecostal churches as sadly deluded on this matter. By 1907 the strong-willed bishop moved her headquarters to New Jersey and built a thriving organization which utilized modern communications techniques. She established congregations from Los Angeles to London, crossing the Atlantic fifty-eight times, and presided over enterprises ranging from radio stations to accredited Bible schools. Her voluminous writings spread the doctrine of personal holiness even farther, so much so that by the time of her death over 4,000 members were counted among the faithful. Her elder son then became senior bishop, directing growth of the fundamentalist sect as it progressed toward full denominational status.

Bibliography:

A. *Looking Back from Beulah* (Denver, CO, 1902); *The New Testament Church* (Denver, CO, 1907); *Demons and Tongues* (Zarephath, NJ, 1910); *The Story of My Life and the Pillar of Fire*, 6 vols. (Zarephath, NJ, 1919–34); *Hymns and Poems* (Zarephath, NJ, 1931); *Modern Miracles and Answers to Prayer* (Zarephath, NJ, 1939).
B. NCAB 35, 151–53; DAB 24, 875–77; NAW 3, 581–83; NYT 27 June 1946, 21.

WHITE, Andrew (1579, London, England—27 December 1656, near London, England). *Career*: entered novitiate of Jesuit order, 1607; at intervals missionary in England and professor of Scripture, Languages, and Theology at Lisbon, Louvain, and Liège, 1610–33; missionary in Colony of MD, 1634–45; missionary in England, 1645–56.

Though White is memorialized by later generations as the ''Apostle of Maryland,'' his availability for missions there arose through unexpected circumstances. He studied principally at St. Alban's College in Valladolid; after more training in Seville and Douai, he became a Catholic priest around the year 1605. In little more than a twelvemonth he became involved in a plot against the British Crown, suffered banishment from his homeland, and applied for entry into the Society of Jesus. Discipline in the order proved amenable to Father White, and he soon warmed to teaching theology as his preferred station in life. But difficulties soon emerged due to his excessively rigid Thomism. As prefect of studies in several houses, he created no little tumult by criticizing those who did not follow Thomas Aquinas rigorously enough to suit him. By 1629 his superiors finally relieved him of all educational duties because it was clear he lacked the prudence or charity to soften his antagonistic ultraconservatism. Thus at the time when *Cecilius Calvert requested Jesuit assistance in his New World colony, the disconsolate professor seized the opportunity. In late 1633 he shipped aboard the *Ark*, together with *John Altham and Thomas Gervase a lay brother, arriving in March of the next year to celebrate the first of many eucharists in the land grant named Terra Mariae.

As superior of the Jesuit mission during its first four years, White organized chapels for white settlers before evangelizing the red man. He received no help from the colonial government in pursuing this ministry and had to work parcels of land as did other gentlemen adventurers for financial support. St. Inigoes

Manor was an early Jesuit enterprise which the father superior established, a prototype of extensive holdings accumulated in subsequent years. By 1639 the apostolate to Indians began in earnest. Living first with the Patuxent nation and then in less dangerous surroundings among the Piscataways, White introduced the gospel to native groups. He wrote a grammar and dictionary of the local Algonkian dialect, translating the catechism into that language as well. Within a year he baptized the Piscataway chief (tayac) and extended considerable influence over native cultural patterns. But successful evangelical efforts proved his undoing to some extent; the growth of Catholicism gave Puritan Virginians an excuse for armed invasion. Forces under William Claiborne captured White and sent him to England in chains (1645) under charges of treason. He was acquitted and banished again but returned to Britain after a few months, spending a final decade in southern counties of the realm. Though unable to return to Maryland, he nourished the secret faith of Catholics who endured in a Protestant land where official policies forbade confessional diversity.

Bibliography:

    B.   DAB 20, 87–88; NCE 14, 892.

WHITE, Ellen Gould Harmon (26 November 1827, Gorham, ME—16 July 1915, St. Helena, CA).

Since her health and nervous condition was seriously impaired by a childhood head injury, Ellen Harmon received virtually no formal education. After responding favorably to Methodist evangelism in 1840, she espoused two years later the more explicit anticipations of Christ's second coming taught by *William Miller. By late 1844 most adventist believers had become bitterly disappointed, but the young girl kept her faith. She began to have visions which helped edify discouraged Millerites; during the course of her lifetime she claimed over 2,000 of these spiritual experiences and used them to strengthen belief in a certain but undetermined return of Christ to earth. In 1846 she married James S. White, an adventist minister responsible for publishing activities among several local churches. The next year both of them became convinced that there was scriptural warrant for designating Saturday as the true day of worship, and so two distinctive features combined by 1860 to comprise their chosen denominational name, Seventh-Day Adventists. Sister White did not claim to be a prophetess, nor was she eager to press her own doctrinal views on others as they studied the Bible for guidance in religious thought. Yet acceptance of her spiritual primacy was so widespread, she exerted among Seventh-Day Adventists the most significant influence of any individual in the nineteenth century. Though acknowledging the authenticity of her visions is not a formal part of that church's belief system, her interpretation of Scriptures has largely determined its notions of orthodoxy. She wrote scores of books, pamphlets, and articles based on intuitional insights over a period of seventy years. In communicating God's messages to others, she rarely broached new ideas but rather shed supplementary light on Scripture, history, and contemporary problems.

Scattered Adventist churches were finally organized into a General Conference in 1863, an achievement due primarily to leadership by both members of the White family. After a strenuous bout with health problems, Mrs. White determined that health reform was an essential part of Christian stewardship. To further that end, she helped establish (1866) the Western Health Reform Institute in Battle Creek, Michigan, a prototype for sanitariums throughout the world. She was also motivated by strong convictions against meat, coffee, tea, alcohol, and other drugs; thousands attended her temperance lectures given in support of the WCTU. She held pronounced views on education which gained implementation in 1874 at Battle Creek College (later Andrews University) and in 1906 at the College of Medical Evangelists (now Loma Linda University), Loma Linda, California. After her husband died, Sister White redoubled her efforts to extend the church. In addition to attending conferences and camp meetings in this country, she conducted significant work in Europe (1885–88) and Australia (1891–99). She was also instrumental in the decision to move the church's national headquarters to Washington, D.C. in 1903. Vigorous until almost the end, she continued to enliven the faith of coreligionists with a compelling insight credited to a source outside her own control.

Bibliography:

A.   *The Great Controversy between Christ and Satan during the Christian Dispensation* (Oakland, CA, 1888); *The Desire of Ages* (Oakland, CA, 1898); *Christ's Object Lessons* (Oakland, CA, 1900); *Education* (Mountain View, CA, 1903); *The Ministry of Healing* (Mountain View, CA, 1905); *Life Sketches of Ellen G. White* (Mountain View, CA, 1915).

B.   DAB 20, 98–99; NAW 3, 585–88; NYT 17 July 1915, 7; Francis D. Nichol, *Ellen G. White and Her Critics* (Washington, DC, 1951); Arthur W. Spalding, *There Shines a Light* (Nashville, 1953); Arthur L. White, *Messenger to the Remnant* (Washington, DC, 1969); Ronald L. Numbers, *The Prophetess of Health: Ellen G. White* (New York, 1976); Roy E. Graham, *Ellen G. White, Co-Founder of the Seventh-day Adventist Church* (New York, 1985).

WHITE, William (4 April 1748, Philadelphia, PA—17 July 1836, Philadelphia, PA). *Education*: graduated from the Coll. of Philadelphia, 1765; studied theology under Richard Peters and Jacob Duché, Philadelphia, 1765–70. *Career*: curate, united parishes of St. Peter's and Christ Church, Philadelphia, 1772–79; rector, same churches, 1779–86; chaplain, Continental and Federal Congresses, 1777–1800; bishop of Pennsylvania, 1787–1836.

After traveling to England and residing there long enough to reach the age required for ordination, White returned to Philadelphia and began a ministry which extended over sixty years. As a native son, he easily sided with the colonies in their search for independence. He had no difficulties in supporting an oath of allegiance to the revolutionary government, and politicians convening in his home town came to trust his political sympathies for American liberty. His actions were at once conciliatory and patriotic, effective in softening the prejudice of those who thought his church hostile to the welfare of the new country. In 1782 White wrote a pamphlet considering the case of the Episcopal church in its current circumstances. His primary concern was to assure a continuation of preaching and worship which was threatened with disruption by new political alignments. Arguing that the office of bishop was compatible with republican government, he nevertheless stated that episcopacy was not necessary for Episcopal churches to continue their essential work. British validation was not requisite, and since it was unobtainable at the moment, it could be waived. Controversies over resident bishops had raged in America for almost a century, and White's ideas were helpful in allaying some of the popular misunderstandings about the relation of office to gospel witness. Constitutional conventions began meeting in several states under his indirect leadership to provide stable, democratic organization.

There were many of Episcopal persuasion, however, who did not agree with White's assertion that bishops were unessential to the church. In 1783 Connecticut clergymen met and nominated *Samuel Seabury as their choice to fill an office which they thought necessary according to Scripture and pragmatic realities. When Seabury returned in 1785 after being consecrated in Scotland, White was tremendously influential in promoting harmonious relations between the general convention of dioceses and the new symbol of authority. He also acquiesced in the church's new constitutional provisions and accepted nomination for the episcopacy himself, beginning in 1787 a long and respected administration. From the start he was the outstanding member of the House of Bishops, and his calm, judicious character of mind made him the natural arbiter of all disputes during the difficult years of reorganization. As presiding bishop after 1795 he aided the steady increase of missionary work, liturgical change, and additional bishoprics (26) while the ancient church grew along with the new nation.

Bibliography:

A.   *Lectures on the Catechism . . . with Supplementary Lectures* (Philadelphia, 1813); *Comparative Views of the Controversy between the Calvinists and the Arminians*, 2 vols. (Philadelphia, 1817); *Memoirs of the Protestant Episcopal Church in the United States of America* (Philadelphia, 1820; New York, 1836).

B.   AAP 5, 280–92; SH 12, 341; NCAB 3, 470; DAB 20, 121–22; Bird Wilson, *Memoir of the Life of the Right Reverend William White* (Philadelphia, 1938); Julius H. Ward, *The Life and Times of Bishop White* (New York, 1892); Walter H. Stowe (ed.), *The Life and Letters of Bishop William White* (New York, 1937).

WHITEFIELD, George (27 December 1714, Gloucester, England—30 September 1770, Newburyport, MA). *Education*: B.A., Pembroke Coll., Oxford Univ., 1736. *Career*: itinerant preacher in England and the American colonies, 1736–70.

It was rare in the 1730s for an Anglican priest not to settle in a local parish, but Whitefield's penchant for evangelism led to wider fields and helped make itinerancy a new form of American clerical activity. As a dramatic preacher who could hold vast audiences spellbound, he embodied the zeal for conversions and precipitated the controversies which are associated with an epoch now called the First Great Awakening. He became known in England quite early for fiery sermons which produced religious fervor in some, animosity in others. Many churches were closed to him, and he resorted to field preaching, as did John Wesley his college friend and adviser. The novelty of hearing extempore addresses delivered in courthouses, barns, or open meadows attracted great crowds on both sides of the Atlantic. In all, Whitefield journeyed to America seven times (1738, 1739–41, 1744–48, 1751–52, 1754–55, 1763–65, 1769–70) to spread salvation as the experience of grace had made itself known to him. While on his second tour he encouraged like-minded revivalists such as *Gilbert Tennent and *Jonathan Edwards, enlarging their circumscribed activities into an interdenominational, intercolonial effort to awaken spiritual lethargy. He became the model of many preachers stirred by pietistic impulses. His excursions had a sensational impact on colonial society from New Hampshire to Georgia, and no one else of his day more forcefully affected people in every class and station.

For all his popularity, Whitefield fared roughly with critics who blamed him for a variety of errors and disorders. Since most of his doctrine remained strictly Calvinistic, he quarreled for a brief time with Wesley over the relative merits of free grace and divine sovereignty. More important than that temporary difference, he was often presumptuous enough to censure anyone who opposed him as spiritually blind and an unworthy minister. Such egotistical attacks stiffened many clergy to resist his methods, if not his message. One divine who denounced both was *Charles Chauncy who began openly criticizing revivals in 1742, leading the faculty of Harvard two years later to reject both the manner and matter of Whitefield's work. Another issue had to do with Bethesda, an orphanage situated near Savannah, Georgia, which he had supported since his first missionary journey. In 1746 he bought a plantation and ran it with slave labor as a source of income for the children. He also collected large sums for this establishment while preaching, but not all the money seems to have made its way to the southern home and school. Questions of theological difference, personal rashness and mismanagement aside, he continued to draw large audiences and impress them with a distinctive gospel witness. Whether in English shires or on Boston Common, the magnetic speaker made the appropriation of religious truth a closer reality for thousands who listened.

Bibliography:

A.   A Journal and A Continuation of the Reverend Mr. Whitefield's Journal, 7 vols. (London, 1739–43); The Works of the Reverend George Whitefield, 6 vols. (London, 1771–72); Fifteen Sermons (Philadelphia, 1794); Eighteen Sermons (Newburyport, MA, 1797).

B.   AAP 5, 94–108; SH 12, 341–42; NCAB 5, 384–85; DAB 20, 124–29; NCE 14,

895–96; John Gillies, *Memoirs of the Rev. George Whitefield* (London, 1772; Hartford, 1853); Luke Tyerman, *The Life of the Rev. George Whitefield*, 2 vols. (New York, 1877); Stuart C. Henry, *George Whitefield: Wayfaring Witness* (Nashville, 1954); John Pollock, *George Whitefield and the Great Awakening* (Garden City, NY, 1972); Harry S. Stout, *The Divine Dramatist: George Whitefield and the Rise of Modern Evangelism* (Grand Rapids, MI, 1991).

WHITMAN, Marcus (4 September 1802, Rushville, NY—29 November 1847, Waiilatpu, Oregon Territory). *Education*: private tutorials in classics, 1814–19; private studies in medicine, 1821–24. *Career*: practiced medicine in Canada, 1825–29; practiced medicine, Wheeler, NY, 1830–34; missionary for American Board of Foreign Missions, 1835–47.

As a young man with strong religious interests, Whitman wanted to prepare for a ministerial career but was persuaded by his family to adopt a more practical profession. After several years as a doctor, however, his earlier inclinations led him to volunteer for missionary service to provide medical, agricultural, and educational benefits for natives in the Far West. In 1836 Whitman married *Narcissa Prentiss, a Presbyterian like himself and one equally dedicated to missions. They made an arduous journey overland with co-workers Henry H. Spalding and wife, using the protection of wagon trains that belonged to the American and Hudson's Bay fur companies. Once they reached the wilds of Oregon, the Whitmans set up a mission among the Cayuse Indians; the Spaldings moved 125 miles away into Nez Percé country. The Cayuse mission situated near Fort Walla Walla, named Waiilatpu, formed part of a long chain of Protestant stations along the Columbia River. Marcus went to work constructing buildings, conducting worship services, practicing medicine, and teaching the Indians about farming and stock raising as well as the rudiments of Christian doctrine.

Life was fearful, thrilling, and grand as the Whitmans sought to do God's work, among an unconverted people. But there were many setbacks, and in 1842 some of the Mission Board commissioners wished to relocate the missions to make them more efficient. Marcus traveled across the continent to oppose this attempt because he feared the growing influence of Roman Catholic missions in Oregon, a flourishing enterprise begun by Jesuit traveler, *Pierre Jean de Smet. The Whitmans stayed at Waiilatpu. Their Indian acquaintances became increasingly alarmed at so many whites entering the area, and they blamed the missionaries for the influx of unwanted settlers. This was not altogether an unwarranted charge because one of the most important aspects of the Whitmans' ministry was to provide comfort, aid, and advice for whites as they arrived from the east. Late in 1847 one wagon train brought an epidemic of measles, a disease annoying to whites but devastating to Indians who had developed no immunity to it. Marcus ministered to native and immigrant alike, but even mild vaccinations caused death in frightening numbers among the red men. This well-intentioned work only confirmed suspicions that the doctor practiced witchcraft and threatened the life of the tribe. A band of vengeful Cayuse retaliated by raiding the mission, killing the Whitmans and twelve other whites who happened to be there.

Bibliography:

    B.   SH 12, 343; NCAB 11, 112; DAB 20, 141–43; Myron Eells, *Marcus Whitman: Pathfinder and Patriot* (Seattle, 1909); Miles Cannon, *Waiilatpu: Its Rise and Fall* (Boise, ID, 1915); Clifford M. Drury, *Marcus Whitman, M.D.* (Caldwell, ID, 1937); Archer B. Hulbert and Dorothy P. Hulbert (eds.), *Marcus Whitman, Crusader*, 3 vols. (Denver, 1936–41).

WHITMAN, Narcissa Prentiss (14 March 1808, Prattsburg, NY—29 November 1847, Waiilatpu, Oregon Territory). *Career*: teacher in district school, Prattsburg, NY, before 1834; missionary for American Board of Foreign Missions, 1836–47.

It was unheard of that an unmarried Protestant woman might become a missionary in foreign parts, and because of such policy Narcissa Prentiss' application was rejected in 1834 despite her earnest desire to serve in that capacity. So in addition to personal affection, religious dedication may have played a role in her decision to marry *Marcus Whitman and spend her life among Indians in Oregon. Together with Eliza Spalding, wife of another missionary bound for the same territory, Narcissa was one of the first white women to cross the Rockies, setting an example for many pioneers to follow. Once the Whitmans were established at Waiilatpu, Narcissa threw herself into the tasks of helping natives understand the gospel message they brought. She conducted the mission school, aiding conversions by giving Indians the nurture she thought necessary for a sound moral, civilized life. She also supervised all domestic affairs of the mission which soon became one of the largest of its kind in Oregon.

At first missionary work seemed to go well, vindicating the decision to sacrifice so much for a spiritual cause. But tragedy and disappointment slowly lessened Narcissa's enthusiasm for the work. Her two year old daughter was accidentally drowned in 1839, causing the mother to enter a period of prolonged depression. Her eyesight began to fail, sometimes almost totally. The daily grind of missionary life could not have been kind to one who loved society and stimulating conversation. The Cayuse Indians and their neighbors, Nez Percés and Flatheads, were not suitable company, nor did they respond in gratifying numbers to the gospel, showing a bewildering preference for Catholic forms instead. Still Narcissa endured and continued faithful until the end. She was killed with her husband at the mission for which she had labored so many years. Her influence was more symbolic than tangible: though there were few lasting results at Waiilatpu, the constancy displayed there set a pattern for those who came after.

Bibliography:

    B.   NAW 3, 595–97; Jeannette Eaton, *Narcissa Whitman* (New York, 1941); Opal S. Allen, *Narcissa Whitman* (Portland, OR, 1959); Clifford M. Drury, *First White Women over the Rockies*, 3 vols. (Glendale, CA, 1963–66); Julie Roy Jeffrey, *Converting the West: A Biography of Narcissa Whitman* (Norman, OK, 1991).

WIEMAN, Henry Nelson (19 August 1884, Rich Hill, MO—19 June 1975, Grinnell, IA). *Education*: B.A., Park Coll., 1907; B.D., San Francisco Sem., 1910; studied at Jena and Heidelberg, 1910–11; Ph.D., Harvard Univ., 1917. *Career*: professor of Philosophy, Occidental Coll., 1917–27; professor of Philosophy and Religion, Chicago Div. Sch., 1927–47; active retirement, 1947–75.

As a philosopher of religion, Wieman developed several categories of thought beneficial to theology. Between 1926 and 1968 he published important works which consistently maintained that religious truths could be verified empirically. Constructing his methodology within a naturalistic framework, he began by observing that the human organism is part of an evolving world, related to other parts by means of knowledge and interaction in a single medium. Religious affirmations derived from that context could be as objectively grounded as general scientific assertions. They could avoid individualistic subjectivism and base all reflective conceptions on an objective referent. Wieman held that God could be perceived in a continuous flow of sense experience. The most important aspect of that temporal process was that values came into being, and men's lives were changed by them. Most people concentrate on subconscious responses, such as emotional warmth, which resulted from such experience. But the philosopher's interest lay not in the content of religious consciousness, a variable and incidental byproduct, but rather in the cause of experience which was in every case objective and verifiable. Wieman called religious experience a "stimulus of the sensorium affecting consciousness," giving persons new energies which could be turned toward good or evil. With a perspective including scientific observation and rational concepts, he laid the basis for metaphysical constructions in religious thought, these built on empirical analysis considered necessary to substantiate it as an area of meaningful discourse.

Drawing on both the unity and universality of creative values in human experience, Wieman defined God as the dynamic process which transforms existence to the greatest good. God was greater than analogical references such as Mind or Person; so too did He transcend human capabilities which depended on divine initiative for their motive force. But for all this God was still objectively established as the factual process of creativity operating to transform men's lives. Much of this terminology is reminiscent of John Dewey, but when Wieman spoke of God as an object of sensory experience, his conception of "experience" was much more comprehensive and sophisticated than that of the earlier empiricist. He also gave more depth to the concept of salvation or creative event. On an emergent level he saw that people received increased awareness, an expanded range of knowing and valuing; then with greater depth in mutually sustaining activities they integrated various perspectives; they also expanded capabilities in a pattern of evolutionary development; finally they deepened interpersonal relationships with the growth of community. All these aspects were present in the single unitive process by which man was led to improved life at God's ubiquitous prompting. Religion or the ultimate human commitment is, he said, to this power which brings all values into mutual support. Within the logical canons of philosophical thought, man's secondary commitment is to seek greater understanding of both the initiating process and the practical decisions which result from it.

Bibliography:

A. *Religious Experience and Scientific Method* (New York, 1926); *The Wrestle of Religion with Truth* (New York, 1927); *Normative Psychology of Religion* (New York, 1935); *The Source of Human Good* (Chicago, 1946); *Man's Ultimate Commitment* (Carbondale, IL, 1958); *Intellectual Foundation of Faith* (New York, 1961).

B. NYT 21 June 1975, 30; William S. Minor, *Creativity in Henry Nelson Wieman* (Metuchen, NJ, 1977); Creighton Peden, *Wieman's Empirical Process Philosophy* (Washington, DC, 1977).

WILDER, Robert Parmalee (2 August 1863, Kolhapur, India—28 March 1938, Oslo, Norway). *Education*: B.A., Princeton Univ., 1886; B.D., Union Sem. (NY), 1891. *Career*: missionary in India, 1892–99; national secretary, Young Men's Christian Associations (YMCA) of India and Ceylon, 1899–1902; secretary, British Student Christian Movement, 1905–16; general secretary, Student Volunteer Movement for Foreign Missions, 1919–27; executive secretary, Near East Christian Council, 1927–33; active retirement, 1933–38.

Missionary activity was a constant theme in Wilder's experience from the start. The example of his parents laid a foundation for interests which were fed by a lifetime of prayerful dedication and found practical expression in work on three continents. While still in college he organized (1883) a small group of students who volunteered for foreign mission fields, adopting as their watchword: "the evangelization of the world in this generation." Three years later his modest beginnings served as the nucleus of a student missionary movement which grew to vast proportions. He attended *Dwight L. Moody's summer Bible school for college students where his personal witness helped launch the Student Volunteer Mission Movement. One hundred persons, including *John R. Mott, declared their intention to spread the Christian message in foreign lands. During the next year Wilder traveled extensively from Maine to Iowa, speaking mostly at colleges on behalf of the new program; because of his efforts the list of volunteers went above 2,000. Such work proved to be his forte. He was an earnest recruiter of missionary personnel for over fifty years, and quickening interest in foreign evangelism was more distinctively his contribution than actual preaching at any particular station. He acquired theological training in order to be effective, but deliberately remained a layman to avoid creating artificial social barriers. In that way he was approachable by concerned persons from all walks of life. And he utilized the informality of private conversations to influence thousands in their decisions to aid mission enterprises.

Work in his native India as an agent of the Presbyterian Foreign Mission Board was succeeded by several posts in Europe and America on an interdenominational level. Wilder embodied the view that effective missions came from those basing their lives on personal faith and Bible study. Christianity was not a matter of theological labels for him but rather a deeply personal commitment where doctrinal issues had no place. While on furlough in the U.S. (1897–99), he worked for the World's Student Christian Federation, visiting seminaries of thirty denominations in efforts to swell the ranks of evangelical volunteers. By 1902 nervous exhaustion forced him to leave India; after slow recuperation he began again (1905) to organize an endless round of conferences for stimulating missionary activity. During World War I he helped direct YMCA programs for enlisted men as well as for the general public. As senior secretary of Religious Work Departments in two councils he tried to further causes of salvation, character building, and national service. For another decade after the war he supervised student mission movements with the same zeal that marked all his labors. Advanced age and faltering health finally brought about a reluctant resignation. But even then he accepted speaking engagements until almost the very end.

Bibliography:

A. *Among India's Students* (New York, 1899); *The Student Volunteer Movement: Its Origin and Early History* (New York, 1935); *Christ and the Student World* (London, 1935); *The Great Commission* (London, 1937).

B. NYT 29 Mar 1938, 21; Ruth W. Braisted, *In This Generation* (New York, 1941).

WILKINSON, Jemima (29 November 1752, Cumberland, RI—1 July 1819, Yates County, NY).

Reared in a well-to-do Quaker family, Wilkinson seemed destined to play the modest role reserved for women in genteel society. During a serious illness in 1776, however, she experienced a vision which radically changed the course of her life. Convinced that she had died and was sent to earth a second time, she spent the next forty years preaching as God's special emissary. After that initial vision, she refused to recognize her legal name, insisting that she be called the "Universal Publick Friend" instead. Her preaching attracted large audiences. Success in evangelistic efforts derived from a magnetic personality and a dramatic presence enhanced by a distinctive dress resembling a priest's cassock. Not least among factors ensuring popularity was the fact that she showed a woman could stand before large crowds and deliver sermons of acceptable quality. As she itinerated between Massachusetts and Pennsylvania, believers gathered around her to form a society of Universal Friends. The group constituted not an organized church but a personal following, entrance into which depended entirely on the Friend's permission. By 1788 she took steps to protect her flock from worldly evil by establishing a settlement in central New York. Two years later a large community flourished west of Seneca Lake; after some disputes over land, Jerusalem Township was founded in 1794 farther west. Loyal followers congregated there in a peaceable manner which encouraged other pioneers to enter the territory.

There was nothing particularly innovative about the doctrine Wilkinson preached. She urged persons to repent and prepare for the day of judgment, following the golden rule in daily affairs. Biblical axioms comprised much of her gospel, but additional elements involved faith healing (soon dropped), prophecies, and mystic interpretations of dreams. Religious behavior included standard Quaker practices of simple clothing, pacifism, and opposition to slavery. Celibacy was encouraged but not enforced. Added to these teachings was Wilkinson's assertion that she had been specially designated by God as divine messenger. Belief in her words necessarily implied acceptance of her person as validation of the truths presented. She did not discourage followers from believing that she was a Messiah, capable of performing miracles. Emotional denunciations and defenses of equal intensity flew in fierce controversy over that point. Out of all the confusion regarding such claims, suffice it to say that she described her mission in terms ambiguous enough to permit a wide variety of interpretations. In her native New England the name of Wilkinson was popularly associated with fraud, spiritual delusion, and physical abandon. Those in the inner circle knew the Friend as a kindly woman who taught biblical principles of virtue and justice. But the group was oriented around a single personality; it declined rapidly in two decades following the leader's death.

Bibliography:

B. NCAB 8, 81; DAB 20, 226–27; NAW 3, 609–10; Herbert A. Wisbey, *Pioneer Prophetess: Jemima Wilkinson, the Publick Universal Friend* (Ithaca, NY, 1964).

WILLARD, Frances Elizabeth Caroline (28 September 1839, Churchville, NY—17 February 1898, New York, NY). *Education*: graduated from North Western Female Coll., Evanston, IL, 1859. *Career*: taught at various female academies in IL, PA, and NY, 1860–67; travel in Europe, 1868–70; president, Evanston Coll. for Ladies, 1871–73; dean of women, Northwestern Univ., 1873–74; secretary, Woman's Christian Temperance Union (WCTU) on state and national levels, 1874–77; president, National WCTU, 1879–98; president, World WCTU, 1891–98.

After four years of formal education in Methodist schools, Willard entered the teaching profession and over the course of fourteen years became prominent as an educator. Acrimonious conflicts with Northwestern's president led to her resignation, and she turned to the increasingly popular antisaloon movement, accepting posts of responsibility on local, state, and national levels of the Woman's Christian Temperance Union (WCTU). It was clear from the beginning that her interest in temperance was part of a general concern to promote reform in several areas and to advance the cause of women while doing so. The main issue was woman's suffrage, and even though the state organization supported Willard's resolutions to secure that end, her efforts met a cool reception at national conventions. Strained relations over the matter led to her resignation in 1877, but she continued to publicize her views through lectures and in the WCTU journal, *Our Union*. Convinced that temperance would come through legislation, she solicited petitions and lobbied in Illinois for reform laws, having some effect on local option results and setting the pattern for similar campaigns in other states. Willard was an earnest and compelling speaker, able to draw crowds, make headlines, and enlist support from local churches. In 1879 she became president of the national WCTU and held that position for the rest of her life.

Under new leadership, the WCTU moved from exclusive concentration on temperance to a full-fledged woman's organization seeking political strength to accomplish reforms not only with alcohol but also with labor conditions, urban welfare, public health, prisons, prostitution, race relations, and narcotics. Under Willard's active guidance the institution achieved national scope in fact as well as in name. Through the 1880s she tried unsuccessfully to introduce prohibition and suffrage planks in the platforms of national political parties. But in that decade she did bring most WCTU members to accept the realistic link between moral and social reform, "gospel politics" as some called it. After failing one last time in 1892 to unite the forces of Populism, labor, prohibition, and woman's suffrage, she spent much of her time in England. While there Willard adopted views akin to socialism and began saying that poverty was the primary cause of intemperance, education rather than prohibition its major cure. Because of her new ideas and frequent absence there was some restlessness in the WCTU, but the rank and file remained loyal. When she died, prohibition once again dominated all issues, and her memory was still a powerful influence in the movement that did not abate with her passing.

Bibliography:

A.   *Woman and Temperance* (Hartford, 1883; New York, 1972); *How to Win* (New York, 1886); *Glimpses of Fifty Years* (Boston, 1889); *Woman in the Pulpit* (Chicago, 1889); *A Great Mother* (Chicago, 1894).

B.   NCAB 1, 376–77; DAB 20, 233–34; NAW 3, 613–19; NYT 18 Feb 1898, 1; Anna A. Gordon, *The Beautiful Life of Frances E. Willard* (Chicago, 1898); Ray Strachey, *Frances Willard: Her Life and Work* (London, 1912); Lydia J. Trowbridge, *Frances Willard of Evanston* (New York, 1938); Mary Earhart, *Frances Willard: From Prayers to Politics* (Chicago, 1944); Ruth Bordin, *Frances Willard: A Biography* (Chapel Hill, NC, 1986).

WILLARD, Samuel (31 January 1640, Concord, MA—12 September 1707, Boston, MA). *Education*: B.A., Harvard Coll., 1659. *Career*: minister, Groton, MA, 1663–76; minister, Third Congregational Church, Boston, 1678–1707.

After moving from Groton to escape the destruction of King Philip's War, Willard was soon installed as teacher at Old South Church in Boston. In that eminent pulpit he typified the major emphases of second generation Puritans, American-born and Harvard-educated, as they tried to maintain original Congregationalist patterns in the face of changing times. His comprehensive theological mind touched on the whole range of traditional ideas, forming at length a complete body of divinity which sought to improve understanding while it renewed the vigor of personal faith. Passages of scripture and recondite doctrines, hermeneutics and polemics, all received meticulous consideration by this representative spokesman who adhered closely to the Westminster Shorter Catechism. Within that framework he declared man to be a rational creature who pursued his own happiness in all circumstances, these controlled by God as author of every contingent reality. As a free moral agent in the created world, man could discern ontological structures and ethical imperatives in nature by the light of reason alone. But beyond that, the fundamental truths regarding man's possible relationships with God came only from the confessional mode of revealed religion.

Rational creatures seeking happiness on their own were, according to Willard, related to God in a covenant of works; they were either sinless as Adam before the Fall or they lived in a state of apostasy, wandering without guidance or favor from creation's deity. But the despair of natural theology was overcome in Christianity through reconciliation provided by the covenant of grace. Healing grace, made possible by Christ the mediator, inaugurated a new level of expectation wherein recipients were directed by divine counsel during this life and looked forward with other saints to a final vision of God in heaven. The rupture between God and man was overcome only on the confessional side of Willard's systematic thought. The active agent there was an interdependent Trinity, undiscernible in nature but essential to the dispensation of grace manifest in an evangelical economy. Such as orientation made the Boston preacher remind audiences that morality was not as important as personal experience of regenerative healing. Legal righteousness was a poor substitute for the supernatural principle which created new life, moving man from a state of rebellion to one of rebirth. But as moralism supplanted piety in the early years of the eighteenth century, his efforts to balance natural and biblical theology did not succeed. One strain of his systematic Puritanism gave sustenance to Enlightenment deism; another major emphasis led directly to the First Great Awakening.

Bibliography:

A. *Covenant-Keeping, the Way to Blessedness* (Boston, 1682); *Mercy Magnified* (Boston, 1684); *A Brief Discourse on Justification* (Boston, 1686); *The Barren Figtree's Doom* (Boston, 1691); *The Truly Blessed Man* (Boston, 1700); *A Compleat Body of Divinity* (Boston, 1726).

B. AAP 1, 164–67; NCAB 6, 413; DAB 20, 237–38; Seymour Van Dyken, *Samuel Willard, 1640–1707: Preacher of Orthodoxy in an Era of Change* (Grand Rapids, MI, 1972); Ernest B. Lowrie, *The Shape of the Puritan Mind* (New Haven, 1974).

WILLETT, Herbert Lockwood (5 May 1864, Ionia, MI—28 March 1944, Winter Park, FL). *Education*: B.A., Bethany Coll., 1886; studied at Yale Univ., 1890–91; Ph.D., Univ. of Chicago, 1896; studied at Berlin, 1898–99. *Career*: minister, North Eaton, OH, 1886–87; minister, Dayton, OH, 1887–90 and 1891–93; minister, Hyde Park Church of the Disciples, Chicago, IL, 1894–97; dean, Disciples House, Univ. of Chicago, 1894–1921; at various ranks, professor of

Oriental Languages and Literature, Univ. of Chicago, 1896–1929; minister, First Christian Church, Chicago, 1905–20; minister, Union Church, Kenilworth, IL, 1926–40; active retirement, 1940–44.

Many religious leaders in late nineteenth-century decades considered evolutionary hypotheses and critical studies of the Bible to be dangerous because the new sciences threatened comfortable assumptions about nature and revelation. Willett became one of the most eminent scholars in his day who succeeded in popularizing new biblical learning to help Christian laymen appreciate its positive qualities. While studying at Yale, he was led by *William R. Harper to specialize in Hebrew; then when Harper became president of the newly formed University of Chicago, he persuaded the young graduate student to complete his work in the midwestern metropolis. This situation placed him near an influential educational institution as well as the geographical center of his denomination, Disciples of Christ, both of which he served effectively for over fifty years. Willett found no difficulty in applying the methods of historical criticism to scriptural materials because he still believed them to be inspired. Holding no theory of supernatural dictation, he embodied with quiet and eloquent power the conviction that God used biblical authors to convey divine truth. He lectured on such topics across the country, liberating thousands from rigid literalism and yet reinforcing their confidence in written sources of God's Word. Expository articles in the *Christian Century*, a journal to which he contributed frequently, also broadcast his persuasive assurances that religious faith was compatible with modern science.

As a popular interpreter of liberal theological ideas Willett also did much to advance an ecumenical spirit during his heyday on the lecture circuit. He thought denominational separatism to be sheer folly and worked in tangible ways to end division. One of his Chicago churches served as a practical example of this attitude, combining formerly Baptist and Disciple groups into one common body. His work at Chicago Divinity School and adjacent Disciples House also affected generations of students with contagious enthusiasm for Christian unity. Willett represented his church at the 1908 meeting which formed the Federal Council of Churches; thereafter he served for a time (1920–25) as executive secretary of its Western Section. He organized the Chicago Federation of Churches, presiding over its early sessions, and also supervised the Disciples Commission on Christian Unity. In addition to attending the 1937 ecumenical conferences at Oxford and Edinburgh, he belonged to innumerable domestic committees on interdenominational cooperation. For the last twenty-five years his activities were slowed, but not stopped, by a heart ailment, an affliction bringing recurrent periods of intense pain. But obstacles could not divert his sense of mission, and he died while delivering yet another series of lectures on the Book of Books.

Bibliography:

A.   *The Prophets of Israel* (Chicago, 1899); *Our Plea for Union and the Present Crisis* (Chicago, 1901); *Basic Truths of the Christian Faith* (Chicago, 1903); *Our Bible: Its Origin, Character and Value* (Chicago, 1917); *The Bible Through the Centuries* (New York, 1929); *The Jew Through the Centuries* (New York, 1932).

B.   DAB 23, 824–25; NYT 29 Mar 1944, 21.

WILLIAMS, Roger (1603?, London, England—? March 1683, Providence, RI). *Education*: B.A., Pembroke Coll., Cambridge Univ., 1627; post-graduate study at Cambridge Univ., 1627–29. *Career*: Anglican chaplain to private family, Essex, 1629–30; minister, Plymouth colony, 1631–33; minister, Salem, 1634–35; founder and resident, Providence (later Rhode Island), 1638–83.

The ship *Lyon* brought among its passengers in 1631 a young dissenter who had taken orders in England but would not associate with public duties of the office. Williams declined preferment at home and upon emigrating refused a ministerial position in Boston because institutions on both sides of the Atlantic represented unacceptable compromise with worldly practices. After he served brief pastorates in Separatist churches at Plymouth and Salem, officers of the Bay Colony hailed him before the General Court in 1635 to answer for opinions dangerous to the state. The gist of Williams' views was that civil magistrates should have no authority over the consciences of men. Governments had no right to regulate what he called "the spiritual Israel," nor could they properly enforce matters of belief. To argue otherwise, in favor of coercion, was to contradict such vital Puritan doctrines as predestination and justification by faith. Ancillary irritants in Williams' preaching were claims that the king had no title to Indian lands, thus granting illegal charters, and that Anglican churches including non-Separatist cadres were essentially un-Christian. Ideas of that sort threatened basic principles on which the colony was founded, and not surprisingly the spokesman for religious liberty was banished. His outline of reasons for toleration, written with unbridled prose in a pamphlet war with *John Cotton (who encouraged an alliance of ecclesiastical and civil power), recorded one of the earliest defenses of religious freedom in American history. Such radicalism did not fit well in a holy commonwealth, and its unyielding exponent was ordered to be "enlarged out of Massachusetts" for his contumacy.

Narragansett Indians befriended Williams who purchased land from them to establish a colony beyond the reach of Puritan law. As settlements grew in the area, he was instrumental in gaining a charter which allowed for self-government and protected them from outside encroachment. Traveling to England twice (1643–44, 1651–54), he was largely responsible in consolidating authority and settling internal disputes, notably with William Coddington. Over the years Rhode Island became a haven for unorthodox thinkers of every stripe because Williams' convictions about religious toleration were incorporated into governmental policy. Even Quakers were tolerated; Williams abhorred their doctrine, but on principle he would not expel or restrict them. Evidence of his zeal, though, is the fact that he challenged *George Fox in 1672 to a debate on the question of Scripture as the only source of saving knowledge. The Bible was constant in Williams' religious quest, but little else had traces of permanency. After changing from Anglican priest to Separatist preacher, by 1639 he was immersed as a Baptist, only to move beyond them in dissatisfaction with all sects. He was known for four decades as a "Seeker," connoting not skepticism but a radically purist conception of the church. True churches were led by apostolic ministers appointed by God; false ones were managed by men appointed by bishops, catering to an unregenerate membership. Williams no longer filled a ministerial post, and he despaired of ever finding the true church on earth. But he continued to search for it with exalted expectations few could match.

Bibliography:

A.   *A Key into the Language of America* (London, 1643; Detroit, 1973); *The Bloudy Tenent of Persecution* (London, 1644); *The Bloudy Tenent of Persecution Yet More Bloudy* (London, 1652); *The Hireling Ministry None of Christs* (London, 1652); *George Fox Digg'd out of His Burrowes* (Boston, 1676); *The Complete Writings of Roger Williams*, 7 vols. (New York, 1963).

B.   AAP 6, 8–21; SH 12, 369–71; NCAB 10, 4–6; DAB 20, 286–89; NCE 14, 944; Samuel H. Brockunier, *The Irrepressible Democrat: Roger Williams* (New York, 1940); Perry Miller, *Roger Williams* (Indianapolis, 1953); Edmund S. Morgan, *Roger Williams: The Church and the State* (New York, 1967); John Garrett, *Roger Williams: Witness Beyond Christendom* (New York, 1970); W. Clark Gilpin, *The Millenarian Piety of Roger Williams* (Chicago, 1979).

WINCHESTER, Elhanan (30 September 1751, Brookline, MA—18 April 1797, Hartford, CT). *Career*: minister, Baptist church, Rehoboth, MA, 1771; preached in many towns including Grafton, Northbridge, Upton, and Hull, MA, 1772–74; minister, Baptist church, Welch Neck, SC, 1774–80; minister, Baptist church, Philadelphia, 1780–81; minister, Universalist church, Philadelphia, 1781–87; Universalist preacher in England, 1787–94; Universalist preacher in U.S., 1794–97.

As a young man with limited schooling but alert mental qualities, Winchester began preaching doctrines he had absorbed from experiences in local churches. His eloquence immediately attracted attention, and great crowds gathered to hear him, no matter what ideas were being elucidated at a given time. He began his first pastorate with Arminian views and the practice of open communion. Within a year his wide reading and restless mind led him to adopt a strict Calvinist theology with corresponding insistence on closed communion. For almost a decade after that he preached in Calvinistic Baptist churches up and down the seacoast, continuing to improve his ministry by studying whatever religious treatises he could find. By 1778 new ideas began to affect his thinking. Over a period of three years he gradually adopted the view that there would be a final end to sin and misery; all fallen creatures would be restored by Christ to a state of happiness. Winchester moved slowly to this position, working his way from soteriologies of limited election to general atonement and finally to universal restoration of all sinful creatures, both men and angels. Most of his Philadelphia congregation followed the young minister in accepting universalist doctrine, or Restorationism, but in 1781 a minority evicted them from the building. Thereafter Winchester drew large audiences to weekly meetings held in facilities of the University of Pennsylvania, where he preached the joyful news of universal reconciliation.

Great Britain appeared a missionary field as willing to receive true doctrine as the new republic; so Winchester extended his ministry to the other side of the Atlantic in 1787. His forensic activities and immensely popular writings made him one of the most notable eighteenth century apologists for universalism. A characteristic pattern of argument was almost propositional in form, resting on the assumption that unless these fundamental tenets were overthrown, they could be trusted implicitly. Winchester's sermons advanced evidences difficult to withstand: God is a loving being who seeks the good for all creatures; His intention in creation was to make all beings happy in the knowledge of His perfections; this design cannot be eternally frustrated by some creatures' remaining unhappy, banished and unreconciled because of sin; Christ died to restore all beings to that intended relationship; His mission to destroy evil will ultimately be successful. All these truths, Winchester claimed, were self-evident as well as being grounded in Scripture. The conclusion of their collective wisdom was that all God's rebellious creatures would suffer punishment in proportion to their offenses and then be restored to the heavenly circle. He thought Restorationism to be an antidote to deistic skepticism, producing a humane system of morality and conceptions of a just God who treated men with loving concern. Though feeble in health, he returned to America and continued to spread the gospel as he understood it until death ended a brief, influential ministry.

Bibliography:

A.   *The Face of Moses Unveiled by the Gospel* (Philadelphia, 1787); *The Universal Restoration, Exhibited in Four Dialogues* (London, 1788); *A Course of Lectures on the Prophecies that Remain to be Fulfilled*, 4 vols. (London, 1789–90); *The Restitution of all Things . . . Defended* (London, 1790); *The Three Woe Trumpets* (London, 1793); *Ten Letters addressed to Mr. Paine* (New York, 1795, 1972).

B.   SH 12, 380; DAB 20, 377–78; William Vidler, *A Sketch of the Life of Elhanan Winchester* (London, 1797); Edwin M. Stone, *Biography of Rev. Elhanan Winchester* (Boston, 1836; New York, 1972).

WINROD, Gerald Burton (1899?, Wichita, KS—12 November 1957, Wichita, KS).

As a self-styled Baptist preacher with deep roots in the prairie farm belt, Winrod first made a name for himself in controversies over evolution. During the 1920s he led fundamentalist elements against teaching modern science in public schools, organizing that opposition in a group known as "Defenders of the Christian Faith." He issued a magazine entitled *The Defender* which used popular topics to build a list of 100,000 subscribers by 1938. He was bitterly opposed to New Deal legislation and attacked everything contrary to his own notions of American freedom. One of the main targets of his vicious denunciations was what he called the international conspiracy of Jewish bankers who were spreading communism into the western hemisphere. In a mixture of Americanist piety and nativistic racism, he declared Jewish communism to be the "scarlet beast," unyielding foe to democratic principles around the world. Though repudiating charges of anti-Semitism on grounds that he did not hate Jews as a race or religious orientation, he repeatedly blamed them for the religious and social ills of this country. Winrod published a great many pamphlets on such topics as the antichrist, Hitler and biblical prophecy or communism, and the Roosevelt brain trust. He also utilized radio broadcasting and developed an impressive following which thought his pro-Fascist ideas had the ring of truth about them. Still his violent rhetoric against Jews, Catholics, and Masons did not sway a majority of the public. In 1938 he was defeated in a campaign for nomination as Senator from the state of Kansas. In 1942 he was indicted for sedition by a federal grand jury, charging that he damaged morale in the nation's armed forces. But legal action could not hide the fact that he spoke for thousands of conservative Christians who expressed their faith within the narrow confines of right wing politics.

Bibliography:

A. *Christ Within* (Wichita, KA, 1925); *Science, Christ and the Bible* (New York, 1929); *The Keystone of Christianity and Other Addresses* (New York, 1930).
B. NYT 13 Nov 1957, 35.

WINTHROP, John (22 January 1588, Edwardstone, England—26 March 1649, Boston, MA). *Education*: studied at Trinity Coll., Cambridge Univ., 1603–05. *Career*: justice of the peace and lord of Groton manor (after 1619), Suffolk, 1609–29; practiced law, London, 1613?–29; governor, Massachusetts Bay Colony, 1629–34, 1637–40, 1642–44, 1646–49.

English Puritans became increasingly pessimistic about successful reform in the Anglican church after William Laud took steps to stifle further agitation for change. As a student at Cambridge, young Winthrop had been influenced by Puritan teachings; while serving in courts of law he developed those spiritual promptings into a religious perspective of deep personal piety. By 1629 he concluded that emigration offered more opportunity for achieving thorough reform in church and state than would ever be possible in a land where vested interests obstructed the process. Because of his legal experience he quickly became a leading executive of the Massachusetts Bay Company, contributing to its basic structure as an independent self-governing colony. Officers in the company had foresight enough to locate the charter, general court, and legal constituents in the new settlement itself rather than leave some components in England. Winthrop was elected first governor, a post renewed on an annual basis, and his recognized services merited frequent re-election. Occasionally he was refused the highest position because of recurring fear that the office might become his for life. But in the last analysis no layman was more important in laying foundations for steady growth as the trading company became a commonwealth. While disclaiming all intention of separating from the Church of

England, he worked tirelessly to establish the Puritan version of it under duly constituted authority.

While on board the *Arbella*, Winthrop recorded his conception of the state as a model of Christian charity. He defined it as a divinely instituted social order where some were appointed to be affluent and others poor, some eminent in power and others placed in subjection. This entire commonwealth, which did not resemble any modern sense of democracy, stood in a covenantal relationship with God as its ultimate governor. All citizens were responsible for assuring universal obedience to God's laws in return for protection in the land given for their inheritance. Winthrop considered the holy enterprise like a city set on a hill, a place where all eyes were fixed to see how thought and behavior could be regulated in final perfection. Massachusetts founded under such expectations was not a theocracy. The clergy had less legal authority there than in any contemporaneous frame of government in the western world. Still ministers had their place, and at times they criticized Winthrop (e.g., 1636) for being too lenient in enforcing ordinances built on divine command. The next year some thought him too severe in banishing *Anne Hutchinson, but on balance his policies were generally wise and humane. He worked till the end in whatever capacity was needed to safeguard physical circumstances for those who sought to embody the covenant in every aspect of community life.

Bibliography:

    A. *The History of New England from 1630 to 1649*, ed. James Savage, 2 vols. (Boston, 1825–26), ed. James K. Hosmer (New York, 1908); *Winthrop Papers*, 5 vols. (Boston, 1929–47).
    B. SH 12, 384–85; NCAB 6, 201–02; DAB 20, 408–11; Robert C. Winthrop, *Life and Letters of John Winthrop*, 2 vols. (Boston, 1864–67); Edmund S. Morgan, *The Puritan Dilemma: The Story of John Winthrop* (Boston, 1958); Robert G. Raymer, *John Winthrop* (New York, 1963).

WISE, Isaac Mayer (29 March 1819, Steingrub, Bohemia—26 March 1900, Cincinnati, OH). *Education*: studied privately and at various yeshivot in Prague, Jenikau, and Vienna, 1835–43. *Career*: rabbi, Radnitz, Bohemia, 1843–45; rabbi, Beth-El Congregation, Albany, NY, 1846–50; rabbi, Anshe Emeth Congregation, Albany, NY, 1850–54; rabbi, B'nai Jeshurun Congregation, Cincinnati, OH, 1854–1900; president, Hebrew Union Coll., 1875–1900.

Probably no name is more closely associated with Reform Judaism in America than that of Rabbi Wise. The modifications in synagogues (mixed pews, choirs, pipe organ, coeducation, confirmation) and his broad vision of Judaism as part of contemporary society embodied the main features of a faith many liberals hoped to transplant from Germany to the New World.

Wise possessed boundless energy and the great organizing ability to give reform sentiments the educational facilities and supportive structures necessary for perpetuating the movement's effectiveness. He was not a great scholar; he read widely but not profoundly. His writing was of a similar nature, but it was influential in disseminating the central themes of Reform. Wise's activities were often criticized by those of conservative persuasion like *Isaac Leeser and also purists with radical tendencies such as *David Einhorn. But his central position as pragmatic mediator made his contributions more important than either of those more polarized advocates.

Wise seems to have been self-conscious in his attempts to unify American synagogues into a comprehensive structure with common standards under his leadership. As early as 1847 he tried to end multiform worship practices by supplying uniform prayers and liturgical usages in a book widely used until the more appealing *Union Prayer Book* was adopted in 1894. In 1848 he began calling for rabbinical synods to regulate the direction of Jewish life. His dream was partially realized in 1873 when the Union of American Hebrew Congregations gave coherence, not rules, to constituents in southern and western parts of the country. Through that body he was largely instrumental in founding Hebrew Union College in 1875, serving as its president until his death. He also presided at the Central Conference of American Rabbis from 1889 to 1900. In addition to these many offices Wise edited two weekly newspapers, *The American Israelite* and *Die Deborah* (English and German, both begun 1854) which spread his views on a host of topics.

In Wise's vision of religion, the serious freedom of Reform extended beyond institutional matters to a universal conception of Jewish identity. He wished to be congruent with the spirit of the age, finding it to contain brotherhood, democracy, and rational behavior, and saw those ideals in turn to be the timeless truths of Judaism. Rather than trying to abandon the essentials of his religion as many conservatives charged, he remained deeply committed to preserving Jewish traditions. He relied upon "historic Judaism," an expansive perspective not confined to any period, place, or class of people and hoped thereby to provide for continuity and flexible change. To him, the enduring values found in Talmud and daily divine guidance could apply to sincere practitioners of Israel's heritage, wherever they resided. For these and other vigorous ideas, Wise is known as the founding father of American Reform, even though it has outdistanced the measures he began.

Bibliography:

A. *History of the Israelitish Nation from Abraham to the Present Time* (Albany, 1854); *Minhag America* (Cincinnati, 1857; rev. eds. 1872, 1876); *The Essence of Judaism* (Cincinnati, 1861); *Judaism and Christianity* (Cincinnati, 1883); *A Defense of Judaism versus Proselytizing Christianity* (Cincinnati, 1889); *Reminiscences*, trans. and ed. David Philipson (Cincinnati, 1900).

B. SH 12, 387–88; NCAB 10, 116; DAB 20, 426–27; UJE 10, 539–41; EJ 16, 563–

65; NYT 27 Mar 1900, 1; Max B. May, *Isaac Mayer Wise* (New York, 1916); Israel Knox, *Rabbi in America* (Boston, 1957); James G. Heller, *Isaac M. Wise: His Life, Work and Thought* (New York, 1965).

WISE, John (August, 1652, Roxbury, MA—8 April 1725, Essex, MA). *Education*: graduated from Harvard Coll., 1673. *Career*: minister, Branford, CT, 1673–77; minister, Hatfield, MA, 1677–83; minister, Chebacco (later Essex), MA, 1683–1725.

After serving as Congregationalist pastor in two New England towns, occasionally supplying pulpits as far away as New Jersey, Wise chose a new parish close to Boston and took part in local affairs as minister and citizen. The spiritual guidance of his charges was the main concern, but he soon became involved in larger controversies as well. Responding to events which he did not initiate, Wise spoke from his own love of independence and reflected that of many others in articulating democratic ideas about civil and ecclesiastical government. In 1688 he was imprisoned, fined, and temporarily suspended from divine office for leading the townspeople of Ipswich against governor Edmund Andros' peremptory tax policy. The following year he represented Ipswich at a convention which framed a new government after Andros' removal, and in 1690 he served as chaplain to those embarking on the hapless military adventure against Quebec. Wise cautioned moderation and reasonableness during the witchcraft troubles and espoused another unpopular cause by defending inoculation as a safe means of combating smallpox. He was, altogether, one who contributed much by teaching and example to the edification of his neighbors.

In 1705 a list of sixteen proposals was circulated by influential ministers such as *Increase and *Cotton Mather, recommending that churches be more centrally organized around a supervisory council. That closer association of clergymen would, it was argued, make it easier to suppress disorder, ensure theological uniformity, and present a united front against worldly temptations. Wise's reaction to the proposals became a classic statement of Congregationalist polity and helped in some measure to prevent the creation of a supererogatory body in Massachusetts. In pungent, satirical analysis he attacked those who sought to improve spiritual matters by adjusting lines of authority; instead of protection for piety, he anticipated descent into presbyterianism. He considered all power exercised over the local congregation to be an abrogation of the original Puritan plan, and he put forth many arguments to defend that position. He appealed to church fathers of the first three centuries in contention that local autonomy had early precedent. Texts of Scripture and the Cambridge Platform (1648) were utilized to show self-rule a continuing good. In a line of argument that was quite rare among American clergymen of that day, Wise also referred to the laws of nature as corroborating the democratic freedom of churches composed of rational men. The proposals for a watchdog association were, in his view, superfluous and potentially tyrannical. Wise was one of the first to combine the covenant idea in federal theology with natural rights philosophy of the Enlightenment period. His ideas marked the emergence of a vigorous train of thought which grew to commanding proportions through the eighteenth century.

Bibliography:

A.   *The Churches Quarrel Espoused* (New York, 1713; Boston, 1715); *A Vindication of the Government of New-England Churches* (Boston, 1717).
B.   AAP 1, 188–89; SH 12, 388; NCAB 1, 177; DAB 20, 427–28; George A. Cook, *John Wise: Early American Democrat* (New York, 1952).

WISE, Stephen Samuel (14 March 1874, Budapest, Hungary—19 April 1949, New York, NY). *Education*: B.A., Columbia Univ., 1892; Ph.D., Columbia, 1902; studied privately for rabbinate in New York, Oxford, and Vienna, 1892–93. *Career*: assistant rabbi, B'nai Jeshurun Congregation, New York, 1893–1900; rabbi, Beth Israel Congregation, Portland, OR, 1900–06; rabbi, Free Synagogue, New York, 1906–49; president, Jewish Institute of Religion, 1922–48; editor, *Opinion*, 1936–49.

The many years of distinguished pastoral service which Wise gave in synagogues on both coasts were eclipsed by his activities on a wider scale. He outgrew Conservative training and became a leading exponent of Reform Judaism, using Sunday services and a popular pulpit to advance causes like interfaith cooperation, social welfare for all citizens, and moral reform in government. The list of institutions and offices with which Wise was associated is phenomenal; just a select number indicates his involvement in the major issues of his day. He was co-founder of the National Association for the Advancement of Colored People (NAACP) in 1909 and of the American Civil Liberties Union (ACLU) in 1920. He established the Jewish Institute of Religion in 1922, a seminary offering training for rabbis of all branches of the faith, and he served as its president until a merger with Hebrew Union College. He was largely responsible for the American Jewish Congress (1916) in its provisional and permanent stages, and the World Jewish Congress (1936), presiding over both from their inception until his death. Always a champion of labor and a foe of political corruption, Wise gained more national publicity along with another New York clergyman, *John H. Holmes, in their exposé of graft in city administration. He was admired and sometimes condemned for discussing controversial topics, but his great oratorical skill left few neutral listeners.

As one who preached and wrote on issues affected by religious commitments among men, Wise was emphatic about none more than that of Zionism. Pogroms in eastern Europe and the Dreyfus case in France were early indications that Jews found little welcome outside a land of their own. Like many other immigrants to America, Wise held a nationalist philosophy regarding Jews as a people even while he remained in the New World. He patterned such convictions after those of his friend, Theodor Herzl, and sustained work in that area for over half a century. There was hardly a Zionist society or program that could not count him among its strong supporters, the most representative being the Zionist Organization of America. He presented the Jewish cause to presidents from Wilson to Roosevelt and was one of the first to raise warnings against the foul and brutal policies of Hitlerism. Wise sometimes disagreed with other leaders about the aims and tactics of securing a homeland for displaced Jews, but he always sought unity within a movement that did not have the full backing of all Jews or the complete sympathy of world opinion. At the time of his death the state of Israel had just been established, fulfilling a dream pursued for so long by an American religious leader.

Bibliography:

A. *Free Synagogue Pulpit: Sermons and Addresses*, 10 vols. (New York, 1908–32); *How to Face Life* (New York, 1917); *The Great Betrayal*, with Jacob de Haas (New York, 1930); *As I See It* (New York, 1944); *Challenging Years: The Autobiography of Stephen Wise* (New York, 1949).

B. UJE 10, 543–44; NCAB 41, 17–18; EJ 16, 566–68; NYT 20 Apr 1949, 1; Justine W. Polier and James W. Wise (eds.), *Personal Letters* (Boston, 1956); Carl H. Voss (ed.), *Stephen S. Wise: Servant of the People, Selected Letters* (Philadelphia, 1969); Melvin I. Urofsky, *A Voice that Spoke for Justice: The Life and Times of Stephen S. Wise* (Albany, NY, 1982).

WISHARD, Luther DeLoraine (April, 1854, Danville, IN—5 August 1925, Indianapolis, IN). *Education*: studied at Indiana Univ., 1870–71; studied at Hanover Coll., 1872–74; B.A., Princeton Univ., 1877; studied at Princeton Sem., 1877–79. *Career*: corresponding secretary of the College Department, International Committee of Young Men's Christian Associations (YMCA), 1877–88; traveling secretary, International YMCA, 1888–92; foreign secretary, International YMCA, 1892–99; director of "Forward Movement," American Board of Foreign Missions, 1899–1902; businessman, 1902–25.

Opportunities for student work with the YMCA caused Wishard to abandon his original plans for seminary training and ordination. His organization efforts in 1877 formed the nucleus of an international student movement which grew to impressive proportions. Though remaining a layman, he supplied energetic leadership for more than two decades and materially enhanced the cause of missions around the world. College campuses were his primary concern. He criss-crossed the country visiting hundreds of colleges, inaugurating revivals in some and organizing Christian students into local cadres of effective religious witness. The aims of intercollegiate work emphasized Bible study, devotional meetings, and a program of missionary outreach that included neighboring towns-people as well as foreign fields. Wishard placed the student movement on a solid foundation by means of constant travel, frequent correspondence, and practical institutional aids. Because of his personal entreaty, *Dwight L. Moody held the first of many student conferences at his school in Northfield, Massachusetts, a means through which great numbers of missionary volunteers were subsequently recruited. By the time he passed the YMCA secretariat over to *John R. Mott, students from almost three hundred campuses had amassed a membership totalling over fifteen thousand.

After 1888 Wishard felt the call of worldwide missions too forcibly to stay in the United States. First in Britain, afterwards in Germany and France, he organized students along lines already firmly established. Then he toured mission stations primarily in Asia to see how the YMCA might sustain or enlarge the work there. In all, he visited 216 missions in twenty countries, wrote sixty reports for home consumption, and helped create greater budgetary support for foreign evangelical enterprises. In 1892 he returned to America but still focused on the international field. Addressing churches, soliciting funds, recruiting personnel, these duties comprised his ministry as he pursued the vision of cumulative revival among the world's youth. By 1899 another project for missionary action attracted his attention. For almost three years he sought to persuade large Protestant congregations to support a specific missionary out of their annual budget. This "forward movement" added 150 more workers to the roll of overseas preachers. At the age of forty-eight Wishard terminated his active participation in evangelistic programs. His decision was lamented by colleagues, but he left them several administrative offices fashioned so well that his own presence was not indispensable to continued efficiency.

Bibliography:

    B.   NYT 7 Aug 1925, 15; Charles K. Ober, *Luther D. Wishard: Projector of World Movements* (New York, 1927).

WITHERSPOON, John (5 February 1723, Yester, Scotland—15 November 1794, Princeton, NJ). *Education*: M.A., Univ. of Edinburgh, 1739; studied theology at Edinburgh, 1739–43. *Career*: minister, Beith, Scotland, 1745–57; minister, Paisley, Scotland, 1757–68; president, Coll. of New Jersey, 1768–94; delegate, Continental Congress, 1776–82; member, New Jersey state legislature, 1783, 1789.

Long before Witherspoon emigrated to this country he was identified with the cause of civil liberty. As a Scots minister allied with the Popular Party, he defended the right of local parishioners to have ultimate authority in choosing clergymen sent them by the national kirk. Fame as an effective public spokesman led New Side Presbyterians to offer (1766) him the presidency of their struggling college in Princeton. After some delay Witherspoon accepted in 1768; his coming marked the turning point of several aspects of Presbyterianism in America. While not a scholar, he was conversant with intellectual trends of his day. He was decidedly opposed to Berkeleian idealistic philosophy and did his utmost to warn students away from such patterns of thought. As an alternative metaphysics he urged Scottish common sense realism, a significant element in later American thought which began with Witherspoon's advocacy. One of the most important human faculties defined by that philosophy was a sense of obligation to group action, and the college president reflected that idea in saying that education was basically preparation for public usefulness. By 1776 he was chosen for such an office himself, arriving as delegate to the Continental Congress just when acceptance of the Declaration of Independence was being debated. While he did not sway reluctant members or save the day with his oratory, he strongly urged its adoption and was the only clergyman to sign that historic document. He also took active part in drafting the Articles of Confederation and helped cement valuable foreign alliances for the new government.

As a religious leader, Witherspoon represented a conservative determination to maintain doctrinal standards of traditional Presbyterianism. Many of his views were amenable to Old Side members of the denomination, and he was able to reconcile factions in the name of greater organizational strength. An irenic spirit made it possible to achieve closer association with Congregationalists while simultaneously increasing the influence of Scotch-Irish divines in the church. He opposed accommodation to changing cultural patterns and worked for years (1785–89) to stabilize his church by uniting it on a national scale. He finally succeeded in creating general acceptance of a common liturgy, confession of faith, constitution, and discipline. In 1789 he was named moderator of the first General Assembly, a body of presbyteries which perpetuated his concern for pure doctrine and even-handed government. Witherspoon continued to serve as college president, even though things were never the same after wartime conditions had ruined his educational advances. The last two years of his life were spent in blindness and serious financial hardship; yet his earlier contributions to church and state lasted far into the nineteenth century.

Bibliography:

A. *Ecclesiastical Characteristics* (Glasgow, 1753); *Essays on Important Subjects*, 3 vols. (London, 1764); *Practical Discourses on the Leading Truths of the Gospel* (Edinburgh, 1768); *Letters on Education* (New York, 1797); *An Essay on Justification and a Treatise on Regeneration* (Edinburgh, 1815); *The Works . . . of John Witherspoon*, 4 vols. (Philadelphia, 1800–01), 9 vols. (Edinburgh, 1815).

B. AAP 3, 288–300; SH 12, 395–96; NCAB 5, 466–67; DAB 20, 435–38; NCE 14, 980; David W. Woods, *John Witherspoon* (New York, 1906); Varnum L. Collins, *President Witherspoon*, 2 vols. (Princeton, 1925; New York, 1969); Lyman B. Butterfield, *John Witherspoon Comes to America* (Princeton, 1953); Martha L. Stohlman, *John Witherspoon: Parson, Politician, Patriot* (Philadelphia, 1976).

WOODROW, James (30 May 1828, Carlisle, England—17 January 1907, Columbia, SC). *Education*: B.A., Jefferson Coll., 1849; studied at Lawrence Scientific Sch., Harvard Coll., 1853; Ph.D., Univ. of Heidelberg, 1856. *Career*: schoolteacher in AL, 1850–53; professor of Natural Science, Oglethorpe Univ., 1853–61; professor of Natural Science in Connection with Revelation, Columbia Presbyterian Sem., 1861–86; professor of sciences, South Carolina Coll., 1869–72, 1880–97; editor, *Southern Presbyterian Review*, 1861–85; editor, *Southern Presbyterian*, 1865–93; president, South Carolina Coll., 1891–97; retirement, 1897–1907.

The son of a Presbyterian minister who emigrated to Canada and then Ohio, Woodrow received his basic education in Pennsylvania before moving south to manage several academies in Alabama. In pursuit of more adequate scientific training he studied briefly with Louis Agassiz and later in Germany where colleagues pressed him to remain as full professor. After a year's post-doctoral work, he returned to this country and soon entered upon a notable experiment in theological education. His task was to demonstrate the harmony of science with written records of Christian faith, especially Scripture, and in so doing refute the criticism of naturalistic detractors. In developing this form of apologetics Woodrow reasoned that the created world is God's work just as the Bible is His word; different products of a single Author cannot contradict each other. The books of nature and revelation are equally true, both being rightly interpreted, and all apparent conflicts between them derive from either faulty understanding of facts or illogical inferences from accurate data. For twenty-five years he taught that the Bible spoke to men not as a handbook of technical information but as a witness to redemption, yielding instruction for faith and duty. From that premise he exhibited a spirit of honest inquiry which never recoiled from truth based on proper evidence. He taught future chemists and prospective ministers alike that men cannot dictate what nature must be or what the Bible must say.

In 1884 Woodrow's seminary requested that he address the question of evolution; his response aroused a storm of controversy in the South and for a time elevated him to national attention as a representative of enlightened religious discussion. True to earlier reasoning, he saw no fundamental conflict between evolutionary hypotheses and biblical references to creation. Scientific theories regarding the material origin of plants or animals were extra-biblical, theologically harmless ideas. They could as easily lead to more profound reverence for God's plan of creation as they might engender doubt. Woodrow observed that the Bible said nothing about the methods, materials, or chronology used by God in natural processes. While not openly advocating evolution as true or even probable, he defended its plausibility because biblical narrative did not explicitly state otherwise. Going further, he argued that it was not the business of the church to teach science. If churches affirmed or denied evolution, they went beyond their proper sphere and weakened their effectiveness by misrepresenting the real focus of gospel truth. Angry reaction to his thoughts ignored such careful distinctions and proceeded to upbraid him for denying assumptions held by the popular majority. As a consequence, he was dismissed from the seminary two years later, though his Presbytery overwhelmingly rejected charges of heresy. Despite this turn of events, he served southern churches for two more decades in offices requiring tact, integrity, and sound personal judgment.

Bibliography:

B.   SH 12, 419–20; NCAB 11, 35–36; DAB 20, 495–96; Marion W. Woodrow (ed.), *Dr. James Woodrow as Seen by His Friends* (Columbia, SC, 1909).

WOODRUFF, Wilford (1 March 1807, Farmington [now Avon], CT—2 September 1898, San Francisco, CA). *Career*: missionary in American states and Great Britain, 1834–40; apostle and elder, 1839–98; president of the Church of Jesus Christ of Latter-day Saints, 1889–98.

After moving to upper New York state with his brother, Woodruff converted to Mormonism in 1833 amid the myriad enthusiasms called the Second Great Awakening. The following year he met the prophet *Joseph Smith in Kirtland, Ohio, and shortly thereafter inaugurated missionary work in Tennessee and Arkansas. Woodruff was not an eloquent speaker, but his honesty and sincerity made him an effective proselytizer. Though he lacked polish, he worked hard, and it was the solid qualities of dedication and drive that helped him spread the faith. His assignments took him to New England, Missouri, England, and the entire Atlantic seaboard. By his own reckoning he traveled more than 170 thousand miles, held more than 7 thousand meetings, delivered well over 3 thousand sermons, and organized more than 50 new branches of the church. When the prophet was assassinated, Woodruff supported *Brigham Young to succeed in leadership. He aided Mormon efforts to evacuate Illinois and in 1847 was one of the first to enter the valley of the Great Salt Lake. There he worked hard for Mormon interests, managing the official publication, *Times and Seasons*, and urging farmers to experiment with scientific agriculture and irrigation. All his life was spent serving his church, its people and its faith.

As early as 1839 Woodruff had been ordained an apostle and thus entered the higher echelons of leadership. In later years he served as assistant historian (beginning 1856) and historian and recorder (beginning 1875) of the church. In 1880 he was made president of the Quorum of Twelve Apostles and in 1889 became the fourth president of the church. This elevation came at a particularly trying time because the U.S. Congress seemed bent at that time on destroying Mormonism. Since the 1850s polygamy had been practiced in Utah Territory over the clamors of non-Mormon agitators. Federal troops in 1857 and the Morrill Law of 1863 were mere preludes to more serious interference. The Edmunds Act of 1883 and the Edmunds-Tucher Act of 1887 threatened legal action to disincorporate the church, dissolve its perpetual emigrating fund, and escheat all church properties. Woodruff, who had been living for years in exile to avoid arrest because he had five wives and thirty-three children, issued a Manifesto in 1890. In it he said that, after prayer and feeling divinely inspired, he was acting for the temporal salvation of the church by submitting to the laws of Congress. In October of 1890 a general conference adopted the Manifesto and thereby declared that Mormonism discontinue teaching on the subject of plural marriages and forbade contracting any further such relationships. This statesmanlike action made it possible for Utah to enter the Union in 1896 and for Mormonism to adjust more fully to the basic contours of modern American culture.

Bibliography:

A. *The Discourses of Wilford Woodruff*, compiled by G. Homer Durham (Salt Lake City, 1946); *Typescript Copy of Wilford Woodruff Journal*, 9 vols., edited by Scott G. Kenney (Midvale, UT, 1983).

B. NCAB 16, 6–7; DAB 20, 498–500; NYT 3 Sep 1898, 12; Matthias F. Cowley, *Wilford Woodruff: History of His Life and Labors* (Salt Lake City, 1909); Francis M. Gibbons, *Wilford Woodruff: Wondrous Worker, Prophet of God* (Salt Lake City, 1988); Thomas G. Alexander, *Things in Heaven and Earth: The Life and Times of Wilford Woodruff* (Salt Lake City, 1991).

WOODS, Leonard (19 June 1774, Princeton, MA—24 August 1854, Andover, MA). *Education*: B.A., Harvard Coll., 1796; studied theology with Charles Backus, Somers, CT, 1797. *Career*: minister, Second Congregational Church, Newbury (now West Newbury), MA, 1798–1808; professor of Christian Theology, Andover Sem., 1808–46; retirement, 1846–54.

Before liberal Congregationalists emerged as a separate party labeled Unitarian, Calvinistic groups in eastern Massachusetts were more prone to argue among themselves than to close ranks and face common problems. Woods played a central role at the turn of the nineteenth century in reconciling trinitarian churchmen to each other. His moderate personality made him acceptable to the Hopkinsian school, allowing participation in its Massachusetts Missionary Society (1799) and attendant *Massachusetts Missionary Magazine* (1803). Similar qualities also recommended him to Old Calvinists, led by *Jedidiah Morse who invited him to join the Massachusetts General Association (1803) and assist in managing the *Panoplist* (1805). By 1808 he succeeded in welding these Calvinistic factions together; their organizations and journals were consolidated while their intellectual energies came to focus at Andover, the oldest American institution specifically devoted to ministerial education. As one of the seminary's first professors, Woods valued union more than abstruse refinements in what he considered secondary matters. He emphasized missionary outreach undergirded by a moderate Edwardsean theology together with a host of agencies intended to influence public life. Among the societies which he helped found were the first foreign missionary society (American Board of Commissioners for Foreign Missions, 1810), the American Tract Society (1814), the Education Society (1815), and the American Temperance Society (1826). For over three decades his conciliatory spirit presided over Congregationalist activity as it turned from inner strife to more evangelical witness.

Andover was established as a deliberate barrier to Unitarian advance, and professor Woods often conducted himself in a manner befitting that purpose. He shaped the minds of a thousand ministerial candidates with lectures noted if not for their brilliance, at least for solid content and earnest delivery. For several years during the 1820s he engaged in a *guerre de plume* with Henry Ware, professor of theology at Harvard, which had become since 1805 the seat of liberal religious tendencies. In a sharp debate over human nature, Ware defended the idea that man is essentially good. Benign feelings predominate in even the worst of men, and salvation proceeds through education, improving the character by developmental degrees. Woods contended on the other hand that humanity is depraved by nature, in need of special elective grace which transforms human character in an event of divine regeneration. There was no clear-cut victory for either side in the "Wood'n Ware Controversy"; after successive rejoinders the only result seemed to be that divisions between theological schools were more sharply drawn. If inventiveness or facility of expression were used as criteria, Woods came off second-best because his argumentation relied on points already clarified by earlier thinkers. Finally at the age of seventy-two he resigned the teaching post in which he labored so long to rally evangelicals and combat the foes of orthodoxy.

Bibliography:

A. *Letters to Unitarians and Reply to Dr. Ware* (Andover, MA, 1822); *Lectures on the Inspiration of the Scriptures* (Andover, MA, 1829); *An Essay on Native Depravity* (Boston, 1835); *Lectures on Church Government* (New York, 1844); *History of the Andover Seminary* (Boston, 1885); *The Works of Leonards Woods*, 5 vols. (Andover, MA, 1850–51).

B. AAP 2, 438–44; SH 12, 420; NCAB 9, 121–22; DAB 20, 502; Madeline Leslie, ed., *Reminiscences and Records of My Father, Rev. Leonard Woods* (Boston, 1887).

WOODWORTH-ETTER, Maria Beulah Underwood (22 July 1844, near Lisbon, OH—16 September 1924, Indianapolis, IN). *Career*: itinerant evangelist, 1880–1924; minister, Woodworth-Etter Tabernacle, Indianapolis, IN, 1918–24.

The day-to-day concerns of Maria Underwood's life included little regard for religious matters, even after she married Philo H. Woodworth in the early 1860s. There may have been nominal church membership in the family, but the future preacher dated her conversion from a revival meeting in 1879 when she was thirty-five years old. Shortly thereafter she experienced visions and calls to begin preaching. Within a year the fifth death among six children apparently released her to respond positively. She affiliated with the United Brethren from 1880 to 1884 and with the Churches of God from 1844 to 1904, declaring herself independent after that but generally associating with Pentecostal congregations. The lack of formal education, theological or otherwise, was an obstacle to success; the novelty of a female evangelist in the pulpit was even more so. But Woodworth slowly won over the doubtful and the curious, moving within five years from successful revivals in the Midwest to evangelical campaigns in the largest cities on both coasts. She spoke with power and authority born of strong convictions. Her dignified, zealous efforts gained national respect for women preachers and made it easier for *Aimee S. McPherson and *Kathryn Kuhlman later to capitalize on precedents thus established.

After a divorce in 1891 and death of the ex-husband a year later, the popular evangelist continued filling countless speaking engagements. In 1902 she married

Samuel P. Etter and thereafter referred to herself with a hyphenated surname. Her fame also brought criticism, most of it pertaining to what she emphasized as important in genuine religious values. Woodworth-Etter encouraged people to be "slain in the spirit" during her worship services. In addition to trances she also emphasized divine healing as a tangible aspect of God's blessing. The "spirit of prophecy" was another important manifestation of spiritual exaltation, and she occasionally foretold events such as earthquakes and tidal waves. Speaking in tongues was an additional phenomenon that occurred when thousands of listeners gathered in meetings under huge tents. This "baptism of the Holy Ghost and of fire" confirmed the truth of her gospel, even when legal challenges (1913, 1915, and 1920) over practicing medicine without a license and obtaining funds under false pretenses threatened her ministry. She was determined to spread healing and salvation as far as possible, and she persisted in limited activities until the end, despite old age, crippling illness and the death of her only surviving child.

Bibliography:

A. *Life, Work and Experience of Maria Beulah Woodworth* (St. Louis, 1894); *Signs and Wonders* (Indianapolis, 1916); *Holy Ghost Sermons* (Indianapolis, 1918); *Spirit-filled Sermons* (Indianapolis, 1921); *Marvels and Miracles* (Indianapolis, 1922).
B. Wayne E. Warner, *The Woman Evangelist: The Life and Times of Charismatic Evangelist, Maria B. Woodworth-Etter* (Metuchen, NJ, 1986).

WOOLMAN, John (19 October 1720, Rancocas, NJ—7 October 1772, York, England). *Career*: assistant shopkeeper and apprentice tailor, Mt. Holly, NJ, 1741–48; tailor, merchant (1748–57), and farmer, Mt. Holly, 1748–72; recorded minister, Society of Friends, 1743–72.

Like other Quaker ministers of his time, Woolman supported himself with a trade, contributing time and services to meetings without remuneration. His diligence did more than supply need, however, and he retired from business, without condemning wealth, to prevent too great a fondness for money. He did not advocate poverty either, but tried to live without those extravagances (even dyed cloth) which distracted men from cultivating spiritual growth. He preferred the leisure time which tailoring gave to pursue his real vocation, counseling those who shared the inner light of God in their lives. Quaker meetings were often silent times of the Spirit, and ministers usually functioned by visiting homes to deal with practical matters instead of preaching at worship services. Woolman made many such visitations, traveling from New England to the Carolinas on thirty separate occasions to confer on Christian principles as he understood them. One of those principles was pacifism, and he supported the cause of peace even to the point of refusing in 1755 to pay taxes marked for the French and Indian War effort. For all his quietism, Woolman spoke movingly of human betterment and valued social justice for the sake of both the oppressed and oppressor. Many of the inequalities which still characterize the relations of capital and labor were noted in his clear analysis. But his self-effacing protest bore no ill will toward those having power and possessions. He sought rather to quicken their consciences and have outer changes mirror inner reformation.

Of all the issues which commanded Woolman's attention, none was as important as slavery, and no one affected Quaker attitudes about that institution more than he. After waiting for divine guidance to show him the way, he served as a medium through which God spoke to his flock regarding this matter. Using the different avenues of preaching, writing, and friendly persuasion he urged that, if one believed in the equality of all men under God, then one's life should bear out this truth in a consistency of profession and practice. Woolman's essays and journal have remained literary classics largely because of eloquence on the question of individual responsibility in an immoral social context. But as far as practical results were concerned, his most effective approach was personal confrontation; in repeated encounters with slaveholders he made them consider their own involvement in the unethical system. By 1758 the Yearly Meeting adopted at his insistence a formal resolution urging Friends to free their slaves and warning further that anyone trading in them would be excluded from the business affairs of the church. In 1776, four years after Woolman died while visiting England, Quakers became the first denomination to prohibit slaveowning among its members.

Bibliography:

A. *Essay on Some Considerations on the Keeping of Negroes*, 2 parts (Philadelphia, 1754–62); *Considerations on the True Harmony of Mankind* (Philadelphia, 1770); *A Plea for the Poor, or A Word of Remembrance and Caution to the Rich* (Dublin, Ireland, 1793); *The Journal and Essays of John Woolman*, ed. Amelia M. Gummere (New York, 1922); *The Journal and Major Essays of John Woolman*, ed. Phillips P. Moulton (New York, 1971).

B.   NCAB 1, 288; DAB 20, 516–17; Janet Whitney, *John Woolman: American Quaker* (Boston, 1942); Edwin H. Cady, *John Woolman* (New York, 1966).

WOVOKA (1856?—20 September 1932, Schurz, NV).

The origins of the Ghost Dance are lost in the mist of conflicting memories, but its general application fits standard observations about religious responses to cultural disorientation. Almost every great Indian nation had been conquered and reduced to reservation life by 1880, and the traditional ways of life for each had begun to decay beyond repair. In that context a new religion arose to bring hope and endurance to many bewildered individuals. The prophet of that new teaching was a Paiute visionary who was born in western Nevada and spent his entire life there. Some claimed that he built on ideas begun in the 1870s by Tavibo, a man who may have been his father. Whatever the origins, the significance of Wovoka, or ''Jack Wilson'' as he was also known because he worked for a family of that name, is that his doctrine spread among peoples eager to receive a glimmer of hope about the future.

Sometime between 1885 and 1889 Wovoka began having visions. At a time when "the sun died" (eclipse), he dreamed of being taken up into a pleasant world full of grass and game. There he saw God and all those who had died, now restored to youth and happiness, engaged in sports and the oldtime occupations. After showing him all this, God told Wovoka to return and tell his people that they must be good and love one another, live in peace with the whites, put away all warlike attitudes, and not lie or steal. If they obeyed, then all Indians would be reunited with their friends and live in a world with no disease, misery, or death. Wovoka was also given a dance to take back to his followers. By performing what came to be called "the ghost dance," the faithful could achieve happiness and hasten the day of final reunion. The essentials were summed up in the prophet's words, "You must not fight. Do no harm to anyone. Do right always." As the religion was originally formulated, no trances were connected with the dancing, there was no special apparel like painted ghost shirts, and no hostility toward non-Indians. The white race simply had no place in the vision of a regenerated earth where all Indian peoples would be restored to vibrant life. God's authority and initiative, not human implementation, were stressed in eschatological expectations. The practical aspect of such a message was that Indians should make themselves worthy of the approaching end by worshipping correctly in the dance and by living peaceably with neighbors of all races.

Wovoka's doctrine of hope and eventual deliverance evoked widespread response from many nations, especially among the Arapaho, Cheyenne, and Kiowa. Others included the Caddo, Wichita, Comanche, Apache, and Sioux on reservations spread from Oklahoma and North Dakota to the Rockies. Delegates from those eastern peoples were sent to learn the new teachings and dances in order to prepare themselves for the coming age.

The prophet's message quickly extended over a great expanse of territory and was incorporated into different tribal cultures with their local colorings. Among the Sioux, certain aspects were emphasized which had no relation to the original vision, emphases leading to a fatal confrontation with white authorities. The Sioux had long been the most warlike of nations on the Great Plains, and Wovoka's ideals of peaceful coexistence with whites were lost on most of them. They believed that their Ghost Dance and special decorated shirt would make them invulnerable to bullets. The new religion and its protection could aid Indian resistance of whites, help exterminate them, and inaugurate a revitalization of pre-contact ways of life. Such bitterness and desperation lay behind the hopes of many disciples who followed the prophet. Thinking themselves invincible, they helped begin the last great slaughter of native Americans, a pathetic spectacle that culminated at Wounded Knee in December of 1890. The Ghost Dance and its millenarian vision survived the massacre and several false predictions regarding the end of the old order. But its popularity waned; its dances and songs blended deeper into the particularities of local cultures. Wovoka's conception of peace, justice, and prosperity remains a challenge to those interested in preparing a better future.

Bibliography:

B. James Mooney, *The Ghost Dance Religion and the Sioux Outbreak of 1890* (Washington, 1896; abr. ed. Chicago, 1965); David H. Miller, *Ghost Dance* (New York, 1959); Paul D. Bailey, *Wovoka the Indian Messiah* (Los Angeles, 1957).

WRIGHT, George Frederick (22 January 1838, Whitehall, NY—20 April 1921, Oberlin, OH). *Education*: B.A., Oberlin Coll., 1859; B.D., Oberlin Sem., 1862. *Career*: Congregational minister, Bakersfield, VT, 1862–72; minister, Andover, MA, 1872–81; professor of New Testament Languages and Literature, Oberlin Sem., 1881–92; professor of Harmony of Science and Revelation, Oberlin Sem., 1892–1907; professor emeritus, 1907–21; editor, *Bibliotheca Sacra*, 1883–1921.

Pastorates in Vermont's Green Mountains and the Massachusetts seacoast gave Wright opportunity for pursuing his geological avocation. His investigation of pleistocene gravel deposits near his Andover church brought recognition from geologists over the world. Thereafter he combined scientific interests with biblical scholarship and embodied for his age a sophisticated correlation of science and religion. In the 1870s he worked with his friend, Harvard botanist Asa Gray, to produce a series of thoughtful articles on Darwinism. For several years he cooperated in a survey which traced the southern edge of terminal glacial moraine from New York to Illinois, yielding information basic to subsequent study of continental ice caps. In 1886 he made the first study of Muir Glacier in Alaska; eight years later he collaborated in similar work on Greenland, and in 1900 conducted geological surveys across the breadth of Russia. By happenstance he brought back a collection of church music, finding later that it contained a liturgy by John Chrysostom with musical settings arranged by Tchaikovsky. He translated the service into English and presented for modern enjoyment a precious relic of early Christian worship. In addition to these activities, Wright also edited the *Bibliotheca Sacra* for almost forty years after it moved to Oberlin, maintaining its reputation as a medium for conservative thought in theology and biblical criticism.

The attitude setting Wright apart from most religious conservatives in his generation was a frank appreciation of inductive reasoning. He understood both theological constructs and scientific hypotheses to be similar patterns in that each sought articulation of man's experience in the world. Instead of condemning science as a threat to deductive systems of religious ideas, he tried to show how fundamental beliefs were compatible with recent discoveries in scientific investigation. He argued that belief in miracles could be juxtaposed with accurate identification of secondary causes to produce congruent views of God and evolution. Further he used specific evidence to support improbable events such as the destruction of Sodom, parting of the Red Sea, and fire falling from the sky to consume Elijah's sacrifice. Throughout his attempts to harmonize modern science and traditional beliefs, Wright held that biblical history was still plausible in light of the most recent scientific knowledge. With his understanding of what constituted proof for empirical minds, he found no reason for abandoning beliefs about theism, biblical authenticity, and central truths giving continuity to the Christian church. Conceptions of providential design in both human and natural history were preserved in an intelligent defense notable for its restraint and balanced judgment.

Bibliography:

A.   *The Logic of Christian Evidences* (Andover, MA, 1880); *Studies in Science and Religion* (Andover, MA, 1882); *The Ice Age in North America and its Bearings on the Antiquity of Man* (New York, 1889); *Scientific Confirmations of Old Testament History* (Oberlin, OH, 1906); *Origin and Antiquity of Man* (Oberlin, OH, 1912); *Story of My Life and Work* (Oberlin, OH, 1916).

B.   SH 12, 445; NCAB 7, 66; DAB 20, 550–51; NYT 21 Apr 1921, 13.

Y

YEATMAN, James Erwin (27 August 1818, near Wartrace, TN—7 July 1901, St. Louis, MO). *Career*: businessman and philanthropist, St. Louis, MO, 1842–95; retirement, 1895–1901.

Raised the son of a well-to-do manufacturer, Yeatman was educated by private tutors before he began managing the family's branch office in St. Louis. There he gained a reputation for energetic administrative skill and probity, attributes which caused many social benevolence groups to seek his aid. When the Civil War broke out, his business experience plus a genuine concern to help the needy led fortunately to his appointment as head of the Western Sanitary Commission. In that capacity he supervised a gigantic five-year effort to supplement medical, sanitation, and welfare facilities for Union forces in the Department of the Mississippi. He fitted out hospitals on railroad cars and river steamers in addition to constructing new ones in the field which provided the most efficient, humane medical treatment found in any of the country's military theaters. Working principally in Missouri, Arkansas, Kentucky, and Tennessee, he shipped vast quantities of sanitary supplies including foodstuffs to ward off typhoid and dysentery, killers which claimed more victims than did battlefield wounds. When it was possible to do so he also improved prison conditions and set up convalescent waystations that serviced over 150,000 soldiers on furlough. Provisions for such extensive charity work came entirely from voluntary contributions; Yeatman proved equally capable in collecting various types of material as he was in distributing it with a minimum of overhead. He made personal inspection tours of camps between St. Louis and Vicksburg, adding the plight of freedmen to his long list of concerns as the war neared its end. While he tried to provide them with rudimentary shelter, adequate food, education, and medical attention, he declined *Abraham Lincoln's suggestion that he preside over the Freedmen's

Bureau. Instead he returned to his place as president of the Merchants' National Bank and supported scores of charities around St. Louis for another three decades. Homes for soldiers, Negroes, orphans, blind girls, and working women—these were examples of his general humanitarian impulse to alleviate suffering with the private resources allotted to him.

Bibliography:

B.   DAB 20, 606–07.

YOGANANDA, Paramhansa (5 January 1893, Gorakhpur, India—7 March 1952, Los Angeles, CA). *Career*: private tutor, Ranchi, India, 1917–20; missionary and founder of Self-Realization Fellowship, Los Angeles, 1920–52.

Mukunda Lal Ghosh became certain quite early in life that he had no capacity for scholarship. Nevertheless he was drawn to vedantic teachings in his country's religious heritage, preferring the devotional aspects of its orientation rather than its philosophical monism. Accordingly he placed himself under the tutelage of a master (guru) at Serampore and began the interior journey to self-discovery. By 1914 he entered an ancient monastic order, adopted the name Yogananda, and concentrated on yoga as the best method for controlling inner turbulence. In 1920 he came to America with the message of yoga and its power to help persons see the true Spirit which animates them. Except for one trip to Europe and India (1935–36), he spent the remainder of his life in this country, first in Boston but principally in southern California, as a missionary of Eastern spiritual insights. Yogananda spread his teachings primarily through personal contact, utilizing the tested methods learned while sitting on a tiger skin before his own guru. His rich, vivid language impressed many and communicated an attractive view of the cosmos to ever-increasing circles of listeners. Through his gentle urging, many westerners claimed the objective of samadhi: emancipation or perfect union of the individual soul with Infinite Spirit. By 1925 he succeeded in establishing headquarters for the Self-Realization Fellowship (Yogoda Sat-Sanga) in Los Angeles; the movement was chartered ten years later and eventually spread to more than 150 centers on four continents.

Though a number of differing means could ultimately lead individuals to the same spiritual goal, Yogananda based his flexible approach on a system known as kriya yoga. This venerable tradition emphasized cultivation of the spirit more than knowledge or intellectual substance; it sought to restrain distractions in body and mind which prevented final union with the source of all life. Seekers after truth had to master five preliminary forms of yoga: moral conduct (yama), religious observances (niyama), correct postures (asana), control of life energy (pranayama), and withdrawal from sense objects (pratyahara). Once an adept had mastered these initial stages, he was qualified to pursue concentration (dharana), meditation (dhyana), and superconscious experience (samadhi). By means of this eightfold path, Yogananda taught that one could reach the final goal of absoluteness wherein a yogi realized the Truth beyond all intellectual apprehension. In America he stressed its compatibility with Christian doctrine. Translating concepts into modern scientific language for illustrative purposes, he argued convincingly that Hinduism and Christianity shared a core of common features. His syncretism impressed many, and he was widely revered as a spiritual giant who embodied the best qualities of both East and West.

Bibliography:

    A.   *Songs of the Soul* (Boston, 1923); *The Science of Religion* (Boston, second edition, 1924); *Scientific Healing Affirmations* (Boston, 1924); *Metaphysical Meditations* (Los Angeles, third edition, 1932); *Whispers from Eternity* (Los Angeles, 1935); *Autobiography of a Yogi* (Los Angeles, 1946).
    B.   NYT 9 Mar 1952, 92.

YOUNG, Brigham (1 June 1801, Whitingham, VT—29 August 1877, Salt Lake City, UT). *Career*: elder, apostle (after 1835), and president (after 1847), Church of Jesus Christ of Latter-day Saints, 1832–77; governor, state of Deseret, 1848–50; governor, territory of Utah, 1850–57.

Born on the outer fringes of American economic and religious patterns, Young sought improvement in both spheres by moving west. In 1830 he became acquainted with the *Book of Mormon* and was baptized into the new church two years later after being convinced by missionaries that God had indeed disclosed himself to latter day prophets. He rose steadily as a church official, giving valuable assistance at settlements in Ohio, Missouri (particularly during their expulsion, 1838–39), and Illinois. His preaching tours along the east coast, in Canada, and England were effective, but his organizational ability proved to be the essential factor which sustained the faithful through one of the most successful colonizing endeavors in American history. Young had long served as a special advisor to prophet *Joseph Smith, and without being designated successor he assumed leadership after Smith's murder in 1844. Many panicked when the church's founder was killed, but Young's strong personal qualities prevented the collapse of community spirit in the face of "Gentile" hostilities. He was certain that Mormons could never receive justice while living among non-believers; so in 1846 he initiated the monumental task of migrating from Nauvoo, Illinois, beyond U.S. borders to find peace in wilderness isolation.

Among primary objectives which Young sought to achieve in the new land of Deseret were safety for the saints and preservation of the faith delivered by Joseph Smith. Not a doctrinal innovator, his loyalty to accepted beliefs included even controversial ones such as plural marriage, which he advocated despite pressure from the federal government to end the practice. Young was adamant in resisting attempts to detract from the body of doctrine. He was also adroit in repressing internal dissent and enjoyed the support of most Mormons while building a cohesive society in the Salt Lake Valley. He encouraged economic cooperation and nurtured the growth of diversified industries. By the time of his death, 70,000 converts had emigrated from Europe, adding their labors to a similar number of native born saints. Under Young's guidance peaceable settlements were reached with Indians and with federal representatives, all of these negotiations retaining the prize of Mormon independence in belief and toleration of most customs. Zion flourished in ever greater numbers, and while denied political autonomy, its socio-religious integrity expanded vigorously along lines envisioned by the church's second president.

Bibliography:

A. *Journal of Discourses*, 26 vols. (Liverpool, 1854–86; not exclusively Young's material, but contains hundreds of his speeches).

B. NCAB 16, 3–5; DAB 20, 620–23; NCE 14, 1075; NYT 30 Aug 1877, 1; Morris R. Werner, *Brigham Young* (New York, 1925); Susa Y. Gates and Leah D. Widtsoe, *The Life Story of Brigham Young* (New York, 1930); Milton R. Hunter, *Brigham Young the Colonizer* (Salt Lake City, 1940); Stanley P. Hirshson, *The Lion of the Lord* (New York, 1969); Leonard J. Arrington, *Brigham Young: American Moses* (New York, 1985).

Z

ZAHM, John Augustine (14 June 1851, New Lexington, OH—10 November 1921, Munich, Germany). *Education*: B.A., Univ. of Notre Dame, 1871; studied at Notre Dame Sem., 1871–75. *Career*: professor of Chemistry and Physics, Univ. of Notre Dame, 1875–92; visiting lecturer in NY, WI, LA, Belgium, and Switzerland, 1893–97; U.S. provincial, Congregation of the Holy Cross, 1898–1906; traveler, lecturer, and author, 1906–21.

Quiet, scholarly efforts at Notre Dame led to an imposing number of responsibilities for Zahm in service to his school and teaching order. Through all his work there he sought to improve Catholic higher education by means of exceptional instruction and the latest scientific equipment. His admiration of modern science combined with this educational objective to make him the most widely known American priest involved in controversies over evolution. Beginning in 1883 he carefully formulated his position and within nine years had gained a national reputation for arguing that evolutionary theories were not contradictory to Catholic dogma. He did not extend himself to defending such hypotheses as scientific truth; it was enough simply to consider them tenable in the light of both geological evidence and traditional theology. On a general level he thought it sufficient to hold that God was the potential cause of natural developments without becoming directly involved in them as biblical narratives seemed to indicate. More particularly he found nothing wrong with the idea that man had descended from earlier forms of anthropoid mammals. Nothing in dogma precluded developmental theories, as long as one also believed that God directly inaugurated human life by infusing a rational soul in the organism at some undetermined point in time. It was possible to view evolution calmly, he held, and to continue investigating empirical evidence with confidence that true science would not destroy the church or belief in the God who was author of both forms of knowledge.

In a wide variety of publications, Zahm tried to lay the foundations of an intelligent believer's response to contemporary science. He pointed out that evolutionary conceptions, as old as Aristotle, had been received positively by church fathers including Thomas Aquinas and were clearly acceptable as part of one's worldview which had to be revised by new knowledge. Still, his position distressed many conservatives who preferred customary assumptions about fixed species, mechanical causation, and biblical literalism. Mounting concern in Europe over "Americanism" focused on Zahm's work in addition to other ideas considered too liberal. By 1898 the Congregation of the Index temporarily prohibited circulation of his books, and in less than a year he forestalled debate by withdrawing Italian translations of his work. For more than eight years he was chief administrator of the American province of his order, during which time he made steady advances in building schools and increasing the number of postulants. But some of his policies were too bold, so he was voted out of office at a time coinciding with serious health problems. Extensive travel was prescribed, and he criss-crossed the Western Hemisphere, recording experiences under the pen name of J. H. Mozans. His books on South America became another outlet for Catholic apologetics, performing essentially the same function as he had done previously in discussions regarding science.

Bibliography:

A. *Catholic Science and Catholic Scientists* (Philadelphia, 1893); *Bible, Science and Faith* (Baltimore, 1894); *Evolution and Dogma* (Chicago, 1896); *Scientific Theory and Catholic Doctrine* (Chicago, 1896); *Science and the Church* (Chicago, 1896); *Great Inspirers* (New York, 1917).

B. NCAB 9, 274; DAB 20, 641–42; NCE 14, 1109; NYT 12 Nov 1921, 13; Ralph E. Weber, *Notre Dame's John Zahm: American Catholic Apologist and Educator* (Notre Dame, IN, 1961).

ZEISBERGER, David (11 April 1721, Zauchtenthal, Moravia—17 November 1808, Goshen, OH). *Career*: missionary to Indians in PA, NY, OH and MI, 1745–1808.

Members of the United Brethren or Moravian church settled early (1734) in Georgia and by 1740 had planted more promising establishments in northeastern Pennsylvania. Young Zeisberger was part of those peregrinations, glad for the freedom to exercise his group's proto-Reformation principles without molestation. At the suggestion of bishop *Augustus G. Spangenberg he volunteered for missionary service among the surrounding Indians, thus inaugurating a ministry of steadfast dedication which lasted more than sixty years. He began learning Iroquoian at the mission school in Bethlehem and improved his schooling by occasionally living with the Onondaga after 1745. Zeisberger was favorably received by the Six Iroquois Nations in whose longhouses he preached the simple gospel of Moravian piety for almost two decades. His most significant missionary efforts, however, concerned Algonkian-speaking tribes in Pennsylvania, especially the Lenni-Lenape, or Delaware. After 1763 he lived in their Wyoming valley towns and strove through education to make them useful members of colonial society. Measures of his work are now more literary than institutional because the white man's wars destroyed much of what he accomplished. But sermons, litanies, and biblical narratives in the Delaware tongue, together with dictionaries, glossaries, and grammars, show how much he labored to share the faith with native Americans.

It was the misfortune of Zeisberger's mission to be associated with tribes directly in the path of westering white population. The Delaware and lesser nations were gradually deprived of their ancestral lands. Armed resistance made life in borderland settlements hazardous while forced treaties gave no guarantees for protecting what remained of native independence. Zeisberger was never blamed for the wrongs experienced with the onslaught of white culture. He lived unpretentiously among his red brothers and was accepted on terms which allowed missions to flourish even when other white values were being rejected. In 1771 he followed his charges farther west and built at Schonbrunn the first church beyond the Ohio River. Four villages were soon constructed; farms and cabins seemed to augur peace. But struggles between Americans and the British on that frontier proved as disastrous for his people as had the earlier wars between England and France. In 1781 Zeisberger was arrested by British authorities on suspicion of revolutionary sympathies. During his absence the following year, American troops perpetrated one of the most senseless massacres in red-white annals. Nearly one hundred Christian Indians from Gnadenhutten and Salem were butchered in cold blood while their villages were burned as a lesson for others. Zeisberger continued to follow his refugee people, in Canada, Michigan, and again in Ohio, faithful to the end among believers whose company he preferred to those who originally sent him.

Bibliography:

A. *Essay of a Delaware Indian and English Spelling Book* (Philadelphia, 1776); *A Collection of Hymns for the Use of the Christian Indians* (Philadelphia, 1803); *Sermons to Children* (Philadelphia, 1803); *The History of our Lord and Saviour Jesus Christ* (New York, 1821); *Diary of David Zeisberger*, ed. Eugene F. Bliss, 2 vols. (Cincinnati, 1885).

B. SH 12, 501–02; NCAB 2, 250–51; DAB 20, 645–47; Edmund A. de Sweinitz, *The Life and Times of David Zeisberger* (Philadelphia, 1871; New York, 1971); William H. Rice, *David Zeisberger and His Brown Brethren* (Bethlehem, PA, 1897); Earl P. Olmstead, *Blackcoats among the Delaware: David Zeisberger on the Ohio Frontier* (Kent, OH, 1991).

ZINZENDORF, Nikolaus Ludwig (26 May 1700, Dresden, Germany—9 May 1760, Herrnhut, Germany). *Education*: studied law at Wittenberg, 1716–19. *Career*: study and travel, 1719–21; royal counselor, Dresden, 1721–28; squire of Berthelsdorf, 1722–60; bishop, Moravian Church, 1737–41; Moravian minister, England and Germany, 1741–60.

Born into Austrian Lutheran nobility, Zinzendorf was influenced quite early by Pietism in both education and example. He was interested in the Christian ministry, but his family prevailed on him to study law preparatory to serving the king of Saxony. By 1722, however, Count Zinzendorf acquired an estate in Lusatia which provided a setting for ecclesiastical events of far reaching significance. He welcomed refugees from Bohemia and Moravia, a small band of underground Protestants whose doctrines stemmed from the fifteenth century church of John Huss. As he lived and worshiped among these simple pietists, he thought of them as constituting an ecclesiola within the Lutheran Ecclesia. By 1727 they formed a more organizational structure, reviving the Unitas Fratrum or Church of the Brethren, more commonly known as Moravians. Zinzendorf was patron and preacher in the flourishing community named Herrnhut (The Lord's Protection); after 1737 the title of bishop allowed him greater authority for directing vigorous missionary activities around the globe. Moravians stressed a life of emotional piety, *Herzensreligion*, one centered on communion with God in prayer, evangelical preaching, songfests, and private devotions. Their emphasis on fellowship instead of creeds led their bishop to pursue many ecumenical ventures. Such an inclusive policy did not reach fruition in his own day, but it kept alive the ideal of Christendom sustained by a common faith.

Moravians began arriving in the New World (Georgia) as early as 1734, due to their own missionary zeal as well as restricted governmental toleration at home. Zinzendorf visited the West Indies (1738–39) and North American colonies (1741–43) to consolidate work already begun there. Leaving episcopal titles behind, he labored as a simple preacher in Pennsylvania to unite all German Protestants into a single association. He dreamed of a comprehensive "Congregation of God in the Spirit," a cooperative blending of denominations allowing for sectarian differences while emphasizing mutual understanding and sympathy. After thirteen months of activity, these plans came to nothing, victim of ecclesiastical inertia, the ecumenist's highhanded manners, plus stiff resistance from more churchly minded spokesmen such as *Henry M. Muhlenberg and *John P. Boehm. While in America the aristocratic pietist ministered to Lutheran and Reformed congregations, but while some converted to Moravian patterns, most aligned with traditional confessions and sent for orthodox ministers from Germany. He also conducted three missionary journeys to Delaware and Iroquois Indians, initiating effective work with native peoples which lasted for another half century. In later years Moravians themselves were torn by theological disputes, but Zinzendorf had provided through material sacrifices a basis for them to endure as a religiously creative group.

Bibliography:

A. *Sixteen Discourses* (London, 1740); *Theologische . . . Bedenken* (Budingen, 1742); *Naturelle Reflexiones* (Ebersdorf, 1746–49); *Nine Publick Discourses* (London, 1748); *Maxims, Theological Ideas and Sentences* (London, 1751); *Peremtorisches Bedenken* (London, 1753).

B. SH 12, 514–16; NCAB 2, 170; DAB 20, 657–58; NCE 14, 1122; August G. Spangenberg, *The Life of Nicholas Lewis Count Zinzendorf* (Eng. transl., London, 1838); John R. Weinlick, *Count Zinzendorf* (Nashville, 1956); Arthur J. Lewis, *Zinzendorf: The Ecumenical Pioneer* (London, 1962).

APPENDIX I

DENOMINATIONAL AFFILIATION

Most individuals in American religious history made their mark in a religious group with which they were long affiliated. They are listed alphabetically under separate denominational titles, as the groups are known at the present time. In cases of converts from one denomination to another, the person is mentioned under the heading where he made the most notable and lasting identification. The name in parenthesis furnishes the denomination to which the person belonged before converting.

BAPTIST

Rufus Babcock
Isaac Backus (Congregationalist)
Richard Henry Boyd
John Albert Broadus
Nannie Helen Burroughs
Lott Cary
Shirley Jackson Case
John Clarke (Congregationalist)
William Newton Clarke
Walter Thomas Connor
Russel Herman Conwell
Amzi Clarence Dixon
Harry Emerson Fosdick
Richard Fuller
Richard Furman
Adoniram Judson Gordon
James Robinson Graves
William Rainey Harper

Charles Richmond Henderson
Adoniram Judson (Congregationalist)
Martin Luther King, Jr.
Kenneth Scott Latourette
John Leland
Douglas Clyde Macintosh
James Manning
Daniel Marshall
Shailer Mathews
Charlotte Digges Moon
Edgar Young Mullins
John Franklyn Norris
Daniel Parker
John Mason Peck (Congregationalist)
Norman Perrin
Walter Rauschenbusch
Luther Rice (Congregationalist)
William Bell Riley

Shubal Stearns
Augustus Hopkins Strong
George Braxton Taylor
Howard Thurman
Crawford Howell Toy
George Washington Truett
Francis Wayland
Gerald Burton Winrod

CHRISTIAN SCIENCE

Mary Baker Eddy
Emma Curtis Hopkins
Augusta Emma Stetson

COMMUNITARIAN

Adin Augustus Ballou, Hopedale
Johan Conrad Beissel, Ephrata
Ann Lee, Shaker communities
John Humphrey Noyes, Oneida
George Rapp, Harmony and Economy
George Ripley, Brook Farm

CONGREGATIONALIST

Lyman Abbott
Leonard Bacon
Roland Herbert Bainton
Edward Beecher
Henry Ward Beecher
Lyman Beecher
Joseph Bellamy
Hiram Bingham
Elias Boudinot
William Bradford
David Brainerd
William Brewster
Horace Bushnell
Charles Chauncy
Francis Edward Clark
Joseph Cook
John Cotton
James Davenport
John Davenport
Henry Dunster
Timothy Dwight

Jonathan Edwards
Jonathan Edwards, Jr.
Cushing Eells
John Eliot
Nathaniel Emmons
Solomon Washington Gladden
George Angier Gordon
Francis Higginson
Edward Hitchcock
Thomas Hooker
Mark Hopkins
Samuel Hopkins
Anne Marbury Hutchinson
Arthur Cushman McGiffert (Presbyterian)
Asa Mahan
James Marsh
Cotton Mather
Increase Mather
Jonathan Mayhew
Samuel John Mills
Jedidiah Morse
Theodore Thorton Munger
Asahel Nettleton
Samson Occom
Elias Benjamin Sanford (Methodist)
Cyrus Ingerson Scofield (Episcopalian)
Charles Monroe Sheldon
Newman Smyth
Ezra Stiles
Solomon Stoddard
Josiah Strong
Moses Stuart
Nathaniel William Taylor
William Jewett Tucker
Joseph Tuckerman
Bennet Tyler
Williston Walker
Luther Allen Weigle (Lutheran)
Eleazer Wheelock
Samuel Willard
John Winthrop
John Wise
Leonard Woods
George Frederick Wright

DISCIPLES OF CHRIST

Peter Ainslie
Edward Scribner Ames

Alexander Campbell (Presbyterian)
Thomas Campbell (Presbyterian)
James Harvey Garrison
David Lipscomb
John William McGarvey
Charles Clayton Morrison
Kirby Page
Walter Scott (Baptist)
Barton Warren Stone (Baptist)
Herbert Lockwood Willet

EPISCOPALIAN

Bernard Iddings Bell
James Blair
William Dwight Porter Bliss
Thomas Bray
James Lloyd Breck
Charles Augustus Briggs (Presbyterian)
Phillips Brooks
Thomas Bradbury Chandler
Philander Chase
Alexander Crummell
George David Cummins (Methodist)
Timothy Cutler (Congregationalist)
William Porcher DuBose
Richard Theodore Ely (Presbyterian)
Alexander Viets Griswold
John Henry Hobart
Frederic Dan Huntington (Unitarian)
William Reed Huntington
Devereux Jarratt
Samuel Johnson (Congregationalist)
George Keith (Quaker)
Charles Pettit McIlvaine
William Augustus Muhlenberg
Joseph Fort Newton (Baptist)
James Albert Pike (Roman Catholic)
Joseph Pilmore (Methodist)
Leonidas Polk
Samuel Provoost (Dutch Reformed)
Thomas Fielding Scott (Presbyterian)
Vida Dutton Scudder
Samuel Seabury
William Smith
John Talbot
Daniel Sylvester Tuttle
Cynthia Clark Wedel

Henry Benjamin Whipple
Alexander Whitaker
William White
George Whitefield

GERMAN-DUTCH REFORMED

John Philip Boehm
Theodorus Jacobus Frelinghuysen
James Isaac Good
John Henry Livingston
Johannes Megapolensis
John Williamson Nevin (Presbyterian)
Philip Wilhelm Otterbein
Friedrich Augustus Rauch
Michael Schlatter

HOLINESS-PENTECOSTAL

Eudorus N. Bell
Charles Harrison Mason
William J. Seymour
Ambrose Jessup Tomlinson
Alma Bridwell White

INDEPENDENT EVANGELISTS

William Morrison Branham
Frank Nathan Daniel Buchman
Charles Cullis
Charles Grandison Finney
Charles Edward Fuller
James Martin Gray
Robert Reynolds Davis Jones
Edward Norris Kirk
Kathryn Kuhlman
Aimee Semple McPherson
Benjamin Fay Mills
Dwight Lyman Moody
Charles Fox Parham
Arthur Tappan Pierson
Homer Alvan Rodeheaver
Ira David Sankey
Amanda Berry Smith
Gerald Lyman Kenneth Smith
Rodney Smith
William Ashley Sunday

David Swing
Reuben Archer Torrey
Maria Beulah Underwood Woodworth-
  Etter

JEWISH

Cyrus Adler
Henry Berkowitz
David Einhorn
Israel Friedlaender
Louis Ginzberg
Rebecca Gratz
Abraham Joshua Heschel
Horace Meyer Kallen
Mordecai Menahem Kaplan
Kaufmann Kohler
Joshua Loth Liebman
Isaac Leeser
Henry Pereira Mendes
Sabato Morais
David Philipson
Solomon Schechter
Gershom Mendez Seixas
Abba Hillel Silver
Eliezer Silver
Milton Steinberg
Henrietta Szold
Isaac Mayer Wise
Stephen Samuel Wise

LUTHERAN

Johan Campanius
Paul Henkel
Charles Porterfield Krauth
Henry Melchior Muhlenberg
William Alfred Passavant
Francis Daniel Pastorius
Samuel Simon Schmucker
Martin Stephan
Carl Ferdinand Wilhelm Walther

MENNONITE

Harold Stauffer Bender

METHODIST

Jacob Albright
William Foxwell Albright
Richard Allen
James Osgood Andrew
Francis Asbury
Nathan Bangs
Mary McLeod Bethune
Borden Parker Bowne
Edgar Sheffield Brightman
Richard Henry Cain
James Cannon, Jr.
Peter Cartwright
Thomas Coke (Episcopalian)
John William Draper
Philip Embury
James Bradley Finley
Wilbur Fisk
Freeborn Garrettson
Georgia Elma Harkness
Gilbert Haven
Atticus Greene Haygood
Barbara Heck
Harry Hosier
Samuel Porter Jones
Albert Cornelius Knudson
Jesse Lee
Charles Cardwell McCabe
Francis John McConnell
William McKendree
John Raleigh Mott
Stephen Olin
James O'Kelly
Phoebe Worrall Palmer
Daniel Alexander Payne
Reverdy Cassius Ransom
Benjamin Titus Roberts
Orange Scott
Matthew Simpson
Ralph Washington Sockman
Abel Stevens
William Warren Sweet
Benjamin Tucker Tanner
Ernest Fremont Tittle
Henry McNeal Turner
James Varick

William Jacob Walls
Harry Frederick Ward
Richard Whatcoat
Frances Elizabeth Willard

MORAVIAN

Benson Young Landis
Augustus Gottlieb Spangenberg
David Zeisberger
Nikolaus Ludwig Zinzendorf

MORMON

Spencer Wooley Kimball
David Oman McKay
Parley Parker Pratt (Baptist)
Sidney Rigdon (Baptist)
Joseph Smith
Joseph Fielding Smith
Wilford Woodruff
Brigham Young

NEW THOUGHT

Francis Ellingwood Abbot (Unitarian)
Edna Ballard
Guy Ballard
Annie Wood Besant
Helena Petrovna Blavatsky
Paul Carus
Andrew Jackson Davis
Warren Felt Evans
Charles Sherlock Fillmore
Myrtle Page Fillmore
Emmet Fox
Ernest Shurtleff Holmes
Henry Steel Olcott
Walter Bowman Russell
Ralph Waldo Trine

PRESBYTERIAN

Archibald Alexander
Robert Baird
Albert Barnes
Gideon Blackburn

Eugene Carson Blake
William Adams Brown
William Jennings Bryan
John Wilbur Chapman
Henry Sloane Coffin
Robert Lewis Dabney
Samuel Davies
Jonathan Dickinson
Finis Ewing
Henry Highland Garnet
Francis James Grimké
Charles Hodge
Sheldon Jackson
Charles Colcock Jones
Elijah Parish Lovejoy
Joseph Ernest McAfee
James McCosh
James McGready
John Gresham Machen
John Alexander MacKay
Francis Mackemie
Samuel Miller
Benjamin Morgan Palmer
Charles Henry Parkhurst
   (Congregationalist)
Francis Landy Patton
James William Charles Pennington
Samuel Irenaeus Prime
David Rice
John Holt Rice
Stephen Return Riggs
Philip Schaff (German Reformed)
Henry Preserved Smith
Robert Elliott Speer
Gardner Spring
Lewis French Stearns
Charles Stelzle
Thomas DeWitt Talmage (Dutch
   Reformed)
Gilbert Tennent
William Tennent
Charles Lemuel Thompson
James Henley Thornwell
William Cameron Townsend
Henry Pitney Van Dusen
Henry Van Dyke
Benjamin Breckinridge Warfield
Marcus Whitman

Narcissa Prentiss Whitman
Robert Parmalee Wilder
John Witherspoon
James Woodrow

QUAKER

Anthony Benezet
Henry Joel Cadbury
Levi Coffin
Mary Dyer (Congregationalist)
George Fox
Elias Hicks
Rufus Matthew Jones
William Penn
Jemima Wilkinson
John Woolman

RATIONALIST-DEIST

Ethan Allen
Thomas Jefferson
Thomas Paine
Elihu Palmer (Presbyterian)
Joseph Priestley
Benjamin Rush
Nathaniel Schmidt (Baptist)

ROMAN CATHOLIC

John Altham
James Roosevelt Bayley (Episcopalian)
Orestes Brownson (Unitarian)
Simon Gabriel Bruté de Rémur
John Joseph Burke
Frances Xavier Cabrini
Patrick Henry Callahan
Cecilius Calvert
John Carroll
Jean Louis Cheverus
John Patrick Cody
Michael Augustine Corrigan
Charles Edward Coughlin
Richard James Cushing
Dorothy Day
Pierre Jean DeSmet
Katharine Drexel

Louis Guillaume Valentine DuBourg
Rose Philippine Duchesne
John England
Patrick Augustine Feehan
Benedict Joseph Flaget
James Gibbons
David Goldstein (Jewish)
Francis Joseph Haas
James Augustine Healy
Isaac Thomas Hecker (Lutheran)
Augustine Francis Hewit
Francis Hodur (Polish National Church)
William Hogan
John Joseph Hughes
John Ireland
Levi Silliman Ives (Episcopalian)
Isaac Jogues
John Joseph Keane
James Patrick Kenrick
Eusebio Francisco Kino
John LaFarge
Jean Baptiste Lamy
Bartolomé de las Casas
Rose Hawthorne Lathrop
Michael Joseph McGivney
James Francis Aloysius McIntyre
Edward McGlynn
Bernard John McQuaid
Ambrose Maréchal
Jacques Marquette
Aristide Peter Maurin
Thomas Merton
Virgil George Michel
George William Mundelein
John Courtney Murray
John Nepomucene Neumann
Denis Joseph O'Connell
Edwin Vincent O'Hara
John Boyle O'Reilly
John Baptist Purcell
Mary Joseph Rogers
John Augustine Ryan
Francesco Satolli
Junípero Serra
Elizabeth Ann Bayley Seton
   (Episcopalian)
Fulton John Sheen
John Lancaster Spalding

Martin John Spalding
Francis Joseph Spellman
Ellen Gates Starr (Unitarian)
Catherine Tekakwitha
Jean-Pierre Augustin Marcellin Verot
Frances Warde
Gustave Weigel
Andrew White
John Augustine Zahm

RUSSIAN ORTHODOX

Veniaminov

UNITARIAN-UNIVERSALIST

Hosea Ballou
Henry Whitney Bellows
Antoinette Louisa Brown Blackwell
 (Congregationalist)
William Ellery Channing
James Freeman Clarke
Ralph Waldo Emerson
Sophia Blanche Lyon Fahs
Octavius Brooks Frothingham
Ezra Stiles Gannett
Dana McLean Greeley

Frederic Henry Hedge
Jenkin Lloyd Jones
Thomas Starr King
Andrews Norton
Theodore Parker
Francis Greenwood Peabody
Minot Judson Savage (Congregationalist)
Henry Nelson Wieman (Presbyterian)
Elhanan Winchester

UNITED BRETHREN

Martin Boehm (Mennonite)

URBAN CULTS

Edgar Cayce
Father Divine
Marcus Mosiah Garvey
Charles Emmanuel Grace
Lafayette Ronald Hubbard
James Warren Jones
Malcolm X
Elijah Muhammad
Charles Taze Russell
Joseph Franklin Rutherford
Alan Wilson Watts

APPENDIX II
LISTING BY BIRTHPLACE

The following lists provide an alphabetical arrangement of persons according to the states in which they were born. Early colonial, territorial, and foreign designations are made contemporary by using modern terminology. Former territories are incorporated into the state names by which they are known at the present time.

The appendix is divided into two groups of persons: those born in the United States and those born in other countries. "Na." indicates that the date or place of birth was not ascertained.

UNITED STATES

ALABAMA

Name	Birthdate	Birthplace
Robert Reynolds Davis Jones	30 October 1883	Skipperville
Samuel Porter Jones	16 October 1847	Chambers County
John Franklyn Norris	18 September 1877	Dadeville

ARKANSAS

Name	Birthdate	Birthplace
Cyrus Adler	13 September 1863	Van Buren
Walter Thomas Connor	19 January 1877	Center (now Rowell)

CALIFORNIA

Name	Birthdate	Birthplace
Charles Edward Fuller	25 April 1887	Los Angeles
Garfield Bromley Oxnam	14 August 1891	Sonora
Josiah Royce	10 November 1855	Grass Valley
William Cameron Townsend	9 July 1896	Downey

CONNECTICUT

Name	Birthdate	Birthplace
Ethan Allen	21 January 1738	Litchfield
Rufus Babcock	18 September 1798	Colebrook
Isaac Backus	9 January 1724	Norwich
Nathan Bangs	2 May 1778	Stratford
Henry Ward Beecher	24 June 1813	Litchfield
Lyman Beecher	12 October 1775	New Haven
Joseph Bellamy	20 February 1719	Cheshire
David Brainerd	20 April 1718	Haddam
Horace Bushnell	14 April 1802	Bantam
Thomas Bradbury Chandler	26 April 1726	Woodstock
James Davenport	1716	Stamford
Jonathan Dickinson	22 April 1688	Hatfield
Jonathan Edwards	5 October 1703	East Windsor
Nathaniel Emmons	1 May 1745	East Haddam
Charles Grandison Finney	29 August 1792	Warren
Alexander Viets Griswold	22 April 1766	Simsbury
Augustine Francis Hewit	27 November 1820	Fairfield
Emma Curtis Hopkins	2 September 1853	Killingly
Samuel Hopkins	17 September 1721	Waterbury
Levi Silliman Ives	16 September 1797	Meridan
Samuel Johnson	14 October 1696	Guilford
Michael Joseph McGivney	12 August 1852	Waterbury
Daniel Marshall	1706	Windsor
Samuel John Mills	21 April 1783	Torringford
Jedidiah Morse	23 August 1761	Woodstock
Asahel Nettleton	21 April 1783	Killingworth
Samson Occom	1723	Mohegan
Elihu Palmer	7 August 1764	Canterbury
John Mason Peck	31 October 1789	Litchfield
Elias Benjamin Sanford	6 June 1843	Westbrook
Samuel Seabury	30 November 1729	Groton
Elias Smith	17 June 1769	Lyme
Ezra Stiles	15 December 1727	North Haven
Harriet Beecher Stowe	14 June 1811	Litchfield
Moses Stuart	26 March 1780	Wilton
Nathaniel William Taylor	23 June 1786	New Milford
William Jewett Tucker	13 July 1839	Griswold
Bennet Tyler	10 July 1783	Middlebury
Theodore Dwight Weld	23 November 1803	Hampton
Eleazar Wheelock	22 April 1711	Windham
Wilford Woodruff	1 March 1807	Avon

DELAWARE

Name	Birthdate	Birthplace
George David Cummins	11 December 1822	near Smyrna

| Samuel Davies | 3 November 1723 | near Summit Ridge |
| Samuel Miller | 31 October 1769 | near Dover |

FLORIDA

| *Name* | *Birthdate* | *Birthplace* |
| Howard Thurman | 18 November 1900 | Daytona Beach |

GEORGIA

Name	*Birthdate*	*Birthplace*
James Osgood Andrew	3 May 1794	Wilkes County
Elias Boudinot	1802?	near Rome
Father Divine	1877?	Hutchinson Island
Atticus Greene Haygood	19 November 1839	Watkinsville
James Augustine Healy	6 April 1830	near Macon
Charles Colcock Jones	20 December 1804	Liberty County
Martin Luther King, Jr.	15 January 1929	Atlanta
Elijah Muhammad	7 October 1897	Sandersville
Albert Cook Outler	17 November 1908	Thomasville

HAWAII

| *Name* | *Birthdate* | *Birthplace* |
| Samuel Chapman Armstrong | 30 January 1839 | na. |

ILLINOIS

Name	*Birthdate*	*Birthplace*
Jane Addams	6 September 1860	Cedarville
William Jennings Bryan	19 March 1860	Salem
Edgar Johnson Goodspeed	23 October 1871	Quincy
Perry Gilbert Eddy Miller	25 February 1905	Chicago
Fulton John Sheen	8 May 1895	El Paso
Ellen Gates Starr	19 March 1859	near Laona
Josiah Strong	19 January 1847	Napierville
Ralph Waldo Trine	9 September 1866	Mt. Morris

INDIANA

Name	*Birthdate*	*Birthplace*
Harold Stauffer Bender	19 July 1897	Elkhart
Samuel Logan Brengle	1 June 1860	Fredericksburg
John Wilbur Chapman	17 June 1859	Richmond
Charles Richmond Henderson	17 December 1848	Covington
George Davis Herron	21 January 1862	Montezuma
James Warren Jones	13 May 1931	Crete
David Philipson	9 August 1862	Wabash
William Bell Riley	22 March 1861	Greene County

Ambrose Jessup Tomlinson	22 September 1865	near Westfield
Luther DeLoraine Wishard	April 1854	Danville

IOWA

Name	Birthdate	Birthplace
Edna Ballard	1886	Burlington
Charles Fox Parham	4 June 1873	near Muscatine
William Ashley Sunday	19 November 1862	Ames

KANSAS

Name	Birthdate	Birthplace
Guy Ballard	28 July 1878	near Newton
William Warren Sweet	15 February 1881	Baldwin
Gerald Burton Winrod	1899?	Wichita

KENTUCKY

Name	Birthdate	Birthplace
James Gillespie Birney	4 February 1792	Danville
William Marrion Branham	6 April 1909	near Burkesville
Edgar Cayce	18 March 1877	near Hopkinsville
Abraham Lincoln	12 February 1809	near Hodgenville
John William McGarvey	1 March 1829	Hopkinsville
John Lancaster Spalding	2 June 1840	Lebanon
Martin John Spalding	23 May 1810	near Lebanon
Benjamin Breckinridge Warfield	5 November 1851	near Lexington
Alma Bridwell White	16 June 1862	Kinniconick

LOUISIANA

Name	Birthdate	Birthplace
William J. Seymour	na.	na.

MAINE

Name	Birthdate	Birthplace
Ernest Shurtleff Holmes	21 January 1887	Lincoln
Rufus Matthew Jones	25 January 1863	South China
Elijah Parish Lovejoy	9 November 1802	Albion
Shailer Mathews	26 May 1863	Portland
Minot Judson Savage	10 June 1841	Norridgewock
Newman Smyth	25 June 1843	Brunswick
Augusta Emma Stetson	12 October 1842	Waldoboro
Williston Walker	1 July 1860	Portland
Ellen Gould Harmon White	26 November 1827	Gorham

MARYLAND

Name	Birthdate	Birthplace
James Cannon, Jr.	13 November 1864	Salisbury

John Carroll	8 January 1735	Upper Marlboro
Henry Highland Garnet	23 December 1815	New Market
Freeborn Garrettson	15 August 1752	Harford County
James Gibbons	23 July 1834	Baltimore
Frances Ellen Watkins Harper	24 September 1825	Baltimore
John Gresham Machen	28 July 1881	Baltimore
Henry Louis Mencken	12 September 1880	Baltimore
James William Charles Pennington	1809	eastern shore
Samuel Simon Schmucker	28 February 1799	Hagerstown
Amanda Berry Smith	23 January 1837	Long Green
Barton Warren Stone	24 December 1772	near Port Tobacco
Henrietta Szold	21 December 1860	Baltimore

MASSACHUSETTS

Name	Birthdate	Birthplace
Francis Ellingwood Abbot	6 November 1836	Boston
Lyman Abbott	18 December 1835	Roxbury
Hannah Adams	20 October 1755	Medfield
Clara Barton	25 December 1821	Oxford
Henry Whitney Bellows	11 June 1814	Boston
Edgar Sheffield Brightman	20 September 1884	Holbrook
Phillips Brooks	13 December 1835	Boston
Charles Chauncy	1 January 1705	Boston
Russell Herman Conwell	15 February 1843	South Worthington
Charles Cullis	7 March 1838	Boston
Richard James Cushing	24 August 1895	Boston
Timothy Cutler	31 May 1684	Charlestown
Jonathan Dickinson	22 April 1688	Hatfield
Timothy Dwight	14 May 1752	Northampton
Jonathan Edwards, Jr.	26 May 1745	Northampton
Cushing Eels	16 February 1810	Blandford
Ralph Waldo Emerson	25 May 1803	Boston
Octavius Brooks Frothingham	28 November 1822	Boston
Sarah Margaret Fuller	23 May 1810	Cambridgeport
Ezra Stiles Gannett	4 May 1801	Cambridge
Dana McLean Greeley	5 July 1908	Lexington
Gilbert Haven	19 September 1821	Malden
Frederic Henry Hedge	12 December 1805	Cambridge
Edward Hitchcock	24 May 1793	Deerfield
Mark Hopkins	4 February 1802	Stockbridge
Frederic Dan Huntington	28 May 1819	Hadley
William Reed Huntington	20 September 1838	Lowell
Adoniram Judson	9 August 1788	Malden
Rose Hawthorne Lathrop	20 May 1851	Lenox
John Leland	14 May 1754	Grafton
Mary Ashton Livermore	19 December 1821	Boston
Horace Mann	4 May 1796	Franklin

Cotton Mather	12 February 1663	Boston
Increase Mather	21 June 1639	Dorchester
Jonathan Mayhew	8 October 1720	Martha's Vineyard
William Miller	15 February 1782	Pittsfield
Dwight Lyman Moody	5 February 1837	Northfield
Lucretia Coffin Mott	3 January 1793	Nantucket
Andrews Norton	31 December 1786	Hingham
Theodore Parker	24 August 1810	Lexington
Charles Henry Parkhurst	17 April 1842	Framingham
Francis Greenwood Peabody	4 December 1847	Boston
Luther Rice	25 March 1783	Northborough
George Ripley	3 October 1802	Greenfield
Mary Joseph Rogers	27 October 1882	Roxbury
Walter Russell	19 May 1871	Boston
Francis Joseph Spellman	4 May 1889	Whitman
Gardiner Spring	24 February 1785	Newburyport
Lewis French Stearns	10 March 1847	Newburyport
Shubal Stearns	28 January 1706	Boston
Solomon Stoddard	27 September 1643	Boston
Arthur Tappan	22 May 1786	Northampton
Lewis Tappan	23 May 1788	Northampton
Joseph Tuckerman	18 January 1778	Boston
Samuel Willard	31 January 1640	Concord
Elhanan Winchester	30 September 1751	Brookline
John Wise	August 1652	Roxbury
Leonard Woods	19 June 1774	Princeton

MICHIGAN

Name	Birthdate	Birthplace
Leonard Bacon	19 February 1802	Detroit
Cyrus Ingerson Scofield	19 August 1843	Lenawee County
Cynthia Clark Wedel	26 August 1908	Dearborn
Herbert Lockwood Willett	5 May 1864	Ionia

MINNESOTA

Name	Birthdate	Birthplace
Charles Sherlock Fillmore	22 August 1854	near St. Cloud
Albert Cornelius Knudson	23 January 1873	Grandmeadow
Virgil Michel	26 June 1890	St. Paul
Edwin Vincent O'Hara	6 September 1881	near Lanesboro
John Augustine Ryan	25 May 1869	Vermillion

MISSISSIPPI

Name	Birthdate	Birthplace
Richard Henry Boyd	15 March 1843	Noxubee County
Edgar Young Mullins	5 January 1860	Franklin County

MISSOURI

Name	Birthdate	Birthplace
Eugene Carson Blake	7 November 1906	St. Louis

John Patrick Cody	24 December 1907	St. Louis
James Harvey Garrison	2 February 1842	near Ozark
Kathryn Kuhlman	9 May 1907	Concordia
Joseph Ernest McAfee	4 April 1870	Louisiana
Helmut Richard Niebuhr	3 September 1894	Wright City
Karl Paul Reinhold Niebuhr	21 June 1892	Wright City
Joseph Franklin Rutherford	8 November 1869	Booneville
Joseph Fielding Smith	13 November 1838	Far West
Henry Nelson Wieman	19 August 1884	Rich Hill

NEBRASKA

Name	Birthdate	Birthplace
Lafayette Ronald Hubbard	13 March 1911	Tilden
Malcolm X	19 May 1925	Omaha

NEVADA

Name	Birthdate	Birthplace
Wovoka	1856?	western Nevada

NEW HAMPSHIRE

Name	Birthdate	Birthplace
Hosea Ballou	30 April 1771	Richmond
Philander Chase	14 December 1775	Cornish
James Freeman Clarke	4 April 1810	Hanover
Mary Baker Eddy	16 July 1821	Bow
Adoniram Judson Gordon	19 April 1836	New Hampton

NEW JERSEY

Name	Birthdate	Birthplace
Borden Parker Bowne	14 January 1847	Leonardville
Michael Augustine Corrigan	13 August 1839	Newark
Lily Hardy Hammond	24 September 1859	Newark
Charles Pettit McIlvaine	18 January 1799	Burlington
James Manning	22 October 1738	Piscataway
Benjamin Fay Mills	4 June 1857	Rahway
Henry Steel Olcott	2 August 1832	Orange
Thomas DeWitt Talmage	7 January 1832	near Bound Brook
Reuben Archer Torrey	28 January 1856	Hoboken
John Woolman	19 October 1720	Rancocas

NEW YORK

Name	Birthdate	Birthplace
Albert Barnes	1 December 1789	Rome
James Roosevelt Bayley	23 August 1814	Rye
Edward Beecher	27 August 1803	East Hampton
Antoinette Louisa Brown Blackwell	20 May 1825	Henrietta
Charles Augustus Briggs	15 January 1841	New York

William Adams Brown	29 December 1865	New York
John Joseph Burke	6 June 1875	New York
William Newton Clarke	2 December 1841	Cazenovia
Henry Sloane Coffin	5 January 1877	New York
Joseph Cook	26 January 1838	Ticonderoga
Frances Jane Crosby	24 March 1820	Southeast
Alexander Crummell	1819	New York
Andrew Jackson Davis	11 August 1826	Blooming Grove
Dorothy Day	8 November 1897	Brooklyn
Richard Theodore Ely	13 April 1854	Ripley
Harry Emerson Fosdick	24 May 1878	Buffalo
Richard Furman	9 October 1755	Esopus
James Martin Gray	1851	New York
Handsome Lake	1735	Gano'wages
Georgia Elma Harkness	21 April 1891	Harkness
Isaac Thomas Hecker	18 December 1819	New York
Elias Hicks	19 March 1748	Hempstead
Robert Green Ingersoll	11 August 1833	Dresden
Sheldon Jackson	18 May 1834	Minaville
William James	11 January 1842	New York
Thomas Starr King	17 December 1824	New York
Edward Norris Kirk	14 August 1802	New York
John Henry Livingston	30 May 1746	Poughkeepsie
Arthur Cushman McGiffert	4 March 1861	Sauquoit
Edward McGlynn	27 September 1837	New York
James Francis Aloysius McIntyre	25 June 1886	New York
Bernard John McQuaid	15 December 1823	New York
Asa Mahan	9 November 1799	Vernon
John Raleigh Mott	25 May 1865	Livingston Manor
George William Mundelein	2 July 1872	New York
Theodore Thornton Munger	5 March 1830	Bainbridge
John Courtney Murray	12 September 1904	New York
Pheobe Worrall Palmer	18 December 1807	New York
Arthur Tappan Peirson	6 March 1837	New York
Parley Parker Pratt	12 April 1807	Burlington
Samuel Irenaeus Prime	4 November 1812	Ballston
Samuel Provoost	9 March 1742	New York
Reverdy Caassius Ransom	4 January 1861	Flushing
Walter Rauschenbusch	4 October 1861	Rochester
Benjamin Titus Roberts	25 July 1823	Gowanda
Gershom Mendez Seixas	15 January 1746	New York
Elizabeth Bayley Seton	28 August 1774	New York
Charles Monroe Sheldon	26 February 1857	Wellsville
Elizabeth Cady Stanton	12 November 1815	Johnstown
Milton Steinberg	25 November 1903	Rochester
Charles Stelzle	4 June 1869	New York
Augustus Hopkins Strong	3 August 1836	Rochester

Catherine Tekakwitha	1656?	Gandahouhague
Sojourner Truth	1797?	Ulster County
Daniel Sylvester Tuttle	26 January 1837	Windham
James Varick	1750?	near Newburgh
Francis Wayland	11 March 1796	New York
Gustave Weigel	15 January 1906	Buffalo
Henry Benjamin Whipple	15 February 1822	Adams
Marcus Whitman	4 September 1802	Rushville
Narcissa Prentiss Whitman	14 March 1808	Prattsburg
Frances Elizabeth Caroline Willard	28 September 1839	Churchville
George Frederick Wright	22 January 1838	Whitehall

NORTH CAROLINA

Name	Birthdate	Birthplace
Levi Coffin	28 October 1789	near New Garden
Amzi Clarence Dixon	6 July 1854	Shelby
James Bradley Finley	1 July 1781	na.
Paul Henkel	15 December 1754	Rowan County
Harry Hosier	1750?	Fayetteville
Leonidas Polk	10 April 1806	Raleigh
Thomas Fielding Scott	12 March 1807	Iredell County
George Washington Truett	6 May 1867	Clay County
William Jacob Walls	8 May 1885	Chimney Rock

OHIO

Name	Birthdate	Birthplace
Bernard Iddings Bell	13 October 1886	Dayton
Patrick Henry Callahan	15 October 1865	Cleveland
Algernon Sidney Crapsey	28 June 1847	Fairmount
Myrtle Page Fillmore	6 August 1845	Pagetown
William Rainey Harper	24 July 1856	New Concord
Joshua Loth Liebman	7 April 1907	Hamilton
Charles Cardwell McCabe	11 October 1836	Athens
Francis John McConnell	18 August 1871	Trinway
Charles Clayton Morrison	4 December 1874	Harrison
Reverdy Cassius Ransom	4 January 1861	Flushing
Stephen Return Riggs	23 March 1812	Steubenville
Homer Alvan Rodeheaver	4 October 1880	Union Furnace
Matthew Simpson	21 June 1811	Cadiz
Henry Preserved Smith	23 October 1847	Troy
Ralph Washington Sockman	1 October 1889	Mt. Vernon
David Swing	23 August 1830	Cincinnati
Tenskwatawa	1768?	Shawnee Territory
Norman Matoon Thomas	20 November 1884	Marion
Ernest Fremont Tittle	21 October 1885	Springfield

Wayne Bidwell Wheeler	10 November 1869	Brookfield
Maria Beulah Underwood Woodworth-Etter	22 July 1844	near Lisbon
John Augustine Zahm	14 June 1851	New Lexington

OKLAHOMA

Name	*Birthdate*	*Birthplace*
James Albert Pike	14 February 1913	Oklahoma City

OREGON

Name	*Birthdate*	*Birthplace*
Kenneth Scott Latourette	9 August 1884	Oregon City

PENNSYLVANIA

Name	*Birthdate*	*Birthplace*
Jacob Albright	1 May 1759	Montgomery County
Richard Allen	14 February 1760	Philadelphia
Robert Baird	6 October 1798	near Pittsburgh
Henry Berkowitz	18 March 1857	Pittsburgh
Martin Boehm	30 November 1724	Lancaster County
James Lloyd Breck	27 June 1818	Philadelphia
Frank Nathan Daniel Buchman	4 June 1878	Pennsburg
Henry Joel Cadbury	1 December 1883	Philadelphia
Katharine Drexel	26 November 1858	Philadelphia
Solomon Washington Gladden	11 February 1836	Pottsgrove
James Isaac Good	31 December 1850	York
Rebecca Gratz	4 March 1781	Philadelphia
John Henry Hobart	14 September 1775	Philadelphia
Charles Hodge	28 December 1797	Philadelphia
John Haynes Holmes	29 November 1879	Philadelphia
Benson Young Landis	12 October 1897	near Coopersburg
James McGready	1758?	western Pennsylvania
William Augustus Muhlenberg	16 September 1796	Philadelphia
John Williamson Nevin	20 February 1803	near Shippensburg
William Alfred Passavant	9 October 1821	Zelienople
Sidney Rigdon	19 February 1793	Piny Fork
Benjamin Rush	4 January 1746	Byberry
Charles Taze Russell	16 February 1852	Allegheny
Ira David Sankey	28 August 1840	Edinburgh
Robert Elliott Speer	10 September 1867	Huntington
Abel Stevens	17 January 1815	Philadelphia
Benjamin Tucker Tanner	25 December 1835	Pittsburgh
Charles Lemuel Thompson	18 August 1839	near Cooperstown
Henry Pitney Van Dusen	11 December 1897	Philadelphia

Henry Van Dyke	10 November 1852	Germantown
Luther Allan Weigle	11 September 1880	Littlestown
William White	4 April 1748	Philadelphia

RHODE ISLAND

Name	Birthdate	Birthplace
Adin Augustus Ballou	23 April 1803	Cumberland
William Ellery Channing	7 April 1780	Newport
John LaFarge	13 February 1880	Newport
Jemima Wilkinson	29 November 1752	Cumberland

SOUTH CAROLINA

Name	Birthdate	Birthplace
Mary McLeod Bethune	10 July 1875	Mayesville
William Porcher DuBose	11 April 1836	near Winnsboro
Richard Fuller	22 April 1804	Beaufort
Angelina Emily Grimké	20 February 1805	Charleston
Francis James Grimké	4 November 1850	near Charleston
Sarah Moore Grimké	26 November 1792	Charleston
Benjamin Elijah Mays	1 August 1895	Epworth
Benjamin Morgan Palmer	25 January 1818	Charleston
Daniel Alexander Payne	24 February 1811	Charleston
James Henley Thornwell	9 December 1812	Marlborough District
Henry McNeal Turner	1 February 1834	Newberry Court House

TENNESSEE

Name	Birthdate	Birthplace
David Lipscomb	21 January 1831	Franklin County
Charles Harrison Mason	8 September 1866	Bartlett
James Erwin Yeatman	27 August 1818	near Wartrace

TEXAS

Name	Birthdate	Birthplace
Joseph Fort Newton	21 July 1876	Decatur
Kirby Page	7 August 1890	Fred
Quanah Parker	1845?	Cedar Lake

UTAH

Name	Birthdate	Birthplace
Spencer Wooley Kimball	28 March 1895	Salt Lake City
David Oman McKay	8 September 1873	Huntsville

VERMONT

Name	Birthdate	Birthplace
Hiram Bingham	30 October 1789	Bennington
Orestes Augustus Brownson	16 September 1803	Stockbridge
Warren Felt Evans	23 December 1817	Rockingham

Wilbur Fisk	31 August 1792	Brattleboro
James Robinson Graves	10 April 1820	Chester
Mary Redington Lyman	24 November 1887	St. Johnsbury
James Marsh	19 July 1794	Hartford
John Humphrey Noyes	3 September 1811	Brattleboro
Stephen Olin	2 March 1797	Leicester
Orange Scott	13 February 1800	Brookfield
Joseph Smith	23 December 1805	near Sharon
Brigham Young	1 June 1801	Whitingham

VIRGINIA

Name	Birthdate	Birthplace
Peter Ainslie	3 June 1867	Dunnsville
Archibald Alexander	17 April 1772	Rockbridge County
Gideon Blackburn	27 August 1772	Augusta County
John Albert Broadus	24 January 1827	Culpeper County
Nannie Helen Burroughs	2 May 1878?	Orange
Richard Harvey Cain	12 April 1825	Greenbrier County
Peter Cartwright	1 September 1785	Amherst County
Lott Cary	1780?	Charles City County
Robert Lewis Dabney	5 March 1820	Louisa County
Finis Ewing	10 June 1773	Bedford County
Devereux Jarratt	17 January 1733	New Kent County
Thomas Jefferson	13 April 1743	Goochland (now Albemarle) County
Charles Porterfield Krauth	17 March 1823	Martinsburg
Jesse Lee	12 March 1758	Prince George County
William McKendree	6 July 1757	King William County
Charlotte Digges Moon	12 December 1840	near Scottsville
Daniel Parker	1781	na.
David Rice	29 December 1733	Hanover County
John Holt Rice	28 November 1777	Bedford County
George Braxton Taylor	25 April 1860	Staunton
Crawford Howell Toy	23 March 1836	Norfolk
Booker Taliaferro Washington	5 April 1856	Hale's Ford

WISCONSIN

Name	Birthdate	Birthplace
Edward Scribner Ames	21 April 1870	Eau Claire
Frederick Clifton Grant	2 February 1891	Beloit
Francis Joseph Haas	18 March 1899	Racine
Gerald Lyman Kenneth Smith	27 February 1898	Pardeeville

OTHER COUNTRIES

BELGIUM

Name	Birthdate	Birthplace
Pierre Jean De Smet	30 January 1801	Termonde

BERMUDA

Name	Birthdate	Birthplace
Francis Landey Patton	22 January 1843	Warwick

BOHEMIA

Name	Birthdate	Birthplace
John Nepomucene Neumann	28 March 1811	Prachatitz
Isaac Mayer Wise	29 March 1819	Steingrub

CANADA

Name	Birthdate	Birthplace
Shirley Jackson Case	28 September 1872	Hatfield Point
Francis Edward Clark	12 September 1851	Aylmer
Charles Edward Coughlin	25 October 1891	Hamilton
Douglas Clyde Macintosh	18 February 1877	Breadalbane
Aimee Semple McPherson	19 October 1890	near Ingersoll

CAPE VERDE ISLANDS

Name	Birthdate	Birthplace
Charles Emmanuel Grace	25 January 1881	Brava

CHILE

Name	Birthdate	Birthplace
William Foxwell Albright	24 May 1891	Coquimbo

CHINA

Name	Birthdate	Birthplace
Sophia Blanche Lyon Fahs	2 August 1876	Hangchow

ENGLAND

Name	Birthdate	Birthplace
John Altham	1589	Warwickshire?
Francis Asbury	20 August 1745	near Hamstead Bridge
Roland Herbert Bainton	30 March 1894	Ikeston
Annie Wood Besant	1 October 1847	London

Evangeline Cory Booth	25 December 1865	London
William Bradford	March 1590	Austerfield
Thomas Bray	1656	Marton
William Brewster	1560	Nottinghamshire
Cecilius Calvert	1606	London
John Clarke	8 October 1609	Westhorpe
John Cotton	4 December 1584	Derby
John Davenport	April 1597	Coventry
John William Draper	5 May 1811	St. Helens
Henry Dunster	1609	Bury
Mary Dyer	na.	na.
John Eliot	August 1604	Widford
George Fox	July 1624	Drayton
David Goldstein	27 July 1870	London
Francis Higginson	1586	Claybrooke
Thomas Hooker	7 July 1586	Marfield
Anne Hutchinson	1591	Alford
Ann Lee	29 February 1736	Manchester
Henry Pereira Mendes	13 April 1852	Birmingham
Thomas Paine	29 January 1737	Thetford
William Penn	14 October 1644	London
Norman Perrin	29 November 1920	Wellingborough
Joseph Pilmore	31 October 1739	Tadmouth
Joseph Priestley	13 March 1733	Fieldhead
Rodney Smith	31 March 1860	Wanstead
John Talbot	1645	Wymondham
Harry Frederick Ward	15 October 1873	Brantford
Alan Wilson Watts	6 January 1915	Chislehurst
Richard Whatcoat	23 February 1736	Quinton
Alexander Whitaker	1585	Cambridge
Andrew White	1579	London
George Whitefield	27 December 1714	Gloucester
Roger Williams	1603?	London
John Winthrop	22 January 1588	Edwardstone
James Woodrow	30 May 1828	Carlisle

FRANCE

Name	Birthdate	Birthplace
Anthony Benezet	31 January 1713	St. Quentin
Simon W. Gabriel Bruté de Rémur	20 March 1799	Rennes
Jean Louis Lefebre de Cheverus	28 January 1768	Mayenne
Rose Philippine Duchesne	29 August 1769	Grenoble
Benedict Joseph Flaget	7 November 1763	Contournat
Isaac Jogues	10 January 1607	Orléans

Jean Baptiste Lamy	11 October 1814	Lempdes
Ambrose Maréchal	28 August 1764	Ingres
Jacques Marquette	1 June 1637	Laon
Aristide Peter Maurin	9 May 1877	Oultet
Thomas Merton	31 January 1915	Prades
J. Augustin M. Verot	23 May 1805	Le Puy

GERMANY

Name	Birthdate	Birthplace
Felix Adler	13 August 1851	Alzey
Johann Conrad Beissel	April 1690	Eberbach
John Philip Boehm	November 1683	Hochstadt
Paul Carus	18 July 1852	Ilsenburg
David Einhorn	10 November 1809	Dispeck
Theodorus Jacobus Frelinghuysen	November 1692	Hagen
Horace Meyer Kallen	11 August 1882	Berenstadt
Kaufmann Kohler	10 May 1843	Fürth
Isaac Leeser	12 December 1806	Neuenkirchen
Henry Melchior Muhlenberg	6 September 1711	Einbeck
Philip Wilhelm Otterbein	3 June 1726	Dillenburg
Francis Daniel Pastorius	26 September 1651	Sommerhausen
George Rapp	1 November 1757	Iptingen
Friedrich Augustus Rauch	22 July 1806	Kirchbracht
Augustus Gottlieb Spangenburg	15 July 1704	Klettenberg
Paul Tillich	20 August 1886	Starzeddel
Carl Ferdinand Wilhelm Walther	25 October 1811	Langenschursdorf
Nikolaus Ludwig Zinzendorf	26 May 1700	Dresden

HOLLAND

Name	Birthdate	Birthplace
Johannes Megapolensis	1603	Keodyck

HUNGARY

Name	Birthdate	Birthplace
Stephen Samuel Wise	14 March 1874	Budapest

INDIA

Name	Birthdate	Birthplace
Vida Dutton Scudder	15 December 1861	Madura
Vivekananda	12 January 1863	Calcutta

| Robert Parmalee Wilder | 2 August 1863 | Kolhapur |
| Paramhansa Yogananda | 5 January 1893 | Gorakhpur |

IRAN

| Name | Birthdate | Birthplace |
| Abdu'l-Baha | 23 May 1844 | Teheran |

IRELAND

Name	Birthdate	Birthplace
Alexander Campbell	12 September 1788	Ballymena
Thomas Campbell	1 February 1763	County Down
Philip Embury	September 1728	Ballingrane
John England	23 September 1786	Cork
Patrick Augustine Feehan	29 August 1829	Killenaule
Emmet Fox	30 July 1886	na.
Barbara Heck	1734	Ballingrane
William Hogan	1788	na.
John Joseph Hughes	24 June 1797	Annaloghan
John Ireland	11 September 1838	Burnchurch
John Joseph Keane	12 September 1839	Ballyshannon
Francis Patrick Kenrick	3 December 1796	Dublin
Francis Makemie	1658	near Ramelton
Denis Joseph O'Connell	28 January 1849	Donoughmore
John Boyle O'Reilly	28 June 1844	near Drogheda
John Baptist Purcell	26 February 1800	Mallow
George Hay Stuart	2 April 1816	County Down
Gilbert Tennent	5 February 1703	County Armagh
William Tennent	1673	na.
Frances Warde	1810	Abbeyleix

ITALY

Name	Birthdate	Birthplace
Frances Xavier Cabrini	1 July 1850	Sant' Angelo Lodigiano
Eusebio Francisco Kino	1 August 1645	Segno
Sabato Morais	13 April 1823	Leghorn
Francesco Satolli	21 July 1839	Marsciano

JAMAICA

| Name | Birthdate | Birthplace |
| Marcus Mosiah Garvey | 17 August 1887 | St Anne's Bay |

JAPAN

| Name | Birthdate | Birthplace |
| Daisetz Teitaro Suzuki | 18 October 1870 | Kanazawa |

LITHUANIA

| Name | Birthdate | Birthplace |
| Louis Ginzberg | 28 November 1873 | Kovno |

Mordecai Menahem Kaplan	11 July 1881	Swenziany
Abba Hillel Silver	28 January 1893	Sirvintus
Eliezer Silver	1882	Abel

MAJORCA

Name	Birthdate	Birthplace
Junípero Serra	24 November 1713	Petra

MORAVIA

Name	Birthdate	Birthplace
Martin Stephan	13 August 1777	Stramberg
David Zeisberger	11 April 1721	Zauchtenthal

POLAND

Name	Birthdate	Birthplace
Israel Friedlaender	8 September 1876	Kovel
Abraham Joshua Heschel	1907	Warsaw
Francis Hodur	2 April 1866	Zarkack

RUMANIA

Name	Birthdate	Birthplace
Solomon Schechter	7 December 1847	Focsani

RUSSIA

Name	Birthdate	Birthplace
Helena Petrovna Blavatsky	12 August 1831	Ekaterinoslav
Veniaminov	26 August 1797	Anga

SANTO DOMINGO

Name	Birthdate	Birthplace
Louis Guillaume Valentin Dubourg	14 February 1766	Cap François

SCOTLAND

Name	Birthdate	Birthplace
James Blair	1655?	Alvah
George Angier Gordon	2 January 1853	Oyne
George Keith	1638?	Peterhead
James McCosh	1 April 1811	Ayrshire
John Alexander Mackay	17 May 1889	Inverness
Walter Scott	31 October 1796	Moffat

William Smith	7 September 1727	Aberdeen
John Witherspoon	5 February 1723	Yester

SPAIN

Name	*Birthdate*	*Birthplace*
Bartolomé de las Casas	1474	Seville

SWEDEN

Name	*Birthdate*	*Birthplace*
Johan Campanius	15 August 1601	Stockholm
Nathaniel Schmidt	22 May 1862	Hudiksvall

SWITZERLAND

Name	*Birthdate*	*Birthplace*
Philip Schaff	1 January 1819	Chur
Michael Schlatter	14 July 1716	St. Gall

TURKEY

Name	*Birthdate*	*Birthplace*
William Dwight Porter Bliss	20 August 1856	Constantinople

WALES

Name	*Birthdate*	*Birthplace*
Thomas Coke	9 October 1747	Brecon
Jenkin Lloyd Jones	14 November 1843	Llandyssil

UNKNOWN

Eudorus N. Bell (United States?)
James O'Kelley (1735? Ireland?)

SELECTED BIBLIOGRAPHY

GENERAL OVERVIEWS

Ahlstrom, Sydney E. *A Religious History of the American People*. New Haven, CT, 1972.

Albanese, Catherine L. *America: Religions and Religion*. Belmont, CA, 1981.

Bednarowski, Mary F. *American Religion: A Cultural Perspective*. Englewood Cliffs, NJ, 1984.

Gaustad, Edwin S. *Historical Atlas of Religion in America*. New York, 1976.

———. *Religion in America: History and Historiography*. Washington, DC, 1973.

———. *A Religious History of America*. New York, 1990.

Hudson, Winthrop S. *Religion in America: An Historical Account of the Development of American Religious Life*. New York, 1987.

Lippy, Charles H., and Peter W. Williams, eds. *Encyclopedia of the American Religious Experience: Studies of Traditions and Movements*. 3 vols. New York, 1988.

Marty, Martin E. *Righteous Empire: The Protestant Experience in America*. New York, 1970.

Olmstead, Clifton E. *History of Religion in the United States*. Englewood Cliffs, NJ, 1960.

Smith, H. Shelton, Robert T. Handy, and Lefferts A. Loetscher, eds. *American Christianity: An Historical Interpretation with Representative Documents*. 2 vols. New York, 1960–63.

Williams, Peter W. *Popular Religion in America: Symbolic Change and the Modernization Process in Historical Perspective*. Englewood Cliffs, NJ, 1980.

PURITAN STUDIES

Bercovitch, Sacvan. *The Puritan Origins of the American Self*. New Haven, CT, 1975.

———. *The American Jeremiad*. Madison WI, 1978.

Demos, John. *Entertaining Satan: Witchcraft and the Culture of Early New England.* New York, 1982.

Fiering, Norman. *Moral Philosophy at Seventeenth-Century Harvard: A Discipline in Transition.* Chapel Hill, NC, 1981.

Greven, Philip. *The Protestant Temperament: Patterns of Childrearing, Religious Experience, and the Self in Early America.* New York, 1977.

Hall, David D. *The Faithful Shepherd: A History of the New England Ministry in the Seventeenth Century.* Chapel Hill, NC, 1972.

Hambrick-Stowe, Charles. *The Practice of Piety: Puritan Devotional Disciplines in Seventeenth-Century New England.* Chapel Hill, NC, 1982.

Lucas, Paul. *Valley of Discord: Church and Society Along the Connecticut River.* New Haven, CT, 1975.

Silverman, Kenneth. *The Life and Times of Cotton Mather.* New York, 1984.

Solberg, Winton U. *Redeem the Time: The Puritan Sabbath in Early America.* Cambridge, MA, 1977.

Stoever, K. B. *"A Faire and Easie Way to Heaven": Covenant Theology and Antinomianism in Early Massachusetts.* Middletown, CT, 1978.

Stout, Harry S. *The New England Soul: Preaching and Religious Culture in Colonial New England.* New York, 1986.

REVIVALS AND MODERN EVANGELICALISM

Anderson, Robert Mapes. *Vision of the Disinherited: The Making of American Pentecostalism.* New York, 1979.

Bruce, Dickson D., Jr. *And They All Sang Hallelujah: Plainfolk Camp-Meeting Religion, 1800–1845.* Knoxville TN, 1974.

Cardwell, Jerry D. *Mass Media Christianity: Televangelism and the Great Commission.* Lanham, MD, 1984.

Flake, Carol. *Redemptorama: Culture, Politics, and the New Evangelicalism.* Garden City, NY, 1984.

Harrell, David Edwin, Jr. *All Things Are Possible: The Healing and Charismatic Revivals in Modern America.* Bloomington, IN, 1976.

McGuire, Meredith B. *Pentecostal Catholics: Power, Charisma, and Order in a Religious Movement.* Philadelphia, 1982.

McLoughlin, William G. *Revivals, Awakenings, and Reform: An Essay on Religious and Social Change in America, 1607–1977.* Chicago, 1978.

Sizer, Sandra S. *Gospel Hymns and Social Religion: The Rhetoric of Nineteenth-Century Revivalism.* Philadelphia, 1978.

Weber, Timothy P. *Living in the Shadow of the Second Coming: American Premillennialism, 1875–1925.* New York, 1979.

SOCIAL GOSPEL STUDIES

Boyer, Paul. *Urban Masses and Moral Order in America.* Cambridge MA, 1978.

Brumberg, Joan Jacobs. *Mission for Life: The Story of the Family of Adoniram Judson . . . and the Course of Evangelical Religion in the Nineteenth Century.* New York, 1980.

Caskey, Marie. *Chariot of Fire: Religion and the Beecher Family*. New Haven, CT, 1978.

Fishburn, Janet Forsythe. *The Fatherhood of God and the Victorian Family: The Social Gospel in America*. Philadelphia, 1981.

Magnuson, Norris. *Salvation in the Slums: Evangelical Social Work, 1865–1920*. Metuchen, NJ, 1977.

Moorhead, James H. *American Apocalypse: Yankee Protestants and the Civil War, 1860–1869*. New Haven, CT, 1978.

ROMAN CATHOLIC STUDIES

Carey, Patrick. *An Immigrant Bishop: John England's Adaptation of Irish Catholicism to American Republicanism*. Yonkers, NY, 1982.

Crosby, Donald F. *God, Church, and Flag: Senator Joseph R. McCarthy and the Catholic Church, 1950–1957*. Chapel Hill, NC, 1978.

Dolan, Jay P. *Catholic Revivalism: The American Experience, 1830–1900*. Notre Dame, IN, 1978.

———. *The American Catholic Experience: A History from Colonial Times to the Present*. Garden City, NY, 1985.

Gleason, Philip, ed. *Catholicism in America*. New York, 1970.

Halsey, William M. *The Survival of American Innocence: Catholicism in an Era of Disillusionment, 1920–1940*. Notre Dame, IN, 1980.

Hennesey, James J. *American Catholics: A History of the Roman Catholic Community in the United States*. New York, 1981.

Linkh, Richard M. *American Catholicism and European Immigrants, 1900–1924*. Staten Island, NY, 1975.

Merwick, Donna. *Boston Priests, 1848–1910: A Study of Social and Intellectual Change*. Cambridge, MA, 1973.

O'Brien, David J. *The Renewal of American Catholicism*. New York, 1972.

Piehl, Mel. *Breaking Bread: The Catholic Worker and the Origin of Catholic Radicalism in America*. Philadelphia, 1982.

JUDAIC STUDIES

Berenbaum, Michael. *After Tragedy and Triumph: Essays in Modern Jewish Thought and the American Experience*. New York, 1990.

Blau, Joseph L. *Judaism in America: From Curiosity to Third Faith*. Chicago, 1976.

———, and Salo W. Baron, eds. *Jews in the United States, 1790–1840: A Documentary History*. New York, 1963.

Karp, Abraham J., ed. *The Jewish Experience in America*. 5 vols. New York, 1969.

Marcus, Jacob R., ed. *American Jewry: Documents, Eighteenth Century*. Cincinnati, 1959.

Raphael, Marc Lee. *Profiles in American Judaism: The Reform, Conservative, Orthodox, and Reconstructionist Traditions in Historical Perspective*. San Francisco, 1984.

Schappes, Morris U., ed. *A Documentary History of the Jews in the United States, 1654–1875*. New York, 1971.

Sosino, Rifat. *Finding God: Ten Jewish Responses*. New York, 1986.

Woocher, Jonathan S. *Sacred Survival: The Civil Religion of American Jews.* Bloomington, IN, 1986.

BLACK STUDIES

Burkett, Randall K. *Garveyism as a Religious Movement: The Institutionalization of a Black Civil Religion.* Metuchen, NJ, 1978.
George, Carol V. R. *Segregated Sabbaths: Richard Allen and the Emergence of Independent Black Churches, 1760–1840.* New York, 1973.
Lincoln, C. Eric, ed. *The Black Experience in Religion.* Garden City, NY, 1974.
Morrison-Reed, Mark D. *Black Pioneers in a White Denomination.* Boston, 1984.
Paris, Arthur E. *Black Pentecostalism: Southern Religion in an Urban World.* Amherst, MA, 1982.
Raboteau, Albert J. *Slave Religion: The "Invisible Institution" in the Antebellum South.* New York, 1978.
Richardson, Harry V. *Dark Salvation: The Story of Methodism as It Developed among Blacks in America.* Garden City, NY, 1976.
Sernett, Milton C., ed. *Afro-American Religious History: A Documentary Witness.* Durham, NC, 1985.
Williams, Walter L. *Black Americans and the Evangelization of Africa, 1877–1900.* Madison, WI, 1982.
Wilmore, Gayraud S. *Black Religion and Black Radicalism: An Examination of the Black Religious Experience.* Garden City, NY, 1972.

WOMEN'S STUDIES

Boyd, Lois, and R. Douglas Brackenridge. *Presbyterian Women in America: Two Centuries of a Quest for Status.* Westport, CT, 1983.
Epstein, Barbara L. *The Politics of Domesticity: Women, Evangelism, and Temperance in Nineteenth-Century America.* Middletown, CT, 1981.
Ewens, Mary. *The Role of the Nun in Nineteenth Century America.* New York, 1978.
Hardesty, Nancy. *Women Called to Witness: Evangelical Feminism in the Nineteenth Century.* Nashville, TN, 1984.
James, Janet W., ed. *Women in American Religion.* Philadelphia, 1980.
Kerber, Linda K. *Women of the Republic: Intellect and Ideology in Revolutionary America.* Chapel Hill, NC, 1980.
Lehman, Edward C. *Women Clergy: Breaking Through Gender Barriers.* New Brunswick, NJ, 1985.
Ruether, Rosemary R., and Rosemary S. Keller, eds. *Women and Religion in America: A Documentary History.* 3 vols. San Francisco, 1981–83.
Sweet, Leonard I. *The Minister's Wife: Her Role in Nineteenth-Century American Evangelicalism.* Philadelphia, 1983.
Weidman, Judith L., ed. *Women Ministers: How Women are Redefining Traditional Roles.* San Francisco, 1981.

NEW MOVEMENTS IN AMERICA

Alexander, Thomas G. *Mormonism in Transition: A History of the Latter-Day Saints, 1890–1930.* Urbana, IL, 1986.

Beckford, James A. *The Trumpet of Prophecy: A Sociological Study of Jehovah's Witnesses.* New York, 1975.

Foster, Lawrence. *Religion and Sexuality: Three American Communal Experiments of the Nineteenth Century.* New York, 1981.

Gottschalk, Stephen. *The Emergence of Christian Science in American Religious Life.* Berkeley, CA, 1973.

Hansen, Klaus J. *Mormonism and the American Experience.* Chicago, 1981.

Shipps, Jan. *Mormonism: The Story of a New Religious Tradition.* Urbana, IL, 1985.

Whitworth, John M. *God's Blueprints: A Sociological Study of Three Utopian Sects.* London, 1975.

INDEX

The page numbers in **boldface** indicate the location of the main entry.

ABOUT THE AUTHOR

HENRY WARNER BOWDEN is Professor of Religion at Rutgers University. He has authored or edited several books on American religious history, and his articles have appeared in the *Journal of Mormon History*, *Church History*, the *Journal of the American Academy of Religion*, and in several encyclopedias. He is the Series Adviser for *Contributions to the Study of Religion* (Greenwood Press).